THEORY OF INTERNATIONAL LAW AT THE THRESHOLD OF THE 21ST CENTURY

edited by
Jerzy Makarczyk

Theory of International Law at the Threshold of the 21st Century

Essays in honour of Krzysztof Skubiszewski

edited by
Jerzy Makarczyk

KLUWER LAW INTERNATIONAL

THE HAGUE - LONDON - BOSTON

A.C.I.P. Catalogue record for this book is available from the Library of Congress.

ISBN 90-411-0296-5

Published by Kluwer Law International.
P.O. Box 85889, 2508 CN The Hague, The Netherlands.

Sold and distributed in the U.S.A. and Canada
by Kluwer Law International,
675 Massachusetts Avenue, Cambridge, MA 02139, U.S.A.

In all other countries, sold and distributed
by Kluwer Law International,
P.O. Box 85889, 2508 CN The Hague, The Netherlands.

Editorial coordination and typesetting
by Wydawnictwo Naukowe SCHOLAR (SCHOLAR Publishing House)

Printed by ELANDERS Poland.

Contents

SECOND PART – SOURCES

Fifth Part – Issues of Theory in the Development of the Law in New Areas

Introduction
Krzysztof Skubiszewski: His Professional and Public Activity

by

Jerzy Makarczyk

The present introduction is in the nature of chronology which, where it seemed necessary or appropriate, is accompanied by brief explanations or comments. It is based on my talks with Professor Skubiszewski and on published or accessible record. Testimony of various people has been equally helpful.

But may I be allowed to begin with some personal remarks.

I first met Professor Skubiszewski in the late fifties, almost forty years ago. I came to Poznań to seek his support for a scholarship at Harvard Law School. He was already a famous international lawyer, I a third year law student. He received me with his usual courtesy and after a conversation of thirty minutes, which indeed was a sort of examination in our common subject, promised to write a letter of recommendation. So he did, but I was never able to use it, as my passport has been withdrawn for the next nine years. In 1973 he left Poznań, where the authorities, his international renown notwithstanding (he was already an associé of the Institut!), decided not to grant him a professorship there, because his influence on students as a professor would grow beyond the limits they considered safe for their ideology. He became a researcher at the Institute of Legal Sciences of the Polish Academy of Sciences, and soon became a professor. It may be added that the Academy Institutes, at least some of them, were permitted to have a much more liberal staff policy, as they were not directly involved in teaching. Our Institute granted employment to a number of distinguished academics, purged after the students' revolt of 1968, including the Rector of the University of Łódź.

And so, employed by the Institute since 1962. I became his younger colleague, and I must say that I am indebted to him in many respects; perhaps the most important was the understanding of international law. He was an official reviewer of both my post-doctoral thesis and the book I have written in order to become a professor. He went through the latter with a fine tooth comb and it took us seven hours, at the final stage, to go though the text, page by page, not forgetting a single misplaced comma.

Then, during the first Solidarity period, I became deputy director of the Institute and organized in 1988, in close collaboration with him, the 63rd Conference of the International Law Association in Warsaw. And then came the fall of communism. I was at that time teaching in Japan and missed the historic days I had been waiting all my life to see. He was there and became the first Foreign Minister of independent Poland.

It was obvious to me that it was my duty to assist him in this new assignment as best I could. I imagined him, all alone, in the jungle of communist bureaucracy. No other Ministry, with the exception perhaps of the Ministries of Interior and Defense, was so politically homogenous under communist rule. Within two months I became Undersecretary of State, and after ten months Secretary of State and deputy of Minister Skubiszewski.

And this is where I owe him a second debt. Indeed, if the period was much shorter (I served under him for two and a half year), its density may only be compared to that of heavy water. Everything had to be started afresh, most of all Poland's relations with its eastern neighbour, the U.S.R.R. And this task, under his guidance, became my responsibility. I negotiated the main political treaty, but also the set of agreements on the withdrawal of Soviet troops from Poland and their transit from Germany to Russia. The task was a formidable one, but the results gave us the greatest possible satisfaction.

It is impossible to make this introduction less personal. In fact, I seek to personalize it even further by speaking about my third debt to him. In reality, in terms of importance, it is the first one. It is thanks to men like him that we, the younger generation of lawyers, during the darkest years of communism, the university purges, the submission of our country to the U.S.S.R. and the communist party, never lost faith in human values, in the primacy of law both in internal and international relations, in the indivisibility of international law, in short – in our belonging to European culture.

FAMILY BACKGROUND

Krzysztof Jan Skubiszewski was born on 8 October 1926 in Poznań, the main city in western Poland, as the second child of Ludwik Skubiszewski, professor at the Faculty of Medicine, Poznań University, and Aniela née Leitgeber.

His father, stemming from the rural region of Lublin in central Poland, came to Poznań in 1922 from Warsaw where he was employed at the University and at a hospital. Before that he was teaching at the University of Kiev. Krzysztof's mother descended from a wealthy family of merchants, established in Poznań since the 18th century.

The backgrounds of his parents were diverse also because, in the 1920's, the differences in outlook and way of life between Poznań, on the one hand, and Warsaw and Lublin, on the other, were considerable; in some respects these were quite distinctive worlds. This situation was the result of the fact that from the Congress of Vienna in 1815 to the end of the Great War in 1918 these Polish cities and regions were artificially separated from each other by the frontier between Prussia (subsequently also the German Reich) and the Russian Empire.[1] So young Krzysztof was growing up in an atmosphere where different influences were present. He has always regarded himself, as he still does, a native and a citizen of Poznań, although he is aware of his links with that part of the country where his father grew up.

His upbringing at home was one of traditional values. His mother was a devout Roman Catholic. She received her secondary education in Austrian Poland (Galicia) at the Society of the Sacred Heart [Sacré Coeur] noted for its fine schools where French was the language of teaching. The influence of French culture and, generally, admiration for things French were strong in his home; that attitude was rather typical among Poles before the Second World War.

There was a firm belief in patriotism and memories of the fight for Poland's independence were vivid. When Krzysztof was a small child a great uncle of his mother's, a veteran of the 1863 uprising against Russia, was still alive. Krzysztof's paternal great grandfather had also taken part in the same uprising. In his maternal grandmother's country house (which was confiscated in 1939 by Nazi Germany and later taken by the Polish Communists) the hung on the wall in the large dining room the portrait of an ancestor, Hipolit Trąmpczyński, who in 1846 led a local military expedition against the Prussian rulers of Poznań; he was wounded, defeated and sentenced to a long imprisonment.

Krzysztof's great uncle, the Reverend Franciszek Skubiszewski, professor of theology, was expelled from Saint Petersburg by the Russian authorities for clandestine anti-tsarist activity; he was confined to a parish near Lublin where he lived under actual police supervision.

---

[1] Between 1772 and 1795 Poland, *i.e.* the combined territory of the Kingdom of Poland and the Grand Duchy of Lithuania (which at that time formed one State), was progressively partitioned by her neighbours Russia, Prussia and Austria; with the third partition (in 1795) Poland was erased from the map of Europe. As a result of Napoleon's victorious campaigns of 1806–1807 Poland's statehood was to some extent revived in the form of the Duchy of Warsaw which comprised, *inter alia*, Poznań, and later Cracow and Lublin. That revival was the beginning of a process in favour of Poland's full reinstatement. The Congress of Vienna brought that process to an end by a new (fourth) partition of the country.

Krzysztof's father belonged to secret Polish youth organisations opposing Russian domination of Poland, distributed illegal publications, took part in the great "school strike" of 1905 and was prohibited to attend any high school (he was later pardoned). As to Krzysztof's mother, she had, as a young girl, participated in the management of a small Polish library (in Prussia this was unlawful) and later, in the Polish cultural activity during the plebiscite in Silesia. After marriage she was working as a volunteer in various community and social organisations.

Some of Krzysztof's maternal relatives actively participated in public life. The example they set was not without influence on him.

A great uncle of his, Władysław Seyda, was a minister in the Ignacy Paderewski[2] Government, an administration of national unity set up in 1919; Seyda was also chairman of the parliamentary commission which drafted the second Polish Constitution (the first dated from 1791), *viz.* that of 1921. He later became First President of the Polish Supreme Court. In the family circle, Seyda often talked about historical events he had witnessed, and these reminiscences made an impression on young Krzysztof.

Another great uncle of his, Roman Leitgeber, was the majority shareholder in Drukarnia Polska S.A. in Poznań which published several newspapers. The editor of one of them, *Kurier Poznański*, was Marian Seyda, a member of the Polish National Committee in Paris during the Great War and former Foreign Minister.[3] Though not holding any high public office (he was a member of the City Council), Leitgeber was rather influential in the National Party, a centre-right political organisation, especially powerful in western Poland.[4]

Still another great uncle and Krzysztof's godfather, Witold Hedinger, was President of the Poznań City Council and senator.

One can also point to another politically active relative, this one rather distant, but quite popular with the family, Wojciech Trąmpczyński, Speaker of the Diet and subsequently President of the Senate.

His uncle Bolesław Leitgeber was in the Polish foreign service both before and during the Second World War, with a stint in journalism in between. In the Thirties he settled in England. After the war, he joined the United Nations Secretariat. He travelled widely and wrote books. He also

---

[2] A famous pianist and an ardent Polish patriot who was on friendly terms with President Woodrow Wilson and his adviser, Colonel House.

[3] He left Poland at the beginning of the Second World War and was a member of the Polish Government first in France and thereafter in London.

[4] After 1945, Leitgeber and Skubiszewski enjoyed discussing politics for hours on end.

spent some years in India and adored that country. Young Krzysztof admired his colourful uncle.

WAR AND OCCUPATION

When the Second World War broke out in 1939, Krzysztof was thirteen. During the German campaign in Poland he found himself in the theatre of war where he survived many airraids and some fighting. The ordeal of that campaign, the wounded, the dead, fires, the sudden and large-scale destruction made a great and lasting impression on the boy. Soon after the fighting was over the Skubiszewski family was expelled by the German occupying authorities: first from their home at Poznań and then from a nearby village. They had to go to central Poland which the Nazis had organised as a dependency of the Reich, the so-called "General Government". Apart from a few items they lost all their property and there was never any compensation.

But the holocaust was the most horrible experience of the war. Skubiszewski had witnessed the forcible rounding up, by the occupant, of the Jewish inhabitants of a small town in central Poland, Międzyrzec Podlaski, and their deportation to one of the death camps set up by Nazi Germany. In 1943 he was in Warsaw when the Jews, locked up in the "Jewish district" created by the occupying authorities, rose up heroically against the Nazi barbarians. He says that he will never forget the sight and smell of the huge columns of smoke rising over and enveloping the "ghetto".

In Warsaw he attended a high school which in 1940–42 was partly and in 1942–1944 entirely clandestine: the occupying authorities allowed Poles to have only elementary and some vocational education.[5] Those caught attending the prohibited schools were severely punished. Once in 1942 he was interrogated by the German security police (the SD). It was only by coincidence that he was not deported to Germany as a forced labourer; his name was on the list of deportees and a summons had already been issued. When the Red Army entered the Podlasie region, where he was staying at that time, he was interrogated by the Soviet security service (the NKVD). During the war several of his relatives were killed, some in Katyń, the place where the NKVD massacred several thousands of Polish officers who were prisoners of war.

---

[5] In the latter period of the occupation the Germans allowed part of the Warsaw Technological University [Politechnika Warszawska] to function.

EDUCATION

Between 1932 and 1938 he attended a private elementary school in Poznań. In the years of 1938–1945 he received his secondary education in Poznań, Warsaw [Szkoła Mazowiecka], and Biała Podlaska where in 1945 he passed the final examination [matura]; he was admitted to that examination already in 1944 in Warsaw, but could not take it because of a long illness and, later, because of war events.

For some time during his high school years he intended to study agriculture and forestry. But towards the end of the war his definitive choice was law, and in particular international law. As early as 1942 he wrote an essay on security and arbitration.

From 1945 to 1949 he read law at the University of Poznań obtaining, in 1949, the degree of *magister iuris*. His graduation paper was a comparative study of the immunities and privileges of government representatives to, and functionaries of, the League of Nations and the United Nations. A year later, in 1950, he submitted his doctoral dissertation at the same Faculty; its title was "Conditions of Admission to Membership in the United Nations". The University accepted it, yet a supervisory organ in Warsaw refused the Poznań publisher the authorization required for its publication. Even a four page summary of the dissertation could be published after some years only although it did bear the date of 1950. Both the graduation paper and the doctoral thesis were written under the formal supervision of Professor Antoni Peretiatkowicz – formal, because the latter, a constitutional lawyer, only deputized for Professor Bohdan Winiarski, who was on leave of absence from Poznań while at The Hague Court.[6] Skubiszewski was a member of Peretiatkowicz's seminar on public law. He also followed the course in private international law by Professor Leon Babiński, the curator of the Chair of International Law when Skubiszewski started working there, as a volunteer. He was in daily contact with Dr. (later Professor) Alfons Klafkowski attending his classes on international law. Skubiszewski owes much to the teachings in the theory of law by Professor Czesław Znamierowski.[7]

As in 1956 the Communist Government of Poland began to allow travel abroad, Skubiszewski chose The Hague as his first foreign destination. He attended the lectures at the Academy of International Law. In early 1957 he went to the European University Centre at Nancy in France, receiving his

---

[6] K.J. Skubiszewski remained in very close contact with Judge Winiarski until his death in 1969.

[7] An important element in Skubiszewski's education in that field was Professor Lon L. Fuller's class in jurisprudence which he attended at Harvard.

Diploma of Higher European Studies, after which he went to Harvard Law School (Master of Laws, 1958).

The happy time of studies abroad was marred by his father's sudden death at the end of 1957.

In 1960 he returned to The Hague, this time to the Research Centre of the Academy. In the same year he completed his "habilitation" at the Faculty of Law, Adam Mickiewicz University in Poznań, becoming Dozent of International Law. That degree[8] would normally open the door to a professorship. His dozentship thesis dealt with the legal aspects of money in occupied territory. This time the book was published without any difficulties from the censor.

ACADEMIC WORK IN COMMUNIST POLAND

Skubiszewski had developed an interest in international law and relations already in his high school years. He maintained that interest while in law school and after graduating from it he concentrated on this discipline. His choice of an academic career was determined not only by his interest in law but there were other reasons as well. He did not feel like joining the bar, and as time went by and Poland's satellite status consolidated, it became clear to him that diplomatic service or journalism (he vaguely harboured such ideas) were excluded. Furthermore, he was, no doubt, greatly affected by his father's devotion to academic work. It may be added that his father's brother Feliks was also an academic teacher: he was professor of surgery and co-founder of the State university at Lublin and of its Faculty of Medicine.

Between 1948 and 1960 Krzysztof Skubiszewski held various teaching posts at the Chair of International Law of Poznań University, starting as a voluntary assistant teacher. He never embraced the Marxist doctrine (and there was a policy of imposing it), nor did he ever join the Communist Party[9] or any of the political organisations affiliated to it. During the Stalinist period, *i.e.* between 1948 and 1954 or thereabouts, he was treated with some suspicion by those in political control of the University: his lectures were interrupted by Communist activists, his teaching was supervised, and his writings criticized as "legalistic" and "formalistic". In 1954, during a confer-

---

[8] Dozent as a degree should be distinguished from dozent as a paid post. Skubiszewski had both. Especially in 1968 and shortly thereafter the Ministry of Higher Education in Warsaw appointed as dozent a number of assistant teachers or lecturers who did not possess the degree of dozent. This policy was dictated by non-academic reasons.

[9] This English term is used here for Polska Partia Robotnicza [PPR] and its successor as of December 1948 Polska Zjednoczona Partia Robotnicza [PZPR].

ence on the history of Gdańsk, his views were described by a Communist dignitary as "scientifically false and politically more than harmful". He would probably have lost his job, were it not for the support and help of Professor Alfons Klafkowski, holder of the Chair. The printing of his first substantial journal article – dealing with the problem of German statehood – was stopped by the censor but was released six months later with its concluding part amputated.

After "habilitation" Skubiszewski was dozent at the same Chair from 1961 to 1973. He was elected Vice-Dean of the Poznañ Faculty of Law for the period 1961–1963. Following completion of his term he went to New York as a Visiting Scholar at the School of International Affairs of Columbia University where he stayed during the academic year 1963–1964. At Columbia he wrote the first draft of a study on the political influence of the U.N. General Assembly. While there, the Carnegie Endowment for International Peace invited him to join a team of jurists from different countries which under the chairmanship of Professor Max Sorensen prepared a collective manual of international law; it was the first endeavour of this kind in the writings on international law. Also while at Columbia University his wish, which he had had since his first private visit to the Secretariat of the United Nations in 1958, seemed to come through: there was a real chance of him being employed by the Office of Legal Affairs. But the matter ended in failure: he did not obtain the necessary permission and authorization from the Polish Government.

He returned to Poznań in 1964 and four years later the Communist authorities refused to appoint him professor at the Adam Mickiewicz University. The reasons were political. Generally, the Communist authorities did not trust him. Occasionally, he would openly criticize their policies; he also refused to accept the relevance of the Communist Party in managing the University and its affairs. More specifically, in 1968, he supported students' demands for liberalization of conditions in the country and condemned the antisemitic government policies and the invasion of Czechoslovakia. The latter point led the Public Prosecutor to consider the possibility of instituting criminal proceedings against Skubiszewski. But the matter was dropped and Skubiszewski could continue teaching as dozent, although the newly created Section [Zakład] of the Law of International Organisations which he headed was liquidated under the guise of Faculty "restructuring".

In 1969 his book on the *Western Frontier of Poland* was held up by the censor. After some wrangling the book did appear but only in a limited number of copies each bearing the inscription "published as manuscript; it was not offered for sale in the book shops but could be ordered directly from the publisher. Then came a surprise. In 1970 talks started between Poland and the Federal Republic of Germany on the normalization of relations, including the issue of the frontier. Skubiszewski's publication turned out to be the most recent and detailed one on that subject. Undersecretary of State Józef Winiewicz found the book very useful during those talks. Professor Resich of Warsaw University, who was the chairman of the Council of the Polish Institute of International Affairs (an agency of the Foreign Ministry), also had a high opinion of the book and was instrumental in the Council then awarding Skubiszewski the Institute's first prize for "the best book of the year on international problems". Soon thereafter, a prize by the Minister of Higher Education followed. The ban on the book was lifted and the remaining 100 copies were sold in four academic book shops in Cracow, Gdańsk, Poznań and Warsaw.

There was another complication in the turbulent years of 1968 and 1969. In Communist Poland lack of housing space was acute; it was, moreover, controlled by the State which determined that an individual could only occupy up to about ten square meters of housing space. For this reason he had to vacate the apartment he shared with his mother and they each moved to different, much smaller, studios. As a result, his conditions of life and work deteriorated considerably. In addition, he had to get rid of the larger pieces of furniture and of many books (he had no office to save them in). The loss of books was especially painful to him.

In 1970 Skubiszewski was offered a visiting professorship at the Faculty of Law, University of Geneva. His friends there thought of it as a means of a quiet relocation from Poland to Switzerland. He could travel to Geneva only at the end of January 1971 after surmounting various difficulties which, however, did not come to an end. Shortly after his departure he was reprimanded by the Rector of the Poznań University for "insulting the Members of the (Communist) Party" and the decision was taken to withdraw his passport (but, fortunately, he was already abroad).[10] There were also some obstacles in regard to his next trip which was to England; from mid-December 1971 to 31 July 1972 he was a Visiting Fellow at All Souls College, Oxford. In the meantime, at the Zagreb Session of 1971, Skubiszewski was elected to the Institut de Droit international. He would soon become rapporteur on the subject of multilateral conventions and internationally enacted norms.

---

[10] In those days, Polish passports were issued for each separate trip. After the trip, the passport, though no longer valid, had to be returned to the Passport Office.

In 1973 Skubiszewski was officially transferred from Poznań University to the Institute of Law, Polish Academy of Sciences in Warsaw and was appointed professor there. The Communists in Poznań did not exactly regret his departure. He missed teaching and the contact with students but the attitude towards him in the capital city was better; the Director of the Institute, Professor Adam Łopatka, was helpful in that respect. And in the Seventies, the Communist Party started to adopt a more open attitude towards the intelligentsia. Although Skubiszewski was not permitted to accept another visiting professorship in Geneva, he was decorated with the Gold Cross of Merit in 1977 and, on his sixtieth birthday, with the Knight's Cross of the Order of Polonia Restitua. In 1979 he could go to Geneva for one semester.

A word should also be said about his teaching abroad. Between 1963 and 1988 he lectured at the Universities of Nottingham and London (1963); International Faculty of Comparative Law, Strasbourg (1966); Graduate Institute of International Studies, Geneva (1966); Student International Law Clubs of Harvard (1964), Duke (1964) and Oxford (1972) Universities; College of Europe, Bruges (Belgium), which he visited three times in the Seventies; Max-Planck Institute of Law, Heidelberg and the Universities of Saarland (in Saarbrücken), Vienna, Graz and Paris II (in the Eighties). He delivered the Hersch Lauterpacht Memorial Lecture, Cambridge (1985). And, as already indicated, he was twice visiting professor at Geneva University.

To sum up his teaching, which at Poznań lasted for twenty five years, it may be said that he has put a lot of time and energy in it. He supported the students in their extra-curricular activities to learn more about international affairs. In the years of 1960–1973 he was the curator of the United Nations Student Association at Poznań.

MORE ABOUT RESEARCH

Turning now specifically to Skubiszewski's research activity, in 1945 he prepared a two-hundred-page manuscript on various historical, political and economic problems of the former German eastern territories which the Potsdam Agreement on the Western Frontier of Poland submitted to the administration of the Polish State. But at the end of that year he had to concentrate on his law studies and found no time to prepare that manuscript for possible publication. His first field of legal research was the United Nations. Difficulties with censorship and political pressures intended to compel authors to write in the vein of Marxism (whatever that meant) and Communist expectations and propaganda made Skubiszewski realize that the field of the United Nations would remain closed to any objective study, in particular if publication of the resulting writings was insisted on. Indeed, he revisited the U.N.-related problems, and generally the law of international organisations as late as the 1960's (in this respect Professor Louis B. Sohn's course in United Nations law which Skubiszewski took while at Harvard was very helpful).

In the meantime, there arose another opportunity. In a sense it was linked to his interest as apparent from the above-mentioned manuscript which he produced in 1945. The Western Institute [Instytut Zachodni] in Poznań was a dynamic body which concentrated on the Polish-German relations in their different aspects and on the newly acquired territories under the Potsdam Agreement. It was in that Institute that Skubiszewski found opportunities for having his writings published thanks to the forthcoming attitudes of the founder of the Institute, Professor Zygmunt Wojciechowski, and of Professor Klafkowski. As a result, he became, through his research and publications on the above topics, part of what was sometimes referred to in Poland as "the Poznań school of international law", that "school" focused in the years 1945–1975 or thereabouts mainly on legal issues of the post-war settlement regarding Germany.

At Nancy, apart from his regular student duties, he worked on the law of concordats. He attended the guest seminars and lectures on this subject by Professor Gabriel Le Bras; also those by Professors Claude-Albert Colliard and Maurice Duverger on religion and politics in Europe. His diploma *mémoire*, submitted to Professor Charles Chaumont, analysed the situation with regard to concordats in the former eastern territories of Germany under Polish administration.

At Harvard Law School he concentrated on classes and examinations, but also did research. It was at Professor Richard R. Baxter's seminar on the legal aspects of economic warfare that he started preparing his book on money in occupied territory.

His long-standing interest in the enactment of law by international organisations and related problems finally developed as a result of suggestions made by Elihu Lauterpacht, then lecturer and later professor at Cambridge University, in his capacity of Director of Studies at the Research Centre of the Hague Academy which Centre Skubiszewski attended in 1960. There was a sequel to this when in 1963–64 he did research at Columbia University on the U.N. General Assembly; there he had the benefit of advice by Professors Leland M. Goodrich and Louis Henkin. And Skubiszewski's reports to the Institut de Droit international have already been mentioned.

Also, his summer trips to Geneva in the Sixties were very useful for his research on international organisations. It is then that he met Professor Krystyna Marek with whom he shared the same deep devotion to international law.

In 1989 the Institute of International Law [Institut für internationales Recht], Kiel University, Germany, appointed Skubiszewski to its Council. It may be added that for the fifteen years between 1974–1989 he was systematically attending the Kiel symposia on international law.

It is true that Skubiszewski has found much inspiration in the centres of learning abroad. Yet most of his research and writing was done at home. Here it is not possible to assess his contribution to the science of international law. The list of Skubiszewski's publications speaks for itself. To put it in a nutshell, Skubiszewski has done ample research on the legal aspects of Polish-German relations, in particular the border between the two countries; on the use of force by states, law of armed conflicts, and belligerent occupation; on the law of international organisations; and on the theory of international law, including sources of that law and the relationship between international law and municipal law.

His research was rewarded by the Polish prizes of 1970 referred to above. In 1984 he was awarded the research prize of the Alexander von Humboldt Foundation.

He was elected as a member of the Society of Friends of Sciences in Poznañ, the Western Institute, the Institut de Droit international, the Société Française pour le Droit International and the Polish Academy of Sciences. This election which took place in 1989 shortly before the political breakthrough was also a sign of the changing wind in the field of learning in Poland. In the earlier circumstances he stood no chance of admittance to that body. He also joined the American Society of International Law (in 1958), the Polish Branch of the International Law Association and the Association Henri Capitant des Amis de la Culture Juridique Française.

To conclude the account covering the years 1945–1989 one question which was sometimes asked should be answered. Why did Skubiszewski not remain in the West? There he would, after all, have had much better conditions of work, and of life in general, than at home. Skubiszewski does not deny that he was thinking of settling down, in the long run, in a Western country. He did have some real opportunities: he had strong links with Geneva; a British friend, supported by others, saw a clear chance for Skubiszewski in a large English university; and a Belgian university was offering him a visiting professorship with a view to future tenure. In these instances the initiative was with foreign quarters. But there was also room for Skubiszewski to take the first step at other places and institutions. Indeed, he had tried to obtain a job with the United Nations.

With regard to the initial period when the Communists authorities first permitted travel abroad – that period covering roughly the time between 1956 and 1960 – Skubiszewski's reply is that he definitely owed the University of Poznań full loyalty and that he had a duty to teach there. In 1956–1957 his University had been more than helpful in his efforts to get passports. The studies in France and in the United States were essential, and the scholarships Skubiszewski obtained at Nancy and at Harvard were far from covering all his expenses; he was receiving the difference from the Ministry of Higher Education through the support of the University (such aid was necessary in view of the foreign currency regulations and the nonconvertibility of the Polish currency).

In the 1960's the situation changed: the University was no longer able to help him in securing exit permits. As private individuals could then open foreign currency accounts, there was more independence in that respect. In addition, he thought that he had worked at the same university long enough and, as every ordinary citizen in those days in Poland, for a rather poor salary at that. Moreover, he was increasingly facing difficulties from the Communist Party and his future was more uncertain than ever. There was, consequently, no moral obstacle to moving elsewhere. But in the meantime his siblings had left Poznań. He was by then the only person to take care of his aging mother and did not like the idea of leaving her behind.

INTEREST IN POLITICS

Professor Skubiszewski's interest in politics was early and systematic. As we have seen, there were some family traditions in this respect.

Throughout the interwar period Poles were divided between the proponents and opponents of Józef Piłsudski.[11] In the 1930's the opposition to the post-Piłsudski régime included the three main political parties in the country: the Peasant Party, the Socialists and the National Party. The controversies were acute and once Krzysztof started going to high school he and his schoolmates often discussed them. But at home no party politics were present, nor did they find any support. The emphasis there was on those fundamentals

[11] A fighter for the country's independence from his early youth, he was the victorious Commander-in-chief in the war against Soviet Russia (1919–20) and the first head of State of the reconstructed Poland in 1918–1922. His *coup d'état* of 1926 progressively gave the system of government an authoritarian flavour, especially under the Constitution and the restrictive electoral law of 1935.

of public life which served best the maintenance of the freshly regained independence of the country.

The process of the political education of young Krzysztof was speeded up by the war and enemy occupation. The armed forces were defeated, though their resistance had been brave and strong, and particularly the struggle of the Poznań Army group was, in Winston Churchill's words, "ever-glorious".[12] Polish administration ceased to exist. The military occupant was ruthless and the Nazis had no regard whatsoever for human life and dignity; neither did they have any respect for Polish property. All this constituted not only a traumatic experience, but also food for thought regarding the state of the country and its future. The conduct of war and the ever-changing international relations became a matter of daily concern to every citizen. Another terrible blow was the unexpected fall of France in 1940. All that prompted Krzysztof to read many books on history and politics. In Warsaw he often visited Władysław Studnicki (whose son, Konrad, was his schoolmate), a well-known, albeit controversial, Polish politician and political writer. During the war clandestine high school classes were held for some time at Studnicki's apartment.

Skubiszewski lived under Soviet occupation from the end of July 1944. While in Biała Podlaska (where he finished his secondary education interrupted by illness and the uprising in Warsaw) he wrote, in the Autumn of 1944, his first contribution to the underground press (the second was to come much later, in 1982, when martial law was introduced in Poland to crush the "Solidarity" movement).

When hostilities in Europe came to an end and he returned to Poznań at the beginning of July 1945 to study law there, the fate of the country was already sealed by the victorious Soviet Union. He took part in the student strike in May 1946 which was organised in protest against the arrest in Cracow by the Red Army of students there. He participated in some activities of the *Caritas Academica*, a student organisation supervised by the Black Friars, later declared illegal by the Communist authorities. In the Association of Students of Law and Economics [Koło Prawników i Ekonomistów] he was chairman of the dispute resolution panel and, for two years, chairman of the general meeting. Especially there did it come to clashes with the Communists.

As a student he found the idea of the United Nations very attractive. So he arranged with the Department of Information of the U.N. Secretariat that

---

[12] W.S. CHURCHILL, THE SECOND WORLD WAR, Vol. 1: THE GATHERING STORM, Houghton Mifflin Co., Boston (1948), p. 445.

he would regularly receive from them various publications which helped him to spread basic knowledge about the Organization, thus presenting a picture of it different from the official Polish-Communist propaganda.

On 28 June 1956 riots broke out in Poznań against the Communist misgovernment and oppression. Skubiszewski who lived close the place of fighting helped to maintain telephone contact with the ambulance service to evacuate the wounded. His sister was later interrogated by the Security police. In the autumn of that year some persons arrested during the riots were put to trial. Skubiszewski accompanied two foreign observers to the trials, Elwyn Jones, Q.C., Labour Member of the House of Commons at that time (he later was Lord Chancellor), and Jules Wolf, a Belgian barrister. Since those memorable days he has remained in touch with the former.

In 1958, while at Harvard, he met Zbigniew Brzeziński. Since that time they have remained in contact. In 1977 Brzeziński became Security Adviser to President Jimmy Carter.

From 1958 on Skubiszewski started to meet exiled Poles abroad who were combating Communist domination and indoctrination of Poland and were endeavouring to have her independence restored. These contacts, which took place mainly in London, but also in Canada, Switzerland and the United States, included Edward Count Raczyński;[13] Kazimierz Sabbat;[14] Wacław Jędrzejewicz[15]; Tadeusz Bielecki, Antoni Dargas, Zygmunt Celichowski and Witold Leitgeber;[16] Józef Lipski;[17] Bolesław Wierzbiański;[18] Zygmunt Kallenbach;[19] and Stanisław Strzetelski.[20] Skubiszewski's brother-in-law, Marek Święszkowski, was director of finance of the Polish Government in exile.

---

13 Polish Ambassador to the Court of St. James, 1934–1945; Head (as Minister of State) of the Ministry of Foreign Affairs, 1941–1943; President of Poland in exile (1979–1986). When Skubiszewski became Foreign Minister Raczyński gave him a lot of support, especially in the crisis of 1992.

14 Premier and, from 1986 until his sudden death in 1989, President of Poland in exile.

15 Minister of Education in the 1930's; he was a long-time collaborator of Józef Piłsudski. It may be added that in Poznań Skubiszewski was between 1950 and 1965 in close touch with another of Piłsudski's Ministers, *viz.* Witold Staniewicz, former Rector of the University of Vilna. That politician's son, Restytut W. Staniewicz, a friend of Skubiszewski's, has been strongly involved in various underground activities in opposition to the Communist *régime* in Poland (1976–1989).

16 At various times leaders of the National Party in exile. The contact with Leitgeber went back to 1956.

17 Ambassador of Poland to Berlin, 1934–1939.

18 A well-known journalist, editor of NOWY DZIENNIK (New York City).

19 A Geneva banker who supported non-Marxist science and culture in Poland.

20 Head of the Polish desk, Committee for Free Europe, New York and Director of the Polish Institute of Arts and Sciences in America.

His short but frequent stays for scholarly purposes in Geneva in the 1960's and 1970's gave him an insight in the diplomatic life in and around the European Office of the United Nations and of several specialized agencies of the U.N.

The visiting fellowship at All Souls College (Oxford, 1971–72), where several former and present British politicians were fellows, created for Skubiszewski a unique opportunity of learning a lot about British politics.

Skubiszewski's reaction to the political disturbances in Poland in 1968 has already been referred to above.

In 1970 Skubiszewski published his first article in *Tygodnik Powszechny*, a weekly which brought together an influential group of Catholic intellectuals, politicians and political writers. Since its inception in 1945 that periodical always opposed Communism, also during those long periods when nobody else, except the Church itself, did so in Poland. Skubiszewski contributed to the *Tygodnik Powszechny* from time to time.

POLITICAL ACTIVITY IN THE 1980's

Skubiszewski joined the "Solidarity" movement in 1980 before that organisation was officially registered. In 1981 he served briefly on the programme council for lectures and adult education of the Poznań Region of "Solidarity". During 1981–1984 he was a member of the Social Council set up by the Primate of Poland to advise him on various public issues. This Council was the first body in the country to draw up specific proposals to solve the crisis resulting from the introduction of martial law by General Jaruzelski on 13 December 1981. Between 1984 and 1989 he represented the Secretariat of the Polish Episcopate on the Coordinating Committee of the German-Polish Forum.

In 1986 Skubiszewski accepted General Wojciech Jaruzelski's invitation to join his newly created Consultative Council. That decision had not been easy: General Jaruzelski was responsible for the introduction of martial law and the delegalization of "Solidarity". Together with a few other members opposing the Communist *régime* (the great majority of that Council was either Communist or their fellow-travellers) Skubiszewski spoke in favour of change in Poland and of her independence. He served on the Council until its dissolution in June 1989. There was no room for the Council after the reinstatement of "Solidarity" and its victory in the general election of the same month. Skubiszewski felt relieved.

Earlier, in 1988, he had taken part in the founding of the Political Club "Order and Freedom" in Poznań. It was the first organisation in opposition to the Communists which they recognized as lawful and it was thus permitted to act openly. Its programme was christian-democratic. Its first chairman was Marek Jurek, soon a well-known right wing member of the Polish Diet.

In the 1980's, Skubiszewski also participated in a group of jurists who advised the delegation of the Church in talks with the Communist Government on a convention with the Holy See. They were Jacek Ambroziak (soon to become Head, in the rank of Cabinet member, of the Office of the Council of Ministers), Professor Wiesław Chrzanowski (Speaker of the Lower House, 1991–1993) and Andrzej Stelmachowski (President of the Senate, 1989–1991). When they were discussing various points arising in Church-State negotiations none ever thought that they would rise to those high offices of the State they did. But the wind of change was already blowing.

In the Summer of 1989, Skubiszewski was not quite well. He felt very tired. Living conditions were rather poor and difficult. With sorrow, he decided not to go to Santiago di Compostella in Spain to attend the session of the Institut de Droit international; up till then he had never been absent from any of the Institut's meetings. At the end of August, he went to Warsaw to read at a conference of historians a paper on the Ribbentrop-Molotov Pact, so far a forbidden subject. Skubiszewski recalls that on his return journey he was thinking of a longer stay abroad to charge his batteries. He thought that he could make use of the prize of the Humboldt Foundation and do research in Germany. There also seemed to be some prospects to visit All Souls College in Oxford again. He was looking forward to these trips and was already planning them on the quiet Sunday of 3 September when the telephone rang. It was the newly appointed Undersecretary of State in the Office of the Council of Ministers: "Would not Professor Skubiszewski mind coming the next day to Warsaw? The Prime Minister wanted to see him urgently. A car would wait at the railway station for him."

Thus began a new chapter in Skubiszewski's life; some would say probably the most significant one.

AT THE HELM OF FOREIGN POLICY

As a result of the political breakthrough in the country a new Government was established on 12 September 1989 at the initiative of Lech Wałęsa who persuaded the United Peasant Party and the Democratic Party[21] to join "Solidarity", thus creating a majority in the Diet. That Government also in-

[21] Up till that moment those parties had been the satellites of the Communist Party.

cluded four ministers from the Communist Party and was presided over by Tadeusz Mazowiecki, a Catholic politician. Prime Minister Mazowiecki had invited Skubiszewski to serve on his cabinet as the Minister of Foreign Affairs, a portfolio Skubiszewski kept for the next four years, *i.e.* till 26 October 1993, in all the Governments made up of political parties originating in "Solidarity".

The task he faced was enormous. Apart from having to inject new blood in the Communist dominated diplomatic service, and that was no small job, Skubiszewski had to devise and pursue the foreign policy of a country which suddenly found itself in the fast lane of the road to regaining its independence after a break of fifty years. He had to meet this challenge not only in the framework of the Government, but also by respecting the powers and functions of the then President, General Jaruzelski, and in collaboration with the Parliament where the Communist Party was still very prominent, the 1989 general election not having been entirely free.

The aims of "Solidarity" and of the new Government were to recover and strengthen Poland's sovereignty, build up the country's internal and external security and bring about the democratic transformation, including a market economy. To fulfil these ambitions Poland's foreign policy was to be firmly set on the course of European priorities while not neglecting co-operation with countries outside of Europe.[22]

The highlights of Skubiszewski's foreign policy were, first of all, the development of strong links with the West, including Poland's association with the European Communities. That association was meant – as it still is – to lead to membership in the European Union.

In 1991 and 1992 Poland concluded new political treaties with six of its seven neighbours (the treaty with the seventh, Lithuania, was signed after Skubiszewski's departure from the Government, but it was practically ready at that moment). These treaties reflected a fundamental change in affairs between Poland and her neighbours. In particular, Poland and Germany eliminated various contentious issues which had accumulated during the 1980's. They signed an agreement confirming the Oder-Neisse frontier. During that time, a very close rapport developed with Germany. Skubiszewski, an ardent advocate of the unification of Germany, made a significant contribution in securing Poland's participation in the Paris session of the "2 + 4" Conference on German unity. It was he who launched the idea

[22] For instance, K.J. Skubiszewski normalized relations with Israel and established them with the Republic of Korea and with Paraguay. He reinvigorated ties not only with Latin America, especially with Argentina, Brazil, Chile and Uruguay but with China, Japan, and Australia as well.

of a German-Polish community of interests. He initiated the treaty of friendship and solidarity with France too. He was also responsible for his country's strong involvement in the tripartite cooperation among France, Germany and Poland, the so-called "Weimar triangle" which resulted from the 1991 initiative taken by the then German Federal Foreign Minister, Hans-Dietrich Genscher. That triangle was a novelty in European diplomacy. After the somewhat inconclusive Bratislava conference in early 1990, Skubiszewski contributed decisively to the revival of the concept of special cooperation between Czechoslovakia, Hungary and Poland and, later, to the activity of what became known as the Visegrad group. He emphasized the need for "new regionalism" in Central Europe which, apart from Visegrad, comprised the Baltic Council and the "Sexagonale" (today the Central European Initiative).

The withdrawal of Russian troops from Poland was eventful. This difficult operation was prepared and negotiated between 1990 and 1992 by the Polish Foreign Ministry, yet it was finally brought about by the personal diplomacy of President Wałęsa. Thus, apart from the short period of time between the World Wars Poland was at last free from foreign troops that had remained on her territory since the second half of the 18th century. The end of Soviet domination in Central Europe enabled Poland to establish new relations with her Eastern neighbours, especially after the dissolution of the Soviet Union. The breakthrough caused by the dissolution was preceded by bold Polish initiatives towards the Ukraine, Russia and Belarus starting as early as 1990 when no one either questioned the coherence of Gorbachov's Soviet Union or was even prepared for its dissolution. In the aftermath of that dissolution and as a result of instability in the former U.S.S.R., Poland raised the issue of the Eastern enlargement of NATO to secure her membership therein.

A word must also be said about the negotiation and signing of the Concordat with the Holy See in 1993. The conclusion of the Concordat was Skubiszewski's last important move as Foreign Minister. The Concordat, a modern instrument adapted to the needs of the 21st century, creates a proper balance between the Church and a State with a long tradition of Catholicism as part of its national and social life. According to Skubiszewski who himself had headed the Polish negotiating team, it could be a model for other countries.

One should equally emphasize Skubiszewski's concern with the conformity of national policies to international law. He regularly spoke of this at the United Nations. Protection and promotion of human rights were high on his agenda, as was the settlement of disputes. Poland became the first country of the defunct Soviet bloc to recognize as compulsory the jurisdiction of the International Court of Justice under Article 36 of its Statute. Poland has joined the small group of CSCE States which drafted the Convention on the Court of Conciliation and Arbitration.

Skubiszewski took advantage of his official trips abroad to lecture all over the world before bodies devoted to the study of international affairs.[23] On these occasions he dealt mainly with the issues of security in Central Europe.

In 1991, when a new Secretary-General of the United Nations was to be elected, Skubiszewski was unofficially considered by some Governments. In forecasts his name was sometimes included among the top few candidates. He himself unequivocally excluded running for that office as he thought himself unprepared for that function; he was definitely in favour of an African candidate and, in particular, fully supported the candidacy of Boutros Boutros-Ghali.

In late Spring 1992, it came to a political crisis which led to the fall of the Government headed by Jan Olszewski. Under the circumstances Skubiszewski had welcome the end of that administration, but the background of the crisis was very difficult for him. But there was continuity: Skubiszewski was appointed to the next Government, presided by Madame Hanna Suchocka, by the way, his former student from Poznań.

In early 1993 Skubiszewski had strong support for his candidacy to the International Court of Justice to fill the vacancy created by Judge Lach's demise. He was nominated by eleven national groups[24] and had the backing of many Governments. He withdrew one day before the voting which took place at the United Nations on 10 May 1993. He did this on the urgent, one can even say, dramatic, appeal of the Prime Minister of Poland. As his election was regarded as a certainty, the Prime Minister feared that if Skubiszewski left there would be a crisis. He decided to stay because he thought that he owed it to his Prime Minister. He had bad luck however: three weeks later, the Government fell anyhow, and, though maintained by the President of the Republic, in less than four months it was out of office as a result of the general election.

During his time at the Foreign Ministry Skubiszewski was probably the least controversial politician in Poland. He enjoyed a large measure of approval and in public opinion polls he was frequently among the top three most popular politicians.

[23] In Europe they included the Cyril Foster Lecture, Oxford (1992) and the Hugh Gaitskell Lecture, Nottingham (1992). He read papers at the Royal Institute of International Affairs (Chatham House), London (1992); at an international conference at All Souls College, Oxford (1992); and at the Institut d'Études Politiques, Paris (1992).

[24] Austria, Belgium, France, Greece, Italy, Luxembourg, Poland, Spain, Switzerland, the United Kingdom and the United States; U.N. document A/47/940 and S/25726, 5 May 1993.

The Holy See and some foreign States recognised Skubiszewski's contribution to mutual causes.[25] On Skubiszewski's departure from the Ministry, President Wałęsa decorated him with the Grand Cross of the Order of Polonia Restituta.

Together with the French and German Foreign Ministers, Roland Dumas and Hans-Dietrich Genscher, Skubiszewski received in 1992 the (German) Wartburg Prize. In the same year he received two Polish prizes, the Organic Work Prize at Poznań and Father Idzi Radziszewski Prize of the Catholic University of Lublin.

The Universities of Ghent, Mainz, Torino, Liège and Geneva conferred upon him their honorary doctorates. He was also made Honorary Master of the Bench, Gray's Inn, London (1990), Honorary Member of the American Society of International Law (1991) and Honorary Professor of the University of Bucharest (1993). He was admitted to the Argentine Council of International Relations as well.

Government duties left him no time for academic work in the field of international law. The rare exceptions gave him much pleasure. He felt honoured when invited to deliver the inaugural Lord Wilberforce Lecture in London in 1990; he accepted and spoke on legal aspects of unilateral acts of States. He also lectured at the Hague Academy of International Law, thirty-six years after he himself had attended the Academy courses. His subject was a classical one: the relationship between international law and municipal law. His task was complicated by the fact that having been unable to prepare a manuscript, he brought with him a suitcase full of papers and notes and after each lecture he would immediately return to the Park Hotel to prepare the lecture for the next day. At the same time, he would also read the dispatches from home and reply to them. Still, in spite of the pressures, he found that week at the Academy a refreshing break from Warsaw politics.

AFTER OCTOBER 1993

When the new Government[26] was sworn in, Skubiszewski was without any offer from the political establishment. He was not expecting any either.

---

[25] He has received the following foreign decorations: Cavaliere di Gran Croce, Ordine Piano (Holy See 1991); Grand Officier de la Légion d'honneur (1991); Gran Cruz de la Orden al Merito de Chile (1991); Grosskreuz des Verdienstordens der Bundesrepublik Deutschland (1991); Order of the Diplomatic Merit of the Republic of Korea (1991); Cross of Merit of the Republic of Hungary (1994).

[26] It consisted of the Alliance of Democratic Left (SLD) and the Polish Peasant Party (PSL).

He was not jobless as he could at any time resume his professorship at the Institute of Law.

First, however, his candidacy for a judgeship at the International Court of Justice had to be clarified. The earlier nomination of the Belgian national group covered not only the 10 May 1993 election to fill one vacancy at the Court, but extended as well to the regular elections which were to be held in the autumn of that same year. Because of that nomination Skubiszewski appeared on the list of candidates. The Polish national group also submitted his candidacy.[27] But to run again when the "East-European" seat had already been filled in May[28] was a mistake and Skubiszewski was doomed to lose. An additional mistake was committed by the Polish Permanent Mission to the United Nations at the time of voting: instead of withdrawing Skubiszewski's candidacy immediately after the first round of voting in the Security Council and the General Assembly, the Mission kept him on the list throughout the elections.[29] Skubiszewski was in hospital at the time; unaware of what was transpiring at the United Nations he could not intervene.

Yet it turned out that there was another prospect at The Hague. When he was still Foreign Minister, he was invited to join the Iran-United States Claims Tribunal there; the proposal was made in view of the resignation of President José María Ruda. In November 1993 Skubiszewski accepted, and, on 4 December 1993, he became a Member of that Tribunal and Chairman of its Chamber Two. Since 16 February 1994 he has been serving as its President. He says that he is glad to be at The Hague.

International adjudication was a field new to Professor Skubiszewski. Nonetheless, his responsibilities soon broadened. In 1994 he was appointed Judge *ad hoc* in the Case of *East Timor*[30] and in the Case of *The Gabcikovo-Nagymaros Project* before the International Court of Justice by Portugal and Slovakia, respectively. In 1994 he became a Member of the Steering Committee of the Permanent Court of Arbitration, The Hague. That Committee deals with various problems of dispute settlement in connection with Hague Convention I of 1899 and 1907. In 1995 the Polish Foreign Minister, Władysław Bartoszewski, appointed him conciliator at the Court of Conciliation and Arbitration of the Organization of Security and Co-operation in

---

27 U.N. documents A/48/433/Rev. 1 and S/26490/Rev. 1.

28 There was, it is true, a vacancy as the term of that particular judgeship would expire on 6 February 1994, but, in that instance, the election of the incumbent for a regular term was a foregone conclusion.

29 *See* especially, U.N. document A/48/PV.53, p. 2, which records the last vote and the termination of elections on 10 November 1993.

30 He wrote a Dissenting Opinion to the Judgement in that Case, *see* ICJ REPORTS 1995, at pp. 224–277.

Europe; that Court has its seat in Geneva. He belongs to the five-Member Bureau of that Court.

All this was, as Skubiszewski says, a welcome development. He also fulfils other functions in the realm of international law. Since 1993 Judge Skubiszewski has been serving on the Curatorium of the Hague Academy of International Law. He was also elected First Vice-President of the Institut de Droit international for the term 1995–1997.

He has been admitted to other scholarly bodies as well: the Académie des Sciences morales et politiques in Paris (as a correspondent), the Polish Academy in Cracow and the Deutsche Gesellschaft für Völkerrecht.

He has also a link with the United Nations. In 1993 the Secretary-General appointed him to the five-member Board of Trustees of the Voluntary Fund for Technical Cooperation, U.N. Centre for Human Rights in Geneva.

Krzysztof Skubiszewski maintains an interest in politics; not as a participant, but rather as a keen observer, interlocutor and commentator, always ready to share his experience and views. He sometimes reads a paper or makes a speech on European problems. He occasionally meets with politicians, including former colleagues. Last year, he presented, at an impressive gathering in Bad Godesberg, the memoirs of his friend Hans-Dietrich Genscher. This year he went to a not less impressive dinner in Munich to attend the launching of the German translation of the book by James A. Baker, III, on his three momentous years at the Department of State. The trip to Munich was also a reunion of five (out of seven)[31] ministers who had taken part in the Paris session of the "2 + 4" Conference on German Unity in 1990 (Poland was invited to that session).

Until 1995 he was serving on the Supervisory Board of the Foundation for German-Polish reconciliation in Warsaw. That Foundation earmarks financial assistance to the surviving Polish victims of the Nazi concentration camps and forced labour. Germany had put DM 500 million at Poland's disposal for that purpose. Skubiszewski had been co-instrumental in negotiating the relevant agreement in 1991. Since 1995 he sits on the Programme Council of the Foundation of Public Affairs in Warsaw.

As to current Polish politics, he, obviously, keeps his distance. On the other hand, there are issues which are of great interest to him. For instance, he takes part in the discussions on foreign service, the ratification of the Concordat (which he signed in 1993) and the relation between international law and Polish law in the future Constitution (for which he has submitted his suggestions to the Parliamentary Commission). In August 1996 he was

---

[31] Roland Dumas and Eduard A. Shevardnadze were unable to come.

elected Chairman of the newly founded Council on Foreign Policy in Warsaw, a nongovernmental body.

At the turn of 1994 the Chairman of the Freedom Union, a centrist political party, requested him to run, in a kind of primary, for the Polish presidency in the 1995 election, possibly on a basis broader than that particular party alone.[32] Skubiszewski refused for two totally unconnected reasons: he was unwilling to run against Lech Wałęsa; and he thought that he could not leave the Iran-United States Claims Tribunal so soon after having been appointed to it; there was work to be done and a certain trust had been placed in him.

In answer to the question to recapitulate Skubiszewski says that he can only thank God. He must also thank his parents and numerous friendly people in Poland and abroad for all that they have done for him. He is convinced that without divine protection and human support he would not have survived the war, Nazi occupation or the Stalinist period. But what is success, he ponders. What he has accomplished, he emphasizes, would not have been possible without the great assistance from others.

Krzysztof Skubiszewski is now seventy and on this anniversary his friends and colleagues wish him well. *Ad multos annos!*

---

[32] The Polish press wrote about this initiative.

Writings of Krzysztof Skubiszewski
published in the period of 1945–1995

PART ONE: INTERNATIONAL LAW

I. Books

1. Pieniądz na terytorium okupowanym. Studium prawnomiędzynarodowe ze szczególnym uwzględnieniem praktyki niemieckiej [Money in Occupied Territory. A Study in International Law with Special Reference to the Occupation Policies of Germany].

   Instytut Zachodni, Poznań 1960, pp. 404.

2. Uchwały prawotwórcze organizacji międzynarodowych. Przegląd zagadnień i analiza wstępna [Law–Making Resolutions of International Organizations].

   Poznańskie Towarzystwo Przyjaciół Nauk, Poznań 1965, pp. 201.

3. Zachodnia granica Polski w świetle traktatów [Western Frontier of Poland in the Light of Treaties].

   Instytut Zachodni, Poznań 1975, pp. 368.

   [The book listed below in Part Three of this bibliography (Zachodnia granica Polski, Gdańsk 1969, pp. 630) contains some two hundred pages on international law].

II. Lectures

1. *Les organisations régionales. Nature et portée juridique des actes des organes non juridictionnels dans les organisations d'intégration économique et de nature politique des pays de l'Est.* Faculté internationale pour l'enseignment du Droit comparé, Strasbourg 1966, pp. 69.

III. Reports to the Institut de Droit international

1. *Les techniques d'élaboration des grandes conventions multilatérales et des normes quasilégislatives internationales* (in collaboration with H. BLIX).

   Institut de Droit international, ANNUAIRE, vol. 57, 1977, PART II, S. Karger, Basel 1978 pp. 36–63 and 96–103.

2. *Resolutions of the General Assembly of the United Nations.*

   Institut de Droit international, ANNUAIRE, vol. 61, 1985, part I, Editions A. Pedone, Paris 1985, pp. 29–249 and 305–334.

IV. Contributions to Collective Manuals or to Encyclopedic Works

1. *Podmioty prawa międzynarodowego* [Subjects of International Law]; *Uznanie międzynarodowe* [International Recognition]; *Odpowiedzialność międzynarodowa* [International Responsibility]; being parts 3, 6 and 10 in: M. MUSZKAT (ed.), ZARYS PRAWA MIĘDZYNARODOWEGO PUBLICZNEGO [Outline of Public International Law].

   Wydawnictwo Prawnicze, Warszawa 1955 and 1956, Vol. I, pp. 141–159 and 169–191, Vol. II, pp. 5–23 and 239–258.

2. *Use of Force by States. Collective Security. Law of War and Neutrality.*

   Chapter XII in: MANUAL OF PUBLIC INTERNATIONAL LAW, (ed.) M. Soerensen. Macmillan, London, Melbourne, Toronto; St. Martin's Press, New York 1968; pp. 739–854. Spanish translation: Fondo de Cultura Economica, Mexico 1973.

3. *Peace and War*, Instalment 4 (1982), pp. 74–78; *International Legislation*, Instalment 5 (1983), pp. 97–104.

   In: ENCYCLOPEDIA OF PUBLIC INTERNATIONAL LAW. Published under the Auspices of the Max Planck Institute for Comparative Public Law and International Law under the Direction of Rudolf Bernhardt. North-Holland, Amsterdam – New York – Oxford.

4. *Les actes unilatéraux des Etats.*

   Chapitre IX in: M. BEDJAOUI (ed.): DROIT INTERNATIONAL. BILAN ET PERSPECTIVES. A. Pedone-UNESCO, Paris 1991, t. 1, pp. 231–251.

Unilateral Acts of States.

Chapter IX in: M. BEDJAOUI (ed.): INTERNATIONAL LAW: ACHIEVEMENTS AND PROSPECTS. Nijhoff-UNESCO, The Hague 1991, pp. 221–240.

5. *Bohdan Winiarski*, in: WIELKOPOLSKI SŁOWNIK BIOGRAFICZNY, Państwowe Wydawnictwo Naukowe, Warszawa–Poznań 1981, pp. 824–825.

V. Contributions to Collective Monographs

1. *Umowy międzynarodowe w świetle Konstytucji Polskiej Rzeczypospolitej Ludowej. Zagadnienia wybrane* [Treaties and the Constitution of the People's Republic of Poland. Selected Problems] (in collaboration with A. KLAFKOWSKI and B. WIEWIÓRA).

In: ZAGADNIENIA PRAWNE KONSTYTUCJI POLSKIEJ RZECZYPOSPOLITEJ LUDOWEJ, Państwowe Wydawnictwo Naukowe, Warszawa 1954, Vol. II, pp. 540–578 and 595–599.

2. *Aspekt prawny zagadnień polsko-niemieckich w Traktacie Wersalskim* [Legal Aspect of Polish-German Problems in the Treaty of Versailles]. Chapter XI in: PROBLEM POLSKO-NIEMIECKI W TRAKTACIE WERSALSKIM, Instytut Zachodni, Poznań 1963, pp. 324–385.

3. *Podstawowe zagadnienia polityczne i prawne w stosunkach międzynarodowych NRF* [Fundamental Political and Legal Problems in the Foreign Relations of the FRG].

Chapter X in: MONOGRAFIA NIEMIEC WSPÓŁCZESNYCH, Vol. II: NIEMIECKA REPUBLIKA FEDERALNA, Instytut Zachodni, Poznań 1965, pp. 305–354.

4. *Die Westgrenze Polens aus der Sicht der Verträge vom Jahre 1970.*

In: VOLKSREPUBLIK POLEN – BUNDESREPUBLIK DEUTSCHLAND. PROBLEME DER NORMALISIERUNG GEGENSEITIGER BEZIEHUNGEN, Instytut Zachodni, Poznań 1972, pp. 59–77.

5. *Can Future International Law Be Developed through the Resolutions of Intergovernmental Bodies?*

In: LE DROIT INTERNATIONAL DEMAIN. INTERNATIONAL LAW TOMORROW, Neuchâtel 1974, pp. 55–66.

6. *Die Empfehlungen des RGW und ihre Rechtswirkungen.*

In: RECHTSFRAGEN DER INTEGRATION UND KOOPERATION IN OST UND WEST, Duncker und Humblot, Berlin 1976, pp. 143–146.

7. Chapter I: *Introduction* and Chapter 14: *Poland and some Eastern European Countries.*

In: INDIVIDUAL RIGHTS AND THE STATE IN FOREIGN AFFAIRS: AN INTERNATIONAL COMPENDIUM. Editors: E. LAUTERPACHT and J.C. COLLIER, Praeger Publishers, New York, London 1977, pp. 1–25 and 416–459.

8. *Konkordat z 10 lutego 1925 roku. Zagadnienia prawnomiędzynarodowe* [Concordat of 10 February 1925: International Legal Problems].

In: KOŚCIÓŁ W II RZECZYPOSPOLITEJ, Wydawnictwo Towarzystwa Naukowego KUL, Lublin 1980, pp. 35–47 (two editions).

9. *Prawo międzynarodowe w porządku prawnym państwa* [International Law in the Legal Order of the State].

In: PRAWO MIĘDZYNARODOWE A PRAWO WEWNĘTRZNE W ŚWIETLE DOŚWIADCZEŃ PAŃSTW SOCJALISTYCZNYCH. Zakład Narodowy im. Ossolińskich, Wrocław–Warszawa–Kraków–Gdańsk 1980, pp. 13–52.

10. *Unity of Christian Europe and Contemporary International Law.*

In: THE COMMON CHRISTIAN ROOTS OF THE EUROPEAN NATIONS. AN INTERNATIONAL COLLOQUIUM IN THE VATICAN, Le Monnier, Florence 1982, Vol. 2, pp. 943–947.

11. *Die Potsdamer Grenze: Politik und Völkerrecht.*

In: W. KUWACZKA (ed.), ENTSPANNUNG VON UNTEN. MÖGLICHKEITEN UND GRENZEN DES DEUTSCH-POLNISCHEN DIALOGS, Burgverlag, Stuttgart–Bonn 1988, pp. 125–135.

12. *The International Court of Justice and the Security Council.*

Chapter 33 in: FIFTY YEARS OF THE INTERNATIONAL COURT OF JUSTICE. ESSAYS IN HONOUR OF SIR ROBERT JENNINGS. Editors: V. LOWE and M. FITZMAURICE. Grotius Publications – Cambridge University Press 1996, pp. 606–629.

VI. Contributions to Collections of Essays (Festschrifts)

1. *A New Source of the Law of Nations: Resolutions of International Organisations.*

RECUEIL D'ÉTUDES DE DROIT INTERNATIONAL EN HOMMAGE À PAUL GUGGENHEIM, Genève 1968, pp. 508–520.

2. *The Problem of the Application of Military Measures by the General Assembly of the United Nations.*

MÉLANGES OFFERTS À JURAJ ANDRASSY, La Haye 1968, pp. 248–268.

3. *Gdańsk and the Dissolution of the Free City.*

RECHT IM DIENST DES FRIEDENS. FESTSCHRIFT FÜR EBERHARD MENZEL ZUM 65. Geburtstag, Duncker und Humblot, Berlin 1975, pp. 469–485.

4. *Das Verhältnis zwischen Völkerrecht und polnischem Recht.*

FESTSCHRIFT FÜR RUDOLF BINDSCHEDLER, Verlag Stämpfli und Cie AG, Bern 1980, pp. 241–259.

5. *Remarks on the Interpretation of the United Nations Charter.*

VÖLKERRECHT ALS RECHTSORDNUNG – INTERNATIONALE GERICHTSBARKEIT – MENSCHENRECHTE. FESTSCHRIFT FÜR HERMANN MOSLER, Springer-Verlag, Berlin –Heidelberg–New York 1983, pp. 891–902.

6. *Quelques remarques sur la notion de force dans la Charte des Nations Unies.*

MÉLANGES GEORGES PERRIN, Payot, Lausanne 1984, s. 293–301.

7. *Europejska geneza prawa międzynarodowego* [The European Origin of International Law].

HISTORIA I WSPÓŁCZESNOŚĆ [essays dedicated to Marian Wojciechowski], Naczelna Dyrekcja Archiwów Państwowych, Warszawa 1987, pp. 33–42.

8. *Rezolucje Zgromadzenia Ogólnego ONZ a powstawanie prawa zwyczajowego* [U.N. General Assembly Resolutions and the Growth of Customary Law].

ACTA UNIVERSITATIS WRATISLAVIENSIS, N° 942, PRAWO CLIX [essays dedicated to Karol Wolfke], Wrocław 1987, pp. 131–140.

9. *Resolutions of the U.N. General Assembly and Evidence of Custom.*

LE DROIT INTERNATIONAL À L'HEURE DE SA CODIFICATION. ÉTUDES EN L'HONNEUR DE ROBERTO AGO, A. Giuffrè Editore, Milano 1987, vol. I, pp. 503–519.

10. *Völkerrecht und Landesrecht: Regelungen und Erfahrungen in Mittel- -und Osteuropa.*

VERFASSUNGSRECHT UND VÖLKERRECHT. GEDÄCHTNISSCHRIFT FÜR WILHELM KARL GECK, Carl Heymanns Verlag, Köln 1989, pp. 777–788.

11. *Implied Powers of International Organizations.*

INTERNATIONAL LAW AT A TIME OF PERPLEXITY. ESSAYS IN HONOUR OF SHABTAI ROSENNE, Nijhoff-Kluwer Academic Publishers, Dordrecht–Boston –London 1989, pp. 855–868.

[See also item 12 in section V above, which is a collection of essays in honour of Sir Robert Jennings. These essays concentrate exclusively on one topic, *viz.* the ICJ, and for that reason they have been placed under the heading of Collective Monographs].

VII. Articles in Journals, Yearbooks and Serial Publications *

1. *Położenie prawno-administracyjne Niemiec po ich bezwarunkowej kapitulacji* [Legal and Administrative Status of Germany after her Unconditional Surrender].

PRZEGLĄD ZACHODNI, Vol. 5, 1949, Part. 2, pp. 318–326.

2. *Zagadnienie państwa niemieckiego w prawie międzynarodowym* [The Question of the German State in International Law].

PRZEGLĄD ZACHODNI, Vol. 6, 1950, Part 1, pp. 331–377.

Some of the contributions in Polish contain summaries in English and/or French, in particular those published in CZASOPISMO PRAWNO-HISTORYCZNE, PAŃSTWO I PRAWO and RUCH PRAWNICZY, EKONOMICZNY I SOCJOLOGICZNY.

3. *Bezwarunkowa kapitulacja z 29 kwietnia 1945 roku* [Unconditional Surrender of 29 April 1945].

PRZEGLĄD ZACHODNI, Vol. 6, 1950, Part 2, pp. 546–548.

4. *Problematyka niemiecka w polskim powojennym piśmiennictwie z dziedziny prawa międzynarodowego* [German Problems in Post-war Polish Writings on International Law].

PRZEGLĄD ZACHODNI, Vol. 6, 1950, Part 2, pp. 559–581.

5. *Warunki uzyskania członkostwa Organizacji Narodów Zjednoczonych* [Conditions of Admission to Membership in the United Nations; being the summary of the writer's unpublished doctoral dissertation].

SPRAWOZDANIA POZNAŃSKIEGO TOWARZYSTWA PRZYJACIÓŁ NAUK, 1950–1951, N° 1, pp. 118–121.

6. *Umowa poczdamska jako jedyna podstawa prawna układu terytorialnego Niemiec* [The Potsdam Agreement as the Sole Basis of the Territorial Arrangement of Germany].

PRZEGLĄD ZACHODNI, Vol. 8, 1952, part 2, pp. 514–530.

7. *Uwagi o zagadnieniach prawa międzynarodowego w Konstytucj Niemieckiej Republiki Demokratycznej* [Observations on Questions of International Law in the Constitution of the German Democratic Republic].

PRZEGLĄD ZACHODNI, Vol. 9, 1953, Part 1, pp. 434–452.

8. *Umowy paryskie z 23 października 1954 r.* [Paris Agreements of 23 October 1954].

PRZEGLĄD ZACHODNI, Vol. 11, 1955, Part 2, pp. 64–131.

9. *Podmiotowość ZSRR w prawie międzynarodowym* [The U.S.S.R. as Subject of International Law].

ZESZYTY NAUKOWE UNIWERSYTETU IM. ADAMA MICKIEWICZA, PRAWO, 1956, N° 1, pp. 77–87.

10. *Gdańsk w prawie międzynarodowym w latach 1919–1939* [Gdańsk in International Law 1919–1939].

CZASOPISMO PRAWNO-HISTORYCZNE, Vol. 8, 1956, pp. 258–272.

11. *Spór o koszty stacjonowania obcych wojsk w Niemieckiej Republice Federalnej* [Dispute relating to the Cost of Stationing of Foreign Troops in the Federal Republic of Germany].

PRZEGLĄD ZACHODNI, Vol. 12, 1956, Part 1, pp. 265–290.

12. *Umowy paryskie i Konstytucja Niemieckiej Republiki Federalnej* [Paris Agreements and the Constitution of the Federal Republic of Germany].

PRZEGLĄD ZACHODNI, Vol. 12, 1956, Part 2, pp. 179–189.

13. *Czy Polska ma umowy sojusznicze z Francją i Anglią?* [Does Poland Still Have Treaties of Alliance with France and Great Britain?].

PRZEGLĄD POLSKI I OBCY, 1957, N° 1, pp. 20–25.

14. *Poland's Constitution and the Conclusion of Treaties.*

JAHRBUCH FÜR INTERNATIONALES RECHT, Vol. 7, 1956, pp. 213–228.

15. *The Present Legal Significance of Poland's Pre-War Alliances.*

ANNUAIRE DE L'A.A.A., 1957, pp. 59–66.

16. *La frontière polono-allemande en droit international.*

REVUE GÉNÉRALE DE DROIT INTERNATIONAL PUBLIC, vol. 61, 1957, pp. 242–258.

17. *Einige Bemerkungen zur Gültigkeit von Eheschliessungen in den Gebieten östlich der Oder und Neisse.*

STANDESAMT, Vol. 12, 1958, p. 107.

18. *Sejm i zawieranie umów międzynarodowych* [The Polish Diet and the Conclusion of Treaties].

PAŃSTWO I PRAWO, Vol. 14, 1959, Part 1, pp. 500–504.

19. *Le transfert de la population allemande était-il conforme au droit international?*

CAHIERS POLOGNE-ALLEMAGNE, 1959, N° 1, pp. 42–56.

20. *The Postwar Alliances of Poland and the United Nations Charter.*

AMERICAN JOURNAL OF INTERNATIONAL LAW, Vol. 53, 1959, pp. 613–634.

21. *Umowy sojusznicze Polski a Karta Narodów Zjednoczonych* [Alliance Agreements of Poland and the Charter of the United Nations].

Ruch Prawniczy i Ekonomiczny, Vol. 21, 1959, N° 3, pp. 1–16.

22. *Kompetencje państwa polskiego w Wolnym Mieście Gdańsku* [Powers of the Polish State in the Free City of Dantzig].

Czasopismo Prawno-Historyczne, Vol. XI, 1959, pp. 145–184.

23. *Odpowiedzialność za pieniądz okupacyjny* [Responsibility for Occupation Currency].

Ruch Prawniczy i Ekonomiczny, Vol. 22, 1960, N° 2, pp. 65–82.

24. *Currency in Occupied Territory and the Law of War.*

Jahrbuch für Internationales Recht, Vol. 9, 1959–1960, pp. 161–197.

25. *Granica polsko-niemiecka* [Polish-German Frontier].

Więź, Vol. III, 1960, N° 4, pp. 19–29.

26. *The Validity of Treaties in Polish Municipal Law.*

Rapports polonais présentés au sixième Congrès International de Droit Comparé, PAN, Varsovie 1962, pp. 109–123.

27. *Uprawnienie państw do samoobrony a Karta Narodów Zjednoczonych* [States' Right to Self-Defence and the Charter of the United Nations].

Ruch Prawniczy, Ekonomiczny i Socjologiczny, Vol. 24, 1962, N°4, pp. 109–120.

28. *Kompetencje prawodawcze Wspólnot Europejskich* [Law-Making Powers of the European Communities].

Przegląd Zachodni, Vol. 18, 1962, Part 3, pp. 8–47 and 212–244.

29. *The General Assembly of the United Nations and Its Power to Influence National Action.*

Proceedings of the American Society of International Law, 1964, pp. 153–162. Reprinted in: The Strategy of World Order, Vol. 3: The United Nations, pp. 238–247.

30. *Forms of Participation of International Organizations in the Lawmaking Process.*

INTERNATIONAL ORGANIZATION, Vol. XVIII, 1964, pp. 790–805.

31. *The Frontier between Poland and Germany as a Problem of International Law and Relations.*

POLISH WESTERN AFFAIRS, Vol. V, 1964, pp. 311–331.

32. *Enactment of Law by International Organizations.*

BRITISH YEAR BOOK OF INTERNATIONAL LAW, Vol. 41, 1965–1966, pp. 198–274.

33. *Granica na Odrze i Nysie i powrót Gdańska do Polski. Aspekty prawnomiędzynarodowe* [The Oder-Neisse Frontier and the Return of Gdańsk to Poland. International Legal Aspects].

KOMUNIKATY INSTYTUTU BAŁTYCKIEGO, 1966, N° 5, pp. 1–31.

34. *Le Conseil d'Entraide Économique et ses actes.*

ANNUAIRE FRAÇAIS DE DROIT INTERNATIONAL, vol. XII, 1966, pp. 544–576.

35. *The Application of Non-Military Measures by the General Assembly of the United Nations.*

POLISH YEARBOOK OF INTERNATIONAL LAW, Vol. I, 1966–67, pp. 110–135.

36. *Wysiedlenie Niemców z Polski jako zagadnienie prawa międzynarodowego* [Deportation of the Germans from Poland as a Problem of International Law].

KOMUNIKATY INSTYTUTU BAŁTYCKIEGO, 1967, N° 6, pp. 18–36.

37. *L'Organisation du Traité de Varsovie.*

REVUE BELGE DE DROIT INTERNATIONAL, 1967, pp. 69–83.

38. *Prawo wojny i neutralności w świecie współczesnym* [Law of War and Neutrality in Contemporary World].

RUCH PRAWNICZY, EKONOMICZNY I SOCJOLOGICZNY, Vol. 29, 1967, N° 1, pp. 105–125.

39. *Powrót Gdańska w granice Rzeczypospolitej* [Return of Gdańsk to Poland].

KOMUNIKATY INSTYTUTU BAŁTYCKIEGO, 1968, N° 9, pp. 3–10.

40. *Resolutions of International Organizations and Municipal Law.*

POLISH YEARBOOK OF INTERNATIONAL LAW, Vol. II, 1968–69, pp. 80–108.

41. *Bohdan Winiarski.*

KRONIKA UNIWERSYTETU IM. ADAMA MICKIEWICZA ZA LATA AKADEMICKIE 1969/70–1971/72, pp. 1076–1077.

42. *Wspomnienie o Bohdanie Winiarskim* [A Reminiscence of Bohdan Winiarski].

TYGODNIK POWSZECHNY, Vol. 24, 1970, N° 3, p. 3.

43. *Bohdan Winiarski 1884–1969.*

RUCH PRAWNICZY, EKONOMICZNY I SOCJOLOGICZNY, Vol. 32, 1970, N° 1, pp. 387–390.

44. *Legal Nature and Domestic Effects of Acts of International Organizations.*

RAPPORTS POLONAIS PRÉSENTÉS AU HUITIÈME CONGRÈS INTERNATIONAL DE DROIT COMPARÉ, Varsovie 1970, pp. 14–26.

45. *The Western Frontier of Poland and the Treaties with Federal Germany.*

POLISH YEARBOOK OF INTERNATIONAL LAW, Vol. III, 1970, pp. 53–68.

46. *Zachodnia granica Polski w świetle układów z 1970 roku* [The Western Frontier of Poland in the Light of the Agreements of 1970].

PAŃSTWO I PRAWO, Vol. 26, 1971, Part 1, N° 3–4, pp. 476–487. Reprinted in: POLSKA – REPUBLIKA FEDERALNA NIEMIEC. PRZESŁANKI I PROCES NORMALIZACJI STOSUNKÓW, Instytut Zachodni, Poznań 1972, pp. 179–194.

47. *Elements of Custom and the Hague Court.*

ZEITSCHRIFT FÜR AUSLÄNDISCHES ÖFFENTLICHES RECHT UND VÖLKERRECHT, Vol. 31, 1971, pp. 810–854.

48. [Review article on D.P. O'Connell's International Law, 2nd edition].

BRITISH YEAR BOOK OF INTERNATIONAL LAW, Vol. 45, 1971, pp. 493–511.

49. *La fin d'un contentieux territorial: l'accord Bonn–Varsovie.*

ANNALES D'ÉTUDES INTERNATIONALES – ANNALS OF INTERNATIONAL STUDIES, vol. 3, 1972, pp. 23–46.

50. *Prawo PRL a traktaty* [The Law of People's Poland and Treaties].

RUCH PRAWNICZY, EKONOMICZNY I SOCJOLOGICZNY, Vol. 34, 1972, N° 3, pp. 1–18.

51. *Recommendations of the United Nations and Municipal Law.*

BRITISH YEAR BOOK OF INTERNATIONAL LAW, Vol. 46, 1972–1973, pp. 353–364.

52. *Miejsce traktatów w porządku prawnym PRL* [The Place of Treaties in the Legal Order of the Polish People's Republic].

SPRAWY MIĘDZYNARODOWE, Vol. 26, 1973, N° 1, pp. 80–91.

53. *Poland's Western Frontier and the 1970 Treaties.*

AMERICAN JOURNAL OF INTERNATIONAL LAW, Vol. 67, 1973, pp. 23–43. Reprinted in: G. DOEKER and J.A. BRÜCKNER (eds.), THE FEDERAL REPUBLIC OF GERMANY AND THE GERMAN DEMOCRATIC REPUBLIC IN INTERNATIONAL RELATIONS, Oceana Publications, Dobbs Ferry, N.Y.; Sijthoff & Noordhoff, Alphen aan den Rijn 1979, Vol. III, pp. 134–154.

54. *Leon Babiński.*

PAŃSTWO I PRAWO, Vol. 28, 1973, N° 4, pp. 117–119.

55. *Nowe traktaty w sprawach niemieckich: problemy terytorialne* [New Treaties on German Questions: Problems of Territory].

PAŃSTWO I PRAWO, Vol. 28, 1973, N° 5, pp. 13–27.

56. *La frontière occidentale de la Pologne et les traités de 1970.*

RES PUBLICA, Vol. XV, 1973, pp. 77–91.

57. *Nowe traktaty w sprawach niemieckich: stosunki RFN–NRD* [New Treaties on German Questions: Relations between the FRG and the GDR].

PAŃSTWO I PRAWO, Vol. 28, 1973, N° 6, pp. 33–46.

58. *La nature juridique de la «Déclaration des principes» sur les fonds marins.*

ANNALES D'ÉTUDES INTERNATIONALES, vol. 4, 1973, pp. 237–248.

59. *Leon Babiński.*

ANNUAIRE DE L'INSTITUT DE DROIT INTERNATIONAL, vol. 55, 1973, pp. 886–888.

60. *Les traités sur les frontières en Europe centrale (1970–1973).*

POLISH YEARBOOK OF INTERNATIONAL LAW, Vol. VI, 1974, pp. 7–26.

61. *Bohdan Winiarski.*

POLISH YEARBOOK OF INTERNATIONAL LAW, Vol. VI, 1974, pp. 311–313.

62. *Uznanie zachodniej granicy Polski* [Recognition of the Western Frontier of Poland].

STUDIA PRAWNICZE, 1974, N° 4, pp. 29–55.

63. *Ochrona dyplomatyczna obywateli* [Diplomatic Protection of Citizens].

PAŃSTWO I PRAWO, Vol. 30, 1975, N° 10, pp. 30–42.

64. *The Great Powers and the Settlement in Central Europe.*

JAHRBUCH FÜR INTERNATIONALES RECHT, Vol. 18, 1975, pp. 92–126.

65. *Der diplomatische Schutz des Staatsbürgers.*

In: STAATSANGEHÖRIGKEIT – SOZIALE GRUNDRECHTE – WIRTSCHAFTLICHE ZUSAMMENARBEIT NACH DEM RECHT DER BUNDESREPUBLIK DEUTSCHLAND UND DER VOLKSREPUBLIK POLEN. REFERATE DES [2. deutsch-polnischen] RECHTSKOLLOQUIUMS, Springer-Verlag, Berlin – Heidelberg – New York; Instytut Śląski, Opole 1976, pp. 82–95.

66. *Akt Końcowy KBWE w świetle prawa międzynarodowego* [Final Act of the CSCE in the Light of International Law].

PAŃSTWO I PRAWO, Vol. 31, 1976, N° 12, pp. 3–16.

67. *Law-Making and Economic Integration in Eastern Europe.*

CURRENT LEGAL PROBLEMS, Vol. 29, 1976, pp. 168–182.

68. *Traktaty a prawo krajowe* [glosa]. [Treaties and Municipal Law. A Note].

PAŃSTWO I PRAWO, Vol. 32, 1977, N° 8–9, pp. 255–265.

69. *Der Rechtscharakter der KSZE-Schlussakte.*

In: DRITTES DEUTSCH-POLNISCHES JURISTEN – KOLLOQUIUM. NOMOS VERLAGSGESELLSCHAFT, Baden–Baden 1977, Vol. 1, pp. 13–30.

70. *Konflikt normy krajowej z międzynarodową* [Conflict between Municipal and International Norms].

PAŃSTWO I PRAWO, Vol. 34, 1979, N° 12, pp. 3–15.

71. *Czy uchwały Zgromadzenia Ogólnego ONZ są źródłem prawa?* [Are Resolutions of the U.N. General Assembly a Source of Law?].

PAŃSTWO I PRAWO, Vol. 36, 1981, N° 2, pp. 19–30.

72. *Prawa jednostki, umowy międzynarodowe i porządek prawny PRL* [Rights of Individuals, International Agreements and the Legal Order of the Polish People's Republic].

PAŃSTWO I PRAWO, Vol. 36, 1981, N° 7, pp. 9–23.

73. *Rechtscharakter der Resolutionen der Generalversammlung der Vereinten Nationen.*

Fünftes deutsch-polnisches Juristen-Kolloquium. Band 2: DIE BEDEUTUNG DER RESOLUTIONEN DER GENERALVERSAMMLUNG DER VEREINTEN NATIONEN. NOMOS VERLAGSGESELLSCHAFT, Baden–Baden 1981, pp. 13–43.

74. *Karta Gospodarczych Uprawnień i Obowiązków Państw* [Charter of Economic Rights and Duties of States].

RUCH PRAWNICZY, EKONOMICZNY I SOCJOLOGICZNY, Vol. 43, 1981, N° 2, pp. 85–99.

75. *Niektóre metody generalnego włączania prawa międzynarodowego w porządek krajowy* [Some Methods of the General Incorporation of International Law into the Municipal Order].

PRZEGLĄD STOSUNKÓW MIĘDZYNARODOWYCH, 1981, N° 2–3, pp. 229–240.

76. *Rapport polonais.*
Le rôle de la pratique dans la formation du droit.

TRAVAUX DE L'ASSOCIATION HENRI CAPITANT DES AMIS DE LA CULTURE JURIDIQUE FRANCAISE. JOURNÉES SUISSES, vol. 34, 1983, pp. 603–614.

77. *Stosowanie i przestrzeganie prawa międzynarodowego w państwie* [Application of and Respect for International Law in the State].

PAŃSTWO I PRAWO, Vol. 39, 1984, N° 9, pp. 18–25.

78. *Administration of Territory and Sovereignty: A Comment on the Potsdam Agreement.*

ARCHIV DES VÖLKERRECHTS, Vol. 23, 1985, pp. 31–41.

79. *Granica poczdamska: polityka i prawo międzynarodowe* [The Potsdam Frontier: Politics and International Law].

TYGODNIK POWSZECHNY, Vol. 39, 1985, N° 25, pp. 1 and 3.

80. *O teorii prawa międzynarodowego* [On the Theory of International Law].

PAŃSTWO I PRAWO, Vol. 40, 1985, N° 7–8, pp. 121–130.

81. *Granica poczdamska* [The Potsdam Frontier].

TYGODNIK POWSZECHNY, Vol. 39, 1985, N° 44.

82. *Rola niewiążących uchwał normatywnych w prawotwórstwie międzynarodowym* [The Role of Non-Binding Normative Resolutions in International Law-Making].

PAŃSTWO I PRAWO, Vol. 41, 1986, N° 1, pp. 34–45.

83. *Wzajemny stosunek i związki pomiędzy prawem międzynarodowym i prawem krajowym* [Relationship and Links between International Law and Municipal Law].

RUCH PRAWNICZY, EKONOMICZNY I SOCJOLOGICZNY, Vol. 48, 1986, N° 1, pp. 1–16.

84. *Pluralism and International Law: The Role of Consensus.*

In: RAPPORTS POLONAIS PRÉSENTÉS AU DOUZIÈME CONGRÈS INTERNATIONAL DU DROIT COMPARÉ, Ossolineum, Wrocław 1986, pp. 171–178.

85. *Non-Binding Resolutions and the Law-Making Process.*

POLISH YEARBOOK OF INTERNATIONAL LAW, Vol. XV, 1986, pp. 135–161.

86. *Konstytucyjne ujęcie stosunku prawa polskiego do prawa międzynarodowego* [Constitutional Framework of the Relation between Polish Law and International Law].

PAŃSTWO I PRAWO, Vol. 42, 1987, N° 10, pp. 138–146.

87. *Nieznane poglądy sędziego Bohdana Winiarskiego na zagadnienia obywatelstwa i opieki dyplomatycznej* [Unknown Views of Judge Winiarski on the Question of Nationality and Diplomatic Protection].

RUCH PRAWNICZY, EKONOMICZNY I SOCJOLOGICZNY, Vol. 49, 1987, N° 4, pp. 103–112.

88. *Law-Making by International Organizations.*

THESAURUS ACROASIUM, Vol. XIX (Session 1988), pp. 357–388.

89. *Umowy międzynarodowe w porządku prawnym PRL* [glosa] [International Agreements in the Legal Order of the People's Republic of Poland. A Note].

PAŃSTWO I PRAWO, Vol. 44, 1989, N° 6, pp. 135–145.

90. *Akcja „Wisła" i prawo międzynarodowe* [Operation "Vistula" and International Law].

TYGODNIK POWSZECHNY, Vol. 44, 1990, N° 10.

91. *Die völkerrechtliche und staatliche Einheit des deutschen Volkes und die Entwicklung in Europa.*

EUROPA-ARCHIV, Vol. 45, 1990, pp. 195–202.

92. *Przyszła Konstytucja RP a miejsce prawa międzynarodowego w krajowym porządku prawnym* [Future Constitution of Poland and the Place of International Law in the Domestic Legal Order].

PAŃSTWO I PRAWO, Vol. 49, 1994, N° 3, pp. 11–17.

VIII. Published Expert Opinions

1. *Opinia w sprawie przystąpienia Polskiej Rzeczypospolitej Ludowej do Konwencji Wiedeńskiej o prawie traktatów* [Opinion on the Accession by the Polish People's Republic to the Vienna Convention on the Law of Treaties].

In: RADA LEGISLACYJNA, MATERIAŁY Z DZIAŁALNOŚCI ZESPOŁU PRAWA MIĘDZYNARODOWEGO, październik 1986 – czerwiec 1987, Warszawa 1987, pp. 42–44.

2. *Skuteczność prawa międzynarodowego w systemie prawnym Polskiej Rzeczypospolitej Ludowej: gwarancje instytucjonalne* [Effectiveness of International Law in the Legal System of the Polish People's Republic: Institutional Guarantees].

In: RADA LEGISLACYJNA, MATERIAŁY Z DZIAŁALNOŚCI ZESPOŁU PRAWA MIĘDZYNARODOWEGO, październik 1986 – czerwiec 1987, Warszawa 1987, pp. 50–68.

IX. Editorial Work and Translations

1. *Materiały do ćwiczeń z prawa międzynarodowego publicznego* [Materials for Classes in Public International Law], N° 1, Państwowe Wydawnictwo Naukowe, Poznań 1951, pp. 157; N° 2, Uniwersytet im. Adama Mickiewicza, Poznań 1961, pp. 180 [mimeographed].

2. Managing editor, ZARYS PRAWA MIĘDZYNARODOWEGO PUBLICZNEGO [Outline of Public International Law].

Wydawnictwo Prawnicze, Warszawa 1955–56, Vols. I and II.

3. Selection and translation of judgments of Polish courts and preparation for publication of some arbitral awards in: E. LAUTERPACHT (ed.), INTERNATIONAL LAW REPORTS:
Vol. 24, pp. 77–82, 223–226, 941–943 and 960–976.
Vol. 25, pp. 33–89, 234–236, 335–360, 495–516 and 522–556.
Vol. 26, pp. 178–180, 714–723 and 728–732.
Vol. 28, pp. 272–274, 515–524 and 544–592.
Vol. 30, pp. 496–511.
Vol. 34, pp. 219–275 and 474–488.
Vol. 47, pp. 24–25, 28–30, 107–108 and 118.
Vol. 51, pp. 423–429.
Vol. 52, pp. 28–29.

4. Translation from Polish into English of an article by Hersch Lauterpacht published in GŁOS PRAWA [Voice of Law], Vol. 5, 1928, N° 5–6, p. 18 et sequentes: Succession of States with Respect to Private Law Obligations.

In: INTERNATIONAL LAW BEING THE COLLECTED PAPERS OF HERSCH LAUTERPACHT. Systematically Arranged and Edited by E. LAUTERPACHT. Vol. 3: THE LAW OF PEACE, Parts II–VI, Cambridge University Press 1977, pp. 121–137.

PART TWO: OTHER FIELDS OF LAW

1. Editor, NAUKA ADMINISTRACJI I POLSKIE PRAWO ADMINISTRACYJNE. WYKŁADY PROF. DR. MARIANA ZIMMERMANNA [Science of Administration and Polish Administrative Law. Lectures by Professor Marian Zimmermann], Koło Prawników i Ekonomistów SUP, Poznań 1949, Part I, pp. 149; Part II, pp. 90 [mimeographed].

2. *Wydział Prawa Uniwersytetu Harwardzkiego* [Harvard Law School].

RUCH PRAWNICZY I EKONOMICZNY, Vol. 21, 1959, N° 4, pp. 303–318.

3. *Studenckie praktyki prawnicze* [Apprenticeship for Law Students].

ŻYCIE SZKOŁY WYŻSZEJ, 1962, N° 7–8, pp. 94–100.

4. Editor (with J. KOKOT), STAATSANGEHÖRIGKEIT – SOZIALE GRUNDRECHTE – WIRTSCHAFTLICHE ZUSAMMENARBEIT NACH DEM RECHT DER BUNDES-

REPUBLIK DEUTSCHLAND UND DER VOLKSREPUBLIK POLEN. Referate der [2. deutsch-polnischen] Rechtskolloquiums 1974, Springer-Verlag, Berlin–Heidelberg–New York; Instytut Śląski, Opole 1976, pp. 293.

5. Co-Editor, PARLAMENT UND AUSSENPOLITIK - ZUSAMMENARBEIT DER OSTSEE – STAATEN – REGELUNG DES VERKEHRS. VIERTES KOLLOQUIUM DER BUNDESDEUTSCHEN UND POLNISCHEN JURISTEN 1978.

INSTYTUT ZACHODNI, Poznań 1980, pp. 241.

PART THREE: CONTEMPORARY HISTORY, INTERNATIONAL RELATIONS, FOREIGN POLICY

I. Books and Pamphlets

1. WYSIEDLENIE NIEMCÓW PO II WOJNIE ŚWIATOWEJ [Transfer of Germans after the Second World War].
Książka i Wiedza, Warszawa 1968, pp. 151.

2. ZACHODNIA GRANICA POLSKI [Western Frontier of Poland].
Instytut Bałtycki, Wydawnictwo Morskie, Gdańsk 1969, pp. 630, 3 maps.

3. POLAND'S FOREIGN POLICY: TRANSFORMATION AND PROSPECTS.
Chilean Council on Foreign Relations, Lecture Series, Santiago 1991, pp. 22.

4. POZYCJA POLSKI W EUROPIE [Poland's Place in Europe].
[A pamphlet edited by D. POPŁAWSKI.] Foundation of International Studies, Warszawa 1994, pp. 5–20.
Also published in the BULLETIN OF THE INTERNATIONAL CENTRE OF CULTURE, Cracow.

II. Contributions to Collective Monographs or Collections of Essays

1. *Adam Stefan Sapieha a zawarcie konkordatu polskiego* [Adam Stefan Sapieha and the Conclusion of the Polish Concordat].
In: KSIĘGA SAPIEŻYŃSKA, Vol. II, Polskie Towarzystwo Teologiczne, Kraków 1986, pp. 9–25.

2. *Europa auf dem Wege zu neuen Institutionen.*

In: EUROPA AUF DEM WEGE ZU NEUEN INSTITUTIONEN, Internationales Symposium, Deutsches Helsinki Menschenrechtskomitee, Berlin, 5–6. Oktober 1990, Bonn 1991, pp. 53–61.

3. *Nationalismus als Gefahr für Europa.*

In: NACHDENKEN ÜBER EUROPA, Vol. I., Verlag Volk und Welt, Berlin 1992, pp. 11–29.

4. *Polens Stellung in einem künftigen Europa.*

E. OBERLÄNDER (ed.), POLEN NACH DEM KOMMUNISMUS, Franz Steiner Verlag, Stuttgart 1993, pp. 12–30.

5. *Europe centrale: coopération et sécurité.*

In: ÉTUDES DE DROIT INTERNATIONAL EN L'HONNEUR DE PIERRE LALIVE, Éditions Helbing & Lichtenhahn, Bâle – Francfort-sur-le-Main 1993, pp. 681–690.

6. *Poland's Political Dialogue with the European Community.*

In: VÖLKERRECHT ZWISCHEN NORMATIVEN ANSPRUCH UND POLITISCHER REALITÄT. FESTSCHRIFT FÜR KARL ZEMANEK, Duncker & Humblot, Berlin 1994, pp. 401–416.

7. *Deutsche Aussenpolitik aus der Sicht von Mitteleuropa: Erwartungen und Möglichkeiten.*

In: 125 JAHRE AUSWÄRTIGES AMT: FESTSCHRIFT, Bonn 1995, pp. 67–73.

8. *Pozycja Polski w Europie* [Poland's Position in Europe].

In: A. TARGOWSKI (ed.), WIZJA POLSKI, P.W., „Com-Tour" S.A., Warszawa 1995, pp. 80–99.

9. *Die Zusammenarbeit der Deutschen und der Polen im Grenzgebiet Mecklenburg-Vorpommern-Pommern und im Ostseeraum.*

In: 1995: 1000 JAHRE MECKLENBURG. REDEN ZUM FESTAKT, Schwerin 1995, pp. 23–34.

III. Articles in Journals, Yearbooks and Serial Publications

1. *Mazowsze Pruskie – przykładem naszej odporności* [Prussian Masovia: A Case in Our Ability to Resist].

   POLSKA ZACHODNIA, Vol. 1, 1945, N° 3, pp. 2–3.

2. *Mazowsze Pruskie w statystyce* [Prussian Masovia in Statistics].

   POLSKA ZACHODNIA, Vol. 1, 1945, N° 6, p. 4 and N° 7, pp. 8–9.

3. *Niemiecka Republika Związkowa i Pakt Atlantycki* [Federal Republic of Germany and the Atlantic Treaty].

   ŻYCIE I MYŚL, 1956, N° 2, pp. 135–158.

4. *Le problème des relations diplomatiques entre la Pologne et la République Fédérale d'Allemagne.*

   CAHIERS POLOGNE – ALLEMAGNE, 1963, N° 4, pp. 8–21.

5. *Wysiedlenie ludności niemieckiej z Europy Środkowowschodniej po drugiej wojnie światowej* [Transfer of German Population from Central-Eastern Europe after the Second World War].

   STUDIA O NIEMCZECH WSPÓŁCZESNYCH, Vol. 2, 1967, pp. 237–255 and 304–306.

6. *Czy Gdańsk był powodem wojny?* [for the English version of this article which is not its mere translation, see item 7 below].

   PRZEGLĄD ZACHODNI, Vol. 25, 1969, Part 2, N° 3, pp. 61–96.
   Reprinted ibidem, Vol. 41, 1995, N° 2, pp. 211–242.

7. *Did the War Start for Danzig?*

   POLISH WESTERN AFFAIRS, Vol. 10, 1969, N° 1, pp. 25–62.

8. *Le Conflit de Dantzig fut-il la cause de la guerre?* [this article is a translation of item 6 above].

   LA POLOGNE ET LES AFFAIRES OCCIDENTALES, Vol. 5, 1969, N° 1, pp. 28–78.

9. *Prawa człowieka – Helsinki – ONZ* [Human Rights, Helsinki, U.N.].

TYGODNIK POWSZECHNY, Vol. 31, 1977, N° 47, p. 1 and Vol. 32, 1978, N° 1, p. 2.

10. *Wojna 1939* [The War of 1939].

TYGODNIK POWSZECHNY, Vol. 38, 1984, N° 12, p. 8.

11. *Wspomnienia Zbigniewa Brzezińskiego* [Zbigniew Brzeziński's Memoirs].

TYGODNIK POWSZECHNY, Vol. 38. 1984, N° 17–18, p. 5.

12. *Change versus Stability in Europe: A Polish View.*

THE WORLD TODAY, Vol. 46, 1990, N° 8–9, pp. 148–151.

13. *Wzglyad iz Varshavy* [Seen from Warsaw].

MEZDUNARODNAYA ZIZN, 1990, N° 12, pp. 52–59.

14. *Neue Probleme der Sicherheit in Mittel- und Osteuropa.*

EUROPA-ARCHIV, Vol. 46, 1991, pp. 351–357.
Also in: EHRENPROMOTION KRZYSZTOF SKUBISZEWSKI [University of Mainz], Mainz 1991, pp. 24–34.

15. *Polska polityka zagraniczna w 1991 roku* [Polish Foreign Policy in 1991].

ROCZNIK POLSKIEJ POLITYKI ZAGRANICZNEJ, 1991, pp. 15–25.

16. *New Problems of Security in Central and Eastern Europe.*

EAST EUROPEAN REPORTER, Vol. 4, 1991, N° 4, pp. 61–64.

17. *Traktat o dobrym sąsiedztwie i przyjaznej współpracy z Niemcami* [German-Polish Treaty on Good Neighbourhood and Friendly Cooperation].

TYGODNIK POWSZECHNY, Vol. 45, 1991, N° 47.

18. *Future Architecture of European Security.*

JANE'S NATO HANDBOOK, 4th edition, 1991–92, pp. 391–393.

19. *Racja stanu z perspektywy polskiej* [Reason of State from Polish Perspective].

ROCZNIK POLSKIEJ POLITYKI ZAGRANICZNEJ, 1992, pp. 35–44.

20. *La coopération franco-allemande. Un modèle pour la Pologne et l'Europe centrale?*

DOCUMENTS, 1993, N° 1, pp. 8–12.

21. *Nacjonalizm w dzisiejszej Europie* [Nationalism in Contemporary Europe].

SPRAWY MIĘDZYNARODOWE, Vol. 46, 1993, N° 3, pp. 11–24.

22. *Nationalism in Europe Today.*

POLISH QUARTERLY OF INTERNATIONAL AFFAIRS, 1993, N° 3, pp. 11–26.

23. *Perspektywy polityki zagranicznej RP w Europie* [For the English Translation of this article, see item 24 *infra*].

ROCZNIK POLSKIEJ POLITYKI ZAGRANICZNEJ, 1993–1994, pp. 21–30.

24. *Perspectives of Poland's Foreign Policy in Europe.*

YEARBOOK OF POLISH FOREIGN POLICY, 1993–1994, pp. 21–30.

25. *Europa central y la Unión Europea.*

POLITICA EXTERIOR, Vol. 8, 1994, N° 39, pp. 18–29.

26. *The National Idea and Nationalism in Contemporary Europe.*

VII INTERNATIONAL AMALDI CONFERENCE, 1994, pp. 349–356.

27. *Das heutige Mitteleuropa und der Westen.*

LIBERAL, Vol. 36, 1994, N° 4, pp. 36.

28. *Development of Czech-Polish Relations and Their Prospects of European Integration.*

The Bohemiae Foundation, Excerpts from Selected Discussion Forums and Lectures [1994–95] [Prague 1995], pp. 66–67.

29. *Der 8. Mai 1945 als Zäsur europäischer Geschichte.*

In: Prokolle. Der 8. Mai 1945 als historische Zäsur. Strukturen – Erfahrungen – Deutungen. Brandenburgische Landeszentrale für politische Bildung, Potsdam 1995, pp. 35–48.

Clarification: The foregoing list of K. Skubiszewski's publications does not contain, with the exception of four review articles, book reviews (which are 53 in number), brief notes on various subjects of international law (35) and published contributions to discussions on such subjects (74). Part Three does not comprise his speeches published in the official records of the Diet and the Senate, Warsaw; newspaper articles; and printed interviews.

First Part

General Theory

De la sanction en droit international
Essai de clarification

par

Georges M. Abi-Saab

C'est en 1960, dans l'enceinte du Palais de la Paix à La Haye que j'ai rencontré Krzysztof Skubiszewski pour la première fois. Nous participions tous deux au Centre de recherches de l'Académie de Droit international. Déjà à cette occasion, comme depuis lors, Krzysztof Skubiszewski s'est intéressé tout particulièrement à l'étude des résolutions de l'Assemblée générale[1] – actes prétendument dépourvus de «sanction juridique» dans le sens de «force obligatoire» – y compris de leur rôle dans l'application des «sanctions» prévues par la Charte[2], dans le sens de «mesures» collectives et coercitives. Il n'est donc pas inapproprié, dans un volume qui lui est dédié, de traiter de la notion même de «sanction» en droit international en général, comme dans le contexte plus particulier des organisations internationales.

La problématique de la sanction a toujours été au centre des débats théoriques sur le fondement et le rôle du droit international, si ce n'est sur la réalité même de son existence en tant que droit. Une bonne part de la confusion qui entoure ces controverses provient du fait que ceux qui les animent procèdent de notions et de prémisses différentes, sans toujours les expliciter pour autant. Cette confusion s'est accrue avec l'apparition récente de nouvelles notions qui évoquent également celle de «sanction», telles les «contre-mesures».

Ce modeste essai n'a d'autre but que d'être un simple exercice de clarification des différentes notions qui gravitent autour de celle de sanction; et cela en vue de déceler les rapports logiques possibles entre elles et de délimiter leurs champs d'application respectifs. Exercice modeste mais non dénué d'intérêt, étant donné que, si l'on en juge par les utilisations doctrinales de ces notions, elles sont toutes à géométrie variable.

---

1 *Voir* notamment son rapport à l'Institut de Droit international, Resolutions of the General Assembly of the United Nations, 61:I Annuaire de l'Institut de Droit international (1985), pp. 29–249.

2 K. Skubiszewski, *The Application of Non-Military Measures by the General Assembly of the United Nations*, 1 Polish Yearbook of International Law (1966/1967), pp. 110–135.

I. ACCEPTIONS DIVERGENTES DE LA NOTION DE SANCTION

En tout premier lieu, nous devons nous arrêter aux diverses acceptions de la notion de sanction et à sa place dans le système juridique international. En fait, l'acception de «sanction» dépend de la conception qu'on a du système juridique. Si nous considérons le droit, par définition, comme un «ordre de contrainte» (comme l'ont fait les positivistes à partir d'Austin, en passant par les volontaristes comme Anzilotti ou les normativistes comme Kelsen), et si l'on ajoute à cela la représentation atomiste (*actor-oriented*) et purement interétatique du système classique (l'Etat maître du jeu des relations internationales, seul sujet et organe du droit international), on est amené à considérer comme sanction tout moyen de contrainte aux mains de l'Etat, les sanctions types étant la guerre et les représailles.

Si on considère en revanche que l'existence de l'ordre juridique (et *a fortiori* de la règle de droit prise isolément) ne repose pas en fin de compte et exclusivement sur la contrainte, ou que l'ordonnancement de la sociabilité a d'autres ressorts que la contrainte sans pour autant l'ignorer, on arrive à une autre acception et à un autre rôle de la sanction.

Dans ces conditions soit on considère, par exemple avec H.L.A. Hart, que la sanction (dans le sens étroit de contrainte presque exclusivement physique ou matérielle) n'est pas un élément nécessaire du système juridique (et *a fortiori* de la règle de droit)[3]; soit on adopte une notion beaucoup plus large de la sanction qui dépasse, et de loin, celle étriquée de contrainte physique ou matérielle et qui ressemble à celle de Santi Romano, suivi par une certaine doctrine italienne[4]; bien qu'on puisse la retrouver également en remontant plus d'un millénaire, chez les jurisconsultes musulmans, qui parlaient de la «garantie des règles» (*damman-ul-ahkam*) et non de leur sanction.

Selon cette conception, la sanction recouvrirait l'ensemble des garanties et moyens dont dispose le système juridique pour assurer sa cohérence et son intégrité normatives (c'est-à-dire la conformité du comportement social avec ses règles), ainsi que son efficacité et, partant, sa crédibilité en tant

---

[3] H.L.A. HART, THE CONCEPT OF LAW, The Clarendon Press, Oxford (1961), pp. 80–81. *Cf.* l'excellent article de CHARLES-ALBERT MORAND, *La sanction*, 35 ARCHIVES DE PHILOSOPHIE DE DROIT (1990), pp. 293–312.

[4] S. ROMANO, L'ORDRE JURIDIQUE (2 éd. Traduite par L. François et P. Gothot), Dalloz, Paris (1975), pp. 15–16, § 8. Il faut relever cependant que l'école italienne, et notamment son chef de file Tomaso Perassi, inclut dans cette panoplie de garanties la «fonction juridictionnelle» (*accertamento juridizionali* ou *del diritto*, en contraste à celle de la production des règles). *Cf.* T. PERASSI, LEZIONI DI DIRITTO INTERNAZIONALE, Partie I, 7ème éd., Padone (1961), p. 18.

qu'ordre juridique; et cela que ces moyens soient matériellement coercitifs ou purement juridiques, négatifs (punitifs) ou positifs (incitatifs). D'où l'importance, comme sanction positive, des bénéfices de la collaboration et de l'exclusion, comme sanction négative, dans le cadre du droit international de coopération, dans le fameux diptyque de Wolfgang Friedmann[5].

Dans cette conception du système juridique et de la sanction, qui est la nôtre, la sanction *lato sensu*, ou génériquement parlant, est un attribut du système et non de la norme prise isolément. Elle relève de sa composante institutionnelle (ou de ses «règles secondaires» selon Hart), et sa manifestation-type est juridique, à savoir la responsabilité ou les conséquences juridiques que le système attache au comportement non conforme à ses prescriptions normatives. L'exécution forcée, impliquant le recours à la contrainte, constitue l'étape ultime et le cas limite, exceptionnel, qui n'est pas toujours atteignable. De plus, elle ne constitue une sanction ou une réaction du système juridique lui-même que quand elle est effectuée à la suite d'une constatation et d'une décision sociales. Ce qui nous amène à une définition *stricto sensu* des sanctions en tant que mesures coercitives prises en application d'une décision d'un organe social compétent. Les mesures coercitives prises individuellement par les Etats en dehors d'une constatation et d'une décision collective, quel que soit le libellé qu'on leur donne (guerre, représailles, contre-mesures), n'entrent évidemment pas dans cette définition. Elles ne sont que les «restes» du pouvoir d'«auto-protection» ou de justice privée, dans les limites étroites encore admises en droit international contemporain.

Cependant, si nous voulons brosser un tableau aussi complet que possible des moyens et des garanties disponibles en droit international contemporain pour assurer l'intégrité normative du système, nous ne pouvons pas exclure les moyens de justice privée, s'agissant d'une communauté internationale loin d'être parfaitement intégrée[6].

L'intégrité normative du système est assurée par la «mise en oeuvre» ou l' «application» de ses règles, en d'autres termes, par la traduction de leurs prescriptions normatives, ou plutôt par leur internalisation ou intégration, dans le comportement des sujets de droit. Cela peut se produire de deux manières différentes:

---

[5] W. FRIEDMANN, THE CHANGING STRUCTURE OF INTERNATIONAL LAW, Stevens, London (1964).

[6] Il faut souligner cependant que la qualification juridique de cette panoplie de moyens ou garanties, ainsi que le découpage ou la délimitation du terrain qu'elle occupe au sein du système juridique, et notamment par rapport à la fonction juridictionnelle, varient dans les différentes traditions juridiques. En *common law* par exemple, des notions telles que *remedies* et *enforcement* recouvrent en grande partie le même champ, tout en ayant un contenu et un champ d'application différents. *Voir* pour ce qui est de l'école italienne, *supra* note 4.

– par l'«application» endogène ou de l'intérieur, par le destinataire de la règle lui-même, ce qui ne pose problème que quand sa conformité à la prescription normative est contestée par un autre sujet de droit, contestation qui peut éventuellement conduire à l'autre type de mise en oeuvre;

– par une «exécution» exogène ou de l'extérieur, par les organes sociaux (mais exceptionnellement, dans les systèmes de justice privée, par les autres sujets de droit à titre individuel), l'«exécution forcée».

II. LES CONSÉQUENCES PUREMENT JURIDIQUES DE LA VIOLATION

Avant d'examiner les moyens d'exécution forcée, il faudrait rappeler les conséquences juridiques que le système attache à la violation de ses normes; conséquences qui participent de la sanction *lato sensu* et qui fournissent les moyens ou titres juridiques justifiant un recours éventuel aux voies d'exécution, tout en déterminant les configurations de la prestation juridique qui fera l'objet de cette exécution. Il s'agit de conséquences qui ne se produisent ou n'ont d'existence que sur un plan ou dans un univers purement juridique et qu'on peut classer en trois catégories, selon les sujets de droit impliqués et la finalité visée:

A. En premier lieu, le système peut attribuer à la violation des conséquences juridiques que son auteur n'aurait pas prévues, et de toute manière n'aurait pas voulues, en commettant son acte ou son omission.

Il s'agit avant tout de la *responsabilité internationale* du sujet du droit qui est engagée par cette violation[7]; mais aussi de la légitimation juridique de la prise des mesures d'exécution forcée individuelles ou collectives à son encontre, dans les limites permises en droit international.

B. En deuxième lieu, le système peut nier ou neutraliser les effets juridiques que l'auteur de la violation aurait voulu produire par son acte ou son omission.

---

[7] Il est intéressant de relever la position de JEAN COMBACAU, dans son excellent ouvrage intitulé LE POUVOIR DE SANCTION DE L'ONU: ÉTUDE THÉORIQUE DE LA COERCITION NON MILITAIRE (Pedone, Paris (1974), p. 44) où il conteste la position de ceux qui considèrent la responsabilité comme une sanction juridique. En effet, selon lui, la responsabilité n'interrompt pas la chaîne normative, mais opère simplement une transformation du contenu des obligations, établissant des rapports nouveaux entre les parties, alors que la sanction vise l'Etat auteur de l'acte comme cible d'une mesure de coercition et non en tant que partie à un rapport normatif, fut-il renouvelé ou transformé. En fait, sa définition de la sanction, si on la limite aux mesures socialement décidées, correspondrait à notre définition de la sanction *stricto sensu*. Cependant, en tant qu'une des garanties dont le système juridique entoure la règle pour assurer son respect, la responsabilité participe de la sanction *lato sensu*, selon notre définition.

Il s'agit de la *nullité* pour ce qui est des violations des conditions de validité d'un acte juridique (à la limite de l' «inexistence», si elle est connue en droit international; ou peut-être est-ce là tout ce qui est connu en droit international, alors que c'est la nullité – qui doit être prononcée par le juge – qui n'existe pas, ou seulement exceptionnellement comme lui)[8]. Mais aussi, s'il y a violation dans l'application d'un acte synallagmatique, elle peut servir de base à des réclamations visant à mettre fin à l'existence juridique de l'acte (abrogation, résiliation, retrait, etc.).

Il faut également signaler dans ce contexte l'*exceptio non adempleti contractus* (se basant sur la réciprocité négative dans la non-exécution); ainsi que, procédant de la même logique mais de manière positive, la «compensation»[9] (bien qu'elle s'opère automatiquement, *ipso jure*, et qu'elle puisse dans ses effets être également rapprochée d'une mesure d'exécution forcée).

C. Enfin et en troisième lieu, le système peut produire certains *effets juridiques à l'égard des tiers*. Il peut ainsi nier ou neutraliser tous les effets juridiques de l'acte ou de l'omission constituant la violation à l'égard des tiers, c'est-à-dire dans la communauté internationale en général.

Pour ce qui est des actes juridiques, cela est subsumé sous la lettre B. ci-dessus, car un accord qui est nul ou qui cesse d'exister, ne l'est pas seulement *inter partes*, mais également et *a fortiori erga omnes*. Il en est de même pour les actes unilatéraux qui ne sont pas conformes aux règles du droit international les régissant et qui ne peuvent produire par conséquent les effets juridiques escomptés par leurs auteurs vis-à-vis des autres sujets du droit international en général, qu'on traite cela sous l'angle de la nullité ou de la non-opposabilité (par exemple la délimitation des zones maritimes de compétence nationale).

En réalité cependant, ce type d'effets à l'égard des tiers va au-delà de la simple neutralisation des effets d'actes juridiques défectueux. Il s'agit surtout ici de faits juridiques constituant non seulement une violation du droit international, mais une violation grave ou qualifiée qui entre dans la catégorie de «crimes internationaux» ou «crimes d'Etat» visés par l'article 19 du projet

---

[8] A nouveau, il ne s'agit pas là de sanction *stricto sensu*. En effet, la nullité ne sanctionne pas nécessairement les parties ou l'une d'elles, par exemple en cas de nullité d'un contrat pour incapacité d'une partie ou pour erreur essentielle, mais peut viser surtout à sauvegarder l'intégrité de la règle. *Voir* CH.-A. MORAND, *op. cit.*, *supra* note 3, p. 295.

[9] La compensation est entendue ici dans le sens de l'article 1289 du Code civil français: «Lorsque deux personnes se trouvent débitrices l'une envers l'autre, il s'opère entre elles une compensation qui éteint les deux dettes...»; c'est-à-dire comme libération de deux personnes débitrices l'une envers l'autre par la balance de leurs dettes réciproques.

d'articles de la CDI sur la responsabilité des Etats (Partie I, préparée par le Professeur Roberto Ago comme Rapporteur spécial)[10].

Ces violations donnent lieu à un rapport triangulaire de responsabilité (et non bilatéral comme pour la responsabilité non qualifiée) entre le sujet actif et deux types de sujets passifs, la victime directe de l'acte (d'une agression par exemple) et la communauté internationale dans son ensemble, qui globalement et à travers chacun de ses membres, a un intérêt juridique direct et une qualité pour agir (*locus standi*) pour défendre la valeur ou l'intérêt commun protégé par la règle violée. Il s'agit donc d'un type de règles qui créent des obligations *erga omnes* à la charge des Etats et qui habilitent tous les autres Etats, même ceux qui ne sont pas directement touchés par la violation, à réagir juridiquement contre leur violation (et dans une certaine mesure leur en imposent même l'obligation)[11].

Ces trois types de conséquences juridiques que le droit attache à la violation, donnent lieu à de nouveaux rapports juridiques en termes de droits, obligations ou habilitations, qui servent à leur tour de titres juridiques aux mesures d'exécution forcée pouvant être prises par la communauté internationale ou les Etats agissant individuellement en vue de les faire valoir.

III. L'EXÉCUTION FORCÉE: «SANCTION» OU «VOIE D'EXÉCUTION»?

L'exécution forcée présuppose un refus d'application de la part du destinataire de la règle; en d'autres termes une violation ou un comportement non conforme à ses prescriptions. Il s'agit donc *grosso modo* de la réaction du système juridique face à une telle violation et des moyens de pression qu'il déploie vis-à-vis du destinataire de la règle afin de le contraindre à revenir à un comportement conforme au droit.

C'est donc dans ce sens large, recouvrant tous les moyens de pression et de contrainte, que nous employons le terme «exécution forcée» et non dans le sens plus étroit, employé quelques fois en droit interne, et signifiant l'exécution de la prestation exigée directement par la puissance publique, à la place du débiteur récalcitrant, là où cela est faisable, ou alternativement par l'emploi de la force à son encontre (en effectuant une éviction par exemple).

Cela nous ramène une fois de plus à la problématique de la sanction. Car beaucoup d'auteurs qualifient l'ensemble des réactions du système juridique de sanctions, ou plus encore de la «sanction» de la règle violée. Alors qu'en

---

10 ANNUAIRE DE LA CDI (1980), vol. 2, part. 2, p. 31.

11 ANNUAIRE DE LA CDI (1984), vol. 2, part. 1, p. 4 (Partie II, Rapporteur spécial W. RIPAGHEN).

droit interne, lorsqu'il s'agit des moyens, ultimement coercitifs, de ramener le destinataire de la règle à un comportement conforme à ses prescriptions, on parle plus concrètement d'«exécution forcée» ou de «voies d'exécution».

Les voies d'exécution relèvent-elles des sanctions ou de la sanction, ou est-ce au contraire la sanction qui fait partie des voies d'exécution? La réponse dépend de la grille des définitions qu'on adopte. Si nous procédons de l'acception *lato sensu* de la sanction, elle engloberait tous les moyens déployés pour assurer l'intégrité normative du système juridique, c'est-à-dire qui contribuent à accroître la probabilité du respect de ses règles, qu'ils soient préventifs ou coercitifs – les derniers étant ceux qui entrent en jeu en cas de violation, en vue d'un redressement rapide du comportement non conforme ou d'un retour rapide à la légalité – on doit admettre que c'est parmi ceux-ci que figurent les voies d'exécution. Si nous procédons, en revanche, de l'acception *stricto sensu* des sanctions, comme mesures prises en application d'une décision d'un organe social compétent pour faire face à la violation, ce sont elles qui figureraient parmi les voies d'exécution.

A cet égard, il faut garder en vue que si les divers moyens juridiques déployés en cas de violation peuvent servir également à d'autres finalités telles la réparation (des dommages causés par la violation, une sorte de responsabilité civile), la punition (évocatrice de la responsabilité pénale) ou la dissuasion (par l'exemple), ces moyens visent tous, en ce faisant, de manière plus ou moins immédiate, la finalité primordiale qui reste la garantie de la conformité, ou de la plus grande conformité du comportement social aux prescriptions des règles, ou le redressement aussi rapide que possible de ce comportement dans ce sens. C'est ce qui compte par dessus tout du point de vue du système juridique, les autres finalités médianes, aussi importantes soient-elles, ne lui sont qu'accessoires. Et c'est cet élément là qu'il faut identifier et jauger en premier lieu dans ces moyens, qu'il convient maintenant de recenser rapidement.

IV. LES VOIES D'EXÉCUTION OUVERTES AUX ÉTATS AGISSANT INDIVIDUELLEMENT (*UTI SINGULI*): VARIATIONS SUR LE THÈME DES «CONTRE-MESURES»

Il s'agit ici des «restes» des institutions de «justice privée», du «droit de se faire justice», ou de l'«auto-protection» (*self-help*), qui sont encore admis en droit international (et dont certains existent dans tous les systèmes juridiques, même les plus évolués, par souci d'efficacité et d'économie de fonction, telle la légitime défense).

Il conviendrait d'emblée et pour éviter toute ambiguïté, de situer ces moyens par rapport aux «contre-mesures», terme qui a fait éruption dans le vocable du droit international dès la fin des années 70. Il s'agit d'un cheminement par transplantation ou emprunts successifs de la terminologie des études stratégiques américaines, appliquées à la stratégie commerciale et, par ce biais, à la formulation de la position juridique des Etats-Unis dans l'arbitrage concernant l'*Accord relatif aux services aériens du 27 mars 1946 entre les Etats-Unis et la France*[12], dont la sentence de 1979 emploie le terme apparemment pour la première fois dans un acte formel de droit international. C'est probablement par le biais des membres de la CDI qui ont servi d'arbitres ou de conseils dans cet arbitrage, que le terme fait son entrée dans les travaux de cette Commission en figurant parmi les causes d'exonération dans son projet d'articles de la même année sur la responsabilité des Etats[13]. Elle est suivie, en 1980, par la CIJ[14], qui achève ainsi d'asseoir le terme et la notion en droit international.

Cette utilisation croissante du terme, notamment par les organes juridictionnels, reflète un souci de ne pas se laisser enfermer dans des classifications juridiques pas trop contraignantes là où le processus de décision n'exige pas une telle spécification, mais demande simplement une référence générale au pouvoir des Etats de réagir aux violations. Le terme peut ainsi être employé génériquement et indifféremment, qu'il s'agisse de responsabilité délictuelle ou contractuelle, d'une violation constatée socialement ou simplement «alléguée» par l'autre ou une autre partie, d'une réaction *uti singulus* ou au contraire collective ou institutionnelle, d'une réaction ne constituant pas en soi une violation du droit international ou une réaction qui aurait constitué en dehors de ce contexte une telle violation, etc.

L'innovation, si innovation il y a, s'inscrit ainsi dans le changement d'optique ou d'approche. Celui-ci repose sur une présentation dynamique de la matière en forme de processus, à mouvement successif, plutôt qu'en forme de propositions normatives intemporelles; ce qui jette une lumière nouvelle sur les finalités, les modalités et les effets juridiques immédiats ou ultimes de ces mouvements et permet de les voir dans une perspective séquentielle et totalisante.

Si tout le monde est d'accord sur ce sens générique et totalisant des contre-mesures, comme englobant toutes les réactions possibles à l'illicite, permises par le droit international, c'est que cette notion remplit ainsi une fonction explicative utile. Mais précisément à cause de ce même caractère

---

12 NATIONS UNIES, RECUEIL DES SENTENCES ARBITRALES, vol. 18, pp. 458–493, § 81.

13 ANNUAIRE DE LA CDI (1979), vol. II, p. 128 (art. 30).

14 *Personnel diplomatique et consulaire des Etats-Unis à Téhéran,* CIJ REC. (1980), p. 3.

générique et compréhensif, elle doit renoncer en même temps à toute valeur opératoire. Car pour évaluer les conditions juridiques dans lesquelles elle peut servir (mis à part son caractère réactif, c'est-à-dire l'existence préalable d'une violation), nous devons préciser la catégorie plus spécifique de réaction couverte par cette acception générique; un niveau auquel les conditions peuvent varier radicalement. Il suffit d'énumérer quelques-unes de ces catégories spécifiques de réaction pour s'en convaincre: la rétorsion, la réciprocité négative, l'*exceptio non adempleti contractus*, l'article 60 de la Convention de Vienne sur le droit des traités, les représailles, les sanctions *stricto sensu*.

Il n'existe cependant pas d'accord général pour confiner le terme à son acception générique; ce qui comporte le double risque de prêter à confusion et de se prêter à manipulation: d'une part, parce qu'on peut utiliser le terme sciemment en lieu et place de la catégorie spécifique des réactions qu'il recouvre dans un cas particulier, afin d'occulter ou d'échapper aux conditions juridiques que doit remplir cette catégorie particulière de contre-mesures; d'autre part, parce qu'elle apparaît comme une notion à géométrie variable, selon le contexte de son emploi ou l'auteur qu'on consulte.

Ainsi, le Professeur Ago, dans son projet d'articles sur la responsabilité des Etats, avait utilisé dans l'article 30 le terme «sanction» pour couvrir (dans le cadre des causes d'exonération) à la fois les réactions des Etats agissant *uti singuli* et les réactions «sociales», prises en application d'une décision ou d'une recommandation d'une organisation internationale compétente. Les discussions au sein de la Commission ont démontré que pour une bonne partie de ses membres, le terme «sanction» a acquis en droit international contemporain un sens plus spécifique, se limitant au deuxième type de réactions seulement. Et c'est ce qui l'a conduite à le remplacer par «contre-mesures», en tant que terme générique couvrant les deux types de réactions[15]. Cependant, pour le Professeur Ago, suivi par la Commission, ce terme ne recouvre pas les mesures de rétorsion, ne s'agissant pas d'actes qui auraient été illicites en soi, en dehors de ce contexte, et n'ayant par conséquent pas besoin d'être justifiés ni exonérés. En revanche, pour une bonne partie de la doctrine, les contre-mesures recouvrent la rétorsion[16], alors que certains de ces mêmes auteurs excluent les sanctions *stricto sensu* des contre-mesures, les limitant ainsi aux réactions des Etats *uti singuli*[17].

---

15 *Voir* Annuaire de la CDI (1979), vol. 1, p. 62 (pour la discussion); vol. II, p. 128 (pour le commentaire de la Commission sur l'article 30, notamment § 21).

16 *E.g.* Ch. Leben, *Les contre-mesures interétatiques et les réactions à l'illicite dans la société internationale*, AFDI (1982), vol. 28, p. 15; O. Schachter, *International Law in Theory and Practice: General Course of International Law*, RCADI (1982-V), vol. 178, p. 180; M. Virally, *Panorama du droit international: Cours général de droit international public*, RCADI (1983-V), vol. 183, p. 217.

17 *E.g.* M. Virally, *op. cit., supra.*

De sorte que le noyau dur de la notion qu'on peut dégager et qui est généralement accepté, se limite en fin de compte aux représailles (comprises dans un sens large pour couvrir leurs dérivés contractuels telle l'*exceptio non adempleti contractus*, ainsi que leurs sous-catégories, telle la réciprocité négative, *reprisals in kind*[18].

V. LES SANCTIONS *STRICTO SENSU*

A. Notion

Comme nous les avons déjà définies, nous entendons par sanctions *stricto sensu* des mesures de contrainte prises à l'encontre d'un Etat ou d'une autre entité en application d'une décision d'un organe social compétent.

Trois éléments sont à retenir dans cette définition:

1) Il s'agit de mesures coercitives, c'est-à-dire de contrainte, quelle soit armée ou non armée, matérielle (militaire, économique, etc.), morale (condamnation) ou purement juridique (suspension ou perte de qualité de membre d'une organisation internationale, bien que de telles sanctions puissent avoir des conséquences matérielles).

Contrainte veut dire également contre la volonté du destinataire, ou du moins sans son consentement; le but ultime de ces mesures étant précisément, comme toutes les voies d'exécution forcée, d'infléchir sa volonté pour le ramener à un comportement conforme au droit. C'est en tant que cible et non pas en tant que partie dans un rapport juridique, qu'il est visé par ces mesures.

2) Ces mesures sont prises à l'encontre, c'est-à-dire au détriment, de leur destinataire, en lui infligeant une valeur négative, une «privation» ou une perte par rapport à sa situation antérieure, en somme une diminution quelconque dans son patrimoine de valeurs matérielles ou morales.

Parallèlement à la distinction connue en matière de responsabilité entre *damnum emergens* et *lucrum cessens*, ces sanctions peuvent être afflictives d'un dommage (telles les mesures de contrainte armée ou non armée des articles 42 et 41 de la Charte) ou privatives d'un avantage. Ce qui correspondrait *grosso modo* aux sanctions des deux catégories de la *summa divisio* du droit international selon le Professeur Wolfgang Friedmann, en «droit international de coexistence» et «droit international de coopération». Les

---

[18] Dans son projet d'articles sur la responsabilité des Etats (Partie II), le Professeur RIPAGHEN a distingué clairement parmi les contre-mesures entre les mesures de réciprocité (art. 8) et celles de représailles (art. 9 et 10) (voir son cinquième rapport, ANNUAIRE DE LA CDI (1984), vol. II, part. 1, p. 3). Cependant, il n'a pas été suivi en cela par la Commission (*voir* pour la discussion, ANNUAIRE DE LA CDI (1985), vol. 1, p. 101 et s.).

premières sont l'issue de ce qui était largement considéré comme les sanctions types *lato sensu* du droit international classique, la guerre et les représailles, même si elles sont par la suite institutionnalisées (par exemple dans le chapitre VII de la Charte). Les secondes ne se conçoivent en revanche que dans un contexte institutionnalisé de coopération, qui devient lui-même l'enjeu des sanctions; celles-ci n'étant en réalité que la privation partielle ou totale des avantages ou bénéfices de la coopération, allant jusqu'à l'exclusion de l'entité sanctionnée du circuit (telle la suspension ou l'exclusion prévue dans les articles 5 et 6 de la Charte)[19].

L'exclusion est une sanction antique qui remonte, comme le bannissement, aux systèmes archaïques de droit. Son rôle était tout autre cependant, car elle signifiait l'exclusion de l'individu de la protection de son groupe social vis-à-vis des autres groupes ou individus, dans des rapports inter-groupes ou inter-tribaux fondés sur le principe de la responsabilité collective. Dans ces conditions, l'exclusion était une sanction hautement afflictive, se rapprochant, du moins partiellement, dans sa visée d'isoler sa cible du groupe, des mesures de contrainte non armée prévues dans l'article 41. Cependant, il faut être conscient que l'«exclusion» peut agir comme une arme à double tranchant, car elle libère l'entité sanctionnée de ses obligations envers la communauté et prive celle-ci, par là même, de certains moyens de pression sur cette entité.

Il faut relever également que cette distinction entre les sanctions du droit de coexistence et celles du droit de coopération, bien que très éclairante au niveau théorique et explicatif, est parfois difficile, si ce n'est impossible, à opérer en pratique.

3) Ces mesures doivent être prises conformément à une décision d'un organe social compétent, c'est-à-dire en dehors ou au-delà des institutions de «justice privée». Car elles présupposent une «constatation» et non seulement une «allégation» ou «prétention» issue d'«auto-interprétation», ainsi qu'une «décision» ordonnant ou recommandant la prise de ces mesures sur la base de cette constatation. Elles sont ainsi fonction du degré d'institutionnalisation du droit international, car elles ne peuvent exister que dans des cadres conventionnels à même d'instituer de tels organes. Il s'agit donc en principe de régimes spéciaux de sanctions, dont le profil juridique et les modalités varient selon l'organisation et le contexte dans lesquels elles sont administrées.

D'habitude ces sanctions sont prises à l'issue d'une procédure de règlement des différends au sein de l'organisation qui n'aboutit pas à un arrange-

---

[19] *Voir* CH. LEBEN, LES SANCTIONS PRIVATIVES DE DROITS OU DE QUALITÉ DANS LES ORGANISATIONS INTERNATIONALES SPÉCIALISÉES, Bruylant, Bruxelles (1979).

ment ramenant le membre en question à un comportement conforme à ses obligations. L'organe compétent «constate» alors la violation et arrête les mesures à prendre selon le traité constitutif, qui peuvent être de le priver de certains avantages ou droits attachés à sa qualité de membre, ou d'autoriser le membre directement lésé à prendre des contre-mesures à son encontre, ou même de le suspendre ou l'exclure de l'organisation.

Cependant, avec l'avènement des organisations internationales générales du XXe siècle (à vocation universelle *ratione personae* et *ratione materiae*) et tout en englobant le même type de sanctions mentionnées ci-dessus, une tendance se fait jour d'abord dans le Pacte de la SdN puis, plus affirmativement, dans la Charte des Nations Unies, de déborder les domaines spécifiques pour s'attaquer à la problématique centrale du droit international (et sa quête séculaire), celle d'apprivoiser la guerre et, par conséquent, d'institutionnaliser la sanction à son égard; d'où leurs systèmes respectifs de sécurité collective.

Le degré d'institutionnalisation, et surtout de centralisation, de la décision n'est cependant pas le même dans les deux systèmes. Cette décision se situe à trois niveaux: celui de constater la violation, celui d'arrêter les mesures à prendre et celui de les exécuter ou de les mettre en oeuvre.

B. La Société des Nations

Ayant inscrit dans son article 10 l'obligation pour chaque membre de «respecter et de maintenir contre toute agression extérieure l'intégrité territoriale et l'indépendance politique» de tous les autres membres, le Pacte établit, à l'article 16, son système de sécurité collective. Le premier alinéa de cet article stipule que tout membre qui «recourt à la guerre en violation des articles 12, 13 et 15 [traitant du règlement pacifique des différends] est *ipso facto* considéré comme ayant commis un acte de guerre contre tous les autres membres», qui s'engagent à lui appliquer immédiatement (c'est-à-dire automatiquement) toutes les sanctions économiques. En plus, aux termes du second alinéa, le Conseil recommande aux membres les mesures militaires à prendre.

L'application de ce système apparemment simple s'est avéré l'être beaucoup moins en pratique. L'obligation d'appliquer automatiquement les sanctions économiques en cas d'agression étant considérée trop contraignante par beaucoup d'Etats membres, la controverse s'est rapidement engagée autour de l'instance compétente pour «constater» l'agression. Plutôt que de suivre la logique du nouveau contexte institutionnel, en reconnaissant cette compétence à l'organe lui-même (en application du principe de la «compétence de la compétence»), un comité de juristes, s'inspirant du droit du XIXe siècle, l'a reconnue aux Etats membres pris individuellement, injectant ainsi l'auto-interprétation au sein du contexte institutionnel.

En ce qui concerne la décision des mesures à prendre, il faut distinguer les sanctions économiques des sanctions militaires. Les premières, comme on l'a vu, sont décrétées dans le Pacte lui-même, car elles devaient être appliquées «automatiquement», c'est-à-dire sans décision spéciale (une fois la violation constatée). Cependant, là aussi, et malgré le texte clair, cette obligation a été interprétée comme laissant aux Etats membres la latitude de décider l'ampleur et le moment de leur application. Quant aux mesures militaires, l'article 16/2 spécifie qu'il est du devoir du Conseil de les *recommander* aux Etats membres intéressés, qui ne sont évidemment pas obligés de suivre cette recommandation. De toute manière, l'application des deux types de sanction est laissée totalement aux Etats. Aucune institutionnalisation ou centralisation n'est prévue à ce niveau-là.

Les piètres résultats de l'unique tentative de la SdN d'appliquer des sanctions (économiques seulement, à l'Italie, dans l'affaire de l'Ethiopie), ont servi de leçon aux rédacteurs de la Charte des Nations Unies.

C. Les Nations Unies

La Charte centralise la décision aux trois niveaux. Ainsi, c'est le Conseil de Sécurité qui «constate», aux termes de l'article 39, «l'existence d'une menace contre la paix, d'une rupture de la paix ou d'un acte d'agression»; et c'est lui aussi, aux termes du même article, qui «fait des recommandations ou décide quelles mesures seront prises conformément aux articles 41 et 42 pour maintenir ou rétablir la paix et la sécurité internationales».

Et si les mesures de contrainte non armées de l'article 41, s'agissant de boycott et d'interruption de relations de toutes sortes, doivent généralement être exécutées par les Etats membres (mais coordonnées par l'Organisation), selon les termes de l'article 42, c'est le Conseil de Sécurité lui-même qui «peut entreprendre» les mesures de contrainte armée prévues dans cet article, en utilisant les forces mises à sa disposition par les Etats membres en vertu des accords prévus à l'article 43 (bien que ces mesures puissent inclure également des «opérations exécutées par les forces aériennes, navales ou terrestres des membres des Nations Unies»)[20].

---

[20] Il faut signaler également deux autres exceptions à cette centralisation au niveau de l'exécution: a) la solution transitoire de l'article 106 – «en attendant l'entrée en vigueur des accords spéciaux mentionnés à l'article 43» – qui autorise des actions menées par les cinq membres

Cependant, ici aussi ce schéma apparemment perfectionné n'a pas résisté à la guerre froide qui allait bientôt éclater et qui l'a grippé à ses deux extrémités: étant donné la division des membres permanents du Conseil de Sécurité, celui-ci n'arrivait pas à faire la «constatation», prémisse de toute «mesure collective», et la guerre froide a mis un terme à tout espoir de conclure les accords prévus par l'article 43, et par là même à la possibilité d'une exécution centralisée. Les rares cas où des décisions ont été prises, ont donné lieu à des mesures «hybrides» ou «a-typiques» par rapport au schéma initial esquissé ci-dessus.

Avant d'essayer de les situer juridiquement par rapport aux sanctions *stricto sensu*, deux clarifications liminaires s'imposent. La première est que l'institutionnalisation ou la centralisation nécessaire pour qualifier juridiquement une mesure de sanction se situe au niveau de la décision et non pas à celui de l'exécution de cette mesure. En d'autres termes, il suffit qu'elle soit prise en application d'une décision sociale, même si son exécution est laissée aux Etats membres ou confiée à l'un ou plusieurs d'entre eux. Car l'Etat ou les Etats (ainsi qu'éventuellement l'entente ou l'organisme régional) agissent dans ce contexte, du moins formellement, non pas à leur compte, *uti singuli*, mais en tant que mandataires de l'organisation qui a pris cette décision. Et cela même si la décision n'est qu'une recommandation, comme l'a fait l'Assemblée générale plus d'une fois, par exemple en recommandant des sanctions contre le Portugal et l'Afrique du Sud.

La seconde clarification porte sur le rôle de l'organe qui prend cette décision. Car il faut garder en vue que dans le schéma de la Charte, le Conseil de Sécurité (pas plus que l'Assemblée générale) n'est pas conçu comme organe d'exécution du droit international général, et que même l'article 94/2 qui prévoit expressément, en cas de non-exécution d'un jugement de la CIJ, le recours au Conseil, lequel, «s'il le juge nécessaire, peut faire des recommandations ou *décider des mesures à prendre* pour faire exécuter l'arrêt» (les mots soulignés étant les mêmes que ceux figurant dans l'article 39), n'a jamais reçu d'application.

La Charte confie plutôt au Conseil «la responsabilité principale du maintien de la paix et de la sécurité internationales» (art. 24/1). Et c'est seulement par leurs effets actuels ou potentiels sur le maintien de la paix que les violations du droit entrent dans le champ d'application des mesures de contrainte armée ou non armée prévues aux articles 41 et 42 de la Charte.

---

permanents du Conseil de Sécurité, avec la possibilité d'y adjoindre d'autres membres; et b) l'utilisation par le Conseil de Sécurité des accords ou organismes régionaux comme agents d'exécution «pour l'application des mesures coercitives prises sous son autorité», aux termes de l'article 53/1.

On pourrait même aller jusqu'à dire qu'il ne s'agit pas là d'une condition nécessaire pour l'application de ces mesures, la «menace contre la paix» n'impliquant pas nécessairement l'existence d'une telle violation. Cependant, comme le remarque très judicieusement le Professeur Jean Combacau, aucune résolution du Conseil de Sécurité ou de l'Assemblée générale ayant décrété de telles mesures, même seulement sur la base d'une menace contre la paix, ne l'a fait qu'après avoir qualifié l'acte contre lequel elle réagissait de violation du droit international[21].

Mais ce propos n'est pas réversible. Car, pas toutes les violations du droit international, même quand elles étaient constatées et condamnées, n'ont été qualifiées de «menace contre la paix», ni assorties de sanctions. Seules les violations de deux principes fondamentaux du droit international contemporain, à savoir l'interdiction du recours à la force et le droit des peuples à disposer d'eux-mêmes (à cause de leur lien étroit avec le maintien de la paix et de la sécurité internationales), quand elles ont pu être constatées (ce qui était rare au Conseil à cause du veto, un peu moins à l'Assemblée), ont été occasionnellement qualifiées de «menaces contre la paix» et assorties de sanctions.

Ces sanctions, lorsqu'elles ont été appliquées, ont rarement suivi fidèlement le schéma initial de la Charte. Ainsi par exemple, des mesures de contrainte non armée (art. 41) ont été décrétées par l'Assemblée générale, c'est-à-dire par des résolutions ayant valeur de recommandation. Quant aux mesures de contrainte armée, dans les rares cas où le Conseil a pu parvenir à les décréter, il l'a toujours fait en demandant aux Etats membres ou en les autorisant à les entreprendre. En d'autres termes, il n'est jamais arrivé à une institutionnalisation et à une centralisation au niveau de l'exécution.

La différence entre ce type d'action et les représailles ou contre-mesures comme nous les avons définies, réside dans le fait que cette action se fonde sur une constatation de violation et une décision l'autorisant; et que l'Etat en l'entreprenant agit ou est censé agir en tant qu'organe social et non pas pour défendre un intérêt particulier, *uti singulus*, comme sujet de droit. En revanche, les représailles se fondent sur l'auto-interprétation du sujet qui les entreprend pour défendre en principe ses intérêts propres; bien que depuis la fin des années soixante-dix, des Etats aient pris des contre-mesures (mais en réalité dans la quasi-totalité des cas il s'agissait simplement de mesures de rétorsion) contre ce qu'ils considéraient des violations des obligations *erga omnes* qui ne les touchaient pas directement (par exemple contre

---

[21] J. COMBACAU, *Sanctions*, ENCYCLOPEDIA OF PUBLIC INTERNATIONAL LAW, vol. 9, p. 339.

l'Union soviétique après l'intervention militaire en Afghanistan ou contre la Pologne après la déclaration de l'état d'exception)[22].

Ce modèle hybride de sanctions, comportant seulement une «légitimation collective» sans «action collective»[23], qui a été qualifié à l'occasion de l'affaire de Corée déjà d'«exécution permise» ou «autorisée» (*permissive enforcement*), a idéalement le mérite, en l'absence de ressources propres de l'Organisation en forme de forces armées mises directement à sa disposition, de mobiliser les ressources et l'action individuelles des Etats membres au service du but collectif. Mais il comporte en même temps, sur un plan plus terre à terre, le risque d'un détournement du cadre et de la légitimation collectifs pour servir des visées privées et inavouées des Etats qui entreprennent l'action; en d'autres termes, de mettre le collectif au service de l'individuel plutôt que l'inverse. Plus l'autorisation est «permissive», c'est-à-dire large et vague, plus grands sont l'ambiguïté qui entoure l'action prise sous sa houlette et les dangers de son détournement à des fins autres que celles de la collectivité[24].

De tels doutes ont toujours plané sur ce type hybride d'opérations, depuis la première en Corée (souvent décrite comme première riposte militaire en

---

22 *Voir* P.-M. DUPUY, *Observations sur la pratique récente des «sanctions» de l'illicite*, RGDIP (1983), vol. 87, pp. 505–548. *Cf.* CH. LEBEN, *op. cit.*, *supra* note 16.

23 Il s'agit de catégories analytiques relevant de la science politique plutôt que du droit. Pour un essai de définition, *voir* G. M. ABI-SAAB, *La notion d'organisation internationale: Essai de synthèse*, dans: LE CONCEPT D'ORGANISATION INTERNATIONALE (G. ABI-SAAB, directeur de publication), UNESCO, Paris (1980).

24 Ainsi par exemple, la rés. 678 du Conseil de Sécurité, adoptée le 24 novembre 1990, qui a servi de base juridique à l'action armée des «coalisés» contre l'Irak, a autorisé «les Etats membres... à user de tous les moyens nécessaires pour faire respecter et appliquer la résolution 660 (1990) et toutes les résolutions pertinentes ultérieures et pour rétablir la paix et la sécurité internationales dans la région».

Il s'agit là d'une abdication totale de la part du Conseil au profit des Etats membres de tout contrôle et de tout pouvoir d'appréciation quant au choix des moyens (le mot «force» n'y figure même pas), et à l'évaluation de leur «nécessité» et de l'ampleur et des limites de leur emploi. Cela a conduit un des conseillers juridiques des Nations Unies à qualifier cette résolution de «renonciation contractuelle aux fonctions coercitives du Conseil de Sécurité», qu'il avait commencé à exercer en imposant des sanctions économiques par sa résolution 661; elle rétablit le droit de légitime défense collective des Etats, qu'ils exercent sous leur propre responsabilité (R. ZACKLIN, *Les Nations Unies et la crise du Golfe*, dans: LES ASPECTS JURIDIQUES DE LA CRISE ET DE LA GUERRE DU GOLFE (sous la direction de B. STERN), Montchrétien, Paris (1991), p. 69.

Cette qualification juridique exclurait ces actions de notre définition des sanctions *stricto sensu*. Il faut noter cependant que dans cette hypothèse, l'exercice du droit de légitime défense reste assujetti aux conditions qui lui sont imposées par le droit international général, notamment la proportionnalité dont on pourrait raisonnablement soutenir qu'elle n'a pas été respectée, mais dont le dépassement a été défendu en l'espèce par la poursuite des objectifs globaux des Nations Unies dans la région. Ce qui ne tiendrait pas juridiquement si l'on fonde l'action militaire sur la légitime défense collective. Toutes ces controverses illustrent bien les grands dangers qui entourent le recours à ce type hybride d'action.

application de la politique d'«endiguement», *containment*) jusqu'à celle en Irak (largement perçue comme devant asseoir un «nouvel ordre mondial» musclé, structuré à partir de l'existence d'une seule super-puissance, et en fonction de ses propres intérêts).

En d'autres termes, pendant la période de la guerre froide, à cause du veto et du blocage du Conseil de Sécurité, le problème en matière de sanctions était que le système ne pouvait pas fonctionner comme prévu dans la Charte. Là où le blocage a pu être évité, de par l'absence fortuite de l'Union soviétique du Conseil (Corée), ou en s'adressant à l'Assemblée générale si la majorité requise pouvait être mobilisée, le maximum atteignable était de constater la violation et d'inviter ou d'autoriser l'action des Etats membres pour y mettre fin[25]. Les résolutions ainsi prises et l'action entreprise par les Etats pour leur exécution reflétaient nécessairement la position des Etats constituant la majorité et notamment ceux qui avaient bien voulu entreprendre l'action.

La fin de la guerre froide rend possible l'institutionnalisation et la centralisation au niveau de l'exécution également. L'absence de forces armées directement disponibles en cas d'urgence n'est pas un obstacle infranchissable à cet égard. Car le Conseil de Sécurité peut conclure rapidement des accords *ad hoc* avec les Etats qui seraient prêts à lui fournir les forces nécessaires, comme il le fait pour les forces de maintien de la paix (*peace-keeping*).

Dans ces conditions, insister à garder l'«action exécutive» en dehors des Nations Unies et au-delà de tout contrôle de la part de l'Organisation augmente les possibilités de détournement de cette action et accroît démesurément le danger de voir le système, enfin dégrippé, fonctionner à rebours en conférant un semblant de légalité et de collégialité à des entreprises et des visées qui le sont beaucoup moins.

---

[25] Une action collective de contrainte armée aurait demandé d'autres décisions du Conseil impossibles à obtenir, et ne pouvait provenir de l'Assemblée générale même si une tentative d'étendre la compétence de l'Assemblée générale aux mesures collectives de contrainte a été entreprise dans la résolution 377 (V) de 1950, dite *Union pour la paix*, qui de par son caractère manifestement exorbitant et des fortes contestations auxquelles elle a donné lieu, n'a jamais trouvé application. On est parvenu par la suite à échaffauder d'autres types de «mesures collectives, mais non coercitives», par l'entremise de l'Assemblée, sous la forme d' «opérations de maintien de la paix» (*peace-keeping operations*).

International Law and the Concept of Law: Why International Law is Law

by

Chittharanjan F. Amerasinghe

There has always been some controversy over the status of international law; whether it is law *stricto sensu*. As is well known, among others, Austin, a positivist theorist, denied to international law the status of law, pointing out that it does not have the characteristics of law, and particularly emphasizing the absence of proper sanctions and enforcement mechanisms. Austinian theory emphasized other aspects of a concept of law, such as command which implied a law-giving legislature and sanctions, but modern legal positivism has come to concentrate more on the elements of sanctions and enforcement. Austin and the legal positivists, however, were not the only theorists to deny international law the status of law. There have been many besides them who have also done so.

Closely associated with the question whether international law can be properly described as law is the issue of the binding force of international law or what makes international law binding. It should be recognized that, while this is a legitimate question, it is different from the primary one whether international law can be characterized as law.[1]

Similarly, the question why international law is generally obeyed or why it is respected or not is of a different nature from the issue of whether international law is law. The answer to that question may depend on a variety of practical considerations which may or may not hinge on the nature of international law.[2] It is much less fundamental.

The jurisprudential search for an answer to the question of the nature of international law may not be entirely an academic pursuit. It is a matter of some practical importance whether the legal system which governs primarily the relations between States and like entities but may also now cover individuals is to be characterized as law or is to be regarded as, for example,

---

[1] On the binding force of international law *see e.g.* O. Schachter, *Towards a Theory of International Obligation*, 8 VaJIL (1968) at 300; M.S. McDougal, H.D. Lasswell and W.M. Reisman, *Theories about International Law: Prologue to a Configurative Jurisprudence*, *ibid.* at 188. *See* also C.F. Amerasinghe, 1 Law of International Civil Service (1994) at 18 ff., and footnote 52 at 22 therein for further references.

[2] *See e.g.* O.Schachter, *op. cit.*, *supra* note 1.

an extension of morality. Apart from the psychological implications of the view taken, its impact on international society could be of considerable importance. It makes a material, and not merely an intangible, difference that a violation of Article 2(4) of the Charter of the United Nations, for instance, is regarded as a breach of a legal obligation not to use force rather than as a mere violation of some socially important norm. Thus, it is significant that the invasion of Kuwait by Iraq was generally treated as an illegal act violating the Charter of the United Nations, and not simply as an unfriendly, immoral or other kind of act.

A brief foray will be made here into considering the questions whether the international law is "law", why it should be so considered and how answers to such questions should be formulated. The purpose is not to provide a concept or definition of "law" but to suggest an approach.

There are many possible approaches to the problems being addressed. Based on a criticism of the theories of law that have evolved up to the present, including the positivist theories of such scholars as Austin, Kelsen and H.L.A. Hart (to mention only a few), it may by concluded that it is necessary to recognize the practical reality of international law and to deny the usefulness of being concerned with concepts or definitions. As has been stated, the view may be taken that the Hart approach,[3] for example, is a result of a priorism and over-simplification, even though it refers to a concept rather than a definition of law, and that, like Austin,[4] Hart offers views primarily related to the way things are ordered in the "more developed" modern States.[5] Not only do these theories *a priori* exclude primitive law and international law from the concept or definition of law, but they may not cover some legal systems of modern States in certain parts of the world, which, of course, would then be relegated to the category of primitive law.

In this connection several realities that have been readily recognized must be conceded. To mention only some of them, first, the fact that rules described as rules of international law by governments are actually used by governments cannot be questioned:

> "All normal governments employ experts to provide routine and other advice on matters of international law and constantly define their relations with other States in terms of international law. Governments and their officials routinely use rules which they have for a very long time

[3] H.L.A. HART, THE CONCEPT OF LAW (1994), Chapter X.

[4] T. AUSTIN, THE PROVINCE OF JURISPRUDENCE DETERMINED (1832); H.L.A. Hart's edition (1954) at 14 ff. For a trenchant criticism of Austin's theory *see* T. NARDIN, LAW, MORALITY AND THE RELATIONS OF STATES (1983) at 121 ff.

[5] I.A. BROWNLIE, *The Reality and Efficacy of International Law*, 52 BYIL (1981) at 6.

> called the 'law of nations' or 'international law.' It is not the case that the resort to law is propagandist – though it sometimes is. The evidence is that reference to international law has been a part of the normal process of decision-making... If States use international law, and they do, then it seems impertinent to question the classification of the rules since even if governments have made some error (according to *academic* categories) the rules still exist and have to be examined."[6]

Secondly, the international system of norms, partly because of the distinctive structure of the society to which it belongs, is, it may be contended, less elaborate and, in a sense, perhaps more rudimentary than national legal orders. It is different from the latter but for that reason does not merit being described as inferior or less legal. What some would describe as structural weaknesses, such as the peculiar nature of its sanctions mechanisms and the mediocrity of norms in many cases, must be recognized.[7] Thirdly, it cannot be denied that there may be breakdowns in the efficacy of the international legal system, such as where terrorism with international implications cannot be controlled or the taking of hostages as an instrument of policy without legal justification is left without sanction. But there have conceivably been similar breakdowns in national systems of law and order, such as where civil wars, wars of secession and *coups d'êtat* have taken place (especially in great numbers since 1945). In a sense it may convincingly be argued that public international law is more efficacious than *public* law within national States. The pertinent observation has been made that:

> "At any rate, whether or not such a judgment is sustainable, those who would judge international law would do well, on ground of logical consistency, to start out by taking a hard look at the performance of *national* legal systems. It is a striking fact that in discussion on the efficacy of sanctions directed at the Smith regime in Rhodesia after U.D.I. it was common for reference to be made to the 'ineffectiveness' of United Nations resolutions. In this context it was unusual to hear reference to the efficacy of the Southern Rhodesia Act of 1965 and the law of treason as applicable in Rhodesia. Logically the Westminster *grundnorm* was as much in issue as the New York *grundnorm*."[8]

---

6 *Ibid.* at 1, 5.

7 P. WEIL, *Towards Relative Normativity in International Law*, 77 AJIL (1983) at 413–414: This author observes that in some areas there are lacunae or the substance of rules are too controversial effectively to govern the conduct of international persons or norms have remained at the stage of abstract general standards on which only what appears to be the slow development of international law can confer concrete substance and precise meaning.

8 I.A. BROWNLIE, *op. cit.*, *supra* note 5, at 2.

There do exist in *national* communities criminal individuals and groups which cannot be brought to justice sometimes, alienated and violent minorities which cannot be controlled and forms of racialism which violates the basic constitutional principles of States. It follows that all legal and political systems, not only the international, are confronted with situations in which the law is not applied inflexibly and rigidly for whatever reasons. In the international legal systems, as in national systems, law is not a substitute for the political will of States or communities, as the case may be, in dealing with situations by reference to cooperation. Criticism, which takes into account the above features, should be directed not at the system but elsewhere.

To look at the matter from another angle, the comparison of international law to primitive law may be examined. Some scholars have concluded that the analogy is very poor and misguided. While, on the one hand, such features as the societal organization behind the law, the authority to apply sanctions, the lack of a central government and of the existence of direct centrally organized sanctions (though not the existence of sanctions *per se*), the lack of a legislature and possibly the lack of courts with compulsory jurisdiction may indicate some similarity between international law and primitive law, there is reason to believe that it is not entirely helpful to generalize about this similarity and certainly unwise to conclude that the identity is complete. At least two reasons have been given for the inadequacy of the comparison:

> "First, consider international law. The rules of international law seem in general to be more articulate, and developed, as (written) rules. There is a 'science' of international law. There are rules of recognition to the extent that the rules of international law can be 'identified' by officials or advisers, apart from authoritative adjudication, although it is not clear the extent to which such rules might also exist in primitive societies, and it can be questioned whether such identification processes allow authoritative 'rules of recognition' so that the international system is here comparable with a modern system. International law may be accepted by modern municipal courts as a modern form of law, and may have municipal sanctions attached to it. It may operate both vertically and horizontally. There may in the courts be a more formal appeal to rules, together with a belief by international lawyers that this is the way forward, rather than to look for reconciliation or compromise. The subjects of the law of nations and primitive society differ, with, possibly, corresponding legal implications.
>
> Second, there is the society. The society in which international law operates is not necessarily comparable to all primitive tribes. It is composed of more independent and powerful units. It may be less stable, and liable to rapid change and potential chaos, given the interaction of technology on cultural differences. The best analogy between international law and

> 'primitive law' is made with the stateless primitive society. If the analogy is most successfully being made with 'stateless' primitive society, rather than with all primitive society – and the 'stateless' is not necessarily co-terminous with 'primitive' – do we learn anything other than the generally disorganized character of the international community which we knew already, rather than indicating that the 'law' is primitive."[9]

The appropriate conclusion is that though international law may share some characteristics with some primitive legal systems, it is really a unique system, different in many respects both from most modern national systems of law, and from primitive legal systems in general. On the other hand, it may upon examination have much in common with modern national systems of law.

With these observations, it is possible to approach the question of definition or concepts. Sometimes a distinction has been made between a definition and a concept. Writers seem today to be more concerned with the latter than the former. There may be some differences between the two but basically the purpose of both is to identify the "essential" abstracted characteristics of the phenomenon for which the word defined or the concept analysed stands. By referring to a concept rather than a definition the fact cannot be hidden that a deliberate choice has to be made in regard to what phenomena are to be included in the concept. As early as 1884 the point was made by Lawrence that the controversy about the definition of law was a logomachy – a dispute about words, not things – and that everything depended upon the definition chosen for adoption.[10] As regards definition it has been observed:

> "Firstly, that a definition need only be a label; secondly, that the same word can be defined differently. Seldom is a definition incorrect (unless it states characteristics not possessed by the thing), nor is there any 'true' or 'only' definition. Thirdly, every definition is governed by the definor's standpoint and purpose and it is either adequate or inadequate for that purpose. One may always question the standpoint and purpose and consider the adequacy of the definition thereby, but criticism of it from other points of view is misconceived. Finally, since a definition is the product of the definor's analysis, it should not be generalized beyond the limits within which it was framed."[11]

The same may be said of concepts. By using the word "concept" instead of "definition", the problems of choice, identification, abstraction and expla-

---

[9] A. CAMPBELL, *International Law and Primitive Law*, 8 OXFORD JOURNAL OF LEGAL STUDIES (1988) at 194.

[10] T.J. LAWRENCE, ESSAYS ON SOME DISPUTED QUESTIONS IN MODERN INTERNATIONAL LAW (1884) at 29.

[11] R.W.M. DIAS, *Mechanism of Definition as Applied to International Law,* 12 CLJ (1954) at 219.

nation are not solved or evaded. There is always a certain subjectivity in definition or conceptualization.

One alternative is to eschew definition or conceptualization. What the result of this would be has been summarized as follows:

> "When jurisprudence comes to shake itself free from verbal controversies, there will still be some questions, hitherto discussed in connection with verbal ones, that may usefully be saved for discussion on their own account. Thus a comparison of international law with municipal law would be a factual, not a verbal discussion. Again, one may usefully hold, debate over the reasons why men observe rules; how far rules are observed; the reasons for non-observance; how far a particular rule-system is adequate to the needs of society; and how its sanctions can be improved. Any of these matters may be discussed in its own right; but to discuss it as incident to the question whether a system of rules is properly called law is to consign the issue to sterility."[12]

This is an eminently sensible option, though some may perhaps regard it either as a counsel of perfection or as the line of least resistance.

Given the relativity of definition or conceptualization in any case and the possibility that the dispute may be about words or a logomachy rather than a useful controversy about realities that need to be addressed and discussed seriously, one may ask why in any event the word, or concept of, "law" must generally be so defined or described as to exclude international law and to include practically and solely "developed" national systems of law. It is clearly possible to adopt a definition or concept which is broad enough to include international law and cover modern national systems of law as well. Then, the question may be asked why should the definition or concept exclude primitive law whose object was undoubtedly similar to, if not identical with, that of international law and modern systems of law. In the last analysis it may be suggested that from one point of view the solution adopted is a matter of taste.

Many explanations of the phenomenon of "law" have been given in the past, whether the search is for a definition or the discussion is about concepts. Two positivist approaches are mentioned here in order to show that the concern is almost solely with developed national systems of law. H.L.A. Hart explains his concept of law by reference to two specific qualities: namely (i) the existence of both primary and secondary rules; the former type are laws concerning human actions and accidents of the usual kind, the latter are concerned

---

12 G. WILLIAMS, *International Law and the Controversy over the Word Law*, 22 BYIL (1954) at 163. On the issue of law and language *see* also N.G. ONUF, WORLD OF OUR MAKING: RULES AND RULE IN SOCIAL THEORY AND INTERNATIONAL RELATIONS (1990) at 67.

with conferring powers and helping to identify those competent to make, and change, the primary rules; and (ii) the existence of an ultimate *rule of recognition* which provides the particular system of rules with its criteria of validity; in other words, a rule which specifies the sources of valid rules.[13] Another writer explained his concept of law as follows: (a) an indefinitely large number of empirically verifiable propositions (the products of "legal thought") alternatively (i) expressing, with a high degree of accuracy, the relation between all possible occurrences or situations and probably consequent court reactions in effectively authorizing or refusing to authorize the use of physical compulsion (sanctions) against persons – in the general form "if situation X then sanction Y" (rules of substantive law), or (ii) affirming the existence of substantive liberties, duties or powers attaching to persons; (b) a limited number of such propositions describing, with a similar degree of accuracy, regularities in the activities of the specified court or court-system in (i) hearing issues (rules of evidence and procedure) and (ii) their mode of reaching conclusions (rules of the judicial process); and (c) a number of true propositions asserting all human activity within a definite area of ordered society and during the above-mentioned time to be either past or present realization of substantive liberties, performance of duties, or wrongs or breaches of duty which have been or will be followed by the above-predicted sanctions to the extent needed to guarantee the maintenance of general order within that area (the society to which the legal system "belongs").[14]

Regardless of how "accurate" or useful these descriptions of the concept of law are as reflections of national legal systems, it is clear that they and others like them, such as Austin's, are a result of concentration solely on national legal systems (or some of them, such as the American, English, French and others like them) as the subject phenomenon to be embraced by the concept. The natural consequence is that international law which does not have the identical characteristics of national laws chosen to be included in these concepts of law will not fit into those concepts. These writers, therefore, exclude international law from their concept of law.

Is this method of proceeding necessary, adequate or acceptable? Would it not be more sensible and realistic to look at the common characteristics of systems of law including international law and so try to formulate a concept of law, if this is the object of the exercise? While definition or formulation of a concept may ultimately be a matter of taste and depend on the purpose or subjective choice of the person defining or formulating the concept, in-

---

13 H.L.A. HART, *op. cit.*, *supra* note 3, at 3 ff.

14 B. KING, *The Concept of a Lawyer's Jurisprudence*, 11 CLJ (1953) at 418.

ternational lawyers and those concerned with international affairs or the welfare of nations would certainly like to see international law included in the definition or concepts of law.

In the light of what has been said above attempts to define international law *per se* as a phenomenon separate from national law, while not being futile or impossible exercises, may not really advance the cause of international law but may tend to reduce the credibility of international law as a "legal system" which there is no denying that it is. For example, international law may be defined as "propositions applicable to, and notional patterns of conduct for, States primarily, which are normally binding on international tribunals and the courts of some countries."[15] As the formulator of this definition points out at the same time, in any case this definition cannot be a magic formula but amounts to no more than a summary of the main points of an analysis made by the formulator. One may question the comprehensiveness, the essence, or lack of essence, even the serviceability of the particular definition. But this is not the point. Such an attempt to define international law *per se*, while being an academic exercise may blur the fact that there are points of similarity between international law and modern national systems of law which make them species of the same genus.

To attempt a definition or conceptualization of law so as to include international law is not the purpose of a short essay of this kind. That would require a much longer and more analytical and exploratory canvass. Suffice it to identify, as has been done here, the possibility, and the advisability from a practical point of view, of incorporating international law in such a definition or concept. For example, without making any prejudgment it may be suggested that a basic idea common to all systems of modern law, including international law, is that law comprises rules which will be recognized and applied by courts or tribunals relevant to the system in the event that such courts or tribunals are called upon to settle disputes involving the application of such rules. Such an approach would take into account the absence of a compulsory system for the settlement of disputes in international law, while relating law to the activity of courts or tribunals. The absence of a central legislature and a compulsory system of sanctions in international law such as exists in national legal systems, would also have to be taken into account in developing a definition or concept rather than raising such absence as a reason for excluding international law from such a definition or concept of law. Many scholars admit that these two features are not basic to their concepts or definitions of law so that it would be easier now to work around them.

---

[15] R.W.M. DIAS, *op. cit.*, *supra* note 11, at 231.

It is not such a great step to work around the absence of a system of compulsory jurisdiction as well.

To move forward from this position, it is difficult to disagree with the observation that:

> "International law as a practical activity does in fact have a great deal in common which municipal law. The language and procedure of the one are closely akin to those of the other. The modern legal profession is one that embraces international law as well as the municipal law of particular countries. The activity of those who are concerned with international law, public and private – statesmen and their legal advisers, national and international courts, and international assemblies – is carried on in terms of the assumption that the rules with which they are dealing are rules of law. If the right and duties asserted under these rules were believed to have the status merely of morality or of etiquette, this whole corpus of activity could not exist. The fact that these rules are believed to have the status of law, whatever theoretical difficulties it might involve, makes possible a corpus of international activity that plays an important part in the working of international society."[16]

It has also been pointed out that, while there may be a certain amount of uncertainty in the content of international legal rules, there is in the international system provision for and the possibility of authoritative determination, whether by public officials or by international courts or tribunals.[17] That international law is different in many respects from national laws cannot be denied, particularly as regards the nature of authoritative determination. At the same time it cannot be assimilated, as has been seen, to primitive law – there are significant differences. Further, it does not seem to be a useful pursuit to determine whether international law is closer to or more like primitive law rather than like national legal systems in terms of its principal characteristics.

In this context, the rule-scepticism which some theorists on international law[18] tend to discern is not a certain feature of international law, as distinguished from national law. There is an element of uncertainty and unforeseeability about the meaning and application of rules in all legal systems – otherwise there would be no need for authoritative determinations or interpretations in the application of the law by bodies such as courts. There may be a question of degree, however. A more pertinent observation re-

16 H. BULL, THE ANARCHICAL SOCIETY (1977) at 130. The theoretical difficulties referred to are the result of emphasizing differences rather than similarities in conceptualization. *See* also above what I.A. Brownlie had to say (at *supra* notes 5 and 6).

17 T. NARDIN, *op. cit.*, *supra* note 4, at 133 ff., and at 158 ff.

18 *See ibid.* at 188 ff.

garding similarities is perhaps to be found in the instrumentalist theories of the policy-oriented school of jurisprudence[19] which describe law as a basis for choosing and implementing policies intended to promote shared purposes. Thus, that similar characteristics can be found cannot be doubted. As already pointed out earlier, the element of recognition or possible recognition by dispute settling organs, such as courts and tribunals, or rules, is a significant common feature, even in the absence of compulsory jurisdiction. What is important is to concentrate on finding similarities which can be developed into an all-embracing concept rather than to identify differences which results in developing separate concepts or definitions.[20] That this is possible, even if without too much detail and elaboration, cannot be denied.[21]

The history of modern legal theory reveals that there have emerged a multiplicity of theories beginning perhaps with the naturalists.[22] These have not really gone beyond focusing on systems of national law, to the exclusion of international law, as the subject to be studied. It is not essential, in encompassing international law as a species of the same genus as national law, to begin by trying to make the former fit the strait-jacket that the positivists have stitched with enforcement and such characteristics as basic requirements,[23] though such characteristics may be examined in order to find what the systems of law have in common. As international law cannot be considered as a phenomenon which is outside a realistic concept of law, a concept could very well be developed which takes into account the basic characteristics of international law and national systems of law. It is one thing to devise a concept of law which does not include systems of primitive law. It is another to develop a concept which includes modern systems of law and international law.

---

19 *See* M.S. MCDOUGAL, STUDIES IN WORLD PUBLIC ORDER (1960) *passim* but particularly at 164 ff.

20 This seems to have been the result of studies such as those of H.L.A. HART, B. KING and R.M.W. DIAS, who may be described as positivists (see references in *supra* notes).

21 In this connection it seems inaccurate to describe international law as solely a "morality". That it is more than this is quite clear. There is a clear difference between morality and international law, not least in the respect that international law is applied by courts and adjudicating bodies, among others: for a consideration of international morality *see* T. NARDIN *op. cit.*, *supra* note 4, at 223 ff.

22 *See e.g.* the account given of legal theories in W.G. FRIEDMANN, LEGAL THEORY (1953) at 17 ff.

23 This is the approach taken by D'AMATO, INTERNATIONAL LAW: PROCESS AND PROSPECTS (1995) at 7 ff. The author tries to find a common element in "enforcement" as a requirement (laid down by, *e.g.* AUSTIN). While it may be possible to find such a common element by redefining the terms as used by Austin, the prior question is whether enforcement in Austin's sense or some other sense is crucial to a concept of law. Then one may ask what is required for the "enforcement" characteristic to be satisfied.

Droit international public et droit international privé: deux identités bien distinctes

par

Maarten Bos

I

Le choix du sujet indiqué dans le titre de cette contribution au *Liber Amicorum* dédié à notre Confrère et Ami Krzysztof Skubiszewski à l'occasion de son soixante-dixième anniversaire nous a été suggéré par le fait que, lui et moi, nous avons été membres de la dix-neuvième Commission de l'Institut de Droit International depuis sa création en 1984 jusqu'à ce jour. La tâche confiée à cette Commission fut celle d'étudier la compétence extraterritoriale de l'Etat. Au cours de ses travaux, la Commission a décidé de se limiter aux aspects de la matière relevant du droit international public et de laisser de côté le droit international privé dans la mesure du possible. Encore a-t-elle voulu se concentrer sur les principes généraux du droit international public que ses recherches révéleraient, tout en réservant l'étude ultérieure de leur applicabilité en toutes circonstances. Trois rapports ont été circulés débouchant sur un projet de résolution comprenant dix articles et soumis à deux séances plénières de l'Institut lors de sa Session de Milan 1993. C'est pendant les discussions consacrées audit projet qu'une certaine dichotomie s'est fait jour entre publicistes et privatistes remontant, à ce qu'il paraît, à des vues opposées de la position qu'occupent droit international public et droit international privé, l'un vis-à-vis de l'autre. Pour éclaircir l'approche suivie dans les rapports autant que dans le projet de résolution, et dont je suis l'auteur en tant que rapporteur de la dix-neuvième Commission, il paraît utile de juxtaposer ici les bases profondes de chacune de ces deux disciplines[1].

II

Commençons par la constatation d'une vérité élémentaire, mais loin d'être superflue dans le présent contexte, savoir que le droit international

---

[1] Pour les développements au sein de l'Institut, *voir* Annuaire de l'Institut de Droit International (1993), vol. 65-I, pp. 13–190, et 65-II (1994), pp. 133–164.

public, en principe, vise les rapports entre Etats, le droit international privé ceux entre des particuliers, qu'il s'agisse de personnes privées ou de sociétés. Il importe, en plus, de se rappeler deux autres vérités fondamentales, celle de l'universalité du droit international public général et celle de l'appartenance du droit international privé au droit national, de sorte que sa validité est, en principe, limitée à l'ordre juridique national auquel il ressort.

Une quatrième vérité n'est pas non plus à négliger. Elle se rapporte à la nature différente de l'ordre juridique international, d'un côte, des ordres juridiques nationaux, de l'autre. C'est ici que je désire faire référence à l'un des passages les plus fameux dans la jurisprudence de la Cour Permanente de Justice Internationale. Il s'agit de l'arrêt du 25 mai 1926 rendu par cette dernière dans l'*Affaire relative à certains intérêts allemands en Haute-Silésie polonaise* (Fond) et où la Cour s'est prononcée de la façon suivante:

> «Au regard du droit international et de la Cour qui en est l'organe, les lois nationales sont de simples faits, manifestations de la volonté et de l'activité des Etats, au même titre que les décisions judiciaires ou les mesures administratives. La Cour n'est certainement pas appelée à interpréter la loi polonaise comme telle; mais rien ne s'oppose à ce qu'elle se prononce sur la question de savoir si, en appliquant ladite loi, la Pologne agit ou non en conformité avec les obligations que la Convention de Genève [conclue le 15 mai 1922 entre l'Allemagne et la Pologne] lui impose envers l'Allemagne»[2].

Passage des plus fameux, je disais, mais aussi des plus controversés. La littérature abonde en commentaires s'opposant à la caractérisation de «simples faits» des lois nationales vis-à-vis du droit international public. Pour ne citer qu'Edvard Hambro dans son cours de 1962 à l'Académie de Droit International, «It is very difficult indeed to know what this statement really means. Since the Court quite clearly has to evaluate facts as well as law, it cannot be said that this statement adds very much to our knowledge»[3].

Il n'est, en réalité, pas difficile du tout d'apprécier ladite caractérisation à sa juste valeur. Pour ce faire, il y a avantage à analyser quelque peu le concept de ce qu'on appelle du «droit». Celui-ci se distingue en deux variétés, un concept général et un concept normatif. Le concept général représente une vision – disons – scientifique ou phénoménologique du droit. Personne ne niera la présence en chaque Etat du monde d'un ordre juridique national. Dans chacun de ces Etats, il y a du «droit». Toutefois, rien que l'extrême

---

[2] C.P.J.I. Série A, RECUEIL DES ARRÊTS, n° 7, p. 19.

[3] E. HAMBRO, *The Relations between International Law and Conflict Law*, Académie de Droit international, RECUEIL DES COURS (1962-I), p. 18.

diversité des ordres juridiques nationaux démontre l'existence quasiment dans chaque Etat d'un concept du droit qui lui est propre et qu'un autre Etat refuserait d'accepter pour lui-même. Chaque Etat, en d'autres termes, a son concept normatif du droit. C'est ce concept-ci qui détermine tout son ordre juridique, et c'est l'ensemble de ces concepts normatifs variés qui répond de l'aspect extraordinairement multicolore qu'offre notre monde juridique. Bien sûr, il y a certaines ressemblances entre les ordres juridiques de certains Etats, et c'est pourquoi les comparatistes distinguent des «familles» parmi les ordres juridiques nationaux, mais cela ne saurait en aucun cas diminuer la valeur de la distinction opérée, celle d'un concept général et d'un concept normatif du droit[4].

Or, ce qui s'applique entre ordres juridiques nationaux s'applique au même titre à ceux-ci d'un côté, l'ordre juridique international de l'autre côté. L'ordre juridique international, tout imprégné de son propre concept normatif du droit qu'il est, ne nie pas pour cela le fait d'ordres juridiques nationaux, mais il les reconnaît seulement sous l'angle du concept général du droit et non pas pour dire qu'ils pourraient l'intéresser d'un point de vue normatif. Le contraire serait plutôt étonnant. Le monde des Etats ne se compare nullement à celui des particuliers. Les deux évoluent en des circonstances historiques tout à fait différentes dans lesquelles il serait impossible de construire un ordre juridique commun autour d'un seul concept normatif du droit. Le concept normatif du droit international public, par la force des choses, est bien plus «primitif» que les concepts normatifs dont les ordres juridiques nationaux font preuve. Ce n'est qu'exceptionnellement qu'ils se recouvrent: voir l'Article 38, premier alinéa, lettre c, du Statut de la Cour Internationale de Justice autorisant la Cour à appliquer les principes généraux de droit reconnus par les nations civilisées.

Revenons maintenant à l'arrêt de 1926. A mon avis, c'est exactement dans l'esprit évoqué à l'alinéa précédent que l'ancienne Cour a voulu s'exprimer au sujet du droit international public et sa perception du droit national. En appelant «de simples faits» les lois nationales, elle a fait ressortir leur appartenance à un monde juridique qui pour elle, la Cour, fut dépourvu de normativité, de telle sorte qu'elle s'estimait en droit de juger de la conformité de ces lois au droit international public, ce dernier étant pour elle l'aune à laquelle mesurer tout fait, y compris les faits législatifs nationaux.

Mais un fait législatif est-il bien un fait comme les autres? L'établissement d'un fait au sens habituel du mot requiert des preuves. Pour savoir si

---

[4] J'ai davantage élaboré la distinction dans ma METHODOLOGY OF INTERNATIONAL LAW (1984), p. 3 et s.

une loi nationale est ou non conforme aux exigences éventuelles posées par le droit international public, il faut l'interpréter. Preuve et interprétation, toutefois, ne sont en somme que la même chose [5] et à cet égard, un fait législatif national, en effet, ne diffère donc en rien d'un «simple fait». La seule question qui reste pour le juge international est comment s'acquitter de son devoir d'interprétation d'une loi nationale. Comment s'y prendre?

La Cour Permanente y a répondu dans son arrêt du 12 juillet 1929 dans l'*Affaire concernant le paiement de divers emprunts serbes émis en France* [6]. Apparemment, dans ce cas – et contrairement à celui relatif à certains intérêts allemands en Haute-Silésie polonaise – la Cour se croyait obligée d'interpréter une loi nationale, et la Cour de conclure que «le sens et la portée» en étaient ceux déterminés par la plus haute cour du pays en question, la France. Renonçant ainsi à «une interprétation personnelle» [7], la Cour ne faisait que confirmer sa propre doctrine du «simple fait». Il en était de même dans l'arrêt rendu le même jour dans l'*Affaire relative au paiement, en or, des emprunts fédéraux brésiliens émis en France*, nonobstant le fait que dans le passage ayant trait au problème la Cour, parlant d'elle-même, se servait de l'expression de «l'application du droit interne» [8]. Il s'agit ici d'une expression malencontreuse. Ce que la Cour «applique» sont les manifestations du droit international public et non pas celles d'un droit national. Si, quand-même, elle se dit «appliquer» le droit interne, elle ne peut qu'envisager le fait d'en tenir compte, tout comme elle tient compte des faits au sens habituel. Aussi est-il incompréhensible de quel droit Hambro a pu dire que ce second arrêt du 12 juillet 1929 «completely undermines the idea that municipal law is a mere fact» [9].

III

Tel étant donc le rapport entre le droit international public et le droit national, il convient de constater ensuite que la même chose vaut pour le droit international public et le droit international privé. Ce dernier, en effet, n'est rien d'autre qu'une branche du droit national. De quoi cette branche s'occupe-t-elle? Du droit national applicable et du juge compétent aux cas où il s'agit d'un rapport juridique entre particuliers montrant des éléments internationaux. Mais si c'est là la vocation du droit international privé, cela ne

---

[5] *Ibid.* p. 228.
[6] C.P.J.I., Série A, RECUEIL DES ARRÊTS, n° 20, pp. 46–47.
[7] *Ibid.* p. 46.
[8] C.P.J.I., Série A, RECUEIL DES ARRÊTS, n° 21, p. 124.
[9] E. HAMBRO, *op. cit.*, *supra* note 3, p. 19.

veut point dire que le droit international public conventionnel soit exclu de s'occuper, lui aussi, de la matière indiquée. J'y reviens plus bas.

Examinons d'abord la question du droit applicable. Une cinquième vérité à relever ici est celle de la différence entre législation et application. Le droit international public général attribue à chaque Etat certains pouvoirs de législation, de juridiction et d'exécution. Ces pouvoirs sont limités, en principe, au territoire des Etats respectifs, de sorte qu'un Etat déterminé est empêché de légiférer pour le territoire d'un autre Etat. Sauf exceptions, donc, le droit néerlandais *n'a pas cours* en territoire belge. Il se peut, toutefois, que le droit néerlandais n'en soit pas moins *appliqué* en Belgique, notamment à un contrat conclu entre un néerlandais et un belge. Dans l'hypothèse d'un pareil contrat, un choix s'impose entre le droit néerlandais et le droit belge. A qui incombe-t-il de faire ce choix? Aux parties en cause, au juge s'il y a procès, au législateur? Voilà une question à laquelle le droit international public ne semble guère s'intéresser. Ce n'est que le pouvoir législatif tel quel qui l'intéresse et non pas le sort réservé aux produits de ce dernier en cas de conflit entre des produits législatifs de différente origine nationale. A cet égard, le droit international public n'intervient pas, laissant une liberté quasi complète aux parties, au juge, au législateur. S'agissant des parties, on a pris l'habitude de parler de «l'autonomie des parties» qu'on voit même s'étendre au choix du juge compétent.

Or, la question se pose s'il s'agit ici d'un principe du droit international public ou bien de ce que j'appellerais une «pratique tolérée» n'ayant qu'un caractère de fait. La première thèse est soutenue, encore, par Hambro, et pour la démontrer il s'en réfère à nouveau à l'arrêt de la Cour Permanente dans l'affaire des emprunts serbes, ainsi qu'à d'autres décisions judiciaires[10]. Quant audit arrêt, il cite le passage suivant:

> «La Cour, saisie d'un différend impliquant la question de savoir quelle est la loi qui régit les obligations contractuelles dont il s'agit, ne saurait déterminer cette loi qu'en s'inspirant de la nature même de ces obligations et des circonstances qui ont accompagné leur création, sauf à tenir compte également de la volonté exprimée ou présumée des Parties. C'est d'ailleurs ce que semblent devoir faire aussi les tribunaux nationaux en l'absence de règles du droit national relatives à la solution des conflits de loi»[11].

Comme le dit Hambro, la Cour recourt ici à trois principes acceptés en droit international privé, savoir celui du *proper law of the contract*, celui de

---

[10] *Ibid.* pp. 20, 34–35 et 44.

[11] C.P.J.K., Série A, RECUEIL DES ARRÊTS, n° 20, p. 41.

l'autonomie des parties, et celui de la pratique judiciaire dans les pays concernés. Rien n'indique, cependant, que la Cour y voie plus que des moyens techniques pour venir à bout d'un problème de droit national considéré comme un «simple fait». Déclarer qu'il s'agit ici de principes du droit international public, ou bien de principes prescrits par celui-ci au droit national, c'est oublier que la Cour en des cas de cette nature sort du monde qui est le sien pour se rendre sur un terrain qui lui est foncièrement étranger et où, pour elle, il n'y a lieu que de s'adapter aux us et coutumes de l'endroit.

Un important argument contre l'autonomie des parties en tant que principe du droit international public est aussi que l'Etat garde, et doit garder, un droit de regard sur son étendue. C'est le droit international public qui confère aux Etats leurs pouvoirs de législation et de juridiction, comme je viens de le constater. Or, s'imagine-t-on que des particuliers puissent les en dérober à leur goût tout en se servant de leur «autonomie»? Ce serait, pourtant, le cas si cette autonomie était un principe du droit international public à invoquer contre l'Etat. Mais ce droit pour des raisons de logique juridique ne saurait être censé contenir deux principes à ce point contradictoires. C'est pourquoi, à juste titre, une Cour fédérale à New York par deux fois a décidé de ne pas pouvoir honorer le choix du droit applicable fait dans un certain contrat de travail, en dans l'un des deux cas a également écarté le choix du for compétent. Il s'agit des jugements rendus le 27 mars 1962 (*Pavlou v. Ocean Traders Marine Corp.* et Al., 33 I.L.R., p. 155) et le 16 décembre 1961 (*Voyiatzis v. National Shipping and Trading Corp.* et Al., 32 I.L.R., p. 103)[12].

Quant à ce second sujet, celui du for compétent, dont je disais qu'il appartient aussi à la sphère d'intérêt du droit international privé, on ne peut que croire que, contrairement à celui de l'application du droit national, l'Etat le prend bien plus à coeur. Car, en effet, la juridiction n'est-t-elle pas gardienne de l'«Etat de droit», et la compétence du juge ne touche-t-elle donc pas au fondement-même de l'Etat? Si l'Etat permet aux particuliers de dévier à l'occasion de ses propres règles à l'égard de cette compétence, saurait-il s'agir d'autre chose que d'une tolérance entièrement facultative n'ayant aucun lien avec le droit international public?

Par rapport aux deux sujets – droit applicable, for compétent – un «droit» peut, certes, se former à l'intérieur de chaque Etat, un droit qu'on intitule droit international privé, mais il est clair d'emblée qu'au regard du droit international public ce droit, tout comme le reste du droit national, ne représente qu'un «simple fait».

---

[12] Comp. ANNUAIRE (1993), vol. 65-I, p. 181.

En est-il autrement quand deux ou plusieurs Etats entre eux concluent un traité sur la matière? Soyons conscients qu'en posant la question on passe du droit international public général au droit international conventionnel et que ce dernier ne vaut que pour les parties au traité. Le droit international général, partant, n'aura pas cure – en principe, bien sûr – de ce que les Hautes Parties Contractantes puissent bien y insérer comme solutions. Mais le contenu du traité, ne constitue-t-il dorénavant une partie du droit international public, ne fût-ce que du droit conventionnel? Nullement, à mon opinion, tant que le traité concerne le droit applicable, et cela pour la simple raison que les Etats parties ont agi en co-législateurs nationaux créant un droit national qui leur est commun. Le seul lien ici avec le droit international public est celui de l'instrument utilisé, le traité. A ce traité en tant qu'instrument s'appliquent les dispositions de la Convention de Vienne du 23 mai 1969, entrée en vigueur le 27 janvier 1980, mais c'est tout. Rappelons aussi le mot de Georges Scelle selon lequel les traités ne sont que des «moules anonymes» capables de contenir n'importe quoi. Leur interprétation doit se plier à la matière qu'ils renferment[13]. Un traité remplaçant le droit international privé de deux ou plusieurs pays appelle donc une interprétation axée sur celle du droit national – et nous voilà de retour au problème discuté au paragraphe précédent. Un traité, par contre, qui réglerait la question du for compétent participerait exclusivement du droit international public conventionnel du fait qu'il concerne le fonctionnement du pouvoir judiciaire – à distinguer de son comportement (quant au droit applicable, par exemple) – prenant origine au droit international public général comme indiqué au début de ce paragraphe. Il remplace toute règle que le droit national des parties au traité ait connue auparavant. C'est à ce traité que les juridictions des Etats en cause sont désormais tenues. Le fait de la «transformation» du traité en droit national par l'entremise d'une loi pratiquée en certains Etats est évidemment sans intérêt dans le présent contexte: ce fait aussi nous ramène au paragraphe II, le statut du droit national ainsi créé n'étant autre que celui du «simple fait».

Des considérations présentées ici il n'y a qu'une conclusion à tirer, savoir que droit international public et droit international privé revêtent deux identités différentes et bien distinctes, voire même nécessairement. Il va presque de soi que d'autres opinions ont été énoncées à cet égard. Hambro, en 1962, s'exprimait en faveur de la thèse selon laquelle le droit international privé n'était que *predominantly national*. Non seulement voyait-il des «liens» entre les deux disciplines, il était aussi d'avis que le droit international public comprenait lui-même des règles de droit international privé[14]. Mais un droit

---

[13] *Voir* M. BOS, *op. cit.*, *supra* note 4, p. 159.

[14] E. HAMBRO, *op. cit.*, *supra* note 3, pp. 10–14, 33 et s., pp. 65–66.

international public, même s'il oblige les Etats – à une échelle universelle ou non – à suivre certaines règles en matière de conflits de loi, par exemple, admet-il par là ces règles dans son propre corps juridique? Ces règles destinées à régler les rapports entre particuliers? L'élément de droit international public ne se limite-t-il pas à ladite obligation, dans ce cas? Qu'on pense aux conséquences de l'optique-Hambro: tout manuel de droit international public devrait contenir une section de droit international privé!

Jetons encore un regard sur d'autres auteurs. Au total, quatre écoles se sont manifestées, à ce qu'il paraît. La première est celle de l'indifférence du droit international public vis-à-vis du droit international privé. Roberto Ago, l'un des plus grands internationalistes de notre siècle, s'y inscrivait, se prévalant d'«une proposition bien caractéristique d'Aubry: savoir que l'on ne peut pas qualifier comme étant des règles du droit des gens des principes dont la violation n'ait provoqué, même une seule fois, le froncement de sourcils d'un diplomate»[15]. J'y compte aussi Paul Heinrich Neuhaus, selon lequel, au fond, le droit international public en matière de conflits de loi ne fait autre chose que d'ordonner aux Etats de suivre la pratique. A son avis, le droit international public et le droit international privé ont chacun leur propre approche des choses. L'apport du premier au second est minimal: le droit international public, bien sûr, est indispensable au droit international privé pour ce qui est de son fondement (*Begründung*), mais en tant que droit privé ce dernier est fondamentalement indépendant (*eigenständig*)[16].

La seconde école est celle d'Henri Batiffol et d'Harold G. Maier, entre autres. Si, en 1957, Batiffol constatait l'existence dans les deux disciplines de notions communes au sujet des conflits de loi ou de juridiction, en 1972 il avait procédé à une «unité sous-jacente des phénomènes et des idées»[17]. Pareille attitude fut adoptée par Maier qui voyait les deux droits se recouper[18]. Batiffol, en plus, admettait la suprématie du droit international public.

Parmi les adhérents d'une troisième école, on compte, à part Hambro déjà signalé ci-dessus, John R. Stevenson, François Rigaux et Fausto Pocar.

---

15 R. AGO, *Régles générales des conflits de lois*, dans: Académie de Droit International, RECUEIL DES COURS (1936-IV), pp. 289–290.

16 P.H. NEUHAUS, *Der Beitrag des Völkerrechts zum Internationalen Privatrecht*, 21 GERMAN YEARBOOK OF INTERNATIONAL LAW (1978), pp. 61, 63–64, 71–72.

17 H. BATIFFOL, *Vers de nouveaux liens entre le droit international public et le droit international privé* (allocution du 5 mai 1957), ANNUAIRE DE L'ASSOCIATION DES AUDITEURS ET ANCIENS AUDITEURS DE L'ACADEMIE DE DROIT INTERNATIONAL DE LA HAYE (1958), p. 199, et *Points de contact entre le droit international public et le droit international privé*, REVISTA ESPAÑOLA DE DERECHO INTERNACIONAL (1972), vol. XXV, p. 91.

18 H. MAIER, *Extraterritorial Jurisdiction at a Crossroads: An Intersection between Public and Private International Law*, 76 AMERICAN JOURNAL OF INTERNATIONAL LAW (1982), p. 280.

Aux yeux de cette école, le droit international général est, en partie, décisif en ce qui concerne le contenu du droit international privé. Rigaux et Pocar – comme Hambro, d'ailleurs – hasardaient même la thèse d'un droit international public contenant des règles de droit international privé[19].

Une fusion totale entre les deux branches du droit est, finalement, soutenue par Mark W. Janis, Friedrich K. Juenger et Ralph G. Steinhardt[20], dont la doctrine mènerait donc tout droit à un seul et unique manuel de droit international autant public que privé. Saisi d'un vrai esprit de négation envers tout traditionnalisme, Juenger plaide même la cause d'un *consensus law* élaboré entre Etats et particuliers agissant d'égal à égal, tout au moins pour des *multistate transactions*. La souveraineté de l'Etat n'y jouerait plus aucun rôle, sa compétence législative tombant dans l'oubli.

Où se situe la prise de position défendue ici par rapport à ces quatre écoles? Il me semble qu'elle réunit en elle des éléments des deux premières. Elle aussi part de l'idée d'une identité distincte du droit international public et du droit international privé (Ago, Neuhaus), reconnaît la distance qui les sépare (Neuhaus), mais admet aussi la présence de certains concepts qu'ils ont en commun (Batiffol, Maier) et l'ultime suprématie du droit international public (Batiffol).

IV

Revenons maintenant au Projet de Milan (paragraphe I). Il repose entièrement sur la doctrine que j'ai faite mienne. S'agissant uniquement de la compétence extraterritoriale de l'Etat en droit international public, il a pu se passer de tout ce qui n'a pas trait à ce problème limité. Aussi, aux Articles 5 à 8, le Projet indique-t-il les personnes à l'étranger auxquelles s'étend le pouvoir législatif, judiciaire et d'exécution de l'Etat, et cherche-t-il, à l'Article 9, comment résoudre ou éviter les conflits de compétence entre Etats. Un article final, l'Article 10, en guise d'extra, réserve au droit international privé la détermination de l'effet de l'exercice de la compétence extrater-

---

19 J. R. STEVENSON, *The Relationship of Private International Law to Public International Law*, dans: ESSAYS ON INTERNATIONAL LAW FROM THE COLUMBIA LAW REVIEW (1965), pp. 64–69; F. RIGAUX, *Réflexions sur les rapports entre le droit international privé et le droit des gens*, REVISTA ESPAÑOLA DE DERECHO INTERNACIONAL (1968), vol. XXI, pp. 573–574; F. POCAR, *Public International Law Solutions for Conflict of Laws Problems*, I THE ITALIAN YEARBOOK OF INTERNATIONAL LAW (1975), p. 179.

20 M.W. JANIS et F.K. JUENGER, observations faites les 25–27 avril 1985 lors de la 79ème réunion annuelle de l'American Society of International Law, PROCEEDINGS 352 et s.; R.G. STEINHARDT, *The Privatization of Public International Law*, 25 THE GEORGE WASHINGTON JOURNAL OF INTERNATIONAL LAW AND ECONOMICS (1991), pp. 526, 551–552.

ritoriale sur le régime juridique des biens, droits et intérêts sur le territoire d'un autre Etat.

Je souligne que lesdits articles se trouvent rangés sous l'en-tête de «Principes *généraux*» et que, dans le rapport final de la dix-neuvième Commission, il est précisé qu'on ne vise que des principes de droit international *public* qui, en plus, tout en étant d'une validité universelle, n'ont d'autre signification que de faire ressortir la conduite à laquelle les Etats *sont en droit de s'attendre* entre eux. Il leur est parfaitement loisible, toutefois, de *renoncer* à pareille conduite si bon leur semble, ce qui explique la grande diversité dont témoigne la pratique. Un certain «bilatéralisme» s'y fait jour, un Etat acceptant d'un autre Etat ce qu'il n'accepte pas d'un tiers.

Si les Etats disposent donc à leur gré de leur droit propre en la matière, il est évident que la situation des particuliers est tout autre. Comme je l'ai déjà observé plus haut (paragraphe III), c'est le droit international public qui confère aux Etats leurs pouvoirs, et partant, ce n'est pas aux particuliers d'en refaire la distribution. C'est, pourtant, ce qui se produit régulièrement par la voie de l'autonomie que, par tolérance, les Etats leur concèdent. Mais il s'entend que cette autonomie ne saurait jamais être entière. Les abus sont à détourner et les deux jugements américains de 1961/1962 cités au paragraphe précédent le démontrent à satisfaction.

Il émane une atmosphère de grande libéralité du Projet de Milan. Pour ce qui est du droit international public, il est modeste, et en se limitant expressément à cette discipline, il ne préjuge en rien des solutions apportées par le droit international privé, sauf un certain droit de regard tout à fait conforme à la nature de ce dernier comme «simple fait» aux yeux du droit international public.

C'est cette vision du rapport entre les deux disciplines que je préfère de loin à celles prônées par les troisième et quatrième écoles évoquées avant et où droit international public et droit international privé, perdant leur indépendance, se trouvent indissolublement et fatalement liés l'un à l'autre.

Reste à voir si l'Institut, lui aussi, estimera que les principes généraux énoncés au Projet de Milan correspondent au droit international public général tel qu'il est vécu de nos jours et le sera à l'avenir.

POUR UN DROIT INTERNATIONAL DE LA DÉMOCRATIE

par
BOUTROS BOUTROS-GHALI

C'est pour moi un plaisir que de contribuer à l'ouvrage par lequel ses amis veulent honorer le Professeur Skubiszewski. Depuis nos premières rencontres à Varsovie, à la fin des années 1950, notre amitié n'a cessé de s'affirmer, au croisement de nos vies diplomatiques et universitaires, et aujourd'hui encore, au sein de l'Institut de Droit international. Qu'il reçoive aussi cette réflexion, consacrée à ce que je voudrais appeler «un Droit international de la démocratie», comme un hommage au combat qu'il n'a cessé de mener – et souvent dans les conditions les plus dures – au service des valeurs démocratiques et des droits de la personne humaine.

L'objet de ce court article est, en effet, de souligner combien un Droit international de la démocratie, encore embryonnaire, est en train de se constituer et de souligner le rôle que l'ONU joue dans cet avènement.

Comme souvent dans la pratique de l'Organisation, ce droit s'affirme aujourd'hui de façon pragmatique et empirique. Il accède à la positivité au travers de règles juridiques et de modalités techniques souvent très disparates. Et pourtant, il constitue déjà un corps de règles qui possède sa cohésion et sa cohérence.

Depuis que j'ai été élu à la tête de l'Organisation mondiale, je n'ai cessé d'agir pour la promotion et le perfectionnement de ce nouveau droit international. Mais ce sera aux théoriciens de l'avenir d'expliciter cette branche du droit et de cerner les contours de son ordonnancement juridique. Mon but n'est donc ici que d'esquisser les grandes lignes de ce droit en gestation et de faire participer les lecteurs à la réflexion prospective qui est la mienne.

A. Le paradoxe d'un Droit international de la démocratie

A vrai dire, tout pouvait laisser penser que l'Organisation des Nations Unies ne pourrait être à même de faire naître ce Droit international de la démocratie. Sur le plan juridique, la Charte repose toute entière sur le principe de la souveraineté de l'Etat dont l'article 2 § 7 constitue, en quelque sorte, la dimension «protectrice». De plus, sur le plan politique, l'antagonisme Est-Ouest et l'affrontement Nord-Sud ont conduit nombre d'Etats à une conception très sourcilleuse de leur souveraineté et à une approche très suspicieuse de l'idée de démocratie.

Et pourtant, seule l'Organisation des Nations Unies était à même de faire apparaître ce corps de règles. Car on sait aujourd'hui le rôle fondamental du multilatéralisme et de l'Organisation mondiale dans la formation des nouvelles règles du droit international. De la même manière que l'ONU a rénové le Droit international de la paix, de la même manière qu'elle a inspiré le Droit international du développement, elle seule pouvait porter vers l'ordre positif le Droit international de la démocratie.

B. L'émergence d'un Droit international de la démocratie

La volonté de transposer les valeurs démocratiques dans l'ordre international est une idée ancienne. Déjà, à la fin du XVIII siècle, Emmanuel Kant soutenait que la démocratie, parce qu'elle peut conduire à une union pacifique entre les Etats libéraux, est un rempart contre les tendances agressives des régimes absolutistes. On retrouve une semblable inspiration dans le Projet de paix perpétuelle de l'Abbé de Saint-Pierre ou dans la Déclaration du Droit des gens proposée, pendant la Révolution française, par l'Abbé Grégoire.

Sans doute trouve-t-on également des traces de cette aspiration démocratique dans la vision wilsonienne du monde et dans les mécanismes de la Société des Nations. De la même manière, l'article 1 de la Charte des Nations Unies, en consacrant le droit des peuples à disposer d'eux-mêmes, a poursuivi cette idée démocratique qu'elle a, d'une certaine manière, institutionnalisée à travers des expériences telles que le plébiscite concernant l'unification du Togoland britannique en 1956, l'avenir du Cameroun entre 1959 et 1961 ou le referendum en Erythrée en 1993.

On pourrait également analyser le long cheminement par lequel la protection internationale des droits de l'homme a contribué à affermir l'idée d'un Droit international de la démocratie.

Mais c'est véritablement, avec l'expérience conduite dans le Sud-Ouest africain et avec l'accession à l'indépendance de la Namibie que ces principes se sont réellement inscrits dans la pratique de l'Organisation.

Depuis lors, selon un principe d'incarnation progressive cher à l'Organisation mondiale, les expériences d'aide à la démocratie et d'assistance technique à la démocratisation se sont multipliées sous des formes diverses. Et l'idée de la conceptualisation d'un Droit international de la démocratie a fait son chemin.

C. Vers la conceptualisation d'un Droit international de la démocratie

Dans mon action à la tête de l'Organisation, j'ai insisté, chaque fois que l'occasion m'en a été donnée, pour que l'impératif démocratique apparaisse comme l'un des grands objectifs de l'ONU. Et j'ai voulu souligner le lien existant entre cet objectif démocratique et les idéaux en faveur de la paix, des droits de l'homme et du développement, tels qu'ils sont inscrits dans la Charte.

Ainsi, dans «l'Agenda pour la Paix» que j'ai présenté aux Etats membres en 1992, j'ai voulu démontrer que la démocratie à tous les niveaux est essentielle à l'instauration de la paix pour une ère nouvelle de prospérité et de justice.

A l'occasion de la Conférence mondiale de Vienne sur les Droits de l'homme, la Déclaration et le Programme d'action adoptés le 25 juin 1993 invitent à la prise de conscience «des relations d'interdépendance entre développement, démocratie et droits de l'homme, chacun de ces éléments contribuant à renforcer l'autre».

De même, dans mon «Agenda pour le Développement» proposé en 1994, j'ai insisté sur le lien naturel qui existe entre développement et démocratie. En effet, la démocratie est un mode de fonctionnement de l'Etat qui influe sur tous les aspects du développement. Sans la démocratie, garantie de la libre concurrence et instrument du changement, le développement reste fragmentaire et perpétuellement menacé.

L'ensemble des Etats membres de l'Organisation a très largement pris en compte cette pénétration de l'idée démocratique dans l'ordre juridique international et convient du rôle croissant que l'ONU doit jouer dans ce domaine. C'est la raison pour laquelle, dans sa résolution 49/30 du 7 décembre 1994, l'Assemblée générale m'a demandé d'étudier «les moyens et les mécanismes grâce auxquels le système des Nations Unies pourrait consolider les démocraties nouvelles ou rétablies».

C'est le sens du Rapport que j'ai soumis le 7 août 1995 à l'Assemblée générale à l'occasion du Cinquantième anniversaire de l'Organisation mondiale.

J'ai bien conscience qu'il faut aujourd'hui aller plus loin, qu'un Agenda pour la démocratisation est sans doute à écrire, que la Communauté universitaire des juristes doit se mobiliser sur cette question.

Car je suis fondamentalement convaincu que le Droit international de la démocratie existe. Et qu'au-delà de **la diversité de ses modalités**, s'affirme de plus en plus nettement **l'unité de ses objectifs**.

I. LA DIVERSITÉ DES MODALITÉS DU DROIT INTERNATIONAL DE LA DÉMOCRATIE

L'action internationale en faveur de la démocratie peut prendre, à l'évidence, les formes les plus diffuses. On peut notamment considérer qu'une grande partie de la diplomatie préventive de l'Organisation participe à cette activité.

Mais, d'une manière plus concrète et juridiquement plus palpable, le Droit international de la démocratie est aujourd'hui mis en oeuvre à travers deux grands types de modalités. Les unes, générales, concernent **la préservation de la paix** (A). Les autres, plus spécifiques, concernent **l'assistance électorale** (B).

A. Le Droit international de la démocratie et la préservation de la paix

1. Les opérations de maintien de la paix conduites depuis quelques années ont sans doute constitué un des apports les plus décisifs à la confirmation d'un Droit international de la démocratie. On sait en effet qu'il s'est produit, dans ce domaine, une évolution quantitative considérable, puisque l'Organisation des Nations Unies a lancé en l'espace de cinq ans plus d'opérations qu'au cours des quarante années précédentes. Mais on sait aussi que cette évolution a été également d'ordre qualitatif. Désormais les opérations de maintien de la paix – celles que j'ai appelé de la deuxième, voire de la troisième génération – sont, dans la plupart des cas, des «opérations polyvalentes». En effet, loin de se borner à la simple interposition entre les belligérants, elles incluent dans le mandat des Casques bleus des actions telles que le déminage, le désarmement des combattants et leur réinsertion dans la vie civile, le rapatriement des réfugiés, la reconstruction des services publics, la protection des droits de l'homme, la réconciliation nationale et le renforcement des institutions, voire le rétablissement de la démocratie.

Ces derniers objectifs ont été particulièrement affirmés dans trois grandes opérations conduites par l'Organisation en El Salvador, au Mozambique et au Cambodge.

a) En El Salvador, le lien entre paix, droits de l'homme et démocratie apparaît clairement dans les Accords de paix signés à Chapultepec entre le Gouvernement et le Front de Libération Nationale, le FMLN, puis dans les Accords sur les Droits de l'homme signés à San José de Costa Rica. Les parties y reconnaissent que l'adhésion aux principes des droits de l'homme est une condition à la fin de la guerre et acceptent que l'ensemble des droits démocratiques qui y sont associés soit garanti et contrôlé par des observateurs internationaux. En conséquence, le Conseil de sécurité dans sa résolution 832 (1993) «décide d'élargir le mandat de la Mission des Nations Unies en El Salvador (ONUSAL) pour y inclure l'observation du processus électoral qui doit se terminer par les élections générales en El Salvador en mars 1994 ... et fait sienne l'opinion du Secrétaire général ... selon laquelle les élections générales de mars 1994 devraient constituer l'aboutissement logique de tout le processus de paix en El Salvador».

b) Au Mozambique, l'accord de paix signé entre les parties à Rome en 1992 prévoyait «l'instauration d'une paix durable et d'une démocratie effective» et demandait son assistance technique à l'ONU, notamment dans le cadre du processus électoral. C'est le sens de la résolution 797 (1992) du Conseil de sécurité «invitant le Secrétaire général à tenir des consultations étroites avec toutes les parties concernant la date exacte et les préparatifs des élections présidentielles et législatives».

c) Au Cambodge, à la suite des Accords de Paris d'octobre 1991, l'ONU a conduit l'une des plus vastes opérations de son histoire en prenant véritablement en charge, pendant plus de deux ans, l'administration et les secteurs clés de la vie publique cambodgienne. Par là même, elle a non seulement contribué à restaurer un Etat en déliquescence, mais elle l'a aussi conforté en mettant en place, dans les conditions difficiles et périlleuses que l'on sait, les élections démocratiques de mai 1993.

2. Il faudrait ajouter à ce rapide panorama, l'usage de **mesures coercitives** mises en oeuvre dans le cadre de l'affaire haïtienne pour restaurer la démocratie dans l'île.

Déjà en 1968, le Conseil de sécurité, dans sa résolution 253, avait évoqué le Chapitre VII pour sanctionner l'indépendance unilatérale de la Rhodésie et avait fermement rejeté tout «accord qui ne tiendrait pas compte des vues du peuple de la Rhodésie du Sud, et en particulier des partis politiques partisans d'un gouvernement représentatif de la majorité».

Vingt-cinq années plus tard, la résolution 940 du Conseil de sécurité du 31 juiller 1994 «agissant en vertu du Chapitre VII de la Charte des Nations Unies, autorise des Etats membres à constituer une force multinationale placée sous un commandement et un contrôle unifiés et à utiliser dans ce cadre tous les moyens nécessaires pour faciliter le départ d'Haïti des dirigeants militaires ... le prompt retour du Président légitimement élu et le rétablissement des autorités légitimes du Gouvernement haïtien...».

B. L'assistance électorale

Elle constitue le deuxième mode, plus spécifique, par lequel le Droit international de la démocratie s'impose comme une des activités importantes de l'Organisation mondiale.

1. A partir de 1992, les **demandes d'assistance électorale** adressées par des Etats membres à l'Organisation n'ont cessé de croître. Auparavant, elles n'avaient pas excédé l'ordre d'une dizaine. En 1992, elles atteignent le chiffre de 33. Ces quatre dernières années, 64 pays ont déposé quelque 94 demandes d'assistance électorale dont 82 ont été honorées, 13 ont été refusées – en général parce qu'elles avaient été déposées trop tardivement – et certaines sont à l'heure actuelle en préparation.

Dans les premiers temps, l'assistance électorale procurée en dehors des opérations de maintien de la paix, a été pris en charge par le Programme des Nations Unies pour le développement (PNUD). Installés dans le pays qu'ils ont charge d'aider à développer, les bureaux du PNUD ont l'avantage d'une bonne connaissance du terrain et de la situation politique. Ils doivent cependant composer avec les autorités puisque leur présence et leur action dépendent du Gouvernement hôte.

2. Ce constat ainsi que la multiplication des demandes ont commandé une **institutionnalisation de l'assistance** et la création d'un Bureau chargé spécifiquement de l'organiser. C'est ainsi que, sur ma recommandation, la résolution A/46/137 de l'Assemblée générale a créé, au sein du Département des Affaires politiques, une Division de l'Assistance électorale. Son rôle est d'examiner la validité des demandes et de proposer aux Etats l'aide la mieux adaptée aux réalités de leur société. Car si l'assistance ne peut être accordée qu'en réponse à une demande expresse émanant d'un gouvernement – exception faite du recours au Chapitre VII – l'ONU est seul juge de la faisabilité et des modalités de l'intervention.

II. L'UNITÉ DES OBJECTIFS DU DROIT INTERNATIONAL DE LA DÉMOCRATIE

Pour éviter toute ambiguïté, il convient de réaffirmer, de la façon la plus nette, que le Droit international de la démocratie n'a évidemment pas pour objectif d'imposer un modèle unique de gouvernement à l'ensemble des Etats de la planète. Bien au contraire. Et j'ai eu l'occasion moi-même de le souligner en de multiples circonstances.

La finalité du Droit international de la démocratie est, tout à l'inverse, de diffuser des valeurs. En effet, je suis convaincu que la démocratie n'appartient à personne, qu'elle est susceptible de s'incarner dans tous les peuples et dans toutes les cultures, et qu'à l'instar des droits de l'homme elle revêt une dimension universelle.

C'est la raison pour laquelle je considère qu'il est essentiel, pour l'ONU, non seulement de **promouvoir un Etat de droit démocratique** (A), mais aussi de **favoriser un environnement planétaire démocratisé** (B).

A. Promouvoir un Etat de droit démocratique

Les mesures mises en oeuvre par l'ONU, ces dernières années, montrent clairement que le Droit international de la démocratie poursuit une double finalité. Il vise tout d'abord à **instaurer des principes démocratiques de gouvernement**.

Mais pour prendre tout son sens, la démocratie doit pouvoir s'appuyer, dans chaque pays, sur un appareil d'Etat viable. Le Droit international de la démocratie vise donc aussi à **affermir l'Etat de droit**.

1. A la lumière de la pratique suivie par l'Organisation, il est possible de dégager trois principes autour desquels l'Organisation des Nations Unies ordonne son action en faveur de la démocratisation: le développement du pluralisme politique, le soutien à la consultation populaire et la promotion de la culture civique.

a) Le développement du pluralisme politique constitue, selon l'Organisation des Nations Unies, un préalable nécessaire à toute consultation électorale véritable. C'est dans cet esprit que l'Organisation des Nations Unies a notamment été conduite à aider à la transformation de mouvements d'opposition armée en véritables partis politiques institutionnalisés. C'est le cas, en particulier, en El Salvador, avec le FMLN, au Mozambique avec la RENAMO et en Angola avec l'UNITA.

Ce passage d'un système de parti unique au multipartisme nécessite souvent une aide technique et financière. Il demande également des modifications constitutionnelles pour lesquelles l'Organisation des Nations Unies a été, là encore, conduite à fournir une assistance.

b) Le soutien à la consultation populaire constitue le deuxième principe fondateur de l'action de l'ONU en faveur de la démocratisation des Etats. Dans mon Rapport du 7 août 1995 à l'Assemblée générale, j'ai eu l'occasion de systématiser les modalités par lesquelles l'Organisation des Nations Unies fournit une assistance technique aux Etats qui en font la demande. Cela a conduit notamment l'ONU à organiser des élections, à les superviser, à les vérifier, à fournir une assistance à des observateurs internationaux et à coordonner leurs activités ou, dans certains cas, à fournir une assistance à des observateurs nationaux.

c) La promotion de la culture civique constitue un troisième champ d'action auquel j'attache, pour ma part, la plus grande importance. Des expériences malheureuses, notamment en Angola et en Haïti, ont montré que le déroulement des élections ne suffit pas. Il faut aussi que le respect du scrutin électoral soit perçu comme un principe impératif. Le Droit international de la démocratie doit donc aussi prendre en charge une assistance de formation des cadres et des citoyens, d'instruction civique, d'enseignement de la démocratie et des droits de l'homme. Cette assistance comprend également l'accès à l'information et la mise en place de médias libres et indépendants.

2. Renforcer l'Etat de droit constitue un complément nécessaire à l'instauration d'un véritable processus démocratique. Là encore, le Droit international de la démocratie a commencé à mettre en oeuvre un ensemble de mesures qu'il est possible d'ordonner autour de trois principes essentiels vers lesquels doivent tendre tous les Etats: des lois publiées, une administration pour les faire exécuter, une justice pour les faire respecter.

a) La publicité donnée à **l'appareil législatif** et réglementaire au sein d'un Etat constitue la base de l'Etat de droit. Dans cette perspective, l'ONU et ses agences spécialisées ont mis sur pied tout un ensemble de programmes destinés notamment à permettre aux Etats de se doter d'une réglementation moderne, d'un ordonnancement juridique cohérent. Elle a notamment créé des programmes d'aide constitutionnelle et législative. Parfois à grande échelle, comme ce fut le cas au Combodge.

b) C'est également au Cambodge que l'ONU a mis en oeuvre l'un de ses plus ambitieux projets de restauration de **l'appareil administratif** national. Chacun sait qu'un Etat n'est pas seulement l'ensemble de ses cadres politiques, mais aussi un appareil administratif compétent, loyal, impartial, transparent, soucieux du service public, attentif à l'intérêt général et respectueux des lois. Dans cette vaste tâche, l'Organisation des Nations Unies travaille en collaboration avec ses agences et notamment le PNUD, mais aussi des institutions spécialisées comme le Fonds Monétaire International, la Banque Mondiale, mais aussi avec des ONG et des instituts ayant un savoir-faire internationalement reconnu en matière d'administration publique. Pour aller plus loin et mieux rationaliser son action, l'ONU a entrepris une vaste réflexion à laquelle elle associe tous les organismes compétents afin de créer une véritable administration publique dans les pays en développement ou en transition.

c) Enfin, il est essentiel d'aider les Etats qui en font la demande à se doter de structures juridictionnelles et d'un **appareil judiciaire** moderne. Dans ce domaine, les programmes mis en oeuvre par l'Organisation des Nations Unies sont très divers: assistance technique en matière de justice pénale, formation des magistrats, assistance à l'élaboration des codes de procédure, renforcement des relations entre la justice et la police, etc. Cette action est menée aujourd'hui à vaste échelle et sur tous les continents.

B. Favoriser un environnement planétaire démocratisé

Je ne voudrais pas terminer cette brève étude consacrée au Droit international de la démocratie sans évoquer une autre dimension, encore largement prospective, mais à laquelle les juristes doivent attacher la plus grande attention, et que les Sommets des Etats Non-Alignés n'ont cessé de réclamer depuis 1961.

En militant pour un Droit international de la démocratie, il ne s'agit pas de prôner l'avènement d'un gouvernement démocratique à l'échelle du monde se superposant à celui des Etats. Au contraire, il s'agit d'affirmer que, parce que les valeurs démocratiques sont universelles, elles ont vocation à se diffuser dans tous les lieux de la société internationale où existent des espaces de pouvoir.

J'ai eu l'occasion de réfléchir, notamment lors du Séminaire de Davos, sur l'idée démocratique dans la société globale d'aujourd'hui et j'ai prôné la nécessité d'ouvrir de nouveaux débats sur les problèmes transnationaux, d'accueillir de nouvelles organisations non gouvernementales, les syndicats, les unions parlementaires, les représentants des organismes locaux, les instituts de recherches. J'ai également souligné la nécessité de former des citoyens du monde.

Pour en rester, ici, à une approche juridique, je voudrais insister sur le fait que, dans l'avenir, le Droit international de la démocratie devra aussi avoir pour vocation de démocratiser l'ensemble du système international.

Démocratiser le système international est une oeuvre à laquelle chaque Etat membre de l'Organisation mondiale doit aujourd'hui s'atteler. Dans «l'Agenda pour la paix», j'ai souligné que «la démocratie dans le concert des nations, c'est l'application des principes qui la régissent à l'Organisation elle-même».

C'est dans cet esprit que j'ai adressé à tous les Etats membres un questionnaire relatif à la question de l'élargissement du Conseil de sécurité. C'est un problème qui ne peut être résolu, en dernier ressort, que par les Etats membres eux-mêmes, dans le cadre de la procédure de révision prévue dans la

Charte. Mais c'est le rôle du Secrétaire général que de tenter de synthétiser ou de systématiser les différentes positions en présence de manière à favoriser les débats et l'éclosion d'une décision.

Par ailleurs, j'ai à plusieurs reprises insisté sur la nécessité de décentraliser et de régionaliser l'action internationale. Dans le domaine du développement économique, j'ai voulu donner plus de poids aux Commissions économiques régionales de l'ONU. Dans le domaine du maintien de la paix, j'ai dit l'importance qu'il convenait, aujourd'hui, d'attacher au Chapitre VIII de la Charte et au rôle des organisations régionales. Et à cette fin, j'ai tenu deux réunions importantes avec les représentants des organisations régionales en 1994 et tout récemment en 1996.

Enfin, le Professeur Skubiszewski est sans doute bien convaincu, comme moi, que la démocratisation du droit international est un élément essentiel pour assurer sa diffusion et sa primauté. A l'occasion de la Session de Milan de l'Institut de Droit international en 1993, j'ai souligné qu'il serait bien réducteur de ne voir le droit international que comme un programme à l'usage des étudiants au sein de l'Université. Le droit international en devenir doit être aussi un vaste manuel d'instruction civique à l'usage de la planète. Un mode de mobilisation de chacune et de chacun vers ce qui est notre destinée commune. Alors le droit international aura atteint, en quelque sorte, son point d'assomption. Et, cessant de n'être que le langage des Etats, il deviendra aussi le patrimoine commun des hommes, des peuples et des nations.

Purposeful Ambiguity as International Legal Strategy: The Two China Problem

by

*Anthony D'Amato**

For every definable term in international law there are clear cases and fuzzy cases. Everyone accepts that the term "State" applies to Paraguay, Poland, Portugal and over a hundred other clear cases, but does it apply to Puerto Rico, Western Samoa, the Isle of Man, the Channel Islands, Gibraltar, or the Vatican City? The word "treaty" has thousands of clear applications, but does it apply to an exchange of faxes between two governments or a handshake between two diplomats at a cocktail party? In addition to ambiguities of this kind, international law is replete with deliberately created ambiguities. Most treaty provisions are ambiguous because the parties were able to agree only on studied ambiguity instead of concrete particularity. Sometimes the treaty itself is deliberately ambiguous: the Helsinki Final Act, with its parts strangely and symbolically called "baskets", is neither clearly a treaty nor clearly a non-treaty. Its signatories were unable to agree on having an actual treaty under international law, but they were able to agree on having some sort of agreement that occupied the nether world between treaty and non-treaty.

One of the most interesting situations in recent years that illustrates in several important ways the role of deliberate ambiguity in international law is the Two China Problem. I will focus primarily upon the purposeful military, political, and legal ambiguities in the incident that has just come to an end as I write these words – the "war games" conducted in the Taiwan Strait in March, 1996. But I will lead up to that situation by a more general account of the history of the ambiguities of the Two China Problem. Even though my account will be general, if one were to dig deeper into the historical facts, one will find further ambiguities underneath the general ones. For each ambiguity uncovered, there is another one inside, like a set of nested Chinese boxes.

The Two China Problem had its origin in the Chinese civil war that began in the 1930s between two competing governmental claimants. By 1949 the

---

* The author wishes to thank Irene Berkey, International Research Librarian at Northwestern Law School, for research assitance on this project.

Communists under Mao Zedong defeated the Nationalists under Chiang Kai Shek, and substantial portions of the Nationalist armed forces and supporters fled to the island province of Taiwan (Formosa), located across the Taiwan Strait from the South China province of Fujian. The mainland Communist government calls itself the People's Republic of China (PRC) and claims Taiwan as part of its territory. The Taiwan government calls itself the Republic of China (ROC) and claims the mainland as part of its territory.[1]

However, the opposing claims are not quite the mirror images of each other. Although there is no doubt that mainland China, considered separately from Taiwan, is an independent sovereign State under international law, there is considerable doubt that Taiwan, considered separately from mainland China, is an independent sovereign State. Prior to 1895 China claimed sovereignty over Taiwan, but then ceded it to Japan following the Sino-Japanese War of 1895. In 1951 Japan relinquished sovereignty over Taiwan as part of the U.S.-Japan peace Treaty of that year, but the treaty was silent as to whom the sovereignty was relinquished. Accordingly there have been, and are, two claimants to sovereignty over Taiwan. Mainland China claims that Taiwan is an "integral part of China",[2] whereas the Taiwanese government's broad claim that its own authority extends to all of China is logically inclusive of its claim of authority over Taiwan.

Whether a territory constitutes a State is not under the territorial government's control; rather, it depends upon the international community's decision to recognize the territory as a State. On this aspect of the Two China Problem there has been a temporal ambiguity. Between 1945 and 1971, the China seat in the United Nations was occupied by the ROC; in 1971, PRC delegates (after complex U.N. resolutions) took the seat. Since both delegations claimed to represent all of China, including Taiwan, we might be led to conclude that that the PRC's claim, coming later in time, trumps that of the ROC. But an equally plausible interpretation is that the world community came to recognize that the ROC was in effective control of Taiwan, the PRC was in effective control of mainland China, and that the latter was bigger and far more important and hence "deserved" the China seat (including its veto in the Security Council) in the U.N. On this interpretation, the fact that the ROC held the China seat from 1945 to 1971 counts in its favour, rather

---

[1] However, in 1991, the ruling Nationalist Party in Taiwan (the Kuomintang) renounced its historical claim to sovereignty over all China and unilaterally recognized the People's Republic of China.

[2] L. ZHAO, *The Main Legal Problems in the Bilateral Relations Between China and the United States*, 16 NEW YORK UNIVERSITY JOURNAL OF INTERNATIONAL LAW & POLITICS (1984) at 543–545. Professor Zao teaches at Peking University.

than against it. Hence the temporal ambiguity: do the years 1971–1996 "trump" the years 1945–1971, or do they validate them?

The role of the United States in the Two China Problem may be viewed more as a spacial ambiguity than as a temporal one. In 1971, Secretary of State Henry Kissinger made a secret visit to China, and President Richard Nixon followed with a formal visit in 1972. The United States, for reasons of its own, decided to tilt toward mainland China; those reasons certainly included creating a buffer in Southeast Asia against the Soviet Union, and a farsighted sense that a more internationally involved China might encourage domestic Chinese pressures toward capitalism and even democracy. The United States terminated its Mutual Defense Treaty with the ROC, and in an ambiguously titled instrument, the "Joint Communique" issued in Shanghai on 28 February 1972, the U.S. and the PRC set forth their views on various issues of mutual interest.[3] The position of the "Chinese side" was stated to be that the PRC is the sole legal government of China, that Taiwan is a province of China, and that the PRC

> "firmly opposes any activities which aim at the creation of 'one China, one Taiwan', 'one China, two governments', 'two Chinas', and 'independent Taiwan' or advocate that 'the status of Taiwan remains to be determined'."

The U.S. side declared:

> "The United States acknowledges that all Chinese on either side of the Taiwan Strait maintain there is but one China and that Taiwan is a part of China. The United States Government does not challenge that position. It reaffirms its interest in a peaceful settlement of the Taiwan question by the Chinese themselves."

The ambiguities in these statements are purposeful and masterful. The underlying ambiguity in the Chinese statement is that no meaning is given to the key phrase "firmly opposes". There is no indication whether this opposition is a matter of ideological preference or military determination, or any shade in between. The first sentence of the U.S. statement makes no commitment; it simply recites the fact, known to all, that both the PRC and the ROC maintain that there is but one China and that Taiwan is part of China. The second sentence is blatantly ambiguous. By saying that the U.S. does not challenge "that position", the statement leaves it indeterminate whether

---

[3] The text of the document can be found in many places, including L.W. KOENIG, J.C. HSIUNG & KNIG-YUH CHANG (eds.), CONGRESS, THE PRESIDENCY, AND THE TAIWAN RELATIONS ACT 169 (1985).

"that position" refers to what the Chinese acknowledge or what the underlying reality is. Finally, if there were any lingering doubts about the ambiguity of the second sentence, the third sentence reinforces the ambiguity by referring to a "peaceful settlement of the Taiwan question". How can there be a "Taiwan question" at all if both sides agree that the first two sentences in the U.S. statement removed all remaining questions?

It is clear that both sides would have been hard pressed to conclude an agreement or a treaty instead of the Shanghai Communique. It would have been very difficult for them to agree on any text addressed to the Taiwan question. Instead, they hit upon an expedient of issuing a "communique" that contained the positions of both sides with all the ambiguities that each side desired. The Shanghai Communique was, in short, an ambiguous instrument replete with ambiguous provisions; in that respect it anticipated the Helsinki Final Act.

But behind the diplomatic double-talk in Shanghai was the reality of the U.S. interest in preventing a Chinese communist take-over of the government of Taiwan. While both the U.S. and the PRC may have created a spatial ambiguity about the competing extent of PRC and ROC claims of governance, from a national security perspective (including the perception that U.S. national security is fostered by the increasing democratization of other countries) there was never any ambiguity in the interests of the U.S. Hence, although the U.S. in 1979 terminated its Mutual Defense Treaty [4] with Taiwan and gradually withdrew its soldiers who were stationed on that island, it continued its policy of arms transfers to Taiwan. Perhaps U.S. military strategists perceived that arming the Taiwanese was more effective in discouraging aggressive impulses by the PRC than leaving U.S. troops on the island as a trip-wire. After all, a future U.S. administration might withdraw the troops; perhaps even in the course of a Chinese invasion the American public would not tolerate the loss of American soldiers defending the Taiwanese, and would want them brought home. Moreover, military self-defense has a huge battlefield advantage. If the PRC were to send fleets of soldiers across the Taiwan Strait, under standard military theory they would need at least 20 attacking personnel for every Taiwanese defender. In addition, the preparations for any such attack from the mainland would be visible months in advance, giving the U.S. and other countries ample opportunity to come to the rescue of Taiwan. The 1992 sale to Taiwan of 150 F-16 advanced jet fighters was dramatic corroboration of this aspect of U.S. policy.

---

4 Mutual Defense Treaty, 2. Dec. 1954, United States-Republic of China (Taiwan), 6 UST at 433, 3178 TIAS.

The PRC repeatedly and bitterly denounced U.S. arms transfers to Taiwan, but could to nothing about it.

If the Shanghai Communique was neither a treaty nor a non-treaty, a new and even more ambiguous instrument was invented by the United States in 1979 to deal with the Taiwan problem: the Taiwan Relations Act.[5] It declares in that it is the policy of the United States

> "to consider any effort to determine the future of Taiwan by other than peaceful means, including boycotts or embargoes, a threat to the peace and security of the Western Pacific area and of grave concern to the United States."[6]

and also

> "to provide Taiwan with arms of a defensive character."[7]

The Act specifies that the United States will make available to Taiwan

> "such defense articles and defense services in such quantity as may be necessary to enable Taiwan to maintain a sufficient self-defense capability."[8]

and further directs the President

> "to inform the Congress promptly of any threat to the security or the social or economic system of the people on Taiwan and any danger to the interests of the United States arising therefrom. The President and the Congress shall determine, in accordance with constitutional processes, appropriate action by the United States in response to any such danger."[9]

Although the Act begins by referring not to Taiwan as a State but to the "people on Taiwan", it goes on to provide that Taiwan is a State in every respect but the name:

> "Whenever the laws of the United States refer or relate to foreign countries, nations, States, governments, or similar entities, such terms shall include and such laws shall apply with respect to Taiwan."[10]

And further:

---

5 93 Stat. 14 (1979), 22 USC § 3301.

6 *Ibid.* at Sec. 2(b)(4).

7 *Ibid.* at Sec. 2(b)(5).

8 *Ibid.* at Sec. 3(a).

9 *Ibid.* at Sec. 3(c).

10 *Ibid.* at Sec. 4(b)(1).

> "The capacity of Taiwan to sue and be sued in courts in the United States, in accordance with the laws of the United States, shall not be abrogated, infringed, modified, denied, or otherwise affected in any way by the absence of diplomatic relations or recognition."[11]

Additionally, the Act permits all relations, programs, and transactions conducted or carried out by the United States and its agencies with respect to Taiwan to be conducted and carried out by or through the American Institute in Taiwan, a nonprofit corporation incorporated under the laws of the District of Columbia. The Act gives the President power to authorize the American Institute in Taiwan to perform all acts that an overseas American consulate might perform.[12]

The Taiwan Relations Act of 1979, in brief, extends to Taiwan the typical rights and privileges that normally are found in a treaty of amity, commerce, and navigation. In addition, it comes close to a mutual defense pact by its allowance of sales to Taiwan of "defense articles and defense services" and its statement that the U.S. will be gravely concerned by any effort to determine the future of Taiwan by other than peaceful means. Most mutual defense pacts signed by the United States do very little more, if at all, than this.[13] And indeed that was the outraged reaction of the PRC. Professor Lihai Zhao wrote that the Taiwan Relations Act

> "is thus merely another version of the Mutual Defense Treaty signed between the United States and Taiwan on 2 December 1954. As such, the Act violates the principles of the Shanghai Communique and unduly interferes with Chinese internal affairs."[14]

My own assessment of the Taiwan Relations Act of 1979 is that it may be the first full-fledged example in international law of a Unilateral Treaty.

Of course, putting it that way underscores the deep and deliberate ambiguity of the Two China Problem. This ambiguity was in the background when PRC in March 1996 began a dramatic and frightening show of force in the Taiwan Strait.

By 13 February 1996, there were some Chinese military maneouvers from inland toward the Chinese coast opposite Taiwan. At a White House Press briefing, the following exchange took place:

---

[11] *Ibid.* at Sec. 4(b)(7).

[12] *Ibid.* at Secs. 6, 7.

[13] A typical mutual defense pact commits the U.S. to act only in accordance with its constitutional processes, which gives the U.S. a Congressional safety valve. Moreover, the pact is in reality a one-way street; the U.S. did not sign it to obtain national security help from its treaty partner.

[14] L. ZHAO, *op. cit.*, *supra* note 1, at 547.

"**Q**. Has China been given an ambiguous answer on what we would do if it did attack Taiwan?

Press Secretary Mike McCurry: Oh, I doubt very much, given the PRC's understanding of the Taiwan Relations Act, that they have much doubt.

Q. I thought you said earlier that we were being deliberately ambiguous.

Mr. McCurry: Well, we have not – we have never specified the exact response consistent with the exact wording of the Taiwan Relations Act. But if you look at that act, if you look at Straits, it is quite clear what the view of the international community would be of any unnecessary provocation.

Q. What would that be?

Mr. McCurry: It is very clearly specified in the Taiwan Relations Act.

Q. Which is?

Mr. McCurry: Which I don't have in front of me."[15]

One may note a theoretical equivalence between a government spokesperson's statements "our policy is ambiguous" and "our policy is clear but I don't know what it is". The important point is that the U.S. was not willing to reveal any of its military contingency plans in advance of China's intentions becoming clearer. At the same time it was sending a message to the Chinese leadership that the Taiwan Relations Act not only indicated what the U.S. response would be, but also incorporated the anticipated response of the international community. Of course, under international law, unilateral legislation does not constitute an international norm. Yet the Press Secretary was making an intentional mistake of law. It was a signal to China not just that the U.S. would adhere to the Taiwan Relations Act, but that the U.S. would actively seek support from other countries in enforcing the principles of the Act.

A month later, the U.S. government, through its spokesperson, opted in favour of calling its policy ambiguous:

"**Q**. Do you think the United States would be bound by the 1979 Act to defend Taiwan against Chinese aggression?

Mr. McCurry The 1979 Taiwan Relations Act does not answer that question specifically and, indeed, there is merit we believe in keeping somewhat ambiguous about the matter."[16]

---

15 Press Briefing by M. MCCURRY, 1996 WL 60961 (White House 1966 – 13 February).

16 Press Briefing by M. MCCURRY, 1996 WL 107147 (White House 1996 – 12 March).

It is not my purpose here to dwell on China's motives for amassing its military forces in the Taiwan Strait. The American media reported that China was trying to influence the upcoming Taiwanese Presidential elections on March 25th, or that China was concerned about the example on the Chinese people of Taiwan's open and democratic elections. Neither of these alleged motives are particularly credible. It seems instead that China was making a statement during the Taiwan election campaign that no matter who was elected, the government should cease its foreign activities seeking to obtain an international personality for Taiwan. I cite as evidence for this proposition a report by CBB on 12 March that the PRC offered to withdraw their military forces from the Taiwan Strait if Taiwan withdrew its overseas compaign for entry into the United Nations – an offer that Taiwan promptly rejected.[17]

By 5 March, the PRC had announced that it was going to conduct war games including missile exercises in the Taiwan Straits. The U.S. reaction, given at its Press Briefing, was restrained:

> "**Mr. McCurry**: We have long felt that military exercises of that nature, specifically these types of missile tests, don't do anything to contribute to peace and stability in the region."[18]

Two days later, the Press Secretary (a) refrained from admitting that there had been tests, (b) said that the PRC had announced missile tests, and (c) characterized them in more forceful language:

> "**Mr. McCurry**: If, indeed, there have been missile tests associated with the military exercises that are underway now adjacent to the Taiwan Straits, they would be consistent with what the People's Republic had previously announced. They have previously announced they would likely include as part of this exercise missile tests. We would be deeply disturbed by any test of that nature, consider that provocative, and consider them reckless."[19]

The United States was speaking from a position of having monitored the Chinese troop movements. It came to the conclusion that the deployment of force in the Taiwan Strait did not have the characteristics of a preparation

---

[17] CNN NEWS REPORT, 6:03 p.m. EST, 12 March 1996. Later, on 12 March 1996, Foreign Minister Qian Qichen denied that the war games were an attempt either to influence the Taiwan presidential campaign or to discourage democracy in Taiwan: "What we oppose are the separatist activities on Taiwan, and the forces working for Taiwan independence." *Tensions Seen as Receding as China Ends War Games*, N.Y. TIMES (1996 – 26 March) at 8.

[18] Press Briefing by M. MCCURRY, 1996 WL 93855 (White House 1996 – 5 March).

[19] Press Briefing by M. MCCURRY, 1996 WL 99450 (White House 1996 – 7 March).

for invasion of Taiwan. Thus there was practically no chance that China intended to start a war with Taiwan. Moreover, intentional aggression against Taiwan would be irrational from the Chinese perspective (although, with Saddam Hussein's invasion of Iraq freshly in mind, one should never rule out the capacity of dictatorial leaders to commence a wholly irrational war). A war against Taiwan would be irrational, first, because several thousand American citizens are present on Taiwan (a number of them working in the quasi-diplomatic American Institute in Taiwan, set up by the Taiwan Relations Act). Chinese aggression against Taiwan would undoubtedly trigger a huge American military response if for no other reason than to protect the lives of American citizens on Taiwan. Second, China continues to count on the support of many Taiwanese residents who are loyal to the PRC. An invasion that would be preceded by artillery and missile fire would not be able to distinguish between these "compatriots" and other Taiwanese citizens, and thus would endanger everyone. In recognition of this problem, Foreign Ministry spokesperson Shen Guofang was quoted on Chinese State radio as saying, "China has never promised to give up the use of force, though of course this is not directed at the Taiwan compatriots."[20] How can artillery and missile fire spare those "compatriots" living in crowded proximity with other Taiwanese citizens? War is simply too blunt an instrument; it would have the effect of immediately turning the "compatriots" against China. Finally, Taiwan has a substantial defense capability. Despite China's overwhelming troop strength (over three million soldiers), its meagre amphibious capability would give Taiwan's beach perimeter defense an almost insuperable advantage.

Yet military hostilities can arise from mistakes and accidents, which is probably one reason Press Secretary McCurry used the words "provocative" and "reckless". In the war of words that was going on, the PRC responded within five days that the U.S. policy "is stupid and reckless".[21] I will now try to show that the fear of error escalating into war was the linchpin in the confrontation between the PRC and the U.S. in March 1996.

The Chinese war games in the Taiwan Strait began on 11 March. More than 150 000 Chinese troops were involved in the live-ammunition exercise, as were a flotilla of ships and at least 300 airplanes.[22] The U.S. responded by deploying significant naval forces to international waters several hundred miles east and southeast of Taiwan, and not in the Taiwan Strait. Included

---

20 CNN WORLD NEWS, 11:20 a.m. EST (1996 – 16 March).

21 Hong Kong newspaper WEN WEI PO, quoting Foreign Minister Qian Qichen, BBC SUMMARY OF WORLD BROADCASTS, EE/D2559/F (1996 – 12 March).

22 CNN NEWS, 6:03 EST (1996 – 12 March).

was the USS Independence, a carrier group out of Yokosuka, Japan, that included several cruisers, destroyers, frigates, and nuclear attack submarines. A second carrier group, the USS Nimitz, was sent from the Persian Gulf to international waters southeast of Taiwan.[23] The U.S. Navy did not conduct live ammunition war games, but engaged in noticeable 24-hour-a-day exercises including 80 sorties daily from the USS Independence.

Rear Admiral James Ellis, Commander of the Seventh Fleet Battle Force, told CNN news:

> "What is our purpose here, and it is not to bully or intimidate. We are here to monitor the ongoing military exercises. The Chinese themselves have said that is a normal naval function. That is what they do with us, that is what we do with them."[24]

It is a classic case of creating an ambiguity between words and actions. The U.S. did not need two huge carrier fleets to "monitor" the Chinese war games; that was already being done by reconnaissance satellites, and in any event the fleets were too far away to see or hear anything connected with the games. However, the PCR, for its part, understood full well that the U.S. was downplaying its naval presence near Taiwan, and rather than contradicting the U.S. characterization, instead chose to downplay it even further. Foreign Minister Qian Qichen was asked by a CNN reporter on Beijing television to react to the American plans to move its carrier forces close to Taiwan. The Minister replied, "It is common for U.S. warships to engage in activities on high seas."[25] Earlier in January 1996 Defense Minister Chiang Chung-ling had downplayed the matter perhaps to the lowest possible level of discourse. Commenting on a rumor about a planned U.S. carrier traversal of the Taiwan Strait during the Taiwan elections in March, the Minister said that he had not heard anything about it: "A minister will not necesarily know every trifling matter such as this. He is in charge of major affairs."[26]

In order to fully analyze these military and diplomatic posturings, they must be seen as interacting with rules of customary international law. One of those rules is that because the Taiwan Strait is approximately a hundred miles wide (and 137 miles long), it is an international waterway. Therefore it is open to vessels of all nations. The Chinese military exercises effectively cut off that waterway, thus temporarily violating international law. Yet I believe it was part of the deliberate Chinese military strategy to violate in-

---

23 CNN WORLDWIDE WEB, posted at 7:10 a.m. EST (1996 – 13 March).

24 CNN NEWS, 10:31 p.m. EST (1996 – 16 March).

25 BBC Summary of World Broadcasts, EE/D2558/G (1996 – 11 March).

26 BBC Summary of World Broadcasts, EE/D2520/F (1996 – 26 January).

ternational law. When any nation uses its military forces in violation of international legal norms, the "intimidation factor" increases. The target of the intimidation - namely, the Taiwanese people – would be insecure whether the PRC might proceed to violate other international norms, such as the norm against aggression.

But this violation of international waters also presented a legal and military challenge to the United States. In December 1995 the USS Nimitz had traversed the Taiwan Strait. Would the U.S. Navy try it again in March 1996 when China was conducting live ammunition and missile tests in those waters? To do so would be to present a frontal challenge to the PCR: either back down, or continue the tests with the high probability of hitting the USS Independence and setting off a war with the United States. Prior to the tests China had issued a warning to international shipping and aviation to stay away from the Taiwan Strait. The PCR chose its language carefully on March 17 when it was still doubtful whether the U.S. Navy would try to navigate the Taiwan Strait. Prime Minister Li Peng said:

> "If someone makes a show of force in the Taiwan Strait, that will not only be a futile act, but it will also make the situation all the more complicated."[27]

The U.S. response was to play down the situation. A *White House Official* said in Washington:

> "Although we don't like the newly announced military exercise, we take note of the fact that there is little to no interference with international shipping or air travel, that they take place far from Taiwan proper so that there is no direct threat, and that the Chinese have been careful in their rhetoric not to issue direct threats."[28]

In fact, the U.S. did not try to navigate the Taiwan Strait, and China brought its war games to an end two days after the presidential election on Taiwan. The entire affair ended peacefully.

Allow me to speculate as to the reasons why the United States decided not to send either or both of its carrier fleets through the Taiwan Strait. First, although the U.S. branded the Chinese war games as "reckless", it has conducted and undoubtedly will continue to conduct similar naval war games of its own, especially in the Persian Gulf and in the Mediterranean (in order to intimidate States like Iraq, Iran, and Libya). Any objection to the Chinese

---

27 *China Warns U.S. to Keep Away from Taiwan Strait*, N.Y. TIMES (1996 – 18 March) at 3.
28 *Ibid.*

war games could come back to haunt the United States the next time it wishes to conduct similar exercises.

Second, the U.S. set the precedent for cordoning off a portion of the high seas when it conducted its nuclear tests in the South Pacific in 1954. At that time it notified international shipping and aviation to stay away from the specified area. However, the magnitude of one of the test explosions was underestimated by half, and there was in addition an erroneous wind prediction. A Japanese fishing vessel, which apparently lay fourteen miles clear off the warning zone, was caught in the radiation; its twenty-seven man crew suffered serious injuries, one of them dying. The U.S. paid Japan two million dollars for the injuries to the crewmen and the damage to the Japanese fishing industry.[29] Japan explicitly refused to demand that the U.S. discontinue its tests.[30] These facts appear to establish that when the international legal norm of freedom of the seas is temporarily violated for the purpose of conducting weapons tests, the norm should be interpreted as a "liability" rather than a "property" norm.[31] Under this interpretation, if the USS Independence were to enter the proclaimed war games zone in the Taiwan Strait, and if it were hit by Chinese artillery fire or a missile, China could restore the situation to the *status quo ante* by promptly offering to pay full damages to the U.S. However, this legal result would be extraordinarily difficult for President Clinton to explain to the American people. There would be cries in Congress to retaliate with full force against China, and the President would be criticized as a weakling for accepting payment from China for the affront to the American Navy. Thus, assuming that lawyers for the Pentagon and the State Department reasoned the matter through to this point, they might very well have advised the President that it was politically a "no-win" situation to send an American carrier force throught the Taiwan Strait.

The preceding two reasons have to do with the relation between rules of customary international law and military strategy. A third reason bears on the relation between political prediction and military strategy. White House political advisers may have come to the conclusion that the PRC made a political miscalculation in deciding to conduct military exercises in the Taiwan Strait. The PRC may have acted out of a sense of frustration that Taiwan was gradually heading toward independence from the mainland; not knowing exactly what to do about it, China may have simply decided to flex its mili-

---

29 N.Y. TIMES (1995 – 5 January), at 6.

30 N.Y. TIMES (1954 – 2 April), at 4.

31 *See* G. CALABRESI & A.D. MELAMED, *Property Rules, Liability Rules, and Inalienability: One View of the Cathedral*, 85 HARVARD LAW REVIEW (1972) at 1089 (explaining property rules and liability rules).

tary muscles – a decision that may have had more to do with fact that the Chinese leadership is aging and nearly senile than with any sound political calculation. But the predictable consequences of a military show of force in the Taiwan Strait would be to drive the Chinese "compatriots" on Taiwan closer to the rest of the Taiwanese citizenry, for reasons I have suggested earlier in this essay. Hence I would not be surprised to see in months to come an acceleration in the overseas activities of Taiwanese officials in the direction of independent statehood for Taiwan, stimulated by the Chinese demonstration in the Taiwan Strait in March 1996. If the White House made a similar assessment, then its best strategy would have been to bring the USS Nimitz and the USS Independence into the area – so as to show support for the people on Taiwan – and at the same time let China go ahead with its war games with only mild remonstrance from the White House Press Secretary. If I am correct about White House strategy, it would simply be the latest example of an ambiguous and hence remarkably flexible policy that has served the U.S. well through the years in preserving peace in the region of the Taiwan Strait and allowing the Two China Problem to work itself out at its own pace.

Some Objective Features in Positive International Law

by

Vladimir-Djuro Degan

Introduction

Since the beginnings of international law as a body of legal rules, two basic tendencies have opposed one another. The solidarist concept takes the existence of the international community as a given fact. The rules of international law are merely derived from the requirements of this community and in order to achieve some established aims of mankind. The voluntarist concept strictly takes all legal rules as a product of the will of sovereign States.

This conflict will persist in the centuries to come. But the main issue are the results of this competition for the positive law of a given time.

This article deals with some shortcomings of the voluntaristic approach, in terms of both the doctrine of international law and the practice of States and international courts and tribunals. Voluntarism – according to which no legal norm can be binding on a State unless accepted by it – has been predominant in the doctrine and practice of States since the 19th century. This voluntaristic approach was best explained by the Permanent Court of International Justice in the *Lotus* case of 7 September 1927:

> "International law governs relations between independent States. The rules of law binding upon States therefore emanate from their own free will as expressed in conventions or by usages generally accepted as expressing principles of law and established in order to regulate the relations between these co-existing independent communities or with a view to the achievement of common aims. Restrictions upon the independence of States cannot therefore be presumed."[1]

---

[1] 10 PCIJ, *Series A,* at 18. On the basis of these arguments the Court upheld that Turkey was right in arresting and prosecuting a French officer for collision of his ship with a Turkish vessel on the high seas. And although the foregoing statement is cited even today as highly authoritative, all subsequent general conventions on this subject-matter rejected the Court's finding in the merits of this case. Hence, Article 97(1) of the 1982 U.N. Law of the Sea Convention States that: "In the event of a collision or any other incident of navigation concerning a ship on the high seas, involving the penal or disciplinary responsibility of the master or of any other person in the service of the ship, no penal or disciplinary proceedings may be instituted against such person except before the judicial or administrative authorities either of the flag State or of State of which such person is national."

Voluntarism was still the leading teaching in the period between the two world wars. But then a number of doctrines appeared contesting it. After 1945 voluntarism became a mark of distinction of the Soviet doctrine of international law with its leading representative Grigory Tunkin.[2]

However, even in the post-war times this approach was not confined by ideological boundaries. It is still widespread among scholars who dispute the existence of fundamental rights and duties of States, who challenge the generation of rules of general international law in customary process by a mere majority of States, and who discard the existence of the rules of *jus cogens* altogether.

This view is thus also the mark of the so-called "moderate" positivists. However, most of them fall into another trap. As a matter of principle, they do not recognize the binding force of a legal norm on a State which did not accept it either expressly or tacitly. But they all refer at the same time to judicial decisions as the proof of existence of actual legal rules, just as in common law. And that in spite of the fact that most States have never recognized the jurisdiction of the Hague Court as obligatory to them. That is mainly because these authors could not otherwise explain the body of international law as a system of legal rules.

One of modern protagonists of the Vattelian concept of the law of nations is Prosper Weil. In his shrewd critical review of what he calls pathology of international normative system, many of his remarks and critical arguments seem to be well-founded.[3]

Prosper Weil, however, consistently advocates the voluntaristic approach in its purest form, arguing that in all times of history the international law bore the stamp of an end, namely "to ensure the coexistence – in peace if possible, in war, if necessary – and the co-operation of basically pluralistic society". In his view the international society has always been, as it will be in future, ideologically pluralistic. He thus implicitly or explicitly repudiates the common moral values of the humanity, and *a fortiori* the existence of the rules of natural law. Therefore, the legal rules between heterogenous and equal States emerge in order to temper this condition of anarchy and to

---

[2] It is likely, however, that after the dissolution of the Soviet Union the attitude of most Russian authors will join the prevailing universalist trend. That was in fact the tradition of the Russian doctrine of international law prior to the 1917 Revolution.

[3] *Cf.* P. WEIL, *Towards Relative Normativity in International Law*?, 3 AMERICAN JOURNAL OF INTERNATIONAL LAW (1983) at 413–442. *See* also the original French version of this article – *Vers une normativité relative en droit international?*, 1 REVUE GÉNÉRALE DE DROIT INTERNATIONAL PUBLIC (1982) at 5–47.

enable them to live side by side, and "to cater to the common interests that did not take long to surface over and above the diversity of States."[4]

According to his words "international law will be unable to carry out its function of co-ordination unless it is neutral."[5] That means religious, as well as ideological neutrality. Thus in a way, a mere absence of any objective rules of law, together with the voluntarism and "positivity" of legal norms (*lex lata*), seem to be for him a condition *sine qua non* that the international normative system can serve its purpose in an international society made up of juxtaposed egoisms.[6]

One should not, however, neglect all dangerous consequences of an outright rejection of all aspects of the voluntaristic doctrine, as signalled by Prosper Weil. He has stressed, *inter alia*, that "as the international community still remains an imprecise entity, the normative power nominally vested in it is in fact entrusted to a directorate of this community, a *de facto* oligarchy". As a consequence: "The sovereign equality of States is in danger of becoming an empty catch phrase; for now some States are more equal than others."[7]

* * *

The voluntaristic approach to international legal order is esteemed by most legal advisors of governments, but on a highly selective basis. In fact, everything depends on whether legal obligations or rights, burdens or advantages of their respective State are at stake. They will refute without much hesitation the specific duties of their State on the basis of voluntaristic arguments which may arise from some alleged rules of general international law. But for the sake of the same arguments they will never deprive their country of new rights arising from that very set of rules of general international law.

Hence, since the time of signature of the respective 1958 Geneva Convention, all coastal States in the world have claimed to be entitled *ipso facto* to their own continental shelf.[8] Its Article 2(3) provides that the rights over it "do not depend on occupation, effective or notional, or on any express proclamation."[9] The actual possession of these new areas of sea-bed and

---

[4] *Ibid.* N° 4, at 418.

[5] *Ibid.* at 420.

[6] *Ibid.* at 422–423.

[7] *Ibid.* at 441.

[8] Prior to that Convention a coastal State which did not expressly proclaim its continental shelf was considered not to possess it, just as is now the case with contiguous zone, exclusive economic zone, or archipelagic waters of archipelagic States.

[9] Exactly this departure from effectiveness and from the effective occupation as being a necessary element for the acquisition of new maritime areas, is the deepest cause of the actual

subsoil thereof by coastal States required neither a formal entry into force of the 1958 Convention, nor the quality of being its party or even its signatory. That "instant custom" appeared by the mere adoption of its text at the 1958 Geneva U.N. Conference on the Law of the Sea.

The same practice continued even before the 1982 U.N. Law of the Convention was signed. Many coastal States which have not the slightest intention to become parties to the 1982 Convention largely use its provisions concerning the exclusive economic zone or new boundaries of the continental shelf, as allegedly being customary rules of general international law already in force, providing such rights to all States.

Strictly speaking, this widespread State practice weakens the exactness of the strict voluntaristic arguments in rejection of specific legal obligations of States arising from the rules of general international law.

* * *

It must be stressed that all concepts of the objective law, like all other doctrinal postulates, must be ultimately proved or rejected by what actually becomes the positive law. Notwithstanding the ingenuity of authors of legal concepts, they have almost no value if not embodied in positive law, and above all, in the rules of positive general international law. The measure of their "positivity" is therefore a test of their trustworthiness.[10]

But the first question is: are there at least some legal principles, the very existence and functioning of which do not depend on a specific agreement of States?

I. GENERAL PRINCIPLES OF LAW

One of the main features of voluntarism is the denial of any unchangeable and everlasting legal principles or precepts. Because, according to this

---

disorder in the legal order of the seas, which ensued after 1958. The 1982 U.N. Law of the Sea Convention has multiplied new legal regimes on the sea, seabed and its subsoil, in addition to the existing ones: archipelagic waters, exclusive economic zone and the International Sea-Bex Area. This plenitude of areas is a source of legal instability in itself. By this trend were reduced the zones under the regime of the high seas, and those which should become parts of the International Sea-Bex Area. This was in fact an example of world-wide law-creating against some legal precepts based on reason.

[10] For this very reason we believe that more than subjective, vague and disparate deductions by Grotius, Pufendorf and Wolff of "everlasting" rules of natural law from reason and from man's social nature, some past legal acts reflected more adequately rules of this kind. They are *inter alia* the American Declaration of Independence of 1776, the US Constitution of 1789, the French Declaration of the Rights of Man and of the Citizen of the same year, and even the Draft Declaration of the Law of Nations by Abbé Grégoire of 1795. And after Justinian's *Corps Juris Civilis* the French and the Austrian Civil Codes were also based on natural legal precepts.

teaching, the sovereign will of States is subject to no superior law, there are no legal rules which States could not modify or abrogate.

On this voluntaristic ground most authors deny the obligatory character for States of such general principles of law which are not embodied either in treaties or in customary law. And *vice versa*, if for a legal norm can be proved its conventional or customary character, even if the matter is of an obvious fiction, such a norm, according to this teaching, ceases to be a "general principle of law, recognized by civilized nations."

On such a reduced basis one cannot ascertain the real nature and scope of this recognized source of positive international law. In fact today there are very few of these principles, if any, which have not already been embodied in the general *corpus* of customary international law.[11]

So far the above dogma has been an obstacle to a rational explanation of the very nature of the general principles of law as an independent source of international law.

In this respect we shall start from some earlier doctrinal views. Besides the *conventional* law proceeding from an *express* consent of States, Emerich de Vattel distinguished between the so-called voluntary law which is based on a *presumed* consent of nations, and customary law properly called, which is based on their tacit consent.[12]

A well-known Italian positivist of this century, Dionisio Anzilotti, almost shared the same view. He argued with a good reason that a treaty does not consist of its written provisions only. Logical implications and necessary logical consequences of its written provisions also form a part of them. The will of parties to comply with a written norm or with a complexity of such norms also suggests their will to comply with logically implied norms, because in their absence written provisions remain senseless. Anzilotti called those implied norms "constructive rules", which are, according to him, essential for any legal order.[13]

Lord McNair was of the same opinion, at least in regard to the basic norm of *pacta sunt servanda*:

---

[11] This topic is discussed in my article – *General Principle of Law (A Source of General International Law)*, The Finnish Yearbook of International Law (1992) at 1–102.

[12] *Cf.* E. de Vattel, The Law of Nations or the Principles of Natural Law Applied to the Conduct and to the Affairs of Nations and Sovereigns, Washington (1916), *Introduction*, para. 27.

[13] *Cf.* D. Anzilotti, Cours de droit international, Paris (1929), Vol. I, at 68. Nevertheless, this author did not consider these "constructive rules" as general principles of law. They were for him parts of a treaty as a formal source of international law. He interpreted, on the contrary, Article 38(1c) of the Statute of the Court as an authorization given to it to resort to analogy, *ibid.* at 115–119.

> "In every uncodified legal system there are certain elements and universally agreed principles for which it is almost impossible to find specific authority. In the Common Law of England and the United States of America, where can you find specific authority for the principle that a man must perform his contracts? Yet almost every decision on a contract presupposes the existence of that principle. The same is true of international law. No Government would decline to accept the principle *pacta sunt servanda*, and the very fact that Governments find it necessary to spend so much effort in explaining in a particular case that the *pactum* has ceased to exist, or that the act complained of is not in breach of it, either by reason or of an implied term of some other reason, is the best acknowledgment of that principle..."[14]

There are other "constructive rules" as well, or, precisely speaking, general principles of law, which apply to agreements and contracts of any kind, be they governed by the municipal law of a State, or be they "transnational contracts", or genuine treaties. They are such as: *pacta tertiis nec nocent nec prosunt*, or *inadimplendi non est adimplendum*. There are, in addition, some well-known vices of consent of parties which may invalidate the agreement, like error, fraud, corruption and coercion.

In addition to it there are some general principles of law which do apply not only to agreements, but also to other legal situations. That is the principle of good faith, or of prescription, or that *nemo plus juris in alium transferre potest quam ipse habet*, or circumstances precluding wrongfulness of an act like *force majeure*, distress, necessity and self-defense.

All these general principles of law operate in international law regardless of the specific will or agreement of States. They are genuine rules of positive law, but not dependent on the consent granted by a sovereign State. In fact, any legal relations of States or of any other kind of juridical persons equal in rights, are impossible if these principles do not function as the rules of positive law. They are a necessary prerequisite for any kind of legal relations.

This means that conventions on codification of a part of international law do not entirely consist of the provisions of declaratory, crystallizing or generating effect of customary rules only. Conventions of this kind, and, above of all the 1969 Vienna Convention on the Law of Treaties, largely codify (or "declare") the existing general principles of law. These codified principles are not merely a *lex ferenda*, they are necessary rules which have always been the rules of positive law.

---

14 *Cf.* Lord McNAIR, THE LAW OF TREATIES, Oxford (1961) at 493.

Similar in nature are the general principles of arbitral and judicial procedure, governed either by municipal, or transnational, or international law. These principles are unchangeable as such. They are absolutely obligatory for judicial organs. But they cannot be binding on sovereign States on their own, simply because according to general international law arbitration and judicial settlement are not obligatory means for settlement of all their disputes.

These universal and perennial procedural principles, which are embodied in the rules of procedure of all permanent judicial bodies, include *inter alia*: the principle of equality of disputing parties in all phases of the procedure; their equal right to produce all kinds of arguments, documents and testimony in support of their claims; the duty of a judicial body to be impartial; the principle *res judicata*; the principle precluding litispendence; etc.

A grave and deliberate violation of these principles by an arbitrator or judge, may make his decision void. On the other hand, a deliberate exclusion or substantial modification of these principles in the compromise of disputing parties – the terms of which are obligatory for the arbitrator – deprive such a procedure of its judicial character.

As already stressed, all these general principles of law, which are a necessary prerequisite for any legal relations or judicial settlement, do not restrain the sovereign will of States. Sovereign States are not legally bound to enter into a treaty or other legal relations with one another. But whenever they conclude a treaty with another State or a foreign juridical person of whatever kind, these prerequisites for the existence of legal order automatically become applicable.

There are, however, some legal principles relating to State responsibility which really affect the freedom of action of sovereign States. They in fact outlaw irresponsible conduct of governments in their mutual relations. Exactly the same can be inferred only in regard to the two provisions from the 1969 Vienna Conventions on the Law of Treaties. These are Articles 53 and 64, invalidating and terminating a treaty conflicting with a peremptory norm of general international law.[15]

The legal validity of all above general principles of law depends on the fact of the very existence of international legal order. The existence of such an order, having at least some features similar to municipal legal orders in modern States, is a precondition for an organized international community of States and legal relations of its members.

---

[15] France has not so far ratified this Convention because it does not recognize the existence of *jus cogens* in international law. The same view is shared by some prominent international lawyers, for instance CH. ROUSSEAU, DROIT INTERNATIONAL PUBLIC, Paris (1971) at 150–151.

There are some experts in international political relations, who with convincing arguments, which are appropriate to them, deny the existence of such an integrated international community of States. If their arguments were valid, all rules on State responsibility and on *jus cogens* are little more than an erroneous and artificial imagination of lawyers, largely based on an analogy with the principles borrowed from the municipal law. In that case all draft articles of the International Law Commission, as well as Articles 53 and 64 from the 1969 Vienna Convention, have little in common with the reality of inter-State relations, even if a future Convention on State responsibility once formally enters into force.

The above problems are essential for the legal nature of international law as a whole, and perhaps even of any law. In this connection J.L. Brierly's explanation will probably not satisfy everybody, but is still worthy of quoting:

> "… The ultimate explanation of the binding force of all law is that man, whether he is a single individual or whether he is associated with other men in a State, is constrained, in so far as he is a reasonable being, to believe that order and not chaos is the governing principle of the world in which he has to live."[16]

Finally, in view of certain physical laws which proved to be valid in the entire universe, in view of the principles of formal logic and of mathematical operations, there is no conclusive evidence that legal rules of alike character are not existent in the relations of equal and autonomous subjects of any kind, as are today sovereign States.

II. FUNDAMENTAL RIGHTS AND DUTIES OF STATES

This set of legal rules is of an entirely different nature than the general principles of law. They do not operate above and beyond the sovereign will of States. Quite on the contrary, unless most States have accepted them of their free will as the rules of positive international law, they will remain at the level of *lex ferenda* and have no significant bearing on international relations as legal rules. As the rules of positive law they are, therefore, a product of historic development.

They are, however, a necessary minimum for the existence of a world political order and for the maintenance of international peace and security.

---

16 *Cf.* J.L. BRIERLY, THE LAW OF NATIONS, Oxford (1963), 6th ed., at 56.

On their actual respect by States as *jus cogens*, directly depends the preservation of these supreme values of humanity.

One should return to the classical doctrine. Following the teachings of his naturalist predecessors, Abbé Grégoire in his 1795 Draft Declaration of the Law of Nations assimilated States with individuals in the society.[17] Just as natural persons, according to the naturalist teaching, are entitled to some inherent and absolute rights due to their birth, States being members of the international community possess on the same grounds some inalienable, indivisible and unassignable rights, resulting from their very existence.

This is the core of all teachings on fundamental rights and duties of States. These rights are therefore based on solidarity and mutual respect by all members in a community of the existence, equality and independence of each of them individually.

Since it is originally based on natural law, the doctrine of fundamental rights of States must necessarily have universal validity. The transformation of its precepts into the positive rules of general international law may take place first by means of some general conventions, which at a latter stage generate into customary rules through a general practice of States and a *communis opinio juris*.

The doctrinal views disagree in the enumeration of these fundamental rights and corresponding correlative duties. The most acceptable seems to be the division into: (i) right of all States to existence, *i.e.* preservation; (ii) their right to independence (sovereignty); (iii) their right to equality in law; (iv) their right to respect; and (v) their right to international communications.[18]

The full enjoyment of all these rights implies the legal obligation of all members of the international community to strictly respect all of them in regard to all other States.[19] From these five fundamental rights and duties a larger number of more specific rights may derive, depending on the development stage of positive international law in a given time.

The core of the same principles is embodied in Article 2 of the United Nations Charter of 1945. What is at stake are the principles of the United

---

17 For more details *see* – V.D. DEGAN, *L'affirmation des principes du droit natural par la Révolution Française, Le Projet de Déclaration du Droit des Gens de l'abbé Grégoire*, ANNUAIRE FRANÇAIS DE DROIT INTERNATIONAL (1989) at 99–116.

18 This enumeration is followed by J. ANDRASSY, MEDJUNARODNO PRAVO [International Law] (1976) at 80–91, 6th ed., and by most other authors from ex-Yugoslavia.

19 The core of the present conflict in the former Yugoslavia lies in the fact that one of its successor States does not recognize all these natural rights of at least some other successor States, which are actually all U.N. Members. Conflicts of this kind cannot be settled through diplomatic mediation. Neither the U.N. Peace Keeping can have any success. Past conflicts of fascist Italy with Abyssinia (Ethiopia) in 1935, and of Nazi Germany with Austria, Czechoslovakia, Poland and the Soviet Union since 1938 were of the same kind.

Nations. They were, however, formulated in that text in the form of specific obligations of member States and of the Organization itself, and still not as universally binding principles of international law. This lacuna was filled by the *Declaration on Principles of International Law concerning Friendly Relations and Co-operation among States in accordance with the Charter of the United Nations*.

In spite of the fact that the U.N. Charter itself does not confer on General Assembly the power to enact rules binding on States, some of its declarations, adopted unanimously or without negative vote, may be declaratory of existing rules of international law, or they may contribute to the creation of new customary rules.[20]

The International Court of Justice in its Judgment of 27 June 1986 on the *Nicaragua* case attached a great importance to some of these declarations, as being a proof of *opinio juris* of the existing general customary rules:

> "... This *opinio juris* may, though with all due caution, be deduced from, *inter alia*, the attitude of the Parties and the attitude of States towards certain General Assembly resolutions, and particularly resolution 2625 (XXV) entitled *Declaration on Principles of International Law concerning Friendly Relations and Cooperation among States in accordance with the Charter of the United Nations*. The effect of consent to the text of such resolutions cannot be understood as merely that of 'reiteration or elucidation' of the treaty commitment undertaken in the Charter. On the contrary, it may be understood as an acceptance of the validity of the rule or set of rules declared by the resolution by themselves..."[21]

The Court largely quoted in that Judgment the said Declaration of 1970 as a proof of the existence of principles prohibiting the use of force and intervention.[22] For the same purpose it quoted the Declaration of the Inadmissibility of Intervention;[23] Definition of Aggression;[24] and even the Helsinki Final Act of 1975.[25]

---

20 *See* the Conclusions of the Commission of the Institute of International Law on *Resolutions of the General Assembly of the United Nations*, TABLEAU DES RÉSOLUTIONS ADOPTÉES (1957–1991), Paris (1992), at 180–192. *See* in particular Conclusions 1, 4 and 5. Exhaustive and scholarly reports on this complex subject-matter were written by KRZYSZTOF SKUBISZEWSKI in volume 61-I of the ANNUAIRE DE L'INSTITUT DE DROIT INTERNATIONAL (1985) at 29–358.

21 ICJ REPORTS 1986 at 99–100, para. 188. The Court added in the same Judgment: "...As already observed, the adoption by States of this text (the said Declaration of 1970) affords an indication of their *opinio juris* as to customary international law on the question...", *ibid.* at 101, para. 191.

22 *Ibid.* at 101, para. 191; at 106, para. 202; at 107, para. 203; at 119, para. 228; and at 133, para. 264.

23 Res. 2131 (XX) of 21 December 1965, *ibid.* at 107, para. 203; and at 134, para. 266.

24 Res. 3314 (XXIX) of 14 December 1974, *ibid.* at 103, para. 195.

25 *Ibid.* at 107, para. 204; at 133, para. 264.

Today there is no doubt at all that even according to the most orthodox and restrictive voluntarist criteria, all above mentioned rights and duties of States have transformed into customary rules of general international law. At present there is virtually no State which has not assumed legal obligation to respect these rights either under the U.N. Charter itself or under some other treaty, or declaration having a law-declaring effect.

But perhaps no other rules of general international law do limit to such an extent the freedom of action of all States, whatever their power and influence can be. Most of these fundamental rights and duties thus consist in far-reaching limitations of arbitrary use of force. It is not surprising that the difference between the normative picture and the reality of international relations is greater here than in other domains of international law.

The common objective, and that is the maintenance of international peace and security, thus requires very precise legal, and at the same time, political obligations of far-reaching importance. These fundamental principles are a kind of axioms on which rests the entire international political order.

Like all other legal rules, they can be respected or ignored in practice. But the stability of international relations depends on their actual and lasting observance as political commitments.[26]

It is worth noting that more than two centuries ago, Abbé Grégoire deduced essentially the same axioms visualizing a harmonious family of human beings.

III. "PRINCIPLES OF INTERNATIONAL LAW" IN PRACTICE OF THE HAGUE COURT

At least a part of this reasoning can be revealed in the deductive approach of the Hague Court to the so-called "fundamental principles of international law".[27] Of course, the Court has never resorted to the concept of natural law in order to prove the existence of these fundamental principles. Nevertheless it applied them occasionally as precepts of objective law, implicitly recognizing them as a part of international legal order.

In its usual practice, the Court has an inductive approach to legal rules of a broad application. It tries to prove their customary origin, namely their use in previous practice of as many States as possible, and, if possible, *com-*

---

[26] *Cf.* J.E.S. FAWCETT, *The Helsinki Act and International Law*, 1–2 REVUE BELGE DE DROIT INTERNATIONAL (1977), at 9.

[27] These principles should not be confused with the already discussed "general principles of law recognized by civilized nations".

munis opinio juris. This second psychological element of customary rules consists in the conviction of participants of a practice that they are fulfilling a legal duty, or at least in their acceptance of such a practice as legally obligatory.[28]

However, already Max Soerensen in his remarkable book on the sources of international law, published in 1946, noticed an important phenomenon in the practice of the former Permanent Court of International Justice. Certain principles are so firmly enshrined in international law and have such a persuasive force that the international judge does not feel obliged to search for their origin and foundation. These axiomatic principles are therefore inherent in international legal order and they are, as he wrote, the spinal column (*épine dorsale*) of the *corpus juris gentium* of our times.[29]

This author believed that this set of "principles of international law" is even different from the customary law itself. That in our view runs a risk of legal subjectivism of judges when deciding on particular cases.

Nevertheless, it is evident that throughout their practice the two Hague Courts have had a deductive rather than inductive approach in regard to some legal rules. From the desired goal, which is the maintenance of international peace and security, or the existence of a world legal order, they deduced some peremptory norms of conduct, obligatory on all subjects of international law, regardless of the acceptance, disapproval or indifference to them by a particular State.

In its actual practice the Court has most often deduced some rules of conduct from the principle of sovereignty of all States, or from juxtaposed sovereignties in relations of several States. Here are some examples, first in the practice of the Permanent Court of International Justice.

In the *Eastern Carelia* case of 23 July 1923, the Court refused to render its advisory opinion because the legal question requested by the Council of the League of Nations related to matters which formed the subject of a pending dispute between Finland and Soviet Russia. Russia refused to accept the obligations of membership in the League for the purposes of that dispute. The Court added:

> "... This rule, moreover, only accepts and applies a principle which is a fundamental principle of international law, namely, the principle of the

[28] Following the same criteria the Court even more often denies in its practice the existence of an alleged general customary rule. But, as mentioned, the Court corroborates most often the existence or lack of existence of customary rules on the basis of its own former practice, which is not fully in agreement with its inductive approach.

[29] *Cf.* M. SOERENSEN, LES SOURCES DU DROIT INTERNATIONAL, Copenhague (1946) at 115, 117.

independence of States. It is well established in international law that no State can, without its consent, be compelled to submit its disputes with other States either to mediation or to arbitration, or to any other kind of pacific settlement..."[30]

In the *Mavrommatis Palestine Concessions* case the Court in its Judgment of 30 August 1924, stressed:

"It is an elementary principle of international law that a State is entitled to protect its subjects, when injured by acts contrary to international law committed by another State, from whom they have been unable to obtain satisfaction through the ordinary channels. By taking up the case of one of its subjects and by resorting to diplomatic action or international judicial proceedings on his behalf, a State is in reality asserting its own rights – its right to ensure, in the person of its subject, respect for the rules of international law."[31]

In the *Brasilian Loans* case of 12 July 1929, the question arose as to whether the applicable law on bonds contracted by the Brazilian government was that of the State borrower or of their bearers. The Court decided the issue on the following ground:

"... Only the identity of the borrower is fixed; in this case it is a sovereign State, which cannot be presumed to have made the substance of its debt and the validity of the obligations accepted by it in respect thereof, subject to any law other than its own."[32]

In the Advisory Opinion on the *Greco-Bulgarian "Communities"* of 31 July 1930, the Court upheld:

"... it is a generally accepted principle of international law that in the relations between Powers who are contracting parties to a treaty, the provisions of municipal law cannot prevail over those of the treaty."[33]

In its first Judgment of 9 April 1949, in the *Corfu Channel* case on Merits, the new International Court of Justice found that the attitude of both disputing parties was contrary to some wider concepts of international law.

On one hand it established the breach of obligation by Albanian authorities to notify the existence of a minefield in Albanian territorial waters, and in warning the approaching British warships of the imminent danger to which

30 5 PCIJ, *Series B*, at 27.
31 2 PCIJ, *Series A*, at 12.
32 20/21 PCIJ, at 121.
33 17 PCIJ, *Series B*, at 32.

the minefield exposed them. Such obligations are based "on certain general and well recognized principles", such as "every State's obligation not to allow knowingly its territory to be used for acts contrary to the rights of other States",[34] namely the right of innocent passage.

On the other hand, the Court found that the British minesweeping operation after the incident happened violated Albanian sovereignty, because it had been carried out against the will of the Albanian Government. It added a well-known passage:

> "... The Court can only regard the alleged right of intervention as the manifestation of a policy of force, such as has in the past, given rise to most serious abuses and such as cannot, whatever be the present defects in international organization, find a place in international law. Intervention is perhaps still less admissible in the particular form it would take here; for, from the nature of things, it would be reserved for the most powerful States, and might easily lead to perverting the administration of international justice itself."[35]

Therefore, the intervention carried out in this particular form violated both concepts of sovereignty and of equality of the State in question.

In a well-known passage from the Advisory Opinion of 28 May 1951, on the *Reservations to the Genocide Convention* the Court stressed *inter alia* that principles underlying that Convention, especially because of extremely cruel consequences in cases of its violation, "are principles which are recognized by civilized nations as binding on States, even without any contractual obligation".[36]

In the Judgment of 24 May 1980, on *U.S. Diplomatic and Consular Staff in Tehran*, after establishing that Iran by holding hostages has violated its obligations under Vienna Conventions of 1961, 1963 and 1973, the Court has stressed the following:

> "... The Vienna Conventions, which codify the law of diplomatic and consular relations, state principles and rules essential for the maintenance of peaceful relations between States and accepted through the world by nations of all creeds, cultures and political complexions..."[37]

With that supplementary argument the Court has condemned in advance as unlawful a possible act of seizure and holding hostages among foreign

---

[34] ICJ REPORTS 1949 at 22.
[35] *Ibid.* at 35.
[36] *Cf.* ICJ REPORTS 1951 at 23.
[37] ICJ REPORTS 1980 at 24, para. 45.

diplomatic or consular staff, even by a State which is not a party to Vienna Conventions.

Iran refused to take part in this procedure and ignored the Judgment rendered in favour of the application by the United States. But in the following case it was the turn of the United States to refuse its participation in the proceedings on merits and to comply with the Judgments.

The matter was of the case concerning *Military and Paramilitary Activities in and against Nicaragua*. The applicant was Nicaragua and the defendant was the United States. The United States claimed on various grounds that the pleas set forth in Nicaragua's application are not within the jurisdiction of the Court, and are inadmissible. One of issues relevant to our topic was the relationship between multilateral treaties and general customary law.

The declaration of acceptance of the jurisdiction of the Court by the United States, given in 1946, literally referred to "all legal disputes" set forth in Article 36(2) of the Statute of the Court, including – "(b) any question of international law". But it specifically provided that this declaration shall not apply *inter alia* to – "(c) disputes arising under a multilateral treaty, unless (1) all parties to the treaty affected by the decision are also parties to the case before the Court, or (2) the United States of America specially agrees to jurisdiction..."

In the proceedings on jurisdiction of the Court, one of complaints by the United States was that – "the Court cannot determine the merits of Nicaragua's claims formulated under customary and general international law without interpreting and applying of the United Nations Charter and the Organization of American States Charter, and since the multilateral treaty reservation bars adjudication of claims based on those treaties, it bars all Nicaragua's claims."[38]

By its Judgment of 26 November 1984 on Jurisdiction and Admissibility, the Court gave effect to the multilateral treaty reservation by the United States, but it found that it had jurisdiction in that case. In regard to the above objection it declared:

> "... The Court cannot dismiss the claims of Nicaragua under principles of customary and general international law, simply because such principles have been enshrined in the texts of conventions relied upon by

[38] ICJ REPORTS 1984 at 423, para. 69. This objection does not seem to be very convincing. If the United States has recognized jurisdiction of the Court in regard to "any question of international law" under specifically multilateral treaty reservation, it seems obvious that the Court had the jurisdiction, on condition of reciprocity, to hear all disputes arising under bilateral treaties, or customary rules of international law, or even general principles of law. Thus the otherwise obsolete principle of interpretation: *expressio unius exclusio alterius est*, cannot apply here.

> Nicaragua. The fact that the above-mentioned principles, recognized as such, have been codified or embodied in multilateral conventions does not mean that they cease to exist and to apply as principles of customary law, even as regards countries that are parties to such conventions. Principles such as those of non-use of force, non-intervention, respect for independence and territorial integrity of States, and the freedom of navigation, continue to be binding as part of customary international law, despite the operation of provisions of conventional law in which they have been incorporated..."[39]

It is not accidental that the Court here insisted on some well-known fundamental principles of international law, although stressing at the same time their customary character.

The United States subsequently declared that the Judgment of 1984 has been "clearly and manifestly erroneous". It refused to comply with it and it did not take part in the proceedings on merits.

In the proceedings on merits, which ensued in the absence of the United States, the main concern of the Court was how to extract general customary rules applicable in that case from the provisions set forth in the U.N. Charter. In the text of its Judgment of 27 June, 1986, it generally adopted the inductive approach to the rules of general application. It put as its task to consider whether a customary rule exists in the *opinio juris* of States, and satisfy itself that it is confirmed by State practice.[40]

But dealing with some legal principles the Court did not renounce to corroborate its statements by deductive considerations as well. At stake was especially the application of principles of non-use of force and of non-intervention. With regard to the first, it stated *inter alia* the following:

> "... The essential consideration is that both the Charter and the customary international law flow from a common fundamental principle outlawing the use of force in international relations..."[41]

It proceeds therefore that this "fundamental principle" deserves its existence in a way apart from the U.N. Charter as conventional instrument, and even apart from customary law.

With regard to the principle of non-intervention, it quoted its own passage from the *Corfu Channel* case of 1949 cited above, and then concluded:

---

39 *Ibid.* at 424, para. 73.

40 *Cf.* ICJ REPORTS 1986 at 97–98, paras. 183–186.

41 *Ibid.* at 97, para. 181.

> "... though examples of trespass against this principle are not infrequent, the Court considers that it is part and parcel of customary international law..."[42]

Important is another passage of this Judgment:

> "... in view of the generally accepted formulations, the principle forbids all States or groups of States to intervene directly or indirectly in internal or external affairs of other States. A prohibited intervention must accordingly be one bearing on matters in which each State is permitted, by the principle of State sovereignty, to decide freely. One of these is the choice of a political, economic, social and cultural system, and formulation of foreign policy. Intervention is wrongful when it uses methods of coercion in regard to such choices, which must remain free ones..."[43]

In that Judgment the following was also emphasized:

> "206. However, before reaching a conclusion on the nature of prohibited intervention, the Court must be satisfied that State practice justifies it. There have been in recent years a number of instances of foreign intervention for the benefit of forces opposed to the government of another State... It has to consider whether there might be indications of a practice illustrative of belief in a kind of general right for States to intervene, directly or indirectly, with or without armed force, in support of an internal opposition in another State, whose cause appeared particularly worthy by reason of political and moral values with which it was identified. For such a general right to come into existence would involve a fundamental modification of the customary law principle of non-intervention."[44]

The above mentioned examples prove the fact that the Court cannot completely give up the deductive approach to the most important legal rules for maintenance of international peace and security.

It seems, however, paradoxical that with the increasing importance of some legal rules for maintenance of world political order, the Court's sense of duty to prove their customary character is being diminished. It would certainly not take the risk simply to deduce a less important rule of general

---

42 *Ibid.* at 106, para. 202.

43 *Ibid.* at 108, para. 205.

44 *Ibid.* at 108, para. 206. Dutch writer P.P. RIJPKEMA, *Customary International Law in the Nicaragua Case*, NETHERLANDS YEARBOOK OF INTERNATIONAL LAW (1989) at 91–116, at 101, comments this statement of the Court, in our view properly: "This passage shows that, in the Court's view, State practice can certainly influence the content of the principle, but that it cannot have an influence of whether it exists. Admittedly, State practice deviating from the principle can 'modify' the principle, but the principle still continues to exist in its modified form." As will be shown in the next Chapter, general international law today allows humanitarian intervention.

customary law – other than *jus cogens* – affecting the subjective rights of one of the parties in a dispute.

Nevertheless it must be admitted that even the authentic inductive method in ascertaining general customary rules which bind all sovereign States, has never met all voluntaristic criteria for their existence. General practice has rarely been tantamount to universal practice of all States. *Communis opinio juris* has been more often than not a legal fiction. Furthermore it has never been proved in actual practice that the existing rules of this kind do not legally bind newly independent States which virtually did not participate in previous law-creating practice. And the references by the Court to its own precedents as a proof of the law in force, have nothing in common with the genuine will of all States to accept the universal validity of a legal rule.

In the light of the above conclusions it must nevertheless be stressed that the deductive approach by the Court – which is not a law-maker in the same sense as are sovereign States – should always be kept under strict control. A rule which the Court itself finds to be a prerequisite for the maintenance of international peace and security, or for the achievement of some other supreme values of the humanity, is not a *lex lata* only for that reason. However, if a predominant practice of States confirms the respect of such a rule, if a number of codification conventions and of the U.N. General Assembly resolutions prove *opinio juris* by a large number of States, such an acceptance can overcome the indifference or opposition on the part a few remaining States. Inductive and deductive operations then usefully complement each other.

That exactly seems to be the attitude of the Court throughout its practice. But it seems likely that the Court, in its own cautious way, has confirmed the validity of fundamental rights and duties of all States as set forth by Abbé Grégoire back in 1795.

IV. HUMAN RIGHTS

Probably the most important deficiency of the voluntaristic approach is still its ideological, or more precisely, "moral neutrality", which in view of Prosper Weil is its main advantage.

Positivism, as well as legal normativism, do not care for probable inhumane consequences of positive laws. For these teachings the most important is the question whether the violation of a legal norm is precluded by a temporary sanction or not. But unlike natural legal concepts, they do not care whether a law as such is just or unjust.

It must be, however, admitted that even the classical teachings on natural law, as preached by St. Thomas Aquinas and Grotius, although pervaded with deep and sincere humanism, did not necessarily advocate the equality and freedom of all human beings. Although inhuman positive laws were in these writings considered as unnatural and sinful, these teachings could not alter the harsh reality of slavery and serfdom over that long period, or even the annihilation of indigenous populations, especially in both Americas.

However, since the second half of the 19th century, mostly under the influence of public opinion, many States have adhered to the conventions prohibiting slavery, slave trade, servitude, and forced labour. After World War I a progress was also made in the protection of minorities in certain States, but equally on the basis of strictly conventional obligations.

The tendency of humanizing the rules of warfare started with the publication of *Un souvenir de Solferino* by the Swiss citizen Henri Dunant, a pamphlet on the battle waged in 1859 in Northern Italy.[45]

But it was only the large-scale crimes committed during World War II, primarily against the civilian population, that shocked the conscience of mankind in a way which lead to sweeping changes in positive international law. These crimes were committed in particular by the implementation of Nazi laws and decisions by German administrative and military bodies.

The outcome of World War II has proved the inadequacy of the voluntaristic doctrine in practice. The judges of the Nuremberg and Tokyo Tribunals were unable to base their verdicts on the rules of international law which were previously consented by either Germany or Japan. That was especially the case with the rules providing the responsibility of individuals for crimes against peace and against humanity. Yet these two judgments were not acts of arbitrariness or revenge against the defeated enemy.

More than the texts of these two judgments, the inadequacy of voluntarism was proved in the Advisory Opinion of the International Court of Justice of 28 May 1951, concerning the *Reservations to the Genocide Convention of 1948*:

> "... The origins of the Convention show that it was the intention of the United Nations to condemn and punish genocide as 'a crime under international law' involving a denial of the right of existence of entire human groups, a denial which shocks the conscience of mankind and results in great losses to humanity, and which is contrary to moral law and to the

45 In 1864 the first Convention for the Amelioration of the Condition of Soldiers Wounded in Armies in the Field was concluded in Brussels. This was followed by conventional regulations on the conduct of hostilities on land and at sea, and for protection of prisoners of war. The common purpose of these convention was to diminish unnecessary human sufferings.

> spirit and aims of the United Nations... The first consequence arising from this conception is that the principles underlying the Convention are principles which are recognized by civilized nations as binding on States, even without any conventional obligation. A second consequence is the universal character both of the condemnation of genocide and of the co-operation required 'in order to liberate mankind from such an odious scourge' (Preamble to the Convention)..."[46]

Therefore, the infamous atrocities committed during World War II, which the new Genocide Convention of 1948 has to prevent and suppress, have proved the simple fact that beyond and above a set of legal rules which were consented by a particular State, there still exist at least some superior principles of what the Court called – moral law. These principles are recognized by civilized nations as binding on all States and, as stressed above, without any conventional obligation. Consequently, the crime of genocide is a crime in itself, and not because specific legal rules, consented by States, prohibited it or not.

This Court has even more departed from the voluntaristic approach in the equally famous passages of its Judgment on *Barcelona Traction Ltd.* case of 5 February 1970, given *obiter dicta* with regard to obligations of States *erga omnes*:

> "... an essential distinction should be drawn between the obligations of a State towards the international community as a whole, and those arising *vis-à-vis* another State in the field of diplomatic protection. By their very nature the former are the concern of all States. In view of the importance of the rights involved, all States can be held to have a legal interest in their protection; they are obligations *erga omnes*.
>
> 34. Such obligations derive, for example, in contemporary international law, from the outlawing of acts of aggression, and of genocide, as also from the principles and rules concerning the basic rights of the human person, including protection from slavery and racial discrimination. Some of corresponding rights of protection have entered into the body of international law ... others are conferred by international instruments of a universal or quasi-universal character."[47]

Being obligations *erga omnes*, they are binding on all States regardless of their conventional character, and even regardless of the participation of an individual State in a customary process. Nevertheless, international instruments can be useful in determining their contents and scope.[48]

---

46 ICJ REPORTS 1951 at 23.

47 ICJ REPORTS 1970 at 32, paras. 33 and 34.

48 *Cf.* critics of this attitude of the Court – P. WEIL, *op.cit., supra* note 3, at 431–433.

Atrocities committed during the recent war on the soil of the former Yugoslavia have resulted in some new developments.

The Arbitration Commission of the Conference on Yugoslavia, in discussing the problems of State succession, declared:

> "... the peremptory norms of general international law and, in particular, respect for the fundamental rights of the individuals and the rights of peoples and minorities, are binding on all the parties to the succession."[49]

Therefore, on no legal basis, such as the clean-slate theory, can successor States release themselves from these obligations, which do not proceed only from treaties of the predecessor State.

On the other hand, by virtue of the U.N. Security Council Resolution 808 (1993) of 22 February 1993 the International Criminal Tribunal for the Former Yugoslavia was established. It has in its competence the prosecution of persons responsible for serious violations of international humanitarian law committed in the territory of former Yugoslavia since the beginning of 1991. Its Statute provides four groups of international crimes: (i) grave breaches of the Geneva Conventions of 1949; (ii) violations of the laws and customs of war; (iii) genocide; and (iv) crimes against humanity.[50]

* * *

Indeed, inhuman municipal laws and their large scale evil consequences produced after 1945 an unprecedented development in positive international law. Thus the U.N. Charter of 1945 already stressed *inter alia* the faith in and respect for fundamental human rights, the worth of the human person, as well as human rights and fundamental freedoms for all without distinction as to race, sex, language or religion.

The Universal Declaration of Human Rights, adopted by the U.N. General Assembly on 10 December 1948, assimilated in fact the substance and standards of the 1789 French Declaration of the Rights of Man and of the

---

[49] *Cf.* Opinion N° 1 of 29 November 1991, para. 1e) and para. 3, 6 INTERNATIONAL LEGAL MATERIALS (1992) at 1496, 1497. In its Opinion N°2 of 11 January 1992, the Commission repeated: "...the – now peremptory – norms of international law require States to ensure respect for the rights of minorities. This requirement applies to all the Republics *vis-à-vis* the minorities on their territory", *ibid.* at 1498.

[50] Also established under the Resolution 955 (1994) of 8 November 1994 was the International Tribunal for Rwanda. Its Statute provides, however, the prosecution of genocide, crimes against humanity and violations of Article 3 common to the 1949 Geneva Conventions and of Additional Protocol II of 1977. Both Tribunals were therefore not established under the treaties between respective States, but on behalf of decisions of the Security Council acting under Chapter VII of the U.N. Charter.

Citizen.[51] But defining particular civil and political rights, the drafters of the 1948 Declaration had in mind the circumstances prevailing in their time. They added to them a number of economic, social and cultural rights, hich mostly remained the long-term aims rather than precise legal obligations for all States.

Therefore, the post-war development of positive international law has the same objectives as the natural law prior to the nineteenth century, and that is the attainment of natural, inalienable and sacred rights of all human beings without discrimination.

There is no doubt that all governments are restrained today by some rules of general international law in their treatment of their own citizens and of any other human beings. These legal obligations no longer depend on their approval or agreement. They are thus above the law consented by a particular State.

This legal development of material rules of international law on human rights has deeply affected the scope of the domestic jurisdiction, as well as the rule of non-intervention.

Thus, the Institute of International Law states in one of its most important resolutions *inter alia*:

> "A State acting in breach of its obligations in the sphere of human rights cannot evade its international responsibility by claiming that such matters are essentially within its domestic jurisdiction."[52]

In its Articles 2 and 3 this Resolution defines the scope of the rights to humanitarian intervention. It says that, without prejudice to the functions and powers which the Charter attributes to the organs of the United Nations in case of violation of the obligations assumed by the members of the Organization:

> "... States, acting individually or collectively, are entitled to take diplomatic, economic and other measures towards any other State which has violated the obligation set forth in Article 1,[53] provided such measures

---

51 The text of the 1789 Declaration, entirely based on reason and on the rational and social nature of man, is perhaps the best sublimation of precepts of natural law and their transformation into the rules of positive law of lasting effect.

52 *Cf.* Article 2(1) of the Resolution of 1989, on *The Protection of Human Rights and the Principle of Non-intervention in Internal Affairs of States*, TABLEAU DES RÉSOLUTIONS ADOPTÉES (1957–1991), Paris (1992) at 206–213.

53 In Article 1 it is provided *inter alia* that: "Human rights are a direct expression of the dignity of human person. The obligation of States to ensure their observance derives from the recognition of this dignity as proclaimed in the Charter of the United Nations and in the Universal

> are permitted under international law and do not involve the use of armed force in violation of the Charter of the United Nations. These measures cannot be considered as unlawful intervention in the internal affairs of that State.
> Violations justifying recourse to the measures referred to above shall be viewed in the light of their gravity and of all the relevant circumstances..."

But on the other side of the medal there is a harsh reality of human sufferings because of the lack of will of international community, including the United Nations, to intervene in order to stop international crimes. In situations like those in Bosnia-Herzegovina, Rwanda, Somalia or Angola, the affirmation of the right to humanitarian intervention does not suffice. What is needed is a duty to intervene. The early prevention of further atrocities is for actual and potential victims of these crimes more important than the prosecution of their perpetrators by newly established international tribunals. The international community thus needs new and much more advanced forms of organization.

Conclusion

It was not our intention to prove in this article the existence of an international legal order entirely based on a set of objective norms, operating beyond and above the sovereign will of States. States remain to be both the main creators and the addressees of international law.

All modern legal doctrines which have underestimated the sovereign will of States, or which have even sought to deny the existence of States and of juridical persons in municipal law, have failed in their aims.[54] These theories were contradicted by the reality of international relations and were all forgotten.

Without in any way contesting the sovereign will of States as the main factor in the creation or termination of the rules of positive law – especially those which are the sources of legal rights and obligations of particular States – some examples were given to show that this will is sometimes dependent on some objective norms. In some situations of the operation of *jus cogens*, these objective norms even determine or at least restrain the law-creating power of sovereign States.

Declaration of Human Rights. – The international obligation, as expressed by the International Court of Justice, is *erga omnes*..."

[54] This was particularly the feature of solidarists and of the objectivist school of law by Leon Duguit and Georges Scelle in France.

What can be expected in the 21st century is a continued expansion of the rules of this kind, deduced from some common goals of mankind. Individual States will not be able to release themselves from these new legal obligations simply by refusing to accede to a convention or even perhaps by protesting against it.

However, if this new law-creating process is not kept under some control of what we now call *communis opinio juris*, as confirmed in practice of most States, it can compromise itself altogether. The same happened in the 16th and 17th centuries when Grotius, Pufendorf and Christian Wolff created "objective" and "everlasting" rules of the law of nature by their simple deductions from reason and social nature of man.

La personnalité juridique dans le système du droit des gens

par

Christian Dominicé

Un coup d'oeil aux traités ou manuels généraux de droit international public révèle, sans que cela soit une surprise, l'importance accordée aux développements consacrés, sous un titre ou un autre, à la question des sujets du droit international. C'est tout à fait légitime, dès lors que, dans tout système juridique, la notion de sujet de droit est essentielle. On peut constater que dans les chapitres réservés à cette question l'on rencontre fréquemment une succession d'analyses portant sur des entités spécifiques – l'Etat au premier chef, les organisations internationales, les insurgés reconnus comme belligérants, etc… – comptées au nombre des personnes juridiques internationales[1]. Il est plus rare de rencontrer un effort de systématisation[2].

La principale controverse concerne la place de l'individu en droit des gens. Tantôt il est inclus dans l'énumération des sujets du droit international, tantôt il se voit attribuer une situation spéciale, parmi ces sujets, ou à l'extérieur de cette définition, mais il est peu fréquent que la place, variable, qui lui est ainsi faite soit expliquée ou justifiée en fonction d'une conception d'ensemble de la personnalité juridique[3]. On observe, il est vrai, que le critère retenu par un certain nombre d'auteurs pour la subjectivité internationale est l'aptitude à présenter une réclamation internationale. Ce n'est cependant pas réellement convaincant si l'on inclut des droits procéduraux institués par des conventions, car la situation de l'individu est alors variable d'un pays à l'autre, en raison du principe de la relativité des traités. Elle peut même

---

1 *Cf. e.g.* Le chapitre rédigé par N. Mugerwa, *Subjects of International Law*, dans: M. Sorensen (éd.), Manual of Public International Law, New York (1968), pp. 247–310; Ch. Rousseau, Droit international public, t. II *Les sujets de droit*, Paris (1974).

2 Il s'agit d'un domaine où, dans la pratique, des vues très variées sont exprimées, *cf.* L. Caflisch, *Les sujets du droit international*, dans: P. Guggenheim (éd.), Répertoire des décisions et des documents de la procédure écrite et orale de la Cour permanente de Justice internationale, Genève, vol. 3 (1973).

3 Pour une revue des diverses opinions à ce sujet; *cf.* Ch. Dominicé, *L'émergence de l'individu en droit international public*, Annales d'études internationales, Genève (1988), vol. 16, pp. 1–16.

varier dans le temps à l'intérieur d'un même Etat au gré de ses engagements conventionnels[4].

En bref, nous avons le sentiment qu'en cette matière il existe un champ de réflexion encore largement ouvert.

Nous n'avons pas la prétention de faire le tour d'une question complexe dans cette modeste étude, mais nous souhaitons nous associer à l'hommage rendu à Krzysztof Skubiszewski, que sa remarquable curiosité intellectuelle a conduit, entre autres, à l'analyse d'importants problèmes de théorie, en tentant de mettre en lumière quelques points de repère.

I. LA NOTION DE LA PERSONNALITÉ JURIDIQUE

A. Définition

Il faut préciser d'emblée que la notion de sujet de droit et celle de personnalité juridique, au sens où nous les utilisons, sont équivalentes. Un sujet de droit revêt cette qualité parce qu'il est doté de la personnalité juridique, et l'on peut dire de même qu'une personne juridique est un sujet de droit.

De plus, il y a lieu de rappeler que la caractéristique première d'un sujet de droit – ou, si l'on préfère, de la personnalité juridique – est l'aptitude à être titulaire de droits et d'obligations. Si l'on ne s'arrête pas à cette définition générale, la notion de sujet de droit n'a pas de sens. Seul un sujet de droit peut être titulaire de droits et assumer des obligations, et tous les sujets de droit sont dans cette situation. De même – c'est le même phénomène appréhendé sous l'angle inverse – les normes juridiques ne peuvent avoir pour destinataires que des sujets de droit, étant entendu qu'à l'intérieur d'une entité collective des règles de fonctionnement ont pour destinataires des organes de cette entité.

Ce n'est pas dire, assurément, que tous les sujets de droit soient identiques. Ils présentent au contraire une très grande diversité[5]. L'exemple des personnes morales dans les droits internes est à cet égard révélateur. La structure, le fonctionnement, le degré d'engagement des associés varient gran-

---

[4] Ainsi, selon qu'une personne se trouverait dans un Etat lié par la Convention européenne de sauvegarde des droits de l'homme et des libertés fondamentales et par son article 25 relatif aux requêtes individuelles, ou dans un Etat étranger à ce système, elle serait, ou ne serait pas, un sujet du droit international.

[5] *Cf.* le *dictum* bien connu de la Cour internationale de Justice dans son avis consultatif du 11 avril 1949 sur la *Réparation des dommages subis au service des Nations Unies,* C.I.J. RECUEIL (1949), pp. 174, 178: «Les sujets de droit, dans un système juridique, ne sont pas nécessairement identiques quant à leur nature ou à l'étendue de leurs droits».

dement selon le type de personne morale, et il faut à chaque fois consulter la loi pertinente. De plus, à diverses fins il s'impose parfois de «percer le voile corporatif»[6]. Cela vaut aussi pour l'application du droit international, par exemple en matière de protection des actionnaires[7], d'identification des biens ennemis, etc. Les sujets du droit international sont eux aussi particulièrement différents les uns des autres. Tout cela est évident et bien connu, mais cependant il demeure que le trait commun, le noyau dur, est l'aptitude à être titulaire de droits et d'obligations.

B. Droit international et droits nationaux

La notion de personnalité juridique est apparue tout d'abord dans les ordres internes, puis elle s'est également imposée en droit international public. Ce n'est pas un phénomène isolé. On le rencontre également pour d'autres notions ou institutions, ainsi par exemple la responsabilité. On sait qu'il s'impose dans des cas de ce genre de procéder à une double démarche intellectuelle.

D'une part, il est important de comprendre ce qu'une notion signifie en droit interne, puisque c'est de là qu'elle vient et que par conséquent la pensée juridique en a reçu une influence importante.

D'autre part, il faut se convaincre que l'analogie entre droit international et droit interne existe sans doute parfois, mais qu'elle est parfois aussi très distante.

Ainsi, il nous paraît nécessaire, pour analyser la question de la personnalité juridique dans le système du droit des gens, d'avoir un regard sur les traits généraux de ce que l'on peut constater dans les droits nationaux, tout en observant une maxime de prudence dès qu'il s'agit de faire état d'éventuelles analogies. Cette méthode comparative paraît d'autant plus indiquée qu'à l'évidence il convient de distinguer, en droit des gens, la personnalité du droit international de la personnalité du droit interne, aspect important de la question sur lequel il y aura lieu de revenir[8].

---

6 On trouve de nombreux exemples dans les rapports nationaux publiés dans l'ouvrage collectif de S. BASTID, R. DAVID, LA PERSONNE MORALE ET SES LIMITES, Paris (1960).

7 L'arrêt de la Cour internationale de Justice dans l'affaire de la *Barcelona Traction*, C.I.J. RECUEIL (1970), p. 3, s'en tient à la structure juridique formelle de la société anonyme, mais des solutions différentes, particulièrement intéressantes, ont été retenues dans des accords internationaux, nous pensons particulièrement à la Convention de Washington de 1965 instituant le CIRDI, et aux accords d'Alger de 1981 instituant le Tribunal des réclamations entre l'Iran et les Etats-Unis.

8 Rappelons que dans l'avis consultatif de 1949 (*supra* note 5), la Cour internationale de Justice a bien marqué la différence entre personnalité juridique du droit international et personnalité

II. ORDRE JURIDIQUE ET SUJETS DE DROIT

A. Les traits spécifiques d'un ordre juridique

L'un des aspects cardinaux de notre interrogation sur la personnalité juridique tient assurément à une bonne compréhension de la relation qui s'établit entre la notion d'ordre juridique et celle de sujet de droit. Il faut s'y arrêter.

Le phénomène juridique se manifeste, comme chacun sait, par l'apparition de ce qu'il est convenu d'appeler des ordres juridiques.

Un ordre juridique est un ensemble de règles ou normes juridiques articulées et coordonnées entre elles. Autrement dit, un ordre juridique se définit par rapport aux normes qui le constituent, mais inversément une norme juridique est identifiée comme telle par son appartenance à un ordre juridique. Il n'existe pas de norme isolée, autonome. Pour constater l'existence d'une règle juridique, il faut pouvoir établir qu'elle est reconnue par un ordre juridique comme lui appartenant, ce qui implique que l'on démontre qu'elle a été valablement créée dans cet ordre juridique. Ainsi, on peut reconnaître l'existence d'une norme du droit français en observant qu'elle figure dans une loi régulièrement édictée en France. De même, une norme du droit international est identifiée par la constatation qu'elle est énoncée par une convention en vigueur, ou qu'elle a suivi le processus de création de la coutume internationale.

En bref, il existe entre ordre juridique et norme juridique un rapport étroit de coexistence. Il y a, à l'évidence, concomitance, car l'un n'apparaît pas sans l'autre. C'est, peut-on dire, comme l'histoire de l'oeuf et de la poule: il est vain de se poser la question de l'antériorité.

C'est à ce stade de l'analyse que surgit la notion de sujet de droit. En effet, la définition retenue de l'ordre juridique – ensemble de normes coordonnées entre elles – n'est qu'une approche initiale, et à certains égards partielle[9]. Un ordre juridique prend naissance dans un milieu social déterminé, les normes qui le composent confèrent des droits ou imposent des obligations à des «destinataires». Qui sont-ils ? Ceux précisément à qui cet ordre juridique reconnaît l'aptitude à être titulaires de droits et d'obligations. C'est ainsi que l'on constate qu'il n'y a pas d'ordre juridique sans sujets de droit.

---

juridique du droit interne, dès lors qu'à juste titre elle n'a pas fait découler la première de l'article 104 de la Charte, qui concerne la seconde. *Cf.* aussi I. SEIDL-HOHENVELDERN, *Das Recht der internationalen Organisationen*, 5. AUFL., Köln (1992), p. 34 et p. 39.

[9] Il y a encore d'autres éléments, auxquels il n'y a pas lieu de s'arrêter ici: ainsi, par exemple, un ordre juridique comporte des normes sur la création de nouvelles règles (sources).

C'est une notion qui apparaît en même temps que celles de droit et d'ordre juridique. Encore faut-il apporter des précisions et voir de plus près comment s'articule cette relation entre sujet de droit et ordre juridique.

B. Sujets primaires et sujets secondaires

La doctrine ayant déjà, dès longtemps, mis en lumière cette distinction, il n'y a pas lieu de s'y arrêter longuement[10]. Le sujet primaire, ou originaire, est celui qui est indispensable à la naissance d'un ordre juridique, et qui, simultanément, lui confère son caractère propre.

Le sujet secondaire, appelé parfois aussi dérivé, est la personne ou l'entité à laquelle un ordre juridique attribue la qualité de sujet de droit, en fixant les conditions ou critères permettant sa création. Le sujet secondaire n'est pas nécessaire à l'existence de l'ordre juridique, mais ce sont les besoins de l'organisation sociale qui poussent à en imaginer la création. Les sociétés commerciales, dans les droits internes, en sont une excellente illustration, ainsi que les associations et fondations[11].

Il n'y a pas de difficulté à constater que les ordres juridiques nationaux ont pour sujet primaire l'être humain, la personne physique, alors que, quant à lui, l'ordre juridique international a l'Etat souverain pour sujet primaire.

Il est important de le souligner, car c'est là l'une des raisons principales voulant que l'ordre juridique international soit distinct des ordres internes. C'est essentiel pour notre propos et il faudra y revenir.

C. Sujets propres et sujets reconnus

Laissant pour l'instant de côté l'ordre juridique international, nous pouvons faire au sujet des ordres internes une constatation importante.

Chaque ordre interne a pour destinataire de ses normes, il va de soi, les sujets primaires que sont les personnes physiques, ainsi que divers types de sujets secondaires qui lui doivent leur existence en qualité d'entités dotées de la personnalité juridique.

Les personnes physiques, elles, sont toutes sujets de droit. L'époque des esclaves est révolue. Il n'est donc plus d'aucun intérêt de se demander à quel ordre juridique une personne déterminée doit sa qualité de sujet de droit. La

---

10 *Cf.* particulièrement H. MOSLER, *Subjects of International Law*, dans: R. BERNHARDT (éd.), ENCYCLOPEDIA OF INTERNATIONAL LAW, Instalment 8 (1984), p. 442.

11 Sur toute l'importante question de la personne morale, *voir* S. BASTID, R. DAVID, *op. cit.*, *supra* note 6.

nationalité, par exemple, peut, selon les cas, revêtir une signification pour l'identification du statut personnel, mais il ne s'agit pas du principe même de la qualité de sujet de droit, acquise à tout être humain.

Quant aux sujets secondaires, les personnes morales, l'ordre juridique auquel elles doivent leur existence les rend titulaires de droits et d'obligations, précisément parce qu'il leur en a donné la capacité.

Cependant, il faut observer un autre phénomène important: une personne morale qui reçoit sa personnalité d'un ordre juridique peut être reconnue comme sujet de droit dans un autre ordre juridique. Dans les rapports horizontaux entre ordres juridiques nationaux, il s'agit d'une situation tout à fait courante. La vie économique et sociale ne serait plus possible si une société commerciale allemande, française, ou italienne, qui a acquis la personnalité juridique dans son ordre juridique d'origine, ne se voyait pas reconnaître la qualité de sujet de droit aux Etats-Unis, au Royaume-Uni ou en Suisse, ce qui lui permet d'être partie à des contrats, d'acquérir des biens ou de participer à une procédure judiciaire. Les principes qui gouvernent la reconnaissance, dans un ordre juridique, des personnes morales étrangères, sont sans doute variables, mais cette reconnaissance intervient dans tous les pays[12]. Autre est la question de la reconnaissance, dans les ordres internes, des personnes juridiques internationales, question qui sera abordée ultérieurement.

Ainsi donc, nous observons qu'à l'intérieur d'un ordre juridique national, les règles générées dans ce système vont avoir pour destinataires, d'une part, les sujets de droit qui reçoivent cette qualité de cet ordre, et, d'autre part, ceux qui reçoivent d'un autre ordre la personnalité juridique et sont reconnus comme sujets de droit. Tout ordre juridique – national pour l'instant – connaît donc ses sujets propres, et les sujets reconnus comme tels venant d'ailleurs.

Tout naturellement, dès lors, on doit se demander ce qu'il en est de l'ordre juridique international.

Comme tout ordre juridique – sinon il n'en serait pas un – le droit international crée ses propres sujets, les sujets du droit international, auxquels nous allons, ci-après, nous arrêter. Comme tout ordre juridique, le droit international peut reconnaître la qualité de sujet de droit à une personne ou entité qui reçoit sa personnalité juridique d'un autre ordre juridique. Du même coup, les normes du droit international, conventionnel principalement, peuvent avoir pour destinataires ces sujets de droit.

---

[12] *Cf. e.g.* l'art. 154 de la loi fédérale suisse sur le droit international privé, qui prescrit, pour les sociétés, qu'elles sont régies par le droit de l'Etat en vertu duquel elles sont organisées, sous réserve de certaines conditions, et de dispositions destinées à la protection des tiers.

C'est à notre avis très exactement ce que l'on peut observer.

En effet, les personnes physiques, les personnes morales qui acquièrent la personnalité juridique dans l'un ou l'autre des ordres internes, sont bien souvent destinataires de normes relevant du droit international. Ces normes leur imposent des obligations – la matière des crimes internationaux en fournit un excellent exemple – et leur confèrent des droits, ce qu'illustrent non seulement les traités relatifs à la protection des droits de l'homme, mais aussi de nombreux autres accords[13]. On peut citer à cet égard les accords relatifs à la double-imposition, à l'établissement, à la reconnaissance et à l'exécution des jugements, d'autres encore, tous accords qui, conclus par des Etats, intéressent en réalité moins ceux-ci que les personnes privées qu'ils concernent.

Il est vrai que ces normes internationales, qui ont pour destinataires autant les individus que les Etats, n'atteignent pas toujours directement les premiers. Il y a, comme on sait, des différences entre les systèmes nationaux lorsqu'il s'agit d'intégrer le droit international au droit interne. Ceci, cependant, est un autre problème. Que les normes du droit international soient immédiatement ou directement insérées dans un ordre interne, ou qu'il soit nécessaire, à cette fin, d'opérer une transformation au moyen d'un acte législatif interne, est une circonstance particulière qui ne modifie pas la nature intrinsèque de la norme internationale lorsque, par hypothèse, elle a pour destinataires, notamment, des personnes privées[14].

Si des normes internationales peuvent avoir pour destinataires des personnes privées, physiques et morales[15], c'est, nous l'avons déjà souligné, parce que la qualité de sujet de droit leur est reconnue, qualité reçue des ordres internes et qui suffit pour que des obligations leur soient imposées ou que des droits leur soient conférés. Cela n'implique pas que ces personnes deviennent des sujets du droit international, question à laquelle il faut maintenant porter attention.

---

[13] *Cf.* pour un examen plus détaillé de cette question, CH. DOMINICÉ, *op. cit.*, *supra* note 3, pp. 4 et s.

[14] Ainsi, par exemple, le statut de la Convention européenne des droits de l'homme n'est pas le même dans les divers ordres juridiques des Etats qui l'ont ratifiée. Elle est directement applicable dans plusieurs systèmes nationaux (France, Suisse, etc.), où le juge peut en faire application, alors qu'elle reste extérieure à d'autres ordres internes (Royaume-Uni, pays scandinaves). Sa nature n'en est pas pour autant affectée, et nombreuses sont celles de ses dispositions qui sans doute obligent les Etats mais ont aussi l'individu pour destinataire.

[15] Rappelons le *dictum* de la Cour permanente de Justice internationale dans son avis consultatif du 3 mars 1928 sur la compétence des tribunaux de Danzig: «... on ne saurait contester que l'objet même d'un accord international, dans l'intention des parties contractantes, puisse être l'adoption, par les parties, de règles déterminées, créant des droits et obligations pour les individus, et susceptibles d'être appliquées par les tribunaux nationaux», (C.P.J.I., série B, n° 15, pp. 17–18).

III. LES SUJETS DU DROIT INTERNATIONAL

A. Distinction entre sujets et destinataires du droit international public

La distinction qu'il y a lieu de faire entre ce que nous avons appelé les sujets propres d'un ordre juridique – ceux qui lui doivent leur personnalité – et les sujets reconnus – ceux qui doivent leur personnalité à un autre ordre juridique – permet d'observer qu'en droit international public il importe de distinguer attentivement les simples destinataires de ses normes, et les sujets du droit international proprement dits.

Ces derniers acquièrent leur personnalité juridique internationale en vertu des règles pertinentes du droit international, qui seront brièvement évoquées ci-après. Ils sont évidemment, au premier chef, les destinataires des règles internationales, titulaires de droits et d'obligations résultant du droit des gens. Mais il y a une autre catégorie de destinataires, les personnes privées, physiques et morales, qui sont des sujets de droit, mais pas des sujets du droit international.

Autrement dit, le seul fait d'être destinataire de règles du droit international n'implique pas l'acquisition de la personnalité juridique internationale.

On s'en rend compte particulièrement lorsque l'analyse plus approfondie de la qualité de sujet du droit international révèle que celle-ci implique des capacités inhérentes (ci-après IV). L'individu, manifestement, même s'il est destinataire de nombreuses règles internationales, n'est pas pourvu de ces capacités.

On peut observer, au demeurant, un phénomène en partie similaire dans les ordres internes. La situation n'est pas la même, car lorsqu'un droit national reconnaît la personnalité d'une personne morale étrangère, cela implique pour celle-ci les mêmes capacités générales – contracter, ester en justice, acquérir des biens – que pour les sujets nés dans l'ordre interne en question. Cependant, cela n'implique pas une transformation de la personne morale en cause. Une société créée en France et qui acquiert dans ce pays la personnalité juridique sera reconnue en Suisse. Elle aura la qualité de sujet de droit *dans* l'ordre juridique suisse, mais ne sera pas pour autant une personne morale *du* droit suisse.

Ainsi, le critère de la personnalité juridique en vertu d'un ordre juridique déterminé n'est pas le fait d'être destinataire de normes issues de cet ordre. Le sujet du droit international acquiert cette qualité en vertu des règles propres de cet ordre.

B. Les diverses catégories de sujets du droit international

Il n'est pas possible d'entrer ici dans les détails d'une question délicate, mais on peut tenter d'identifier quelques perspectives.

1. Les *sujets primaires* de l'ordre juridique international sont les Etats souverains. Il ne peut exister sans eux. Mais, dès lors qu'il existe, le droit des gens fixe lui-même les critères selon lesquels un nouvel Etat va être reconnu comme tel dans la communauté internationale. Il n'y a pas lieu d'insister davantage.

Rappelons que l'on rencontre des entités territoriales non-souveraines, comme les démembrements d'un Etat fédéral ou des territoires non-autonomes, qui réunissent généralement les qualités de l'Etat, mais qui, dépourvues de souveraineté, agissent par l'intermédiaire d'un Etat souverain.

2. La question des *sujets secondaires* est plus complexe. Faut-il considérer qu'il n'y a aucun système en cette matière ? Les diverses entités qui sont mentionnées par les auteurs comme sujets du droit international sont-elles là uniquement parce que la pratique les fait apparaître, sans qu'il en résulte aucune cohérence?

Nous ne pouvons prétendre répondre à ces questions en quelques lignes. La pratique n'est pas toujours substantielle et elle est incertaine. Nous voulons tout de même nous demander s'il y a certaines techniques juridiques selon lesquelles la création des sujets de droit est ordonnée et si l'on peut en discerner les linéaments en droit international.

Ici aussi, un coup d'oeil aux droits internes peut être intéressant, mais il faut répéter la mise en garde contre des analogies injustifiées.

Il faudrait une analyse approfondie des systèmes nationaux pour prétendre en présenter les traits les plus saillants. Ce ne peut être l'ambition de la présente étude[16]. Il nous paraît intéressant d'indiquer que l'on peut identifier, à tout le moins dans les systèmes qui nous sont les plus familiers, diverses techniques en matière de création de personnes morales, dont deux sont évoquées ici.

L'une consiste à énoncer dans une loi les conditions qui doivent être réunies pour qu'une personne morale soit créée, répondant à un certain type. C'est la technique, bien connue, qui vaut pour les sociétés commerciales, notamment les sociétés anonymes, et parfois certains types d'associations, avec des diversités selon les systèmes nationaux. Ces dispositions législatives s'appliquent à un nombre indéterminé de cas. Il suffit que les fondateurs

---

[16] Il faut renvoyer à l'ouvrage de S. BASTID, R. DAVID, déjà cité (*supra* note 6).

accomplissent tout ce qui est requis par la loi pour créer une nouvelle personne morale.

Une autre technique est bien différente. Elle est utilisée lorsque, par l'adoption d'une loi, le législateur crée une personne morale nettement individualisée, ou éventuellement plusieurs, mais aussi individualisées. On peut reconnaître ici ce qui vaut, par exemple, pour certains types d'établissements, lorsque la loi tout à la fois décide leur création et leur attribue la personnalité juridique.

Peut-on déceler, en droit international, et tout en procédant avec prudence face à une pratique souvent incertaine, quelques éléments qui pourraient indiquer des similitudes? De très brèves remarques paraissent appropriées.

3. De manière générale, on reconnaît à quelques entités politiques la qualité de sujets du droit international. Nous pensons particulièrement aux insurgés reconnus comme belligérants et aux gouvernements en exil, dont sont assez proches, parfois, les mouvements de libération nationale.

Il faut dire qu'en cette matière la reconnaissance joue un rôle primordial, mais ce n'est pas inédit car pour les nouveaux Etats la reconnaissance joue aussi un rôle[17]. Il nous paraît que, pour qu'une telle reconnaissance puisse produire ses effets, certaines conditions d'autorité, d'effectivité et d'organisation doivent être réunies, toutes conditions qui résultent du droit international. On est proche de l'acquisition de la personnalité juridique du fait de la réunion de critères énoncés par le droit, la reconnaissance étant d'ailleurs l'une de ces conditions.

On observera au demeurant que ces entités politiques ont une sorte d'aspiration ou de vocation à devenir un Etat, ou à s'identifier à un Etat[18].

4. Les associations d'Etats que sont les organisations internationales gouvernementales sont, elles aussi, des sujets du droit international[19]. On

---

17 *Cf.* plus particulièrement JENNINGS-WATTS (éd.), OPPENHEIM'S INTERNATIONAL LAW, 9th éd. (1992), p. 126.

18 Ces entités politiques ont l'un ou l'autre des éléments de l'Etat, mais non pas tous les éléments constitutifs. Autre est la question des entités territoriales non-autonomes ou des subdivisions d'Etats, car ce qui leur manque est la souveraineté, c'est-à-dire l'immédiateté par rapport au droit international.

19 La littérature est abondante, *voir* notamment l'article de H. MOSLER dans: L'ENCYCLOPEDIA OF INTERNATIONAL LAW *(supra* note 10); D.W. BOWETT, THE LAW OF INTERNATIONAL INSTITUTIONS, London (1982), p. 335; M. DIEZ DE VALASCO, LAS ORGANIZACIONES INTERNATIONALES, 8ème éd., Madrid (1994), p. 59; H. SCHERMERS, *Les organisations internationales*, dans: M. BEDJAOUI (réd. général), DROIT INTERNATIONAL BILAN ET PERSPECTIVES, t. I, Paris (1991), p. 69; P.M. DUPUY, DROIT INTERNATIONAL PUBLIC, 3ème éd., Paris (1993), p. 130; S. MULLER, INTERNATIONAL ORGANIZATIONS AND THEIR HOST STATES (1995), Chapter 3: *Legal Personality of International Organizations* (p. 69).

sait que si, pour des motifs tout à fait compréhensibles, la Cour internationale de Justice, dans son avis consultatif de 1949 sur la *Réparation des dommages subis au service des Nations Unies*, a préféré s'en tenir à la lecture de la Charte et à la théorie des pouvoirs implicites pour constater l'existence de la personnalité juridique de l'ONU [20], un courant important de la doctrine estime aujourd'hui que c'est en vertu du droit international général qu'une organisation internationale acquiert la personnalité juridique, dès lors que certaines conditions sont réunies – association d'Etats, fondée sur un traité international, et dotée d'organes susceptibles d'exprimer sa volonté propre [21]. Nous pensons que c'est une doctrine plus solide que celle des pouvoirs inhérents [22], pour autant cependant que les critères objectifs soient complétés par un élément subjectif: la volonté des Etats fondateurs de créer une entité autonome sur le plan international. On peut observer en effet que des Etats s'associent parfois par traité pour créer un organisme qu'ils ne veulent opérationnel que dans la sphère de leurs droits internes - entreprise commune, par exemple[23].

Toujours est-il que l'acquisition de la personnalité juridique internationale résulte à nos yeux d'une création opérée selon certains principes fixés par le droit.

5. C'est un phénomène bien différent qui, à notre avis, caractérise d'autres situations dont la pratique offre l'exemple.

Ainsi, le Saint-Siège est revêtu de la personnalité juridique internationale. Bien que l'on rencontre plusieurs doctrines à ce sujet, celle qui est la plus convaincante voit ici l'existence d'une coutume internationale particulière relative au Saint-Siège, qui est d'origine ancienne et trouve ses racines à l'époque où le Pape était aussi un souverain temporel [24].

---

[20] C.I.J. RECUEIL (1949), p. 174.

[21] *Cf.* F. SEYERSTED, OBJECTIVE INTERNATIONAL PERSONALITY OF INTERGOVERNMENTAL ORGANIZATIONS, Copenhagen (1963).

[22] Elle a reçu la consécration, notamment, du Tribunal fédéral suisse qui, dans une cause *Groupement d'entreprises Fougerolle* c. *CERN*, s'est exprimé comme suit: «a) Acquérant leur personnalité juridique interne par une disposition de leurs actes constitutifs, les organisations interétatiques disposent de la personnalité juridique internationale en vertu d'une règle de droit international général, à condition cependant de réunir un ensemble de critères objectifs». ATF 118 Ib, p. 564, reproduit dans: L. CAFLISCH, *La pratique suisse en 1992,* RSDIE (1993), p. 691.

[23] Sur les entreprises communes, *voir* notamment les travaux de l'Institut de Droit international, dont les rapports du Professeur I., SEIDL-HOHENVELDERN, ANNUAIRE DE L'INSTITUT DE DROIT INTERNATIONAL, vol. 60–I, p. 1 et vol. 6l-II, p. 268.

[24] *Cf.* notamment H. OECHSLIN, DIE VÖLKERRECHTSSUBJEKTIVITÄT DES APOSTOLISCHEN STUHLS UND DER KATHOLISCHEN KIRCHE, Freiburg (1974). Lier cette personnalité à l'Etat du Vatican tel que résultant des accords du Latran de 1929 n'est pas convaincant, car on ne voit pas ce qu'aurait été la situation juridique entre la disparition des Etats pontificaux et la conclusion de ces accords.

Il y aurait donc là un exemple de personnalité juridique internationale due à une règle spécifique du droit international coutumier, visant une entité particulière.

A notre avis, à une époque tout à fait récente, une coutume internationale du même genre, générée par la pratique des Etats, a attribué la personnalité juridique internationale au Comité international de la Croix-Rouge[25].

6. Ce survol, très sommaire et incomplet, pourrait donner à penser – ce qui devrait encore être confirmé – qu'à côté des sujets primaires du droit des gens, il existe des sujets qui acquièrent cette qualité en vertu du droit international lorsque diverses conditions sont réunies. Ce sont des entités politiques à vocation étatique, d'une part, et d'autre part des associations d'Etats. De plus, dans de rares cas, une norme coutumière spécifique attribue la personnalité juridique internationale à une entité particulière.

IV. LES CAPACITÉS INHÉRENTES À LA PERSONNALITÉ INTERNATIONALE

A. Les diverses facettes de la personnalité

La définition de la qualité de sujet de droit - l'aptitude à être titulaire de droits et d'obligations – n'est qu'un point de départ.

Nous l'avons vu, il faut tout d'abord distinguer le droit international des ordres juridiques internes, et s'interroger sur les modalités de création des sujets du droit international.

Ce n'est pas tout. D'autres questions se posent.

1. Le régime des entités collectives

Ainsi, s'agissant des entités collectives, un problème fondamental est celui du *régime* qui les gouverne. C'est important à plusieurs égards, et notamment pour la question de savoir si les membres d'une telle entité sont responsables, solidairement, ou subsidiairement, des obligations qui lui incombent, ou ne le sont pas du tout.

Les personnes morales du droit interne sont un exemple très éclairant à cet égard. Le régime des diverses catégories de sociétés n'est pas identique.

---

[25] *Cf.* les études consacrées à ce sujet par J.A. BARBERIS, CH. DOMINICÉ, P. REUTER, dans: ETUDES ET ESSAIS SUR LE DROIT INTERNATIONAL HUMANITAIRE ET SUR LES PRINCIPES DE LA CROIX-ROUGE EN L'HONNEUR DE JEAN PICTET, Genève (1984), pp. 635, 663, 783, ainsi que CH. DOMINICÉ, *L'accord de siège conclu par le Comité international de la Croix-Rouge avec la Suisse,* RGDIP (1995), p. 5.

Ainsi, la même qualité de personne morale recouvre des régimes juridiques très différents.

La question est posée en droit international. Sur la question des dettes d'une organisation internationale, elle a été projetée en plein éclairage par l'affaire du *Conseil international de l'étain*[26]. Elle a fait l'objet, tout récemment, d'une Résolution de l'Institut de Droit international[27].

On n'éprouvera pas de difficulté à s'accorder sur le principe selon lequel ce sont les textes particuliers et le droit auxquels elle doit son existence qui constituent le régime d'une entité collective. Pour une organisation internationale, l'instrument constitutif, et le droit international à la mesure des règles qu'il énonce, vont être déterminants, alors que pour une société commerciale, la *lex societatis*, et ses statuts, vont indiquer ce qu'est la position juridique des «membres» (actionnaires, associés, etc.) et les obligations qu'ils assument, qui varient selon le type de société.

Cette question du régime gouvernant une entité collective est évoquée ici pour en souligner l'importance, mais c'est à vrai dire un autre aspect de la signification de la personnalité qui doit retenir notre attention. Il s'agit du problème des capacités.

2. Les capacités

La question posée est celle de savoir si la personnalité juridique implique nécessairement des attributs particuliers, sous forme de *capacités*[28].

Une capacité est une *aptitude de principe*. Elle est distincte d'un simple droit. Ainsi, lorsqu'une organisation internationale est mise au bénéfice de l'exemption des impôts directs, elle est titulaire d'un droit (résultant généralement de l'accord de siège), un droit précis dont elle peut exiger le respect. Alors que lorsqu'elle se lie à un Etat par un accord international, elle exerce une capacité, la capacité de conclure des traités.

Dans les droits internes, la personnalité juridique est assurément liée à des capacités, et nous en trouvons l'indication, entre autres, dans de très nombreux accords internationaux relatifs à la situation juridique des organi-

---

[26] Le Conseil international de l'étain, qui devait assurer la régulation du marché de l'étain, tomba en cessation de payement en 1985, présentant un important découvert. Diverses procédures judiciaires furent ouvertes par les créanciers. On en trouve la description dans l'arrêt rendu le 26 octobre 1989 par la Chambre des Lords, 81 I.L.R., p. 670.

[27] Les travaux préparatoires (Rapporteur: Madame ROSALYN HIGGINS) sont publiés dans L'ANNUAIRE DE L'INSTITUT DE DROIT INTERNATIONAL, vol. 66-I, pp. 250 et s. Le texte de la Résolution paraîtra dans le vol. 66-II (1996).

[28] *Cf.* particulièrement l'étude de H. MOSLER, *op. cit.*, *supra* note 10.

sations internationales dans les Etats membres, singulièrement l'Etat du siège[29].

Dès que l'on s'attache à préciser ce qu'implique la personnalité juridique, ou la capacité civile, reconnue à une organisation internationale dans un système juridique national, ce sont toujours et sans exception les trois mêmes capacités qui sont énoncées: contracter, acquérir et vendre des biens, ester en justice. La notion de personnalité juridique aurait peu de sens si elle n'impliquait pas ces capacités. C'est ainsi que lorsqu'on veut déterminer si une entité peut agir en justice ou faire l'objet d'une action, il faut examiner si cette entité a la personnalité juridique[30].

Le principe d'une capacité, il faut le rappeler, est sans préjudice des restrictions qui peuvent être apportées à son exercice. C'est cependant un autre problème[31].

En droit international, la situation est moins claire. Avant même d'aborder la question des capacités attachées à la personnalité juridique internationale, il faut rappeler que pour la plupart des auteurs, les sujets du droit international, à l'exception des Etats, sont bien souvent décrits comme des sujets partiels. Cela vaut notamment pour les organisations internationales: leur personnalité ne vaut que dans les limites de leurs fonctions, il s'agit d'une personnalité fonctionnelle, affirme-t-on[32].

A cet égard, il faut dire qu'à l'évidence l'ensemble des droits dont un sujet de droit est susceptible d'être titulaire varie grandement selon les sujets de droit, mais nous préférons y reconnaître un problème de compétence. Autrement dit, il nous paraît plus exact de considérer que la personnalité juridique n'est pas divisible – elle est ou elle n'est pas – mais qu'en revanche le faisceau de droits, facultés, compétences, est très variable selon les catégories de sujets du droit international[33].

---

[29] On en trouve l'expression plus particulièrement dans la *Convention sur les privilèges et immunités des Nations Unies*, du 13.2.1946, RTNU, vol. I, p. 17, art. 1er, section 1 et la *Convention sur les privilèges et immunités des institutions spécialisées*, du 21.11.1947, RTNU, vol. 33, p. 263, art. II, section 3. De très nombreux accords de siège ont une disposition de contenu identique.

[30] Un exemple spectaculaire est celui de l'*Arab Monetary Fund*, que le juge anglais a éprouvé une certaine difficulté à pouvoir considérer comme revêtu la personnalité juridique, voir *Arab Monetary Rund v. Hashim* (n° 3) (1991) 1 A11 ER 871. La reconnaissance de cette personnalité juridique était nécessaire pour que *AMF* puisse agir en justice.

[31] Les restrictions à l'exercice d'une capacité peuvent résulter, par exemple, des statuts d'une société, s'ils interdisent certaines opérations, ou de la loi, comme c'est le cas lorsque les sociétés étrangères n'ont pas le droit d'acquérir des immeubles. La capacité, dans son principe, n'est pas en cause.

[32] Pour un bon exemple de cette manière de voir I. SEIDL-HOHENVELDERN, *op.cit.*, *supra* note 8, p. 39, pour qui les organisations internationales «... sind nur partielle Völkerrechtssubjekte».

[33] On observera qu'en droit interne les personnes morales ne peuvent pas contracter mariage, faire un testament, etc. Faut-il pour autant les tenir pour des sujets de droit partiels? Il s'agit de

Quoi qu'il en soit, la question de savoir si la personnalité internationale implique des capacités inhérentes est importante. Des indications intéressantes dans ce sens peuvent être trouvées dans la doctrine, confirmées à notre avis par la pratique[34]. Il s'agit des trois capacités de conclure des traités, d'établir des relations diplomatiques, et de participer aux mécanismes généraux de la responsabilité internationale.

Notons à ce propos que ce sont précisément ces trois capacités, distinctes de celles qui valent dans les ordres internes, qui confirment la pertinence de la distinction entre sujets du droit international et sujets du droit interne.

B. Les trois capacités internationales

1. Conclure des traités

Il paraît exact de constater que les sujets du droit international sont investis, du fait de cette qualité, de la capacité de conclure des traités internationaux.

C'est au niveau de l'exercice de cette capacité que des différences vont se manifester. Il s'agit alors, non plus de la capacité dans son principe, mais de questions de compétence.

Ainsi, des insurgés reconnus comme belligérants, des gouvernements en exil, n'ont la possibilité d'exercer leur capacité que d'une manière limitée[35], alors qu'une organisation internationale va conclure des traités lui permettant d'assurer son fonctionnement (accord de siège, *e.g.*) ou s'inscrivant dans le cadre de la réalisation de ses buts. C'est cette compétence qui est fonctionnelle, c'est-à-dire définie par les buts de l'organisation et non pas la personnalité ou la capacité[36].

---

sujets de droit à part entière, mais qui en raison de leur nature n'ont pas accès à certaines catégories de droits.

[34] *Cf.* H. SCHMERMERS, *op. cit.*, *supra* note 19, p. 86; P.M. DUPUY, *op. cit.*, *supra* note 19, p. 136; M. DIEZ DE VELASCO, *op. cit.*, *supra* note 19, p. 66; M. RAMA-MONTALDO, *International Legal Personality and Implied Powers of International Organizations*, BYIL (1970), p. 111. vol. XLIV,

[35] Ainsi, des belligérants qui exercent leur contrôle et leur autorité sur un territoire peuvent sans doute conclure des accords avec les voisins sur des questions d'intérêt pratique. Ce sont les compétences qui sont variables selon les circonstances, mais la capacité, dans son principe, ne varie pas.

[36] On admettra que l'ONU peut conclure des traités dans une gamme de domaines beaucoup plus vaste que l'OMS, l'OIT, l'UIT, etc. La personnalité juridique – incluant la capacité de conclure des traités – de ces organisations nous paraît être cependant la même. Il s'agit d'une question de compétences.

2. Etablir des relations diplomatiques

Cette capacité diplomatique nous paraît également être liée à la personnalité juridique internationale. Si puissantes qu'elles puissent être, les sociétés multinationales n'ont pas cette capacité, attribut réservé aux sujets du droit international.

Il s'agit de l'aptitude à accréditer des représentants diplomatiques, ou à en recevoi[37].

Cette capacité – qui est bien celle d'établir des relations diplomatiques – ne doit pas être confondue avec certains droits qui sont institués au bénéfice de la fonction diplomatique ou en raison de facteurs particuliers, mais ne sont sans doute pas liés à la personnalité juridique internationale en tant que telle.

Ainsi, par exemple, l'immunité de juridiction des organisations internationales n'est pas un attribut de leur personnalité juridique, mais elle est instituée, avec une étendue qui peut varier, par une convention, bien souvent l'accord de siège[38].

3. Participer aux mécanismes généraux de la responsabilité internationale

Lorsque la Cour internationale de Justice fut priée, en 1949, d'indiquer si l'Organisation des Nations Unies avait la qualité (texte anglais «capacity») pour présenter une réclamation internationale, elle fut très logiquement amenée à s'interroger tout d'abord sur la personnalité internationale de l'Organisation[39]. Elle souligna du même coup le rapport étroit qui s'établit entre la qualité de sujet du droit international et la capacité de présenter une réclamation internationale[40].

Il n'est pas nécessaire d'insister longuement sur cette évidence, sinon pour souligner la raison pour laquelle il est opportun d'utiliser l'expression «mécanismes généraux de la responsabilité internationale».

---

37 Nous visons bien ici la relation diplomatique à proprement parler; une série de questions connexes, relatives au statut des missions diplomatiques, impliquent un tiers, l'Etat hôte.

38 *Voir* dans ce sens l'arrêt *Fougerolles*, déjà cité (*supra* note 22) du Tribunal fédéral suisse: «L'immunité de juridiction des organisations internationales ne découle pas directement de leur personnalité internationale». (RSDIE 1993, p. 692). A défaut d'accord, l'organisation internationale ne bénéficie pas de l'immunité de juridiction, comme l'affirment au sujet du Conseil international de l'étain des arrêts rendus en Malaisie (*Bank Bumiputra Malaysia Bhd. v. International Tin Council and Another*, I.L.R., vol. 80, p. 24), et aux Etats-Unis (*International Tin Council v. Amalgamet Inc.*, I.L.R., vol. 80, p. 30).

39 C.I.J. RECUEIL (1949), pp. 177–178.

40 «Cela signifie que l'Organisation est un sujet de droit international, qu'elle a capacité d'être titulaire de droits et devoirs internationaux et qu'elle a capacité de se prévaloir de ses droits par voie de réclamation internationale». (C.I.J. RECUEIL (1949), p. 179).

Une vue d'ensemble de la responsabilité internationale montre, notamment, qu'il existe quelques procédures particulières en vertu desquelles des personnes privées sont mises en mesure de faire valoir la violation du droit international, à leur détriment, par un Etat.

C'est ce que l'on observe en matière de protection des droits de l'homme, lorsque des requêtes individuelles sont admises, qui constituent des mécanismes de mise en oeuvre de la responsabilité internationale des Etats, comme peuvent l'être aussi, le cas échéant, d'autres procédures instituées par traité international pour permettre l'action directe d'un particulier contre un Etat. Ce sont cependant des procédures ponctuelles, et précaires dans la mesure où il suffit pourqu'elles disparaissent qu'un accord international cesse d'être en vigueur à l'égard d'un Etat particulier.

Les mécanismes généraux comprennent l'action diplomatique, la présentation de prétentions internationales de manière libre et indépendamment de l'existence d'un traité, et même, au besoin, la faculté de recourir à des contre-mesures.

Seuls les sujets du droit international sont au bénéfice d'une telle capacité, qui est inhérente à la personnalité juridique internationale.

V. LA PERSONNALITÉ INTERNATIONALE DANS LES DROITS INTERNES

A. Une importante asymétrie

Une question mérite encore l'attention, qui est intéressante du point de vue théorique et importante dans la pratique. Il s'agit de déterminer quelle place tiennent les sujets du droit international dans les ordres juridiques nationaux.

On peut voir dans cette question un aspect particulier des relations entre l'ordre juridique international et les ordres juridiques internes.

Il faudrait, à vrai dire, une investigation approfondie dans les jurisprudences nationales pour prendre la mesure exacte des diverses conceptions qui se sont révélées à ce jour. Les quelques observations qui sont présentées ici ne sont pas exhaustives. Elles n'ont d'autre prétention que de nourrir la réflexion.

A vrai dire, l'interaction entre les ordres juridiques se développe dans deux sens, de l'ordre international vers les ordres internes et inversément. On observe à cet égard, à notre avis, une asymétrie manifeste.

D'une part, comme nous l'avons déjà souligné, l'ordre juridique international reconnaît l'existence des sujets de droit qui reçoivent cette qualité dans les ordres internes – personnes physiques et morales. Grâce à cela, ces personnes peuvent être destinataires de normes du droit international qui leur imposent des obligations ou leur confèrent des droits, y compris des droits de procédure les mettant en mesure d'agir devant des juridictions internationales[41]. Cependant, cela n'implique pas pour autant que ces sujets de droit des droits internes revêtent du même coup la qualité de sujets du droit international. Ce n'est pas nécessaire pour qu'ils puissent être destinataires de normes internationales. Et la pratique montre manifestement que les personnes privées, tout en étant titulaires de droits «internationaux», ne sont pas au bénéfice des capacités qui caractérisent les sujets du droit international. Elles ne peuvent pas conclure des traités, ni établir des relations diplomatiques, ni participer aux mécanismes généraux de la responsabilité internationale. Les individus ne sont pas maîtres de leurs droits internationaux[42].

D'autre part, dans le sens inverse si l'on peut dire, il faut constater que la reconnaissance dans les ordres internes de l'existence des sujets du droit international ne peut avoir une signification juridique si cette reconnaissance n'a pas pour effet que ces personnes internationales bénéficient dans l'ordre interne des capacités inhérentes à la personnalité juridique interne. Reconnaître à un Etat étranger, à une organisation internationale, sa qualité de sujet de droit a pour objectif principal de constater son aptitude à contracter, à acquérir des biens, à être partie à une procédure judiciaire.

Il n'y a donc pas un exact parallélisme des situations en droit international pour les sujets des droits internes, et dans les droits internes pour les sujets du droit international. Cela tient pour une bonne part à la nature différente des personnalités et des capacités qui leur sont attachées.

Ces réflexions de caractère théorique peuvent être utilement complétées par quelques remarques fondées sur l'observation de la pratique.

---

41 On peut observer qu'une norme du droit international peut conférer aux sujets du droit interne des facultés ou capacités particulières, qui n'en font pas pour autant des sujets du droit international. Ainsi, en vertu d'une règle du droit international coutumier générée par l'abondante pratique des contrats d'Etat et la jurisprudence, les investisseurs peuvent conclure des contrats d'investissement ancrés dans le droit international public, *cf.* la sentence rendue par R.J. DUPUY dans l'affaire *Texaco/Calasiatic c. Gouvernement Libyen*: «... Déclarer qu'un contrat entre un Etat et une personne privée se situe dans l'ordre juridique international signifie qu'aux fins de l'interprétation et de l'exécution du contrat, il convient de reconnaître au contractant privé des capacités internationales spécifiques» (JOURNAL DU DROIT INTERNATIONAL (1977), p. 361, par. 47).

42 Il suffit qu'un traité cesse d'être en vigueur, ou qu'un Etat s'en retire, pour que des personnes privées qui étaient destinataires de certaines de ses dispositions en perdent le bénéfice.

B. Quelques indications concrètes

On pourrait se demander si les sujets du droit international sont automatiquement reconnus comme tels dans les ordres internes et s'y voient reconnaître les capacités des sujets de droit.

La réponse est sans doute très nuancée.

Sans prétendre faire le tour de la question, nous nous proposons de prendre en considération trois illustrations du problème qui nous intéresse ici, à savoir le cas des Etats étrangers, celui des organisations internationales, et le cas particulier de quelques organes sans personnalité internationale autonome.

1. L'Etat étranger

Il paraît acquis, à première vue tout au moins, que l'Etat étranger se voit reconnaître la qualité de sujet de droit dans les droits internes, où il contracte, acquiert des biens, agit et défend en justice[43].

Pour autant que nous en puissions juger, les systèmes nationaux tiennent compte de l'existence des Etats étrangers et leur reconnaissent les capacités classiques sans qu'une loi ou tout autre acte du droit interne soit nécessaire à cet effet. On peut à cet égard présenter deux observations:

i.

L'exemple de l'Etat, contrairement à celui des organisations internationales, dont la situation est beaucoup plus incertaine, paraît montrer que les sujets du droit international ont une vocation naturelle à bénéficier dans les droits internes de la qualité de personnes juridiques. Faut-il y voir un reflet de leur personnalité internationale? On pourrait être tenté de l'affirmer en rappelant que c'est en vertu du droit international coutumier que l'Etat revêt la qualité de sujet du droit international, de sorte que, logiquement, dans les droits internes il doit se voir reconnaître ou accorder pleine capacité.

ii.

On peut aussi observer, brièvement, que l'ordre interne, soit l'administration et le juge, tiennent compte du droit qui régit l'Etat étranger et sa structure organique, soit son droit public et aussi, à certains égards, le droit international. C'est ainsi qu'une mission diplomatique se voit reconnaître – dans des procédures judiciaires notamment – la qualité d'organe de l'Etat

43 Demeure réservé le cas particulier de l'Etat non-reconnu, *cf.* N. MUGERWA, *op. cit.*, *supra* note 1, p. 273.

qu'elle représente, avec pour effet, entre autres, que l'on applique à cette mission les règles relatives à l'immunité de juridiction de l'Etat.

2. Les organisations internationales

La situation est ici hétérogène. Elle varie d'un pays à l'autre. Ce n'est pas surprenant, dès lors que les organisations gouvernementales sont fondées sur un traité international. Or, l'attitude des ordres juridiques nationaux à l'égard du droit conventionnel international n'est pas uniforme.

Ainsi, dans les pays où les traités internationaux font partie, sans procédure spéciale, de l'ensemble des règles juridiques susceptibles d'être appliquées par le juge, celui-ci va tenir compte des dispositions qui, le cas échéant, reconnaissent ou attribuent à l'organisation la qualité de sujet de droit. A vrai dire, ce qui va intéresser le juge est essentiellement la question de savoir si l'organisation bénéficie de la qualité de sujet de droit dans l'ordre interne, avec les capacités «civiles» qui lui sont attachées.

Dans les systèmes juridiques où les traités internationaux ne peuvent pas être appliqués s'il n'y a pas eu insertion des obligations qu'ils contiennent dans la législation interne, la situation est évidemment différente.

Nous devons, ici, limiter notre propos à de brefs exemples, qui sont instructifs.

On se rappelle que dans l'importante affaire du *Conseil international de l'étain (International Tin Council)*, la question de la personnalité juridique a été sérieusement étudiée et discutée[44]. Le juge anglais n'a pas manqué d'observer que l'organisation était investie de la personnalité juridique internationale, mais cet élément, à lui seul, ne lui permettait pas de trancher par l'affirmative la question, essentielle, de la capacité juridique en droit interne. Il se référa, à cet égard, à l'*Order in Council* édicté en application de l'accord de siège conclu entre le Conseil international de l'étain et le Royaume-Uni, *Order* précisant que le Conseil «... shall have the legal capacities of a body corporate»[45]. C'est donc bien le texte interne qui est déterminant. De plus, il faut noter qu'il a été souligné à juste titre que le Conseil n'était pas une personne morale du droit anglais, mais que son régime relevait du droit international public[46].

---

[44] Le jugement de la Chambre des Lords du 26 octobre 1989 (I.L.R., vol. 81, p. 671) rappelle les diverses procédures antérieures et se prononce sur la question de la personnalité juridique. *Voir* aussi BYIL (1989), vol. LX, p. 461.

[45] International Tin Council (Immunities and Privileges) Order 1972, S.I. (1972), n° 120, *voir* I.L.R., vol. 81, p. 677.

[46] *Voir* notamment: «Consistently with the treaty, the United Kingdom could not convert the I.T.C. into a *United Kingdom* organization» (I.L.R., vol. 81, p. 678).

Il est intéressant de rappeler également deux autres affaires connues, celles de l'*Arab Monetary Fund*[47] et de l'*Arab Organization for Industrialization*[48]. Le juge anglais, ne pouvant s'appuyer sur aucun texte du droit interne, ne fut pas en mesure de constater la personnalité juridique de ces deux organisations – question particulièrement importante – en se référant à leurs instruments constitutifs. Il dut avoir recours aux principes du droit international privé anglais relatifs à la reconnaissance de la capacité juridique des sociétés étrangères. C'est en observant que ces organisations avaient acquis, dans des ordres juridiques étrangers, le statut de sujet de droit, qu'il put leur reconnaître la personnalité juridique au Royaume-Uni, donc la capacité d'ester en justice.

En comparaison, on remarquera qu'aux Etats-Unis d'Amérique, où les traités font partie du droit du pays, la capacité d'agir en justice du Conseil international de l'étain n'a pas été mise en doute, quand bien même les Etats-Unis n'étaient pas membre de l'organisation[49].

De même, en Suisse, le juge prend en compte les accords internationaux, ce qu'illustre un intéressant arrêt du Tribunal fédéral concernant l'*Arab Organization for Industrialization*, que nous avons déjà rencontrée devant le juge anglais. La haute juridiction helvétique analysa très attentivement l'accord instituant l'Organisation – auquel la Suisse n'était pas partie – pour conclure à l'existence d'une personnalité juridique distincte[50]. Ce qui intéressait ici le juge suisse était la capacité de conclure un accord commercial contenant une clause d'arbitrage.

Autre pays où le droit international est intégré à l'ordre interne sans transformation ni procédure particulière, les Pays-Bas offrent, dans une jurisprudence intéressante, un arrêt de la Cour suprême qui reconnaît la qualité d'organisation internationale au Tribunal arbitral des réclamations entre l'Iran et les Etats-Unis, en se fondant sur les accords d'Alger[51]. On peut se demander si le Tribunal irano-américain n'est pas un organe commun des

---

47 *Voir supra* note 30.

48 *Westland Helicopters Ltd v. Arab Organization for Industrialization* (1995), ALL ER, vol. 1, p. 387. Ce jugement fait de larges emprunts à la décision rendue au sujet de l'*Arab Monetary Fund.*

49 *Voir* l'arrêt déjà cité *International Tin Council v. Amalgamet Inc.* (I.L.R., vol. 80, p. 30).

50 L'accord concernant l'AOI avait été conclu par quatre Etats arabes, et le Tribunal fédéral estima qu'à teneur de son texte il instituait une organisation pourvue de la personnalité juridique, arrêt du 19 juillet 1988, et *voir* CH. DOMINICÉ, *Le Tribunal fédéral face à la personnalité juridique d'un organisme international*, REVUE DE DROIT SUISSE (1989), p. 517, BULLETIN DE L'ASSOCIATION SUISSE DE L'ARBITRAGE (1989), p. 48.

51 *Iran-United States Claims Tribunal v. AS*, I.L.R., vol. 94, p. 321: «The Tribunal ... must be regarded as an international organization which derives its legal personnality from international law» (p. 327).

deux Etats plutôt qu'une organisation internationale, mais l'essentiel est de constater que la Cour s'est référée aux accords d'Alger, auxquels les Pays-Bas ne sont pas liés.

En bref, l'aperçu très sommaire que nous venons de présenter, limité à quelques exemples tirés de jurisprudences nationales, permet deux observations.

Tout d'abord, la structure d'accueil du droit international conventionnel dans les droits internes n'étant pas la même partout, on rencontre diverses situations quant à l'identification de la personnalité juridique d'une organisation internationale par le juge national. Cependant, on observe que ce qui importe pour celui-ci est la capacité dans l'ordre interne, de sorte qu'il examine si cette capacité existe en vertu des textes et principes qu'il lui est loisible d'appliquer, sans être préoccupé par la question de la relation entre cette capacité interne et la personnalité juridique internationale.

En second lieu, on peut dire aussi que, quels que soient les principes ou la méthode lui permettant de constater qu'un organisme international dispose de la personnalité juridique en droit interne, le juge national est bien conscient du fait qu'en aucune manière cette personnalité, essentiellement génératrice de capacités, ne correspond à l'un des types de personnes morales du droit interne. Le régime juridique de l'organisation est déterminé par le droit international public, au premier chef l'accord international par lequel l'organisation est créée.

3. La personnalité juridique d'organes particuliers

Un trait particulier de la pratique mérite encore d'être signalé, car il donne un éclairage intéressant à la question de la personnalité juridique dans la relation entre droit international et ordres juridiques internes.

i.

On observe que, d'une manière assez fréquente, des organisations internationales concluent avec un Etat une sorte d'accord de siège concernant le statut dans cet Etat d'un siège secondaire, office régional, bureau, laboratoire, etc. Cet accord porte sur le régime des immunités, des privilèges fiscaux, etc. Il est intéressant de constater qu'il contient souvent une disposition accordant à cette unité administrative la personnalité juridique sur le territoire de l'Etat contractant, à savoir les capacités civiles traditionnelles.

On comprend les motifs qui sont à l'origine d'une telle pratique. Il s'agit de faciliter les transactions courantes de l'entité en question et d'éviter des incertitudes en ce qui concerne sa capacité d'agir, diverses questions relatives au droit applicable, au for, etc. Il demeure que le régime de cette entité est bien celui qui résulte du droit international. Il s'agit bien d'un organe d'une organisation internationale, dépourvu en tant que tel de personnalité juridique internationale autonome. Si cet organe devait à un moment donné se révéler incapable de faire face à ses obligations, financières notamment, c'est l'organisation internationale qui devrait les assumer, car la personnalité juridique dans le droit interne attribuée dans de telles conditions ne crée en aucune manière une entité autonome[52].

Qu'est-ce à dire?

Il semble bien que, par traité international, il soit possible d'attribuer la personnalité juridique dans un droit interne à une entité qui n'est pas, en tant que telle, un sujet du droit international, mais il faut souligner que son régime – notamment la question des responsabilités – demeure celui qui résulte de son statut international, ce qui vaut particulièrement lorsqu'il s'agit d'un organe d'une organisation internationale.

ii.

On doit également admettre, et constater que le même principe peut être appliqué à l'*organe commun* de deux ou plusieurs Etats. Par exemple, si deux Etats mettent sur pied un tribunal arbitral pour venir à bout d'un contentieux qui les oppose, il leur est possible de conclure avec l'Etat du siège du tribunal un accord pour fixer son statut dans cet Etat, notamment son régime de privilèges et immunités. Conférer à ce tribunal la personnalité juridique du droit interne peut être utile, car cela lui permet de louer des locaux, d'engager du personnel administratif, bref d'effectuer les transactions quotidiennes nécessaires à son bon fonctionnement.

Il n'en demeure pas moins que l'on ne voit pas apparaître, pour autant, une nouvelle entité juridique. Un tel tribunal arbitral, à notre avis, est un organe commun des deux Etats, qui sont liés par ses actes en vertu du droit international. L'arrêt néerlandais concernant le tribunal irano-américain, que nous avons déjà mentionné, s'explique peut-être par des circonstances spéciales[53].

---

52 De son côté, l'ONU a conclu des accords de siège (particulièrement avec les Etats-Unis, la Suisse, l'Autriche) qui reconnaissent sa personnalité juridique, mais de manière plus générale elle a pour habitude de rendre applicables à ses organes dans d'autres pays les dispositions de la Convention sur les privilèges et immunités des Nations Unies, du 13.2.1946, R.T.N.U., vol. 1, p. 17). Cela vaut par exemple pour la Cour internationale de Justice (*cf.* A.S. MULLER, *op. cit.*, *supra* note 19, p. 47), le Tribunal pénal international pour l'ex-Yougoslavie (*ibid.* p. 269), etc. Cette convention reconnaît la personnalité juridique de l'ONU (Art. Premier, section 1), de sorte que la qualité d'organe apparaît bien.

53 *Voir* ci-dessus, note 51. Lorsque le Tribunal fut assigné en justice par un ancien employé (un traducteur), la question de son statut n'avait pas encore été réglée par un accord entre les

VI. SYNTHÈSE

Sur une matière délicate et complexe, il faut éviter de se livrer à des conclusions schématiques, ou trop dogmatiques. Cependant, tenter de dessiner une vision générale d'un phénomène n'est dépourvu ni d'intérêt, ni d'utilité.

Les quelques observations qui viennent d'être présentées conduisent aux propositions suivantes:

1. Comme tout ordre juridique, le droit international public accorde une place centrale aux sujets de droit, titulaires des droits et devoirs qu'il institue. Fondé sur la juxtaposition d'Etats souverains, il a les Etats pour sujets primaires. Il a également, comme les ordres internes, développé quelques principes relatifs à l'apparition de sujets secondaires.

De même que les sujets en droit interne ne sont pas tous identiques, les sujets du droit international sont différents les uns des autres.

2. En très large approximation, on observe qu'en règle générale les sujets secondaires du droit international gravitent dans la mouvance de l'Etat. On y trouve des entités partiellement étatiques, et surtout, de plus en plus, des associations d'Etats. Il y a donc une certaine cohérence.

Font exception les entités qui reçoivent la personnalité juridique internationale d'une norme coutumière individualisée. Le cas est très rare.

3. La qualité de sujet du droit international implique trois capacités inhérentes: conclure des traités, établir des relations diplomatiques, participer aux mécanismes généraux de la responsabilité internationale. L'exercice de ces capacités est déterminé par les compétences propres à chaque sujet et peut être limité par des règles du droit international.

4. Dans l'ordre juridique international, la personnalité juridique des sujets de droit qui doivent cette qualité aux droits internes est reconnue, de sorte que des normes du droit international peuvent en faire leurs destinataires, sans pour autant leur conférer le statut de sujets du droit international.

5. Dans les ordres juridiques internes, les sujets du droit international peuvent agir seulement si on leur reconnaît la personnalité juridique et ses trois capacités de contracter, d'acquérir des biens et d'ester en justice. Il ne s'agit pas d'une transformation en une personne morale du droit interne, mais

---

Pays-Bas et les deux Etats intéressés. C'est ainsi que le juge eut recours à une construction fondée (i) sur l'idée que le tribunal était une organisation internationale, et (ii) sur l'idée que le droit international coutumier accorde l'immunité de juridiction aux organisations internationales. Il eut mieux valu constater l'existence d'un organe commun, et appliquer les règles relatives à l'immunité de juridiction des Etats. Il est intéressant de noter que l'échange de lettres qui, depuis lors, a fixé le statut du Tribunal ne paraît pas en faire une organisation internationale, (*cf.* A.S. MULLER, *op. cit.*, *supra* note 19, p. 113).

uniquement de la reconnaissance de la capacité civile. Le régime demeure celui que fixe le droit international.

Cette reconnaissance n'intervient pas d'une manière uniforme. Elle paraît aller de soi pour les Etats, alors que pour les organisations internationales elle dépend essentiellement de la manière dont le droit conventionnel international reçoit application dans l'ordre interne.

6. Il est loisible aux Etats, aux organisations internationales, de conclure avec un Etat un accord selon lequel un organe reçoit la personnalité juridique dans l'ordre interne de cet Etat. Cela permet à cet organe d'agir sous son propre nom, mais cela ne modifie pas sa qualité d'organe telle que déterminée par le droit international.

Some Observations on the Inter-Temporal Rule in International Law

by

Rosalyn Higgins

These comments are offered in tribute to Krzysztof Skubiszewski. His independence of mind and scholarly vigour are admired by all. As the vagaries of time and unfolding history have had such an impact upon his professional life, I have thought that some observations on the contemporary status of the so-called rule of inter-temporal law might be appropriate.

* * *

Few arbitral *dicta* have been more widely cited, or have come to assume a more important place in international law, than the *dictum* of Judge Huber in the *Island of Palmas* case.[1] It will be recalled that the *dictum* consists of two elements. The first part provides:

> "A judicial fact must be appreciated in the light of the law contemporary with it, and not of the law in force at the time such a dispute in regard to it arises or falls to be settled."

The observation was directed towards the question of the legal requirements, at a certain era, for the establishment of sovereign title – hence the reference to "appreciation" of a "juridical fact" (which latter term must be taken to mean "a fact with juridical relevance"). The question Max Huber was addressing was whether mere discovery had allowed Spain to acquire and retain title. It has been understood, without difficulty, that this first limb of the doctrine required one to look at the law of the era (which in the particular case allowed the establishment of title through mere discovery) and not at the law as it may have later developed, or as it stood at the time any dispute arose or fell to be resolved.

The second element of Huber's doctrine has caused much more difficulty. He distinguished "between the creation of rights and the existence of rights" and spoke of a principle by virtue of which:

---

1 II UNRIAA at 845.

> "the existence of the right, in other words, its continued manifestation, shall follow the conditions required by the evolution of the law."[2]

Some have interpreted this second limb as providing that a right, even if lawfully obtained by reference to the law of the era, will be lost if a later rule of international law evolves by reference to which the basis of the "right" would no longer be lawful. But to give such an understanding to the second limb of the Huber *dictum* is essentially to wipe out the legal consequences of the first. Our understanding of it should flow from the realization that it was a *dictum* offered in the context of establishing and maintaining territorial title. The second element may then be seen as providing that the creation of an initial right does not suffice of itself to maintain it up to the moment of the claim. Perpetuation of that right, demonstrated by effective occupation (as required by later law) is necessary. The Huber *dictum*, taken in its entirety, may be taken as providing that by virtue of the principles of inter-temporal law a State must continue to maintain a title, validly won, in an effective manner – no more and no less.

It has, however, been read in the most remarkably extensive fashion, as providing obligatory rules in circumstances that it never addressed, with consequences that it never intended.[3]

Even the first limb of the Huber *dictum*, apparently so well-established, seems to have its exceptions.

There are good reasons for thinking that treaties that guarantee human rights – whether expressly or as an incident of their subject-matter – fall into a special category so far as inter-temporal law is concerned. The matter still cannot be better put than it was by Judge Tanaka in the *South West Africa* cases (1966). There it has been suggested by South Africa that the Mandate was to be interpreted by reference to the law as it stood in 1920, without reference to the much more recently formulated notion of self-determination. The reason why Judge Tanaka believed that contemporary law should be applied was because:

> "In the present case, the protection of the acquired right of the Respondent is not the issue, but its obligations, because the main purposes of the mandate system are ethical and humanitarian. The Respondent has no right to behave in an inhuman way today as well as during these 40 years."[4]

---

[2] *Ibid.*

[3] The meaning and scope of the inter-temporal rules was the subject of contending pleadings, written and oral, in the case *Concerning the Territorial Dispute (Libyan Arab Jamahiriya/Chad)*, but the Court's judgment turns on different issues and thus never had need to pronounce upon these arguments.

[4] ICJ REPORTS 1966 at 294.

As we shall see, the European Court of Justice has taken an approach based on the same starting point. But Judge Tanaka then pushed the matter to its limits, saying:

> "... the recognition of the generation of a new customary international law on the matter of non-discrimination is not to be regarded as detrimental to the mandatory, but as an authentic interpretation of the already existing provisions of Article 2, paragraph 2, of the Mandate and the Covenant. It is nothing other than a simple clarification of what was not so clear 40 years ago. What ought to have been clear 40 years ago has been revealed by the creation of a new customary law which plays the role of authentic interpretation the effect of which is retroactive."

This goes further than is perhaps necessary and is not reflected in the practice of the European Court of Human Rights, which has been content to emphasize the need to interpret human rights by reference to developing ideas, without pretence that each new judgment is a retrospective relevation of what in reality had been true before.

The classic statement of the European Court of Human Rights remains that enunciated in the *Tyrer* case, which concerned judicial corporal punishment on a youth. In that case that Court stated that it:

> "... must also recall that the Convention is a living instrument which ... must be interpreted in the light of present-day conditions. In the case now before it the Court cannot but be influenced by the developments and commonly accepted standards in general policy of the member States of the Council of Europe in this field."[5]

Whereas for the International Court the issue was the application of contemporary international law to the international human rights obligations undertaken in a treaty, for the European Court of Human Rights the issue has rather been the insistence on the European Convention on Human Rights as a living instrument, which is to be achieved by interpreting its provisions "in the light of present day conditions". Those "present day conditions", in turn, are largely to be found by reference to the developing practice of the member States themselves, in an approach that is now well established.[6] This

---

[5] Judgment of the Court, *Tyrer* case, 25 April 1978, para. 31, publ. Court A, Vol. 26 at 15, 16.

[6] *See* also *Marckx* case, Series A, N° 31, p. 19, para. 41; *Winterwerp v. Netherlands*, Series A, N° 33, para. 37; *Cossey v. United Kingdom*, Series A, N° 184, para. 35. This reliance on the changing attitude of States parties to the Covenant may also be seen as an approximation to the doctrine of revision by reference to the subsequent practice – though it is never articulated in this way.

is not identical to the interpretation of obligations by reference to contemporary customary international law, but the underlying approach is very similar. It can well be understood that, facing such issues as discrimination in property rights between legitimate and illegitimate children, or the request by transsexuals for the alteration of their birth certificates, the European Court has found more help in reference to contemporary European conditions than to customary international law. Again, in reference to the interpretation to be given to "persons of unsound mind" in Article 5(1)(e) of the Convention, the Court said "this term cannot be given a definitive interpretation ... it is a term whose meaning is continually evolving as research in psychiatry progresses..."[7]

But the fact that the European Court has not followed the *dictum* of Judge Tanaka in his dissenting opinion in 1966, to the effect that the application of contemporary law merely reveals existing hitherto hidden truths, is not without significance. This view implies that the specific interpretation of the rights existed from the outset. But an approach that merely requires human rights treaties, because of their nature, to be interpreted in accordance with contemporary international law or conditions in society, avoids any suggestion that the States upon whom the obligations fall are required to reopen legal acts or pay compensation for "incorrect applications" of the obligation in the past.

If it is clear that the inter-temporal principle of international law, as it is commonly understood, does not apply in the interpretation of human rights obligations,[8] what can be said of treaties in general? The International Court of Justice, in the *Namibia* case – still looking at the Mandate for South West Africa – opined that:

> "an international instrument must be interpreted and applied within the overall framework of the juridical system in force at the time of the interpretation."[9]

But the instrument in question was a provision for the protection of the rights of the inhabitants of South West Africa and the Court appears not to

[7] *Winterwerp* case, Series A, N° 33, para. 37.

[8] The same approach has been taken by the Inter-American Court of Human Rights, which has stated that "... it is necessary to point out that to determine the legal status of the American Declaration it is appropriate to look to the Inter-American system of today in the light of the evolution it has undergone since the adoption of the Declaration, rather than to examine the normative value and significance which that instrument was believed to have had in 1948." Advisory Opinion OC/10/89 of 14 July 1989, 29:378 ILM (1990) at 387.

[9] *Legal Consequences for States of the Continued Presence of South Africa in Namibia (South West Africa)* notwithstanding Security Council resolution 276 (1970), Advisory Opinion, ICJ REPORTS 1971 at 31.

have addressed the treaty issue more deeply. The reality is that the inter-temporal issue as it arises for treaties generally is very much more complex.

It will be recalled that Judge Huber's *dictum* in the *Island of Palmas* case referred to the need for a "juridical fact" to be "appreciated" in the light of the law contemporary with it. How does this bear, if at all, upon the need to interpret treaties and pronounce upon their validity? What is the relationship between "appreciation", "interpretation" and "validation"?

The International Court of Justice certainly has indicated that the doctrine of international law does apply to treaties. In the *Rights of Passage* case it said:

> "the validity of a treaty concluded as long ago as the last quarter of the eighteenth century, in the conditions then prevailing in the Indian Peninsula, should not be judged upon the basis of practices and procedures which have since developed only gradually."[10]

The International Court has accepted the inter-temporal doctrine also in *Rights of Nationals of the United States of America in Morocco*;[11] and it was recognized also by the Tribunal in the *Guinea Bissau v. Senegal* arbitration. But the matter is not as straightforward as it might seem. In the *Rights of Passage* case the Court spoke of the **validity** of a treaty being determined by the law at the time it was concluded. Is a distinction to be made in the application of the inter-temporal principle between **validity** and **interpretation**? In the *Aegean Sea* case in 1978 the issue arose in the context of an agreement made by Greece in 1931 to accept compulsory procedures of settlement for disputes including those relating to "the territorial status of Greece". How was that term to be understood? Could it include contested rights in the Aegean Sea? The Court said:

> "Once it is established that the expression 'the territorial status of Greece' was used in Greece's instrument of accession as a generic term denoting any matters comprises within the concept of territorial status under general international law, the presumption necessarily arises that its meaning was intended to follow the evolution of the law and to correspond with the meaning attached to the expression by the law in force at any given time."

The apparent exception to the Huber rule in the interpretation of human rights obligations now has added to it the "generic" exception. How are these

10 ICJ REPORTS 1960 at 37.
11 ICJ REPORTS 1952 at 176, 185–187.

exceptions to be tied together, and what is the general rule of inter-temporal law as it applies to treaties?

Sir Humphrey Waldock, when preparing his draft articles for the International Law Commission on the Law of Treaties, simply assumed the relevance of the doctrine of inter-temporal law to the realm of treaties. In preparing his Third Report, he offered an article (draft article 56) appropriately entitled *The Inter-Temporal Law*, which provided:

> "1. A treaty is to be interpreted in the light of the law in force at the time when the treaty was drawn up.
>
> 2. Subject to paragraph 12, the application of a treaty shall be governed by the rules of international law in force at the time when the treaty is applied."

Waldock regarded the two paragraphs as the articulation of the two elements in the inter-temporal rule as stated by Judge Huber – though, in the view of this writer, whether **appreciation** and **continued manifestation** (the two elements mentioned by Huber) are at all the same as **interpretation** and **application** is doubtful. The Special Rapporteur's Commentary says:

> "The solution proposed in paragraph 2 is that for purposes of interpretation, the law in force at the time of the conclusion of the treaty prevails. But, the interpretation of the treaty having been ascertained in accordance with the law, the application of the treaty, as interpreted, is subject to the law in force at the date of application."

This seems not to have been a true "match" of the inter-temporal rule articulated by Huber. In the event, the proposal met considerable opposition. Some thought the distinction between interpretation and application artificial, and proposed that paragraph 2 of the draft Article 56 simply State that "if international law changed after the conclusion of a treaty, the obligations arising from the treaty were thenceforth governed by the subsequent rule of international law."[12] Others raised a more fundamental objection, noting that not only was the relationship between interpretation and application intertwined, but that the very basis of the proposal was debateable. In particular, Jiménez de Aréchaga took the view that the issue was not really one of the application of an inter-temporal rule to the law of treaties at all. Rather, what was important to look at was the intention of the parties. The question to ask was whether it had been the intention of the parties, in settling their obligations, that those obligations should be determined by

---

12 A. VERDROSS, 1 YBILC (1964) at 33.

reference to the law as it then stood or as it might stand when any controversy later arose. He put it thus:

> "The intention of the parties should be controlling, and there seemed to be two possibilities as far as that intention was concerned: either they had meant to incorporate in the treaty some legal concepts that would remain unchanged, or if they had no such intention, the legal concept might be subject to change and would then have to be interpreted not only in the context of the instrument, but also within the framework of the entire legal order to which they belonged."[13]

This perspective had in fact been adopted by the International Court in the *Namibia* Advisory Opinion, when it found that the notions guaranteed in Article 22 had to be read against the background that the Mandate was a "sacred trust for civilization". Accordingly, it was to be assumed that the parties to the Covenant accepted that the content of Article 22 was evolutionary, and not static.[14] In the *Aegean Sea* case the Court had also dealt with the inter-temporal factor by reference to the presumed intention of the parties.

Presumed intention was also the basis that the Court relied on to distinguish the finding in the *Abu Dhabi* arbitration,[15] on which the Greek Government relied. From that it proceeded to render in the *Aegean Sea* case. In that case the Sheikh of Abu Dhabi had granted to Petroleum Development Ltd. the right to explore and exploit the oil in the territory, islands and waters belonging to him. Did this give Petroleum Development Ltd. rights over the continental shelf, whose existence as a doctrine in international law at the time of the grant was in doubt? Lord Asquith stated that "it would seem a most artificial refinement to read back into a contract the implications of a doctrine not mooted till seven years later."[16]

The International Court distinguished these facts from those it was facing in the *Aegean Sea*. It found that there was an essential difference between the two cases. The Court stated:

> "While there may be a presumption that a person transferring valuable property rights to another intends to transfer the rights which he possesses at that time, the case appears to the Court to be quite otherwise when a State, in agreeing to subject to compulsory procedures of pacific set-

---

13 1 YBILC (1964) at 34, para. 10.

14 *Legal Consequences for States of the Continued Presence of South Africa in Namibia (South West Africa)*, ICJ Reports 1971 at 31.

15 *Petroleum Development Ltd. v. Sheikh of Abu Dhabi*, 18 ILR (1951) at 144.

16 *Ibid.* at 152.

tlement, excepts from that agreement a category of disputes which, though covering clearly specified subject matters, is of a generic kind."[17]

We may not begin to see that the intention of the parties is often to be deduced from the object and purpose of the agreement. In the recent case of *Commission v. United Kingdom* the European Court was faced with inter-temporal law issues in relation to fishing limits under Regulation 170/83. Certain derogations were permitted from EC regulations providing for equal fishing rights with the waters of member States. Article 6 and Annex 1 of Council Regulation 170/83 specified the waters within which these temporary derogating arrangements could be made. For the United Kingdom the areas concerned were certain specified waters lying between six and twelve miles from the baselines from which the territorial sea was measured. In 1987 the United Kingdom extended its territorial sea from 3 to 12 miles and announced that since the fisheries limits under Regulation 170/83 were measured from the baselines of the territorial sea, certain new lines, further out to sea, would now be used. This had the effect of excluding fisherman from other EC States from waters in which they had hitherto fished. In ensuing litigation, the Court rejected the United Kingdom argument that the Regulation was to be interpreted in accordance with developing international law, in conformity with which each State was lawfully entitled to determine its baselines. The Court found that the Regulation was to be interpreted in accordance with its object and purpose, which was directed to providing stability of fishing conditions and not to enlarging exclusions. Thus, although a reference to baselines could in many circumstances be to baselines as they existed from time to time, in this particular case it must be understood as a reference to the baselines existing at the time the Regulation was passed. In other words, the European Court here thought the reference to baselines was **not** a "generic term".[18]

That the intention of the parties to a treaty (perhaps revealed by the objects and purposes) should be controlling was also the approach approved by the Institut de Droit international in its resolution on the Inter-temporal Problem in International Law. After restating the first lines of the Huber *dictum* as a general principle, the resolution[19] then addressed the inter-temporal issue as it arose in treaties. It found:

---

[17] ICJ REPORTS 1978 at 32, para. 77.

[18] *Commission v. United Kingdom*, 100 ILR at 114.

[19] 56 ANNUAIRE DE L'INSTITUT DE DROIT INTERNATIONAL at 536. Nothing that detracts from this approach is to be found in the Institut's 1995 Resolution on Problems arising from a Succession of Codification Conventions on a particular subject.

"4. Whereas a provision of a treaty refers to a legal or other concept without defining it, it is appropriate to have recourse to the usual methods of interpretation in order to determine whether the concept concerned is to be interpreted as understood at the time when the provision was drawn up or as understood at the time of its application. Any interpretation of a treaty must take into account all the relevant rules of international law which apply between the parties at the time of application."

Faced with these and comparable arguments concerning the application of inter-temporal law in treaties, the Special Rapporteur of the International Law Commission was not able to maintain his original proposals. Very much less ambitious proposals on the topic were then offered. At the Conference for the drafting of the Vienna Convention on the Law of Treaties, he stated that the ILC draft, at the end of the day, made no attempt to solve the problem of inter-temporal law, as the Commission felt it was not on safe ground. The Vienna Convention itself contains no general rule on the inter-temporal question. The only hint one gets is in Article 31, which simply provides that treaties are to be interpreted in accordance with any relevant rules of law.[20] There also exist certain disparate clauses that bear indirectly on inter-temporal law. Thus Article 64, while making no pronouncement of general application, does stipulate that a treaty becomes void if it conflicts with a later emergent rule of *jus cogens*. (Article 53 provides that a treaty is also void if, at the time of its conclusion, it conflicts with a rule of *jus cogens*. No element of inter-temporal law is engaged here.) And Article 52 provides that a treaty is void if its conclusion has been procured by the threat or use of force contrary to the Charter of the United Nations.

* * *

In conclusion, we may suggest that the Huber rule should not be extended beyond its proper confines. In the law of treaties – notwithstanding judicial indications that the Huber rule is applicable thereto – the intention of the parties is really the key. Attention to that point allows one to see that "generic clauses" and human rights provisions are not really random exceptions to a general rule. They are an application of a wider principle – intention of the parties, reflected by reference to the objects and purpose – that guides the law of treaties.

---

20 Committee of the Whole, 103rd meeting at 337, paras. 78-81.

Réflexions sur la souveraineté

par

Jerzy Kranz

I

La notion de souveraineté se trouvait toujours au centre de l'intérêt du Professeur Skubiszewski. Il suffit de rappeler à cet égard ses travaux consacrés au problème allemand et aux relations polono-allemandes après la deuxième guerre mondiale, à la monnaie sur le territoire occupé, aux nouvelles sources de droit créées par les organisations internationales ainsi qu'aux rapports entre le droit international et le droit national[1].

La souveraineté[2] fait partie des notions les plus controversées et les plus ambiguës en droit international. Pour éviter des malentendus, toute discussion concernant la souveraineté doit distinguer entre ses divers aspects (politiques et juridiques, constitutionnel et international)[3]. Il est aussi à retenir que, dans son évolution historique, la notion de souveraineté n'exclut pas la soumission au droit (naturel ou positif, national ou international).

---

1 Selon K. Skubiszewski, dans: Zarys prawa międzynarodowego publicznego [Précis du droit international public], t. I, Warszawa 1955, p. 158, la souveraineté signifie «l'indépendance de l'Etat à l'égard de tout autre pouvoir dans ses relations avec les autres sujets du droit international et sa liberté [samodzielność] dans la réglementation des affaires internes, c'est-à-dire le droit de l'Etat de décider de ses affaires internes et de ses relations extérieures sans restriction par les facteurs externes, mais sans enfreindre les droits des autres Etats et en conformité avec les principes fondamentaux du droit international» [trad. de l'auteur – J.K.].

2 Pour la bibliographie *voir* H. Steinberger, *Sovereignty*, dans: Encyclopedia of Public International Law, sous la réd. de R. Bernhardt (ci-après EPIL), t. 10 (1987), p. 408. *Voir* aussi N. Politis, *Le problème des limitations de la souveraineté et la théorie de l'abus des droits dans les rapports internationaux*, Recueil des cours de l'Académie de Droit international (RCADI), vol. 6, (1925–I); G. Schwarzenberger, *The Forms of Sovereignty*, 10 Current Legal Problems, (1957), pp. 264–295; Ch. Rousseau, *L'indépendance de l'Etat dans l'ordre international*, RCADI, vol. 73, (1948–II), pp. 171–253; H. Kelsen, *Souveränität*, dans: Wörterbuch des Völkerrechts (sous la réd. de Strupp et de Schlochauer), t. 3, Berlin (1962); D. Carreau, Souveraineté et coopération monétaire internationale, Paris (1970); Ch. Rousseau, Droit international public, t. II, Paris (1974), pp. 55–95.

3 Il convient notamment de distinguer entre la souveraineté de l'Etat (notion concernant la définition et la position de l'Etat dans les relations internationales) et la souveraineté dans l'Etat (qualifiée souvent de souveraineté nationale ou populaire).

II

Dans la pratique, il n'est pas toujours facile de préciser d'avance le moment à partir duquel une entité territoriale devient l'Etat ou cesse de l'être. Si les faits jouent à cet égard un rôle primordial, le droit international ne se désintéresse pas totalement à ce phénomène et il contient des règles qui protègent l'existence de l'Etat et qui établissent certains critères de sa naissance et de sa reconnaissance internationale.

Il n'existe pas en droit international une définition juridique universelle de l'Etat[4], mais on admet généralement dans la doctrine que trois éléments font partie de la notion de l'Etat à savoir une population, un territoire et une structure politique capable d'exercer un pouvoir suprême (gouvernement) à l'égard de cette population et de ce territoire. Le premier but de l'Etat consiste à assurer son existence (l'ordre social et les intérêts propres à l'Etat et à sa population), notamment par l'exercice d'une politique intérieure et extérieure.

La naissance de l'Etat étant une question de fait (y compris du rapport des forces), elle se traduit par la capacité d'exercer des fonctions étatiques (et notamment celles de commandement et de contrainte) indépendamment des autres sujets du droit des gens[5]. Cette donnée factuelle constitue la prémisse de la reconnaissance internationale d'une entité territoriale en tant qu'Etat, de son statut et de son rôle dans l'ordre juridique international. Au point de vue du droit international, qui régit les relations entre les Etats et auquel ceux-ci sont soumis à partir de leur naissance, cette capacité s'exprime en la notion (mais pas une norme) juridique[6] de souveraineté. Sur le plan de la terminologie du droit des gens, on assimile souvent les notions de souveraineté et d'indépendance[7], ce dernier terme servant parfois d'élément de définition de la souveraineté.

---

[4] *Voir e.g.* G. ARANGIO-RUIZ, *L'Etat dans le sens du droit des gens et la notion du droit international*, 26 ÖSTERREICHISCHE ZEITSCHRIFT FÜR ÖFFENTLICHES RECHT (1976), p. 281 et s.

[5] *Voir* notamment J. CRAWFORD, THE CREATION OF STATES IN INTERNATIONAL LAW, Oxford (1979), pp. 10–76; K. MAREK, IDENTITY AND CONTINUITY OF STATES IN PUBLIC INTERNATIONAL LAW, Genève (1968); J. CRAWFORD, *Islands as Sovereign Nations*, INTERNATIONAL AND COMPARATIVE LAW QUARTERLY (April 1989), vol. 38, p. 281; J. CRAWFORD, *The Creation of the State of Palestine: Too Much Too Soon*, JOURNAL EUROPÉEN DE DROIT INTERNATIONAL, vol. 1 (1990), n° 1/2, p. 309.

[6] *E.g.*, la mort d'une personne constitue un fait qui engendre des conséquences juridiques dans les systèmes juridiques nationaux et qui peut être mentionné ou défini dans une norme juridique. Dans ce sens, la mort est une notion juridique, mais pas une norme juridique.

[7] Cette assimilation est connue de la jurisprudence internationale, *voir e.g.* M. HUBER (arbitre unique) dans l'affaire de l'île de Palmas (1928), RECUEIL DES SENTENCES ARBITRALES, vol. 2, p. 838; l'arrêt de la CPJI dans l'affaire du *Lotus* (1927), série A, n° 10, pp. 18–19; l'avis consultatif de la CPJI concernant le régime douanier entre l'Allemagne et l'Autriche (1931), série A/B, n° 41, pp. 45–46, et l'opinion individuelle sur cet avis de D. ANZILOTTI, *ibid.* p. 57.

Une situation factuelle (qualifiée souvent de souveraineté) se reflète ainsi dans la notion juridique de souveraineté qui – sur le pan juridique – constitue l'élément décisif de la définition de l'Etat et de son statut en droit international[8]. La capacité originaire et factuelle de l'Etat s'inscrit de cette manière dans l'ordre juridique international et elle se traduit par la capacité de jouissance et par la capacité d'exercice selon le droit international. La souveraineté constitue donc le fondement de sa personnalité juridique internationale, mais elle ne s'y confond pas, car c'est bien la souveraineté qui permet de distinguer l'Etat parmi les autres entités territoriales et parmi les autres sujets du droit des gens (*e.g.* organisations internationales ou Etats fédérés d'une fédération)[9] qui ne sont pas souverains. Elle implique en même temps plusieurs conséquences juridiques concernant la protection de l'Etat par le droit des gens ainsi que certaines limitations que celui-ci impose à l'Etat.

Le droit international ne créé pas l'Etat, mais il le protège. En l'absence du droit international, l'existence des Etats et leurs relations seraient déterminées seulement par le rapport des forces. La souveraineté, en tant que notion juridique, ne peut exister qu'à condition de la proclamation par le droit international (créé par les Etats) du principe de l'égalité des souverainetés[10]. Il faut donc considérer la souveraineté dans l'optique de ce principe et non dans celle d'une liberté illimitée. Autrement dit, les rapports internationaux se fondent non seulement sur la souveraineté des Etats, mais sur l'égalité de ces souverainetés. Il en résulte que la soumission au droit international constitue un élément essentiel de la protection de la souveraineté de tous les Etats.

III

Le terme «souveraineté» est le plus souvent employé dans deux acceptions: en premier lieu, pour désigner la condition (statut) de l'Etat dans les relations internationales et, en deuxième lieu, pour exprimer la liberté dans l'exercice par l'Etat de ses compétences (en conformité avec le droit des gens). Ces deux acceptions restent liées.

---

[8] H. KELSEN, *op. cit.*, *supra* note 2, p. 279, est d'un autre avis lorsqu'il estime que le problème de la souveraineté (en tant que notion juridique) est celui de la relation entre le droit international et le droit national.

[9] Ceux-ci exercent un pouvoir suprême dans des domaines particuliers et jouissent parfois d'une personnalité juridique internationale limitée, mais ils sont organisés et agissent en vertu du droit national (constitution fédérale) auquel ils sont soumis.

[10] Ce principe est connu sous le nom d'égalité souveraine des Etats, terme mal formulé, puisqu'il s'agit de l'égalité des souverainetés ou de l'égalité des Etats quant à leur souveraineté.

La notion juridique de souveraineté de l'Etat se définit à travers l'étendue, la nature et les modalités d'exercice de ses compétences[11]. Notons cependant, en anticipant sur les développements ultérieurs, que la souveraineté n'équivaut pas à un catalogue de compétences. La souveraineté en droit international signifie que la compétence de l'Etat est exclusive, pleine et autonome[12].

L'exclusivité implique que sur le territoire d'un Etat fonctionne une structure politique du pouvoir, distincte et indépendante de celle des autres Etats. Sa principale expression consiste à exclure les activités des autres sujets du droit des gens sur le territoire en question. Cela signifie que la compétence de l'Etat sur son territoire et à l'égard de ce territoire (*e.g.* droit de cession), à l'égard des personnes relevant de son pouvoir et en ce qui concerne l'établissement et la protection de son ordre social est unique et prédominante, exception faite des limitations résultant du droit international[13].

La plénitude veut dire que, par opposition aux autres sujets du droit international (*e.g.* aux compétences d'attribution des organisations internationales), la compétence *ratione materiae* de l'Etat n'est pas limitée d'avance et ne dépend pas chaque fois d'une norme attributive particulière du droit international. On dit parfois que l'Etat dispose de la compétence de sa compétence.

Cependant, l'étendue et l'exercice par l'Etat des compétences qui comportent un aspect extérieur trouvent leur limite dans la souveraineté des autres Etats, dans la réglementation internationale et dans la responsabilité juridique internationale de chaque Etat. Pour ce qui est des compétences de l'Etat dirigées à l'intérieur, le droit international peut aussi mettre certaines limites

---

[11] La notion de compétence est étroitement liée au principe de la légalité et elle est le contraire de l'arbitraire, de l'omnipotence et de l'absolutisme. Elle est «un ensemble de virtualitées juridiques dont le droit ne dit pas, et ne 'sait' pas, quel usage (correct) en sera fait par le sujet», V. CONSTANTINESCO, COMPÉTENCES ET POUVOIRS DANS LES COMMUNAUTÉS EUROPÉENNES, Paris (1974), p. 70. La compétence a sa source dans une norme juridique (la compétence dite originaire mise à part).

La notion de pouvoir est liée à l'exercice de la compétence à tel point qu'on les tient parfois pour synonymes (ce qui n'est exact). Une compétence se réalise par l'action d'un organe sous une forme juridique. Autrement dit, dans le cadre d'une compétence l'organe exerce divers pouvoirs pour prendre divers actes juridiques. Par conséquent, chacune des deux notions est une condition d'existence et d'efficacité de l'autre: «une compétence sans pouvoir est inefficace, un pouvoir se développant en dehors ou en l'absence d'une compétence est illégal», V. CONSTANTINESCO, *op. cit.*, *supra* note 5, p. 83.

[12] CH. ROUSSEAU, DROIT, *op. cit.*, *supra* note 2, pp. 72–93; J. CRAWFORD, THE CREATION OF STATES..., *op. cit.*, *supra* note 5, p. 53 et 56.

[13] Dans l'affaire de l'île de Palmas (1928), M. HUBER (arbitre unique) souligne que la «souveraineté, dans les relations entre Etats, signifie l'indépendance» et que «l'indépendance, relativement à une partie du globe, est le droit d'y exercer, à l'exclusion de tout autre Etat, les fonctions étatiques», RECUEIL DES SENTENCES ARBITRALES, vol. II, p. 838. Selon la CIJ, *Entre Etats indépendants, le respect de la souveraineté territoriale est une des bases essentielles des rapports internationaux*, l'affaire du détroit de Corfou, RECUEIL (1949), p. 35.

à leur exercice. Autrement dit, la plénitude des compétences de l'Etat ne constitue pas le fondement de l'arbitraire ou un titre suffisant pour n'importe quelle action de l'Etat ou pour le changement unilatéral des normes juridiques internationales qui le lient. En ce sens, le terme «plénitude» (qui peut induire en erreur) doit être interprété avec prudence[14].

L'autonomie signifie que l'Etat exerce ses compétences sans subir des injonctions d'un autre sujet du droit des gens, tout en étant lié par les normes juridiques internationales. L'autonomie se traduit notamment par la liberté de l'Etat de contracter des obligations juridiques internationales (*e.g.* l'absence d'une juridiction internationale universelle en est la conséquence). Ce caractère de la compétence étatique est surtout perceptible dans les cas où son exercice n'est pas délimité par le droit international particulier. Ces compétences sont qualifiées de discrétionnaires[15] ou comme faisant partie du domaine réservé d'un Etat.

La souveraineté se présente ainsi dans son aspect positif et négatif, externe et interne. Positif, car on met l'accent sur l'étendue et la nature de la compétence de l'Etat ou, autrement dit, sur sa capacité de commandement. Négatif, parce qu'on souligne que l'Etat est maître de ses actes et qu'il n'a au-dessus de lui aucune autre autorité (mis à part sa responsabilité internationale et la soumission au droit des gens)[16]; il s'agit donc de la liberté devant le commandement de la part des autres Etats. Si l'Etat dispose d'un pouvoir qualifié souvent de suprême, c'est bien dans ce sens et non dans celui qu'il puisse toujours s'imposer aux autres sujets du droit des gens. Externe – parce qu'il s'agit des rapports ou des situations contenant un aspect extérieur,

---

[14] Prenons, à titre d'exemple, le vocabulaire confus de la Convention sur le droit de la mer (1982), selon laquelle, dans des espaces particuliers, les Etats ont: la pleine souveraineté, la souveraineté, les droits souverains ou la juridiction.

[15] S. Jovanović, Restriction des compétences discrétionnaires des Etats en droit international, Paris (1988). La distinction entre le pouvoir discrétionnaire et le pouvoir lié est connue de plusieurs systèmes juridiques nationaux, bien que les définitions du pouvoir discrétionnaire ne soient pas toujours identiques. *Cf.* A. de Laubadère, Traité de droit administratif, Paris (1980), t. 1er, §§ 443–448; dans la théorie allemande (Ermessenslehre), *voir* H. Maurer, Allgemeines Verwaltungsrecht, München (1988), pp. 98–105; pour une étude de droit comparé – J. Schwarze, Europäisches Verwaltungsrecht, t. 1er, Baden–Baden (1988), p. 198 et s.

[16] Dans son opinion individuelle sur l'avis consultatif de la CPJI concernant le régime douanier entre l'Allemagne et l'Autriche (1931), le juge D. Anzilotti s'est exprimé à ce propos de la manière suivante: «l'indépendance ... n'est, au fond, que la condition normale des Etats d'après le droit international: elle peut être aussi qualifiée comme souveraineté (*suprema potestas*) ou souveraineté extérieure, si l'on entend par cela que l'Etat n'a au-dessus de soi aucune autorité, si ce n'est celle du droit international», série A/B, nº 41, p. 57.

Selon la sentence du Tribunal arbitral dans l'affaire du lac Lanoux (16 novembre 1957), «La souveraineté territoriale joue à la manière d'une présomption. Elle doit fléchir devant toutes les obligations internationales..., mais elle ne fléchit que devant elles», Recueil des sentences arbitrales, vol. XII, p. 301.

interne – en ce qui concerne l'établissement, la réglementation et la protection de l'ordre juridique propre à chaque Etat[17].

Ces aspects de la souveraineté sont complémentaires et expriment diverses perspectives du même phénomène. Essentiellement, il s'agit de la capacité de commandement de l'Etat et, d'autre part, de l'exercice des compétences et pouvoirs qui en découlent, sans subir le commandement des autres Etats, sous réserve toutefois de respecter les normes juridiques internationales qui le lient[18].

IV

Le rapport entre l'Etat et sa souveraineté d'une part et le droit international de l'autre fait partie des problèmes essentiels de la théorie du droit des gens. Il s'agit notamment de savoir quelle est la source des compétences des Etats et quelle est, dans ce contexte, la fonction du droit des gens[19]. La question principale est de savoir si le droit international attribue les compétences aux Etats ou bien s'il sert seulement à contrôler leur exercice.

Dans l'affaire du *Lotus*, la CPJI a notamment constaté que: «tout ce qu'on peut demander à un Etat, c'est de ne pas dépasser les limites que le droit international trace à sa compétence; en deçà de ces limites, le titre à la juridiction qu'il exerce se trouve dans sa souveraineté»[20]. Ce passage fut l'objet de sévères critiques d'une partie de la doctrine[21]. Cette critique ne semble pas entièrement convaincante et appelle un commentaire.

---

17 G. ARANGIO-RUIZ, *op. cit.*, *supra* note 4, pp. 364–367, «La souveraineté interne indique tout d'abord la *suprema potestas* en tant que qualité de l'Etat du droit interne ou de cette 'portion' de l'Etat qui d'après l'ordre établi detient le pouvoir suprême» (p. 364); «la souveraineté extérieure se présente, de même que l'indépendance (son synonyme), comme une qualité ou situation factuelle. Elle indique le fait de la non subordination à autrui. Par conséquent, la souveraineté … ne saurait pas dépendre du droit international. Dans la mesure où celui-ci régit les relations d'entités factuelles indépendantes, il ne saurait pas leur attribuer cette qualité» (p. 365).

18 N. POLITIS, *op. cit.*, *supra* note 2, p. 20, constate: «Si, débarrassée des dogmes et des fictions, on regarde la réalité bien en face, on s'aperçoit que ce qu'il y a derrière la prétendue souveraineté, c'est le libre exercice, dans les limites du droit, des diverses activités dévolues aux gouvernements».

19 Selon CH. ROUSSEAU, DROIT…, *op. cit.*, *supra* note 2, p. 65, trois principales conclusions résultent de la jurisprudence internationale: «1° en l'absence de dispositions internationales ou coutumières habilitant l'Etat à agir, la jurisprudence internationale estime que celui-ci possède un titre suffisant dans sa souveraineté; 2° d'après la jurisprudence internationale, la souveraineté de l'Etat doit toujours être présumée, même en l'absence de disposition positive la prévoyant expressément; 3° la jurisprudence internationale décide enfin que toute atteinte apportée par voie conventionnelle à la souveraineté de l'Etat doit être interprétée restrictivement».

20 L'arrêt de la CPJI du 7 septembre 1927 dans l'affaire du *Lotus*, série A, n° 10, p. 19.

21 *E.g.* CH. ROUSSEAU, DROIT…, *op. cit.*, *supra* note 2, pp. 65–66 estime que le passage précité de l'arrêt dans l'affaire du *Lotus* repose sur une analyse erronée, car «la notion de

Il existe une différence entre l'ordre juridique international dont la nature penche vers la coordination et les systèmes juridiques nationaux basés sur la subordination. Un organe public national, qui agit dans le cadre du droit national, doit toujours fonder son action (sa compétence) sur une norme législative qui, pour sa part, dépend des normes constitutionnelles. La nature de la communauté internationale est différente parce que les Etats sont des sujets originaires qui créent en commun le droit international, celui-ci les proclamant égaux quant à leur souveraineté. En ce sens, leurs compétences résultent non seulement d'une norme attributive du droit des gens, mais aussi de leur souveraineté.

S'il est vrai que certaines compétences de l'Etat résultent de leur attribution directe par les normes particulières du droit des gens[22], d'autres sont reconnues[23] par ce droit qui les légitime ainsi de manière générale. Toutefois, cette reconnaissance n'est pas absolue, car l'existence de la compétence d'un Etat qui concerne la compétence territoriale, personnelle ou l'ordre juridique d'un autre Etat n'est pas acquise d'avance et elle nécessite des rattachements particuliers, reconnus par le droit des gens. Une fois prouvée l'existence d'une telle compétence, son exercice n'est pas toujours libre.

La soumission des Etats au droit international et l'égalité des souverainetés se conditionnent réciproquement[24]. Ce droit se fonde sur la nécessité de la coexistence des Etats (y compris le maintien de la paix internationale) et sur leur volonté, ce qui implique normalement leur consentement (ou acquiescement)[25]. Cependant, dans leurs actes, même s'ils traduisent une liberté incorporée dans la notion de compétence discrétionnaire, les Etats ne peuvent pas agir de manière contraire au droit international[26]. Autrement dit, aussi bien l'existence que l'exercice de la compétence de l'Etat est à exa-

---

souveraineté ... ne sert nullement à distribuer les compétences, mais seulement à préciser leur mode d'exercice. Elle est également dangereuse en ce qu'elle équivaut à l'affirmation que tout ce qui n'est pas défendu est permis: admissible à la rigueur en droit interne..., ce prétendu principe ne trouve au contraire pas d'application normale dans les rapports internationaux, où l'on ne saurait conclure de l'absence d'une règle prohibitive à l'existence d'une règle permissive».

[22] *E.g.* un accord sur le désarmement peut attribuer à un Etat la compétence de contrôler la réduction des armements d'un autre Etat. En l'absence d'une telle norme internationale, la compétence serait inexistante et se réduirait à une possibilité de fait.

[23] Convaincantes sont à cet égard les observations de S. JOVANOVIĆ, *op. cit.*, *supra* note 15, surtout pp. 59–88.

[24] Selon l'opinion dissidente du juge Weiss concernant l'arrêt de la CPJI dans l'affaire du *Lotus* (1927), «si les Etats ne sont pas souverains, il n'y a pas de droit international possible, puisque l'objet de ce droit est précisément d'accorder et de concilier les diverses souverainetés sur lesquelles il exerce son empire», série A, n° 10, p. 44.

[25] *Voir* l'arrêt de la CPJI dans l'affaire du *Lotus* (1927), série A, n° 10, p. 18.

[26] La notion de *jus cogens* vient notamment à l'esprit. Selon NGUYEN QUOC DINH, P. DAILLIER, A. PELLET, DROIT INTERNATIONAL PUBLIC, 5ème éd., Paris (1994), «aucun Etat ne prétend, et nul ne saurait admettre, qu'un traité pourrait rendre licites des pratiques esclavagistes ou un génocide.

miner sous l'angle des normes particulières, des principes généraux ou des normes prohibitives du droit international universel[27].

La fonction du droit international est donc de nature coordinatrice et elle consiste surtout à assurer l'égalité des souverainetés étatiques et à contrôler l'exercice par les Etats de leurs compétences (y compris les conflits de compétences)[28]. L'étendue et la forme de ce contrôle dépendent du développement du droit international. Dans ce contexte, la contradiction entre la soumission de l'Etat au droit international et sa souveraineté semble apparente et trompeuse, et elle résulte d'un malentendu conceptuel.

V

L'exercice d'une compétence peut subir certaines limitations. A leur origine se trouvent le plus souvent des contraintes qui résultent de la coopération internationale et de la coexistence des Etats. Ces limitations peuvent avoir leur origine dans les faits ou dans une norme juridique internationale, être conformes au droit des gens ou illégales, de nature volontaire ou coercitive. On peut les percevoir dans la perspective d'une limite imposée à l'action d'un Etat ou dans celle de la protection d'un autre Etat contre les actes du premier.

A. Les limitations juridiques (conformes au droit des gens) sont surtout de nature volontaire et elles résultent normalement du consentement de l'Etat concerné[29]. Cependant, dans des situations exceptionnelles, elles sont parfois imposées. L'invocation par l'Etat visé de sa souveraineté aboutirait notam-

---

La notion de *jus cogens*, qui est la timide transposition de celle d'ordre public dans la sphère internationale, est la traduction juridique de cette idée» (p. 103); il en est de même pour la reconnaissance par un Etat d'une situation contraire à une norme de *jus cogens* (p. 530).

27 Selon S. JOVANOVIĆ, *op. cit.*, *supra* note 15, p. 87, «De l'inexistence de règles de répartition dans une matière, il est impossible de conclure à l'incompétence de l'Etat, car la souveraineté se caractérise par la plénitude des compétences ... Dans cette hypothèse de la non-réglementation juridique, l'Etat possède un pouvoir discrétionnaire. Dans les cas concrets, le juge international n'a jamais déclaré que l'Etat, qui ne peut pas légitimer son action par une règle attributive, est *ipso facto* incompétent. Il a toujours cherché à établir si l'Etat n'a pas outrepassé des limites de droit international».

28 Selon CH. DE VISSCHER, THÉORIES ET RÉALITÉS EN DROIT INTERNATIONAL, 4ème éd., Paris (1970), p. 127, «la théorie qui ramène les droits étatiques à des compétences attribuées et réparties par le droit international s'est trouvée en avance sur les faits».

29 Les nouveaux Etats sont soumis (c'est en quelque sorte la condition *sine qua non* de leur souveraineté) au droit international universel en vigueur (la succession d'Etats et ses problèmes ne suppriment pas cette règle). La souveraineté reste certes une donnée essentielle à cet égard, mais la liberté de l'Etat successeur se trouve souvent restreinte par des exceptions résultant du droit conventionnel ou coutumier. Il n'existe cependant pas un régime universel et complet de la succession d'Etats.

ment à contester la légalité des traités de paix ou des sanctions adoptées ou autorisées par le Conseil de sécurité de l'ONU.

1. Les limitations juridiques volontaires résultent des obligations internationales (normes du droit des gens universel et particulier – conventionnelles et coutumières, et certaines déclarations unilatérales)[30]. Elles semblent assez évidentes[31].

i. Un exemple – aujourd'hui historique, mais controversé – constituent les protectorats internationaux. Les entités protégées ont été considérées comme des Etats (qualifiés parfois de dépendants), l'approche en question se fondant sur le critère formel à savoir la conclusion d'un traité de protectorat[32]. Celui-ci prévoyait notamment l'exercice permanent par l'Etat protecteur de certaines compétences au nom de l'entité protégée, donc sa partielle interdiction (incapacité). Cependant, «compte tenu de ce que la conclusion des traités de protectorat est rarement libre, mais résulte toujours d'une pression politique et militaire», le protectorat constituait l'expression de «l'éthique de l'époque coloniale»[33]. Ce commentaire jette une ombre sur le statut étatique des entités protégées[34].

---

[30] Selon la CIJ, l'engagement international résultant d'une déclaration unilatérale «ne saurait être interprété comme ayant comporté l'invocation d'un pouvoir arbitraire de révision», *cf.* l'arrêt du 20 décembre 1974 dans l'affaire concernant les essais nucléaires, RECUEIL (1974), p. 270.

[31] Dans l'affaire du vapeur «Wimbledon» (1923), la CPJI a constaté dans son arrêt: «La Cour se refuse à voir dans la conclusion d'un traité, par lequel l'Etat s'engage à faire ou à ne pas faire quelque chose, un abandon de sa souveraineté. Sans doute, toute convention engendrant une obligation de ce genre, apporte une restriction à l'exercice des droits souverains de l'Etat, en ce sens qu'elle imprime à cet exercice une direction déterminée. Mais la faculté de contracter des engagements internationaux est précisément un attribut de la souveraineté de l'Etat», série A, n° 1, p. 25.

Selon l'opinion individuelle du juge D. ANZILOTTI sur l'avis consultatif de la CPJI concernant le régime douanier entre l'Allemagne et l'Autriche (1931), «la notion juridique de l'indépendance n'a rien à faire, ni avec la soumission de l'Etat au droit international, ni avec les nombreuses et toujours croissantes dépendances de fait, dans lesquelles un Etat se trouve par rapport aux autres Etats»; Anzilotti estime également que «les limitations de la liberté d'un Etat, qu'elles dérivent du droit international commun, ou d'engagements contractés, n'affectent aucunement, en tant que telles, son indépendance. Tant que ces limitations n'ont pas pour effet de mettre l'Etat sous l'autorité légale d'un autre Etat, le premier reste un Etat indépendant, pour onéreuses et étendues que soient lesdites obligations», série A/B, n° 41, p. 58. *Voir* aussi G. ARANGIO-RUIZ, *op. cit.*, *supra* note 4, pp. 366–367.

[32] L'avis consultatif de la CPJI du 7 février 1923 concernant les décrets de nationalité promulgués en Tunisie et au Maroc, série B, n° 4, p. 27; l'arrêt de la CIJ du 27 août 1952 dans l'affaire relative aux droits des ressortissants des Etats-Unis d'Amérique au Maroc, RECUEIL (1952), p. 188.

[33] CH. ROUSSEAU, DROIT..., *op. cit.*, *supra* note 2, p. 279.

[34] Pour ce qui est du droit des peuples à disposer d'eux-mêmes, il existe une sorte de tension entre la souveraineté de l'Etat et le droit en question. Si le contenu de ce droit et la notion de peuple ne sont pas toujours évidents, il reste que l'argument de souveraineté ne suffit pas pour contester le droit en question. Cependant, ce droit ne doit pas être automatiquement assimilé au droit à la sécession, surtout lorsque le peuple concerné vit dans un Etat démocratique (*cf.* la

ii. Dans certains cas, en vertu d'un traité, l'administration par un Etat d'une partie du territoire d'un autre Etat aboutit à l'exercice, par la Puissance administrante, sur le territoire en question des compétences étatiques, l'autre Etat conservant seulement un aspect de sa compétence à savoir le droit de disposer du territoire (donc le droit d'une éventuelle cession).

Ces situations sont assez rares et concernent surtout le passé. Si l'on excepte Chypre et la Bosnie-Herzégovine, annexés par les Puissances administrantes au début du XXème siècle, les autres cas concernent surtout des petits territoires, souvent cédés à bail ou administrés à titre de compensation, la plupart du temps l'administration ayant été confiée pour une période fixe, contre de l'argent et en admettant le retour de l'administration à l'Etat qui conserve la compétence de disposer du territoire[35]. Le plus souvent, le traité confiant l'administration exclut de manière expresse la souveraineté de la Puissance administrante sur le territoire administré. Dans ce contexte, certains auteurs distinguent entre la souveraineté (terme plus large qui englobe notamment la compétence de disposer du territoire) et la compétence territoriale[36].

iii. Les Communautés européennes (CE) sont des organisations internationales spécifiques en ce qui concerne les limitations de l'exercice par les Etats membres de leurs compétences. Malgré leur spécificité, les CE ne sont pas des entités souveraines (ne sont pas un Etat – unitaire ou fédéral). Les critiques prétendent que l'évolution des CE, et notamment le Traité de Maastricht établissant l'Union européenne (1992), mène à la suppression de la souveraineté populaire[37] et, finalement, menace la souveraineté des Etats membres.

---

résolution 2625 (XX) de l'Assemblée générale des Nations unies de 1970). *Voir* à ce sujet quelques observations de K. SKUBISZEWSKI dans son opinion dissidente dans l'affaire relative au Timor oriental, CIJ, RECUEIL (1995), pp. 224–277.

Par son souci de préserver la stabilité internationale et notamment l'existence des Etats déjà reconnus, le droit des gens contemporain et la politique des Etats ne facilitent pas toujours (sauf événements plutôt rares, *e.g.* une guerre ou l'époque de décolonisation) la naissance de nouveaux Etats. On peut même penser que, dans le contexte du droit des peuples à disposer d'eux-mêmes, le droit international remplit parfois une fonction conservatrice.

[35] K. SKUBISZEWSKI, *Administration and Sovereignty*, ARCHIV DES VÖLKERRECHTS (1985), n° 1–2; A. VERDROSS, B. SIMMA, *op. cit.*, *supra* note 13, pp. 655–662.

[36] A. VERDROSS, B. SIMMA, *ibid.*, pp. 658–659, ont profité de cette distinction pour souligner le caractère non définitif de la frontière occidentale de la Pologne et l'absence – jusqu'à la conclusion d'un traité de paix avec l'Allemagne – de la souveraineté de la Pologne sur les territoires qui lui ont été attribués par l'accord de Potsdam de 1945.

Sans entrer dans les détails de ce débat (déjà historique), contrairement à la pratique dominante antérieure (précitée) en matière d'administration d'une partie du territoire, l'accord de Potsdam ne mentionnait pas la souveraineté allemande sur les territoires en question et les qualifiait de «former German territories». On doit également estimer que le but et la fonction de la réglementation de Potsdam diffèrent des exemples précités de l'administration d'un territoire.

[37] *Cf.* S. OETER, *Souveränität und Demokratie als Probleme in der «Verfassungsentwicklung» der Europäischen Union*, ZEITSCHRIFT FÜR AUSLÄNDISCHES ÖFFENTLICHES RECHT UND

Les Etats membres des CE, qui restent actifs comme sujets du droit des gens dans plusieurs autres domaines, renoncent non seulement à l'exercice de certaines compétences, mais ils transfèrent aussi certaines compétences au profit des organes communautaires qui les exercent au nom de chaque Communauté (pas au nom de leurs membres). Il s'agit en l'occurrence d'un acte volontaire qui trouve sa confirmation dans les ratifications successives des traités européens et de leurs amendements.

Les impulsions de la construction communautaire ont leur source dans la volonté politique et dans les actes des Etats et des organes communautaires interétatiques. Ces Etats gardent en même temps leurs organes législatifs, exécutifs et judiciaires, le pouvoir de contrainte restant toujours dans leur compétence exclusive. Ils déterminent aussi, en commun, le contenu et le mode d'exercice des compétences par les organes communautaires. Grâce à leur participation au processus décisionnel, les Etats membres obtiennent une influence sur l'exercice des compétences par ces organes.

Une des plus grandes controverses entoure l'union économique et monétaire, prévue dans le cadre de la Communauté européenne par le Traité de Maastricht. Les Etats membres y envisagent notamment le transfert de certaines de leurs compétences en matière de politique monétaire au profit des organes communautaires[38]. Il n'existe pas de doute que les problèmes posés par l'union monétaire sont bien réels et d'une dimension incomparable avec certaines autres limitations, mais les étudier dans l'hypothèse d'un abandon de la «souveraineté monétaire» (comme s'il existait une souveraineté militaire, commerciale, douanière etc.) mène nulle part. Si les compétences des Etats membres des CE ne cessent de se réduire au profit des organes communautaires, procéder dans ce contexte à des gradations de la souveraineté s'avère peu utile (sauf pour alimenter des querelles politiques). L'exemple des CE montre ainsi les faiblesses de la définition de la souveraineté à travers le contenu de la compétence étatique.

VÖLKERRECHT (1995), n° 3, pp. 659–712. Le problème de la souveraineté populaire porte notamment sur la légitimité démocratique des organes des CE. La solution du problème pourrait consister à rendre plus transparent le processus décisionnel communautaire et à renforcer le contrôle du Parlement européen (élu au suffrage universel) sur les organes communautaires (technocrates ou intergouvernementaux). Cette opinion se heurte cependant à la tendance (en partie contradictoire) vers le renforcement du contrôle de la part des parlements nationaux en vue de sauvegarder la tradition démocratique et l'identité nationale de chaque Etat membre. Les controverses peu fructueuses et très politisées relatives à la (prétendue) division de la souveraineté populaire remplacent le vrai débat.

[38] N'oublions pas que la liberté des Etats membres en la matière fut déjà réduite à partir de 1979 avec l'établissement du système monétaire européen (sans que celui-ci soit prévu par le Traité de Rome). Dans ce système (modifié en partie en 1993 et rendu moins efficace), le réajustement des parités des monnaies nationales ne peut s'effectuer que de manière concertée entre les pays participants.

Ce qui, par contre, peut être discuté, ce sont les questions politiques et juridiques liées à l'opportunité de l'évolution des CE et de l'UE (choix politique important), aux formes de consultation des parlements nationaux, au contrôle national et/ou communautaire du processus décisionnel des CE et de l'UE et à la conformité des traités européens successifs avec la constitution de chaque Etat membre.

Il serait en tout cas paradoxal si les Etats membres invoquaient la défense de leur souveraineté contre les formes et objectifs d'une coopération internationale qui leur est profitable ou, autrement dit, contre la liberté d'exercice de leurs compétences. Pour compléter cette argumentation, il semble indispensable de rappeler que l'intégration en question résulte des contraintes économiques et politiques. Les avantages de l'intégration constituent une contrepartie essentielle des limitations dans l'exercice des compétences, ce qui représente une donnée fondamentale du débat. La forme juridique de l'intégration répond aux buts politiques que se fixent les Etats membres.

iv. Un conflit relatif aux effets extraterritoriaux[39] de l'exercice des compétences étatiques ne met pas directement en jeu le statut de l'Etat visé.

La tentative d'influencer par un Etat les rapports juridiques dans un autre Etat, sans le consentement de ce dernier et en l'absence d'un titre particulier du droit des gens, conduit néanmoins à contester le caractère unique et prédominant (exclusivité) de la compétence de celui-ci (donc de sa souveraineté). Le principe de l'égalité des Etats interdit normalement d'étendre la compétence législative, exécutive ou judiciaire d'un Etat au territoire d'un autre ou aux personnes relevant de la compétence de celui-ci. Il existe cependant des situations ou certains rattachements – reconnus par le droit international – rendent plausible l'existence de la compétence d'un Etat tiers[40].

Le problème qui se pose dans ce contexte consiste non seulement à constater l'existence réelle d'un conflit de compétences, mais aussi à examiner la légalité de leur exercice. On s'accorde généralement à reconnaître que la

---

[39] W. MENG, *Extraterritorial Effects of Administrative, Judicial and Legislative Acts*, dans: EPIL, t. 10 (1987), pp. 155–156. *Voir* aussi l'ouvrage de W. MENG, EXTRATERRITORIALE JURISDIKTION IM ÖFFENTLICHEN WIRTSCHAFTSRECHT, Berlin (1994).

[40] Selon le § 402 du RESTATEMENT OF THE LAW (Third). The Foreign Relations Law of the United States. The American Law Institute, May 14, 1986: «a state has jurisdiction to prescribe with respect to

(1) (a) conduct that, wholly or in substantial part, takes place within its territory; (b) the status of persons, or interests in things, present within its territory; (c) conduct outside its territory that has or is intended to have substantial effect within its territory;

(2) the activities, interests, status, or relations of its nationals outside as well as within its territory; and

(3) certain conduct outside its territory by persons not its nationals that is directed against the security of the state or against a limited class of other state interests».

compétence d'un Etat tiers doit se fonder sur un rattachement raisonnable[41] tandis que son exercice doit s'accompagner de la pondération des intérêts des parties (principe de proportionnalité). L'interdiction de l'intervention de même que l'interdiction du détournement de pouvoir[42] peuvent également servir d'instrument d'appréciation.

Le problème des effets extraterritoriaux prouve en tout cas que la souveraineté d'un Etat trouve ses limites dans celle d'un autre Etat et que le caractère exclusif, plein et autonome de la compétence étatique ne s'assimile pas à l'omnipotence. D'un autre côté, il ne suffit pas de contester les effets extraterritoriaux de certains actes uniquement en invoquant la souveraineté ou la compétence territoriale d'un Etat.

2. Les limitations juridiques peuvent également être de nature coercitive et résulter *e.g.* d'un traité de paix ou des sanctions internationales. Elles n'aboutissent normalement pas à la disparition d'un Etat (tout en pouvant modifier sa politique, ses frontières ou son régime constitutionnel).

i. Si tout Etat peut décider de sa disparition et s'unir avec un autre Etat, l'article 88 du Traité de paix conclu en 1919, à Saint-Germain, avec l'Autriche supprimait cette possibilité en proclamant que «l'indépendance de l'Autriche est inaliénable, si ce n'est du consentement du Conseil de la Société des Nations» (il s'agissait à l'époque d'empêcher une éventuelle unification de l'Autriche et de l'Allemagne). Cette réglementation n'a pas été considérée comme portant atteinte à la souveraineté de l'Autriche[43].

L'interdiction d'une union de l'Autriche avec l'Allemagne, ainsi que certaines autres prohibitions, figurent également dans le Traité du 15 mai 1955 portant rétablissement d'une Autriche indépendante et démocratique.

---

41 Selon, *ibid.* la *reasonableness* est non seulement "a basis for requiring states to consider moderating their enforcement of law that they are authorized to prescribe, but as an essential element in determining whether, as a matter of international law, the state may exercise jurisdiction to prescribe" (§ 403, Reporters' Note 10).

Le § 403 (1) du Restatement précise que "Even when one of the bases for jurisdiction under § 402 (n. 40) is present, a state may not exercise jurisdiction to prescribe law with respect to a person or activity having connections with another state when the exercise of such jurisdiction is unreasonable."

42 Le droit et la doctrine juridique témoignent d'une grande diversité (qui frôle la confusion) dans l'emploi des termes abus (de droit, de pouvoir) et détournement (de pouvoir). *Cf.* A. DE LAUBADÈRE, *op. cit*, *supra* note 15, §§ 945–959; pour le détournement de pouvoir en droit international *voir* S. JOVANOVIĆ, *op. cit.*, *supra* note 15, pp. 169–200; CH. KISS, *Abuse of Rights*, dans: EPIL, t. 7 (1984); N. POLITIS, *op. cit.*, *supra* note 2, pp. 77–116.

43 En ce sens l'avis consultatif de la CPJI concernant le régime douanier entre l'Allemagne et l'Autriche (1931), série A/B, n° 41, pp. 45–46; l'opinion individuelle du juge D. ANZILOTTI sur l'avis précité ne s'en écarte pas (*ibid.* p. 58).

ii. Le cas de l'Autriche fait penser à la situation exceptionnelle de l'Allemagne en 1945 qui reste notamment en rapport avec la responsabilité de l'agresseur. Les Puissances victorieuses y ont pris, le 5 juin 1945, l'autorité suprême et, en excluant de manière explicite l'annexion, y ont exercé d'importantes fonctions étatiques.

Cette situation résultait non seulement de la nature et de l'étendue des crimes du troisième Reich et de la capitulation inconditionnelle de ses troupes, mais surtout de l'absence en Allemagne, en 1945, de forces politiques internes organisées et d'organes nationaux capables d'assurer l'ordre, l'administration du pays et l'exécution des prescriptions des Puissances. La prise par les Puissances de l'autorité suprême n'avait pas pour but de soumettre l'Allemagne en permanence à une sorte de tutelle internationale, car il s'agissait des limitations temporaires en vue d'établir un régime démocratique dans ce pays. On situe ainsi le problème de la souveraineté allemande sous un autre éclairage.

Entre 1945 et 1949 (jusqu'à la création des deux Etats allemands) l'existence de l'Allemagne en tant qu'Etat n'était pas sérieusement mise en doute. En admettant (hypothèse d'école) que l'Allemagne (ensuite les deux Etats allemands) n'était pas souveraine, qu'est-ce qu'elle était? La qualifier d'Etat non souverain ou non entièrement souverain conduit, à notre avis, à une *contradictio in adiecto*. Elle n'était ni un protectorat international, ni un condominium. Il faut plutôt estimer qu'il s'agissait d'un Etat à condition juridique particulière soumis à un régime d'occupation internationale spécifique, mais non à une occupation de guerre. En tenant compte du caractère exceptionnel de cette situation, l'Etat allemand a conservé dans cette période sa personnalité juridique et sa capacité de jouissance, tout en étant privé (provisoirement, mais légalement) de sa capacité d'exercice[44].

Certains droits des quatre Puissances relatifs à l'Allemagne dans son ensemble – y compris la possibilité de l'unification des deux Etats allemands seulement avec le consentement des Puissances – ont été retenus en attendant le règlement de paix (*peace settlement*). Il s'agissait donc d'une limitation provisoire, mais légale au point de vue du droit international, qui ne privait cependant pas la RFA et la RDA de leur statut étatique. Les deux Etats allemands étaient reconnus, agissaient en cette qualité sur le plan international, poursuivaient leurs politiques étrangères et concluaient, en leur propre nom, d'importants traités. La thèse selon laquelle, après l'incorporation de la RDA à la RFA en 1990, l'Allemagne aurait recouvré la pleine souve-

---

44 *Voir* aussi *infra*, note 64.

raineté[45] semble artificielle et implique l'existence des deux Etats allemands «mi-souverains».

iii. Pour prendre l'exemple de l'agression du Koweït par l'Irak en 1990, la résolution 678 (1990) du Conseil de sécurité de l'ONU autorise les Etats membres

> «à user de tous les moyens nécessaires pour faire respecter et appliquer la résolution 660 (1990) du Conseil de sécurité et toutes les résolutions pertinentes ultérieures, ainsi que pour rétablir la paix et la sécurité internationales dans la région.»

Dans sa résolution 687 (1991), le Conseil de sécurité de l'ONU a notamment imposé à l'Irak l'obligation de détruire toutes ses armes chimiques et biologiques ainsi que les missiles balistiques d'une portée de plus de 150 kilomètres. Il a également autorisé une commission spéciale de l'ONU à effectuer à cet égard des inspections sur place. La même résolution interdit aux Etats membres (sans fixer un délai) de livrer à l'Irak certaines armes et certains équipements militaires[46].

Le statut international de l'Irak reste intact, mais l'exercice de ses compétences est limité. Il semble donc erroné de considérer *a priori* les sanctions imposées ou approuvées par le Conseil de sécurité comme une atteinte à la souveraineté[47], celle-ci n'étant pas un titre suffisant pour autoriser l'Etat à violer les normes du droit international[48].

---

[45] En mettant fin aux droits et responsabilités des quatre Puissances relatifs à l'Allemagne dans son ensemble (§ 1), le paragraphe 2 de l'article 7 du Traité du 12 septembre 1990 portant règlement définitif concernant l'Allemagne (Traité 2+4) précise que «l'Allemagne unie jouira, en conséquence, de la pleine souveraineté sur ses affaires intérieures et extérieures». Cette formule nous semble conceptuellement fausse.

[46] Dans ce contexte, les Etats tiers perdent, en raison de ces sanctions, une part de liberté dans l'exercice de leurs compétences (l'interdiction des ventes d'armes à l'Irak).

[47] H. MEYROWITZ, *La guerre du Golfe et le droit des conflits armés*, REVUE GÉNÉRALE DE DROIT INTERNATIONAL PUBLIC (1992), n° 3, p. 595, estime à juste titre que le fondement juridique et la justification politique et morale de l'action de l'ONU dans le conflit entre l'Irak et le Koweït se trouvent «dans la fonction d'ordre public international, assumée, conformément à la mission que lui a assignée la Charte, par le Conseil de sécurité» (chapitre VII). Il soutient cette thèse notamment en rapport avec le désarmement partiel de l'Irak décidé par le Conseil de sécurité dans sa résolution 687 (1991).

Les doutes exprimés à ce propos par F. L. KIRGIS, Jr., *The Security Council's First Fifty Years*, AMERICAN JOURNAL OF INTERNATIONAL LAW (1995), n° 3, pp. 535–536, nous semblent peu convaincants. En effet, si la souveraineté de tous les Etats est égale, la souveraineté ne s'assimile pas à l'égalité dans la menace de la paix et de la sécurité internationales. En outre, le désarmement partiel imposé à l'Irak doit être considéré comme une part de sa responsabilité internationale pour une grave violation du droit des gens.

[48] Tel est notamment le cas de la responsabilité internationale de l'Etat et de celle de ses agents pour les crimes internationaux (*e.g.* les procès de Nürnberg au lendemain de la deuxième

Le cas irakien met néanmoins à l'ordre du jour le problème général des mesures prises par le Conseil de sécurité dans le cadre du chapitre VII de la Charte de l'ONU, et notamment de leurs limites juridiques. Le problème s'est posé récemment avec l'interprétation (extensive) par le Conseil de sécurité du chapitre VII (notion de «menace contre la paix») en rapport avec les troubles internes, la violation des principes démocratiques dans certains Etats, les migrations des populations ou le terrorisme international[49].

Si le Conseil de sécurité, responsable du maintien de la paix et de la sécurité internationales (art. 24), possède la compétence pour constater l'existence d'une menace contre la paix, d'une rupture de la paix ou d'un acte d'agression (art. 39), la Charte ne préjuge pas quels actes ou quelles situations sont susceptibles d'être constitutifs de cette norme. Cependant, si le Conseil de sécurité constate une telle menace, les mesures de coercition[50], adoptées dans le cadre du chapitre VII, ne constituent pas (art. 2 (7) de la Charte) une intervention dans les affaires relevant essentiellement de la compétence nationale d'un Etat.

La compétence du Conseil de sécurité dans le cadre du chapitre VII est large et repose dans une grande partie sur les jugements de caractère subjectif et politique tandis que le contrôle par la CIJ reste (et doit plutôt rester) très limité[51]. Même dans l'hypothèse d'un amendement de la Charte, un contrôle de l'appréciation politique semble peu réel et seules les questions de droit

---

guerre mondiale ou les tribunaux internationaux établis au début des années 1990 par l'ONU en rapport avec les conflits yougoslave ou rwandais).

49 On admet de plus en plus souvent, dans la théorie et dans la pratique, que l'existence d'une menace contre la paix ou d'une rupture de la paix peut résulter non seulement d'un conflit armé entre deux Etats, mais aussi des conflits internes ou des violations de droits de l'homme dans un Etat, celui-ci étant parfois privé d'un pouvoir central et efficace. Il reste cependant que cette évolution suit les méandres des réactions politiques sélectives des membres du Conseil de sécurité.

Cette tendance s'accentue depuis le début des années 1990, *voir* les références à la situation des droits de l'homme dans le contexte de la menace contre la paix et la sécurité internationales dans les résolutions du Conseil de sécurité concernant l'Irak – rés. 688 (1991), le Libéria – rés. 788 (1992), la Somalie – rés. 794 (1992), la Bosnie-Herzégovine rés. 836 (1993), Haïti – rés. 841 (1993) et 940 (1994), l'Angola – rés. 864 (1993), le Rwanda – rés. 929 (1994). Pour les crimes internationaux en Yougoslavie et au Rwanda et la création des tribunaux internationaux *voir* les résolutions 827 (1993) et 955 (1994).

50 La définition des mesures de coercition pose parfois des problèmes, *cf.* F.L. KIRGIS, Jr., *op. cit.*, *supra* note 47, pp. 529–532. Cet auteur met notamment en doute la légalité de certaines mesures (concernant la frontière irako-koweïtienne et la nullité de la répudiation par l'Irak de sa dette extérieure) adoptées par le Conseil de sécurité et mentionne dans ce contexte le principe de l'égalité souveraine (art. 2, par. 1, de la Charte). Tout en appréciant cette réflexion, il faudrait réfléchir si elle ne restreint pas trop la mission du Conseil dans les cas d'une rupture de la paix internationale.

51 *Voir* à cet égard M. HERDEGEN, *The «Constitutionalization» of the UN Security System*, VANDERBILT JOURNAL OF TRANSNATIONAL LAW, vol. 27 (1994), n° 1, pp. 135–159; F. L. KIRGIS, Jr., *op. cit.*, *supra* note 47.

pourraient éventuellement en faire l'objet[52]. Malgré le risque d'une sélectivité politique dans les réactions du Conseil, il semble que la règle de l'unanimité, applicable aux membres permanents, garantit actuellement un contrôle le plus réaliste.

3. Compte tenu du fait que la réglementation internationale pénètre de plus en plus dans les ordres juridiques internes des Etats (et notamment en ce qui concerne les droits et obligations des personnes physiques et morales), le rapport entre le droit international et le droit national revêt une importance pour la notion de souveraineté. Notons dans ce contexte que l'évolution du droit international s'oriente vers des limitations qui ont de plus en plus en vue la protection des valeurs communes à tous les Etats et à leur population (*e.g.* l'environnement, la dignité et les droits de l'individu). Il n'en résulte cependant pas qu'il s'agisse d'atteinte à la souveraineté.

L'application du droit des gens dans le système national nécessite le plus souvent des actes nationaux supplémentaires. C'est au droit national de préciser les méthodes d'application ainsi que la place des normes internationales dans l'ordre interne. Cependant, il est un principe du droit international qu'un Etat ne peut pas invoquer son droit interne pour se soustraire aux obligations que lui impose le droit des gens[53]. Cette règle engendre la responsabilité internationale de l'Etat, mais elle n'assure pas automatiquement la primauté des règles juridiques internationales dans l'ordre interne.

B. Les limitations dans l'exercice par les Etats de leurs compétences ont également leur origine dans les faits. Le rôle de ces limitations dans la vie internationale ne cesse de croître, elles sont de plus en plus sophistiquées et difficiles à prouver. Le problème essentiel consiste à apprécier leur légalité à la lumière des normes du droit des gens. Cela est important dans la mesure ou le choix du régime politique, économique et social de chaque Etat ainsi que la liberté dans la poursuite de sa politique étrangère sont des composants essentiels de l'exercice des fonctions étatiques (et, par conséquent, de la souveraineté).

---

52 On peut notamment penser à la violation des normes de *jus cogens* ou se demander si les mesures de coercition prises dans le cadre du chapitre VII puissent aboutir directement à la disparition d'un Etat. Il est à noter que l'embargo, décidé par le Conseil de sécurité, sur les livraisons d'armes à destination de Bosnie-Herzégovine (membre de l'ONU et victime d'une agression) pouvait impliquer une telle menace.

53 L'affaire du traitement des nationaux polonais dans le territoire de Dantzig, CPJI, série A/B, n° 44, p. 24. *Voir* aussi les articles 27 et 46 de la Convention de Vienne sur le droit des traités (1969). Cette Convention limite aussi l'extinction ou la suspension unilatérale par un Etat des traités de caractère humanitaire comme conséquence de leur violation par l'une des parties (art. 60, para. 5).

1. Les limitations factuelles résultent souvent des situations structurelles et objectives. Les différences concernant le potentiel économique, militaire, démographique ou territorial des Etats[54] ainsi que l'interdépendance qui caractérise les relations internationales contemporaines restent sans effet direct pour le statut international de l'Etat, mais elles ne sont pas sans importance pour les possibilités réelles de l'exercice des compétences et pour le rôle international de chaque Etat. Il semble toutefois erroné, au moins sur le plan juridique international, de considérer que l'interdépendance politique et économique des Etats conduit à une dilution (sinon suppression) de leur souveraineté.

Les différences en question échappent à l'appréciation de la légalité en droit international, mais ce dernier peut tout de même contribuer à les aplanir. L'indépendance dans l'exercice des compétences apparaît ainsi comme une capacité limitée par les possibilités objectives.

2. En dehors des facteurs objectifs, il existe toute une gamme d'instruments politiques, militaires et économiques utilisés en vue d'influencer les Etats dans l'exercice de leurs compétences.

L'emploi de la force ou la menace de son emploi sans un titre juridique sont interdits par le droit des gens. Par conséquent, il faut considérer de tels actes comme des faits qui engendrent des conséquences juridiques. Le problème essentiel consiste non seulement à interdire l'emploi de la force ou de sa menace, mais aussi à apprécier la légalité de son emploi (surtout comme réaction à une violation du droit international). Ce problème ne se pose pas uniquement dans le contexte d'une action unilatérale (*e.g.* intervention humanitaire[55] ou défense légitime), mais aussi dans le cas de l'action de l'ONU dans le cadre du chapitre VII.

L'emploi de la force contre un Etat peut limiter ou supprimer l'exercice de ses compétences sur l'ensemble ou sur une partie de son territoire, mais il n'aboutit pas automatiquement au remplacement de sa souveraineté ou à la disparition de cet Etat. D'ailleurs, plusieurs violations n'ont pas pour but la disparition d'un Etat, mais seulement l'élimination de son gouvernement ou la modification de sa politique.

En évoquant des atteintes à la souveraineté d'un Etat, il semble préférable mettre l'accent non sur la souveraineté (qui n'est pas une norme juridique), mais sur la violation des normes du droit des gens (*e.g.* des normes pro-

---

[54] «In the eyes of many developing states, the big powers intervene in their affairs simply by existing», D.A. BALDWIN, *Foreign Aid, Intervention and Influence*, WORLD POLITICS (1969), nº 3, p. 427.

[55] Il est préférable de parler dans ce contexte d'action humanitaire sans préjuger de sa légalité, car l'intervention est un acte illégal par définition.

hibitives comme l'interdiction de l'emploi de la force ou l'interdiction de l'intervention) qui protègent la souveraineté.

La vie internationale connaît aussi la notion de zone d'influence d'un Etat, reconnue informellement par certains autres Etats. Les aspects de politique étrangère s'y mêlent souvent avec des considérations de nature économique. Il s'agit des cas où, souvent en raison de leur situation géopolitique, les pays visés par la politique d'une Puissance sont en fait limités dans la liberté du choix de leur régime politique, économique ou social ainsi que dans la conduite de leur politique étrangère[56]. On applique diverses méthodes pour maintenir une telle dépendance. La doctrine de Brejnev fait ici concurrence à celle de *big stick* ou aux accords de défense conclus entre la France et certains pays africains.

Si certains traités contiennent la formule qui invite à respecter la souveraineté, l'intégrité territoriale et l'indépendance politique des Etats, cela témoigne que le statut international d'un Etat peut rester intact, mais son intégrité territoriale et son indépendance politique peuvent être menacées ou réduites par des actes illicites d'un autre Etat[57].

Dans la pratique, la réduction des effets juridiques des actes illicites, dangereux pour l'existence d'un Etat, n'est pas tout à fait évidente (la *Realpolitik* est toujours présente). La nature, le but de l'acte illicite, sa durée et son effectivité ne sont pas sans importance à cet égard, mais la violation du droit des gens rend la reconnaissance internationale plus difficile. L'évolution du droit des gens contemporaine penche en faveur de la continuité de l'Etat et de sa souveraineté[58].

3. Les relations économiques internationales constituent un espace où l'influence entraîne souvent une sorte de dépendance (contrairement aux phénomènes objectifs et structurels).

La résolution 1803 (XVII) de l'Assemblée générale de l'ONU du 14 décembre 1962, intitulée *Souveraineté permanente sur les ressources naturelles*, constitue une bonne illustration des malentendus concernant la notion même.

---

[56] Une bonne illustration de cette situation figure dans une annonce parue, en 1956, dans un journal satirique polonais: j'accepte de changer la souveraineté pour une meilleure position géographique.

[57] Pour prendre l'exemple des pays d'Europe centrale, soumis – après 1945 – à la domination soviétique, on peut penser à une sorte d'intervention (acte illégal par définition) quasi-permanente. L'indépendance politique de ces pays fut limitée, mais contester leur souveraineté pourrait conduire à mettre en doute la validité de leurs engagements internationaux (*e.g.* des traités qu'ils ont conclus).

[58] Pour une analyse de ces problèmes en rapport avec les Malouines *voir* R. DOLZER, THE TERRITORIAL STATUS OF THE FALKLAND ISLANDS (MALVINAS): PAST AND PRESENT, New York (1993).

Elle établit en effet un «droit de souveraineté permanente (dans un autre passage: des droits souverains, JK) des peuples et des nations sur leurs richesses et leurs ressources naturelles». Elle implique ainsi l'existence d'un nombre illimité des droits souverains sur d'autres domaines. En outre, la qualification «souveraineté permanente» admet indirectement l'existence d'une souveraineté non permanente.

Cette critique n'enlève rien à l'importance du problème, elle vise seulement son fondement. En réalité, la controverse porte sur la validité des actes de nationalisation de la propriété étrangère, sur les conditions d'indemnisation et sur le rôle du droit international.

D'un autre côté, si la référence à la de souveraineté semble dans ce contexte utile, c'est à la souveraineté tout court. En effet, indépendamment du problème des nationalisations, il existe une autre face de la médaille à savoir la légalité de l'influence du capital étranger sur l'Etat d'accueil. En l'absence des normes particulières applicables, l'interdiction de l'intervention peut servir d'instrument de protection contre certaines pressions.

Dans le domaine monétaire[59], malgré une grande marge de liberté en la matière, les Etats sont tout de même liés par les règles conventionnelles et coutumières[60]. Dans tous ces cas, il serait difficile de prétendre que les normes en question (pour importantes que soient parfois les limitations qu'elles apportent) portent atteinte à la souveraineté des Etats concernés.

Sur un autre plan, sans que le droit des gens réglemente nécessairement ce domaine,

> «L'Etat qui adopte une complète convertibilité externe renonce par la même à tout contrôle des changes et prend le risque par conséquent de voir sa monnaie utilisée en dehors de son contrôle. Or il y a là un paradoxe: en effet la libre convertibilité externe de la monnaie est un atout économique qui est normalement le fait d'une monnaie forte. Mais en abandonnant tout contrôle des changes, l'Etat perd tout moyen de contrôle sur l'utilisation qui est faite de sa monnaie en dehors de ses frontières et notamment sur le développement des crédits bancaires consentis en dehors de son territoire dans sa monnaie»[61].

---

59 *Voir* notamment G. BURDEAU, *L'exercice des compétences monétaires par les Etats*, RCADI (1988–V), t. 212; J. GOLD, EXCHANGE RATES IN INTERNATIONAL LAW AND ORGANIZATION (1988) (American Bar Association); F.A. MANN, THE LEGAL ASPECTS OF MONEY, Oxford (1982); D. CARREAU, *op. cit.*, *supra* note 2.

60 Avant la naissance du Fonds Monétaire International (FMI), les tribunaux nationaux et internationaux ont souvent considéré que des inflations organisées en vue d'éviter le paiement réel des dettes extérieures, des réglementations de changes discriminatoires et odieuses ainsi que des taux de change spoliateurs constituaient un détournement de pouvoir, *cf.* D. CARREAU, *op. cit.*, *supra* note 2, pp. 119–127. *Voir* aussi G. BURDEAU, *op. cit.*, *supra* note 59, p. 255; F.A. MANN, *op. cit.*, *supra* note 59, p. 477.

61 G. BURDEAU, *op. cit.*, *supra* note 59, p. 254.

Il est vrai que l'abolition ou l'affaiblissement du contrôle de la masse monétaire d'un pays résulte d'une décision volontaire, mais celle-ci est imposée par des contraintes de l'économie internationale. L'alternative serait de rétablir ou de renforcer le contrôle des changes par les Etats-Unis ou par l'Allemagne, ce qui est en principe possible, mais non sans de sérieuses perturbations de l'économie nationale de ces pays et des marchés mondiaux. Ces pays, restent-ils souverains? La question est rhétorique. Cet exemple montre bien la différence entre la capacité et les possibilités réelles, et il témoigne que le débat à propos des soi disant limitations de la souveraineté n'explique pas de manière satisfaisante la complexité de la réalité internationale.

C. Quelques observations générales s'imposent dans le contexte de cette analyse.

Certains malentendus semblent caractéristiques pour le problème débattu: assimiler la souveraineté de l'Etat à une liberté absolue (omnipotence) dans l'extension et dans l'exercice des compétences qui ne sont pas réglementées par les normes particulières du droit des gens, considérer la souveraineté comme une notion ayant un contenu matériel fixe et percevoir le développement et l'influence croissante du droit des gens dans la perspective d'une réduction de la souveraineté.

1. La nature et l'étendue de la compétence de l'Etat n'excluent pas que celle-ci trouve ses limites dans la compétence d'un autre Etat (égalité des souverainetés), que l'Etat renonce à l'exercice de certaines compétences ou qu'il y soit contraint – toujours en conformité avec les normes du droit international particulier ou universel. L'évolution de ce droit témoigne d'ailleurs que son influence ne vise pas uniquement la protection croissante de la souveraineté, mais aussi qu'il impose certaines limitations à l'exercice par les Etats de leurs compétences, ceci au nom des valeurs communes.

Dans la doctrine, on distingue parfois entre les limitations de la souveraineté et les limitations dans l'exercice de la souveraineté (exercice des compétences). On avance comme critère essentiel des limitations de la souveraineté la suppression partielle (mais durable et formelle) de la capacité d'un Etat d'agir dans certains domaines en tant que sujet du droit des gens, cette capacité ayant été transférée à une autre entité souveraine (Etat) qui agit au nom de l'Etat concerné (pas en son propre nom)[62]. L'idée de limitations de la souveraineté conduit à admettre l'existence des Etats qualifiés de dépendants ou mi-souverains (cas des protectorats), donc à admettre

---

[62] Notons dans ce contexte qu'une organisation internationale (y compris les CE) exerce normalement ses compétences en son propre nom.

l'existence des entités souveraines à 99 ou à 50 pour cent (avec toutes les conséquences juridiques qui puissent en résulter). De telles gradations de la souveraineté sont difficilement concevables, car celle-ci – en tant que notion qualitative et non quantitative – ne préjuge pas d'avance de la portée exacte des compétences de l'Etat.

Il est par contre possible de parler des limitations dans l'exercice des compétences d'un Etat. Si la norme fondamentale est celle de l'égalité des souverainetés étatiques (et non une souveraineté absolue), les limitations apportées par le droit des gens ne doivent pas être assimilées aux limitations de la souveraineté, car autrement la réglementation internationale et l'évolution du droit des gens équivaudrait à réduire la souveraineté, ce qui semble conceptuellement faux. Il convient donc de distinguer entre les limitations (légales) de l'exercice des compétences des Etats et les atteintes (illégales) à la souveraineté qui résultent des violations de certaines normes internationales.

Sur le plan juridique, le problème essentiel consiste à se prononcer sur la conformité des limitations débattues avec le droit des gens, à se mettre d'accord sur les critères d'application et d'interprétation de ce droit et à assurer une protection adéquate et efficace contre ses violations. La dépendance croissante entre les Etats prenant souvent une forme sophistiquée et indirecte, elle ne facilite pas l'appréciation des limitations (juridiques et factuelles).

En renversant un peu l'ordre habituel, il est préférable de percevoir la souveraineté non pas dans la perspective de la plénitude de la compétence, mais plutôt dans l'optique d'une capacité d'exercer des fonctions étatiques. La capacité ne s'assimile pas toujours à la possibilité et les limitations factuelles ou juridiques peuvent réduire les compétences de l'Etat et leur exercice. Cependant, comme la souveraineté ne se traduit pas par un contenu fixe, cela ne supprime pas automatiquement la capacité même.

Le débat de la souveraineté rappelle parfois le dilemme d'un verre à moitié plein ou à moitié vide. Or, dans la mesure où la plénitude de la compétence étatique (ainsi que son exclusivité et son autonomie) n'est pas absolue, il faudrait plutôt estimer que le verre est à moitié plein, car il convient de mettre l'accent sur les compétences dont l'Etat dispose (en admettant des limitations de droit et de fait) et non sur celles dont il ne dispose pas ou qu'il n'exerce pas. C'est, à notre avis, une approche plus adéquate et plus nuancée de la réalité.

On doit en conclure qu'une entité territoriale est souveraine ou ne l'est pas (est un Etat ou ne l'est pas), tout en admettant que, en raison de la complexité de diverses situations[63], la qualification de certaines collectivités

---

[63] *E.g.* le condominium (phénomène marginal) doit être envisagé plutôt comme l'absence de souveraineté de chaque partie et non comme l'expression d'une souveraineté commune.

internationales ou de certaines situations peut poser des problèmes. Sauf circonstances évidentes, mais plutôt rares (*e.g.* la fusion des deux Etats), il semble extrêmement difficile d'établir d'avance un seuil fixe à partir duquel naît ou disparaît l'Etat et sa souveraineté. La pratique internationale connaît des exemples dans lesquels l'existence d'un Etat est assurée entièrement ou en grande partie seulement par le fait que les autres Etats continuent à le reconnaître et qu'il jouit de la protection résultant du droit des gens[64]. Chaque cas, y compris les conséquences des actes internationalement illicites, nécessite un examen distinct[65].

2. Les relations internationales sont de plus en plus marquées par une sorte de tension entre la souveraineté de l'Etat d'une part et la souveraineté populaire de l'autre.

On prétend souvent que la souveraineté de l'Etat ainsi que la souveraineté nationale (populaire) sont indivisibles. Cette affirmation semble admissible à condition de se mettre d'accord sur le sens du terme «souveraineté» et sur celui de l'adjectif «indivisible». En effet, certaines limitations sont possibles surtout lorsqu'elles résultent du consentement des organes compétents et restent conformes au droit applicable. Le débat sur le caractère indivisible ou inaliénable de la souveraineté comporte en tout cas un risque accru de politisation et de manipulation.

Les notions de souveraineté de l'Etat et de souveraineté populaire étant distinctes, elles restent néanmoins dans un certain rapport. L'expression de la volonté populaire se trouve normalement à l'origine de la naissance de l'Etat; en d'autres mots, la souveraineté de l'Etat et la souveraineté populaire apparaissent parallèlement. Il arrive cependant que l'Etat se transforme en

---

[64] Un Etat peut continuer à exister et être reconnu malgré l'impossibilité d'exercer certaines de ses fonctions. Il est caractéristique que la résolution 794 (1992) du Conseil de sécurité de l'ONU ne s'adresse pas aux autorités somaliennes, mais aux «all parties, movements and factions in Somalia». Selon le Rapport du Secrétaire général sur la situation en Somalie du 22 juillet 1992 (S/24343), «Somalia is today a country without central, regional or local administration, and without services». La situation au Libéria au début des années 1990 ou au Rwanda en 1994 ressemblait à beaucoup d'égards à celle de la Somalie. Ces pays conservent cependant leur statut d'Etat et restent membres de l'ONU, leur situation étant considérée comme transitoire et exceptionnelle.

L'Etat polonais a existé pendant la deuxième guerre mondiale malgré l'annexion ou l'occupation de l'ensemble de son territoire par l'Allemagne et l'Union soviétique. De même, l'Allemagne n'a pas cessé d'exister en 1945 malgré la prise du pouvoir suprême dans ce pays par les Puissances (*voir supra* V.A.2.ii.).

[65] Il faut notamment prendre en considération le caractère effectif du pouvoir, la reconnaissance internationale (même si l'on considère celle-ci comme non constitutive), la conformité avec le droit des gens de la naissance d'un Etat (*e.g.* problème de la sécession) ou de l'extension de la compétence d'un Etat à un autre territoire (*e.g.* l'agression). Pour certains aspects voir *e.g.* J. Abr. FROWEIN, DAS DE FACTO-REGIME IM VÖLKERRECHT (1968).

une dictature ou se trouve sous une domination (dépendance) politique ou économique extérieure qui suppriment ou limitent sensiblement la souveraineté du peuple. Cependant, selon le droit international, la suppression de la souveraineté populaire n'aboutit pas automatiquement à la disparition de la souveraineté de l'Etat.

Les Etats – en se référant à la notion de domaine réservé – ont souvent tendance à invoquer leur souveraineté pour justifier les violations du droit international. Celui-ci évolue cependant vers la protection plus efficace non seulement de l'Etat (donc de sa souveraineté), mais aussi de sa population et des valeurs communes de l'humanité (*e.g.* le problème de la destruction, ayant des conséquences internationales, de l'environnement ou celui des droits de l'homme). On affronte ainsi le problème de la légitimité démocratique des Etats et, dans ce contexte, celui de la souveraineté de l'Etat et du rôle du droit international[66]. Pour louable que soit la tendance à prendre en compte cet aspect, elle comporte un risque de manipulation politique ou de sélectivité abusive[67] qui résulte du rapport des forces international, des faiblesses du contrôle international et de la nature du droit des gens.

Notons cependant que – contrairement à certaines opinions – la souveraineté de l'Etat n'est pas en train de se dissoudre avec l'intensité croissante des relations internationales et avec l'évolution du droit des gens. Nous sommes plutôt témoins d'une nouvelle perception de cette notion, de même que de la fonction de l'Etat et du rôle du droit international[68]. On peut même penser que le droit des gens s'oriente vers un droit de finalités largement conçues.

---

[66] TH.M. FRANCK, *The Emerging Right to Democratic Governance*, AMERICAN JOURNAL OF INTERNATIONAL LAW, vol. 86 (1992), n° 1, pp. 46–91. Le caractère démocratique d'un Etat ou la légitimité démocratique de son gouvernement ont longtemps été négligé par le droit des gens. Notons, par exemple, qu'il n'existe pas en droit des gens un droit (du peuple ou de l'individu) au régime démocratique (sur le plan politique interne on pourrait éventuellement déduire ce droit de la notion de souveraineté populaire). Dans ce, contexte, la notion de souveraineté de l'Etat renforce non seulement le *status quo* international, mais aussi certains régimes dictatoriaux qui ne cessent pas de se prévaloir de leur domaine réservé. Parmi les exceptions figure l'action (critiquée) du Conseil de sécurité de l'ONU contre le régime illégitime d'Haïti, *voir* ses résolutions 904 (1994), 917 (1994) et 940 (1994). *Voir* aussi *infra*, note 76.

[67] Il faut notamment penser à l'application de critères supplémentaires dans les cas de reconnaissance (sélective) de certains Etats ou gouvernements ou à la condamnation seulement de certains régimes.

[68] *Voir* S. SUR, *Sur quelques tribulations de l'Etat dans la société internationale*, REVUE GÉNÉRALE DE DROIT INTERNATIONAL PUBLIC (1993), n° 3, p. 885; CH. SCHREUER, *The Waning of the Sovereign State: Towards a New Paradigm for International Law?*, JOURNAL EUROPÉEN DE DROIT INTERNATIONAL, vol. 4 (1993), n° 4, pp. 447–471; A.-M. SLAUGHTER, *International Law in a World of Liberal States*, JOURNAL EUROPÉEN DE DROIT INTERNATIONAL, vol. 6 (1995), n° 4, pp. 503–538.

VI

La souveraineté de l'Etat est protégée par le droit des gens. Cette protection résulte, bien entendu, de plusieurs normes particulières dont le nombre et la teneur changent selon le cas. Parmi les normes du droit universel, une importance essentielle incombe à l'établissement de l'égalité des souverainetés, à l'interdiction de l'emploi de la force et à l'interdiction de l'intervention. Cependant, le vrai problème porte non seulement sur la protection et sa portée, mais aussi sur l'étendue et l'efficacité du contrôle international. C'est là que se situe le point névralgique du système des relations internationales.

A. L'égalité des deux ou plusieurs sujets, objets ou situations signifie qu'ils appartiennent à la même classe, celle-ci étant distinguée en fonction d'un ou de plusieurs caractères (traits) choisis à cet effet. Les critères de distinction sont parfois subjectifs et se fondent sur certaines valeurs. Certains sujets sont égaux à certains égards, mais – en même temps – inégaux à certains autres. Le principe d'égalité ne signifie donc autre chose que la nécessité de traiter de manière égale des situations définies comme égales et de façon inégale les situations inégales[69].

En droit international universel, le principe d'égalité[70] concerne surtout la souveraineté des Etats. En dehors de ce principe, le droit des gens ne connaît pas une règle universelle d'égalité des Etats, ce qui n'exclut pas que, à certains égards, la réglementation internationale particulière (*e.g.* les statuts d'une organisation internationale) puisse établir certaines préférences ou l'égalité entre divers groupes de pays et tenter d'aplanir ainsi les différences de fait.

B. La catégorie des compétences de l'Etat dont l'exercice n'est pas réglementé par les normes particulières du droit international porte le nom – pas tout à fait précis – de domaine réservé (on parle aussi d'affaires intérieures d'un Etat).

L'étendue de ce domaine n'est pas facile à définir[71]. La difficulté consiste à déterminer l'état de la réglementation internationale et à désigner les

---

[69] Le problème essentiel se ramène à la question de savoir qui (quoi) est (ou doit être) égal, par rapport à qui (à quoi), à quel égard, en raison de quels buts ou valeurs et qui doit en décider. L'obligation de traiter de manière égale les situations égales ne nous fournit pas de réponse générale à ces questions, elle est seulement une directive juridique.

[70] *Voir* notamment l'article 2 (1) de la Charte des Nations unies et la résolution 2625 (XXV) de l'Assemblée générale de l'ONU du 24 octobre 1970.

[71] Aux termes de la résolution de l'Institut de Droit international, «le domaine réservé est celui des activités étatiques où la compétence de l'Etat n'est pas liée par le droit international. L'étendue de ce domaine dépend du droit international et varie suivant son développement», ANNUAIRE DE L'INSTITUT DE DROIT INTERNATIONAL, vol. 45, t. II, p. 293 (session d'Aix-en-Provence en 1954).

organes et les procédures pour trancher les controverses qui apparaissent dans ce contexte. Notons cependant que la notion d'affaires internes ne se définit pas en fonction de la nature même d'une question, mais selon que celle-ci soit ou non réglementée (pour un Etat) par le droit international. Le fait que, pour un Etat donné et à un moment donné, une matière relève de la réglementation internationale fait sortir cette matière du domaine réservé de celui-ci.

La notion de domaine réservé est inséparable de celle de souveraineté, car en mettant l'accent sur l'absence des obligations internationales particulières d'un Etat, on souligne en même temps son indépendance dans la détermination et dans l'exercice de ses compétences. Il s'agit d'un domaine où l'Etat doit rester libre dans ses actes et, dans une autre perspective, où un autre Etat doit être protégé contre les actes du premier, lesquels – sans être interdits – sont légaux seulement jusqu'à un certain degré, déterminé par les normes prohibitives du droit international universel.

Selon Politis, «le droit international reconnaît l'existence d'un domaine réservé», mais «il en ignore le contenu»[72]. Si ce droit est la seule référence pour définir l'étendue du domaine réservé, il ne fournit pas de critères qui permettent de la faire *in abstracto*. En effet, il n'existe pas un domaine réservé commun à tous les Etats, mais seulement le domaine réservé d'un Etat concret, à un moment donné et dans un contexte donné.

L'absence d'une règle juridique internationale particulière ne signifie point que le droit des gens réserve – d'avance et définitivement – certaines matières à la compétence nationale et exclut ainsi la possibilité de leur réglementation internationale, «mais seulement que, en fait, aucune obligation internationale n'a encore été créée» dans un domaine, une situation qui peut changer à tout moment[73]. Le domaine réservé constitue donc un reflet de la souveraineté.

Le domaine réservé est connu des documents internationaux et de la doctrine du droit international sous diverses appellations. Les textes internationaux témoignent de l'absence d'une cohérence terminologique dans les termes utilisés pour désigner les compétences étatiques dont l'exercice n'est pas réglementé par le droit international particulier[74]. Cette confusion ne semble pas grave aussi longtemps que l'essence des notions employées

---

[72] N. POLITIS, *op. cit., supra* note 2, p. 48.

[73] M. VIRALLY dans son cours général à La Haye, RCADI, t. 183 (1983–V), p. 82; dans le même sens G. ARANGIO-RUIZ, *op. cit., supra* note 4, pp. 368, 370–371; N. POLITIS, *op. cit., supra* note 2, p. 48; CH. ROUSSEAU, DROIT…, *op. cit., supra* note 2, p. 88; S. JOVANOVIĆ, *op. cit., supra* note 15, p. 97.

[74] *Voir* J. KRANZ, ENTRE L'INFLUENCE ET L'INTERVENTION. CERTAINS ASPECTS JURIDIQUES DE L'ASSISTANCE FINANCIÈRE MULTILATÉRALE, Frankfurt/M (1994), pp. 69–74.

ne fait pas l'objet de controverse. Cependant, certains auteurs tentent de distinguer entre la notion apparemment plus restreinte de domaine réservé et celle, plus large, d'affaires intérieures et extérieures. Cette opinion est difficile à partager[75].

La qualification d'une affaire comme faisant partie de la compétence nationale exclusive pose de nombreux problèmes. La pratique internationale, assez courante et peu satisfaisante à cet égard, consiste souvent en ce que les Etats définissent unilatéralement l'étendue de leur domaine réservé.

Une autre difficulté porte sur la question de savoir s'il existe des matières qui ne peuvent pas relever de la réglementation internationale. Il est vrai que certains domaines sensibles font rarement l'objet de la réglementation internationale, *e.g.* le système politique, économique et social de l'Etat[76]. Il n'existe cependant pas un catalogue de matières qui seraient *a priori* exclues de la réglementation internationale, bien que – à un moment – on puisse prétendre qu'une question relève du domaine non réglementé par le droit des gens.

---

[75] Elle s'inspire, au moins en partie, de l'article 15, paragraphe 8, du Pacte de la Société des Nations et de l'avis consultatif de la CPJI du 7 février 1923 au sujet des décrets de nationalité promulgués en Tunisie et au Maroc (série B, n° 4). Pour la discussion de ce sujet *voir* J. KRANZ, *op. cit.*, *supra* note 74, pp. 93–95.

[76] Notons cependant que les dispositions de certains traités et l'évolution des normes juridiques internationales relatives à la protection des droits de l'homme limitent la liberté des Etats dans le choix des éléments de leur régime interne. Par exemple, le traité de Versailles (1919) et certains traités conclus dans son exécution imposaient notamment à quelques pays d'Europe centrale (*e.g.* à la Pologne) des obligations relatives à leur droit interne en matière de protection des minorités nationales. L'établissement d'un régime démocratique en Allemagne ou des élections libres en Pologne furent l'objet de l'accord des Alliés conclu à Potsdam, le 2 août 1945. Pour certains engagements du Nicaragua concernant son régime étatique après la chute du dictateur Somoza, *voir* l'opinion dissidente du juge Schwebel sur l'arrêt de la CIJ dans l'affaire *Nicaragua c. Etats-Unis d'Amérique*, RECUEIL (1986), pp. 398–402. L'assistance financière multilatérale est parfois expressément conditionnée par le respect des droits de l'homme, de la démocratie pluraliste et de l'économie de marché – *e.g.* l'article 5 de la Convention CEE-ACP (Lomé IV) de 1990 ou l'article 1er des statuts de la Banque européenne pour la reconstruction et le développement (1990). L'accord de Paris sur le Cambodge du 23 octobre 1991, conclu par plusieurs pays avec le Cambodge, imposait à ce pays (avec son consentement) certains éléments de sa future constitution (y compris la neutralité du Cambodge et la protection constitutionnelle de certains droits de l'homme) et plaçait (pour une période transitoire) les autorités administratives de ce pays sous le «contrôle direct» de «United Nations Transitional Authority in Cambodia», celle-ci étant entre autres compétente à organiser des élections et à suspendre ou abroger (en consultation avec le Conseil national suprême cambodgien) des lois contraires aux buts de l'Accord. Le régime démocratique d'un Etat peut avoir une influence sur sa reconnaissance internationale par certains Etats, cf. à cet égard la déclaration de la Communauté européenne et de ses Etats membres sur les lignes directrices sur la reconnaissance des nouveaux Etats en Europe orientale et en Union soviétique (16 décembre 1991) et leur déclaration sur la Yougoslavie (16 décembre 1991) ainsi que l'avis de la Commission d'arbitrage de la Conférence européenne pour la paix en Yougoslavie (29 novembre 1991). *Voir supra*, note 49 et note 66.

C. La délimitation des compétences relevant du domaine réservé d'un Etat ne résout pas toutes les difficultés, car les actes de l'Etat, accomplis dans le cadre de son domaine réservé, posent le problème de l'intervention. En droit international, l'intervention signifie, toujours et par définition, un acte illicite, interdit par le principe juridique de non-intervention. Par conséquent, il n'existe pas d'intervention légale, comme il n'existe pas d'agression légale[77].

Si l'intervention se traduit par une pression sur le domaine réservé de l'Etat visé, l'un des plus grands malentendus, au moins sur le plan juridique, consiste à croire que toute tentative (qui ne se fonde pas sur un titre du droit des gens) d'influencer le comportement d'un Etat dans son domaine réservé constitue l'intervention.

Un autre malentendu consiste à estimer que, en l'absence d'une norme juridique internationale particulière, les Etats – en invoquant leur souveraineté ou leur pouvoir discrétionnaire – puissent agir comme ils entendent. Cette approche rendrait vain le principe de non-intervention.

Pourtant, c'est bien ce principe (norme prohibitive du droit international universel) qui protège les domaines non protégés par le droit international particulier, mais il ne les protège pas contre toute sorte de pression. Le principe de non-intervention a pour fonction d'établir une balance entre l'exercice par un Etat de ses compétences non réglementées par les normes particulières du droit international et le domaine réservé d'un autre Etat.

Pour garder un certain réalisme, la définition de l'intervention doit laisser un espace suffisant au développement des influences internationales (y compris des actes considérés comme inamicaux). Pour que la pression d'un Etat sur le domaine réservé d'un autre se transforme en intervention, il faut envisager l'existence de conditions supplémentaires. On s'approche ainsi de la définition du verbe «intervenir».

L'examen de la pression sur le domaine réservé doit prendre en considération deux aspects. En premier lieu, il faut que la pression d'un Etat, exercée sans titre particulier du droit des gens, s'accompagne de l'éventualité d'un effet négatif pour l'exercice par l'Etat visé de ses fonctions étatiques (certains effets négatifs sont également possibles chez l'Etat qui agit, mais celui-ci les admet souvent d'avance). En deuxième lieu, l'application de la pression (toujours sans titre juridique international) se caractérise par un rapport déraisonnable (reprochable) entre le but poursuivi et les moyens appliqués[78].

---

[77] Les actes conformes au droit des gens ne constituent pas une intervention. C'est notamment le cas de la réaction à l'illicite, sous réserve de respecter les conditions d'application des normes particulières sur lesquelles elle se fonde (*e.g.* les conditions d'application des représailles).

[78] D.W. BOWETT, *International Law and Economic Coercion*, VIRGINIA JOURNAL OF INTERNATIONAL LAW, vol. 16 (1976), p. 249, avance notamment le concept de *conspiracy*, connu du

Que la pression aboutisse effectivement, qu'on l'annonce seulement ou qu'on essaie de l'appliquer est sans importance pour la définition de l'intervention. Considérer les pressions sur le domaine réservé comme illégales seulement lorsqu'elles ont atteint leur but n'est pas pertinent, car on déplace ainsi le problème vers les possibilités réelles de défense de l'Etat visé et vers l'efficacité de sa résistance à la pression. Il faut plutôt estimer que l'intervention est – pour utiliser la terminologie allemande – un *Handlungsdelikt*[79] et que le principe de non-intervention est, comme son nom l'indique, une obligation négative consistant à ne pas exercer certaines pressions.

La difficulté essentielle consiste à trouver des mesures juridiques adéquates qui permettent de déterminer si, dans une situation concrète, la pression sur le domaine réservé est légale. A cet égard, la nature des moyens appliqués sera déterminante dans le cas des pressions militaires. La relation entre les motifs, le but poursuivi et les moyens appliqués sera d'une importance primordiale dans le cas des pressions non militaires.

L'intervention, en tant que notion du droit international, se caractérise par les traits suivants:

- elle est l'oeuvre d'un Etat ou d'un groupe d'Etats;
- elle consiste en une pression intentionnelle qui ne s'appuie pas sur une norme du droit des gens;
- la pression concerne l'orientation de l'exercice par l'Etat visé de ses compétences non réglementées par les normes particulières du droit des gens; elle a donc pour but d'influencer (changement ou conservation) l'Etat dans son domaine réservé;
- la pression consiste dans l'application illégale des moyens de pression militaires (interdits par le principe de non-emploi de la force et, dans certains cas, par celui de non-intervention) ou non militaires (interdits par le principe de non-intervention et mesurés à l'aide des standards juridiques de proportionnalité et de *reasonableness*);
- que le but envisagé soit atteint ou non est sans importance pour la définition.

Cette définition prend en considération le bien protégé (le domaine réservé ou, de manière plus générale, la souveraineté), la nature des moyens

---

droit britannique, comme critère de la légalité des pressions économiques exercées sans titre du droit des gens. Selon lui, «in English law a necessary element of the tort of 'economic conspiracy' is that the defendant's predominant purpose or motive be to cause injury to the plaintiff rather than to advance or protect his own interests».

79 K. BOCKSLAFF, DAS VÖLKERRECHTLICHE INTERVENTIONSVERBOT ALS SCHRANKE AUßENPOLITISCH MOTIVIERTER HANDELSBESCHRÄNKUNGEN, Berlin (1987), p. 85; A. VAN WYNEN THOMAS, A.J. THOMAS, NON-INTERVENTION. THE LAW AND ITS IMPORT IN THE AMERICAS, Dallas (1956), p. 72; D.W. BOWETT, *op. cit.*, *supra* note 78, p. 249.

utilisés ainsi que la relation entre les motifs, le but poursuivi et les moyens appliqués. La constatation d'une intervention relève donc d'une qualification des circonstances de droit et de fait ainsi que de leur appréciation en fonction de certaines valeurs, avec toutes les difficultés que comporte une telle opération. Par conséquent, les tentatives visant à déterminer un seuil fixe de l'intervention semblent vouées à l'échec.

Cette définition englobe aussi l'élément dit dictatorial[80], souvent cité dans ce contexte. Le caractère dictatorial de l'acte d'un Etat à l'égard d'un autre constitue un élément important de l'appréciation. Cependant, sauf pour l'application des moyens militaires, il ne suffit pas de dire que l'intervention consiste en une pression dictatoriale, car ce caractère est une chose relative qui change selon les circonstances. En cherchant un instrument de mesure, il faut prendre en considération la relation entre les motifs, le but et les moyens. A cet égard, les principes de proportionnalité et de *reasonableness*, bien établis en droit national et international[81], semblent des outils appropriés pour déceler les pressions illégales.

Cette conception du principe de non-intervention vise surtout à ne pas l'appliquer comme une norme caoutchouc. D'une part, il s'agit d'éviter de qualifier d'intervention tout acte inamical ou toute pression sur le domaine réservé d'un Etat. D'autre part, la notion d'intervention ne doit pas s'appliquer automatiquement à des situations où l'auteur de l'acte dépasse les compétences et pouvoirs fondés sur une norme particulière du droit des gens et notamment agit pour un motif inexistant ou erroné, poursuit un but illégal (détournement de pouvoir), ne respecte pas la forme ou les procédures requises, car cela sont des sources autonomes de l'illégalité qu'il faudrait appliquer en première ligne. Cependant, on ne doit pas considérer cette approche comme un soutien sans réserve apporté au concept de *self-contained regimes*.

Le principe de non-intervention est une obligation négative (ne pas faire). Sa fonction consiste à protéger contre les pressions spécifiquement qualifiées les domaines non protégés par les normes particulières du droit des gens. La non-intervention constitue un standard minimum de protection et un contrepoids nécessaire à l'exercice du pouvoir discrétionnaire des Etats. Ce principe joue donc un rôle correcteur général en vue de prévenir l'arbitraire

---

[80] On pense surtout à la définition suivante: «intervention is dictatorial interference by a State in the affairs of another State for the purpose of maintaining or altering the actual condition of things», L. OPPENHEIM, H. LAUTERPACHT, INTERNATIONAL LAW. A TREATISE, London, New York, Toronto (1955), t. Ier, p. 305.

[81] *Voir e.g.* J. DELBRÜCK, *Proportionality*, dans: EPIL, t. 7 (1984), pp. 396–400; J. SALMON, *Le concept de raisonnable en droit international public*, dans: MÉLANGES OFFERTS À PAUL REUTER, Paris (1981), pp. 447–478; S. JOVANOVIĆ, *op. cit.*, *supra* note 15, pp. 147–168.

et d'éliminer la transmission directe du rapport des forces aux relations internationales. La conception précitée du principe de non-intervention revêt ainsi un caractère subsidiaire.

VII

Notre analyse mène à la conclusion que – au point de vue du droit des gens – la souveraineté est une qualité particulière (attribut) de l'Etat et une notion du droit des gens qui distinguent l'Etat parmi les autres sujets de ce droit.

La souveraineté est une situation factuelle qui trouve son reflet dans le droit international. Cette notion du droit des gens n'est cependant pas une norme de ce droit, comme on le prétend souvent. S'il s'agissait d'une norme, il faudrait préciser son contenu. Cela (au moins à la lumière de notre conception) est difficilement concevable. On doit plutôt estimer que la norme fondamentale à cet égard est celle qui proclame l'égalité des souverainetés étatiques, avec toutes les conséquences qui en découlent.

La souveraineté n'énonce aucune règle juridique qui aurait un contenu matériel fixe et précis. Il n'existe pas un minimum formel de souveraineté dans le sens d'un catalogue de matières ou compétences fixé d'avance.

L'essence de la souveraineté consiste en l'aptitude (capacité) d'une organisation politique de fonctionner (d'exercer ses compétences relatives au territoire, aux personnes et à l'ordre juridique et social relevant de la compétence de l'Etat) en tant que centre de direction et système décisionnel indépendants des autres Etats.

La souveraineté n'a pas un caractère absolu, car l'exercice des compétences d'un Etat trouve ses limites dans les compétences des autres Etats (égalité des souverainetés établie par le droit des gens) et dans les normes du droit international qui lient chaque Etat. Evoquer la souveraineté limitée, la nécessité de recouvrer la pleine souveraineté ou bien diviser la souveraineté en politique, économique etc. témoigne d'une fausse conception de cette notion. Les divisions de ce genre sont insatisfaisantes et sèment la confusion, car la souveraineté est une notion qualitative et non quantitative.

Le problème essentiel consiste à déterminer si et dans quelle mesure les limitations subies par l'Etat dans l'exercice de ses compétences restent en conformité avec le droit international et quels en sont d'éventuelles conséquences juridiques.

En admettant que la souveraineté n'est pas une norme juridique et que le droit international ne la crée pas, celui-ci la protège à travers ses normes particulières et universelles. Parmi ces dernières, le principe de l'égalité des souverainetés, l'interdiction de l'intervention ou l'interdiction de l'emploi de la force jouent un rôle essentiel. Par conséquent, les atteintes à la souveraineté se définissent à travers les violations des normes du droit international qui la protègent et non par la violation du prétendu principe juridique de souveraineté. Il faut donc distinguer entre les limitations (légales) dans l'exercice des compétences étatiques et les atteintes (illégales) à la souveraineté.

Même si la souveraineté devient souvent un slogan ou un mot magique, cela ne veut pas dire qu'elle soit devenue obsolète, mais plutôt que l'emploi de ce terme est trop arbitraire et peu uniforme. L'interdépendance croissante dans les relations internationales ne supprime pas la valeur de cette notion. Les problèmes que cache la souveraineté sont nombreux, importants et actuels, aussi bien pour la théorie que pour la pratique, pour le droit des gens et pour les relations internationales.

The Juridical and the Meta-Juridical in International Law

by

Elihu Lauterpacht

On 13 October 1994, the President of the International Court of Justice ("the ICJ"), M. Mohammed Bedjaoui, made a statement in the United Nations General Assembly which has an important bearing on a perennial problem in the judicial application of law: to what extent should a court be influenced in its judgment by other than strictly legal considerations?

As will be immediately apparent, to state the issue in this way is hardly jurisprudentially elegant. It assumes something that is itself highly debatable, namely, that it is possible in the judicial sphere to distinguish between considerations which are "strictly legal" and considerations which are not. A judgment that may strike one reader as admirably "legal" in its premises and conclusions may appear to another to be riddled by a whole range of extra-legal elements. While in each case the analysis may seem to be entirely "objective" in character, its outcome will necessarily depend upon the analyst's own preconceptions, some of which may be "objective" and others "subjective", according to the stance of the critic.

Subject, however, to the reservation just expressed it can hardly be gainsaid that there is a spectrum of judicial approaches ranging from, at one extreme, a narrowly technical approach to, at the other, a deliberately law-creative approach. The question is where on this spectrum should the work of an international tribunal and, in particular, of the ICJ fall?

The present reference to a problem which has occupied so large a place in legal literature[1] is occasioned by the terms of the President's address in

---

[1] So extensive is the literature that only a few items can be mentioned below, with apologies to the authors of the many equally interesting titles which have been omitted: C.K. Allen, Law in the Making (1964) 7th ed.; A. Barak, Judicial Discretion (1989); D. Bethlehem, *The Proper Role of International Adjudication*, paper delivered at a meeting of the British Branch of the International Law Association, May 1996 (not yet published); A.R. Brewer-Carias, Judicial Review in Comparative Law (1989); M. Cappelletti, The Judicial Process in Comparative Perspective (1989); B.N. Cardozo, The Nature of the Judicial Process; T.M. Franck, Fairness in International Law and Institutions (1995), esp. Chapter 10, *Judicial Fairness: The International Court of Justice*; K.M. Holland (ed.), Judicial Activism in Comparative Perspective (1991); Lauterpacht, The Development of International Law by the International Court (1958); S. Shetreet (ed.), The Role of Courts in Society (1988); M. Shahabuddeen, *Municipal Reason-*

1994 to the General Assembly in connection with the submission to that body of the Annual Report of the Court. The President's concern was to encourage States to refer to the Court not merely more, but more significant, legal disputes. In developing the theme that the Court "is perfectly able, for all the modest material resources at its command, simply and effectively to fulfil the functions entrusted to it by the Charter", the President referred to the order for provisional measures made in 1986 in the *Burkina Faso/Mali*[2] case and to the acceptance by the Parties of the 1994 judgment of the Court in the *Libya/Chad*[3] case. The President suggested that

> "some States may perhaps tend to have misgivings about judicial settlement on the grounds that, unlike a political settlement, it would be completely outside their control and hence, given the reputed rigidity of legal rules, always liable in the end to turn out less favourably to themselves."

To meet this supposed concern of States the President continued:

> "I think I can safely say here that such fears are largely groundless. The Court, by the nature of the law it applies, by the role it fulfils and by its composition, is better able than any other judicial institution to withstand blind applications of the law. While being sufficiently precise to offer those who come before it all the legal security to which they legitimately aspire, international law remains at the same time and in essence a flexible and open law."

After mentioning that the Court by no means rules out "due regard for equity *infra legem*" and noting particularly the application of equitable principles in connection with the law of the sea, the President concluded:

> "The Court takes its decisions on the basis of law, following a most minute and meticulous examination of each case, **without failing to take account of the meta-juridical factors, the expectations of the parties and the imperative requirements of peace and justice.**"[4]

ing in International Law, in: V. LOWE & M. FITZMAURICE (eds.), FIFTY YEARS OF THE INTERNATIONAL COURT OF JUSTICE (1996), p. 90; P. WEIL, *L'Equité dans la jurisprudence de la Cour Internationale de Justice*, *ibid.* p. 121.

[2] *Frontier Dispute, Provisional Measures*, Order of 10 January 1986, ICJ REPORTS 1986, p. 3.

[3] *Territorial Dispute (Libyan Arab Jamahiriya/Chad)*, Judgment, ICJ REPORTS 1994, p. 6.

[4] To do full justice to the President's speech it should be read as a whole. *See* U.N. General Assembly, Official Records, Forty-ninth session, 29th Meeting, 13 October, 1994.

It is to the meaning and implication of this last sentence that the present essay is particularly directed.

The statement that the Court takes its decisions on the basis of law, following a most minute and meticulous examination of each case is, of course, unexceptionable. This is exactly what one would expect of the principal judicial organ of the United Nations. The real problem arises from the continuation of the statement with its reference to the Court taking account of the "meta-juridical factors". What are we to make of this expression?

There are two possible approaches. One involves attributing a specific meaning to the expression. However, the critical reader need only turn his attention to the article on *Métathéorie* in the *Dictionnaire encyclopédique de théorie et de sociologie du droit* (1993) to appreciate the difficulty that exists for anyone seeking to define "metajuridical" in simple objective terms.

It seems more effective, therefore, to adopt another approach, that of assessing the impact of the word relative to the rest of the sentence in which it appears. As the expression was used in seeming contrast with the word "juridical", the reader may reasonably conclude that "meta-juridical" is something outside the ordinary legal order.

According to commonly accepted doctrine relating to the functioning of the Court, a clear distinction is to be maintained between the application by the Court of "law" and the application of any other, non-legal, criterion to the determination of a case. Thus, Article 38(1) of the Statute of the Court specifically declares that it is the "function" of the Court to decide cases "in accordance with law". It is in elaboration of that principle that that paragraph then refers to treaties, custom, general principles of law, judicial decisions and the writings of publicists.

The second paragraph of that Article, on the other hand, permits the Court to decide a case *ex aequo et bono*, that is to say, by reference to non-legal considerations – but only if the parties expressly so request.

Given this clear distinction between the primary duty of the Court to decide by reference to law and its reserve power to decide by reference to considerations other than law at the request of the parties, it seems perfectly justifiable to associate the word "juridical" with the primary duty. The implication then follows that something that is not "juridical" falls outside the scope of the exercise by the Court of its function to decide cases in accordance with law. On that basis, it would not matter whether this other concept is called "meta-juridical" or any other kind of "juridical". The very fact that it is not equated with "juridical" must mean that it embraces considerations outside the law. Approached in this way, the absolute or objective meaning of "meta-juridical" is not so important. As used in the President's statement it must mean "something other than strictly legal".

To this clear dichotomy between legal or "juridical" considerations, on the one hand, and non-legal or "meta-juridical" considerations, on the other, there have hitherto appeared to be only two, not easily distinguishable, exceptions on, so to speak, the "legal" side of the line – the side which for its use does **not** require the additional express request of the parties. The first is the general power of the Court to apply existing rules of law to new situations and thereby to extend and develop the law in a manner familiar to all systems of jurisprudence whether codified or decision-led. But this process, though undoubtedly one which involves change in the law, in the sense that the law after the decision is no longer the same as the law before it, is not **avowedly** an exercise in law-making. It does not involve going outside or beyond the law. It is merely the development of the law inherent in the proper application of the normal judicial process. The extent to which the law is changed as a result depends in part upon the imagination, ingenuity and sense of direction of the judge who makes the "new" rule and in part upon the extent to which the quality of the new rule commends itself generally to the international community and particularly to the judges before whom it is subsequently invoked.

The second exception involves the use "within the law" of "equity". In this sense, equity is the application by the Court not of "rules" of equity but of equitable "principles" or "criteria", the contents of which are not predetermined but are variable according to the needs of the case. The principal illustration of this kind of equity is to be found in the law that has been developed in relation to the delimitation of the continental shelf in and since the judgment of the Court in the *North Sea Continental Shelf* cases.[5]

If the President's reference to "meta-juridical" was intended to refer to either of these two aspects of the application of "law", then evidently there can be no objection to it – save for the fact that it may raise expectations, which could possibly be disappointed, of a more dynamic and, therefore, more controversial use of its powers by the Court.

This possibility, that the President did not intend his words to go beyond the traditional, accepted, understanding of the scope of Article 38(1) of the Statute, is not necessarily to be excluded. It would be supported by the fact that the reference to "meta-juridical factors" was immediately followed by the words "... the expectations of the parties and the imperative requirements of justice and peace". Mention of "the expectation of the parties" must necessarily refer to the **common** expectations of the parties since it is not to be

---

[5] *North Sea Continental Shelf* cases, Judgment, ICJ REPORTS 1969, p. 3.

contemplated that the Court would pay heed to the expectation of one party in preference to that of the other – unless there was some legal reason for doing so. And the only common expectation that the parties could share in going to the Court would, in the absence of special agreement, be that the Court would apply the law. Moreover, few would dissent from the view that the associated invocation of "the imperative requirements of justice and peace" is so general as not to suggest, on the basis of this sole mention of them, that the President had in mind something outside the law.

Yet the fact remains that use was made of the expression "meta-juridical factors" in what could only have been a considered manner on an important occasion, in the most comprehensive of international assemblies. One must, therefore, probe further the significance of the observation.

There are at least two ways in which one may attempt to give content to the concept. First, one may seek examples of specific ideas or approaches (outside the rules of law strictly applicable to the problem) which the Court has specifically declared may **not** be taken into consideration in the determination of the **legal** position. For example, economic factors, such as the absence of energy resources in the territory of one party, the relatively limited development of its economy and industry, as well as considerations of security were all held in the *Libya/Malta Continental Shelf* case[6] **not** to be relevant to the Court's determination of the continental shelf boundary, despite the Court's recourse, on the basis of established precedent, to "equitable principles". Earlier, in the *Barcelona Traction* case (*Second Phase*),[7] the Court had rejected the argument, based on "equity", that Belgium was entitled to protect Belgian shareholders in a Canadian company despite the fact that they had suffered clear economic loss as a result of measures taken against the company by Spain. Given the fact of that rejection, the Belgian arguments about the economic reality of the loss and the fact that such losses had been regarded in State practice as entitled to recognition and remedial action would also presumably fall to be classified as non-legal or "meta-juridical". Again, if the Court or, indeed, any other international tribunal, were confronted by the question of whether the maintenance by one State of certain tariffs violated agreed limits, such factors as the burden upon one party of paying the tariffs under challenge or the effect upon employment in the other of the elimination of the tariffs would be "meta-juridical factors" not properly to be considered by the tribunal.

---

6 *Continental Shelf (Libyan Arab Jamahiriya/Malta)*, Judgment, ICJ REPORTS 1985, p. 13.

7 *Barcelona Traction, Light and Power Company, Limited (Second Phase)*, Judgment, ICJ REPORTS 1970, p. 3.

A second way in which one may attempt to give the "meta-juridical" concept a meaning is to look at it in terms of tendencies discernible in the jurisprudence of the Court. Evidently this is not the occasion on which to attempt a comprehensive survey of the Court's practice. However, one need examine no more than three relatively recent judgments of the Court to perceive the limited support there to be found for any suggestion that during the period covered by these cases, the Court has looked at matters in a "non-legal", "broad" or "liberal" manner. The remainder of this small essay will, therefore, be devoted to a scrutiny of the judgments of the Court in the jurisdictional phase of *Qatar v. Bahrain*,[8] the *East Timor*[9] case and in what has come to be called *Nuclear Tests II*.[10] Only in the first of these does one find a flexibility of approach that begins to approach the concept of "meta-juridical" referred to by President Bedjaoui.[11]

The decision in the *Qatar v. Bahrain* case may be read as providing general support for the identification of an inclination of the Court to approach procedural matters in a relatively fluid manner. In providing a further illustration of the principle that in procedural matters the Court will not insist on rigid formalism, this judgment adds weight to the view that the Court's approach goes beyond the juridical towards the meta-juridical. In the field of procedure, this can hardly be made the subject of adverse comment – except in so far as this approach contributes further to a general sense of unpredictability in the Court's jurisprudence.

The specific contribution of this case lies in its elaboration of the procedural significance (or insignificance) of the application instituting proceedings. Article 40(1) of the Statute provides:

> "Cases are brought before the Court, as the case may be, either by the notification of the special agreement or by a written application addressed to the Registrar. In either case the subject of the dispute and the parties shall be indicated."

The received wisdom has been that the existence of the Court's jurisdiction must be determined by reference to the moment of the filing of the

[8] *Maritime Delimitation and Territorial Questions between Qatar and Bahrain, Jurisdiction and Admissibility*, Judgment, ICJ REPORTS 1995, p. 6.

[9] *East Timor (Portugal v. Australia)*, Judgment, ICJ REPORTS 1995, p. 90.

[10] *Request for an Examination of the Situation in Accordance with Paragraph 63 of the Court's Judgment of 20 December 1974 in the Nuclear Tests (New Zealand v. France)* case, ICJ REPORTS 1995, p. 288. The decision takes the form of an Order, albeit an extended one, rather than of a Judgment.

[11] At the time of writing, the Court has under deliberation two further matters: the requests of the U.N. General Assembly and of the World Health Organization for advisory opinions on the

application. Thus, in the *Nottebohm*[12] case the existence of the jurisdictional link between Liechtenstein as applicant and Guatemala as respondent was assessed at the moment of the application. The fact that Guatemala's acceptance of the Optional Clause expired only a short time afterwards and before any significant procedural step had been taken in the case was held not to deprive the Court of the jurisdiction that it acquired at the moment of the application. Once the jurisdiction of the Court was invoked on the basis of two concordant declarations effective at the moment of the application, such jurisdiction remained effective notwithstanding the little delayed change in the position of the respondent.

On the basis of this decision, it was widely believed that the jurisdictional relationship between the parties was fixed at the moment of the application. By the same token, the application was to be regarded as having fixed the substantive scope of the case. This assessment of the role of the application was confirmed by the wording of paragraphs (1) and (2) of Article 38 of the Court's Rules. Moreover, in the absence of any provision in the Rules regarding the amendment of applications, it was understood that the content of an application could only be changed with the consent of the respondent – as was shown in the manner in which the Court permitted the Cameroons to amend the application in its case against Nigeria.[13]

In *Qatar v. Bahrain*,[14] the Court adopted a more relaxed approach to these procedural matters. The case was commenced on the basis of an application filed by Qatar in respect of specific disputes relating to sovereignty over certain islands, sovereign rights over two named maritime features and the delimitation of the maritime areas lying between the two States. As the basis of jurisdiction Qatar invoked two agreements with Bahrain of December 1987 and December 1990. Bahrain objected to the Court's jurisdiction partly because it contested the quality as an agreement of one of the texts upon which Qatar relied and partly because the Qatar Application did not bring into issue one substantive matter (a question relating to a locality called Zubarah) which, in Bahrain's view, formed part of the dispute. Bahrain contended that the Parties had agreed that the whole of the dispute would be

legality of the use of nuclear weapons; and the jurisdictional phase of the case brought by Bosnia-Herzegovina against Yugoslavia regarding the Application of the Genocide Convention. The decisions in both of them are likely to contribute significantly to further discussion of this subject.

12 *Nottebohm* case *(Preliminary Objection)*, Judgment of 18 November 1953, ICJ REPORTS 1953, p. 111.

13 *Land and Maritime Boundary between Cameroon and Nigeria*, Order of 16 June 1994, ICJ REPORTS 1994, p. 105.

14 The author must declare an interest in this case, having been one of the counsel for Bahrain.

submitted to the Court and that the omission of the question of Zubarah breached that agreement. Qatar acknowledged that only part of the dispute had been submitted to the Court by its Application. In other words, the Application did not reflect the whole of the relevant agreements and was, therefore, defective. However, instead of rejecting the Application, as would have been permissible and appropriate, the Court took the unprecedented step of deciding to afford the Parties the opportunity to ensure the submission to it of the entire dispute as foreseen in the pertinent agreement, gave them five months for this purpose and reserved for subsequent decision all such matters as had not been decided in that Judgment.

The Parties failed to reach agreement within the time limit, whereupon Qatar addressed to the Court an "Act to comply"[15] with the relevant paragraphs of the operative part of the Court's previous order. In effect, this was a unilateral amendment of Qatar's original application intended to bring within the scope of the proceedings the question of Zubarah. In commenting upon this Act, Bahrain observed that the Court had not by its initial Judgment found that it had jurisdiction. "Consequently", said Bahrain, "if the Court did not have jurisdiction at that time, then the Qatari separate Act of 30th November, even when considered in the light of the [initial] Judgment, cannot create that jurisdiction or effect a valid submission in the absence of Bahrain's consent."[16]

The Court resumed its consideration of the case without further argument by the Parties. On 15 February 1995 the Court gave a Judgment on Jurisdiction and Admissibility in which it held that it had jurisdiction "to adjudicate upon the dispute submitted to it" between Qatar and Bahrain.[17] The Court did not specify the instruments by which the dispute had been "submitted" to it. Nor, if the Court was of the opinion that submission had not taken place at the date of the original Application, did it explain how it was procedurally possible for the applicant State validly to submit the case afresh at a later date without either discontinuing the proceedings initially commenced or securing the consent of the respondent State. In effect, either the Court treated Qatar's original application as valid, and as having been validly amended by Qatar's subsequent "Act to comply", or the Court treated the Qatari "Act to comply" as a fresh and valid application. Evidently, therefore, we have here an instance of a highly flexible and, in the eyes of some, a liberal or constructive approach to matters of procedure, the end result

15 ICJ REPORTS 1995, pp. 9 and 14.

16 *Ibid.* p. 11.

17 *Ibid.* p. 26.

of which was that the Court found that consent had been given to its jurisdiction despite the fact that the respondent State, Bahrain, was emphatic that it had not given any such consent. For those who favour generally the extension of the Court's jurisdiction, this is no doubt a welcome development. For those who seek a significant degree of predictability in the Court's approach to procedure, it will be less welcome. But certainly the episode may be seen as falling within the scope of the President's concept of being "meta-juridical", in the sense that it was beyond the law as theretofore perceived.[18]

Another respect in which the Court extended its procedural law in this case was in its earlier decision in July 1994 to render a "partial" or interim judgment,[19] giving the Parties an opportunity to reach agreement to submit to the Court the whole of the dispute between them.[20]

The other two cases that will be discussed here – being the remaining decisions of substantive significance decided in the year proceeding this essay – reveal a significantly different tendency on the part of the Court. Neither case can in any way be seen as reflecting a "meta-juridical" approach. Rather, each case appears to represent a decision by the Court to take a narrow and technical view of the matter, thus foregoing the opportunity of developing the law in a significant manner.

The first of these cases is the *East Timor* case.

For many years the eastern part of the Island of Timor was a Portuguese colony. In 1960 Timor was determined by the General Assembly of the United Nations to be a non-self governing territory. In 1975 Portugal sought to negotiate with the rival popular movements in the Territory, of which there were principally two – favouring respectively either complete independence or integration with Indonesia. Fighting broke out between the rival parties and in August 1975 the Portuguese authorities moved from the capital to the adjacent island of Atauro. On 7 December 1975 Indonesian forces invaded East Timor and the Portuguese authorities left on the next day.

On 22 December 1975 the Security Council called upon Indonesia to withdraw all its forces from the Territory and upon Portugal "as the admin-

---

18 Important dissenting opinions were filed by Vice-President SCHWEBEL; Judges ODA, SHAHABUDDEEN and KOROMA; and Judge *ad hoc* VALTICOS. *See* ICJ REPORTS 1995, p. 27 and following, but only Judge ODA (at 43), Judge SHAHABUDDEEN (pp. 51–55) and Judge VALTICOS (at 74–78) dealt in any detail with the procedural issues. Vice-President SCHWEBEL had at an earlier stage expressed his views on the procedure (ICJ REPORTS 1994, pp. 130–131), as had Judges ODA and VALTICOS.

19 *Maritime Delimitation and Territorial Questions between Bahrain and Qatar, Jurisdiction and Admissibility*, Judgment, ICJ REPORTS 1994, p. 114.

20 *See* this author's article on *Partial Judgments, and the Inherent Jurisdiction of the International Court of Justice*, in V. LOWE and M. FITZMAURICE (eds.), *op. cit., supra* note 1, p. 465.

istering power" to cooperate fully with the United Nations so as to enable the people of East Timor to exercise freely their right of self-determination. The call to Indonesia to withdraw was reiterated by a further Security Council resolution in April 1976. Portugal continued to be acknowledged as the administering power of the territory, as is shown by a number of, but not all, subsequent resolutions of the General Assembly bearing on the question. Indonesia's claim to have integrated East Timor into its territory was rejected, for example by General Assembly resolutions in 1976 and 1977. A limited number of States recognised the incorporation of the territory into Indonesia. Amongst these was Australia which subsequently, in 1989, concluded a treaty with Indonesia regarding the delimitation and joint exploitation of part of the continental shelf lying between Australia and East Timor. Australia declined to negotiate on this matter with Portugal and the latter began as early as 1985 to protest against Australia's negotiations with Indonesia.

In February 1991 Portugal commenced proceedings against Australia in the International Court. The Court's jurisdiction was invoked on the basis of the acceptances by Australia and Portugal of the Court's compulsory jurisdiction under the Optional Clause.

Portugal submitted, first, that the rights of the people of East Timor to self-determination, as well as the rights of Portugal as administering Power, were opposable to Australia which was under an obligation to respect them. Secondly, Portugal maintained that the negotiation, conclusion and implementation of the 1989 Treaty infringed the rights both of the people of East Timor and of Portugal as administering Power and, in contravening Security Council Resolutions 384 and 389, breached Australia's obligations to accept and carry out Security Council resolutions.

Australia's principal objection[21] was that the Court was being asked to rule on the rights and obligations of a State which was not a party to the proceedings, namely, Indonesia; and it is upon the Court's treatment of this objection that consideration of the case will be focussed.

The essence of Australia's case was that the decision sought by Portugal would inevitably require the Court to rule on the lawfulness of Indonesia's conduct in the absence of that State's consent. The argument rested upon the decision of the Court in the *Monetary Gold*[22] case between Italy, France, the United Kingdom and the United States, in which the Court had held that it could not proceed with the case because this would involve a considera-

21 Australia also contended that there was no dispute between itself and Portugal. The Court dismissed this objection and no more need be said about it now.

22 *Monetary Gold* case (*Preliminary Objection*), Judgment, ICJ REPORTS 1954, p. 19.

tion of the international responsibility of Albania and the latter had not consented to the jurisdiction of the Court. The Court stated that "Albania's legal interests would not only be affected by a decision, but would form the very subject matter of the decision."[23]

In response, Portugal contended that its Application was concerned exclusively with the conduct of Australia in negotiating the 1989 Treaty with Indonesia. This, so Portugal argued, amounted to a denial by Australia of the rights of the people of East Timor to self-determination, of East Timor's status as a non-self governing territory and of Portugal's position as administering Power. In relation to this submission it was not, in Portugal's view, necessary for the Court to consider the position of Indonesia.

The Court decided that it could not exercise the jurisdiction that the parties had conferred on it by their Optional Clause declarations because "it would have to rule, as a pre-requisite, on the lawfulness of Indonesia's conduct in the absence of that State's consent." The Court stated that its conclusion applied to all of Portugal's submissions because all of them raised a common question: "whether the power to make treaties concerning the continental shelf resources of East Timor belongs to Portugal or Indonesia, and, therefore, whether Indonesia's entry into and continued presence in the Territory are lawful."[24]

Having regard to the fact that the Security Council has deplored the intervention of the armed forces of Indonesia in East Timor and has twice called upon Indonesia to withdraw its forces from that territory, it is necessary to scrutinise with special care a judgment which in effect gives a wrongdoer the opportunity to frustrate proceedings brought by the lawful administration against a State which has disregarded the legal status of that administration.

The decision of the Court appears to involve four specific propositions:

1. It is a fundamental principle that the Court cannot decide a dispute between States without the consent of those States to its jurisdiction.[25] As a general statement, this cannot be denied – though in the view of some, perhaps many, the principle is one that should be re-examined by international lawmakers, in the light of the seeming willingness of States to accept quasi--judicial consideration of their conduct without specific consent.[26]

---

23 *Ibid.* p. 32.

24 ICJ REPORTS 1995, p. 105, para. 35.

25 *Ibid.* p. 101, para. 26.

26 *See e.g.* this author's ASPECTS OF THE ADMINISTRATION OF INTERNATIONAL JUSTICE (1991), Chapter III.

2. The Court then stated that it had "carefully considered the argument advanced by Portugal which seeks to separate Australia's behaviour from that of Indonesia." But without further elaboration of the elements entering into that consideration, the Court proceeded to state its conclusion:

> "However, in the view of the Court, Australia's behaviour cannot be assessed without first entering into the question why it is that Indonesia could not lawfully have concluded the 1989 Treaty, while Portugal allegedly could have done so; the very subject of the Court's decision would necessarily be a determination whether, having regard to the circumstances in which Indonesia entered and remained in East Timor, it could or could not have acquired the power to enter into treaties on behalf of East Timor relating to the resources of its continental shelf. The Court could not make such a determination in the absence of the consent of Indonesia."[27]

It is difficult to understand why a lawful administrator (and possibly even sovereign) of a territory should have to show why a third party, whose conduct has previously been determined by the Security Council to be unlawful, did not have a right to make a treaty in respect of the occupied territory or, if it is obliged so to show, why it should then be frustrated in this endeavour by the fact that the third party has not consented to the exercise of the Court's jurisdiction. It would seem to be more consistent with legal principle that the lawful administrator should be entitled to rely on its known lawful authority; and if the respondent or the third party wish to show that that authority is at an end, it is up to them to present to the Court arguments which deal with that matter, rather than invoke the Court's lack of jurisdiction over the third party to prevent a proper consideration of the matter. Any suggestion that the Court performs a meta-juridical function or is inclined to develop the law in a manner contributing to the effective enforcement of the legal rights of States must founder upon the rock of the Court's decision in the *East Timor* case.

3. In response to Portugal's argument that the right of the people of East Timor to self-determination was a right *erga omnes* and that, therefore, Portugal could require Australia to respect it regardless of whether or not another State had conducted itself in an unlawful manner, the Court concluded that "whatever the nature of the obligations involved, the **Court could not rule on the lawfulness of the conduct of a State when its judgment would imply an evaluation of the lawfulness of the conduct of another State which is not a party to the case**. Where this is so the Court cannot act, even if the right in question is a right *erga omnes*" (emphasis supplied).

---

[27] ICJ REPORTS 1995, p. 102, para. 28.

A similar comment may be made upon this element in the Court's decision to that just made in relation to the previous one. Why did the Court feel impelled to adopt so restrictive a view of its own competence as is conveyed in the words emphasised in the passage just quoted? The protection thus accorded to the position of the non-party seems excessive in that it prevents the rights of the applicant State being determined as against the respondent State. Why, one may ask, should the interests of a non-party be put above those of a party? And why should the mere **implication** of an evaluation of the lawfulness of the conduct of the non-party be seen as undermining the requirement of consent, properly conceived? The position of the non-party in this case is only incidental to the main complaint of Portugal, which is directed against the conduct of Australia. If the approach adopted by the Court is generalised, it would lead to the proposition that, despite the acceptance by a State of the Court's jurisdiction, its conduct, if carried out in association with another State not subject to the Court's jurisdiction, will be protected from judicial scrutiny – a conclusion made even more unsatisfactory in this case because it involved an *erga omnes* obligation.

This pampering of third-party interests on the grounds that the State concerned has not consented to the Court's jurisdiction is to be contrasted with the more expansive manner in which the Court has dealt with comparable problems in two other relatively recent cases.

Thus, in the related (though obviously different) context of intervention, the Chamber of the Court in *El Salvador/Honduras* (*Application by Nicaragua for Permission to Intervene*)[28] permitted Nicaragua to intervene despite the absence of any jurisdictional link between it and either of the principal parties. Although Nicaragua did not thereby become a "party" to the case in the strict sense, the fact remains that without the specific consent – indeed, against the opposition – of the principal parties, it was enabled to present its views to the Court and seek to influence the outcome of the proceedings. True, the Chamber found an element of consent by the principal parties in the very fact of their acceptance of the Court's Statute, including especially Articles 62 and 63. But this willingness to find in the Statute authority to permit intervention (albeit as a non-party) without a jurisdictional link suggests that one could find, by a comparable process of statutory construction, an indication of consent by third States to the exercise by the Court of its competence in a case in which the issues between the two principal parties touched the interests of the non-party. Or, to the extent that the decision in the *East Timor*

---

[28] *Land, Island and Maritime Frontier Dispute (El Salvador/Honduras), Application to Intervene,* Judgment, ICJ REPORTS 1990, p. 92.

case stemmed from the Court's finding that the position of Indonesia was the very subject matter of the case, the more flexible attitude evinced in the *El Salvador/Honduras* intervention decision could, if constructively followed, have led the Court to show a lesser concern with the preservation of Indonesia's position.

Also pertinent are certain observations by the Court in the *Nauru* case:[29]

> "The Court does not consider that any reason has been shown why a claim brought against only one of the three States should be declared inadmissible *in limine litis* merely because that claim raises questions of the administration of the Territory, which was shared with two other States. It cannot be denied that Australia had obligations under the Trusteeship Agreement, in its capacity as one of the three States forming the Administering Authority, and there is nothing in the character of that Agreement which debars the Court from considering a claim of a breach of those obligations."[30]

It is not easy to see why, if the Court did not regard itself as debarred from considering Australia's position on its own in the *Nauru* case, it should have felt precluded from considering Australia's position on its own in the *East Timor* case.

One may compare with the emphasised words quoted at the beginning of this sub-section[31] the following words in the *Nauru* judgment:

> "In the present case, a finding by the Court regarding the existence or the content of the responsibility attributed to Australia by Nauru **might well have implications** for the legal situation of the two other States concerned, but no finding in respect of that legal situation will be needed as a basis for the Court's decision on Nauru's claims against Australia."[32]

Why should the "implications" for Indonesia in the *East Timor* case have been regarded as more legally significant than those for New Zealand and the United Kingdom in the *Nauru* case? Though the Court provides some answer to this question in paragraph 34 of the *East Timor* judgment, it does so by way of assertion rather than reasoned elaboration.

4. Finally, mention should be made of the manner in which the Court approached the role and effect of the General Assembly and Security Council resolutions adopted in relation to East Timor. Portugal contended, as part

---

29 *Certain Phosphate Lands in Nauru (Nauru v. Australia), Preliminary Objections*, Judgment, ICJ REPORTS 1992, p. 240.

30 *Ibid.* pp. 258–259.

31 *Supra*, p. 226.

32 *Ibid.* pp. 261–262.

of its argument, that the *Monetary Gold* case was inapplicable; that the status of East Timor as a non-self-governing territory and its own capacity as the Administering Power had already been decided by the Security Council and the General Assembly; that the Court could decide on Portugal's claims without deciding *de novo* on the questions covered by those decisions; and that therefore the Court need not pronounce on the question of the use of force by Indonesia in East Timor or upon the lawfulness of its presence in the Territory.[33]

The Court noted that the Portuguese argument rested on the premise that the U.N. resolutions, especially those of the Security Council, could be read as imposing an obligation on States not to recognise any authority on the part of Indonesia over the Territory and in relation thereto to deal only with Portugal. The Court then stated that it "is not persuaded … that the relevant resolutions went so far."[34]

However, the manner in which the Court supported this conclusion is far from compelling. It acknowledged, first, that East Timor remained a non-self-governing territory and that the General Assembly resolutions expressly referred to Portugal as the "administering Power". But it found

> "that it cannot be inferred from the sole fact that the [relevant] resolutions of the General Assembly and the Security Council refer to Portugal as the administering Power of East Timor that they intended to establish an obligation on third States to treat exclusively with Portugal as regards the continental shelf of East Timor."

Accordingly the Court concluded that the resolutions could not be regarded as "givens" capable of constituting a sufficient basis for determining the dispute between the Parties. It followed, said the Court, that it

> "would necessarily have to rule upon the lawfulness of Indonesia's conduct as a pre-requisite for deciding on Portugal's contention that Australia violated its obligation to respect Portugal's status as administering Power."[35]

There are at least two ways of looking at this section of the Judgment. One is to regret the Court's reluctance to accept the resolutions of the Security Council and of the General Assembly at their face value as determining that Indonesia's presence in East Timor was unlawful and that Portugal re-

---

33 ICJ REPORTS 1995, p. 103.

34 *Ibid.*

35 *Ibid.* p. 104. The important dissenting opinions of Judge WEERAMANTRY and Judge *ad hoc* SKUBISZEWSKI also call for detailed consideration.

mained the "administering Power" and, as such, alone had the capacity to represent the Territory in its international affairs.

The other is to approve of the seeming reservation by the Court of a power to interpret the resolutions of the Security Council and the General Assembly to the point even of depriving them of legal effect. However, the awkwardness of this position is that it appears to imply that the Court saw merit, though it did not expressly say so, in the Australian arguments that the Security Council resolutions went back to 1976 and those of the General Assembly to 1982, that Portugal took no account of the passage of time and that the Security Council resolutions were not binding and were not framed in mandatory terms. One is thus left with a decision which appears to run counter to contemporary doctrine denying the legal effect of the use of force in the acquisition of territory. The decision in this respect conveys the impression of reflecting the maxim *ex factis ius oritur*. In the circumstances, much more was called for from the Court than a judgment that appears in many important features to be a rather peremptory and surprising dismissal of Portugal's complaint.

The remaining case for consideration is the *Nuclear Tests* case, decided by the Court on 22 September 1995.[36] This arose out of an announcement by the French Government in June 1995 that it proposed to renew underground nuclear testing at Mururoa Atoll in the Pacific Ocean in August 1995. The New Zealand Government requested the Court to examine the situation in the light of the Court's Judgment in the *Nuclear Tests* case of 1974.[37] The New Zealand Government also requested interim measures of protection.

It is, therefore, necessary first to refer briefly to the 1974 *Nuclear Tests* Judgment. This brought to an end proceedings which had been begun by New Zealand in 1973 in an attempt to secure an order of the Court requiring France to terminate atmospheric nuclear testing in the Pacific. The jurisdictional basis of the New Zealand Application was the fact that both France and New Zealand had made declarations accepting the Court's jurisdiction under the General Act for the Pacific Settlement of Disputes, 1928. The substantive basis of the Application was not only the infringement of New Zealand's sovereignty arising from the deposit of radioactive fall-out on its territory but also New Zealand's concern to ensure the protection of the marine environment. New Zealand sought and obtained from the Court in June 1973[38]

---

[36] The author must declare an interest in this case by reason of having been one of the counsel appearing for New Zealand.

[37] *Nuclear Tests (New Zealand v. France)*, Judgment of 20 December 1974, ICJ REPORTS 1974, p. 457.

[38] ICJ REPORTS 1973, p. 135.

an indication of interim measures of protection. The Court then ordered the Parties to argue, in the first instance, questions of jurisdiction and admissibility. In the period between the making of this Order and the hearing which the Court held on the matter in July 1974 a number of public statements were made by high authorities in the French Government to the effect that, after the series of atmospheric tests to be conducted in 1974, France would no longer need to conduct nuclear tests in the atmosphere and would thenceforth conduct only underground tests.

The Court held that these statements constituted unilateral declarations binding on France under international law and that they amounted to an undertaking by France to hold no further atmospheric tests in the South Pacific. In consequence New Zealand's objective had in effect been accomplished. The Court accordingly concluded that "the dispute having disappeared, the claim advanced by New Zealand no longer has any object."[39] "There was nothing on which to give judgment."[40] The operative words of the Judgment were that "the claim of New Zealand no longer has any object and that the Court is therefore not called upon to give a decision thereon."[41]

However, the Court added an important qualification to its decision:

> "63. Once the Court has found that a State has entered into a commitment concerning its future conduct it is not the Court's function to contemplate that it will not comply with it. Moreover, the Court observes that if the basis of this Judgment were to be affected, the Applicant could request an examination of the situation in accordance with the provisions of the Statute; the denunciation by France, by letter dated 2 January 1974, of the General Act for the Pacific Settlement of International Disputes, which is relied on as a basis of jurisdiction in the present case, cannot constitute by itself an obstacle to the presentation of such a request."[42]

From 1974 to 1992 France conducted a significant number of underground nuclear tests at Mururoa and Fangataufa Atolls. France then joined in the moratorium declared by the major nuclear powers on the further testing of nuclear weapons, whether in the atmosphere or underground. In June 1995 France announced its intention to resume underground testing.

The position taken by New Zealand was based upon an accumulation of evidence that the underground testing that had taken place within Mururoa Atoll over the years since 1974 had led to a significant weakening of the struc-

---

39 ICJ REPORTS 1974, p. 476, para. 59.
40 *Ibid.* p. 477, para. 62.
41 *Ibid.* p. 478, para. 65.
42 *Ibid.* p. 477, para. 63.

ture of that atoll and some pollution of the surrounding seas. There was, therefore, a risk that further testing, even though underground, might lead to a major fracture in the atoll and the direct escape into the sea of radioactive material. Although such testing might actually take place underground, it could lead to precisely the kind of damage to the marine environment that it had been one of the principal objectives of the 1973 proceedings to terminate. New Zealand saw the situation as one which fell within the terms of paragraph 63 of the 1974 Judgment quoted above in that the possibility of nuclear contamination was something which could affect the basis of that Judgment. Accordingly, in 1995 New Zealand requested the Court to examine the situation and, at the same time, requested the Court to indicate interim measures of protection.

New Zealand also contended that developments in international law had taken place in the intervening twenty years that were capable of affecting the 1974 Judgment. New Zealand pointed to the Noumea Convention of 1986 for the Protection of the Natural Resources and Environment of the South Pacific Region. It argued that France was under an obligation to conduct an environmental impact assessment before carrying out any further nuclear tests at Mururoa and Fangataufa; that France's conduct was illegal in that it caused, or was likely to cause, the introduction into the marine environment of radioactive material; and that France was bound by the "precautionary principle" to provide evidence, before carrying out any further underground test, that they would not result in the introduction of radioactive material into the environment. As to the fact that the undertakings given by France in 1974 had been limited to the abandonment of atmospheric testing and had expressly stated that France would henceforth only test underground, New Zealand argued that in 1974, and in the period before 1974, only atmospheric testing had taken place, that it was that kind of testing alone that had occasioned nuclear contamination and that it had not been foreseen that underground testing might lead to the same kind of damage as it was thought that the abandonment of atmospheric testing would bring to an end.

The Court thus had before it a case which posed in stark terms the choice between a juridical and a meta-juridical approach. If the Court had treated the case in strictly formalistic terms, it could have adopted the line of argument advanced by France: that France has in 1974 undertaken to give up atmospheric testing and had done so; and that the Court in 1974 had regarded the French undertaking as meeting the essence of the complaint then advanced by New Zealand. If, on the other hand, the Court had looked at the essentials of the New Zealand complaints of 1973 as well as of 1995, had accepted that New Zealand's concern had been with **any** nuclear testing that might affect the environment, had appreciated that New Zealand had in 1973–74 only used the adjective "atmospheric" to qualify "nuclear testing" because at that time that was the only kind of testing that had taken place, had recalled that the limitation to "atmospheric" testing had not been uniformly used in all pertinent places, had understood that the development of the concepts of environmental impact assessment and of the "precautionary principle" were progressive elements in the growth of international environmental law which merited judicial consideration and support, it could easily and cogently have put a quite different gloss upon the crucial paragraph 29 of the 1974 Judgment and its seeming limitation to atmospheric nuclear testing.[43]

For present purposes it is not necessary to express a firm view as to whether the Court was "right" or "wrong" in the conclusion which it reached. Indeed, as hardly needs saying, whatever conclusion the majority of the Court reaches in any case is necessarily "right" as between the parties and, in most circumstances, also for the world at large. For present purposes it is only necessary to identify the choice that was open to the Court – the juridical or the meta-juridical, the rigid or the flexible, the static or the dynamic, the narrow or the wide – and to suggest that in each of these last two cases it was the first alternative which the Court chose. If the choice which the Court made will be regretted in some quarters, it will not be in others. But it does matter that, for the sound administration of the law, the considerations, not always expressed, which underlay the Court's choice should be consistently applied.

In conclusion, there is room for a word of caution. This essay has been entirely devoted to a consideration of certain activity of the Court as a collegiate institution. Such an exercise can be valuable as an aid to predicting the possible direction which future decisions of the Court may take. It assists also in the necessary task of assessing the sufficiency of the Court's performance.

There is, however, a danger that in thus speaking of the Court as a collective body one may foster the impression that at any given moment it is a unified body and that over time it is an unchanging one. Such an impression would be incorrect. Rarely does a judgment secure the unanimous support of all members of the Court and certainly not in any case of substantive significance. Article 10 of the Statute prescribes "that in the body as a whole the representation of the main forms of civilization and of the principal legal systems of the world should be assured". And so it is – but the

---

[43] On all these points, reference should be made to the full and important dissenting opinions of Judges WEERAMANTRY and KOROMA and of Judge *ad hoc* Sir GEOFFREY PALMER.

consequence is that the decisions of the Court are subject to diverse and often conflicting tendencies that reflect the differences in legal traditions of the fifteen titular judges, not to mention the one or two *ad hoc* judges that also sit in most cases. Moreover, not only is the Court a body of diverse composition; it is one of constantly changing composition – ever absorbing new talent, ever extruding old talent. Although the changes that may occur at one election will not by themselves secure a radical alteration in the collective judicial attitude, two or three elections may cumulatively have such an effect, so that the Court of today is not the same as the Court of yesteryear. Nor is the direction of change always uniform. Depending upon the individual personalities involved, the Court may at one moment be predominantly "conservative" and "juridical", at another "liberal" or "meta-juridical", and thereafter may revert again to its former outlook.

There is nothing unnatural or improper about this. It is just a fact of life that can have a significant influence on the outcome of litigation before the Court. One cannot change it, but one needs ever to bear it in mind. At the same time, it is important to recall that the merit of the Court is not dependent upon establishing that it acts in a "flexible" manner or that it sees its task as not merely "juridical" but also as "meta-juridical". One nation's meat may be another nation's poison. A judicial approach which may suit the interests of one State may well not suit the interests of its opponent. For such reasons, the attempt to identify the underlying judicial approach of the Court may be interesting but the result is unavoidably inexact and ever exposed to change.

The Widening Scope of International Law

by

Gerardo E. do Nascimento e Silva

Of all the branches of law, international law stands out as the most dynamic and one that has shown the greatest capacity to adapt itself to a changing world. The advances in the field of science and technology always influenced international law, but after World War Two technology has reached a stage in which scientific discovery can be transformed almost overnight into reality.

I. THE NEW DIMENSIONS OF INTERNATIONAL LAW

Science and technology opened up new dimensions and new domains in the field of international law. Until the beginning of the twentieth century, International Law was limited to a two-dimensional plane, *i.e.* the sea and the land. In 1902, Paul Fauchille called attention to a new field, namely air space. The Parisian exploits of Alberto Santos Dumont, a young Brazilian engineer, probably influenced him. In 1898 he flew in a balloon, to which he had attached a propeller, successfully rose 400 meters into the air, manoeuvred for several minutes and then descended to the exact spot of his take-off. On 19 October 1901 he won the *Deutsch de La Meurthe* prize given to the first man to take off from a pre-established point, fly around the Eiffel Tower and return to the starting point in less that 30 minutes. His greatest achievement occurred on October 23, 1906, when, after a 200 meter run, his 350 ton plane took off and flew over a 100 meter course in Bagatelle near Paris. He was immediately acclaimed by the European press as the sole inventor of the heavier than air flying machine.

When in 1908 the Wright Brothers claimed that on 17 December 1903 they had flewn for the first time their claim was greeted with indignation in Europe, where it was pointed out that no officially accredited person witnessed the flight, that the *Kitty Hawk* didn't take off but was pushed along an inclined rail which permitted it to remain above the ground for a few seconds. The fact is that the *Kitty Hawk* never managed to get off the ground on its own, while Santos Dumont's planes were well known in Paris. The power of the American media, however, slowly but surely pushed Santos Dumont's exploit into the background and transformed the claim of the Wright Brothers into a fact.

Be it as it may, in 1902 Paul Fauchille submitted to the Institut de Droit international a report on the legal aspects of airplanes; the first important document on air law was approved during a session in Gand in 1906. The 1906 resolution embraced Fauchille's approach to the subject, namely that the space above the States should be free, subject to the right of self-defense. Westlake, on the contrary, defended the idea of the sovereignty of the subjacent State limited by the right of innocent passage.

The Paris Convention for the Regulation of Aerial Navigation of 13 October 1919 recognized the sovereignty of States over the air space. The 1944 Convention on International Civil Aviation (the *Chicago Convention*) also provides that "The contracting States recognize that every State has complete and exclusive sovereignty over the airspace above its territory."

With the launching of *Sputnik I* on 4 October 1957, followed by *Sputnik II* on 3 November 1957, a new dimension was added to international law. Yuri Gagarin's epic flight around the Earth on 12 April 1961 was another proof of the need to elaborate rules governing outer-space. To deal with the relevant law-making, the United Nations established a Committee for the Peaceful Use of Outer Space, with the understanding that outer space and celestial bodies are not susceptible to appropriation by States.

On 13 December 1963, the General Assembly unanimously adopted a declaration on the legal principles governing activities of States in the exploration and use of outer space. As a sequel to this resolution, the Treaty of Principles Governing the Activities of States in the Exploration and Use of Outer Space, Including the Moon and Other Celestial Bodies (known as the *Space Treaty*) was signed in 1967, undoubted one of the major legal documents adopted after the second world war. This basic Treaty was followed by four other treaties and a considerable number of recommendations of the United Nations and other inter-governmental organizations. Manfred Lachs sums up the paramount provision of the Space Treaty as follows: "Outer space, including the Moon and other celestial bodies, is not subject to national appropriation by claims of sovereignty, by means of use or occupation, or by any other means."

With Arvid Pardo's speech in the General Assembly in 1967 international law was faced with the challenge to adopt rules aimed at governing the sea-bed and the ocean floor as well as the subsoil thereof beyond the limits of national jurisdiction. In short a fifth dimension of international law had been opened up.

In his speech the delegate from Malta called attention to studies and the latest technological progress in the exploration of the seas, principally the sea-bed and ocean floor where enormous quantities of minerals such as manganese, nickel, copper and iron could be found.

The speech caught the attention of the delegates from developing countries who realized the necessity of immediately adopting strict norms in order to avoid a situation in which the major industrialized nations should start the exploitation of these riches by creating a *fait accompli*, aimed at creating a right over the sea-bed and ocean floor. An *ad hoc* committee was installed in the General Assembly with the task of preparing a report on the use of the sea-bed beyond national jurisdiction. On 17 December 1970 a Declaration was adopted that pronounced *inter alia* that the sea-bed, ocean floor and the subsoil thereof were the **common heritage of mankind** as such.

The legal framework of the common heritage of mankind was duly codified by the Convention on the Law of the Sea that provides that "No State shall claim or exercise sovereignty or sovereign rights over any part of the Area or its resources, nor shall any State or natural or juridical person appropriate any part thereof. No such claim or exercise of sovereignty or sovereign rights nor such appropriations shall be recognized" (art. 137, 2).

II. THE CONTRIBUTION OF THE UNITED NATIONS

The new international order created after 1945 took into account all the changes caused by science and technology, and the United Nations and the specialized international organizations were entrusted with the task of drafting legal documents aimed at regulating the new issues that had been raised.

It is worthwhile noting that the authors of the Dumbarton Oaks draft attempted to push international law into the background. The basic document drafted by the Department of State simply ignored its existence, even though its purpose was to put before the world a document aimed at the consolidation of peace and the peaceful settlement of international disputes. In other words, it simply ignored the efforts of many generations aimed at solving these and other problems that up till then could be found in the teachings of international law. One can only presume that the idea behind this approach was to adopt a *tabula rasa* that would continue to give the three Powers a free hand in the destiny of the world. Under existing international law, all States had the same rights and duties, and such a situation might eventually hinder them.

Or to cite the words of Oscar Schacht "in contrast to the emphasis given to the Security Council in the Charter, little attention was paid to the potential legislative capacity of the international organs. Indeed, the term **legislation** was taboo. There were strong strictures against its application to the U.N. bodies which on the surface looked and behaved in many ways like legislatures."

A proposal by China aimed "at encouraging the progressive development of international law and its codification" by the General Assembly (Art. 13) was considered harmless and duly accepted. This provision became the basis for the International Law Commission that was responsible for an important contribution to the codification of international law.

The increase in the membership of the U.N., however, was not beneficial to the work of the ILC since political and economic considerations became an important element in the formulation of most of the conventions dealing with international law.

In the 1960's many of the ex-colonies that had become members of the United Nations showed a desire to modify existing international law arguing that it was purely European in its conception, and that it did not take into account the valuable contribution of all the other legal systems of the world. In other words they defended the idea of a truly **global** international law.

This was far from being a new idea since at the beginning of the 20th century some Latin American jurists spoke of the existence of an **American International Law**, although the majority who took up the issue rejected the idea. According to Hildebrando Accioly,

> "In fact, there can be no doubt that all the world recognizes the same superior principles of justice, that is the same essential or fundamental juridical principles. This does not mean that in certain geographic regions, social, economical or political circumstances may result in the adoption of certain norms of conduct peculiar to that region, but which are not contrary to general or universal international law."

The principal example used to justify the idea of American international law was the right of asylum in diplomatic missions recognized by all Latin American countries, but criticized in Europe and the United States. One can reasonably assert that asylum in diplomatic missions cannot be considered as contrary to universally recognized human rights. In the *Haya de la Torre* case Alejandre Alvarez, the staunchest defender of a Latin American international law, adopted years later in his capacity as Judge of the International Court of Justice, a different approach "one cannot think, like many have done, of an International Law peculiar to the New World and entirely different from universal International Law".

III. THE CONFERENCE ON THE LAW OF TREATIES

During the Conference on the Law of Treaties held in Vienna in 1968 and 1969, the newly independent States, notably those from Africa, were able to put forward their ideas regarding the new international law in a multi--cultural world. Many of the positions taken in Vienna repeated arguments put forward during the debates in the 6th Committee and in the ILC. To begin with, the whole philosophy was changed. Until 1939, in the study of the law of treaties doctrine worked on the conditions that lead towards the validity of treaties; the idea behind the 1969 Convention is that of invalidity, termination and suspension of the operation of treaties. Although the rules adopted in 1969 are very near to those of the pre-war era, the basic idea behind *pacta sunt serrvanda* has changed: the idea behind many of the rules that were codified was that under certain conditions the validity of pre-existent treaties could be challenged.

A perfunctory reference to some of the interventions made in 1968 can give an idea of the attitude of some delegations to the matters raised, with emphasis on unequal treaties signed in the past and those imposed on weaker States.

Article 49 of the draft states that "A treaty is void if its conclusion has been procured by the threat or use of force in violation of the principles of the Charter of the United Nations." As the ILC pointed out in its commentary, "The traditional doctrine prior to the Convenant of the League of Nations was that the validity of a treaty was not affected by the fact that it had been brought about by the threat or use of force." Even though some jurists still hesitated to accept it, the ILC had no doubt as to its legal value.

Two amendments, aimed at mentioning after the words "threat" or "use of force" the words "including economic or political preassure", received the backing of various delegations that in some cases mentioned examples from their own past. The delegation of China which adopted a low-profile attitude during the Conference insisted that it attached great importance to the article "since over a hundred years China had been bound by treaties procured by the threat or the use of force." The delegate from Zambia recalled that "no jurist had denied the moral value of inserting such a principle in the convention, though some delegations had exponded the traditional view that business should not be mixed up with politics or morality." In his view, all progressive lawyers admitted that the term "force" included economic and political as well as other forms of pressure or coercion failing short of armed force. The delegate from Kenya insisted that "the principle of sovereign equality of States made it necessary to reject any provision which might help one State dominate another. The road to equality was rugged and the vestiges of degradation and humiliation resulting from oppression could not be eradicated overnight; but nothing should be done to encourage their perpetuation."

In order to defuse a rather delicate situation, the delegate from the Netherlands suggested that representatives of the various groups should meet in order to reach an agreement. The result of this compromise was the adoption by the Conference of a resolution solemnly condemning "the threat or use of pressure in any form, military, political or economic, by any State, in order the coerce another State to perform any act relating to the conclusion of a treaty in violation of the principles of sovereign equality of States and freedom of consent." With the adoption of this resolution, amendments aimed at mentioning the use of political or economic pressure were withdrawn.

The article codifying the *rebus sic stantibus* principle was also the object of lengthy debates. Almost most jurists accepted the principle prior to 1969, but hesitated as to its applicability. There was consensus as to the acceptance of the rule, although some delegations were opposed to paragraph 2 under which the rule cannot be invoked "as a ground for terminating or withdrawing from a treaty establishing a boundary." In spite of the fact that the African representatives did not hesitate in condemning the policy of the colonial powers that had divided the African continent without taking into account tribal traditions, they fully realized the importance of the rule. The opposition, curiously enough, came from some Latin-American States that in the past had lost part of their territories.

A special reference must be made regarding the provisions to be found in the Vienna Convention on Succession of States in respect of State Property, Archives and Debts, of 8 April 1983. From the very beginning, M. Bedjaoui, who had been chosen as Raporteur by the ILC, made it quite clear that he would not follow traditional patterns on the subject and that the situation of newly independent States would receive a completely new approach. In his first report he declared that "priority should be given to succession resulting from the elimination of colonialism, rather than to succession of the traditional style." In consequence, he continued "efforts should not be limited to codifying solutions provided by texts which have fallen into disuse, much less than those derived from texts which have remained a dead letter, for that would not be a faithful reflection of actual international practice." And, "since decolonization is a phenomenon that tends to rapid development ... the International Law Commission should not concern itself with abortive or precarious solutions." Even though the draft managed to receive the necessary votes, none of the States present at the 1983 Conference signed it, a phenomenon which had never been witnessed before.

The articles on *jus cogens* adopted in the 1989 Convention undoubtedly stand out as its most important innovation.

The atrocities perpetrated by Nazi Germany shocked the whole world and the idea of special norms of international law from which no derogation could be permitted began to take shape. The initial reaction was of a negative nature, yet with the passing of time the idea of *jus cogens* began to carry weight, in spite of the fact that doctrine did not seem to come up with a satisfactory definition. One of the main difficulties was the identification of those rules which could qualify as *jus cogens*. In some cases, such as slavery, genocide and racial discrimination, there is general agreement that they qualify as such in spite of the fact that they continue to exist, and in the war in former Yugoslavia the clamorous cases of a violation of human rights due to racial reasons still have to be analysed.

In spite of the almost unanimous declaration in favour of *jus cogens*, during the Vienna Conference of 1968–69, many delegation insisted that the ILC draft was unsatisfactory. Some feared that the principle could provide a new argument aimed at ending a treaty unilaterally, even though the ILC in its commentary insisted that *jus cogens* could not be applied retroactivly or unilaterally.

There is an exaggerated tendency on the part of some writers to consider as *jus cogens* rules that do not qualify as such and by so doing to weaken the notion of *jus cogens*. In his report, Sir Humphrey was quite adamant that the examples of *jus cogens* were very few, and those mentioned cannot be discussed. The difficulty arises in the case of some examples that have been raised such as self-determination, unequal treaties and the freedom of the high seas.

The study of the discussions in the International Law Commission can be helpful, but when the members of the Commission took up the issue for the first time, many of them were still in doubt as to what *jus cogens* really meant. Gilberto Amado had the opportunity to say jokingly that he envied one of the members that had declared that the notion of *jus cogens* was crystal clear. The same occurred in Vienna, and although all the delegates, with one exception, declared that their countries were in favour of the norm, there was obviously quite a few who did not wish to see the draft article approved. The fact is that the two articles are vague and the idea of including some examples was put aside.

It is important to remember that the provisions of a treaty can be modified by subsequent practice. In other words, if mankind were to restrict itself to applying the legal conception that always existed, the legal system would not develop and the law would not have fulfilled its social functions. Article 38 of the International Law Commission draft proposed an article along these lines: "A treaty may be modified by subsequent practice in the application of the treaty establishing the agreement of the parties to modify its provisions."

In Vienna, in 1968, article 38 was deleted since in the opinion of some delegates it was not advisable to take up the complex problem of relations between customary law and written law. Other delegates also argued that the adoption of the article raised problems of a constitutional nature, since any modification of a treaty should be submitted to parliament for approval.

It must be stressed that the ILC is not the only organ operative in the law-making process of the U.N. In many cases, due to the technical nature of the problems under consideration, the task of working out a draft convention is entrusted to scientific and legal working groups under the supervision of the U.N. itself or of one of the specialized agencies. In this respect, most of the recent and important conventions aimed at the protection of the environment were drafted by specialized groups, as in the case of the conventions on the ozone layer, transport of hazardous waste, climatic change and biological diversity, to quote a few recent ones.

It should also be pointed out that alongside the legal, economic, technical and social factors that influence the international law maker, political considerations can be decisive. The Convention on the Law of the Sea is the best example. When the General Assembly decided to convene a conference to re-open the issue, it was decided that it would not be forwarded to the ILC, as had occurred previously, but that a special group would be entrusted with the task. This was a cumbersome approach, but after more than ten years it was possible to adopt the Convention in Montego Bay in 1982.

One cannot ignore the fact that even though the great majority of discoveries are advantageous to mankind, in some cases the impact of science and technology had serious side-effects with the consequential degradation and pollution of the ecosystem. The list of pollutants, such as sewers, oil, persistent organic pollutants, radioactive waste and plastics represent a permanent threat to the world environment. The simple fact is that in spite of the improvements in modern living, many of the advantages are momentary and in the long run represent a serious threat. Some of the risks pass unnoticed since the threat is not immediate, the damage to the ozone layer being a good example.

Be it as it may, the negative effects of science and technology are also responsible for the opening up of some of the most challenging issues facing mankind which are being studied in the field of international environmental law.

La détermination de l'Etat lésé. Les régimes dissociables et les régimes indissociables

par

Georges Perrin

I

Point n'est besoin de rappeler que la violation d'une règle bilatérale ne crée un nouveau rapport juridique qu'entre l'Etat auteur du fait internationalement illicite et l'Etat lésé. Le premier a l'obligation de réparer le dommage subi par le second, lequel a le droit corrélatif d'obtenir réparation[1]. Quant au manquement à une règle miltilatérale, il donne naissance, selon la conception traditionnelle, à un rapport juridique bilatéral entre l'Etat auteur de ce comportement et l'Etat lésé[2]. Cette opinion s'explique par le fait que lorsque se sont formées les règles de la responsabilité, les différends étudiés par la doctrine portaient presque toujours sur les règles relatives à la condition des étrangers, règles qui créent des régimes dissociables. Ces derniers sont en effet constitués par un faisceau de rapports bilatéraux indépendants les uns des autres. La violation de la règle porte donc atteinte à l'un de ces rapports, celui qui existe entre l'Etat auteur du fait internationalement illicite et l'Etat dont le ressortissant a été maltraité, si bien que ce n'est qu'entre eux que naît un nouveau rapport entraînant l'obligation de réparer et le droit à réparation.

II

Les règles multilatérales dont découlent des régimes dissociables demeurent de loin les plus nombreuses. Aussi les auteurs ne sont-ils pas rares

---

[1] Nous entendons ici le terme «réparation» dans son sens large. Il désigne tout ce que l'Etat auteur du fait internationalement illicite peut être tenu de faire et – ou – de cesser de faire. On sait que nombre d'auteurs ont adopté une conception essentiellement patrimoniale du dommage. Aussi emploient-ils le terme «réparation» dans un sens restrictif, à savoir la remise matérielle des choses en l'état ou le versement de dommages-intérêts.

[2] *Cf.* D. Anzilotti, Cours de droit international public, Paris (1929), p. 467; C. Eagleton, The Responsibility of States in International Law, New York (1928), p. 182; K. Strupp, Handbuch des Völkerrecht, vol. III: Das völkerrechtliche Delikt, Stuttgart (1920), p. 217; Ch. De Visscher, Aspects récents du droit procédural de la Cour internationale de Justice, cité Droit procédural, Paris (1966), pp. 115–116.

questiment que le fait internationalement illicite a pour seule conséquence un rapport bilatéral entre l'Etat coupable et l'Etat victime. D'où la définition de Rousseau: «On entend par responsabilité internationale l'institution juridique en vertu de laquelle l'Etat auquel est imputable un acte illicite selon le droit international doit réparation à l'Etat à l'encontre duquel cet acte a été commis»[3].

III

Cette analyse ne correspond plus aujourd'hui à toutes les hypothèses. La transgression d'un régime indissociable ne lèse pas seulement l'Etat qui en est la cible. Elle porte atteinte au droit des Etats soumis à ce régime à ce qu'il soit respecté. D'où la naissance d'une série de nouveaux rapports juridiques entre d'une part l'auteur du fait internationalement illicite et d'autre part chacun de ses partenaires[4].

IV

Il convient de s'interroger sur la nature du droit invoqué par l'Etat lésé.

A. Lorsque les conséquences juridiques du fait internationalement illicite se manifestent dans un cadre bilatéral – comme c'est le cas dans tous les régimes dissociables – il n'a jamais été contesté que la violation de l'obligation portait atteinte à un droit de l'Etat qui lui appartenait en propre, c'est-à-dire à un droit subjectif[5]. Il faut entendre par là un droit conféré par une règle coutumière ou conventionnelle à la personne internationale que constitue l'Etat, droit que l'on peut qualifier de primaire.

B. Le droit primaire qui n'a pas été respecté ayant un caractère subjectif, le même caractère appartient au droit secondaire d'exiger réparation. Il s'agit en effet d'un droit qui est propre à l'Etat lésé et qu'il est seul à pouvoir exercer[6].

---

[3] CH. ROUSSEAU, DROIT INTERNATIONAL PUBLIC, t. V, Paris (1983), p. 6.

[4] Lorsque l'Etat qui est la cible de la violation a subi un dommage matériel ou une atteinte à son honneur, c'est naturellement lui qui doit bénéficier de la remise des choses en l'état et – ou – recevoir une indemnité et – ou – des excuses. Les autres Etats soumis ou régime indissociable n'ont droit qu'à voir effectuer cette réparation.

[5] L'expression «droit subjectif» désigne un concept qui a soulevé dans la doctrine du droit interne de nombreux débats. *Cf.* J. DABIN, LE DROIT SUBJECTIF, Paris (1952), p. 55; P. ROUBIER, DROITS SUBJECTIFS ET SITUATIONS JURIDIQUES, Paris (1963), p. 67. L'existence de tels droits a même été contestée. Sur les thèses de Duguit et de Kelsen, *cf.* J. DABIN, *op. cit.*, *supra* note 5, p. 5. Il n'en demeure pas moins que le concept de droit subjectif est communément employé en droit interne et en droit international.

[6] Sur le caractère subjectif du droit secondaire, *cf.* E. DECAUX, *Responsabilité et réparation, Société française pour le droit international*, dans: LA RESPONSABILITÉ DANS LE SYSTÈME INTERNA-

V

A. Chaque Etat lié par un régime indissociable a un droit subjectif au respect de ce régime non seulement à son égard, mais à celui de ses partenaires. L'existence de ce droit se trouve en germe dans la jurisprudence de la Cour de La Haye. Dans l'affaire du Wimbledon, elle a admis que des Etats parties au Traité de Versailles étaient en droit d'exiger le respect de la liberté de navigation dans le canal de Kiel sans avoir besoin de justifier d'un intérêt pécuniaire lésé[7]. Dans l'affaire du Sud-ouest africain, la Cour a reconnu que, parmi les Etats parties à un traité multilatéral, d'autres que celui qui a subi un dommage matériel pouvent mettre en cause la responsabilité de l'Etat auteur du fait illicite[8]. Enfin, selon l'arrêt *Barcelona Traction*, chaque Etat a «un intérêt juridique» à ce que les règles universelles ou quasi universelles qui consacrent des valeurs communes soient respectées non seulement à son égard, mais à celui de tous les autres Etats[9]. Toutefois les obligations découlant de ces règles existent, aux yeux de la Cour, «envers la communauté internationale dans son ensemble»[10]. Il semble donc qu'elle n'ait pas envisagé l'existence en cette matière d'un droit subjectif de chaque Etat, d'autant plus qu'elle oppose l'hypothèse de la défense des valeurs communes à celle où, dans le cadre de la protection diplomatique, le fait internationalement illicite affecte le droit subjectif d'un seul Etat[11].

B. Lorsque certains Etats occidentaux ont pris des mesures à l'encontre de pays qui avaient commis des agressions ou avaient très gravement violé les droits de l'homme[12], ils semblent s'être considérés comme agissant au nom de la légalité internationale et n'ont jamais invoqué une atteinte à leur droit subjectif au respect des règles en cause.

C. Plusieurs auteurs ne voient pas les choses différemment. «Parfois, écrit Basdevant, un Etat qui n'a subi et dont les nationaux n'ont subi aucun dommage se plaint, d'une manière en quelque sorte objective, du manquement au droit; c'est ce que faisaient la Grande-Bretagne et plus encore l'Italie et

---

TIONAL, Paris (1991), p. 155; P.-M. DUPUY, *Responsabilité et légalité, Société française pour le droit international*, dans: *ibid.* p. 265.

[7] 1 CPIJ, Série A, p. 20.

[8] *Cf.* CIJ (1966), p. 32.

[9] *Cf.* CIJ (1970), p. 32, ch. 33 et 34. L'expression «intérêt juridique» est ici synonyme de droit.

[10] CIJ (1970), p. 32, ch. 33.

[11] *Cf. ibid.* ch. 33.

[12] Sur leurs diverses actions *cf.* P.-M. DUPUY, *op. cit.*, *supra* note 6, p. 285. Selon cet auteur, les mesures prises par ces Etats étaient destinées à sanctionner l'atteinte à des règles internationales «jugées par eux-mêmes cardinales», *ibid.* p. 285.

le Japon dans l'affaire du Wimbledon»[13]. De son côté Ch. De Visscher n'exclut pas qu'il puisse y avoir une action individuelle si des conventions collectives conclues dans l'intérêt général de l'humanité et de la civilisation ne sont pas respectées. Mais il s'agit à ses yeux d'une action «en contrôle de la légalité»[14]. L'analyse à laquelle se livre P.M. Dupuy nous paraît beaucoup plus proche de la réalité. Prenant comme exemple l'agression, il estime qu'en pareil cas, les Etats sont tous lésés, mais dans des intérêts et des droits différents. Celui qui est la cible de cette attaque «est évidemment atteint dans son droit *subjectif* au respect de sa souveraineté. Les autres sont tout aussi directement atteints dans leur droit, mais ce dernier est différent. Il s'agit du droit de chacun des membres de la communauté internationale à voir respecter les 'obligations essentielles' pour la survie, l'intégrité et le développement harmonieux de la communauté. Ou peut ainsi dire ... qu'ils sont atteints dans leur droit *objectif*, puisque identique pour tous»[15].

VI

A. Comme P.M. Dupuy, nous estimons que, dans une hypothèse telle que l'agression, tous les Etats sont lésés. Mais contrairement à lui, nous estimons qu'ils sont atteints dans leur droit subjectif et non pas objectif. Ainsi que nous l'avons vu, lorsqu'il est lié par une règle multilatérale qui crée un régime indissociable, l'Etat assume individuellement l'obligation de respecter cette règle à l'égard de chacun des autres Etats soumis à l'empire de ce régime[16]. A cette obligation correspond nécessairement le droit de chaque Etat au respect de la règle, droit qui lui appartient en propre et dont il nous paraît ainsi difficile de contester le caractère subjectif[17]. Les droits découlant

---

[13] J. BASDEVANT, *Règles générales du droit de la paix*, dans: IV RCADI (1936), p. 471.

[14] DROIT PROCÉDURAL, *op. cit.*, *supra* note 2, p. 71. On notera qu'il ne reconnaît pas cependant aux Etats en termes généraux une sorte d'*actio popularis* pour la défense du droit international, conception assurément étrangère à l'état actuel de l'organisation internationale, *ibid.* p. 71.

[15] P.-M. DUPUY, *op. cit.*, *supra* note 6, pp. 289–290. SALMON ne se réfère pas à un droit, mais à un intérêt. Il admet que, lors de graves violations du droit international, des mesures peuvent être prises par des tiers non directement touchés et sans y être autorisés ou invités par une organisation internationale. J. SALMON, *Les circonstances excluant l'illicéité*, dans: K. ZEMANEK et J. SALMON, RESPONSABILITÉ INTERNATIONALE, Paris (1987), p. 89. Il cite à cet égard les mesures prises par des Etats occidentaux à l'encontre de l'Union soviétique, l'Iran, l'Argentine, le Vietnam et la Libye. Il s'agit à ses yeux de «sanctions ... fondées sur une conception élargie de l'intérêt à agir», *ibid.* p. 176.

[16] Il n'est guère besoin de rappeler que cette obligation ne peut pas exister envers la communauté internationale, laquelle n'est titulaire de droits et d'obligations sur le plan du droit international.

[17] G.I. TUNKIN, THEORY OF INTERNATIONAL LAW, London (1974), p. 222.

de régimes indissociables ne forment donc pas une exception au système général du droit international, système qui a été défini par la Commission du droit international de la manière suivante: «... en droit international, l'idée de violation d'une obligation peut être considérée comme l'équivalent absolu de celle de lésion du droit subjectif d'autrui»[18]. Il s'agit non pas d'une vue théorique, mais de la constatation d'un phénomène qui découle de la structure de la communauté internationale. Ainsi que le dit Barile, le droit international «est obligé d'opérer, même lorsqu'il vise à la protection d'intérêts généraux, suivant le mécanisme classique 'droit-obligation' qui lie réciproquement les membres de la communauté internationale et qui par les membres mêmes est mis en mouvement et géré selon leurs propres intérêts politiques»[19].

B. Il serait faux de croire que les règles qui créent des régimes indissociables sont nécessairement universelles ou à vocation universelle et qu'elles défendent toujours les valeurs fondamentales de la communauté des Etats. Nombre de régimes indissociables appartiennent au droit particulier et concernent des domaines sans rapport avec lesdites valeurs. Il serait donc tout à fait inexact de croire que le principe de la relativité des règles internationales ne s'applique pas, dans toute sa rigueur, à celles qui créent des régimes indissociables.

C. Les règles créant des régimes indissociables ont un effet impératif au sens de l'article 53 de la Convention de Vienne sur le droit des traités. De tels régimes interdisent en effet par leur nature même des accords particuliers dérogatoires.

---

[18] ACDI (1973), vol. II, p. 184, ch. 9. *Voir* également J. Cottereau, *Système juridique et notion de responsabilité, Société française pour le droit international*, dans: La responsabilité dans le système international, *op. cit., supra* note 6, p. 329.

[19] G. Barile, *La structure de l'ordre juridique international*, dans: RCADI (1978), vol. III, p. 9.

"Common Heritage of Mankind": From Metaphor to Myth, and the Consequences of Constructive Ambiguity

by

Moragodage C.W. Pinto

Introduction

Words are the elementary particles that make up the fabric of any law. In international law, words make up communications between governments, declarations, resolutions, treaties, the judgements of international tribunals, and the opinions of jurists. For the lawyer the use of words in the course of argument, or to define or interpret legal concepts is an essential function of professional life. In the process of creating international law through the interaction of sovereign States that are juridically equal, the need to reach compromise with respect to the meaning or scope of some rule and to embody that compromise in words, is nearly always present, frequently eroding clarity of expression. Moreover, this interaction calls for communication between persons from different cultures and different legal systems or philosophies. Often conducted through intermediaries, *viz*. intepreters and translators, this is a feature that may both increase the risk of failure to achieve a meeting of minds, and reduce the likelihood that the resulting text would have a single agreed interpretation.

At conferences convened to formulate treaties or other instruments intended to codify or develop international law, time constraints, fatigue, even personal ambition, are among factors that may heighten pressures toward agreement on a form of words. When opposing views on substance cannot be reconciled, participants may be persuaded to vote in favour of texts so worded as to attract support from opposing groups, even while fundamental differences among them persist, rather than abandon the negotiating effort in which so much labour and resources have been invested. The texts of treaties or resolutions produced under such conditions may not represent true compromise in the sense of trade-offs properly understood, and freely made. Almost inevitably they lack the minimum of precision required for efficient application. They are bridges of paper, unable to support the regulatory structures to come. The price of such diplomatic and organizational "successes" is high indeed. They may foreshadow costly commitments of human and other resources by States, affluent and poor alike, to protracted negotiations only to have it revealed that there had in fact been no meeting of minds, no fundamental agreement on substance, and that the endeavour had been of little consequence.

Conference participants have had recourse to this type of negotiating strategy, involving the use of what has been called "constructive ambiguity" often because the idea that first fired the collective imagination and mobilized legislative effort, was contained in some captivating phrase capable of widely different interpretations: "new international economic order", "common heritage of mankind", "sustainable development". The concept conveyed by the phrase has generally promised immediate transfers of resources to the majority of States, to the poor, while being sufficiently plastic as to tempt the affluent to experiment with it in the hope that the process of its realization might be so controlled as to ensure that the resources to be transferred would not be theirs. Under the pressures of the moment all sides may be willing to take up the challenge, considering it politically expedient that negotiations should continue despite disagreement on fundamentals.

All this would seem to place upon international negotiators, and lawyers in particular, a special duty of care to ensure that words and phrases are used responsibly and with as much precision as possible; that the relation of fact and experience to the inspiring central phrase is clear and demonstrable at all times; and that formulation of a treaty should be undertaken only when there is a manifest meeting of minds on the scope and content of basic principles, and that it should, in fact, be abandoned or postponed where basic agreement has not been reached; and finally, that they not apply their skills to papering over differences, and thus condone the use of "constructive ambiguity".

This essay is about the search made over a quarter of a century for the meaning of one such inspiring phrase, a metaphor, "the common heritage of mankind". It may illustrate some of the perils associated with emotive ambiguity and indefinitely postponed agreement on fundamentals. Here, it will be contended, lack of agreement on the meaning of the concept contained in a charismatic original metaphor, and thus on its legal potential, fostered the emergence of a measure of illusion or self-deception among the participants, the growth of a mythology which the majority came to believe in. It may be useful first to examine briefly a theory of the origin of myth in metaphor, that may help to explain why rule-making on the basis of metaphor is a risky enterprise.

I. LANGUAGE, METAPHOR AND MYTH

Words are used to describe facts, both of the world outside, and within our minds, and to direct our own and other people's actions. Words derive from human sounds made far back in time in response to certain specific impressions of natural objects and phenomena. Over the millennia, language developed through a process that included the formulation of general concepts out of these specific impressions, aimed at breaking the isolation of the individual impression, relating it to other things, and gathering it and them in some inclusive order or system.[1] An impression was fixed in, and by, the word; and the word, in time became informed with a spiritual quality. So powerful was that spiritual potential, that one authority was moved to refer to words as "momentary gods".[2]

Philosophers have often commented upon the power of words to influence thought.[3] Wilhelm von Humboldt has said:

> "Man lives with his objects chiefly ... one may say exclusively – as language presents them to him. By the same process whereby he spins his language out of his own being, he ensnares himself in it; and each language draws a magic circle round the people to which it belongs, a circle from which there is no escape save by stepping out of it into another."[4]

Max Müller referred to:

> "the dark shadow which language throws upon thought, and which can never disappear till language becomes entirely commensurate with thought, which it never will..."[5]

---

1 E. CASSIRER, LANGUAGE AND MYTH (1946) at 25. Extensive use of this translation of CASSIRER's brilliant essay SPRACHE UND MYTHOS (1924), and works therein cited, is respectfully and gratefully acknowledged.

2 USENER (GÖTTERNAMEN. VERSUCH EINER LEHRE VON DER RELIGIÖSEN BEGRIFFSBILDUNG (1896)) cited by E. CASSIRER, *ibid.* at 15, and quoted at 18–23, 33.

3 The theory that a language influences the user's thought should be distinguished from the theory that particular languages shape their users' thoughts in ways that differ dramatically from one another *i.e.* linguistic determinism. For a review and criticism of linguistic determinism, *see* the recent outstanding work by S. PINKER, THE LANGUAGE INSTINCT: HOW THE MIND CREATES LANGUAGE (1994), Chapter 3 entitled *Mentalese*.

4 English translation quoted in E. CASSIRER, *op. cit., supra* note 1, at 9.

5 M. MÜLLER, THE PHILOSOPHY OF MYTHOLOGY, APPENDED to INTRODUCTION TO THE SCIENCE OF RELIGION (1873) quoted in E. CASSIRER, *op. cit., supra* note 1, at 5.

Ernst Cassirer speaks of the self-deception rooted in language:

> "which is forever making game of the human mind, ever ensnaring it in that iridescent play of meanings that is its own heritage...,"[6]

while Wittgenstein described "philosophy" as "a battle against the 'bewitchment' of our intelligence by means of language."[7]

Contributing to this phenomenon of "bewitchment" or "ensnaring" of the mind, is the fact that words, as symbols uttered by one and interpreted by others, do not always convey meanings precisely. Words are affected by what Cassirer calls "the curse of mediacy". He observes:

> "All linguistic denotation is essentially ambiguous – and in its ambiguity, this 'paronymia' of words lies the source of all myths."[8]

As more complex thought evolved, the use of analogy, of metaphor, became necessary, for the purpose of informing more graphically, to persuade or compel. Metaphor abounds in all our thinking about abstract matters. While clearly a useful tool, the attractive power of metaphor may present a hazard to precise verbal communication, as when analogy is not recognized as such, or is interpreted variously. Going beyond mere communication, metaphor has also the power to induce conviction, sometimes taking the form of an effective slogan.[9]

Compounding the effects of the "curse of mediacy", the hazard posed by the use of analogy is its potential for generating myth as a by-product. That hazard is well expressed in this passage from a work by Müller quoted by Cassirer:

> "Whenever any word, that was at first used metaphorically, is used without a clear conception of the steps that led from its original to its metaphorical meaning, there is danger of mythology; whenever those steps are forgotten and artificial steps put in their places, we have mythology, or, if I may say so, we have diseased language, whether that language refers to religious or secular interests..."[10]

---

6 *Ibid.* at 6.

7 L. WITTGENSTEIN, PHILOSOPHICAL INVESTIGATIONS, Part I, paragraph 109.

8 E. CASSIRER, *op. cit.*, *supra* note 1, at 4, *see* also at 7.

9 AS TO THE FUNCTION OF SLOGANS, *see* R.H. THOULESS, STRAIGHT AND CROOKED THINKING (1953). In a chapter entitled *Predigested Thinking*, he observes: "Thus, the second Russian revolution was directed not by a preaching of the subtleties of Marx to the people, but by the slogan 'All Power to the Soviets.' This was a legitimate use of a slogan; **slogans can reasonably and properly be used to stir people to action, but not to induce belief**." (emphasis added) P. 133. According to E. PARTRIDGE, the word "slogan" is derived from a Gaelic term meaning "battle cry" ORIGINS (1966).

10 E. CASSIRER, *op. cit.*, *supra* note 1, at 86, quoting MÜLLER, LECTURES ON THE SCIENCE OF LANGUAGE (1875). *See* also R.H. THOULESS, *op. cit.*, *supra* note 9, at p. 133: "Analogies are

Of course, myths have their place, in every respect as important as any other motivating element within our consciousness. But there are good reasons for guarding against the formation of myths in the context of rule-making among States. Here a measure of the common understanding of concepts and of the factual context in which they must be interpreted is nothing less than essential to achieving more or less precise formulations, which themselves become the basis for acceptance of rules and, ultimately, compliance with them. The incautious, careless or expedient use of metaphor in such contexts can be shown to result in an enormous waste of time, of funds and creative energy, all scarce resources that might be applied in pursuit of more beneficial aims.

II. UNDERSTANDING THE "COMMON HERITAGE OF MANKIND": A CLASH OF IDEOLOGIES

The idea, expounded by Malta's Arvid Pardo in a three-hour address to the United Nations General Assembly in 1967,[11] that the area of the sea-bed beyond the then narrow limits of a coastal States' national jurisdiction, and its resources, should be declared "the common heritage of mankind", captured the imagination of diplomats and scholars of the developing countries of the time. The phrase had an intrinsic emotive appeal, conveying the notion of new wealth acquired automatically as of a right, held in common by all countries without distinction on grounds of technological capability and political influence; notions of equal rights and distributive justice.

Pardo's phrase was, of course, a metaphor. There was, after all, no ancestor who had died and bequeathed rights to the sea-bed to all countries; no law of intestate succession on which they might base a claim, and no court to supervise the distribution of such a "heritage". Inspiring to many, the metaphor had no obvious connection with real experience, conveyed no precise meaning, and was, as the industrialized countries were quick to point out, "of uncertain legal content". However, swept along by the enthusiasms of the post-colonial period and by contemporary scientific writing interpreted by some to mean that "the Area" held limitless mineral wealth,[12] Pardo's

---

a valuable guide as to what facts we may expect, **but are never final evidence as to what we shall discover**. A guide whose reliability is certain to give out at some point must obviously be accepted with caution. We can never feel certain of a conclusion which rests only on analogy, and we must always look for more direct proof. Also we must examine all our methods of thought carefully, because thinking by analogy is much more extensive than many of us are inclined to suppose." (emphasis added)

[11] A. PARDO, THE COMMON HERITAGE: SELECTED PAPERS ON OCEANS AND WORLD ORDER (Introduction by E. MANN BORGESE – 1975).

[12] *E.g.* J. MERO, THE MINERAL RESOURCES OF THE SEA (1965).

idea of the sea-bed as "the common heritage of mankind" became the subject of the well known Declaration of Principles by the General Assembly, adopted without dissent (but with some fourteen industrialized and socialist country abstentions) at its Twenty-fifth Anniversary Session in 1970.[13]

The essential elements of the "common heritage" concept as set out in the Declaration were (1) **common sovereignty**, the area (and its resources) *in situ* could never become private property, or be subjected to the sovereignty of any State; (2) **common benefit**, the exploration of the area and the exploitation of its resources should be "carried out for the benefit of mankind as a whole"; (3) **common management**, an "international treaty of a universal character generally agreed upon" would establish "an international regime applying to the area and its resources and including appropriate international machinery to give effect to its provisions;" and (4) reservation of the area "exclusively for peaceful purposes". It was the first step taken by governments toward agreement on the "legal content" of the new term.[14] Much scholarly writing would attempt to document the antecedents of the concept, to establish its roots in previously recognized legal principle,[15] and to legitimize its reception into customary international law.[16] Some declared

---

[13] General Assembly resolution 2749 (XXV) adopted 17 December 1970 by 108 votes in favour, none against, with 14 abstentions.

[14] Similarly, romantic phrases conveying an emotive appeal on behalf of "all mankind" had indeed, been incorporated in internationally negotiated resource related treaties before. References to "the interest of all mankind" and "the progress of all mankind" occur in the preambular paragraphs of the 1959 Antarctic Treaty, and of some of its related instruments. Article 1 of the 1967 Treaty on Principles governing the Activities of States in the Exploration and Use of Outer Space, including the Moon and Other Celestial Bodies, had declared exploration of outer space and celestial bodies to be "the province of all mankind". Subsequent to the Declaration, the 1979 Agreement Governing the Activities of States on the Moon and Other Celestial Bodies, elaborating upon the 1967 Treaty, declared that "The Moon and its natural resources are the common heritage of mankind" (article 11).

[15] *See* for example A. PARDO and E. BORGESE *supra* note 11; E. LUARD, THE CONTROL OF THE SEA-BED: A NEW INTERNATIONAL ISSUE (1974); A. DOLMAN (ed.), RESOURCES, REGIMES, WORLD ORDER (1981); A.M. POST, DEEPSEA MINING AND THE LAW OF THE SEA (1983); R.C. OGLEY, INTERNATIONALIZING THE SEABED (1984); S. MAHMOUDI, THE LAW OF DEEP SEA-BED MINING (1987).

[16] In this connection, *see* the statements of the representative of Mexico before the Sea-bed Committee in 1971, U.N. doc. A/AC.138/SR.58 at 184–185; of Iraq U.N. doc. A/AC.138/SR.44 at 130; and of Trinidad and Tobago, U.N. doc. A/AC.138/SR.50 at 61; and "The Legal Position of the Group of 77, etc." U.N. doc. A/CONF.62/106 of 23 September 1980. For a review and analysis of the views of delegates and of scholars on the significance of the Declaration of Principles, *see* K. SKUBISZEWSKI, *La nature juridique de la 'Declaration des principes' sur les fonds marins*, 4 ANNALES D'ÉTUDES INTERNATIONALES (1973) at 237–248. "Nous pouvons donc conclure que dans son ensemble la Déclaration formule des principes non obligatoires au sens juridique. Elle établit en revance un programme qui doit guider les négociateurs dans l'élaboration et la concrétisation du concept du 'patrimoine commun.' La differance fondamentale entre les principes recommandés par l'Assemblée Générale et les règles juridiques d'un futur traité-loi demeure

it to be *jus cogens*[17] even before the outlines of the concept could be "generally agreed upon".

To the developing countries "common heritage" meant that sovereignty or ownership in the area and its resources was common and indivisible. It followed that exploration for and exploitation of the area and its resources had to be carried out collectively, through an intergovernmental organization of universal membership that would plan and manage all activities, and eventually distribute the benefits to all States (and even to other collectivities) on the basis of need. The poor would thus benefit in inverse proportion to their investment in these activities and in maintenance of the organization. As far as the poorer countries were concerned, the value of that "investment" would be thought of as augmented by their undivided entitlement to a share in the sea-bed's mineral wealth, and as giving them rights to participate in the organization's decisions on the basis of equality with all other States.

As conceived by the developing countries, the organization (named by them the "International Seabed Authority") would carry out these activities through service contracts with private firms (or the State entities of the socialist countries) chosen on a competitive basis, to execute the different phases of projects from prospecting, and recovery of minerals, to transportation, processing and marketing of the extracted metals. Being thus in control of all such activities, the Authority would also regulate production of minerals from the sea-bed, if necessary, restricting access to the area. This would at once prevent sea-bed minerals from being exploited exclusively by the industrialized countries which currently had the technological capability to do so; ensure the preservation of the sea-bed's resources for use by future generations, and prevent the marketing of metals from this new source from adversely affecting the export earnings of the many poor countries which produced the same metals from within their own territories. If such regulation were to fail to prevent the latter category of adverse effects, the Authority would be empowered to arrange economic "adjustment assistance" for the affected country, until protective "commodity agreements" could be established.

---

entière. Pourtant, le premier pas a été fait et la Déclaration, si générale qu'elle soit, délimite le contenu doctrinal et conceptuel du régime futur des fonds marins. Après l'adoption de la Déclaration, il serait très difficile de renverser la vapeur et d'orienter les travaux sur le droit nouveau selon des principes autres que ceux de la Déclaration" (at 247–148).

[17] This view is based on an interpretation of the provisions of articles 136, 155 paragraph 2, and 311 paragraph 6 of the draft Convention on the Law of the Sea. However, a proposal to recognize the "common heritage" concept expressly as having the character of *jus cogens*, was not adopted. UNCLOS III, Official Records, Vol. XIV at 129.

In addition, the Authority would be empowered to collect and disseminate scientific knowledge from the exploration and exploitation of the sea--bed, and to facilitate the transfer of technology associated with sea-bed mining to developing countries which wished to enter the field, inspired by their undivided share in sovereignty over the minerals. Science and technology were seen as being among the "benefits" to be distributed, along with profits, in accomplishing what the Declaration of Principles (paragraph 9) appeared to treat as the central purpose of the international regime, *viz*. to provide for

> "the orderly and safe development and rational management of the area and its resources and for expanding opportunities for the use thereof and ensure the equitable sharing by States in the benefits derived therefrom, taking into particular consideration the interests and needs of the developing countries..."

The industrialized countries saw the concept of "common heritage" in a very different light. Anticipating in the decade of the 1970's a dwindling of land sources of the metals available from "the Area", the emergence of producer cartels, and a sharp increase in the prices of those metals, the sea-bed seemed to offer timely release from dependence on developing country land-based producers, and the political pressures and entanglements that such dependence might entail. Secure in the knowledge that they alone possessed the technology and other resources to recover the Area's minerals, they sought to realise the concept of the "common heritage" not through establishing a giant regulatory bureaucracy with a monopoly over sea-bed mining, but by an extention to the sea-bed of the well-recognized principle of the "freedom of the seas". To them, "common heritage" implied that there should be freedom of access to the area for sea-bed miners from all participating States on an equal footing under a system of licensing. There should be minimal technical, financial and environmental supervision, administered by an organization in which the industrialized countries, by virtue of superior economic capacity, financial input, technical competence and mining experience would become entitled to a position of ultimate control. The regime would cover only the recovery of minerals from the sea-bed, and no other related subsequent activity, such as transportation and processing. It would provide adequate protection for proprietary rights in the technology employed, and there would be no interference with market forces. "Benefits" from the system would take the form of a portion of the profits from each mining operation being paid by each licensee to be agreed, but according to conditions and criteria not dissimilar to those currently applied by multilateral aid institutions like the World Bank and the International Monetary Fund.

The developing countries recognized early that it would not be feasible to reach "general" agreement on an organization that would be both regulator and sole sea-bed miner as such a scheme would not be consistent with fairness as interpreted by the advocates of the free market. Accordingly, they modified their proposals by limiting the functions of the Authority to supervising sea--bed activities, and establishing a separate intergovernmental entity, the "Enterprise", that would engage in sea-bed mining. The Enterprise was conceived as an organ of the International Sea-bed Authority, but at the same time an autonomous corporate entity with its own directorate – a unique legal creation – required to operate on commercial lines, in competing with other sea-bed miners for contracts with the Authority.[18]

In the negotiations that ensued, the "dirigistic" policies favoured by the majority, the developing countries, were opposed by a relatively small group of economically and politically influential industrialized countries certain of the efficacy of the free market and private enterprise. Another relatively small group, the socialist countries, adopted a third position. While they might have been expected to fully support the "dirigistic" stance of the developing countries which had much in common with their own domestic policies, they did not do so. Recognizing the contradictions inherent in trying to administer a "dirigistic" regime in collaboration with the capitalist West, they chose to give only qualified support to the developing countries' initiatives while ensuring that group representation and impact would be maintained in any future organization. Moreover, negotiation of these issues seemed to offer opportunities for expanding their influence, and for promoting mechanisms that would channel to themselves some of the advanced mining technologies developed by private enterprise.

The attempt to give legal content to the "common heritage" metaphor and to resolve the many issues arising in the process was carried out over a quarter of a century within United Nations in four main phases, the need for each succeeding phase becoming apparent in the course of the preceding one. Between 1967–1973 the subject was dealt with in the Committee (initially an *ad hoc* Committee) of the General Assembly on the Peaceful Uses of the Sea-Bed and the Ocean Floor beyond the Limits of National Jurisdiction; from 1973–1982 it was dealt with by Committee I of the Third United Nations Conference on the Law of the Sea, which incorporated the results of its labours in part XI of

---

[18] Not all economists from the developing countries viewed the positions taken up by their governments' representatives with enthusiasm. One of them, P.N. KIRTHISINGHA, then a senior official with UNCTED, subjected those positions in general, and the idea of an Enterprise in particular, to frank and penetrating criticism. *See* his article *The Enterprise: An Expendable Triumph*, MARINE POLICY (1981), July.

the United Nations Convention on the Law of the Sea; from 1982–1994 measures for effective operation of the International Sea-bed Authority were discussed by the Preparatory Commission established by the Conference; and from 1990–1994 a dialogue aimed at achieving universal participation in the Convention was conducted by the Secretary-General of the United Nations, resulting in the adoption of an Agreement relating to the Implementation of Part XI of the U.N. Convention on the Law of the Sea.

The history of the negotiations has been amply described and documented elsewhere.[19] The outline that follows is only intended to recall salient features of the protracted efforts that were made to interpret a metaphor, efforts that seemed inexorably to carry the participants away from the lessons of experience – primarily those connected with the exercise of power, and into the realm of myth.

III. NEGOTIATING AGREEMENT: EVOLUTION OF A MYTH

The Third U.N. Conference on the Law of the Sea, having made substantial progress toward resolving most of the complex issues before it, remained unable to bridge the essentially ideological gap that persisted within its First Committee between a "common heritage" realized through "dirigism" and one driven by the free market, concerning the provisions of part XI of a draft Convention on the Law of the Sea. What appeared to be emerging was the compromise that both "dirigism" and the free market would have their roles referred to as the "parallel system". The mining corporations of member States would be allowed access to sea-bed minerals upon satisfying agreed criteria and giving specified undertakings as to the conduct of exploration and mining operations, including those concerning transfer of technology and payment of royalties and other revenues to the Authority. Access would thus not, in terms, be guaranteed, but virtually certain, subject to agreed mineral production limits. In parallel with these entities, the Enterprise would mine the sea-bed acting on behalf of "mankind as a whole", and would be assisted in its operations through receiving from each miner a fully prospected mine site of prime quality, as well as other preferential treatment as part of the conditions for award of a mining contract by the Authority. However, negotiations remained dead-locked regarding a range of issues concerning the structure and powers of the Authority and the favoured

---

[19] *See* for example, M.G. SCHMIDT, COMMON HERITAGE OR COMMON BURDEN? (1989); R.C. OGLEY, *op. cit.*, *supra* note 15; S. MAHMOUDI, *op. cit.*, *supra* note 15; A.M. POST, *op. cit.*, *supra* note 15; and J.K. SEBENIUS, NEGOTIATING THE LAW OF THE SEA (1984), all of which have extensive bibliographies.

position foreseen for the Enterprise. In 1976 a bold initiative by then Secretary of State Henry Kissinger seemed to complement the parallel system and pave the way to general agreement. Kissinger's initiative, which nevertheless left considerable room for negotiation in matters of detail, had three elements which seemed directed toward meeting the expressed concerns of the developing countries: (1) his government would be willing to "see to the financing" of the Enterprise and its establishment as a viable, functioning entity by the time any other entity was in a position to commence sea-bed mining on a commercial scale; (2) his government would be willing to adopt practical measures for the transfer of sea-bed mining technology to the Enterprise; and (3) assuming the "parallel system" (as opposed to the Authority's monopoly advocated by the developing countries) were to be written into the treaty, his government would be willing to have the whole system reviewed after, say, 25 years of its operation.

Intensive negotiations, in which the representatives of the industrialized countries participated fully, led to the elaboration of provisions which appeared to reflect the Kissinger proposals in a generally acceptable way. Having been deemed by the officers of the Conference to have received "widespread and substantial support" indicating that they offered a "substantially improved prospect of consensus",[20] those provisions were incorporated in part XI and its annexes to become, so it was generally believed, part of the "package deal"[21] established as an element of the culture of the Conference. While there were indeed those among the United States' representatives who remained convinced that inclusion of such provisions in part XI would result in eventual rejection of the entire Convention by their legislature, irrespective of the dominant party or the President in office, others believed that rules, regulations and procedures could be worked out at the

---

[20] These were the agreed conditions on which texts elaborated according to the Conference's working methods were to be admitted by the President's "collegium" into the emerging composite draft of the Convention. *See* U.N. doc. A/CONF.62/62.

[21] M.G. SCHMIDT, *op. cit.* (*supra* note 19) suggests that the following passage from a statement by U.S. Ambassador Phillips in the First Committee of the U.N. General Assembly: "We do not seek priorities ... It is not our desire to deal in the context of an international conference in 'manageable packages' ... The conference should deal concurrently with all the issues that could be expected to come before it." (*op. cit.* at 28–29) was "public endorsement of the notion of UNCLOS as a 'package deal.'" Ambassador T.T.B. KOH, who presided over the final stages of the Conference, referred to the "package deal" as among the "major themes" to emerge from the Conference: "The second theme that emerged from statements is that the provisions of the Convention are closely interrelated and form an integral package. Thus it is not possible for a State to pick what it likes and to disregard what it does not like. It was also said that rights and obligations go hand in hand and it is not permissible to claim rights under the Convention without being willing to shoulder the corresponding obligations." (Ambassador KOH's remarks appearing in *A Constitution for the Oceans* published with the official text of the Convention.)

stage of a Preparatory Commission that would meet the United States' objectives and so neutralize any offensive ideological colour perceived in the parent text. It might thus be feasible, having conceded the ideological trappings to the developing countries, to secure the United States' (and the industrialized countries') objectives at the stage of implementation, thus making the Convention universally acceptable.

The political changes that swept President Reagan into office, and the review of United States law of the sea policies that followed, resulted in the President's announcing some six objectives to be achieved by the newly appointed delegation to the Conference so as to make part XI of the Convention acceptable to the United States. The Convention's provisions (a) should not deter the development of any deep sea-bed mineral resources to meet national and world demand; (b) should assure national access to those resources by ... qualified entities to enhance United States security of supply, avoid monopolization of the resources by the Enterprise, and promote the economic development of the resources; (c) should provide a decision-making role in the deep sea-bed regime that reflects the political and economic interests and financial contributions of participating States; (d) should not allow for amendments to come into force without approval of the participating States, including ... the advice and consent of the United States Senate; (e) should not set other undesirable precedents for international organizations; and (f) should be likely to receive the advice and consent of the Senate; the Convention should not contain provisions for the mandatory transfer of technology and participation by and funding for national liberation movements.[22]

These views regarding part XI, although articulated by the United States and maintained by it to the point of voting against the adoption of the text of the Convention, were shared by the industrialized countries as a whole. The issues raised were not new, and although these objectives were presented subsequently by the United States as informal proposals in various stages of elaboration, they failed to halt the inexorable march of the Conference toward concluding its decade-long negotiation. Despite the efforts of a "Group of 11" of industrialized countries to work out proposals for compromise at that late stage, it seemed that a generalized terminal inertia had foreclosed the possibility of an universally agreed outcome. Some industrialized countries did, indeed, vote in favour of the Convention[23] and sign it as well. Relying on a strategy of post-Conference adjustment, all of them but the United States

---

[22] 371 U.S. STATE DEPT. CURRENT POLICY (1982), January–February.

[23] On 29 April 1982 the draft Convention as a whole was adopted by a vote of 130 in favour (most of the developing countries, Canada, France, Japan, the Nordic countries, Australia and

participated actively, if warily, in the next phase, the work of the Preparatory Commission established by Annex I to the Final Act of the Convention.

The developing countries, on the other hand, hailed the Convention, and the provisions of part XI, as a major achievement of an emerging international "community". Painstakingly negotiated by all participants irrespective of level of economic development or ideological persuasion, part XI in particular seemed to them to reflect the fundamentals of a New International Economic Order which placed emphasis on "full and effective participation on the basis of equality, of all countries in solving the world's economic problems." Other elements of the NIEO reflected in part XI interpreting the "common heritage" concept, included application of the "equality of States" principle (one-state-one-vote) in the decision-making procedures of the International Sea-bed Authority including its executive organ, the Council; "Just and equitable relationship between prices of exports from the developing countries, and prices of imports by them," which had inspired a formulation of the Authority's production policies, and economic adjustment assistance to adversely affected land-based mineral producers; and "giving developing countries access to the achievements of science and technology," reflected in provisions on the transfer of technology and dissemination of scientific knowledge. More general provisions based on other NIEO principles such as the international "duty" of co-operation, and "preferential treatment of the developing countries" were to be found in part XI, as elsewhere in the Convention.[24] Moreover, the range and variety of topics dealt with by the Conference, and its negotiating mechanisms and working methods, concerning which the industrialized countries had expressed reservations, seemed to the developing countries consistent with efficiency as well as equity, in that they enabled the individual and collective bargaining strengths among them to be used to full effect. To them, in contrast to the attitude of the industrialized countries, the scope, mechanisms and procedures of the Conference added up to a model to be emulated in future "legislative" initiatives.

New Zealand), to 4 against (the United States, Israel, Venezuela and Turkey), with 18 abstentions (nine socialist countries, Britain, W. Germany, Belgium, the Netherlands, Luxembourg, Italy, Spain and Thailand).

24 The words and phrases quoted in this paragraph are from the Declaration on the Establishment of the New International Economic Order, U.N. General Assembly resolution 3201 of the Sixth Special Session, adopted 1 May 1974.

IV. IMPLEMENTING THE REGIME: DISMANTLING THE MYTH

The developing countries embarked on the work of the Preparatory Commission as though it were a continuation of the Conference itself, tending to ignore, it seemed, the persistent critical stance of the industrialized countries. The adopted text of the Convention, including part XI and related provisions were to them immutable, and the efforts of some industrialized country representatives to secure adjustments that might have garnered some support within their ranks, were met with legal and moral arguments that were difficult to counter: the sanctity to be attached to a carefully negotiated text that had been formally adopted by an overwhelming majority, and had already been presented to national parliaments with a view to ratification; and the commitment of all to treat the outcome of the Conference as a "package deal" which a former participant might accept or reject, but from which no selective withdrawal would be acceptable. It seemed that if any radical surgery affecting part XI were to be attempted, this should be done outside the Preparatory Commission, in a forum less prone to be influenced by the history and the aspirations that had brought the Convention into existence.

Commencing in July 1990, the Secretary-General of the United Nations provided just such a forum by inviting concerned States to informal consultations aimed at making acceptance of the Convention "universal", a coded reference to facilitating ratification by the United States and the other industrialized countries by making significant changes to part XI and related provisions[25] of the Convention. Driven by a variety of global changes, including wider acceptance of market-oriented policies and dwindling reliance on dirigism and central planning world-wide, the dissolution of the Soviet Union and its consequences for the direction and level of influence exercised by the States of Eastern Europe, and an industry forecast that deep sea-bed mining was only likely to commence in the next century, the course of the consultations seemed promising enough to induce the United States to begin to take part in them in April 1993. The result was the preparation and submission to the U.N. General Assembly during its 48th extended session in July 1994, of the Agreement Relating to the Implementation of Part XI of the United Nations Convention on the Law of the Sea.[26] When in force, that Agreement "interpreted and applied together with part XI of the Con-

[25] Essentially, Annex III: *Basic Conditions of Prospecting Exploration and Exploitation*, and Annex IV *The Enterprise*.

[26] The Report of the Secretary-General on the result of his consultations, including the draft resolution and AGREEMENT and its Annex is contained in U.N. Doc. A/48/950.

vention as a single instrument," would nullify those provisions in the original text of part XI that had not been universally acceptable, and pave the way for ratification of the Convention by the industrialized countries, including the United States.

The resolution containing the Draft Implementing Agreement and a detailed Annex was adopted on 28 July 1994 by 121 votes in favour, with no opposition, and with some 7 abstentions.[27] The Agreement and its Annex would have the effect of suppressing those provisions of part XI that had been inspired by the NIEO and put in place at the decade-long insistence of the developing countries in the belief that the vote of the majority of State representatives at a conference signified a "democratic" decision that would sooner or later compel or induce democracies within individual States, however powerful, to comply and to assume the obligations imposed by that decision. The provisions of the Annex to the implementing Agreement ensure expeditious, non-discriminatory Council approval of an application for a plan of work/contract to explore or exploit sea-bed minerals,[28] thus guaranteeing access to sea-bed minerals for all. New production policies[29] designed to promote the exploitation of sea-bed minerals, replace the old which would have limited exploitation in order to protect land-based mineral producers pending the elaboration of one or more commodity agreements which would then take on that role.[30] The possibility of compensation or economic adjustment assistance for the latter is circumscribed, if not virtually excluded by limiting funds available for the purpose to the amount of a surplus after expenditure on the administrative expenses of the Authority.[31]

While the Assembly retains its plenary role it is now required, as a rule, to act by consensus.[32] The Agreement shifts emphasis to the recommendatory role of the Council,[33] itself re-designed[34] to ensure that decisions perceived as

---

27 U.N. Doc. A/48/263 reprinted 33 (1994) ILM 1309.

28 Annex, Section 1, paras. 6–11 and Section 3, paras. 11 and 12.

29 Annex, Section 6.

30 By para. 7 of Section 6 the following provisions of the Convention no longer apply: article 151, paras. 1–7 (production ceiling) and other provisions on the selection of applicants for contracts by reference to production limits: article 162, para. 2(q); article 165, para. 2(n); Annex III, article 6, para. 5, and article 7. Also suppressed is Convention article 151, para. 9, which empowered the Authority to limit the production from the Area of minerals other than those from polymetallic nodules.

31 Annex, Section 7. While the power to establish a "system of compensation or ... other measures of adjustment assistance" remains with the Assembly (Convention article 151, para. 10) the Agreement makes it clear that all critical decisions are to be taken by the Council on the recommendation of the newly constituted Finance Committee.

32 Annex, Section 3 (Decision-making), paras. 2, 3 and 4.

33 Annex, Section 3, paras. 1 and 4.

34 Annex, Section 3, paras. 9, 10 and 15.

inconsistent with the interests of major contributors, would not be adopted.[35] To protect those interests even further, the Agreement establishes a Finance Committee of 15 members, in which, for the foreseeable future, "the five largest financial contributors to the administrative budget of the Authority" will have assured representation.[36] The Assembly and the Council, when taking decisions on specified financial issues are to "take into account the recommendations of the Finance Committee." The Finance Committee's decisions on matters of substance are to be taken by consensus. Elaborate provisions in part XI of the Convention intended to enable the Authority to obtain the best possible revenues from mines, are abandoned, and are substituted essentially by an instruction to the Authority to adopt rules, regulations and procedures for financial terms of contracts that are "fair both to the contractor and to the Authority," to apply them in a non-discriminatory manner, and to revise them periodically.[37] The power conferred on the Authority by article 174, paragraph 1 of the Convention, to borrow funds to finance its administrative budget, is withdrawn.[38]

The Enterprise, the unique inter-governmental mining arm of the Authority, conceived as having a favoured position as a kind of standard-bearer of the New International Economic Order, is reduced to a shadow of the original concept. It will have no staff of its own, but would use the staff of the Authority to carry out a modest range of functions, essentially the monitoring and review of trends and developments relating to deep sea-bed mining, and the study and evaluation of specified categories of related information.[39] The obligation earlier undertaken by states parties "to fund one mine site of the Enterprise" is suppressed.[40] If and when the Enterprise is made operative, it must conduct its operations through joint ventures, and be subject to the Council's directives. It is required to adhere to "sound commercial principles", and will not receive preferential treatment. In particular, certain obligations concerning the transfer of technology, to have been undertaken by contractors, are not to apply.[41] Finally, the offending provisions of article

---

35 Annex, Section 3, paras. 5, 9(a).

36 Annex, Section 9, paras. 3 and 8. The Finance Committee is the subsidiary organ of the Council foreseen in article 162, para. 2(y) of the Convention.

37 Annex, Section 8. The provisions of the Convention's Annex III, article 13, paras. 3–10, which were the subject of protracted and complex negotiations during the Conference, are suppressed.

38 Annex, Section 1, para. 14.

39 Annex, Section 2.

40 Annex, Section 2, para. 3, declaring Convention Annex IV, article 11, para. 3 not to apply.

41 Annex, Section 2, para. 4, declaring Convention Annex III, article 3, para. 5 not to apply.

155 of the Convention (the "Review Clause") on mandatory entry into force of amendments adopted following review, are declared not to apply.[42]

V. THE FORTUNES OF A METAPHOR

Intensive study of the "common heritage" concept with a view to determining its legal content commenced in 1967 with the establishment of an *ad hoc* Committee of the General Assembly to deal with the matter. Fifteen years later, in December 1982 part XI of the Convention, inspired as we have seen, by the tenets of the New International Economic Order, was adopted by an overwhelming majority of States, and signed by an unprecedented number of them within a year. The task of elaborating "all possible measures to ensure the entry into effective operation without undue delay of the Authority ... and to make the necessary arrangement for the commencement of [its] functions" was carried out over another 11 years, before those negotiations were overtaken by events. The focus of activity then shifted to the Secretary-General's consultations, from which resulted the suppression of large sections of part XI, indeed those very sections that had been the subject of the most protracted and complex negotiations in the first place. Thus, it had taken a **quarter of a century** and countless millions in various currencies from the budget of the United Nations and, equally importantly, from all of the budgets of participating States, to determine by near-consensus the legal content of the "common heritage", only to have that legal content radically altered in the **two years** that followed.

What caused this colossal expenditure of funds, time and human creativity was, it seems, the emergence of a myth generated in the course of efforts, however dedicated and sincere, to give legal content to an emotive metaphor: "common heritage of mankind". The meaning of the metaphor may well have been clear to Arvid Pardo and his collaborators when making their presentation to the General Assembly in 1967. But the analogy they used generated different meanings among groups of their listeners. The "curse of mediacy" which, as we saw at the outset, besets all language, was compounded here through the use of an emotive metaphor whose original meaning was lost over time, if it was ever clearly apprehended. To the majority of participants at the Third U.N. Conference on the Law of the Sea

42 Annex, Section 4, suppressing Convention article 155, paras. 1, 3 and 4, but requiring any Review Conference to maintain the "principles, regime and other terms referred to in article 155" which include the "common heritage of mankind", its legal content now interpreted in the Implementation Agreement so as to be generally agreed upon.

"common heritage of mankind" came to imply distributive justice, co-operation and preferential treatment for the poor. This was the myth embodied in part XI of the Convention on the Law of the Sea. It was believed, moreover, that that understanding of the metaphor, collectively expressed and given legal value through agreed procedural rules could, on the analogy of a national legislature, form the basis of a regime and institutions that would bring about compliance by all States, including those whose resources would be vital to its operation. Such a belief could only have been based on the grave misunderstanding that law-making at the inter-state level was a mere matter of pluralities. Little thought seems to have been given to the complexities of the process through which compliance with international law is to be achieved. Little thought seems to have been given to the central fact of that process, a fact which all had surely learned from experience: **disparities of power**.

A remarkable aspect of the adoption of the Implementing Agreement which in effect destroyed the myth and modified part XI, was the welcome accorded to it by the developing countries whose statist and dirigistic positions had been reflected in many provisions of part XI as it stood originally. There were no tears for aspirations denied, no words of regret much less of defiance, at having to accept features of the sea-bed regime **which they had resolutely opposed during the 15 years from 1968 to 1982, some for as long as a quarter of a century**. In particular, there was no epitaph for the demise of the New International Economic Order, the fountain of inspiration during much of the Conference. On the contrary, the enthusiasm with which representative after representative from the developing countries rose to welcome the Implementing Agreement, and extol the anticipated "universality" of the Convention could only be taken to imply that there had been a complete *volte-face* on their part, individually and collectively. In fact, the draft resolution containing the text of the Implementing Agreement was introduced by a representative from a developing country,[43] and given firm endorsement by the developing countries as a whole, in the following terms:

> "As Chairman of the Group of 77 on the Law of the Sea, it is a distinct honour and pleasure to welcome the draft Resolution and the Agreement with its Annexes. The Group of 77 has also authorized me to state that it accepts and endorses the Resolution and the Agreement. It encourages all States to participate actively in the adoption of the Resolution and whenever possible to co-sponsor those documents. Furthermore, it encourages all States to sign the Agreement as soon as possible within the

43 The representative of Fiji. U.N. Doc. A/48/L.60.

time-frame mentioned in the Agreement. Finally, it encourages all States to take immediate steps, and if necessary, to ratify the Agreement and the Convention as soon as possible."[44]

To characterise the application of funds, time and creativity during a quarter of a century on the elaboration of an international regime for sea-bed mining as a "waste", might be an exaggeration. There were certainly collateral benefits in information and insights gained, skills developed and acquaintanceships established. However, it would be difficult to deny that not one cent has been won for "mankind" through the mining of sea-bed metals as a return on its investment in this initiative, nor does there seem to be any immediate prospect of such a return. Moreover, funds and qualified human resources, more scarce in the developing countries than elsewhere, might surely have been deployed in activities more immediately beneficial than protracted and arcane negotiations over resources which were effectively so remote as to be those of another planet.

How was it possible that so many States should have committed themselves year after year to such a venture? No doubt many reasons can be adduced, among them the *hubris* generated by newly won sovereignty, ill-considered notions of the role of democracy in international relations, ideological commitments of the political leadership of the time, group solidarities and, indeed, some of the early scientific literature on polymetallic modules, which led some to imagine a bonanza at the bottom of the sea. But lawyers too should accept part of the responsibility. They might have insisted to the policy-makers that the legal content of the "common heritage" concept, including its institutional implications, be definitively agreed upon before embarking on the drafting of texts which would focus minds on myths gradually accumulating in the interstices between differences in interpretation of the central metaphor. In fact, the "common heritage" for all the ink and paper used in attempting its elucidation, may never have had an "original meaning" capable of being given legal form. It was an inspiring vision offered to a world at a time when it seemed feasible to establish a "new international economic order" founded on distributive justice and co-operation that would replace an old order of exploitative relationships based essentially on power disparities and competition. Like many visions, its very lack of precision tended to enhance its inspirational capability and reach. Its lack of precision permitted the evolution of a costly myth.

Visions have an honoured place in schemes for the ordering of human affairs, and ancient wisdom attests that "Where there is no vision, the peo-

44 Statement of the representative of Indonesia on 28 July 1994.

ple perish".[45] However, the author of that very epigram goes on to say "... but he that keepeth the law, happy is he." The law, on any reckoning, is the outcome of experience, and perhaps these words are a warning: when pursuing our visions, we must avoid being ensnared by wasteful and profitless illusion; to achieve this, discipline must keep us ever in touch with the facts, with experience, with reality.

[45] "Where there is no vision, the people perish: but he that keepeth the law, happy is he." PROVERBS XXIX.18.

Sur le fondement du droit des gens

par

Francisco Rezek

Ne serait-ce que par élimination – si la logique la plus simple n'apportait elle-même son soutien à cette thèse – il nous faudrait reconnaître dans le consentement des Etats le seul fondement possible des règles, conventionnelles ou non, du droit des gens. Quelle pourrait être l'alternative? Si l'on écarte toute inspiration théologique pour la science du droit et si l'on refuse, *a fortiori*, l'idée que la volonté d'un groupe choisi d'Etats, ou bien les convictions de l'olympe doctrinal puissent générer des normes obligatoires pour l'ensemble de la société internationale, il résulte assez clairement que le fondement de la validité des règles non conventionnelles, y compris les plus éminents des principes généraux du droit des gens, ne diffère pas, dans l'essentiel, du fondement sur lequel reposent la légitimité et le caractère obligatoire des traités internationaux.

Dirait-on que plusieurs des grands principes jaillissent d'une manière aussi naturelle et inexorable de l'esprit humain qu'on aurait du mal à les placer à coté des traités, voire même de la coutume, dans le terrain de la création volontaire des sujets du droit international. Cette proposition, apparemment bien fondée, résulte d'une simplification assez courante: elle ignore la circonstance que le consentement peut assumer aussi bien une forme **créative** qu'une forme tout simplement **perceptive**. Cela détermine la distinction entre le droit libre et originalement forgé par les Etats souverains et le droit qu'ils ne font plus que reconnaître et proclamer.

Il paraît, à ce propos, que la vigueur de la critique à la pensée positiviste s'explique souvent par la fixation de l'analyste dans la formule qui révèle un droit international résultant de rien d'autre que la volonté des Etats. Le terme **volonté** a l'inconvénient grave de faire penser au consentement créatif, et à lui seul. Néanmoins on n'ignore pas qu'au long des siècles les Etats se sont mis à consentir sur des normes qu'ils estiment, d'une part, en provenance d'un domaine autre que celui de leur propre et discrétionnaire fécondité créatrice et, d'autre part – et par conséquent – immunes à leur pouvoir de manipulation.

D'une perspective opérationnelle, il s'avère peu important de distinguer, entre les principes généraux du droit des gens, ceux qui ne sont qu'une manifestation de la raison humaine – si l'on préfère, de la logique juridique – et ceux qui reposent principalement sur une valeur éthique.

Prenons par exemple la règle *nemo plus iuris*. Affirmer que personne ne peut transférer à autrui plus de droits que ceux qu'elle ne possède revient à dire la même chose que personne ne peut diviser un tout en trois moitiés. Cette consistance purement logique caractérise, parmi d'autres hypothèses notoires en droit, l'exception de litispendance et les principes suivant lesquels le conflit entre deux règles provenant d'une même source légiférante doit être résolu par la primauté du spécial sur le général et du postérieur sur l'antérieur. La raison cède de l'espace plus ou moins grand au sens éthique des créatures humaines et coexiste avec lui dans le soutien de principes tels que *pacta sunt servanda*, le contradictoire, la responsabilité, la condamnation de l'abus de droit.

Les traités, suivant une thèse aussi ancienne qu'incontestée, trouvent leur fondement dans la règle *pacta sunt servanda*, une formule classique pour signifier l'accord de volontés et ses conséquences. L'Etat est tenu de procéder conformément aux accords dont il est partie précisément parce qu'il a convenu, et ce qui a été convenu doit être exécuté en bonne foi. Pour ce qui est de la coutume, la recherche de son fondement conduit depuis longtemps à une conclusion similaire. Ainsi, Hugo Grotius y voyait le produit de l'assentiment des Etats[1]. Cette idée, partagée par Vattel[2], deviendrait plus tard un des apanages des écoles positivistes d'Allemagne et d'Italie; elle aurait aussi le soutien de la doctrine socialiste et d'un nombre d'auteurs n'appartenant à aucun courant déterminé[3].

Cependant d'autres publicistes, à partir de Savigny, ont préféré percevoir la coutume comme un ensemble de règles objectives, extérieures et supérieures à la volonté des Etats[4]. Inspirés à l'évidence par la théorie du droit naturel, ils n'ont néanmoins pas démontré la raison pour laquelle la règle coutumière, ainsi comprise, serait en mesure d'obliger aussi des Etats non engagés dans sa pratique et moins encore convaincus de sa validité en tant qu'impératif de la raison.

La théorie du consentement ou théorie **volontariste**, suivant beaucoup de partisans de l'objectivisme, n'expliquerait point la force obligatoire des règles coutumières pour les Etats nouveaux, ceux qui dès leur accès à l'in-

---

1 *Voir* CH. ROUSSEAU, DROIT INTERNATIONAL PUBLIC, Paris (1984), p. 79.

2 E. DE VATTEL, LE DROIT DES GENS – OU PRINCIPES DE LA LOI NATURELLE APPLIQUÉS À LA CONDUITE ET AUX AFFAIRES DES NATIONS ET DES SOUVERAINS, Guillaumin & Cie, Paris (1863), p. 66.

3 *Voir e.g.* le cours général de droit international public donné par CH. CHAUMONT à l'Académie de La Haye en 1970, RCADI (1970), vol. 129, p. 333 et s.

4 *Voir* CH. ROUSSEAU, *op. cit.*, *supra* note 1, p. 79.

dépendance se trouveraient automatiquement engagés par l'ensemble du droit coutumier préexistant. Mais il résulte inévitablement qu'on se demande quelle est la base sur laquelle on peut faire état de cette force obligatoire.

Il a été même possible de témoigner au sein de la doctrine objectiviste une certaine sympathie envers la distinction entre les Etats nouveaux, pour lesquels les règles coutumières établies avant leur existence indépendante seraient irrécusables, et les autres Etats, auxquels on reconnaît la prérogative de se préserver à l'écart d'une coutume donnée moyennant l'assomption d'attitudes signifiant le refus. On cite à ce propos la décision de la Cour internationale de Justice dans l'affaire des **Pêcheries** (*Royaume-Uni c. Norvège*), où, une fois établie l'existence d'une certaine norme coutumière, celle-ci a été estimée inapplicable à la Norvège qui s'était «... toujours élevée contre toute tentative de l'appliquer à la côte norvégienne»[5]. Il paraît qu'une telle doctrine ne dénie qu'aux nouveaux Etats, lors de la première occasion dont ils disposent pour faire connaître leur opinion souveraine, le droit de refuser leur soutien à une règle coutumière. De ce chef, l'objectivité de la coutume aurait une destination politiquement circonscrite, à l'instar de quelques autres institutions du droit international classique.

Paul Guggenheim, après avoir admis que l'exigence de l'*opinio iuris* présuppose l'évidence de la reconnaissance de la norme par l'Etat que l'on veuille obliger, a fait état de ses doutes sur le besoin même de l'*opinio iuris*[6]. Alfred Verdross a suggéré que la volonté majoritaire peut imposer des règles de droit à l'ensemble, comme si l'on était déjà arrivés à une société internationale forgée dans le moule des ordres juridiques internes, marquées par la centralisation de l'autorité[7]. Rolando Quadri, à son tour, devant le fait que la majorité numérique n'arbore plus le profil qu'elle montrait dans le passé, disserta sur l'objectivité – et de là l'universalité – de toute règle coutumière dictée par les forces prépondérantes sur la scène internationale, soit les Etats qualifiés pour faire entendre leurs propositions d'une manière efficace[8].

En statuant sur l'affaire du **Lotus**, en 1927, la Cour Permanente de Justice Internationale rappela que:

---

[5] Recueil des arrêts, avis consultatifs et ordonnances de la COUR INTERNATIONALE DE JUSTICE (1951), p. 131. *Voir* aussi M. AKEHURST, A MODERN INTRODUCTION TO INTERNATIONAL LAW, Allen & Unwin, London (1990), pp. 40–41.

[6] P. GUGGENHEIM, *Les deux éléments de la coutume en droit international public*, ETUDES SCELLE, Paris (1950), vol. 1, pp. 275–280.

[7] A. VERDROSS, DERECHO INTERNATIONAL PÚBLICO (traduction espagnole de A. Truyol y Serra), Aguilar, Madrid (1969), pp. 160–162.

[8] R. QUADRI, *Le fondement du caractère obligatoire du droit international public*, RCADI (1952), vol. 80, p. 625.

> «Les règles de droit liant les Etats procèdent donc de la volonté de ceux-ci, volonté manifestée dans des conventions ou dans des usages acceptés généralement comme consacrant des principes de droit...»[9].

Longtemps plus tard, dans l'affaire de la **Barcelona Traction**, la CIJ a produit un enseignement précieux en se référant à la création du droit sur des matières politiquement difficiles. Le droit coutumier au sujet de la protection diplomatique, dit la Cour,

> «... s'est formé en une période d'intense conflit de systèmes et d'intérêts. Des rapports essentiellement bilatéraux sont en cause, où les droits des Etats qui exercent la protection diplomatique et des Etats à l'égard desquels une protection est demandée ont dû être également sauvegardés. Dans ce domaine comme dans d'autres, un ensemble de règles n'aurait pu mûrir qu'avec l'assentiment des intéressés»[10].

À plusieurs auteurs, cependant, il a paru que l'arrêt de la CIJ dans l'affaire du **Plateau continental de la Mer du Nord** rejeta de manière implicite la théorie du consentement[11]. Mais cet arrêt, il vaut bien la remarque, précède d'une année celui de l'affaire de la **Barcelona Traction**.

* * *

Toute réflexion exempte de dogmatisme mène de nos jours à percevoir que la théorie du consentement nécessaire et la doctrine objectiviste, ne s'opposent pas vraiment sur l'essentiel. Ce qu'il faut reprocher à l'objectivisme c'est plutôt ce trait d'arrogance sans lequel il serait impensable de suggérer qu'un Etat souverain, même au stade actuel des relations internationales, puisse être obligé malgré lui – c'est dire, faute de toute sorte d'argument autorisant à l'entendre **consentant** – par une règle de droit, qu'il s'agisse d'une règle conventionnelle, d'une règle coutumière ou d'un principe général.

Il y a bien sûr, pour les Etats comme pour les hommes, de ces normes qui échappent à leur prérogative de refus ou de remaniement, mais, car les uns et les autres le reconnaissent, dans l'exercice de la raison qui leur est propre – et jamais, parce que tel est l'avis des publicistes ou parce que soit la majorité, soit l'élite l'estime ainsi nécessaire.

Dès que l'on évite les ambiguïtés de l'expression **volontarisme**, toujours suggestive de l'arbitraire, il devient simple d'accepter l'idée que sans le

---

9 CPJI RECEUIL (1927), A-10, p. 18.
10 CIJ RECUEIL (1970), p. 48.
11 E.J. DE ARÉCHAGA, EL DERECHO INTERNACIONAL CONTEMPORÁNEO, Madrid (1980), pp. 34–35.

consentement de l'Etat aucune norme ne l'oblige. Vattel évoquait Justinien pour rappeler, sur les hommes, que

> «... la droite raison leur a dicté certaines maximes de droit, tellement fondées sur la nature des choses, qu'elles ont été reconnues et admises partout»[12].

Tel est aussi le soustrait des grands principes du droit des gens. Ils ne seraient pas **généraux** si des voix souveraines, aussi peu nombreuses qu'elles fussent, en déniaient la force obligatoire.

Tunkin, d'autre part, en affirmant que tout nouvel Etat peut répudier des règles coutumières établies avant son indépendance, pondère que son silence dans le contexte des rapports qu'il entretiendra avec les autres Etats justifiera bientôt la présomption de son consentement sur le droit coutumier, en tout ce qui n'aura pas fait l'objet de son refus manifeste[13].

En effet, on n'a jamais prétendu que le consentement doit être toujours exprès, et moins encore qu'il obéisse à une liturgie donnée. Dans les rapports entre Etats comme dans les rapports entre individus, il est raisonnable d'admettre l'assentiement **tacite**, ainsi que la validité, dans certaines circonstances, d'une **présomption** d'assentiment. Voici pourquoi la thèse de l'opposabilité du droit coutumier préexistant aux Etats nouveaux n'est une insolence que lorsqu'on la soutient en l'absence de tout argument susceptible de les engager, d'une façon ou d'une autre, dans le processus de formation d'un tel droit. Les Etat nouveaux ne surgissent pas abruptement du néant. Ce qu'ils ont de nouveau, c'est l'indépendance: le territoire existait déjà, et sur le territoire la dimension humaine. Il y a là une histoire dont l'analyse permettra d'évaluer l'engagement de cette communauté devenue souveraine avec les pratiques internationales soutenues par la puissance à laquelle elle se rattachait[14].

Tout ce que l'on trouve donc à l'origine de l'idée d'opposabilité des principes généraux du droit et de la coutume internationale aux nouveaux Etats, c'est le phénomène du consentement tacite, voire du consentement présumé,

---

12 E. DE VATTEL, *op. cit.*, *supra* note 2, p. 49.

13 G. TUNKIN, DROIT INTERNATIONAL PUBLIC: PROBLÈMES THÉORIQUES, Pedone, Paris (1965), p. 87.

14 Cela devient particulièrement visible dans le cas des règles coutumières à portée régionale. Lors de son indépendance au début du siècle, le Panama, résultant d'une sécession en Colombie, préserva la coutume de l'asile diplomatique. Dans la même région géographique les anciennes colonies britanniques n'avaient à ce propos aucun héritage lors de leur accès à l'indépendance. Les jeunes républiques des Caraïbes se sont gardées, par leur pratique ultérieure, à l'écart de cette coutume latino-américaine.

associé à quelques règles élémentaires du droit des gens ayant trait à la succession d'Etats. Rien n'existe d'**extérieur et supérieur** à la conscience à laquelle les Etats souverains, au nom de leurs peuples, produisent ou simplement reconnaissent les règles du droit des gens.

Le problème de l'efficacité du droit international

par

Milan Šahović

Un des grands problèmes du droit international est celui de son efficacité. Du point de vue de la doctrine il est fondamental parce qu'il soulève la question de sa nature et force juridique ainsi que des moyens et méthodes de la mise en oeuvre de ses normes. Sur le plan pratique il se présente comme conséquence du caractère de l'application de ses règles et principes et des obligations des états et autres sujets de la vie internationale. Il est évident que ces deux aspects sont interdépendants. Aucune réponse théorique ne peut être formulée ne tenant pas compte de l'expérience de la réalisation du droit international qui est le seul critère de son efficacité.

Cette constatation peut être considérée comme un truisme. Mais, en ce moment, son importance est exceptionnelle et peut difficilement être contestée. Il paraît indispensable d'insister sur le rapport entre la doctrine et la pratique en voulant parler du problème de l'efficacité du droit international. Pour une double raison. Premièrement, il est évident, que le débat et la recherche des voies du renforcement de son efficacité et du respect de ses normes s'imposent à la doctrine sous la pression des perturbations et des conflits qui ont suivi la fin de la guerre froide. Deuxièmement, leur influence sur l'évolution contemporaine du droit international est de plus en plus visible.

Le problème de l'efficacité du droit international n'est pas nouveau. Cependant, les réponses de la doctrine et de la pratique à ses aspects actuels ne peuvent plus se limiter aux thèses traditionnelles. L'efficacité et l'inefficacité de ses normes ont été expliquées habituellement par sa nature juridique imparfaite. Le rôle prépondérant de la volonté des états et l'inexistence d'une force superétatique ont été l'argument majeur exploité par les sceptiques et les négateurs du caractère juridique du droit international. Pour eux le droit ne peut être constitué qu'à la base du modèle du droit interne. Etant donné que ce n'est pas le cas du droit international c'est l'obstacle insurmontable qui limite, d'après leur opinion, substanstiellement la possibilité d'atteindre un niveau satisfaisant de son efficacité.

Mon propos n'est pas de se lancer dans un débat pro ou contre cet argument. C'est une donnée préalable qui sur le plan théorique restreint et peut même rendre impossible une tentative de clarification des conditions dans lesquelles se manifeste ce problème. En effet, tout en respectant les particularités du droit international, à cause desquelles il ne pourrait jamais être identique avec le droit interne, le problème de son efficacité doit être examiné dans un nouveau contexte en partant du niveau de son développement actuel. Ce n'est qu'à la lumière de la totalité des changements qu'il a subi au cours des dernières décénies que le problème de son efficacité peut être clarifié aujourd'hui.

Il est évident que l'évolution récente n'a pas pu avoir comme résultat la construction d'un système complet garantissant le respect stricte et l'application absolument efficace des normes juridiques internationales et des obligations des états. Les éléments constitutifs du droit international, normatifs et institutionnels, n'évoluent pas uniformement, également, en même temps et avec la même intensité. Leur caractère et viabilité sont l'expression du jeu des facteurs extrajuridiques, en premier lieu du rapport de forces entre les états. On peut en déduire facilement qu'effectivement le problème de l'efficacité du droit international ne pourra jamais être résolu une fois pour toujours. C'est d'ailleurs le cas de tous les autres domaines du droit et des rapports sociaux en général.

Malgré ce fait, il est difficile à nier qu'en ce qui concerne son efficacité l'évolution du droit international suit une ligne bien déterminée. Elle est présente sur les deux plans de sa formation – normatif et institutionnel. Mais, indépendamment de degré différent de sa présence sur ces deux plans cette ligne reflète un même but, à savoir: la tendance du renforcement de l'efficacité du droit international par une «libération» de son application des intérêts particuliers des états en faveur de la protection des besoins de la communauté internationale confiée aux organisations et organes internationaux. Une «objectivisation» de la force juridique obligatoire des normes du droit international en est une des conséquences essentielles de cette «libération» de la volonté subjective des états. La défense de leurs intérêts individuels ne devrait être traitée en dehors des droits légitimes des autres états et de la communauté internationale toute entière. Le problème de l'efficacité du droit internationale se manifeste un ce moment dans une nouvelle forme.

Les répercussions de l'évolution dans cette direction sont à la fois qualitatives et quantitatives. L'état du droit international positif actuel le démontre. D'une part, une hierarchisation des obligations des états et un renforcement du caractère obligatoire de ses normes fondamentales commencent à s'affirmer. D'autre part, la législation internationale a pratiquement englobé tous les domaines des relations internationales en y incluant dans la plus grande mesure du possible la vie interne des états. Le résultat final est la cristallisation progressive d'un système de normes plus ou moins integrées et harmonisées qui commence à s'imposer aux états comme un ordre juridique objectif. Sa force juridique n'est pas encore satisfaisante mais un nombre d'éléments de ce système indique assez clairement dans quelle direction l'évolution du droit international pourrait se dérouler en avenir.

L'adoption de l'art. 103 de la Charte des Nations Unies a ouvert la voie d'un tel développement. En insistant: «Qu'en cas de conflit entre les obligations des Membres des Nations Unies en vertu de la présente Charte et leurs obligations en vertu de tout accord international, le premières prévaudront», la hierarchisation des obligations juridiques des états a été formellement sanctionnée. C'est une des prémisses de la légalité internationale actuelle. Elle a été maintes fois reconfirmée par les conventions universelles et régionales ainsi que des accords bilatéraux qui se réfèrent à la Charte en insistant que ses buts et principes représentent le fondement de leurs textes. Le point culminant de l'affirmation de cet approche est l'approbation de l'existence des règles impératives (*jus cogens*) par la Convention de Vienne sur le droit des traités. Dans l'art. 53 les états ont reconnu qu': «Est nul tout traité qui au moment de sa conclusion, est en conflit avec une norme impérative du droit international général. Aux fins de la présente Convention, une norme impérative du droit international général est une norme acceptée et reconnue par la communauté internationale des Etats dans son ensemble en tant que norme à laquelle aucune dérogation n'est permise et qui ne peut être modifiée que par une nouvelle norme du droit international général ayant le même caractère». En plus, l'art. 64 insiste: «Si une nouvelle norme impérative survient, tout traité existant qui est en conflit avec cette norme devient nul et prend fin». De cette manière le droit international positif a fondamentalement changé. Les critères de l'appréciation du comportement des états sont devenus plus fermes et clairs. On a réussi à poser la base de construction d'un ordre juridique international profondément différent de celui qui a existé du début jusqu'à la moitié du 20ème siècle.

Les conséquences de ce développement sur le plan normatif dont l'influence sur l'affermissement de l'efficacité du droit international peut difficilement être mise en doute, se sont directement reflétées sur la conception de la responsabilité des états. Un nouvel approche qui n'est pas encore formellement confirmé s'est cristallisé grâce aux travaux de la Commission du Droit international sur la codification et développement progressif des règles sur la responsabilité des états pour faits internationalement illicites.

C'est à la base des rapports de Roberto Ago que la Commission a confirmé la règle de la responsabilité objective des états dans le cadre de la première partie de son Projet d'articles en négligeant la théorie de la responsabilité subjective. Les principes généraux évoqués du premier au 4ème article démontrent qu'il s'agit d'une attitude qui élève l'autorité du droit international à un niveau supérieur par rapport aux états dans le cas de leur violation des obligations internationales. C'est ainsi que l'art. 3 souligne: «Il y a fait international illicite lorsque: a) un comportement consistant en une action ou en une ommission est attribuable d'après le droit international à l'Etat; et b) ce comportement constitue une violation d'une obligation internationale de l'Etat». Et d'après l'art. 16: «Il y a violation d'une obligation internationale par un Etat lorsqu'un fait dudit Etat n'est pas conforme à ce qui est requis de lui par cette obligation». L'idée d'une «objectivisation» de la force juridique du droit international a ainsi été également évoquée. Pourtant, la Commission se n'est pas arrêtée dans son élaboration d'une nouvelle conception de la responsabilité des états. Elle a fait un pas en avant en reconnaissant la nécessité de gradation du degré de leur responsabilité dans l'art. 19 du Projet qui conserne à côté des délits l'existence des crimes internationaux des états. En partant des règles juridiques du *jus cogens* la Commission a, en les adaptant à la matière de la responsabilité, défini la notion de ces crimes d'après laquelle: «Le fait internationalement illicite qui résulte d'une violation par un état d'une obligation internationale si essentielle pour la sauvegarde d'intérêts fondamentaux de la communauté internationale que sa violation est reconnue comme un crime par cette communauté dans son ensemble constitue un crime internationa». Les exemples des violations qui entrent dans cette catégorie que citent ces articles (l'agression, droit des peuples à disposer d'eux-mêmes, l'esclavage, le génocide, l'*apartheid*, la préservation de l'environnement humain tout particulièrement la pollution massive de l'atmosphère ou des mers) permettent de tirer cette conclusion. La hiérarchisation des normes du droit international qui est un des éléments fondamentaux du renforcement de l'efficacité de son application a par cette disposition du Projet sur la responsabilité été encore une fois fortement reconfirmée en ouvrant la porte à une évolution dont tous les aspects ne sont pas encore étudiés à fond.

En ce qui concerne le droit international positif dans les domaines humanitaire ainsi que de la protection des droits de l'homme l'évolution de l'efficacité de leur application a pris une autre orientation. Après l'adoption des Principes de Nuremberg et les Conventions de Genève sur la protection des victimes de guerre ainsi que des deux Protocoles additionnels de 1977 sur la protection des victimes des conflits armés internationaux et non-internationaux, la responsabilité individuelle est devenue une des normes fondamentales de l'ordre juridique international. Avec le Code de crimes contre la paix et la sécurité de l'humanité dont l'approbation devrait avoir lieu dans un avenir pas très lointain cette orientation sera confirmée encore une fois. Quant à la protection des droits de l'homme, la reconnaissance du droit de l'individu de chercher la protection des instances internationales pour les violations de ses droits perpétrées par les autorités de son pays ne peut pas être interprétée autrement que comme reflêt de l'aspiration de la communauté internationale de voir que les normes juridiques générales et les obligations des états soient appliquées plus efficacement. Toutes les conventions internationales universelles ou régionales tiennent compte de cet aspect de la protection des droits de l'homme, et d'une ou autre manière et mesure, prévoient des mécanismes juridictionnels ou politiques respectifs.

On peut constater, en parlant du progrès auquel on a abouti sur le plan normatif que les états ont pratiquement dû renoncer jusqu'à un certain degré à un nombre de leurs droits inhérants à leur souveraineté en tant que conséquence du renforcement de l'efficacité du droit international. Les pouvoirs dont ils disposent, leurs competénces ne découlent plus exclusivement de leur souveraineté et dépendent de plus en plus des normes approuvées par la communauté internationale dans le cadre de laquelle ils participent à leur adoption. En effet, les états sont aujourd'hui d'après le système des normes fondamentales de l'ordre juridique international dans une situation qui demande qu'ils remplissent leurs obligations juridiques internationales en respectant, entre autres facteurs, les compétences des institutions, mécanismes et procédures constitués par la communauté internationale.

Cette remarque permet d'aborder la question de l'évolution sur le plan institutionnel et son influence sur l'efficacité du droit international. La base normative peut avoir un niveau très élevé mais sans existence des méthodes et moyens appropriés, l'expériences nous le montre, la réalisation de sa mise en oeuvre effective ne serait que platonique. C'est pourquoi il est évident qu'avec toutes les acquisitions ci-dessus mentionnées, qui ont renforcé le caractère obligatoire de ses normes, les voies du contrôle de leur application et de repression de leurs violations ont dû être parallèlement développées.

Tout ce qui c'est passé au cours des dernières décénies indique que l'orientation générale prise dans ce but vise l'augmentation de l'autorité de la communauté internationale et de ses organes. Un nombre de tendances positives reflètent le progrès atteint en deux directions.

D'une part, on peut voir qu'un mouvement en faveur du recours à la juridiction internationale est présent. En dépit du fait que la clause facultative du Statut de la Cour internationale de La Haye n'est pas adoptée par la majorité des états, son activité extrêmement intense est l'expression évidente d'un renforcement de confiance envers cette instance juridictionnelle suprême internationale et de la possibilité de la solution des conflits interétatiques à la base du niveau contemporain du développement du droit international. La création des juridictions spécialisées en est une preuve de l'existence de ce mouvement. La constitution des Tribunaux internationaux pour juger les personnes présumées responsables de violations graves du droit international humanitaire sur les territoires de l'ex-Yugoslavie et de Rouanda, ainsi que les travaux sur l'adoption du Statut d'un Tribunal criminel international permanent et du Tribunal international pour le droit de la mer doivent être mentionnés dans ce contexte.

D'autre part, c'est une intensification du contrôle de l'application des obligations des états par intermédiaire des mécanismes appropriés constitués par les conventions internationales et dans le cadre des organisations universelles et régionales qui caractérise les efforts déployés en faveur du renforcement de l'efficacité du droit international. Ayant comme point de départ la présentation des rapports et leur considération du point de vue politique, en passant par l'établissement des commissions d'enquête et des représentants spéciaux, en terminant par la constitution des Cours pour la protection des droits de l'homme à l'échelle régionale ce domaine en est le meilleur exemple. Enfin, une participation de plus en plus active des organisations internationales, des Nations Unies et organisations régionales, dans l'application des divers moyens du réglement pacifique des différends internationaux, commence à contribuer à leur efficacité. On peut attirer l'attention sur le phénomène d'une utilisation combinée des méthodes de négociation, médiation et conciliation qui se déroule sous l'auspice et dans le cadre de l'activité des organisations internationales qui est de plus en plus visible dans la vie internationale. Mais c'est surtout dans le cadre de l'OESC qu'on a réussi d'aboutir à un résultat remarquable en adoptant dans la Convention sur la conciliation et l'arbitrage un système de règles qui réduit dans une bonne mesure le pouvoir discrétionnaire des états par rapport de la procédure de l'arbitrage en insistant sur le rôle des organes de cette organisation et des tiers.

Tout en ayant en vue cette évolution positive sur le plan institutionnel on peut estimer, d'après les besoins objectifs, qu'elle est en certain retard en comparaison avec le plan normatif. Cette lenteur s'explique par le fait qui démontre que le progrès sur le plan institutionnel présuppose une limitation de plus en plus grande de la souveraineté des états et de la liberté de leur comportement dans les relations internationales. Mais, en même temps, il faut souligner qu'il sera possible d'atteindre ce niveau de développement qu'au moment de la création d'une communauté internationale organisée dans laquelle les droits et devoirs des états, grands et petits, développés et en voie de développement seront coordonnés et harmonisés à la base de l'égalité souveraine en tant que règle impérative du droit international. Dans une communauté internationale pleine de contradictions politiques, économiques et autres, le fétichisme de la souveraineté ne sera jamais dépassé. Le scepticisme et le manque de confiance des états déterminera leur rapport envers les moyens et methodes qui pourraient être créés en vue du renforcement de l'efficacité du droit international.

* * *

Il paraît que la porte est entreouverte pour une évolution plus ambitieuse dans la recherche des voies nouvelles de l'affermissement de l'efficacité du droit international. Un débat théorique, suivi d'une tentative de transposition de ses résultats sur le plan pratique, pourra contribuer indubitablement à la réalisation de ce but. Pourtant, une condition préalable devrait être remplie.

Il s'agit du besoin que la doctrine se libère dans la plus grande mesure du possible de l'influence de la politique des états et de leurs intérêts diplomatiques quotidiens. Il peut paraître que c'est une demande trop idéaliste, donc, irréalisable. Cependant, pour tous ceux qui ont contribué ou étudié l'évolution du droit international pendant la seconde partie du 20ème siècle, et qui se souviennent de la contribution de la doctrine, une telle demande devrait être beaucoup plus d'un rappel historique. Elle pourrait être considérée comme un stimulant pour que l'expérience positive du passé soit utilisée en vue de lever dans les conditions actuelles à un niveau plus haut l'efficacité du droit international.

State Responsibility and International Liability in Transnational Relations

by

Sompong Sucharitkul

Introduction

This essay is principally concerned with the theory of State responsibility under international law and the closeness of its connection or even possible marginal overlap with the notion of international liability of States in respect of injurious consequences, arising out of activities within their jurisdiction or control, and affecting other States or nationals of other States. It is a reflection of a personal assessment of the pertinent relations between two of the topics under active studies by the International Law Commission, namely, "State responsibility"[1] and "International Liability for Injurious Consequences Arising out of Acts not Prohibited by International Law."[2]

There appears to have been, at least initially, some confusion in theory between the two topics selected for codification by the International Law Commission. "International Liability," as a newly emerged topic was carved out of the main topic of "State responsibility," while both topics deal essentially with the obligations and duties incumbent upon States under international law. Notionally the task of delineating the scope of international liability of a State from that of "State responsibility" is prefaced by a major conceptual difficulty. Preclusion of wrongfulness of an act of a State by virtue of consent,[3] *force majeure* or fortuitous event,[4] distress[5] or state of necessity[6] "does not prejudge any question that may arise in regard to compensation for damage caused by that act."[7] International liability to pay com-

---

1 *See* in particular II Yearbook of the International Law Commission (1975) at 55–59, document A/10010/Rev.1, paras. 38–51; *ibid.* (1980), Part Two at 26–63, document A/35/10, Chap. III.

2 *See* in particular II Yearbook of the International Law Commission (1980), Part Two at 150–152; *ibid.* II (1980), Part One at 247, document A/CN.4/334 and Add. 1 and 2.

3 Article 29: *consent, of the Draft Articles on State Responsibility Provisionally Adopted on First Reading by the International Law Commission*, GE.81-61731.

4 *Ibid.* Article 31: *Force Majeure and Fortuitous Event.*

5 *Ibid.* Article 32: *Distress.*

6 *Ibid.* Article 33: *State of Necessity.*

7 *Ibid.* Article 35: *Reservation as to Compensation for Damage.*

pensation for damage may be engaged regardless of the existence of an international wrongful act. In more ways than one, international liability of a State is constituted by proof of injurious consequences independent of wrongfulness of an act attributable to that State.

The difficulty in any attempt to distinguish between "State responsibility" and "international liability" of a State is further compounded by linguistic deficiency in languages other than English to differentiate between "responsibility" and "liability." In civil-law vocabularies, the notion of "liability " is expressed in terms of "responsibility" or at best "civil responsibility." Thus, "State responsibility" refers to the responsibility of States under international law in general, whereas "international liability" denotes the "civil responsibility" of States or the obligation of a State to pay appropriate compensation or to make reparation for injuries suffered by non-nationals outside its national boundaries resulting from activities within its territory or under its control. This international liability or "civil responsibility" of a State is engaged not only under international law, but also, it would seem, within the national dimension of municipal legal systems in circumstances involving transnational relations.

In the sections that follow an endeavor will be made to reveal some of the salient features of what may appear to be very close similarities between various components of "State responsibility" and "international liability" of a State. The exercise is expected to demonstrate elements of contrast as well as ingredients of comparable analytical compounds between the two international legal concepts.

I. HISTORICAL DEVELOPMENTS

It is not unnatural that in the practice of States legal principles have developed through historical accidents. International norms continue to evolve in response to the exigencies of the time. Legal norms regarding State responsibility and international liability are no exceptions. A glance at their respective origins and historical developments will disclose some convergence in the paths of their evolution which appear to have crossed, intersected and coincided at various junctions.

A. State Responsibility

As a topic for codification by the International Law Commission, "State responsibility" was originally conceived as a set of rules of international law governing the international obligations of States in their relations with other States, primarily the duty incumbent upon a State to make reparation or to pay compensation for the injuries suffered by nationals of other States. In traditional international law, this topic constituted a classic example of violations of customary international law. From the point of view of the injured State, it represented the exercise of the right and duty or even the power of a mighty developed State to protect its citizens outside its national frontier. A State is traditionally empowered to extend its diplomatic protection to all its citizens or nationals wherever they might be, including their presence in the territory of another State. This aspect of the customary rule of international is known as "diplomatic protection of citizens abroad." Conversely, the exercise of diplomatic protection by one State *vis-à-vis* an offending State was predicated upon the failure of that other State to meet the minimum international standard in "the treatment of aliens." In other words, the injured State or complainant State is exercising its power of diplomatic protection, to demand compensation or reparation in respect of injuries which could be physical personal injuries, loss of life, as well as economic or financial injuries, loss of property, assets, or damage to property, such as loss of investments, expropriation, nationalization and requisition or confiscation of properties belonging to foreigners.

The term "diplomatic protection" was never confined to the use of diplomacy or recourse to diplomatic channels to negotiate a settlement of international claims. Rather the adjective "diplomatic" refers to the "governmental" level of protection, which could entail any means adopted by the injured State. Thus, under traditional international law a State could resort to the use of force to compel payment of debts owed by another State to one of its nationals, including natural as well as juridical persons, *i.e.* corporations or enterprises. The collection of private debts from another State by the State whose citizens could not secure repayment of their loans was prevalent in the Western hemisphere until the Hague Peace Conferences in 1899 and 1907, and ultimately prohibited when the use of force or war as an instrument of national policy was denounced by States, following the close of World War I.

Indeed for some States, notably the United States, the law of State responsibility for all practical purposes meant responsibility of States for injuries to aliens or conversely diplomatic protection of citizens abroad. The topic so conceived, in its initial stages, was not only considered to constitute the major component of international law, but was also regarded by many as the exclusive domain of the law of nations. In its primitive stages, international law had condoned the use of force to enforce payment of compensation or repayment of loan even on an international scene. The practice of European and Inter-American nations was abound with instances of settlement of disputes relating to injuries suffered by aliens by mixed claims commissions and other types of international arbitration, conciliation and mediation including good offices and fact-finding missions.

Personal injuries and economic losses suffered by aliens at the hands of the territorial State were recoverable in the first instance through the availability of local remedies. There soon developed the requirement that local remedies be exhausted before the injured State could espouse or take up the claims of its nationals against another State, responsible for the injuries, physical or economic, suffered by victims who were non-nationals of the offending State. This requirement came to be known as exhaustion of the local remedies rule,[8] forming an integral part of the law of State responsibility for injuries suffered by aliens. The American Society of International Law published in 1929 Draft Conventions and Comments, *inter alia*, on "Responsibility of States for Damage Done in Their Territory to the Person or Property of Foreigners."[9] This Draft of the Harvard Research was revised, on a smaller scale, by the preparation of a subsequent Draft Convention on the "International Responsibility of States for Injuries to Aliens."[10]

According to the first Harvard Draft of 1929, "A State is responsible, when it has a duty to make reparation to another State for the injury sustained by the latter State as a consequence of an injury to its national."[11] This earlier Draft went on to prescribe some of the general principles and defined the circumstances in which a State is responsible. The Institut de Droit international at its session in Lausanne in 1927 also adopted a resolution on the same topic to the effect that "The State is responsible for injuries caused to foreigners by any action or omission contrary to its international obligations."[12]

The revised Harvard Draft of 1961 likewise stipulated that "A State is internationally responsible for an act or omission which, under international

---

[8] *See* also *International Case, Switzerland v. U.S.A.*, ICJ REPORTS 1959 at 6; and the *Ambatielos Arbitration, Greece v. U.K.*, 23:306 ILR (1956) . *See Anglo-Iranian Oil Co. Case*, ICJ REPORTS 1952; *see* also ICJ REPORT 1951 at 89. Compare Article 22: *Exhaustion of Local Remedies of the Draft Articles on State Responsibility..., op. cit., supra* note 3.

[9] Supplement to 23 AJIL (1929), Special number (April), Research in International Law, Harvard Law School, Director, Manley O. Hudson, Rapporteur, Edwin M. Borchard, assisted by such renowned publicists as Philip Marshall Brown, Clyde Eagleton, Charles Hughes, Charles Cheney Hyde and Quency Wright.

[10] *Responsibility of States for Injuries to the Economic Interests of Aliens*, 55 AJIL (1961) at 545–584, by Louis B. Sohn and Richard R. Baxter of the Board of Editors.

[11] *See* Article 1 of the Harvard Draft, (in:) 23 AJIL (1929), Supplement Special Number (April) at 133 ff.

[12] *See* Appendix N° 3, 22 AJIL, Special Supplement, at 330.

law, is wrongful, is attributable to that State, and causes an injury to an alien."[13] Thus, earlier attempts at a codification of the law of State responsibility by the Harvard Research, as well as the Institute of International Law during the period of the League of Nations and the revised Harvard Draft of 1961, concentrated on the rules of international law regarding violation of a primary international obligation, giving rise to a secondary obligation to make reparation for injury suffered by aliens.

In the meantime, the General Assembly of the United Nations decided in 1953 that "It is desirable for the maintenance and development of peaceful relations between States that the principles of international law governing State responsibility be codified."[14] Dr. F.V. Garcia-Amador, a national of Cuba, was appointed Special Rapporteur, who submitted six reports from 1956 to 1961 on various aspects of State responsibility.[15] By this time, Dr. Garcia-Amador began to notice the one-sided trend in the various drafts proposed by the developed world in favour of excessive protection of economic interests of the advanced countries in the exploitation of natural resources and raw materials within the developing countries. A compromise was suggested, whereby the so-called minimum standard should have a double application, both in the treatment of aliens and in the treatment of individuals in international law. In other words, a minimum standard of human rights or guarantee against racial discrimination should be included as a counterpart of the required international standard of treatment of foreigners. Any endeavour to enforce a minimum standard of treatment of individuals or minimum guarantee of human rights and fundamental freedoms was doomed to failure, considering strong opposition from the West which regarded the requirement of a minimum standard as interference in its domestic affairs.

The second generation of reports presented by the Special Rapporteur, the late Judge Roberto Ago, followed the general plan adopted by the International Law Commission in 1975 which envisaged the structure of the draft articles as follow: Part One concerning the origin of international responsibility; Part Two on the content, forms and degrees of international responsibility; and a possible Part Three concerning the settlement of disputes and the implementation (*mis en oeuvre*) of international responsibility.[16] In 1980, the Commission provisionally adopted, on first reading, Part One of the draft

---

[13] *See* 55 AJIL at 548–584, Article 1: *Basic Principles of State Responsibility*.

[14] Resolution 799 (VIII), December 7, 1953, U.N. Doc. A/2630 at 52.

[15] U.N. Doc. A/CN.4/96, 106, 111, 119, 125 and 134 (1956–61).

[16] II YEARBOOK OF THE INTERNATIONAL LAW COMMISSION (1975) at 55–59, document A/10010 Rev.1, paras. 38–51.

articles, containing 35 articles on "the origin of international responsibility," concerning I: General Principles; II: The "Act of State" under International Law; III: The Breach of an International Obligation; IV: Implication of a State in the Internationally Wrongful Act of Another State; and V: Circumstances Precluding Wrongfulness.[17]

Following Judge Ago's election to the International Court of Justice, a third Special Rapporteur, Professor Willem Riphagen, was appointed, who succeeded in presenting a series of seven reports with reference to Part Two and Part Three of the draft articles from 1980 to 1986.[18]

In 1986, the Commission provisionally adopted draft articles 1 to 5 of Part Two.[19] In 1987, Professor Gaetano Arangio-Ruiz was appointed the fourth and current Special Rapporteur on the topic, and began submitting reports to the Commission since 1988,[20] several reports have been considered and draft articles referred to the Drafting Committee.[21]

Pending further consideration and elaboration of the draft articles by the International Law Commission, it is to be observed at this point that since 1975 the scope of the law on State responsibility has expanded far beyond the traditional notion as contained in the various draft Conventions prepared by national and international institutions of higher learning, such as the Harvard Research, the Institut de Droit international, the International Law Association, or even the first generation of the reports submitted by Dr. Garcia-Amador, Special Rapporteur of the International Law Commission.

The current notion of "State responsibility" is all-embracing, covering general principles of international responsibility of States in the sense of a comprehensive *régime* of the law of obligations, including all types of internationally wrongful acts attributable to the State and the entire series of

---

17 II YEARBOOK OF THE INTERNATIONAL LAW COMMISSION (1980) (Part Two) at 26–63, document A.35/6, Chap. III.

18 II YEARBOOK OF THE INTERNATIONAL LAW COMMISSION (1980), Part One at 107, document A/CN.4/330; 1980, Vol. II Part One at 79, document A/CN.4/334; 1982, Vol. II, Part One at 22, document A/CN.4/354; 1983, Vol. II, Part One at 3, document A/CN.4/336 and Add. 1; 1984, Vol. II, Part One at 2, document A/CN.4/380; 1985, Vol. II, Part One at 3, document A/CN. 4/389; and 1986, Vol. II, Part One at 1, document A/CN.4/49; and Add. 1.

19 YEARBOOK OF THE INTERNATIONAL LAW COMMISSION (1986), Vol. II, Part Two at 35, note 86. The five articles of Part Three and its Annex were referred to the Drafting Committee in 1986, *ibid.* para. 63.

20 YEARBOOK OF THE INTERNATIONAL LAW COMMISSION (1987), Vol. II, Part Two, para. 220.

21 For text of Articles 6 and 7, *see* REPORT OF THE INTERNATIONAL LAW COMMISSION, document A/44/10 at 191–193, paras. 229–230, and for Articles 8, 9 and 10, *see* REPORT OF THE INTERNATIONAL LAW COMMISSION, document A/45/10, notes 247 and 263. YEARBOOK OF THE INTERNATIONAL LAW COMMISSION (1988), Vol. II, Part Two at 20, note 61. *See* REPORT OF THE INTERNATIONAL LAW COMMISSION, A/46/10, paras. 311–322, third and fourth reports; and a/47/10, paras. 112–276.

secondary rules flowing as legal consequences of a breach of an international obligation binding on the State, regardless of its origin.

"State responsibility" as a topic for codification has thus come a long way from the notion of a special *régime* of responsibility of States for injuries suffered by aliens on their territories to a comprehensive system of "international responsibility" of States whether or not involving aliens or individuals, and regardless of injuries.

B. International Liability for Injurious Consequences Arising out of Acts not Prohibited by International Law

"International liability" as conceived by the International Law Commission was an off-shoot of Article 35 of the draft articles on State responsibility based on the proposition that absence of wrongfulness does not prejudge any question that may arise in regard to compensation for damage caused by the act of that State. The basis for liability lies neither in any fault or wrongfulness of an act attributable to the State but is to be found in the injurious consequences suffered by persons beyond its boundary. Its origin is traceable to the Roman law, and indeed common law, Latin maxim: *sic tuo utere ut alienum non laedas* (use your property in such a way as not to harm others). This is a concept of liability based on restrictive enjoyment of one's own property, or limited and regulated use of proprietary rights subject to the prevention of harm to one's neighbors.

This theory of international liability finds expression in State practice, as exemplified in the *Trail Smelter Arbitration*, (1938 and 1941),[22] the *Lake Lanoux Arbitration*, (1957),[23] the *Corfu Channel Case* (*Merits*), (1949),[24] and the *Gut Dam Arbitration*, (1969).[25] In all these cases, the primary rule that a State must refrain from harming its neighbor has received further application with far wider implications. Not only is a State bound by an obligation not to harm or to hurt another State, but the obligation appears to encompass also the duty to prevent harm from occurring in the territory of its neighboring States.

---

22 *U.S.A. v. Canada* (1938 and 1941), 3 REPORT OF INTERNATIONAL ARBITRATION AWARDS (RIAA 1905).

23 *Spain v. France* (1957), 24:101 INTERNATIONAL LAW REPORT (ILR).

24 *U.K. v. Albania*, ICJ REPORTS 1949 at 4; *see* also assessment of compensation, *ibid.* at 244, damages were awarded in a separate judgement. The Court held Albania responsible: "... nothing was attempted by the Albanian authorities to prevent the disaster. These grave omissions involve the international responsibility of Albania..." Failure to take steps to warn ships near the danger zone was the basis for Albania's responsibility.

25 *USA v. Canada*, 8:118 INTERNATIONAL LEGAL MATERIALS (ILM) (1969).

Apart from elaborating primary rules specifying the content of obligation incumbent on every State in the enjoyment of its sovereign rights, in the exploration and exploitation of natural resources within its own national boundaries, the International Law Commission has attempted to conceptualize and circumscribe the set of rules or draft articles on international liability for injurious consequences arising out of acts not prohibited by international law. This topic was included in its programme of work in 1978 when Professor Quentin Quentin-Baxter was appointed Special Rapporteur.[26] Five reports were submitted and considered by the Commission between 1980 and 1984.[27] The Commission also had before it a study prepared by the Secretariat entitled *Survey of State practice relevant to international liability for injurious consequences arising out of acts not prohibited by international law*.[28]

Following the untimely death of Professor Quentin-Baxter, Ambassador Julio Barboza was appointed succeeding Special Rapporteur in 1985. No fewer than seven reports were received by the Commission from the second Special Rapporteur from 1985 to 1992.[29]

The Commission continues to consider succeeding reports from the Special Rapporteurs. An open-ended working group was established in 1992 to consider some general issues relating to the scope, the approach to be taken at the possible direction of the future work on the topic. The Commission had identified the broad area and outer limits of the topic but no final decision has been taken on its set of draft articles dealing with primary rules regarding international obligations of States, which appear to favor a more or less strict doctrine of international liability of States together with the primary duty to undertake precautionary measures consistent with its obligation to prevent harm.

This topic appears to have developed into various specialized *régimes* of strict or even absolute liability providing for international fund to cover

---

[26] II YEARBOOK OF THE INTERNATIONAL LAW COMMISSION (1978), Part One at 103, document A/CN.4/334 and Add. 1 and 2.

[27] II YEARBOOK OF THE INTERNATIONAL LAW COMMISSION (1980–84), Part One at 247, document A/CN.4/334 and Add. 1 and 2 (1980); at 103, A/CN.4/346 and Add. 1 and 2 (1981); at 51, document A/CN.4/(1982); at 201, document A/CN.4/373 (1983); and at 155, A/CN.4/383 and Add. 1 (1984).

[28] II YEARBOOK OF THE INTERNATIONAL LAW COMMISSION (1984) Part One at 129, document A/CN.4/378.

[29] For the seven reports of the Special Rapporteur, *see* II YEARBOOK OF THE INTERNATIONAL LAW COMMISSION (1985), (1986) (1987), (1988), Part One at 97, document A/CN.4/394 (1985) at 145, document A/CN.4/402 (1986) at 47, document A/CN.4/405 (1987); and at 251, document A/CN.4/413, and Corr. 1, Corr. 2, documents A/CN.4/423, A/CN.4/426, and A/CN.4/437, and Corrs. (1988).

expenses for clearing up of environmental pollution and compensation for personal losses and injuries suffered, including the establishment of international agencies to organize, manage and regulate procedures to ensure the safety and security of the international community in various fields of human endeavours and activities, such as maritime transport, oil pollution, marine environment, resource-sharing, and long-range transboundary air pollution.

Not unlike State responsibility which in its inception started off as a set of primary rules regulating State responsibility for injuries suffered by aliens, international liability prescribes also primary rules of State liability for harms to non-nationals which the State fails to prevent or to give necessary warning to avoid and abate harmful effects. But unlike State responsibility, international liability continues to be concerned with primary rules, while the expanded scope of State responsibility is no longer concerned with primary rules of international law generating primary obligations incumbent upon States but will deal more particularly with the consequences of breaches of such primary rules or obligations already subsisting in international law regardless of origin, whether derived from a treaty or from customary international law.

Thus, on several occasions, both in their origin and in the course of their developments, the two topics started off as primary rules and primary obligations and their paths continue to cross from time to time, thereby necessitating occasional comments on the relevance of their mutual relations.

II. ANALYTICAL EXAMINATION

A comparative analysis of the constitutive elements of "State responsibility" and "international liability" may clarify further the similarities and differences that are pertinent between the two topics now under our analytical examination.

A. Nature of the Rules of International Law

As has been disclosed in our examination of the historical developments and origin of the two topics, the current trends that have clearly emerged indicate that "State responsibility" is a comprehensive part of international law, embracing all aspects of obligations incumbent upon States *vis-à-vis* other States whether voluntarily contracted or imposed by customs, including the general principle that an internationally wrongful act engaging State responsibility entails legal consequences in international law, whereas "international liability" is a set of primary rules concerning primary obligations of States. It follows that the breach of a primary obligation contained in the topic of "international liability" inevitably sets in motion all the secondary rules prescribed under the topic of "State responsibility." The obligation not to cause harm to others, or in its wider version, the obligation to prevent harmful effects to others, would be a primary rule of international law, a breach of which would engage State responsibility.

However, this does not preclude the possibility that under the topic "international liability," there are several areas in which specialized *régimes* of implementation of secondary rights and obligations have been created by international conventions or multilateral treaties. Just as the Vienna Convention on the Law of Treaties 1969 provides for all the legal consequences of a breach of a treaty obligation, a set of draft articles on "international liability" may create a residuary general *régime* with provisions for implementation of secondary obligations, consistent with but containing further detailed regulations different from the implementation rules provided by the draft articles on State responsibility, which in any event would always operate as the residual secondary rules in the absence of any special arrangements under the "international liability" draft articles which may contain stricter rules of liability, and more flexible criteria of attributability or imputation.

While "State responsibility" presupposes the existence of primary rules and primary obligations, breaches of which entail the application of secondary rules provided by "State responsibility," the rules and obligations elaborated under "international liability" constitute precisely such primary rules and obligations, untouched by State responsibility, but the breach of which will generate secondary obligations to be fulfilled under the law of State responsibility, such as the obligation to take measures *ex nunc*, *ex tunc*, and *ex ante*, including cessation of the wrongful acts or harmful effects, restitution or reparation, and satisfaction or adoption of precautionary measures to prevent repetition of the harmful effects or the injurious consequences of activities whether or not inconsistent with international law.

B. The Relevance of Wrongfulness

To reconcile the law of "international liability" with the law of "State responsibility" by permitting the application of the residual rules of State responsibility to all breaches of the duties to prevent harm which entail international liability is to assimilate the consequences of "international liability" to those generated by State responsibility.

However, the general rule of State responsibility requires the existence, by commission or omission, of an internationally wrongful act, whereas international liability is regardless of unlawfulness or prohibition by international law. In this particular connection, Article 35 of the draft articles on State responsibility has paved the way to this reconciliation. There are circumstances precluding wrongfulness under the draft articles, but in at least four provisions, Articles 29, 31, 32 and 33, absence of wrongfulness does not prejudge the question that may arise regarding compensation. Thus, the obligation to compensate in the absence of wrongfulness is not inconsistent with the law of State responsibility. Nor would special requirements to prevent future harms be viewed as necessarily rejected by the law of State responsibility. Thus, wrongfulness may be a constitutive element for State responsibility. There are exceptions to this general proposition where absence of wrongfulness will not preclude the application of some aspects of the secondary rules which impose an obligation to compensate for the loss or damage or harm suffered.

In any event, the relevance of wrongfulness is relatively insignificant in the context of absolute and strict liability. The basis for international liability being the existence of injurious consequences or harm. This relative insignificance of the requirement of wrongfulness is reflected in the continuing evolution of international law itself. What was not prohibited yesterday may be prohibited tomorrow, and what was disallowed today may be permitted in the future. The bottom line for international liability is that a State is liable for harmful effects of activities under its control or within its jurisdiction. It is control or jurisdiction which gives rise to liability of the State, irrespective of whether the activities in questions are prohibited by international law or are permitted or not tolerated by the law of nations.

The law of "international liability" regardless of wrongfulness also opens the way for international law to evolve and develop its proscriptive rules without prejudice to the obligation to compensate for harmful consequences generated by a State or the obligation incumbent on every State to prevent, avoid and abate all injurious consequences to others. In this fashion, the moving frontier of international law progresses.

C. The Relative Irrelevance of Damage or Injury

One of the areas of contrast or difference of emphasis between "State responsibility" and "international liability" may be seen in the absence of requirement of injury or damage as a constitutive element of State responsibility, whereas under "international liability," there is no breach of a primary obligation if no appreciable harm results from activities which a State either permits, condones or fails to prevent.

On the other hand, to engage State responsibility, there is no need to prove any damage or injury, so long only as it is established that an internationally wrongful act has been committed which is attributable to the State. Although the gravity of damage or seriousness of injury may be a relevant factor in the assessment of the amount of compensation to be awarded to the injured State, it is not relevant to the establishment of State responsibility as such. A shift of emphasis is readily visible from the need for proof of wrongfulness to found State responsibility to a total disregard of lawfulness of activities in the case of international liability. There is another shift of relevance from absence of any requirement of injury to constitute State responsibility to the necessity of at least an appreciable harm or injurious consequence to establish a violation of the duty not to cause harm or a breach of the primary obligation to prevent harm as an element of international liability of a State.

D. Differences in the Test of Attributability to the State of an Action or Omission

As demonstrated in the draft articles on State responsibility, it is important to trace the commission of an internationally wrongful act, which could be by action or omission but which must be attributable to the State to engage the responsibility of that State. On the other hand, the international liability of a State in regard to its obligation not to cause harm to others requires no such close tie or attributability of an act to the State. Indeed, there is no requirement of an act at all, let alone an internationally wrongful act. International liability is created by injurious consequences which according to the natural law of causation must result from activities over which the State has or should have direct or indirect control, or which lies within its jurisdiction.

More often than not, a State may be held internationally liable for harmful effects caused by activities occurring or emanating from within its territory, hence under its jurisdiction or from a sea-going vessel or spacecraft carrying its flag or registered in its territory; liability in this sense may be said to be strict or almost absolute, regardless of fault or intention or even negligence. The test is whether the State could have prevented the harm but has failed to take necessary steps to pre-empt or abate it. Such failure is the source of its international liability. The test of attributability is more negative or less positive, in the sense that the act in question need not be attributable to the State. It is sufficient if the activities giving rise to the harm, although not prohibited by international law, and although not performed by the State or any of its organs or agencies, were nevertheless conducted within its territory or under its jurisdiction or control.

E. Breach of an Obligation to Prevent a Given Event

Article 23 of the draft articles on State responsibility provides that: "When the result required of a State by an international obligation is the prevention, by means of its own choice, of the occurrence of a given event, there is a breach of that obligation only if, by the conduct adopted, the State does not achieve that result."

This is one of the four articles dealing with different types of international obligations incumbent upon a State, namely, Article 20: Obligation of Conduct; Article 21: Obligation of Result; Article 22: Exhaustion of Local Remedies; and Article 23: Obligation to Prevent a Given Event. Article 23 therefore refers essentially to a special type of obligation of result which is also intrinsically related to the adoption of conduct by the State, a mixed obligation of result and conduct.

In general, Part I of the draft articles deals with general principles and Chapter III with the Breach of an International Obligation. Articles 23 is part of Chapter III and envisages cases of breach of obligation to prevent a given event, such as the taking of hostages of accredited diplomats, the seizure of an accredited embassy or consulate, the assassination of a visiting dignitary and the prevention of harm to another State.

Events which in principle should be prevented or are required to be prevented by international law may include the occurrence of injurious consequences caused by activities which are otherwise lawful within one's territory but the harmful effects occur in the neighboring country, such as in the *Trail Smelter Case*, or the diversion of water from the river in one territory which could adversely affect the flow of water, its quantity and quality, into a lake bordering another State, as in the *Lake Lanoux Arbitration*; or indeed failure to warn about imminent danger in an area within the jurisdiction of a State normally safe for international navigation, as in the *Corfu Channel Case*. Thus, rules of international law relating to international liability constitute the type of primary obligations envisaged in Article 23: Obligation to Prevent a Given Event, which whenever breaches, would call for the application of another series of rules of international law on State responsibility giving rise to a host of secondary obligations to be fulfilled by the breaching State.

There appears to be a natural flow of consequential connections between all international obligations including the rule *sic tuo utere ut alienum non laedas* and State responsibility.

F. Duality of International Obligations

In general, an international obligation is owed by one State towards another State, or it is incumbent upon one State to be discharged *vis-à-vis* another State. However, there are also obligations which a State owes to the whole world or to all alike, an *obligatio erga omnes*, such as an obligation to maintain the minimum standard of human rights, or the non-discriminatory treatment of all aliens, or an obligation to co-operate with one's neighbors or to prevent harm to an adjacent community. By their very nature, *obligationes erga omnes* are the concern of all States, and as such all States can be held to have a legal interest in their protection.[30]

To acknowledge the existence of this type of obligation *erga omnes* which is the concern of all States, does not imply the availability of a right of action or *jus standi* for every State. *Actio popularis* is not admitted in the international forum. Indeed, the International Court of Justice distinguished between the obligation of a State towards the international community as a whole, and those arising *vis-à-vis* another State in the field of diplomatic protection[31] or air pollution. It is difficult to designate a State or anyone else to represent the international community, examples closest to an *actio popularis* would be the requests for advisory opinions of the International Court of Justice by the General Assembly of the United Nations.

State responsibility in its original concept represented an aspect of diplomatic protection, covering two different dimensions of victims, *i.e.* personal victims or the persons, natural or juridical, suffering the injury inflicted by the territorial State and the victim State whose nationals suffered personal injury or economic loss. This particular aspect of State responsibility in its classical form related to the treatment of aliens and its minimum standard. Likewise, the occurrence of environmental damage suffered by neighboring States and their nationals as the result of activities conducted in the offending State contains two dimensions of victims, namely, the individuals exposed to harmful effects and the States of which the victims are nation-

---

30 Barcelona Traction, Light & Power Co., case *Belgium v. Spain*, ICJ REPORTS 1970 at 3.

31 *Ibid.* paras. 33–35.

als. The damage, injury or injurious consequences constitute the special or particular interest needed to make room for a *locus standi* or the victim State.[32]

The injury to aliens is represented by Article 22 of the draft articles on State responsibility requiring exhaustion of local remedies and implying the existence of two-fold measures of redress: the first dimension under the national law of the territorial State as reflected in the availability of local remedies, and the second dimension under international law, once the claim is espoused by the State of which the victims are nationals.

Similarly, State responsibility flowing from its international liability or a breach of an obligation to prevent a given event, also contains two distinct dimensions, *i.e.* the domestic-law remedies which do not normally exist and the international liability attached to the State *vis-à-vis* the victim State.

While no local remedies are readily available in respect of injurious consequences arising out of activities causing transboundary air pollution, in the absence of a treaty *régime*, the victim State could only find a solution through negotiations, arbitration, conciliation or good offices, if not litigation at an international as distinguished from national level.

Article 23 of the draft articles on State responsibility: Breach of a international obligation to prevent a given event, in as much as it comprehends international liability may end up with the settlement of claims by paying compensation to the victim State or directly to the individuals suffering from the breach of the international obligation to prevent a given event, such as flooding as a consequence of the construction of a dam.[33]

Both categories of cases: (i) diplomatic protection; and (ii) international liability are concerned with claims that could be settled under national law through local remedies, or amicable settlement, failing which international methods of dispute settlement may be invoked.

Conclusion

Whatever the theory adopted in any examination of the topic of State responsibility as a major basic part of public international law and the topic of international liability for injurious consequences arising out of acts not prohibited by international law, it is clear that the two topics are closely related if not intrinsically interconnected.

---

[32] *See e.g. Nuclear Test Cases, Australia v. France, New Zealand v. France,* ICJ REPORTS 1974 at 253, 457.

[33] As in the Gut Dam Arbitration, *U.S.A. v. Canada*, 8:118 ILM (1969).

It has not been simple to sever international liability completely from State responsibility, although both topics are undergoing an intensive process of investigation, deliberation and codification by international norms – formulating agencies, such as the International Law Commission and non-governmental institutions of academic and professional importance such as the Institut de Droit international.

Pending consideration of the topics by the international bodies, which may take decades if not scores of years before final completion and adoption, independent studies should be continued and encouraged to throw more light on the subjects.

State responsibility which has grown more fully from a narrow confine of injury to aliens will receive much further studies and more thorough scrutiny. The topic appears now to be all inclusive, comprehending all aspects of international obligations, whether created by treaties or by customs, including obligations of conduct as well as obligations of result and a mixture of both.

Meanwhile, what was originally conceived as the narrowest of State responsibility has received further attention from the international financial circles to provide further incentives and more exhaustive guarantees of foreign investments, as against possible expropriation, nationalization, requisition, or the taking of property with the widest notion of the most effective measures to protect international investments and to pre-empt or prevent expropriation without appropriate or adequate compensation under the new international economic order. Different groups of States, such as Group 77, Group 7 and OECD[34] have endeavoured to assert their views of the rule of international law as it ought to be, *de lege ferenda*. Divergent views appear to have emerged with further efforts to converge them through various resolutions of the United Nations.[35] In the ultimate analysis, a more balanced set of rules may prevail through consensus if not a gradual and progressive implementation by international conventions, bilateral, regional and global.

On the whole, State responsibility for breaches of all types of international obligations, amounting to international delicts or torts or indeed crimes under international law will continue to retain our serious attention in the years ahead. The next century which begins the third millennium in the

---

[34] *See* Vol. I, SURVEY OF EXISTING INSTRUMENTS, PROGRESS REPORT AND BACKGROUND STUDIES BY THE WORLD BANK GROUP, *Legal Framework for the Treatment of Foreign Investment* (1990).

[35] *See e.g.* United Nations General Assembly Resolutions 626, 1803, 2158, 3171, 3201 and 3281. Compare ICC Code (1949), Harvard Draft (1961), ICC Guidelines (1972), Agreement among Arab Countries (1973), OPIC Investment Agreement (1981), ASEAN Agreement on Investment Compnesation, Promotion and Protection (1987), and INCTC Code of Conduct (1990).

Christian era may portend a clearer picture of future progressive developments of international law on this topic. International liability also continues to grow with further redresses beyond restitution or payment of compensation with a view to preventing harm to human beings and the environment whenever a State exercises its legitimate right to explore and exploit its natural resources.

Pluralité des ordres juridiques internationaux et unité du droit international

par

Nicolas Valticos

L'histoire du droit international est celle de son expansion et de sa diversification. Dans ce processus, le droit international a, pour l'essentiel, conservé son unité, ce qui, du reste, est fondamental pour son efficacité.

Cependant, à côté de sa croissance générale, il a connu, dans certains domaines, des avancées qui ont fini par constituer différents types d'ordres juridiques particuliers, de branches plus ou moins distinctes de cette discipline. L'évolution a été stimulée par une certaine transformation et un enrichissement du droit international lui-même qui, de droit presque uniquement relationnel[1], est devenu aussi, dans une large mesure, non seulement un droit institutionnel, mais aussi un droit matériel, réglementant plusieurs domaines dorénavant couverts, généralement, par des organisations internationales, qu'il s'agisse de l'Organisation des Nations Unies et de ses institutions spécialisées ou d'autres organisations, universelles, régionales ou spécifiques.

Ce mouvement est nettement plus accentué qu'en droit interne où, à l'exception des systèmes de la *common law*, la majeure partie des ordres juridiques est fondée sur des règles écrites de droit positif, et cela quelle qu'ait été l'évolution considérable qu'ont connue les méthodes d'interprétation depuis l'époque de l'exégèse et de la «déduction pure»[2]. En droit international, par contre, des restrictions de ce type n'ont pas joué et le mouvement s'est donc précipité depuis la fin de la Deuxième Guerre mondiale, de sorte qu'à côté de l'ordre juridique international général se sont développés des ordres juridiques particuliers, ce terme étant pris dans le sens d'ensemble de normes coordonnées portant sur un domaine spécifique du droit et ayant un développement propre mais non nécessairement indépendant de l'ordre juridique général ou d'autres ordres juridiques particuliers de cette discipline.

A cet égard, deux écueils sont à éviter: l'un serait de considérer le droit international général comme une discipline tutélaire régissant souverainement l'ensemble de ces mouvements, d'ailleurs très inégaux; l'autre consisterait à considérer ces développements comme ayant une pleine autonomie et constituant des rameaux pratiquement détachés du tronc du droit international.

---

1 La formule, on le sait, est de R.-J. Dupuy, Le droit international, Paris (1966).

2 V.F. Gény, Méthodes d'interprétation et sources en droit privé positif, Paris (1952), vol. I, p. 54 et s.

Il ne saurait y avoir, dans le domaine du droit international, d'ordre juridique particulier qui pourrait être considéré comme totalement détaché de l'ordre juridique général.

Entre le large tronc et les diverses branches, robustes ou frêles, du droit international, les liens restent plus ou moins étroits et la sève circule avec plus ou moins de fluidité, allant du tronc aux branches – qui connaissent du reste un développement propre – et revenant, enrichie, pour alimenter à son tour le tronc.

Ces relations et ces échanges n'empêchent cependant pas une certaine autonomie des ordres particuliers et même la possibilité qu'une norme d'un ordre dérivé puisse parfois prendre rang de norme de l'ordre général.

Un exemple en est la règle de la majorité des deux tiers qui, depuis 1919, était la règle pour l'adoption des conventions internationales du travail, et qui, en vertu de la Convention de Vienne sur le droit des traités de 1969, a remplacé la règle de l'unanimité pour l'adoption des décisions des Conférences internationales.

Il s'agit ici d'un domaine dans lequel la notion, fort répandue, d'«ordre juridique», qui a été approfondie et enrichie par Santi Romano[3] et qui est très proche de la théorie des institutions d'Hauriou[4], peut contribuer sensiblement à comprendre et à analyser le phénomène. Ainsi conçu[5], l'ordre juridique n'est pas seulement un ensemble statique de normes constituant un système juridique plus ou moins cohérent, mais il constitue, en outre, une entité dynamique qui, dans une certaine mesure, conduit les normes elles-mêmes dans un développement dynamique cohérent.

A cet égard, il faut d'ailleurs préciser que la notion d'ordre juridique ne constitue pas simplement un concept susceptible de clarifier les idées et de préciser les rapports entre les diverses normes et institutions. En plus de cet incontestable avantage théorique, le recours à la catégorie d'ordre juridique

---

[3] S. ROMANO, L'ORDRE JURIDIQUE, Paris (1975) (trad. française par L. François et P. Gothot, introduction de Ph. Francescakis). Comme il est observé dans cette introduction (p. VIII), l'apport de Santi Romano «paraît épouser le temps présent encore mieux que le sien». Pour l'ordre international, *voir* p. 34 et s. Et pour ce qui est de l'actualité des conceptions de Santi Romano dans le domaine du droit international, on peut rappeler qu'entre 1945 et 1984, le nombre des organisations internationales est passé d'une dizaine à plus de 500 (*voir* P.M. DUPUY, DROIT INTERNATIONAL PUBLIC, Paris, 3e éd. (1995), p. 153). Cet auteur utilise par ailleurs largement la notion d'«ordre juridique» (*ibid.* p. 10 et s.).

[4] En ce qui concerne l'influence des travaux D'HAURIOU, *voir* LA PENSÉE DU DOYEN HAURIOU ET SON INFLUENCE, Paris (1969).

[5] *Voir* S. ROMANO, *op. cit.*, *supra* note 3, pp. 9–10. On a aussi défini l'ordre juridique des communautés internationales comme «un ensemble de normes organisées et unies dans un tout harmonieux et autonome en vue de réglementer une société donnée» (PH. CAHIER, *L'ordre juridique interne des organisations internationales*, dans: R.-J. DUPUY (direction), MANUEL SUR LES ORGANISATIONS INTERNATIONALES, Dordrecht (1988), p. 237.

présente, en matière d'interprétation – disons même de la dynamique du développement du droit – un avantage incontestable par rapport à l'approche classique du droit des traités.

En effet, le droit des traités classique ne peut fournir que des solutions formelles et statiques aux problèmes d'interprétation juridique. Or, l'évolution du droit international, et notamment le développement, souvent complexe, des Organisations internationales et de leur droit dérivé constituent des phénomènes dynamiques qui appellent une analyse parallèle et comparée des ordres juridiques concernés et de leur développement, une évaluation de leurs rapports et de leur plus ou moins proche parenté, et en conséquence une appréciation de la légitimité d'emprunts réciproques en vue de compléter ces ordres et d'en faciliter le développement dans le respect de leur finalité et non par une simple opération de logique formelle.

Pour en venir plus spécialement à l'ordre juridique international, disons, pour le moment, que les liens entre l'ordre juridique international général et les ordres juridiques internationaux particuliers peuvent varier sensiblement, mais qu'il ne saurait y avoir de cas, si spécifique soit-il, qui puisse être complètement autonome dans ce domaine.

Ceci dit, ce qui distingue l'ordre juridique international général des ordres particuliers est naturellement le fait que ceux-ci visent des domaines spécifiques dans lesquels ils comportent des ensembles de normes portant réglementation des domaines en question, les règles et techniques juridiques ainsi adoptées n'étant pas – normalement – partie du droit international général, sans pour cela que ces règles, généralement plus spécifiques et plus avancées, lui soient pour cela contraires.

L'exposé, nécessairement schématique, qui suivra partira de l'ordre juridique fondamental, qui est celui du droit international général, et traitera ensuite de certains ordres internationaux plus ou moins complets et spécialisés et liés de plus ou moins près à l'ordre international général. Il portera aussi sur les relations entre les différents ordres considérés. Il convient cependant de préciser auparavant certaines considérations générales.

* * *

Que l'unité, autant que la diversité, caractérisent de plus en plus le droit international, il n'est, pour en avoir confirmation, que de se référer au titre choisi pour les *Mélanges* offerts à l'un des maîtres du droit international de notre époque, le regretté Paul Reuter[6].

---

[6] MÉLANGES OFFERTS À PAUL REUTER – LE DROIT INTERNATIONAL: UNITÉ ET DIVERSITÉ, Paris (1981).

Les deux phénomènes de l'évolution du droit international qui ont largement contribué à ce développement ont été, avons-nous dit, le développement du droit de la société «institutionnelle» et celui d'un droit matériel issu des institutions et des accords internationaux et portant sur le fond des questions dont ces accords traitaient et que ces institutions étaient appelées à développer.

Certes, le droit des siècles précédents n'était pas uniquement relationnel. Il comportait aussi certaines règles de fond, mais était loin des véritables systèmes de dispositions matérielles qui se sont développées, à notre époque, surtout à partir de la création et du développement des organisations internationales[7], universelles ou régionales, tissant chacune un réseau de règles liant – ou visant à lier – les Etats concernés dans le domaine qui leur est propre.

Ces règles varient d'un domaine à l'autre. Elles peuvent aussi se différencier plus ou moins du droit commun international. Plus spéciales, par définition, elles prolongent celui-ci dans la matière dont elles traitent, ou le complètent, ou encore l'approfondissent. Elles n'en sont pas moins consacrées à une finalité qui leur est propre et qui leur donne la spécificité d'un ordre juridique particulier. Ces règles diffèrent cependant entre elles d'après le degré de leur développement et, partant, de leur autonomie. Certains des ordres juridiques qu'elles constituent sont plus ou moins complets et autonomes, pour ne pas dire fermés (car aucun ordre juridique particulier ne peut ignorer l'ordre juridique général du droit international). D'autres ordres sont plus limités, en quelque sorte élémentaires, incomplets et largement ouverts, mais peuvent progressivement, si la matière couverte l'exige et l'amène à se développer, prendre les proportions d'un ordre juridique véritable.

Santi Romano[8], pour sa part, distinguait, en ce qui concerne le droit international, plusieurs catégories, et ses distinctions, toutes systématiques qu'elles fussent, avaient un côté prophétique pour notre époque. Traitant d'abord de la notion proche d'*institution*, il en observait de parfaites ou d'imparfaites, d'indépendantes, de coordonnées, de subordonnées. Il signalait aussi la notion de «relevance» d'un ordre pour un autre et observait la relation dans laguelle un ordre se situe par rapport à un autre, ainsi que celle dans laquelle plusieurs ordres indépendants entre eux dépendent d'un autre. Nous aurons l'occasion d'y revenir, bien que moins systématiquement que le subtil maître italien.

---

[7] Sur les organisations internationales, *voir* notamment, sous la direction de G. ABI-SAAB, LE CONCEPT D'ORGANISATION INTERNATIONALE, Paris (1980); P. GERBET, LES ORGANISATIONS INTERNATIONALES, Paris (1972); R.-J. DUPUY, *Le droit des relations entre les organisations internationales*, 100 RCADI (1960), pp. 457–589; M. BETTATI, LE DROIT DES ORGANISATIONS INTERNATIONALES, Paris (1987); et R.-J. DUPUY (direction), MANUEL SUR LES ORGANISATIONS INTERNATIONALES, *op. cit.*, *supra* note 5.

[8] S. ROMANO, *op. cit.*, *supra* note 3, p. 101 et s.

L'objet de la présente étude sera d'exposer les grandes subdivisions et les relations des ordres juridiques internationaux[9] et de rechercher de quelle manière ils peuvent, si nécessaire, être complétés.

Les principales catégories d'ordres juridiques internationaux que nous nous proposons d'examiner sont constituées à partir d'organisations internationales étatiques établies par traités et dotées d'une Constitution qui en définit la composition, les objectifs et les pouvoirs, possédant des organes communs et une personnalité juridique distincte de celles des Etats qui les composent et, généralement, adoptant des règles qui précisent leur mode de fonctionnement et des normes internationales visant à atteindre leurs objectifs. Cette définition vise cependant des ordres juridiques complets, ce qui ne veut pas dire clos. Il existe aussi divers ordres juridiques imparfaits n'ayant pas tous ces caractéristiques, comme dans le cas de la CSCE (actuellement OSCE) qui commença par constituer un ordre juridique avant de devenir une organisation.

* * *

L'exposé qui suivra portera successivement sur l'ordre juridique international général et l'ordre juridique des Nations Unies, les ordres juridiques particuliers des institutions spécialisées du système des Nations Unies, les ordres juridiques internationaux spéciaux, les ordres juridiques régionaux et les ordres juridiques non gouvernementaux. Cet exposé sera entrecoupé et complété par des aperçus sur la question des relations entre les ordres et à l'intérieur des grandes catégories d'ordres.

I. L'ORDRE JURIDIQUE INTERNATIONAL GÉNÉRAL ET CEUX DES INSTITUTIONS DU SYSTÈME DES NATIONS UNIES

A. L'ordre juridique international général et l'ordre juridique des Nations Unies

1. L'ordre juridique international général

L'ordre juridique international général est celui qui recouvre essentiellement la formule «droit international (public)» (auparavant «droit des

9 Le problème des relations entre les différents ordres a été étudié dans une large mesure par R.-J. DUPUY dans son cours *Le droit des relations entre les organisations internationales*, *op. cit.*, *supra* note 7.

gens»). Il englobe les règles juridiques, coutumières ou conventionnelles, qui régissent la communauté internationale.

Il n'est plus possible, à cet égard, d'établir une cloison étanche entre l'ordre juridique général ainsi conçu et celui des Nations Unies, c'est-à-dire celui qui a été établi dans le cadre des Nations Unies, car c'est dans ce cadre que sont souvent élaborées, depuis un demi-siècle, la plupart des normes qui font partie de l'ordre international général[10].

La question, il est vrai, n'est pas aussi simple qu'elle pourrait le paraître, car les auteurs classiques avaient tracé une délimitation nette entre le droit et la pratique des organisations internationales, d'une part, et le droit international coutumier, de l'autre. Plus récemment, cependant, il a été admis, notamment, que la position adoptée par les Etats dans le cadre des organisations internationales revêt une portée juridique en tant qu'expression de l'état du droit international public[11].

De toute manière, on ne peut contester – et il s'agit d'un élément significatif en l'occurrence – qu'une catégorie importante, bien qu'imprécise, de l'ordre juridique international est la notion du *jus cogens* ou «règles impératives», introduite par la Convention de Vienne sur le droit des traités (art. 53).

On doit également, et surtout, admettre la place occupée dans l'ordre juridique général établi dans le cadre des Nations Unies par les différents textes, largement ratifiés, concernant la protection des droits de l'homme, alors qu'un autre exemple bien connu est celui de droit de la mer, droit que la Cour internationale de Justice, relevant elle aussi du système juridique des Nations Unies, a progressivement façonné, sur la base de critères d'ailleurs évolutifs.

On a aussi pu parler de règles coutumières nouvelles, établies par la repétition de recommandations émanant des Nations Unies[12].

2. L'ordre juridique propre des Nations Unies

L'Organisation des Nations Unies n'est cependant pas uniquement, ni même principalement, une institution dont l'activité comporte la formulation de règles générales de droit. Elle est aussi et surtout une organisation

---

[10] A. PELLET, *La formation du droit international dans le cadre des Nations Unies* JOURNAL EUROPÉEN DE DROIT INTERNATIONAL (1995), vol. 6, n° 3, pp. 401–425.

[11] G. ARANGIO-RUIZ, *The Normative Role of the General Assembly of the United Nations, etc.*, RCADI (1972), pp. 407–742; R. HIGGINS, *Interprétations occidentales du concept d'organisation internationale,* dans: LE CONCEPT D'ORGANISATION INTERNATIONALE, *op. cit.*, *supra* note 7, pp. 211–212.

[12] A. PELLET, *op. cit.*, *supra* note 10, p. 404.

qui a son *ordre juridique propre*[13]. Elle est en particulier chargée – et c'est notamment le cas du Conseil de Sécurité – du maintien de la paix. En tant que telle, elle prend, quand elle le peut ou le veut, des décisions conformément au Chapitre VII de la Charte, qu'elle considère appropriées à cet effet[14] et établit des pratiques qu façonnent un ordre juridique propre mais marquent aussi plus largement le droit international général.

Cet ordre juridique propre des Nations Unies comprend naturellement aussi des règles concernant le fonctionnement même de cette organisation comme, notamment, l'admission et les droits et obligations des Etats membres, la composition et les pouvoirs de ses organes (ainsi le cas, fort discuté, du Conseil de Sécurité).

Par ailleurs, cet ordre juridique recouvre différents types d'ordres subordonnés ou annexes qui, tout en lui étant rattachés, ont une plus ou moins large mesure d'autonomie. Tels sont, entre autres, les domaines couverts par des organes, unités ou institutions comme l'UNDP, la CNUCED, le Haut-Commissariat pour les réfugiés.

En outre, des ordres disposant d'une plus grande autonomie sont ceux des institutions dites spécialisées qui maintiennent certains liens avec les Nations Unies et sur lesquels nous reviendrons dans la section suivante.

Enfin – et il conviendra aussi d'y revenir – diverses organisations internationales ou régionales sont complètement autonomes par rapport à l'ordre juridique des Nations Unies, mais des liens peuvent être établis par des accords particuliers sur des points concrets.

Pour préciser les relations éventuelles entre ces différents types d'ordres juridiques, il y aura lieu d'examiner de plus près les compétences de chacun d'eux aussi bien que les liens juridiques ou même pratiques qui les rattachent avec l'ordre des Nations Unies. Dans la suite de cet exposé, nous essaierons de donner quelques indications générales à ce sujet.

---

13 PH. CAHIER, *Le droit interne des organisations internationales*, REVUE GÉNÉRALE DE DROIT INTERNATIONAL PUBLIC (1963), pp. 563–602; *idem*, *L'ordre juridique interne des organisations internationales*, *op. cit.*, *supra* note 5; G. BALLADORE-PALLIERI, *Le droit interne des organisations internationales*, RCADI (1969-II), pp. 1–38.

14 La littérature est très abondante à ce sujet. *Voir* ainsi les travaux du colloque de Rennes de la SOCIÉTÉ FRANÇAISE POUR LE DROIT INTERNATIONAL, Paris (1995) et les diverses études citées dans: N. VALTICOS, *L'expansion du droit international et le Conseil de Sécurité – A la pénible recherche du maintien de la paix*, à paraître dans les MÉLANGES ŠAHOVIĆ.

B. Les ordres juridiques des institutions spécialisées du système des Nations Unies et leurs relations avec l'ordre juridique international général et celui des Nations Unies

Parmi les nombreuses organisations internationales, les institutions spécialisées du système des Nations Unies telles que l'OIT, l'OMS, la FAO (OAA), l'UNESCO, l'ONUDI, notamment, et, pour les institutions économiques, la Banque mondiale et le Fonds monétaire, sont des plus importantes. Elles diffèrent d'ailleurs sensiblement entre elles et les ordres juridiques qui émanent d'elles s'en ressentent, notamment en raison de leur objet, très différent de l'une à l'autre, du type de leur activité, qui est tantôt en grande partie normatif et tantôt essentiellement pratique. Ces institutions ont un caractère – ou une vocation – universel, mais leur composition étatique effective varie selon les cas et l'époque[15]. De toute manière, chacune de ces institutions est fondée sur une Constitution définissant sa compétence, ses méthodes d'action et les obligations des Etats qui en sont membres.

Ainsi pour ce qui est de l'OIT qui, fondée en 1919, est la plus ancienne organisation et celle qui a adopté le plus grand nombre de textes normatifs (176 conventions qui ont fait l'objet de plus de 6000 ratifications) – raisons pour lesquelles nous nous référerons plus d'une fois à cet ordre juridique – les Etats membres sont tenus d'appliquer non seulement les textes qu'ils ont ratifiés, mais aussi certains principes fondamentaux, ainsi que de se soumettre au système de contrôle établi par l'Organisation[16].

Il peut parfois se poser une question de relations entre l'ordre juridique des institutions spécialiseés et celui des Nations Unies, comme avec l'ordre juridique international général, de même qu'entre les ordres juridiques de ces diverses institutions elles-mêmes ou – mais on le verra aussi par la suite – avec ceux d'organisations internationales indépendantes.

D'une manière générale, aucun de ces ordres juridiques particuliers ne saurait ignorer l'ordre juridique international général, et, en outre, quel que soit son degré d'autonomie, ne saurait être complètement détaché de l'ordre juridique propre des Nations Unies ni s'écarter de ses principes et de ses objectifs considérés dans leurs grandes lignes. Du reste, des accords, assez généraux il est vrai, rattachent les institutions spécialisées aux Nations Unies[17], et le Conseil économique et social des Nations Unies peut coor-

---

[15] Le cas des Etats-Unis et de ses entrées et sorties dans l'une ou l'autre organisation est bien connu.

[16] *Voir* N. VALTICOS, DROIT INTERNATIONAL DU TRAVAIL, Paris (1981), p. 581 et s.

[17] *Voir* R.-J. DUPUY, *Le droit des relations entre organisations internationales*, *op. cit.*, *supra* note 7, p. 563.

donner leur action à propos de questions d'intérêt commun, de même que l'Assemblée générale des Nations Unies peut leur adresser des recommandations. En outre, les chefs exécutifs de ces institutions se rencontrent régulièrement avec le Secrétaire général des Nations Unies pour assurer la coordination des activités de celles-ci.

Ceci dit, encore faut-il tenir compte d'une différence souvent sensible entre ces deux types d'ordres juridiques: c'est que les ordres particuliers ont été créés pour approfondir et développer des domaines que l'ordre juridique général des Nations Unies ne recouvre pas, du moins pas expressément ni, en tout cas, complètement. Ces ordres particuliers peuvent donc porter sur des matières qui relèvent de leur compétence propre et qui, en tant que telles, pouvent ne pas être couvertes, du moins précisément, par l'ordre des Nations Unies.

On a donc considéré que l'ordre des Nations Unies n'est pas vraiment hiérarchiquement supérieur à celui des institutions spécialisées et qu'il ne doit pas toujours l'emporter, mais qu'il s'agit, généralement, d'une liason latérale[18] sous réserve de questions politiques dont il sera question un peu plus loin.

Par ailleurs, il peut aussi y avoir, dans certains cas, similitude de compétence entre deux organisations sur certains points. Certes, en principe, chaque organisation de la «famille» des Nations Unies, du reste qualifiée de «spécialisée», est compétente pour traiter de questions de son ressort. Il y a cependant des cas dans lesquels la compétence générale des Nations Unies peut couvrir des questions relevant également de celle, plus spécifique, d'une institution spécialisée. Il peut y avoir alors compétence de deux ordres juridiques sur la même question, même si celle-ci est envisagée sous un angle quelque peu différent.

Le cas le plus connu est celui des droits de l'homme, dans lequel les Nations Unies ont adopté les célèbres pactes et conventions sur les droits en question et l'OIT des conventions sur les droits des travailleurs qui, notamment s'agissant de droit d'association, vont plus loin en matière de protection que les normes générales des Nations Unies. Dans ce cas, en cas de conflit, ce serait la norme de l'institution spécialisée qui, plus avancée, devrait avoir le pas (ce qui donnerait, en même temps, satisfaction aussi à la norme la plus générale).

En revanche, la primauté politique de l'ordre de l'Organisation des Nations Unies doit s'imposer lorsqu'il s'agit de questions de caractère politique

---

[18] *Ibid.*

et notamment de la légitimité de chaque délégation étatique qui prétend représenter un Etat membre.

C'est ce qui a été décidé, à propos de la Chine, en 1966[19]. L'Assemblée générale des Nations Unies ayant adopté une résolution (396 [VI]) énonçant que, compte tenu du caractère essentiellement politique de la question, celle-ci devait être subordonnée à une décision de l'Assemblée générale, il s'ensuivit qu'en octobre 1971, à la suite de la décision de l'Assemblée de reconnaître les représentants de la République populaire de Chine comme les seuls représentants légitimes de la Chine, le Conseil d'administration du BIT décida de prendre, de son côté, une décision semblable.

Ceci dit, chaque Organisation a ses activités et ses procédures propres et développe son ordre juridique de manière autonome dans l'exercice de ses compétences.

Ainsi l'OIT a non seulement une compétence établie par sa Constitution mais, comme on le sait, une composition (dite tripartite) et des procédures bien à elles qui ont marqué l'évolution du droit international[20].

Parmi les plus significatifs de ces traits[21], on peut rappeler le cas, signalé au début de la présente étude, de la majorité des deux tiers considérée, à l'origine, comme suffisante pour l'adoption d'une convention de l'OIT et étendue, en 1963, par la Convention de Vienne sur le droit des traités, à l'ensemble des conférences internationales. Un autre cas concerne la règle en vertu de laquelle les Etats sont tenus de soumettre à leurs autorités «compétentes» (en principe leur Parlement) les conventions adoptées par la Conférence internationale du Travail, en vue de leurs application et ratification, règle dont Roberto Ago[22] avait souhaité la généralisation aux autres textes adoptés par les institutions internationales, notamment celles de la famille des Nations Unies. Du reste, l'Acte constitutif de l'UNESCO contient une disposition semblable (art. IV.4).

Ainsi, entre l'ordre juridique des Nations Unies et ceux des institutions spécialisées, il y a, sur certains points, des liens étroits et une coordination systématique, parfois fondée sur la primauté politique de l'ordre des Nations Unies, mais aussi, plus généralement, une large autonomie. C'est souvent

---

19 *Voir* N. VALTICOS, *op. cit.*, *supra* note 16, pp. 82–83.

20 *Voir* N. VALTICOS, *L'OIT et le droit international*, REVUE FRANÇAISE DES AFFAIRES SOCIALES. 75E ANNIVERSAIRE DE L'OIT (1994, novembre), pp. 81–91.

21 Nous n'insisterons pas ici sur la composition tripartite (gouvernement, employeurs et travailleurs) de chaque délégation nationale à la Conférence internationale du travail et le système de vote des conventions internationales du travail, car ces traits sont spécifiques à l'OIT.

22 R. AGO, *La codification du droit international et les problèmes de sa réalisation*, RECUEIL D'ÉTUDES DE DROIT INTERNATIONAL EN HOMMAGE À PAUL GUGGENHEIM, Genève (1968), p. 118 et s.

le politique, d'une part, et, d'autre part, le technique qui constitueront les critères pour ce qui est de la primauté ou de l'autonomie.

C. Les relations des ordres juridiques particuliers des institutions spécialisées du système des Nations Unies entre elles

La différence essentielle qui distingue les relations entre les ordres juridiques des institutions spécialisées et celui des Nations Unies, que nous venons d'examiner, d'une part, et, d'autre part, les relations réciproques entre ces institutions mêmes est qu'il n'y a pas, dans ce dernier cas, d'institution ayant une certaine primauté.

A première vue, chacune de ces institutions et chacun des ordres qui relèvent d'elles ont une compétence et une autonomie propres et il ne saurait, en principe du moins, s'élever de contestations de frontières. Il ne faut cependant pas exclure qu'il ait des questions de répartition précise des compétences ou de compétence commune. On peut ainsi rappeler que l'OIT a formulé des normes relatives aux maladies professionnelles. Dans de tels cas, il y a normalement coopération et consultation entre les Organisations intéressées dans le domaine de leurs compétences respectives. La norme qui sera ainsi adoptée dans le cadre de l'Organisation qui est principalement intéressée tiendra sans doute compte de l'avis de celle qui y a aussi une compétence technique. Ce fut le cas, ainsi, pour une liste mise à jour des maladies professionnelles, figurant dans la Convention de l'OIT en cette matière et élaborée, en 1980, par des experts réunis par l'OIT en coopération avec l'Organisation Mondiale de la Santé[23]. C'est une coopération analogue qui s'était établie lorsque l'OIT a élaboré, en 1977, la Convention (N° 157) sur le personnel infirmier[24].

Un élément particulièrement important de la coopération entre organisations du système des Nations Unies est ce qu'on appelle les activités conjointes[25] qui comportent une division du travail entre Organisations telles que les Nations Unies ou la Banque mondiale, d'une part, et, d'autre part, diverses institutions spécialisées notamment, au sujet de travaux d'une importance considérable.

Ces cas de coopération positive ne doivent cependant pas faire perdre de vue certaines divergences importantes quant aux priorités différentes que peuvent s'assigner certaines des Organisations concernées dans l'orientation

---

23 *Voir* N. VALTICOS, *op. cit.*, *supra* note 16, p. 378.

24 *Ibid.* para. 676, p. 512.

25 *Voir* V. UMBRICHT, *Joint Activities of International Organizations*, dans: MANUEL SUR LES ORGANISATIONS INTERNATIONALES, *op. cit.*, *supra* note 5, pp. 362–378.

de leur ordre juridique. Ainsi, les grandes institutions économiques et financières comme la Banque mondiale et le Fonds monétaire accordent, comme elles estiment devoir le faire, la priorité à la remise sur pied économique des Etats concernés, même au prix d'une dure période d'austérité, alors que, pour l'Organisation internationale du Travail, un minimum de justice sociale doit même alors être assuré. Cette différence de critère s'est plus d'une fois manifestée à propos de pays du Tiers-monde et elle a donné lieu à des échanges de vues entre responsables, mais l'ordre juridique des institutions spécialisées est fondé essentiellement sur la coopération entre celles-ci et il comporte ainsi parfois de sérieuses différences d'appréciation. La décentralisation des ordres juridiques des institutions spécialisées, qui a certes de grands avantages, comporte ainsi parfois aussi l'inconvénient sérieux d'une vue partielle des problèmes et de leurs priorités. Lorsqu'il se pose des questions de principe, une concertation plus étroite paraît indispensable.

D. Les relations des ordres juridiques des institutions spécialisées du système des Nations Unies avec des ordres juridiques indépendants de ce système

Dans le cas où l'ordre juridique des Nations Unies ou l'un des ordres de ce système se trouve en relation ou en conflit avec un ordre juridique international ne relevant pas dudit système, il n'existe pas, à première vue, de critère ou de ligne directrice permettant de résoudre le problème. Une solution pourrait cependant intervenir si l'on tient compte des compétences respectives des organisations concernées et, naturellement, en faisant preuve de bonne volonté et d'imagination.

Ainsi, lorsque le Conseil de l'Europe, organisation régionale autonome, décida d'établir une «Charte sociale européenne», il s'entendit avec l'Organisation internationale du Travail pour convoquer, en 1958, une conférence conjointe qui exprima son avis sur le niveau des normes à adopter. En outre, il demanda à cette Organisation de déléguer un représentant qui suivit l'établissement du texte de la Charte et donna un avis consultatif sur les dispositions à adopter. Les résultats de cette coordination furent certainement positifs[26].

Pour ce qui est de L'Union européenne, il s'agit d'un ordre juridique plus clos et du reste plus particulier[27]. Étant donné notamment ses finalités

---

26 *Voir* N. VALTICOS, *op. cit.*, *supra* note 16, p. 143 et s.

27 *Voir* notamment J. GROUX et PH. MANIN, LES COMMUNAUTÉS EUROPÉENNES DANS L'ORDRE INTERNATIONAL, Bruxelles (1984); G. ISAAC, DROIT COMMUNAUTAIRE GÉNÉRAL, Paris (1994); PH. MANIN, LES COMMUNAUTÉS EUROPÉENNES. L'UNION EUROPÉENNE, Paris (1993).

d'intégration. Ces particularités ont parfois conduit à des conflits avec des normes juridiques établies dans d'autres ordres internationaux, par exemple en matière de travail des femmes.

II. LES ORDRES JURIDIQUES INTERNATIONAUX NE DEPENDANT PAS DU SYSTÈME DES NATIONS UNIES

Il existe de nombreux ordres juridiques internationaux ne se rattachant pas à celui du système des Nations Unies. Ces ordres sont très variés quant à leur objet et à leur composition étatique. Cette diversité même empêche d'établir un classement rigoureux, mais on s'efforcera d'en donner un aperçu général.

On peut ainsi, d'une manière générale, distinguer entre les ordres juridiques établis en fonction de leurs objectifs et ceux fondés sur des critères régionaux.

A. Les ordres juridiques établis en fonction de leurs objectifs

D'importants ordres juridiques internationaux ont été établis en fonction des objectifs qu'ils visent. Ils peuvent englober des Etats situés dans différentes régions du monde sans que le critère géographique soit généralement déterminant. Dans certains cas, l'objectif poursuivi est d'ordre économique, financier ou commercial, comme dans le cas de l'OCDE, l'Organisation mondiale du Commerce, qui a remplacé le GATT et, plus spécialement, l'OPEP, le Conseil international de l'Etain, l'Organisation internationale du Café. L'objectif vise aussi parfois les questions maritimes (Organisation maritime internationale) ou encore – et on connaît leur importance – il concerne les problèmes de la défense (OTAN, UEO).

Certaines de ces organisations sont récentes, comme l'Organisation pour la Sécurité et la Coopération en Europe (précédemment CSCE), dont l'objectif, comme l'indique son titre, est la sécurité en Europe sans que sa composition soit uniquement européenne.

Enfin, on ne peut passer sous silence le Comité international de la Croix-Rouge, ordre humanitaire dont la composition n'est pas interétatique et dont on parlera plus loin.

B. Les ordres juridiques régionaux

Parallèlement aux divers ordres cités plus haut, on sait bien qu'il existe diverses organisations établies sur le plan régional en vue de développer les questions d'intérêt commun pour les pays de la région. L'Europe, on le sait, en a le plus, l'Asie le moins[28], l'Afrique[29] et l'Amérique[30] une principale chacune, et il existe en outre des associations groupant un ensemble géographique d'Etats plus limité dans certains des continents.

Ce type d'organisations ne pose pas, à première vue, de problèmes de dépendance par rapport à d'autres ordres juridiques. Elles n'en soulèvent pas moins parfois des questions complexes, soit que leur ordre juridique, imparfait, doive être complété, soit du fait d'un certain chevauchement, notamment en Europe, où coexistent Conseil de l'Europe (groupant à l'origine des pays d'Europe de l'Ouest et maintenant, depuis l'effondrement du bloc soviétique, s'étendant rapidement à l'Est), Union européenne (elle aussi s'élargissant vers le Centre et l'Est du continent, mais plus lentement et plus attentivement en raison notamment des conséquences économiques qu'entraîne la participation à l'Union), l'UEO, et de petites organisations du genre AELE et pays nordiques, sans compter l'OSCE, déjà citée. Les inconvénients de ce type de chevauchement sont dans une certaine mesure limités par les différences que présentent les divers ordres juridiques quant à leur plus ou moins grande rigidité et à leur plus ou moins large compétence. Un aspect significatif de cette différence est le problème, discuté depuis de nombreuses années, de l'acceptation éventuelle, par l'Union européenne, de la Convention européenne des droits de l'homme qu'a adoptée le Conseil de l'Europe.

De toute manière, il n'existe pas de lien organique entre ces diverses organisations, pas plus qu'elles n'en ont avec les Nations Unies et leurs institutions spécialisées. Leur ordre juridique est autonome, mais limité aux problèmes – et même à certains problèmes – de la région. Il se développe cependant en fonction de l'activité des organisations concernées. Dans le cas du Conseil de l'Europe, une des activités principales a visé à promouvoir la protection des droits de l'homme, alors que, pour l'Union européenne, l'objectif essentiel a été d'ordre économique et une intégration plus poussée est visée.

Un problème sérieux pour ces ordres juridiques régionaux est le risque d'une différence de contenu, ou d'interprétation entre les normes qu'ils établissent et certains textes universels. La question des droits de l'homme, déjà mentionnée, en est un exemple, mais pas le seul. La coordination s'impose naturellement alors, mais, si l'on excepte certains cas cités plus haut (comme

---

[28] Et couvrant le Sud-Est asiatique.

[29] L'Organisation de l'Unité africaine.

[30] L'Organisation des Etats d'Amérique.

la Charte sociale européenne), elle est loin d'être organisée de manière systématique. L'inconvénient, réel, comme l'ont montré certains cas, est limité du fait que les différentes normes régionales sur les droits de l'homme et les droits sociaux ont été fortement inspirées, du moins pour ce qui est du Conseil de l'Europe, par les textes préexistants on parallèles des Nations Unies et de l'OIT en la matière.

Certes, on peut aussi estimer qu'un élément indirect de coordination des textes adoptés dans ces différents types d'institutions peut résulter du fait que les Etats faisant partie des organisations régionales sont aussi membres de l'ONU et des institutions spécialisées. Cela peut avoir un certain effet, mais il advient aussi que, dans le cadre régional, les points de vue diffèrent, comme les majorités, et l'on en a eu des illustrations avec des textes aussi différents que la Charte africaine et certaines normes des Communautés européennes.

Il reste, en outre, le problème fréquent de la jurisprudence des organes chargés du contrôle de l'application de ces textes, et ce problème laisse encore à désirer, même à propos de textes semblables. C'est notamment le cas en matière de liberté syndicale où certaines différences d'interprétation ont apparu, encore récemment, entre les organes de contrôle de l'OIT et la Cour européenne des droits de l'homme (notamment au sujet du droit de ne pas se syndiquer).

De tels risques sont réduits – car ils ne peuvent être complètement éliminés – par des mesures comme celles qui ont été rappelées plus haut et qui ont visé à assurer la coordination entre les textes adoptés, les uns sur le plan universel et les autres sur le plan régional, ainsi que pour le contrôle de leur application (notamment pour la Charte sociale européenne).

Pour ce qui est cependant de l'Union européenne, déjà citée et dont on connaît l'importance et les finalités, elle a développé un ordre juridique certes inégal mais en expansion. Il s'agit, comme on le sait, d'une institution à l'origine et toujours essentiellement économique. Cette institution présente la particularité de constituer un ordre à la fois incomplet et généralement fermé, parfois même rigide. Cependant, elle pratique parfois des activités communes avec d'autres institutions, comme le Conseil de l'Europe. Elle se distingue des autres ordres par un caractère plus resserré et un pouvoir plus contraignant à certains égards.

* * *

Heureusement, les différents ordres régionaux dont il vient d'être question ne sont nullement opposés comme l'étaient naguère ceux de l'Europe occidentale et celui, disparu, de l'Europe orientale (dit Pacte de Varsovie).

Les organisations européennes actuelles s'entremêlent et les liens entre les Etats qui les composent se combinent selon des modalités pragmatiques autant que fondées sur leurs compétences. Ainsi un Etat relève souvent de plus d'une organisation régionale européenne, en plus des organisations universelles.

C. Les relations entre les ordres juridiques ne dépendant pas du système des Nations Unies avec d'autres ordres juridiques

Les deux catégories d'ordres indépendants dont il vient d'être question n'ont, par définition, pas de liens juridiques – du moins institutionnels et réguliers, avec d'autres ordres. Si, cependant, leur autonomie constitue une caractéristique évidente de leur nature, cette autonomie connaît des limitations de fait et même de droit. Aucun ordre, même si les responsables le voulaient, ne peut être absolument une île, comme écrivait le poète pour l'homme. Du reste, des ordres juridiques comme le GATT et l'OMC, qui lui a succédé, ont tenu compte de mesures d'embargo, notamment, décidées par le Conseil de Sécurité.

Il y a aussi, là encore, de nombreux cas de ces activités conjointes, par exemple entre le Conseil de l'Europe et l'Union européenne ou encore avec des institutions spécialisées des Nations Unies dont il a été question plus haut et qui concernent des montants parfois considérables. Ces opérations portent généralement sur des problèmes de développement. Il y a eu en outre, récemment, un cas différent concernant le conflit récent dans l'ex-Yougoslavie, où les circonstances ont conduit à une coopération *ad hoc* entre organisations: ce fut le cas, en 1995, entre le Conseil de Sécurité des Nations Unies et l'OTAN, qui fit fonction, si l'on peut dire, de «bras séculier» dans cette triste affaire.

Plus généralement, comme on l'a déjà observé, les ordres juridiques internationaux sont souvent animés par des Etats relevant aussi d'autres ordres et même si, parfois, un Etat est représenté par une administration différente d'un cas à l'autre, il existe naturellement, sur des points importants, un souci de consistance et de coordination de la politique nationale. Il en est ainsi même si la position de l'agent est influencée par la finalité de l'ordre dans le cadre duquel il agit et s'il manifeste, à cette occasion, un certain dédoublement fonctionnel, et enfin si la composition étatique de l'ordre concerné varie parfois sensiblement.

En outre, il y a parfois, comme on l'a vu à propos du Conseil de l'Europe, un souci exprès de coordination avec d'autres organisations, et cela ne peut être que bénéfique pour l'efficacité de chacun des ordres concernés et la cohérence de l'action internationale. Des cas inverses d'isolement délibéré, plus ou moins splendide, et de tours d'ivoire sont bien connus et, sans être la règle, ils posent parfois des problèmes sérieux.

On peut enfin observer qu'ici aussi, même s'il n'y a pas eu consultation ou coopération expresse, certains textes régionaux ont été manifestement élaborés compte tenu de normes traitant de la même question et adoptées antérieurement – ou en voie d'élaboration – dans le cadre d'un ordre juridique différent. Tels sont les cas des conventions sur les droits de l'homme émanant d'organisations européenne, américaine et africaine et établies manifestement sous l'inspiration des textes élaborés au sein des Nations Unies.

Il va de soi que de telles préoccupations d'harmonisation ne peuvent être que souhaitables dans l'ordre juridique international. Encore faut-il que, si les Etats d'une région souhaitent établir, à l'intention de leur région, des textes sur une matière déjà couverte sur le plan universel, ces textes se distinguent d'une certaine manière de ceux déjà existants, soit quant au fond (et alors dans le sens d'une protection accrue), soit quant à la procédure de mise en oeuvre. Tout le problème de la coexistence d'ordres juridiques différents est celui de leur compatibilité et de leur cohérence.

III. LES ORDRES JURIDIQUES NON ÉTATIQUES

On considère généralement qu'un ordre juridique international ne peut émaner que d'un ensemble interétatique, plus précisément d'institutions qui ont pour membres des Etats ou des organismes publics. Cette conception, certes justifiée dans la plupart des cas, découle, dans son principe, d'une vue trop limitée de la notion de norme juridique. Déjà Santi Romano[31] avait évoqué le droit international lui-même et l'Eglise comme des cas d'ordres juridiques non étatiques. Il avait aussi évoqué les diverses communautés qui élaborent des règlements intérieurs, les contrats collectifs et, plus généralement, la tendance de l'ordre formé par les groupes professionnels à élever la règle *intra partes* au rang de précepte *supra partes*.

Plus spécialement, il nous semble difficile de contester, à cet égard, qu'il y a certaines sources sociologiques du droit et qu'une partie, en tout cas, du droit a un caractère spontané, comme l'a notamment exposé Roberto Ago[32], proche en cela de Georges Scelle et de Santi Romano. Il peut ainsi y avoir des ordres juridiques internationaux – et en tout cas des commencements

---

[31] S. ROMANO, *op. cit.*, *supra* note 3, p. 83 et s., p. 92 et s.

[32] *Voir* A. MIGLIAZZA, *L'oeuvre scientifique de Roberto Ago*, dans: LE DROIT INTERNATIONAL À L'HEURE DE SA CODIFICATION – ETUDES EN L'HONNEUR DE ROBERTO AGO, Milan (1987), pp. 26–29.

de formation de tels ordres – qui sont constitués par l'action de ce qu'on appelle les organisations non gouvernementales («non étatiques», devrait-on plutôt dire, ainsi que l'avait observé Michel Virally)[33].

L'exemple le plus frappant de ce type d'ordre non étatique est celui du Comité international de la Croix-Rouge[34] dont on sait qu'il a eu l'initiative des diverses conventions et protocoles de Genève, et plus généralement du droit international humanitaire dont il est à juste titre considéré le «promoteur»[35].

Ce type d'influence est, certes, exceptionnel. En revanche, on ne saurait assez souligner l'influence grandissante des organisations internationales non gouvernementales sur le fonctionnement des organisations internationales intergouvernementales[36] et la position des Etats qui y participent. Même en mettant à part le rôle exceptionnel des organisations d'employeurs et de travailleurs dans l'action normative de l'OIT, on a relevé que les différents types d'organisations non gouvernementales jouent un rôle croissant dans la formation et l'application des normes internationales, qu'il s'agisse d'organisations corporatives, techniques, savantes ou humanitaires et sociales. L'art. 71 de la Charte des Nations Unies a d'ailleurs contribué à légitimer ce rôle.

Qu'il s'agisse d'organisations aussi différentes que Amnesty International, la Commission internationale de Juristes, l'Institut de Droit international (sans reparler du CICR) et bien d'autres, ces organisations jouent un rôle désormais reconnu dans l'ordre juridique international par la part qu'elles prennent à la formation et à l'application de normes internationales et, comme l'observe P.-M. Dupuy, par leur contribution au respect de la règle de droit, et cela qu'on admette ou pas encore que certaines au moins de ces organisations possèdent maintenant, comme se le demandait Paul Reuter[37], la personnalité juridique internationale.

---

33 M. VIRALLY, *Définition et classification des organisations internationales*, dans: LE CONCEPT D'ORGANISATION INTERNATIONALE, *op. cit.*, *supra* note 7, p. 53.

34 *Voir* P. REUTER, *La personnalité internationale du CICR*, ETUDES ET ESSAIS SUR LE DROIT INTERNATIONAL HUMANITAIRE ET SUR LES PRINCIPES DE LA CROIX-ROUGE EN L'HONNEUR DE JEAN PICTET, Genève et La Haye (1984), pp. 783 à 293 (*voir* aussi les contributions de CH. DOMINICÉ et D. PLATTNER, pp. 663 à 675 et 761 à 771).

35 J. FREYMOND (avec la collaboration de G. WILLEMIN et R. HEACOCK), LE COMITÉ INTERNATIONAL DE LA CROIX-ROUGE, Genève (1984), p. 24.

36 On doit consulter à ce sujet l'importante publication de M. BETTATI et P.-M. DUPUY, LES ONG ET LE DROIT INTERNATIONAL, Paris (1986), qui rend compte d'un colloque sur cette question et, à part les diverses contributions, le rapport introductif de M. BETTATI et les conclusions générales par P.-M. DUPUY, tous deux remarquables.

37 *Voir* étude citée à la note 34 ci-dessus.

Il n'est donc pas contestable que certaines, en tout cas, des organisations internationales non gouvernementales apportent une contribution substantielle à l'évolution de l'ordre juridique international.

IV. EXTENSION D'UNE NORME D'UN ORDRE JURIDIQUE À UN ORDRE DIFFÉRENT

Indépendamment de l'influence que les normes d'un certain ordre juridique peuvent exercer sur celles d'un autre, il y a des cas dans lesquels une norme présentant des potentialités plus larges est elle-même étendue et incorporée dans un ordre différent et même supérieur.

Une telle situation est loin d'être simple. En effet, l'extension – on peut dire la transplantation – d'une norme dans un ordre juridique différent peut entraîner une modification plus ou moins importante de son contenu dans son nouveau milieu juridique, du fait de son adaptation et de son interprétation dans un cadre différent.

Ici intervient encore parfois le facteur de diversification que peut constituer l'étape de la jurisprudence qui sera édifiée par les organes de contrôle respectifs des institutions concernées. Le cas des normes sur la liberté syndicale qui figurent dans les textes des Nations Unies, de l'OIT et des conventions européenne et autres peut ici encore être signalé à cet égard.

On ne saurait donc assez insister sur la nécessité de veiller, dans de pareils cas, à éviter des contradictions et des conflits entre ordres juridiques à propos d'une norme d'origine identique.

Naturellement, la question est aisée lorsqu'il s'agit d'une norme n'appelant pas d'interprétation étant donné sa simplicité[38].

Qu'en aurait-il été si la règle de la soumission des conventions aux Parlements nationaux, propre à l'OIT dès sa création en 1919 et suivie, après la Deuxième Guerre mondiale, par l'UNESCO dans sa propre Constitution, règle qui avait fait l'objet d'une importante jurisprudence de la part des organes de contrôle de l'OIT[39], avait pu, comme nous avons rappelé que l'avait proposé Roberto Ago[40], être généralisée aux conventions des Nations Unies et des diverses institutions spécialisées? Certes, la règle aurait pu alors faire l'objet de différences d'interprétation d'une organisation à l'autre, mais on peut estimer que, dans l'ensemble, une telle extension aurait constitué

---

[38] *E.g.* la règle de la majorité des deux tiers étendue en principe à toutes les conférences internationales par la Convention de Vienne de 1969.

[39] *Voir* N. VALTICOS, *op. cit.*, *supra* note 16, pp. 538–548.

[40] R. AGO, *op. cit.*, *supra* note 22.

un progrès, à moins d'interprétation tellement restrictive dans l'ensemble qu'elle aurait pu affecter la règle originale elle-même. Il y a là un cas du conflit classique entre le souci de perfection et la voie du progrès par étapes.

V. OBSERVATIONS GÉNÉRALES SUR LES RELATIONS ENTRE LES DIFFÉRENTS ORDRES

Nous avons eu l'occasion d'exposer certains types de relations entre des ordres juridiques analogues ou différents. Il reste encore à rechercher s'il existe des critères plus généraux applicables aux rapports entre les différents ordres dans leur ensemble.

Les exposés qui ont précédé ont montré que les relations entre ordres juridiques peuvent être, *grosso modo*, de trois types, à savoir celles avec un ordre supérieur dans la même catégorie, celles avec un ordre de niveau analogue de la même famille, et enfin celles avec un ordre non apparenté.

Santi Romano, toujours lui, a établi à cet égard des subdivisions raffinées et complexes[41]. Dans le cadre moins théorique de la présente étude, on peut proposer un certain nombre de principes directeurs plus simples.

Ainsi, dans le cas d'un ordre juridique incomplet, on pourrait se tourner d'abord vers l'ordre supérieur, bien que celui-ci soit parfois moins détaillé – du moins sur certains points. Une telle opération permettrait de maintenir la cohérence de l'ensemble des ordres juridiques concernés. Cependant le problème sera souvent qu'il n'y a pas pleine similitude entre l'ordre supérieur et ceux, distincts, qui en sont issus, car autrement il n'y aurait pas eu de raisons d'établir ceux-ci. En outre, cela ne signifie pas que l'ordre juridique des Nations Unies doive alors toujours l'emporter sur un ordre spécial qui lui est attaché[42]. Ce qui importe est que, tout en tenant compte des finalités propres à chaque ordre, on s'efforce d'éviter à la fois la contradiction et le vide juridique.

A défaut cependant de solution par le haut, ou encore si d'autres facteurs (tels que la similitude de certaines normes ou la commodité pratique) le justifient, c'est à un ordre voisin qu'on pourra recourir.

On peut enfin penser qu'à défaut d'une solution plus voisine, il ne serait pas impossible de se référer par analogie à un ordre présentant certaines simi-

---

[41] Sans entrer dans le détail de cette analyse, on peut citer le jeu, en la matière, de principes ou critères tels que les institutions simples ou complexes, parfaites ou imparfaites, avec ou sans personnalité, leur substrat, etc. Ici intervient l'importante notion de «relevance» d'un ordre par rapport à un autre.

[42] R.-J. DUPUY, *op. cit.*, *supra* note 7, pp. 563–564.

litudes, bien que non apparenté à celui en cause. Il faudrait cependant alors se méfier des dangers des transplantations, mentionnés plus haut, et prendre les mesures propres à assurer la saine adaptation de la norme et à éviter les risques de rejet.

On en arrive ainsi à observer qu'au-delà de la multiplication et de la complexité croissante des ordres juridiques internationaux, il importe de plus en plus de sauvegarder et de développer l'ordre juridique général du droit international. Seul celui-ci pourra maintenir une certaine coordination et une unité entre les différents ordres internationaux particuliers.

On ne saurait du reste concevoir un ordre international fragmenté en ordres distincts complétement indépendants et imperméables.

Certes, les normes qui relèvent d'ordres différents n'ont pas d'effets juridiques au-delà de leur domaine propre mais diverses formules peuvent permettre de jeter des ponts et d'établir des relations entre les ordres juridiques des organisations internationales de différents types.

Ainsi, au-delà des techniques relationnelles existantes, on pourrait arriver à des rapports conceptuels susceptibles de créer une cohésion accrue entre le contenu même des ordres juridiques internationaux.

Conclusion

Le développement constant, tantôt systématique et tantôt pragmatique, des différents types d'ordres internationaux crée une situation qui ne se prête ni aux généralisations faciles ni aux solutions miracles.

Dans ces constellations où figurent des astres de première grandeur mais aussi des étoiles, moyennes et petites, à l'avenir incertain, et même des météores qui ne font qu'un temps, il ne serait pas possible de tenter d'établir des règles qui se voudraient générales ou précises. Il ne faudrait cependant pas pour cela renoncer à formuler certains principes, nécessairement simples, qui les rapprochent et à dégager quelques critères forcément généraux, qui aident à en combler les lacunes.

Si hétérogène que soit le monde des ordres juridiques internationaux, il ne saurait s'agir d'un univers compartimenté, composé de pièces indépendantes, ni, par contre, d'une sorte de puzzle dont les pièces doivent finalement s'imbriquer sans défaut. Néanmoins, l'unité plus profonde du droit international doit rester le principe fondamental de la société mondiale et de l'ordre juridique universel.

Certes, cette société est toujours en mouvement, et nous savons maintenant que les ordres juridiques, comme les Etats mêmes (malgré la célèbre et d'ailleurs prudente expression de Grotius[43]) – et les civilisations, ajouteront les littéraires – sont mortels. A travers eux, cependant, le rôle du droit international et des principaux ordres qui le composent reste de permettre la coexistence, la coopération même et le fonctionnement satisfaisant des divers ordres juridiques internationaux. Quelle que soit la variété de ces ordres, le droit international général reste un droit tutélaire qui, sans pouvoir les suivre dans leurs divers développements, est susceptible, dans une certaine mesure, de fournir des solutions en cas de contradiction ou d'impasse entre des ordres particuliers.

Certes, le droit international général risque de couvrir un ensemble disparate d'ordres juridiques privé de toute ligne directrice. Ariane plutôt qu'Arlequin, il doit pouvoir fournir le fil conducteur de l'évolution et les clefs de la cohérence des ordres juridiques particuliers. Jusqu'où va l'ordre juridique propre à une entité internationale, dans quelle mesure cet ordre est-il ouvert ou soumis à certains autres, quelle est la portée des normes qui le constituent, ce sont là des questions auxquelles seule une analyse des ordres concernés pourrait permettre de répondre. La tâche ne serait d'ailleurs pas simple car les ordres juridiques combinent stabilité et mouvement, et leurs frontières sont mouvantes.

Cependant, même si l'ordre international général ne va pas aussi loin dans la spécialisation que les ordres particuliers, il peut dégager les principes directeurs qui établissent les priorités et orientent vers les solutions. Pour ne citer qu'un des critères évidents, ce sont les dispositions sur les droits de l'homme consacrés par les Pactes que l'on doit considérer comme une sorte de Charte mondiale s'imposant aux ordres particuliers.

Aussi, tout en faisant la part de situations encore mouvantes, on ne saurait finalement contester qu'à travers la pluralité des ordres juridiques internationaux transparaît, certes encore bien imparfaite, la profonde unité du droit international. Tout juriste se doit d'y contribuer.

---

[43] *De jure belli ac pacis*, Livre II, chap. IX, section 3.

Monism and Dualism at Present

by

Andrzej Wasilkowski

I

This article is devoted to the relation between international and municipal law. A new phenomenon of community law may not be, however, omitted in this context. It is this very branch of law that puts into question the traditional dichotomy of legal order comprising municipal law and international law.

It must be recalled here, however, that the concept of dichotomous division of law is acceptable only if we conceive law as an aspect of State activity. Such a link between State and law is widely recognized and it is in conformity with the popular vision of the legal order. It is worth remembering that such a definition of law will not comprise several normative acts not originating from any State or a group of States, but at the same time playing a very important practical role. This can be said about norms of religious groups (*e.g.* canonical law), unless there is no separation of State and religion. Also normative acts of international corporations cannot be regarded as part of law, no regard being made to the very fact, that they regulate the status and activities of the component enterprises, their managers and employees in several countries. It must be borne in mind, however, that the present concept of "law" may still evolve in the future.

The concept of dichotomy of law (its division into municipal and international law) emerged at the end of the mediaeval system, just at the time of the emergence of a new international community in Europe.[1] The mediaeval universalism did not differentiate between "municipal" (internal) and "international" elements. It was, however, replaced by a concept of a community of independent (sovereign) States regulating their mutual relations on the basis of equality. This led to the formulation of international law as an international system based on different principles than those underlying municipal legal systems.

---

1 *See* A. Nussbaum, A Concise History of the Law of Nations, New York (1947) at 86 ff.

II

It should be pointed out that for a long time the relation between international law and municipal law had not been in the centre of interest. It resulted from different scopes of application of the two legal orders. Municipal law regulated internal affairs of States. International law was mainly the law of war, peace treaties, alliances and additionally it regulated the scope of State jurisdiction. This resulted in hardly any room for potential conflicts of norms belonging to different legal systems. In such a situation the considerations of actual relations between international and municipal law lacked practical and political inspiration.

On the other hand, a theoretical inspiration for such considerations was present. It was based, however, on philosophical premises. They were related to what we would call now "material sources of law"[2] or in other words: the reasons of law as such. In this respect differences between international and municipal law were not material. A general question "why a given set of norms is to be recognized as law?" necessitated a general answer. In fact not one but several answers were given by representatives of different schools of thought. Paradoxically enough, the general character of these answers was one if not the only common characteristic thereof. The doctrines in question did not attach decisive importance to separation between municipal and international law. This was especially evident in the case of the natural law doctrines. According to them both international and municipal law were to reflect and protect the same values.[3] In consequence the difference between them was not easily conceivable.

Moreover, even positivists and representatives of voluntarist doctrines recognized only one material source of law – common to both international and municipal law – namely the will of States. Also in this context the dif-

---

[2] Several authors reject the term "sources of law" as unnecessary or even misleading. *See e.g.*: G. SCHWARZENBERGER, THE INDUCTIVE APPROACH TO INTERNATIONAL LAW, London (1965) at 2; A.A. D'AMATO, THE CONCEPT OF CUSTOM IN INTERNATIONAL LAW, London (1971) at 268. According to others this term should be reserved for formal sources of law. *See e.g.* CH. ROUSSEAU, I DROIT INTERNATIONAL PUBLIC, Paris (1970) at 37. Critical remarks are quite convincing, but they are not accompanied by positive proposals that would be widely adopted. So, we must share the opinion of proponents of the wide meaning of this term – denoting especially material sources of law. *See* R. BIERZANEK, STUDIA NAD SPOŁECZNOŚCIĄ MIĘDZYNARODOWĄ. ŹRÓDŁA PRAWA MIĘDZYNARODOWEGO [Studies on the International Community. Sources of International Law], Lublin (1991) at 15–20. *See* also: H.W.A. THRILWAY, INTERNATIONAL CUSTOMARY LAW AND CODIFICATION, Leiden (1979) at 17.

[3] H. GROTIUS in Prolegomena to his fundamental work DE JURE BELLI AC PACIS names four general principles of natural law: 1) respect for the property of others, 2) *pacta sunt servanda*, 3) an obligation to repair damage resulting from own fault and 4) recognition that certain acts must be punished. Those four principles are a point of departure for more detailed rules.

ferences between municipal and international law were only of secondary importance. Generally speaking – the will of States was expressed either unilaterally – in case of municipal law – or together with the will of others States– in case of international law.[4]

It was only when the analysis of material sources of law was replaced by the analysis of the formal ones that the orthodox positivism was able to distinguish definitely the two legal orders. Till then, however, the difference between them was not of decisive importance.

This was also the case with other schools of thought. All of them looked for one material source of law – expressing itself on both international and internal planes. The sociological school of thought pointed at social interdependencies as a reason of law, the psychological school referred to legal consciousness and the feeling of justice as elements underlying legal order as such. Others looked for other elements that both international and national law were to serve, fulfill or protect.

In general, all those concepts of material sources of law (actual reasons thereof) may be arguments in favour of monism – according to which international and municipal law form together one legal order.[5] From this point of view also European Community law – though formally separate – would be only a part of this legal order harmonizing really well with the other elements thereof.

III

However, the relation between international and municipal law became subsequently more and more a problem in a practical and political dimension. The reason was the coincidation of the subject matters of both systems. This resulted in the attention being shifted from material sources of law to formal ones. It was on this ground that the problem of the effectiveness (applicability) of international instruments within internal legal orders was to be soived. Also the strong position of positivist and voluntarist doctrines was conducive to the analysis of formal and not material sources of law being undertaken.

It was only in the context of formal sources of law that the differences between international law and municipal law and not their similarities were

---

4 Some modifications in this respect are due to the theory of "group will" developed by G. JELLINEK, H. TRIEPEL AND D. ANZILOTTI.

5 A. VERDROSS in the very title of his work, DIE EINHEIT DES RECHTLICHES WELTBILDES AUF GRUNDLAGE DE VOELKERRECHTS- VERFASSUNG, Tuebingen (1923), presented his idea of the unity of the world legal order.

accentuated. Actually, from the formal point of view these two legal orders are without any doubt separate from each other. This very fact gave and still gives rise to dualistic doctrines. However the actual differences justifying those doctrines are diminishing, what cannot be without influence upon the strength of the arguments of their representatives.

This evolution may be examined in detail. To this end we can choose as a point of departure the view of an eminent representative of dualist doctrine – H. Triepel.[6] According to him, international law and municipal law had 1) **different sources**, 2) **different subjects** and 3) **different objects**. The passage of almost one hundred years from the time when those words had been written obliges us to verify their correctness.

As regards different sources, the statement by Triepel is still actual, although some exceptions may be pointed out.

As regards different subjects, the thesis by Triepel is still correct. However some different concepts are to be seen.

As to differences of objects (subject matters) regulated by both legal orders, the thesis by Triepel was not completely actual even at the very time of writing (1899). However, it is competely outdated now and must be denied if we assume at least a mimimal degree of respect for facts in our considerations.

This important evolution of the two systems should be examined more carefully.

IV

Generally speaking, the differences of formal sources of municipal and international law are evident. While acts of parliament and regulations (or other by-laws) form municipal law, the sources of international law include treaties and custom. It is, however, sufficient to analyse contemporary tendencies in this field to put into question such a simplified version.

A. First of all, international law is applied by courts and other State organs and as such it is present within national legal systems of several States. If such an inclusion of international law into the sphere of municipal law is only of a functional nature (*e.g.* internal acts refer to international law) or takes a form of transformation or other method of reception, it does not automatically deny the concept of the separate character of both legal orders

---

6 The theory of H. TRIEPEL was presented in his work, VOELKERRECHT UND LANDSRECHT, Leipzig (1899).

(international norms simply become municipal ones). But where is exactly the boundary between a general transformation – turning international norms into municipal ones automatically – and the direct applicability of international norms as such?

Poland faces this very question now in the context of preparatory works on the new constitution. The sources of law are to be regulated in chapter III of the draft already accepted by the Constitutional Commission of the National Assembly. The first article of this chapter (namely art. 67 of the draft) provides that: "The law of the Polish Republic consists of the Constitution, ratified international treaties, acts of Parliament and normative acts based upon and aimed at the implementation of acts of Parliament." The position of treaties in the future Polish legal order must be considered now. Of course, it may be also pleaded that in this case we have to do with a general transformation. It cannot change, however, the very fact that treaties are recognized as sources of municipal law. Instead of strict separation of international and municipal law, an intensive interaction of the two is to be seen. It should be also remembered that treaties do not lose the character of the source of international law bacause of the act of transformation.

B. Secondly, the emergence of international organizations and their diversified law-making activities complicate the so far clear vision of the legal order presented by dualists. Some organizations utilize the method of contracting-out while taking decisions.[7] *E.g.* the International Civil Aviation Organization (ICAO) Council adopts decisions establishing technical standards of international civil aviation by the majority of 2/3 of votes. Such decisions are binding for all member States except those which inform the Council in due time about their incapacity to conform to them. In the absence of such a notification decisions of the Council are self-executing and form part of the municipal law of member States. The question of the position of resolutions adopted by international organizations in the system of international law is another subject that may not be discussed here.

This is on the regional level that new tendencies can be easily distinguished and examined. It is especially true with regard to the European organizations.[8]

---

[7] K. SKUBISZEWSKI, UCHWAŁY PRAWOTWÓRCZE ORGANIZACJI MIĘDZYNARODOWYCH. PRZEGLĄD ZAGADNIEŃ I ANALIZA WSTĘPNA [Law-Making Decisions of International Organizations. The Survey of the Subject and Introductory Analysis], Poznań (1965). The author was one of the first publicists who analysed the procedure of contracting-out and its role in the strengthening of the law-making function of international organizations.

[8] Similar tendencies are to be seen in other regions of the world, especially in Latin America. *See First Interim Report, Committee on Regional Economic Development,* (in:) THE INTERNATIONAL LAW ASSOCIATION. REPORT OF THE SIXTY-SIXTH CONFERENCE, Buenos Aires (1994) at 510–517.

Whatever are our views about the European Community law, its very emergence and subsequent development were a serious blow to the dualistic concept of law. If we accept the opinion according to which the Community law is an exceptional legal order stemming from international law (the view that was presented much more frequently just after the creation of the EC than nowadays), the abovementioned separation of formal sources of international and municipal law will be put into question. The best proof thereof is the wide scope and the complexity of the judicial functions of the Court of Justice of the European Communities. In the context of our considerations we should first of all point to the judgments in which the Court referred to constitutions of member States in search of the principles governing the Communities as such.[9]

On the other hand, if we insist upon the separation of Community law from both international and municipal law (Community law being a third, *sui generis* legal order) the very foundation of dualistic concept – namely the dichotomy of law – is put aside. This puts into doubt the usefulness of dualistic doctrines as such.

V

Although it would be difficult to ignore differences between the subjects of municipal and international law and the above-mentioned statement by Triepel in this part seems to be correct even now, it would be still more difficult to neglect the process of the inclusion of individuals (*i.e.* natural and legal persons) into the sphere of international law. They are to a very high extent the addressees of international norms (suffice to invoke here human rights covenants, International Labour Organization [ILO] conventions, treaties on environmental and intellectual propery rights protection and so on). It results in a controversy as to if one may qualify individuals as subjects of international law.[10] *E.g.* an individual challenging his own country before the European Court of Human Rights is no longer a mere addressee of international norms, but a subject of international law as he is authorized to act himself on the international plane.

What is more – formal agreements are nowadays concluded between individuals (in practice legal persons, companies) and States. As a rule such agreements relate to international investments. Especially if the agreements

[9] *See* ECR (1974) at 491.

[10] More on this subject, M. JANIS, *Individuals and International Law*, Chapter 8, (in:) AN INTRODUCTION TO INTERNATIONAL LAW, 2nd edition, Boston (1993).

in question contain provisions referring to international law, they give considerable support to those writers who admit that individuals are to some extent subjects of international law, although their personality is of a limited character (usually international corporations are at stake).[11] Such a view can be supported additionally by a few examples that emerged in the context of activities of international organizations. For example in INMARSAT not only States but also public or private entities indicated by the respective States were admitted to the so-called exploitation agreement. In consequence persons of private law (among them American Communications Satellite Corporation) became parties to an international agreement. One should treat it as evidence of a limited international law personality.[12]

If we apply the same criteria on the level of the European Communities, we will arrive at extremely astounding conclusions. Certainly, there can be no doubt as to the personality of member States themselves and international organizations with their participation. However, the scope of Community law subjects is wider. It will also comprise organs of the Communities – at least to the extent to which they can initiate proceedings against other persons before the Court of Justice. As a consequence, we would have to admit such a personality – though of a narrower scope – to natural and legal persons enjoying a similar right. In such a case we would have to do with a dual personality – the one of Community law and international law (and possibly also municipal law) or only of Community law and municipal law. Such constructions are evidence of the evolution of the European structures. The best symbol thereof is the institution of the citizenship of the European Union, which functions parallel to the citizenship of member States.

VI

The differences of the object of the two legal systems are no longer to be attributed the decisive importance. Our conclusions in this respect depend upon the meaning of the very notion of "object". It may denote either a function of law or substance thereof (that is subject matters regulated). In the first case we will arrive at the general conclusion that while the function of municipal law is the regulation of intra-state relations, international law governs

---

[11] More on this subject (in:) I. SEIDL-HOHENVELDERN, CORPORATIONS IN AND UNDER INTERNATIONAL LAW, Cambridge (1987).

[12] Such a view was substantiated by W. GÓRALCZYK, *Satelitarna radiokomunikacja morska* [Sattelite Maritime Radio-Communication], (in:) A. WASILKOWSKI (ed.), DZIAŁALNOŚĆ KOSMICZNA W ŚWIETLE PRAWA MIĘDZYNARODOWEGO [Outer Space Activities under International Law], Warszawa (1991).

international ones (mainly inter-state ones). However, even such an assumption will not result in the full separation of the objects – as demonstrated in section IV and V above.

On the other hand, if an "object" means the substance of norms (actual relations to which they refer), the lack of major differences between municipal and international law is evident. Municipal and international law regulate nowadays the same subject matters. What is more, such a meaning of the word "object" seems to be well suited and will be utilized in our subsequent considerations. It will help us explain the intensity of changes that have taken place in this respect. The process of inclusion into the sphere of international law of matters that have been traditionally regulated by the provisions of municipal law has influence upon the very relation between the two legal orders. It depends now exclusively upon one's point of view to qualify this change as: an important element of the evolution of contemporary international community, as a substantial enrichment of international law, as strengthening of the influence of international law upon municipal law or, last but not least, as the emergence of potential conflicts between the two legal regimes.

The European Community law regulates matters traditionally regulated on the one hand by municipal and on the other hand by international law. We should, however, wonder if it does not have its own subject matters that can be associated neither with municipal nor international regulation. The answer seems to be affirmative. It is just the case of European institutional law. Special mention should be made in this context of the European Parliament as a unique Community institution.

VII

When the question of relation between municipal and international law is considered, much more attention is paid to formal aspects of the both systems than to material ones. It is, however, in the latter field that both systems affect each other. The forms of this influence are: reception of several institutions functioning in the other system of law, the application of the same methods of interpretation and legal argumentation and, lastly, the regulation of the same subject matters by both systems of law. The latter affects judgments of both national and international courts.

International law was developed later than municipal systems. It has overtaken from them several legal institutions. It was in the Roman law that the very notion of an "agreement" (treaty) and the basic rule of *pacta servanda sunt* were developed. Civil (private) law influenced such international law institutions as the acquisition of territory, State succession and State responsibility.[13]

Nowadays we can see a somehow analogous influence of municipal public (constitutional, criminal and administrative) law upon international instruments. Suffice here to invoke the human rights covenants. Here the situation amounts to a symbol as it was the law of one group of States (that is from the West) that determined the content of the Covenant on Civil and Political Rights while the law of the other group influenced the norms of the Covenant on Economic, Social and Cultural Rights.

At present, however, international law is no longer only a recipient of municipal law institutions. It plays a role of a donor as well. It often brings about changes of the municipal law of several States. It is also here that several forms of pressure aimed at such changes are looked for. However, the influence is in no case one-sided, especially in a longer time.

This is true also with respect to legal reasoning. The way of understanding of such rules as "protection of acquired rights", "abuse of rights" or "equity" in either of the legal systems is likely to influence the other. The same may be said about the rules of interpretation.[14]

In this context we must recall article 38(1)(c) of the Statute of the International Court of Justice, according to which the Court applies general principles of law recognized by civilized nations. We will not discuss here all the controversies that emerged in the context of this provision.[15] Suffice here to say that if that provision is to be given any significance it must be interpreted as an authorization to apply on the international plane some principles developed within the internal legal systems and common to different States with sufficiently high legal culture. It seems acceptable to plead that such a provision assumes the existence of a set of rules common to both municipal and international law, though such a view is likely to meet with protests from orthodox positivists.

The European Communities law in this respect reveals dependence upon both municipal and international law. The founding treaties belong as such to international law, the secondary legislation of the Communities are to some extent an equivalent of municipal law. But it was the European law itself that soon became a factor of influence and inspiration for other legal systems – especially municipal ones. What is more – this influence is not limited

---

13 *See* G. RIPPERT, *Les regles du droit civil applicables aux rapports internationaux*, 44 RCADI.

14 More on this subject: L. EHRLICH, *L'interpratation des traites*, 24 RCADI.

15 *See* R. BIERZANEK, *op. cit., supra* note 2, at 44-52; H. KELSEN: PRINCIPLES OF INTERNATIONAL LAW, New York (1966) at 146; G. TUNKIN, *General Principles of International Law*, (in:) FESTSCHRIFT VERDROSS, Muenchen-Salzburg (1971) at 530 ff.

to member States themselves. Several treaties of association provide for approximation of law of the associated States with the EC law. It seems moreover that this approximation, if not reception, is to a high extent not dependent upon formal treaty obligations in this respect and is the consequence of the will of the interested States themselves.

The influence of the EC law upon international law is not so evident. It is, however, demonstrated by a trend of strengthening the rights of international organizations *vis-à-vis* member States. It is deemed to result in the enlarged effectiveness of the organizations concerned. However, the actual results of the transformation of EC patterns (*e.g.* in Latin America) are not always fully satisfactory.

VIII

Great theories can be cast with good effect during the time of fundamental changes. However, the dispute between monists and dualists is no longer in the centre of interest. What is looked for are pragmatic, practical solutions to the question of relation between international and municipal law which would be well suited in the situation of permanent changes and developments.

However, from our perspective it seems that dualism is nowadays worse off than monism.

One of the reasons is the weak position of positivist doctrines that were the foundations of dualism itself. This can be attributed to the practice of totalitarian States which used law – even made in due form – against justice and fundamental humanitarian and human values. That is why attempts to verify law from the point of view of certain values were made (it is a kind of evaluation from outside). Such attempts can hardly be compromised with the premises of positivism and *nolens volens* produce a concept of law related somehow to the doctrines of natural law.[16] The monistic inclinations of the latter are beyond doubt.

Secondly, the evolution of international law was such as to weaken several arguments of the representatives of dualist schools. This can also be said about the constitutional norms of democratic States that reveal eagerness to apply international law as such, though changes in this respect are of a gradual nature. However, it is still the existence of different sources of international

---

[16] *See* A. WASILKOWSKI, *The Position of the International Court of Justice on the Foundation of the Principle of Equity in International Law. Comments*, (in:) A. BLOED and P. VAN DIJK (eds.), FOURTY YEARS. INTERNATIONAL COURT OF JUSTICE: JURISDICTION, EQUITY AND EQUALITY, Utrecht (1988).

and municipal law that is the ground for some less orthodox versions of dualist doctrines.

Monist doctrines seem to be well suited to the facts of life and we cannot exclude that they will dominate in the future. Of course, this does not relate to such versions which claim the primacy of municipal norms within the legal system. The primacy of international law norms is widely accepted now and a concept of the primacy of the European law in the Communities may give support to the followers of it.

However, it is enough to take a more careful look at the practice of States and their constitutional provisions (special mention being made with respect to court judgments) to find out that even if monist doctrines will put aside dualist ones in the future, they still do not reflect the actual contemporary State of affairs.[17]

IX

In this part of our essay we will deal with the fundamental question of the character of the European Community law. In other words: we will try to answer whether the similarities or differences thereof *vis-à-vis* international law are to be given priority.

This very question is in no case a new one. The present author encountered it twenty-five years ago during a comparative law colloqium dealing with international law aspects of international economic integration.[18] The dispute about the very classification of the European law was not devoid of emotions, as it was not strictly theoretical argumentation, but rather a general vision of the problem that was at stake.

According to some participants, integration and the European law amounted to a mere example of dynamic changes of international law and were an indication of its future development.[19] That it why the representatives of this view strongly opposed to any attempts to separate the European law from international law. In their opinion such attempts were a mere acceptance of the stagnation of international law, the latter remaining with no changes and still founded on the orthodox understanding of inter-state cooperation and sovereignty.

---

[17] This author has used comparative materials collected by the Legislative Council of the Prime Minister in connection with preparatory work on the project of the Polish constitution.

[18] Hague Academy of International Law, Colloquium (1971). LEGAL ASPECTS OF ECONOMIC INTEGRATION, Stijhoff, Leiden (1972).

[19] *See* W. FRIEDMANN, *ibid.* at 476–478.

Their opponents, however, attempted rather to keep the integration process beyond the influence of classical international law. The main characterists of international law were suspected to adversely affect the development of communities and especially their identity and separation from traditional inter-state co-operation.[20] That was why new premises were necessary rather than those underlying international law.

There is no reason to repeat the details of this dispute which are generally known; suffice here to recall that the very dispute had in its background the controversy as to if the Community was to be a federation or rather *l'Europe des patries*. So the political aspect was at least present in the disputes of lawyers. Unfortunately, it did not remain without impact upon the impartiality and value of the views presented.

The formula of supranationality was really attractive for the adherents of the view about the separateness of the European law. With this very notion it is possible to defend the assertion about the existence of three and not two legal orders: municipal, supranational and international. However, it cannot release us from a more careful examination of the sources of the European law and their connections with the other legal orders.

Generally speaking, the sources of the European law comprise:
- the founding treaties as amended,
- the treaties on accession of new members,
- treaties on the approximation of the national laws,
- general rules of law,
- secondary legislation of the Communities.

It would not be easy to claim homogenity of these sources. The treaties are part of international law. The general rules of law – having a distinct character – are usually deducted by the Court of Justice from municipal regimes of member States. At last, secondary legislation is made by the organs of the Community on the bases of the treaty provisions.

However, there is one unifying factor for all of them – namely the jurisdiction of the Court of Justice. It is only this factor that gives the EC law the character of a system. The more abundant is the case-law of the Court in Luxembourg, the stronger is the identity of EC law as such. The Court endeavours to provide for a coherence of various elements of this very system. The competence of the Court is determined by treaties themselves, but the Court has been always very creative while determining its scope.

We may only wonder if the existence of the Court is a sufficiently strong argument in favour of the separateness of the European law. The latter amounts to denial of the traditional dichotomous division of legal order.

---

20 *See* P.H. TEITGEN, *ibid.* at 478–480.

One should answer in the affirmative, if one considers the very fact that the communities are empowered to make law directly applicable in member States and availing itself of the priority over their municipal systems. However, it must be remembered that the European law cannot as such make national laws null and void. It only excludes the application of norms conflicting with norms of Community law. It is worth remembering that several constitutions provide for a priority of treaty provisions *vis-à-vis* domestic regulations. There is no such a great discrepancy between the EC law and international law as is sometimes believed to exist.

Special mention should be made with respect to the possibility of making decisions by a qualified majority of votes. This means that States outvoted are bound by legal instruments adopted within the framework of Community institutions. In fact, however, all member States have accepted such a solution. In practice the possibility of outvoting other States is not frequently used, consensus being always looked for. In consequence, the procedure of making decisions in the EC reveals similarities to negotiating treaties. It relates especially to consultations conducted within the Committee of Permanent Representatives (COREPER).[21]

Thus Community law is more a common legal system than a really supranational order. It is first of all an effective instrument for the achievement of the goals indicated in the treaty by the means of the approximation or even unification of laws. Traditional methods (*i.e.* international treaties) would not be sufficient in this field. However, the application of the powers of the Community is now to conform to the principle of subsidiarity.

The specific characteristics of the EC law as compared with other branches of law are so evident that the temptation to accentuate its specificity is fully justified. However, this distinct character is of a functional and not of an essential (ontological) nature. The EC law stems from international law, but it enjoys a considerable autonomy *vis-à-vis* international law and it is the Court of Justice which is to guard this autonomy. However, each example of "autonomy" *ex definitio* excludes "independence".

Such a cautious opinion is supported by the analysis of the contemporary development of international law. A tendency to strengthen international legal order and widen its substantive coverage is to be seen nowadays. International law regulates fields that traditionally have been reserved for municipal law. It is the very concept of State sovereignty that evolves. The European Communities model has followers in different regions of the globe.

---

[21] *See* F. HAYES-RENSHAW, CH. LEQUESNE, P. MAYOR LOPEZ, *The Permanent Representation of Member States to the European Communities*, XXVIII:2 JOURNAL OF MARKET STUDIES (1989 – December).

Certainly, the similarities do not mean identity and it seems really difficult to compete with EC in terms of speed of integration. However, the general direction is the same. From this perspective, the EC law may be seen as a precursory experience for the international community as such. EC law is not only an automous branch thereof and a functional solution. It indicates the evolution of the international community and of its law.

Justice among Individuals and Justice among Nations*

by

† *Zygmunt Ziembiński*

I

The way of understanding such words as "juste", "just", "justice" – in Polish *sprawiedliwy, sprawiedliwość* – is of the utmost importance. It is very complicated, however. To some extent this is due to the fact that the notion of justice has several meanings which still tend to change. Sometimes "justice" is equalized with legalism, with the care of the public interest or with respect for the binding patterns of behaviour.[1] Secondly, the word "justice" is used in relation to such different areas that in each of them the meaning of this term can be affected in a subtle or even imperceptible way. The problem is also that the very notion of justice is so closely bound with emotions that any attempt to define justice may be qualified as a persuasive definition.[2] As Chaim Perelman wrote: "Several wars are fought for justice, but this justice is differently understood by the fighting parties."[3]

In this article we will use the term "justice" as referring to inter-personal relations. It was Aristotle who qualified such a meaning as a basic one[4] which is widely used nowadays. It is sufficient to take a look at any dictionary to find out that the Polish term for "just" no longer can be attributed to any behaviour conforming to a given set of rules (legal, moral or religious ones). It is reserved exclusively for acts taken with respect to other persons. The ancient Polish translations of the Bible characterized as "just" those people who were religious, obedient to God or generally good, no difference being made if in a given case the norms *suum cuique* were engaged or not.

---

* This article is an abridged and partly modified version of a paper presented at the plenary session of the VI Polish Congress of Philosophy held in Toruń in 1995.

1 *See e.g.* O.A. Bird, The Idea of Justice, N. York–Washington–London (1967) at 3–5.

2 On the concept of "persuasive definitions" *see* Ch.L. Stevenson, Persuasive Definitions, Mind (1950).

3 Ch. Perelman, O sprawiedliwości [Justice], Warszawa (1959).

4 Aristotle, Nicomachean Ethics – in citations I refer not to pages but to verses, according to the Polish edition: Arystoteles, Etyka Nikomachejska, Warszawa (1956).

The present – much narrower – meaning of the term "just" may be attributed only to such behaviour towards others which is in conformity with the principle of the good co-operation and equal treatment of all subjects which are identical from a given point of view – the latter being of sufficient significance. So we can speak about just individuals (*i.a.* persons who usually act in a just way), about just law (*i.a.* a legal order based on the principle of equal treatment of persons equal in a given respect),[5] about a just State order (an order in which just norms are enacted and actually respected). In the same way we can qualify a just society, a just judgment and so on.

The justice of behaviour determines moral qualifications and moral norms. The moral thought of perfectionism recognizes the ability to act in a just way as a basic virtue. On the other hand, according to "third current of moral thought" – as it was called by Maria Ossowska[6] – what determines the moral qualification of a given act is the friendliness of behaviour towards others. However, it is not an individual friendliness what matters, but a general one, the justice of the latter being demonstrated by the equal treatment in a given respect of all subjects (persons) finding themselves in the some position. It is the qualification of differences between those subjects as important, or not important, ones which is likely to give rise to disputes. A given choice will determine the scope of persons who can expect our friendliness. Some concepts of justice may recommend just behaviour towards the entire world population. However, in some other systems justice (and morality as well) may be reserved only for the members of a given race, nation, social or religious group. The group of subjects entitled to justice may include only individuals already born or may be extended to include even unborn ones. It may differentiate or not between people living in a normal way and persons being already in a State of clinical death. The differences of the underlying concepts of justice are evident. It is obvious that nobody will approve a concept of justice in a group of criminals, according to which each of the members is to participate equally in the profits of their activities. The reasons for our disapproval are both the character of the members of the group and the kind of matters involved. So it would be shocking to invoke this situation as an example of justice, the latter being associated with respect for decent rules governing relations among decent persons and morality being envisaged as "honourable morality."

Despite all the problems with casting one universal definition of "justice" and the complexity of the very question of the qualification of different

---

5 ARISTOTLE, *op. cit.*, *supra* note 4, V. 2 at 1130b–1131a.

6 M. OSSOWSKA, PODSTAWY NAUKI O MORALNOŚCI [The Bases of the Moral Science], Warszawa (1963), Chapter X at 345–354.

human acts as "just" or "unjust" from a given point of view, there is still a possibility at least to classify the problems connected with the way of understanding "just" behaviour in inter-personal relations. As a result, we will be able to determine what is really the subject-matter of several never-ending disputes as to the qualification of a given act as just or unjust and what is the real difference of the views presented by the followers of both contradicting opinions. In Poland a seminar paradigm of discussing the problem of justice is to be seen. The same order is, however, lacking in considerations of "justice" in relations between groups and especially between nations. The latter are of the utmost importance – being the very sore point of inter-state relations. This is true not only with respect to diplomatic relations but also with regard to several conflicts.

This article is to point out the simple fact that even the best elaborated concepts of interpersonal relations cannot be always applied on the international (interstate) plane. It seems, however, that the moralizing of publicists is not sufficient in this field and it is up to the moral scientists to elaborate the very criteria of discussions to be held with regard to those matters.

II

It is a long tradition[7] to begin discussions about justice with the differentiation of compensatory and distributive justice. However this differentiation does not seem to me to be especially important. Compensatory justice is based on returning good for good and evil for evil, in both cases the intensity of the latter being measured by the former. On the other hand distributive justice is to lead to such a distribution of benefits or burdens which will leave individuals possessing the same decisive characteristic with the same share of those benefits or burdens. If the decisive characteristic is subject to graduation, this graduation must be reflected at the level of distribution. However, because of the positive tinge of the notion of justice, it is only ironical to use this term with respect to persons who harm others actually without any discrimination, but without any reason as well.

Compensatory justice is invoked in a different social and political context than distributive justice. So *e.g.* in the last period of so called "real socialism" distributive justice was invoked much more frequently than the compensatory one, and several claims being made with respect to the public weal found not sufficient for all. In the market economy the emphasis is,

---

7 ARISTOTLE, *op. cit.*, *supra* note 4, V. 2 at 1130b–1131a.

however, on the basic questions of compensatory justice – who owes something, to whom and for what. From the formal point of view it is, however, possible, though a little artificial, to put the idea of compensatory justice in the distributive way: "equally to everybody, respectively to the good or evil he produced for us." To tell the truth, such a way of understanding justice would require the adoption of several formulas thereof with very narrow scope of application, or even individual ones. On the other hand, it may be pointed out that also typical formulas of distributive justice granting privileges to persons who have produced something good, contain an element of compensatory justice.

While formulas of both distributive and compensatory justice may be classified as substantive formulas of justice, the procedural ones are to ensure the interested persons an equal access to legal measures (or other means of intervention) for the vindication of what they are entitled to. This is a very important question, but in our article we will satisfy ourselves with discussing only the former category of formulas.

The formulas of distributive justice indicate not only who is entitled to something, but also – and this is very important – from whom we are to expect something and what is exactly to be expected. Those two kinds of formulas are sometimes merged in a phraze "From everybody ... to everybody..." and much more complex formulas are often built from several one-aspect ones – the latter being used in changing combinations. The formulas of distributive justice may be divided into egalitarist and meritorial ones. The former give individuals a title to participate in the benefits, no regard being made to their personal contributions to the common wealfare. The latter make benefits dependent upon the contributions of an individual to the common weal.

Different formulas of justice have different virtues and vices from the point of view of the organization of public life. That is why complex formulas (combinations of single or one-aspect ones) are widely utilized to achieve optimum solutions.

So *e.g.* the formula "equally from everybody" – apparently simple – in fact cannot be put into life, considering the different abilities, powers, knowledge, skills and resources of different people. The other formula – "from everybody according to his abilities" – is difficult to be executed, as it is impossible to assess if somebody has utilized his abilities to the full extent. The formula "from everybody according to his origin" may be of a positive character, if we assume that nobility entails more obligations, but much more frequently it would be used to diminish the burdens placed upon persons claiming nobility.

On the other hand, the formula "equally to everyone" may be temporarily used even with good effects, but when applied for a longer time, it brings about the so called effect of equalization (*uravnilowka*). Though it may sometimes relieve social tensions, it is likely to produce the same situation as that - described in the Gospel – in which people working the entire day achieve the same wage as those working for a mere hour.[8] This formula is also wasteful, as for some persons the amount granted is too small, and for others – too big. The latter fact brought about the emergence of another formula "to everyone according to his needs." Its utopist character is beyond any doubt. It is also possible to propose measuring benefits in accordance with the results of work or efforts made by several individuals. It was, however, much easier to apply this rule in the past with respect to shoemakers, joiners or builders – the examples given by Aristotle – than nowadays, when group work is widely utilized, the share of an individual member being both indispensable and impossible to be quantified. As regards the choice of individual efforts as a decisive factor from the point of view of distribution, it may be pointed that it would be hardly possible to differentiate the prices of corn cut with a sickle and with a combine-harvester – the differences of efforts in both cases being evident. The other formula "to everyone according to his deserts" sounds reasonable. It is only problematic what will be qualified as deserts (merits, accomplishments). After the changes of social order, *e.g.* in Poland, people engaged in the consolidation of the former political order may be despised, and former political criminals may suddenly become national heroes. Another formula "to everybody according to his birth" may sound retrograde if understood in a heraldic meaning, but may be of great value if applied so as to procure equal chances to individuals who have had worse chances at the very beginning than others. The very formula utilized by lawyers "to everybody according to what the law adduces him" is nothing but a blanket form. It has no substance of its own, unless it is determined which one of the substantive formulas of justice has been adopted by the lawmaker in a given system.

Those problems may be said to be banal, but we will never say this about the resulting question – to what extent and how to utilize particular one-aspect, simple formulas while constructing complex ones. The latter are usually a kind of compromise, being capable of practical use. This is the problem defined in Greek as *epiekeia*. Even if in a particular field a simple one-aspect formula is believed to be sufficient, it must be all the same concretized and differs from its own version to be found on banners.

---

[8] Gospel according to Saint Matthew 20, 10–12.

The ensuing question of the utmost importance is the global appreciation of different solutions of multi-aspect problems. This question will emerge *e.g.* in a situation in which a reference to "the rules of social justice" is made – as in art. 1 of the Polish Constitution. Both the subject and the criteria of this appreciation are very complicated.[9]

Nowadays a new aspect of inter-personal and inter-group justice has become strongly accentuated. This is the problem of inter-generation justice and the significance of time for the materialization of justice.[10] Such problems as the conciseness of the world, ecological dangers and the economy of non-renewable resources having been generally recognized as important, it is still necessary to determine what is to be reserved for fathers, children and grandchildren. The element of time is present not only in the above-mentioned "macro-justice" context but also in the "micro-justice" one. Such phenomena as the prolongation of the education period, the later attainment by young persons of self-sufficiency but also the longer period of life after the end of ability to work taken together influence several changes in family life. The best examples thereof are such financial instruments as social security schemes and grant systems.

A new concept of justice would be necessary to solve the question of the professional activation of women, the problems of disabled persons, of social participation in risk through the system of insurance and first of all the question of unemployment. It would be very easy to invoke several other groups of problems, with respect to which sociologists and economists would be more competent than the moral scientists.

We cannot forget the importance of the question who is to appreciate the possible results of the adoption of particular formulas of justice in a given field. The idea presented by J. Rawls in this respect seems to be very far-reaching fiction. According to this idea the appropriate formulas would be those indicated by individuals asked "from behind the blind of ignorance" about what the social position they themselves would acquire.[11] However, it is impossible to effect such a global appraisal with no reference being made to our views and social experience. In social life there is no "zero point" in which people would be able to consider very abstract problems in this regard with no social experience.

---

9 *See* J. WRÓBLEWSKI, *Z zagadnień pojęcia i ideologii państwa prawnego (analiza teoretyczna)* [The Notion and the Ideology of State Based on Law (Theoretical Analysis)], 6 PAŃSTWO I PRAWO [State and Law] (1990) at 14.

10 J. RAWLS, A THEORY OF JUSTICE, Oxford (1972), pages cited according to the Polish edition J. RAWLS, TEORIA SPRAWIEDLIWOŚCI, Warszawa (1994) at 195 ff.

11 *Ibid.* at 2, 190 ff.

This very style of thinking about justice – used widely by moral scientists, who consider problems of people while forgetting their past – results in the little practical significance of their considerations. At most they can be partly utilized in a practical arrangement of inter-personal relations.

The notion of justice refers to goods which are not in abundance and which are capable of being transferred. It would be difficult to speak about a "just" transfer of something which is in abundance for everybody, but this can change in the future. We cannot qualify as unjust a lack of appreciation for poems which conform to the recognized canons of art but were written by a forgotten poet. This is the normal consequence of the lack of a possibility to demand an aesthetic approval for something which is not approved in fact. This is true even though perhaps there is a duty of demonstrating social approval for events deserving such an approval.

Despite the exact number of questions relating to inter-personal justice that are still to be considered by the moral scientists and sociologists, this field is much better examined than the field of international justice.

III

This field involves especially complicated problems. Also the chances for arriving at the *communis opinio doctorum* or consensus of politicians dealing with international affairs – the latter being even more difficult – are much smaller than in the field of inter-personal relations. We will concentrate on some of those specific difficulties.

First of all – group subjects whose relations would be regulated are difficult to identify. Sometimes it is difficult to establish if the notion of a "nation" is used in political or ethnic meaning. If the former is true – "nation" being simply a group of citizens of a given State – the concept would be formally not so difficult. However, it sometimes happens that a State, acting contrary to the interests of its own nation, deprives its best soldiers of citizenship and forgets the fate of its own nationals on territories captured by a foreign power.

Important problems are likely to emerge in States inhabited by different nationalities, and ethnic groups, especially if the legal position of the majority and minority is different (including cases in which it is a minority that dominates the government). The situation is much more complicated if a minority looks for support from neighbouring States or aims at separation from the existing State. The "political nation" becomes in such situations a mere apparent sovereign, being at the same time split. The ethnic majority is ready to conceive the minority as a group of traitors, while the minority can see in the majority mere political oppressors. In regions with ethnic diversification, the split of national identity may affect even the life of single families. Any success of a given nation is sufficient to attract to it cosmopolitic individuals and people with no stable national identity. Any disaster or moral discredit on the part of this nation is, however, likely to diminish the number of people identifying themselves with it and to increase the number of those for whom this nation is more often referred to as "they" than as "we".

Secondly, even if we determine the personal scope of the word "nation", it remains to be determined what is actually so frequently invoked as the common good of the nation, which is to be protected. This protection is, as we remember, the basis of the qualification of a given behaviour as just or unjust. As regards material goods, an appropriate individualization on the level of nations is possible. It is only to be determined how to distribute wealth among the individual members of a given nation. Following J. Bentham in his "calculus of pleasure" we can wonder what is better: a situation in which all individuals are provided with a social minimum or in which they all as a group get a bigger amount of wealth, but unequally distributed among the poor and the rich.

Not only material goods are at stake, spiritual ones are important as well. How should we refer to the question of the preservation of the language and culture of small nations, if this results in the isolation and marginalization of such nations. The good of a nation may require sacrifice of individual good, the only indirect compensation being the feeling of participation in a determined ethnic culture, the lack of which would amount to a feeling of inferiority. The primitive Bentham calculation seems to be incapable of solving such problems.

The country of ancestors, the homeland – understood as an ideological homeland or even as a group of private homelands – is no doubt the good of a given nation. There are, however, two aspects of such a good. It is first of all an element of spiritual culture that can be shared by representatives of different nations – demonstrated by the sentiments towards the old country of the Polish Jews who left Poland. On the other hand – it is a geographic region in which different ethnic nations are expected to co-operate, but only one political nation is to rule, according to the doctrine of State sovereignty from the first part of the 20th century. Still there is always a possibility of considering the question: whose land is a given territory, to whom and by whom was it promised, by whom settled and who left it under physical, political or economical pressure.

Thirdly, referring to the categories of inter-personal justice, it would be difficult to assess what should be attributed to a given nation. Such a consideration may amount to historiography – suspicious from the intellectual point of view. But we should not overlook the simple fact that there are nations settled on a given territory since time immemorial, which managed it with great effort, which turned the sea into fertile land and protected the latter from deserts and floods; there are also nations which blatantly wasted their own resources or subjugating lands to the best economical prospects, limited their management activities to ousting the small populations of those territories. There are also nations which demonstrate an inclination to subjugate others and attribute themselves the right to everything that had ever found itself in their hands, looking only for ever new reasons for invasions. Still others have the simple ambition of preserving the land of their fathers.

While basing the claims to justice on the deserts of a given nation to the mankind, it is difficult to abstain from national megalomania. If "our nation gave the world…", we expect more for us now. This may be sometimes really funny, but not always – especially when national megalomania turns into aggressive nationalism, much more dangerous than the nationalism of nations which justify their negative relation towards other nations with real or imaginary harms suffered due to the latter.

It is not only the question of the participation of nations in the profits from their celebrated past and the achievements of their famous nationals, but also a much more important problem of responsibility for crimes committed by their nationals. We should accept the view of K. Jaspers according to which passive members of the nation of criminals are not responsible for the crimes of genocide, but must accept the responsibility of the entire nation as such.[12] One cannot blame sons for the crimes of their fathers, but can expect their condemnation of such crimes and first of all a renunciation of profits resulting from them.

The fourth question is that it would be necessary to accept – both in inter-personal and international relations – a date from which to begin counting mutual benefits and harms. There are several one-sided or two-sided detriments following one another and it is very difficult to point at the first of them, the others being mere responses to it and responses to responses. The situation with inter-personal relations is much easier – the time period taken into account must be limited. At most it comprises the harms effected upon the parents of the respective individual, which adversely influenced his start into life. Such a limitation is not to be found in international relations. Nations exist outside the time and cannot be equalized with generations passing

---

12 K. JASPERS, *Problem winy* [The Problem of Blame], 17 ETYKA [Ethics] (1979) at 145–206.

one after another. It must be remembered that stereotypes of other nations are much more influenced by the harms effected by them than by aid granted. It is the basis of prejudice in the eyes of the nation believing itself to have been harmed.

Despite the fact that such prejudice is only partly transmitted to the next generations, especially if the political situation tends to change, it forms part of the national culture, even if we do not accept it.

It must be also pointed out that appeals to justice are usually made by those nations which expect something from them. It happens very rarely in international relations that gratuitous acts of aid are presented not as acts of mercy given *ex gratia*, but as acts of international justice. When aid is actually given in cases of natural disasters or other calamities, such acts of assistance are to be treated as evidence of good will and a special kind of a feeling of justice.

Certain new aspects are to be dealt with if we consider the application in inter-group (especially international) relations of the principles of justice expressing themselves in the distribution of benefits or burdens according to a given formula, as is the case in relations of individuals and individuals *vis-à-vis* groups. On the one hand, we can ask what mechanisms of the transfer of goods are to be utilized. Should we rely on the State organs of the recipients or should external bodies be created? On the other hand, the question is who would determine the distribution of both burdens and benefits. In this respect we should bear in mind the sensitivity of nations – especially small ones – as regards their sovereignty and limitations thereof in favour of supranational organizations. This is also why regionalization or integration utilizing supranational organs are not always welcome.

The first of the above-mentioned solutions according to which the organs of recipient States are to be used for the administration of international assistance may be very controversial. It may strengthen the elites who are themselves responsible for the state of affairs that is deemed to be eliminated by the assistance in question. Several examples of international aid wasted by the elites of the recipient States are well known. On the other hand, assistance administered by a foreign international organization may not only be perceived as a peril to the sovereignty of the recipient State, but it may be really ineffective, especially if the cultural systems of donors and recipients differ substantially from each other.

In the context of justice in relations among different nations, it seems to be necessary to pay some attention to how the parties to those relations are conceived. For example, we may wonder if a certain conflict is an aspect of relations between the Irish people and Unionists in Ulster, local relations between Catholics and Protestants or a fragment of relations between the poor and the rich. As those characteristics may coincide, it is more difficult to identify the decisive factor. We may choose among ethnic, religious, social and many other denominators of different groups, the mutual relations of which are actually at stake.

Whatever shape we choose for relations among ethnic groups and their political representations (States), two basic requirements of justice are always to be taken into account. The first of them is abstention from the use of force. The second is respect for incurred obligations.

The first requirement is connected with the widely discussed question of the admissibility of so called "just war." Several problems may be discussed in this context *e.g.* the limits of "self-defence", the intensity of unfriendly acts justifying the use of force by the other party, the level of exploitation justifying self-liberation struggle and so on. Because of the abundancy of aspects this problem may not be considered in full here. It seems to us that such questions cannot be solved *a priori*. This is possible only in a given situation when a general legal norm is interpreted in the factual context and is in fact reconstructed (it becomes a particular norm). Such a reconstructed norm may be subsequently applied as such only in a very limited number of analogical situations.

The second requirement – *pacta sunt servanda* – applies to partners of any kind. From a formal point of view, this rule applies only to agreements which were concluded properly and, to be exact, to inter-state treaties. In fact – the principle is much wider, and amounts to a general requirement of fairness (loyalty) in relations of members of State societies which approve or disapprove their governmental representatives. In democratic States the pressure of the public opinion is not to be neglected even during international crises.

Two problems emerge at once in this context. First of all, governments are to protect the interests of their own citizens. However, it is still to be determined to what extent they can sacrifice to this end the good of other, also sovereign and equal, nations, if at all. This is not only the question of nationalism, the latter being an extreme example, but of a more general problem of fairness towards other participants of international relations. In fact the needs of weaker nations tend to be neglected by their stronger partners, when the former are no longer necessary or even disturbing.

The dilemma – to respect an ally as far as possible or to leave an ally in need – is the basic one from the point of view of international justice. In this respect it is much more honest to declare actual intents towards partners than to conduct a diplomatic game aimed at a selfish exploitation of the illusions of weaker partners. The breach of treaty obligations is a much heavier international delict than a simple declaration of indifference towards the fate of weaker nations.

Fortunately, or maybe unfortunately, Poland has always been a country acting fairly rather than unfairly towards other partners. This must be, however, taken into account while defining relations with other nations.

The last to be discussed is a crucial question of just economic relations among nations. It is not reserved for "political nations" represented by States, but ethnic groups and even individuals also have a say in this respect. Economic rules govern such matters as national and international labour markets, the exploitation of natural resources, capital investments, effects of ecological dangers and many others.

In such matters any references to international justice are as a rule of a mere rhetorical nature. There is no chance for international intervention, unless oil or strategic bases are at stake. In other cases States are not ready to risk as many soldiers as the number of victims of traffic accidents per month. Even J. Rawls noticed the lack of international consensus as to international justice.[13]

The benefits of foreign investments, international migrations and other elements of international economic co-operation are well known. However, not only economists but also philosophers of law have something to say on the subject. The unjustice is inherent in the above-mentioned processes. *E.g.* a country admitting immigrants, when and as long as they are necessary, gets hold of skilled people ready to work. However, these persons have been only recipients of public goods in their native country for more than ten years. The same is to be said about the "brain drain", owing to which the social costs of specialists' education incurred by poor nations benefit the rich ones.

IV

It is very pleasant that the ideals of international justice are so frequently invoked during international conferences. Without those references the language of international law would be too hard if not brutal. It would be, however, much better had those declarations been supported by a certain agreement as to their meaning, as to what justice among free, independent and civilized nations actually meant; had the people invoking international

---

[13] PH. VAN PARIJS, *Social Justice and Individual Ethics*, 8:1 RATIO JURIS at 60–62 – about the concepts of J. RAWLS.

justice determined the criteria (formulas) thereof and the factual elements putting into motion those formulas.

Briefly, what is necessary is to change the heretofore emotional character of references to international justice and give them a strong substantive foundation.

Second Part

Sources

Le rôle du juge dans l'élaboration du droit international

par

Philippe Cahier

I

L'article 38 du Statut de la Cour, qui énumère les sources du droit international, mentionne à son paragraphe premier, alinéa b) «Les décisions judiciaires et la doctrine des publicistes les plus qualifiés des différentes nations comme moyen auxiliaire de détermination des règles du droit».

Ainsi, la jurisprudence et la doctrine semblent être placées au même niveau juridique, ce qui est difficilement admissible. Il n'y a, en effet, aucune commune mesure entre l'autorité qui se dégage d'un arrêt d'un Tribunal international et celle qui découle de l'ouvrage d'une personne, fut-elle «la plus qualifiée» en la matière.

D'après l'article 38, la jurisprudence ne saurait donc être à proprement parler une véritable source du droit international. A première vue on ne peut que souscrire à une telle affirmation. La tâche du juge est d'appliquer le droit existant et non de le créer. Si le praticien se réfère, dans ses écrits ou ses plaidoiries, à la jurisprudence, c'est bien en vue de prouver l'existence d'une règle de droit ainsi que son contenu, ou de connaître l'interprétation qui lui est donnée par un Tribunal, mais ce dernier n'a pu le faire que dans la mesure où la règle était préexistante à sa décision.

II

Telle est la théorie, mais la réalité est beaucoup plus complexe; et le rôle du juge dans l'élaboration du droit international est d'autant plus décisif que son arrêt, fondé ou non, fera obligatoirement jurisprudence. Le cadre très limité de cette étude ne va pas nous permettre d'examiner de manière exhaustive le problème considéré, mais simplement de montrer, à l'aide de quelques exemples, que la jurisprudence mériterait une place différente de celle qui lui a été attribuée au sein de l'article 38 du Statut de la Cour.

III

Même si on limitait le rôle d'un Tribunal international à la détermination de l'existence et du contenu d'une règle de droit, l'apport de la jurisprudence serait considérable. Cela est particulièrement vrai en ce qui concerne les normes coutumières. Comme on l'a fait observer:

> «La démarche du juge appelé à se prononcer sur une règle coutumière ne se réduit donc pas à une analyse neutre et objective d'un ensemble de faits. Les faits seraient incapables par eux-mêmes de lui fournir la solution du problème. Aussi bien doit-il les disséquer, les qualifier, les valoriser ou les minimiser, à l'instar de ce que font les plaideurs, en fonction d'une thèse dont le choix relève pour une part considérable de son appréciation»[1].

C'est justement cette appréciation, inhérente à tout juge, qui lui permet de dire si, à son avis, tel comportement des Etats doit être considéré comme obéissant à une coutume.

On connaît l'importance que la Cour a donné aux éléments matériel et psychologique de la coutume. Dans l'affaire du Plateau continental de la mer du Nord, elle a estimé que l'existence d'une quinzaine de traités qui appliquaient la méthode de l'équidistance, circonstances spéciales, pour la délimitation du plateau continental: «ne suffisait pas à établir, comme on le voudrait, une pratique constante»[2].

On peut souscrire à ce point de vue de la Cour, tout en gardant à l'esprit que

> «A practice followed by a very small number of States can create a rule of customary law if there is no practice which conflicts with the rule»[3].

C'était à peu près la situation existante à l'époque.

Il devient par contre plus difficile de suivre cette même Cour lorsque, seize ans plus tard, elle refuse de prendre en considération, comme élément matériel de la coutume, soixante-dix traités, en déclarant:

> «Cette pratique ne suffit pas à prouver l'existence d'une règle prescrivant le recours à l'équidistance ou toute autre méthode tenue pour obligatoire»[4].

---

[1] P. HAGGENMACHER, *La doctrine des deux éléments du droit coutumier dans la pratique de la Cour internationale*, RGDIP (1986), p. 118.

[2] CIJ RECUEIL (1969), p. 45.

[3] M. AKEHURST, *Custom As a Source of International Law*, BYBIL (1974–1975), p. 18.

[4] CIJ RECUEIL (1985), p. 38.

Cette manière hâtive d'écarter ainsi une pratique, pourtant considérable, fut d'ailleurs critiquée par Valticos, Juge *ad hoc* dans cette affaire[5].

Bien que la Cour ait réaffirmé, à plusieurs reprises, la nécessité d'une pratique uniforme et constante, elle se contentera d'indiquer, dans l'affaire des activités militaires des Etats-Unis au Nicaragua:

> «La Cour ne pense pas que, pour qu'une règle soit coutumièrement établie, la pratique correspondante doive être rigoureusement conforme à cette règle»[6].

Ces deux exemples montrent bien l'importance de la jurisprudence dans la détermination de l'existence d'une règle coutumière[7].

IV

Mais la Cour n'hésite pas à aller pluc loin et à donner à certaines règles coutumières un rang supérieur aux autres, sans toutefois que l'on puisse en distinguer clairement les conséquences, puisqu'elle n'ose pas vraiment les baptiser de normes impératives, dont certaines n'en ont sûrement pas la caractéristique.

On se souvient du célèbre passage de son arrêt dans l'affaire de la Barcelona Traction concernant les obligations *erga omnes*[8]. En 1980, dans son arrêt relatif au personnel diplomatique et consulaire des Etats-Unis à Téhéran, elle souligne, à propos de certaines règles du droit diplomatique «... l'extrême importance des principes de droit dont elle est amenée à faire application dans la présente affaire»[9].

Dans l'affaire Burkina-Faso/Mali elle estime que:

> «Le principe de l'*uti possidetis* s'est maintenu au rang des principes juridiques les plus importants»[10].

Enfin, on ne sera pas étonné de son affirmation, dans son arrêt relatif aux activités militaires des Etats-Unis au Nicaragua, que les principes généraux

---

5 *Ibid.* p. 108.
6 CIJ Recueil (1986), p. 98.
7 *Voir* aussi dans ce domaine l'existence de l'excellente article de P.M. Dupuy, *Le juge et la règle générale*, RGDIP (1989), pp. 570–598.
8 CIJ Recueil (1970), p. 32.
9 CIJ Recueil (1980), p. 42.
10 CIJ Recueil (1986), p. 566.

du droit humanitaire doivent être respectés «en toute circonstance»[11], ce qui les rend insusceptibles de dérogation.

Il convient de noter que, dans ces différents exemples, la Cour n'a aucunement essayé de démontrer en quoi, juridiquement, une telle norme serait supérieure aux autres. Il apparaît qu'en indiquant aux Etats l'existence de règles qui lui paraissent fondamentales pour le bon fonctionnement de la société internationale, la Cour, dans sa fonction interprétative du droit international, se place davantage sur un plan éthique que juridique. Cependant, ce faisant, la Cour ne nous semble pas sortir de sa fonction judiciaire, mais elle montre combien cette dernière est importante dans l'étude des sources.

V

Mais le but de ces quelques réflexions est de montrer que, malgré l'article 38, la jurisprudence est une véritable source de droit, car le juge, tout en s'en défendant, n'hésite pas à en créer.

VI

Un premier exemple nous est donné par l'avis consultatif de la Cour sur la réparation des dommages subis au service des Nations Unies.

Contrairement à ce que certains ont pu affirmer, la contribution de la Cour ne porte pas sur la reconnaissance de la personnalité juridique des organisations internationales. Cette question avait déjà été tranchée entre les deux guerres en ce qui concerne l'Institut international d'Agriculture et la Société des Nations[12].

L'apport de la Cour au droit international est double. Il concerne, tout d'abord, la théorie des pouvoirs implicites. Face à la question de savoir si l'ONU pouvait présenter une réclamation internationale, non prévue par la Charte, la Cour a déclaré:

> «Selon le droit international, l'Organisation doit être considérée comme possédant ces pouvoirs qui, s'ils ne sont pas expressément énoncés dans la Charte, sont, par une conséquence nécessaire, conférés à l'Organisation en tant qu'essentiels à l'exercice des fonctions de celle-ci»[13].

---

11 CIJ RECUEIL (1986), p. 114.

12 PH. CAHIER, ETUDE DES ACCORDS DE SIÈGES, Giuffrè, Milan (1959), pp. 65 et s.

13 CIJ RECUEIL (1949), p. 182.

Il est vrai que la Cour s'est référée à l'avis N° 13 de la CPJI (Série B, N° 13, p. 18) mais comme l'a fait remarquer Badawi Pacha[14], dans son opinion dissidente, il ne contenait pas une portée générale de principe, comme semble vouloir dire la Cour.

La théorie des pouvoirs implicites est sans doute indispensable au bon fonctionnement des organisations internationales. Elle ne comporte guère d'inconvénients dans le cas des organisations de coopération, les Etats conservant leurs compétences parallèlement à celles de l'organisation. Il en va par contre tout autrement dans le cas des organisations d'intégration. Ainsi la Cour de l'Union européenne a utilisé à plusieurs reprises une telle théorie pour élargir les compétences de l'Union en matière de conclusion des traités[15], avec pour résultat de transférer celles-ci à l'Union au détriment des Etats membres qui perdaient ainsi toute compétence dans ces domaines.

C'est toujours en se basant sur le principe des pouvoirs implicites que la Cour, face à une «situation nouvelle»[16], a cru bon d'introduire une nouvelle notion de droit international: «la protection fonctionnelle de ses agents»[17]. A savoir, la possibilité pour l'ONU de présenter une réclamation au cas où un de ses agents subit, dans l'exercice de ses fonctions, un dommage dans des conditions de nature à engager la responsabilité d'un Etat.

Sur ce point l'avis de la Cour est loin d'être clair, et, à en juger d'après des opinions dissidentes, les discussions en son sein ont dû être confuses. Il est possible d'interpréter cet avis de deux manières.

D'après la première, le fait illicite en venant frapper un agent de l'organisation (à savoir un organe) touche directement l'organisation. Dans ce cas il ne saurait être question d'une protection fonctionnelle, de la même manière qu'un fait illicite touchant le diplomate d'un Etat ne met pas en jeu le mécanisme de la protection diplomatique.

En faveur de cette thèse, on peut citer le passage suivant de cet avis:

> «En demandant une réparation fondée sur le préjudice subi par son agent, l'Organisation ne représente pas cet agent; elle affirme son propre droit, le droit de garantir le respect des engagements contractés envers l'Organisation»[18].

Toutefois, le soin pris par la Cour pour montrer que les règles relatives à la protection diplomatique ne font pas obstacle à la présentation d'une

---

14 *Ibid.* p. 214.

15 Affaire AETR, Recueil de la jurisprudence de la Cour des Communautés (1971), pp. 273–284; Avis I-76, *ibid.* (1977), pp. 741–762.

16 CIJ Recueil (1949), p. 182.

17 *Ibid.* p. 184.

18 *Ibid.*

réclamation de la part de l'Organisation en faveur d'un de ses agents; le fait que la Cour, en répondant à la deuxième question posée par l'Assemblée générale, se soit efforcée de concilier la protection diplomatique de l'Etat et la protection «fonctionnelle» de l'Organisation semble indiquer que cette première innterprétation de l'Avis consultatif n'est pas la bonne.

En réalité il apparaît que la Cour a voulu dire que l'Organisation était atteinte dans ses droits à travers la personne de son agent. Si cette deuxième interprétation est exacte, et elle semble être reconnue par certains juges dans leurs opinions dissidentes, il faut alors reconnaître avec le Juge Krylov qu'il s'agit d'une «règle nouvelle du droit international»[19].

VII

Si des doutes peuvent subsister en ce qui concerne l'interprétation à donner à l'Avis de la Cour de 1949, il n'y en a guère pour l'Avis consultatif de 1951 sur les réserves à la Convention pour la répression du crime de génocide.

La question posée à la Cour, toujours par l'Assemblée générale des Nations Unies, était de savoir dans quelle mesure un Etat ayant formulé des réserves à cette Convention, qui n'en prévoyait pas, pouvait être considéré partie à celle-ci, malgré l'objection d'autres Etats.

Il n'y pas lieu ici d'examiner le problème des réserves aux traités, mais personne n'a jamais contesté qu'il existait, avant 1950, une «pratique» résumée d'ailleurs dans un avis d'une Commission d'experts, et repris par le Conseil de la Société des Nations en 1927, qui prévoyait pour qu'un Etat réservataire puisse devenir partie à une Convention soit le consentement de tous les Etats signataires, soit celui de tous les Etats liés à la Convention.

Sans aucune démonstration, la Cour l'a baptisée d'une «pratique administrative». Elle a dès lors indiqué c'est:

> «... la compatibilité de la réserve avec l'objet et le but de la convention qui doit fournir le critère de l'attitude de l'Etat qui joint une réserve à son adhésion et de l'Etat qui estime devoir y faire une objection»[20].

En conséquence l'objection d'un ou plusieurs Etats n'empêche pas l'Etat réservataire de devenir partie à la Convention.

---

[19] *Ibid.* p. 217.
[20] CIJ RECUEIL (1951), p. 24.

Deux enseignements se dégagent de cet avis. Tout d'abord, face à une pratique constante et uniforme[21], la Cour n'a pas essayé de rechercher une *opinio juris* qui lui aurait permis d'individualiser une norme juridique. Ensuite, elle pose, comme l'indique l'opinion dissidente collective de certains juges:

> «... une règle nouvelle qui, selon nous, manque de fondement juridique. Nous n'apercevons ni dans la jurisprudence de notre Cour, de la Cour permanente de Justice internationale ou de toute autre juridiction internationale, ni dans les ouvrages des auteurs, aucune autorité qui vienne confirmer l'existence, en matière de réserves d'une distinction de cet ordre»[22].

VIII

L'affaire Nottebohm est encore un exemple de l'activité prétorienne de la Cour. Dans son arrêt, elle a estimé qu'il appartient à chaque Etat de régler par sa propre législation l'acquisition de sa nationalité. Toutefois, cette dernière ne saurait être opposable, au regard de la protection diplomatique à un Etat tiers que dans la mesure où elle serait effective, où il y aurait concordance entre le lien juridique et le rattachement réel de l'individu à l'Etat.

A première vue logique, ce raisonnement de la Cour n'est pas fondé juridiquement. Elle invoque l'article premier de la Convention de La Haye de 1930 relative aux conflits de lois en matière de nationalité qui déclare que la législation étatique en la matière «doit être admise par les autres Etats pourvu qu'elle soit en accord avec ... la coutume internationale et les principes de droit généralement reconnus en matière de nationalité».

Mais justement, rien n'indique que cette coutume ou ces principes se réfèrent à la nationalité effective. Il est vrai que l'article 5 de cette même convention mentionne le rattachement effectif en cas de double nationalité. Dès lors, la Cour ajoute:

> «L'arbitre international a tranché de la même façon de nombreux cas de double nationalité où la question se posait à propos de l'exercice de la protection. Il a fait prévaloir la nationalité effective»[23].

Cependant Nottebohm ne possédant qu'une seule nationalité, on est en droit de se demander si la Cour pouvait lui appliquer, par analogie, une règle

---

[21] *Cf.* l'analyse très fouillée de la doctrine et de la pratique qui se trouve dans l'opinion dissidente collective, *ibid.* pp. 32–39.

[22] *Ibid.* pp. 42–43.

[23] CIJ RECUEIL (1955), p. 22.

valable pour une situation différente. Certains juges ont répondu par la négative[24].

IX

On s'en doute c'est dans le domaine du droit de la mer que la Cour aura surtout fait oeuvre novatrice.

Dans l'affaire du Plateau continental de la mer du Nord, la Cour a estimé que l'article 6 de la Convention de Genève de 1958, qui préconisait pour la délimitation du plateau continental le principe de l'équidistance – circonstances spéciales – n'était pas une règle coutumière. Il convient de souligner que le raisonnement de la Cour, dans cet arrêt, s'explique par le but poursuivi: la délimitation du plateau continental doit aboutir à un résultat équitable:

> «Quel que soit le raisonnement juridique du juge, ses décisions doivent par définition être justes, donc en un sens équitables»[25].

Tout en étant conscient du danger d'une telle afirmation – la notion de justice comportant inévitablement une part de subjectivité – on peut sur ce point se rallier au raisonnement de la Cour, tant il est vrai que l'équité devrait imprégner toute règle de droit. Encore faut-il que la règle existe. Or c'est là que la Cour va innover de toute pièce. L'équidistance – circonstances spéciales – va être remplacée par des «principes équitables». Et la Cour de préciser:

> «Il s'agit là, sur la base de préceptes très généraux de justice et de bonne foi, de véritables règles de droit en matière de délimitation des plateaux continentaux limitrophes, c'est-à-dire, de règles obligatoires pour les Etats pour toute délimitation ... d'appliquer une règle de droit prescrivant le recours à des principes équitables»[26].

Plus loin elle insistera sur le fait qu'il n'est «pas question en l'espèce d'une décision *ex aequo et bono*»[27].

Ayant consacré plusieurs pages de son arrêt à démontrer que, faute d'une pratique suffisante et d'une *opinio juris*, le principe de l'équidistance n'était pas une règle coutumière, le lecteur aurait pu s'attendre à ce que la Cour prouve l'existence d'une norme exigeant en la matière l'application des

---

24 *Ibid.* pp. 31, 42, 54.
25 CIJ RECUEIL (1969), pp. 48.
26 *Ibid.* pp. 46-47.
27 *Ibid.* p. 48.

principes équitables. Cette démonstration fait défaut, hormis une référence à la proclamation du Président Truman de 1945 et à quelques opinions au sein de la Commission du droit international. L'activité prétorienne de la Cour est donc évidente.

X

La Cour procédera de la même manière en ce qui concerne le contenu de ces fameux principes équitables. Il est vrai que par moments il est difficile de distinguer les règles de droit, des simples méthodes de délimitation.

Une règle est certaine:

> «... le plateau continental de tout Etat doit être le prolongement naturel de son territoire et ne doit pas empiéter sur ce qui est le prolongement naturel du territoire d'un autre Etat»[28].

L'arrêt précisait cette notion:

> «Ce n'est pas vraiment ou pas seulement parce qu'elles sont proches de son territoire que les zones sous-marines relèvent d'un Etat riverain ...; le titre que le droit international attribue *ipso jure* à l'Etat riverain sur son plateau continental procède de ce que les zones sous-marines en cause peuvent être considérées comme faisant véritablement partie du territoire sur lequel l'Etat riverain exerce déjà son autorité: on peut dire que, tout en étant recouvertes d'eau, elles sont un prolongement, une continuation, une extension de ce territoire sous la mer»[29].

Ainsi si le plateau continental appartient à un Etat c'est parce qu'il consiste dans le prolongement immergé de son territoire. Si tel est le cas, on peut dire qu'à la limite il n'y a plus à appliquer d'autres critères de délimitation, puisque celle-ci se borne à rechercher les limites du prolongement naturel du territoire terrestre. On a pu dire avec raison qu'il s'agissait d'une «délimitation déclarative»[30].

Ce principe, apparemment simple, soulève toutefois des difficultés. En effet, dans le cas où il s'agit d'un plateau continental ayant la même histoire géologique et présentant les mêmes caractéristiques physiques, comment déterminer si le plateau relève du prolongement naturel d'un Etat plutôt que

---

28 *Ibid.* p. 47.

29 *Ibid.* p. 31.

30 P. WEIL, PERSPECTIVES DU DROIT DE LA DÉLIMITATION MARITIME, Pedone, Paris (1988), pp. 26–27.

de l'autre? En fait, il prolonge le territoire des deux. De plus, si la délimitation est basée sur des facteurs physiques et géographiques, il appartient alors aux experts d'y procéder et non plus aux juristes. Malgré ces inconvénients, les juridictions internationales se sont référées à ce principe sans toutefois vraiment l'appliquer. Quant aux Etats, ils ont invoqué souvent ce principe dans leurs plaidoiries devant les tribunaux internationaux.

Cependant, dans son arrêt Libye/Malte de 1985, la Cour abandonnait ce principe. Dans cette affaire, les deux parties avaient soumis à la Cour un grand nombre d'expertises sur les particularités géologiques ou géomorphologiques de la zone dite d'effondrement.

Après avoir déclaré: «La Cour ne peut accepter l'idée que, pour statuer en l'espèce, elle devrait d'abord trancher un désaccord entre des hommes de science réputés sur l'interprétation plus ou moins plausible de données apparemment incomplète», elle ajoutait: «Du fait que la zone du plateau continental qui se trouve relever de chaque Partie ne s'étend pas à plus de 200 milles de la côte de la Partie concernée, aucun critère de délimitation des zones du plateau ne saurait être tiré du principe du prolongement naturel»[31].

L'abandon de ce principe est dû sans doute à la nécessité d'affirmer sans ambages le caractère juridique du processus de délimitation – ce qui avait d'ailleurs déjà été fait dans le passé – mais aussi à l'existence de la Convention de 1982 sur le droit de la mer. Son article 76 définit le plateau continental en fonction de la distance de 200 milles et ce n'est qu'au-delà que la notion du prolongement naturel pourrait trouver application. Si donc ce principe n'a pas totalement disparu, son effet pratique ne pourra être que fort limité.

Voilà donc une règle de droit créée par la Cour dont l'existence aura été bien éphémère.

Il a été indiqué ci-dessus qu'hormis la règle du prolongement naturel, il était difficile en examinant l'arrêt de la Cour de 1969 de distinguer les principes – règles de droit – des simples méthodes de délimitation.

En 1985, cependant, la Cour a été amenée à dégager certaines règles de droit, dans la mesure où l'application de la justice doit être marquée par la cohérence et une certaine prévisibilité. Après avoir mentionné le caractère normatif des principes équitables, susceptibles d'application générales, elle en a fait l'énumération: «… Le principe qu'il ne saurait être question de refaire complètement la géographie ni de rectifier les inégalités de la nature; le principe voisin du non-empiètement d'une partie sur le prolongement naturel de l'autre…; le principe du respect dû à toutes ces circonstances

---

[31] CIJ RECUEIL (1985), p. 57.

pertinentes; le principe suivant lequel, bien que tous les Etats soient égaux en droit et puissent prétendre à un traitement égal, „l'équité n'implique pas nécessairement l'égalité" … Ni ne vise à rendre égal ce que la nature a fait inégal; et le principe qu'il ne saurait être question de justice distributive»[32].

Il est toutefois curieux de constater qu'un an auparavant la Cour avait estimé que le principe de non-empiètement n'était qu'un critère équitable susceptible d'être pris en considération aux fins d'une délimitation maritime internationale. Or, toujours d'après la Cour dans cette affaire, «les critères en question ne sont pas eux-mêmes des règles de droit et donc d'application obligatoire»[33].

On constate donc combien est mouvant ce droit de la délimitation du plateau continental: en une année le non-empiètement, critère non obligatoire, est promu au rang de principe équitable sans que l'on sache trop pourquoi.

Ainsi donc, en 1985, il existe, d'après la Cour, un corps de principes obligatoires mais il importe de souligner que celle-ci n'a en aucune manière essayé de faire la preuve de leur existence.

XI

Il n'y a pas lieu ici de se pencher sur le problème des délimitations maritimes. Le but de cette étude étant de montrer l'importance de la jurisprudence, il est certain que dans ce domaine, le juge se sert de principes – considérés comme obligatoires – critères ou méthodes dans le seul but d'arriver à un résultat équitable. Cette grande liberté du juge a d'ailleurs été soulignée par le Tribunal arbitral dans l'affaire de la délimitation de la frontière maritime entre la Guinée et la Guinée-Bissau, qui indiquait que chaque litige relatif au plateau continental est un cas unique et doit être résolu en fonction des circonstances qui lui sont propres et que ces dernières ne sont prises en considération par le Tribunal que quand celui-ci les juge pertinentes dans le cas d'espèce[34].

On aurait tort cependant de penser que l'opération de la délimitation du plateau continental trouve davantage sa source dans l'équité, au sens de l'article 38, chiffre 2 du Statut de la Cour, que dans le droit proprement dit. La jurisprudence a affirmé à plusieurs reprises que la délimitation du plateau continental était une opération juridique.

---

32 *Ibid.* pp. 39–40.
33 CIJ RECUEIL (1984), p. 313.
34 Sentence arbitrale du 14 février 1985, paragraphe 89.

Cette grande liberté d'appréciation du juge trouve peut-être son explication dans l'opinion conjointe des juges Bedjaoui, Jiménez de Arechaga et Ruda, en 1985. D'après eux la difficulté provient de ce que le droit de la délimitation est marqué d'une «certaine indétermination», que le droit de la mer est encore «assez rudimentaire» et comporte peu de règles. De plus: «... Le processus entier du droit de la délimitation maritime est dominé par une „norme fondamentale", celle du résultat équitable, qui dit tout et rien à la fois». Dès lors: «il [le juge] ne sait comment échapper à la frustrante tyrannie d'un certain „subjectivisme prétorien", alors même que la marge d'indétermination qui cause celui-ci trouve sa source dans un droit encore neuf, pétri d'équité, c'est-à-dire d'une notion certes juridique et éminente, mais inévitablement mesurable à „l'aune humaine". Les plus belles dissertations juridiques sur l'équité ne parviendront pas à éliminer une part peut-être irréductible de ce subjectivisme prétorien»[35].

Il nous paraît inutile d'ajouter quoi que ce soit à l'opinion de ces illustres juges.

XII

Cette modeste étude a pour but de démontrer que la jurisprudence mériterait une place à part dans l'énumération des sources prévues à l'article 38 du Statut de la Cour. Sans doute, permettre à celle-ci de créer des règles de droit n'est pas sans danger pour la sécurité juridique des relations internationales. On ne saurait, toutefois, nier à la Cour internationale de Justice le caractère de Cour suprême de l'ordre juridique international.

Dès lors, il lui revient d'adapter les règles existantes aux nouveaux besoins de la société internationale, sans attendre que celles-ci soient modifiées par le processus relativement lent qui est celui de la création de nouvelles normes coutumières. Non seulement la Cour n'a pas abusé de ce pouvoir, mais les règles dégagées par sa jurisprudence ont été acceptées par la suite, même si au début elles ont pu rencontrer certaines réticences.

La théorie des pouvoirs implicites était, sans doute, indispensable au bon fonctionnement des organisations internationales. En matière de réserves, la Cour a fait oeuvre de précurseur et, malgré une longue résistance de la Commission du droit international, le contenu de son avis consultatif est passé dans la Convention de Vienne sur le droit des Traités. Sans doute, il est possible de critiquer le point de vue de la Cour dans l'affaire Nottebohm mais,

---

35 CIJ RECUEIL (1985), p. 90.

là aussi, l'Institut de Droit international, après maintes discussions, a fini par accepter, en 1965, le principe de la nationalité effective dans le domaine de la protection diplomatique.

On l'a vu, la prépondérance de la jurisprudence comme source de droit de la délimitation du plateau continental était inévitable dans le cas d'un droit en formation. Toute proportion gardée on la retrouve aussi dans le droit commercial international.

En définitive, l'augmentation du nombre d'affaires devant la Cour montre que celle-ci répond aux attentes de ces sujets de l'ordre juridique international que sont les Etats.

ENGAGEMENTS UNILATÉRAUX ET ENGAGEMENTS CONVENTIONNELS: DIFFÉRENCES ET CONVERGENCES

par

JEAN CHARPENTIER

1. Que l'Etat puisse, en dehors de ses obligations conventionnelles, s'engager unilatéralement semble aujourd'hui bien admis, tant par la jurisprudence[1] que par la doctrine[2]; la présente étude ne saurait apporter sur ce sujet ni révélation ni remise en cause fondamentale; tout au plus se propose-t-elle de faire le point sur un aspect des engagements de l'Etat dont la raison d'être, la base juridique et la portée n'ont peut être pas été précisés avec toute la rigueur qu'il mérite; il semble que le moyen d'y parvenir soit de comparer les engagements unilatéraux aux engagements conventionnels: on sera peut être surpris de constater que la distance entre les deux est moindre qu'on ne le pensait.

2. Il faut d'abord s'entendre sur ce dont on parle.

En traitant des engagements unilatéraux, on écarte tout d'abord de l'étude un certain nombre de phénomènes qui sont souvent rangés dans la catégorie des actes unilatéraux, mais qui sont en réalité des faits juridiques. Le fait juridique (international) est un fait auquel l'ordre international attache des effets de droit; l'acte juridique est une manifestation de volonté (d'un ou de plusieurs sujets de droit international) qui donne naissance à une norme nouvelle[3]. Le même phénomène peut d'ailleurs être un acte juridique dans l'ordre interne et un fait juridique dans l'ordre international; ainsi une loi de nationalité ou une extension territoriale. On écarte également les «prétentions» ou «revendications», qui cherchent à faire acquérir des droits à leur auteur mais n'en ont pas la capacité puisque, comme on le dira, un Etat ne peut unilatéralement imposer des obligations à un autre Etat, et qui se ramènent donc à la catégorie des faits juridiques internationaux.

---

[1] CIJ Affaire des essais nucléaires français, arrêt du 20 décembre 1974.

[2] E. SUY, LES ACTES JURIDIQUES UNILATÉRAUX EN DROIT INTERNATIONAL PUBLIC, LGDJ, Paris (1962), p. 290; G. VENTURINI, *La portée et les effets juridiques des attitudes et des actes unilatéraux des Etats*, RCADI (1964), t. 112, pp. 363–467; A.P. RUBIN, *The international legal effects of unilateral Declarations*, AJIL (1977), pp. 1–30; J.P. JACQUÉ, *A propos de la promesse unilatérale*, dans: MÉLANGES REUTER, Paris (1981), pp. 327–346; J.D. SICAULT, *Du caractère obligatoire des engagements unilatéraux en droit international public*, RGDIP (1979), pp. 633–688.

[3] Sur ce point, *cf.* J.P. JACQUÉ, *Eléments pour une théorie de l'acte juridique en droit international public*, LGDJ, Paris (1972), pp. 188–189.

3. On écarte également les actes des organisations internationales dirigés vers l'ordre interne de ces organisations – ce qui inclut les Etats membres. Ces actes, sur lesquels le dédicataire de cet ouvrage a apporté de pénétrantes réflexions[4], répondent à un principe hiérarchique voulu par leurs fondateurs qui les rapproche de l'acte public étatique et en fait une catégorie tout à fait spécifique du droit international. En revanche, il n'y a aucune raison d'exclure de notre étude les engagements unilatéraux qu'une organisation internationale peut prendre vis-à-vis d'une autre organisation internationale ou d'un Etat tiers, dans les mêmes conditions que le ferait un Etat.

4. Rentrent donc dans notre étude, tout d'abord ce qu'il est convenu d'appeler la «promesse»: si le terme employé traditionnellement est contestable, car il laisse entendre que l'effet juridique de cet acte est subordonné à son acceptation par son destinataire, ce qui tend à l'assimiler à un élément d'une opération conventionnelle, la notion est claire: c'est l'intention exprimée par un Etat (ou plus généralement par un sujet de droit international) de suivre une ligne de conduite déterminée; cette définition s'applique parfaitement à un cas particulièrement important de «promesse»: la déclaration d'acceptation de la juridiction obligatoire de la CIJ[5]. A côté de la promesse, une autre manifestation importante d'engagement unilatéral est la reconnaissance qui, à travers ses nombreuses applications, exprime l'intention par un Etat (ou par une organisation internationale) de ne pas contester une modification de l'ordre juridique international à laquelle il n'avait pas participé[6]. Enfin, la renonciation, si elle est exprimée de façon autonome, apparaît aussi comme une forme – négative – d'engagement. En revanche, nous excluons la protestation qui n'est pas, comme on le dit trop facilement, l'inverse de la reconnaissance, mais plutôt l'inverse de la notification; en effet, la protestation ne produit pas d'effet par elle-même, si ce n'est de faire connaître officiellement son refus d'admettre une prétention donnée; son effet recherché – maintenir les droits de celui qui proteste – dépend d'une comparaison entre ces droits et ceux de l'Etat que l'on conteste; ce n'est pas un engagement.

5. Ces trois manifestations d'engagement unilatéral sont retenues dans le cadre de cette étude à condition d'être … unilatérales, c'est-à-dire, comme on le précisera plus loin, d'être imputables à un seul sujet de droit; il se

---

4 K. SKUBISZEWSKI, *Le Conseil d'entr'aide économique et ses actes*, AFDI (1966), pp. 574–576. *A New Source of the Law of Nations: Resolutions of International Organisations*, dans: MÉLANGES GUGGENHEIM, Genève (1968), pp. 508–520.

5 Sur ce point, *cf. infra* note 8. Y ajouter, bien sûr, les déclarations établies sur le même modèle, comme celle de l'article 46 de la Convention européenne des Droits de l'Homme.

6 *Cf.* J. CHARPENTIER, LA RECONNAISSANCE INTERNATIONALE ET L'ÉVOLUTION DU DROIT DES GENS, Paris (1956), p. 315.

peut que des intentions de reconnaître – sans même parler de promesses – ou des renonciations soient exprimées dans des instruments conventionnels (qu'on pense, par exemple à la reconnaissance respective de la RFA et de la RDA par le «Traité fondamental» du 21 décembre 1972); elles acquièrent alors un caractère conventionnel qui les rattache à la méthodologie des traités et non plus des actes unilatéraux. Remarque banale, certes, mais dont on peut déjà retenir que l'opposition entre l'engagement unilatéral et l'engagement conventionnel dépend davantage d'élements circonstantiels que d'une différence de nature.

I. DES PERSPECTIVES DIFFÉRENTES

6. Dans l'esprit des gouvernants, la sécurité des relations internationales est liée à l'adoption d'engagements conventionnels; à partir d'intérêts divergents, une franche négociation permet de dégager un accord équilibré qui définira la ligne de conduite à venir des protagonistes. Telle était, avec la parenthèse des solutions imposées par la force, la seule méthode envisageable au temps du «concert européen», lorsque les princes n'hésitaient pas, après quelques brouilles passagères et éventuellement sanglantes, à reprendre le chemin de la table de négociations pour régler ensemble leurs affaires.

Ce n'est plus toujours le cas, et le fait que le recours à la force soit interdit n'incite pas nécessairement les Gouvernements à se rencontrer. Ils peuvent être alors tentés de proclamer unilatéralement leur position, faute de pouvoir, pour des raisons diverses, en faire l'enjeu d'une négociation. L'engagement unilatéral apparaît comme un substitut de l'engagement conventionnel. N'était-ce pas déjà la raison d'être de la déclaration d'acceptation de la juridiction obligatorie de la Cour internationale? Faute d'espérer réunir dans un même instrument multilatéral tous les plaideurs potentiels, on faisait éclater leur assentiment à la compétence obligatoire de la Cour en un nombre indéterminé d'engagements unilatéraux. Mais cette substitution de l'unilatéral au conventionnel a trouvé des perspectives d'extentions considérables avec la mondialisation et le fractionnement simultané de la société internationale; tandis que les progrès technologiques obligent les Etats à coopérer, des obstacles idéologiques les séparent et les pressions médiatiques les amènent souvent à sacrifier la raison à la passion: ils s'isolent alors et tentent de résoudre leurs difficultés extérieures par la voie unilatérale. C'est ainsi que dans la tension nord-sud aggravée par l'affaire du canal de Suez, l'Egypte trouve dans sa déclaration unilatérale du 24 avril 1957 le moyen de rétablir la confiance dans la libre circulation dans le canal de Suez, que, dans la tension est-ouest, un premier pas vers la détente est attendu de la déclaration soviétique du 15 juillet 1982 sur le non usage en premier de l'arme nucléaire, que la France, pour suivre la même voie sans donner l'impression d'être inféodée à l'OTAN s'engage à respecter les principes du traité de non prolifération sans pour autant y adhérer[7].

7. L'engagement unilatéral entretient donc avec l'engagement conventionnel des rapports subtils de substitution qu'il est, comme toute, assez facile de cerner; les rapports juridiques entre les deux types d'engagements sont plus stricts, mais parfois plus difficiles à délimiter: les engagements unilatéraux sont et doivent être autonomes par rapport aux engagements conventionnels.

L'autonomie des engagements unilatéraux a été longtemps contestée, d'abord parce que les exemples incontestables de ce genre d'engagement manquaient, et surtout parce que la doctrine n'était pas prête à admettre qu'une norme juridique internationale puisse découler d'autre chose que d'un accord entre Etats. Le positivisme juridique dominant en doctrine n'aboutissait-il pas à fonder le caractère obligatoire du droit international sur le principe *Pacta sunt servanda*? On verra plus loin ce qu'il faut penser de cette équation; remarquons simplement qu'elle se justifiait au regard de l'objet de l'enquête, à savoir la valeur obligatoire du droit objectif, des principes généraux du droit internationaux. Mais la perspective change si, au lieu de s'intéresser à la norme objective, on étudie la norme subjective, celle qui définit les obligations auxquelles s'astreignent un ou plusieurs sujets de droit; c'est l'accent mis sur la théorie de l'acte juridique international qui va mettre en lumière l'acte unilatéral, à côté de l'acte conventionnel comme sources des obligations de l'Etat, des normes juridiques subjectives étatiques[8]. Désormais, il n'est plus nécessaire de présenter les engagements unilatéraux comme les éléments d'un accord étalé dans le temps qui tirent leur valeur de la réponse qu'ils reçoivent ou de la réponse qu'ils donnent[9]. On peut étudier leurs effets propres. A condition qu'ils soient effectivement autonomes.

---

[7] Déclaration de principes du Conseil de politique nucléaire extérieure, du 11 octobre 1976, AFDI (1976), p. 1006.

[8] C'est PAUL REUTER qui a ouvert la voie, dans son cours général à l'Académie de La Haye, RCADI (1961), vol. II, pp. 531 et s., voie explorée ensuite par J.P. JACQUÉ, *Eléments pour une théorie de l'acte juridique en droit international public*, *op. cit.*, *supra* note 3, p. 505.

[9] C'était encore la position de BRIERLY (*Rapport sur le droit des traités*, Ann. CDI (1950), vol. II, p. 227) ou de QUADRI (*Cours général de DIP*, RCADI (1964), t. 113, p. 363); (*voir* l'analyse de SICAULT, *op. cit.*, *supra* note 2, pp. 636 et s.). Elle a été définitivement écartée par la CIJ, dans son arrêt précité du 20 décembre 1974, qui, parlant de la déclaration française de ne plus procéder à des essais nucléaires dans l'atmosphère, précise: «Un engagement de cette nature, exprimé publiquement et dans l'intention de se lier, même hors du cadre des négociations internationales, a un effet obligatoire. Dans ces conditions, aucune contrepartie n'est nécessaire pour que la déclaration prenne effet, non plus qu'une acceptation ultérieure ni même une réplique

8. Il faut en effet exclure de la notion d'engagement unilatéral les actes qui ont pour objet de créer ou de moduler un lien conventionnel. Tel est le cas de la ratification, ou celui de la réserve: tel est le cas de l'adhésion, qui mérite qu'on s'y arrête un instant. L'adhésion est formellement un acte unilatéral, qui intervient bien après qu'un traité donné soit entré en vigueur entre ses signataires; mais il a pour objet, de la part de son auteur, de se joindre à eux, de devenir partie contractante au traité en question; il se distingue ainsi très nettement de l'acte par lequel un Etat, ou une organisation internationale, déclare accepter les dispositions d'un traité auquel il ne veut ou ne peut adhérer: il est alors lié unilatéralement par cette obligation mais ne devient pas partie à ce traité. Tel a été le cas, déjà évoqué, de la France vis-à-vis du TNP[10], tel est celui de l'Agence spatiale européenne qui, par une déclaration en date du 12 décembre 1978, a accepté les droits et les obligations de la Convention du 12 novembre 1974 sur l'immatriculation des objects lancés dans l'espace extra-atmosphérique.

En revanche, ce n'est pas parce qu'un engagement unilatéral produit des effets déterminés par un statut conventionnel général qu'il perd son autonomie: on pense à la déclaration d'acceptation de la juridiction de la CIJ; elle ne pourrait à elle seule, sans l'article 36 du statut de la CIJ, fonder la compétence obligatoire de la Cour, mais c'est l'Etat qui la fait qui en détermine seul la portée, la requête d'un adversaire créant ensuite, si les conditions prévues sont réunies (réciprocité des engagements unilatéraux) le lien d'instance irrévocable[11]. De même, et ceci est plus facile à admettre, des engagements unilatéraux peuvent être conjoints sans perdre pour autant leur caractère unilatéral: telles ont été les reconnaissances adoptées par les Douze en application de la Déclaration sur les lignes directrices sur la reconnaissance de nouveaux Etats en Europe orientale et en Union soviétique du 16 décembre 1991[12].

9. Dire que l'engagement unilatéral est autonome, c'est donc dire que sa valeur juridique ne s'apprécie qu'en fonction de ses caractères propres, en fonction de l'intention normative de son auteur: il doit avoir l'intention

---

ou une réaction d'autres Etats, car ce serait incompatible avec la nature strictement unilatérale de l'acte juridique par lequel l'Etat s'est prononcé» (REC. (1974), p. 267). Comme le dit très bien G. VENTURINI (*op. cit.*, *supra* note 2, p. 400) l'acte unilatéral «se suffit à lui-même pour atteindre ses propres effets juridiques».

[10] Depuis, la France a changé d'attitude et, le 3 août 1992, a déposé ses instruments d'adhésion au TNP, ce qui ne lui impose aucune obligation nouvelle, mais la rend partie à ce traité.

[11] Face à la position négative de E. SUY (*op. cit.*, *supra* note 2, pp. 142 et s.) et de G. VENTURINI (*op. cit.*, *supra* note 2, p. 398), on renvoie à l'excellente argumentation de J.P. JACQUÉ (*Elements pour une théorie de l'acte juridique...*, *op. cit.*, *supra* note 3, p. 333).

[12] *Voir* sur ce texte notre étude à la RGDIP (1992), pp. 343–355.

de s'engager et de s'imposer une ligne de conduite obligatoire, et pas seulement d'annoncer le comportement qu'il envisage de suivre; l'interprétation correcte de cette intention normative peut être d'autant plus difficile à établir qu'elle n'est pas habituellement enserrée dans des formes imposées par le droit constitutionnel; la seule condition de forme, imposée par le droit international, est d'être officiellement portée – pas forcément par une notification[13] – à la connaissance de son destinataire, ou de ses destinataires. Il en résulte une certaine latitude dans le pouvoir d'interprétation, dont la Cour a su jouer dans l'affaire des essais nucléaires français pour présenter comme un engagement de la France ce que beaucoup d'exégètes n'avaient considéré que comme une déclaration politique[14].

10. En tout cas, aucun problème spécifique de validité de l'engagement unilatéral par rapport aux obligations conventionnelles antérieures de son auteur ne se pose. Certes un engagement unilatéral peut se révéler en contradiction avec un engagement conventionnel antérieur auquel l'auteur de l'acte unilatéral est partie; en ce cas son partenaire est en droit d'obtenir l'application de la convention en question car il est un tiers par rapport à l'engagement unilatéral postérieur selon le principe même de l'article 30 § 4 de la Convention de Vienne[15]; mais la situation qui se présente plus fréquemment est autre: c'est celle où un comportement unilatéral d'un Etat est en contradiction avec un engagement conventionnel pris antérieurement; ce comportement est bien unilatéral, mais ce n'est pas un engagement, c'est un fait juridique qui, s'il est contraire à un traité, est évidemment illicite; c'est – entre autres – l'hypothèse classique de la dénonciation unilatérale d'un traité qui est licite si elle est prévue par le traité, illicite au cas contraire. Autonome, l'engagement unilatéral se détache donc de tout contexte conventionnel, et il produit seul, comme le fait un engagement conventionnel, des effets juridiques obligatoires; mais ce qui va le différencier finalement de ce dernier, c'est qu'il produit ces effets sans contrepartie.

---

[13] On aura noté que la CIJ, dans le passage de son arrêt dans l'affaire des essais nucléaires français, reproduit en note 9, se contente d'exiger qu'un engagement de ce genre soit «exprimé publiquement». Il ne pourrait d'ailleurs en aller autrement, s'agissant d'un engagement de portée générale.

[14] *Voir* le commentaire d'H. THIERRY, dans: AFDI (1974), pp. 286–298.

[15] Sous peine de mettre en jeu la responsabilité de l'Etat qui aurait manqué, unilatéralement, à ses obligations conventionnelles. Bien entendu, si l'engagement unilatéral est en contradiction avec un principe, conventionnel ou coutumier, de *jus cogens*, la contradiction se résoudra non en terme d'inopposabilité mais en terme de nullité de l'engagement unilatéral, solution qui est exactement la même que pour un engagement conventionnel. *Voir* sur ce point, J.D. SICAULT, *op. cit.*, *supra* note 2, pp. 662–663.

11. Un engagement sans contrepartie. Par un engagement unilatéral, un Etat ne peut se créer d'obligations qu'à lui-même; il en est ainsi pour la bonne raison qu'il n'a aucune qualité pour imposer des obligations à un autre Etat; il n'est pas nécessaire de faire appel à la souveraineté pour justifier cela: la personnalité juridique y suffit, de sorte que ce principe s'applique aussi aux relations entre Etats et organisations internationales, ou entre organisations internationales.

La situation n'est pas, par nature, différente, dans l'engagement conventionnel: aucune Partie contractante n'a qualité pour imposer aux autres Parties contractantes des obligations; mais chaque Etat s'engage vis-à-vis de chacun de ses partenaires en fonction des obligations que celui-ci a déclaré assumer à son égard; les obligations des uns sont la cause des obligations des autres, qui acquièrent ainsi un droit à les voir respectées. On constate alors que l'engagement unilatéral se distingue de l'engagement conventionnel par l'absence de contrepartie, ou, dans un langage plus juridique, l'absence de réciprocité[16]. On comprend mieux, dès lors, que les engagements unilatéraux soient relativement rares, car les Etats ne sont normalement prêts à assumer des obligations que pour obtenir des contreparties équilibrées, et qu'ils ne s'y résolvent que dans un contexte politique qui exclut toute négociation. C'est ce manque de contrepartie, plus qu'une différence de nature, qui explique que l'engagement unilatéral produise des effets juridiques plus fragiles que l'engagement conventionnel.

II. UN FONDEMENT COMMUN

12. En proclamant, dans son arrêt sur les Essais nucléaires français, que «le caractère obligatoire d'un engagement international assumé par déclaration unilatérale repose sur la bonne foi», la Cour semble avoir tranché définitivement la question du fondement du caractère obligatoire de l'enga-

---

[16] Cette distinction est particulièrement nette s'agissant des traités bilatéraux. Comme le note M. VIRALLY (*Le principe de réciprocité dans le droit international contemporain,* RCADI (1967), t. 112, p. 54), la réciprocité «établit un lien juridique direct entre les engagements respectivement pris par les parties à un traité ou, plus largement, entre les obligations internationales respectives des deux Etats dans leurs rapports mutuels, et a donc des effets sur l'existence, la portée et l'exigibilité de ces engagements et obligations». C'est à ces engagements que le langage du droit privé réserve la qualification de synallagmatiques. Dans les traités multilatéraux, dit encore M. VIRALLY, la réciprocité n'est qu'une forme de l'égalité devant la loi. Mais même pour ceux des traités multilatéraux qui n'exigent pas la réciprocité au niveau de l'application (ceux qui proclament des droits de l'homme, notamment), en ce sens que l'inexécution des obligations du traité par un des signataires n'autorise pas les autres à se dégager de leurs obligations, la réciprocité est prise en compte par les Etats au moment où ils s'engagent, en ce sens que l'engagement des autres Etats, et parfois de tel ou tel d'entre eux, est une condition de leur propre engagement.

gement unilatéral. Certains[17] ont cependant fait remarquer que la bonne foi pouvait expliquer l'obligation de l'auteur de l'engagement de ne pas revenir sur l'obligation qu'il avait contractée mais non pas fonder l'obligation initiale. A première vue, l'observation peut paraître oiseuse: n'est-ce pas dire autrement la même chose[18]? A la réflexion, elle est beaucoup plus profonde et ouvre des perspectives importantes. Elle revient à dire que la bonne foi – comme l'estoppel qui exprime la perception que le destinataire d'un engagement se fait de la bonne foi de son auteur[19] – porte sur l'exécution de l'obligation, et non sur sa naissance. Une conséquence immédiate de cette remarque, c'est que la bonne foi s'applique également aux obligations nées d'un traité; l'article 26 de la Convention de Vienne, intitulé *Pacta sunt servanda* et placé dans la section consacrée au respect des traités proclame d'ailleurs: «Tout traité en vigueur lie les parties et doit être exécuté par elles de bonne foi», et la Cour elle-même, dans le même arrêt, a fait précéder le passage cité plus haut de ces mots: «tout comme la règle du droit des traités *Pacta sunt servanda* elle-même ...». Le problème reste alors entier pour les engagements unilatéraux, qui ne peuvent s'appuyer sur *Pacta sunt servanda*: si la bonne foi n'est qu'une condition de leur exécution, quel est le fondement de leur caractère obligatoire?

13. La réponse ne peut être trouvée que dans l'autonomie de la volonté: le propre d'une personne juridique est de pouvoir s'engager valablement par une manifestation libre de sa volonté. Cela est vrai des personnes physiques, car cette autonomie de la volonté repose sur une réalité qui est à la fois physique et morale: la dignité de la personne humaine; pour les personnes morales, elle est un corollaire de cette personnalité et repose sur l'idée qu'en conférant à un groupement donné cette personnalité qui le distingue de ses membres, la société dans laquelle il se meut a jugé bon de lui conférer les moyens d'action nécessaires à la défense d'intérêts qu'elle estime conformes à la bonne organisation des rapports sociaux. Il est à remarquer d'ailleurs que les théoriciens du droit privé, après avoir longtemps assimilé le principe de l'autonomie de la volonté à celui du consensualisme, en tant qu'il justifie la valeur obligatoire des contrats, admettent aujourd'hui «qu'une personne par sa seule volonté fasse naître une obligation à sa charge»[20], l'exemple donné étant celui de la promesse de récompense.

---

17 *Cf.* A.P. RUBIN, *op. cit*, *supra* note 2, pp. 2 et 10.

18 C'est l'opinion de J.D. SICAULT, *op. cit.*, *supra* note 2, p. 678.

19 Sur les rapports entre la „promesse" unilatérale, l'estoppel et la bonne foi, *voir* J.P. JACQUÉ, *op. cit.*, *supra* note 2, pp. 335–339.

20 PLANIOL et RIPERT, DROIT CIVIL, vol. 6 par P. ESMEIN (1952), § 9, 10 35; J. MARTIN DE LA MOUTTE, L'ACTE JURIDIQUE UNILATÉRAL. ESSAI SUR SA NATURE ET SA TECHNIQUE EN DROIT PRIVÉ, Toulouse (1949), p. 343.

Pour ce qui est de l'Etat, la tentation est grande de faire reposer l'autonomie de sa volonté sur sa souveraineté, en s'appuyant sur le passage célèbre de l'arrêt de la C.P.J.I. dans l'affaire du Wimbledon[21]: «la faculté de contracter des engagements internationaux est précisément un attribut de la souveraineté de l'Etat». Le rapprochement est légitime, si l'on entend par souveraineté[22] l'identité d'un Etat qui prend en charge une population donnée sur un territoire donné; il ne l'est plus si l'on veut mettre l'accent sur le refus de l'Etat d'être soumis à toute autorité supérieure, avec ses corollaires qui sont la compétence de la compétence et l'exclusivité de la compétence. En effet, l'autonomie de la volonté, qui est un attribut de la personnalité morale, justifie aussi le caractère obligatoire des engagements souscrits par les Organisations internationales, soumises, comme on le sait, au principe antinomique de spécialité[23].

Fonder le caractère obligatoire des engagements unilatéraux de l'Etat sur l'autonomie de la volonté et celle-ci sur la personnalité juridique ne va sans doute pas tout à fait au fond des choses, car l'Etat est une réalité changeante qui ne justifie pas de façon absolue la qualité que l'on attribue ainsi à sa volonté. On peut alors avancer des explications plus profondes: dire que c'est la société internationale, ou le Droit international, qui lui confère cette qualité; c'est là un postulat théorique qui cherche à assimiler la société internationale à la société interne, et qui est parfaitement artificiel. On peut plutôt – et c'est peut être une autre façon de dire la même chose – dire que le principe de l'autonomie de la volonté de l'Etat entraînant la confiance que ses partenaires sont en droit d'avoir en sa parole, répond à une exigence de stabilité des rapports internationaux[24]; c'est sans doute vrai, mais c'est une explication métajuridique qui montre que le problème du fondement du caractère obligatoire du droit ne peut être fourni par le droit lui-même.

14. Le fondement, ainsi limité à ce qui peut être perçu par le droit – à savoir l'autonomie de la volonté a en tout cas une conséquence importante: il vaut aussi bien pour les engagements conventionnels que pour les engagements unilatéraux. *Pacta sunt servanda* n'aurait aucun sens si les signataires du Pacte n'avaient la capacité de s'engager par une libre manifestation de

---

[21] Arrêt du 17 août 1923, Série A, nº 1, p. 25.

[22] *Voir* C. CHAUMONT, *Recherche du contenu irréductible du concept de souveraineté internationale de l'Etat*, dans: MÉLANGES BASDEVANT, Paris (1960), pp. 114–151.

[23] C. CHAUMONT, *La signification du principe de spécialité des organisations internationales*, dans: MÉLANGES HENRI ROLIN, Paris (1964), pp. 55–66.

[24] En ce sens, la Cour, dans le même arrêt (269) dit: «La validité de telles déclarations (unilatérales) et leurs conséquences juridiques doivent être envisagées dans le cadre général de la sécurité des relations internationales et de la confiance mutuelle si indispensable dans les rapports entre Etats».

leur volonté. Comme le dit très bien Venturini[25], le caractère obligatoire de la promesse unilatérale se justifie de la même façon que le caractère obligatoire du traité, «car l'une et l'autre sont une expression du pouvoir général de s'obliger, fondé sur la même norme constitutionnelle de l'ordre juridique international relative à la production juridique volontaire». Et Elisabeth Zoller ne dit pas autre chose lorsqu'elle admet que «*Pacta sunt servanda* ne doit pas être distingué de *Promissio est servanda*; dans un cas comme dans l'autre, c'est une parole qui a été donnée»[26]. Ainsi, le fondement du caractère obligatoire des engagements souscrits par l'Etat repose sur l'autonomie de la volonté, que ces engagements soient pris unilatéralement ou dans un cadre conventionnel. Une différence essentielle distingue cependant les seconds des premiers: seuls les engagements conventionnels sont soumis au principe de réciprocité, et c'est cette réciprocité qui va justifier leur caractère irrévocable dont, à première vue, les engagements unilatéraux semblent dépourvus[27]. Il nous reste donc à apprécier la portée réelle de cette différence touchant à l'irrévocabilité des engagements de l'Etat.

15. Avant d'y procéder, toutefois, on voudrait ajouter une remarque. *Pacta sunt servanda* est un principe relationnel qui est immergé, par sa nature, dans l'ordre juridique international. Le principe d'autonomie de la volonté des Etats, qui justifie, on l'a vu, le caractère obligatoire de tous leurs engagements, est situé, lui, à la charnière de l'ordre juridique interne et de l'ordre juridique international. Il peut être modulé dans son exercice par la constitution de l'Etat qui fixe les conditions de sa validité. Il ne s'agit pas, bien entendu, de faire du droit international une projection du droit interne et de prôner la supériorité du second sur le premier, mais de réduire l'opposition entre les deux en mettant l'accent sur un principe unique – l'autonomie de la volonté – qui est à la fois le fondement des engagements internationaux et l'expression de la personnalité de l'Etat, laquelle, encadrée par sa constitution, repose finalement sur la souveraineté du peuple.

III. UNE SOLIDITÉ COMPARABLE

16. La question de la révocabilité de l'engagement unilatéral de l'Etat embarrasse tous ceux, théoriciens autant que praticiens du droit international,

---

[25] G. VENTURINI, *op. cit.*, *supra* note 2, p. 403.

[26] E. ZOLLER, LA BONNE FOI EN DROIT INTERNATIONAL PUBLIC, Paris (1977), p. 343.

[27] Nous nous séparons ici totalement d'E. ZOLLER (*op. cit*, *supra* note 26, pp. 345–346) pour qui «c'est la réciprocité qui fonde le caractère obligatoire de tout engagement mais non la volonté», ce qui semble par ailleurs en contradiction avec le passage cité précédemment.

qui admettent son caractère obligatoire; si un tel engagement n'est obligatoire que pour autant que son auteur ne l'ait pas révoqué, quelle confiance lui accorder? En dernière analyse, mérite-t-il même d'être tenu pour obligatoire? Certains auteurs, parmi les meilleurs, en arrivent à se débarrasser du problème en prétendant, d'autorité, que la révocation des actes unilatéraux est exclue «faute de normes générales qui l'admettent»[28] argument assez surprenant dans un monde où les limitations à la souveraineté de l'Etat ne se présument pas. Toute aussi spécieuse est la position de J.D. Sicault[29] selon laquelle «l'obligation de ne pas abroger un engagement unilatéral ... découle du caractère obligatorie dudit engagement». Il faudrait préciser (*cf. infra* n° 17) «l'obligation de ne pas abroger arbitrairement ...».

17. Pourtant, la logique a des exigences dont on ne peut pas se débarrasser d'un trait de plume: si la volonté unilatérale d'un Etat lui a permis de s'imposer des obligations, la volonté unilatérale ultérieure du même Etat doit lui permettre de s'en dégager. La CIJ a d'ailleurs expressément admis cette révocabilité à propos de la déclaration d'acceptation de sa juridiction obligatoire en reconnaissant, dans l'affaire du droit de passage en territoire indien «le droit pour de nombreux signataires de la disposition facultative, l'Inde y comprise, de mettre fin à leur déclaration d'acceptation par simple notification sans préavis obligatoire»[30]. Et la même Cour, dans l'affaire des essais nucléaires, ne se départit pas de cette logique, implicitement cette fois, lorsqu'elle indique qu'un engagement unilatéral «ne saurait être interprété comme ayant comporté l'invocation d'un pouvoir arbitraire de révision»[31]. «Arbitraire» ... la Cour se place, à juste titre, sur le terrain de l'abus de droit: l'Etat pourrait, logiquement, révoquer un engagement unilatéral, mais compte tenu de diverses considérations liées à la sécurité des relations internationales, son pouvoir doit être limité. Suivons la donc sur ce terrain.

18. Une première limite à la révocabilité de l'engagement unilatéral tient à la nature même de l'engagement: fondé sur l'effet attribué à la volonté exprimée par l'Etat, il doit correspondre à une véritable intention de s'engager, ce qui exclut toute liberté de revenir arbitrairement sur cette intention: un engagement potestatif n'est pas un engagement.

---

[28] G. VENTURINI, *op. cit.*, *supra* note 2, p. 422.

[29] J.D. SICAULT, *op. cit.*, *supra* note 2, p. 678.

[30] Arrêt du 26 novembre 1957, REC., p. 143. J.D. SICAULT méconnait la portée, très claire, de cet arrêt, lorsqu'il prétend (*op. cit.*, *supra* note 2, p. 655) que «toute révision qui aurait pour but de diminuer tant soit peu les obligations contractées dans l'engagement unilatéral n'est pas plus admissible qu'une abrogation».

[31] Arrêt du 20 décembre 1974, REC., p. 270.

Plus précisément, la solidité de l'engagement pris unilatéralement est garantie par le principe de bonne foi. C'est ici, au niveau de l'exécution, que la bonne foi intervient, pour interdire à l'Etat qui s'est engagé unilatéralement de se déjuger sans raison. Que la bonne foi réponde à un souci moral de respecter la parole donnée ou à une exigence sociale d'assurer la stabilité des relations internationales, qu'elle joue à travers la sincérité du déclarant, ou à travers la perception que s'en fait le bénéficiaire pour y ajuster sa propre conduite (c'est le sens de l'estoppel), peu importe[32]. L'essentiel, c'est de considérer la bonne foi comme un principe de droit international imposant aux Etats le respect de leurs engagements[33]. Finalement, l'Etat qui s'engage unilatéralement, et avant même que cet engagement ait été accepté, ne peut légitimement révoquer ou modifier cet engagement qu'en cas de changement fondamental de circonstances[34]. On se retrouve ainsi pratiquement dans la même situation que celle concernant la modification unilatérale d'un engagement conventionnel, à ceci près que l'invocation – de bonne foi – d'un changement de circonstances par l'auteur d'un engagement unilatéral n'a pas à être suivie d'une concertation avec des partenaires qui n'existent pas.

19. Ainsi, la différence entre la révocabilité de principe des engagements unilatéraux et l'irrévocabilité des engagements conventionnels, liée à leur réciprocité, s'estompe-t-elle singulièrement. Ce rapprochement, dû, dans une perspective juridique, à l'application commune du principe de bonne foi dans l'exécution des uns et des autres, se renforce encore si l'on veut bien prendre en considération certaines données d'ordre politique. Dans cet ordre d'idées, on doit constater que l'hésitation d'un Etat à enfreindre une obligation conventionnelle tient moins à la crainte d'engager sa responsabilité qu'à celle de perdre la confiance de son partenaire. C'est aussi la confiance qui donne toute sa valeur aux accords politiques, une valeur parfois supérieure à celle des traités formels[35]. C'est elle, de la même manière, qui donne tout

---

[32] La Cour, dans l'arrêt précité, s'est d'ailleurs appuyée aussi bien sur l'une que l'autre de ces fonctions, comme l'a démontré E. ZOLLER (*op. cit.*, *supra* note 26, pp. 340–342).

[33] Appliquant ces principes dans l'affaire des activités militaires et para-militaires au Nicaragua à propos de la déclaration américaine d'acceptation de sa juridiction obligatoire, la CIJ (arrêt du 26 novembre 1984, REC., p. 419), tout en rappelant „le droit, inhérent à tout acte unilatéral, d'un Etat de changer la teneur de sa déclaration ou d'y mettre fin" a conclu que „les Etats-Unis ont néanmoins assumé une obligation irrévocable à l'égard des autres Etats qui acceptent la clause facultative, en déclarant formellement et solennellement que tout changement semblable ne prendrait effet qu'après l'expiration des six mois de préavis". Elle n'a pas hésité par ailleurs à transposer aux engagements unilatéraux le régime des traités par application du principe de bonne foi (REC., p. 420).

[34] En ce sens, J.D. SICAULT, *op. cit.*, *supra* note 2, p. 654.

[35] M. VIRALLY (*Sur la notion d'accord*, dans: FESTCHRIFT FÜR RUDOLF BINDSCHEDLER, pp. 159–172) écrit très justement: «Dans les ingrédients du jeu politique, la confiance joue un rôle

son prix aux engagements unilatéraux, et qui fait que l'Etat hésitera à revenir sans raison majeure (le changement fondamental de circonstances, notamment) sur un engagement unilatéral.

La publicité qu'il peut donner à cet engagement a non seulement pour objet de porter à la connaissance des intéressés un engagement dont ils peuvent tirer avantage, mais d'attester publiquement de sa sincérité. C'est dans ce but qu'il peut être tenté de renforcer la crédibilité de son engagement en l'entourant de formes solennelles qui, en vertu du principe de parallélisme des formes, l'obligerait à suivre la même procédure s'il lui venait à l'esprit de la révoquer (on pense à la déclaration égyptienne de 1957 sur le canal de Suez enregistrée auprès du Secrétaire général des Nations-Unies). Mais de toute façon, il est des engagements unilatéraux qu'il est politiquement inconcevable de révoquer, sauf à se mettre au ban de la Communauté internationale, par exemple l'engagement de ne pas user le premier de l'arme nucléaire.

20. La révocabilité théorique de l'engagement unilatéral se trouve ainsi, dans la pratique, réduite à peu de choses et la différence sur ce point avec l'engagement conventionnel s'estompe, d'autant plus qu'il se développe, dans les milieux politiques, un courant de pensée, regrettable mais persistant, selon lequel les traités en vigueur sont en permanence «renégociables». Il reste, malgré tout, que souvent on cherche à consolider l'engagement unilatéral en l'insérant dans un lien conventionnel, l'acceptation par son bénéficiaire d'une «promesse» unilatérale créant entre eux un lien conventionnel irrévocable. On notera que cette interprétation n'est pas en contradiction avec l'idée de base selon laquelle la valeur obligatoire de l'engagement unilatéral n'est pas subordonnée à son acceptation mais découle de la volonté de son auteur: dans l'hypothèse de la consolidation, l'engagement était unilatéral; par son acceptation il devient conventionnel; on notera également que cette situation est plus plausible pour les engagements à portée individuelle que pour les engagements à portée générale, comme la renonciation aux essais nucléaires, censée promise à la communauté internationale toute entière; on notera enfin que l'intérêt de cette consolidation pour l'auteur de l'engagement unilatéral est sans doute moins de la rendre irrévocable que d'obtenir par cette contractualisation des contreparties que le caractère initialement unilatéral de son engagement ne lui avait pas permis de négocier.

---

considérable. C'est sa présence qui convainc chaque acteur de la probalité que la promesse donnée sera tenue, parce qu'il croit à l'existence chez son auteur d'une volonté en ce sens».

* * *

21. Ainsi, par rapport à l'exigence fondamentale de la stabilité des rapports internationaux, l'engagement unilatéral assure des garanties de solidité comparables à celles de l'engagement conventionnel. Si la voie conventionnelle, forte de l'irrévocabilité que lui confère la réciprocité des engagements souscrits, reste «la voie normale»[36] des actes internationaux, c'est essentiellement parce que seule elle permet, par la négociation, de concilier les intérêts divergents des Etats. La voie unilatérale n'est qu'un palliatif lorsque la négociation n'apparaît pas possible. Mais le régime des engagements unilatéraux, emprunté à celui, plus élaboré, des traités, n'en est pas très différent[37]. Ce rapprochement n'est pas seulement le fruit d'une propension de l'interprète à la facilité, appliquant aux situations moins connues ce qui est déjà établi pour les situations plus connues. Il correspond à une inspiration commune, les deux types d'engagement trouvant leur fondement, comme on a essayé de la démontrer, dans le principe d'autonomie de la volonté, et leur garantie dans celui de la bonne foi. Faut-il aller plus loin et, à la suite d'une étude récente[38], «voir dans le droit des traités une partie ... du droit des actes étatiques unilatéraux»? Le présent article aidera peut être le lecteur à se faire une opinion sur cette question, volontairement provocatrice.

---

36 Selon la Chambre de la CIJ dans l'affaire du Différend frontalier entre le Burkina Faso et le Mali, arrêt du 22 décembre 1986, REC., p. 574.

37 Comme le reconnaissent P. DAILLIER et A. PELLET, DROIT INTERNATIONAL PUBLIC, LGDIP, Paris (1994), p. 358. Sur les aspects de ce régime, non abordés dans cette étude, relatifs à l'interprétation et aux conditions de validité des engagements unilatéraux, *voir* J.D. SICAULT, *op. cit.*, *supra* note 2.

38 J. COMBACAU, LE DROIT DES TRAITÉS, Paris (1991), p. 122.

THE EFFECT OF RESOLUTIONS OF INTERNATIONAL ORGANIZATIONS

by

INGRID DETTER

There is one subject which is much overlooked by international lawyers and yet which I personally always found fascinating. This is the subject of the legal effect of the resolutions of international organizations.

When I worked on my second doctoral thesis on *Law Making of International Organizations*,[1] I realized that there was one inspiring lawyer, an eminent professor, who had analyzed and considered various legal implications of such resolutions; this eminent lawyer was Professor Krzysztof Skubiszewski. I sought to find everything I could that this famous professor had written, a task which was not always easy. Much was published in Polish, a language which I read with difficulty. However, there was an important article in the *British Yearbook* that Professor Skubiszewski had written on the subject.[2] Later, Professor Skubiszewski produced some important reports in the publications of the *Institut*.[3]

There had been some early articles by Sloan,[4] Virally,[5] and Vallat,[6] but the subject had, on the whole, escaped attention. This is all the more surprising considering that numerous powerful and important organizations had been created in 1945 to form the United Nations system with all its specialized agencies. Even earlier, the subject had certainly deserved some attention as other organizations, like the Universal Postal Union and the International Telecommunications Union, had existed for nearly a hundred years and had considerable powers to bind the member States by their resolutions. In 1945 these organizations, such as the International Labour Organization created in 1919, were incorporated into to the United Nations network as specialized agencies.

---

1 Published by Norstedt, Stockholm (1965).

2 BRITISH YEARBOOK OF INTERNATIONAL LAW (1965–1966).

3 II ANNUAIRE DE L'INSTITUT (1977) at 36–103; I ANNUAIRE DE L'INSTITUT (1985) at 29–358.

4 B. SLOAN, *The Binding Force of a "Recommendation" of the General Assembly*, BRITISH YEARBOOK OF INTERNATIONAL LAW (1948).

5 *La valeur juridique des recommendations des organisations internationales*, ANNUAIRE FRANÇAIS DE DROIT INTERNATIONAL (1960).

6 *The Competence of the United Nations General Assembly*, 97 RECUEIL DES COURS DE L'ACADÉMIE DE DROIT INTERNATIONAL DE LA HAYE (1959) at 230.

Later, other international lawyers, academics like Seidl-Hohenveldern[7] and Dupuy,[8] took an interest in this subject and their writings contributed to renewed discussion.

When the European Communities were created in 1952 (the European Coal and Steel Community by the Paris Treaty), and in 1958 (the European Economic Community and Euratom by the Rome Treaties), the subject of the effect of the resolutions of organization became even more pertinent as the Communities, later the Community and, later still, the European Union, enjoyed considerable power to bind the member States and even individuals and enterprises in the territories of the member States. Floods of books and articles appeared, largely on the so called "supranational character" of the European organization(s), but rarely on the qualities and characteristics of the regulatory power.

I. UNILATERAL CHARACTER OF RESOLUTIONS

What is then so fascinating about decisions and resolutions of international organizations? Why was it that I found it even more inspiring and rewarding than my first doctoral thesis, the one written at Oxford, which had dealt with the treaties of international organizations,[9] another a subject of great theoretical and practical interest.

The reason that makes resolutions of organizations warrant special attention may be that it is resolutions which are unilateral measures, taken *vis-à-vis* the member States, and it is such measures which may acquire an authoritative character. In other words, resolutions of international organizations belong to a field where an organization, created by some States, may gain a position of authority with regard to its own founders; this in itself is an intriguing phenomenon, almost as if a company in its capacity as a legal person would acquire the power to order its own founders to pursue certain action.

From a legal point of view with a focus on the root of an obligation, resolutions are *unilateral*, that is to say, they emanate from one body, from the

---

7 *International Economic Soft Law*, 163 RECUEIL DES COURS DE L'ACADÉMIE DE DROIT INTERNATIONAL DE LA HAYE (1979) at 176.

8 R.J. DUPUY, *Droit déclaratoire et droit programmatoire: de la coutume "sauvage" à la "soft law"*, L'ÉLABORATION DU DROIT INTERNATIONAL PUBLIC (1974) at 140.

9 This first doctoral thesis concerned the *Treaty Making Power of International Organizations*, and was partly published in BRITISH YEARBOOK OF INTERNATIONAL LAW (1962); it dealt with bilateral acts of organizations and specifically with the question as to which organ is invested with the capacity to bind organizations by agreements and treaties.

organization, and they are directed to States. This means that such acts cannot be reduced, as some did in the early phase of the theory of organizations, to mere disguised treaties.[10]

II. IMPLIED POWERS

Another reason why the legal effects of resolutions of international organizations are of practical, and not only theoretical interest is that States themselves appear to overlook the power that an organization enjoys – by the treaty that the States have concluded for its establishment or by the so called "implied powers" which may authorize any act reasonably necessary for the fulfilment of the objectives of the organization, and which thus cover a considerable field of action.

III. FINANCIAL IMPLICATIONS

The third reason why it is interesting to assess the legal effect of resolutions is that such acts may engage States to *financially* defray any cost incurred by such resolutions – although such effects are often far away from the consideration of States as they hear, or take part in, decisions of organizations.

IV. EMPOWERED ORGAN

When we discuss resolutions of international organizations, the turn of phrase may be important: which organ does, in fact, take decisions and resolutions of international organizations? Of course, all this depends on the constituent document of the organization, usually a treaty which serves both as a Treaty between the Contracting States, and as a Constitution of the organization itself.[11]

If the organ which makes resolutions is one where all member States are represented, it would seem to some, that the representatives of States are just taking a self-binding measure. But when a restricted organ passes the resolution, the unilateral character becomes more pronounced and it is clear that the resolution is directly imputed to the organization and not to the member States.

---

[10] As does, for example, H. BLIX, in his TREATY MAKING POWER, Norstedt (1960).

[11] *See* I. DETTER, LAW MAKING BY INTERNATIONAL ORGANIZATIONS, Norstedt (1965) at 23 on the two-fold function of the Constitution of an organization.

V. PRIMARY AND OPERATIVE ACTS

There are a number of distinctions to be made at the outset of any discussion about acts of an organization. First of all, some acts obviously concern the staff, headquarters and budget. Numerous acts concerning the very functioning of an organization bind the member States as any organization must have the implied power to organize its own affairs so that it can function. Secondly – and I think this is an important point – questions concerning the budget can be dealt with by decisions which, of course, must bind the member States although such decisions can hardly been called "internal": they are directly addressed to the member States.

In one of my works[12] I introduced the term *primary* acts for these initial and recurring decisions, on headquarters, staff and budget that all organizations have to take to carry out their functions. *Internal* did not seem to be an appropriate and adequate term as some resolutions, like those on the budget, are directed to member States. **Primary acts** would perhaps be a useful label, implying that these were acts that *all* organizations have to take before they start acting; further characteristics of these acts are that they are extremely similar and quasi-identical in their *type* in *all* organizations.

Once organizations have been set up and arranged their headquarters, their staff and, in principle at least, their budget, they will begin taking another form of decisions. These are the decisions which bring the organizations nearer to the objectives. I have called them **operative acts**, since they are precisely designed to further the operations of the organizations. By definition –as organizations have different and heterogeneous objectives – operative acts will be *different* in all organizations and rarely similar. For example, the World Health Organization will promote, by its operative acts, the regulation and improvement of health in the world coupled with the prevention of disease and epidemics; the Universal Postal Union will, by its operative acts, further a coherent and functional system of transmitting mail from and to the various countries of the world.

One would perhaps have expected the term **secondary acts** to follow **primary acts**. **Secondary acts** conveys a sense of hierarchically less important acts, subordinated, in some sense, to the **primary acts**. But this is not so in the case of international organizations: although the primary acts form the framework within which the organizations will work, it is the operative acts which are, by far, the most important ones. Therefore, they must

---

12 *See ibid.*

be given an appropriate name which indicates that it is these which make the organizations achieve their objective, *i.e. operative acts*.

VI. COMPULSORY DECISIONS AND OPTIONAL RECOMMENDATIONS

We may consider whether the act appears to be a **decision** or a **recommendation**. Naturally, the terminology is not decisive. Yet, if an act *pretends* to be a decision it can only, in my opinion, be binding if there is provision for such binding effect in the constitutive document.

My point is based on the simple but often overlooked argument that the member States cannot ever be bound by an act when they have not been aware – or at least did not have what we may call constructive knowledge of – that they could be bound by such an act. Thus, they are bound by acts authorized in their constitution and by acts implied in that document. States which found an international organization are therefore bound by all reasonable decisions, taken within the constituent document, even if such acts fall within the implied powers and were not specifically enumerated in the constitution. However, in all cases States must be reasonably able to foresee by which acts they will be bound. If that is a summary of how one may view the two main types of acts of international organizations, it remains to analyze the numerous subcategories of acts.

The most rewarding field of inquiry is found among the operative acts. These fall into two broad types: those which are, on the face, **binding** and **compulsory** and those which are mere **recommendations** and thus consist of facultative measures. This would seem to imply the rapid deduction that the first group is binding and the second group is not. However, the situation is not so simple and numerous writers have pretended to find a source of obligation also for the so called recommendations.

A wave of articles appeared,[13] referring to **soft law**, or a sort of "not quite binding law" which seemed to flow from recommendations. Dupuy called it "green law" (*droit vert*), or "fluid law" (*droit flou*). But how could this happen and how could it be that measures, named in the records as recommendations, become binding. In a pragmatic way, writers studied the behaviour of States and noted that in many cases States actually followed these recommendations as if they had been binding.

It became important to clear up some misunderstandings: by obeying an act one cannot deduce its compulsory nature. In other words, States, and

---

13 *See* for example, the articles cited in the initial *supra* notes 7–8.

others, may abide by a facultative measure but this does not prove that they were under any obligation to do so; a facultative measure still remains facultative and is not binding in law.

However, there are many other occasions when so called "recommendations" imply binding measures, and other situations when they clearly lead to a development of binding law.

VII. ARE RECOMMENDATIONS EVER BINDING?

The most difficult problem, on which there is little consensus among international lawyers, is whether recommendations actually entail legal obligations. To me, it seems that this can never be the case as the constitution of organizations[14] never uses this term for binding measures. There are normally other ways to explain why the recommendations **appear** binding.

A. Resolutions on Primary Matters

Resolutions on *primary* matters are generally obligatory. By implied powers enjoyed by the organization, there is always a right to arrange the internal and budget questions by decisions which clearly have binding legal effect. The founders of an organization must intend to give that organization the necessary means to start functioning. Even if such powers are not spelt out in the treaty which sets up the organization, resolutions on such matters are binding. As mentioned above, the matters dealt with are not merely **internal** as budgetary question – of the utmost direct relevance to the contributing members States – are included in this category.

If then an organization uses the term "recommendation" to organize some primary matters, the measure is still binding since it concerns such ordinary matters although the wrong term may have been used. Like in the law of treaties, it is not the term employed which is decisive but the contents; and measures concerning all primary matters may certainly be compulsory and entail legal effects within the organization and *vis-à-vis* the member States.

B. Resolutions Reflecting *lex lata*

One basis for subsequent, or even immediate obligation of States, is that they **recognize** that the subject matter of the recommendation concerns, or

[14] Except for the now discarded terminology of the European Coal and Steel Community under the Paris Treaty of 1952. *See* LAW MAKING, *op. cit., supra* note 11, Chapter VI.

forms part of, rules of *lex lata*, that is to say they already form part of the binding body of law in international society, for example by repeating what is already embodied in treaties.[15] One particular group of resolutions, now increasingly frequent in organizations like the United Nations, consists in acts designed to make States cease a particular action. These resolutions may concern restraint of specific action in a specific situation. Such resolutions are often taken in the case of war or aggression, demanding that States refrain from military action.

Other resolutions, often in the form of explicit recommendations, concern exhortations to undertake specific action, and these are thus acts which have a positive aspect, as those which concern restraint could be viewed as negative.

An important distinction must be made: if the act is taken as a recommendation it is not binding, since States must be able to rely on the ordinary meaning of words.[16] It will appear to be binding if, for example, it states that "aggression is forbidden". On the other hand, beyond such reflection of *lex lata* if the act is called a "decision" it will be binding but only on the condition that the constitution of the organization confers such binding effect on certain acts: again this is important for the paramount requirement of the foreseeability of the law that States enjoy, as all subjects do under any legal system; they must **know** by which acts they become bound.

Recommendations may also reflect customary law.[17] An overwhelming vote of the General Assembly may be an indication that a legal rule exists but it is no conclusive proof:[18] all situations must be examined on their merit.

If the recommendations in these cases reflect already existing law it is, naturally, not recommendations which are binding in these cases, by their own force: they are binding by the underlying source of obligation in treaties or in customary law.

---

[15] As for example, the Declaration on Rights and Duties of States, or the Friendly Relations Declaration; *see* further I. DETTER, FINANCE AND PROTECTION OF INVESTMENT IN DEVELOPING COUNTRIES, Gower (1987) 2nd ed.

[16] As emphasized also in the CONVENTION ON TREATIES (1960).

[17] *See* R.-J. Dupuy in the *Texaco Case*, JDI (1977) at 376, 379, speaking of an *opinio juris* reflecting already existing law, in the event of the existence of customary law. Note that I myself have adopted a very limited view of the contents customary law, virtually restricting it to cases where there is a *territorial connection*, such as in rights of passage, law of the sea, etc. Most other cases of alleged "customary law" can often be better explained by reference to categories like "natural law", *see infra*, and, further, I. DETTER, INTERNATIONAL LEGAL ORDER, Dartmouth at 197 ff.

[18] *Contra, M. Sørensen Principes de droit international public*, RCADI (1960) at 99: "une preuve concluante de l'existence de la norme juridique qu'elle formule". But elsewhere, on the following page, 100, in the same Hague Course, Sørensen states "it faut se mettren garde contre toute tendance à attribuer à l'Assemblée Générale un pouvoir législatif."

C. Resolutions Reflecting Natural Law

An important, and grossly overlooked, possibility, is that recommendations reflect rules of **natural law**, which are always binding. Such rules are few, but certainly are an important source of law. This is not a category which, as some think, is inflexible but one which may change with the social needs of different time, in other words, this is what is necessary for States to live together in international society.[19] This case is particularly important if, for example, the United Nations recommends action or restraint in the field of humanitarian law in armed conflict. Few such rules can be explained as binding unless we resort to the basis of natural law: the category of customary law appears as particularly inappropriate as we would have to rely on **negative custom**, that is to say, proof that belligerents have not normally committed, for example, atrocities in the field to explain why certain action is forbidden by International Law.[20]

In my view, natural law forms an important source of law and contains the necessary general principles, maxims, and certainly rules on ethics which so often form part of so called recommendations of international organizations, especially of the General Assembly of the United Nations. But if a recommendation of the General Assembly deals with fundamental human rights or basic rules of humanitarian rules in war, such a recommendation may be binding albeit the basis of obligation is the *natural law*, and not the recommendation itself.

Resolutions on apartheid, regarded as binding long before any conventions were concluded on the matter, may illustrate that the content of natural law is not a stationary, but a dynamic category, which adapts to the needs of the times.

D. The Relevance of Interpretation

Some writers claim that organizations are entitled to authoritative interpretation of their own powers.[21] But an organization obviously cannot enlarge its own competence by anything beyond what is implied[22] or results from the *compétence de la compétence*.[23] States can **accept** such interpre-

---

19 *See* in detail, I. DETTER, *op. cit., supra* note 17, at 197.
20 *See* I. DETTER, LAW OF WAR, Cambridge (1987), 2nd ed. forthcoming 1996.
21 *E.g.* I. BROWNLIE, PRINCIPLES OF PUBLIC INTERNATIONAL LAW, 4th ed. OUP at 696.
22 *See* I. DETTER, LAW MAKING, *op. cit., supra* note 11, at 24, Chapter I.
23 *Ibid.*

tations and then become bound by their own *unilateral pledge*,[24] an important source of law often overlooked by international lawyers. Interpretations alone can never be binding unless subsumed under an already binding framework.

E. Later Unilateral Pledges

1. Behaviour

It is less certain whether States can later be bound by their mere behaviour which somehow would be absorbed by **custom**.[25] I have often criticized[26] the notion of customary law which has increasingly become a "dustbin" for rules that international lawyers know are binding but for which they cannot find a convenient slot or for the binding force of which they cannot find a reasonable explanation.

Some claim that acts of this category **become** binding if they are repeated, or even cited,[27] and especially if they are repeated frequently. As often before, some rely heavily on custom. A recommendation in this field, often repeated, may **reflect** custom,[28] but is more appropriately viewed as an expression for a law which is to be made, *de ferenda*, and not for a *lex lata*. To see things otherwise would be to ignore the right of States to make disclaimers.[29]

2. Unilateral Pledges

It is clear that States can often bind themselves by a unilateral declaration: such a declaration with regard to the interpretation of the Constitution of an organization is clearly binding in law.

Thus, there are situations when States can become bound by repeated recommendations but not by virtue of the force of the recommendation, which remains facultative, but by virtue of subsequent acts with effect in law.

---

24 *See* I. DETTER, THE CONCEPT OF INTERNATIONAL LAW, Norstedt (1994), 2nd ed. (1995), at 102 and 105, and *infra* text to note 30.

25 As *see supra* note 17 and claims G.I. TUNKIN, TEORIA MEZHDUNARONOGO PRAVA (171); *cf.* N.A. KRYLOV, MEZHDUNARODNOE PRAVA (1947) at 24.

26 *See* I. DETTER, THE CONCEPT, *op. cit., supra* note 24.

27 O. SCHACHTER, *The Quasi-Juridical Role of the Security Council and the General Assembly*, AJIL (1969) at 96; D. JOHNSON, *The Effect of Resolutions of the General Assembly of the United Nations*, GYIL (1955–1956) at 97.

28 B. SLOAN, *The Binding Force of a Recommendation of the General Assembly of the United Nations*, BYIL (1948) at 19.

29 *Cf.* SEIDL-HOHENVELDERN, INTERNATIONAL ECONOMIC LAW, I at 196.

By ignoring the common and convenient way that States can bind themselves by unilateral pledges,[30] some international lawyers have difficulty identifying **at which point** States become bound by repeated recommendations, but clear, unequivocal acceptance ought to provide some guidance.

i. Technical Standards

Such unilateral pledges are most common when organizations propose or **recommend certain technical rules**, such as Codes for economic behaviour,[31] especially for multinational enterprises,[32] but also for commodity problems,[33] preferences,[34] Liner Conferences,[35] and **standards**, very common and hardly noticed by international lawyers as an important source of law. By such standards States may accept blinding obligations through what is essentially mere recommendations or proposals. Other standards have a high technical contents. We are thus thinking of standards like the size of a metre, the weight of a kilo,[36] and to give more modern examples, the ISO standards set up by the International Organization of Standardization in Geneva, food standards adopted by the Food and Agriculture Organization or by the World Health Organization, both specialized agencies of the United Nations,[37] or even the type of standard required by ISBN for the allocation of a specific number to this book.

---

30 *See* in detail, I. DETTER, THE INTERNATIONAL LEGAL ORDER, *op. cit., supra* note 17, at 191 ff. For example, *see* the acceptance of recommendations by France within the Trusteeship framework in 1946, *ibid.* at 233; the acceptance by Austria of the League of Nation recommendation concerning the Hungarian border, 9 LNTS (1923) at 209 and ff. *Cf.* I. DETTER, THE MOGUL case, 27 PCIJ (1923) at 122.

31 Some of these recommendations belong to a more nebulous category, and concern declarations of targets to be reached by programmatic declarations on general action.

32 For example, Resolution 3281 (XXIX) of the General Assembly of the U.N. on the Charter of Economic Rights and Duties of 1974; for comments in literature on this resolution, *see* I. DETTER, THE INTERNATIONAL LEGAL ORDER, *op. cit., supra* note 17 at 218. *See* also, the *ILO Tripartite Declaration on Principles Concerning Multinational Enterprises and Social Policy* (1978), E/C.10/AC2/8 1978; 15 ILM (1976) at 969, 17 ILM (1979) at 1527; the EC Code for Subsidies of Multinational Enterprises 1977, 1986 and later revisions, KEESING'S ARCHIVES (1977) 21256; and *the ICC Principles Regarding Multinational Enterprises* (1974) with later revisions, 191/93.

33 UNCTAD's General Code for Commodities, TD/CODE TOT/197.

34 For example, by GATT Resolutions. On GATT, *see* T. FLORY, LE GATT (1968) at 282.

35 UNCTAD Code of Conduct for Liner Conferences, 13 ILM (1974) at 917, with later revisions.

36 Set by the International Institute of Weights and Measures which does not enjoy any proper power of "decision."

37 FAO issues the ALINORM standards; FAO has no power of decision; FAO and WHO issue jointly the *codex alimentarius*; again, WHO has regulatory powers, *see* I. Detter, LAW MAKING, *op. cit., supra* note 17. Chapter IV, but this power is not allocated for this field but other matters.

Such standards tend to become immediately effective. The reason why such standards are generally accepted by unilateral undertaking of States without much ado and without much problem is that such standards, of a prevailing technical nature, are necessary or, at least, most useful, for the efficient functioning of international society.

ii. Pre-Standards

Other types of recommendations appear to form a pool from which States can draw if they wish to accept a proposal as binding by their own individual unilateral pledge. Such a pool of recommendations may be called pre-standards.

F. Irrelevance of Voting Patterns

In certain cases writers have argued that recommendations would, somehow, be binding as they reflect the views of the world,[38] and would have law making effect.[39] Numerous writers have subscribed to these theories and yet these represent a most dangerous attitude to the security of law in international society. The reason for special caution is that it is necessary to restrict compulsory acts of organizations to those which actually have such effect by virtue of their constitution. But what is so important to refute with regard to the importance of voting and the quantity of votes, is the simple fact, so often overlooked by writers, that at the moment when a State is voting it does not know the outcome of the voting. Not until afterwards will a State realize that its vote coincided with an "overwhelming" majority. But how can that affect the obligatory nature of the act on which it has voted? Perhaps many States would have voted differently if they knew they risked being bound by the resolution? In other words, we will only undermine the work of international organizations if we impute binding force to resolutions on the mere technical basis of quantity of votes.

Thus, not even a unanimous vote can create legal obligations in the case where there is no provision for binding acts under the constitution.[40] Consensus is sometimes mistaken for unanimity,[41] but it rather hints at even less legal obligations as there is no basis for any legal obligation in the constitu-

---

38 MARCOFF, *Sources de droit international de l'espace*, 168 RCADI (1980) at 79.

39 I. BROWNLIE, *op. cit., supra* note 21, at 14.

40 S. BASTID, *Observations sur une étape dans le développement progressif et la codification des principes du droit international*, RECUEIL GUGGENHEIM (1968) at 144.

41 A. CASSESE, *Consensus and Some of Its Pit-Falls*, 58 RIVDI (1975) at 760.

ent document.[42] Nor can individual voting be a substitute for the unilateral pledge which I claim may bind a State: by its vote the State does not conclude any form of contract with the organization or with other States.[43] To take any other view, we would again ignore the fact that the State is not aware of entering into any contract or into any other legal obligations *at the time of voting*. In other words, as confirmed by France after a discussion on the legal value of the voting in the case of Klaus Barbie, a vote in the General Assembly is not opposable to any State.[44]

Nor does subsequent behaviour entail obligations of States unless they make any form of formal unilateral pledge, as mentioned above.[45] But estoppel,[46] a devise occasionally useful in English law, may not be widely known or widely used in international law;[47] it may be useful to explain the value of a subsequent unilateral undertaking, but not of behaviour in general. As this principle is not known, or little known, in States which have not to any degree accepted the English legal system, it would also lead to further legal uncertainty if such a national legal device were relied on to suggest a further legal obligation in international society.

It would thus seem that recommendations of organizations are binding only by *appearance*, or because the wrong term has been suggested, or because they reflect *lex lata* or natural law, or, after proposals have been accepted by unilateral formal pledges by States.

To impute greater legal force to recommendations is to distort the valuable firm set of rules of international law. If we dilute the law by categories which are *nearly binding*, we will only create legal uncertainty, general confusion among States and, eventually, contempt for our own discipline, that of international law.

---

42 *Contra*, LASSAN, *Le consensus dans la pratique des Nations Unies*, AF (1974).

43 *Contra*, ASAMOAH, THE LEGAL SIGNIFICANCE OF DECLARATIONS OF THE GENERAL ASSEMBLY (1966) at 70.

44 *See* further I. DETTER, INTERNATIONAL LEGAL ORDER, *op. cit., supra* note 17, at 241.

45 *See supra*, text to notes 21–24 and 30.

46 A simplified explanation of this legal term may suggest that it is a principle of self-exclusion by which a party may not contradict the veracity of statements or facts made public by statements, especially if others have changed their behaviour in reliance of these statements.

47 *See* D. BOWETT, *Estoppel before International Tribunals and its Relation to Requiescence*, BYIL (1957) at 176 ff.

Formalisme juridique et Cour internationale de justice

par

René Jean Dupuy

Une remarque préalable s'impose: il ne convient pas de donner à l'expression de formalisme juridique un sens forcément péjoratif. Le droit est une forme. Par conséquent nombreux sont les cas où faire du formalisme, c'est tout simplement appliquer le droit lorsqu'il est clair. Le piège serait de penser, comme les non spécialistes le reprochent aux juristes, que ce comportement judiciaire est toujours critiquable. Comme si l'attention rigoureuse attachée à la lettre du droit aboutissait toujours et nécessairement à en trahir l'esprit. Tout dépend des cas à résoudre et des époques qui inspirent la politique judiciaire d'une juridiction. La Cour internationale de justice n'échappe pas à ce choix.

Confromément à une conception souple de sa politique judiciaire, elle adoptera une démarche plus ou moins stricte dans l'application des normes juridiques à une affaire: soit elle limite son rôle au règlement du différend sans tenter de donner à sa décision une portée jurisprudentielle susceptible de dépasser le cadre de l'affaire, soit elle en profitera pour étendre sa mission au plan de la *juris dictio*. Le juge G. Guillaume a très clairement exposé cette alternance[1]. Il a montré l'opposition de deux grandes écoles de pensée. Pour les unes, la Cour, compte tenu du petit nombre d'affaires qu'elle a à connaître, se doit d'examiner, dans chaque cas, tous les problèmes de droit soulevés et de développer son raisonnement de manière plus élaborée que ne le font les tribunaux nationaux, et même de ne pas s'interdire des *obliter dicta*. Pour les tenants de cette méthode, elle seule permettrait le progrès du droit international.

Cette approche didactique est contestée par ceux qui considèrent que la juridiction internationale ne saurait s'écarter de la base purement consensuelle qui est la sienne. «Elle doit répondre avant tout aux préoccupations des Etats, c'est-à-dire trancher les différends qui lui sont soumis avec une autorité incontestée. Pour ce faire, la Cour doit user de prudence judiciaire à titre

---

[1] G. Guillaume, Transformations du droit international et jurisprudence de la Cour internationale de justice, in Les nouveaux aspects du droit international, Colloque de Tunis, Pedone, Paris (1994), pp. 175–192.

principal, elle n'a pas à examiner les arguments avancés à titre alternatif ou subsidiaire».

De fait, ces deux comportements se retrouvent à la C.I.J. mais on ne saurait soutenir qu'ils alternent au hasard des cas. Chacun d'eux s'est montré prédominant dans une période où des conditions d'ordre culturel encourageaient l'un ou l'autre.

Durant ces dernières décennies, la Cour de La Haye est passée par ces tendances opposées dans l'exercice de sa fonction contentieuse. Elle est partie de l'image qu'elle croyait devoir respecter d'une juridiction sourcilleuse, défenseur du droit pour lui-même, et poussant la volonté d'indépendance jusqu'à oublier qu'elle a été établie par son statut comme «l'organe judiciaire principal des Nations Unies». Telle est l'impression qu'elle donna en 1966 par son arrêt dans l'affaire du Sud Ouest Africain.

Le Liberia et l'Ethiopie, anciens membres de la Société des Nations, attaquaient le maintien de la présence de l'Union sud africaine sur ce territoire placé par la SDN sous le mandat de ce pays.

La Cour n'a pas reconnu le *locus standi* aux deux Etats requérants. La Cour se déclara compétente, mais la requête ne lui parut pas recevable faute d'intérêt pour agir du Liberia et de l'Ethiopie, ces deux Etats n'ayant pas ressenti de dommages propres, personnels et directs du fait de la présence de l'Union sud africaine. Cette décision n'avait été acquise que grâce à la voix du Président, sept juges s'étant prononcés pour le rejet de la requête et les sept autres, dont Philipp C. Jessup, ayant voté pour son admission. Le formalisme ainsi manifesté par la Cour était d'autant plus choquant que le Liberia et l'Ethiopie avaient un intérêt juridique incontestable à l'égard de la situation du Sud Ouest africain puisqu'ils étaient parties à l'accord de tutelle le concernant.

Cet arrêt causa une manière de scandale qui ne se limita pas au Tiers monde dont la Cour semblait ainsi se couper. En fait, la situation devait se débloquer avec les modifications intervenues dans la composition de la haute juridiction et l'entrée de juges issus de la Commission du droit international des Nations Unies et plus proches des courants d'idées qui les animaient. Tel était le cas, notamment, des juges Eduardo Jimenez de Arechaga et Manfred Lachs. La présidence de ce dernier fut décisive. Dès 1970, sous la présidence du Péruvien Bustamante y Rivero, la Cour entama un virage significatif. Dès lors, durant les années 70 et 80, elle va, dans son activité contentieuse, se faire l'écho des stratégies normatives déployées par le groupe des 77 à l'Assemblée générale. Celle-ci votera ainsi de nombreuses résolutions tendant à faire évoluer le droit international dans un sens répondant aux voeux des pays en recherche de développement.

I. LE COURANT NORMATIF

A. A vrai dire, le rejet du formalisme en vue de la consécration de la fonction prétorienne de la Cour et de son action dans le développement normatif s'est manifesté d'abord dans l'exercice de son activité consultative. Dès le début de celle-ci elle a donné des avis ayant pour objectif de consolider l'organisation mondiale et d'activer son dynamisme.

Très illustrant à cet égard l'Avis consultatif de 1949 sur l'aptitude de l'Organisation des Nations Unies à réclamer réparation à la suite de l'assassinat du Comte Bernadotte, médiateur envoyé par elle en Palestine. La Cour a reconnu la personnalité juridique internationale au bénéfice de l'ONU, en l'absence pourtant d'énonciation expresse de la Charte dans ce sens.

De même l'Avis de 1962 sur les dépenses qui refuse d'effectuer une sorte de contrôle de constitutionnalité interne des actes par lesquels l'ONU a décidé la création des premières forces du maintien de la paix (FUNU). La Cour n'a pas voulu débattre de la répartition des compétences entre l'Assemblée générale et le Conseil de sécurité, se contenant de constater que cette création répondait aux buts de l'ONU.

Dans les deux cas, la Cour s'affranchit de la lettre de la Charte et ne tient pas davantage compte de ses silences. Elle consacre ainsi une vision dynamique de la Charte et de l'Organisation elle-même, donnant à celle-ci les plus larges facultés d'action.

On doit rappeler que la position de la Cour dans l'exercice de sa fonction consultative s'inscrivait dans un contexte différent de celui de son rôle au contentieux. En effet, lorsqu'elle donne un avis, la Cour agit en tant qu'organe de l'Organisation (on est au sein de l'institutionnel), alors qu'elle n'est pas tout à fait dans la même situation lorsqu'elle remplit sa fonction contentieuse. Sans doute la Cour est-elle encore dans le système des Nations Unies mais, tout en y restant, elle est alors au service du règlement des différends interétatiques: l'institutionnel se met ici au service du relationnel.

B. Dans sa fonction contentieuse, justement, dans la période 1970–1986, on a pu avoir le sentiment que la Cour était une sorte de relais de la grande effervescence normative manifestée au sein de l'Assemblée générale pour adapter le droit international classique aux grandes tendances réformistes animées par les pays en recherche de développement. C'est ce qui explique que pendant cette période qui correspond à la phase durant laquelle ces pays définissaient des stratégies normatives, autour des concepts de communauté internationale et de droit au développement, notamment, la Cour a tenu à veiller à ce que ne s'introduise pas de hiatus entre le contenu de ses décisions jurisprudentielles et les orientations dégagées par ailleurs au sein de l'Assemblée générale. Révélateurs à cet égard sont les paragraphes 33 et 34 de l'arrêt rendu en 1970 dans l'affaire de la Barcelona Traction. Présence insolite de dispositions introduites dans une sentence qui ne semblait pas devoir la comporter, dans le souci évident de rassurer les pays en développement et d'effacer le souvenir humiliant de l'arrête sur le Sud Ouest Africain. Ces paragraphes font référence à des obligations *erga omnes* qui pèsent sur les Etats envers la communauté internationale dans son ensemble. On peut voir ici un coup de pouce donné par la Cour au *ius cogens* sans le dire expressément. Attitude de la Cour que l'on observe aussi dans certains égards, dans l'arrêt de 1980 sur le personnel diplomatique et consulaire des Etats-Unis à Téhéran.

On ne retrouve pas davantage, quoi qu'on en ait dit, de référence formelle au *ius cogens* dans l'arrêt Nicarague-Etats-Unis de 1986, même si la Cour est arrivée très près de cette évocation par la consécration qu'elle a reconnue aux principes particulièrement appréciés par le groupe des 77.

Le point d'orgue de cette évolution de la Cour vers une conception très ouverte de sa fonction normative a été certainement atteint dans cette affaire. Il faut rappeler que le Nicaragua invoquait la responsabilité directe des Etats-Unis soit pour un certain nombre de faits d'assistance à l'opposition intérieure (les contra), soit même pour des actes de guerre directe, comme le minage du port de Managua.

Cette affaire a donné lieu à deux arrêts, l'un de 1984 sur la compétence, l'autre de 1986 sur le fond.

En 1984, la Cour, selon une conception très peu formaliste, avait considéré que la Déclaration nicaraguayenne de reconnaissance de sa juridiction était valable, interprétation qui peut paraître contestable mais qui répondait au désir de la C.I.J. de se prononcer sur le fond. De surcroît, en 1986, la Cour, développant une conception dynamique de sa fonction, s'est dégagée de tout formalisme en donnant une acception très large à quelques principes, il est vrai, fondamentaux, du droit international contemporain. Sans doute ces principes sont-ils consacrés dans la Charte, mais ils ne pouvaient pas être considérés comme applicables comme tels au différend entre les deux pays en raison d'une réserve unilatérale des Etats-Unis frappant l'invocabilité des conventions multilatérales, réserve qui se trouvait placée dans la Déclaration américaine de la juridiction de la Cour.

Se trouvaient en cause les normes de non recours à la force, de non-ingérence et certains «principes élémentaires de droit humanitaire», selon la formulation de la Cour.

La C.I.J. a privilégié l'esprit par rapport à la lettre. Elle a tout d'abord déclaré que ces divers principes font partie du droit coutumier. On peut considérer qu'une telle position est légitime, mais il faut convenir qu'elle était assez audacieuse et qu'elle contrastait avec les positions beaucoup plus prudentes dont la Cour s'inspire à l'époque actuelle. En 1986, la Cour, avec beaucoup d'habileté, a contourné l'objection d'après laquelle on ne pouvait pas voir dans le non-recours à la force une règle coutumière compte tenu des violations multiples que la pratique apporte à son application.

La Cour a remarqué que chacune des atteintes à cette règle était accompagnée par les Etats qui s'y livraient, d'une reconnaissance explicite du caractère de principe du non-recours à la force dans les relations internationales. Elle observe dès lors que l'on ne peut soutenir que les violations du principe portent atteinte à son autorité. L'hommage rendu à la règle par ceux-là même qui la violent lui a donc paru exprimer l'*opinio juris*. Ainsi l'impossibilité de se référer à cette norme dans l'ordre conventionnel n'empêchait nullement, aux yeux de la Cour, d'y faire appel sur le plan coutumier dès lors que chaque fois qu'ils ont recours à la force, les Etats ont soin, soit de s'abriter derrière l'article 51 reconnaissant la légitime défense, soit derrière d'autres considérations, comme la légitimité des luttes de libération nationaliste.

On retrouve ici dans la démarche de la C.I.J. un thème cher à l'Assemblée générale des Nations Unies, laquelle a privilégié, dans le processus coutumier, l'*opinio juris* sur l'élément matériel constitué par la pratique effective. La répétition d'une idée dans des résolutions successives, est considérée comme portant témoignage de sa consécration par la conscience universelle.

La C.I.J. se livre, à propos du principe de non-ingérence, à une analyse qui permet également de l'asseoir dans le droit coutumier et de ne pas le limiter à une valeur conventionnelle puisée dans la Charte.

Parmi les principes que la Cour situe dans le droit coutumier, encore qu'ils soient proclamés dans la Charte, on relève aussi la légitime défense. L'autonomie de ce principe, en dehors de la lettre de l'article 51, trouve d'ailleurs une confirmation dans ce dernier qui le désigne comme «un droit naturel». Quant aux «principes élémentaires de droit humanitaire», le Cour les puise dans l'article 3 commun aux quatre Conventions de Genève de 1949, disposition à laquelle la Cour trouve un caractère non consitutif mais déclaratoire de principe existant préalablement. Elle avait déjà retenu ce type d'arguments dans son Avis consultatif de 1951 sur l'interdiction des réserves à la Convention sur le génocide de 1948.

Il y a lieu de souligner l'importance de l'arrêt de 1986 dans l'affaire Nicarague-Etats-Unis pour la consolidation des principes que la C.I.J. considère comme constituant les pierres d'angle du système juridique international contemporain. Dans cette décision, la Cour donnait un appui très sérieux à l'affermissement de ces règles et on a pu considérer qu'elle avait ainsi manifesté l'ampleur de la fonction normative de l'activité judiciaire.

On est donc dans cette jurisprudence aux antipodes du formalisme. Et l'on voit bien que la même Cour se détermine en fonction de sa composition et de la nature des affaires, certes, mais aussi suivant l'évolution de la communauté internationale au sein de laquelle elle a à régler des différends. Elle est conduite à adapter sa jurisprudence selon une conception variable de l'étendue de sa fonction judiciaire. Elle l'élargit ou la restreint en fonction de l'appréciation qu'elle fait de son rôle à un moment déterminé des relations internationales.

II. LE COURANT RESTRICTIF

Si la Cour, dans les années 70 et 80, a montré une tendance à donner à sa mission une portée extensive, elle semble, en revanche, durant ces dernières années, montrer une prudente réserve. Deux affaires témoignent de cette nouvelle préoccupation, celle de la Zone d'Aouzou, en 1993, et celle du Timor oriental, en 1995.

A. Dans la première, la zone, objet du différend, présente du point de vue spatial et économique un grand intérêt.

Dans leurs pièces écrites, et dans leurs plaidoiries, les parties ont insisté sur la qualification du litige.

Pour la Libye, aucune frontière n'existant à l'Est de Toummo, le rôle de la Cour était de décider de l'attribution des territoires respectifs, sur la base des meilleurs titres avancés de part et d'autre.

Pour le Tchad, en revanche, il existait déjà une frontière, celle qui résulte du Traité d'amitié et de bon voisinage conclu entre la Libye et la France, le 10 août 1955.

Aux yeux de la Libye, il s'agissait d'un conflit d'attribution territoriale, pour le Tchad, d'un conflit de délimitation.

La C.I.J. a déclaré: «Le différend soumis à la Cour, qu'on le qualifie de différend territorial ou de différend frontalier, est réglé de manière concluante par un traité auquel la Libye est une partie originelle et le Tchad, une partie ayant succédé à la France».

Le premier réflexe d'un juge avisé, face à un différend territorial sera logiquement d'examiner s'il existe entre les parties un traité réglant la question. Dans l'affirmative, il s'interrogera sur la validité et sur l'interprétation de ce traité.

La Cour a refusé de s'engager dans une appréciation approfondie des titres ou de l'effectivité, et s'est contentée de s'appuyer sur un instrument juridique formalisé, le Traité de 1955. Cet examen lui a suffi pour donner raison au Tchad parce que ce pays a pu prouver que l'accord était valide et que lui-même était successeur de la France, signataire originel. La Cour ne croyant pas utile ici de rechercher d'autres titres, souvent aléatoires, s'en tient à une méthode juridique stricte. Cette attitude est parfaitement fondée.

B. La Cour fait du formalisme juridique lorsqu'elle entend se prémunir contre la tentation de «faire du droit». Elle souhaite alors donner à sa fonction judiciaire une acception très restrictive par répugnance à rentrer dans des questions dont le traitement supposerait qu'elle s'engageât dans une oeuvre normative. Une interprétation restrictive de sa compétence s'inspire du refus de développer le droit, de céder à la séduction prétorienne. Dès lors plusieurs affaires de ce type se décident, dès le stade de l'appréciation de la compétence; tant il est clair que la meilleure façon pour la Cour d'éviter d'avoir à rentrer dans les débats substantiels qui solliciteraient la pulsion normative de sa fonction judiciaire, consiste, tout simplement, *in limine litis*, à se déclarer incompétente.

Il ne s'agit pas pour nous de se prononcer sur la légitimité de cette démarche, mais de constater que l'une des illustrations les plus nettes de cette tendance a été donnée par l'arrêt rendu par la Cour dans l'affaire du Timor oriental.

Sur la base d'une requête unilatérale, le Portugal avait mis en cause la responsabilité internationale de l'Australie au motif qu'elle avait conclu avec un Etat tiers, l'Indonésie, par ailleurs non lié par la clause facultative de juridiction obligatoire, un accord d'exploration et d'exploitation du pétrole dans la zone maritime comprise entre les côtes méridionales du Timor Est et de l'Australie septentrionale.

Sans s'engager dans les détails de l'affaire, on doit relever que si la Cour s'était déclarée compétente, elle aurait été amenée à se prononcer sur certaines implications du droit des peuples à disposer d'eux-mêmes et elle aurait dû, également, statuer sur le maintien de la qualité de puissance administrante du Portugal à l'égard du territoire du Timor oriental, envahi par l'Indonésie en décembre 1975.

On peut considérer que le fait, pour la Cour, de se prononcer sur l'extension et les applications du droit des peuples, à une époque où il est invoqué hors des situations coloniales ou post-coloniales, notamment en Europe centrale et orientale, pouvait présenter quelques aléas politiques.

Toujours est-il que, sans avoir à prendre parti sur le bien fondé de cet arrêt, on doit observer que la Cour a saisi l'occasion d'un argument d'incompétence soulevé par l'Australie, ce qui lui a permis d'éviter de rentrer dans l'examen du fond de l'affaire. La Cour n'a pas hésité à prendre des positions difficilement conciliables avec sa jurisprudence récente sur la même question, intervenue dans l'affaire du Nauru. Elle a considéré qu'elle ne pouvait connaître de la requête du Portugal sans impliquer la responsabilité internationale d'un Etat, tiers à l'instance, à savoir l'Indonésie dont on a déjà indiqué qu'elle n'avait pas reconnu sa juridiction.

Il s'agit là de l'argument dit «de la partie indispensable» d'après lequel, en l'absence d'un Etat tiers dont la responsabilité constituerait l'objet même du différend, la Cour ne peut pas statuer au fond.

Deux ans auparavant cependant, dans l'affaire de Nauru, la C.I.J. avait adopté une solution différente. Dans cette espèce, l'Australie avait tenté de se défendre en arguant de l'incompétence de la Cour, comme elle le fera en 1994 à propos du Timor. Dans les deux cas, l'Australie a utilisé le même argument, celui de la «partie indispensable», en se fondant sur la jurisprudence de **l'or monétaire à Rome**. Pour elle, admettre la compétence de la Cour à propos du Nauru, aurait eu pour effet de mettre directement en cause la responsabilité de deux autres Etats, la Nouvelle-Zélande et la Grande-Bretagne, alors qu'aucun d'eux n'avait accepté, pour cette affaire, la juridiction de la Cour. Manquaient donc à l'instance, deux parties indispensables dont on ne pouvait nier qu'elles fussent également impliquées dans l'affaire, étant toutes deux co-tuteurs. En fait, seule l'Australie entreprenait sur le terrain l'exploitation de phosphates. La Cour, en acceptant de n'examiner que la responsabilité de l'Australie, a déclaré pouvoir identifier clairement ce qui était imputable à ce pays et n'a pas retenu l'objection tirée de l'absence de deux autres Etats et a donc admis la recevabilité de la requête en responsabilité introduite par Nauru à l'encontre de l'Australie pour les dommages de caractère économique et écologique que ce pays lui avait causés du fait de l'exploitation du phosphate de l'île.

La Grande-Bretagne et la Nouvelle-Zélande, les deux Etats cités, limitaient leur participation à la tutelle à une réunion qu'ils tenaient annuellement avec l'Australie pour examiner les conditions d'exploitation des ressources naturelles de Nauru que seule l'Australie exploitait effectivement.

Dans cette affaire, contrairement à la position qu'elle adoptera deux ans plus tard à propos du Timor, la Cour a jugé que la qualité de cocontractants de la Nouvelle-Zélande et de la Grande-Bretagne, au même titre que l'Australie, ne l'empêchait nullement de connaître de la responsabilité australienne. La Cour a déclaré à l'Australie qu'elle pouvait isoler sa responsabilité de celle des deux autres Etats qui, eux, n'étaient pas parties à l'instance.

Dans l'affaire du Timor oriental, c'est en vain que le Portugal a repris cette argumentation en soutenant qu'il était possible d'examiner dans cette nouvelle affaire la responsabilité de l'Australie qui, en concluant un accord maritime avec l'Indonésie, a porté atteinte aux droits du peuple du Timor sur ses ressources naturelles. Les faits reprochés à l'Australie étaient en effet totalement indépendants de ceux pour lesquels l'Indonésie avait déjà été condamnée par le Conseil de sécurité et l'Assemblée générale des Nations Unies, après l'invasion et à s'être livrée à l'occupation par la force du territoire du Timor. Or la Cour n'a pas suivi cette argumentation du Portugal, a priori convaincante. Elle a, cette fois, considéré que la mise en cause de la responsabilité de l'Australie ne pouvait pas aller sans celle de l'Indonésie, alors pourtant que les faits reprochés à l'un et à l'autre Etat, étaient totalement distincts.

Cette contradiction de jurisprudence démontre que le recours au formalisme n'est ni une fin en soi, ni un travers systématique de la Cour; c'est un instrument de la politique judiciaire que, pour des raisons qui lui appartiennent (et qui peuvent ne pas être exclusivement juridiques) elle a décidé d'adopter dans une affaire déterminée.

Ainsi le formalisme juridique apparaît bien comme un moyen de la politique judiciaire de la Cour.

On peut notamment comprendre sa position dans l'affaire du Timor comme un refus d'envisager également la portée de certaines normes et notamment le caractère *erga omnes* de certains droits dont le droit des peuples à disposer d'eux-mêmes (encore que dans l'un des paragraphes de son arrêt, elle ait tenu à marquer qu'elle n'avait pas eu à l'égard de l'affirmation de ce caractère, de difficultés juridiques particulières).

Il est permis de considérer cette prudence judiciaire comme excessive étant donné le contexte général de l'affaire, et on ne peut s'empêcher de constater le très vif contraste de cette conception de la politique judiciaire de la Cour, avec celle qui prévalait naguère dans son sein, en particulier entre 1970 (*Barcelona Traction*) et 1986 (Aff. *Nicaragua-Etats-Unis*).

La Cour aurait-elle fait sien le sage conseil de Jules Renard: «Il faut avoir des idées arrêtées, mais pas toujours au même endroit»?

RESERVATIONS AND THE INTERNATIONAL *ORDRE PUBLIC*

by

JOCHEN ABR. FROWEIN

Introduction

Long before he became responsible for the foreign policy of his country Krzysztof Skubiszewski has been dealing with problems of international law-making. In the Encyclopedia of Public International Law he was responsible for the important entry *International Legislation.*[1] In the Institut de Droit international he did admirable research on the effect of resolutions by international organizations, particularly resolutions of the General Assembly of the United Nations.[2] With the changes brought about by the re-establishment of free and independent democracies in Central and Eastern Europe international law entered into a new phase. Skubiszewski has explained in detail how important a fabric of international treaties concluded by his country was for the stabilization of this new period.[3] This author, who advised the German delegation in 1970 at the conclusion of the Warsaw treaty, has witnessed the important development of German–Polish treaty relations since this first step in 1970 to the border treaty and the treaty on good neighbourliness of 1991.[4] Not only is the final treaty on the German question which came into force on 15 March 1991 part of the public order of Europe, but also the treaties between Germany and Poland.[5]

I. THE WILL OF THE STATE AND THE BINDING FORCE OF TREATIES

Treaties are commonly seen to be based on the will of the State, this will very much equated with the will of a human personality in concluding

---

1 R. BERNHARDT (ed.), ENCYCLOPEDIA OF PUBLIC INTERNATIONAL LAW, Vol. 2 (1985) at 1255–1262, appeared originally in: 5 *Instalment* (1983) at 97–104.

2 61:I ANNUAIRE IDI, Session of Helsinki (1985) at 29–358.

3 K. SKUBISZEWSKI, *Poland, Germany and Europe After 1989*, in: RECHT ZWISCHEN UMBRUCH UND BEWAHRUNG, FESTSCHRIFT FÜR R. BERNHARDT (1995) at 1305–1312.

4 J.A. Frowein, *Zur verfassungsrechtlichen Beurteilung des Warschauer Vertrages*, 18 JAHRBUCH FÜR INTERNATIONALES RECHT (1975) at 11–61.

5 J.A. FROWEIN, *Germany Reunited*, 51 ZAÖRV (1991) at 333, 339.

a contract under private law. For contracts under private law it is not doubtful that they remain binding even if the will of the person having concluded the contract later changes. This is of course likewise true for treaties under public international law, well expressed by the famous notion *pacta sunt servanda*. As the Vienna Convention on the Law of Treaties states in Article 26, every treaty in force is binding upon the parties to it and must be performed by them in good faith. Already this fundamental rule that a treaty remains binding even if the will of the State should later change is, although self-evident, an important restriction of "sovereignty" as sometimes used in political rhetoric.

Treaties as internal legislation develop in the course of time. There are different categories of treaties as to their dependence on the time factor. An extradition treaty or a treaty on friendship commerce and navigation may hardly be influenced by the time factor, at least in most of the technical provisions. This is quite different with treaties as the United Nations Charter, human rights treaties or other law-making treaties.

We have recently witnessed a strange phenomenon where States tried to protect themselves against the development of treaty rights through later evolutions. Under Article 3 para. 2 of the dispute settlement rules under the new WTO treaty the dispute settlement system is described as a central element in providing security and predictability to the multilateral trading system. The provision then adds:[6]

> "The Members recognize that it serves to preserve the rights and obligations of Members under the covered agreements, and to clarify the existing provisions of those agreements in accordance with customary rules of interpretation of public international law. Recommendations and rulings of the DSB cannot add to or diminish the rights and obligations provided in the covered agreements."

It would seem that particularly powerful States, as the United States, have insisted on this clause limiting what is sometimes considered to be the rather broad discretion of courts or other dispute settlement organs when they make use of rules of dynamic or evolutive interpretation.[7] However, even with the

---

[6] *Annex 2, Understanding on Rules and Procedures Governing the Settlement of Disputes*, 33 ILM (1994) at 1226.

[7] The European Court of Human Rights puts it as follows: "That the Convention is a living instrument which must be interpreted in the light of present day conditions is firmly rooted in the Court's case-law ... Such an approach, in the Court's view, is not confined to the substantive provisions of the Convention, but also applies to those provisions, such as Articles 25 and 46, which govern the operation of the Convention's enforcement machinery. It follows that these provisions cannot be interpreted solely in accordance with the intentions of their authors as ex-

rule indicated it is certainly beyond human possibilities to avoid evolutive interpretation with new facts and social conditions arising. The problem is well-known in internal law with the rules concerning interpretation included in special legislation. Particularly the history of the Preußisches Allgemeines Landrecht of 1794 confirms this position. The idea that there should be a formal prohibition to interpret the rules of the Landrecht had to be given up already before the codification came into force.[8]

II. INADMISSIBLE RESERVATIONS AND THEIR CONSEQUENCES

The Vienna Convention on the Law of Treaties has tried to find a compromise between the diverging views concerning the admissibility of reservations to multilateral treaties. Of particular importance is Article 19 which excludes reservations which are incompatible with the object and purpose of the treaty. However, since it is rare that an international court may decide on whether or not a reservation is admissible it is mostly left to the individual State to judge to what extent a reservation is in fact compatible with the object and purpose of the treaty. Although the matter is not fully clear from Article 20 of the Vienna Convention, in practice the rules concerning objections are also applied for reservations which are seen as incompatible with the object and purpose of the treaty.[9] Only where the State formulating an objection expresses the intention not to be bound *vis-à-vis* the State making the reservation the objection will exclude membership of both parties in their bilateral relations. In all other cases the consequence of the objection will be that the provisions to which the reservation relates will not apply as between the two States to the extent of the reservation as Article 21 para. 3 lays down.

The case of *Belilos v. Switzerland* decided by the European Court of Human Rights was the first case decided by an international tribunal where a reservation was declared to be null and void because it did not satisfy the specific requirements of Article 64 of the Convention. The European Court

pressed more than forty years ago." *Case of Loizidou v. Turkey*, 310 ECHR para. 71. The judgment dates of 23 March 1995.

[8] The judge was limited by the introduction of the ALR as follows: "Bei Entscheidungen streitiger Rechtsfälle darf der Richter den Gesetzen keinen anderen Sinn beilegen, als welcher aus den Worten und dem Zusammenhange derselben, in Beziehung auf den streitigen Gegenstand, oder aus dem nächsten unzweifelhaften Grunde des Gesetzes, deutlich erhellt."

[9] R. KÜHNER, VORBEHALTE ZU MULTILATERALEN VÖLKERRECHTLICHEN VERTRÄGEN (1986) at 220 ff.

of Human Rights held that the reservation entered by Switzerland was of a general nature prohibited by Art. 64 para. 1 and did not comply with the formalities laid down by Article 64 para. 2 of the European Convention on Human Rights providing for the enumeration of the provisions concerned. The Court held that the declaration by the Swiss government did not satisfy two of the requirements of Article 64 of the Convention, with the result that it must be held to be invalid. The Court then added the following:[10]

> "At the same time, it is beyond doubt that Switzerland is, and regards itself as, bound by the Convention irrespective of the validity of the declaration. Moreover, the Swiss Government recognised the Court's competence to determine the latter issue, which they argued before it."

With this short explanation the Court rejected the idea that a finding of invalidity concerning the reservation would result in the invalidity of the Swiss ratification of the European Convention on Human Rights. The dogma of the paramount will of the State when concluding the treaty might lead to that result.

In an even more dramatic context the European Court of Human Rights confirmed the Commission's position that Turkey had validly recognized the jurisdiction of the Commission and the Court under Articles 25 and 46 of the Convention and that specific restrictions added by Turkey to her declarations were null and void. Commission and Court based themselves on the character of the Convention as a public order treaty of Europe and both organs underlined the quality of the European Convention on Human Rights as a constitutional instrument of the European order.[11]

The Commission emphasized that Turkey had recognized the Commission's jurisdiction to decide on the validity of the Turkish restrictions and relied on the main intention of Turkey to be bound by the system.[12] The Court was even more outspoken. It stated that the respondent government must have been aware, in view of the consistent practice of Contracting Parties under Articles 25 and 46 to accept unconditionally the competence of the Commission and Court, that the impugned restrictive clauses were of questionable validity under the Convention system and might be deemed impermissible by the Convention organs. The fact that Turkey continued to file declarations indicated according to the Court a willingness on her part to run the risk that the limitation clauses at issue would be declared invalid by the

[10] *Belilos Case*, 132 ECHR, at 28, para. 60.

[11] *Case of Loizidou v. Turkey*, 310 ECHR; *Decision of the European Commission of Human Rights*, 68 DR at 216–253.

[12] *Ibid.* at 249.

Convention institutions without affecting the validity of the declarations themselves. *Ex post facto* statements by Turkish representatives according to which the declaration would be null and void could not, according to the Court, be relied upon to detract from the respondent government's basic intention to accept the competence of the Commission and Court.[13]

Within the European system for the protection of Human Rights the examples of Belilos and Loizidou stand for a clear recognition that States are not entitled to rely on their will to an extent which would undermine the public order system established by the Convention.

III. THE GENERAL COMMENT ADOPTED BY THE HUMAN RIGHTS COMMITTEE ON 11 NOVEMBER 1994

The Human Rights Committee under the Covenant on Civil and Political Rights adopted a General Comment on issues relating to reservations in 1994. This comment states that reservations are only admissible where they respect the fundamental rules of the Covenant on Civil and Political Rights. For reservations which are inadmissible the Committee indicates that they may be without legal effect.[14]

> "The normal consequence of an unacceptable reservation is not that the Covenant will not be in effect at all for a reserving party. Rather, such a reservation will generally be severable, in the sense that the Covenant will be operative for the reserving party without benefit of the reservation."

The Committee under the Covenant, by this statement, endorsed the rule confirmed by the European Commission and Court of Human Rights in the cases of Belilos and Loizidou. Several countries objected to the General Comment formulated by the Human Rights Committee. The United States underlined:[15]

> "The reservations contained in the United States instrument of ratification are integral parts of its consent to be bound by the Covenant and are not severable. If it were to be determined that anyone or more of them were ineffective, the ratification as a whole could thereby be nullified."

---

13 310 ECHR, para. 95.

14 CCPR/C/21/Rev. 1/Add. 6, 11 November 1994, at 7, para. 18.

15 Observations on General Comment 24 at 5 under 5, 16 HUMAN RIGHTS LAW JOURNAL (1995) at 422, 423.

The United Kingdom, without referring to the European developments, suggested that the only sound approach be the one adopted by the International Court of Justice in the Genocide case:[16]

> "A State which purports to ratify a human rights treaty subject to a reservation which is fundamentally incompatible with participation in the treaty regime cannot be regarded as having become a party at all – unless it withdraws the reservation."

This shows that on the worldwide level there is still a great reluctance by States to adopt the line now established within the system of the European Convention on Human Rights. This would have the consequence that participation in the global human rights treaties would be a matter of great uncertainty. Since there are many reservations which may raise difficult issues it is doubtful whether the position taken by the United States and Britain can be upheld.

IV. STATE PRACTICE AS TO INVALID RESERVATIONS

It is not generally taken into account that there is State practice available showing that there is a wide consensus among States of very different traditions to treat reservations as invalid under specific circumstances. To start with a rather recent example, Finland on 5 September 1995 objected to the Iranian reservation made upon the ratification of the Convention of the Rights of the Child and stated expressly:[17]

> "The Government of Finland further notes that the reservation made by the Government of the Islamic Republic of Iran is devoid of legal effect."

This is by no means a unique occurrence. When the Philippines entered a declaration to the U.N. Convention on the Law of the Sea, Australia declared that it cannot accept that this statement has any legal effect or will have any legal effect when the Convention comes into force. Australia added that it considers that the provisions of the Convention should be observed without being made subject to the restrictions asserted in the declaration of the Republic of the Philippines.[18] This example may be explained because the United Nations Convention on the Law of the Sea expressly prohibits any

---

[16] Observations by the United Kingdom on General Comment 24, para. 15, 16 HUMAN RIGHTS LAW JOURNAL (1995) at 424, 426.

[17] BUNDESGESETZBLATT [BGBl.] 1996, Part II at 232.

[18] BGBl. 1996, Part II at 622, 623.

sort of reservation in Art. 309. However, State practice as to invalid reservation occurs also where the reservation is not expressly prohibited by treaty.

The practice of rejecting reservations as null and void is not only of recent origin. When the Geneva Red Cross Conventions were ratified soon after 1949 many of the then communist countries made reservations to specific articles in the Convention on Prisoners and on the Protection of Civilian Persons in time of war. These reservations concerned the protection of the Prisoners Convention after conviction and the protection of both conventions as to the handing over of people to other powers. The United Kingdom government took the following position as to reservations concerning both conventions:[19]

> "I am instructed by Her Majesty's Government to state that whilst they regard all the above mentioned States as being parties to the above-mentioned Conventions, they do not regard the above-mentioned reservations thereto made by those States as valid, and will therefore regard any application of any of those reservations as constituting a breach of the Convention to which the reservation relates."

Similar declarations were made by Australia and New Zealand.[20] The declarations concerned are not open to any interpretation. The United Kingdom Government took the view that a State having ratified these fundamental rules for the protection of war victims cannot, by a reservation added to the instrument of ratification, validly limit the protection of the treaty.[21]

In the area of human rights treaties there are several examples of objections against reservations which make it clear that the objecting State considers the reservation as null and void and the State fully bound by its ratification. For the International Covenant on the Elimination of all Forms of Racial Discrimination objections formulated in that manner have been entered by Finland, France and Mexico.[22] Finland gave a detailed reasoning for its position amounting to the conclusion: "By making a reservation

---

19 BGBl. 1958, Part II at 66.

20 BGBl. 1959, Part II at 1078, 1079.

21 In 1985 the United Kingdom formulated its objection to similar reservations by Angola in a less clear manner, BGBl. 1986, Part II at 1030: "With reference to the reservation made by the Government of the People's Republic of Angola to Article 85 of the Convention relative to the Treatment of Prisoners of War, Her Majesty's Government, recalling their previous declarations in relation to similar reservations by other States, wish to state that, whilst they do not oppose the entry into force of the Convention in question between the United Kingdom and the People's Republic of Angola, they are unable to accept the reservation, because, in the view of the Government of the United Kingdom, this reservation is not of the kind which intending parties to the Convention are entitled to make."

22 *See* MULTILATERAL TREATIES DEPOSITED WITH THE SECRETARY-GENERAL, Status as at 31 December 1994 at 99, 100.

a State cannot contract out from universally binding human rights standards." France and Italy expressed the view that the U.S. reservation to the International Covenant on Civil and Political Rights by which the United States excluded the prohibition of the death penalty for persons under 18 years is not valid.[23] While France used the formula "not valid", Italy stated: "Therefore this reservation is null and void..."

The State practice indicated here is not limited to human rights treaties, however. Another area where many States have taken the view that incompatible reservations are null and void and do not modify the obligations undertaken by the ratification is the Vienna Convention on Diplomatic Relations of 1961. Declarations by Australia, Belgium, Canada, Denmark, France, Hungary, Ireland, New Zealand, Poland, Great Britain, to mention just some, clearly indicated that reservations were seen to be incompatible and therefore null and void.[24]

As the last example may be mentioned the reaction by Mexico to the reservation entered by the United States when ratifying the Genocide Convention. The U.S. reservation to Article IX stated that before any dispute may be submitted to the jurisdiction of the International Court of Justice the specific consent of the United States is required in each case but it added that nothing in the Convention requires or authorizes legislation or other action by the United States of America prohibited by the Constitution of the United States as interpreted by the United States.

Mexico, on 4 June 1990, objected in the following terms:[25]

> "The Government of Mexico believes that the reservation made by the United States Government to Article IX of the aforesaid Convention should by considered invalid because it is not in keeping with the object and purpose of the Convention, nor with the principle governing the interpretation of treaties whereby no State can invoke provisions of its domestic law as a reason for not complying with a treaty.
>
> If the aforementioned reservation were applied, it would give rise to a situation of uncertainty as to the scope of the obligations which the United States Government would assume with respect to the Convention. Mexico's objection to the reservation in question should not be interpreted as preventing the entry into force of the 1948 Convention between the [Mexico] Government and the United States Government."

---

[23] *Ibid.* at 128.

[24] *Ibid.* at 56, 57, 58, 59, 60 61.

[25] *Ibid.* at 1.

Evaluation

The survey carried out shows that there is a growing practice by the community of States to reject reservations as invalid where they are, according to the view of the State concerned, clearly incompatible with the fundamental rules of the treaty. There is one State which has never taken the position that a reservation can be treated as invalid. That is the United States, as far as matters could be researched.[26] However, the wide range of practice shows that many States will rely on the binding force of treaty rules and leave aside a reservation which they consider to be null and void. With the cases of Belilos and Loizidou decided by the European Court of Human Rights there exists important international case-law confirming the State practice referred to.

Where the rules of a treaty can be considered to form part of customary international law or even of *jus cogens* it is clear that States cannot, by ratifying the treaty and entering a reservation, derogate from these rules. This recognition is the basis of some of the objections concerned, particularly where they relate to human rights treaties. A good example is the Finnish position as to reservations concerning the Convention against Racial Discrimination quoted above.[27] However, many examples cannot be explained in this way. Neither specific rules concerning the treatment of prisoners of war nor of diplomatic relations fall into this category. The State practice indicated here must rather be understood as a recognition of the paramount importance of ordre public in public international law.

International legislation has become an important activity in present day international law. Whether one refers to law-making treaties, to law--making by majority decision in international organizations or to the enactment of law by international organizations through resolutions and other procedures there is a tendency towards more international legislation. The practice concerning invalid reservations should be seen in that context. It is a contribution to upholding the international ordre public created by the treaties at issue. A State, when ratifying such a treaty, adheres to the legislative act worked out by the international community of States. It cannot by a reservation incompatible with the object and purpose of the treaty unilaterally withdraw from that legislation.

The solution, traditionally proposed in this context, to treat the whole ratification as invalid should be rejected where it is not in line with the nature of the treaty, the international ordre public and a fair evaluation of the

---

26 *See* R. KÜHNER, *op. cit.*, *supra* note 9, at 225–227; DIGEST OF THE UNITED STATES PRACTICE IN INTERNATIONAL LAW (1975) at 263 ff.

27 *See supra* note 22.

State's behaviour.[28] What should be avoided by all means is a situation where it remains open and unclear for a prolonged period of time whether or not a State is bound by one of the important treaties protecting the international ordre public.

It should not be overlooked that reservations to human rights treaties carry an element of contradiction within them. Human rights treaties want to guarantee common minimum standards. A permanent reservation lowering the minimum standard is incompatible with this basic idea.[29] It is a different matter where States use reservations to bring their legislation in line with the standards set up by the treaty. It would seem that the rejection of reservations as null and void by courts, independent treaty-organs and States is a phenomenon going hand in hand with the development of a more sophisticated system of international legislation.[30]

---

28 In the same sense for human rights treaties T. GIEGERICH, *Vorbehalte zu Menschenrechtsabkommen: Zulässigkeit, Gütigkeit und Prüfungskompetenzen von Vertragsgremien*, 55 ZAÖRV (1995) at 713, 774–778; *see* also W.A. SCHABAS, *Invalid Reservations to the International Covenant on Civil and Political Rights: Is the United States Still a Party?*, XXI BROOKLYN JOURNAL OF INTERNATIONAL LAW (1995) at 277–325; L. LIJNZAAD, RESERVATIONS TO U.N.-HUMAN RIGHTS TREATIES (1995); E.F. SHERMAN, Jr., *The U.S. Death Penalty Reservation to the International Covenant on Civil and Political Rights: Exposing the Limitations of the Flexible System Governing Treaty Formation*, 29 TEXAS INTERNATIONAL LAW JOURNAL (1994) at 69–93.

29 J.A. FROWEIN, *Reservations to the European Convention on Human Rights*, in: F. MATSCHER, H. PETZOLD (eds.), PROTECTING HUMAN RIGHTS: THE EUROPEAN DIMENSION, STUDIES IN HONOUR OF G. WIARDA (1988) at 193–200.

30 *See* K. SKUBISZEWSKI, *op. cit.*, *supra* note 3.

International Lawyers and the Progressive Development of International Law

by

Sir Robert Jennings

This brief article is about the influence that international legal scholars have over the shape and direction of the progressive development of international law; and some ideas about how that influence might best be used. The term "progressive development" is not used here just in the special sense in which it appears in Article 13.1(a) of the Charter of the United Nations, but in the broader sense comprising the many and varied opportunities that international lawyers enjoy to influence and sometimes to determine the direction to be taken by, and sometimes even the content of, developing international law. These opportunities arise especially for members of such bodies as the International Law Commission, or the Sixth Committee of the United Nations, and for members of international courts and tribunals. But the full range of such possibilities is impressive, for it also includes the work of writers who may aspire to be the authors of "the teachings of the most highly qualified publicists of the various nations". In fact it is safe to say that there is probably no other system of law in which individual workers and scholars enjoy such telling influence over the shaping of the content of the rules and even of the principles of law. A major reason for this is evident: there is no international legislature; and moreover it is unlikely that there will be one in the foreseeable future. Accordingly international legal scholars have an influence probably unparalleled since the jurisconsults of classical Roman law. Perhaps the writer might be permitted to recall something he said more than thirty years ago in an article about the International Law Commission, concerning "the persistent assumption that the great need of international law is for some procedures for legislation; and the resulting tendency to look for and therefore to find what may be called statute-substitutes, more especially in treaties:" "Is it possible" it was asked, "that this search for the statute substitute has obscured from us not only that international law may develop law-making processes of a quite different kind but even that this development is happening under our very eyes?"[1]

---

1 13 ICLQ (1964) at 388.

That this surmise was not far wide of the mark is now clear enough, for although there is still no legislature for international law, the last four or five decades have seen more changes and more international law being created than probably any other period in the history of the subject. One need only think of the developments in the law of the sea, which has recently seen changes not only to the rules but to the fundamental principles. To be sure the Third United Nations Conference on the Law of the Sea brought about most of this new law; but a delegate to that ten year conference who supposed that the changes would be brought about by the kind of procedures to be expected in a domestic law legislature would have found himself much mistaken.

There is one particular difference between domestic legislation and the ways in which international law is made, that is significant for the purposes of the present article. In domestic legislation the determination of legislative policy would be pretty firmly in the hands of politicians; and the part of the lawyers would be drafting. In international law, the international lawyer has a much broader remit. Situations of course vary. At the Conference on the Law of the Sea, for example, delegations would have been working under instructions from their governments; and might also have included expert representatives of interests involved, such as oil, defence, shipping and so on. Yet it remains broadly true that the professional international lawyers, including academics, have much more say in the shaping of international law, whether in treaty or in customary law form, than do their counterparts in domestic law making and changing. This is a very important competence and responsibility.

This position prompts, however, a question about how the structure and organisation of international law provides for the making of those determinations and the bringing about of those changes in law, or other kinds of decisions, which need to be made not on the basis of the application of legal rules but on the basis of quite other grounds such as political considerations, or reasons of expediency, or technology or even of keeping the peace? Such decisions plainly require quite different skills from those of the international lawyer; although his skills may be useful or even necessary in an ancillary capacity. The need for other kinds of skills and knowledge varies no doubt from one part of the law to another. The law of treaties is very much lawyers' law; but other departments, such as those parts of the law of the sea which concern fish stocks and fishing, mineral exploitation, security and defence, or pollution and conservation, require, if the law is to be good law, a major input from other disciplines. What is needed in fact is an interdisciplinary team; and this government delegations at diplomatic conferences usually provide.

What one is sometimes left wishing for, however, is a greater appreciation amongst international lawyers and their organisations and schools that the art of law making and law developing is an interdisciplinary art; and that this is especially true of making and developing public international law. It is interesting that the International law Commission has been up against this problem, has indeed used experts in one way or another, but that their use has been relatively infrequent and has met with opposition.[2] It is not easy to understand the opposition when one remembers the important part played by Commander Kennedy and his team at the 1958 Geneva Conference on the Law of the Sea.

Perhaps the part of international law where those other than lawyers have had the most influence on the making of the law is in outer space. Ever since the launch of the "sputnik", that part of the law has been driven by science and technology. It quite quickly engendered the ultimate contradiction in terms, when the rubric "instant custom" was coined. One recollects the incredulity with which some distinguished international lawyers greeted the late Wilfred Jenks's prophetic, pioneering article launched some time before the sputnik; and their alarm on finding Jenks actually citing the works of scientists and mathematicians.[3] But even Wilfred Jenks was not able to foresee that his new law would before long be the vector of a revolutionary technology of communication the significance of which for mankind in general is almost frightening to contemplate. It is interesting to note that the International Institute of Space Law is one of the international lawyers' organisations which, already at the level of the academic study of the law, involves scientists, geographers and mathematicians at its conferences; very much to the benefit of the discussions.

This contrasts with the Institute of International Law which, in its Reports and Resolutions, seems not to have seen any need to involve, officially at least, any others than international lawyers in its work. But there are dangers in regarding expertise in international law as a sufficient qualification for making and developing, or sometimes even for interpreting and applying international law. An instructive illustration comes to mind. Tribunals faced with the task of drawing a maritime boundary have sometimes dealt with the distorting effect of an island upon an equidistance line by holding that the island should have "half-effect" on the boundary line. But we learn from a hydrographer, Cmdr. P.B. Beazley, that this expression is inexact to the extent that it can result in several quite different lines de-

---

2 *See* H.W. BRIGGS, THE INTERNATIONAL LAW COMMISSION (1965) at 147 ff.

3 *See* W. JENKS, *International Law – Activities in Space*, 5 ICLQ (1956) at 99–114.

pending upon the precise meaning to be given to the expression half-effect. Moreover he adds, after describing and drawing these several lines, that:

> "Care has been taken throughout this article to avoid prejudicial terms like 'the true half-effect line', for it is not possible to describe one of the lines illustrated as being more correct than another."[4]

Admittedly these cases have usually resulted in an agreed line; probably because the hydrographers on both sides have got together to pick up the pieces left by the tribunal. But would it not have been better if the members of the tribunal had themselves been aware of these problems arising from their own formula?

It is not suggested, nor could it be, that this usefulness of some other disciplines to the work of international lawyers is in any way a new revelation. The situation is recognised in Article 50 of the Statute of the International Court of Justice; and that Court has indeed not infrequently employed cartographers, hydrographers, geographers, linguists, and even very specialised legal experts to assist in the understanding of the issues in a case before it; and has not on the whole felt any need to make this public knowledge or even to apprise the parties.

There is, however, a more serious question: what provision is made in the general structure of international law for those questions and matters where it is better that decisions should be firmly in the hands of people other than international lawyers and where international lawyers as such, if they have a role at all, will have one which is ancillary to the role of decision makers with quite other skills?

It is now some years ago that the present writer attempted to give a series of lectures on the acquisition of territory in international law.[5] What one found in the legal sources was a system of developed law all right; but it was essentially analogous to a private law system of conveyancing of land between subjects of the system, *i.e.* in this case sovereign States. It was assumed that the point at issue in disputes would be one of legal title; which should be decided if not by negotiation then by a court or tribunal, which would apply that conveyancing law (which law would also comprise a set of legal rules called the law of state succession where there had been change in the *persona* of a State).

Yet if one looks at the legal history of territorial title one finds very quickly that this international conveyancing law has played an important and yet

---

[4] P.B. BEAZLEY, *Half-effect Applied to Equidistance Lines*, LVI INTERNATIONAL HYDROGRAPHIC REVIEW (1979) – January.

[5] R.Y. JENNINGS, THE ACQUISITION OF TERRITORY IN INTERNATIONAL LAW (1963).

almost ancillary role mainly in relatively minor disputes about boundaries or small parcels of territory subject to rival claims; the big changes of title have been brought about by the use of force. One thinks of the great territorial settlements of 1648, 1815, 1918 and 1946; and one thinks of the great periods in which force played a part. Certainly the law governing the use of force and its consequences has been entirely changed by the Charter of the United Nations. But this does not of itself solve questions of territorial title, for the root of title to territory – as of land in private law – is most often to be found in the past, and difficult questions of the intertemporal law arise. The effectiveness of such titles was indeed accommodated by the conveyancing system by such devices as the special position of the peace treaty; and the doctrine of *uti possidetis*, which the International Court of Justice has pronounced to be now a general principle.[6]

The question, however, to which there is no very clear or definite answer, is what are now the legal procedures of peaceful change of territory in those instances which require not the skill of the international lawyer applying his system of conveyancing law, but the creation of a legal title conferred by a decision, made indeed lawfully and giving rise to legal obligations and to good title to territory, but made because the international community has judged the change to be required in order to bring about a just and stable settlement or indeed in order to keep or restore peace and order in a region? Here what has to be brought into play is the knowledge and wisdom of those such as statesmen, historians, cultural experts, geographers and so on. Some time ago it might have been possible to hope that the conveyancing system would suffice. But that system assumes stability. And the present turmoil produced by the tendency of States to fragmentation has destroyed that illusion. Who can possibly suppose that a court's judgment applying the basic conveyancing-style law of territory could have had any crucial part to play in the settlement of the territorial question in former Yugoslavia? Perhaps the writer might be allowed to recall a passage from his lectures of 1963:[7]

> "... it is most important to bear constantly in mind the distinction between the question who presently has title and the question whether there ought for this or that reason to be a transfer of title to another. The first question is purely legal and requires a legal answer; the second is essentially a political question – though it may involve a number of ancillary legal questions concerning procedures, the status of certain decisions and so on."

---

6 *See Frontier Dispute* case, ICJ REPORTS 1986 at 554, 565.
7 R.Y. JENNINGS, *op. cit.*, *supra* note 5, at 71.

Now of course there are indeed procedures for such decisions: there are the resolutions of the Security Council or of the General Assembly; the work of Ambassador Badinter for European security showed at least appreciation of the need for flexibility in procedures; there are other regional organisations; and there are the traditional procedures of diplomacy which have been dealing with these sorts of problems during the entire history of international law. Yet these many devices and procedures do not yet form part of a developed and clearly structured framework of international constitutional and administrative law. There is, to say the least, a great deal of room for improvement. The recent attempts to deal with the Yugoslavian situation showed the international community improvising and trying this or that, but without any clear procedure laid down. This contrasts quite strongly with the clear procedures for dealing with legal questions through the ICJ or other tribunals.

The Security Council does indeed have competences under Chapter VII of the Charter for dealing with threats to the peace, breaches of the peace and acts of aggression. But by that stage it is by definition rather late in the day. At a stage prior to that there are the powers under chapter VI for securing the pacific settlement of disputes. But this rather illustrates the problem. If the dispute is a legal dispute there is of course the International Court (Art. 36.6). But if it is not a legal dispute the provisions of the Charter are comprehensive but vague. There is no clear routine to follow. In any event it is not always what an international lawyer would call a "dispute" that is at the core of a problem.

There is indeed also another kind of decision-making besides those by courts of law and those by political organs; namely, the task of management. The peace-keeping sections of the United Nations are not inexperienced in this activity, nor are they in any need of conversion to its importance. Again it demands institutions, skills and competences that do not loom very large in the general international lawyers' syllabus. Certainly it is not primarily a task for lawyers, though a lawyer might also possess management skills, and some knowledge of the legal framework within which management has to operate may be essential. For a domestic system of law this element of good government would be tought as an important part of constitutional law. In works on international law it tends to get less of a showing. It is true that efficient international management mechanisms will be regarded with suspicion by state governments which might be apprehensive about trespass on their own powers and discretions. Nevertheless, one need only think of the international problem of the conservation of fish stocks to appreciate that the only hope of averting disaster is to devise international systems of management. There will of course be legal "disputes" about fishing areas and about fish stocks and quotas; and this will doubtless engender traditional-type work for international lawyers and international courts; but important as the settlement of legal disputes undoubtedly is, it is doubtful whether the eventual settlement of these disputes will do enough for the protection of fish stocks.

It is true that the devising of new institutional mechanisms for political, administrative or executive, rather than forensic legal decisions is a formidable proposition. It may be that for the time being one must get along with such assistance as the tragically underfunded organs of the United Nations can provide to supplement the traditional methods of diplomacy. What is discouraging, however, is the relatively small attention being given to this problem by international lawyers in general who seem still to be more interested in the proliferation of courts and tribunals, and in a misguided pressure to try to fill the constitutional gap by expansionist policies for the existing law. One sometimes regrets that modern international law does not seem to breed law reformers, but rather those who want more of the same, apparently under a conviction that to have more, and more comprehensive, legal rules is *per se* a good thing.

Yet, decisions by courts of law, and decisions by legally competent organs, for making political or administrative decisions should in a society subject to the rule of law, be complementary to each other and necessary to each other. Each should reign in its own proper sphere and the competence and importance of the other kind of decision-making should be recognised and respected. The establishment of the rule of law does not mean the establishment of a hegemony of the judges.

Although we have here two quite different modes of decision making, they are both a concern to the lawyer. This is partly because, as mentioned already, the administrative decision has to be made within the parameters permitted by constitutional or administrative law; but also because both kinds of decision-making are necessary to a developed and healthy regime of law. Accordingly the machinery for administrative decision is a necessary complement of judicial decision. So much so that it is the conviction of the writer of this article that the existence of a developed system of administrative law is probably a *sine qua non* for the establishment of courts with full compulsory jurisdiction.

Thus, in the area of domestic law analogous to our international territorial law, there is as a matter of course a property law which enables different kinds of decisions to be made. Besides the private law conveyancing rules applied by the courts one can have governmental or local authority compulsory purchase orders for certain purposes; planning decisions made by planning authorities; governmental powers of statutory or delegated legislation for carrying out policies on the ownership, use of disposition of land, and so on. Yet for decades now international lawyers have been demanding an international court with more or less full compulsory jurisdiction and yet relatively little in the way of the necessary complementary institutions for making decisions of a different kind on policy or good administration grounds. How can it seriously be supposed that it might be possible to establish in the international community a court which would then have a scope of competence far exceeding that of the highest courts in domestic law systems.[8]

Nevertheless it is finally the well-being of international litigation and in particular of the International Court of Justice that the writer is concerned for in this article. The intention, in calling attention to other kinds of decision making and to the importance of other skills than those of international lawyers, is not at all to try to relegate the work of the World Court and of other international tribunals for trying legal claims to a secondary role. The intention is quite the contrary. The consensual character of the competence of almost all kinds of international litigation has, at least since 1920, very rightly, been a matter of grave concern and regret to international lawyers. It is manifestly a damaging defect not only of international forensic recourse but also of substantive international law. Anyone who doubts the latter observation might try the exercise of trying to construct, or even imagine, a domestic law of contract without the assurance of unilateral recourse to a court if need be. The relative lack of it in international law is probably the only aspect of modern international law which still may be used to question with some cogency whether international law is truly a system of law at all.

One result of this very well founded anxiety has been that internationalists for many decades have expended great energy and much dedicated work in trying to persuade governments to accept some measure of compulsory jurisdiction, of the ICJ in particular, whether through declarations under Article 36.2. of the Statute or otherwise. This policy has had some measure of new and welcome success recently. The Court has been having some cases successfully begun by unilateral application. It is, however, an unattractive aspect of the optional clause system that a government accepting compulsory jurisdiction puts itself into a weak position as against governments that

---

[8] This is the problem much discussed in the inter-war years under the rubric of "peaceful change." *See e.g.* PEACEFUL CHANGES, MANNING (1937); the important essay on *The Legal Aspect* was by Dr. H. LAUTERPACHT as he then was. The writings are forgotten but the problem is still a real one.

have not yet done so, unless the accepting government fences its declaration by formidable reservations.

Again these strivings with the optional clause seem to the writer to be ameliorating the effect of the symptoms of the disease rather than identifying the root cause of the general reluctance to create a system of general compulsory jurisdiction. And again it is instructive to look at the paradigm of the usual legal structure of a developed independent state. Its high court and its supreme court will be found indeed to enjoy that compulsory jurisdiction which international lawyers have so long dreamed of for the World Court. But this is possible within the state legal structure precisely because the courts work alongside equally developed organs with competence to make, where needed, decisions governed by criteria other than the law, though of course they will work within the legal framework and competence allotted to them by constitutional and administrative public law. The criteria on which decisions are based, instead of on legal rules, will be various: what good and wise government appears to require at the moment; experience and common sense: administrative convenience and efficiency; and of course also the possibility in some cases of legislation to change the rules of law, the possibilities ranging from a general statute to limited powers of delegated legislation. Here one may cite a passage from Professor Sir William Wade's treaties on administrative law, where he describes the difference between a judicial decision and an administrative decision:

> "A judicial decision is made according to law. An administrative decision is made according to administrative policy. A judge attempts to find out what is the correct solution according to legal rules and principles. An administrator attempts to find out what is the most expedient and desirable solution in the public interest. It is true, of course, that many decisions of the courts can be said to be made on grounds of legal policy and that the courts sometimes have to choose between alternative solutions with little else than the public interest to guide them. There will always be grey areas. Nevertheless, the mental exercises of judge and administrator are fundamentally different. The judge's approach is objective, guided by his idea of the law. The administrator's approach is empirical, guided merely by expediency."

It is true, therefore, that the tasks of judge, political expert or administrative expert are different. That is precisely the point; they involve different skills and different training. But the fully working system of the rule of law requires both. And accordingly it is not permissible for the lawyer to deny responsibility for the political side of things; partly because of the "grey areas" as Sir William calls them; partly because the political side must work within the permissible parameters set by the law; and partly because even the legal side is seen in a distorted and less useful form unless it is seen in the context of the entire system of the rule of law, of which the political and administrative side is an essential and complementary part. This is especially so if, as the writer believes, it is the relatively underdeveloped political and administrative side in international law which inevitably inhibits the full development of the legal side.

It was at one time the orthodox, or at any rate seemingly the most influential, view amongst academic international lawyers that the extension of obligatory judicial or arbitral settlement of "disputes" would of itself be a safeguard of peace. The late Hans Kelsen still astonishes by his apparent ability to believe, even in 1944, that the 1928 Peace Pact of Paris was ineffective because it "undertook too little by obliging States to seek pacific settlement of their disputes without obliging them to submit all their conflicts without any exception to the compulsory jurisdiction of an international court."[9] This insouciant notion lingers still in the "go to law, not to war" school of thought.

It cannot indeed be doubted that courts have a crucial part to play in the establishing and safeguarding of peace. But the true role of courts is more accurately delineated in the works of two great international lawyer sages and prophets of the same generation, Charles De Visscher and James Brierly. Charles De Visscher dealt very faithfully with the matter in his *Théories et Réalités en Droit International Public* in 1953. One quotation must suffice:

> "There was a time when the possible contribution of international tribunals to the maintenance of peace was exaggerated. At the end of the nineteenth century, the anxieties aroused by changes in the European balance, combined with some discrediting of the diplomatic methods employed to sustain it, led some minds to look to the development of the jurisdictional function, and more particularly to the extension of obligatory arbitration, for the most effective safeguards to peace. At the same time the somewhat confused ideal of 'the primacy of law over force' promoted the view that the establishment of a permanent international tribunal of fixed composition must be the principle and centre of all international organization.
>
> Yet nothing in the past history of arbitration justified such hopes. Rare in all ages were wars arising out of pure disputes as to rights. In the immense majority of cases wars sprang from conflicts of interest. Their motives were political, even though a legal discussion furnished the pretext to recourse to arms." [Corbett's English translation 1957][10]

---

[9] H. KELSEN, PEACE THROUGH LAW (1944) at 18.

[10] *See* translation from the French by P.E. CORBETT (1957) at 327; but the whole of BOOK IV on *The Judicial Settlement of Disputes* is pertinent.

One may couple that with one quotation from Brierly's little book *The Law of Nations*:

> "The dissatisfaction of a State with the *status quo* raises a question which is not a judicial one, and cannot be turned into a judicial question by adopting judicial methods of procedure ..."[11]

* * *

International law has now for some decades been developing rapidly. In particular the classical orthodoxy that it is a law only between states and does not apply to other entities and to individuals has gone for good. Public international law nowadays is a matter of personal concern to everybody whether they are aware of it or not. It is symptomatic of the splendid changes of international law for the better that the International Court of Justice is now *mirabile dictu* steadily occupied with important cases under its contentious jurisdiction. It is the purpose of this article to suggest that, in this relatively very happy situation for international lawyers, it behoves us, no doubt amongst many other things, to attend to what seem to the writer to be two weaknesses as we try to cope with new challenges.

First, there should be a much greater, and a practical, recognition by international lawyers that the rule of law in international affairs, and the establishment of international justice, are inter-disciplinary subjects. International lawyers usually cannot become more than dilettantes in these other approaches (and the *North Sea Continental Shelf* cases showed the dangers of succumbing to the temptation to become amateur geologists); but international lawyers can at least speak to, and try to involve in their work, students of international relations, diplomatic historians, geographers and geologists, cartographers and hydrographers. International lawyers have many organizations where they discuss with each other; but there is relatively little in the way of organizations or even conferences where international lawyers can speak to experts in other disciplines about international legal problems. Here, as has been indicated above, some of the more venerable associations of international lawyers have something to learn here from the younger International Institute of Space Law.

Secondly, looking now at matters which are the direct concern and responsibility of international lawyers, this writer wishes that more attention could be given to the significance of the way in which the development of international law has lagged – relatively to the development of courts and tribunals and of lawyers' law – in the development of means for other kinds

[11] THE LAW OF NATIONS, 5th ed. by the author (1955) at 292.

of international decision-making, for management, and for executive action, in which considerations of policy, statesmanlike wisdom, convenience, efficiency and expediency could take their proper place. One is conscious that this is an exceedingly difficult and delicate problem. But at least it could attract more academic attention; and greater realization that until this side of the organization of international relations can become more developed, it is not very sensible to demand a general acceptance of compulsory jurisdiction as a panacea. This writer wishes to say that he makes these suggestions in all humility, fully recognizing that he is himself one who has in his own career been happy to specialize in traditional international law and has himself made very little if any contribution to the improvement of the mechanics of political and administrative work in the international field. But truths sometimes dawn in the mind rather later than would have been ideal.

Finally, let it be said that the writer feels that these suggestions for a generally broader approach to international legal problems cannot be said to be inappropriate in a tribute to President Skubiszewski who is not only one of the very best of our professional international lawyers, but he has also been an outstanding Foreign Minister of his country, has taken a consistently important part in precisely that area of international affairs and law to the significance and importance of which this article has sought to call attention; and thinking of an interdisciplinary approach, let it also be said that President Skubiszewski is equipped with a quite remarkable and detailed knowledge and understanding of diplomatic history.

Some Thoughts on the Relation between Extra-Legal Agreements and the Law-Creating Process

by

Peter H. Kooijmans

Introductory Remarks

The phenomenon of extra- or non-legal agreements between States has always intrigued the international lawyer. For a lawyer, much more so than for a politician, it seems illogical that States enter into commitments which are considered by them to be no less binding than legal commitments, which are often even drafted in similar language but which nevertheless are seen as lacking the consent to be bound, which according to treaty law (*e.g.* contained in art. 2,1 of the Vienna Convention on the Law of Treaties) is a precondition for the establishment of legally binding relations. And even this last phrase seems to be in itself illogical. For there is a consent to be bound, be it that by implicit or explicit expression of the parties, this consent does not entail a legal relationship between them.

The issue has become the subject of lively debate, in particular in connection with the CSCE Final Act of Helsinki of 1975 and the ensuing CSCE (now OSCE) documents.[1] Here the lack of the consent to be bound in the legal sense is expressed in one of the final clauses (a formulation which has become standard in CSCE documents) stating that the act is not eligible for registration under article 102 of the Charter of the United Nations. Nevertheless the participating States (not Contracting Parties) declare their resolve to pay due regard to and implement the provisions of the Final Act. In more recent documents the language is less circumspect. In the Code of Conduct on Politico-Military Aspects of Security, adopted at the Budapest Summit of December 1994, the sentence about the non-eligibility of the document for registration under art. 102 of the Charter is preceded by the rather blunt statement that the provisions of the Code are politically binding (para. 39).

---

[1] *See* for a comprehensive survey of literature R. Szafarz, *CSCE Contribution to the Establishment of the European Legal Order*, 21 Polish Yearbook of International Law (1994) at 7, note 2.

It is, therefore, beyond doubt that such extra-legal agreements may be binding; consequently it is incorrect to call such agreements non-binding, as is sometimes done. In this respect they differ from the so-called gentlemen's agreements which usually are no more than declarations of intent. That CSCE-commitments are more than declarations of intent is clear, *e.g.* by the fact that during the CSCE process several mechanisms were established in order to enforce and monitor compliance by the participating States with their commitments.[2]

A few years after the Final Act had been concluded, the Institut de Droit international established a commission to study the subject of international texts of legal import in the mutual relations of their authors and texts devoid of such import. In his final conclusions submitted to the Cambridge session of 1983, the Commission's Rapporteur, Professor Michel Virally, distinguished between texts containing legal commitments, texts containing political commitments and texts merely formulating declarations of intent. The Rapporteur called the last category devoid of any legal import. Whether a text belongs to the first or the second category is in his view dependent "upon the intention of the parties as may be established by the usual rules of interpretation, including an examination of the terms used to express such intention, the circumstances in which the text was adopted and the subsequent behaviour of the parties." Clearly, as will be shown, the Rapporteur considered the second category, that of the extra-legal agreements, as having legal import just like the first category, albeit that this legal import is of a different character. Although the Institut did not approve Professor Virally's conclusions (it recommended the subject for further study in the future dependent upon further development of State practice and more profound doctrinal thought), the Rapporteur's reports and his conclusions[3] provide a highly useful point of departure. It is this second category which will be the subject of the following remarks. For this purpose we will deal first with the reasons why States (or rather politicians) prefer in certain cases to conclude political agreements rather than legal agreements; secondly, we will look into the legal effects of these non-legal commitments, their legal import therefore; and finally we will consider the question whether such non-legal commitments may develop into legal obligations without an explicit change of their status, *i.e.* by transforming them into a treaty.

---

2 The Vienna and Moscow mechanisms on the human dimension and the Vienna mechanism regarding unusual military activities may be mentioned in this respect.

3 ANNUAIRE DE L'INSTITUT DE DROIT INTERNATIONAL (1984) at 285–291.

I. THE INTENT OF THE PARTIES

The preference for a non-legal agreement may be caused by a variety of reasons. In the case of the CSCE Final Act the rather unstable relationship between East and West was initially given as an explanation. Skubiszewski was of the opinion that the political division for the time being made it impossible to agree on concrete legal mutual obligations. The maximum that could be achieved was agreement on an ambitious political programme.[4] Likewise, Bothe feels that "the process of political *detente* between Eastern and Western Europe had not developed to an extent which would have allowed the States to make a prognosis of correct behaviour *vis-à-vis* one another sufficient to have prompted them to enter into a stable legal relationship." According to him a State will not be able to enter into legal commitments if the prognosis of an ability or willingness to honour the engagements is not safe enough, either on the own side or on that of the other party or parties.[5] Van Dijk, also, points out that "it is precisely in the fields in which there are great contradictions in the interests and opinions, but where self-interest demands international co-operation (and thus international agreement on the basic principles and further regulation of the co-operation), that the contradictions make it so difficult to lay down these basic principles and this further regulation in a treaty."[6] The Final Act, which he characterizes as a declaration with legally binding principles and a politically binding programme, in his opinion is an adequate starting point for co-operation between countries with very different political and societal ideologies and systems. According to the three authors mentioned (and a number of other authors could be added), it is the political situation that led the participating States to the decision to refrain from entering into clear legal commitments. Both Skubiszewski and Van Dijk expect that in a later stage – when the political *ambiance* has become less tense – these political commitments may be transformed into legal arrangements. Van Dijk qualifies the process, set into motion by the Final Act, as a "growth situation" which requires a flexible juridical machinery in which there is room for "growth norms", dependent upon the measure of consensus which comes to light in the implementation of politically binding agreements, up to the time that the

---

[4] K. SKUBISZEWSKI, *Der Rechtscharacter der KSZE-Schluszakte*, (in:) R. BERNHARDT, I. VON MÜNCH, W. RUDOLF (eds.), DRITTES DEUTSCH-POLNISCHES JURISTEN KOLLOQUIUM, Baden-Baden (1977) at 28.

[5] M. BOTHE, *Legal and Non-legal Norms – a Meaningful Distinction in International Relations?*, (in:) XI NETHERLANDS YEARBOOK OF INTERNATIONAL LAW (1980) at 91.

[6] P. VAN DIJK, *The Final Act of Helsinki-Basis for a Pan-European System*, (in:) XI NETHERLANDS YEARBOOK OF INTERNATIONAL LAW (1980) at 115.

consensus on goals and their achievement is sufficiently concrete and tested to allow "petrification" in a legally binding agreement.[7]

It is remarkable that these expectations did not materialize even when the political situation had radically changed after the collapse of the Soviet Empire. The Charter of Paris for a New Europe of 21 November 1990 solemnly declared that the era of confrontation and division of Europe had ended and that henceforth the relations between the participating States would be founded on respect and co-operation. Since that moment nothing seems to stand in the way of a stable legal relationship but the preference for non-legal relations has remained as strong as before. The "non-eligibility" clause of the Final Act has become standard. Obviously, there are other reasons for this preference.

For OSCE commitments one of these may be what is called by Bloed the principle of "universalism" which means that all CSCE commitments are fully applicable to all CSCE States[8] from the very start.[9]

Entering into legally binding agreements would require most participating States to submit such agreements to parliamentary approval with all the risks involved. Doubts whether the document will be able to obtain parliamentary approval or fear that the effect of the agreement will be counter-productive if parliamentary approval is withheld in a number of participating States may also explain the clear preference for political agreements. But even the mere fact of conducting negotiations on the conclusion of a treaty may adversely affect this principle of universalism as is evidenced by the outcome of the negotiations on the Convention on Conciliation and Arbitration within the CSCE, adopted during the meeting of the CSCE Council in Stockholm in December 1992. At the time this treaty was signed by only 29 of the 53 attending Foreign Ministers. Of more importance is the fact that a number of participating States (amongst them the United States and the United Kingdom) made clear that they did not intend to become a party.[10] Until now this convention is the only exception to the non-legal character of OSCE commitments.[11]

---

[7] *Ibid.* at 120.

[8] A. BLOED (ed.), THE CONFERENCE ON SECURITY AND CO-OPERATION IN EUROPE. ANALYSIS AND BASIC DOCUMENTS, 1972–1993, Dordrecht (1993) at 24.

[9] The Code of Conduct on Politico-Military Aspects of Security, adopted at 6 December 1994, proudly states that it will come into effect on 1 January 1995.

[10] *See* R. SZAFARZ, *CSCE Procedures for Peaceful Settlement of International Disputes*, (in:) O. BRING AND S. MAHMOUDI (eds.), CURRENT INTERNATIONAL LAW ISSUES. NORDIC PERSPECTIVES. ESSAYS IN HONOUR OF JERZY STUCKI, Göteborg (1994) at 183–193.

[11] Two other conventions, the Treaty on Conventional Armed Forces in Europe (CFE Treaty) of 1990 and the Open Skies Treaty of 1992, have only a weak link with the CSCE process and have, therefore, a *sui generis* character.

The most probable reason to opt for a non-legal arrangement may well be that it enables the parties involved to include in it provisions which do not yet reflect legal norms but are deemed desirable as norms for future behaviour. A good example in this respect is the OSCE Code of Conduct on Politico-Military Aspects of Security of 1994. "The nature of the Code is a set of norms, not a codification of rules," a U.S. Conference document pointedly says. The Code of Conduct partly reflects existing norms of international law, either treaty law or customary law, as many other CSCE documents do. Other provisions, in particular those of Chapters VII and VIII are, however, truly revolutionary from the view-point of international law. This may be illustrated by merely quoting para. 20: "The participating States consider the democratic political control of military, paramilitary and internal security forces as well as of intelligence services and the police to be an indispensable element of stability and security. They will further the integration of their armed forces with civil society as an important expression of democracy." According to present international law the control of security forces forms the hard core of what are considered to be "matters falling essentially within the domestic jurisdiction of a State". Nevertheless, the commitments of the participating States in this field are cast in terms of obligations and rights. "The specific content of the Code should stress certain rights and obligations of participating States toward each other, both in times of peace and in times of conflict, and should establish clear norms regarding democratic control over the armed forces as well as the use of armed force," the U.S. document states. It would have been completely impossible to reach agreement on a legally binding document, containing such far-reaching commitments. Nevertheless the Code explicitly states that each participating State is responsible for its implementation and on request shall provide appropriate clarification regarding this implementation (the so-called inspection by challenge) (para. 38), whereas para. 39 frankly states: "The provisions adopted in this Code of Conduct are politically binding". There is, therefore, a shared expectation of compliance. This brings us to our second question: if such commitments are not legally binding, do they have any legal import, *e.g.*, in case of non-compliance?

II. THE EFFECTS IN LAW OF EXTRA-LEGAL AGREEMENTS

"Non-compliance by a party with an extra-legal commitment is not a ground for a claim for reparation in the legal sense or for judicial remedies." This is about as much as can be said with absolute certainty about the legal effects of non-legal commitments. The above sentence which is a slightly adapted quotation from Oscar Schachter's article *The Twilight Existence of Non-Binding (sic!) International Agreements*[12] is logical since a non-legal agreement is not governed by international law (art. 2, 1(a) Vienna Convention on the Law of Treaties). According to Schachter the conclusion that a non-binding agreement (by which he understands non-legal agreements including the Helsinki Final Act) does not give rise to legal responsibility is not an analytical proposition but an empirical conclusion based on State practice. He points to the fact that there have been more than a few of such agreements, but that there has been no indication that the parties have treated non-performance as a ground for reparations of legal sanctions. I wonder whether this conclusion, made only two years after the adoption of the Final Act, can be maintained unconditionally in the light of more recent State-practice. After the crackdown on Solidarność by the Polish government in December 1981, Western and other CSCE-States accused that government of violation of CSCE commitments and demanded that these measures be revoked; when the Polish government refused to do so, economic sanctions were imposed by a number of these States. This State-practice bears evidence of a prevailing opinion that a violation of politically binding agreements is as inadmissible as a violation of norms of international law[13] and that the other parties are entitled to react vigorously in case of non-compliance. If there is no legal responsibility, there certainly is political accountability; if there is no ground for legal reparation, there surely is ground for political redress.

Since, however, such agreements are not governed by international law, counter-measures have to remain within the limits of what is legally permitted. This means that only retorsions are allowed and that reprisals cannot be justified. Non-compliance with such commitments does not put aside the general rules of international law. This opinion is shared by a number of authors; in this respect in particular the Institut de Droit international's Rap-

---

12 81 AMERICAN JOURNAL OF INTERNATIONAL LAW (1977) at 300.

13 *Cf.* A. BLOED, *op. cit.*, *supra* note 8, at 22.

porteur, Virally, may be mentioned.[14] He maintains that the violation of a purely political engagement entitles the party which is the victim of such violation to take any measure to stop such violation or to obtain redress, in so far as such measures are not prohibited by international law.

But international law does not only impose negative limits with regard to the implementation of politically binding agreements. The fact that such agreements are not governed by international law does not mean that they are devoid of any legal import.

First, there is wide agreement that the principle of good faith, itself of a non-legal origin, governs the interpretation and application both of legal and non-legal agreements. One of Virally's conclusions is that a State which has accepted a purely political commitment is subject to the general obligation of good faith which governs the conduct of subjects of international law in their mutual relations. But does it in both cases have the same meaning and purport? Here Virally seems to hesitate. In his provisional report he suggests that maybe the application of the *clausula rebus sic stantibus* and the principle of necessity should be interpreted in a more liberal way in the case of politically binding agreements. And he adds: *Ce pourrait même être là la différence fondamentale qui existe, d'un point de vue pratique, entre eux et les traités*. I wonder whether this line of thought would be acceptable since it would imply that political commitments are less binding than legal commitments in so far as it is easier to evade them for political reasons. The fact that it is easier to terminate political agreement than legal agreements (which seems to be widely accepted) should not lead to the conclusion that it is easier to evade them.

Much more sceptical about the applicability of the principle of good faith on non-legal obligations is Bothe. "Good faith is a legal concept, and basing respect for non-legal obligations on a legal concept would not seem to be appropriate."[15]

The reverse question, whether non-compliance with an extra-legal commitment entitles the "injured" State to invoke the *clausula rebus sic stantibus* with regard to a legally binding obligation, is not explicitly dealt with by Virally.[16] Delbrück denies – at least for the Helsinki Final Act – that this is the case, both for treaties concluded before and after its adoption;[17] this holds

---

14 M. Virally, Annuaire de l'Institut de Droit international (1983) at 254. In the same sense, but more cautiously phrased J. Delbrück, *Die völkerrechtliche Bedeutung der Schluszakte der Konferenz über Sicherheit und Zusammenarbeit in Europa*, (in:) R. Bernhardt, I. von Münch und W. Rudolf, *op. cit.*, *supra* note 4, at 45.

15 M. Bothe, *op. cit.*, *supra* note 5, at 95.

16 M. Virally, *op. cit.*, *supra* note 14, at 236.

17 J. Delbrück, *op. cit.*, *supra* note 14, at 45–46.

true even if, in the latter case, such treaties are concluded as a follow-up of the Final Act, since this document can never be the legal basis of such a consecutive treaty. This approach seems to be too restrictive. With all cautiousness which has to be taken into account in the case of the *clausula*, a fundamental change of political circumstances which may be the result of a serious violation of binding political commitments is not by definition excluded by the language of art. 62 of the Vienna Convention on the Law of Treaties, provided all other conditions are met.

Another important legal effect of the conclusion of extra-legal agreements relates to estoppel. Rapporteur Virally concludes that a State which has accepted a purely political commitment is deemed to have waived the right to invoke possible pleas under international law (including the objection related to domestic jurisdiction) against an action for enforcement of its commitment brought by someone in relation to whom it has bound itself. Consequently, such an action cannot be regarded as unlawful interference.[18] Schachter is of the same opinion even in the case of a non-binding gentlemen's agreement.[19]

This conclusion seems to be sound. From a legal point of view the conclusion of a legally non-binding agreement is at any rate State-conduct which may which lead to estoppel. A State which has entered into an explicit politically binding agreement on the internal use of force by its security forces, is no longer entitled to invoke the plea of domestic jurisdiction if this use is questioned by other parties to such commitments. This may well be the most important aspect of the Code of Conduct on Politico-Military Aspects of Security and provides a forceful legal argument for the political interference by other OSCE-States in the case of the war in Chechnya.

Schachter is also correct when he says that disputes about extra-legal agreements cannot be submitted to judicial settlement. Two comments, however, have to be made.

First, Virally rightly submits that art. 33 of the Charter of the United Nations is applicable to all disputes which may endanger international peace and security and that therefore such disputes must be submitted to a peaceful settlement procedure, even if they do not lend themselves to judicial settlement.

Secondly, it is by no means excluded that in a legal dispute before the International Court of Justice or an arbitration tribunal a politically binding agreement may be invoked by one of the parties as a legally relevant fact.

---

[18] M. VIRALLY, *op. cit.*, *supra* note 3, at 290–291. Contrary J. DELBRÜCK, *op. cit.*, *supra* note 14, at 49 and M. BOTHE, *op. cit.*, *supra* note 5, at 99.

[19] O. SCHACHTER, *op. cit.*, *supra* note 12, at 301. *See* also his INTERNATIONAL LAW IN THEORY AND PRACTICE, Dordrecht (1991) at 101.

From the foregoing it will be clear that policitally binding agreements are not devoid of all legal import. However, we find ourselves in a twilight-zone. For this reason it is understandable that the Institut de Droit international did not yet approve the conclusions of its Commission and the Rapporteur – persuasive as they may be – but preferred to reserve the subject for further study; State practice is ambiguous and far from unequivocal; the increasing intensity of inter-State relations may lead to new forms of arrangements; doctrine is still in flux.

This stock-taking of new trends, however, does not discharge the international lawyer from dealing with another question with which he is by tradition much more familiar: how does this State-behaviour relate to the law-creating process, in particular the formation of customary law? Is there a strict parallel with non-binding *usus* and binding customary law or is the situation more complex? Here we have arrived at our third question.

III. THE RELATION BETWEEN EXTRA-LEGAL AGREEMENTS AND THE LAW-CREATING PROCESS

Before going into this question one is well-advised to keep in mind the warning, given by Karol Wolfke thirty years ago, but as topical today as it was then: "The intangibleness of the process of formation of international customary law is precisely one of the reasons why it is so difficult to State authoritatively if at all, and how, such new rules are arising."[20]

At first sight, it may seem attractive to draw a parallel between the law-creating effect of resolutions of international organizations, in particular those of the General Assembly of the United Nations, and that of politically binding agreements and there certainly are a number of similarities, apart from the fact that both are non-legally binding texts. Just like resolutions of international organizations, non-legal agreements may contain elements which reflect already existing rules of international law. The Declaration of Principles of the Helsinki Final Act, the so-called Decalogue, is may be the most well-known example and can be compared with the Declaration of Friendly Relations and Peaceful Co-operation between States adopted by the General Assembly in 1970 (GA Res. 2625 (XXV)). Both reflect the views of the States which have participated in their adoption on the way in which their obligations under international law must be interpreted.

---

[20] K. WOLFKE, *Practice of International Organizations and Customary Law*, (in:) I POLISH YEARBOOK OF INTERNATIONAL LAW (1966/67) at 185.

Such obligations, however, are binding either under a previous treaty or under general international law independent of the document (resolution or non-legal agreement) which enumerates them. This in itself is not controversial.

Of greater relevance is whether a parallel can be drawn between the elements in such documents which have not yet legally binding force. We have touched here upon the problem of "soft law". In doctrine and in State practice it is nowadays widely recognized that, if certain conditions are met, provisions of non-binding resolutions of international organizations may gradually '"crystallize" into "hard" norms of international law.[21] In this respect the Declaration on the Right of Self-Determination (GA Res. 1514 (XV)) or the early resolutions of the General Assembly on the regime of outer space are often mentioned; in the latter case we may even speak of "instant custom".

It is questionable, however, if the same reasoning can be applied to non-legal agreements. In this respect it is of importance to keep in mind what the International Court of Justice said in the *North Sea Continental Shelf* cases with regard to the conduct of States which were not a party to the 1958 Geneva Convention on the Continental Self. The Court said: "The essential point ... is that even if these instances of action by non-parties to the Convention were much more numerous than they in fact are, they would not, even in the aggregate, suffice in themselves to constitute the *opinio juris*; ... not only must the acts concerned amount to a settled practice, but they must also be such, or be carried out in such a way, as to be evidence of a belief that this practice is rendered obligatory by the existence of a rule of law requiring it."[22]

It is exactly this belief that the practice is rendered obligatory by the existence of a rule of law requiring it, the *opinio juris*, which is lacking in the case of politically binding agreements, as is evidenced by the fact that the parties refused to enter into a legally binding agreement. The lack of consent to be bound at the moment of the agreement's conclusion translates itself – so to say – in a lack of *opinio juris* during its performance unless there are strong indications that the parties have changed their views. The persistent use of the term "politically binding" in the context of OCSE-commitments seems to be a clear contrary indication. Although the parties acknowledge that norm-conform conduct is required by virtue of the agreement laying down such norms and although they feel entitled to protest vehemently in

---

21 *See* the thorough study of Professor Skubiszewski on Resolutions of the General Assembly of the United Nations for the Institut de Droit international, ANNUAIRE (1985) at 29–358.

22 ICJ REPORTS 1969, para. 77.

case of non-compliance (deviating conduct is not tolerated), they also agree that such conduct is not required by law. "L'accord politique constitue alors une solution d'attente, qui 'gèle' la situation jusqu'au moment où les conditions d'un règlement juridique acceptable par toutes les parties intéressées seront réunies."[23] The "freezing-process prevents the crystallization into hard law.

This does not, however, exclude the possibility that the setting of political norms may be an impetus for the creation of legal norms elsewhere. In this respect it is noteworthy that minority rights, which were developed as political norms during the various CSCE conferences on the human dimension in a remarkably audacious way, have become a matter for consideration within the Council of Europe for treaty-making purposes. The experience gained until now in this respect, however, also shows that States are considerably more restrictive in accepting legal obligations than in entering into non-legal commitments. It may therefore be asked whether Renata Szafarz's forecast that one cannot exclude the emergence in the future of certain European customary norms, or more precisely: customary norms of the CSCE, (in particular in the field of the human dimension)[24] is not – in spite of her cautious wording – already too ambitious.

This conclusion, which seems to be sound both from a view-point of doctrine and from that of State-practice, nevertheless has one highly unsatisfactory element. From the view-point of a legal *order* it is unsatisfactory that States obviously can prevent the establishment of the shared conviction that the behaviour, prescribed by an agreement, is required by a rule of law by just calling these commitments "political". Or, to put it in a different way, what is the difference between a norm of soft law, which is allowed to crystallize into a hard legal norm and a politically binding norm, which is supposed to remain political for an indeterminate period unless it is formally transformed into a legally binding treaty? Is not in reality the distinction between legal norms and non-legal norms more blurred?

Let me illustrate this by referring to another potential source of legal obligations: the unilateral act. In the *Nuclear Tests* cases the International Court of Justice states: "It is well recognized that declarations made by way of unilateral acts, concerning legal or factual situations, may have the effect of creating legal obligations... When it is the intention of the State making the declaration that it should become bound according to its terms, that intention confers on the declaration the character of a *legal* undertaking, the

23 M. VIRALLY, *op. cit.*, *supra* note 14, at 235.

24 R. SZAFARZ, *op. cit.*, *supra* note 1, at 27.

State being thenceforth *legally* required to follow a course of conduct consistent with the declaration" (emphasis added).[25] Whether there is in fact an intention to be bound is – according to the Court – to be ascertained by interpretation of the act. The Court applies to such unilateral acts the principle of good faith and concludes: "Thus interested States may take cognizance of unilateral declarations and place confidence in them and are entitled to require that the obligation thus created be respected" (para. 46).

Now it is quite clear that the various statements by high French authorities, which formed the basis of the Court's decision, were made in a political context. If it can be assumed that there was an intention to be bound, it may also be assumed that these statements had more the character of a political declaration of intent,[26] may be even a political commitment, than that of an intention to become legally bound. Nowhere, however, does the Court make a distinction between the intention to become politically bound and that to become legally bound and – in all fairness – it would have set itself an impossible task had it tried to do so. As Schachter says "Chiefs of State and foreign ministers do enter into 'non-binding' (=political) arrangements and lower officials may, if authorized, act for a State in incurring legally binding obligations."[27] The same goes true for unilateral declarations.

But if, in the case of unilateral acts, it is impossible to distinguish between political and legal commitments, a too rigid distinction between such commitments which are contained in written texts (where such a distinction usually *is* possible) may lead to rather unbalanced results. Maybe this is the reason why Virally included in his conclusions a sentence which at first sight seems rather bewildering: "(a State which has accepted a purely political commitment) is subject to all legal obligations resulting from such a commitment, in particular when it has created the appearance of a legal commitment upon which another person has relied and if the conditions required by international law for the creation of such obligations are fulfilled."[28] One wonders whether in a twilight zone clear and unequivocal rules and guidelines can be discerned.

---

25 ICJ REPORTS 1974 at 267, para. 43.

26 This at least seems to have been the view of the Australian Government, which submitted that a statement by the French Minister of Foreign Affairs "falls far short of an undertaking that there will be no more atmospheric tests conducted by the French Government" (para. 47).

27 O. SCHACHTER, *op. cit., supra* note 12, at 299.

28 M. VIRALLY, *op. cit., supra* note 3, at 289.

Concluding Remarks

When the Commission of the Institut de Droit international started its work, Judge Manfred Lachs warned against a too thorough study of the concept of moral or political obligations. In hindsight, it may be called fortunate that the Commission did not heed his advice, even if it has to be admitted that complete clarity has not been obtained. Maybe the situation is best illustrated by Bothe who at one place says that the line between legal and non-legal obligations becomes blurred, whereas at another place he says that the differences between legal and non-legal norms should caution against doctrinal approaches which bring them into too close proximity.[29] In all probability, in both cases he is right. Scylla and Charybdis are both omnipresent in the borderland between legally-binding and non-binding agreements. The existence of the borderland, however, cannot be denied. It is in this borderland that, to use another expression of Bothe, non-legal steps are set on the way to legal change. For the international lawyer, exploring this process may sometimes lead to annoying obfuscation but from time to time it also opens new and fascinating horizons.

---

[29] M. BOTHE, *op. cit.*, *supra* note 5, at 88, 94.

THE INTERNATIONAL COURT OF JUSTICE AND THE LAW OF THE SEA – SOME REFLECTIONS

by

BARBARA KWIATKOWSKA

> "A court of justice need not be and, indeed, should not be an exponent of the law-making opinion of 'yesterday' or still worse – to use Albert V. Dicey's expression – 'the opinion of the day before yesterday.' The Court should and can look ahead. Otherwise there would not be decisions such as the one in the case concerning *Reparation for Injuries Suffered in the Service of the United Nations*."
>
> Dissenting Opinion of Judge *ad hoc* Krzysztof Skubiszewski from the *Portugal v. Australia East Timor* Judgment of 30 June, ICJ REPORTS 1995, 90, 224–77, at 238 [citing A.V. DICEY, LECTURES ON THE RELATION BETWEEN LAW AND PUBLIC OPINION IN ENGLAND DURING THE NINETEENTH CENTUR 32 and 367 (1905)].

The law and practice of the International Court of Justice (ICJ) and its predecessor, Permanent Court of International Justice (PCIJ), have always been of particular interest to Professor Krzysztof Jan Skubiszewski as a prominent scholar[1] and practitioner (Minister, arbitrator and Judge *ad hoc*) of international law. His Foreign Ministership, which contributed to his image as the greatest diplomat of modern Poland, was marked by a Polish Declaration accepting the compulsory jurisdiction of the Court under Article 36(2) of the Statute which was signed by the then Minister Skubiszewski on 21 September 1990, and which was followed two years later by such Declarations of two other former members of the Warsaw Pact – Bulgaria and Hungary.[2] Hungary and Slovakia filed subsequently in the Court their 1993

---

[1] *See e.g.* an excellent early article by K.J. SKUBISZEWSKI, *Elements of Custom and the Hague Court*, 31 ZEITSCHRIFT FÜR AUSLÄNDISCHES ÖFFENTLICHES RECHT UND VÖLKERRECHT (ZAÖRV) (1971) at 810–54; and of his more recent writings, *see* K. SKUBISZEWSKI, *The International Court of Justice and the Security Council*, (in:) A.V. LOWE and M. FITZMAURICE (eds.)), FIFTY YEARS OF THE INTERNATIONAL COURT OF JUSTICE – ESSAYS IN HONOUR OF SIR ROBERT JENNINGS (1996) at 606–29.

[2] ICJ YEARBOOK (1993–1994), 86 [Bulgaria], 95 [Hungary], 112 [Poland] (N° 48). *Cf.* R. SZAFARZ, THE COMPULSORY JURISDICTION OF THE INTERNATIONAL COURT OF JUSTICE (1993) at 86–8; S. ROSENNE, *The Cold War and the International Court of Justice: A Review Essay of Stephen M. Schwebel's*, JUSTICE IN INTERNATIONAL LAW, 35 VIRGINIA JOURNAL OF INTERNATIONAL LAW (VJIL) (1995) at 669, 681. For Professor Skubiszewski's perception of the post-Cold War Europe and Poland's role (in the context of its prospective NATO membership) therein, *see* his interview on *No Buffer Zone Between Germany and Russia*, NRC HANDELSBLAD (in Dutch) of 26 June 1995, at 7.

compromis in the currently pending *Gabcikovo-Nagymoros Project* case,[3] with Professor Skubiszewski (as we are used to address him notwithstanding his actual affiliations), by then already a President of Iran-United States Claims Tribunal in the Hague, having been chosen by Slovakia as Judge *ad hoc*.[4] Meanwhile, he also was designated as Judge *ad hoc* by Portugal[5] and inaugurated his appearance in the Great Hall of Justice in the *East Timor* case.[6] At the magnificent celebration of the 50th ICJ Anniversary, Krzysztof J. Skubiszewski shared with us his perceptions of this experience in an exchange of views with eminent Professor Elihu Lauterpacht, QC,[7] in a Panel on The Role of *Ad Hoc* Judges, gracefully Chaired by Judge Shi Jiuyong through the ensuing vivid discussion.[8]

It seemed therefore appropriate, in an essay in Professor Skubiszewski's honour, to reflect on an area of this author's expertise in the context of the contentious and advisory practice of the Court. The prominent place of international law of the sea in the Court's annals makes no exception to judicial practice of other courts and tribunals, whether national or international. This is evident from a glance at space which law of the sea-related cases take (in sections ranging through foundations of international law, recognition, international and municipal law, immunities, State territory,

---

3 ICJ REPORTS 1993 at 319; 1994 at 151. *Cf.* S. ROSENNE, THE WORLD COURT: WHAT IT IS AND HOW IT WORKS, at 115, 242 (Fifth Completely Revised Edition, 1995).

4 REPORT OF THE INTERNATIONAL COURT OF JUSTICE, U.N. Doc.A/50/4, para.124 at 27 (1995). On initiation by the *Corfu Channel* case of choosing by States of non-nationals as Judges *ad hoc*, *see* S. ROSENNE, *op. cit.*, *supra* note 3, at 249.

5 *Cf.* the glamorous JUBILEE BOOK by A. EYFFINGER, THE INTERNATIONAL COURT OF JUSTICE 1946–1996 (1996) at 164, reporting that Judge *ad hoc* Skubiszewski from Poland was called in twice by different foreign nations, Portugal and Slovakia respectively.

6 ICJ REPORTS 1995 at 90, 93, noting that by its Letter of 14 July 1994, the Agent of Portugal informed the Court that it had chosen Krzysztof J. Skubiszewski to replace António de Arruda Ferrer-CORREIA as Judge *ad hoc*. For Dissenting Opinion of Judge *ad hoc* Skubiszewski, *see ibid.* at 224–77, as referred to in main text accompanying *infra* notes 7, at 99–103, 151, 221. For references to passage of that Opinion chosen as motto of this essay, *see* main text accompanying *infra* notes 153, at 188, 230 and 256.

7 For Biography of Judge *ad hoc* Lauterpacht, designated by Bosnia-Herzegovina in the APPLICATION OF THE CONVENTION ON THE PREVENTION AND PUNISHMENT OF THE CRIME OF GENOCIDE case (ICJ REPORTS 1993 at 325, 335), *see* 48 ICJ Yearbook (1993–1994) at 58. For invocation of Judge Lauterpacht's Separate Opinion (ICJ REPORTS 1993 at 408) in the *East Timor* Dissenting Opinion of Judge Skubiszewski, *see* ICJ REPORTS 1995 at 238–9; and for further discussion of Lauterpacht's views, *see* K.J. SKUBISZEWSKI, *The Role of* ***Ad Hoc*** *Judges, Panel of Judge Shi*, *infra* note 8.

8 K.J. SKUBISZEWSKI and E. LAUTERPACHT, QC, *The Role of* ***Ad Hoc*** *Judges*, and statements in discussion by Sir IAN SINCLAIR, KCMG, QC, Vice-President SCHWEBEL, G. ABI-SAAB, C.K. HARPER and Judge SHAHABUDDEEN, (in:) R. HIGGINS and CH.G. WEERAMANTRY (eds.), INCREASING THE EFFECTIVENESS OF THE COURT – AN ICJ/UNITAR COLLOQUIUM TO CELEBRATE THE 50TH ANNIVERSARY OF THE INTERNATIONAL COURT OF JUSTICE, PEACE PALACE, The Hague, 16–18 April 1996 (in press).

treaties, unilateral acts, warfare and neutrality, etc.) in voluminous cases on international law compiled for the past century. The experts of this important branch of law take special pride from recognition of the 1872 *G.B./U.S.A. The Alabama (The Kaersage)* arbitration,[9] which dealt with the law of neutrality and of warfare at sea, as the watershed of modern international litigation and as the source of the underlying principle of the consent of the parties which is governing the jurisdiction of the Court.[10] Many other, though less spectacular, law of the sea-related cases remained of notable importance from the viewpoint of various substantial and procedural solutions concerning, *e.g.* international servitudes,[11] exhaustion of local remedies,[12] or *ad hoc*

---

[9] A.M. STUYT, 94 SURVEY OF INTERNATIONAL ARBITRATIONS 1794–1989 (1990). For reliance on the *Alabama* pronouncements, *see* the 1953 *Nottebohm* Judgment (Preliminary Objection), ICJ REPORTS 1953 at 111, 119; repeated in the *Arbitral Award of 31 July 1989* Judgment, ICJ REPORTS 1991 at 53, 68–9. *See* also the *Corfu Channel* Dissenting Opinion (Merits) of Judge Azevedo, ICJ REPORTS 1949 at 78, 96; the *Anglo/Norwegian Fisheries* Dissenting Opinion of Judge Sir Arnold McNair, ICJ REPORTS 1951 at 158, 181; the *Rights of Nationals of the U.S.A. in Morocco* Pleadings, Vol. II, at 147 (Agent Gros/France); the *Fisheries Jurisdiction* Pleadings (U.K.), at 249; the *East Timor* Dissenting Opinion of Judge Weeramantry, ICJ REPORTS 1995 at 139, 158–9.

[10] *See* S. ROSENNE, *L'Affaire de l'**Alabama, Tribune de Gen ve***, le 14 septembre 1972 (cent ans apr s la sentence du 14 septembre 1872), reprinted (in:) S. ROSENNE, AN INTERNATIONAL LAW MISCELLANY (1993) at 125–31; M.O. HUDSON, THE PERMANENT COURT OF INTERNATIONAL JUSTICE 1920–1942 (1943) at 601; J. SETTE-CAMARA, *Methods of Obligatory Settlement of Disputes*, (in:) M. BEDJAOUI (ed.), INTERNATIONAL LAW: ACHIEVEMENTS AND PROSPECTS (1991) at 519, 527; S. ROSENNE, INTERVENTION IN THE INTERNATIONAL COURT OF JUSTICE (1993) at 7; S. ROSENNE, THE WORLD COURT, *op. cit.*, *supra* note 3, at 5.

[11] The rejection (in accordance with British contention) of the concept of international servitudes by the 1910 *G.B./U.S.A. North Atlantic Coast Fisheries* Award [RIAA XI, at 167; 7 AJIL 1, at 140, and Supp. 41 (1913); N° 291/Stuyt] was not referred to in the 1923 *S.S. Wimbledon* Judgment (Merits), PCIJ Series A, N° 1, 15. But the PCIJ did not accept German contention as to applicability of this concept to the Kiel Canal. *Cf.* H.D. REID, INTERNATIONAL SERVITUDES IN LAW AND PRACTICE (1932) at 32–5, 138–40.

For invocation of rejection of the servitudes by the 1910 Award, *see* the RIGHTS OF NATIONALS OF THE U.S.A. IN MOROCCO Pleadings, Vol. I, at 66 (Memorial of France), Vol. II, at 173 (Agent Gros, 16 July 1952); the *Minquiers* Pleadings, Vol. II, at 88 (Counsel Fitzmaurice, 21 September 1953). On the concept of servitudes, *see* the ***Corfu** Dissenting Opinion (Merits) of Judge Azevedo*, ICJ REPORTS 1949 at 104; the *Minquiers* Pleadings, Vol. I, at 473, 477 and 487 (Reply of U.K.), 716 (Rejoinder of France).

[12] The classical rule of exhaustion of local remedies, as expounded in the 1934 *Finland v. U.K. Finnish Ships* Award of Judge Bagge (Sweden) [RIAA III, at 1479; N° 397/Stuyt], was applied in the 1956 *Greece v. U.K. Ambatielos Claim* Award [RIAA XII, at 91; 24 ILR, at 291; N° 422/Stuyt], which settled the merits of the claim itself in a follow-up to the *Ambatielos* Judgment (Merits: Obligation to Arbitrate), ICJ REPORTS 1953 at 10. *Cf.* main text accompanying *infra* note 132. For comparative analysis of the *Ambatielos Claim* and the *Finnish Ships* Awards, *see* D.R. MUMMERY, *The Content of the Duty to Exhaust Local Judicial Remedies*, 58 AJIL (1964) at 389, 398–414.

For reliance on the *Finnish Ships* Award, *see* the *Ambatielos* Pleadings, 16 (Memorial of Greece), at 266–7 (Rejoinder[Merits] of U.K.), at 427–33 (27 March, Counsel Fawcett), at 442–4 (28 March,

Chambers.[13] In the field of State immunity, the national case law and domestic enactments, including their major part related to maritime shipping,[14] continue to provide a rare insight into national decision-making as a source of international law.[15]

I. IDENTTIFYING THE LAW OF THE SEA-RELATED CASES

Both the Permanent Court and International Court of Justice initiated their practice by the law of the sea contentious cases, *i.e.* the 1923 *S.S. Wimbledon (France, Great Britain, Italy, Japan v. Germany: Poland Intervening)* and the 1947/49 *Corfu Channel (U.K. v. Albania)* cases respectively. The classification into law of the sea-category of cases which followed in both Courts might in some instances be a matter of controversy. The precious

Counsel Sir Frank Soskice), at 492–4 (30 March 1953, Fawcett); and on both *Finnish Ships* and *Ambatielos Claim* Awards, *see* the *Certain Norwegian Loans* Pleadings, Vol. II, at 74 (15 May, Agent Gros), at 161–5 (22 May 1957, Advocate Bourquin). In the *Elettronica Sicula S.p.A. (ELSI)* case, objection to the admissibility of Italy, which (in part) relied on both Awards along with the *Interhandel* Judgment (Preliminary Objections) [ICJ REPORTS 1959 at 27], in the *ELSI* Pleadings, Vol. II, at 27–9, 264–7 (Counter-Memorial of Italy), at 417–18 (Rejoinder of Italy), was contested by the United States, *ibid.* at 374–6 (Reply of the U.S.A.), and it was rejected unanimously in the *ELSI* Judgment, ICJ REPORTS 1989 at 15. On contribution of this Judgment to the elucidation of the local remedies rule, *see* the *ELSI* Dissenting Opinion of Judge Schwebel, ICJ REPORTS 1989 at 94, 94; S.M. SCHWEBEL, *The Treatment of Human Rights and of Aliens in the ICJ*, (in:) ESSAYS IN HONOUR OF SIR ROBERT JENNINGS, *op. cit.*, *supra* note 1, at 327, 350.

13 The composition of the *Argentina/Chile Beagle Channel* Court of Arbitration of five members, who all were the ICJ Judges (H. Dillard, Sir Gerald Fitzmaurice, A. Gros, Ch.D. Onyeama and S. Petrén) [17 ILM (1978) at 634; 71 AJIL (1977) at 733; N°435/Stuyt], provided a stimulus for amending Article 26(2) of the ICJ Statute with respect to composition of *ad hoc* Chambers. *Cf.* S.M. SCHWEBEL, *New Life for World Court*, 23 VJIL (1983) at 375–8; G. ABI-SAAB, *De l'evolution de la Cour Internationale: Reflexions sur quelques tendances recentes*, 96 REVUE GÉNÉRALE DE DROIT INTERNATIONAL PUBLIC (RGDIP) (1992) at 274, 287; S.M. SCHWEBEL, JUSTICE IN INTERNATIONAL LAW – SELECTED WRITINGS OF JUDGE STEPHEN M. SCHWEBEL, (1994) Chapter 6: *Chambers of the International Court of Justice Formed for Particular Cases*, at 93, 101–2; E. VALENCIA-OSPINA, *The Use of Chambers of the ICJ*, (in:) ESSAYS IN HONOUR OF SIR ROBERT JENNINGS, *op. cit.*, *supra* note 1, at 503, 506–7.

14 Absolute immunity for a sovereign required by English law since 1873 *The Charkieh (The Batavier)* [L.R. 4 A. & E. 59; 42 L.J.Q.B. 75] and 1879/80 *The Parlament Belge* [L.R. (1879) 4 P.D. 129; (1880) 5 P.D. 197] cases was reversed only by 1977 *The Owners of the Philippine Admiral v. Wallem Shipping (Hong Kong)* Judgment [A.C. 373; 64 ILR 90], which initiated restrictive doctrine of immunity in respect of actions *in rem* (as followed by the extension in the 1977 *Trendtex Trading Corporation v. Central Bank of Nigeria* [Q.B. 529; 16 ILM (1977) at 471] of the restrictive doctrine to actions *in personam* as well).

15 R. HIGGINS, *Certain Unresolved Aspects of the Law of State Immunity*, 29 NETHERLANDS INTERNATIONAL LAW REVIEW (1982) at 265–76, 265. *Cf.* M. BYERS, *State Immunity: Article 18 of the ILC's Draft*, 44 INTERNATIONAL & COMPARATIVE LAW QUARTERLY (ICLQ) (1995) at 882–93.

Unofficial Summaries published by the ICJ Registry in 1986[16] and the splendid *Jubilee Book* of 1996[17] cover only such cases *sensu stricto*. From among cases brought before the PCIJ, apart from the *Wimbledon*, this category covers the *S.S. Lotus (France v. Turkey)* and the [discontined] *Delimitation of the Territorial Waters Between the Island of Castellorizo and the Coast of Anatolia (Italy/Turkey)* cases. From among cases instituted in the ICJ after the *Corfu Channel*, both publications referred to above include into law of the sea-category: the *Fisheries (U.K. v. Norway)*, the *North Sea Continental Shelf (F.R.G./Denmark; F.R.G./Netherlands)*, pair of the *Fisheries Jurisdiction (U.K. v. Iceland* and *F.R.G. v. Iceland)*, the *Aegean Sea Continental Shelf (Greece v. Turkey)*, the *Tunisia/Libya Continental Shelf*, the *Libya/Malta Continental Shelf* and the *Delimitation of the Maritime Boundary in the Gulf of Maine (Canada/U.S.A.)* cases. The more recent cases added thereto by the *Jubilee Book* are: the [discontinued] *Passage Through the Great Belt (Finland v. Denmark)*, the *Maritime Delimitation in the Area Between Greenland and Jan Mayen (Denmark v. Norway)*, the *Arbitral Award of 31 July 1989 (Guinea-Bissau v. Senegal)*[18] and the [discontinued] *Maritime Delimitation Between Guinea-Bissau and Senegal (Guinea-Bissau v. Senegal)*, as well as the pending *Maritime Delimitation and Territorial Questions Between Qatar and Bahrain (Qatar v. Bahrain)* and the *Fisheries Jurisdiction [The Estai] (Spain v. Canada)* cases.

We could, however, *sensu largo*, consider as law of the sea-related also some cases which primarily involved territorial disputes, the law of international organizations, issues of decolonization, and international peace and security. In particular, commencing with the 1933 *Legal Status of Eastern Greenland (Denmark v. Norway)* Judgment (as paralleled by the [discontinued] *Legal Status of Southeastern Territory of Greenland (Denmark/Norway)* case), a number of cases – including the *Minquiers and Ecrehos (U.K./France)*, the [discontinued] pair of *Antarctica (U.K. v. Argentina* and *U.K. v. Chile)*, the *Land, Island and Maritime Frontier Dispute (El Salvador/Honduras: Nicaragua Intervening*, hereinafter: *Gulf of Fonseca*),[19] the

---

16 BACKGROUND NOTE VI: COLLECTED UNOFFICIAL SUMMARIES OF DECISIONS CONCERNING THE LAW OF THE SEA 1946–1986 (ICJ, July 1986).

17 The *Jubilee Book, op. cit., supra* note 5, A. WITTEVEEN, Chapter 10: *A Review of the Court's Case-Law*, at 342–58, 344–9 (Disputes Concerning the Law of the Sea, including maps).

18 The two *Arbitral Award of 31 July 1989* decisions (1990 and 1991) of the Court are exceptional in this category of law of the sea cases in that this case concerned the validity of the *Guinea-Bissau/Senegal* Arbitral Award. But the 1991 Court's Judgment was of direct relevance to future delimitation through reaffirming the findings of the 1989 Award concerning the validity of the 1960 Franco-Portuguese Delimitation Agreement.

19 The *Jubilee Book, op. cit., supra* note 5, at 343, refers to the *Gulf of Fonseca* in section on Territorial and Boundary Disputes. The case was reported in the *Reports of the Secretary-*

East Timor (Portugal v. Australia)[20] and the pending *Qatar v. Bahrain* cases – involved the question of sovereignty over island territory, dealing with certain law of the sea-related aspects in this context. Apart from the *Gulf of Fonseca*, maritime delimitation also forms a part of the pending *Land and Maritime Boundary Between Cameroon and Nigeria (Cameroon v. Nigeria)* case.[21] The Court's decisions in the *South West Africa (Namibia)* (1966 and 1971)[22] and the 1975 *Western Sahara*[23] cases concerned, moreover, (both West African) territories whose long coastlines determine their major interests in ocean governance.

The law of the sea cases *sensu largo* which dealt with various aspects pertaining to shipping and navigation include the 1931 *Access to, or Anchorage in, the Port of Danzig of Polish War Vessels* and the 1960 *Constitution of the Maritime Safety Committee of the IMCO*[24] Advisory Opinions of the PCIJ and ICJ respectively, as well as the 1952/3 *Ambatielos (Greece v. U.K.)*

General – Law of the Sea, U.N. Docs A/43/718, 9 (1988), A/44/650, 11 (1989), A/46/724, 13, A/45/721, 13 and Corr.1 [*El Salvador v. Honduras*] (1990), A/47/623, 12 (1992), in section on Maritime Disputes and Conflicts. The Reports are prepared annually by the Division for Ocean Affairs and the Law of the Sea (DOALOS/OLA), U.N./New York, under the Directorship of presently Dr. Moritaka Hayashi (Japan) who succeeded, in 1996, Dr. Jean-Pierre Lévy (France). *See* also *infra* note 67.

20 The *Jubilee Book*, *op. cit.*, *supra* note 5, at 355, refers to the *East Timor* case in section on Issues of Decolonization. The 1995 *East Timor* Judgment was reported in the *Report of the Secretary-General – Law of the Sea*, U.N. Doc. A/50/713, 34–5 (1995), in section on Maritime Disputes and Conflicts. For reference to the 1989 Australia/Indonesia Timor Gap Treaty [29 ILM (1990) at 469], *see ibid.* at 39, and; Doc. A/45/721 (1990), *op. cit.*, *supra* note 19, at 12.

21 The *Jubilee Book*, *op. cit.*, *supra* note 5, at 343–4, refers to the *Cameroon v. Nigeria* case in section on Territorial and Boundary Disputes. Institution of this case was referred to in the *Report of the Secretary-General – Law of the Sea*, U.N. Doc. A/49/631, 15 (1994), in section on Maritime Delimitation Disputes.

22 *South West Africa (Ethiopia v. South Africa; Liberia v. South Africa)* and *Legal Consequences for States of the Continued Presence of South Africa in Namibia (South West Africa) Notwithstanding Security Council Resolution 276 (1970)* cases; main text accompanying *infra* note 44. *Cf. Namibia, South Africa, and the Walvis Bay Dispute*, 89 YALE LAW JOURNAL (1980) at 903–22; 1992 Namibia/South Africa Agreement on the Joint Administration of Walvis Bay and the Offshore Islands, 32 ILM (1993) at 1152, 1470; D.B. HAMMAN, *A Solution for Maritime Delimitation Between Namibia and South Africa*, 10 INTERNATIONAL JOURNAL OF MARINE AND COASTAL LAW (1995) at 369–88.

23 *Cf.* main text accompanying *infra* note 242; M. SHAW, *The **Western Sahara** Case*, 49 BRITISH YEARBOOK OF INTERNATIONAL LAW (BYIL) (1978) at 119–54; UNGA Resolutions 48/49 and 50/36 on Question of Western Sahara of 10 December 1993 and 6 December 1995 respectively; *Reports of the Secretary-General on the Work of the Organization* (Western Sahara), U.N. Docs A/49/1, 78–9 (1994) and A/50/1, 108–9 (1995); Security Council Resolution 1042 (1996).

24 The JUBILEE BOOK, *op. cit.*, *supra* note 5, at 353, refers to the *IMCO* case in section on The Law of International Organizations.

case.[25] The 1955 *Nottebohm (Liechtenstein v. Guatemala)* (Second Phase) Judgment was unique in its unintended impact, *i.e.* application by the International Law Commission (ILC) of the genuine link concept to ships,[26] as endorsed in the 1958 U.N. Geneva Convention on the High Seas,[27] and as underlying the events which led to the *IMCO* case. The matter found further reflection in the 1970 *Barcelona Traction, Light and Power Company, Ltd. (Belgium v. Spain)* Separate Opinion (Second Phase) of Judge Jessup. Some important issues related to navigation and the use of force were, moreover, involved in the *Military and Paramilitary Activities in and Against Nicaragua (Nicaragua v. U.S.A.)*,[28] the [discontinued] *Aerial Incident of 3 July 1988 (Iran v. U.S.A.)* and the pending *Oil Platforms (Iran v. U.S.A.)* cases. In addition, navigational matters in combination with the marine environment protection played an important role in the pair of the 1973/4 *Nuclear Tests (Australia v. France* and *New Zealand v. France)* cases, with New Zealand's attempt to reopen its case on environmental grounds having failed twenty years later in the 1995 *Request for an Examination of the Situation in Accordance with Paragraph 63 of the Court's Judgment of 20 December 1974 in the Nuclear Tests (New Zealand v. France)* case.[29]

Given their numerosity and the magnitude of procedural and substantial issues involved, a systematic analysis of the cases related to the law of the sea *sensu stricto* and *sensu largo* would exceed limited space available to this essay. The preceding remarks and some reflections drawn below are, therefore, meant as but framework for such an analysis to be hopefully continued elsewhere.[30]

---

25 *Ibid.* at 357, refers to the *Ambatielos* case in section on Protection of Private Interests. *See* also *supra* note 12.

26 ILC YEARBOOK (1956-II) at 15 and 278–9. *Cf. infra* notes 223–229.

27 *See infra* note 31.

28 The JUBILEE BOOK, *op. cit., supra* note 5, at 356, refers to the *Nicaragua v. U.S.A.* case in section on International Peace and Security, the Use of Force and Intervention; and Thirlway, *infra* note 62, Part VI, 88–90, analyzes this case in Division A on The Law of the Sea.

29 The JUBILEE BOOK, *op. cit., supra* note 5, at 356, refers to 1995 *New Zealand v. France Nuclear Tests* Order, jointly with the 1973/4 *Nuclear Tests* cases, in section on International Peace and Security, the Use of Force and Intervention. The 1973/4 *Nuclear Tests* cases are analyzed by Thirlway, *infra* note 62, Part VI, 87–8, in Division A on The Law of the Sea; and the 1995 *NZ v. France* Order is reported upon in the *Report of the Secretary-General – Law of the Sea*, U.N. Doc. A/50/713, *supra* note 20, at 40, in section on Peace and Security.

30 It has been this author's hope to undertake a comprehensive work on *The International Court of Justice and the Law of the Sea, with Reference to Other Courts and Tribunals.*

II. THE WORLD COURT AND THE TRADITIONAL AND THE NEW LAW OF THE SEA

It would seem appropriate to preliminary reflect at first on the critical importance of the contribution of the World Court to the law of the sea development in the context of: traditional and the new law of the sea; the law of the sea as an indispensable part of the global system of peace and security; and the law of the sea as an inherent part of general international law.

Through its consistent pronouncements, the World Court has been indeed contributing significantly to the development of both the traditional (through the 1923 *Wimbledon*, the 1927 *Lotus*, the 1949 *Corfu Channel* [Merits], the 1951 *Anglo/Norwegian Fisheries*, and the 1955 *Nottebohm* [Second Phase] Judgments) and the new (through the 1960 *IMCO*, the 1969 *North Sea*, pair of the 1974 *Nuclear Tests*, pair of the 1974 *Fisheries Jurisdiction* [Merits], and the 1978 *Aegean Sea* [Jurisdiction] Judgments) law of the sea, as codified and progressively developed in the four U.N. Geneva Conventions of 29 April 1958[31] and the U.N. Montego Bay Convention on the Law of the Sea of 10 December 1982,[32] respectively. The *Lotus* case was perhaps settled in the most difficult time, given the controversies concerning the criminal jurisdiction which the League of Nations Committee of Experts for the Progressive Codification of International Law found itself unable to decide prior to that case.[33] The subsequent Draft Convention of the Second Committee (Territorial Waters) of the 1930 Hague Conference for the Codification of International Law[34] was not referred to in either the *Corfu* (Merits) or the *Anglo/Norwegian Fisheries* Judgments. But the 1930 Draft[35] was extensively discussed by the parties in the pleadings in these two

31 Conventions on: Territorial Sea and the Contiguous Zone (in force: 10 September 1964), 516 UNTS at 205; High Seas (in force: 30 September 1962), 450 UNTS at 11; Fishing and Conservation of the Living Resources of the High Seas (in force: 20 March 1966), 559 UNTS at 285; Continental Shelf (in force: 10 June 1964), 499 UNTS, at 311; Optional Protocol of Signature Concerning the Compulsory Settlement of Disputes (in force: 30 September 1982), 450 UNTS at 169. *Cf.* U.N. Doc. ST/LEG/SER.E/13 (Multilateral Treaties as of 31 December 1994), at 831–49 (1995).

32 For the 1982 U.N. Montego Bay Convention, which entered into force on 16 November 1994, *see* 21 ILM (1982) at 1245, and for the U.N. Agreement of 28 July 1994 Relating to the Implementation of the Convention's Part XI, *see* 33 ILM (1994) at 1309. For status of the Convention and the Agreement, as of 29 February 1996, *see U.N./DOALOS Law of the Sea Bulletin* (1996 N° 30). *Cf.* M. HAYASHI, *The 1994 Agreement for the Universalization of the Law of the Sea Convention*, 27 OCEAN DEVELOPMENT AND INTERNATIONAL LAW (1996) at 31–9.

33 20 AJIL Supp. (1926). *Cf.* main text accompanying *infra* notes 214–218.

34 24 AJIL Supp. (1930). *Cf.* M.O. HUDSON, *The First Conference for the Codification of International Law*, 24 AJIL (1930) at 447–66, 784 [*erratum*].

35 *Cf.* the *Anglo/Norwegian* Pleadings, Vol. I, at 395–6 (Counter-Memorial of Norway), invoking the *Corfu* Pleadings [Vol. III, at 269–71 (11 November 1948, Agent Sir Eric Beckett)]

cases which, along with the preceding *Lotus*, provided notable early instances of the Court's reliance on customary international law.

During the *Anglo/Norwegian Fisheries* proceedings, the U.N. General Assembly included in 1949 (on Iceland's initiative) the regime of Territorial Sea into the ILC *travaux préparatoires* to the First U.N. Conference on the Law of the Sea (UNCLOS I), whereas the *North Sea* cases were the first to overlap with preparation since 1967 of the UNCLOS III. The new law of the sea as embodied in the 1982 U.N. Montego Bay Convention and its voluminous legislative history found therefore important reflection in the *North Sea* and all subsequent Judgments, including their Opinions (especially the *Tunisia/Libya* and *Libya/Malta* Dissenting Opinions [Merits] of Judge Shigeru Oda).[36] The 1958 U.N. Geneva Conventions and their legislative history featured prominently in all cases since the *Anglo/Norwegian Fisheries* until today. Upon adoption of the Montego Bay Convention, the Court's Judgments delieverd in the 1982 *Tunisia/Libya* (Merits), 1984 *Gulf of Maine*, 1985 *Libya/Malta* (Merits), 1986 *Nicaragua v. U.S.A.* (Merits), 1991 *Guinea-Bissau v. Senegal*, 1991 *Great Belt* (Provisional Measures), 1992 *Gulf of Fonseca* (Merits), and 1993 *Jan Mayen* cases, have continued to retain the highest authority in determining the State of law regarding various law of the sea issues and concepts.[37]

This also relates to individual Opinions attached by the members of the Court to the respective Judgments. The overestimating of such (especially Dissenting) Opinions – as is evident in both the classic writings[38] and (too) many current commentaries on the Court's practice – seems to underestimate fundamental rules of the Court's functioning. The role of Judges' Opinions as properly construed[39] does not, however, affect the fact that some of

to the effect that international conventions, referred to under Article 38(1)(a) of the ICJ Statute, "are finally agreed and ratified conventions," and that the Court is not entitled to apply as law in case before it conventions which are only signed, and still less a mere 1930 Draft Convention; Vol. II, at 432–9 (Reply of U.K.), Vol. III, at 301–2 (Rejoinder of Norway). *Cf.* main text accompanying *infra* note 206.

36 *See infra* notes 41, 61, 67 and 186. *Cf.* S. Rosennne et al. (eds.), UNITED NATIONS CONVENTION ON THE LAW OF THE SEA 1982 – A COMMENTARY, Vol. I (1985), Vol. II (1993), Vol. III (1995), Vol. IV (1991), Vol. V (1989), Vol. VI (in press); *Problems Arising From a Succession of Codification Conventions on a Particular Subject*, Rapporteur: Sir IAN SINCLAIR, 66 ANNUAIRE INSTITUT DE DROIT INTERNATIONAL (Annuaire IDI) [Session de Lisbonne] (1995-I) at 15–248.

37 *Cf.* R. HIGGINS, QC, PROBLEMS AND PROCESS: INTERNATIONAL LAW AND HOW WE USE IT 18 (1994), referring to submission of H. THIRLWAY, INTERNATIONAL CUSTOMARY LAW AND CODIFICATION (1972), that international law is defined as that which the Court would apply in a given case.

38 *Cf.* J.H.W. VERZIJL, *The Jurisprudence of the World Court – A Case By Case Commentary*, Vol. I: PCIJ (1965) at 1922–40 and Vol. II: ICJ (1966) at 1947–65.

39 *See* S. ROSENNE, THE LAW AND PRACTICE OF THE INTERNATIONAL COURT (1965/1985) at 595–9; Sir ROBERT JENNINGS, *The Internal Judicial Practice of the International Court of Justice*,

these Opinions turned to be precursory of such basic concepts as, *e.g.*, the unity of archipelagic State,[40] or the parallelism between 200-mile exclusive economic zone (EEZ) and the continental shelf (CS).[41] In some instances Opinions of Judges may be instrumental for appreciation of the essential points underlying the majority's reasoning.[42] The views expressed in the three searching *New Zealand v. France* Dissenting Opinions (Request for an Examination of the Situation) on impacts of nuclear weapon tests on the marine environment perhaps carry particular weight in a situation where these views do not oppose those of the Court's majority which did not pronounce itself on these questions.[43]

III. THE WORLD COURT AND THE LAW OF THE SEA AS PART OF THE GLOBAL SYSTEM OF PEACE AND SECURITY AND AS PART OF GENERAL INTERNATIONAL LAW

The development of law of the sea (as that of international law generally) through jurisprudence of the International Court profited importantly from detour of developing countries from their distrust to by now well-es-

59 BYIL (1988) at 31–47; R.Y. JENNINGS, *The Collegiate Responsibility and Authority of the International Court of Justice*, (in:) INTERNATIONAL LAW AT A TIME OF PERPLEXITY, EASSAYS IN HONOUR OF SHABTAI ROSENNE (1989) at 343–53.

40 *Minquiers and Ecrehos* Separate Opinions of Judges Basdevant and Levi Carneiro, ICJ REPORTS 1953 at 74, 78; 85, 97–102, 108; the *Minquiers* Pleadings, Vol. II, 196–7 (28 September 1953, Agent Gros).

41 On precedential exposition of the EEZ/CS parallelism by Judge Oda, *see* B. KWIATKOWSKA, *Judge Shigeru Oda's Opinions in Law-of-the-Sea Cases: Equitable Maritime Boundary Delimitation*, 36 GERMAN YEARBOOK OF INTERNATIONAL LAW (1993) at 225–94. The article covers Judge Oda's *Tunisia/Libya, Libya/Malta, Guinea-Bissau v. Senegal* and *Gulf of Fonseca* Opinions. Not covered are subsequent Judge Oda's Opinions in the *Denmark v. Norway (Jan Mayen), East Timor*, and the pending *Qatar v. Bahrain* and *Cameroon v. Nigeria* cases.

42 *See e.g.* the *Denmark v. Norway (Jan Mayen)* Separate Opinion of Judge Schwebel, ICJ REPORTS 1993 at 118, 127, remarking that, "Yet it may be said in defence of the approach of Denmark, if not of the Court, that however extreme Denmark's claim appears in legal terms, in political terms it is perfectly understandable. Once Norway had extended to Iceland a 200-mile zone in relation to Jan Mayen, naturally Denmark sought no less on behalf of Greenland." *Cf.* also important procedural points raised in the *New Zealand v. France Nuclear Tests* Declaration (Request for an Examination of the Situation) of Vice-President Schwebel, ICJ REPORTS 1995 at 309. On the 1937 Opinion of Judge Hudson, *see infra* notes 178 and 185.

43 *New Zealand v. France Nuclear Tests* Dissenting Opinions (Request for an Examination of the Situation) of Judges Weeramantry, ICJ REPORTS 1995 at 317–62, and Koroma, *ibid.* 363–80, and Judge *ad hoc* Sir Geoffrey Palmer, *ibid.* 381–421. *Cf.* Sir KENNETH KEITH, *QC, The ICJ and Nuclear Weapons*, 21 NEW ZEALAND INTERNATIONAL REVIEW (1996 N° 1) at 20–3; B. KWIATKOWSKA, *New Zealand v. France Nuclear Tests Case: The Dismissed Case of Lasting Significance*, 36 VIJL (1996, in press).

tablished confidence in the Court. The former attitude, especially disappointment with the 1963 *Northern Cameroons (Cameroon v. U.K.)* Judgment and that *bête noir* of Court's jurisprudence, the 1966 *South West Africa (Ethiopia v. South Africa; Liberia v. South Africa)* Judgment (taken by a casting vote of President Sir Percy Spender) were in fact – in spite of the Court having "redeemed" itself by its 1971 *South West Africa (Namibia)* Advisory Opinion[44] – the main reason of support exerted by the Third World States during UNCLOS III in favour of the new International Tribunal for the Law of the Sea (ITLOS).[45] As the United Nations Legal Counsel, Mr. Hans Corell, stated on the occasion of the Court's 50th Anniversary:

> "The past 50 years have been marked by significant political and economic changes in the world and the ICJ has firmly established itself during that period as one of the most important international institutions which plays a crucial role in maintaining international peace and security and in ensuring that international disputes are settled in accordance with the principles of justice, international law and through peaceful means."[46]

At the same time, the Court became used in the general context of *An Agenda for Peace*,[47] assuming a new role unimagined by earlier commentators on the adjudication process in international matters which is reflected by becoming by the Court, as the then its President Sir Robert Jennings put it, "a component of the scheme of preventive diplomacy" in terms of the "tendency to use the Court, acting under its contentious jurisdiction, as a partner in preventive diplomacy rather than as a last-resort alternative...".[48] In

---

[44] *Cf.* L. GROSS, *Review of the Role of the International Court of Justice*, 66 AJIL (1972) at 479, 488; S.M. SCHWEBEL, *The Treatment of Human Rights and of Aliens in the ICJ*, *op. cit.*, *supra* note 12, at 333–6.

[45] *Cf.* S. ODA, *The International Court of Justice Viewed From the Bench (1976–1993)*, 244 RECUEIL DES COURS (RCADI) (1993-VII) at 12, 145.

[46] Statement by Mr. HANS CORELL, U.N. Under Secretary-General and the Legal Counsel of 16 April 1996, (in:) R. HIGGINS and CH.G. WEERAMANTRY, *op. cit.*, *supra* note 8. *Cf.* S.M. SCHWEBEL, *Fifty Years of the World Court: A Critical Appraisal*, (in:) ARE INTERNATIONAL INSTITUTIONS DOING THEIR JOB?, PROCEEDINGS OF THE 90TH ASIL ANNUAL MEETING, WASHINGTON D.C., 27–30 MARCH 1996 (in press):

[47] *An Agenda for Peace: Preventive Diplomacy, Peacemaking and Peace-Keeping*, U.N. Doc. A/47/277-S/24111 (1992); *Implementation of the Recommendations Contained in "An Agenda for Peace"*, Doc. A/47/965-S/25944 (1993); *Supplement to An Agenda for Peace*, Doc. A/50/60-S/1995/1 (1995).

[48] Speeches by Sir ROBERT JENNINGS, ICJ President, to the UNGA, 21 October 1992, (in:) U.N. Doc. A/47/PV.43, 6–16, 11 (1992); 15 October 1993, (in:) Doc. A/48/PV.31, 2–4 (1993) and 88 AJIL (1994) at 422; *infra* notes 80 and 197–198. *Cf.* R.Y. JENNINGS, *Note préliminaire, Comité restreint sur le r glement pacifique des différends*, 65 ANNUAIRE IDI (Session de Milan) (1993-II) at 279, 281–2; C.-A. FLEISCHHAUER (the then U.N. Legal Counsel), *The U.N. Decade of International Law – The Role and Work of the Secretariat of the United Nations and of Its*

the field of the law of the sea, an immeasurable contribution of the U.N. Montego Bay Convention to the global system of peace and security, of which the Charter of the United Nations is the foundation, is widely recognized as consisting in the fact that even before its entry into force (on 16 November 1994) the Convention has become the basis for the decisions of the Court as the principal judicial organ of the United Nations.[49]

The significance of the 1982 U.N. Montego Bay Convention and the 1994 Part XI Agreement[50] as part of the global system of peace and security is a logical consequence of the fact that the law of the sea forms an (if not the most) important part of general international law. Consequently, universally accepted Convention and the Part XI Agreement will count among major events in the development of public international law as a whole (and not just the law of the sea).[51] This is evidenced by space devoted to the law of the sea by Judge Carl-August Fleischhauer (as the then United Nations Legal Counsel) in his precious Commentary on Article 13 of the U.N. Charter.[52] While referring at the Milan Session of the Institut de Droit international (IDI) to proliferation of various specialized courts and tribunals, Sir Robert Jennings, QC, remarked that the creation of tribunals for modish subjects such as the environment may obscure the fact that the problems of the environment will only be adequately addressed when they are seen to be a part of the problems of general international law.[53] This argument has been also widely relied upon by commentators favouring the ICJ over the ITLOS[54] with respect to the law of the sea-related disputes.[55] While the result of ITLOS'

System of Organizations, (in:) N. AL-NAUIMI (ed.), INTERNATIONAL LEGAL ISSUES ARISING UNDER THE U.N. DECADE OF INTERNATIONAL LAW (1995).

49 *See* Statements of Ambassador S.N. Nandan (Fiji), U.N. Docs A/48/PV.99, 1–6, at 2 (1994), and A/49/PV.77, at 1–5 (1994); and of the U.N. Legal Counsel H. Corell (Sweden), on behalf of the U.N. Secretary-General Boutros-Ghali, Doc. A/48/PV.101, 19–1, at 20 (1994).

50 *See supra* note 32.

51 *See* Statement of Deputy Legal Adviser D. Anderson (U.K.), U.N. Doc. A/48/PV.100, at 12–14, 13 (1994); J.-P. LÉVY, *infra* note 186; B.H. OXMAN, *infra* note 84.

52 C.-A. FLEISCHHAUER, Article 13, (in:) B. SIMMA et al. (eds.), THE CHARTER OF THE UNITED NATIONS – A COMMENTARY (1994) at 265–79.

53 R.Y. JENNINGS, *Note préliminaire*, *op. cit.*, *supra* note 48, at 282. *See* also Speech by Sir Robert Jennings (U.K.), President of the International Court of Justice, to the UNCED, 3–14 June 1992, read on behalf of President by the ICJ Registrar, Eduardo Valencia-Ospina, (in:) ICJ YEARBOOK 1991–1992, N° 46, at 212–8.

54 The initial (August 1996/December 1997) budget of the ITLOS totals over US $ 6 million. The first election of ITLOS' Judges was postponed until 1 August 1996, to be followed by the swearing-in ceremony on 18 October 1996. *Cf.* S. ROSENNE, *Establishing the International Tribunal for the Law of the Sea*, 89 AJIL (1995) at 806–14.

55 *See* esp. E. LAUTERPACHT, QC, ASPECTS OF THE ADMINISTRATION OF INTERNATIONAL JUSTICE 19–22 (Grotius Publications Limited: Cambridge 1991); G. GUILLAUME, *The Future of International Judicial Institutions*, 44 ICLQ (1995) at 848, 854–5, concluding his remarks on ITLOS

establishment is yet to be awaited, most what could be anticipated at present is that, as the Court's Vice-President, Judge Stephen M. Schwebel remarked, a large part of the traditional docket of the ICJ *may eventually* be removed to the ITLOS.[56]

Shortly prior to her election to the Court on 12 July 1995 as the first woman Member in the history of both the PCIJ and the ICJ, the then Professor Rosalyn Higgins, QC, within her treatment of international law as "a process, a system of authoritative decision-making," wished that students would understand better, *e.g.* "that competence over events on vessels is part of the law of jurisdiction and not the law of the sea, notwithstanding its customary placement under the latter heading in textbooks."[57] While this Judge Higgins' hope should strongly be supported, we may keep in mind that separation of the law of the sea as a branch of international law, whether "as a set of rules, with exceptions, or as complementary norms,"[58] is unavoidable. Therefore, given that the linkages are not always apparent both ways, we could extend Judge Higgins' hope to that for better *mutual* understanding, *e.g.* – as Judge John Bassett Moore seemed to appreciate so adequately in his 1927 *Lotus* Dissenting Opinion[59] – that piracy at sea is a notable instance of universal jurisdiction, and vice versa, that universal jurisdiction over piracy forms an inherent and important part of State jurisdiction at sea.

In the context of critical importance of mutuality of these linkages in the Court's practice, it is of gratifying comfort that it finds such an outstanding reflection in the works of that distinguished commentator on the jurisprudence of the Court, Ambassador Shabtai Rosenne who, at the same time, belongs to the principal architects of both the traditional and the new law of the sea.[60] We have also been fortunate to benefit from a unique experience

---

that "*errare humanum est, perseverare diabolicum*"; S. ODA, *op. cit.*, *supra* note 45, at 139–55, and S. ODA, *Dispute Settlement Prospects in the Law of the Sea*, 44 ICLQ (1995) at 863–72, as replied to by J.I. CHARNEY, *The Implications of Expanding International Dispute Settlement Systems*, 90 AJIL (1996) at 69–75, as rejoined by S. ODA, *ibid.* (in press). For more moderate views, *see* R. RANJEVA, *L'Environnement, la Cour Internationale de Justice et sa Chambre spéciale pour les questions d'environnement*, 40 ANNUAIRE FRANÇAIS DE DROIT INTERNATIONAL (AFDI) (1994) at 433–41; A.G. KOROMA, *Interpretation of International Law*, (in:) CONTEMPORARY INTERNATIONAL LAW ISSUES, PROCEEDINGS OF THE 3RD ASIL/NVIL JOINT CONFERENCE, THE HAGUE, 13–15 JULY 1995 (1996) at 154–7.

56 S.M. SCHWEBEL, JUSTICE IN INTERNATIONAL LAW, *op. cit.*, *supra* note 13, Chapter 2: *Relations between the ICJ and the United Nations*, at 14, 18.

57 R. HIGGINS, Problems and Pocess, *op. cit.*, *supra* note 37, at 267.

58 *Ibid.* at 58.

59 *Lotus* Dissenting Opinion of Judge Moore, PCIJ Series A, N° 10, at 65, 70–2.

60 S. ROSENNE, THE LAW AND PRACTICE (1965/1985), *op. cit.*, *supra* note 39, with magnificent revision of this work forthcoming (1997); THE WORLD COURT (1995), *op. cit.*, *supra* note 3; AN INTERNATIONAL LAW MISCELLANY (1993) and INTERVENTION (1993), both *op. cit.*, *supra* note 10;

of Judge Shigeru Oda – serving presently his already third term on the Bench (1976–2003) – as both an excellent generalist and a remarkable law of the sea expert.[61] Competent insights into maritime boundary delimitation and other law of the sea issues may be found in Parts V and VI of an invaluable series by the former ICJ Principal Legal Secretary, presently Professor Hugh Thirlway on The Law and Procedure of the Court, whose all (by now six) Parts testify to the significant contributions of the law of the sea-related cases to international law generally.[62] It also is rewarding that so much attention has been devoted to the law of the sea in writings of such distinguished generalists and experienced pleaders before the Court as Elihu Lauterpacht, QC, Jean-Pierre Quéneudec, Prosper Weil, Keith Highet, or Derek W. Bowett, QC.

Yet, and despite of writings by also a number of the leading law of the sea scholars (*e.g.* Bernard H. Oxman, Moritaka Hayashi, Jonathan I. Charney, L.D.M. Nelson, Edward D. Brown, Francisco Orrego Vicuña, Tullio Treves, David H. Anderson and Jean-Pierre Lévy) who possess adequate background in general international law, appreciation of the Court's practice and its treatment of the law of the sea, and likewise environmental law, as part of international law could still be enhanced. This may be exemplified by an appeal of environmentalists that the Court should yet give attention to the issue of indigenous population, which appeal shows unawareness of the Court's recognition of an importance of that issue as early as in the *Eastern Greenland* and the *Anglo/Norwegian Fisheries* cases. More serious instance are the continuing laments (especially in the context of maritime delimitation Judgments) that the Court would not take account of the law of the sea practice of States, which laments may result from unawareness of the stage of pleadings and the Court's internal deliberations when such practice is thoroughly presented and examined. Equally regrettable are instances of opposing mechanistically the Dissenting Opinions to the views of major-

---

UNITED NATIONS CONVENTION, *op. cit.*, *supra* note 36; and of his other works, *see e.g.* S. ROSENNE, *op. cit.*, *supra* notes 2, 54, and *infra* notes 69, 72, 82, 85, 134, 140 and 174. For innumerable citations of Ambassador Rosenne's authoritative views – which are also apparent in the Pleadings and Opinions of the Judges in virtually all cases – *see* Index of Names, in the JUBILEE BOOK, *op. cit.*, *supra* note 5; and most of the 50th ICJ presentations, (in:) R. HIGGINS and CH.G. WEERAMANTRY, *op. cit.*, *supra* note 8.

61 *See supra* notes 36, 41 and 45.

62 H. THIRLWAY, *The Law and Procedure of the International Court of Justice 1960–1989*, Part I, 60 BYIL (1989) at 1–157; Part II, 61 BYIL (1990) at 1–133; Part III, 62 BYIL (1991) at 1–75; Part IV, 63 BYIL (1992) at 1–96; Part V, 64 BYIL (1993) at 1–54; Part VI, 65 BYIL (1994) at 1–102. Professor Thirlway's series is designed in continuation of a series of articles published by Sir Gerald Fitzmaurice in the BYIL in 1950–1959, and then in tribute to Sir Hersch

ity[63] with a view to maintaining that the Court missed an opportunity of developing the law in a way it did so in, *e.g.* the *Corfu Channel* or *Anglo/Norwegian Fisheries* cases. When such criticism concerns, *e.g.* avoiding by the Court of pronouncing on the validity of Icelandic 50-mile fisheries zone,[64] it may be a result of disappreciation by the author of the stage of development of the law of the sea at the time of the *Fisheries Jurisdiction* cases, and perhaps also of the pleadings.[65] And when dismissal by the Court of New Zealand's *Nuclear Tests* Request (Examination of the Situation) is criticized,[66] it appears to testify to underestimating by the author of procedural restraints imposed on the Court by the basic requirement of impartiality. In both instances, the criticism could also be aligned to unawareness on the part of scholars concerned of the complexity of entirely different circumstances which led to the respective decisions of the Court.

It would, therefore, perhaps be useful to undertake a survey of specifically law of the sea-related cases of both the Permanent and International Courts, in continuation of approaches found in *The World Court* by Ambassador Rosenne and in The Hague Academy Lectures of Judge Shigeru Oda, and taking account of the Registry's *Unofficial Summaries of Decisions Concerning The Law of the Sea*.[67] The potential usefulness of such a survey seems to be underlined by importance of preserving judicial consistency of pronouncements concerning law of the sea, which seems especially timely given the forthcoming establishment of an ITLOS in Hamburg, Germany. in this context, Ambassador Rosenne finds no evidence to support an eventual impairment of the unity of jurisprudence, which he considers "a difficult proposition at the best of times."[68] On another occasion, he stresses that although the ITLOS Statute is drawn up along the lines of the ICJ Statute, the ITLOS is characteristically a different type of judicial organ from the ICJ

Lauterpacht in 1961–1963. *See* also G. ZICCARDI CAPALDO, REPERTORY OF DECISIONS OF THE INTERNATIONAL COURT OF JUSTICE (1947–1992), Vols. I and II (1995).

63 *Cf.* main text accompanying *supra* notes 38–43.

64 E. LANGAVANT et O. PIROTTE, *L'Affaire des Pêcheries islandaises*, 80 RGDIP (1976) at 55, 80.

65 *Cf.* H. THIRLWAY, *Reflections on the Articulation of International Judicial Decisions and the Problem of "Mootness"*, (in:) R.ST.J. MACDONALD (ed.), ESSAYS IN HONOUR OF WANG TIEYA (1994) at 789, 805–6; *infra* notes 157, 232.

66 M. FITZMAURICE, *Environmental Law*, (in:) R. HIGGINS and CH.G. WEERAMANTRY, *op. cit.*, *supra* note 8; main text accompanying *supra* note 43, and *infra* notes 126–127.

67 *See supra* notes 3 (S. ROSENNE), 16 (UNOFFICIAL SUMMARIES), and 45, (S. ODA, Chapter V); also *supra* note 30. Significantly, the REPORT OF THE SECRETARY-GENERAL – LAW OF THE SEA prepared annually by the U.N. DOALOS/OLA (*supra* note 19, and elsewhere in this essay) reports not only on the phase of Merits of the respective cases, but also on those of Provisional Measures, Jurisdiction, Intervention and Discontinuance as appropriate.

68 S. ROSENNE, *op. cit.*, *supra* note 54, at 814.

and it will have to chart its own course.[69] There has, however, been recently at least one disquieting example of decision taken by the Strasbourg Court of Human Rights in the 1995 *Loizidou v. Turkey* case, whose insistence on separateness Sir Robert Jennings, QC, found to be "disturbing" and adding "a whole new dimension to the art of distinguishing."[70] We may but hope that such "a new dimension" would indeed not be echoed by ITLOS in the process of "charting its own course."

IV. SOME PROCEDURAL ISSUES

Whereas proper appreciation of law of the sea-related cases necessarily includes the procedural aspects involved therein, magnitude of these aspects would necessitate a selective approach. The Court's jurisdiction in the cases concerned was rested both on compromissory, whether bilateral or multilateral, clauses under Article 36(1) and on Optional Clause under Article 36(2) of the Statute. The *Corfu Channel* (early stage) and the [discontinued] pair of *Antarctica* cases provided instances of the *forum prorogatum*, with precautions against its any possible application having been taken, *inter alia*, by Turkey in the *Aegean Sea* and by New Zealand in the *Nuclear Tests* (Request for an Examination of the Situation) cases.[71] In the latter case, France's contention that if the NZ Request were a matter of a new Application under Article 40(1) of the Statute, it would be precluded from entering in the General List by virtue of Article 38(5) of the Rules of Court, was contested by New Zealand on the ground that its Request did not invoke *forum prorogatum*. And this French submission was rejected by the Court when it took its unprecedented decision that the NZ Request for an Examination of the Situation had to be entered in the General List (under a new N° 97) for "the sole purpose" of enabling the Court to determine whether this Request ful-

---

69 S. ROSENNE, *The International Tribunal for the Law of the Sea and the International Court of Justice*, obtained in 1994 through kindness of Ambassador Rosenne (on the file with the author). *Cf.* T. TREVES, *The Law of the Sea Tribunal: Its Status and Scope of Jurisdiction After November 16, 1994*, 55 ZAöRV (1995) at 421–51; T. TREVES, *Aspects of the Relationship Between the Jurisdiction of the ITLOS and the ICJ*, (in:) CONTEMPORARY INTERNATIONAL LAW ISSUES, *supra* note 55, at 305–9; K. HIGHET, *Maritime Boundary Disputes and Settlement*, (in:) MOCHTAR KUSUMAATMADJA (ed.), SUSTAINABLE DEVELOPMENT AND PRESERVATION OF THE OCEANS, 29TH LSI PROCEEDINGS, BALI, INDONESIA, 19–22 JUNE 1995 (in press).

70 Sir R.Y. JENNINGS, *The Judiciary, International and National, and the Development of International Law*, 45 ICLQ (1996) at 1, 5–6, invoking the *Loizidou v. Turkey* Ser.A, N° 310, 23 March 1995; meanwhile reported in 90 AJIL (1996) at 98, **without** reference to the Strasbourg Court's holding that the World Court's precedents were inapposite to it.

71 *Cf.* the *Qatar v. Bahrain* Dissenting Opinion (Jurisdiction and Admissibility) of Judge Shahabuddeen, ICJ REPORTS 1995 at 51, 61–2.

filled the conditions set in Paragraph 63 of the 1974 *New Zealand v. France* Judgment.[72]

The Court's reliance, in the *Aegean Sea* Judgment (Jurisdiction), on the "territorial status" clause in Greece's reservation to the 1928 Geneva General Act for the Pacific Settlement of International Disputes provided, by analogy, significant contribution to the interpretation that a "territorial status/disputes" reservation in the Optional Clause declarations covers the continental shelf.[73] Reservations *ratione materiae* concerning specifically matters of the law of the sea were exemplified by Declaration made during the *Libya/Malta* case (which was instituted by a *compromis*) by Malta in 1981, as withdrawn in 1983 when Malta modified – by another law of the sea reservation – its original Declaration of 1966 which remains in force.[74] A reservation entered by Canada to its Optional Clause Declaration in connection with enactment of its spectacular 1970 Arctic Waters Pollution Prevention Act,[75] in combination with extension by Canada of its fisheries zone beyond the then permissible limit of 12 miles, might have encouraged Iceland to non-appearing in the two simultaneous *Fisheries Jurisdiction* cases.[76] The current fisheries-related reservation was entered by Canada to its Optional Clause Declaration two days prior to enactment of the 1994 Canadian Coastal Fisheries Protection Act,[77] which as a result of the *Estai* incident, led to institution by Spain, in reliance of Article 36(2) of the Statute, of the pending *Fisheries Jurisdiction (The Estai)* case against Canada.[78]

---

72 ICJ REPORTS 1995 at 302. Given its dismissal by the Court, the NZ Request was subsequently removed from the General List as of the date of the Order, *ibid.* at 306. *Cf.* B. KWIATKOWSKA, *op. cit., supra* note 43. For somewhat different interpretation of the Court's treatment of French submission regarding Article 38(5) of the Rules, *see* S. ROSENNE, *The General List of the International Court of Justice* (contained in this volume).

73 ICJ REPORTS 1978 at 3, 29–37. *Cf.* main text accompanying *infra* note 222.

74 ICJ YEARBOOK 1993–1994, at 102 [Malta] (N° 48); the *Libya/Malta* Pleadings, Vol. II, at 621 (30 January 1984, Counsel Lauterpacht). On this and other law of the sea reservations (including that of Canada), *see* the *Nicaragua v. U.S.A.* Separate Opinions (Jurisdiction and Admissibility) of Judges S. ODA, ICJ REPORTS 1984 at 471, 490–4, and Sir ROBERT JENNINGS, *ibid.* at 533, 551–2.

75 9 ILM (1970) at 598–9, and related documents, *ibid.* at 600–15. Following Canadian Arctic Waters Act (*ibid.* at 543), the 1971 Policy Statement of Iceland, which announced its 50-mile fisheries zone, also envisaged establishment of a 100-mile pollution prevention zone. *See* the *Fisheries Jurisdiction* Pleadings (U.K.), 6 [Application], 13 [U.K. *Aide-Mémoire*]; (F.R.G.), 6 [Application]; *U.K. v. Iceland* Separate Opinion (Merits) of Judge Onyeama, ICJ REPORTS 1974 at 168.

76 *See* main text accompanying *infra* note 124.

77 ICJ YEARBOOK 1993–1994 88 [Canada] (N° 48); *U.N./DOALOS Law of the Sea Bulletin* 19 [Declaration], 20 [Fisheries Act] (1994 N° 26).

78 ICJ REPORTS 1995 at 87; Order of 8 May 1996, ICJ REPORTS 1996 at 58. *Cf.* U.N. Doc. A/50/713 (1995), *op. cit., supra* note 20, at 35–6; B. KWIATKOWSKA, *The **Spain v. Canada***

As regards compromissory clauses, it is gratifying that the *North Sea* cases initiated the renewed importance of the *compromis* (providing the first tripartite instance thereof), which after its broad use in the Permanent Court, was used only three times in the first twenty years of the International Court (in the *Corfu*'s later stage, the *Minquiers and Ecrehos* and the *Honduras/ Nicaragua Arbitral Award of 23 December 1906* cases). The method used in the *North Sea* cases of submitting portions of disputes by mutual agreement to the Court (or variations on this theme) combines, in Ambassador Rosenne's view, "some of the best features inherent in both judicial and diplomatic means of dispute settlement."[79] This was reaffirmed in the speech of the then Court's President Sir Robert Jennings to the UNGA when he indicated that the *North Sea* cases provided a successful foretaste of the new tendency, initiated in the 1990s in the context of *An Agenda for Peace*, to use the Court as a partner in preventive diplomacy.[80] Whereas the *Tunisia/ Libya* and the next maritime boundary delimitation cases continued importance of this method by reliance on a *compromis*, in the *Denmark v. Norway (Jan Mayen)* case jurisdiction was founded on Article 36(2) of the Statute, thus establishing that the Court can effect delimitation on a unilateral request, provided that it has jurisdiction to do so.[81] The *Gulf of Fonseca* and the pending *Qatar v. Bahrain* cases exemplify, moreover, reliance (initiated in the [discontinued] *Southeastern Greenland* case) on the "framework agreement" as a method of conferring jurisdiction on the Court which is distinct from a *compromis*.[82]

Although the compromissory clauses of the 1958 U.N. Geneva Optional Protocol were never relied upon, they provided a model for similar Optional Protocols concluded to some other treaties.[83] The complex compromissory

Fisheries Jurisdiction (The Estai) Case, presented at the Asser Round Table Session, The Hague, 29 June 1995.

79 S. ROSENNE, THE WORLD COURT, *op. cit.*, *supra* note 3, at 86 (confirming his view expressed in the previous edition of THE WORLD COURT 85 [1989]).

80 UN Doc. A/48/PV.31, 2–4 (1993), *op. cit.*, *supra* note 48.

81 S. Rosenne, THE WORLD COURT, *op. cit.*, *supra* note 3, at 231. Reliance on Article 36(2) of the Statute in the *Denmark v. Norway (Jan Mayen)* case was reported in U.N. Doc. A/43/718 (1988), *op. cit.*, *supra* note 19, at 9, and the Court's 1993 Judgment, (in:) the *Report of the Secretary-General – Law of the Sea*, Doc. A/48/527, 12 (1993).

82 *See* S. ROSENNE, *The **Qatar/Bahrain** Case: What Is a Treaty? A Framework Agreement and the Sesing of the Court*, 8 LEIDEN JOURNAL OF INTERNATIONAL LAW (LJIL) (1995) at 161–80, at 171–6. The two *Qatar v. Bahrain* Judgments (Jurisdiction and Admissibility), ICJ REPORTS 1994 at 112, 1995 at 6, are reported in U.N. Docs A/49/631 (1994), *op. cit.*, *supra* note 21, at 16, and A/50/713 (1995), *op. cit.*, *supra* note 20, at 33–4, respectively.

83 For the Geneva Protocol, *see supra* note 31. *Cf.* the *North Sea* Dissenting Opinion of Judge Sorensen, ICJ REPORTS 1969 at 241, 256; and the *Qatar v. Bahrain* Dissenting Opinion (Jurisdiction and Admissibility) of Judge Koroma, ICJ REPORTS 1995 at 67, 70.

clauses of the 1982 U.N. Montego Bay Convention (Part XV) remain yet to be tested as well. At the same time, an important aspect of turning this Convention (including the Part XI Agreement), as a result of a wide ratification, into "a monument to the possibilities of global multilateral diplomacy", consists in the fact that no comparable treaty with such broad mandatory compromissory clauses has ever been widely ratified.[84] The significance of these clauses appears to be illustrated by Ambassador Rosenne's suggestion to consider, for the purposes of review of the whole ICJ Statute, the innovations introduced in the ITLOS Statute with respect to: intervention [Annex VI (Article 31) of the Montego Bay Convention and Article 62 of the ICJ Statute]; provisional measures [Article 290 of the Convention and its Annex VI (Article 25), and Article 41 of the ICJ Statute]; and participation clause for semi-independent territories and peoples [Article 305(1)(c)–(e) of the Convention and Article 34 of the ICJ Statute].[85]

Whereas the 1923 *Wimbledon* (Question of Intervention by Poland) Judgment initiated intervention under Article 63 of the Statute,[86] the 1933 *Eastern Greenland* Judgment turned significant due to articulation of an important factor of territorial adjudication, *i.e.* "the extent to which sovereignty is also claimed by some other Power."[87] This pronouncement resulted presumably from Iceland's intention (as later abandoned) to intervene in the

[84] J.R. STEVENSON and B.H. OXMAN, *The Future of the United Nations Convention on the Law of the Sea*, 88 AJIL (1994) at 488, 499. *Cf.* S. ROSENNE et al., *op. cit.*, *supra* note 36, Vol. V (1989).

[85] S. ROSENNE, as Moderator of Round-Table on Settlement of Disputes, (in:) PROCEEDINGS OF THE UNITED NATIONS CONGRESS ON PUBLIC INTERNATIONAL LAW, NEW YORK, 13–17 MARCH 1995 (in press). *Cf.* S. ROSENNE, *The International Tribunal, op. cit., supra* note 69; S. ROSENNE, *The International Court of Justice: Lessons of the Past and the Needs of the Future*, (in:) R. HIGGINS and CH.G. WEERAMANTRY, *op. cit., supra* note 8. On participation clause of the Montego Bay Convention (Article 305), *see* also S. ROSENNE, INTERVENTION, *op. cit., supra* note 10, at 82–3.

[86] PCIJ Series A, N° 1, at 11. in its Application, Poland sought permission to intervene under Article 62 of the Statute, but shifted to Article 63 during the Oral Hearings as a result of the initiative of the British Agent Sir Cecil Hurst. *See* the *Wimbledon* Pleadings, PCIJ Series C, N° 3–I, at, 106. Permission to intervene under Article 63 was also requested by Cuba in the *Colombia/Peru Haya de la Torre*, ICJ REPORTS 1951 at 71; by El Salvador in the *Nicaragua v. U.S.A.* (Intervention), ICJ REPORTS 1984 at 215, Separate Opinion of Judges Ruda, Mosler, Ago, Sir Robert Jennings and de Lacharri re, *ibid.* at 219, Separate Opinions of Judges Oda and Bedjaoui, *ibid.* at 220, 222, and Dissenting Opinion of Judge Schwebel, *ibid.* at 223–44; and by four Pacific island states in the *New Zealand v. France Nuclear Tests*, ICJ REPORTS 1995 at 288; cases. *Cf.* review by S.M. SCHWEBEL of CH. CHINKIN, THIRD PARTIES IN INTERNATIONAL LAW (1993), 89 AJIL (1995) at 835–7.

[87] PCIJ Series A/B, N° 53, at 46. For reliance thereon, *see* the *Libya/Malta* Judgment (Intervention), ICJ REPORTS 1984 at 26, and Dissenting Opinion of Judge Sir ROBERT JENNINGS, *ibid.* at 158–9. *See* also the *Anglo/Norwegian Fisheries* Pleadings, Vol. IV, at 523 (26 October 1951, Counsel Bourquin); the *Minquiers* Pleadings, Vol. I, at 543, 553 (Reply of U.K.), Vol. II, at 55 (18 September 1953, Counsel Sir Lionel Heald), at 270 (30 September, Agent Gros).

Eastern Greenland proceedings under Article 62 of the Statute.[88] The *Corfu Channel* (Merits)[89] and the *Monetary Gold Removed from Rome in 1943 (Italy v. France, U.K. and U.S.A.)* (Preliminary Question)[90] cases involved actions classified by Ambassador Rosenne as exemplifying one category of "actions falling short of intervention", in particular actions by third States (Yugoslavia and Albania respectively) in relation to pending proceedings in which these States were not participating and in regard to which they were not requesting permission to intervene.[91] However, the two cases differed importantly in that in the *Corfu* there were no direct allegations *in the submissions* that the international responsibility of Yugoslavia was in some way engaged, and there was no claim against that country, whereas in the *Monetary Gold*, Albania's conduct was the very subject-matter of the principal claim of Italy to the gold.[92] The *Corfu* Judgment (Merits) was interpreted in the *Certain Phosphate Lands in Nauru (Nauru v. Australia)* Dissenting Opinion (Preliminary Objections) of Judge Stephen M. Schwebel as permitting proceedings against a named State and other States unknown.[93]

The *Monetary Gold* Judgment (Preliminary Question) – including its authoritative "proposition of continuing vitality, namely, that where a third State's legal interests would not only be affected by a decision but form the very subject-matter of the decision, proceedings may not be maintained in the absence of that third State"[94] – played an important role in a number of subsequent cases, including the [discontinued] *Nauru* and those which involved a third-State intervention in maritime delimitation proceedings.[95] The *Monetary Gold* pronouncements were also heavily relied upon by both Australia and Portugal in the *East Timor* case, where the Court (by 14:2 majority vote) found itself unable to exercise the jurisdiction it possessed

[88] *Eastern Greenland* Pleadings, PCIJ Series C, N° 67, at 4081–2 [Iceland's Letter of 19 August 1931], at 4118–9 [Iceland's Letter of 25 October 1932].

[89] ICJ REPORTS 1949 at 1.

[90] ICJ REPORTS 1954 at 19. The *Monetary Gold* (Preliminary Question) case concerned the possible implementation of the *Corfu* (Compensation) Judgment, ICJ REPORTS 1949 at 244, and was preceded by the 1953 *Monetary Gold Looted by Germany from Rome (France, U.K., U.S.A. v. Italy)* Arbitral Advice of Georges Sauser Hall, RIAA XII, at 19; 20 ILR, at 441; N°415/Stuyt.

[91] S. ROSENNE, INTERVENTION, *op. cit., supra* note 10, at 160–76 (169–74).

[92] *Ibid.* at 173–4.

[93] *Nauru* Dissenting Opinion (Preliminary Objections) of Judge Schwebel, ICJ REPORTS 1992 at 329, 330. *Cf.* the *East Timor* Separate Opinion of Judge Shahabuddeen, ICJ REPORTS 1995 at 119, 121–2, and Dissenting Opinion of Judge Weeramantry, *ibid.* at 158, 164–7.

[94] *Nauru* Dissenting Opinion (Preliminary Objections) of Judge Schwebel, ICJ REPORTS 1992, 330–1. *See* also *Nauru* Judgment, *ibid.* at 259, citing *Monetary Gold* Judgment (Preliminary Question), ICJ REPORTS 1954 at 32.

[95] *See supra* note 91.

because, in order to decide the claims of Portugal, it would have to rule, as a prerequisite, on the lawfulness of Indonesia's conduct in the absence of that State's consent.[96] Such a judgment would run directly counter to the "well-established principle of international law embodied in the Court's Statute, namely that the Court can only exercise jurisdiction over a State with its consent."[97]

In his important and searching *East Timor* Dissenting Opinion,[98] Judge *ad hoc* Krzysztof J. Skubiszewski, basing himself on distinction between involvement of interests and determination of rights or duties, was of the view that had the Court assumed jurisdiction, it would not, and could not, pass on any rights and/or duties of Indonesia, which country was protected by Article 59 of the Statute (whatever the possible broader effects of the Judgment).[99] The Court should see whether it could decide on the claim without ruling on the interests of a third State. In the triangle Portugal-Australia-Indonesia such separation was, in his view, not only possible but already existed, since Portugal did not put at issue the legal interests of Indonesia. While relying on interpretation of the *Monetary Gold* Judgment (Preliminary Question) by the *Gulf of Fonseca* Judgment (Intervention), Judge Skubiszewski considered that the criterion of the "very subject-matter of the decision" was conclusive in establishing the Court's jurisdiction when the interests of a third State were or seemed to be at stake.[100] There was, in his opinion, room for applying the concept inherent in the *Nauru* (Preliminary Objections) dictum to the *East Timor* case.[101] As in the present case the separation of the rights and/or duties of Australia and Indonesia was both possible and necessary, and Indonesia's interests did not constitute "the very subject-matter of the decision", the Court should and could decide on the merits and the

---

[96] *East Timor* Judgment, ICJ REPORTS 1995 at 90, 100–5.

[97] *Ibid.* at 105, citing *Monetary Gold* Judgment (Preliminary Question), ICJ REPORTS 1954 at 32. *Cf. supra* note 20, and *infra* note 221.

[98] *Cf.* statement of Vice-President Schwebel, *supra* note 8, noting that a vote and the *Tunisia v. Libya* Separate Opinion (Revision and Interpretation), ICJ REPORTS 1985 at 192, 247–52, of Judge *ad hoc* Mrs. Suzanne Bastid remains an exceptional example of a Judge *ad hoc* taking a position against that of the appointing state (in this case Tunisia).

[99] *East Timor* Dissenting Opinion of Judge *ad hoc* Skubiszewski, ICJ REPORTS 1995 at 224–77, 241–53, at 242.

[100] *East Timor* Dissenting Opinion of Judge *ad hoc* Skubiszewski, *ibid.* at 243, citing *Gulf of Fonseca* Judgment (Intervention), ICJ REPORTS 1990 at 115–16 and 122. *Cf.* the *Nauru* Dissenting Opinion (Preliminary Objections) of Judge S.M. SCHWEBEL, ICJ REPORTS 1992 at 335–7, interpreting these *Gulf of Fonseca* pronouncements as supporting the position of Australia (and not that of Nauru) in the *Nauru* case.

[101] *East Timor* Dissenting Opinion of Judge *ad hoc* Skubiszewski, ICJ REPORTS 1995 at 243–4, citing *Nauru* Judgment (Preliminary Objections), ICJ REPORTS 1992 at 261–2.

Monetary Gold rule excluding jurisdiction could not be invoked.[102] Given the entirely different position of Indonesia than that of Albania, Judge *ad hoc* Skubiszewski respectfully considered that in the *East Timor* case the Court has gone beyond the limit of the operation of *Monetary Gold*.[103] The view that the circumstances of *East Timor* case rendered the *Monetary Gold* rule inapplicable was also shared (for different reasons) in the Separate Opinion of Judge Shigeru Oda and Dissenting Opinion of Judge Christopher G. Weeramantry,[104] as well as in a recent ASIL Address of Judge *ad hoc* (in the *Cameroon v. Nigeria* case[105]) Bola Ajibola.[106]

As regards third-State intervention under Article 62 of the Court's Statute, there was an indication in the *Anglo/Norwegian Fisheries* case that Iceland might have been contemplating again (after having previously abandoned to do so in the *Eastern Greenland* case[107]) such an intervention, but no measures to this effect were initiated.[108] The first actual attempt to intervene under Article 62 was illustrated by two requests of Fiji which the Court did not find necessary to deal with in the pair of the 1973/4 *Nuclear Tests* cases.[109] The 1981 *Tunisia/Libya* (Intervention)[110] and the 1984 *Libya/Malta* (Intervention)[111] Judgments thus provided the first instances of consideration by the Court of the requests made under Article 62 by Malta and Italy respectively. Although in neither of the two Libyan instances was permission to intervene (opposed by each of the respective principal parties) granted, the would-be interveners had to an important extent achieve their objectives. Judges Shigeru Oda and Stephen M. Schwebel, who appended their Separate Opinions to the unanimous 1981 *Tunisia/Libya* Judgment (Intervention),

---

102 *East Timor* Dissenting Opinion of Judge *ad hoc* Skubiszewski, ICJ REPORTS 1995 at 245.

103 *Ibid.* at 250–1.

104 *East Timor* Separate Opinion of Judge Oda, *ibid.* at 107, 113, and Dissenting Opinion of Judge Weeramantry, *ibid.* at 139–223, 150–78.

105 *Cameroon v. Nigeria* Order (Provisional Measures) of 15 March 1996, para.15; Declarations of Judges Oda, Shahabuddeen, Ranjeva, Koroma, Joint Declaration of Judges Weeramantry, Shi and Vereshchetin, Declaration of Judge *ad hoc* Kéba Mbaye, and Separate Opinion of Judge Ajibola, ICJ REPORTS 1996 at 13.

106 B. AJIBOLA, *Third Parties in ICJ Proceedings*, (in:) ARE INTERNATIONAL INSTITUTIONS DOING THEIR JOB?, *op. cit.*, *supra* note 46.

107 *See supra* note 88.

108 *Anglo/Norwegian Fisheries* Pleadings, Vol. IV, at 671–2.

109 ICJ REPORTS 1973 at 320, 324 (Intervention), and 1974 at 530, 535 (Intervention).

110 ICJ REPORTS 1981 at 3 (Intervention); Separate Opinions of Judges Morozov, *ibid.* at 22, S. ODA, *ibid.* at 23–34, and S.M. Schwebel, *ibid.* at 35–40.

111 ICJ REPORTS 1984 at 3 (Intervention); Separate Opinions of Judges Morozov, Nagendra Singh and Mbaye and Judge *ad hoc* JIMÉNEZ DE ARÉCHAGA, *ibid.* at 30–70; Dissenting Opinions of Vice-President SETTE-CAMARA, *ibid.* at 71–89, and Judges S. ODA, *ibid.* at 90–114, R. AGO, *ibid.* at 115–30, S.M. SCHWEBEL, *ibid.* at 131–47, and Sir ROBERT Y. JENNINGS, *ibid.* at 148–60.

dissented subsequently from the majority 1984 *Libya/Malta* Judgment (Intervention). A more liberal approach to third State intervention in maritime boundary delimitation, culminated in the unanimous 1990 *Gulf of Fonseca* Judgment (Intervention) of the ICJ Chamber which, for the first time in the history of the World Court, granted a State (Nicaragua) permission to intervene as a non-party under Article 62 of the Statute.[112] Three *Fonseca* Chamber's members, Judges José Sette-Camara, Shigeru Oda and Sir Robert Jennings, all filed previously Opinions in the two negative Libyan decisions. Subsequently, the requests of Australia and other Pacific States to intervene under Article 62 (and likewise 63) were all dismissed in the *New Zealand v. France Nuclear Tests* (Request for an Examination of the Situation) case.[113]

It was in the *Libya/Malta* (Intervention) case that Vice-President José Sette-Camara and Judge *ad hoc* Eduardo Jiménez de Aréchaga (designated by Libya) referred for the first time to the ITLOS in their Dissenting and Separate Opinions respectively. Vice-President Sette-Camara stressed, in his Dissenting Opinion, that intervention was an important device of procedural law in all legal systems of the world, and that, significantly, the respective provisions of the ITLOS Statute [Annex VI (Articles 31/32) of the U.N. Montego Bay Convention] were closely aligned with Articles 62 and 63 of the Court's Statute.[114] The Vice-President did not mention that there also are important differences between the ITLOS and the ICJ Statutes in this respect. One of those differences was signalled in the *Libya/Malta* Separate Opinion (Intervention) of Judge *ad hoc* Jiménez de Aréchaga who – while reciting the 1981 *Tunisia/Libya* Separate Opinions of Judges Shigeru Oda and Stephen M. Schwebel[115] – considered that granting intervention despite the absence of a jurisdictional link would involve disadvantages for the future work of the Court.[116] He believed that the risk would be all the greater in the case of maritime delimitation, so that States might prefer to resort to the ITLOS where the intervener and the principal parties must all have accepted its jurisdiction [Article 287(1) and (3)–(5) of the Montego Bay Convention].

---

112 ICJ REPORTS 1990 at 92 (Intervention); Separate Opinion of Judge S. ODA, *ibid.* at 138–44.

113 ICJ REPORTS 1995 at 288. *Cf. supra* note 43 and 86.

114 *Libya/Malta* Dissenting Opinion (Intervention) of Vice-President SETTE-CAMARA, ICJ REPORTS 1984 at 71, 88.

115 *Tunisia/Libya* Separate Opinions (Intervention) of Judge Oda, ICJ REPORTS 1981 at 27, and Judge SCHWEBEL, *ibid.* at 40.

116 *Libya/Malta* Separate Opinion (Intervention) of Judge *ad hoc* de Aréchaga, ICJ REPORTS 1984 at 55, 64.

The risk indicated by Judge Jiménez de Aréchaga results from the fact that intervention under the ITLOS Statute [Annex VI (Article 31) of the Montego Bay Convention] applies – not as under Article 62 of the Court's Statute to any State, not necessarily a party to the ICJ Statute – but that it applies only to "States Parties" to the Montego Bay Convention. This, in turn, would seem to exclude the notion of non-party intervener in the proceedings before ITLOS. A suggestion of Ambassador Rosenne to consider – for the purpose of reviewing Article 62 of the ICJ Statute – the innovations introduced in the ITLOS Statute with respect to intervention, appears therefore to testify to his reluctance with regard to non-party intervention.[117] Sir Robert Jennings – who dissented from the *Libya/Malta* Judgment (Intervention) and was the member of the *Gulf of Fonseca* Chamber – [118] believes that by permitting non-party intervention, the Chamber found a *tertium quid* concerning the jurisdictional link point. In particular, although it decided that the absence of a jurisdictional link was "no bar to permission being given for intervention", the Chamber nevertheless observed and indeed applied the jurisdictional link principle.[119]

After rejection by the Court of request to this effect in the 1950 *Haya de la Torre (Colombia v. Peru)* Judgment (Interpretation),[120] the 1985 *Tunisia v. Libya* Judgment (Revision and Interpretation) found Tunisian request for interpretation of the 1982 *Tunisia/Libya* Judgment (Merits), under Article 60 of the ICJ Statute, to be partly admissible.[121] The *Tunisia v. Libya* Judgment (Revision and Interpretation) also found a simultaneous Tunisia's request for revision, under Article 61 of the Statute, to be inadmissible. The Judgment remains the only instance of revision in the Court's history, with the issues pertaining to both interpretation and revision having subsequently resurfaced in the 1995 *New Zealand v. France Nuclear Tests* case.[122] The *Tunisia/Libya* (Intervention) and the *Tunisia v. Libya* (Revision and Inter-

---

117 *See* main text accompanying *supra* note 85; S. Rosenne, INTERVENTION, *op. cit.*, *supra* note 10, at 105–15, 148–55, 177–83. For doubts on non-party intervention, *see* also E. LAUTERPACHT, *op. cit.*, *supra* note 55, at 26–30; and the *EL Salvador/Honuras* Oral Hearings, C 4/CR 90/3, at 80–4 (6 June 1990, Counsel Lauterpacht).

118 *See supra* notes 111–112.

119 ICJ REPORTS 1990 at 135–6, discussed by Sir R.Y. JENNINGS, *The International Court of Justice After Fifty Years*, 89 AJIL (1995) at 493, 500. *Cf.* B. KWIATKOWSKA, *Equitable Maritime Boundary Delimitation – As Exemplified in the Work of the World Court During the Presidency of Sir Robert Yewdall Jennings*, (in:) ESSAYS IN HONOUR OF SIR ROBERT JENNINGS, *op. cit.*, *supra* note 1, at 264, 273–6.

120 ICJ REPORTS 1950 at 395.

121 ICJ REPORTS 1985 at 192.

122 ICJ REPORTS 1995 at 299–304. *See* main text accompanying, *infra* note 126.

pretation)[123] Judgments, decided under Presidency of Sir Humphrey Waldock and Acting Presidency of Nagendra Singh respectively, exemplify – along with the 1953 *Minquiers* [Acting President Gustavo Guerrero] and the 1990 *Gulf of Fonseca* (Intervention) [Chamber's President José Sette-Camara] Judgments – unanimous decisions which are not being reached frequently by the Court.

By contrast to the *Corfu Channel*, the *Anglo/Iranian Oil Co. (U.K. v. Iran)*, the *Nottebohm* and the *Nicaragua v. U.S.A.* cases where the respondents only partly did not participate in the proceedings, the two parallel *Fisheries Jurisdiction* cases initiated practice of non-appearance throughout the whole proceedings, which was subsequently followed in the *Nuclear Tests*, the *Trial of Pakistani Prisoners of War (Pakistan v. India)*, the *Aegean Sea* and the *US Diplomatic and Consular Staff in Tehran (U.S.A. v. Iran)* cases.[124] In the *Fisheries Jurisdiction* (Provisional Measures) cases, as echoed by the pair of *Nuclear Tests* (Provisional Measures) cases (where respondent was a permanent member of the U.N. Security Council), the Court upheld its *prima facie* jurisdiction to indicate provisional measures in spite of non-recognition of the Court's jurisdiction by the non-appearing respondent. In the *Nuclear Tests* cases, after these measures were indicated (as preceded by unexplained leak in Australia concerning the Court's voting), France provided the first instance of withdrawal of its Optional Clause Declaration during the actual proceedings.[125] Along with the *Northern Cameroons* case, the *Nuclear Tests* cases also exemplify an unusual instance where the Court declined (though on the basis of different reasoning) to give any decision on the merits at all.

In the 1974 *Nuclear Tests* Judgments, the Court contemplated the possibility of non-compliance with its decision and made unique provision accordingly (in identical Paragraphs 60 and 63 of the two Judgments), notwithstanding the fact that by then France both denounced the 1928 General Act and terminated its Optional Clause Declaration. This provision was relied upon two decades later by New Zealand in its no less unique attempt to reopen its own *Nuclear Tests* case. This uniqueness resulted in the unprecedented way in which the Court actually proceeded in the new case, as well

---

123 On Judge *ad hoc* in the *Tunisia v. Libya* case, *see op. cit.*, *supra* note 98. *See* also main text accompanying *infra* note 237.

124 *Cf.* Non-Appearance Before the International Court of Justice, Rapporteur: G. ARANGIO-RUIZ, 64 ANNUAIRE IDI [Session de Bâle], (1991-I) at 193–376. On Iceland's non-appearance, *see* main text accompanying *supra* note 76.

125 *Cf.* A. Gros, *La Cour Internationale de Justice 1946–1986*, (in:) EASSAYS IN HONOUR OF SHABTAI ROSENNE, *op. cit.*, *supra* note 39, at 289, 299.

as the unprecedented nature of a "special procedure" (distinct from interpretation and revision under Articles 60 and 61 of the Statute) which is envisaged by the 1995 Order (Request for an Examination of the Situation) for the purpose of the possible future action in pursuance of the 1974 *New Zealand v. France* Judgment (Paragraph 63).[126] The 1995 Order dismissed the NZ Request (Examination of the Situation) on the sole and cogent ground that it did not fall within Paragraph 63 of the 1974 Judgment whose "basis" involved exclusively (as France contended) atmospheric nuclear tests in the South Pacific. The *New Zealand v. France* case, as that of *Australia v. France*, will remain moot unless the hypothesis of resumption by France of atmospheric testing materializes. New Zealand's argument to the contrary was inventive and ingenious: namely, that even though the 1974 *NZ v. France Nuclear Tests* Judgment confined New Zealand's claims to atmospheric testing, its true intendment was to interdict nuclear contamination; and it has been only recently that it has become known that underground testing in the Mururoa and Fangataufa Atolls could contaminate.[127] But it was not an argument which could move the majority to go beyond the clear terms of the 1974 Judgment.

Unusual instances regarding implementation of Judgments were also provided by the 1951 U.K./France Fishery Agreement concluded by the parties in advance (and separately from their *compromis*) to the *Minquiers and Ecrehos* Judgment with a view to determining the modalities of this Judgment's implementation,[128] and, perhaps first and foremost, by the post-adjudicative history of the 1947/9 *Corfu Channel* case. Implementation of the 1949 *Corfu* Judgment (Compensation) became intertwined with the *Monetary Gold* Arbitral Advice and Judgment[129] and was ultimately effected

---

126 ICJ REPORTS 1995 at 288, 303–4 (Request for an Examination of the Situation); Declaration of Vice-President SCHWEBEL, *ibid.* at 309; Declarations of Judges ODA and RANJEVA, *ibid.* at 310–11; Separate Opinion of Judge SHAHABUDDEEN, *ibid.* at 312–16; Dissenting Opinions, *supra* note 43. *Cf.* also *supra* notes 42, 72, 86, 113, 122 and 126, and *infra* notes 165, 172, 233 and 252–255.

127 *Cf.* Written Reply by New Zealand of 15 September 1995 (on the file with the author), to Question 2 of Vice-President Schwebel, *NZ v. France* Oral Hearings, CR 95/20, 45 (12 September 1995).

128 121 UNTS 97. *Cf.* the *Minquiers* Pleadings, Vol. II, at 20 (17 September 1953, Counsel Sir Lionel Heald), at 62–3 (18 September, Counsel Fitzmaurice). *Cf.* also statement of Britain that neither the status of Ecrehos (remaining within the jurisdiction of Jersey) nor fishing rights around Ecrehos were in any way affected by the 1994 U.K./France Agreement on Fishing Rights in Waters Between Guernsey and French Coast. *See* 65 BYIL, at 649–51 [incl. map] (1994). *Cf.* main text accompanying *infra* notes 203–204, 241–244.

129 *See supra* note 90.

only by the 1992 Albania/UK[130] and the 1995 Albania/USA[131] Agreements. The 1951/3 *Ambatielos* case, as followed by the 1956 *Ambatielos Claim* Award,[132] exemplified (along with the *Applicability of the Obligation to Arbitrate under Section 21 of the U.N. Headquarters Agreement of 26 June 1947* Advisory Opinion[133]) the issues arbitrability of the dispute and the Court's jurisdiction to decide the matter.[134] The 1990/1 *Guinea-Bissau v. Senegal Arbitral Award of 31 July 1989*[135] case was the second (after the *Honduras/Nicaragua Arbitral Award Made by the King of Spain on 23 December 1906*[136]) instance of upholding by the Court the validity of an arbitral award,[137] whereas the *Gulf of Fonseca* Chamber regarded the 1917 *El Salvador v. Nicaragua* Judgment of Central American Court of Justice as a subsidiary source of the law.[138]

The *Gulf of Maine* was the first case decided by an *ad hoc* Chamber, constituted under Article 26(2) of the ICJ Statute,[139] as followed by the *Burkina Faso/Mali*, the *ELSI* and the *Gulf of Fonseca* Chambers. The successful use of an *ad hoc* Chamber in the *Gulf of Maine* case, coupled with the *Nicaragua v. U.S.A.* case, commenced, according to Ambassador Rosenne, in the years 1984/6, fifth period of the history of the World Court[140] which is yet continuing. The election during the *Tunisia/Libya* proceedings of the

---

130 *See* the 1992 UNCED Speech by President Sir ROBERT JENNINGS, *op. cit.*, *supra* note 53, at 217.

131 34 ILM (1995) at 595.

132 ICJ REPORTS 1952 at 28 (Preliminary Objection), 1953 at 10 (Merits: Obligation to Arbitrate). For the *Ambatielos Claim* Award, *see supra* note 12.

133 ICJ REPORTS 1988 at 12.

134 *Cf.* S. ROSENNE, *The International Court of Justice and International Arbitration*, 6 LJIL (1993) at 297–323; S.M. SCHWEBEL, Justice in International Law, *op. cit.*, *supra* note 13, Chapter 26: *On Whether the Breach by a State of a Contract with an Alien is a Breach of International Law*, at 425–35.

135 ICJ REPORTS 1990 at 64 (Provisional Measures), 1991 at 53. For the 1989 *Guinea-Bissau/Senegal* Award, *see* 94 RGDIP (1990) at 204; 83 ILR, at 1; N° 443/Stuyt.

136 ICJ REPORTS 1960 at 192.

137 *See supra* note 134; S.M. SCHWEBEL, JUSTICE IN INTERNATIONAL LAW, *supra* note 13, Chapter 13: *The Majority Vote of an International Arbitral Tribunal*, at 213–22; S.M. SCHWEBEL, *The Creation and Operation of an International Court of Arbitral Awards*, (in:) THE INTERNATIONALIZATION OF INTERNATIONAL ARBITRATION, THE LCIA CENTENARY CONFERENCE (1995) at 115–23.

138 ICJ REPORTS 1992 at 351, 600–4. For the 1917 *Gulf of Fonseca* Judgment, *see* 11 AJIL (1917) at 674. *Cf.* HUDSON, *op. cit.*, *supra* note 10, at 60–2; S. ROSENNE, *op. cit.*, *supra* note 134, at 321 n. 43.

139 *Gulf of Maine* Order (Constitution of Chamber), ICJ REPORTS 1982 at 1. The Chamber was composed of Judges GROS, MOSLER, AGO (Chamber's President) and SCHWEBEL, and Judge *ad hoc* Cohen (designated by Canada). *See* also the GULF OF MAINE Judgment, ICJ REPORTS 1984 at 246; *Technical Report of Commander Beazley*, *ibid.* at 347–52; *Separate Opinion of Judge Schwebel*, *ibid.* at 353–59; Dissenting Opinion of Judge GROS, *ibid.* at 360–90.

140 S. ROSENNE, *The Role of the International Court of Justice in Inter-State Relations Today*, 20 REVUE BELGE DE DROIT INTERNATIONAL (RBDI) (1987) at 275, 277. *Cf. supra* note 13.

first African Judge, Taslim O. Elias (Nigeria) to the Court's Presidency (1982/5) was "widely perceived as symbolizing the emergence of a decolonized continent into parity of regard".[141] The *Nicaragua v. U.S.A.* case, as partly overlapping with Judge Elias' Presidency and as discontinued (in Compensation Phase) during Presidency of Sir Robert Jennings,[142] raised more controversy than any other case brought before the Court, with four Dissenting Opinions (Provisional Measures, Intervention, Jurisdiction and Admissiblity, and Merits) of Judge Stephen M. Schwebel in this case ranking "among the more remarkable judicial pronouncements of this century".[143] Judge Schwebel's strong criticism of profoundly puzzling handling by the Court of some aspects of the facts was substantiated by the recently disclosed revelations, which would necessitate re-examination – in light of the facts as now known – of these *Nicaragua v. U.S.A.* dicta which are directly the outcome of the Court's statement of the facts.[144]

In connection with the pending pair of *Interpretation and Application of the 1971 Montreal Convention Arising From the Aerial Incident at Lockerbie (Libya v. U.K.* and *Libya v. U.S.A.)*[145] and the *Application of the Convention on the Prevention and Punishment of the Crime of Genocide (Bosnia and Herzegovina v. Yugoslavia [Serbia and Montenegro])*[146] cases, the beginning of the 1990s also witnessed a revival of the issues pertaning to the relationship between the Court and the Security Council (SC) as the principal organs of the United Nations. In the preceding three cases which involved the ICJ/SC parallelism of action,[147] *i.e.* the *Corfu Channel* (SC Resolution 22 of 9 April 1947), the *Aegean Sea* (SC

---

[141] S. ODA, *op. cit.*, *supra* note 45, at 114.

[142] ICJ REPORTS 1991 at 47.

[143] S. ROSENNE, *A Review Essay of Stephen M. Schwebel's* ***Justice in International Law***, *op. cit.*, *supra* note 2, at 678–80 (679). *Cf.* S. ROSENNE, THE WORLD COURT, *op. cit.*, *supra* note 3, at 251–4, and on Questions put to the witnesses by Judge Schwebel, *see ibid.* at 141, 142–3. For more philosophical perception of the *Nicaragua v. U.S.A.* case, *see* G. ABI-SAAB, *supra* note 13, at 293–5.

[144] S. ROSENNE, *A Review Essay of Stephen M. Schwebel's* ***Justice in International Law***, *op. cit.*, *supra* note 2, at 680; S. ROSENNE, *Lessons of the Past and the Needs of the Future*, *op. cit.*, *supra* note 85; and on the revelations disclosed in a follow-up to an explosion in Managua on 23 May 1993, *see* S. ROSENNE, THE WORLD COURT, *op. cit.*, *supra* note 3, at 152–3 (Postscript).

[145] ICJ REPORTS 1992 at 3, 114 (Provisional Measures).

[146] ICJ REPORTS 1993 at 325 (Provisional Measures).

[147] Note that during the *Fisheries Jurisdiction (U.K. v. Iceland)* case (May 1973) and thereafter (December 1975), the British/Icelandic incidents were brought to the attention of the Security Council, which took no decision on either occasion. Nor did the SC take decision when prior to the institution of the *Libya/Malta* proceedings, the dispute was brought to its attention in 1980/1. In this case, the good offices of the Secretary-General Kurt Waldheim were instrumental in persuading Libya and Malta to bring their dispute to the Court. A draft resolution submitted by Nicaragua on 4 April 1984 was not adopted by the SC following the negative vote of the United States, what triggered Nicaragua's decision to bring the case to the Court.

Resolution 395 of 25 August 1976) and the *US Diplomatic and Consular Staff in Tehran* (SC Resolution 457 of 4 December 1979), there did not arise, as Professor Krzysztof J. Skubiszewski showed, jurisdictional conflict between the two organs and there even was a measure of coordination, including complementarity.[148] In the *Lockerbie* cases, while the Declarations and Opinions appended to the (11:5) majority Orders (Provisional Measures) indicate the discomfort felt by the Court at the issues which it faced, the Court, according to Ambassador Rosenne, was careful not to trespass on the competence of the Security Council, and the Court's decision to deny the Libyan requests for provisional measures avoided a direct conflict between these two principal organs of the United Nations.[149] In Professor Skubiszewski's view, the *Lockerbie* Orders by applying Article 103 of the U.N. Charter, thus recognizing the primacy of obligations resulting from the SC Resolution 748 of 31 March 1992 (under Chapter VII of the Charter), appear to testify that the Council has brought about a change that had a direct effect on the Court's jurisdiction – there was concurrent competence of the two organs and the action of the Security Council cut down the Court's competence.[150] Given that SC Resolution 748 (1992) left the Court practically with no choice other than inaction and that the Court did not elaborate in its *Lockerbie* Orders on the issue, Professor Skubiszewski tends to believe that this was perhaps a situation where jurisdiction was at stake rather than a situation of judicial restraint.[151]

V. SOME SUBSTANTIAL ISSUES: "THE COURT SHOULD AND CAN LOOK AHEAD"

The proposition found in the *East Timor* Dissenting Opinion of Judge *ad hoc* Krzysztof J. Skubiszewski that, "The Court should and can look ahead",

---

148 K. SKUBISZEWSKI, *The International Court of..., op. cit., supra* note 1, at 606–15, 610. *Cf.* S.M. SCHWEBEL, JUSTICE IN INTERNATIONAL LAW, *op. cit., supra* note 13, Chapter 2: *Relations between the International Court of Justice and the United Nations*, at 14, 21–3.

149 S. ROSENNE, THE WORLD COURT, *op. cit., supra* note 3, at 239, 251.

150 K. SKUBISZEWSKI, *The International..., op. cit., supra* note 1, at 615–22, 618.

151 *Ibid.* at 622, noting that in the *Lockerbie* cases the SC came rather close to the proposition advanced in the *Anglo/Iranian Oil Co.* Dissenting Opinion of Judge Alvarez, ICJ REPORTS 1952 at 124, 134, for which S. ROSENNE, THE LAW AND PRACTICE, *op. cit., supra* note 39, at 73, found no express authority in the Charter or in the Court's Statute. For citation of this Rosenne's view, *see* the *Lockerbie* Dissenting Opinions (Provisional Measures) of Judge Weeramantry, ICJ REPORTS 1992 at 56–7, 166–7. *Cf.* remarks on the *Lockerbie* Orders (Provisional Measures) in the *East Timor* Dissenting Opinion of Judge *ad hoc* Skubiszewski, ICJ REPORTS 1995, at 247–8. *Cf.* also T.M. FRANCK, *The "Powers of Appreciation"*, 86 AJIL (1992) at 519–23; W.M. REISMAN, *The Constitutional Crisis in the United Nations*, 87 AJIL (1993) at 83–100; R.ST.J. MACDONALD, *Changing Relations Between the ICJ and the Security Council*, 31 CANADIAN YEARBOOK OF INTERNATIONAL LAW (1993) at 3–32.

which was chosen as a motto of this essay, could – in addition to the *Reparation for Injuries Suffered in the Service of the United Nations* Advisory Opinion[152] which he invokes[153] – be substantiated by a number of cases which involved the issues of the law of the sea as part of general international law.

Some examples of contributions made by the Court in those cases to international law generally[154] include abandonment in the 1923 *Wimbledon* Judgment (Merits) of the concept of international servitudes,[155] or exposition in the 1927 *Lotus* Judgment of metaprinciple of sovereign liberty,[156] as relied upon by Norway in justifying its straight baselines system in the *Anglo/Norwegian Fisheries* case, and by (non-appearing) Iceland in extending its 50-mile fisheries zone which led to the 1972/4 *Fisheries Jurisdiction* cases.[157] During the *Nuclear Weapons* Oral Hearings in 1995, the *Lotus* principle that limitations on sovereignty cannot be presumed was relied upon by France which argued that, in the absence of rules expressly prohibiting recourse to the threat or use of nuclear weapons in any circumstances, such recourse must be considered lawful, except in particular circumstances in which it would be prohibited.[158] This France's position was strongly objected to by the Philippines and Samoa (also on behalf of the Marshall Islands and Solomon Islands) on the ground of fundamental changes which occurred in the nature and structure of international law since the *Lotus* case.[159] The *Lotus* Judgment initiated, moreover, the requirement of a very high standard of proof of the issue of *opinio juris sive necessitatis*,[160] as confirmed by the 1969

---

152 ICJ REPORTS 1949 at 174. On significance of the *Reparation* Advisory Opinion, *see* S.M. SCHWEBEL, JUSTICE IN INTERNATIONAL LAW, *op. cit.*, *supra* note 13, Chapter 16: *The International Character of the Secretariat of the United Nations*, at 248, 258–60.

153 *East Timor* Dissenting Opinion of Judge *ad hoc* Skubiszewski, ICJ REPORTS 1995 at 238. For full citation, *see supra* motto to this essay, and note 6.

154 On concerns with such contributions in the context of the ITLOS, *see* main text accompanying *supra* notes 55 and 68–70.

155 *See supra* note 11.

156 PCIJ Series A, N°, at 10, 4, 18. For a view that this *Lotus* passage was no more than an *obiter dictum* which could have been omitted without affecting the Judgment, *see* Sir HERSCH LAUTERPACHT, QC, LLD, FBA, THE DEVELOPMENT OF INTERNATIONAL LAW BY THE INTERNATIONAL COURT (1934/1982) at 359–61. *Cf.* R.Y. JENNINGS, *General Course on Principles of International Law*, RCADI (1967-II) at 327, 515–26.

157 *Cf.* the *Fisheries Jurisdiction (U.K. v. Iceland)* Separate Opinion (Merits) of Judge Dillard, ICJ REPORTS 1974 at 53, 58–60.

158 *Nuclear Weapons* Oral Pleadings, CR 95/23 [transl.], 65 (1 November 1995, de Brichambaut/France). *See* also *ibid.* CR 95/29, at 47 (10 November, Khodakov/Russia).

159 *Ibid.* CR 95/28, at 69–71 (9 November 1995, Advocate Sanchez/Philippines), CR 95/31, at 59–61 (13 November, Clark/Samoa, also on behalf of the Marshall Islands and Solomon Islands), CR 95/32, at 81 (14 November 1995, Crawford/Solomon Islands).

160 *Cf.* K. SKUBISZEWSKI, *Elements of Custom*, *op. cit.*, *supra* note 1, at 816, 824, 830–1, 840–2, 852–3; R.Y. JENNINGS, *op. cit.*, *supra* note 70, at 2.

North Sea[161] and the 1986 *Nicaragua v. U.S.A.* (Merits)[162] Judgments. The transformation of a conventional rule into customary one was contended, by analogy to the *North Sea* Judgment, in the *Nuclear Tests* cases by Australia which invoked the 1963 Partial Nuclear Test Ban Treaty in support of illegality of atmospheric nuclear weapon tests under customary international law.[163]

Another instance provides the innovative recognition by the 1933 *Eastern Greenland* Judgment of the international binding force of the unilateral act (verbal Ihlen Declaration of 1919),[164] as confirmed in the pair of the 1974 *Nuclear Tests* Judgments and the 1995 *New Zealand v. France Nuclear Tests* Order (Request for an Examination of the Situation) with respect to the written French statements on the cessation of atmospheric nuclear tests.[165] Although the 1974 Judgments have been criticized, the Court's dictum on unilateral declarations, especially the express emphasis on the role of the State's intention to be bound by its unilateral act (as now confirmed by the 1995 Order) constitutes, according to Professor Krzysztof J. Skubiszewski, a contribution to the understanding of the law on the subject.[166] The 1974 *Nuclear Tests* pronouncements were invoked in the *Aegean Sea* case by Greece hoping that since the Court found a statement of President Giscard D'Estaing to be legally binding, it would also ascribe the nature of a legal commitment to a solemn statement made by Prime Ministers of Greece and Turkey in their 1975 Brussels Joint Communiqué.[167] But the Court did not accept the Greece/Turkey Communiqué as providing a valid basis for establishing its jurisdiction.[168] In view of subsequent holding in the 1986 *Nicaragua* Judgment (Merits) that a formal communication which had been

---

[161] ICJ REPORTS 1969 at 44–5. *Cf.* the *North Sea* Pleadings, Vol. I, 58 (Memorial of F.R.G.[D]), Vol. II, at 200 (5 November 1968, Counsel Shigeru Oda).

[162] ICJ REPORTS 1986 at 108–9, citing the *North Sea* Judgment, ICJ REPORTS 1969 at 44.

[163] *Nuclear Tests* Pleadings (Australia), 333. *See* also *Fisheries Jurisdiction* Pleadings (U.K.), 351 [Memorial (Merits)]; the *Nuclear Weapons* Oral Hearings, CR 95/28, at 38 (9 November 1995, New Zealand), CR 95/34, at 77, 78 (15 November, U.K.).

[164] PCIJ Series A/B, N° 53, at 22, 71–3.

[165] ICJ REPORTS 1995 at 305–6 (Order), citing ICJ REPORTS 1974 at 474 (*NZ v. France* Judgment). *See* also the *Nicaragua v. U.S.A.* Judgment (Jurisdiction and Admissibility), ICJ REPORTS 1984 at 418; the *Burkina Faso/Mali Frontier Dispute* Judgment, ICJ REPORTS 1986 at 573–4; the *Nicaragua v. Honduras* Judgment (Jurisdiction), ICJ REPORTS 1988 at 105–6. *Cf.* the *Nuclear Weapons* Oral Hearings, CR 95/28, at 50 (9 November 1995, New Zealand).

[166] K.J. SKUBISZEWSKI, *Unilateral Acts of States, in Bedjaoui, op. cit. supra* note 10, at 221, 225; also 231–2, 235. *Cf.* E. JIMÉNEZ DE ARÉCHAGA, *The Work and Jurisprudence of the ICJ 1947/1986*, 48 BYIL (1987) at 1, 10–11.

[167] *Aegean Sea* Pleadings, at 111–12 (25 August 1976, Counsel O'Connell), at 266 (Memorial [Jurisdiction] of Greece); Separate Opinion (Jurisdiction) of Judge Lachs, ICJ REPORTS 1978 at 50, 51.

[168] ICJ REPORTS 1978 at 3, 39–44.

committed to the Organization of American States was not to be a formal undertaking, but rather a political pledge,[169] Judge Rosalyn Higgins, QC, stresses that an appreciation of all the circumstances will have to be made in every case: "The law can signal the criteria, but the difficult problem of application of the criteria remains and cannot be short-circuited."[170]

The innumerous other pronouncements of lasting importance can be exemplified by those made by the Court in the 1949 *Corfu* Judgment (Merits) on "elementary considerations of humanity"[171] and the principle *sic utere tuo ut alienum non laedas*,[172] or in the *Fisheries Jurisdiction* cases on the doctrine *rebus sic stantibus* and the issue of coercion as invalidating State's consent,[173] whereas the 1960 *IMCO* Advisory Opinion remained important as the first instance in which the Court held action taken by an international organization to be unconstitutional.[174] It is also in the context of its law of the sea-related Judgments that the Court has been making an invaluable contribution to the fundamental concept of equity for the past half a century. The 1949 *Corfu* Judgment (Compensation) provided the first instance of applying by the Court of equity in the field of the quantification of monetary sums due in reparation claims and related types of cases.[175] This appears to be confirmed by reference to this case in the 1956 *Judgments of the Administrative Tribunal of the I.L.O. Upon Complaints Made Against UNESCO*

---

169 ICJ REPORTS 1986 at 132.

170 R. HIGGINS, *Problems and Process*, *op. cit.*, *supra* note 37, at 35.

171 ICJ REPORTS 1949 at 22, repeated in the *Nicaragua v. U.S.A.* Judgment (Merits), ICJ REPORTS 1986 at 112. *Cf.* S.M. SCHWEBEL, *The Treatment of Human Rights*, *op. cit.*, *supra* note 12, at 330 and 339. For invocation of this *Corfu* pronouncement, *see* also the *Nuclear Weapons* Oral Hearings, CR 95/22, at 44 (30 October 1995, Australia), CR 95/25, at 29 (3 November, Indonesia), CR 95/28, at 28 (9 November, New Zealand), CR 95/32, at 18 (14 November, Marshall Islands), CR 95/34, at 55–6 (15 November 1995, U.K.).

172 ICJ REPORTS 1949 at 22. For reliance thereupon, *see* the *Australia v. France Nuclear Tests* Joint Dissenting Opinion, and Dissenting Opinion of Judge de Castro, ICJ REPORTS 1974 at 361, 388; the *New Zealand v. France Nuclear Tests* Dissenting Opinions (Request for an Examination of the Situation) of Judge Weeramantry, ICJ REPORTS 1995 at 346–7, 362 n. 1, and Judge *ad hoc* Sir Geoffrey Palmer, *ibid.* at 408. *See* also the *Anglo/Norwegian Fisheries* Pleadings, Vol. II, at 427, 430 (Reply of U.K.); the *North Sea* Pleadings, Vol. II, at 200 (5 November 1968, Counsel Shigeru Oda); the *Nuclear Weapons* Oral Hearings, CR 95/34, at 55 (15 November 1995, U.K.). *Cf.* VALENCIA-OSPINA, *op. cit.*, *supra* note 13, at 523.

173 *Cf.* CH. GREENWOOD, *The ICJ and the Use of Force*, (in:) ESSAYS IN HONOUR OF SIR ROBERT JENNINGS, *op. cit.*, *supra* note 1, at 373, 373–4.

174 ICJ REPORTS 1960 at 150. *Cf.* S. ROSENNE, *La Cour Internationale de Justice en 1960*, 65 RGDIP (1961) at 473, 515–17. *Cf.* also main text accompanying *infra* notes 223–229.

175 See S. ROSENNE, AN INTERNATIONAL LAW MISCELLANY, *op. cit.*, *supra* note 10, Chapter 7: *The Position of the ICJ on the Foundations of the Principle of Equity in International Law*, at 201, 220.

Advisory Opinion which, in turn, was relied upon in the 1969 *North Sea* Judgment.[176]

Following a preliminary step taken to this effect in the *Anglo/Norwegian Fisheries* case, the 1969 *North Sea* Judgment, including its Opinions, contained a significant exposition of the concept of equity as part of international law applicable to maritime boundary delimitation, and became one of the most widely debatable decisions in the history of the World Court.[177] No express reference was made in the *North Sea* Judgment to precedential application of equity within the framework of law in the 1937 *Diversion of Water from the Meuse* Judgment, as affirmed in Dissenting Opinion of Judge Hudson therefrom,[178] and in the 1951 *Anglo/Norwegian Fisheries* Judgment.[179] Both these precedents were, however, relied upon in the *North Sea* Oral Hearings by the F.R.G., and were invoked – along with some relevant arbitrations[180] – in Separate Opinions of Judges Philip C. Jessup and Fouad Ammoun.[181] The 1982 *Tunisia/Libya* Judgment and Opinions (Merits), along with all the next decisions rendered in maritime delimitation cases, entailed a significant restatement and further crystallization of the Court's doctrine of equity. In addition, whereas considerations of equity invoked by

---

[176] ICJ REPORTS 1956 at 100 (*Judgments of the Administrative Tribunal*), invoking to ICJ REPORTS 1949 at 249 (*Corfu* [Compensation]); as cited in the *North Sea* Judgment, ICJ REPORTS 1969 at 48–9.

[177] *Cf.* main text accompanying *supra* notes 79–80; *infra* notes 231 and 236.

[178] PCIJ Series A/B, N° 70, at 25. According to Dissenting Opinion of Judge HUDSON, *ibid.* at 77, "under Article 38 of the Statute, if not independently of that article, the Court has some freedom to consider principles of equity as part of the international law which it must apply." Judge Hudson's Opinion, *ibid.* at 76, was invoked in the *Tunisia/Libya* Dissenting Opinion (Merits) of Judge *ad hoc* Evensen, ICJ REPORTS 1982 at 290–1; and *infra* notes 183 and 185. *See* also the *North Sea* Pleadings, Vol. II, at 200 (Counsel Shigeru Oda, 5 November 1968); the *Fisheries Jurisdiction* Pleadings (U.K.), at 473 (25 March 1974, Counsel Silkin); the *Tunisia/Libya* Pleadings Vol. I, at 166–7 (Memorial of Tunisia), Vol. IV, at 417 (16 September 1981, Counsel Sir Robert Jennings). *Cf.* M.O. HUDSON, THE PERMANENT COURT, *op. cit.*, *supra* note 10, at 618.

[179] ICJ REPORTS 1951 at 128–9, 132. *Cf.* the *North Sea* Pleadings Vol. II, at 179–80 (4 November 1968, Agent Jaenicke), at 194–5 (5 November, Counsel Shigeru Oda), at 271–2 (11 November 1968, Counsel Sir Humphrey Waldock).

[180] Including: 1902 *France/Venezuela Frederick & Co.* [N° 260/Stuyt], 1914 *Netherlands/Portugal Island of Timor* [9 AJIL (1915) at 240 and Suppl. 107; N° 275/Stuyt] and 1928 *U.K./Turkey W.J. Armstrong & Co. Ltd. v. Vickers Ltd.* decisions. Other examples are: 1922 *Norway/U.S.A. Norwegian Shipowners' Claim* [RIAA I, at 339; 16 AJIL (1922) at 81 and Suppl. 16; 17 AJIL (1923) at 287, 362; N° 339/Stuyt], 1926 *G.B. v. U.S.A. Cayuga Indians* [20 AJIL (1926) at 574; N° 303/Stuyt], and 1968 *India/Pakistan Rann of Kutch* [50 ILR, at 2; 7 ILM (1968) at 633; J. Gillis Wetter, 65 AJIL (1971) at 346–57; N° 433/Stuyt].

[181] ***North Sea*** *Separate Opinions of Judge Jessup*, ICJ REPORTS 1969 at 66, 84, and Judge AMMOUN, *ibid.* at 100, 138, 142, 145.

Belgium in the *Barcelona Traction* (Second Phase) case[182] did not cause the Court to modify its views, the Court (and its Chamber) had regard to equity *infra legem* (as expounded in the *North Sea* cases) in the 1974 *Fisheries Jurisdiction* (Merits)[183] and the 1986 *Burkina Faso/Mali Frontier Dispute*[184] Judgments. It was also relied upon by Judge Stephen M. Schwebel in his Dissenting Opinions from the *Nicaragua v. U.S.A.* Order (Provisional Measures) and Judgment (Merits), where while reinforcing his conclusions of law with considerations of equity, he referred to the Dissenting Opinion of Judge Hudson from the 1937 *Diversion of Water from the Meuse* Judgment.[185]

The richness of the issues of general international law dealt with by the Court in the context of law of the sea-related cases, as exemplified above, including a prominent place of equity among them, could, to important extent, be aligned to the very nature of international law of the sea which was adequately seized in the pair of *Fisheries Jurisdiction* Judgments (Merits) as follows:

> "The very fact of convening the Third Conference on the Law of the Sea evidences a manifest desire on the part of all States to proceed to the codification of the law of the sea on a universal basis, including the question of fisheries and conservation of the living resources of the sea. Such a general desire is understandable since *the rules of international maritime law have been the product of mutual accomodation, reasonableness and cooperation*. So it was in the past, and so it necessarily is today."[186] (emphasis added)

The continuing actuality of this pronouncement found reflection in an admirable recent survey of Dr. Jean-Pierre Lévy welcoming the ever progressing evolution of the law of the sea and concluding that, "The world

---

182 ICJ REPORTS 1970 at 48–50. For invocation of the *Barcelona Traction* Separate Opinion (Second Phase) of Judge Sir Gerald Fitzmaurice, *ibid.* at 85–6, *see* the *Libya/Malta* Pleadings, Vol. II, at 316 n. 3 (Counter-Memorial of Malta).

183 ICJ REPORTS 1974 at 33, 34 (para. 79(3)), and 202, 205 (para. 77(3)); Separate Opinion (Merits) of Judge Dillard, *ibid.* at 63–6, invoking the 1937 *Diversion of Water from the Meuse* Dissenting Opinion of Judge Hudson (PCIJ Series A/B, N° 70, at 76); Separate Opinion of Judge DE CASTRO, *ibid.* at 99, 103–4; Dissenting Opinion of Judge GROS, *ibid.* at 146. *Cf.* R. HIGGINS, PROBLEMS AND PROCESS, *op. cit.*, *supra* note 37, at 224–5.

184 ICJ REPORTS 1986 at 567–8, 631–3, and Separate Opinion of Judge *ad hoc* G. ABI-SAAB, *ibid.* at 659, 662.

185 *Nicaragua v. U.S.A.* Dissenting Opinions of Judge SCHWEBEL, ICJ REPORTS 1984 at 190, 198–9 (Provisional Measures), and (1986) at 259, 392–3 (Merits). For Judge Hudson's Opinion, *see supra* note 178.

186 *Fisheries Jurisdiction* Judgments (Merits), ICJ REPORTS 1974 at 23–4, 192. *Cf.* Declarations of Judge IGNACIO-PINTO, *ibid.* at 38, 211, where he agreed with J.-P. LÉVY, *La troisi me Conférence sur le droit de la mer*, 17 AFDI (1971) at 828, in thinking that the UNCLOS III could only succeed "by moderation, mutual understanding, and the spirit of compromise."

evolves, international relations change and international law continues to but reflect the respective stage in the history of these international relations".[187] Consequently, appreciation of a given stage of codification and development of international law of the sea is of primordial importance for assessing properly whether and why the Court, which "should look ahead", actually could or could not, and did or did not do so in the respective cases.[188] Such an appreciation may also facilitate comprehension of the impacts of the respective Judgments on the development of the law of the sea as a result of both taking (*e.g.*, in the *Lotus*, the *Corfu Channel*, the *Anglo/Norwegian Fisheries* or the *North Sea* and all subsequent maritime delimitation cases) and not taking (*e.g.* in the *IMCO*, the *Fisheries Jurisdiction* or the *Nuclear Tests* cases) by the Court of decisions on the issues concerned. In addition, certain impacts (in some instances overlapping with either of the former two) perhaps neither were intended nor could be overseen by the Court at the time of taking or non-taking its decisions (*e.g.* in the *Anglo/Norwegian Fisheries*, the *Nottebohm* [Second Phase] or the *IMCO* cases). All these impacts resulted in the context of both the very issues submitted for the Court's settlement and questions dealt with by the Court in this connection. This may be exemplified by importance of all maritime boundary delimitation cases from the viewpoint of also the development of legal regimes of the continental shelf, islands, 200-mile zones and many other issues.

At the same time, a number of cases were of important impacts on the law of the sea development notwithstanding the fact that they did not (for different reasons) proceed to the phase of merits and/or involved non-appearance of the respondent. The pair of *Nuclear Tests* and the *Agean Sea* cases exemplify disadvantages of both these factors, while the pair of *Fisheries Jurisdiction* – those of non-appearance only. Two recent cases, which could have been of more pronounced law of the sea-related impacts if they proceeded to the next phases, include the *East Timor* and the *New Zealand v. France Nuclear Tests* cases.[189] Two other pending *Fisheries Jurisdiction (The Estai)* and the *Cameroon v. Nigeria* cases might yet end in the phase of jurisdiction if the Court upholds preliminary objections of Canada and Nigeria respectively.[190] This also applies to the *Iran v. U.S.A. Oil Platforms*

---

[187] J.-P. LÉVY (Former Director of the DOALOS/OLA, *supra* note 19), Les Nations Unies et la Convention de 1982 sur le droit de la mer, 28 RBDI (1995) at 11–35, 31.

[188] *Cf.* the *East Timor* Dissenting Opinion of Judge *ad hoc* Skubiszewski, ICJ REPORTS 1995 at 238, referred to *supra* note 153.

[189] *See* main text accompanying *supra* notes 96–106 (*East Timor*) and 126–127 (*NZ v. France*).

[190] *See supra* notes 78 (*The Estai*) and 105 (*Cameroon v. Nigeria*).

case, in which certain preliminary objections to the Court's jurisdiction were filed by the United States.[191]

The law of the sea-related cases which were discontinued include the *Castellorizo*,[192] the *Southeastern Greenland*,[193] the pair of *Antarctica (forum prorogatum)*, the *Great Belt*, the *Guinea-Bissau v. Senegal Maritime Delimitation*[194] and the *Iran v. U.S.A. Aerial Incident*[195] cases. From the viewpoint of their prospective impacts, this is particularly regrettable in the case of the *Great Belt* which would otherwise be the second (after the *Corfu*) case contributing to the critical regime of international straits, including the new transit passage regime and the question of bridges over straits.[196] The *Great Belt* and two other recently discontinued cases referred to above provide notable examples of using the Court, in the context of *An Agenda for Peace*, as a partner in preventive diplomacy,[197] which found such a notable precursory expression in the view of eminent Elihu Root that "the value of a Court is not to be measured solely by the cases it decides, but also by the vastly greater number of cases which are settled because the Court is there to decide".[198]

This Court's role is continuously also reflected by tensions and conflicts (*e.g.*, recently those between Singapore/Malaysia [Horsburgh Light], Turkey/Greece [Imia/Kardak Island],[199] Japan/South Korea [Takeshima/Tokdo Islands][200] or Iran/U.A.E. [Abu Musa and Tunbs Islands]),[201] in which intentions of bringing the respective disputes to the Court are being expressed, though not (yet) materialized.[202] In case of the Horsburgh Light, position of Singapore (which has reportedly chose Counsel in 1995) would perhaps be weakened by the precedential rejection by the Court in the *Minquiers and Ecrehos* case of the French argument based on maintenance of an extensive

---

191 ICJ REPORTS 1982 at 763, and 1994 at 3; ICJ COMMUNIQUÉ N° 96/4.

192 PCIJ Series A/B, N° 51, at 1.

193 PCIJ Series A/B, N° 55, at 157; main text accompanying *supra* note 82.

194 ICJ REPORTS 1995 at 423.

195 ICJ REPORTS 1996 at 9.

196 *Great Belt* Order (Provisional Measures), ICJ REPORTS 1991 at 12; ICJ COMMUNIQUÉ N° 92/23.

197 *See* main text accompanying *supra* notes 47–48 and 80.

198 E. ROOT, *The Codification of International Law*, 19 AJIL (1925) at 675, 678.

199 *See* main text accompanying *infra* notes 247–251.

200 Interview with Japan's Vice-Foreign Minister, Hisashi Owada, *The Korea Times* of 14 July 1993, 3; Japan Rules Out Force Over Disputed Islands, *International Herald Tribune* (IHT) of 14 February 1996, at 4, and 21 February, at 4; Korean Plan for Isles Risks Japanese Anger, *ibid.* at 23 February, 4, and 14 March 1996, at 4.

201 UN Doc. A/50/713 (1995), *supra* note 20, at 38.

202 Of earlier instances, *see* the 1974 US Senate Resolution 74 on ICJ – Territorial Disputes (Sec.2), 69 AJIL (1975) at 246; L.B. SOHN, *ibid.* at 92–6.

and costly system of navigational aids (lights and buoys) for more than 75 years. Without invoking similar pronouncement of the 1909 *Grisbadarna Maritime Frontier (Norway v. Sweden)* Award,[203] the 1953 *Minquiers* Judgment held that this France's system simply purported to ensure safety of navigation and was not sufficient to show that France had a valid title to the Minquiers.[204]

The decisions taken by the Court in the *Anglo/Norwegian Fisheries* case on baselines (normal and straight) and bays (including rejection of a 10-mile rule[205]) and in the *Corfu* (Merits) case – on innocent passage of commercial ships and warships through the territorial sea and the regime of international straits were expressly relied upon in the 1956 ILC Draft, wherefrom they were carried to the 1958 U.N. Geneva Convention on the Territorial Sea and Contiguous Zone (TSC), and subsequently to the respective provisions of the 1982 U.N. Montego Bay Convention on the Law of the Sea.[206] The 1923 *Wimbledon* Judgment (Merits) remained an authority for the right of free navigation through inter-oceanic canals,[207] whereas 1931 *Polish War Vessels in Danzig* Advisory Opinion[208] was of incidental importance for access

---

[203] RIAA XI, at 155; 4 AJIL (1910) at 226; N°288/Stuyt. For invocation of the *Grisabadarna* Award in this context, *see* the *Eastern Greenland* Pleadings [PCIJ Series C, N°63], 817 (Reply of Denmark), at 1314–15 (Rejoinder of Norway); the *Minquiers* Pleadings, Vol. II, at 177–8 (24 September 1953, Counsel Harrison), at 274 (30 September, Agent Gros).

[204] ICJ REPORTS 1953 at 47, 70–1. On the Horsburgh Light, *see* G. KENT and M.J. VALENCIA, MARINE POLICY IN SOUTHEAST ASIA (1985) at 93.

[205] Article 7(5) of the 1958 TSC, as repeated in Article 10(5) of the 1982 MBC, introduced a 24-mile closing line for bays, as a result of rejection by the *Anglo/Norwegian Fisheries* Judgment, ICJ REPORTS 1951 at 131, of a 10-mile rule, despite its previous affirmation in state practice and the 1853 *G.B./U.S.A. The Washington (The Julia; Bay of Fundy)* [N°47/Stuyt] and the 1910 *G.B./U.S.A. North Atlantic Coast Fisheries* [*supra* note 11] Awards. The Awards were referred to in Dissenting Opinions of Judge Sir ARNOLD MCNAIR, ICJ REPORTS 1951 at 158, 165, and Judge READ, *ibid.* 186, 188, respectively. *See* also references to the *Fisheries* Judgment in main text accompanying *supra* notes 108 and 157.

[206] ILC YEARBOOK (1956-II) at 266–8 (*Anglo/Norwegian Fisheries* [ICJ REPORTS 1951 at 116]: normal and straight baselines), at 268–9 (*ibid.*: bays), at 273 (*Corfu* [Merits, ICJ REPORTS 1949 at 1]: innocent passage through TS and regime of straits), at 277 (*ibid.*: innocent passage of warships).

Normal and straight baselines: 1958 TSC – Articles 3, 4 and 5, 1982 MBC – Articles 5, 7 and 8; *Bays*: 1958 TSC – Article 7, 1982 MBC – Article 10; *Innocent passage through TS*: 1958 TSC – Articles 15 and 16, 1982 MBC – Articles 24 and 25; *Regime of Straits*: 1958 TSC – Article 16(4), 1982 MBC – Articles 37 (definition of strait) and 45 (innocent passage); *Innocent passage of warships*: 1958 TSC – Article 23, 1982 MBC – Article 30. For the 1958 TSC and 1982 MBC, *see supra* notes 31 and 32; also *supra* note 35.

[207] PCIJ Series A, N° 1, at 15. *Cf.* main text accompanying *supra* note 155.

[208] PCIJ Series A/B, N° 43, at 128; Dissenting Opinion of Count Michel Jean César ROSTWOROWSKI (Poland), *ibid.* at 151–61, and Statements of Dissent of Judges FROMAGEOT (France) and URRUTIA (Colombia), *ibid.* 149–50. *Cf.* M.O. HUDSON, *op. cit.*, *supra* note 10, at 657; Sir HERSCH LAUTERPACHT, *op. cit.*, *supra* note 156, at 119–20, also at 29–30, 80, 304 n. 20.

of warships to foreign ports.[209] The *Corfu* (Merits), along with the *Nicaragua v. U.S.A.* (Merits) Judgments, formed moreover the important contribution to the law concerning the use of mines at sea.[210]

In addition, whereas the *Corfu* Judgment (Merits) rejected the Albanian contention that Britain has violated Albania's sovereignty by sending the warships through the Corfu Strait without prior authorization of Albania, the aphorism of eminent Elihu Root in his oral argument in the *North Atlantic Coast Fisheries* proceedings that, "Warships may not pass without consent into this zone [territorial waters – B.K.], because they threaten; merchantmen may pass and repass because they do not threaten", featured prominently in the *Corfu* pleadings,[211] and was supported in the Dissenting Opinions (Merits) of Judges S.B. Krylov (U.S.S.R.) and Philadelpho Azevedo (Brazil).[212] Although it amounted to unconsidered *obiter dictum* outweighing the settled practice of Mr. Root's own government and other States, it has ever since overshadowed the right of innocent passage of warships without prior notification and/or authorization, which, despite the 1989 U.S.A./U.S.R.R. Wyoming Joint Statement,[213] remains one of the most sensitive and controversial issues of the law of the sea.

The 1927 *Lotus* Judgment, which was the only PCIJ decision taken by a casting vote of the President (Judge Hans Max Huber),[214] was referred to in the 1956 ILC Draft only in the context of reversal of the *Lotus* rule by the 1952 Brussels International Convention for the Unification of Certain Rules Relating to Penal Jurisdiction in Matters of Collision or Other Incidents of

---

209 For invocation of the *Polish War Vessels in Danzig* Advisory Opinion in this context, *see* the *Corfu* Dissenting Opinion (Merits) of Judge Azevedo, ICJ REPORTS 1949 at 75, 100.

210 *See* the *Nicaragua v. U.S.A.* Dissenting Opinion (Merits) of Judge Schwebel, ICJ REPORTS 1986 at 259, 378–81; as discussed by W. HEINTSCHEL VON HEINEGG, *The International Law of Mine Warfare at Sea*, 23 ISRAEL YEARBOOK OF HUMAN RIGHTS (1993) at 53–76, at 67–8. *Cf.* main text accompanying *supra* notes 142–144. On US mining of Haipong, Vietnam in 1972, *see* the *Nuclear Tests* Pleadings (Australia), at 517 (9 July 1974, Solicitor-General Byers).

211 For reliance on Elihu Root's *dictum* from the *North Atlantic Coast Fisheries* Proceedings, Vol. II, at 2006 (*supra* note 11), *see* the *Corfu* Pleadings, Vol. II, at 137 (Counter-Memorial of Albania), 293 (Reply of U.K.), Vol. III, at 274–5 and 276 (11 November 1948, Agent Sir Eric Beckett), at 377, 382 and 386 (18 November 1948, Counsel Cot), Vol. IV, at 543 and 553 (18 January 1949, Agent Beckett), at 673 (22 January 1949, Counsel Cot).

212 *Corfu* Dissenting Opinions (Merits) of Judge Krylov, ICJ REPORTS 1949 at 68, 74, and Judge Azevedo, *ibid.* at 8, 101.

213 28 ILM (1989) at 1444; U.N. Doc.A/44/650 (1989), *supra* note 19, at 8.

214 PCIJ Series A, N° 10, at 4. Dissenting Opinions were appended by all six minority Judges, including Former President Loder, Vice-President Weiss, and Judges Lord FINLAY, NYHOLM, ALTAMIRA and MOORE, *ibid.* at 34–107. Since Judge Moore (U.S.A.) concurred in the *Lotus* Judgment as to question submitted in France/Turkey *compromis*, this made "a definitely ascertained majority" of 7:5, *ibid.* at 65. *Cf.* PCIJ Series E, N° 4, at 165–6; M.O. HUDSON, *op, cit,. supra* note 10, at 359–60. *Cf.* also main text accompanying *supra* notes 33, 59 and 156–160.

Navigation,[215] as confirmed by both the 1958 Geneva Convention on the High Seas [HSC] (Article 11) and the 1982 Montego Bay Convention (Article 97). However, it was the *Lotus* Judgment itself which by underlining the then unresolved controversies regarding criminal jurisdiction over collisions on the high seas, led to reversal of its ruling in the Brussels Convention in favour of primacy of the flag State jurisdiction over such collisions. Moreover, the *Lotus* principle that "vessels on the high seas are subject to no authority except that of the State whose flag they fly",[216] was codified in the 1958 HSC (Article 6), indirectly confirmed by the *IMCO* Advisory Opinion, and restated in the Montego Bay Convention (Article 92). The *Lotus* case was also important due to emphasizing that the exclusiveness of the flag State jurisdiction is not absolute, as is evidenced by a number of ever-evolving exceptions thereto, and due to suggesting, as solution *de lege ferenda*, the concurrent jurisdiction over collisions. As was argued by the United States in the *IMCO* case, the six minority Judges were divided in the *Lotus* case on the question of concurrent criminal jurisdiction in a collision involving vessels of different flags on the high seas which was at issue in this case.[217] However, and most importantly, all the six dissenting Judges recognized the basic principle of the jurisdiction of the law of the flag State of registry regarding acts done on board ships, as enunciated in the *Lotus* Judgment.[218]

The 1960 *IMCO* Advisory Opinion, along with the 1951 *Anglo/Norwegian Fisheries* Judgment, both effected impacts reaching farther than the Members of the Court might have realized at the time. Sir Hersch Lauterpacht, QC, saw the inarticulate major premise of the decision reached by the Court's (12:2) majority in the *Fisheries* case in the unsatisfactory nature of pre-existing preponderant rules on baselines (and bays) from the viewpoint of modern "realities" which involved certain geographical and economic circumstances. Significantly, Sir Hersch considered such "realities" – which underline the very essence of the development of international law of the sea – as not being irrelevant, since, as he put it, "the full appreciation of these realities constitutes the hallmark of the reasonableness – or the continued reasonableness – of the rule".[219] The accomodation within such appreciation of claims advanced for over four past decades by coastal States

---

215 439 UNTS 233; referred to in the ILC Yearbook 1956-II, at 281.

216 PCIJ Series A, N° 10, at 1, 25.

217 *IMCO* Pleadings, at 132–6 (U.S.A.).

218 *IMCO* Pleadings, at 136 (U.S.A.). *See* also *ibid.* at 44 (Liberia), at 182–3 (Panama), at 256 (India), at 317 (27 April 1960, Panama).

219 Sir HERSCH LAUTERPACHT, *op. cit., supra* note 156, at 192–3. *Cf.* main text accompanying *supra* notes 186–187.

to by now the 200-mile limit and beyond, does not appear to affect the "continued reasonableness" of the respective rules.[220] These rules include those applying to mid-ocean archipelagos, for the development of which the *Anglo/Norwegian Fisheries* Judgment was of essential encouragement. As a result, the archipelagic State regime has now been legitimized in the U.N. Montego Bay Convention (Part IV), with some familiar aspects thereof having resurfaced in the *East Timor* case.[221] Far-reaching implications in favour of the coastal states' rights could also result from inclusion by the *Aegean Sea* Judgment (Jurisdiction) of the continental shelf (as now extending beyond 200 miles) into the notion of "territorial status" of State, what may lead logically to the same propensity in the case of the 200-mile EEZ.[222]

In the *IMCO* advisory case – which given its quasi-contentious character, could be considered as having been won by Liberia and Panama as supported by the United States due to its strategic interest in the continued existence of "open registry" fleets – the Court did not decide on any substantial issue of the law of the sea. But the *IMCO* case testified to difficulties surrounding application of the elusive concept of "genuine link" to nationality of ships, as transposed by the ILC from the 1955 *Nottebohm* Judgment (Second Phase)[223] into the 1958 HSC (Article 5). During the *IMCO* proceedings, the open registry fleet States argued against,[224] while the maritime powers fearing competition of those fleets argued in favour,[225] of applying the *Nottebohm* analogy to the open registry fleets. In its 1960 *IMCO* Advisory Opinion the Court found that examination of the contention based on a genuine link, as provided for in the then unratified 1958 HSC (Article 5), was irrelevant for the purpose of answering the question submitted to the

220 For opposite view, *see* W.M. REISMAN and G.G. WESTERMAN, STRAIGHT BASELINES IN MARITIME BOUNDARY DELIMITATION (1992) at 34.

221 The 1989 Australia/Indonesia Timor Gap Treaty, whose validity was questioned in the *East Timor* case by Portugal, ICJ REPORTS 1995 at 98, 100, 102, 105, and Dissenting Opinion of Judge *ad hoc* SKUBISZEWSKI, *ibid.* at 233–4, 253–5, exemplified Indonesia's policy of concluding some 15 maritime delimitation and other treaties [*e.g.* 1988 Indonesia/U.S.A. Income Tax Treaty, 83 AJIL (1989) at 559] with a view to securing international recognition of the archipelagic concept. *See* also *East Timor* Separate Opinion of Judge ODA, *ibid.* at 107–18. *Cf.* main text accompanying *supra* notes 20, 40 and 96–106.

222 *See* main text accompanying *supra* note 73.

223 ICJ REPORTS 1955 at 4, 23; *supra* note 26.

224 *IMCO* Pleadings, at 71 (Liberia), at 298–9 (27 April 1960, L), at 317 (27 June, Panama), at 404–5, 407 (3 May, L). *See* also *supra* notes 217–218.

225 *IMCO* Pleadings, at 335, 344 (28 April 1960, Italy), at 355–9 (29 April, Netherlands), at 365–8 (Norway), at 374, 383 (U.K.). *Cf.* the *North Sea* Pleadings, Vol. II, at 242 (8 November 1969, Counsel Sir Humphrey Waldock); the *ELSI* Pleadings, Vol. II, at 250 n. 4 (Counter-Memorial of Italy).

Court.[226] The far-reaching wisdom of this Court's position, despite criticism which it raised in the 1970 *Barcelona Traction* Separate Opinion (Second Phase) of Judge Philip C. Jessup[227] and despite restatement of the genuine link concept in the 1982 Montego Bay Convention (Article 91), has been confirmed by so far scarce prospects for entry into force of the 1986 UNCTAD Convention on Conditions for Registration of Ships.[228] On the whole, the developments since surprising importation of the genuine link from the *Nottebohm* Judgment to the rules governing nationality of ships, confirmed prediction of Sir Robert Jennings, QC, as to perils inherent in such, by its very nature inappropriate, transposition.[229]

Another instance exemplifying that, as Judge *ad hoc* Skubiszewski put it, "The Court should and can look ahead",[230] is a tremendous impact which the Court's doctrine of applying equity to maritime boundary delimitation has effected on State practice as well as jurisprudence of other courts and tribunals. Commencing with the critical Caracas Session (20 June-29 August 1974), the 1969 *North Sea* Judgment underlain the debates of UNCLOS III concerning both delimitation of the continental shelf and other maritime spaces between adjacent/opposite States and the legal regimes of these spaces,[231] and found a notable reflection in Articles 74/83 and other respective provisions of the Montego Bay Convention. Equally pronounced was the impact – especially on the regime of fisheries in 200-mile zones and on the high seas, as laid down in the Montego Bay Convention (Parts V and VII) – of decisions which were both taken and wisely avoided (regarding the validity of Iceland's 50-mile EFZ) by the Court in the pair of *Fisheries Juris-*

---

226 ICJ Reports 1960, at 150, 171. For support of genuine link concept, *see* Dissenting Opinion of Judge Moreno Quintana, *ibid.* at 177, 178. *Cf.* also *supra* note 174.

227 ICJ REPORTS 1970 at 182, 183–4.

228 26 ILM (1987) at 1229.

229 R.Y. JENNINGS, *General Course*, *op. cit.*, *supra* note 156, at 463–5.

230 *East Timor* Dissenting Opinion of Judge *ad hoc* Skubiszewski, ICJ REPORTS 1995 at 238, referred to *supra* note 153.

231 For reliance on the *North Sea* Judgment, ICJ REPORTS 1969 at 3, *see* Statements of: Orion (Israel), 16th Meeting-26 July 1974, (in:) UNCLOS III Off. Rec. Vol. II, at 144 (1975); HERRERA CACERES (Honduras), *ibid.* at 145; GALINDO POHL (El Salvador), 18th M-29 July, *ibid.* at 149; KELLY DE GUIBOURG (Argentina), at 150; CHAO (Singapore), at 151; LUPINACCI (Uruguay), at 153; MIRCEA (Romania), 19th M-30 July, *ibid.* at 156; CAFLISCH (Switzerland), at 157; YOLGA (Turkey), at 158; ARAIM (Iraq), at 159; PANUPONG (Thailand), at 159–60; KEDADI (Tunisia), 20th Meeting-30 July, *ibid.* at 163; GAYAN (Mauritius), at 163; JACOVIDES (Cyprus), at 163; LYSAGHT (Ireland), at 165; SOBARZO (Mexico), at 166; ROBINSON (Jamaica), at 167–8; BELLIZZI (Malta), at 168–9; AL-NIMER (Bahrain), 22nd M-31 July 1974, *ibid.* at 171. *Cf.* also YOLGA (Turkey), 140th M-27 August 1980, *ibid.* Vol. XIV, at 79 (1982); *Libya/Malta* Pleadings Vol. I, at 105–7 (Memorial of Libya).

diction Judgments (Merits).[232] Many other notable examples include the essential impact effected on the 200-mile EEZ/EFZ regime by pronouncements made by the Court (and its Chamber) in the 1982 *Tunisia/Libya* (Merits) and all subsequent maritime delimitation cases, whereas the 1995 *New Zealand v. France* Order (Request for an Examination of the Situation) was the first to recognize the critical "obligations of States to respect and protect the natural environment",[233] as codified in the Montego Bay Convention (Part XII) and many other treaties.

A notable feature of the law of equitable maritime delimitation which, as Judge Stephen M. Schwebel put it, "is more plastic than formed",[234] has been the mutually reinforcing relationship[235] between jurisprudence of the Court and that of other, especially arbitral courts and tribunals. The 1977 *Anglo/French Delimitation of the Continental Shelf* Decision (para.70) of the Court of Arbitration, which was the first to address the *North Sea*-introduced distinction between conventional and customary rules, was significant in its outright identification of these two categories of rules, namely the equidistance/special circumstances rule of the 1958 U.N. Geneva Convention on the Continental Shelf [CSC] (Article 6) and the customary norm of equitable principles enunciated by the *North Sea* Judgment.[236] It is, therefore, equally significant that in its almost unanimous (14:1 majority) Judgment delivered under Presidency of Sir Robert Jennings in the *Denmark v. Norway (Jan Mayen)* case, the Court ascertained that an equidistance/special circumstances rule under the 1958 CSC (Article 6) "produces much the same

232 For reliance on the *Fisheries Jurisdiction* Judgments (Merits), ICJ REPORTS 1974 at 3, 175, *see* Statements of: Ambassador ROSENNE (Israel), 22nd Meeting-31 July 1974, (in:) UNCLOS III Off. Rec. Vol. II, at 178 (1975); Ambassador Andersen (Iceland), 30th M-7 August 1974, *ibid.* at 229 (1975). *See* also Working Paper co-sponsored by Iceland jointly with Canada, Chile, India, Indonesia, Mauritius, Mexico, New Zealand and Norway one day after the delivery of the 1974 Judgments, Doc. A/CONF.62/L.4 of 26 July 1974, *ibid.* Vol. III, at 81 (1975). For invocation of the Court's Judgments in support of traditional rights, *see* Statements of: Goerner (GDR), 22nd M-31 July 1974, *ibid.* Vol. II, at 173; JAENICKE (F.R.G.), 24th M-1 August, *ibid.* at 191–2; Sir ROGER JACKLING (U.K.), 25th M-5 August, *ibid.* at 200; OGISO (Japan), 28th M-6 August 1974, *ibid.* at 217–18.

233 ICJ REPORTS 1995 at 306.

234 *Gulf of Maine* Separate Opinion of Judge Schwebel, ICJ REPORTS 1984 at 353, 357. *Cf.* main text accompanying *supra* notes 175–185.

235 An exception thereto seems to be provided by the 1992 *Delimitation of Maritime Areas Between Canada and France (St. Pierre and Miquelon)* Award, 31 ILM (1992) at 1165; 96 RGDIP (1992) at 673; N° 450/Stuyt. *Cf.* E. ZOLLER, *L'Affaire de la* ***Délimitation des espaces maritimes entre le Canada et la République Française***, 38 AFDI (1992) at 480–500.

236 RIAA XVIII, at 3; 54 ILR, at 139; 18 ILM (1979) at 397. For the 1958 CSC, *see supra* note 31. For the first attempt to combine the application of equitable principles with equidistance, *see* Doc. A/CONF.62/C.2/L.14 (Netherlands), 19 July 1974, in UNCLOS III Off. Rec. Vol. III, at 190 (1975), and Statement of Riphagen (NL), 28th Meeting-6 August 1974, *ibid.* Vol. II, at 218 (1975).

result" as an equitable principles/relevant circumstances rule under customary law in the case of opposite coasts.[237]

The events in a follow-up to three cases, which for different reasons were prevented from proceeding to the merits, *i.e.* the pair of *Antarctica (U.K. v. Argentina* and *U.K. v. Chile)*, the *Aegean Sea* (as preceded by [discontinued] 1931/3 *Italy/Turkey Castellorizo* case) and the *Nuclear Tests* cases, have been continuing until today and may yet lead to third-party settlements. While the two *Antarctica* cases have mainly attracted attention as instances of *forum prorogatum*,[238] the 1955 British Applications contributed to the development of rules governing acquisition of territorial sovereignty in continuation of the 1928 *Palmas (Miangas) Island (U.S.A./Netherlands)*[239] and the 1931 *Clipperton Island (France/Mexico)*[240] Awards, as well as the 1933 *Eastern Greenland* and the 1953 *Minquiers* Judgments.[241] The *Eastern Greenland* decision was invoked by Morocco in the *Western Sahara* case and was, along with the *Minquiers* pronouncements, addressed by the Court in its 1975 Advisory Opinion.[242] The position (especially on the critical date) taken by Britain in the *Minquiers* case (decided fully in its favour) was relied heavily upon by Sharjah in the 1981 *Land and Maritime Boundary (Dubai/Sharjah)* arbitration.[243] The pre-eminence of evidence of actual and effective occupation as a source of title to territory over claims to historic title, as developed by this jurisprudence, particularly as it related to unsettled territory (which was especially made clear in the *Eastern Greenland* case), has provided the conceptual foundation for the expansionist claims effected subsequently over Spratly Islands in the South China Sea. The Spratly – along with the Aegean and Caspian disputes – are considered by the US Department of Defence as three "real-world examples" where the principles embodied in the 1982 U.N. Montego Bay Convention are being used to enhance international peace and security by defusing part or all of a dispute.[244]

---

237 ICJ REPORTS 1993 at 38, 62–3.

238 ICJ REPORTS 1956 at 12, 15 (Removal from the List). *Cf.* main text accompanying *supra* note 71.

239 RIAA II, 829; N° 366/Stuyt. *Cf.* Ph.C. JESSUP, *The **Palmas Island** Arbitration*, 22 AJIL (1928) at 735–52.

240 RIAA II, 1105; 26 AJIL (1932) at 390; 27 AJIL (1933) at 130; N° 293/Stuyt.

241 *Antarctica* Pleadings, 8–47, 48–77, and a map at the end of volume. *Cf.* Sir HUMPHREY WALDOCK, *Disputed Sovereignty in the Falkland Islands Dependencies*, 25 BYIL (1948) at 311–53.

242 ICJ REPORTS 1975 at 12, 38–9, 42–3. *Cf. supra* note 23.

243 N° 438/Stuyt; 91 ILR, at 543. *Cf.* D.W. Bowett, 65 BYIL (1994) at 103–33.

244 *National Security and the Convention on the Law of the Sea* 16–20 (US Department of Defence, 1996). *Cf.* G.M.C. VALERO, *Spratly Archipelago Dispute*, 18 MARINE POLICY (1994) at 314–44; U.N. Doc. A/50/713 (1995), *supra* note 20, at 37–8.

The conflicting claims to the islands originally called the Falkland Islands (Malvinas) Dependencies, especially the South Georgia and South Sandwich Islands, and to the Falklands (Malvinas) themselves have continued, with a varied intensity, during the four decades since the *Antarctica* Applications were filed, against the background of the opening of the Antarctic Treaty System, evolution of modern concepts of the law of the sea, the 1982 Anglo/Argentine Falklands (Malvinas) War, and other developments in the region. On the whole, the situation has continued to develop in a manner similar to that described in the British *Antarctica* Application; *i.e.* instead of actively displaying and exercising its authority, Argentina has attempted by diplomatic moves – through the United Nations and other fora, including in the context of law of the sea debates – to throw doubt upon the existing British titles.[245] Whereas the resort to the ICJ seems, however, in this case, as in that of Japan/South Korea dispute over the Takeshima (Tokdo) Islands,[246] improbable, such a resort in the case of Turkey/Greece dispute could not with certainty be excluded.

After the Court declined to indicate interim measures against non-appearing Turkey in the 1976 *Aegean Sea* Order (Provisional Measures) and upheld Turkey's preliminary objections in the 1978 *Aegean Sea* Judgment (Jurisdiction),[247] the Turkish/Greek dispute over the continental shelf delimitation and sovereignty over Aegean islands, paralleled by the controversy over Cyprus question, continued to influence the conflicting positions taken by two States during the UNCLOS III. Thereafter, the unresolved conflict has continued to complicate Turkey/Greece relations, including through crises in 1987, 1991 and 1995/6, as reflected by leverage diplomacy pursued by the two States (both of them NATO members) within the United Nations, the European Union (in the context of the 1995 EU/Turkey Customs Union) and other fora in support of their respective claims.[248] In a follow-up to

---

245 *Antarctica* Pleadings, at 27. *See* also Letter of the U.K. Agent Sir Gerald Fitzmaurice of 31 August 1955 to the Court's Registrar, *ibid.* at 97–100. For some recent exchanges, *see e.g.* U.N./DOALOS LAW OF THE SEA BULLETIN (1987 N° 9) at 40–52; (1995 N° 27) at 81. *See* also Declaration made by Argentina upon ratification of the U.N. Montego Bay Convention and the Part XI Agreement on 1 December 1995, *ibid.* at 6–8 (1996 N° 30); Working Paper of the Secretariat on Falkland Islands (Malvinas), U.N. Doc. A/AC.109/2027 (1995).

246 *See supra* note 200.

247 *Cf.* main text accompanying *supra* notes 71, 73, 124 and 148.

248 For some recent exchanges, *see* U.N. Docs A/50/216-S/1995/476, A/50/256-S/1995/505, A/50/264-S/1995/526, A/50/279-S/1995/568, A/50/303-S/1995/603. *See* also Declaration made by Greece upon ratification of the U.N. Montego Bay Convention and the Part XI Agreement on 21 July 1995, U.N./DOALOS LAW OF THE SEA BULLETIN (1995 N° 29) at 6–7, and Objection of Turkey of 19 December 1995 to Greece's Declaration, *ibid.* at 9–10 (1996 N° 30).

the latest incident related to the Imia (Kardak) Island, including intervention of President Bill Clinton,[249] the United States and the EU have reportedly endorsed Greek suggestion that the two States seek a ruling from the ICJ, with Turkey having opposed the idea.[250] Were this idea to materialize, it is clear as a result of the 1978 *Aegean Sea* Judgment (Jurisdiction) that this will have to be on the basis of a joint submission by Greece and Turkey of their dispute to the Court.[251]

The unique and highly politicized history of the pair of *Nuclear Tests* cases which were mooted by the Court in 1974, and which remain moot given New Zealand's failure to reopen its own case in 1995,[252] may yet continue despite the fact that France meanwhile ended (with the sixth explosion in the current series effected on 27 January 1996) its underground nuclear weapon tests at the Mururoa and Fangataufa Atolls. In response to announcement made by President Jacques Chirac to this effect on 29 January 1996, both Foreign Minister of Australia, Gareth Evans, and Prime Minister of New Zealand, Jim Bolger, stated that the matter was not to be closed until there would be no environmental damage as a result of French testing in the South Pacific.[253] On 1 March 1996, the IAEA undertook (on France's request) the major 18-month Radiological Study of Mururoa and Fangataufa Atolls, covering an evaluation of not only the current, but also of the long-term, radiological situation at the Atolls.[254] Were a damage as a result of French tests to be substantiated, the resort to the ICJ would, however, be precluded unless France (as is unlikely) consented to the Court's jurisdiction. Nor could the 1982 U.N. Montego Bay Convention (Part XV) be relied upon (including resort to the ITLOS), given possibilities of excepting "disputes concer-

---

249 UN Calls on Greece and Turkey for Calm in Aegean, IHT of 31 January 1996, at 1 and 5; Greek-Turkish Crisis, *ibid.* 1 February, at 1, and 2 February, at 5; Turkey Urges Greece to Repair Relations, *ibid.* 7 February 1996, at 5.

250 Turkey Will Lobby Europe, IHT of 13 February 1996, at 5 and 7; Deputies Fault EU's Handling of Aegean Turmoil, *ibid.* 16 February, at 5, and 17/18 February, at 1; Athens Seeks Ruling on Isle Feud, *ibid.* 24/25 February, at 2, and 27 February, at 7; Clinton Cautious on Aegean Islets, *ibid.* 11 April, at 5; Greek Vessel Opens Fire, *ibid.* 23 April, at 2, and 24 April, at 5; Greece-Turkey Ministers Meet, *ibid.* 29 April 1996, at 7.

251 S. ROSENNE, THE WORLD COURT, *op. cit.*, *supra* note 3, at 213.

252 *See* main text accompanying *supra* notes 126–127.

253 W. DROZDIAK, *Nuclear Tests Over, Chirac Announces*, IHT of 30 January 1996, at 1; M. RICHARDSON, *ibid.* 31 January 1996, at 4. *See* also *Report of the Third Ordinary Meeting of the Contracting Parties to the SPREP Convention, Apia, Western Samoa, 6–7 October 1995*, Agenda Item 6, at 2–4 [Declaration], Annexes 5 [AUS], at 6 [NZ], at 7 [U.S.A., abstaining] (SPREP 1995); the *Nuclear Weapons* Oral Hearings, CR 95/22, at 67–8 (30 October, Counsel Evans), CR 95/28, at 19–62, at 20 and 53–8 (9 November 1995, Attorney-General East).

254 *IAEA Press Release* PR 96/3 (1996).

ning military activities" from compulsory procedures (Article 298(1)(b)) and of withholding information essential to security interests of States (Article 302). However, the worldwide support for New Zealand and other Pacific States which was apparent in connection with the 1995 *New Zealand v. France* (Request for an Examination of the Situation) case, and the fact of "the Court being there",[255] would most likely contribute to settlement of any eventual claims for damage through direct negotiations between France and the claimant States concerned.

* * *

A half-century achievement of the International Court, coupled with the accepted success of its predecessor, the Permanent Court, illustrate adequacy, in relation to law of the sea cases surveyed in this essay, of the view expressed by Professor Krzysztof J. Skubiszewski as Judge *ad hoc* in the *East Timor* case that, "The Court should and can look ahead".[256] Whereas the Court, as its current Vice-President, Judge Stephen M. Schwebel remarked, "is not a body of uniformly high achievement or unlimited potential",[257] it seems encouraging that some law of the sea-related cases provided instances of the *major* impact effected by the Court upon the global system of international law and relations. Significantly, Sir Robert Jennings, QC, includes in such cases – along with the *Reparation for Injuries* Advisory Opinion[258] which is invoked by Judge *ad hoc* Skubiszewski as illustrating his view quoted above – the *Anglo/Norwegian Fisheries* case and maritime boundary delimitation cases[259] which have given a new and lasting direction to the law of the sea in general.[260] The considerable impact of the Court's practice on international law of the sea also covers procedural aspects of its functioning which provided such a notable model for dispute settlement scheme of the U.N. Montego Bay Convention on the Law of the Sea (Part XV), including

---

255 E. ROOT, *op. cit., supra* note 198.

256 *East Timor* Dissenting Opinion of Judge *ad hoc* SKUBISZEWSKI, ICJ REPORTS 1995 at 238, referred to *supra* note 153.

257 S.M. SCHWEBEL, JUSTICE IN INTERNATIONAL LAW, *supra* note 13, Chapter 1: *Reflections on the Role of the ICJ*, at 3–13, at 4; as cited in the JUBILEE BOOK, *op. cit., supra* note 5, Chapter Nine: *The Judges, Stephen M. Schwebel*, at 323.

258 *See supra* note 152.

259 Of maritime delimitation cases, Sir Robert, *infra* note 260, refers only to the first three which involved *Continental Shelf, i.e.* the *North Sea*, the *Tunisia/Libya* and the *Libya/Malta* cases. But it is assumed that he would consent in adding thereto the *Gulf of Maine* and the *Denmark v. Norway (Jan Mayen)*, and perhaps also the *Gulf of Fonseca*, cases.

260 R.Y. JENNINGS, *The ICJ After Fifty Years*, *op. cit., supra* note 119, at 493.

the ITLOS Statute.[261] All these impacts will undoubtedly continue to shape evolution of the law of the sea as part of general international law and, it is hoped, will be further enhanced by the decisions of the Court and other courts and tribunals in the years to come.

---

[261] *Cf.* ROSENNE, *Establishing the ITLOS, op. cit., supra* note 54; S. ROSENNE, *The ITLOS and the ICJ, op. cit., supra* note 69; and S. ROSENNE, as Moderator of Round-Table on Settlement of Disputes, *op. cit., supra* notes 85 and 117.

Customary Norms in Contemporary International Law

by

Igor I. Lukashuk

The computer brought to light a long list of works by Professor K. Skubiszewski. Some of them, especially among those published outside Poland, turned out to be unknown to me despite the fact that I had always carefully followed the writings of this outstanding jurist. More important, however, is not the volume, but the high professionalism of the writings which distinguish themselves by the quality of juridical logic and attention to realities. The writings often touched on the problem of customary norms which today enjoy a new lease on life. All that is determined by choice of topic.

There is no point in engaging in detailed analysis of the numerous doctrinal concepts of customary norms since this had already been done more than once. Let me comment on only the most recent and, moreover, the most original. True, such examples are not plentiful. I could cite, for instance, the theory advanced by Z. Slouka, professor of political science at Columbia University. In his opinion, the secret of international customary law will never be solved until the traditional theory has been replaced by a new ensemble of conceptual techniques. He believes that the traditional approach, premised on a definition of these norms as common or universal, is unrealistic and that it operates to obscure the dynamic nature of the development of customary norms. To serve as a new ensemble of conceptual techniques, the author opted for the theory of the Yale school which views international law as a process of adoption of imperative decisions. Accordingly, customary norms too are understood as a process by medium of which the political judgment calls of States gradually draw closer, moving toward ever more constraining, inevitable and, ultimately, mandatory models.[1]

These propositions speak for themselves. I shall therefore comment on just a few points. The creation and application of norms of law is in effect a process of adoption of imperative decisions. But, the same can be said for politics. As a result, this approach does not help elucidate the specific na-

---

[1] Z. Slouka, International Custom and the Continental Shelf: A Study in the Dynamics of Customary Rules of International Law (1968) at 4.

ture of law, including customary law. A telling fact also is that even Z. Slouka in the end cannot dispense with the concept of the mandatory model, *i.e.* a legal norm the significance of which is disputed by the theory of the adoption of imperative decisions.

Let us begin our consideration of the concept of custom by elucidating its essence. In the absence of a supranational authority, the consent of independent subjects lies at the root of every international legal norm. It is the only means of creating norms. That is the only way to set the content of the norm and vest it with legal force. Consent has two modes of expression. One of them is in the clearly expressed, generally written, shape of a treaty. The other entails the unwritten form of custom which in the majority of cases is generated not by clearly expressed, but by tacit consent (*tacitum pactum*). Consequently, the customary norm differs from the contractual not in essence, but in the method of achieving agreement and the form of expressing the latter.

It is highly indicative that all this was very clearly spelled out already by H. Grotius who tapped the rich experience of Roman law. He wrote of law that governed relations among many nations and one of the sources of which was tacit consent. H. Grotius substantiated the existence of this law on the grounds that particular laws could arise by virtue of mutual agreement both among all States and a majority of them. And it even turns out that such laws arose in the interests not of each community of people separately, but in the interests of a large concert of all such communities. In his words, this is precisely what constitutes the law that is called the law of nations.[2] These thoughts have lost none of their import even today. An old truth is by no means always an outmoded one.

Nevertheless, this concept has long been the object of criticism in which authoritative jurists have also joined. Here, they cite the fact that customary norms represent an independent form of law, distinct from the norms created by agreement.[3] Hardly anyone will bother to deny that a custom represents a special form of law (*consuetudo est altera lex*). But a special form does not controvert the unitary essence of norms.

---

[2] G. GROTSII (H. GROTIUS), O PRAVE VOINY I MIRA, Moscow (1956) at 44, 48.

[3] The well-known English jurist, H. Waldock, has written that in the opinion of most international lawyers, customary law is not a form of tacit agreement, but an independent form of law. H. WALDOCK, *General Course of Public International Law*, 106 RDC (1962–II) at 49. In his detailed study of custom, the Belgian jurist, P. Haggenmacher, comes to the conclusion that, as distinct from treaty norms, custom is not the result of concert of the sovereign wills of States. P. HAGGENMACHER, *Doctrine des deux élèments du droit coutumier dans la pratique de la Cour Internationale*, 90:1 REVUE GÉNÈRALE DE DROIT INTERN. PUBLIC, Paris (1986).

Those who deny custom's consensual character maintain that its genesis entails not tacit agreement, but something completely different, namely, a series of unilateral acts.[4] However, a series of unilateral acts amounts to nothing else than a series of acts of consent by individual States to recognize a particular rule as a norm of international custom. An analogous process, except in clearly expressed guise, occurs when States adhere to a convention by medium of unilateral acts.

The consideration is also adduced that, once a custom has become a general norm of international law, it binds all States that do not object thereto.[5] But, in order to become a norm of general international law, a custom must win the consent of States and it will not be binding for a State that has not given such consent of that objects.

A significant number of authoritative jurists, who furthermore have extensive experience in practical work, consider custom a form of agreement; in that connection, G.I. Tunkin marks a point of no small importance: "The concept whereby customary, as well as contractual, norms of international law are created by medium of concert of the wills of States comports with the fundamental principles of international law."[6]

G. Fizmaurice's compromise position is highly instructive: he was legal advisor to the British Foreign Office, a member of the International Law Commission and a member of the International Court. As he saw it, when a general norm of customary international law was formed by the matching practice of States, then, although it may be somewhat inexpedient to resort to the concept of agreement, it would nonetheless be correct to say that agreement lurks in the mutual tolerance that allows practice to form in the first place.[7] In other words without some form of consent, customary norms could not be formed at all. Note that G. Fitzmaurice arrived at his opinion on the basis of analysis of the practice of the International Court recorded during its first years of operation. And, in effect, the concept of consent as the basis for international customary law was quite widely reflected in a number of the Court's decisions.[8]

---

[4] *See* J. KUNZ, *The Nature of Customary International Law*, 47:4 AJIL (1953) at 666; T. GIHL, THE LEGAL CHARACTER AND SOURCES OF INTERNATIONAL LAW, Stockholm (1957) at 77.

[5] H. WALDOCK, *op. cit., supra* note 3, at 50.

[6] KURS MEZHDUNARODNOGO PRAVA V SEMI TOMAKH, T. 1, Moscow (1989) at 197 [hereafter abbr. as KURS].

[7] G. FITZMAURICE, *The Law and Procedure of the International Court of Justice, 1951–1954*, 30 BYIL (1955) at 68.

[8] Asylum, Judgment, ICJ REPORTS 1950 at 266; Fisheries, Judgment ICJ REPORTS 1951 at 116; Right of Passage over Indian Territory, Merits, Judgment, ICJ REPORTS 1960 at 4.

To some extent, the concept whereby both customary and contractual norms are created as a result of the consent of States also found reflection in the doctrinal codification of international law prepared by the American Law Institute.[9]

The concept of the consensual nature of customary norms commands the advantage that it comports with the practice of States and the nature of international law and furnishes answers to the cardinal questions of theory and practice regarding not only the nature, but also the creation and mode of operation of custom. O. Schachter notes that the theory that became dominant in the nineteenth century and continues to prevail today provides clear criteria for the creation and establishment of the legal force of prescriptions. He adds that these criteria call for the clear manifestation of the wills of the States in the process in the course of which norms are formed, to wit, in treaty and the practice of States accepted as law.

Revealing the reasons behind this proposition. O. Schachter writes that the ideas of natural law based on the principles of morality which ran counter to the aforecited theory were increasingly perceived as at odds with the political regime of sovereign States. This theory was seen as designed to make international law realistic and definite. It satisfied those who were worried about the realities of State power and the meaning of sovereignty and, he observes, also met the intellectual demands of the analytical theoreticians of law who strove to place jurisprudence on a scientific footing.[10]

Such an admission is also valuable in that it comes from an author who does not have much sympathy for the prevalent theory. Even so, one must take issue with one of the propositions in the above reasoning. In common with many other jurists, O. Schachter contraposes morality to the theory of positive law. In effect, such an approach has been characteristic of many proponents of this theory, especially in the past. However, today, no brand whatever of theory of positive law could be considered tenable if it ignored morality or, worse yet, contraposed it to law. It is hard to imagine amoral customs taking root in general international law. They would inevitably collide with the fundamental principles of international law which reflect the prime ethical principles of the international community. Based as it is on universal human values, international law cannot stand opposed to universal human morality.

---

9 RESTATEMENT OF THE LAW. FOREIGN RELATIONS LAW OF THE UNITED STATES (REVISED) (1986), Vol. 1, para. 102, the authors define a norm of international law as one that has been accepted as such by the international community of States in the form of customary law or by international agreement.

10 O. SCHACHTER, *International Law in Theory and Practice*, 178 RDC (1982–V) at 60–61.

Let us now turn to the concept of custom in positive law. The most authoritative source on this question is Article 38 of the Statute of the International Court. The reference there is to international custom as evidence of "general [in the Russian text – universal. I.L.][11] practice recognized as a legal norm."

As we know, the Statute of the International Court on the whole modeled itself on the Statute of its predecessor, the Permanent Court of International Justice. One of the few innovations touched on point "b" of Art. 38. It had previously pronounced that general practice, accepted as law, constitutes evidence of a customary norm. Both formulas are far from ideal in that they do not set sufficiently precise criteria for defining customary norms. Nevertheless, of the two formulas, the Statute of the Permanent Court seems preferable, given that it visualizes practice as evidence of a customary norm. As concerns the formula in the Statute of the International Court, there international custom is classified as evidence of practice that it recognized as a legal norm. The result is that one norm serves as proof of another norm.

Jurists have on several occasions pointed out the deficiencies of both formulas.[12] Analyzing the formula in the Statute of the International Court, they noted its illogicality that primarily entails reversal of the logical coupling of phenomena since it is precisely general practice, accepted as law, that constitutes evidence of a customary norm.[13] However, even this formula is not entirely logical, as has already been pointed out.

The illogicality of the formulations betrays not an accidental, but a conceptual, strain and offers merely another piece of evidence to the effect that the very widespread, especially in Anglo-Saxon doctrine, version of custom not only adds complications to its precise definition, but also difficulties to its operation. The corresponding formulations took shape under the influence of the doctrinal views shared by a majority of the parties drafting the statutes. The authors proceeded from the very widely accepted version of customary law as factual practice that mirrored legal consciousness.[14]

---

[11] That what was at stake here was indeed general, and not universal, practice was noted by the Court already in one of its earls decisions, letting it be known that what was meant was not universal acceptance, but "the generally accepted practice of States". Fisheries, Judgment, ICJ REPORTS 1951 at 128.

[12] This was already discussed in the preparatory committee working on the draft of the Statute of the Permanent Court of International Justice. *See* H. GUENTHER, ZUR ENTSTEHUNG VON VÖLKERGEWONHEITSRECHT, Berlin (1970) at 64 ff. After thoroughly studying the materials relating to the origins of the corresponding formula of Art. 38 of the Statute of the International Court, P. Haggenmacher reached the conclusion that it does not represent a definition of custom at all. P. HAGGENMACHER, *op. cit., supra* note 3, at 30.

[13] M. VILLIGER, CUSTOMARY INTERNATIONAL LAW AND TREATIES, Dordrecht (1985) at 3.

[14] *See* F. LIST, MEZHDUNARODNOE PRAVO V SISTEMATICHESKOM IZLOZHENII (1917) at 13.

The same sort of concept continued to prevail even among members of the International Court and that is why its practice did not contribute much to clarifying the matter. Its decisions sent the message that practice must be such or be implemented in such a way as to afford proof of conviction that this practice has become mandatory thanks to the existence of a norm to law to that effect.[15]

A positive element is that the Court reverted to the proposition that practice is proof of conviction as to the legal force of the norm. As regards the point that practice became mandatory thanks to an already existing norm, here the Court has uncritically echoed the proposition well known to doctrine which has already been branded as an unanswerable paradox.[16] An Indian professor, K. Vankata Raman, has correctly observed that the so-called "prior existing norm of law" which begot the legal compulsoriness of customary practice is itself the product of customary practice.[17] Given such an approach, law could never come into existence.

Therefore, it is not surprising that the corresponding proposition in the Court's decision has incurred criticism. Especially telling in this sense is the separate opinion by judge M. Lachs who, *inter alia*, marked that to claim that all States, even those that were the initiators of a given practice, believed that they were acting in accordance with a legal duty, means to resort to fiction and in fact deny the possibility of development of such a norm. It was further stressed that international *entente* is formed only at a later stage.[18] Such a point of view would seem more sound than the version recorded in the decision of the Court. One would like to believe that it will in time be adopted by the Court as well. As witness thereto, in particular, is the fact that in its latest decisions practice is treated as proof of the existence of a customary norm.[19]

The aforecited facts show how thoroughly vague is the conceptual approach to custom even on the part of an organ of such stature as the Court that is called upon to apply to all subjects customary norms constituting general international law.

What has been said above, as well as what follows, prompts the conclusion that in contemporary international law there exist two types of customary norms. Some represent unwritten rules that have crystallized in practice to which the subjects ascribe legal force. Others are also unwritten rules

---

15 North Sea Continental Shelf, Judgment, ICJ REPORTS 1969 at 44.

16 H. THIRLWAY, INTERNATIONAL CUSTOMARY LAW AND CODIFICATION, Leiden (1972) at 47.

17 K. VENKATA RAMAN, *Toward a General Theory of International Customary Law*, TOWARD WORLD ORDER AND HUMAN DIGNITY, New York (1976) at 367.

18 ICJ REPORTS 1969 at 232.

19 Case *Concerning Military and Paramilitary Activities In and Against Nicaragua*, ICJ REPORTS 1986, para. 186.

to which is ascribed legal force, except that they are created not as a result of prolonged practice, but by medium of recognition of several preceding acts or even just one.

Norms of the second type are initially articulated either in international treaties or in non-legal acts, such as those adopted by international organs and organizations, and they subsequently win recognition as a norm of general international law. As a result, in a legal sense they exist in unwritten form, and the respective international acts, including legal acts, afford proof of their content.

What these norms have in common with traditional customary norms consists of unwritten form and *opinio juris*. What distinguishes them is that they do not solidify an already existing practice, but are called upon to launch one. In comparison with norms of the first type, they attach greater relative weight to what ought to be than to what is. Herein indeed lies the basic reason for the widespread incidence of norms of the second type in international relations that require increasingly affirmative legal regulation. Hence, the differences between the two types of customary norms mainly concern the process of their genesis; as for other juridical attributes, they coincide, and this entitles one to talk about two varieties of customary norms.

Doctrine espoused a closely similar point of view.[20] But, it also has quite a number of opponents.[21] One cannot agree with the opinion of jurists who contrapose traditional customary norms to their new strain.[22] The gist of the matter is not that some norms are being squeezed out by others, but that they interact. At stake here is a *sui generis* division of labor. The traditional customary norms are called upon to safeguard stability and their new strain to guarantee the dynamism of international legal regulation.

In our domestic literature, custom is in most cases visualized as a rule that has been evolved through practice to which subjects of international law ascribe legally binding force.[23] Practically all authors proceed from the premise that a customary norm reflects to consent of the subjects.

---

[20] G. Arangio-Ruiz speaks of so-called customary law which he prefers to call "unwritten or common law". G. ARANGIO-RUIZ, *Voluntarism v. Majority Rule*, CHANGE AND STABILITY IN INTERNATIONAL LAW-MAKING, Berlin (1988) at 102.

[21] *E.g.* A. KOERS, *The Third United Nations Conference on the Law of the Sea*, INTERNATIONAL LAW AND ITS SOURCES, Deventer (1989) at 45; I. DE LUPIS, THE CONCEPT OF INTERNATIONAL LAW, Uppsala (1987) at 112–113.

[22] Judge A. Alvarez already back in 1951 expressed the opinion that custom has a tendency to disappear as a result of rapid changes in contemporary international life and because a firmly established new case may be enough to render obsolete an old custom. Fisheries, Judgment, ICJ REPORTS 1951 at 148–149.

[23] MEZHDUNARODNOE PRAVO, Moscow (1974) at 57. *See* to P.I. LUKIN, ISTOCHNIKI MEZHDUNARODNOGO PRAVA, Moscow (1960) at 70 ff.; MEZHDUNARODNOE PRAVO, Moscow (1978) at 57; KURS, *op. cit.*, *supra* note 6, Vol. 1 at 190, 196.

On the whole, one can consider that in our literature the traditional version of custom prevails while, where the second species of customar norm is concerned, *i.e.* "instant law", the attitude thereto is generally reserved. G.I. Tunkin notes that a customary norm can spring up quickly, but at the same time presumes the indispensability of the existence of a rule of conduct previously set in the practice of States.[24]

G.M. Danilenko also underlines that without practice customary law cannot arise. In accordance with his notion of practice, he concludes that "custom cannot serve as a vehicle of anterior legal regulation."[25] Such an approach means either ignoring new factors in the formation of custom and the role of norms engendered in this manner, or relegating them not to customary, but to other kind of norms. Either way, it would be desirable to define their interrelationship with traditional norms.

From what has been said above, one can see that in all concepts of international law custom two elements occupy the central spot: practice and the attribution of legal force (*opinio juris*) to a rule set in practice.[26] Actually, the interpretation of these elements and their interrelationship determines the gist of the concepts of custom and their legal consequences.

We also know of concepts that reject the very idea of necessity of the two elements. In one case, only *opinio juris* is considered indispensable and, in the other only practice. Finally, there are those who deny the need for either. The latter position is typical of the natural school of law according to which customary law is determined by the laws of nature and not the will of States. Note that in the seventies there emerged a new constellation of young international lawyers who champion the natural law concept of the objective nature of customary international law.[27]

There also exist intermediate concepts of different kinds which recognize the relative supremacy of one of the elements. The position of the previously cited P. Haggenmacher may serve as a sample. He recognizes that the doctrine of the two elements of custom supplies practice with relatively clear-cut criteria that allow one to discover the content of a customary norm. Even so, he ends by expressing doubt about the value of the schematic plan proposed by the two-elements doctrine. In the author's opinion, it finds no confirmation in international practice which, in his words, "constitutes ... a com-

---

[24] *Ibid.* at 193, 196.

[25] G.M. DANILENKO, OBYCHAI V SOVREMENNOM MEZHDUNARODNOM PRAVE, Moscow (1988) at 37, 106.

[26] In our domestic literature, these phenomena have been most thoroughly studied by G.M. DANILENKO, *see ibid.* Chap. 2.

[27] On that question, *see* P. HAGGENMACHER, *op. cit.*, *supra* note 3.

pound element, *sui generis*, vested with 'material' and 'psychological' aspects."[28]

The foregoing testifies to the wide divergence of opinion concerning the role of each of the elements of custom and the dissentience among the existing conceptions. All of this compels us in examining the concept of custom to focus, be it but briefly, on the concept of both elements.

Let us begin with practice. Jurists have noted that the term "practice" is one of the most fundamental and, at the same time, one of the most general and indefinite terms used in connection with international custom.[29] Two basic versions of practice as an element of custom are encountered in the doctrinal canon. According to one, it represents action or abstention from action on the part of States or their organs.[30] According to the other, practice is understood as a rule set in the conduct of States coupled with conviction on the part of the States that such conduct comports with international law and is legally binding.[31]

The second version, as we have seen, is widespread not only in doctrine, but also in practice, including the practice of the International Court. It has its proponents in our domestic literature as well. P.I. Lukin has written that "the practice of States may generate international custom when a definite course of conduct on their part is accompanied by the realization that such conduct is legally necessary."[32]

Both versions strike us as insufficiently precise. In the first case, one must remember that the conduct of States can serve as basis for a norm only in those instances where it represents not only an action or an abstention therefrom, but a definite rule. The authors who see practice as the conduct of States realize this as well.[33] When a rule set in practice is being talked about, this is already no longer just conduct, but a generalized strain thereof, a model, a designated abstraction which does not match actual conduct. Such a model acquires relative independence, it does not automatically follow the conduct of States and, even before being ascribed legal force, it regulates international relations in the sense of usage. The conduct itself operates as a factor in forming a practice-norm, and then as evidence of its existence and content.[34]

---

28 *Ibid.* at 11, 113, 114.

29 K. WOLFKE, CUSTOM IN PRESENT INTERNATIONAL LAW, Wrocław (1964) at 14.

30 *See* KURS, *op. cit., supra* note 6, Vol. 1 at 192–193; K. WOLFKE, *op. cit., supra* at 14.

31 *See* L. OPPENHEIM, INTERNATIONAL LAW, Vol. 1, London (1967) at 26.

32 P.I. LUKIN, *op. cit.*, at 81. *See* G.M. DANILENKO, *op. cit., supra* note 25, at 64.

33 G.I. TUNKIN writes that for the genesis of a customary norm, there needs "to be a definite practice, a rule of conduct set in the practice of states." KURS, *op. cit., supra* note 6, Vol. 1 at 196.

34 The American jurist, R. Baxter, observed that the actual conduct of States in their relations with other countries represents only an ancillary technique by means of which are revealed

As regards the second version of practice, it was spawned primarily by the jurisprudence of common law countries where under practice are understood to fall not only recurrent actions, but also customs and usages.[35] As a matter of fact, in order to generate a custom, there is no need for the process of formation in practice of a distinct rule to unfold in tandem with the conviction that a legal norm is being created. It is widely recognized that a norm can initially coalesce as usages and only later be recognized as having legal status.

Thus, there exist two versions of practice. In one case, what is meant here is a rule set through the interaction of subjects which they prefer to follow despite its lack of legal force. This is precisely the sort of practice contemplated in diplomatic acts containing references to accepted or established practice. By recognition of such practice as legally binding, a customary law is created. In the other case, practice is equated with the *de facto* actions of subjects which serve the environment in which the practice-norm takes form. The two types of practice can coincide in those instances where a customary norm is born as the result of attribution of legal force to a single precedent.

What has been said above dictates one of the main demands addressed to practice. It must be sufficiently definite and uniform so as to enable one to deduce from it a general rule. Custom must be definite (*consuetude debet esse certa).* The International Court has pointed out that custom may be moot in case of marked vagueness and discrepancies.[36]

The problem of certainty is among the crucial ones for customary law which chronically suffers from insufficient precision and vagueness of content.[37] There lies one of the reasons why, in hatching a custom and defining its content, an increasingly important role is assumed by those forms of practice where the position of States is expressed precisely enough (statements, notes, communiquées, resolutions of international organs and organizations).

At the same time, one cannot expect absolute certainty from customary law, since that would significantly hinder the inception and development of

---

norms directing the conduct of States. R. BAXTER, *Multilateral Treaties as Evidence of Customary International Law*, 41 BYIL (1966), London (1968) at 300.

35 BLACK'S LAW DICTIONARY, St. Paul (1983) at 611.

36 Asylum, Judgment, ICJ REPORTS 1950 at 277. The significance of definiteness and uniformity of practice was underscored more than once both in the decisions of the International Court and the separate opinions of its members. *See* Heya de la Torre, Judgment, ICJ REPORTS 1969 at 42; Fisheries Jurisdiction, Judgment, ICJ REPORTS 1974 at 90.

37 The significance of the problem of vagueness in customary law is quite frequently noted in doctrine. In this connection, the practice of States is named as the main reason. As has been remarked, insofar as State practice is incomplete, inaccessible or inadequately recorded, even the established norms of legal custom are often unclear in their details. M. MERRILLS, ANATOMY OF INTERNATIONAL LAW, London (1976) at 3.

customary norms. Besides, even treaty texts do not guarantee certainty. Touching on this issue, the International Court observed that one should not attach too much weight to some vagueness or discrepancies, real or imagined.[38]

The requirement of certainty, which is extremely important to law, is currently being put to a serious test by the growing activity of States and the dynamism of international life. In these processes, rules continuously crop up which, although lacking the requisite definiteness, nonetheless regulate international relations. It seems to us that there are no grounds for rushing to ascribe legal force to such norms without adequate reason for doing so. It would be better to let this type of norm congealing in practice to continue to regulate international relations in a non-legal capacity. Only after they have demonstrated their *rationale* and the advisability of vesting them with legal force becomes manifest can they then be converted into norms of legal custom. One should keep in mind that insufficient definiteness as to the content and status of norms being set in practice is to a considerable degree the result of the conscious positions of States.

Practice must also be sufficiently consistent and stable. Talking of acts needed to engender a customary norm, the International Court indicated that they must rise to the level of established practice.[39] Even so, in this case as well, the requirement of consistency is not absolute and does not mean that the conduct of States must fully comport with the norm being set. In the decision in the case of *Nicaragua v. the United States*, the Court said that it did not consider that, in order to establish a customary norm, the corresponding practice had to conform to the norm in every last detail and, instead, was of the opinion that it would be enough for the conduct of States on the whole to follow these norms.[40]

The forms of practice are diverse. They have substantial legal meaning and serve as evidence of or testimony to customary law.[41] All these forms may be divided into two basic types. The first encompasses the actual conduct of States which is not reflected in any sort of formal paperwork (the basic form of passive practice). The second concerns documents that reflect in more or less precise form the positions of States.

---

[38] Fisheries, Judgment, ICJ REPORTS 1951 at 138.

[39] North Sea Continental Shelf, Judgment, ICJ REPORTS 1969 at 44.

[40] Case *Concerning Military and Paramilitary Activities In and Against Nicaragua*, ICJ REPORTS 1986 para. 186.

[41] It is noteworthy that among the surveys on international law prepared by the U.N. Secretariat, one of the first was a memorandum devoted to evidences of customary law submitted to the International Law Commission. WAYS AND MEANS OF TAKING EVIDENCE OF CUSTOMARY INTERNATIONAL LAW, New York (1949).

Opinions differ in the matter of evaluating the significance of these two forms of practice. We know of one point of view according to which only actual behavior, "physical actions", are taken into account in setting a custom. As regards other forms, they can formulate legal norms, but cannot serve as the material element of custom.[42] However, the fact alone of formulating a legal norm constitutes part of practice and plays an important role in defining the positions of States.

Many jurists subscribe to the opposite point of view, justifiably assuming that a State's *de facto* conduct represents only a secondary means for setting customary norms. A State's clear declaration of what it considers to be a norm offers better evidence as to its position than what can be deduced in most cases from the actions of that State on varying occasions and under different circumstances.[43] A source of complications is the fact that many official acts of governments pursue primarily propaganda aims and do not reflect their actual positions. That is why for the formulation of a custom the combination of both forms of practice is important, so as to ensure that official acts are confirmed and not refuted by *de facto* conduct.

It would appear that such an approach is to some extent also confirmed by the latest practice of the International Court. On the one hand, the Court as previously proceeds to treat as axiomatic the proposition that the materials of customary international law must be sought above all in real practice.[44] But, on the other hand, this pronouncement was not substantiated by appropriate efforts by the Court to identify the corresponding real practice. To a considerable extent, it focuses attention not on analysis of the *de facto* conduct of States, but on their positions as enunciated in official documents, including resolutions and declarations of international organizations. In the case of *Nicaragua v. the United States*, the Court made exceptionally wide use of such acts as the Declaration on principles of international law of 1970 and the Definition of aggression of 1974 in order to ascertain the content of customary norms. On the whole, one can say that this decision contributed toward strengthening the position of resolutions of the General Assembly in the mechanics of creating customary norms.[45] Coincidentally, it contributed toward downgrading the significance of real conduct. I believe the tendency is natural. One cannot condone the abuse of official acts and their use

[42] A. D'AMATO, THE CONCEPT OF CUSTOM IN INTERNATIONAL LAW, Ithaca (1971) at 88.

[43] *See* R. BAXTER, *op. cit., supra* note 34, at 300; M. AKEHURST, *Custom as a Source of International Law*, BYIL 1974–1975 (1975) at 38.

[44] Continental Shelf, Judgment, ICJ REPORTS 1977 at 38.

[45] This circumstance did not escape the attention of jurists; *see* T. FRANCK, *Some Observations on the ICJ's Procedural Innovations*, 81:1 AJIL (1987) at 116, 119.

for purposes of deceiving other States and peoples. From the point of view of international legality, divergence between word and deed is becoming increasingly less tolerable.

From the aforementioned facts, one can see how large and complicated is the problem of forms of the practice of States wherein customary norms crystallize and operate. The unwritten form of custom determines the special importance and complexity, the high practical significance of what is denominated evidence of or testimony to the existence of international customary law. Not accidentally, art. 24 of the Statute of the International Law Commission assigned it the task to study ways and means to facilitate access to evidence of international customary law. Already in 1950, the Commission discussed this question and submitted a corresponding report to the General Assembly.[46]

The Statute of the Commission included among such evidence the practice of States, as well as decisions by national and international courts on questions of international law (art. 24). In its report, the Commission noted that this did not preclude the existence of other sources.[47] It felt that the task of drawing up a roster of all the many kinds of materials which recorded the practice of States was unrealistic and proposed the following array of evidence: a) texts of treaties; b) decisions by international courts; c) decisions by national courts; d) national legislation e) diplomatic correspondence; f) the opinion of national legal advisors; g) the practice of international organizations.

I believe that treaties were justifiably put at the head of the line. The content of multilateral and bilateral treaties represents the most lucid and authoritative evidence specifically of legal practice. The Commission noted that even multilateral conventions that have not entered into force can be valuable as evidence of customary law. We know that, with the intensification of codification, acts of this type have started to play a very important role in this venue. In that capacity, they have on more than one occasion been cited by the International Court. This looks to me like one of the novelties.

An important role in setting and interpreting customary norms belongs to international judicial organs, especially when what is at stake is one such as the International Court. Not accidentally, in all the works devoted to custom, including the present one, the practice of the Court is quarried quite vigorously. This state of affairs is explained by the high authority of this organ, the qualifications of its members and the representative nature of its composition. It strikes me that the role of this function of the Court will grow

[46] II YILC, 1950 (1957) at 26 ff.
[47] *Ibid.* Vol. I, at 367.

still further. True, much will depend on how well-grounded juridically its decisions turn out to be.

The opinion has been expressed in literature to the effect that the International Law Commission and other organs engaged in codification always considered national law, resolutions and court decisions as the chief proof of the practice of States.[48] National legislation does indeed constitute an authoritative statement of the positions of a State. As an example, one can point to the constitutional enshrinement of the fundamental principles of international law in the U.S.S.R. The problem, however, lies in that the concept of national legislation is very broad and for that reason there exist differing opinions about what the concept encompasses. The International Law Commission drew the circle of corresponding acts quite wide, including among them the constitution, acts of legislative organs, as well as resolutions and even declarations by executive and administrative organs. It was stipulated that none of the forms or normative prescription issued by State authority was precluded.

That the latter proposition is correct cannot be doubted. It is also true that declarations by State organs exercise a not insignificant role in defining the positions of a State. However, from the juridical point of view, it is hardly expedient to include them in the concept of national legislation. They constitute a separate category.

The growth of the role of national courts in effectuating norms of international law is evident.[49] Some authors view them as organs of the international legal order.[50] The growth of their role in interpreting international norms is also inevitably tied thereto and, consequently, the decision of national courts will begin to assume an increasingly prominent role as attestations to customary norms. National courts not only interpret international norms, but also apply them in concrete cases which lends them particular importance. Touching on this question, the American Law Institute voiced the opinion that the decisions of courts of other countries likewise possess significance for purposes of defining and interpreting international law.[51]

---

48 M. AKEHURST, *op. cit., supra* note 43, at 9.

49 *See* R. FERDINAND, DIE RECHTSPRECHUNG DER GERICHTE DER BUNDESREPUBLIK DEUTSCHALND ZUM VÖLKERGEWOHNHEITSRECHT, Frankfurt/M. (1985); E. ALKEMA, EEN MEERKEUZETOETS, Zwolle (1985); P. PICONE, B. CONFORTI, LA GIURISPRUDENZA ITALIANA DI DIRITTO INTERNAZIONALE PUBLICO, Napoli (1988).

50 F. KRATOCHWIL, *The Role of Domestic Courts as Agencies of the International Legal Order*, INTERNATIONAL LAW: A CONTEMPORARY PERSPECTIVE, London (1985).

51 RESTATEMENT OF THE LAW. FOREIGN RELATIONS LAW OF THE UNITED STATES (REVISED), Vol. 1, para. 132 "b".

At the same time, serious obstacles lie in the path of this trend. National legal systems have still not settled the question of application by the courts of international customary law. The majority of judges do not have sufficient training in the field of international law.[52] Finally, ascertaining the content of a customary norm, collecting and analyzing the corresponding materials requires major working skills.[53] That is why judges in deciding such cases rely on the opinion of the foreign affairs branch and the conclusions of experts.

Taking the aforementioned factors into account, the International Law Commission had noted, not without reason, the relative value of decisions of national courts compared with other types of attestations to customary international law.

As for the significance of the opinions of national legal advisors, the International Law Commission indicated that in evaluating them caution must be exercised inasmuch as the efforts of legal advisors are inevitably aimed at giving effect to policy.

This last proposition has a bearing on clarifying the status of such acts as speeches, interviews and analogous documents emanating from top officials of the State. The Commission has, on the whole, passed this type of acts over in silence, given that they can hardly fit under the heading of "diplomatic correspondence". Meanwhile, public diplomacy has caused such acts to proliferate. One often has to hear the opinion claiming that such acts cannot be ascribed to international law practice because they display a political and even a propaganda character and their authors far from always possess the necessary knowledge in the field of law. All these circumstances must, to be sure, be taken into consideration and, yet, acts of this type express the official position of the State and cannot be ignored.

Very noteworthy is the fact that the Commission almost entirely excluded resolutions of international organs and organizations from the array of attestations to customary law. All that was said here was that the generalized practice of organizations can be considered as evidence of customary international law in the relations of States with international organizations. That kind of position can be explained if one takes into account that it was formulated

52 The Italian professor, A. La Pergola, and the member of the Constitutional Court of Italy, P. Del Duca, consider it self-evident that the ordinary court cannot be trusted with the discovery of changes in customary international law and their outcome. A. LA PERGOLA, P. DEL DUCA, *Community Law and the Italian Constitution*, 79:3 AJIL (1985) at 601.

53 The American Law Institute has noted that national courts, when called upon to decide questions of international law, are forced to do so by unreliable means on the basis of uncertain materials and to analyze a process that encompasses the entire world and includes the actions and decisions of foreign actors. *Introductory note*, RESTATEMENT.

in 1950. Since then, the role of resolutions of international organs and organizations not only in the regulation of international relations, but also in the formation of customary norms has undergone radical change. Today, as has already been noted, even in the practice of the International Court they operate as one of the chief attestations to customary law.

In the past, unilateral and bilateral attestations predominated. Today, when the process of creation of customary norms has to an increasing degree become collective attestations have moved to the fore – primarily conventions, as well as resolutions of international organizations and conferences. Everyone knows the significance that attaches to the Helsinki Final Act as evidence of the content of fundamental principles of international law.

On the whole, one can draw the conclusion that the increasing level of activity in the interrelationships of States as well as the need to regulate it spelled corresponding changes in the forms of practice. The diversity and growing complexity of international relations dictate analogous tendencies in the development of forms of practice as well. This process must not escape the attention of jurists inasmuch as otherwise a conception of contemporary custom cannot be elaborated. A professor at the University of Rome, F. Bravo, has correctly observed: "Scholars in the field of international law must expand analysis of the practice of States in order to create definitions and rules that would reflect the rapidly changing forms of practice."[54]

Let us now touch upon the question of subjects of practice. It would seem that the answer thereto must be unambiguous. Only subjects of international law can have that status. However, in doctrine one quite often encounters the opinion according to which the activity of private persons and corporations, along with many other factors, exerts influence on the process of formation of customary norms.[55] However, only the position, the practice of States themselves with respect to such activity has juridical significance.

In our times, the role of the practice of international organizations in the formation of customary norms has substantially risen. From that point of view, it can be divided into two types. To the first type we will consign the practice of organizations as subjects of international law. The second type features the practice of organizations as collective organs of States. In such cases, the organizations express in the resolutions they adopt the opinion of the member States or even of the international community of States as a whole.

---

[54] F. BRAVO, *Méthodes de recherche de la coutume internationale dans la pratique des Etats*, 1 RDC 1985 (1986) at 267.

[55] *See* DICTIONNAIRE DE LA TERMINOLOGIE DU DROIT INTERNATIONAL, Paris (1960) at 465; K. WOLFKE, *op. cit., supra* note 29, at 14; R. BERNHARDT, *Ungeschribenes Völkerrecht*, 36:1 ZAÖRV (1976) at 76.

That last proposition also applies to the acts of international conferences whose significance in the formation of customary norms is also increasing. However, such acts do not *per se* create customary norms. They figure as authoritative evidence of the positions, the practice of States.

The International Court occupies a special position among other organs. It has an important role in the general process of the formation of customary norms. It is capable of furthering the inception of some norms and the determination of others. Its role in shedding light on the content of customary norms is also great. Nevertheless, no decision of the Court can *per se* create a norm; it also operates to attest to the practice of States. The Court has noted on several occasions that it represents an organ charged with applying the law and not making law. There are reasons to assume that the significance of the practice of the International Court in the designated capacity will continue to grow. The development of this tendency depends also on the extent to which and how well the Court will manage to reflect the practice of States and their exigencies.

Inasmuch as custom is formed in the practice of States, the question naturally arises concerning the duration required for the debut of a norm.[56] It seems to us that, on the whole, the duration of practice never had any decisive significance, although it did lend custom an added authority. When we talk of customs, it is not the length of time, but the sound grounds for their existence that must be taken into consideration (*inconsuetudinibus, non diuturnitas temporis sed soliditas rationis est consideranda*).

Jurists have noted for several decades now that the duration of practice was not of decisive importance.[57] The time necessary to generate custom depends on concrete circumstances and may vary from case to case. Given abrupt changes and the emergence of new problems calling for immediate decisions, customary norms can sprout without preceding practice. Not accidentally, the idea of "instant" customary law meets with ever widening recognition in doctrine.[58] True, as has already been said, it also has not a few opponents.

---

[56] A. CHEMILLIER, B. GENDREAU, ROLE DU TEMPS DANS LA FORMATION DU DROIT INTERNATIONAL, Paris (1988).

[57] *See* G.I. TUNKIN, VOPROSY TEORII MEZHDUNARODNOGO PRAVA, Moscow (1962) at 85; M. SORENSEN, LES SOURCES DU DROIT INTERNATIONAL, Copenhague (1946) at 101.

[58] The German jurist, H. Strebel, has written: "General international law can also come into existence as a spontaneous reaction on the part of States to new, exceptionally dangerous problems precipitated by States or individuals. Thus, as a result only of the collective will of the majority of States can in such circumstances general international law be forged instantly ('instant law'), without any practice whatever." H. STREBEL, *Quellen des Völkerrechts als Rechtsordnung*, 36/1 ZAÖRV (1976) at 345.

To clarify this question, let us look at the practice of international organs, the activity of which has major significance for shedding light on the mode of conception of customary norms in contemporary international law. In the course of the very first discussion in the International Law Commission devoted to customary norms, the well-known English jurist, J. Brierly, claimed that for custom to be formed what was needed was specifically *opinio juris*. It is known that customary norms have sprung up instantly as well. As an example, J. Brierly pointed to the principle of sovereignty over air space which originated with the beginning of the war in 1914 and prior to that existed only in theoretical guise. Generally speaking, the inception of *opinio juris* takes a long time, but exceptions from the rule likewise occur.[59]

The aforecited pronouncement testifies that the idea of "instant" law originated considerably earlier than when Bin Cheng proposed the term. However, neither can J. Brierly himself be considered its author.[60] It is indicative that this idea was not endorsed by the International Law Commission. From among those who spoke on that occasion, only the Syrian jurist, F. El--Khouri, seconded it, citing in support of his thesis the forging of the Nuremberg principles. The circumstance that in enunciating the customary norms of law of armed conflict the Nuremberg tribunal attributed decisive importance not to practice, but to *opinio juris*, was also subsequently noted more than once by jurists.[61]

Let us next look at the position of the International Court. It was most clearly articulated in the decision on the North Sea Continental Shelf in 1969.[62] The Court observed that a brief length of time does not necessarily or of itself offer an obstacle to the genesis of a new norm of international customary law. Hence, the possibility can exist that norms will be created over a short span of time. However, this proposition is in considerable measure undercut by the demand that practice be widespread. In its later practice, as has already been mentioned, the Court repeatedly cited resolutions of the U.N. General Assembly as attestations to the existence of customary norms

---

59 1 YILC (1950) at 5.

60 Attesting to that is the fact that in his book published in 1942, this idea is missing. J. BRIERLY, THE LAW OF NATIONS, Oxford (1942) at 47–49. In addition, at the same session of the International Law Commission, even before, J. Brierly's address, the Brazilian jurist, J. Amado, firmly spoke against the conception already articulated in literature to the effect that the factor of duration does not play an important role and a single precedent may be enough to beget international custom. 1 YILC (1950) at 5.

61 TH. MERON, HUMAN RIGHTS AND HUMANITARIAN NORMS OF CUSTOMARY LAW, Oxford (1989) at 38.

62 North Sea Continental Shelf, Judgment, ICJ REPORTS 1969 at 42–43.

and thereby drew closer to the position of recognizing the possibility of creating custom without preceding practice.[63]

Thus, in the doctrine as well as practice of international organs a tendency can be seen toward recognizing the possibility of inception of custom without preceding "widespread" practice. This tendency is occasioned by the need to insure the kind of situation where customary norms do not lag or do not lag too far behind the development of international life. By virtue of this, the relative weight of new types of unwritten norms that are not set in practice, but appear as a result of attribution by States of legal force to rules articulated in various international acts, is growing. As a result, the key role in creating customary norms is plainly shifting to *opinio juris*. What had previously been perceived as evidence of practice, now to an increasing degree is becoming evidence of *opinio juris*.

In doctrine, there exist differing versions of *opinio juris*. Three of them may be regarded as staple. Depending on what role is assigned to *opinio juris*, they can be arrayed in the following order. We will put in first place the concept that is very widespread in both theory and practice according to which *opinio juris* is viewed as conviction on the part of States that they are following a particular practice by dint of operation of the law and that, if they were to deviate from this practice, they could incur definite sanctions.[64] The main shortcoming of this concept, in our opinion, lies in that it strips *opinio juris* of juridical meaning, converts the formation of custom into mysticism. The result is that customary law crystallizes in practice without any *opinio juris*. The latter boils down to mere conviction on the part of the State that it is following an already existing norm.

Different authors vest the present concept with its own nuances. In the Encyclopedic Dictionary of International Law by Parry and Grant, *opinio juris* is defined as an understanding that the respective practice is prescribed by or comports with prevailing law.[65] This proposition deserves attention in the sense that *opinio juris* and customary norms take form not in a normative vacuum, but within a system of positive international law. That is why in creating new norms the subjects must take into account the requirements of that law, and the new norm must be compatible therewith.

The second traditional concept, which at any rate predominated in the past, sprang from the perception of *opinio juris* as an element of custom personifying attribution by the State of juridical force to a rule set in prac-

---

63 TH. MERON, *The Geneva Conventions as Customary Law*, 81 AJIL (1987) at 362.

64 M. VILLIGER, *op. cit., supra* note 13, at 26.

65 PARRY and GRANT, *Encyclopedic Dictionary of International Law*, New York (1986) at 82.

tice.[66] Hence, it is as though we were talking here about the parity of two elements. In that context, the presence of a rule set in practice constitutes an essential prior condition for the inception of a customary law norm.

Finally, the third concept is a new one; pursuant thereto, for the creation of a customary norm no preceding practice is needed. The sole element of such a norm can be *opinio juris*. Bin Cheng has written that the role of habit in the inception of a norm of international customary law is purely evidential. Hence, according to him, international customary law to all intents and purposes has only one constitutive element – *opinio juris*.[67]

In light of everything that has previously been said, it would seem correct to define *opinio juris* as an attribution by subjects of international law of the character of a juridical norm to a rule set in practice or formulated in some other fashion. Such recognition can be effected in the clearly expressed form of a declaration or through some other official act. But, the most common is the form of silent or tacit recognition. In connection with the inception of norms of customary international law, the key role is played by the absence of objections.

There also exists an *opinio juris* that can be described as negative. One runs into the opinion alleging that a negative customary law likewise exists.[68] However, it strikes one that in this case it would be more correct to speak of *opinio juris* since what is at stake is not a norm, but recognition of the absence thereof. This is not a matter of theoretical niceties, but of different legal consequences. If we were talking about negative law, then the latter would not only deny the existence of the norm, but also prohibit the corresponding behavior. As distinct therefrom negative *opinio juris* does not make illegal neither the respective action nor the rule set in practice, confining itself to not recognizing the legal character thereof.

What has been said is also confirmed by the opinion of another German jurist, a well-known specialist in the field of customary law, R. Bernhardt, who writes that if the community of States unambiguously and without any reservations considers particular actions that have not previously been en-

---

66 In our domestic literature, it is most fully elaborated by G.M. Danilenko; G.M. DANILENKO, *op. cit., supra* note 25, at 99 ff.

67 BIN CHENG, *United Nations Resolutions on Outer Space: "Instant" International Customary Law?*, 5:1 IND. JIL *(1965)* at 36. In one of his other works he wrote that *opinio juris* is merely what the subjects who act as law makers recognize at any given moment as law; BIN CHENG, *On the Nature and Sources of International Law*, INTERNATIONAL LAW/ TEACHING AND PRACTICE, London (1982) at 223.

68 The German jurist, A. Beckmann, has written: "Negative customary international law arises when the unanimous practice of States based on legal conviction proceeds from the premise that a designated general norm of customary international law does not exist." A. BECKMANN, *Zur Feststellung und Auslegung von Völkergewonheitsrecht*, 37:3–4 ZAÖRV (1977) at 511.

countered unlawful, then *opinio juris* may be sufficient, even in the total absence of practice.[69] Note that this pronouncement once again confirms the independent juridical meaning of *opinio juris* in a particular sense.

We have had to dwell on negative *opinio juris* primarily in order to show that the proper definition of each of the elements of custom and their interrelationships can have substantial legal consequences, a fact that assumes special significance as the role of customary norms is enhanced.

To round off our examination of *opinio juris*, let us touch on the current position of the International Court on this question.[70] One must keep in mind that the Court is bound to comply with the corresponding provisions of art. 38 of its Statute. The significance of this point is underscored in its decisions, leaving it with no option but to apply, *inter alia*, international custom as "evidence of general practice accepted as law" and prompting it to go on record as saying that the Court cannot but take into account the substantial role exercised by practice.[71]

On that basis, the Court did not recognize the existence of *opinio juris* not ratified by practice as adequate either for the purpose of creating norms or spelling out their content, reasoning that the fact alone of declarations by the States that they recognize particular norms is not enough for the Court to consider them part of customary law and also applicable as such to these States. In the same vein, the Court held that in the field of international customary law, the existence of a common point of view among the parties regarding the content of what they consider a norm is not enough. The Court let it be known that it shall be satisfied whenever the existence of a norm in the *opinio juris* of States is corroborated by practice.

Meanwhile, though, in the latest decisions of the Court one also discovers a different, non-traditional approach toward practice and *opinio juris*. In the same decision in the case of *Nicaragua v. the United States*, the Court noted that *opinio juris* can, as long as every precaution is taken, be distilled from the attitude of States toward designated resolutions of the U.N. General Assembly. Agreement with such resolutions, it added, had to be understood as attribution of legal force to the norm or the ensemble of norms enunciated by the resolution itself.[72]

---

[69] R. BERNHARDT, *Customary International Law*, ENCYCLOPEDIA OF PUBLIC INTERNATIONAL LAW, Vol. 7, Amsterdam (1984) at 65.

[70] For a thorough analysis of previous practice, *see* K. SKUBISZEWSKI, *Elements of Custom and the Hague Court*, 31:4 ZAöRV (1971).

[71] Case *Concerning Military and Paramilitary Activities in and Against Nicaragua*, Judgment, ICJ REPORTS 1986, para. 184.

[72] *Ibid.* paras. 188, 189.

The aforecited propositions amount to a recognition of the existence of the second type of customary norms and the mechanism for their manufacture. There is no need for previous widespread practice. The norm is created as a result of attribution by the States of legal force to rules contained in the resolution. As agreement with the resolutions, to which the decision of the Court refers, must, in our opinion, be understood not the fact proper of voting for them, but subsequent attribution of legal force to their provisions, procured tacitly in the main.

Thus, substantial changes in the interrelationship of the two elements of custom have taken place. Preceding widespread practice ceased being indispensable for the creation of customary norms, and *opinio juris* assumed prime significance. It is capable of creating norms on international customary law even in the absence of preceding practice and in some cases also in the presence of a marked level of deviation from practice (as witness, the norms of humanitarian law). However, all this in no way means the downgrading of the significance of traditional customary norms set in the practice of States which, as hitherto, will continue to occupy a very important place in the system of general international law.

The International Court and Judicial Law-Making. Nuclear Tests Re-visited

by

Edward McWhinney

The recognition of the 70th birthday of Krzysztof Skubiszewski draws attention to the signal contribution to international law and its progressive development made by Polish jurists, in a number of different arenas – academic, diplomatic and judicial. There are special ties between Poland and the World Court throughout most of that institution's history. A Polish judge was elected and served on the old Permanent Court of International Justice from 1931 to his death in 1940 – M.C.J. Rostworowski. With the International Court of Justice, reconstituted in 1946 within the new United Nations system, a Polish jurist, Bohdan Winiarski, was chosen in the first multiple ballots, for a three-year term, 1946-49; then re-elected for a full nine-year term, 1949–58; and re-elected again for a further full nine-year term, 1958–67, serving also as Court President for the period 1961–64. His immediate successor, without any break in the continuity, was Manfred Lachs, elected for a nine-year term, 1967–76, serving also as Court President for the period 1973–76; re-elected for a further nine-year term, 1976–85; and re-elected again, for a further nine-year term, in 1985. By the time of his death in January 1993, Judge Lachs had become the longest serving member of the World Court, in its seventy years of history.[1]

Reference to the continuity of Polish membership of the World Court, based on the rich intellectual-legal training and experience of the successive Polish incumbents, should not veil the basic fact of deep-seated differences in judicial philosophy and the individual judges' conceptions of the role and missions of a judge of the International Court. These differences mirror the intellectual-legal antinomies within the International Court which have, at various times, threatened the internal harmony of the Court and put strains on that element of collegiality necessary for its effective function *qua*

---

[1] The present essay draws, generally, upon the author's earlier-published trilogy on the International Court: The World Court and the Contemporary International Law-Making Process (1979); The International Court of Justice and the Western Tradition of International Law (1987); Judicial Settlement of International Disputes (1991). More specifically in relation to Judge Lachs, reference should be made to the author's Judge Manfred Lachs and Judicial Law-Making (1995).

multi-member tribunal. A Court, as Mr. Justice Felix Frankfurter of the United States Supreme Court once reminded us, is (or should be) an orchestra and not a series of solo performances. Nevertheless, the differences in judicial attitudinal approaches to decision-making, amply demonstrated in the clear contrasts between Judge Winiarski and Judge Lachs, are vital to an understanding of current dilemmas within the International Court in a period of historical transition and far-reaching societal and institutional change in the world community as a whole.

Judge Winiarski's philosophy of law and his basic conception of the international judicial process is perhaps best demonstrated in his Dissenting Opinion, rendered at a time when he was, in fact, President of the Court, in the Advisory Opinion on *Certain Expenses of the United Nations*,[2] handed down by the World Court on 20 July 1962. The Court majority position, rendered by a 9-to-5 vote, precipitated the Western-sponsored action within the United Nations to use Article 19 of the U.N. Charter to deprive France and the Soviet Union of their votes in the U.N. General Assembly because of their refusal to pay the special financial assessments that had been levied by the General Assembly in support of the politically-contested U.N. peace-keeping operations in the then newly-decolonised Belgian Congo, according to the plan devised by U.N. Secretary-General Hammarskjöld. In his Dissenting Opinion in *Certain Expenses of the United Nations*, President Winiarski formulated basic principles of legal interpretation to be applied to the U.N. Charter:

> "The Charter, a multilateral Treaty which was the result of prolonged and laborious negotiations, carefully created organs and determined their competence and means of action.
>
> The intention of those who drafted it was clearly to abandon the possibility of useful action rather than to sacrifice the balance of carefully established fields of competence, as can be seen, for example, in the case of voting in the Security Council. It is only by such procedures, which were clearly defined, that the United Nations can seek to achieve its purposes. It may be that the United Nations is sometimes not in a position to undertake action which would by useful for the maintenance of international peace and security or for one or another of the purposes indicated in Article 1 of the Charter, but that is the way in which the Organisation was conceived and brought into being."[3]

Since the majority of the World Court upheld the validity of the expenditures authorised by the U.N. General Assembly as legitimate "expenses

---

[2] ICJ REPORTS 1962 at 151.

[3] *Ibid.* at 230.

of the Organisation" within the meaning of Article 17(2) of the Charter, it might have been tempting, in *Realpolitk* terms, to try to explain President Winiarski's Dissenting Opinion and his vote within the Court as an *ad hoc* judicial response to the then conceived political self-interest of Poland as a Warsaw Pact member-country. Certainly, President Winiarski was joined in his vote by the Soviet member of the Court, Judge Koretsky, who filed his own Dissenting Opinion which accorded very closely with President Winiarski's mode of legal interpretation. But the other Dissentes included the distinguished French jurist, Judge Basdevant and two Latin-Americans, Judge Moreno Quintana and Judge (and later President) Bustamante y Rivero. The intellectual-legal antinomy within the Court in *Certain Expenses of the United Nations* seems better explained as involving, on the one hand, the more traditional, and certainly civil law-favoured, canons of interpretation, with the U.N. Charter conceived as a treaty and to be strictly interpreted as such; and, on the other hand, the more free-wheeling, law-making or "policy-making" conceptions of the international judicial process favoured by the United States and its associated States in the period prior to the massive wave of decolonisation and admission of new States to the United Nations, when the Western bloc could still command an effective working political majority in the U.N. General Assembly and the main U.N. organs. On this view – best reflected in the celebrated Uniting for Peace Resolution adopted by the U.N. General Assembly in November, 1950, in the Korean crisis – the U.N. Charter was no mere treaty or contract *inter partes*, to be interpreted restrictively and against any new assertions of power, but a Constitution, to be interpreted (in the spirit of the great early Chief Justice of the United States Supreme Court, John Marshall), broadly and permissively so as to authorise new actions to meet new societal needs hardly envisaged by the original Founding Fathers. This creative, optimistic, "living Constitution" approach to the U.N. Charter, strongly influenced by the doctrinal writings of Professors Myres McDougal and Harold Lasswell of the Yale Law School, was to yield very quickly, in Western-based legal circles within the United Nations, to the more traditional, positivistic, strict-and-literal interpretative approaches generally favoured in Western law schools outside the United States, and this in seeming response to the changing balances of political forces and the political balance-of-power within the United Nations General Assembly. In his last case within the International Court, *South West Africa. Second Phase*[4] in 1966, Judge Winiarski was part of a Court majority, created 8-to-7 with the exercise of a second, tie-breaking

---

4 ICJ REPORTS 1966 at 6.

vote by the Court President, that included representatives of the major Western countries (other than the United States, whose member, Judge Jessup, dissented strongly). The Opinion of the Court, signed by the Court President, Judge Spender of Australia, is generally considered, on stylistic and other grounds, to have been written by the British judge on the Court, Sir Gerald Fitzmaurice. In rejecting (on the basis of a purported logical distinction that the Canadian Prime Minister of the day, Lester Pearson, said would have baffled the ingenuity of the mediaeval schoolmen), the claims to *locus standi* of Ethiopia and Liberia in order to gain judgment condemning the white minority government of South Africa's extension of its apartheid *régime* to the former League of Nations mandate over South West Africa, the Court majority brought down a hail of political criticism on itself at the immediately succeeding Annual Session of the U.N. General Assembly. Judge Winiarski, as part of the Court majority, was part of the target of that political criticism; yet his legal position was intellectually fully consistent with his earlier position as advanced in *Certain Expenses of the United Nations*, four years earlier. What had happened, by 1966, was that he had been joined by a politically and legal-systemically plural Court majority in his positivistic, black-letter-law approach to judicial interpretation of the U.N. Charter.

The political back-lash against the Court majority in *South West Africa. Second Phase*, was reflected in the triennial Court elections of 1966 when an outstanding candidate of the same nationality as retiring Court President Spender, who had signed the majority Opinion, was defeated in the votes in the U.N. General Assembly and Security Council. It was not, however, sufficient to defeat the new Polish candidate, Manfred Lachs, whose demonstrated legal activism in special committees of the U.N. General Assembly over a number of years was evidently felt to outweigh any resentment against Judge Winiarski for his part in the majority Opinion. As it turned out, the new political majority in the U.N. General Assembly, reacting against the *South West Africa. Second Phase* majority, had opted correctly in voting for Judge Lachs if what was desired, henceforward, was legal change and creative adjustment of old legal jurisprudence and doctrines to rapidly evolving new societal conditions and needs in the world community.

A practical problem for the new group of judges elected in October, 1966, in reaction to the legal positivism of *South West Africa. Second Phase*, was how to build a new, working majority in a tribunal in transition with many carry-overs, still, from the earlier dominant legal philosophy. The long road back from the judicial abdication of *South West Africa. Second Phase* was certainly assisted by political activism in both the Security Council and General Assembly, directed against the apartheid *régime*. The Court ruling in *Namibia*, 1971, generally thought to be the work of Judge Lachs, reflects a new, instrumental philosophy of law, and an evolutionary approach to world history to which legal doctrines should properly be accommodated.

More difficult, in terms of the antinomy or opposition between the "old" and the "new" wings of the Court and their differing attitudes to changes in the positive law in response in turn to changes in underlying societal facts, was *Nuclear Tests*, over which Judge Lachs presided in his role as Court President (1973–76). The handling of the case, within the Court, was undoubtedly exacerbated by personality conflicts, superimposed on the legal--philosophical problems surviving from the divisions among the judges manifested both in *South West Africa. Second Phase* in 1966 and in its effective overruling in *Namibia* in 1971. In its preliminary phase, the International Court decided, by an 8-to-6 majority, to grant interim measures of protection, though without canvassing in depth the issue of whether jurisdiction existed in the first place.[5] This had been the key objection made by the respondent State, France, which, in pursuance of its denial of any Court jurisdiction, limited its own participation to filing a written memorandum or White Paper, but took no part in the actual proceedings before the Court. The French member of the Court, Judge Gros, however, as a regularly elected judge of the Court, sat on the case and participated fully in the *interim* and final judgments. There is a certain mystery surrounding the actual vote on the preliminary issue. We know, because he signed the Interim Protection Order, that Vice-President Ammoun was part of the 8-member majority, and we can identify four other majority judges (Jiménez de Aréchaga, Waldock, Nagendra Singh, and *ad hoc* Judge Barwick), simply because they filed individual Separate, concurring Opinions. But the three other majority judges remained unidentified. Similarly with the 6-member minority, while four judges (Forster, Gros, Petrén, and Ignacio-Pinto) can be identified because they filed individual Dissenting Opinions, the two other minority judges remained unidentified. President Lachs and the U.S. Judge, Dillard, were both absent from the final vote on the Interim Protection Order, with suggestions from two of the dissenters, Judge Petrén and Judge Gros, that President Lachs' absence was a diplomatic absence only and that arrangements could have been made to record his vote in any case. In the end result, President Lachs' absence may have facilitated coalition-building for a new majority within the Court, for the purposes of its final, substantive ruling. In *Nuclear Tests. Judgment*[6] in 1974, the Court, by a 9-to-6 majority, ruled that the is-

---

[5] *Nuclear Tests (Australia v. France), Interim Protection, Order*, ICJ REPORTS 1973 at 99; ICJ Reports 1973 at 135.

[6] *Nuclear Test (Australia v. France), Judgment*, ICJ REPORTS 1974 at 253; *(New Zealand v. France)*, ICJ REPORTS 1974 at 457.

sue of French nuclear tests in the South Pacific had become moot because of unilateral declarations of intention made by President Giscard d'Estaing, and by the French Foreign Minister and Defence Minister, of France's intention to terminate any further above-the-ground nuclear tests in the South Pacific. The Opinion of the Court was signed by President Lachs, and the majority included the four identified dissenting judges to the Interim Protection Order of 1973 – Judges Forster, Gros, Petrén, and Ignacio-Pinto – who each, once again, filed individual, Separate Opinions.

The intellectual-legal foundations of the Opinion of Court in *Nuclear Tests. Judgment* were strongly criticised at the time of the rendering in 1974, with some of the sharpest questions raised in the individual Separate, concurring Opinions. The Court's recognition, in effect, of a doctrine of estoppel as applying to unilateral declarations of State intervention was certainly innovatory for its time, in accepting new sources of international law; but it emerges, clearly, as the lowest common denominator of possible agreement among disparate judicial personalities, with conflicting judicial philosophies, necessary to build a coalition majority in support of a substantive ruling that effectively ended French above-the-ground nuclear tests in the South Pacific. There were, certainly, academic critics of the 1974 judgment who attacked the Court for its failure to come out boldly with a ruling that nuclear test explosions of any form would be, *per se*, illegal. The most persuasive response to those particular academic critics was, I think, given by the Dutch Foreign Minister, Professor Kooijmans, in his memorial tribute to Judge Lachs in 1993:[7]

> "By applying the law strictly and basing itself faithfully on the closed categories of formal sources of law, the Court could easily – and from a legal point of view not incorrectly – have come to the conclusion that there was no legal impediment for France to continue to carry out its nuclear atmospheric tests. But maybe more than anyone else, Manfred Lachs was aware of the devastating effects such a decision could have for the reputation of the Court, as the General Assembly had pleaded in numerous resolutions for a discontinuance of such tests. Esteem for the Court in the international community could plummet to a new low. He realised that a repetition of 1966 could be fatal for the Court and as the Court's President he hoped to avoid such an outcome. So he looked for other venues..."

President Lachs' practical resolution of the dilemma was to embrace a new formal source of law in aid of an adjectival-law based decision that could

[7] P.H. KOOIJMANS, *In Memoriam Manfred Lachs',* 6:2 LEIDEN JOURNAL OF INTERNATIONAL LAW (1993) at ix.

manage to reconcile, within the Court, enough judges who might support the general principle of the illegality of nuclear tests, and enough judges who were clearly firmly opposed to the enunciation of any such principle. As Professor Kooijmans, quoting the present writer, concluded, the Opinion of the Court

> "stands as exercise in judicial pragmatism by a Court President trying carefully to build a majority among judges, who were then even more cautious than today, as to venturing on the avant-garde in doctrinal-legal terms (into law-making through jurisprudence)."[8]

The 1974 Court judgment ended French above-the-ground nuclear tests in the South Pacific. *Nuclear Tests. Judgment* was, however, to be resurrected in 1995, two years after Judge Lachs' death, with the decision by the new French President Chirac, to open a further series of eight nuclear weapons tests in the South Pacific – this time, however, underground nuclear weapons tests. One of the original complainant States from 1973–74, New Zealand, invoked the specific terms of the Court's 1974 ruling to ask the Court to rule, anew, on the substantive issue of the legality of nuclear test explosions, this time in the context of underground nuclear test explosions. Paragraph 63 of the 1974 Judgment was what was now relied upon:

> "Once the Court has found that a State has entered into a commitment concerning its future conduct it is not the Court's function to contemplate that it will not comply with it. However, the Court observes that if the basis of Judgment were to be affected, the Applicant could request an examination of the situation in accordance with the provisions of the Statute; the denunciation by France, by letter dated 2 January 1974, of the General Act for the Pacific Settlement of International Disputes which is relied on as a basis of jurisdiction in the present case, cannot constitute by itself an obstacle to the presentation of such a request."[9]

In the 1995 case,[10] the applicant, New Zealand, focused upon the key passage in paragraph 63 – "if the basis of this Judgment were to be affected" – as the foundation for its request for reopening of the 1974 judgment. As the Opinion of Court in 1995 noted, the applicant State's argument proceeded now on the basis that the original, 1973 Application had concerned nuclear contamination of the environment arising from nuclear testing of whatever nature; and that the 1974 Court judgment must be measured not by refer-

---

8 *Ibid.* at x.

9 *Nuclear Tests (New Zealand v. France), Judgment,* ICJ REPORTS 1974 at 457, 477.

10 *Request for an examination of the situation in accordance with Paragraph 63 of the Court's Judgment of 20 December 1974 in the Nuclear Tests Case (New Zealand v. France),* ICJ REPORTS 1995.

ence to atmospheric testing, as such, but rather by reference to the resulting nuclear contamination, since in 1974 the only mode of testing used by France in the Pacific had been atmospheric. It was an interesting argument though it did not persuade the International Court which rejected, by a 12-to-3 vote, the New Zealand application. The three dissenting judges, Weeramantry and Koroma and *ad hoc* Judge Palmer, and particularly Judge Weeramantry, advert to the larger, evolutionary, law-in-the-making conceptions of the international judicial process which were at the core of Judge Lachs' judicial philosophy but which, for fully pragmatic reasons, he had subordinated to an essentially adjectival law, procedurally-based argumentation in order to build a Court majority ending the particular French nuclear test explosions involved in the early 1970's. The intellectual-legal dilemma involved in the judicial positivism/judicial policy-making antinomy thus continues after Judge Lach's death, and is perhaps best reflected in the special Declaration which one of the Court majority, Judge Oda, filed to accompany the 1995 Court judgment:

> "As the Member of the Court from the only country which has suffered the devastating effects of nuclear weapons, I feel bound to express my personal hope that no further tests of any kind of nuclear weapons will be carried out under any circumstances in future."

Réflexions sur la théorie des sources du droit international

par

Riccardo Monaco

I. PRÉMISSE

A. Je me demande souvent pourquoi une partie importante de la doctrine juridique internationale, c'est à dire celle qui étudie l'évolution constante de l'ordre juridique international, s'attache à la critique de la théorie des sources du droit international. Je crois que tout cela se produit à cause de deux facteurs importants: le premier est celui de l'élargissement de la communauté internationale et le deuxième celui qui voit s'accroître les différents systèmes de création des règles qui la régissent. Un grand exemple provient du fait que dans le Liber Amicorum en l'honneur de Eduardo Jimenez d'Arechaga[1], qui pour sa part a donné une grande contribution à l'étude des sources, il y a trois essais qui méritent toute notre attention. Tout d'abord l'excellent confrère Georges Abi-Saab a écrit un article dont le titre: *Les sources du droit international; essai de déconstruction* est assez impressionant. Le sujet traité par Abi-Saab[2] reflète très bien le style et le caractère génial de l'Auteur. Il, nous le savons bien, préfère les analyses dogmatiques aux exposés de mineur envergure: c'est pour cela qu'il nous présente un essai très brillant de déconstruction du système des sources traditionnelles. Vu l'importance de cette contribution je préfère pour le moment de la laisser de côté.

Pierre Marie Dupuy[3] analyse à nouveau la théorie des sources à travers un examen très approfondi: il s'agit vraiment d'un effort qui nous conduit sur un terrain très difficile: d'ailleurs il nous signale qu'on ne peut pas ignorer, à côté de la théorie des sources, l'influence de la coutume en tant que facteur déterminant d'autres sources de droit.

Je vous déclare d'ores et déjà que mon discours aura comme objet le travail de Dupuy essentiellement parce-qu'il fonde sa critique sur plusieurs

---

1 Le droit international dans un monde en mutation, Montevideo (1994), vol. 1, p. 29 et s.

2 G. Abi-Saab, Les sources du droit international: essai de deconstruction, p. 29 et s.

3 P.M. Dupuy, Theorie des sources et coutume en droit international contemporain, p. 51 et s.

éléments qui méritent bien toute notre attention, compte tenu aussi des difficultés nouvelles auxquelles il se refère.

Enfin je voudrais féliciter notre collègue José Maria Gamio pour avoir complété d'une façon magistrale les différents aspects que la coutume présente lorsqu'elle commence par son universalité et joue ensuite son rôle d'une façon très concrète sur le plan régional et local.

B. Je reviens à Dupuy, bien convaincu de la pertinence de l'analyse très détaillée qu'il développe. Elle tourne autour de trois conséquences que la doctrine actuelle semble tirer de ses prémisses.

Tout d'abord elle aboutit à un **équivoque**, parce-que Dupuy affirme que la première cause de cela est à rechercher dans le caractère métaphorique du terme de sources du droit. Il ajoute que plusieurs auteurs s'en montrent conscients mais tous n'échappent pas également à la tentation de substituer l'image à l'analyse, même si l'expression a le mérite de suggérer la superposition de divers niveaux normatifs. En outre elle va créer un **malentendu** dont l'origine est la suivante. En effet la théorie des sources du droit international a été conçue par référence à celles que l'on trouve pour expliquer les modes de formation des droits internes. Cette origine interiste a profondement marqué sa structure générale. Il en résulte qu'on perd de vue trop souvent les approximations au prix dequelles on a voulu faire correspondre les catégories normatives et les schémas d'explication des sources du droit international à celles du droit interne.

En droit interne le système des sources du droit est à la fois différencié, organisé et hierarchisé. Le droit écrit y occupe une place prépondérante. C'est évident dans les pays de tradition continentale. Mais c'est de plus en plus manifeste dans les pays de *common law* dans lesquels le nombre, l'importance, et la proportion des **actes** et **statuts** n'a pas cessé et ne cessera pas d'augmenter. Cette prédominance générale de la loi est évidemment liée au privilège normatif de l'Etat, exercé par la voie des organes investis de l'autorité législative (Parlement) et du pouvoir réglementaire (exécutif). Certes le rôle joué par la coutume interne n'est pas pour autant totalement inexistant. Je ne voudrais pas vous amener sur le terrain, tout à fait différent, de celle que Dupuy appelle la désillusion. Autrement dit je ne voudrais pas vous conduire à faire une analyse supplémentaire, mais, de toute façon, l'espace qu'il concède à cette désillusion, m'apparait de première importance et de toute actualité.

C. Il s'agit de fixer en termes tout à fait claires le phénomène de la transformation de l'origine de règles générales du droit international. Elles ne surgissent pas d'un procédé destiné en particulier à leur création, mais, étant facilités par le système actuel des communications, trouvent leur place dans les conférences à vocation normative tenues le plus souvent dans le cadre et sous les auspices des organisations internationales, parmi lesquelles agissent de façon déterminante l'ONU et certaines institutions spécialisées. Les contributions tout à fait récentes à la théorie des sources du droit international, dont nous avons fait mention au début de notre discours, nous apportent la preuve que l'ensemble des problèmes demandent une réflexion de plus en plus attentive et approfondie. Etant donné que tout récemment j'ai eu l'occasion définitive, car dans la matière qui est la nôtre il est impossible de mettre un point final à la recherche, je voudrais mettre les résultats de ma synthèse à comparaison de critiques et des solutions nouvelles qui ont été suggérées. Cela dit, je n'ai pas la prétention de passer en revue les différentes solutions. En effet je crois que je me bornerai à souligner l'essentiel de la matière.

D. Après les interventions multiples de la doctrine et les évaluations de la pratique je crois qu'il faudra choisir les sujets les plus marquants. Certainement un des secteurs les plus importants de la production normative internationale est celui des règles produites par les institutions d'organisations internationales.

Le production juridique en question est d'autant plus importante à cause du fait qu'elle est due à l'activité de la Commission des Nations Unies pour le droit international. On se trouve déjà, depuis la longue activité de la Commission, en présence d'un ensemble très important de projets de codification. Une certaine partie de ces textes a donné lieu à des Conférences internationales, lesquelles ont défini le texte de plusieurs secteurs du droit. La conception particulière que nous venons d'exposer est en outre renforcée par la pratique à laquelle on a imposé le nom significatif **d'attitude de l'Etat qui se présente en tant qu'objecteur systématique**[4]. En effet il arrive qu'un Etat, qui n'a pas l'intention de s'opposer à la formation d'une règle coutumière, tâche quand même de se soustraire à l'application d'une telle règle. De la sorte cet Etat tend à créer une exception à la règle elle-même.

E. Pour mieux expliquer la portée du droit international non écrit il faut faire une comparaison entre le droit écrit, c'est-à-dire celui qui est créé par voie de traité, et celui qui est créé en vertu d'une coutume.

Cela dit, la conséquence qu'on peut tirer est la suivante: tandis que les règles des traités rentrent toujours dans le droit international particulier, alors même qu'un nombre très élevé d'Etats y a participé, les normes du droit international non écrit peuvent apparaître comme règles pleinement générales.

---

[4] Esempio di Stato obiettore della consuetudine desunto da GIULIANO, SCOVAZZI, TREVES, DIRITTO INTERNAZIONALE, PARTE GENERALE, Milano (1991), p. 209.

A ce point de notre analyse il faut souligner que la distinction entre **droit non écrit général** et **droit écrit particulier** a perdu beaucoup de son importance à cause du fait que récemment le nombre des traités à tendance universelle a multiplié son domaine d'application.

Il faut aussi tenir compte du fait que le grand développement du droit des organisations internationales ainsi que l'énorme série des accords bilatéraux, qui ont couvert les relations économiques entre les Etats, ont modéré l'influence du droit international non écrit.

F. A ce point de mon exposé qu'il me soit permis de souligner à nouveau le peu de confiance que les Auteurs les plus récents dont nous avons resumé les prises de position, ont à l'égard de la théorie actuelle des sources du droit international. Elle est due aux différentes coutumes qui surgissent en même temps que les règles du droit international écrit.

La coutume au stade actuel ne peut pas, à cause de cela, avoir la même autorité de la règle écrite. Cela fait qu'elle demeure une source de droit suspecte à l'autorité publique. Etant donné qu'elle émane directement des personnes privées elle remet en cause le fondement étatique de la création normative. Au contraire, dans l'ordre juridique international, le créateur quasi exclusif de la coutume demeure l'Etat.

Etant donné qu'il existe une identité d'origines il devient impossible de transposer en droit international la distinction loi-coutume. Cette affirmation est renforcée par l'analyse qui est développée ultérieurement afin d'affaiblir la portée de la coutume. On souligne en outre, en particulier, que l'on doit tenir compte des différences existantes à l'intérieur de la catégorie des sources écrites, entre d'une part la loi, source émanant d'une autorité centralisée disposant le plus souvent sur habilitation constitutionnelle de pouvoir normatif et d'autre part par le traité, par essence contractuel, même quand on dit abusivement de lui qu'il est un traité loi, alors qu'il procède de toute façon de la rencontre des volontés de deux Etats.

Les remarques que nous avons faites jusqu'ici n'enlèvent toutefois pas au droit non écrit sa grande influence. Ainsi entre autre demeurent toujours confiées à ce droit nonobstant les dispositions des traités multilatéraux et bilatéraux destinées à les compléter ou bien à lui déroger, les matières qui n'ont pas encore fait l'objet de codification.

Il faut aussi noter que, même dans les matières codifiées, restent encore soumises au droit non écrit, sauf dérogation expresse, les relations entre les Etats non participants et en outre celles entre les Etats participants suivent le même sort. Il faut encore ajouter, et cela vaut pour toutes les matières et toutes les règles créées en vertu des traités ou conventions, et en outre les relations de ces Etats avec Etats participants sont régies en ce qui concerne leur validité, efficacité, interprétation, application, exécution par des règles internationales non écrites. En laissant de côté d'autres problèmes de moindre valeur il faut souligner un phénomène de grande importance. Il amène à reconnaître que droit écrit et droit non écrit s'intègrent et se conditionnent de façon variée. Cela a comme conséquence que le droit créé avec traité peut validement déroger, dans les relations entre les parties, à n'importe quelle règle du droit non écrit, tandis que celui-ci, à son tour peut modifier les régles du droit écrit. Les recherches qui ont été développées jusqu'ici pour vérifier la formation des règles coutumières ont montré que le facteur temporel n'est pas décisif à cet égard. Bien que la plupart des règles internationales de nature coutumière se soient affirmées à travers un long et difficile procès historique, il est parfois arrivé que l'expression **droit international coutumier**, bien qu'elle signale l'influence du facteur temporel aux fins de l'existence et de la formation de telles règles, l'on peut signaler que la pratique internationale n'attribue pas au facteur temporel une influence décisive. Tout cela doit être tenu en compte aux fins de la preuve de l'existence d'une coutume.

D'autre part il faut rappeler que la Cour internationale de Justice dans son arrêt du 20 février 1969 dans les deux affaires sur le plateau continental de la Mer du Nord, a établi que le fait qu'il soit passé une brève période de temps ne constitue pas nécessairement en lui-même un obstacle à la formation d'une nouvelle règle de droit international coutumier. Ces prémisses ont comme conséquence que l'on ne peut pas parler d'une véritable charge de la preuve de ces règles générales à l'égard d'un Etat qui les invoque. La même solution s'impose aussi dans le cas où le juge soit un arbitre ou bien une instance judiciaire internationale, parce que le principe *jura novit curia* serait valable en l'espèce pourvu que la décision doive être prise sur la base du droit international.

Dans l'ensemble des évaluations qu'il faut faire avant de proclamer l'existence d'une nouvelle règle coutumière on peut arriver à la conclusion qu'une règle donnée peut être considérée comme universellement reconnue seulement si elle a été suivie par un nombre suffisant d'Etats qui sont intéressés à cette règle. Il va sans dire que la dite situation doit être évaluée avec une certaine prudence. En effet doivent entrer en ligne de compte aussi les données évolutives concernant les groupes auxquels nous avons fait allusion. D'autres facteurs acquièrent en outre un leur poids sur le processus de formation et d'évolution du droit international coutumier. A cet égard les Etats ont la tendance à influencer actuellement ce processus. En effet en 1970 le premier ministre du Canada publiait une Déclaration en vertu de laquelle, contrairement à la coutume en vigueur qui limitait à douze milles la largeur de la mer territoriale, étendait à cent milles le domaine d'application des règles canadiennes relatives à la protection de l'environnement dans la région arctique. Il s'agit toutefois d'un cas exceptionnel, de sorte qu'il ne faut pas penser qu'il s'agisse d'un changement du système des moyens en vertu desquels le droit coutumier visait à changer. Normalement ce changement est graduel et il ne comporte pas des affirmations qui soient fondées sur la force.

II. LA CONTRIBUTION DE L'INSTITUT DE DROIT INTERNATIONAL

Je dois avouer que le sujet de cette étude a grandi en dépassant mes prévisions initiales: au départ il s'agissait simplement de présenter certaines réflexions sur la théorie des sources du droit international. Cela voulait signifier que j'aurais dû me tenir à un simple discours théorique. Mais je n'avais pas tenu compte du fait que dans la matière en question la théorie se trouve beaucoup conditionnée par la pratique. Et alors il fallait se borner à un discours plus concret et plus réaliste. Un événement tout à fait particulier m'a conduit à mieux apprécier la contribution qui aurait pu amener mon étude vers une conception plus exacte de la tâche que je me suis imposée. En effet j'ai constaté que tout récemment l'Institut de Droit international, sur la base de l'organisation de ses travaux, a confié a sa première Commission dont le Rapporteur était l'illustre juriste Sir Ian Sinclair la tâche d'étudier les problèmes découlant de la succession de conventions de codification ayant le même objet particulier.

L'Institut a considéré que le problème en question incluait à la fois des matières appartenant à la loi des traités et des problèmes concernant les relations entre les traités et la coutume.

L'Institut a étudié ces problèmes qui ont été débattus au sein de la Première Commission et aussi de l'Assemblée de l'Institut pendant la session que l'Institut a tenue à Lisbonne en 1995.

Le premier septembre 1995 l'Institut a adopté la Résolution avec laquelle les travaux ont pris fin. La troisième partie de la Résolution a pour objet les relations entre droit conventionnel et coutume.

Voila donc que ce document d'une grande importance m'oblige à reconsidérer le grand thème de la coutume qui encore une fois s'impose à l'attention de tous ceux qui poursuivent l'étude de cette matière, qui est devenue aussi la mienne, vu les prémisses desquelles je suis parti.

Et alors comme premier pas il me faut donner connaissance du contenu de la Résolution.

Le premier article de la IIIème Partie de la Résolution concerne le traité et la coutume en tant que sources de droit international; il établit: «Traité et coutume constituent des sources distinctes, reliées entre elles, de droit international. Une norme issue de l'une de ces deux sources peut avoir une incidence sur le contenu et l'interprétation d'une norme issue de l'autre source». En principe, cependant, chacune continue à exister séparément en tant que, respectivement, norme du droit conventionnel ou norme du droit coutumier.

Le deuxième article traite de la hiérarchie des sources: «il n'existe pas de hiérarchie *a priori* entre traité et coutume en tant que sources du droit international. Toutefois, dans l'application du droit international, les normes pertinentes résultant d'un traité l'emportent dans les relations entre les parties sur les norme issues du droit coutumier».

Le troisième article a pour objet la pratique des Etats par rapport au processus de création de droit coutumier par une convention de codification. Il affirme ce qui suit: «pour apprécier l'élément que présente la pratique des Etats dans le processus de création, par une convention de codification, d'une règle de droit coutumier, il convient de tenir compte de la pratique, tant de ceux qui sont partie à cette convention que des tiers. Le comportement à titre de pratique d'Etat d'une partie à cette convention dans ses relations avec une autre partie ou avec un tiers se trouvera significativement renforcé s'il est établi que l'Etat concerné a agi avec la conviction que la pratique était, en tout état de cause déterminante.

Le quatorzième article dispose: «un prononcé judiciaire établissant qu'une disposition particulière d'une convention de codification est ou n'est déclaratoire d'une règle de droit coutumier ou a un n'a pas cristallisé, on a ou n'a pas créé une règle de droit coutumier dit le droit en vigueur à la date de ce prononcé».

La Résolution de l'Institut est déstinée à avoir une très grande influence parce qu'elle met en évidence les effets possibles des prononcés judiciaires ainsi que la contribution de la jurisprudence à la formation du droit coutumier.

Avec ces références concrètes nous avons donc repris notre contact théorique et pratique avec les facteurs de ce grand phénomène normatif qui est la coutume. Nos réflexions précédentes nous obligent en outre à reprendre le discours sur les aspects théoriques de la coutume qui sont les facteurs permanents qui s'insèrent dans le processus de formation de la coutume ellemême. Comme nous le savons, la coutume, dans la variété de ses connexions avec la théorie des sources du droit international, a fait l'objet d'une littérature juridique enorme, à laquelle il serait impossible de se référer dans ce bref commentaire.

Pour suivre certaines orientations dans l'ensemble des contributions dont nous avons eu connaissance, qu'il me soit permis de faire un choix simple et pratique.

Je voudrais tout d'abord citer une synthèse de grande clarté et en même temps de caractère très concret. J'ai pensé que cela pouvait provenir d'un grand théoricien non seulement du droit international, mais aussi de la philosophie du droit et des problèmes de la sociologie internationale: Michel Virally qui malheureusement nous a quitté trop tôt, alors qu'il pouvait encore nous faire don de sa culture, de son géni juridique, de sa sagesse et de son grand équilibre[5].

III. HIÉRARCHIE DES SOURCES

A ce point de notre exposé on a établi certaines règles qui régissent les relations entre la coutume et le traité, en tenant compte aussi de récents travaux de l'Institut de Droit international. Mais l'analyse générale des problèmes des sources du droit international dans la mesure où elle a été transferée sur un plan largement critique par une partie de la doctrine, qui mérite toute notre attention, nous signale qu'il faut approfondir davantage le problème de base qui est celui de la hiérarchie des sources du droit international. Cela est devenu indispensable, parce que pour arriver à des conclusions concrètes et satisfaisantes il faut venir au clair d'un certain nombre de problèmes qui continuent à subsister dans la matière.

A partir de ce moment devient possible procéder à la fixation de la hiérarchie des véritables sources du droit international. On pourrait quand même se demander si la hiérarchie en question concerne seulement les sources typiques et non les sources atypiques.

En prévoyant cette graduation on doit faire un choix important, parce que les règles constitutionnelles de l'ordre juridique international peuvent rentrer dans la catégorie des règles de *jus cogens*.

En effet les deux catégories sont semblables parce qu'elles possèdent toutes les deux le caractère de l'impérativité. Il en découle qu'il est impossible d'établir si les normes constitutionnelles ont prééminence sur les règles

---

[5] On trouve un résumé magistral de la pensée de VIRALLY dans le Cours général de droit international public qu'il a donné en 1983 à l'Académie de Droit international de La Haye et qui a été publié comme tiré à part. Il s'agit d'un volume qui restera dans l'historie du droit international. Il est intitulé PANORAMA DU DROIT INTERNATIONAL CONTEMPORAIN et il reflète la façon géniale d'aprés laquelle VIRALLY a traité le sujet.

de *jus cogens* ou vice versa. Cela fait que les unes et les autres peuvent être placées au premier rang ou vice versa.

Le deuxième rang appartient à toutes les normes créées en vertu d'un accord international; par conséquent elles, comme nous l'avous déjà expliqué, ont prééminence sur les normes créées d'une coutume. Il s'agit d'un résultat généralement reconnu.

Sur cette base il sera possible de parvenir à une solution en tenant compte en voie exceptionelle et en procédant à l'interprétation des éléments qui appartiennent au cas particulier.

Après la troixième place attribuée à la coutume, au quatrième rang se placent les principes généraux de l'ordre international. A ces derniers peuvent être assimilés, en utilisant une formule bien connue par la pratique et par la doctrine internationale, les principes généraux reconnus par les nations civilisées.

A cet égard l'on pourrait observer qu'une telle assimilation n'est pas possible étant donné qu'il s'agit de deux catégories différentes de principes généraux.

Toutefois, compte tenu de la situation actuelle, il est prudent d'accepter la solution qui été créée par l'évolution progressive de la matière. En réalité les principes dont à l'art. 38 du Statut de la Cour internationale de Justice sont réservés en tant que moyen dont peut faire usage la Cour elle-même.

Au contraire les principes généraux de l'ordre international correspondent à la structure de celui-ci. Ce qui fait que la portée normative qui leur appartient est différente, et exerce une influence majeure à l'égard de la position de la Cour. Celle-ci en effet utilise ces principes, auxquels elle attribue la fonction, indispensable pour le progrès de l'ordre international, d'un des piliers portants du mouvement qui a pour fonction l'évolution progressive de l'ordre international. Ceci signifie qu'un traité prévaut sur une coutume antérieure et que, à son tour, une coutume postérieure a la primauté sur le traité. Mais ce principe ne s'applique pas lorsque la norme coutumière antérieure a le caractère de *jus cogens* à laquelle un traité postérieur ne peut déroger.

Il en résulte que la primauté d'une norme par rapport à une autre peut avoir pour conséquence que l'application de l'une d'elles exclue entièrement l'application de l'autre. Toutefois il peut arriver aussi que les normes antérieures et postérieures aient des contenus divers et que, dans une certaine mesure, elles soient compatibles entre elles. Dans ce cas la norme postérieure prévaudra, mais les dispositions de la norme antérieure s'appliqueront dans la mesure où elle n'auront pas été modifées par la norme postérieure.

La primauté d'une coutume par rapport à un traité antérieur a été examinée par référence à l'art. 42 de la Convention de Vienne sur le droit des traités. Cet article établit que la terminaison d'un traité ne pourra avoir lieu que comme résultat de l'application des dispositions du traité et de la Convention elle-même.

Etant donné que celle-ci ne contient aucune clause à cet égard il arriverait que la coutume postérieure ne pourrait être cause de la terminaison d'un traité. La matière de la hiérarchie des sources est abordée très rapidement dans la conclusion no 11 du document de l'Institut de droit international.

Elle est formulée de la façon suivante: «Il n'existe pas de hiérarchie *a priori* entre traité et coutume. Toutefois, dans l'application du droit international, les normes pertinentes résultant d'un traité l'emportent dans les relations entre les parties sur les normes issues du droit coutumier».

A notre avis ce thème demande d'être exposé dans la complexité de sa nature.

La première catégorie des normes appartenant à l'ordre international est celle des règles constitutionnelles. Elles peuvent être comprises et assimilées aux règles de *jus cogens*. Cela dit, il semble impossible établir si les règles constitutionnelles priment celles de *jus cogens* ou vice versa.

Une appréciation plus ou moins complète de la matière peut résulter d'un aperçu élémentaire comme celui qui suit.

La conclusion 10 de l'Institut de Droit international statue très brièvement en ce qui concerne l'application des sources existantes. Etant donné qu'il s'agit des relations entre droit conventionnel et coutume, une norme issue de l'une de ces deux sources peut avoir une incidence sur la coutume et l'interprétation d'une norme issue de l'autre source. En principe, cependant, chacune continue à exister séparément en tant que, respectivement, norme du droit conventionnel ou norme du droit coutumier.

La conclusion 11 aborde ensuite le problème de la hiérarchie des sources en constatant qu'il n'existe pas de hiérarchie *a priori* entre traité et coutume en tant que sources du droit international.

Après cette référence rapide aux solutions possibles qui peuvent être adoptées pendant la codification du droit international, il faut analyser d'une façon plus approfondie les différents problèmes du côté de la coutume.

Souvent la doctrine part du principe qui semble être désormais bien reconnu, de la parité entre traité et coutume; ce qui conduit à des conclusions qui, à première vue, sont très simples: selon Barberis[6] entre les deux, compte tenu de leur origine, il n'existe de différence de degré.

---

[6] Il s'agit de J. BARBERIS excellent diplomate et juriste. Son travail intitulé *Reflexions sur la coutume internationale*, ANNUAIRE FRANÇAIS DE DROIT INTERNATIONAL (1990), pp. 9–46 est l'oeuvre la plus complète qui a été produite récemment.

Si l'on se réfère à un conflit d'application, dans un cas concret, entre une coutume et un traité, ce conflit doit être resolu selon le principe *lex posterior derogat legi priori*.

La conclusion 12 affirme ce qui suit: il n'existe pas *a priori* une hiérarchie entre les différentes sources du droit international.

Toutefois en ce qui concerne l'application du droit international dans le cadre d'un différend, les règles en question découlant d'un traité liant les parties à une dispute prévalent sur les normes découlant du droit coutumier, sauf le cas où la norme dérivant d'un traité soit contraire à une règle de **droit cogens**.

La conclusion 14 a pour objet la pratique des Etats en ce qui concerne le processus de création du droit coutumier par les traités: donc la pratique de tous les Etats parties ou non à un traité, doit être tenue en considération.

L'Institut de Droit international, dans ses conclusions que nous avons rappelées tout à l'heure, a reconnu la nécessité de considérer **l'apport de la pratique des Etats**, dans son ampleur, au processus de formation des règles coutumières. A cette fin il a recommandé de tenir compte tant de ceux qui sont parties à une procédure dans ses relations avec une autre partie ou avec un tiers.

Cela comporte la nécessité de se référer aux différents organes et sujets qui sont les véritables auteurs de la pratique dans ses multiples expressions. Sur la base d'un auteur qui a accompli divers études sur ce sujet on peut résumer comme suit les plus importantes expressions de cette activité[7].

Tout d'abord les organes extérieurs de l'Etat, ce qui non seulement est évident, mais qui en outre souligne l'apport essentiel de l'Etat. Parmi ces organes on peut distinguer ceux qui représentent l'Etat au plan international et que l'on peut appeler organes extérieurs. En outre ceux qui fonctionnent dans le domaine interne, comme les tribunaux, le Parlement et la majeure partie de l'administration publique.

Il faut souligner qu'une partie importante de cette activité est réalisée par des organisations internationales. A cet égard il faut distinguer entre la création de normes coutumières relevant de l'ordre juridique interne d'une organisation donnée et les règles de la même nature qui, à cause de leur efficacité seulement interne à l'organisation, ne font pas partie de l'ordre international.

Le droit coutumier en outre peut être créé en vertu de l'activité de certains tribunaux internationaux.

---

[7] Il s'agit encore de J. BARBERIS que nous avons déjà cité, *supra* note 6.

Le problème qui se pose parfois dans la doctrine et qui consiste à établir si les traités internationaux peuvent donner vie à des règles coutumières pourrait être résolu sur la base de certaines prémisses logiques qui semblent être très claires.

Tout d'abord il faut admettre que la nécessité fondamentale devant laquelle les Etats se trouvent normalement est celle de parvenir à la formulation de textes de droit écrit. Cela signifie que, dans la mesure où l'activité des Etats est destinée à arriver à une convention internationale, la règle coutumière n'entre pas en ligne de compte. D'ailleurs il est certain que la règle générale reconnue par tous le Etats est celle qui proclame que le droit conventionnel l'emporte sur la coutume.

Si les Etats qui sont d'accord entre eux en vertu d'une volonté commune pour consacrer cette volonté dans une convention pourraient penser que dans le temps le traité sera depassé par une règle coutumière future, ils ne renonceront pas à faire un traité pour les avantages que celui-ci aurait à l'égard d'une coutume future dont on ne connait pas les possibilités de naissance.

On répond à cette objection en disant que l'augmentation constante du nombre des traités internationaux exerce une certaine influence sur la formation de nouvelles normes coutumières.

Il y a au contraire un phénomène qui grandit toujours à l'heure actuelle. En effet les nouveaux Etats y compris ceux qui vivent à l'ombre de règles coutumières, participeront de plus en plus aux conférences internationales pour profiter des avantages qu'elles donnent à ces Etats, c'est-à-dire les avantages découlant de la protection collective qui provient de l'existence des grandes conférences internationales et des resultats normatifs qu'elles réprésentent.

Conclusion

Les problèmes concernant les sources du droit international ont toujours attiré mon attention; c'est à cause de cela que depuis longtemps j'ai commencé à réflechir sur ce grand thème.

Depuis lors, nonobstant que l'étude du droit, dans ses différentes expressions, commence naturellement par ses sources, l'intérêt des auteurs pour cet ensemble de problèmes, n'a fait que grandir.

La matière est devenue plus ample et plus complexe, à partir du moment qu'on a constaté l'existence d'une pluralité de systèmes juridiques et, par conséquent, d'ordres juridiques. C'est pour cela que le monopole de l'ordre étatique en ce qui concerne la création de règles juridiques a perdu sa prépondérance. En effet à l'heure actuelle la porte est largement ouverte à l'étude de la naissance et du développement d'une pluralité d'ordres juridiques.

Ces remarques font suite à certaines contributions qui figurent parmi mes premiers écrits en la matière. Ainsi j'ai commencé par un exposé critique: *Fonti e pseudo fonti del diritto internazionale*, dans: RIVISTA DI DIRITTO INTERNAZIONALE (1978), p. 740; ensuite on peut voir *Observations sur la hiérarchie des sources du droit international*, dans: FESTSCHRIFT FÜR HERMANN MOSLER, Berlin (1983), p. 599; *Sources of International Law*, dans: ENCYCLOPEDIA OF PUBLIC INTERNATIONAL LAW (1984), vol. 7; *Fonti del diritto internazionale*, dans: ENCICLOPEDIA GURIDICA TRECCANI (1989), vol. XIV; *Fonti del diritto comunitario*, dans: MANUALE DI DIRITTO COMUNITARIO, Torino (1984).

L'ordre juridique international a largement contribué à ce phénomène; et c'est sourtout grâce à la naissance des grandes organisations internationales que celles ci ont donné vie à plusieurs catégories de règles juridiques qui proviennent des organisations internationales elles-mêmes. De la sorte a pris naissance le droit des organisations internationales auquel l'illustre juriste auquel nous rendons honneur aussi en tant que promoteur de l'étude du grande monde des organisations internationales a beaucoup contribué. Pour ma part, avant de me lancer dans cette nouvelle direction, je dois avouer que les considérations qui ont formé l'objet de notre exposé pourraient, je l'espère, être simplement une mise à point necéssaire des tendances de la doctrine actuelle en matière de sources du droit international.

Cette doctrine s'est développée très lentement, avec la prudence qui devient nécessaire quand l'objectif qui est poursuivi n'est pas celui d'une révision critique, peut être sans limites, mais seulement celui de l'adaptation de la doctrine aux situations nouvelles résultant des faits et de la structure des formations sociales qui se trouvent normalement à la base du droit.

Dans les affirmations critiques récentes des auteurs dont nous avons tâché de mieux interpréter la pensée, nous avons remarqué l'intention de rébatir la doctrine des sources comme s'il s'agisait de quelque chose dépassé.

Dans ces conditions il apparaît inopportune et sans mérite toute tentative de formuler des conclusions comme en général il arrive lorsqu'on est juste à la fin d'un discours qui, de toute façon, tâche de se référer à des idées claires et à des situations concrètes.

New Custom: Power, *Opinio Juris* and Contrary Practice

by

Oscar Schachter

I am honored to write this essay in homage to Krzysztof Skubiszewski, an old friend who has served the international community with distinction as legal scholar, Foreign Minister and currently international judge.

My topic addresses some basic – and troubling – issues of contemporary international law. It has both theoretical and practical significance. I had the opportunity to discuss some aspects of the subject with Professor Skubiszewski during the ten years or so when he was the Rapporteur of a commission of the Institut de Droit international that considered the implications of U.N. General Assembly resolutions for the formation and application of international law. In the course of the many debates on this broad subject, we had to face the problem raised by pronouncements of States asserting rules and principles as customary international law even if they were not supported by general and consistent State practice.

The fact that governments do not always practice what they preach comes as no surprise; indeed, we would be surprised if they did, at least in some areas. Still, under the canons of positivist international law, we lawyers are called upon to determine whether a putative rule of customary law meets the requirements of general and consistent practice followed by States from a sense of legal obligation. The latter requirement – the *opinio juris sive necessitatis* – calls for a "belief" by States that the practice in question is obligatory by virtue of a rule of law requiring it. In the words of an International Court of Justice judgment, "Not only must the acts concerned amount to a settled practice, they must also be such, or be carried out in such a way, as to be evidence of a belief that this practice is rendered obligatory by the existence of a rule of law requiring it."[1] As this passage indicates, custom begins with "acts" that become a "settled practice;" that practice may then give rise to the belief that it had become obligatory.

This generally accepted view of the relation of practice and *opinio juris* was indirectly challenged by the International Court in its 1986 Judgment

---

1 *North Sea Continental Shelf* Cases, ICJ Rep. 1969 at 3, 44 (para. 77).

in the *Nicaragua* Case.[2] In that judgment, the Court first found the *opinio juris communis* on the non-use of force in the unanimous acceptance of relevant U.N. General Assembly resolutions that defined aggression. It then declared that the Court "must satisfy itself that the existence of the rule in the *opinio juris* of States is confirmed by practice."[3] This sentence was seen by some critics as standing custom on its head. In place of a practice that began with the gradual accretion of acts and subsequently received the imprimatur of *opinio juris*, the Court reversed the process: an *opinio juris* expressed first as a declaration would become law if confirmed by general practice. While this passage seemed to some commentators to show a profound misunderstanding of custom,[4] it is fair to say that it reflected a widespread professional opinion that law-declaring resolutions particularly when adopted by unanimous decisions of the General Assembly could have a creative role in the formation of custom. Professor Skubiszewski in his studies and the pertinent discussions in the Institut de Droit international on his Commission's report confirmed this though they avoided the conclusion that General Assembly resolutions created new law.[5]

Perhaps the principal question faced by the Skubiszewski Commission and by the Institut was whether General Assembly law-declaring resolutions evidenced the *opinio juris communis* and, if so, should be accepted as presumptive evidence of existing law even if contrary State practice existed.

The Commission was cautious in its conclusions. The Institut more so. The main conclusions of the Commission pertaining to international customary law can be summarized as follows:[6]

- a law-declaring resolution adopted by the General Assembly without negative vote or abstention creates a rebuttable presumption that the resolution contains a correct statement of law;
- a resolution may constitute evidence of customary law or of one of its ingredients (*opinio juris*, custom-creating practice), in particular when that has been the intention of States;
- the authority of a resolution is enhanced when adopted by consensus or by "a representative majority that includes the main legal systems;"
- principles and rules proclaimed in a resolution may influence State practice or initiate a new practice that constitutes an ingredient of new cus-

---

2 *Military and Paramilitary Activities in and against Nicaragua, Merits*, ICJ REP. 1986 at 14 (hereinafter referred to as the *Nicaragua* case).

3 *Ibid.* at 97–98 (para. 184).

4 *See* A. D'AMATO, *Trashing Customary Law*, 81AJIL (1987), at 101.

5 61 ANN. INST. DE DR. INT., PART I (HELSINKI SESS.) (1985) at 29–358; 62 ANN. INST. DE DR. INT., PART II (CAIRO SESS) (1987) at 274–289.

6 *Ibid.* at 282–286.

tomary law. They may also contribute to the formation of the *opinio juris communis*.

Although these conclusions and the others in the Skubiszewski Commission report were endorsed by all of its members, the plenary body of the Institut refrained from adopting them as its views. Instead, it congratulated the Rapporteur and the Commission for "elucidating the numerous factors which, depending on the circumstances, allow the General Assembly resolutions to contribute to a better knowledge of international law, to hasten its development, to enhance its authority and to ensure stricter compliance therewith."

With these conclusions as background, I will comment briefly on three aspects of the contemporary customary law process, as follows:

1. The demand for customary law.
2. The role of power in the formation and application of custom.
3. The problem of *opinio juris* and contrary practice.

I. THE DEMAND FOR NEW CUSTOM

We would laugh at a notice that read "this custom will take effect tomorrow." For much the same reason, it seems anomalous to speak of a "demand" for new customary law. We are expected to recognize custom only after it has come into existence through the accretion of acts that are perceived *ex post facto* as the basis of a new legal rule or principle. However, in the contemporary international milieu governments have felt a need for new law which, for one reason or another, could not be fully realized through multilateral treaties. Treaties are still important and there are good reasons to consider them as the best way to create new law. This is shown by the numerous law-making treaties of a multilateral character adopted in the past half-century. As scholars have noted, virtually every field of human activity has been significantly affected by such "legislative" treaties.[7]

However, treaties have not fully met the needs for new law. For one thing, the processes of treaty negotiation are often slow and cumbersome. It is easy to see why. The increase in the number of States, the diversity of interests, the novelty of the problems faced, the shortage of competent officials are factors which combine to delay and complicate the treaty-drafting negotiations and ratifications. The difficulty of obtaining ratifications and accessions even from States that had supported and signed the treaties has been a dis-

---

[7] *See* O. SCHACHTER and C. JOYNER (eds.), UNITED NATIONS LEGAL ORDER (1994), Vol. I, at 135–168.

couraging feature. Even when multilateral treaties obtained the requisite number of parties, a substantial number of countries remained outside of the treaty, though they had no significant substantive objections and voted for its adoption by the drafting conference.[8]

In these circumstances, it has been natural for States to turn to law-declaring resolutions of the General Assembly. They did recognize that the Assembly had not been empowered to create law binding on States (except regarding same internal matters) and that its resolutions were not a "source" under article 38(1) of the Statute of the International Court. But this did not prevent the General Assembly at its very first session in 1946 from adopting – without dissent – a resolution that declared genocide to be an international crime[9] and another that "affirmed" the Nuremberg Principles as law.[10] This unexpected use of the recommendatory power of the General Assembly produced doctrinal controversy among international lawyers and political controversy among governments. Nonetheless, it clearly emerged that law-declaring resolutions served political objectives of States and that many were accepted as evidence of a general *opinio juris* that either reflected State practice or was expected to be followed in future practice.[11] Even if the latter seemed to place the cart before the horse, it did not depart in principle from the basic postulate that binding custom was the result of the two elements: State practice and *opinio juris*.

Significantly, most U.N. law-declaring resolutions were adopted by consensus or without negative votes; in some cases with a few abstentions. The preponderant legal opinion (as reflected in the Skubiszewski report) considered that such unanimous resolutions created a presumption that the statements of law therein are accepted as existing law. These resolutions fall mainly within two major areas of international law: one concerns force and intervention (the security area); the other human rights. As the former involves principles of the Charter they were often viewed as interpretations of the Charter, rather than as customary law. However, this has changed somewhat since the *Nicaragua* Case ruled that resolutions such as those on aggression are evidence of customary law as well as Charter interpretation.[12]

The expanding area of international human rights has been an even more fertile area for the law-declaring resolutions. If the oxymoronic term "instant

---

[8] *See* O. SCHACHTER, M. NAWAZ, J. FRIED, TOWARD THE WIDER ACCEPTANCE OF UN TREATIES (1970).

[9] G.A. RES. 96(I), (1946 – 11 December).

[10] G.A. RES. 95(I), (1946 – 11 December).

[11] Numerous supporting references are in the reports of Skubiszewski to the Commission of the Institut. *See op. cit., supra* note 5.

[12] *Supra* note 2, paras. 188–193.

custom" can be used at all it would fit the resolutions on torture and genocide. Such law-declaring resolutions have never been opposed in the General Assembly but whether they have been "confirmed" by general practice is more debatable. I shall return to this problem later.

Not all law-declaring resolutions have been unanimous or without significant dissent. In two notable instances, a majority of members succeeded in adopting far-reaching law-declaring resolutions over the negative votes of a significant minority. The first example is a resolution in 1961 that declared the use of nuclear weapons to be illegal.[13] This resolution was opposed by the nuclear powers and their allies. The other resolution adopted in 1974 contained a "Charter on Economic Rights and Duties of States." It received the support of a large majority but was strongly opposed by the most important economic powers.[14] Both of these resolutions lacked support of the States needed to give them effect. Consequently, there was no expectation that they would seriously influence practice. These examples while significant do not mean that non-unanimous resolutions in the General Assembly are without some influence or that the General Assembly will no longer adopt law-declaring resolutions by majority votes. It is likely they will increase since new subjects of international concern will attract such law-declaring resolutions. The consensus resolution on non-appropriation of outer space and celestial bodies and the nearly unanimous resolution on the non-appropriation of the sea-bed are precedents.[15] Both have been "confirmed" by practice and are regarded generally as part of customary law.

Demands for new customary law have also been made to meet environmental concerns. The principles adopted in the Stockholm and Rio conferences on the environment have been characterized as new law by some governments and by a few international lawyers.[16] However the novelty of the principles and the qualifications accompanying them raise doubts as to whether the governments intended them to express existing law. An important political factor is that governments are deeply divided on the critical issue of whether the proposed international environmental law should supersede national policies on economic development. The demand for new binding environmental law is strongly expressed by some non-governmental groups but governments on the whole prefer to seek solutions through negotiated

---

13 GEN. ASS. RES. 1953 (XVI) (1961 – 24 November).

14 GEN. ASS. RES. 3281 (XXIX) (1974 – 12 December).

15 GEN. ASS. RES. 1962 (XVIII) (1963 – 13 December) (on outer space); GEN. ASS. RES. 2749 (XXV), 17 Dec. (1970) (Sea-Bed).

16 AMERICAN LAW INSTITUTE, RESTATEMENT OF FOREIGN RELATIONS LAW OF THE UNITED STATES (Third), sec. 601 (1987).

agreements. However, we may expect that as the treaty process proves inadequate (for reasons such as those noted earlier) the demand for environmental protection will probably lead to declarations that purport to express nascent custom.

II. THE ROLE OF POWER IN CUSTOMARY LAW

This last observation is a reminder – if one is needed – that customary law, new and old, are products of political aims and conditions. Doctrinal discussions by international lawyers may acknowledge this in general terms but rarely consider its implications. The Skubiszewski Commission touched on the problem by stating that the authority of a resolution is enhanced when it is adopted by a "representative majority that includes the main legal systems."[17] The phrase "main legal systems" had a special meaning in U.N. usage. It was a "code" term to refer during the Cold War to the three major groupings: Developed Capitalist, Communist and Non-Aligned. Its special function in the U.N. and other global bodies was to ensure that the majority (*i.e.* the non-aligned developing States) did not control the outcome of contested decisions. In this way, the realities of political power were recognized. With the end of the Cold War and the new divisions within the former "non--aligned" group the "troika" of so-called "legal systems" no longer has its old significance.

However, the problems of relating law and power remain. International law doctrine on customary law tends to obscure the problems by its emphasis on the consent of all States, whether explicitly or by implication, and by its postulate of formal equality of States. These principles do have a role in both the creation and use of custom. Reciprocity of treatment, and the right of every State to make claims are important in the customary process; so is the right of all States to vote and to join in blocs and alliances.

Still, power is crucial. Judge Charles De Visscher put the point strongly: "Every international custom is the work of power."[18] As a historical fact, the great body of customary international law was made by remarkably few States. Only the States with navies – perhaps 3 or 4 made most of the law of the sea. Military power, exercised on land and sea, shaped the customary law of war and, to a large degree, the customary rules on territorial rights

---

17 62 ANN. INST. DE DR. INT., PART II at 284 (Conclusion 15).

18 CH. DE VISSCHER, THEORY AND REALITY IN PUBLIC INTERNATIONAL LAW (2d ed. P.E. CORBETT, Trans.) at 154.

and principles of State responsibility. "Gunboat diplomacy" was only the most obvious form of coercive law-making.

Economic power, like military power, is applied often through implicit, if not open, threats in support of claims over a broad range of inter-State action. The more powerful the economy, the greater the presence of its government and nationals in international transactions. Trade, foreign investment, and technical know-how emanate disproportionately from the advanced economic powers; they carry with them, as a rule, the political views of their respective States, together with social attitudes bearing on international relations. Moreover, for these reasons the affluent States are objects of attention by others. Their views and positions are noticed and usually respected. Their official legal opinions and digests of State practice are available along with international law treatises that influence professional opinion and practical outcomes. In De Visscher's words, "the great powers after imprinting a definite direction upon a usage make themselves its guarantors and defenders."[19]

In addition to the sources of power, relative "resistances" matter. As pointed out by Michael Byers, the resistances to power vary with the territorial jurisdiction in question.[20] A State can most easily apply international law to foreign persons and conduct within its own territory, as for example, denying sovereign immunity to foreign State entities in its jurisdiction. A State faces more resistance in respect of issues that involve boundaries or geographic proximity to an outside jurisdiction. Coastal States succeeded in adopting a 200-mile economic zone but failed to win acceptance of a territorial sea of that width. Even more resistance can be expected to rules that would restrict a foreign State in regard to persons and events in its own territory. This would apply to human rights or environmental rules. The variation in "resistances" is but one factor bearing on the role of power in international law. The whole subject warrants empirical study by international lawyers and political scientists.

III. *OPINIO JURIS* AND INCONSISTENT PRACTICE

I turn now to the problem raised by newly-declared norms of international law that prohibit certain State conduct but are in fact often violated. If

---

19 *Ibid.* at 155. De Visscher referring to the "Great Powers" says: "Their role which was always decisive in the formation of customary law, is to confer upon usages that degree of effectiveness without which the legal conviction, condition of general assent, would find no sufficient basis in social reality."

20 *See* M. BYERS, *Custom, Power and the Power of Rules*, 17 MICH. J. INT'L L. (1995) at 109, 147–155.

we accept the conclusion that a law-declaring resolution adopted unanimously by the U.N. General Assembly constitutes presumptive evidence of *opinio juris*, we must consider whether widespread violations of the declared rules impugn their recognition as customary law. It will be recalled that in the *Nicaragua* Case the International Court pointed out that the "instances of conduct" inconsistent with the *opinio juris* prohibiting force and intervention were generally treated as breaches of the rules and consequently did not override the finding of general practice confirming the *opinio juris*.[21]

The problem of inconsistent practice (*i.e.* violations) comes up sharply in respect of declared norms of international human rights. A pertinent example is the 1975 Declaration on the Protection of All Persons from Being Subjected to Torture and Other Cruel, Inhuman and Degrading Treatment.[22] There is little doubt, as responsible studies show, that torture and cruel, degrading treatment occur often under colour of State authority.[23] In the face of these facts, it is hard to conclude that the declared norms are confirmed by general and consistent practice. A similar problem arises in regard to other declared rules that prohibit State conduct in violation of basic human rights including, not least, the humanitarian law of armed conflict.[24]

Most international lawyers seek to minimize the violations by emphasizing strong verbal condemnations and denials. The fact that *opinio juris* is manifested in international forums (usually in general terms) is regarded by some as sufficient to sustain the customary law status of the prohibition.[25] However this conclusion requires some discrimination with respect to kinds of customary law involved. The notion that contrary practice should yield to *opinio juris* challenges the basic premise of customary law. It would not be acceptable in respect of the great body of customary rules – as for example, the law on jurisdiction, immunities, State responsibility, diplomatic privileges. In these areas, pertinent changes in State conduct usually create expectations of future behavior that modify the *opinio juris* on applicable law.

The legal perception is quite different in regard to prohibitions of State conduct that are strongly supported and important to international order and human values. Examples are the prohibitions of aggression, genocide, slavery, torture and systematic racial discrimination. We would also include the

---

21 *See op. cit., supra* note 3.

22 GEN. ASS. RES. 3452 (XXX), 9 Dec. (1975).

23 Amnesty International reports that in more than 100 countries torture is carried out under colour of state authority.

24 Discrimination against women, and discrimination on racial or religious grounds are conspicuous examples of practices in violation of proclaimed rights.

25 *See* for example, R. HIGGINS, *General Course in Public International Law*, 230 REC. DES COURS (1991-V) at 9, 48; F. KIRGIS, *Custom on a Sliding Scale*, 81:146 AJIL (1980).

humanitarian law of armed conflict as a prime example of norms generally accepted as customary law (as well as treaty law) even though often violated in practice. This basic issue was considered in 1995 by the International Tribunal for war crimes in the former Yugoslavia in its first judgment.[26] The Court noted the difficulties of ascertaining actual military conduct to ascertain the degree of compliance with legal norms. It concluded that reliance must be placed on such elements as official pronouncements, military manuals and judicial decisions. These evidences of *opinio juris* include not only general propositions of existing law but also references to particular cases in regard to which States have condemned actions or denied that they had occurred under State authority.

It is worth noting that a characteristic of this category of legal norms is that they are brittle in the sense that violations are likely. For that very reason, the norm has to be maintained despite violations. The difference between international *opinio juris* in these cases and that in the other areas of customary law is empirically evident. It is a fact of international life evidenced by formal pronouncements of a general character and also by statements condemning conduct in particular cases.

From the standpoint of legal doctrine, a proposal has been made by Simma and Alston to regard this category of norms not as custom but as "general principles of law" in the sense of article 38(1) of the Statute of the Court.[27] This has the advantage, it is noted, of minimizing the problem of inconsistent practice. As "general principles of law," their authority would be based on their acceptance by the generality of States rather than on "practices" in the sense of customary law. A variation of this approach proposed by Henkin would characterize many of these norms as a "new law of fundamental values adopted by the international system" which "would not derive from or depend on State practice or on law made purposefully by the consent of States.[28] They would come within the concept of a *jus cogens*, adopted by all the "essential components of the international community."[29]

It is sufficient, in my view, to recognize that there is a category of norms that are part of "general international law" which governments in general regard as obligatory despite violations, even if widespread. This conception

---

26 *Prosecutor v. Tadic'*, APPEAL ON JURISDICTION (Oct. 2, 1995) 35 INT. LEGAL MATERIALS 32 (1996). *See* also, T. MERON, *The Continuing Role of Custom in the Formation of International Humanitarian Law*, 90 AJIL (1996) at 238.

27 *See* E. SIMMA and P. ALSTON, *The Sources of Human Rights Law; Custom, jus cogens and General Principles*, 12 AUSTRALIAN Y.B. INT. L at 82–108.

28 L. HENKIN, INTERNATIONAL LAW: POLITICS AND VALUES (1992) at 39.

29 *Ibid.*

of general international law is reflected in several International Court of Justice opinions and decisions of national courts.[30] It would not be inappropriate to consider these norms as a species of "higher law" evidenced by the positions taken by the generality of governments and by juridical bodies.

[30] The International Court of Justice tends to use the term "general international law" in cases of a human rights character. *See* B. SIMMA and P. ALSTON, *op. cit, supra* note 27, at 105–106 for references. In many domestic jurisdictions however, customary law rules will be given effect more easily than general principles. T. MERON, *The Geneva Conventions As a Customary Law*, 81 AJIL 348 (1987). *See* also *Filartiga v. Pena-Trala U.S.C.C.A.* 630 F. 2d 876 (1980).

May Preparatory Work be Used to Correct Rather than Confirm the "Clear" Meaning of a Treaty Provision?

by

Stephen M. Schwebel

The Vienna Convention on the Law of Treaties, which entered into force in 1980, has been adopted at this writing by some 80 States, *i.e.* under half of the membership of the United Nations; and the States not party include a variety of States large and small, including such major States as the United States of America, China, Brazil, India and Pakistan. It nevertheless has been treated more than once by the International Court of Justice as expressive of customary international law binding upon States parties and non-parties alike. Thus in the case concerning the *Territorial Dispute (Libyan Arab Jamahariya/ Chad)*,[1] the Court held:

> "in accordance with customary international law, reflected in Article 31 of the 1969 Vienna Convention on the Law of Treaties, a treaty must be interpreted in good faith in accordance with the ordinary meaning to be given to its terms in their context and in the light of its object and purpose. Interpretation must be based above all upon the text of the treaty. As a supplementary measure recourse may be had to means of interpretation such as the preparatory work of the treaty and the circumstances of its conclusion."

In the case concerning *Maritime Delimitation and Territorial Questions between Qatar and Bahrain: Jurisdiction and Admissibility*,[2] the Court applied (or, it may be argued, misapplied) the Vienna Convention's provisions on the interpretation of treaties to determine the rights of the parties to the dispute though neither Bahrain nor Qatar were party to the Convention. In so doing it again brought to bear Articles 31 and 32 of the Convention, which were among those whose adoption in the terms adopted was most vigorously contested at Vienna.

---

1 ICJ Reports 1994 at 21–22.

2 ICJ Reports 1995 at 21–22. *See* also, the author's dissent, *ibid.* at 27–39; that of Judge Shahabuddeen, *ibid.* at 56–58; that of Judge Koroma, *ibid.* at 69–73; and that of Judge Valticos, *ibid.* at 75–76.

Articles 31 and 32 of the Vienna Convention provide:

"*Article 31*

General rule of interpretation

1. A treaty shall be interpreted in good faith in accordance with the ordinary meaning to be given to the terms of the treaty in their context and in the light of its object and purpose.

2. The context for the purpose of the interpretation of a treaty shall comprise, in addition to the text, including its preamble and annexes:

(a) any agreement relating to the treaty which was made between all the parties in connexion with the conclusion of the treaty;

(b) any instrument which was made by one or more parties in connexion with the conclusion of the treaty and accepted by the other parties as an instrument related to the treaty.

3. There shall be taken into account, together with the context:

(a) any subsequent agreement between the parties regarding the interpretation of the treaty or the application of its provisions;

(b) any subsequent practice in the application of the treaty which establishes the agreement of the parties regarding its interpretation;

(c) any relevant rules of international law applicable in the relations between the parties.

4. A special meaning shall be given to a term if it is established that the parties so intended.

Article 32

Supplementary means of interpretation

Recourse may be had to supplementary means of interpretation, including the preparatory work of the treaty and the circumstances of its conclusion, in order to confirm the meaning resulting from the application of article 31, or to determine the meaning when the interpretation according to article 31:

(a) leaves the meaning ambiguous or obscure; or

(b) leads to a result which is manifestly absurd or unreasonable."

The problem to which this essay is devoted is this. Suppose that the Court or another interpreter of a treaty arrives at an interpretation of the terms of a treaty at issue "in accordance with the ordinary meaning to be given to the terms of the treaty in their context and in the light of its object and purpose." Suppose as well that the parties to the treaty have argued and placed before the Court the preparatory work of the treaty and the circumstances of its conclusion, as they customarily do. Suppose that the Court has, as it invariably must, read, listened to and weighed the evidence and arguments of the parties respecting the preparatory work as it has their other evidence and arguments. May it bring to bear in arriving at its interpretation of the treaty the *travaux préparatoires* only "to confirm the meaning resulting from the application of Article 31?" Or may it bring to bear the *travaux* to correct – or indeed from the outset to inform and influence – what otherwise would be its understanding of the meaning of the treaty provisions at issue?

Of course these questions assume that the Court or other treaty interpreter has not found that the interpretation according to Article 31 leaves the meaning of the treaty provision "ambiguous or obscure" or "leads to a result which is manifestly absurd or unreasonable." If it has so found, by the terms of Article 32 it is plain that the interpreter may employ preparatory work "to determine the meaning." In point of fact, the terms of a treaty which come before the Court for interpretation, if not usually obscure, are often "ambiguous." If this were not so, that is, if they did not lend themselves to argument attaching different meaning to their terms, they would not likely be legally contested at all. Moreover, it is not infrequent that the "ordinary meaning" of the terms of a treaty, even if found to be unambiguously such, leads to a result which, if not "manifestly absurd" is "unreasonable" – at any rate, in the view of one of the parties to the dispute.

But let us put all that aside, and concentrate on the assumption that the Court or interpreter has found the "ordinary meaning" and proposes to have recourse to the preparatory work of the treaty "in order to confirm" it, in circumstances in which that meaning is not ambiguous or obscure or in which it will not lead to a result which is manifestly absurd or unreasonable.

It will at once be objected that the assumption – and hence the hierarchical structure of Articles 31 and 32 of the Vienna Convention – is unreal. Since the parties to the case have argued (or so often argued) that the preparatory work shows this or that, and since the Court perforce has had to consider any such arguments and the evidence on which they rely before arriving at even a provisional interpretation of the treaty, how can it be that recourse to the *travaux* is only a "supplementary" way of confirming the meaning resulting from the application of Article 31?

The answer to that objection is that it is unanswerable. Three quotations of statements of leading members of the International Law Commission made in the course of the Commission's preparation of the draft of the Vienna Convention are telling. Shabtai Rosenne:

> "It was true that there existed a number of apparently consistent pronouncements by the International Court of Justice and arbitral tribunals to the effect that *travaux préparatoires* had only been used to confirm what had been found to be the clear meaning of the text of a treaty. However, that case-law would be much more convincing if from the outset

the Court or tribunal had refused to admit consideration of *travaux préparatoires* until it had first established whether or not the text was clear, but in fact, what had happened was that on all those occasions the *travaux préparatoires* had been fully and extensively placed before the Court or arbitral tribunal by one or other of the parties, if not by both. In the circumstances, to State that the *travaux préparatoires* had been used only to confirm an opinion already arrived at on the basis of the text of the treaty was coming close to a legal fiction. It was impossible to know by what process judges reached their decisions and it was particularly difficult to accept the proposition that the *travaux préparatoires* had not actually contributed to form their opinion as to the meaning of a treaty which, nevertheless, they stated to be clear from its text, but which, as the pleadings in fact showed, was not so. At all events, it could be supposed that all practitioners of international law were free in their use of *travaux préparatoires*."[3]

Mustafa Yasseen:

"The clearness or ambiguity of a provision was a relative matter; sometimes one had to refer to the preparatory work or look to the circumstances surrounding the conclusion of the treaty in order to determine whether the text was really clear and whether the seeming clarity was not simply a deceptive appearance. He could not accept an article which would impose a chronological order and which would permit reference to preparatory work only after it had been decided that the text was not clear, that decision itself being often influenced by the consultation of the same sources."[4]

Sir Humphrey Waldock:

"It was unrealistic to imagine that the preparatory work was not really consulted by States, organizations and tribunals whenever they saw fit, before or at any stage of the proceedings, even though they might afterwards pretend that they had not given it much attention ... the reference to confirmation and, *a fortiori*, verification tended to undermine the text of a treaty in the sense that there was an express authorization to interpret it in the light of something else; nevertheless that was what happened in practice."[5]

(It may be recalled that Sir Humphrey Waldock was the Commission's last Special Rapporteur on the topic.)

---

[3] I YEARBOOK OF THE INTERNATIONAL LAW COMMISSION (1964) at 283, para. 17. (The quotation is from the summary record.)

[4] *Ibid.* at 313, para. 56.

[5] *Ibid.* at 314, para. 65.

Nevertheless, in view of the persistence of the pretence that recourse to preparatory work may be had "in order to confirm" the meaning otherwise arrived at, what if that allegedly postponed and purely supplementary means of interpretation when applied fails to confirm that "ordinary meaning?"

Two possibilities present themselves. Either the preparatory work must be discarded and its import set aside; or "the meaning resulting from the application of Article 31" may or must be corrected to take account of the distinctive light shed on the meaning of the treaty provisions at issue by the preparatory work. Which is the better interpretation?

If one takes the ordinary meaning of the word, "confirm," that is, in this context, to make firmer, to strengthen, to settle, to verify, it follows that, where the preparatory work is consistent with the "ordinary" meaning, it may be invoked to buttress the interpretation otherwise arrived at; but where the preparatory work undermines, detracts from or otherwise fails to sustain this ordinary meaning, it may not be taken into account to correct it.

That, of course, is one more illustration of the inadequacy of reliance upon the "ordinary" or "plain" or "clear" meaning of a treaty provision.[6] So interpreted, the reference to preparatory work is unnecessary; the ordinary meaning stands without it. Why have recourse to that which is merely confirmatory of what is already so plain? Especially why so, if preparatory work is subject to the disabilities which its critics attribute to it? (It is claimed that preparatory work is misleading, fragmentary, too difficult to find or – somewhat inconsistently – too ample, or is "merged" in the final text which then has a life of its own. These criticisms may be merited in some cases, unmerited in others.)

Interpreted in this fashion, this provision of Article 32 is essentially without purpose. It follows that it may not be so interpreted, since it is a canon of treaty interpretation that clauses may not be interpreted to be surplusage. That is all the more so in a treaty prepared and adopted with the extraordinary care that went into the preparation and adoption of the Vienna Convention on the Law of Treaties. The Vienna Convention does not reproduce boilerplate as so many contracts routinely do. It is rather the product of a line of British Spe-

---

6 For a vigorous analysis of the "obscurantist tautology" inherent in "plain" or "ordinary" or "clear" meaning, *see* the statement of Professor MYRES S. MCDOUGAL of the United States Delegation to the Committee of the Whole of the Vienna Conference on the Law of Treaties, printed *verbatim* in the 62 AMERICAN JOURNAL OF INTERNATIONAL LAW (1968) at 433, and reprinted M.S. MCDOUGAL, H.D. LASSWELL and V.C. MILLER, THE INTERPRETATION OF INTERNATIONAL AGREEMENTS AND WORLD PUBLIC ORDER (1994) at 433. As Lord MCNAIR put it, the maxim of clear meaning "is in truth a *petitio principii* because it begs the question whether the words are, or are not clear – a subjective matter because they may be clear to one man and not clear to another, and frequently to one or more judges and not to their colleagues." MCNAIR, THE LAW OF TREATIES (1961) at 372.

cial Rapporteurs of the International Law Commission of quite exceptional distinction; of a Commission which then was at the peak of its powers; and of two extended sessions of plenipotentiary conferences at which every provision of the draft convention was subjected to careful consideration. If, as Article 31 itself prescribes, a treaty is to be interpreted "in good faith," surely the provision of Article 32 respecting recourse to preparatory work must be understood to be meaningful rather than meaningless. If preparatory work may be invoked only when it confirms the ordinary meaning otherwise deduced, the provision for its application in Article 32 approaches the meaningless. But if preparatory work may be invoked to correct the ordinary meaning otherwise deduced (if not to inform and influence the interpretation of the treaty from the outset), it and the provision of Article 32 are accorded a meaningful place.

What light does the preparatory work of the Vienna Convention itself shed on this very issue? Not much, because surprisingly little was said on the point. But what little there is supports the approach of this writer.

The views of the Special Rapporteur of the International Law Commission at the time of the Vienna Conference, Sir Humphrey Waldock, were quoted above in terms that indicate that he understood "confirmation" as tending to permit the "undermining" of the text of a treaty. The most direct answer to the question addressed in this essay appears to have been that offered by the representative of Portugal at the Vienna Conference:

> "What would happen if, though the text of a treaty was apparently clear, in seeking confirmation in the preparatory work and other surrounding circumstances a divergent meaning came to light? It was impossible to be sure in advance that those circumstances would confirm the textual meaning of the treaty. If the emphasis were placed on good faith, it would appear that in such a case those circumstances should be taken into consideration, although they did not lead to the confirmation of the meaning..."[7]

As far as the writer is aware, nothing in the record of the Vienna Conference counters this eminently reasonable position.

There is a further consideration, allied with that of good faith, which supports the interpretation set out above, namely, that the provisions of the Vienna Convention must be interpreted to be effective rather than ineffective. To confine preparatory work to the place to which a literal interpretation of the term, "to confirm," consigns it, hardly renders Article 32 effective.[8]

---

[7] United Nations Conference on the Law of Treaties, First Session (1968), OFFICIAL RECORDS at 183.

[8] For the classic and compelling exposition of the principle of effectiveness, *see* H. LAUTERPACHT, *Restrictive Interpretation and the Principle of Effectiveness in the interpretation of treaties*, XXVI BRITISH YEAR BOOK OF INTERNATIONAL LAW (1949) at 73.

It should finally be recalled that the provisions of the Vienna Convention were seen by the International Law Commission and its Special Rapporteurs, and were adopted by the Conference, largely (though not entirely) as a codification of international law, as a crystallization of State practice. That certainly was true of Articles 31 and 32, which were thought not wholly to embrace one or another school of treaty interpretation but as articles which encompassed and balanced them. The balance heavily inclined towards the text of the treaty as the authentic expression of the intentions of the parties, and away from the intentions of the parties as an element distinct from the text and away from the declared objects and purposes of the treaty as guides to interpretation. But it included all these elements. It was seen as a compromise text designed to reflect the differing approaches and to attract the maximum adherence of the international community.

However, if the reference in Article 32 to recourse to preparatory work is to be marginalized by a literal interpretation of the term, "to confirm," that compromise vanishes; the ascendancy of the plain meaning school is complete. In that event, the Vienna Convention could hardly be said, in its provisions for treaty interpretation, to be reflective of customary international law, for there is simply too much State practice and too much judicial precedent that accords preparatory work a greater place.[9] A treaty, even a great law-making convention such as the treaty on treaties, can hardly be said to be reflective of customary international law if it does not in fact fairly reflect State practice and judicial precedent. That practice and that precedent demonstrate that preparatory work is often brought to bear in the interpretation of treaties, by the parties to those treaties and by their interpreters, and this whether the *travaux préparatoires* confirm or correct an interpretation otherwise arrived at.

---

[9] For an analysis of precedent in the use of preparatory work in the Permanent Court of International Justice and the International Court of Justice, *see* Sir Hersch Lauterpacht, The Development of International Law by the International Court (1958) at 116–141. For a discerning discussion of the place of preparatory work in treaty interpretation, *see* M.S. McDougal, H.D. Lasswell and V.C. Miller, *op. cit., supra* note 6, at 122–132.

Enhancing the Role of the General Assembly of the United Nations in Crystallizing International Law

by

Louis B. Sohn

I. PROFESSOR SKUBISZEWSKI'S ROLE IN DEFINING THE ROLE OF THE GENERAL ASSEMBLY IN DEVELOPING INTERNATIONAL LAW

I had the pleasure of becoming acquainted with Krzysztof Skubiszewski in 1958, when he was working on his LL.M. degree at Harvard. Since then he has become one of the leaders of world-wide renown in the teaching and practice of international law. Having been asked to contribute to a volume in his honour dealing with the status of public international law at this crucial time when we shall observe not only the end of a century but also the beginning of a new millennium, I would like to discuss a topic dear to Professor Skubiszewski, namely the increasing role which the General Assembly of the United Nations has played in the development of international law.

Already in 1968, Professor Skubiszewski published an essay on *A New Source of the Law of Nations: Resolutions of International Organizations* in the volume in honour of Paul Guggenheim.[1] He pointed out that during the first twenty years of the United Nations only a few of the more than 2000 resolutions of the General Assembly could be regarded as law making.[2] He noted, however, the binding character of regulations being enacted by various international organizations, starting with the commissions established in the 19th century for controlling the navigation on the Rhine and the Danube,[3] continuing with several specialized agencies of the United Nations,[4]

---

[1] Faculté de Droit de l'Université de Genève et Institut Universitaire de Hautes Études Internationales, Genève, RECUEIL D'ÉTUDES DE DROIT INTERNATIONAL EN HOMMAGE À PAUL GUGGENHEIM (1968) at 508–520.

[2] *Ibid.* at 508.

[3] *Ibid.* at 508, 511.

[4] *Ibid.* at 512–513. He considered, in particular, the International Civil Aviation Organization, the World Health Organization and the World Meteoreological Organization, which have the power to enact regulations, but allow a State to contract-out of specific provisions with which it is not yet able to comply.

and ending with the then still embryonic powers of the three European Communities.[5] In his conclusions, Professor Skubiszewski, on the one hand, refused to agree with the authors who consider resolutions, especially unanimous ones, as equivalent to treaties, but, on the other hand, he accepted "the making of international law by international organizations" as "an accomplished fact of contemporary international law," and "a new source of the law of nations".[6]

In 1977, Professor Skubiszewski was assigned by the Institute of International Law (Geneva) the enormous task of preparing a report on "non-contractual instruments having a normative functions."[7] The subject was originally suggested by Professor Balladore Pallieri, who called attention to the existence of instruments, usually in the form of declarations, which were different from treaties containing contractual obligations among parties to them, and noted the inability of contemporary legal theory to determine the status of this new development.[8] He prepared several voluminous reports on the Part of the topic that related to the resolutions of the General Assembly of the United Nations, taking into account a large number of comments on each of them by members of the Thirteenth Commission that was assigned this topic. Professor Skubiszewski presented finally all this documentation to the Institute at its Helsinki session in 1985.[9] Faced with this tremendous set of materials, the Institute postponed the decision to the Cairo session in 1987, which adopted a carefully worded final resolution on the subject which congratulated the Rapporteur and the Members of the Commission on "having succeeded in elucidating the numerous factors which, depending on circumstances, allow the resolutions of the General Assembly of the United Nations to contribute to a better knowledge of international law, to hasten its development, to enhance its authority and to ensure stricter compliance therewith."[10] Annexes to this resolution were the twenty-six conclusions of the Thirteenth Commission. These conclusions were carefully drafted and to better understand their importance, it would be necessary to read this interrelated text as a whole. It is possible to summarize here – in a slightly simplified language that takes also into account both the French and English versions of the text – only some crucial points:

---

5 *Ibid.* at 511–512.

6 *Ibid.* at 517–519.

7 57 ANNUAIRE DE L'INSTITUT DE DROIT INTERNATIONAL, Part II at 96, 102–103 (items 26–36).

8 G. BALLADORE PALLIERI, *La formation des traités dans la pratique internationale contemporaine*, 74:1 HAGUE ACADEMY, RECUEIL DES COURS (1949) at 465, 541–542.

9 61 ANNUAIRE, *op. cit.*, *supra* note 7, Part I at 29–358.

10 62 *ibid.* Part II at 204–205.

The Commission, in its conclusions, recognized that the Charter of the United Nations did not confer on the General Assembly the power to enact rules binding on States in their relations *inter se*, but concluded that the Assembly may nevertheless "made recommendations contributing to the progressive development of international law, its consolidation and codification."[11]

Some of the resolutions of the Assembly are law-creating and constitute a restatement of (*réaffirment*) the existing law; they do this by: determining the content of a rule of international law; providing evidence of an international custom; or setting forth some general principles of law.[12] Other resolutions are law-developing, crystallizing or generating new law by such means as: contributing to the creation of a customary rule or emergence of general principles; facilitating negotiation of a multilateral treaty by setting forth rules to be included in that treaty; or "laying down policies (*arrêtent des politiques*) that determine the substance of future law, whether customary or treaty".[13]

Declarations are used to emphasize the importance of the norms enunciated. They are suitable for a comprehensive treatment of a subject, or for expressing "principles the purpose of which is to influence the progressive development of international law".[14]

"A law-declaring resolution, adopted without negative vote or abstention creates a presumption that the resolution contains a correct statement of the law."[15] A resolution adopted by such unanimity is especially effective in situations "where a rule of customary law is emerging from State practice or where there is still doubt whether a rule, though already applied by an international organ or by some States, is a rule of law." Such resolution "may consolidate the custom or remove doubts that might have existed."[16] The authority of a resolution is enhanced when it is adopted by consensus,[17] or at least "by a representative majority that includes the main legal systems."[18] On the other hand, if "the number of negative votes or abstentions is large, or qualitatively significant, the law-stating or rule-developing effect of the resolution is weakened."[19]

---

11 Conclusion 1, *ibid.* at 276.
12 Conclusions 3(2*), ibid.* at 276.
13 Conclusions 3(2) and 5, *ibid.* at 278.
14 Conclusion 12, *ibid.* at 282.
15 Conclusion 13, *ibid.* at 282. That presumption is, however "subject to rebuttal".
16 Conclusion 16, *ibid.* at 284.
17 Conclusion 16, *ibid.* at 284.
18 Conclusion 15(1), *ibid.* at 284.
19 Conclusion 15(2), *ibid.* at 284.

II. THE INTERNATIONAL COURT OF JUSTICE AND THE ROLE OF ASSEMBLY RESOLUTIONS

The Skubiszewski report constituted an important step in the direction of consolidating the theoretical basis for enhancing the role of the General Assembly in the process of crystallizing new rules of international law. Until then, many international lawyers were rejecting the idea of law-making decisions of the General Assembly. A strong rebuttal of this negative approach came, however, near the end of the Institute's deliberations, in 1986, when the International Court of Justice, in the *Nicaragua v. United States* case,[20] endorsed several principles relating to the use of force on the basis that they were contained in one of the most important declarations of the General Assembly, the "Declaration on Principles of International Law Concerning the Friendly Relations and Cooperation among States in Accordance with the Charter of the United Nations". The Court pointed out:

> "The effect of consent to the text of such resolution cannot be understood as merely that of a 'reiteration or elucidation' of the treaty commitment undertaken in the Charter. On the contrary it may be understood as an acceptance of the validity of the rule or set of rules declared by the resolution by themselves ... It would therefore seem apparent that the attitude referred to expresses an *opinio juris* respecting such rule (or set of rules), to be henceforth treated separately from the provisions, especially those of institutional kind, to which it is subject on the treaty-law plane of the Charter."[21]

This statement by the Court made it clear that it is the consensus in the General Assembly that establishes the more precise principles, not the fact that the power of the Assembly is based on the Charter. It is also from the Declaration on Friendly Relations that the Court has drawn the distinction between "the most grave forms of the use of force (those constituting an armed attack) from other less grave forms", and included some kinds of intervention in one group rather than the other.[22]

---

[20] Case concerning Military and Paramilitary Activities in and against Nicarague (*Nicaragua v. U.S.A.*) (Merits), Judgement of 27 June 1986, ICJ REPORTS 1986 at 14.

[21] *Ibid.* para. 188, at 99–100.

[22] *See e.g. ibid.* para. 192 at 101, and para. 205 at 108.

III. THE SHIFT IN THE IMPORTANCE OF VARIOUS SOURCES OF INTERNATIONAL LAW

The views of Professor Skubiszewski and of his Commission, which included several eminent leaders of the Institute of International Law, and the almost contemporaneous statement of the International Court of Justice, reflect the growing acceptance by the community of nations of a new theory of sources of international law that is more appropriate for the third millennium than its predecessors. It is the purpose of this essay to describe the path that the science of international law took to arrive at this result.

The rules relating to the creation of international law have changed many times during the second millennium, and they have changed even more drastically during the last fifty years of the twentieth century. Early Italian jurists such as Bartolus de Sassoferrato and Baldus de Ubaldis,[23] relied mostly on Roman codes, and prepared long "glosses" interpreting provisions of the Pandecta and the Justinian Code. For several centuries thereafter international law experts started to take into account also official pronouncements by governments and views expressed in diplomatic correspondence, organized them in accordance with various topics, and distilled from them numerous principles. For instance, the three fathers of international law, Vitoria,[24] Suarez,[25] and Grotius,[26] found their precedents in the Bible and in various Greek, Roman and medieval history books. Their successors discovered also that there were many references to international law in contemporaneous diplomatic documents, in international treaties and arbitral decisions, and collections of these documents soon were made.[27] Building on

---

[23] *See e.g.* T.A. WALKER, A HISTORY OF THE LAW OF NATIONS (1899), Vol. I, at 203–204. Bartolus (1313–59) taught successively in Pisa, Perugia and Bologna, and his equally famous student, Baldus, started in Bologna and taught later in Florence, Padua and Pavia. In their commentaries on Roman texts they dealt with such international law topics as war, reprisals, diplomatic service and law of the sea. For instance, Bartolus anticipated some twentieth century developments by arguing that the jurisdiction of a coastal State over the adjacent sea extends to the distance of one hundred miles. *See* A.P. SERENI, THE ITALIAN CONCEPTION OF INTERNATIONAL LAW (1943) at 72.

[24] F. DE VITORIA, DE INDIS ET DE JURE BELLI (1557), reprinted and edited, with English translation, by E. NYS (1917). *See* also J. BROWN SCOTT, THE SPANISH ORIGIN OF INTERNATIONAL LAW: FRANCISCO DE VITORIA AND HIS LAW OF NATIONS (1934).

[25] F. SUAREZ, TRACTATUS DE LEGIBUS AC DEO LEGISLATORE (1612), reprinted and edited with English translation, by J. BROWN SCOTT (1944).

[26] H. GROTIUS, DE JURE BELLI AC PACIS LIBRI TRES (1625), reprinted, with English translation by Kalsey and introduction by J. BROWN SCOTT (1913), Vol. 1 and Vol. 2 (1925).

[27] With respect to treaties, *see* e.g. T. RYMER, FOEDERA, CONVENTIONES, LITTERAE, 20 Volumes (1704–1718), reprinted (1816–1830); J. DUMONT, CORPS UNIVERSEL DIPLOMATIQUE DU DROIT DES GENS, 8 vols (1726–1731); G.F. DE MARTENS, RECUEIL DES PRINCIPAUX TRAITÉSD D'ALLIANCE, DE PAIX, etc. (since 1791, several series, including treaties since 1761 to 1942).

these new-found treasures, Wolff[28] and Vattel[29] provided the models for modern textbooks of international law in which the views of their predecessors and these new sources of international law were woven together. Vattel's condensation of Wolff proved to be a best-seller and was quickly translated from French into several languages including English, and became especially popular in American and British courts. During the nineteenth century, many international arbitrations were held, domestic courts rendered judgments on international topics, and the production of compilations of the interstate correspondence and of treaties, especially those dealing with international trade, greatly increased. All of them became important additional sources for the use by authors of treatises on the subject, and for an increasing number of doctoral dissertations on particular topics. While diplomats were still the ones who made the law, the lawyers of Foreign Offices and the eminent legal professors were the ones who continued to decide which rules are becoming customary international law.

While most treaties continued to be bilateral, multilateral treaties on various topics, especially on communications and transportation, made their appearance in the second half of the nineteenth century and were followed by international organizations monitoring the implementation of some of these treaties. The two Hague Conferences of 1899 and 1907 codified the rules for the pacific settlement of disputes and for waging wars in a more civilized way. Nevertheless, the First World War led to many gross violations of international law and the League of Nations was established to prevent future wars. Many important multilateral treaties were concluded under the auspices of the League,[30] but its efforts to codify international law largely failed. After the Second World War, the United Nations established

---

With respect to arbitrations, *see e.g.* A. RAEDER, L'ARBITRAGE INTERNATIONAL CHEZ LES HELLENES (1912); M.N. TOD, INTERNATIONAL ARBITRATION AMONGST THE GREEKS (1913); H. LAFONTAINE, PASICRISIE INTERNATIONALE: HISTOIRE DOCUMENTAIRE DES ARBITRAGES INTERNATIONAUX (1902); J.H. RALSTON, INTERNATIONAL ARBITRATION FROM ATHENS TO LOCARNO (1929); A.M. STUYT, SURVEY OF INTERNATIONAL ARBITRATIONS, 1794–1989 (3d ed. 1990).

[28] CH. VON WOLFF (1679–1754) wrote two books: JUS GENTIUM METHODO SCIENTIFICO PERTRACTATUM (1749), reprinted with English translation by J.H. DRAKE and introduction by Nippold (1934), and INSTITUTIONES JURIS NATURAE AC GENTIUM (1750).

[29] E. DE VATTEL (1714–1764), LE DROIT DES GENS, OU PRINCIPES DE LA LOI NATURELLE (1758), reprinted with English translation by CH.G. FENWICK and editorial comments by A. DE LA PRADELLE (1916). The books cited in notes 24–26 and 28–29 belong to the series of 16 CLASSICS OF INTERNATIONAL LAW, prepared under the direction of J. BROWN SCOTT and published by the Carnegie Endowment of International Law. Unfortunately the series was discontinued and many other classics are not as easily accessible.

[30] They may be found in M.O. HUDSON, INTERNATIONAL LEGISLATION, 9 Volumes (1931–1950). This collection contained also an increasing number of agreements concluded under the auspices of other international organizations.

a special commission of experts to revive the codification effort, and the International Law Commission did succeed in preparing a number of treaties on such basic areas of international law as the law of treaties and the privileges and immunities of diplomats and consuls. Its pace was, however slow, and the United Nations General Assembly started arranging special working groups on a broad variety of subjects, which resulted in a substantial increase in multilateral treaty making. While special diplomatic conferences were called usually to adopt the final documents, the General Assembly itself started to approve international conventions on human rights and a variety of other subjects. More often the preparatory work on a new set of international rules is done now by General Assembly's working groups, and the Assembly either decides itself the few remaining national issues or arranges for a short diplomatic conference to give final approval to its committees' work.

IV. THE NEW ROLE OF THE RESOLUTIONS OF THE GENERAL ASSEMBLY

Originally, the resolutions of the General Assembly were considered merely as recommendations which a State could follow when it was convenient but which would not lead to some undesirable consequences. As a result, however, of a rapid growth in United Nations membership, the governments became slowly more conscious of the fact that the General Assembly was no longer merely a group of victors in a war, who were also the major colonial powers ruling a majority of the world's peoples. Instead, the Assembly became a more democratic institution in which practically all peoples of the world were directly represented by their own governments, rather than by foreign rulers. By the end of the twentieth century, the General Assembly became entitled to speak in the name of all the States of the world, and its decisions became the decisions of the world community, of mankind as a whole. Even the few countries which are not officially members of the United Nations, were permitted to participate in most United Nations activities dealing with economic, social and cultural matters, including the major global conferences such as those on the protection of the environment and the law of the sea, as well as on human rights and women's rights. They participate also in the work of the specialized agencies of the United Nations relating to health, food production, telecommunications, postal service, international sea and air transportation, financial assistance for reconstruction and development, and monetary problems. Even in the political field, while they do not vote in the General Assembly or the Security Council, these few non-members usually comply with the important decisions against States that were found by the United Nations to have committed gross violations of international law.

Consequently, practically all important decisions of the General Assembly, and in matters of international peace and security, also decisions of the Security Council, have become enforceable throughout the world. There is only one important condition – that the decision had been adopted unanimously or by consensus. In some cases, it might be sufficient if the decision represents the views of both all the major powers and a majority in each regional group. It is less likely that a decision will be enforceable against a major power or a majority of a regional group. There is, however, also the possibility that a generally acceptable decision would become binding on all those that have voted for it, but that the dissenting State or regional group would not be obliged to comply with it, as long as this noncompliance does not affect the execution of the decision by the other States willing to enforce it *inter se*.

It may be noted that the developments of the 1990s, which were to some extent foreseen by the Skubiszewski report, were not approved by any solemn act, a revision of the Charter of the United Nations, or the adoption of an express decision by the General Assembly on the legal status of its important resolutions or declarations. It is simply the result of the general recognition that for the first time in human history there is a world-wide institution accepted directly by almost all States, and less formally by the remaining ones. This result is consistent with the traditional view that international law is made by States or by those individuals who are acting on behalf of States. In the past, however, it was made haphazardly, by bits and pieces, and by relatively small groups of States. A large amount of research was required to ascertain what has been agreed upon and by whom, and what was the reaction of those not participating in the decision. Once the United Nations decided to admit almost every country applying for membership, and in effect practically everyone was able and willing to join it, or at least respect its decisions, the international law making became simplified. Two decisions were needed. First, an agreement, direct or implied, that the General Assembly, acting unanimously, with the consent of all the States, large or small, is authorized to adopt decisions crystallizing rules of international law. Second, any decision leading to the crystallization of a rule or set of rules must be adopted by a process that has been specially designed to obtain a general acceptance of a rule or set of rules.

The first rule is the result of the practice of the General Assembly asserting in important resolutions, usually in the form of declarations, that they shall be observed. For instance, the 1963 Declaration on the Elimination of All Forms of Racial Discrimination boldly asserted in Article 11 that not only every State shall promote respect for and observance of human rights and fundamental freedoms in accordance with the Charter of the United Nations, but also that it "shall fully and faithfully observe the provisions of the present Declaration, the Universal Declaration of Human Rights and the Declaration on the Granting Independence to Colonial Countries and Peoples."[31] Similarly, the International Conference on Human Rights at Teheran, Iran, proclaimed in para. 2 that

> "The Universal Declaration of Human Rights states a common understanding of the peoples of the world concerning the inalienable and inviolable rights of all members of the human family and constitutes an obligation for members of the international community."[32]

In several of its decisions relating to boundary delimitation with respect to the continental shelf, the International Court of Justice has asserted its power to decide whether an international customary rule has become crystallized. Similarly, the Skubiszewski report concluded that the General Assembly can adopt decisions that are law-developing or crystallizing.[33]

Neither the Court nor the Assembly can create instant international law. In the Court, the decision is preceded by briefs of the parties, oral hearings, and the preparation of a text that can be discussed and revised several times. If the Court's decision is unanimous, it is generally accepted; if it less than that, its effect is weaker; and if the decision is approved by a majority of one, there may be reluctance to comply with it, and later attempts are likely to be made to reverse it.

In the General Assembly, there is a similar situation, though at least a two-thirds majority is required for a substantive decision. This means, however, that even if some sixty States disagree, they can be overruled. They usually do not take it kindly; they are not likely to comply with it; and wait for an occasion when they might revenge themselves by overruling the objections of those who were primarily responsible for the previous decision. As a result of that situation, the General Assembly operates, in principle, on the basis of a different principle. It has developed a procedure that enables it

---

31 Approved by Resolution 1904 (XVIII) of the General Assembly, 20 November 1963, 18 GAOR, Supp. N° 18 (A/5515), para. 35, at 37.

32 U.N.Doc.A/CONF.32/41 (13 May 1968), U.N. Pub.E.68.XIV.2. *See* also General Assembly Resolution 2442, 19 December 1968, 23 GAOR, Supp. N° 18 (A/7218) para. 49, endorsing this declaration.

33 *See supra* text preceding note 13.

to reach consensus decisions. It relies not on negotiations which are usually between two groups intent on winning, but on consultations that are based on the idea that the enemy is not the other side but the difficult problem that affects both of them. This requires a joint effort to find a solution, not an adversary, antagonistic duel. It is relatively easy to vote an opponent down, and it is more difficult to make the effort to understand the point of view of the other party and to find a solution that would provide as much satisfaction for all States concerned as may be possible to achieve. This approach requires patience, perseverance, ingenuity and persuasiveness. Sometimes, it is important to encourage the other side to find a solution and to guide it in that direction rather than to insist that your own solution is the best. Once a joint solution is found it should be one enabling each protagonist to discover in it some of his or her own proposals. Such solution is more likely to establish a better atmosphere for future relationship between the parties, and may lead to using consultation not only for solving a problem but also for preventing future disputes.

Early in the history of the United Nations, Judge Lauterpacht noted the beginning of this process in the *South West Africa-Voting Procedure* case when he pointed out that a resolution recommending "a specific course of action creates *some* legal obligations" however "rudimentary, elastic and imperfect" they might be. The addressee State, "while not bound to accept the recommendation, is bound to give it due consideration in good faith." Should it decide to disregard it, "it is bound to explain the reasons for its decision". A State

> "may not be acting illegally by declining to act upon a recommendation or series of recommendations on the same subject. But in doing so it acts at its peril when a point is reached when the cumulative effect of the persistent disregard of the articulate opinion of the Organization is such as to foster the conviction that the State in question has become guilty of disloyalty to the Principles and Purposes of the Charter."

Consequently, a State which

> "consistently sets itself above the solemnly and repeatedly expressed judgment of the Organization, in particular in proportion as that judgment approximates to unanimity, may find that it had overstepped the imperceptible line between impropriety and illegality, between discretion and arbitrariness, between the exercise of the legal right to disregard the recommendation and the abuse of that right, and that it has exposed itself to consequences legitimately following as a legal sanction."[34]

[34] *Voting Procedures Relating to Reports and Petitions Concerning the Territory of South West Africa*, Advisory Opinion of 7 June 1955, ICJ REPORTS 1955 at 67, 118–120.

A few years later, Professor Tammes in his Hague lecture suggested in a parallel situation that

> "the gradualness of the decision making process provides continuous opportunities for the presentation of various views in working groups, both informal and formal, in subcommittees and committees. The final product embodies many amendments suggested to meet the views of various minorities, and contains many compromises between divergent approaches. It is the work of the Conference as a whole, rather than of any particular majority, and minorities usually find it difficult to reject completely a text to the elaboration of which they have in fact contributed. Consensus thus can be reached, with remaining objections being merely recorded in the minutes, without impairing the final adoption of a generally agreed text."[35]

As it was noted before, this process requires patience, perseverance, ingenuity and persuasiveness. A skillful chairperson or rapporteur needs to blend disparate views into a generally accepted compromise. The result may not be perfect, but is much more useful than a decision imposed by a majority on an angry minority. It requires also a willingness of the minority to accept the final product; otherwise the tyranny of the majority is replaced by the tyranny of the minority. Thus, unreasonable requests must be avoided by both majority and minority, and a consensus can be achieved by watchful chairperson. The combined consultation and consensus process can be long and arduous but the result is likely to endure.

Conclusions

In the last few years, the General Assembly of the United Nations has been able to reach agreement on a variety of important documents, to approve them itself or through a special conference. Very often these new instruments are accompanied by agendas for action and by a follow-up commission or a special representative that would supervise the implementation of the agreed rules and of the agenda.

As most of these documents represent a large measure of consensus, and the implementation of the rules and the agenda is in the common interest, the compliance is voluntary and any difficulties that arise can be resolved by further consultations. Thus the process really never ends, the achievement of an agreement is a temporary high point, and preventive watchfulness is

---

[35] A.J.P. TAMMES, *Decisions of International Organs as a Source of International Law*, 94:II HAGUE ACADEMY, RECUEIL DES COURS (1958) at 261, 287.

needed to ensure that the agreement does not disintegrate. It is not surprising, therefore that the daily "Journal" issued at the United Nations headquarters in New York (and there are parallel ones in Geneva and Vienna) ordinarily includes not only notices of meeting of the Security Council, the General Assembly and their subsidiary bodies, but also of a considerable number of "consultations" on various topics by *ad hoc* committees or working groups. Some of them are "closed", and open only to invited participants. Many of them are, however, open-ended, and any member of the United Nations may be admitted on its request. Next day a little note may be published about any result reached, which is rather cryptic, merely mentioning that a document was approved, the document number of which is given, but there is no indication of its content or even topic. Nevertheless, the work progresses, and at some point an excellent document emerges, solving a problem, big or small, or stopping a crisis before it explodes. Usually, most of these preventive diplomatic activities have little publicity; only the States concerned are happy that they have avoided another confrontation, and the peace of the world is saved one more time.

As far as international law is concerned, this continuous process of consultations leads to a slow accretion of new rules, or agreed interpretations of old rules, which can be discovered by diligent research in the *Repertory of Practice of United Nations Organs* or in a set of General Assembly resolutions or, surprisingly, even in documents prepared by one of the Assembly's subsidiary organs or working groups, that were quietly endorsed by the Assembly by a short resolution, to which the new regulations or guidelines are annexed. I have found long ago that United Nations law is not created only by the General Assembly, but is made practically every day by this continuing consultation and decision making process; and that no one is able to keep track of all that is being done. Enough, however, gets into more readily available documents that can provide as much material for doctoral dissertations as diplomatic correspondence provided in the past. Many of the relevant documents exist now in a computerized form and it should be possible to make these materials available to researchers.

In the meantime, it would be desirable to start working on collecting and systematizing at least those documents approved by the General Assembly itself that have crystallized international law. There is more of it than even experts realize, and they could be made available in a format of a "code" that would present them not by date and number, as has been done until now, but in well organized volumes, with a good index, and a CD-ROM disc that would provide greater accessibility.

If we really believe in the rule of law, this should be done, and should be done soon, as with every passing year the job becomes more difficult. It is not enough to crystallize international law, if the crystals remain invisible. It is the duty of the international legal profession to see to it that this is somehow done, and done well.

THE CONCLUDING DOCUMENTS OF WORLD ORDER CONFERENCES

by

CHRISTIAN TOMUSCHAT

Introduction

In recent years, a number of world conferences with universal participation have taken place, each of which dealt with a vast array or issues transcending the realm of national jurisdiction. As such, the phenomenon of world conferences is not new. Suffice it to give a few examples. The era of the United Nations started with the Conference on International Organization, the founding conference of the world organization. Population questions were studied and discussed in former years by two meetings, the Bucharest World Population Conference of 1974 and the International Conference on Population, held at Mexico City in 1984. Two vast conferences reviewing the status of women took place in 1975 (Mexico City) and 1985 (Nairobi). A major international event was the Third U.N. Conference on the Law of the Sea, whose different rounds of negotiations took place between 1973 and 1982. But what is unprecedented is the rapid sequence of such jamborees of mankind and the fact that on most occasions there was no intention to adopt specific legal instruments for well-defined purposes; rather, the conferences were designed to put on the agenda the most pressing global problems in their entirety and to create awareness for the need to seriously cope with them in the interest of mankind as a whole. Nonetheless, it would be shortsighted to dismiss the outcome of all of these gatherings, to the extent that they have not materialized in binding legal instruments in the traditional sense, as pure political rhetoric not being susceptible of producing legal effects. One simply has to note that voluminous international documents were adopted and that these documents reflect in any event an international understanding of what conduct should be pursued by States with a view to reaching the specific goals universally approved. It would almost be bizarre if such consensus statements about world order, peace and human rights lacked any legal relevance. The following reflections seek to shed some light on this issue.

The current round of world order conferences started with the U.N. Conference on Environment and Development (Rio de Janeiro, 3 to 14 June

1992). This meeting was particularly productive. It brought into being the Rio Declaration on Environment and Development as well as a Statement of Principles for a Global Consensus on the Management, Conservation and Sustainable Development of All Types of Forests.[1] Additionally, it opened for Signature the Framework Convention on Climate Change and the Convention on Biological Diversity.[2] Lastly, Agenda 21 was adopted, a far-reaching plan of action designed to provide guidelines for national policies aiming to protect the environment and promote development.[3] The next in line was the World Conference on Human Rights (Vienna, 14 to 25 June 1993), whose concluding document, if compared with the bulky volumes put together at Rio de Janeiro, looks fairly modest.[4] In 1994, attention was focused on the International Conference on Population and Development (Cairo, 5 to 13 September 1994).[5] 1995 witnessed not less than two world order conferences, the World Summit for Social Development (Copenhagen, 6 to 12 March 1995)[6] as well as the Fourth World Conference on Women (Beijing, 4 to 15 September 1995).[7] Thus, within a relatively short span of time, a great part of the "international problems of an economic, social, cultural or humanitarian character" (Article 1, paragraph 3 of the U.N. Charter) that currently besiege mankind and, if unresolved, could in the long run threaten international peace and security, were addressed and received detailed answers, in any event at the level of political – and maybe even legal – discourse.

I. BACKGROUND

It is not easy to define clearly the rationale underlying the convening of all of these conferences at such an accelerated rhythm. It is a matter of public knowledge that every year the General Assembly looks into the broad range of issues that have repercussions beyond national boundaries. Environment and development, human rights, population issues, social development and the situation of women belong to its standard menu. And yet, as it appears, it was felt that a debate held solely among all-purpose diplomats

---

1 U.N. doc. A/CONF.151/26 REV. 1 (Vol. I) at 3 and 480.

2 All four instruments are reprinted (in:) 31:814 ILM (1992).

3 U.N. doc. A/CONF.151/26 I REV. 1 at 9.

4 *Vienna Declaration and Programme of Action*, U.N. doc. A/CONF.157/23, also reprinted (in:) 32:1663 ILM (1993).

5 *Report of the International Conference on Population and Development*, U.N. doc. A/CONF.171/13.

6 *Report of the World Summit for Social Development*, U.N. doc. A/CONF.166/9.

7 *Report of the Fourth World Conference on Women*, U.N. doc. A/CONF.177/20.

without any specific qualification for each one of the topics was not enough to obtain well-founded insights into the complexities of the many interrelated questions and that therefore broader participation of experts from all walks of life concerned was necessary. It may even be that governments wished to be able to mobilize and activate non-governmental organizations for a meaningful discussion of issues deeply impacting upon national policies and therefore requiring solid support from societies for their successful solution. It has indeed become a routine pattern that parallel to an official governmental conference a meeting of non-governmental organizations is held. Though at times disturbing and irritating for diplomats, these parallel meetings have the great advantage of focusing public attention on the tasks and objectives of the official agenda and thus providing a thrust to the negotiations which official delegations alone could not generate.

The fact, on the other hand, that in most instances no major ambition was pursued as far as tangible legal results are concerned has different reasons. In the first place, many problems tabled at the world conferences were so difficult, even thorny and almost unassailable, that no hope could be nurtured as to bringing about an agreed draft text of an international treaty. In particular, anything relating to population issues is rooted in such deep-seated national, ethical and religious convictions that the most that could ever be expected was to create awareness and understanding, coupled perhaps with some general formulae more suited to hide than to address the real questions. Additionally, the venerated international treaty looks fairly outdated as an instrument whose function it would be to address the complexities of societal development at the universal level. On one hand, it would be clearly impossible to lay down in conventional form every principle, recommendation or suggestion that has found its way into the concluding documents. Low legal profile was the price to be paid for the tremendous reach of these documents. On the other hand, since our time is moving faster than ever before in history, a legal instrument that may take years and decades to come into force would be overtaken by events even before that date. Urgent problems affecting humankind cannot be resolved through the traditional procedures of norm-setting at the international level. Conference documents as well as resolutions of the General Assembly therefore assume the functions which in today's nation State are discharged by legislative bodies in the form of statutory enactments.

II. COMPONENT ELEMENTS OF CONCLUDING DOCUMENTS

The output of the different conferences is characterized by certain common features and lends itself therefore easily to a classification according to those characteristics.

A. International Treaties

In some instances, new international treaties were drafted or adopted. As already mentioned, the Rio Conference opened for signature two new international conventions which had been finalized shortly before. However, this was an exceptional occurrence. Generally, the purpose of the conferences was not directed at creating new binding legal instruments as such. None of the subsequent conferences counts among its concrete results an international convention. Indeed, with regard to a great many of the issues considered by the conferences international treaties do exist already. Other issues are of such difficulty that it would hardly be possible to establish a legal regime in treaty form. As far as the draft agreements approved by the Rio Conference are concerned, in any event, no particular legal problems arise. These texts require to be put into force according to the procedures generally applicable for that purpose.

B. Declarations of Principles

A second component of many of the concluding documents are declarations of principles. In that regard, the Vienna Conference produced the simplest and most straightforward structure. Its concluding document, the Vienna Declaration and Programme of Action, consists, exactly as the name indicates, of two parts, namely a declaration, which sets forth a number of guiding principles, and a programme of action, which seeks to identify mechanisms and procedures suited to effectuate better than in the past the existing law on the books. A similar pattern underlies the report of the Rio Conference, where the Rio Declaration on Environment and Development sets forth the basic tenets whereas Agenda 21 deals with implementation issues. The subsequent documents all have slight particularities. At Copenhagen, a Declaration on Social Development was adopted alongside a Plan of Action. Within the Declaration, one finds a section on "Principles and goals" (B.)[8] as well as a section entitled "Commitments."[9] The World Conference on Women adopted the Beijing Declaration, a statement made up of the most diverse propositions,[10] as well as a Platform for Action.[11] At Cairo, a different technique was resorted to. Here, 15 principles constitute an integral part of the Programme of Action adopted by the International Conference on Population and Development.[12]

C. Plans of Action

The plans of action generally delineate strategies of implementation for the promotion of the manifold goals identified in the preceding declarations of principles. The reader is confronted with an almost dazzling mass of statements that request, claim, admonish, exhort and recommend. In general, the plans of action have been constructed according to a principle of accumulation. As it would appear at first sight, no great measure of control was exercised. The reader feels compelled to conclude that almost uninhibited leeway was given to every delegation to insert into the text any amendment it considered useful notwithstanding the fact that many times the same idea was already expressed somewhere else, maybe even in different places. Thus, a playground was opened to national delegations to cast into a common construction what essentially corresponded to individual wishes, and often exclusively to such individual wishes.

III. LEGAL ASSESSMENT

A. General

It need not be explicitly emphasized that conference resolutions as such do not count among the sources of positive international law as listed in Article 38, paragraph 1 of the Statute of the International Court of Justice. This proposition applies independently of the modalities of adoption. It stands to reason that a resolution objected to by a State cannot bind it notwithstanding its opposition. But even if a State has joined a general consensus, it is, in principle, not bound by a mere conference resolution. International confer-

---

8 *Op. cit., supra* note 6, at 9–11, paras. 25–27.

9 *Ibid.* at 11–26, paras. 28–29.

10 *Op. cit., supra* note 7, at 5.

11 *Ibid.* at 9.

12 *Op. cit., supra* note 5, at 14–17.

ences do not qualify as law-making bodies. When governments draft a text summarizing the results of a conference, they generally do not act with the intention to create binding law. Rather, their aim is to indicate a political course of action to be pursued in the future. Conferences are stepping stones for further international action. Even if agreement is reached in a final document, binding legal effects come into being solely if so wished by the parties concerned. Indeed, if governments intend to enter into a legal commitment, they always have the possibility to opt for an unequivocal treaty instrument. If they do not envisage the conclusion of a treaty, this reluctance shows that they are not prepared to obligate themselves in strict legal terms. The Final Act of the Conference on Security and Cooperation in Europe (Helsinki, 1975) – as well as the subsequent documents having emerged from the CSCE process – still today provide the most prominent examples of international instruments deliberately kept outside the realm of law.

B. Disclaimers and Reservations

And yet, in spite of what has been said, it is not too difficult for a lawyer to turn around the reasoning just expounded, arguing that if a government makes a formal statement, it must be held to comply with its own words. In fact, it can be shown that there was at times some uneasiness among States with regard to the conference documents reviewed here. As some of the formulations reveal, delegations did not always blindly trust the general characterization of conference resolutions, believing it necessary to shield themselves against their possible interpretation as constituting legally binding commitments.

The most instructive example of such a defensive strategy is provided by the Authoritative Statement of Principles for a Global Consensus on the Management, Conservation and Sustainable Development of All Types of Forests.[13] Although such a statement of principles, following the orthodoxy of Article 38 of the Statute of the International Court of Justice, could in no way be characterized as establishing true legal obligations, the Conference found it necessary to qualify the Statement by the words "Non-Legally Binding." Here, two goals were pursued at the same time in apparent contradiction. On one hand, the Statement is called "authoritative," on the other, every effort is made to relegate it to the field of politics. The fact that the diminishing characterization was considered desirable indicates that it would

13 *Op. cit., supra* note 1.

not be totally ludicrous to take the Statement as a point of departure for legal reasoning.

A similar strategy was pursued in Chapter 9 of Agenda 21, dealing with the protection of the atmosphere. Here, it was felt necessary to clarify the relationship between the relevant treaties (1985 Vienna Convention for the Protection of the Ozone Layer, etc.) and the propositions enunciated by the Chapter. In a specific sentence addressed to the issue, it is provided:

> "In the case of activities covered by such agreements, it is understood that the recommendations contained in this chapter do not oblige any Government to take measures which exceed the provisions of these legal instruments."[14]

In other instances, formal reservations were entered. Two categories of such reservations can be distinguished. On one hand, a number of representatives objected simply to the substance of certain paragraphs or chapters of the conference resolutions without caring too much for the legal or political character of the propositions set forth in the relevant document. Very quickly, the objections expressed by the Holy See to the concluding documents of the Cairo Conference on Population and Development[15] and the Beijing World Conference on Women[16] have acquired a certain notoriety. For the Holy See, it matters little what kind of preceptive value – legal or political – is attributable to the resolutions at stake. Even if every word pertained exclusively to the realm of political statements, a reservation made sense for it because it wished to neutralize the effects which any official statement, irrespective of its precise characterization, may or will have on societies. Many governments, on their part, also criticized the substance of the agreed formulae mainly on political grounds.

But some States specifically attempted to shield themselves against any undesired overspill of the resolutions at stake into the legal field. First and foremost, reference has to be made in this connection to the United States. At the closure of the Copenhagen Conference, the United States declared that it

> "understands and accepts that ... the Programme of Action, like the Declaration, is not legally binding and that it consists of recommendations concerning how States can and should promote social development."[17]

---

14 *Op. cit., supra* note 3, at 111, para. 9.2.
15 *Op. cit., supra* note 5, at 146–149.
16 *Op. cit., supra* note 7, at 161–165.
17 *Op. cit., supra* note 6, at 111.

A similar statement was made on the occasion of the adoption of the Beijing Declaration and Platform for Action:

> "The United States understands the phrase 'hereby adopt and commit ourselves as Governments to implement the ... Platform for Action' contained in the Beijing Declaration, and other similar references throughout the texts, are consistent with the fact that the Platform, Declaration and commitments made by States (unless such States indicate to the contrary) are not legally binding, and that they consist of recommendations concerning how States can and should promote the objectives of the Conference."[18]

A somewhat different approach was followed by the Government of Guatemala. It stated at Copenhagen that the "positions and commitments" of the country as set forth in its constitutional principles and domestic law could not be adversely affected by the concluding resolution, and at Beijing it declared that

> "Guatemala has the sovereign right to implement the recommendations contained in the Platform for Action in accordance with the provisions of its Political Constitution, national legislation and international treaties and conventions to which it is a party."[19]

Obviously, like the United States Guatemala feared that its approval of the concluding documents might be interpreted as a legal obligation taking precedence over any earlier national statutory provision or international commitment.

C. Bases of Legal Relevance

The reasons for this uneasiness, which was not shared as explicitly by the other delegations, are not difficult to identify. First of all, the language used does not differ much from expressions which are currently employed in drafting genuine legal instruments. The most challenging instrument in this regard is the Copenhagen Declaration on Social Development. Here, in section C. ten "Commitments" are listed, invariably structured in a well-organized manner. In an introductory sentence, the first words are: "We commit ourselves to..." Every such commitment is couched in brief and succinct language. Mostly, a specific goal is indicated. Thus, Commitment 1 reads:

---

[18] *Op. cit., supra* note 7, at 173.

[19] *Ibid.* at 160.

> "We commit ourselves to creating an economic, political, social, cultural and legal environment that will enable people to achieve social development."

As such, this formulation could also figure in a legal text, were it not for the breadth of its terms which shove it out of the field of legal thinking. In some of the inferences from the different commitments, however, a high degree of precision is attained. Thus, for instance, paragraph (I) under Commitment 9 specifies:

> "(At the international level, we will:)
>
> (I) Strive for the fulfilment of the agreed target of 0.7 per cent of gross national product for overall official development assistance as soon as possible…"

It is precisely this formulation which intrigued the United States, prompting it to enter the reservation already referred to.

Other documents are less categorical and do not lend themselves as easily to an interpretation that has legal connotations. One may note, however, the sentences in the Beijing Declaration whereby the governments participating in the World Conference on Women "reaffirm our (= their) commitment to" certain values and "are determined to" undertake specific actions. Additionally, whenever reference is made to principles, it is certainly not an arbitrary conclusion to assume that such principles reside on legal ground, all the more so if and when the language employed is phrased in clear and sober terms. Mention should be made, in this connection, of the Declaration of the U.N. Conference on the Human Environment, held at Stockholm in June 1972,[20] which set forth 26 "Principles" with such foresightedness and clarity that until today these principles have survived as the focal point of all efforts to promote environmental goals. Indeed, the Stockholm principles were integrated, with only slight variations, into the Rio Declaration on Environment and Development which, in order to take into account development needs, had to undergo a revision process and could not remain unchanged. A similar role could possibly be played by the "Principles and goals" of the Copenhagen world summit or by the "Principles" included in the Programme of Action of the Cairo Conference.

Every student of the sources of international law will be immediately reminded of the debate held on the legal significance of the resolutions of the General Assembly, which was masterfully summarized and synthetized

---

[20] U.N. doc. A/CONF.48/14 REV. 1.

by Krzysztof Skubiszewski in his reports to the Institut de Droit international.[21] Having become the numerically dominant element in the world forum, third world countries for a while attempted to use resolutions as an instrument of law-making. Many justifications were adduced to support the thesis that the General Assembly was a true international legislator. All of this has faded away. Politically, everyone has become aware of the fact that an alliance of like-minded countries is not in a position to overpower another group of States with a different ideological and political outlook to the world. Juridically, on the other hand, the position is not different inasmuch as a State or a group of States opposes a resolution or other legal act supported by a majority. As yet, majoritarianism has no right of abode in international law, except where specifically stipulated by international treaty. However, things are less clear when a State unequivocally manifests its agreement with a common position.

The judgment of the International Court of Justice in the *Nuclear Test* cases is a well-known judicial pronouncement.[22] But the consequences of the Court's characterization of unilateral declarations have never been fully explored. The Court held:

> "When it is the intention of the State making the declaration that it should become bound according to its terms, that intention confers on the declaration the character of a legal undertaking, the State being thenceforth legally required to follow a course of conduct consistent with the declaration. An undertaking of this kind, if given publicly, and with an intent to be bound, even though not made within the context of international negotiations, is binding."[23]

The logic underlying this explanation applies equally to declarations made by States not in isolation, but in conjunction with other States. Of course, the Court insists upon an important requirement. A legally binding effect is dependent upon the intention pursued by the declaring State. But when trying to identify the intention underlying a given declaration, recourse must be had primarily to its text because the Court derives its binding force essentially from the principle of good faith. It held:

---

21 *Preliminary Expose* 61:1 ANNUAIRE DE L'INSTITUT DE DROIT INTERNATIONAL (1985) at 29 ff.; *Provisional Report, ibid.* at 85 ff.; *Definitive Report, ibid.* at 305 ff. For the resolution of the Institut, adopted at the Cairo session in 1987, *see* 62-II ANNUAIRE (1987) at 274.

22 *Nuclear Test cases* (*Australia v. France*), ICJ REPORTS 1974 at 253; (*New Zealand v. France*), ICJ REPORTS 1974 at 457.

23 *Op. cit.,* at 267 resp. 472.

> "Thus interested States may take cognizance of unilateral declarations and place confidence in them, and are entitled to require that the obligation thus created be respected."[24]

If it is the legitimate expectation of a third State that deserves protection, then the manner in which a statement is drafted is the primary element to be taken into account and to be weighed. There may be many intentions which are pursued through a public declaration addressed to other States. Yet their governments cannot possibly start an investigation into the relevant motives. They must be able to rely on the plain meaning of the words that have been expressed. Otherwise, the declaring State would always find an easy way out to evade the obligations which the principle of good faith makes incumbent upon it.

Consequently, in order to rebut the presumption of a juridical connotation of what has been said, in particular of expressions like "commitment," solid arguments are required. As far as the parallel example of resolutions of the General Assembly is concerned, reference may simply be made to the provisions of the U.N. Charter which, in general, characterize acts of the main body of the world organization as mere recommendations. This characterization makes clear that States, when participating in a vote on a draft resolution in the General Assembly, do not act under the assumption that binding effects could result for them from their support of the substance of the text before them. However, there is no such clear-cut rule with regard to the resolutions of an international conference. As long as only the three sources listed in Article 38, paragraph 1 of the Statute of the International Court of Justice were recognized as possible bases of legal obligations, governments could be sure that anything outside those three categories could at the most be evaluated as an element of practice capable of being drawn upon in the search for a customary rule of international law. Inasmuch as even an informal declaration can now bring into being a juridical commitment, the distance from a political to a legally relevant statement has shrunk considerably.[25]

Yet, formalities have not totally lost their value as indicators of the intention of a State when making statements with regard to matters of foreign policy. One may safely assume that the less formal, the more spontaneous government representatives express themselves, the less an intention can be imputed to them to commit their country in a legally binding fashion. To be

---

[24] *Op. cit.* at 268 resp. 473.

[25] Formalism was also rejected by the Court in the *Aegean Sea Continental Shelf* case, 3 ICJ REPORTS 1978 at 39 ff. (even a joint communiqué can be characterized as an international treaty).

sure, concluding documents of international conferences are in a certain sense formal documents. Every delegation knows perfectly well what the real issues are. For that reason, a lot of care is invested in finding appropriate language which would reflect the existing consensus or at least paper over the remaining divergences that could not be bridged. In general, conference resolutions contain no element of surprise for delegations that have been actively participating in the drafting process.

It is another element which invites caution in assessing conference resolutions. Although there is no lack of formality, any outcome of a State conference is largely considered as provisional by all participating actors. Conference proceedings are generally crammed into a short span of time. There is no real opportunity to fully explore the scope and meaning of the formulations suggested for the concluding document – which pursuant to diplomatic usages is an absolute necessity in order to show that at least some progress has been reached. Only in exceptional circumstances, if a truly disastrous confrontation has arisen among the participants, do delegations refrain from publishing a joint communiqué. Additionally, all participants know that any commitment of major significance, designed to become legally binding in a true sense, is subject to parliamentary approval in almost every State. Thus, nobody really expects that the propositions enunciated in a conference document will be scrupulously heeded by all the States expressing their consent. The principle of good faith, the main basis of legal effects outside the scheme acknowledged by Article 38 of the Statute of the ICJ, does not apply under such circumstances.

A further consideration buttresses what has already been said. Generally, in drafting an international treaty, States display a large measure of caution. They invariably attempt to identify in the most precise manner their rights and obligations. Never do they enter into commitments which would tie their hands in all fields of life, wherever they may act at the domestic level to satisfy the needs of their citizens. Even a short glance at any one of the documents reviewed in this article, shows, however, that here almost any limitation *ratione materiae* has disappeared. The Copenhagen document is the most drastic instrument in this regard. There is hardly any area of governmental activity which is not affected by the requests and recommendations contained therein. The breadth of the "commitments" undertaken is so overwhelming that almost no room for sovereign decisions would be left if one had to conclude that the substance of the document pertains to the realm of law instead of falling under the rubric of politics.

Generally, account is furthermore taken of implementation procedures in assessing the relevance of statements whose legal or other nature may be in doubt. The documents under review all devote considerable attention to that issue. But it is never one single body which is entrusted with ensuring execution of, or monitoring compliance with, the conference resolutions. Invariably, all the competent bodies, including also private organizations, are invited to take an active part in the process. Indeed, in many fields there is no lack of institutions charged with responsibilities for the matters concerned. This is true, in particular, of human rights where under the aegis of the United Nations a whole network of international agencies has emerged. It is only the environment which would require more robust institutional support from a centralized agency vested with true decision-making powers. This deplorable lacuna was not filled in by the Rio documents, not with – standing the establishment of the Commision on Sustainable Development.

D. Indirect Legal Consequences

1. But legal reasoning cannot stop at this stage. Even if it must be acknowledged that none of the concluding documents is to be considered *per se* as a legal instrument giving rise to legal rights and obligations, the multitude of the propositions assembled therein could gain legal relevance as an elaboration of legal principles having their legal roots elsewhere, in documents of unchallengeable legal value. Thus, in particular, the Vienna Declaration has solid foundations in the two international Covenants on human rights of 1966 and the vast array of other treaties existing in the field of human rights. Likewise, the Beijing Declaration is in large part derived from the Convention on the Elimination of All Forms of Discrimination against Women. It is precisely under such circumstances that stimulating issues arise. Each time, the reader is summoned to put the question whether a given statement is just a political pledge or whether, in the last analysis, it can be traced back to one of the relevant treaties. It is one of the most salient characteristics of all the concluding documents that governments are invited to take action for the protection of the rights of individuals at the domestic level. None of the treaties underlying one of the conference documents referred to is as specific in this respect. Mostly, one finds broad statements of principles which leave it open whether governments are just prohibited from interfering with the rights set forth or whether the corresponding obligation has a wider scope in that governments are additionally required actively to ensure not only full enjoyment of a given right, but also full opportunity of enjoyment concerning the factual elements conditioning its actual accessibility. A current question in this regard is whether States have the obligation to protect a specific right also against negative societal influences. If it is not the State as such that engages in discrimination but if instead powerful private actors so behave – is then the governmental apparatus nonetheless required to take measures with a view to putting an end to such discriminatory practices?

An example may serve better to illustrate the meaning of the present train of thought. The International Covenant on Civil and Political Rights provides (Article 3) that the States parties "undertake to ensure the equal right of men and women to the enjoyment of all civil and political rights set forth in the present Covenant." This rule, no matter how generously it is framed, provides no clear answer to the issue of equality of men and women in society, inasmuch as the Covenant deals essentially with rights that are directed against the State as a complex of institutions vested with governmental power. In a bold step, the Human Rights Committee, already in one of its first General Comments under Article 40, paragraph 4 of the Covenant, expressed its opinion that Article 3 "requires not only measures of protection, but also affirmative action designed to ensure the positive enjoyment of rights."[26] Still, given the relatedness of this comment to the rights under the Covenant, one may wonder how far the Human Rights Committee would wish governments to interfere with relationships that exist between members of society without any involvement of the State. The Convention on the Elimination of All Forms of Discrimination conspicuously expands the scope of the obligation to fight patterns of discrimination by identifying a large number of fields of social activity where even private individuals should be debarred from discriminating against women. This applies, in particular, with regard to education (Article 10), employment (Article 11) and health care (Article 12). But none of the provisions of the Convention is as straightforward and in a way "radical" as paragraph 24 of the Beijing Declaration according to which all participating States are determined to "take all necessary measures to eliminate all forms of discrimination against women and the girl child and remove all obstacles to gender equality and the advancement and empowerment of women." Here, the scope of the statement is all-embracing and limitless. No boundary line *ratione materiae* is defined. Gender equality seems to become a general yardstick not only for States, but also for societies, without any distinction as to the inherent differences between these two forms of organization of human beings.

This is not the appropriate place to make an enquiry into the specific issue just referred to. Our aim is confined to demonstrating that declarations of

---

[26] General comment 4(13), II YEARBOOK OF THE HUMAN RIGHTS COMMITTEE (1981–1982) at 299.

principles can be used as an auxiliary means of interpretation that may provide helpful clues in the search for the meaning of rules set forth in an international treaty. Indeed, if all States agree that for the purpose of reaching certain goals laid down in such an instrument measures of a specific nature should or must be taken, one is almost compelled to conclude that they view these measures as a necessary inference from the premises which they themselves have established on the legal plane. Only one major counter-argument is easily available and can be relied upon. It is the realistic – or even cynical – observation that when adopting concluding documents of world conferences States are much more careless than when drafting the texts of international treaties. Whenever the language of an international convention is being negotiated, the general direction is clear. The final stage is to be the creation of a binding commitment. Accordingly, everyone involved in the process knows from the very first moment that the matter dealt with requires the utmost attention. At a conference which limits its ambitions to creating awareness for a certain problem and alerting public opinion, governments more often than not do not feel it worthwhile to resist the political pressures exerted upon them in particular from domestic groups to subscribe to the "agenda for a better future," as one could call by a common denominator most of the documents at stake.

In other fields, the relationship between established principles of positive international law and "principles" enunciated by a concluding document is even more openly visible. Principle 21 of the Stockholm Conference on the Human Environment has become one of the essential foundations of international environmental law. Its statement to the effect that on the one hand States have the sovereign right to exploit their own resources but that, on the other hand, they must ensure that such activities do not cause damage to other States is an accurate reflection of the difficult balance that must be established between two neighbouring States, each of whom is sovereign. Whereas the State engaged in an activity with physical repercussions beyond its borders can invoke its territorial sovereignty, the victim State can claim that its territorial integrity is in the same way protected by the basic premise of sovereignty. Accordingly, since sovereignty must always be qualified by the attribute "equal," some mutual arrangement is necessary. No State can be allowed to subject the territory of neighbouring States to its determinations as to the appropriate uses. Yet, on the other hand no State can expect that on the other side of the border any human activity that might to some slight extent affect the natural condition of its territory will stop. It is significant, in this regard, that principle 2 of the Rio Declaration has left principle 21 of the Stockholm Declaration virtually unchanged. There can be no doubt that the proposition formulated in 1972 and confirmed in 1992 can be directly derived from Article 2, paragraph 1 of the U.N. Charter and receives therefrom a legally binding character.

It is not a particularly original finding to note that even instruments which, *per se*, do not constitute acts vested with binding force, may contribute to elucidating the meaning and scope of legal norms enshrined in one of the groups of sources recognized as positive international law.[27] However, it seems to be worth stressing the particular suitability of conference documents adopted by consensus to be relied upon for that purpose. If no objections have been raised against a proposition set out in such a document, one may safely assume that the proposition describes or prescribes a form of conduct considered by all States not only as desirable, but also as just and practicable. When it then comes to interpreting the legal principle itself, the student will almost necessarily have to turn to an available elaboration whose legal value as such is certainly open to doubt. But the fact of its general approval makes it a powerful piece of legal argument. It is for that reason that, from time to time, clarifications have been inserted into the relevant texts with regard to particularly delicate issues.

2. While some of the conferences have broken new ground, others have been essentially confined to "reconfirming" legal rules already in existence. The Vienna World Conference on Human Rights belongs to the latter category. Indeed, the Declaration starts out with the words:

> "The World Conference on Human Rights reaffirms the solemn commitment of all States to fulfil their obligation to promote universal respect for, and observance and protection of, all human rights and fundamental freedoms for all…"

Legally, a rule or principle of international law requires no confirmation. In particular, legal prescriptions like those contained in the two human rights Covenants of 1966 have been conceived of as cornerstones of a world order based on peace and justice. And yet, the international community obviously considers it appropriate to recall the existence of those treaties and the commitments undertaken by ratifying them. This reflects the State of mind of a world where, in law as in any other field, developments have assumed such a fast pace that the past has to be recalled constantly in order to remain a living force capable to influence the present. For many developing countries, in particular, 1966 lies far back in a time when they had just ac-

[27] K. Skubiszewski has analyzed in great detail the distinction between law-declaring and law-generating resolutions, *see* his conclusion 5, *Definitive Report*, *supra* note 21, at 314.

ceded to statehood and independence. Although they may have joined the now massive group of States supporting the Covenants, their main concerns are generally directed towards other issues. For other reasons, industrialized countries, too, have a short-lived memory. Acceleration with its rejection of the past is a current phenomenon of the contemporary world. Declarations of reaffirmation or reconfirmation seek to counteract that pernicious trend. Although in a strict legal scheme there is no room for them, they play a vital role within a larger context focused not only on the existence of a legal rule, but also on its effectiveness.

3. It may be more of a political observation to note that all of the documents examined in the present study indicate a clear shift away from traditional ways of handling international law. In the past, legal methods were largely dominated by Anglo-Saxon thinking. Of course, none of the great writers ignored or could afford to ignore the basic principles of the international legal order. And yet, when it came to identifying specific rules for application in a given case, it was normally preferred to look for precedents that would provide a confirmation of an abstract principle. There existed a noticeable fear to resort to such principles directly, without having seen them stand the test of time and practice. The concluding documents reviewed here show a different trend. Of course, to the extent that they constitute nothing else than political statements it is fully legitimate for governments to use the grandiose words that constitute the central building blocks also in other political fora. Justice and peace belong to those core elements of political discourse everywhere in the world, whenever a group of human beings defines its political objectives. But there are also other parts that have a clear juridical connotation. One of the concepts stressed and highlighted like a leitmotiv is democracy. The Vienna Declaration mentions it several times (paras. 8, 9). But it appears even more frequently in the Copenhagen Declaration (paras. 3, 26(f) (= principles and goals), commitment 4(a)) and Programme of Action (paras. 7, 14(b), 15(d), 66, 67, 70, 71, 73(h)). Indeed, a notion like "democracy" cannot be reduced to a purely political slogan. If in a document of the kind discussed here emphasis is put on democracy and democratic institutions as the only acceptable form of government, this cannot be discarded as a *façon de parler* without any substantive importance. It means, stated in unambiguous terms, that any other form of government, given the specific circumstances of the contemporary world, lacks legitimacy and should not receive international recognition. In other words, the traditional rule according to which it was left to every State to organize itself internally according to the prevailing power relationships, has become obsolete. To be sure, many other hints and clues in international instruments point in the same direction.[28] The key provision in this regard may be Article 25 of the International Covenant on Civil and Political Rights. Yet, the Covenant confines itself to setting forth an individual entitlement which only through systematic integration hardens into a general principle of democracy. Therefore, the enunciations in the conference documents at issue push the pre-existing trend at least some inches further. They may constitute the one supplementary straw under whose weight dictatorships and authoritarian monarchies break down – unfortunately not as factual phenomena, but at least as juridically consolidated institutions.

An even more striking example is provided by the concept of "sustainable development." As is well known, sustainable development stays at the centre of all the resolutions adopted by the Rio Conference in 1992. In a true sense, sustainable development was understood there as a legal notion that formed the cornerstone of international environmental law and which, although its precise scope and meaning was to be elaborated and set out in greater detail, was *grosso modo* defined by the connotation of the word itself. In Chapter 21 of Agenda 21, the "basis for action" with regard to international legal instruments and mechanisms is identified as the "recognition that the following vital aspects of the" international "treaty-making process should be taken into account: (a) the further development of international law on sustainable development..." Somewhat later, reference is made to the necessity of examining "the feasibility of elaborating general rights and obligations of States, as appropriate, in the field of sustainable development." Of course it must be acknowledged that this sentence contains many provisos, caveats and reservations. One thing remains nonetheless clear. The task envisaged is to specify the legal regime of "sustainable" development, a notion which cannot be interpreted freely, but implies a definite political choice, namely that in framing the desired rules account must be taken of the long-term viability of any political project.

E. Matters under Domestic Jurisdiction

The statements enunciated in concluding documents of world order conferences may additionally have consequences that were not aimed at by participants but which nonetheless may be considered necessary inferences

[28] *See* for instance, TH. FRANCK, *The Emerging Right to Democratic Governance*, 86:46 AJIL (1992) ff.; C. TOMUSCHAT, *Democratic Pluralism: The Right to Political Opposition*, (in:) A. ROSAS, J. HELGESEN (eds.), THE STRENGTH OF DIVERSITY. HUMAN RIGHTS AND PLURALIST DEMOCRACY (1992) at 27 (40 ff.).

from the agreement manifested by all the participating States. What is tabled, discussed and determined by an international conference is or becomes a matter of international relevance. Otherwise, governments would have refrained from putting the matters concerned on an international agenda. Even the layman knows today that the field of activity of international institutions has considerably broadened over the last decades. The great turning point was the founding of the United Nations when human rights were placed under international care, although originally with some degree of reluctance (Article, paragraph 3 of the U.N. Chapter: "promoting and encouraging respect for human rights..."). The developments shown by the five concluding documents cannot be called revolutionary. But their intensity and the breadth *ratione materiae* by which they are characterized mean that a new dimension has been reached where the notion of matters under domestic jurisdiction tends to disappear altogether.

The resolutions adopted at the Rio Conference may in a certain way still constitute the most traditional ones of all the five documents. It has long since become an evident truth that many human activities produce effects outside the national territory where they are carried out. Water and air do not recognize national boundaries as man-made creations. Even destruction of ecosystems located within national territory may affect humankind as a whole. Already at Stockholm in 1972 many consequences were drawn from these undisputable facts. To construe the world in terms of isolated national sovereignties is a hopelessly outdated approach to the pressing problems of our time. Action directed at natural resources acquires almost necessarily an international dimension. To attempt to reach internationally agreed solutions for environmental problems remains therefore fully within the traditional logic of the inter-State framework of the international legal order.

Human rights issues are of a different nature. Notwithstanding the fact that the U.N. Charter made human rights a matter to be taken care of by the international community, actual implementation of human rights remains essentially under national competence. If violations take place, other States as well as the institutions of the organized international community are today recognized as actors entitled to intervene in varying forms and procedures. Suffice it to mention, on one hand, ECOSOC resolution 1503 (XLVIII) of 27 May 1970 with its notorious formula authorizing the Sub-Commission on Prevention of Discrimination and Protection of Minorities to take cognizance of complaints revealing "a consistent pattern of gross and reliably attested violations of human rights," and, on the other, Article 5 of the Second Part of the ILC's draft articles on State responsibility pursuant to which any State is to be considered an "injured State" if a right that has been breached "had been created or is established for the protection of human rights and fundamental freedoms" (paragraph 2(e)(iii).[29] Given the vast scope of the human rights instruments adopted by the United Nations in the course of five decades, the areas of unrestricted sovereign freedom have considerably shrunk, contrary to the general assumption that sovereignty constitutes the rule in the relationship between national and international competence, whereas matters falling under international jurisdiction make up for some rare exceptions from that rule. On the whole, therefore, nobody could have been surprised if the Vienna Declaration had been drastically more comprehensive in scope and substance than is actually the case. On the other hand, the Beijing Declaration and Platform for Action, although taking up a theme that was already addressed in 1945 by the Charter of the United Nations, namely gender equality, may indeed be a surprise for the reader. With a meticulousness of the utmost resolve, equality of the sexes is pursued into its tiniest ramifications and root causes. As it appears, the knowledge of all the women of the world about open and hidden discriminations was present at the Beijing Conference and was addressed to the greatest possible extent so that the Beijing document would seem to contain recipes for any ill to be cured.

Even more radical is the approach taken by the Copenhagen Declaration and Programme of Action. Here, the world is constructed anew from the premise that every individual has a right to lead a life in dignity without too much hardship imposed by negative external circumstances. There is hardly any spot of governmental activity in the economic and social field that is not covered by the statements in the Copenhagen document. In particular, the document seeks to explore all the necessary preconditions of material well-being, going as far as requesting

> "a stable legal framework, in accordance with our constitutions, laws and procedures, and consistent with international law and obligations, which includes and promotes equality and equity between women and men, full respect for all human rights and fundamental freedoms and the rule of law, access to justice, the elimination of all forms of discrimination, transparent and accountable governance and administration and the encouragement of partnership with free and representative organizations of civil society."

(Commitment 1(1))[30] as well as "democracy, the rule of law, pluralism and diversity, tolerance and responsibility" (Commitment 4(a)). In other words, a comprehensive catalogue of requirements of legitimate governance is established under the innocuous heading of "social development."

---

[29] II YEARBOOK OF THE INTERNATIONAL LAW COMMISSION (1993), Part 2, at 54.

[30] *Op. cit., supra* note 6, at 11.

Only one area of governmental activity has been left out from the Copenhagen document, namely armament and disarmament. Here, governments apparently saw a barrier that a social summit should not attempt to surmount. On the other hand, based on the premise that employment is the core theme of an economy centred on the human being, generous advice is given on how economies should be run in order to provide ample employment opportunities (Programme of Action, Chapter III, sub-section A: The centrality of employment in policy formulation). Unfortunately, the long lists of requests and recommendations confine themselves to formulating policy goals, without being able to indicate the strategies permitting to reach those goals.

The fact that States have more or less abandoned the notion that there exist specific fields of governmental activity exclusively under domestic jurisdiction does not mean that any State would be allowed to interfere with matters falling essentially under the jurisdiction of another State. The distinction between the principle of non-interference in inter-State relationships and the analogous principle applicable to the United Nations (Article 2, paragraph 7 of the U.N. Charter) acquires its full significance here. All the concluding documents create an opening for the international community, in whatever form it may be organized. They do not intend to remove the shield of national sovereignty *vis-à-vis* other States. Actions which the international community may legitimately undertake may still be off-limits for individual governments interested in a given issue. Notwithstanding this general observation, it is clear that, by letting grow and expand the scope of matters discussed on the international plane, a climate of greater openness has been ushered in which makes it difficult for governments to maintain that specific issues relating to their economic, social or even constitutional order may under no circumstances be touched upon by a foreign State.

IV. THE ROLE OF THE STATE

Essentially, the concluding documents assign to governments the task of implementing the manifold blueprints for action delineated by them. Throughout the texts, the State appears as the great provider able to deliver anything that is demanded of it. Yet, at the same time, and certainly under the influence of the many non-governmental organizations involved in the conferences, it has been acknowledged that without a massive involvement of societal forces all efforts would be vain. Agenda 21 identifies the actors whose co-operation is necessary in a most careful manner, each time with regard to the specific activity at hand. Although the Vienna documents, too, mention active participation by all sectors of the population here and there, the most far-reaching statements to that effect can be read in the Copenhagen Declaration on Social Development: "Our challenge is to establish a people-centred framework for social development to guide us now and in the future..."[31]

In the Beijing Platform for Action, reliance on co-operation of non-governmental organizations has at times been expressed in such strong and demanding terms that the United States saw fit to clarify its attitude to that approach by specifying that

> "when the Platform mentions the actions these other actors may take, it thereby invites and encourages the suggested actions; it does not, and cannot, require such actions."[32]

Thus, the tradition-honoured concept of a State that, seen from the outside, is impenetrable and impermeable, has lost its validity. States present themselves with all their internal complexities and fissures. Some day, this acknowledgement must have legal consequences in the field of State responsibility. Hitherto, the general assumption is that a system of governance, because of the state's internal sovereignty, can do anything that is not physically impossible. All of the concluding documents are based on a different perception. They view State and society as a co-operative configuration, the governmental machinery depending heavily on the output provided by societal forces.

Conclusion

Of all the concluding documents of the five world conferences examined in this article, the Vienna Declaration and Programme of Action contain the most modest statements, notwithstanding the importance of human rights as one of the pillars of international peace and justice. With the other documents, a new dimension of international intrusion into matters traditionally assigned to domestic jurisdiction has been attained. Agenda 21, the plan of action of the Rio Conference, first indicated the general direction. Its 470 pages set out a complete blueprint for the survival of mankind. If taken seriously, Agenda 21 would in many States absorb all the administrative capac-

---

31 *Ibid.* at 9 para. 24. *See* also, para. 26(a), as well as *the Programme of Action*, para. 8 (at 31).

32 *Op. cit., supra* note 7, at 175.

ities of the governmental system. Cairo, Copenhagen and Beijing continued on that route. According to our assessment, the highpoint was reached with the World Summit for Social Development at Copenhagen.

Some first commentators establish an overwhelmingly positive balance sheet of these conferences.[33] They seem to believe that the task consisted of tackling as many issues as possible in the concluding documents, listing all the sources of injustices, defects and malfunctions and proposing remedies for every single one of them. It is not the task of the lawyer to assess the effectiveness of this strategy. Yet it springs to the eyes that the means recommended are so demanding and far-reaching that even the best organized system of governance must have difficulties in trying to heed the recommendations in their entirety. Again, although in many places emphasis is placed on the necessary involvement of societies, *i.e.* of ordinary people, the State is conceived of as a bureaucratic machine of unlimited potential and capabilities. Just reading the Copenhagen and Beijing documents is a challenging undertaking which not many readers will succeed in carrying on to its end. Given the weakness of governmental structures in many Third World countries, the documents bear the appearance of typical products of the industrialized world with its huge bureaucracies that are masters in the art of producing heaps of printed paper which, more often than not, end up nowhere else than in a dust bin. It would certainly have been wiser to concentrate efforts on the most flagrant ills. But the specific dynamics of universal conferences apparently made it impossible to sort out the issues, differentiating between grave and urgent, on one hand, and less important issues, on the other. For the international lawyer, it is precisely this wealth of statements of all kinds that will lead him or her to believe that generally the concluding documents pertain to the field of policy and not of law.

---

33 *See* for instance, the evaluation by the International Commission of Jurists, 54 THE REVIEW OF THE INTERNATIONAL COMMISSION OF JURISTS (1995) at 111 (113); C. NICOLETTI, *Ripensare lo sviluppo partendo dalla gente. Riflessioni sul vertice sociale di Copenaghe*,. 617:V LA SOCIETA (1995) at 638.

Some Reflections on Kinds of Rules and International Law-Making by Practice

by

Karol Wolfke

In my contribution to the volume in honour of my eminent colleague and friend, Krzysztof Skubiszewski, I wish to refer to a few problems of our common subject of interest: international law-making.

Reflections on this subject are of necessity always connected with the supplementing of the generally criticized, but still recognized as basic, Article 38 of the Statute of the International Court of Justice.[1]

In 1945 to its original text of 1920 only one important phrase was added: [The Court] "whose function is to decide in accordance with international law," without any other additions or ameliorations. The Rapporteur of the United Nations Committee of Jurists, Basdevant, merely noted that "Article 38 was not well drafted," but "it would be difficult to make a better draft in the time at the disposal of the Committee."[2]

At present, however, in face of the amassed practice, it is already undisputable that to the triad (conventional and customary rules and general principles) at least yet rules made by international organizations must be added.[3]

Justified may be also to consider unilateral declarations of States creating legal obligations, referred to in the *Nuclear Test* Cases of 1974.[4] Decisive seems to be here the general argument that unilateral promises of States should be binding in virtue of the fundamental principle of good faith. Doubts arise only as regards some more detailed aspects, for example, the unilat-

---

1 *E.g.* in the *Delimitation of the Maritime Boundary of the Gulf of Maine Area Case* the Chamber of the Court stated: "... a chamber of the Court, in its reasoning of the matter, must obviously begin by referring to Article 38, paragraph 1...," ICJ Reports 1984 at 290.

2 United Nations, Documents of the United Nations Conference on International Organization, San Francisco (1945), Vol. XIV at 176.

3 The manifold law-making by international organizations is already undisputable and has been broadly discussed, among others, in several publications by Krzysztof Skubiszewski, *e.g.* (in:) *Forms of Participation of International Organizations in the Law Making Process*, 18:4 International Organization (1964), 790–805; and (in:) *Provisional and Definitive Report and Draft Resolutions, Thirteenth Commission, Resolutions of the General Assembly of the United Nations*, 61:I IDI, Session d'Helsinki (1985) at 85–325.

4 ICJ Reports 1974 at 22.

eral character of such obligations, consisting, in fact, merely in lack of any reciprocal obligation on the part of the beneficiaries of the declaration.[5]

As regards the broadly accepted by the drafters of the Vienna Convention on the Law of Treaties and in the literature norms of *ius cogens*, disregarding their very far from precision definition in Article 53 of the mentioned convention, they cannot, from the point of view of law-making, be classified as a separate kind of rules because they will always belong to one of the basic three kinds of rules of international law.

Numerous rules, which might be called mixed or intermediary ones, composed of both conventional and customary elements, deserve mentioning. They originate from treaties or customs.

Treaties with time become overgrown with practice of their implementation, more or less changing their original content. Whereas customs with time undergo various formulations and at least attempts at codification which unavoidably introduces new elements to the original custom-making practice. In both cases, then, new mixed rules arise, often essentially differing from the original ones. It should be noted that, in fact, every description of a live practice of necessity constitutes only its very approximate replica, like a picture of a living person.[6] Looking for examples, it suffices to remind the development of all the oldest branches of international law.

A separate consideration of such mixed rules, for example, in a possible amendment of Article 38, would be, of course, difficult. One must, however, at least be always aware of their existence and importance.

Whatever the chances for a formal amendment of Article 38 are, it is already certain that it must be changed, otherwise it is inapplicable by the Court.[7] May we, however, assert that this article has not been already amended somehow?

To give a positive answer to this question, it suffices to point to the law-making power of practice or even of single precedents, created by the conduct of States and their common organs, that is, mainly international organiza-

---

[5] *E.g.* Franck called the decision of the Court "a most useful step forward in international jurisprudence," T.M. FRANCK, *Word Made Law: The Decision of the ICJ in the Test Cases*, 69 AJIL (1975) at 617–618. Rather critical is, *e.g.* A.P. RUBIN, *The International Legal Aspects of Unilateral Declarations*, 71 AJIL (1977), 1–30. On promises in general, *see e.g.* A. VERDROSS, B. SIMMA, UNIVERSELLES VÖLKERRECHT, 3rd ed., Berlin (1984) at 430–431.

[6] The comparison was used by R.R. BAXTER, *Multilateral Treaties as Evidence of Customary International Law*, 41 BYBIL (1965–1966) at 299.

[7] *E.g.* the late President of the International Court of Justice, Sir ROBERT JENNINGS even stated that "to use Article 38 as it stands ... has a strong element of absurdity. *See The Identification of International Law*, (in:) B. CHENG (ed.), INTERNATIONAL LAW: TEACHING AND PRACTICE, London (1982) at 9.

tions. Precisely the already abundant practice of the latter, because of its easy accessibility thanks to special publications, is very instructive. As an example, one may mention the Repertory of Practice of the United Nations Organs where practice has not only been described, analysed and evaluated, but also recommended for codification. In several cases the arising of a precedent has been, however, expressly precluded, which, in fact, confirms the significance for law-making of even single precedents.[8]

One may, of course, question whether such accepted practice of the organs of the United Nations may always be qualified as true customary rules of international law. In certain cases doubts are certainly justified. The criteria should not be, however, too rigid. When a practice is followed and accepted by the organization and its members, there is no ground for hesitation to give a positive answer. More legitimate may be doubts about the category of such arising customary rules. In a considerable number of cases, however, they will fulfil the criteria of customary international law, binding the organization and its members at least for two reasons.

Firstly, there is a legitimate presumption that the practice of the international organization is known to all its members, and, in absence of evidence to the contrary, acquiesced in as law by all of them. Secondly, such rules, though in many cases merely procedural in character, but often very important, create, at least indirectly, rights and obligations also in respect to the member-States.

As a confirmation, the history of the customary amendment of the important Article 27, paragraph 3 of the United Nations Charter deserves to be reminded here as a, so far, not sufficiently appreciated illustration of the custom-making process in general.

The above mentioned Repertory reported:

> "During the period 1946–1954, sixty four decisions of seemingly non-procedural character were adopted by the [Security] Council by a vote in which one or more of the permanent members abstained. That the abstention of a permanent member otherwise than in accordance with the proviso of Article 27(3) does not preclude fulfilment of the requirement of Article 27(3) concerning affirmative decisions by the Council has been affirmed in the presidential rulings and by each of the permanent members. One permanent member has placed before the committee of Experts a proposal to embody this practice in a rule of procedure."[9]

---

8 REPERTORY OF PRACTICE OF THE UNITED NATIONS ORGANS, Vols. I–V, New York (1955) and SUPPLEMENTS N° 1–2, New York (1957, 1964). *See* also, J. KOLASA, RULES OF PROCEDURE OF THE UNITED NATIONS GENERAL ASSEMBLY, Wrocław (1967), 142–163.

9 *Ibid.* Vol. II at 81.

It has been stated in the same volume:

> "On certain occasions some elected members have expressed doubts regarding the legality of decisions taken when a permanent member has abstained. One instant is cited in the proceedings of the Council when such an objection was raised."[10]

In the Supplement of the Repertory no more opposition or reservations were recorded. We read there only that the practice "continued unchanged".[11]

In Supplement 2, Vol. II of the Repertory it is stated:

> "During the period under review, the Council adopted six decisions by a vote in which one of the permanent members abstained" and "such abstention did not preclude the fulfilment of the requirement of Article 27(3)... This was affirmed in the presidential rulings and by each of the permanent members."[12]

This practice has been acquiesced in also by other members of the United States and, for example, as Stavrapoulos stated in his article of 1967, "it can now be considered as a firm part of the constitutional law of the United Nations."[13]

A confirmation of this amendment of Article 27(3) may be found also in the Advisory Opinion of the International Court of Justice on *Legal Consequences for States of the Continued Presence of South Africa in Namibia (South West Africa)*. The Court stated, *inter alia*:

> "The proceedings of the Security Council extending over a long period of time supply abundant evidence that presidential rulings and the position taken by the members of the Council ... have consistently and uniformly interpreted the practice of voluntary abstention by a permanent member as not constituting a bar to the adoption of resolutions... This procedure followed by the Security Council ... has been generally accepted by Members of the United Nations and evidences a general practice of the Organization".[14]

It should be added yet that this practice, being clearly at variance with the text of Article 27(3), cannot be considered merely as its interpretation, but also is its amendment by accepted practice, that is, custom.

---

10 *Ibid.*

11 *Ibid.* SUPPLEMENT N° 1, Vol. I at 86, 272.

12 *Ibid.* SUPPLEMENT N° 2, Vol. II at 310.

13 C.A. STAVRAPOULOS, *The Practice of Voluntary Abstentions by Permanent Members of the Security Council under Article 27, paragraph 3, of the Charter of the United Nations*, 61 AJIL (1967), 737–752, at 752; F.L. KIRGIS, JR., *The Security Council First Fifty Years*, 89 AJIL (1995), 506–539, at 510–511.

14 ICJ REPORTS 1971 at 22.

The just reminded mechanism of law-making by means of acquiesced in practice certainly has been already applied to many other cases not yet expressly reported, among others, to the amendment of Article 38 of the ICJ Statute.

It should be remarked, in this connection, that customary rules need no express formulation for their arising and functioning. Such formulation, in fact, is indispensable only in cases of disputes and codification. Custom as ripe accepted practice is simply followed.

One must conclude, then, that precisely law-making by custom still constitutes an invaluable means for the development of international law in the present multiplied and divided society of States.

It exceeds, of course, the scope of this article to analyse the latest practice in order to ascertain new developing customs. Just for illustration, the rich activity of the Security Council described by F.L. Kirgis, Jr. in his recent article will be mentioned here.[15]

In the conclusion he states, among others, that the Security Council has in its history several times, in various ways, transgressed its competences. Lately this happened, for example, by establishing war crimes tribunals and by making quasi-judicial determinations "beyond those inherent in (the Council's) authority to determine threats of peace, breaches of peace and acts of agression."[16]

The Council has also gone beyond its authority to interpret and apply relevant Charter provisions. It has done so despite of its nonjudicial character and without procedural safeguards. The invented by the Council peacekeeping "has no even clearly implied basis in the Charter." Nevertheless, as Kirgis underlines, and what is particularly important in this case, "it has been widely accepted by the membership."[17]

More disturbing, according to the author, has been "the Council's tendency to invoke Chapter VII of the Charter without demonstrating who the threat of the peace is; the recent instances of quasi-legislation establishing norms for particular situations that go beyond what international law already required without any recognition by the Council, and the making of quasi-judicial pronouncements regarding the conduct of designated States or entities."[18]

In Kirgis's convincing opinion, "without the development of new justification for its acts, the Council would hardly have even the prospects of ful-

---

[15] L. Kirgis, *op. cit.*, *supra* note 13.

[16] *Ibid.* at 538.

[17] *Ibid.*

[18] *Ibid.*

filling its primary responsibility – the maintaining of international peace and security".

The author ends his article by stating that "the Charter continues to evolve, and so does the Security Council, not to the complete satisfaction of all legal or political observers, but it evolves inevitably nonetheless."[19]

One might only throw in here that this evolution, of necessity, takes place mainly by means of tolerated practice, namely by customs.

Lately, one may observe in the literature a growing criticism of the traditional requirement of State consent in international law-making.[20] As an example, also referring to the practice of recent decades, one may mention the interesting paper entitled *The Waning of the Requirement of Consent* by Elihu Lauterpacht.[21]

The author, writing on the Security Council, states that today "there are certain highly significant respects in which States have acted in a manner that shows in certain crucial areas an indifference to the need for consent." As an example he mentions the activities of the Council "acting as quasi-judicial body."[22] In particular, according to him, "it is not the task of the Council to pass judgment on the legality or validity of the conduct of the parties involved." Neither is it within the competence of the Council to pass a general judgment on a State, or a party to a situation, describing its relevant conduct as illegal or null and void. As examples, several cases have been mentioned, adding that "no evidence can be found of the specific consent of the interested parties to the exercise of that jurisdiction, nor any warrant in the United Nations Charter for the Security Council to pass such a judgment."[23]

The consent which may be derived from the membership in the United Nations, Lauterpacht considers "very remote from the occasion on which it was actually exercised" and that "such consent would apply only to members." The author adds, however, which is again very essential here, "that all the members of the United Nations have either participated or acquiesced in this conduct, since under Article 24 of the Charter the Security Council acts on behalf of all."[24]

---

19 *Ibid.* at 538–539.

20 *See e.g.* A. PELLET, *The Normative Dilemma: Will and Consent in International Law-Making*, 12 THE AUSTRALIAN YEAR BOOK OF INTERNATIONAL LAW (1992), 22–53; J.I. CHARNEY, *Universal International Law*, 87 AJIL (1993), 529–551; CH. TOMUSCHAT, *Obligations Arising for States Without or Against Their Will*, 241:IV RECUEIL DES COURS, ACADÉMIE DE DROIT INTERNATIONAL (1993), 195–374.

21 ASIL PROCEEDINGS (1991), 38–41.

22 *Ibid.* at 38.

23 *Ibid.* at 39.

24 *Ibid.* at 40.

The second example mentioned by Lauterpacht is no less striking. It is the manner in which the International American Commission on Human Rights (IACHR) has asserted a jurisdiction in respect to human rights violations "over a number of states that are not parties to the Inter-American Convention on Human Rights," *inter alia*, the United States. Nevertheless, as Lauterpacht states, "there have been at least four occasions on which IACHR has exercised jurisdiction over the United States." What is noteworthy here, however, that "for its part the United States has not objected to this exercise of jurisdiction, but merely has not participated in the procedure."[25]

So, in Lauterpacht's opinion, the consent must be again "traced to the United States' acceptance of the amendment of the Charter of the Organizations of American States and a resolution of the OAS General Assembly." But, according Lauterpacht, "these origins are very remote from the episodes in which the jurisdiction was exercised."[26]

The author mentions also other examples "contemplating comparable slender indications of consent."[27]

In his conclusion E. Lauterpach as "a real point" considers that all this practice is of a kind that States will find difficult to explain in the traditional language of consent. He thinks, therefore, that

> "... a fresh ... debate on the question of consent ... must not be conducted ... on the assumption that the requirement of consent is a political axiom resting on solid formulations of State practice. Any new debate must take the new and growing practice into account. That, in turn, means that we may have to change, or at the very least significantly qualify, our views on the assumed necessity for consent in all cases."[28]

This certainly interesting and original argument with the final conclusion do not seem, however, entirely convincing in the light of the present international reality and even of the above presented fresh practice.

The requirement of consent, whether we like it or not, remains not only a political, but also a solemnly accepted legal axiom, still resting on solid foundations of general State practice. The strong attachment of all States to their traditional sovereignty, manifested repeatedly on various occasions, confirm it. To neglect this fact in a debate on the question of consent would, therefore, inevitably result in its failure.

---

25 *Ibid.*

26 *Ibid.*

27 *Ibid.*

28 *Ibid.* at 40–41.

The misunderstanding probably consists here in the underestimation of the difference between the consent required in conventional and customary international law. In the former, the bulk of present international law, as we know, even active will of the State-parties is invariably required. Whereas in the latter one, as a rule, tacit acceptance of a practice as law, that is, consent mainly presumed on the circumstances of the practice, suffices.

The above discussed "fresh practice" has been in fact even expressly consented to even in treaties. The repeated by Lauterpacht argument that the old acts of consent, like consent derived from the membership in the United Nations, "were too remote from the occasion it was actually exercised"[29] is hardly tenable. States, nowadays, as a rule represented by expert lawyers, fully realize the importance and durability of the consequences of their consent given to treaties or to membership in international organizations.

From this point of view, the discussed fresh practice in fact does not constitute a striking novelty, nor any symptom of "waning requirement of consent". It is, however, a symptom of an important new trend of further considerable liberalization of the conditions of presumed consent to law-making practice, that is, a noteworthy progress in the present international law-arising process.

The reasons for such progress in all international law are easy to explain. They consist in growing understanding by States of their interdependence and hence necessity to consent to co-operation in more and more numerous fields.

In law-making by practice the liberalization is caused by modern means of communication and better knowledge of the international relations in general. States simply better and better know the practice and, what is even more important, know the growing presumption of their consent to it, when they do not in time react against it.

One should add yet that this growing law-making effect of tolerated practice is not confined to secondary matters, but, as could be seen above, to such important ones as peace or amendment of the U.N. Charter.

A final remark in connection with international law-making should be made yet as regards the frequent present concepts of replacing the allegedly no more tenable requirement of individual consent of States by a vague, still too abstract authority like the "international community as a whole" or even "mankind."[30] Such concepts, recalling the old ideal of *civitas maxima*, seem

---

29 *See ibid.* at 6 and 7.

30 *See* interesting arguments for such concepts in, *e.g.* CH. TOMUSCHAT, *op. cit.*, *supra* note 20, at 209–240. For critical remarks: P. WEIL, *Towards Relative Normativity in International Law*, 77 AJIL (1983), 413–442, esp. at 422–433 and 440–442.

to be still far from any legal usefulness. They in fact divert the world opinion from the actually developing perspectives for progress, consisting in voluntary solidary co-operation of States, among others, by creating by them common organs with the necessary competences.

The recent law-making by means of tacitly accepted practice seems to warrant some optimism in this respect.

Third Part

International Institutions

Ultra vires Activities of International Organizations

by

Rudolf Bernhardt

In the East Timor Judgement of the International Court of Justice of 30 June 1995,[1] Krzysztof Skubiszewski acted as judge *ad hoc* for Portugal. In his Dissenting Opinion he made several remarks concerning the problem of *ultra vires* acts of international organizations. In para. 70 of the Dissenting Opinion, he states: "Unless the Court finds that the Organization acted *ultra vires*, the Court's opinion cannot diverge from that law…" [the law of the United Nations]. In para. 85 we read: "The Court … cannot ignore the law of the United Nations as applied by the Organization's other principal organs provided they act within their Charter powers." And para. 86 concludes:

> "The Court is competent to make findings on their lawfulness [of the resolutions of the Organization], in particular whether they were *intra vires*. This competence follows from its function as the principal judicial organ of the United Nations. The decisions of the Organization … are subject to scrutiny by the Court with regard to their legality, validity and effect."

In the present short contribution dedicated to an outstanding international lawyer and an old friend,[2] some remarks will be made on the general problem of *ultra vires* activities of international organizations and their organs. We have to do with an extremely complex problem, and it is only possible to formulate some relevant questions which, however, still await convincing answers.

I

The existence and the competences of international organizations are based on legal norms, as a rule on a treaty concluded by States. The relevant

---

[1] ICJ Reports 1995 at 90; Dissenting Opinion of Judge K. Skubiszewski, *ibid.* at 224.

[2] Over many years, since 1972, Krzysztof Skubiszewski and the author of this article have been regular participants in Polish-German colloquies on problems of public international law and comparative public law.

treaty always attributes limited competences to the organization and its organs. Theoretically, one could imagine a treaty which leaves an organization entirely free to determine its own jurisdiction, but this does not occur in reality, and it would be hardly compatible with State sovereignty. No government and no national parliament would probably accept a treaty which gives an international entity unlimited regulatory powers. International organizations are and remain for the foreseeable future legal persons with limited competences. This holds true also for so-called supranational organizations like the European Community; the recent discussion on the principle of subsidiarity is one example of the reluctance of States to sacrifice their residual sovereignty by conceding more or less unlimited powers to international institutions.

These general considerations lead to our next question: Who determines the extent and the limits of the competences of an international organization and its organs? In the first place, the constitutive treaty is decisive, but its norms may be and are often vague and unclear; they need interpretation, clarification and implementation. There are good reasons for considering that the organization and its organs themselves are in principle called upon to determine their own competences as circumscribed in the treaty. But this power cannot be unlimited, and even a unanimous vote in an international organ cannot always be the last word. If in a given organ not all member States are represented, it is at least doubtful that the organ can take decisions to the disadvantage of all member States of the organization without any control. All organs have limited powers; they may be competent to take first steps in circumscribing their powers when taking decisions on the basis of the constitutive treaty. But the question remains whether States or other organs of the organization concerned can challenge such decisions as being *ultra vires*. The same question must be answered by an international court or tribunal which is asked to rule on the legality and validity of a decision of an international organization.

In a considerable number of cases, international courts have been asked to rule on the competences of an international organization. This started in the early years of the Permanent Court of International Justice when the Court was asked to determine the competences of the International Labour Organisation in the area of agriculture.[3] The International Court of Justice gave the famous Advisory Opinion on "Certain Expenses of the United Nations" in 1962,[4] and some years before it had already been asked to give its opinion

---

3 *See* the two Advisory Opinions of 12 August 1922, 2 and 3 PCIJ, Series B.

4 ICJ REPORTS 1962 at 151.

on the "Competence of the General Assembly for the Admission of a State to the United Nations."[5] Many other decisions and advisory opinions can be quoted in which international courts considered themselves competent to rule on the limits of the powers of international organizations.

What are the consequences of *ultra vires* activities of an international organization and its organs? Do the relevant acts remain valid; are they void or voidable? This question has found some interest in legal writings,[6] but much less in judicial decisions and opinions. The special problem of the validity and nullity of judicial and arbitral decisions has often been discussed,[7] but the questions connected with this problem can hardly be compared with the powers of international organizations and their organs. In the latter respect, recent developments may reveal a new dimension of an old problem. The Security Council of the United Nations has adopted under Chapter VII of the Charter binding decisions which have become possible only in the new international climate and because of the co-operation of the great powers.[8] Decisions taken in connection with and in the aftermath of the occupation of Kuwait by Iraq, especially the compensation rules against Iraq, appear to some commentators to be legally doubtful and *ultra vires*, beyond the competences of the Security Council.[9] The same problem arises with respect to the creation of tribunals for the prosecution of those who have committed crimes in the former Yugoslavia and in Rwanda. Do the provisions of Chapter VII of the U.N. Charter cover measures after the end of all hostilities? It is not the intention of the present remarks to give answers to these concrete questions.[10] But these new developments highlight the possibility and the problem of eventual consequences of *ultra vires* activities of international organizations.

---

5 ICJ REPORTS 1950 at 4.

6 *See* the basic article of E. LAUTERPACHT, *The Legal Effect of Illegal Acts of International Organisations*, (in:) ESSAYS IN HONOUR OF LORD MCNAIR (1965) at 88.

7 *See* K. OELLERS-FRAHM, *Judicial and Arbitral Decisions: Validity and Nullity*, (in:) R. BERNHARDT (ed.), ENCYCLOPEDIA OF PUBLIC INTERNATIONAL LAW (EPIL), Instalment 1 (1981) at 11; and Vol. III (1996) at 38, with further references.

8 *See* P.-M. DUPUY, *Sécurité collective et construction de la paix dans la pratique contemporaine du Conseil de Sécurité*, (in:) RECHT ZWISCHEN UMBRUCH UND BEWAHRUNG, FESTSCHRIFT FÜR RUDOLF BERNHARDT (1995) at 41; M. HERDEGEN, *Der Sicherheitsrat und die autoritative Konkretisierung des VII. Kapitels der UN-Charta*, *ibid.* at 103; E. MCWHINNEY, *Judicial Wisdom and the World Court as Special Constitutional Court*, *ibid.* at 705.

9 *See* B. GRAEFRATH, *Iraqi Reparations and the Security Council*, ZEITSCHRIFT FÜR AUSLÄNDISCHES ÖFFENTLICHES RECHT UND VÖLKERRECHT (1995), Vol. 55, at 1.

10 For the problems connected with the *Lockerbie* case *see* V. GOWLLAND-DEBBAS, *The Relationship between the International Court of Justice and the Security Council in the Light of the Lockerbie Case*, 88 AJIL (1994) at 643–5677. In respect of parallel activities of the Security Council and the ICJ, the competence of the Court to review decisions of the Council can become relevant; *See ibid.* at 663 ff. *See* also T. FRANCK, *The "Powers of Appreciation": Who Is the Ultimate Guardian of U.N. Legality?*, 66 AJIL (1992) at 519.

The main questions which arise in this context can be summarized as follows:

1) What are *ultra vires* – acts of international organizations?
2) Who decides whether an act is *intra* or *ultra vires*?
3) What are the legal effects of *ultra vires* acts?
4) What other consequences can follow from *ultra vires* acts?

In the following sections, we try to describe relevant factors in answering these questions. One word of caution may be added: Any abstract discussion of relevant principles must take into account that the interpretation of each constituent treaty and all relevant internal rules of a given organization may lead to different results. If an organization like the European Community comprises binding dispute settlement procedures with a court giving final decisions on acts of Community organs, the answers to the questions summarized above can possibly be deduced without difficulties from the text of the organization's "constitution." To give another example: In the context of the Law of the Sea Convention of 1982, the provisions on the Sea-Bed Disputes Chamber and its competences[11] can lead to results which are hardly possible in and for other organizations. In sum: The interpretation of a given treaty takes always precedence over general and abstract principles.

II

When are acts of an international organization *ultra vires*? A simple answer: When they fall outside the competence of the organization as determined by the constituent treaty (the "constitution") of the organization concerned. The general rules of treaty interpretation are applicable when one tries to delimit the competences under the treaty. These rules are codified in the Vienna conventions on the law of treaties,[12] but it must also be taken into account that treaties and among them especially "constitutions" of organizations are "living instruments" under which the organs develop the law of the organization beyond the original intentions of the authors. The greater the consensus among the member States of an organization, the easier is an evolutive interpretation of the constituent treaty. Much depends on the concrete circumstances.

The International Court of Justice has indicated, in the *Certain Expenses* Advisory Opinion, a possible distinction between *ultra vires* acts of the United Nations Organization and acts of its organs which fall inside the

[11] *Cf.* esp. Article 187 of the Law of the Sea Convention.

[12] Vienna Convention on the Law of Treaties (between States) of 1969 and Vienna Convention on the Law of Treaties between States and International Organizations and between International Organizations of 1986.

competence of the Organization, but outside the competence of the organ concerned.[13] Thus, the General Assembly of the United Nations may adopt measures which can only be taken by the Security Council. The distinction is interesting and important, but it is uncertain what consequences can be drawn.

Since the constituent treaty is the basis of all activities of an organization, and since this treaty determines and limits not only the competences of the organization, but also of its organs, it is difficult to draw different conclusions for acts which are *ultra vires* of the organization and acts which may fall inside the power of the organization, but outside the jurisdiction of the organ concerned. Both categories of acts violate the "constitution" of the organization, and the member States (eventually also third States) as well as other actors can claim that the organization and all its organs must respect the constitution. Therefore, the distinction indicated in the *Certain Expenses* Advisory Opinion of the International Court of Justice is of doubtful value. Good reasons can probably be invoked for the opinion that the distinction between acts beyond the powers of the organization and acts inside these powers, but outside the competence of the organ which has acted, does not lead to different legal consequences. Both categories pose the same or at least similar problems and require similar answers.

As already stated, it is the constituent treaty of the organization which determines the competences, and this treaty has to be interpreted in accordance with the general rules of treaty interpretation, as codified in the Vienna Conventions on the Law of Treaties. Of special importance is Art. 31(3) of the Convention which provides: "There shall be taken into account ... (b) any subsequent practice in the application of the treaty which establishes the agreement of the parties regarding its interpretation..." This includes the practice of an international organization and its organs. The precarious borderline between evolutive treaty interpretation, implicit and legally valid changes of the original treaty and *ultra vires* acts incompatible with existing law may require careful investigation in many cases.

III

Who can challenge an act of an international organization as being *ultra vires*, and who can finally decide this question? At least four alternatives or possibilities can be considered:

---

13 *See* ICJ REPORTS 1962 at 168.

1) The organ concerned determines its competence conclusively, and nobody can challenge the decision taken.
2) Other organs of the same organization may be entitled to challenge the decision taken by an organ as being *ultra vires*.
3) An international court or tribunal may declare an act to be *ultra vires*.
4) States may claim the right to neglect a decision which they consider *ultra vires*. For all these alternatives, arguments can be found; let us consider some of the arguments and some implications.

A. One can argue that each main organ of an international organization determines its own jurisdiction and competences with binding force, and nobody else has the right to challenge such a decision as being *ultra vires*. This would be an extraordinary solution because the organ could act like a sovereign, in spite of the fact that the constituent treaty concluded by sovereign States is the basis of the organization's activity and confers only limited competences to the organ. Therefore, it is hardly acceptable that an organ has always the final word in the determination of its competence.

An intermediate or compromise solution could be that the organ concerned decides finally and with binding force whenever it is not obvious that the decision is *ultra* or *intra vires*, and that only decisions which fall clearly outside the organ's competence can be challenged.[14] There are, in my view, good reasons for such a position, especially in relation to member States of an organization which should not be permitted to disregard decisions which they do not like by invoking the *ultra vires* doctrine. But it must be conceded that the distinction proposed – between obvious and doubtful *ultra vires* activities – carries with it uncertainties, and it will often remain controversial whether an act is obviously *ultra vires*.

In sum, international organizations and their organs are legally bound by the basic treaty or "constitution" of the organization, and this excludes an unlimited power to interpret the "constitution" with binding force in all circumstances. But it remains doubtful whether and how far "other actors" can challenge *ultra vires* decisions.

---

[14] *See e.g.* the *Certain Expenses* Advisory Opinion, ICJ REPORTS 1962 at 168: "When the Organization takes action which warrants the assertion that it was appropriate for the fulfilment of one of the stated purposes of the United Nations, the presumption is [*sic*!] that such action is not *ultra vires* of the Organization." The same should be valid for acts of the individual organs of the organization. *See* recently J.A. FROWEIN, *Reactions by Not Directly Affected States to Breaches of Public International Law*, 248–IV RECUEIL DES COURS (1994) at 349 at. 385: "Only in extreme cases could States argue that decisions by the Security Council under Chapter VII are null and void." *Cf.* M. HERDEGEN, *op. cit., supra* note 8, at 119.

B. Can organs of the same organization challenge a decision taken by one of them as being *ultra vires*? A first distinction can and must certainly be drawn: The principal organs of an organization have as a rule the possibility to create subsidiary organs, and it is hardly conceivable that *ultra vires* acts of a subsidiary organ are binding for the "mother" organ. Whenever a clear hierarchy between the organs exists, the higher organ is not bound by acts of the inferior organ considered *ultra vires*. (We come back to the special position of courts or tribunals created as "subsidiary" organs, see *infra*.)

Another rule should also be accepted: Whenever the law of an organization provides for a special procedure to resolve disputes between the organs, no organ should be permitted to challenge the decisions of another organ outside the prescribed procedure. This principle should apply, *e.g.* in the European Community.

No clear answer can be given for other disputes between the organs of an organization when their mutual competences are controversial. Can the General Assembly of the United Nations consider acts of the Security Council as being *ultra vires* and invalid? Has the Security Council a similar right to neglect decisions of the General Assembly? There are good reasons for assuming that each organ is competent to determine its own "constitutional" powers, and that the other organs are in principle bound to respect the determination. But is it not necessary to make exceptions? Must the General Assembly always approve the financial means necessary for an action decided under Chapter VII by the Security Council? We can only articulate some doubts without giving clear answers. Only the basic principle should be acceptable: Each organ of an organization is competent to determine its own jurisdiction, and other organs have in principle to accept this determination. But some limits do exist and must be recognized, even if the borderline is difficult to draw.

C. The existence and the limits of competences of an international organization and its organs are legal questions, and it is the proper role of courts and tribunals under all legal systems to decide legal questions with binding force. Therefore, whenever the law of an international organization provides for or permits a decision-making power of a court or tribunal, it must be assumed that this judicial institution possesses also the competence to scrutinize acts of the organization and to find acts of its organs *ultra vires* and therefore not binding.

The International Court of Justice has recognized the competence of the General Assembly to create an administrative tribunal which is competent to decide certain disputes with binding force, not only for the parties, but also for the organs of the United Nations Organization.[15] Similar competences of similar tribunals exist now in many international organizations,[16] and to all of them the rule should apply that any legal questions including that of *ultra vires* activities can and must be decided by the tribunal concerned. This is an exceptional competence of a "subsidiary organ" to adopt decisions which are binding also for the "higher" organ, an exception which is justified by the special role of judicial institutions. In the internal order of all States recognizing the rule of law, the situation is the same: Courts are competent to decide cases with binding force for those organs which have created these courts.

Some statutes of international administrative tribunals provide that certain questions can be submitted to the International Court of Justice, which adopts a binding ruling in the form of an advisory opinion.[17] Also in such a procedure, the ICJ must be competent to control acts of other organs and to find them eventually *ultra vires*.

More controversial may be the question whether the International Court of Justice may declare acts of other organs, especially decisions of the Security Council under Chapter VII of the U.N. Charter, *ultra vires*. Such a competence of the highest judicial organ of the world organization should and must be recognized.[18] It has already been mentioned that since the League of Nations in many cases the Permanent Court of International Justice and the present World Court have been invited to state their opinion on the extent and the limits of the competences of an organization. Nothing else should apply in relation to the powers of the Security Council. Its powers under Chapter VII are not unlimited, but bound by legal norms to be finally determined by the ICJ.

This competence of the Court can become relevant in different procedures. In inter-State disputes, a preliminary question can arise concerning the binding force of a decision of the Security Council. This is a question to be decided by the Court. The same competence to control acts of the organs of the organization exists in proceedings on advisory opinions. Such opinions are not legally binding, but other organs and States must be entitled to act on the basis of the Court's opinion.

---

15 Effect of Awards of Compensation Made by the United Nations Administrative Tribunal, Advisory Opinion, ICJ REPORTS 1954 at 47.

16 *See* G. VANDERSANDEN, *Administrative Tribunals, Boards and Commissions in International Organizations*, I(A–D) EPIL (1992) at 27.

17 *See* Judgements of the Administrative Tribunal of the ILO upon Complaints Made by UNESCO Advisory Opinion, ICJ REPORTS 1956 at 77.

18 *See* V. GOWLLAND-DEBBAS, *op. cit.*, *supra* note 10, at 663 ff., 669 ff., with further references. *See* also *supra* note 14.

The competence of the Court does obviously not mean that also the mere expediency of acts of other organs can be controlled by the Court, nor does it mean that the Security Council (like other organs) does not possess a certain autonomy and discretion when interpreting and applying the relevant provisions of the Charter. We are here only concerned with the legal (or "constitutional") limits of the competences attributed to the organs of the world organization by the United Nations Charter.

D. Probably the most difficult question concerns the right of the member States of an international organization to challenge acts alleging that they are *ultra vires*. A real problem exists only if decisions can be taken by majority vote or without the participation of all member States of the organization, and if such decisions are binding. Non-binding recommendations or binding decisions approved by all members may produce difficulties only in exceptional cases. A State is probably also estopped from challenging a decision which has been taken with its own consent.

Let us again take the United Nations Organization for illustrating the problem. The General Assembly takes decisions under the Charter by majority vote, and as far as such decisions (*e.g.* in budget matters) are legally binding and not only recommendations, all member States are bound even if they have voted against the decision. In the Security Council, less than 10% of the present member States of the Organization are represented, and only five States have a veto. It would hardly be compatible with the Charter system if member States could always challenge decisions of the two organs mentioned by arguing that the decisions are *ultra vires*. Majority rule and decision-making powers of the Security Council imply that all member States are in principle bound by rules and decisions adopted without their approval. This must, in the opinion of the present author, also apply with respect to the conformity of an act with the Charter. Were it otherwise, each State could reject a decision with the argument that it had been taken *ultra vires*.

On the other hand, the competences of all organs are limited. If, for instance, the General Assembly would order an armed intervention in one of the member States (or a third State), or if the Security Council tried to decide a boundary dispute pending, with the consent of the parties, before the International Court of Justice, would such measures be binding for the State concerned? This can hardly be correct. We come back to our tentative proposal that acts which are obviously *ultra vires* are not binding, but the others are.[19]

---

19 *See* also *ibid.* at 662 ("... under Article 25 members are obliged to carry out the decisions of the Security Council only if they are taken in accordance with the Charter") and *ibid.* note 103 with further references.

Some political scientists and other sceptical observers will probably ask whether these legal considerations are of any relevance in the political process where actual power and not judicial arguments are finally decisive. But the international lawyer cannot deny the existence of important legal questions which need legal answers.

IV

Are illegal acts nevertheless valid? Are they invalid *ab initio*? Or can they be valid until they are declared void by a competent organ? E. Lauterpacht has written the outstanding article on this subject, entitled *The Legal Effect of Illegal Acts of International Organisations*,[20] and he has investigated a considerable amount of material.

I must confess that, again, I do not see convincing general or abstract answers. Distinctions and differentiations are necessary. If one accepts a distinction between acts which are obviously *ultra vires* and acts where good arguments can be invoked both for and against their conformity with the law of the organization, only the first category of acts can and must be considered invalid or void *ab initio*. Where a special procedure exists for the control of certain acts, as in the case of the dismissal of international civil servants, acts pronouncing the dismissal are probably only voidable but not void. Other examples can be imagined: When the members of an organ have been appointed in violation of the constituent treaty, requirement of legal certainty can be invoked for the validity – at least transitory – of acts adopted by such an organ.

Our tentative conclusion has already been mentioned: Different cases require different considerations, and the consequences may also be different. In some cases, the invalidity of an act *ab initio* may be necessary, while in other cases more flexible solutions are advisable, in the interest of justice and legal certainty.

V

Finally, a few remarks should be made with respect to other consequences of *ultra vires* acts of international organizations.

The following problem has been widely discussed: Can or must the General Assembly of the United Nations insert in the budget means neces-

---

[20] *See supra* note 6.

sary for carrying out decisions of the Security Council (or other organs including the Assembly itself) even if these decisions are challenged as being *ultra vires*? Again, one and the same answer for all cases is hardly possible. The General Assembly must in principle accept the decisions taken by other organs, especially the Security Council, and insofar as these decisions have legal consequences for the Organization, the necessary means must be approved. On the other hand, if the Assembly is firmly convinced that acts are clearly *ultra vires*, it can hardly be bound to approve all expenditures connected therewith.

International organizations are legal persons and subjects of international law, and as such they have rights and duties not only towards their member States. They are responsible for their *ultra vires* activities, and an organization may be obliged to pay damages or to make other reparations. But the old question arises again: Who decides finally whether an act is *ultra vires*?

The final decision in a dispute should be left neither to the organization concerned nor to any other party to the dispute. Here again, international (and also national) courts should be the final arbiters. Otherwise, the dispute may continue to exist forever.

Les organisations internationales, entre gestion publique et gestion privée

par

Geneviève Burdeau

L'histoire des organisations internationales montre que leur apparition progressive au cours du XIXème siècle sous forme d'unions administratives, puis leur épanouissement dans la première moitié du XIXème siècle sont contemporains du développement, dans l'ordre interne, des services publics. Les premières unions administratives étaient, comme leur appellation générique l'évoque, des groupements internationaux d'administrations nationales. A partir de 1920, et plus encore au lendemain de la seconde guerre mondiale, le développement des organisations internationales est concomitante d'une extension, sur le plan interne, de l'intervention de l'Etat et du mode de gestion publique. Cette extension est particulièrement spectaculaire dans les Etats socialistes dans lesquels elle gagne tous les secteurs de la vie économique et sociale, mais elle est également significative dans bon nombre d'Etats à économie de marché, en Europe, en Amérique Latine et en Afrique, et même, jusqu'à un certain point, dans des Etats traditionnellement très libéraux comme les Etats Unis.

Il n'est donc pas étonnant qu'au cours de la phase d'intensification des relations internationales qui marque le milieu du XXème siècle, les organisations intergouvernementales se soient développées sous l'influence de droits publics internes marqué par l'édification de la théorie du service public, telle qu'elle a pu s'édifier en Europe et particulièrement en France, ou de ses équivalents dans d'autres pays du monde. La notion d'activité ou de mission d'intérêt général qui fonde la notion de service public en droit administratif français par exemple est au coeur des définitions proposées par les internationalistes pour les organisations integrouvernementales, même si les principes fondamentaux du régime juridique du service public en droit interne – adaptation, continuité, égalité, neutralité – n'ont pas été systématiquement transposés dans le cadre des organisations internationales. Il est clair cependant que nombre de principes, de règles, de méthodes administratives et de modes de gestion utilisés dans les organisations internationales se sont inspirés de ceux pratiqués dans les administrations nationales, qu'il s'agisse de la gestion du personnel, de l'organisation des services, de la gestion budgétaire et financière.

Sous l'influence des idées libérales qui prévalent depuis le début des années 80, les Etats ont adopté sur tous les continents des politiques nouvelles qui ont conduit dans le cadre interne à d'innombrables opérations de privatisation, à la remise en cause des modes de gestion publique et à la réduction spectaculaire du secteur public, non seulement dans les Etats socialistes mais aussi plus largement dans tous ceux qui étaient adeptes de l'économie mixte. Ce mouvement n'a fait que s'accélérer depuis le début des années 90. Dès lors que les Etats remettent en question très largement les modes de gestion publique sur le plan interne, il était inévitable que des interrogations et des remises en cause surgissent à propos des organisations internationales qui sont traditionnellement étrangères à la logique de l'organisation et des modes de gestion privés. Certes, même les organisations qui ont un objet technique ou économique, présentent également un aspect diplomatique qui peut freiner les velléités de remise en cause. Pourtant cette caractéristique n'est pas toujours décisive et, dans le cadre des efforts désespérés auxquels se livrent les gouvernements pour réduire les déficits publics, bien peu d'organisations peuvent échapper à une évaluation de leur «efficacité».

Au delà des difficultés budgétaires, qui ne sont pas forcément nouvelles, et des «crises financières» spectaculairement mises en avant dans la presse, on peut se demander si, compte tenu d'un particularisme d'organisation qu'il ne faut jamais perdre de vue, toute une série de caractéristiques traditionnelles du régime juridique des organisations intergouvernementales ne sont pas en train d'être remises en cause.

Les organisations internationales, notamment celles qui ont une vocation économique, ont joué un rôle non négligeable dans la diffusion des idées du libéralisme économique, qu'elle ont parfois imposées aux Etats lorsqu'elles en avaient les moyens.

Le rôle du Fonds Monétaire International et de la Banque Mondiale dans la mise en place par les Etats de politiques de privatisation et de réduction du secteur public est à cet égard bien connu. Paradoxalement, c'est l'extension de l'interventionnisme et du pouvoir de surveillance du Fonds consécutifs au 2ème amendement aux Statuts du Fonds Monétaire qui a indirectement favorisé cette action en faveur de la réduction du rôle du secteur public dans les économies nationales. Initialement en effet, le Fonds Monétaire ne pouvait offrir aux Etats qui en faisaient la demande que des facilités financières de faible durée (1 à 3 ans) moyennant des mesures correctrices désignées sous le terme de conditionnalité. C'est à la suite du 2ème amendement entré en vigueur en 1978 et notamment à la faveur de la mise en place à partir de 1986 de la facilité d'ajustement structurel (FAS), puis de la facilité d'ajustement structurel renforcée (FASR) rendues possibles par les ventes d'or du Fonds, que l'organisation a étendu le champ de la conditionnalité de ses prêts à des réformes de structures et a pu jouer un rôle accru en faveur de la réduction du secteur public et des privatisations. La Banque Mondiale, qui, depuis le début des années 80 a également développé les prêts d'ajustements structurels a oeuvré dans le même sens.

On pourrait également citer l'action de la Communauté européenne en faveur du développement de la concurrence, qui a largement contribué au cours des dix dernières années à réduire le champ des activités dites de service public soustraites par là-même aux règles de concurrence, à tel point que la notion même de service public ou de service universel en devient problématique, et qui s'est efforcée par l'élimination des subventions de soumettre les entreprises publiques à un régime comparable à celui des entreprises privées.

Dans le nouveau cours de la vie internationale qui s'est instauré depuis le début des années 90 le libéralisme va de pair avec la mondialisation accélérée de l'économie, c'est à dire le jeu de plus en plus libre des forces économiques internationales indépendamment de l'emprise des Etats.

Il était inévitable que les organisations intergouvernementales soient à leur tour touchées par ce mouvement d'idées et que leur régime juridique, leurs méthodes, leur place par rapport aux sociétés privées, voire l'existence de certaines d'entre elles s'en trouvent affectés. Les critiques, les doutes, voire la suspicion qui entourent aujourd'hui les méthodes de gestion publique et l'engouement corrélatif suscité par la gestion privée jugée plus efficace, ont des répercussions observables déjà depuis plusieurs années. Il est probable que la réflexion sur ces thèmes ne fait que commencer et s'amplifiera dans les années à venir, entraînant probablement de profondes mutations dans la structure et le droit des organisations. Pour l'heure il est sans doute trop tôt pour esquisser des tendances générales, d'autant que la diversité des situations des organisations, selon qu'elles ont un caractère technique ou politique, une vocation régionale ou universelle doit inciter à la plus grande prudence. L'objet des propos qui suivent sera plus modestement d'évoquer quelques questions récemment apparues en liaison avec le développement de la gestion privée et de la mondialisation, auxquelles certaines organisations ont été confrontées et qui pourraient s'étendre à d'autres organisations.

On évoquera ainsi d'abord la question de l'existence même de l'organisation, puis celle de sa participation à des activités privées et enfin celle de ses méthodes.

I. LA REMISE EN CAUSE DE L'EXISTENCE DE CERTAINES ORGANISATIONS AU NOM DU LIBÉRALISME ÉCONOMIQUE

Il n'est pas douteux que la mondialisation et l'affirmation de la supériorité de la gestion privée ont entraîné ou susciteront pour un certain nombre d'organisations des problèmes existentiels. On ne s'attardera pas sur la première organisation victime du «retournement du monde», pour reprendre la formule évocatrice de M.C. Smouts[1]: la transformation en économie de marché de l'ensemble de l'espace est-européen a eu en effet raison du Conseil d'Assistance Economique Mutuelle (COMECON) dont la disparition n'a guère suscité d'émotion ni d'ailleurs de commentaires juridiques. Peut-on y voir un exemple d'application à une organisation internationale de la théorie du changement fondamental de circonstances (article 62 de la Convention de Vienne) ou de la terminaison d'un traité par décision collective de toutes les parties contractantes (article 54b de la Convention de Vienne)?

En revanche les interrogations s'appesantissent sur le sort d'une organisation universelle comme l'ONUDI dont l'opportunité de la création avait, il est vrai, été sérieusement contestée par certains Etats comme les Etats-Unis. Cette organisation, dont la mission est d'intervenir en vue de favoriser l'industrialisation des pays du tiers monde est à l'heure actuelle l'objet d'une remise en cause fondamentale: au delà de l'efficacité de ses méthodes dans la promotion du développement industriel, c'est en réalité le principe même de son rôle qui est en cause. Les partenariats et coentreprises établis entre entreprises privées du Nord et entreprises publiques ou privées du Sud établis à l'initiative de l'ONUDI, qui pouvaient apparaître comme l'expression d'une sorte de pédagogie des méthodes de gestion privée et qui présentaient une assez grande originalité dans la panoplie des modes d'aide au développement, sont aujourd'hui discutés, tant en raison de leur bilan concret que sur leur opportunité en général. C'est l'existence même de l'organisation qui est actuellement en discussion.

---

[1] M.C. SMOUTS, LE RETOURNEMENT DU MONDE, SOCIOLOGIE DE LA SCÈNE INTERNATIONALE, 2ème éd. Presses de la FNSP et Dalloz (1995).

II. LES INTERROGATIONS SUR LES COMPÉTENCES ET LE STATUT JURIDIQUE DES ORGANISATIONS

A. Participation à des activités commerciales

Dans la palette des activités auxquelles les organisations internationales sont amenées à se livrer, la participation à des activités de nature commerciale n'est pas une hypothèse d'école. Etant donné la très grande liberté qui préside la définition du statut des organisations internationales, aucun principe de droit international n'interdit aux Etats fondateurs d'une organisation de doter celle-ci d'un statut adapté à ce genre d'activité. C'est ainsi par exemple que l'accord du 25 mai 1955 créant la Société Financière Internationale a eu précisément pour but d'autoriser cette organisation «en association avec des investissements privés, à financer l'établissement, l'amélioration et l'expansion d'entreprises privées de caractère productif de nature à contribuer au développement de ses Etats membres» (article 1). A cet égard, le rôle de la SFI, qui peut ainsi directement participer au capital d'entreprises privées, constitue une innovation par rapport aux modalités d'intervention de la Banque Mondiale, dont les prêts sont consentis aux Etats membres sur la base d'accords qui ont le caractère de véritables traités internationaux. Les statuts plus récents de la BERD (1990) autorisent le même type d'opérations[2]. Toutefois le statut classique de l'organisation internationale n'est pas complètement abandonné, notamment sur le plan des immunités. En effet si les statuts de la SFI prévoient (article VI) la possibilité de poursuites devant un tribunal d'un Etat sur le territoire duquel se trouve une succursale de la SFI, elle reste couverte, ainsi que ses biens et avoirs par une immunité absolue d'exécution. Les mêmes dispositions se retrouvent dans les statuts de la BERD (articles 46 et 47).

En revanche, la participation directe à des activités privées à but lucratif d'organisations internationales dont les statuts n'ont rien prévu à cet égard de manière expresse paraît plus problématique, même si la Charte constitutive n'édicte aucune interdiction formelle. Pour ne prendre qu'un exemple, l'Organisation des Nations Unies a été confrontée à plusieurs reprises à ce problème, notamment pour la participation à des activités d'édition. Plusieurs avis émanant du service juridique des Nations Unies se sont prononcés négativement sur la possibilité pour l'organisation ou certains de ses organes

---

[2] Statuts de la SFI et de la BERD à jour au 1er janvier 1994, reproduits dans: P. SABOURIN (éd.), ORGANISMES ÉCONOMIQUES INTERNATIONAUX. Documentation française, coll. Retour aux textes, Paris (1994).

comme l'UNICEFF ou le PNUD de prendre une participation ou de s'associer avec un entreprise privée d'édition ou autre[3], soit en vue de l'édition de cartes de voeux ou de publications, soit pour d'autres activités de nature privée. Dans tous les cas, les activités envisagées avaient un lien non discuté avec la spécialité de l'organisation.

Les arguments qui ont été invoqués à l'encontre de la participation de l'organisation tenaient d'abord à la soumission qu'entraînerait une telle participation au droit des sociétés de l'Etat de rattachement de la société privée. Cette soumission au droit interne d'un Etat membre a été jugée par le Conseiller juridique de l'organisation comme incompatible avec «le caractère et le statut» de l'organisation, essentiellement dans la mesure où, en général, le droit des sociétés implique la soumission, dans l'intérêt de la protection des tiers, à des contrôles (comptables, fiscaux etc...) et à des responsabilités spécifiques. Par ailleurs, la participation d'agents de l'organisation aux organes de gestion exposerait ceux-ci à des obligations également incompatibles avec les privilèges et immunités dont ils bénéficient.

Toutefois, si la participation au capital de sociétés privées est exclue, dès lors qu'elle n'est pas expressément autorisée par la charte constitutive[4], on a admis, notamment dans le cas de Nations Unies la licéité d'une activité fondée sur une base contractuelle par exemple pour des activités éditoriales ou de production de films. Pour cette dernière activité, la production est financée par l'organisation qui conserve les droits de propriété intellectuelle et de reproduction. Dans tous les cas où l'organisation conclut de tels contrats, elle veille à conserver un contrôle très strict des conditions d'exercice de l'activité concernée.

B. Soumission aux règles de concurrence

Beaucoup d'organisations ont comme fonction de fournir des prestations soit à leurs Etats membres, soit même à des particuliers. La question s'est posée récomment de savoir si ces activités de prestation de service qui, au départ avaient pu être organisées dans un esprit de service public, ne tombaient pas, compte tenu de leur nature économique, sous le coup des règles de concurrence. Inconcevable il ya quelque dizanes d'années, une telle question a été récemment examinée par la Cour de Justice des Communautés, s'agissant des activités d'Eurocontrol[5].

---

[3] ANNUAIRE JURIDIQUE DES NATIONS UNIES (1990), p. 256 et s.

[4] Les activités philatéliques de l'administration postale des Nations Unies ont été établies expressément par l'Assemblée générale.

[5] Affaire *SAT Fluggesellschaft*, Arrêt du 19 janvier 1994, Aff. 364/92.

Eurocontrol, organisation internationale instituée par une convention du 13 décembre 1960, modifiée par un protocole du 12 février 1981, se voit reconnaître par ces textes le pouvoir d'établir et de percevoir les redevances imposées aux usagers des services de navigation aérienne. La compagnie aérienne SAT Fluggesellschaft reprochait à Eurocontrol d'avoir méconnu les dispositions des articles 86 et 90 du Traité de Rome relatifs à l'abus de position dominante et à l'interdiction des aides d'Etat dans l'établissement des tarifs de redevances qui, pour des prestations équivalentes, variaient selon les Etat et les années. Posée par voie de question préjudicielle sur la question était de savoir si Eurocontrol devait être considérée comme une entreprise au sens des articles 86 et 90 du traité de Rome. Parmi les arguments invoqués, SAT faisait valoir que dans le droit communautaire de la concurrence, la notion d'entreprise désigne toute entité exerçant une activité économique, indépendamment du statut juridique de celle-ci et de son mode de financement, ainsi que cela a été admis par la jurisprudence de la Cour à propos d'entreprises publiques de droit interne.

Il est vrai que la jurisprudence antérieure pouvait prêter à interrogation et que la question de la soumission au droit de la concurrence de certaines activités menées par des organisations internationales, notamment dans le domaine spatial, a déjà pu prêter à discussion. Néanmoins la Cour n'a pas entendu franchir le pas: elle relève qu'Eurocontrol assure «pour le compte des Etats contractants des missions d'intérêt général dont l'objet est de contribuer au maintien et à l'amélioration de la sécurité de la navigation aérienne» et que l'activité relative à la perception des redevances de route «n'est pas détachable des autres activités de l'organisation». Elle ajoute que

> «prises dans leur ensemble, les activités d'Eurocontrol, par leur nature, par leur objet et par les règles auxquelles elles sont soumises, se rattachent à l'exercice de prérogatives, relatives au contrôle et à la police de l'espace aérien, qui sont typiquement des prérogatives de puissance publique. Elle ne présentent pas un caractère économique justifiant l'application des règles de concurrence du traité».

Elle en conclut qu «une organisation internationale comme Eurocontrol ne constitue pas, dès lors, une entreprise assujettie aux dispositions des articles 86 et 90 du traité».

Cet arrêt présente un intérêt tout particulier, tant par la définition qu'il fournit des organisations internationales que par la manière dont il aborde les activités économiques gérées par celles-ci. On retrouve en effet dans cette définition les éléments caractéristiques de la définition classique du service public: nature (mission d'intérêt général), objet (maintien et amélioration de la sécurité des personnes et des biens), régime juridique impliquant des prérogatives de puissance publique. Mais en outre la Cour se range à une vision globale de l'organisation, refusant de dissocier certaines activités qui pourraient, prises individuellement, être considérées comme comparables à des activités économiques ordinaires.

Ainsi le statut de l'organisation internationale en tant que statut public conserve son caractère attractif et, si l'on suit le raisonnement de la Cour, on peut douter qu'aucune activité conduite par une organisation intergouvernementale puisse jamais tomber sous le coup des règles de concurrence. En effet une organisation intergouvernementale ne saurait agir que dans son domaine de spécialité, si bien que l'on voit mal quelle activité menée dans un tel cadre pourrait être considérée comme «détachable des autres activités de l'organisation». En réalité il semble bien, qu'eu égard aux règles de concurrence, la prise en considération de la *nature* des activités de l'organisation s'efface devant celle du *statut* de celle-ci. Cette position est d'autant plus intéressante qu'elle diffère de celle adoptée par la jurisprudence européenne, tant communautaire que nationale, à l'égard des personnes publiques nationales (établissements public, collectivités trerritoriales).

Toutefois cette position de la Cour de Justice des Communautés européennes ne correspond pas à la position adoptée par la Commission dans le domaine des télécommunications par satellite à propos d'Eutelsat. Dans le livre vert du 20 novembre 1990 intitulé «Une approche commune dans le domaine des communications par satellites», il est souligné que la libéralisation du secteur spatial interfère directement avec les activités d'Eutelsat. La situation de monopole de fait occupé par l'organisation, puisque le secteur spatial d'Eutelsat est seul en mesure d'être utilisé pour la diffusion transfrontière par satellite entre pays européens, est assimilée par la Commission à un cartel tombant sous le coup de l'article 85 du Traité. Dans ses recommandations, la Commission préconise une révision de l'article XVI de la Convention Eutelsat afin d'ouvrir l'accès aux opérateurs, de manières non-discriminatoire et sur la base des coûts réels, du secteur spatial d'Eutelsat.

C. Structure de l'organisation

Une caractéristique traditionnelle des organisations internationales est de regrouper des membres qui sont des Etats. Ceci correspond à la vocation habituelle de l'organisation intergouvernementale qui est d'être un instrument de coopération entre Etats ou éventuellement entre administrations nationales. Cette caractéristique n'a pas soulevé de difficultés tant qu'un consensus a prévalu sur le caractère d'intérêt général de la mission de l'organisation. Normalement, ce caractère d'intérêt général consacré dans le cadre de l'organisation n'était que la projection sur le plan international de la conception que l'on se faisait de la mission en cause sur le plan interne. Ainsi, la météorologie ou le tourisme ont pu devenir l'objet d'une mission confiée à des organisations internationales dès lors que leur promotion au rang de mission d'intérêt général a été reconnue sur le plan interne.

A partir du moment où le caractère de service public de certaines missions traditionnelles se trouve remis en cause dans le cadre national, quelle va en être la conséquence sur le plan du statut de l'organisation? En particulier comment vont se traduire sur le plan de la structure interne de l'organisation intergouvernementale les conséquences du transfert à des sociétés privées d'activités précédemment considérées comme de service public ou l'admission du rôle d'opérateurs privés agissant en concurrence avec les opérateurs publics? Ces questions se posent essentiellement dans les organisations internationales à vocation technique.

La question, ici encore, est loin d'être théorique et se pose par exemple aussi bien à propos d'une activité traditionnelle comme le service postal que d'une activité d'apparition récente mais qui, pour des raisons de coût et de lien avec les aspects militaires, a été au départ gérée par les Etats dans un cadre de droit public, comme le lancement de satellites.

Dans ces deux domaines, qui seront sans doute suivis par d'autres, les organisations intergouvernementales se trouvent confrontées à la nécessité de tenir compte de l'évolution du statut des entités participantes. S'agissant de l'Union Postale Universelle, qui est une de plus anciennes organisations internationales, reposant traditionnellement sur la coopération entre des administrations nationales, l'autonomisation des activités postales dans un premier temps, telle qu'elle fut initiée il y a une vingtaine d'années par les Etats Unis et le Royaume Uni, avec la création d'entreprises publiques, puis la privatisation amorcée au début des années 90 avec la création de sociétés privées[6], risque de modifier sensiblement les conditions de la concertation internationale. La solidarité traditionnelle entre administrations postales nationales se trouvera confrontée à la concurrence entre organismes privés.

Cette dualité d'intervenants et la distinction entre le rôle dévolu aux *régulateurs*, qui, dans la société internationale demeurent les Etats, et aux *opérateurs* qui peuvent aussi être des Etats ou des administrations inter-

---

[6] En Europe, un des premiers exemples d'une telle privatisation de la poste est celle des Pays Bas dont les actions de la holding ont été placées dans le public en juin 1994, mais d'autres Etats, comme l'Allemagne sont en train de suivre la même voie avec la création d'une société anonyme dont les actions devraient être placées dans le public dans les prochaines années. Ce mouvement de privatisation se retrouve également sur les autres continents.

nationales mais qui sont déjà souvent et seront de plus en plus des entreprises privées, n'est certes pas une nouveauté: dans le domaine de la navigation aérienne par exemple, la distinction déjà ancienne entre la rôle dévolu à l'OACI et le rôle dévolu à l'IATA en est une illustration. Cette distinction organique a d'ailleurs permis au secteur de la navigation aérienne d'aborder en souplesse le tournant de l'ouverture à la concurrence des services aériens internationaux. Mais dans cet exemple il ya une nette distinction organique entre l'organisation non gouvernementale qu'est l'IATA, association de droit canadien regroupant les compagnies (publiques ou privées et plus ou moins distinctes des administrations d'Etats) et l'organisation intergouvernementale regroupant les Etats.

Cette distinction entre régulateurs et opérateurs paraît vouée à un certain avenir dans le domaine des organisations internationales et s'est traduite par des modifications institutionnelles récentes dans différents secteurs, mais les exemples suivants montrent que l'on tend à admettre plus facilement une coexistence des Etats régulateurs et des opérateurs souvent privés au sein même de l'organisation intergouvernementale.

Dans le domaine des services postaux, une vingtaine de grandes postes du monde, représentant plus de 60% du trafic mondial se sont regroupées dans une société commune, l'International Post Corporation (IPC) afin de lutter contre la perte de leurs parts de marché et d'améliorer la qualité du courrier international. Celle-ci s'efforce de définir quelle devrait être la voie à suivre pour les postes participantes entre la concurrence et l'esprit de service public.

L'IPC évoque naturellement le précédent déjà ancien, dans le domaine du trafic aérien, de l'IATA.

Mais c'est aussi l'Union Postale Universelle[7] elle-même qui s'est trouvée affectée par cette évolution: lors de son congrès de Séoul en 1994, elle a révisé sa charte constitutive afin de faire apparaître la dualité des intervenants dans le domaine postal, avec la dissociation entre les Etats régulateurs et les opérateurs, ces derniers étant de plus en plus constitués, dans le domaine postal, par des entités distinctes des Etats, notamment sous forme de sociétés privées. Il en est résulté la création d'une dualité organes nouveaux, Conseil d'administration et Conseil d'exploitation, en remplacement du Conseil exécutif.

La même dualité entre régulateurs et opérateurs avait été reconnue dès l'origine dans les statuts d'Eutelsat. Elle apparaît même dans la dualité d'instruments juridiques qui fondent l'existence et le fonctionnement de l'organisation, à l'image de ce qui avait été imaginé pour Intelsat. La con-

---

7 Créée en 1874, l'organisation regroupe 189 Etats.

vention portant création de l'Organisation européenne de télécommunications par satellite (entrée en vigueur le 1er septembre 1985) est en effet une charte constitutive classique d'organisation intergouvernementale conclue entre Etats souverains, cependant que l'accord d'exploitation signé de manière concomittante est conclu entre «les signataires», c'est à dire selon les cas des organismes nationaux de télévision ou des Etats parties à la convention. Ces deux instruments sont étroitement imbriqués juridiquement et l'accord d'exploitation est généralement considéré comme assimilable à un véritable traité international.

Dans le système d'Eutelsat, le capital de l'Organisation, nécessaire au financement de la construction et du lancement des satellites est souscrit par les «signataires», parties à l'accord d'exploitation qui, jusqu'à une date récente étaient des entités nationales (France Télécom, British Telecom, Deutsche Telekom, etc...) jouissant dans leurs pays respectifs d'une situation de monopole. Les signataires reçoivent, en contrepartie et en fonction de leur participation financière, un accès à un segment plus ou moins important du secteur spatial d'Eutelsat, avec la possibilité de sous-traiter éventuellement à d'autres opérateurs une partie de leur capacité de transmission par satellite. Le principe de l'investissement financier lié à l'utilisation du secteur spatial est un des principes de base du système et, chaque année, la part d'investissement de chaque signataire est réajustée en fonction de son pourcentage utilisation effective du secteur spatial d'Eutelsat au cours de l'année précédente.

Dès lors qu'Eutelsat est tenue, du fait de l'ouverture à la concurrence imposée par le droit communautaire comme on l'a vu plus haut, d'admettre un accès direct au secteur spatial au profit d'opérateurs autres que les signataires, se pose naturellement d'une part la question des relations de ces opérateurs non-signataires, qui sont en général des entreprises privées, avec Eutelsat, et d'autre part la question de leur participation au capital de l'organisation, dès lors que le principe du lien entre l'investissement et la capacité d'utilisation est maintenue. Ainsi cette évolution en cours devrait conduire à la participation financière d'entreprises privées au capital d'une organisation intergouvernementale.

Comme on le voit, les organisations internationales à vocation technique seront probablement confrontées, du fait de l'extension de la portée des règles de concurrence internationale, à imaginer des solutions nouvelles pour permettre l'accès de plus en plus fréquent d'opérateurs privés à leurs activités. Tout laisse à penser que cette tendance devrait se traduire par la mise en place de formules institutionnelles nouvelles et originales, dans lesquelles la frontière entre l'organisation intergouvernementale traditionnelle, constituée par des Etats et régie par des principes issus du droit public international et l'organisation non gouvernementale, devrait s'effacer pour donner le jour à des formules hybrides dans lesquelles agiront de concert Etats et opérateurs publics et privés.

III. LA RÉVISION DES MÉTHODES ET DES PRINCIPES DE GESTION

Les organisations internationales non-techniques ne sont pas non plus restées à l'écart des idées découlant du courant de libéralisme économique. Les idées de rationalisation et de recherche d'une meilleure efficacité des administrations internationales sont probablement presqu'aussi anciennes que les organisations elles-mêmes. Les innombrables rapports consacrés à ces thèmes, qui jalonnent par exemple l'histoire de l'Organisation des Nations Unies sont là pour en témoigner. Toutefois il semble que jusqu'à ces dernières années, les propositions d'amélioration et de réforme se rattachaient à un effort de rénovation administrative et à un souci d'adaptation de l'outil institutionnel aux évolutions de sa mission qui ne remettaient pas en cause un certain nombre de principes que l'on peut, certes approximativement, rattacher à l'idée de service public.

On peut se demander si, sous la pression de l'aggravation de la crise financière que connaissent beaucoup d'organisations, qui vient renforcer le poids des idées du temps en matière de gestion, les méthodes de gestion ne s'orientent pas de plus en plus vers les méthodes du secteur privé.

Certaines organisations techniques, en raison de leur objet même et de leur mode de financement, ont déjà adopté depuis longtemps des méthodes de gestion commerciale. Certaines y sont invitées par les dispositions de leur statut. Ainsi le préambule de la convention Eutelsat, dont il a déjà été question, prévoit que l'organisation doit fournir

> «grâce aux techniques disponibles de télécommunications spatiales les plus appropriées, les moyens les plus efficaces et les plus économiques, dans toute la mesure compatible avec l'utilisation la plus efficace et la plus équitable du spectre des fréquences radioélectriques ainsi que de l'espace orbital».

Toutes les organisations intergouvernementales à caractère bancaire ont également à respecter des impératifs de bonne gestion et de rentabilité. On connaît les critiques qui se sont déchaînées à l'égard de la BERD dans ses premières années d'existence, avant que celle-ci ne révise sérieusement ses méthodes et ne donne des gages de bonne gestion à ses actionnaires.

Les organisations internationales, ou du moins certaines d'entre elles ne sont pas non plus forcément à l'abri du mouvement de privatisation, aujourd'hui si répandu dans le monde entier. Tel a été le cas lors de la création de la société anonyme de droit français Arianespace, en conséquence d'une résolution du Conseil de l'Agence Spatiale Européenne du 3 juillet 1979, à laquelle les gouvernements concernés ont, par une déclaration du 4 octobre 1990, confié l'exécution de la fusée Ariane et transféré à titre gratuit l'ensemble des installations et équipements appartenant à l'ASE qui avaient été acquis ou construits dans le cadre des programmes de développement d'Ariane, ainsi que les dossiers industriels et les droits de propriété intellectuelle découlant des programmes de développement d'Ariane[8].

Des efforts importants d'amélioration de gestion et de plus grande efficacité ont également été déployés dans les organisations non-techniques, notamment depuis le début des années 90. Il est frappant de constater que ces préoccupations sont de plus en plus souvent évoquées dans les rapports des organisations, et particulièrement aux Nations Unies où il n'est guère de rapport du Secrétaire Général qui n'aborde ces questions. En pratique, le rapprochement avec les méthodes du secteur privé, qui paraissent devoir constituer le modèle de référence, se traduit par le recours généralisé aux outils et techniques d'évaluation et d'audit permettant de quantifier les gains d'efficacité des services[9], à la sensibilisation du personnel aux problèmes de gestion[10], à la réduction des «frais généraux», c'est à dire des coûts administratifs par rapport aux dépenses opérationnelles, à la réduction des effectifs et à l'introduction de nouvelles méthodes de gestion du personnel. C'est ainsi que lors de sa 49ème session, l'Assemblée générale des Nations Unies a adopté une nouvelle stratégie de gestion des ressources humaines qui met l'accent sur l'évaluation des performances de gestion des personnels de direction, sur la nécessité d'une formation plus complète, mais aussi sur la possibilité de procéder à des réductions de personnel par mise à la retraite anticipée et par la généralisation des contrats à durée déterminée. L'annonce récente de la suppression d'un millier de postes aux Nations Unies est la traduction concrète de cette nouvelle politique.

---

[8] J. CHAPPEZ, *Arianespace: première société commerciale de transport spatial*, JOURNAL DU DROIT INTERNATIONAL (1983), n° 4, p. 695.

[9] Ainsi dans une lettre adressée le 29 avril 1995 aux chefs d'Etats et de Gouvernements, le Secrétaire général des Nations Unies mettait en avant que «Plus de 30% de gains d'efficacité globaux ont été atteints dans le secteur des services d'appui communs. Les coûts de l'administration centrale inclus dans les services d'appui commun représenteront moins de 10% du budget total biennal ... L'installation mondiale du nouveau Système d'Information de Gestion Intégré doit être finalisée afin de fournir les données fiables nécessaires à la gestion de l'Organisation».

[10] Ce que le Secrétaire général dans la lettre pécitée appelle l'amélioration de la «culture de gestion du Secrétariat», afin de «renforcer sa performance et sa productivité».

Personne ne saurait contester sérieusement le droit pour les Etats, qui sont maîtres du budget de l'Organisation, de décider d'en réduire les dépenses et en conséquence de chercher à améliorer l'efficacité des moyens financiers qu'ils consacrent à celle-ci et d'éviter les gaspillages inutiles. On peut néanmoins se demander jusqu'où l'idée d'efficacité peut trouver à s'appliquer à des organisations intergouvernementales qui ne sont pas chargées de la gestion d'une activité précise comme c'est le cas pour les organisations à caractère technique ou financier. Il n'existe pas, jusqu'à plus ample informé, de méthode d'évaluation de l'efficacité économique des sommes que les Etats consacrent à leur diplomatie. L'époque contemporaine qui a tendance à généraliser l'évaluation des coûts et de la rentabilité[11] commence à prendre en considération l'efficacité économique indirecte de la démocratie, ce qui peut chagriner ceux qui estiment qu'elle n'a de prix. A quand une évaluation économique du coût de la non-existence des Nations Unies?

Ainsi il est probable que les organisations internationales ne resteront pas à l'écart du grand vent de libéralisme actuel et que leurs règles de fonctionnement en seront directement affectées. La souplesse et l'absence de formalisme du droit international autorise toutes sortes de formules possibles: l'existence et la variété de ce que l'on a pu appeler les établissements publics internationaux ou les sociétés internationales montrent qu'une grande diversité existe déjà et rien n'interdit de penser que toutes sortes de formes d'hybridation puissent gagner également les organisations intergouvernementales. Rien ne s'oppose à de telles évolutions, mais elles risquent de faire surgir de délicats problèmes de statut et de responsabilité: pourra-t-on continuer à faire bénéficier de privilèges et d'immunités absolus des organisations qui utilisent de plus en plus les procédés du droit privé? Pourra-t-on exclure la responsabilité des entités privées participant à de tels systèmes comme on l'admet aujourd'hui pour les Etats membres d'une organisation internationale?[12] Autant de questions que soulèvent ces évolutions.

---

[11] Ainsi des évaluations ont été avancées au cours de ces dernières années de la non-réalisation de l'achèvement du marché unique européen ou de la non-conclusion des accords mettant fin au Cycle de l'Uruguay.

[12] L'exemple de la failite du Conseil International de l'Etain montre que les règles du droit international public devraient dans doute être adaptées dans le cas d'organisations opérant dans le domaine économique. *Cf.* P.M. EISEMANN, *Crise du Conseil International de l'Etain et insolvabilité d'une organisation internationale*, AFDI (1985), p. 730 et s.

On the Procedural and Organizational Law Adopted by the Organs of the European Union

by

Jan Kolasa

I. THE PROBLEM

The speedy development of international organizations after the Second World War resulted in the abundance of problems connected with international law – both in its theoretical and practical dimension. First of all – international organizations as subjects of international law began to participate together with States in the creation of international law *i.e.* treaties and custom. As an entirely new element they introduced another form of law-making – that is their decisions of collective organs. As a result, the third source of international law emerged to embrace norms adopted by unilateral acts of collective organs of international organizations.

These resolutions can be divided into two groups. The first one would comprise norms addressed to member States of a given organization, giving them rights or imposing obligations upon them. The second group would contain organizational and procedural norms, binding exclusively within an individual organization. While the norms of the first group are rather an exception than a rule in practice, the decisions of the second type are unexpectedly abundant and their importance can hardly be overestimated within the scope of general international organizations.[1] The doctrine of international law has already recognized the significance of this new body of law. Several names have been cast for it. It is sometimes called "parliamentary law", "adjective law", but the most widely accepted name is "internal law of international organizations".[2]

---

[1] In the Polish doctrine the first scholar to take up and develop this problem was Prof. K. Skubiszewski, Uchwały prawotwórcze organizacji międzynarodowych [Lawmaking Resolutions of International Organizations], Poznań (1965) at 30–36 and *Forms of Participation of International Organizations in the Lawmaking Processes*, XVIII:4 International Organization (1964) *passim*.

[2] *See e.g.* P.C. Jessup, *Parliamentary Diplomacy. An Examination of the Legal Quality of the Rules of Procedure of Organs of the United Nations*, 89:I RCADI (1956) at 204; K.P.E. Lasok, The European Court of Justice. Practice and Procedure, London (1984), para.

The founding treaties of general international organizations limit themselves to determining general directions and means of the activity of their organs. It is usually only the most general procedural and organizational norms that are prescribed directly in the treaties. Their interpretation, development and even supplementing is left for the organs of a given organization. The scope of this competence determines the significance and substance of organizational and procedural norms (internal law of an organization in question).

Special mention must be made with respect to the so-called "rules of procedure".[3] They may be looked at as the most important sources of law of a given organization, just after founding treaties themselves. Rules of procedure form direct bases for the functioning of international organizations. Though such rules are not usually addressed directly to States (but to organs of an organization), they often influence their important interests.[4]

The subject of internal law of international organizations happened to attract a considerable interest of scholars dealing with international law. It is, however, true only with respect to the general international organizations. Strangely enough this cannot be said with respect to the internal law of the European Union. What we can observe here is the lack of publications on the matter. It is the aim of the present essay to attract more interest to this very subject, being understood that our considerations – devoted in a major part to "rules of procedure" – will limit themselves to general remarks.

II. NON-TREATY OR *SUI GENERIS* ACTS

The system of law of the European Union consists of two groups of norms. They are namely: primary law (we can describe its norms as constitutional norms) and secondary or derived law. While the norms of the first group are to be found in the treaties, the secondary law is made by the institutions of the European Union themselves, according to the rules prescribed in the founding treaties. In other words, the norms of primary law are con-

---

VII; P. CAHIER, *Le droit interne des organisations internationales*, 34:3 RGDIP (1963) at 563–602; W. MORAWIECKI, *Prawo wewnętrzne organizacji międzynarodowych* [The Internal Law of International Organizations], 1 PAŃSTWO I PRAWO (1969) at 36–46; J. KOLASA, *La notion de droit interne des organisations internationales*, III POLISH YEARBOOK OF INTERNATIONAL LAW (PYIL) (1970) at 95–110.

[3] J. KOLASA, RULES OF PROCEDURE OF THE UNITED NATIONS GENERAL ASSEMBLY. A LEGAL ANALYSIS, Wrocław (1967).

[4] *See* K. SKUBISZEWSKI, UCHWAŁY..., *op. cit.*, *supra* note 1, at 25–26.

tractual, treaty ones, the norms of secondary law result from unilateral resolutions adopted by various organs of the European Union.

The founding treaties of the European Communities contain provisions authorizing various organs thereof to make law. The three treaties determine exactly how and in what form this law is to be shaped. Both binding and non-binding acts may be adopted. The former ones may take the form of regulations, directives and decisions, the latter ones comprise resolutions and opinions.[5] Generally speaking, three institutions of the European Union are involved in the process of legislation: the Council, the Commission and the European Parliament cooperating with the Council. Their relative importance in a given case depends upon the procedure that is to be followed for the adoption of an act in question, but it is the Council that plays the dominant role in the process of the European Union law-making.

In practice, however, the legislation of the European Union is not limited to the process of the adoption of the above mentioned acts – which are defined in the founding treaties. There is still a group of norms escaping such a classification. They are usually called "innominate acts", "non-treaty acts" and simply "*sui generis* acts".[6] Among them "decisions" deserve special mention. Despite the very definition thereof inserted into the founding treaties, decisions are in practice made in different matters and do not confine themselves to the limits indicated in the treaties.

Among them we can easily find decisions regulating procedural and organizational matters. They determine the functioning of various organs of the European Union and the cooperation among them. D. Lasok called these decisions "the internal acts of the Community" that is "organizational law" thereof.[7] According to P.H. Houben "tous les actes relatifs à l'organisation interne des Communautés ... sont dénommés arrêtés" that is *sui generis* decisions.[8] R.H. Lauwaars observed that decisions dealing with the internal organization of the organs of the European Union were examples of "*sui generis* decisions".[9] Another eminent publicist J.V. Louis noticed that certain innominate acts had a purely internal character, forming "internal measures" concerned with the organization and workings of the

---

[5] *See* art. 189 of the EC Treaty.

[6] P.H.J. HOUBEN, LE CONSEIL DES MINISTRES DES COMMUNAUTÉS EUROPÉENNES, Leyden (1964) at 87–88; J.-V. LOUIS, THE COMMUNITY LEGAL ORDER, 2nd ed., Brussels (1990) at 88–91; D. LASOK AND J.W. BRIDGE, LAW AND INSTITUTIONS OF THE EUROPEAN COMMUNITY, 5th ed., London (1991) at 152–153; K.P.E. LASOK, *op. cit.*, *supra* note 2, at VII.

[7] D. LASOK AND J.W. BRIDGE, *op. cit.*, *supra*, at 152.

[8] P.H.J. HOUBEN, *op. cit*, supra note 6, at 83–84 and 87–88.

[9] R.H. LAUWAARS, LAWFULNESS AND LEGAL FORCE OF COMMUNITY DECISIONS, Leyden (1973) at 50–54.

institutions and subordinate bodies.[10] According to this author "innominate acts" are all acts that cannot be identified with any of the instruments provided for in article 189 of the Rome Treaty. Here we must cite once again P.H.J. Houben, who has expressed an opinion that not only regulations and directives, but also decisions named in art. 189 of the Rome Treaty "ont le caractère d'actes normatifs destinés à l'usage externe". So, they cannot include "des dispositions d'ordre interne régissant le fonctionnement ou l'organisation des institutions communautaires".[11]

What is missing, however, in the doctrine of international law is a more broad outlook at the very subject that would let us formulate a concept of the internal law of the European Union.

III. THE SOURCES OF COMPETENCE TO MAKE ORGANIZATIONAL AND PROCEDURAL NORMS

The founding treaties of contemporary international organizations usually contain provisions expressly authorizing their main organs or even subsidiary ones to make their own rules of procedure. This does not, however, mean that lack of such an express authorization is to be seen as a lack of competence in this matter. Both practice and theory share the widely accepted view that the right to make rules of procedure, or generally to adopt internal law, results from implied powers of international organizations. What is more, according to some authors such competences result from a norm of international customary law.[12]

There is, however, no unanimity among scholars dealing with the EC law in these matters. Additionally, what we find in their publications are only references – more or less elaborated. So *e.g.* Ch.-A. Morand expressed the opinion that the founding treaties of the European Union rarely make any provisions authorizing expressly the organs thereof to make rules for their internal order and functioning. According to this author, such competences are to be inferred from the whole body of norms concerning a given organ of the European Union and specially the powers of this organ.[13] Such a view is similar to the well-know concept of implied powers of international organizations for making their own internal law, though the author himself does not refer to it.

---

10 J.-V. Louis, *op. cit.*, *supra* note 6, at 89–91.

11 P.H.J. Houben, *op. cit.*, *supra* note 6, at 83–84, and 87–88.

12 *See* J. Kolasa, *La notion...*, *op. cit.*, *supra* note 2, at 101–105.

13 Ch.-A. Morand, La législation dans les Communautés Européennes, Paris (1968) at 185.

As regards the Communities, we must emphasize that it was already in the first of the founding treaties (*i.e.* the Paris Treaty on the European Coal and Steel Community) that express authorizations for the organs to adopt internal law were inserted. Article 25 of this Treaty reads: "The Assembly shall make its own rules of procedure by a vote of a majority of its total membership". Similar formulas are to be found in art. 142 of the European Community Treaty and art. 112 of the European Atomic Energy Community. It is just the Parliament that is expressly authorized to make its own rules of procedure. The doctrine, however, is of the opinion that "l'Assemblée, en vertu du principe de son indepédence, se reconnut competént pur établir son ordre de jour et fixer, dans son règlement interieur, la procédure de ses travaux."[14] It is also stressed that it is the basic characteristic of Community law that the organs of the Communities enjoy the right to determine independently their own internal activities.[15]

It is not only the European Parliament but also the Council and the Commission that are expressly authorized by the founding treaties to adopt their own rules of procedure. As regards the Council the respective provision is very succinct. It reads: "The Council shall establish its own rules of procedure."[16] The provision dealing with such a right of the Commission is more complex. According to it: "The Commission shall adopt its rules of procedure so as to ensure that both it and its departments operate in accordance with the provisions of the treaties."[17] As we can see, here also the aim of the rules of procedure is indicated. What is more, it is compulsory for the Commission to get its rules of procedure published.[18]

The respective powers of the Court of Justice are regulated in two treaties: the EC Treaty and EAEC Treaty. They provide that "The Court of Justice shall adopt its rules of procedure. These shall require the unanimous approval of the Council."[19] The lack of such a provision in the Paris Treaty is due to the fact that it was concluded together with the Statute of the Court (an international agreement) attached to it. The first version of the Statute (from 1951) provided that: "The Court shall establish its own rules of procedure. These rules shall contain all the provisions necessary for the application and, when necessary, the complementation of the present code" (that is of the Statute).

---

14 H. Manzanares, Le Parlement Européen, Paris (1964) at 132.

15 K.C. Bradley, *Maintaining the Balance. The Role of the Court of Justice in Defining the Institutional Position of the European Parliament*, 24 CMLRev. (1987) at 58–61; R. Bieber, *Achievements of the European Parliament 1979–1984*, 21 CMLRev. (1984) at 202–203.

16 Art. 30 ESCC, art. 151 EEC, art. 121 EAEC.

17 Art. 16 ESCC, art. 162 EEC, art. 131 EAEC.

18 Published in the Official Journal of the European Communities.

19 Art. 188 para. 3 EEC, art. 160 para. 3 EAEC.

It is astounding that the rules of procedure of the Court are to be approved also by the Council (by unanimous vote). The situation of dependence of the rules of procedure of one basic organ upon the consent of the other is familiar neither for international law nor for international practice. It is contrary to the principle of the independence of the basic organs of the European Communities and their autonomy with respect to the other organs in matters of internal functioning, procedure and organization. It is much more astounding if we realize that the very organ that happens not to be independent in these matters is an international court – in the full meaning of the term. On the contrary, even international arbitration courts or conciliatory commissions usually determine their rules of procedure themselves, this being understood that their freedom in those matters is determined by the respective international instruments.[20]

The early publications concerning the Court of Justice tended to concentrate on its freedom to determine its internal organization and procedure. It was believed to be a normal rule, as such a competence of international judges and arbiters was "traditionellement reconnue". The scholars emphasized that the Court of Justice determined its own procedure itself and that its competence in this regard was respected ("est respectée comme il se doit").[21]

The abovementioned opinions were fomulated with respect to the initial period of the activity of the Court of Justice – to be exact within the framework of the European Coal and Steel Community. Today such remarks are devoid of purpose and additionally almost completely forgotten.

IV. THE SUBJECTIVE SCOPE OF THE RULES OF PROCEDURE

A. General Introduction

The competence to adopt internal legislation (no difference as to whether it results from express treaty provisions, from implied powers or from the autonomy of organ) must, however, remain within the treaty limits. Such a competence must not only conform to the latter and should be aimed at the achievement of treaty objectives. The problem is that there is no indication

---

[20] *See* J. KOLASA, *Some Reflections Concerning the Evolution of International Arbitral and Judicial Rules of Procedure*, XIV PYIL (1985) *passim*.

[21] G. KNAUB, *La procédure devant la Cour de Justice de Communautés Européennes*, 3 REVUE TRIMESTRIELE DE DROIT EUROPÉEN (RTDE) (1967) at 271; L. DELVAUX, LA COUR DE JUSTICE DE COMMUNAUTÉ EUROPÉENNE DU CHARBON ET DE L'ACIER, Paris (1956) at 18; E.H. WALL, THE COURT OF JUSTICE OF THE EUROPEAN COMMUNITIES. JURISDICTION AND PROCEDURE, London (1966) at 181.

what procedural and organizational matters should be reserved for treaty regulation and which may or even should be left for the regulations of appropriate organs themselves. This problem is solved in a different way in different organizations and the diversities between organizations in this respect may not always be indicative as to the differences of the very character of a given organization or of a given organ. A matter regulated in a founding treaty of one organization may be recognized as a question to be determined by the interested organs themselves within the framework of another organization. It is the case with such important questions as: quorum, membership of organs, the choice of their members, presidents and vicepresidents, the creation of subsidiary organs and even voting procedures and the rules of arriving at respective majority of votes.

In practice, the relation and interdependence between the treaties and respective rules of procedure may be also very remote. In some cases there is hardly any direct relation between them. To illustrate this we should invoke here the example of the rules of procedure of the United Nations General Assembly as compared with the provisions of the U.N. Charter. We can easily distinguish three groups of provisions of the rules of procedure, the denominator being the relation thereof to the Charter. They are namely: a) provisions repeating U.N. Charter provisions *verbatim* or with slight modifications (there are seven such provisions), b) provisions based directly and expressly on appropriate provisions of the Charter (there are only thirteen such provisions), c) the rest of the rules of procedure. There are more than one hundred and fifty provisions of the latter kind. They are autonomous procedural and organizational rules, and their task is to interpret, develop and supplement certain Charter provisions or the Charter as such. Their common characteristic is that they neither repeat any articles of the Charter nor even invoke any of them as their bases.[22]

B. The Procedural Matters in the Practice of the Communities

The abovementioned practice of general international organizations with respect to their internal law is not reflected in the practice of the three Communities or – at present – in the European Union. The views presented by some scholars as to a considerable freedom of the Communities' organs with respect to their internal legislation are also not convincing. It is sufficient to have a look at the three founding treaties to find out that there is hardly any differentiation between the substantive and procedural matters, this differen-

22 *See* J. KOLASA, *op. cit*, *supra* note 3, at 72–110.

tiation being highly celebrated both in practice and in the theory of international law. What is specially astounding is the lack of a general voting majority for procedural decisions – analogous to the one to be found in the United Nations (*i.e.* simple majority of members present and voting).

The founding treaties of the three Communities themselves regulate several matters, traditionally regarded as procedural ones *i.e.* forming part of the internal law of the organizations, this regulation being often very casuistic. So *e.g.* article 161 of the European Community Treaty provides that the Commission may nominate its vicepresident or two vicepresidents. In the European Communities even staff regulations – usually forming part of the internal law of the majority of international organizations – are a product of a formal process of legislation and are issued in the form of regulations. What is very characteristic is the interference of the Council in the procedural and organizational matters of other organs of the Union.

C. The Content of the Rules of Procedure

There is no universal pattern of the rules of procedure of the organs of the European Union. While the rules of procedure of the Court of Justice are complex and detailed, the ones of the Council and the Commission are succinct and generally worded. The reason thereof is that the procedure of these latter organs has been already determined by the Treaties.

1. The European Parliament

Only a few provisions of the three founding treaties are devoted to procedural and organizational matters of the European Parliament. It was, however, sufficient to form the basis for the rules of procedure – comprising more than 130 articles. If we add to them also a few annexes, we will arrive at a brochure of more than 170 pages with the European Parliament procedural and organizational law.[23] It is the best evidence of the activity of the Parliament in this field. Only a negligible fraction of these provisions finds an express and direct basis in the Treaties themselves.

To prove this we will refer to an extremely important subject – namely the voting procedures – as regulated in the treaties and in the rules of procedure. The treaties merely provide that: "Save as otherwise provided in this Treaty, the Assembly shall act by an absolute majority of votes cast. The rules of procedure shall determine the quorum."[24] This short article is the basis

23 EUROPEAN PARLIAMENT. RULES OF PROCEDURE, 6th ed. (1991), at 1–169.

24 Art. 141 EEC.

of Chapter IX of the Rules of Procedure: "Quorum and Voting". In the subsequent articles (89–99) of this Chapter there are regulated the following matters related to the voting "Quorum", "Voting Procedure", "Separate Votes", "Order of Voting on Amendments", "Rights to Vote", "Voting", "Voting by Roll Call", "Electronic Voting", "Voting by Secret Ballot", "Explanations of Vote", "Disputes on Voting". Some chapters of the Rules of Procedure have, however, no direct connection with the Treaty provisions. This is *e.g.* the case of the chapter dealing with the Bureau of the Parliament (art. 21–25) or with political groups in the Parliament (art. 26–28).

It was just the Rules of Procedure of the European Parliament that formally sanctioned the activities of political groups in it, and prescribed the rules of their membership. These latter rules were published in the Official Journal of the European Communities. The Rules of Procedure not only recognized those groups but also gave them some rights. They include the right to nominate candidates for the President, vicepresidents and questors of the Parliament (art. 12), the right to representation in the broadened Bureau of the Parliament (art. 23 par. 1) and to interpellate the Commission, the Council and the Foreign Ministers meeting in the European Political Cooperation (art. 58). The political groups may also request the President of the Parliament to initiate a debate on matters believed by them to be of special importance (art. 61 par. 1). Those are only a few examples of the matters regulated exclusively in the rules of procedure.

Certainly, several provisions of the rules of procedure have only a formal character, but many others have an impact upon the results of the work of the Parliament. There are also a few rules that influence even the very rights and obligations of member States. It is sometimes said that some provisions of the rules of procedure "are specifically aimed at increasing the Parliament's influence in the legislative process and have been used to this end on a number of occassions".[25]

2. The European Court of Justice

The rules of procedure of the European Court of Justice are slightly shorter than the ones of the European Parliament. Its consolidated version published in 1982 has 133 articles grouped in 11 chapters and several annexes, additional regulations, instructions and so on.[26] As opposed to the Parliament, the Court

---

[25] E. KIRCHNER AND K. WILLIAMS, *The Legal, Political and Institutional Implications of the Isoglucose Judgment 1980*, XXII:2 JOURNAL OF COMMUNITY LAW STUDIES (JCLS) (1983) at 174.

[26] Published in OJ N° C 39/1 of 15 February 1982.

was able to base its rules of procedure not only on the founding treaties but also on the other treaty instrument – the Statute.

Of course, the scope of matters regulated by the rules of procedure could not coincide with the one of the treaties. So *e.g.* only one provision of the Statute (art. 21 – "Stages of Procedure") found its counterparts in two chapters of the Rules of Procedure – "Written Procedure" (art. 37–44) and "Oral Procedure" (art. 55–62). Even such an important question as the procedure of the preparation and issuance of judgments was regulated in the rules of procedure without any direct basis in the treaty provisions (art. 63–69 of the rules of procedure). As opposed to the other organs of the Communities, the Court was attributed a wide scope of powers in matters of internal legislation. Article 44 of the Statute provides that the rules of procedure of the Court "shall contain all the provisions necessary for applying and, where required, supplementing this Statute".

However, the rules of procedure of the Court are the result of a cooperation of two organs of the European Union – the Court itself and the Council, and their respective powers are not even on the par. It is the political organ – the Council that has reserved for itself the superior position by means of the right of approval of the Court rules of procedure.

3. The Council and the Commission

The rules of procedure of both the Commission and the Council are much less complex than the ones of the Parliament or the Court. Their rules of procedure formulate a few most fundamental and general principles. They happen to be both indispensable and insufficient for the smooth conduct of debate and voting procedure.

The Rules of Procedure of the Council count not more than 20 articles. All the same they usually have no counterparts in the treaty provisions. They regulate *i.a.* the summoning of the Council, preparation of the list of topics to be dealt with, the non-public category of the meetings of the Council, the procedure of inviting representatives of the Commission, voting by proxy, the procedure of voting, written procedure of voting on specially important and urgent matters, protocols of the Council meetings, the ways of signature and publication of legal acts of the Council, formation of committees and working groups, nominations and tasks of the Secretariat and Secretary General, representation of the Council in the European Parliament and in its committees.[27] The Rules of Procedure of the Commission regulate simi-

[27] Rules of Procedure of the Council of 24 July 1979, amended on 20 July 1987 (OJ N° L 268/1, 25.10.79, N° L 291, 15.10.1987).

lar matters and additionallly the question of substitution of members of the Commission and the possibility thereof to delegate powers.[28]

It was quite normal that such a narrow scope of regulation of the respective rules of procedure resulted in the abundance of loose procedural resolutions. What is more, in some cases it is the respective rules of procedure themselves that provide for such a way of supplementing the loopholes in the rules. *E.g.* art. 11 of the Rules of Procedure of the Commission provides for a further development of the procedure of its application. Also written rules of procedure are gradually accompanied by usages and customs.

D. General Conclusions

What should be remarked here is the narrow scope of the content of the rules of procedure of the Council and the Commission. Even despite the fact that several aspects of their activities are regulated directly in the treaties themselves, the importance of the Council as the main legislative organ of the Communities calls for more detailed official rules of procedure. The present ones are not sufficient for the normal operation of the organ. In practice unofficial collections of rules are utilized. They are to be found in procedural and organizational manuals of not quite clear legal character.[29]

It seems that the exceptionally wide scope of lawmaking competences of the Communities as compared with other contemporary international organizations should not lead to the disappearance of the differences between substantive and procedural norms, but on the other hand to the accentuation of such differences, the broadening of the content and significance of procedural norms. The more complex the system of substantive law is, the deeper interest and the need to develop procedure in the form of procedural resolutions (decisions) should be. In the practice of the Communities, however, not only treaties themselves regulate many procedural aspects, but also the normal process of legislation – the same as for substantive law – is widely utilized for the adoption of procedural decisions. Though the measures even when adopted in such a way but dealing with procedure must be classified as "procedural" and not "substantive" law, we cannot overlook the simple fact that the procedure of the adoption of acts classified in the treaties founding the Communities is more rigid and of a different legal character than the

---

28 *Règlement intérieur provisoire de la Commission,* OJ 181/6, 31.01.63, amended in 1967, 1970 and 1973 (OJ N° L 7/1, 06.01.73).

29 *E.g.* MANUAL OF OPERATIONAL PROCEDURES, 6th updating, February 1992 (Commission) at 166 and 24 annexes.

one involving only the interested organ shaping its own procedure in the form of *sui generis* acts.

V. LEGAL CHARACTER AND IMPLEMENTATION OF RULES OF PROCEDURE

A. A General View

Though the internal law of international organizations seems attractive for scholars, there is no unanimity among them as to the legal character of this law.[30] Avoiding a more detailed discussion on this subject, we can divide the views presented in this respect into three basic groups: a) treating the norms of internal law as treaty law[31], b) placing internal law within the broadened concept of international law[32], c) treating it as a new autonomous branch of law.[33] For some scholars the internal law of international organizations is simply an extension of treaty law, for others – a new branch and source of international law and for the rest of scholars – a new branch of law distinct both from international law and municipal law. There is, however, one common denominator of all these positions – namely they respect the binding force of this branch of law.

It seems, however, that the discussion of the same problem on the European Communities ground must take a different formula. This context of the question may even seem to be more simple than the former considerations. But it is not so.

First of all, we must remind that the Community law – as opposed to international law – disposes of a sophisticated system of sources of law. While international law is based on treaties and custom, the Communities law derives to a high extent from decisions of their organs. In consequence one may doubt if there is any need to distinguish another group of norms – *i.e.* proce-

---

30 *See e.g.* J. KOLASA, *op. cit.*, *supra* note 2, at 105–109 and literature quoted there.

31 D. ANZILOTTI, COURS DE DROIT INTERNATIONAL, Paris (1929) at 295–296 and P.C. JESSUP, *op. cit.*, *supra* note 2, at 213–221 and S. ROSENNE, THE INTERNATIONAL COURT OF JUSTICE, Leyden (1957) at 213–221.

32 H. KELSEN, THE LAW OF THE UNITED NATIONS, London (1951) at 193–194 and 703; H. WALDOCK, *General Course of Public International Law*, 106:II RCADI (1962) at 99–103; C.W. JENKS, *The Scope of International Law*, 31 BYIL (1954) at 46–47; P. CAHIER, *op. cit.*, *supra* note 2, at 571–590; K. SKUBISZEWSKI, UCHWAŁY..., *op. cit.*, *supra* note 1, at 30–31; P. REUTER, *Organizations internationales et evolution du droit public,* ÉTUDES OFFERTES À ACHILLE MEASTRE, Paris (1956) at 458.

33 L. FOCSANEANU, *Le droit interne de l'Organisation des Nations Unies*, 3 ANNUAIRE FRANÇAIS DE DROIT INTERNATIONAL (1957) at 325–344.

dural ones. Though unilateral acts, as a souce of substantive law, in other international organizations still amount to exceptions rather than to principles, the situation in the Communities is just the opposite. Here decisions (in a wide meaning of the word) are normal, every-day sources of substantive law. *A fortiori* – they may apply to procedural and organizational matters. So, we can satisfy ourselves with the conclusion that procedural and organizational norms form a part of the secondary law of the Communities. However, this is not so simple, as we will demonstrate. To this end a few introductory remarks must be made.

First of all, the secondary law of the Communities may be made only on the bases of an express authorization of the founding treaties. Secondly, there is no concept of a resolution as such in the Community law. Contrary, there are concepts of regulations, decisions and directives – each of them with determined objectives, forms, contents and addressees. The latter may be member States, physical or legal persons. Neither of these characteristics is possessed by resolutions being the sources of procedural and organizational norms of the particular organs. Such norms are not classified by the respective treaties but what is more – do not require any express treaty authorization. Various organs may make them on the bases of implied powers, excluded in the case of the adoption of acts named by the Treaty. Also the addressees of such norms are neither States, nor persons (physical or legal) as such. These norms namely concern the process of the functioning of various organs and are binding only in the internal sphere of their activity, this being understood that the effects of them may indirectly extend to States and individuals.

Last but not least, the way of adoption of organizational and procedural resolutions is different than the ones indicated for decisions, regulations and directives of the Communities. The latter require cooperation of two if not three organs, while *sui generis* decisions are adopted exclusively by the interested organ and their application is limited to the functioning of this very organ. The only exception here is the abovementioned right of the Council to approve the rules of procedure of the Court of Justice.

Consequently, the organizational and procedural norms of the Communities originate from *sui generis* decisions – distinct from the acts named by the treaties. Such norms result from different procedures and possess different legal characteristics than the nominated acts. From this point of view, organizational and procedural norms form a separate branch of law in the legal system of the Communities.

B. Interpretation and Application

The legal character of procedural and organizational norms is not uniform. Not all *sui generis* acts are binding. They may take the form of non-binding guidelines or recommendations. In this essay, however, we will concentrate our attention on rules of procedure, the binding force of which is beyond any doubt. Such acts are just made to be binding upon organs as such and their members as well. This view is generally shared both by scholars and practitioners. Sometimes, however, the internal law of international organizations is characterized as a soft law – with a doubtful binding force. A reservation should be made here.

Both practice and normative acts evidence that one of the basic tasks of the presidents (chairmen) of collective organs is to ensure observance of the rules of procedure. *E.g.* art. 18 para. 1 and 2 of the Rules of Procedure of the European Parliament read as follows: "The President shall direct all the activities of the Parliament and of its bodies under the conditions laid down in these rules. ... The duties of the President shall be ... to ensure observance of these rules...". To this end different measures may be used – *e.g.* the limitation of a pronouncement (pleadings) or even putting it to an end. The presidents are, however, subordinated to organs which they conduct. It is the interested organ and not its president that has the last word as to the interpretation and application of the rules of procedure. If the interpretation by the president is not correct, the other members of an organ may oppose to it and refer the question to the organ as such. So *e.g.* rule 131 of the Rules of Procedure of the European Parliament reads as follows:

"1. Should doubt arise over the application or interpretation of these Rules of Procedure, the President may ... refer the matter to the committee responsible for examination...

4. Should a political group or at least thirteen Members contest the committee's interpretation, the matter shall be put to the vote in Parliament."

In the European Communities an infringement of procedural norms may be ground for an action for the annulment of an act adopted in such a way. Art. 173 of the EC Treaty provides that the Court of Justice shall be able to review the legality of acts adopted by the Communities and "shall for this purpose have jurisdiction in actions brought by a Member State, the Council or the Commission on grounds of lack of competence, infringement of an essential procedural requirement ... or of any rule of law relating to its application...". It seems to us that both references to "essential procedural requirement" and to "any rule of law" apply also to organizational and procedural norms adopted by the organs of the Communities. Such a conclusion is additionally supported by the practice.

The Court of Justice annuled *e.g.* a directive adopted by the Council of Ministers in breach of art. 6 par. 1 of its Rules of Procedure. The Court stated that: "... Le Conseil est tenu de respecter la règle de procedure qu'il a lui même fixée à l'article 6, paragraph 1, de son règlement intérieur. Il ne saurait s'en écarter, même à une majorité plus forte que celle exigée pour l'adoption ou la modification du règlement intérieur, sans modifier formellement ce règlement ... La Cour déclare et arrête: 1. La Directive 85/649 du Conseil ... est annulée."[34]

Essential procedural requirement need not be based on any specially important substantial provision of the rules of procedure concerning the legislative process itself. The Court *e.g.* requires strict adherence to the provisions of the rules of procedure dealing with terms for filing official documents. The Court even ruled that an application filed not in conformity with art. 37 par. 3 of its Rules of Procedure is a defect that could not be rectified.[35]

The Court also questioned the competence of the Commission to delegate some of its rights. In one of the cases the Court distinguished, however, the delegation of the powers from a mere authorization to sign an act given by a member of the Commission to a Director General. In the opinion of the Court the latter is a matter of the internal rules of the Commission. In fact the authorization in question was found to be in conformity with art. 27 of the Provisional Rules of Procedure of the Commission and the application for annulment was dismissed.[36] On the other hand an actual infringement of procedure – a mistake in the communication of a document – was not believed by the Court to constitute an infringement of an essential procedural requirement. In consequence the Court did not annul the act in question and denied the application.[37]

However, procedural and organizational norms should be flexible, sensitive to changes of situation in order to adapt themselves to the requirements of the day. Provisions providing for such a flexibility are inserted into the

---

34 Affair 68/86 *Royaume-Uni de Grands-Britagne et d'Irlande du Nord contre le Conseil des Communautés Européennes*, II Recueil (1988) at 902–903.

35 *See* XI ILM (1972) at 1215 and 1117. *See* some other cases of this kind, (in:) J.A. Uscher, European Court Practice, London (1983) at 59.

36 *European Court of Justice Decision in Imperial Chemical Industries v. Commission* (Restrictive Business Practices in Dyestuff Industries), July 14, 1972, XI ILM (1972) at 1208–1209.

37 The decision of the Commission was incorrectly titled as a directive when published but it was sent to the addressee with a correct name (*i.e.* "decision"). Court of Justice, *Decision in Consten and Grundig v. EEC Commission*, V:1 ILM (1966) at 891–930.

rules of procedure themselves. For example, a chapter of the Rules of Procedure of the European Parliament is devoted to such matters ("Application and Amendment of the Rules"). In case of doubts as to a correct application of a given rule the President may initiate a procedure leading to the interpretation or, if necessary, to the modification of provisions concerned (rule 131–132).

Generally speaking, rules of procedure often undergo changes. They are attributable partly to the development of practice and partly to general amendments undertaken from time to time.[38] Amendments are effected according to the same procedure that is utilized for the adoption of the rules in question. So *e.g.* art. 132 par. 2 of the Rules of Procedure of the Parliament reads as follows: "Amendments to these Rules shall be adopted only if they secure the votes of the majority of the current members of the Parliament."

In practice international organizations often suspend the application of their rules of procedure for a determined period or even for time unlimited. It was the organs of the United Nations that widely utilized such a possibility.[39] This phenomenon is also to be seen in the practice of the European Communities. On July 6, 1967 the Council of Ministers suspended a few provisions of its Rules of Procedure for time unlimited.[40]

Some difficulties and misunderstandings in the relations of various organs of the European Union emerge as a result of the application of their procedural rules. These rules on the one hand impose upon the organs concerned a duty of mutual cooperation, while on the other hand they must respect the autonomy of individual organs in matters of their internal procedure and organization. The question is of the utmost importance, as procedural norms of the kind are regarded as "essential procedural requirements" within the meaning of art. 173 of the EC Treaty *i.e.* an infringement thereof may result in the annulment of an act concerned. That is why the Court of Justice was requested several times to rule on the limits of the competence of a given organ to rule on the powers of other organs. We must invoke in this context the ruling of the Court from February 10, 1983. It contains several carefully balanced statements with respect to mutual rights and duties of various member States and institutions. Among others this one should be cited *in extenso*: "Lorsque les gouvernements des États Membres prennet

---

[38] *See e.g.* 36 REVIEW OF THE COUNCIL'S WORK, 1 January–31 December (1988), Luxembourg, Office for Official Publications of the European Communities (1991) at 14.

[39] *See* J. KOLASA, *op. cit.*, *supra* note 3, at 179–187 and B. CONFORTI, *The Legal Effect of Non-Compliance with the Rules of Procedure in the United Nations General Assembly and Security Council*, 63 AJIL (1969) at 479–489.

[40] *See e.g. Règlement interieur provisoire de la Commission*, art. 1; OJ N° 147/1, 11.07.67.

des décisions fixant des lieux de travail provisoires des institutions ils doivent, ... respecter la compétence du Parlement européen de régler son organisation interne et veiller à ce que de telles décisions n'entravent pas son bon fonctionnement."[41]

Still the legal character of various organizational and procedural acts of the Communities is discussed by both practitioners and scholars. *E.g.* as regards the well-known Joint Declaration of the European Parliament, the Council and the Commission of a Conciliation Procedure (March 1975) the opinion of the majority is in favour of the non-binding character of this very act, usually defined as a purely political document. However, a few scholars defend the opinion that the Declaration amounts to a kind of "soft law" or a custom *in statu nascendi*.[42] Both opinions are, however, very doubtful. There is namely no uniform definition of "soft law" and custom may originate from any practice if it is stable and is not put into question.

It is worth-while to cite here the opinion of R. Bieber. According to this opinion the intercourse between the organs of a given organization is determined by the character of this organization and their arrangements are as a rule legal norms. So, in a case in which a few organs agree to follow a given procedure in their mutual relations, they are under an obligation to follow this procedure.[43] It seems, however, to be difficult to accept this general conclusion. The very character of the legal obligation of co-operation with other organs – imposed by the Treaties – is not sufficient to determine the character of other instruments dealing with inter-organizational co-operation also as binding ones. This latter question may be solved independently from the question of the underlying treaty provisions or the content of the norms concerned. It is the will of organs concerned that determines the binding or non-binding character of acts adopted by them in common. Their will may be express (then we can find in the instruments concerned such clauses as: "enter into force" or "are binding" from the day...), or it may be inferred from other provisions of an instrument in question.

In practice certain rules of procedure are binding, while others are of non-binding guidelines or mere indications as to the future course of action. As

---

[41] Affair 230/81, *Grand-Duché de Luxembourg contre Parlement Européen* (*Siegie et lieu de travail du Parlement*), Arrêt de la Cour du 10 Février 1983, 2 RECUEIL (1983) at 255–256; *see* also R. BIEBER, *The Settlement of Institutional Conflicts on the Basis of Article 4 of the EEC Treaty*, 21 CMLREV. (1984) at 517.

[42] M. BOTHE, *Soft Law in den Europäischen Gemeinschaften, Staatsrecht-Völkerrecht-Europäischenrecht*, FESTSCHRIFT FÜR H.J. SCHOCHAUER, Berlin (1981) at 761 and R. BIEBER, *op. cit.*, *supra* at 520–523.

[43] R. BIEBER, *ibid.* at 521–522.

the example of the latter we can invoke the interpretations of several Rules of Procedure of the European Parliament. Though they fall within the scope of the competence of the Parliament and are published in its "Rules of Procedure", what is missing is the will to give them binding force. Also various regulations contained in the annexes to the Rules of Procedure are not binding. In conclusion, we can see that the practice of the European Union as to its internal law is in no case uniform and different solutions are possible.

LA «PRÉÉMINENCE DU DROIT» DANS L'ORDRE JURIDIQUE EUROPÉEN

par

JACQUES-YVAN MORIN

À l'heure où les droits de l'homme, l'État de droit et la démocratie sont inscrits à l'ordre du jour des Nations Unies et de nombreux États sur tous les continents, il n'est pas sans intérêt de mesurer la portée donnée en Europe, depuis une vingtaine d'années, aux notions de prééminence du droit et de *rule of law*, telles que le Statut du Conseil de l'Europe et la Convention de sauvegarde des droits de l'homme les ont consacrées[1]. Quelle est l'origine de ces notions et comment ont été appliqués les principes qu'elles recèlent, vers lesquels tendent aujourd'hui la plupart des pays d'Europe centrale et orientale[2], naguère si méfiants à l'égard les idées libérales venues d'Occident, et de nombreux pays du Tiers-Monde, qui prennent conscience des rapports subtils qui lient le développement socio-économique à la démocratie, au respect des droits fondamentaux et à l'État de droit? Il n'est pas jusqu'à l'Assemblée générale des Nations Unies qui n'ait recommandé à ses membres depuis trois ans d'oeuvrer au «renforcement de l'État de droit» en vue de «prendre les mesures de caractère civil, pénal et administratif qui conviennent pour remédier aux violations des droits de l'homme»[3].

Ces notions de prééminence du droit et d'État de droit, toutes deux rendues en anglais par l'expression *rule of law*, s'exposent à être frappées d'ambiguïté lorsque, détachées des contextes nationaux qui les ont vu naître, elles passent dans l'ordre international. Non sans hésiter parfois, les traducteurs de l'ONU ont choisi les termes *gospodsvo prava, Fa Zhi, Estado de derecho* et *Siyadat-ul-Qanoun*, lesquels ne présentent pas toujours un sens précis dans les traditions juridiques des États concernés. Sans doute ces

---

1 Statut du 5 mai 1949, reproduit dans Conseil de l'Europe, DROITS DE L'HOMME EN DROIT INTERNATIONAL (1992), p. 163; Convention du 4 nov. 1950, reproduite dans: *ibid.* p. 166.

2 Dès 1988, la XIXe Conférence du Parti communiste de l'Union Soviétique, sous la conduite de M.S. Gorbatchev, approuvait des réformes en vue de faire de la Fédération un «État socialiste de droit». Le rapport de la Conférence a été publié dans DOCUMENTS ET MATÉRIAUX, Agence Novosti, Moscou, (1988), pp. 68–69; *voir* M. LESAGE (dir.), L'URSS. VERS UN ÉTAT DE DROIT, Paris (1988), pp. 3, 6, 9.

3 AG RÉS. 48/132, 20 déc. 1993, Doc. off. AG, 48e sess., supp. nº 49, p. 265; AG RÉS. 49/194, 23 déc. 1994, Doc. off. AG, 49e sess., supp. nº 49, v. Ier, p. 225.

expressions tendent-elles à acquérir une signification autonome, propre à l'ordre international, bien qu'elles ne puissent être entièrement détachées des contextes étatiques dans lesquels elles sont appelées à régir les comportements des gouvernants et de leurs agents. Aussi a-t-il paru utile d'étudier l'origine des principes de la prééminence du droit et du *rule of law* ainsi que la signification et la portée nouvelles que leur a valu leur inclusion dans les instruments européens destinés à protéger effectivement les grands principes énoncés en 1948 dans la Déclaration universelle des droits de l'homme[4].

Que le modèle européen de garantie des droits fondamentaux, tel que mis en oeuvre par les institutions de Strasbourg et la Cour de justice des Communautés européennes, ait exercé depuis quelques années une influence considérable sur les autres systèmes régionaux, notamment dans l'Hémisphère occidental et en Afrique, ne saurait faire de doute. Même s'il se heurte à la diversité des cultures politiques et juridiques dans plusieurs pays du Tiers-Monde, particulièrement en Asie[5], on ne peut nier que ce modèle et l'accent qu'il met sur la prééminence du droit sont d'une grande importance pour l'avenir des droits de l'homme dans le monde, pour peu que l'on puisse éviter que les divergences au sujet de leur universalité et de leur application pratique n'entraînent des conflits. Dans la mesure, en effet, où les États réussiront à former une authentique «communauté», fondée à la fois sur un juste équilibre entre une conception largement partagée de l'homme et le respect de l'identité des nations, les idées européennes, imprégnées de la diversité qui caractérise le continent mais également d'une longue tradition intellectuelle et spirituelle commune, ne peuvent manquer d'exercer un attrait croissant. C'est pourquoi les notions d'État de droit et de *rule of law*, qui synthétisent en quelque sorte l'ensemble des moyens concrets que les pays européens ont élaborés pour la protection des droits et libertés à l'encontre du pouvoir étatique, méritent d'être approfondies, non seulement dans les traditions nationales, qui demeurent vivaces et diverses, mais dans leur version européanisée, qui déjà paraît se détacher des matrices étatiques pour former, dans le cadre de la Convention de sauvegarde, ce que la Cour européenne appelle, dans l'arrêt *Loizidou*, un «instrument constitutionnel de l'ordre public européen»[6].

---

[4] AG RÉS. 217A (III), 10 déc. 1948, reproduite dans: *op. cit.*, *supra* note 1, p. 11.

[5] *Voir e.g.* Y. KUSHALANI, *Human Rights in Asia and Africa*, dans: F.E. SNYDER et S. SATHIRATAI, THIRD WORLD ATTITUDES TOWARD INTERNATIONAL LAW, Nijhoff, Boston (1987), p. 331: cet auteur met en relief l'origine occidentale du concept de droits de l'homme et estime que, dans le plus grand nombre des États aujourd'hui, l'expérience enseigne qu'il est non seulement rejeté, mais, plus exactement, *dénué de sens*.

[6] ARRÊT du 23 mars 1995, série A, n° 310, p. 31, § 93.

Cette démarche analytique paraît d'autant plus pertinente aujourd'hui qu'elle révèle au passage combien a été ardue et longue la conquête des libertés et de l'État de droit en Occident depuis qu'Aristote a posé, dans le cadre particulier des Cités grecques, la question fondamentale et intemporelle des rapports entre le pouvoir et le droit: «Est-il préférable d'être gouverné par le meilleur homme ou par les meilleures lois?»[7]. Les réponses antinomiques que donnent à cette question le Stagirite et son maître Platon marquent encore aujourd'hui les bornes entre lesquelles la philosophie politique et le droit oscillent: ou bien doit régner, selon Platon, l'homme dont la «vertu» et le savoir font un philosophe-roi, qui prend place pour ainsi dire naturellement au-dessus des lois et des opinions contradictoires des gouvernés, ou bien, au contraire, la stabilité des régimes politiques repose sur un partage du pouvoir garanti par le droit, les gouvernants n'étant plus que les «gardiens et ministres des lois»[8]. Il a fallu beaucoup de temps à l'Europe et bien des péripéties, parfois d'une extrême violence, pour en arriver à la prééminence du droit, telle que pratiquée dans les États et interprétée par les Cours de Strasbourg et de Luxembourg, et ce fait doit nous rendre conscients à la fois des obstacles qui jonchent le chemin vers l'universalité de l'État de droit et de la nécessité d'éviter, s'il se peut, de répéter sur la scène internationale les erreurs de parcours des pays occidentaux.

Pour rendre compte de ce cheminement et des difficultés qu'il a rencontrées en Europe ainsi que des étapes que les institutions régionales ont franchi dans l'affirmation du principe de la prééminence du droit, nous étudierons tout d'abord l'évolution du *rule of law* et de l'État de droit dans quelques pays qui les ont vu naître (I) pour nous pencher ensuite sur la portée de ces principes dans la jurisprudence par laquelle les Cours de Strasbourg et de Luxembourg ont interprété les obligations des États parties à la Convention de sauvegarde ainsi que celles des pays membres des Communautés européennes (II).

---

[7] ARISTOTE, POLITIQUE, III, XV, 3, n° 1285b; III, XVI, 1 et 2, n° 1286b, (1991), t. II, pp. 90–91, 94.

[8] PLATON, *La République*, IX, n° 875c, dans: OEUVRES COMPLÈTES, Belles-Lettres, Paris (1956), t. XII, I^e^ partie, p. 131; ARISTOTE, *op. cit.*, *supra* note 7, III, XVI, 3 et 5, n° 1287a, pp. 95–96. *Voir* D. GRISONI, *Platon, Aristote, les frères ennemis*, MAGAZINE LITTÉRAIRE n° 183 (1982), pp. 16–17. Cependant, la pensée de Platon a beaucoup évolué sur ce point, dans: *Les Lois*, oeuvre de maturité, la vertu fait une place au «fil d'or» du droit: *voir* n° 645a, dans: *ibid.*, t. XI, 2e partie, p. 30.

I. LES ORIGINES NATIONALES DE LA NOTION DE PRÉÉMINENCE DU DROIT

Bien avant que la pensée libérale du XVIIIe siècle ne fît des droits individuels la raison d'être de tout régime politique légitime et même avant l'apparition de l'État des Temps modernes, la limitation du pouvoir avait été un thème de réflexion en Europe. Apparaît déjà dans la réforme du gouvernement de l'Église, à la fin du XIe siècle, la volonté de soumettre toute autorité, y compris celle du pontife romain, au principe de la légalité: ce *ius novum*, issu de la Querelle des Investitures, produit une structure dont les nombreux rouages, et particulièrement ceux qui administrent la justice canonique, se voient attribuer des compétences précises et limitées, constituant ainsi, selon le pr H.J. Berman, une manière de *Rechtsstaat* avant la lettre[9]. Bientôt, cependant, la revendication de la suprématie politique par la papauté à l'encontre des monarchies encore féodales amène celles-ci à contester la *plenitudo potestatis* du Souverain pontife en même temps que les administrations royales s'inspirent de l'État romain. Si Jean de Salisbury a pu écrire au XIIe siècle que le prince temporel est le «ministre des prêtres», assujetti à la suprématie inhérente au pouvoir spirituel[10], les légistes du Roi de France, formés au droit de l'Empire romain, lui répondront au siècle suivant: *Rex est imperator in regni suo*.

À la fin du Moyen-Âge et notamment avec la Réforme, il est clair que l'Europe chrétienne ne formera pas un seul État de droit. Les grands désordres du XVe et du XVIe siècles conduisent chaque monarque à revendiquer pour lui-même la *plenitudo potestatis*, pouvoir suprême dont Jean Bodin fera la souveraineté[11]. Les peuples de chaque royaume ou principauté devront conquérir, au prix de révolutions parfois sanglantes et de guerres civiles ou étrangères, la limitation et le contrôle du pouvoir qu'exercent les princes sur leurs sujets. Il faudra quelques siècles pour que ce processus historique, fusionnant en quelque sorte les anciennes coutumes de participation au pouvoir politique (notamment chez les peuples du Nord), l'héritage judéo-chrétien de la dignité humaine, le droit naturel laïcisé des émules de Grotius[12] et les libertés proclamées par le siècle des Lumières, aboutissent à l'État

---

9 LAW AND REVOLUTION. THE FORMATION OF THE WESTERN LEGAL TRADITION, Harvard University Press, Boston (1983), pp. 530–532.

10 POLICRATICUS (1159); éd. C.J. Nederman, Cambridge University Press (1990), p. 32.

11 LES SIX LIVRES DE LA RÉPUBLIQUE DE J. BODIN ANGEVIN, J. du Puys, Paris (1576), p. iij.

12 H. GROTIUS, DE JURE BELLI AC PACIS LIBRI TRES (1625), éd. franç. Barbeyrac, Bâle, Thourneisen (1746), t. Ier, p. 10, § XI; S. DE PUFENDORF, LE DROIT DE LA NATURE ET DES GENS (1670; éd. Barbeyrac, Amsterdam, P. du Coup (1712), p. 169 et s.; E. DE VATTEL, LE DROIT DES GENS (1758), éd. Harrevelt, Amsterdam (1775), t. Ier, p. 3.

de droit, au *rule of law,* au *Rechtsstaat,* au *Stato di diritto* ou à l'*Estado de derecho* tels que nous les connaissons aujourd'hui chez les États membres du Conseil de l'Europe. Cette évolution ne se déroule pas au même rythme dans tous les pays: elle se manifeste d'abord aux Pays-Bas et en Angleterre, marqués par l'ouverture précoce aux échanges commerciaux avec le monde extérieur et la montée des classes moyennes, puis dans les colonies britanniques de l'Amérique du Nord pour s'étendre ensuite à l'Europe continentale dans la foulée des révolutions libérales en France, en Allemagne, en Italie et ailleurs. On ne saurait non plus ignorer la remarquable contribution à l'État de droit qu'ont été les *remedios* proposés par un Bartolomé de Las Casas contre l'asservissement des Indiens d'Amérique[13], qui anticipent la pensée européenne au sujet du colonialisme, lequel fut l'antithèse même des droits de l'homme et de l'État de droit.

Pour identifier ces origines diverses du principe de la prééminence du droit, nous nous attacherons à son développement en Angleterre, en Allemagne et en France, non pas que ce soient là les seuls pays qui y aient contribué, mais parce que ce sont avant tout les traditions de ces pays et le dialogue, parfois contradictoire, qui s'est noué entre leurs philosophes et juristes depuis le dernier quart du XIXe siècle, qui en ont posé les fondements.

A. Les traditions nationales

1. L'Angleterre et le *rule of law*

L'histoire constitutionnelle de l'Angleterre a pour fil conducteur la lutte incessante contre la prérogative royale. Déjà en 1215, la *Magna Carta* arrachée au roi Jean par les barons et leurs alliés des villes interdit à ses agents d'accuser un homme libre sans produire de témoins dignes de foi, de se substituer au juge compétent et de réquisitionner des biens sans le consentement du propriétaire; le Roi s'engage à réparer les dénis de justice du passé et à rendre celle-ci de telle manière qu'aucun homme libre ne soit arrêté ou détenu, privé de ses droits, mis hors la loi ou exilé si ce n'est par le jugement licite de ses pairs et selon la loi du pays[14]. Cette *Grande Charte* ne fut pas le

---

13 Du plaidoyer sans fin du PROCURADOR DE LOS INDIOS, on retiendra avant tout la TRÈS BRÈVE RELATION SUR LA DESTRUCTION DES INDES, suivie de TRENTE PROPOSITIONS TRÈS JURIDIQUES, Mouton, Paris (1974), pp. 121 et s.; *Apologética Historia Sumaria II*, dans: FRAY B. DE LAS CASAS, OBRAS COMPLETAS, V. ABRIL CASTELLO (ed.) Alianza, Madrid (1992), v. 7, p. 536; *voir* A. LOSADA, FRAY BARTOLOMÉ DE LAS CASAS A LA LUZ DE LA MODERNA CRITICA HISTORICA, Tecnos, Madrid (1970), pp. 105, 334; PH.I. ANDRÉ-VINCENT, DROIT DES INDIENS ET DÉVELOPPEMENT EN AMÉRIQUE LATINE, Paris (1971), p. 40.

14 G.R.C. DAVIS, MAGNA CARTA, (Br. Museum 1971), art. 9, 24, 28, 30, 31 et 38, pp. 16–25.

seul instrument du genre au Moyen-Âge – on songe à la *Bulle d'or* hongroise de 1222 – mais c'est l'exemple le plus probant qui nous soit parvenu de ce que la pensée politique appellera *pactum subjectionis*, ancêtre du «contrat social» qui jouera un rôle si important dans la philosophie d'un Locke ou d'un Rousseau.

Du XIIIe au XVIIe siècles, à l'exception de l'époque des Tudor, il ne se passe pas deux générations sans que le pouvoir royal ne soit l'objet de contestations violentes. Nul n'a mieux exprimé ce refus opiniâtre du pays profond de s'incliner devant l'autorité arbitraire du prince que le juriste Henry de Bracton, lorsqu'il écrit, au XIIIe siècle, que le Roi doit être assujetti à Dieu et au droit, «puisque c'est la loi qui fait le Roi (*quia lex facit regem*)»; il lui faut donc, ajoute-t-il, tempérer son pouvoir par le droit[15]. Ce «pouvoir de droit» n'est encore, à cette époque, qu'un grand dessein de juriste, mais il est appelé à devenir, à compter du siècle suivant, le projet du parlementarisme naissant et la raison d'être des magistrats anglais.

Les Guerres de religion du XVIe siècle ne sont guère propices à l'instauration d'États de droit en Europe; les institutions représentatives, qui vont de pair avec le règne du droit, disparaissent presque partout. Même en Angleterre, elles sont menacées: sous les Stuart, le conflit entre la prérogative royale et le droit entre dans une phase critique. C'est en 1610 que la Chambre des communes adopte la *Petition of Grievances*, par laquelle elle proteste contre les agissements de l'Exécutif et revendique pour les sujets anglais le droit d'être gouvernés «*by the certain rule of law* ... et non par quelque forme de gouvernement incertaine et arbitraire»[16]. C'est à cette occasion que l'expression *rule of law* apparaît pour ainsi dire officiellement dans le vocabulaire politique anglais, mais il faudra bien des protestations semblables contre les emprisonnements sans procès, les violations du recours d'*habeas corpus*, la condamnation à mort de sujets par des commissaires royaux et les exactions fiscales, pour venir à bout de l'absolutisme. Quand le Parlement, écarté des affaires pendant de longues années, se réunit à nouveau en 1640, il s'engage dans une révolution dont il perdra d'ailleurs le contrôle: la guerre civile conduit le Roi à l'échafaud, un siècle et demi avant la Révolution française. Mais les peuples se lassent du désordre et l'Angleterre voit en 1660 la restauration de la dynastie: il faudra attendre que le dernier Stuart soit chassé du trône et que le Parlement invite la Maison d'Orange à l'occuper pour que la suprématie du législateur soit assurée. Ces événements sont

---

15 *De legibus et consuetudinibus Angliae*, dans: S. THORNE, BRACTON AND THE LAWS AND CUSTOMS OF ENGLAND (1977), vol. II, p. 33, et s.

16 *Voir* J.R. TANNER, CONSTITUTIONAL DOCUMENTS OF THE REIGN OF JAMES I, 1603–1625, (1960), pp. 153–154.

à l'origine de deux sources importantes du *rule of law*, dont l'influence s'étendra bien au-delà de la Grande-Bretagne: le *Bill of Rights* de 1689 et la pensée de John Locke.

Le *Bill of Rights* établit avant tout les droits du Parlement en limitant la prérogative royale, mais on y a joint quelques garanties pour les sujets: il ne sera pas imposé de peines «cruelles et inhabituelles», ni d'amendes excessives et la création de tribunaux spéciaux est interdite[17]. Ce sont là des éléments fondateurs de la prééminence du droit telle que l'Europe la conçoit aujourd'hui, prééminence dont Locke sera le défenseur devant un continent qui s'étonne du caractère insolite de ces nouveautés. Les sujets ont le droit de s'insurger contre un souverain qui manque à ses devoirs de «fiduciaire» du gouvernement (*trusteeship*): l'ordre juridique, les magistrats et les sanctions sont fondées sur un pacte social et les individus ont conservé de l'état antérieur à ce pacte – l'état de nature – des droits inaliénables qu'ils peuvent opposer au pouvoir et dont celui-ci est garant[18]. La doctrine lockienne ne va pas, cependant, jusqu'à imposer pareilles limites au pouvoir du Parlement: celui-ci est sorti vainqueur du conflit avec la monarchie et il est difficile pour notre philosophe de concevoir qu'un contrôle quelconque puisse lui être imposé. Même les juges, qui avaient joué un rôle important sous les Stuart en rappelant au Roi qu'il ne pouvait juger lui-même les procès entre ses sujets ou créer de nouveaux crimes par proclamation[19], n'ont d'autre fonction, selon Locke, que d'appliquer la loi et non de se prononcer sur sa validité: les magistrats peuvent contrôler les actes de l'Exécutif, non ceux du Parlement. Contre les abus que celui-ci ferait de sa suprématie, «il ne peut exister aucun juge sur terre» et, à la limite, on retombe dans l'état de nature, chaque sujet recouvrant son droit naturel de résistance[20]. Ces idées, dont le rayonnement sera immense dans les colonies britanniques rebelles de l'Amérique et dans la pensée européenne – chez un Montesquieu, par exemple – ont cependant figé en quelque sorte l'évolution du *rule of law* dans le pays qui l'a vu naître: il faudra attendre le dernier quart du XXe siècle pour que des juristes proposent de limiter le pouvoir du Parlement lui-même par les moyens d'une constitution formelle et d'un contrôle de constitutionnalité des lois; nous

---

[17] *An Act Declaring the Rights and Liberties of the Subject and the Settling of the Succession of the Crown*, 1 GUL. & MAR., Sess. 2, c. 2 (1688), dans: V STATUTES OF THE REALM (1819), p. 142.

[18] SECOND TREATISE ON CIVIL GOVERNMENT (1690); trad. B. Gilson, Vrin, Paris (1967), *sub. tit.* DEUXIÈME TRAITÉ DU GOUVERNEMENT CIVIL.

[19] *Prohibitions del Roy* (1607), 12 CO. REP. 63; *Case of Proclamations* (1610), 12 CO. REP. 74, dans: 77 ENGLISH REPORTS (K.B.), pp. 1342 et s.

[20] *Supra* note 18, II, n° 20, p. 85; XIV, n° 168; XIX, n°s 222, 240, 242–243; *voir* R. POLIN, LA POLITIQUE MORALE DE JOHN LOCKE, PUF, Paris (1953).

y reviendrons après avoir étudié les origines de l'État de droit en France et en Allemagne.

2. L'État de droit en France

Si la lutte contre l'absolutisme du Roi s'apaise en Angleterre avec le triomphe du Parlement et des nouvelles classes dirigeantes, il n'en va pas de même en France, où la protection des sujets contre les féodaux, puis les désordres religieux, aboutissent à légitimer diverses formes de pouvoir absolu. Non pas que la théorie politique ait consacré l'autorité royale sans discussion: aux XVe et XVIe siècles, un vigoureux courant de pensée veut la tempérer par des «freins»[21]; mais les populations et les théoriciens ont trop souvent à choisir entre un pouvoir fort et ce que Bodin appelle la «licentieuse anarchie»: pendant les Guerres de religion, le pays connaît huit conflits armés et l'assassinat de deux Rois. Au lendemain de la Saint-Barthélemy (1572), si les «Monarchomaques», Hotman par exemple, reprennent à leur compte la notion de monarchie soumise au droit et y ajoutent l'idée de consentement du peuple, les «Politiques» répondent que la souveraineté n'est limitée «ny en puissance, ny en charge, ny à certain temps», encore que Bodin prennent soin d'ajouter que le Roi doit néanmoins demeurer soumis aux «lois fondamentales du royaume» et aux «lois communes à tous peuples»[22].

Louis XIV lui-même entend bien affirmer sa «volonté bien absolue» et son autorité «n'est limitée ni contrôlée par aucun organe doté de pouvoirs propres»[23], mais il doit néanmoins tenir compte des institutions: s'il prend soin d'annuler les concessions, inspirées à la fois de la *Grande Charte* anglaise et de l'*habeas corpus*, que les Chambres souveraines lui ont arrachées à la faveur de la Fronde, pendant sa minorité[24], en revanche, l'*Ordonnance criminelle* de 1670 montre son souci de rendre bonne justice à ses sujets, par exemple en atténuant les rigueurs de la «question» et en réglementant rigoureusement les «lettres de justice», par lesquelles il peut intervenir dans les

---

21 *V.g.* C. DE SEYSSEL, LA GRAND' MONARCHIE DE FRANCE (1519, éd. Galiot du Pré, Paris 1558), pp. 9–13.

22 J.-F. HOTMAN, LA GAULE FRANÇAISE (1573; éd. Fayard, Paris 1991), pp. 91, 111–112; J. BODIN, *op. cit.*, *supra* note 11, pp. 89, 125, 129.

23 MÉMOIRES POUR L'INSTRUCTION DU DAUPHIN (1661–1666; éd. C. Dreyss, Didier, Paris 1860), t. II, p. 382; *voir* F. OLIVIER-MARTIN, HISTOIRE DU DROIT FRANÇAIS DES ORIGINES À LA RÉVOLUTION, éd. CNRS, Paris (1992), p. 301, § 235.

24 DÉCLARATION DU ROY. DU VINGT-DEUXIÈME OCTOBRE 1648, vérifiée en Parlement, Chambre des Comptes et Cour des Aydes, B.N., doc. F. 23611 (944), art. XV: «Voulons … qu'aucuns de nos Subjets de quelque qualité & condition qu'ils soient ne soient à l'advenir traités criminellement que selon les formes prescrites par les Loix de notre Royaume & Ordonnances; & non par Commissaires & Juges choisis». Cette Déclaration est abrogée avec d'autres actes le 22 oct. 1652: B.N., doc. F. 23612 (115).

affaires soumises aux tribunaux[25]. L'évolution des mentalités et de la culture juridique permet ainsi, en dépit de l'absolutisme, de franchir de modestes étapes sur le chemin sinueux qui mène à l'État de droit. La torture institutionnalisée soulèvera bientôt un débat d'envergure européenne, surtout avec la parution en 1765 de l'ouvrage de C. Beccaria, *Des délits et des peines*; relayée par Voltaire, ce mouvement d'opinion conduit aux Ordonnances de 1780 et 1788, par lesquelles Louis XVI abolit la question.

Cette humanisation du droit pénal est le fruit des idées libérales du siècle des Lumières, qui débordent le cadre de la limitation du pouvoir telle qu'on l'avait conçue du Moyen-Âge au XVIIe siècle. S'affirme en effet à cette époque, avant tout en France, mais bientôt dans toute l'Europe occidentale, la philosophie selon laquelle l'individu possède comme tel des libertés et droits antérieurs et supérieurs au pouvoir, donc opposables à l'État. Chez Montesquieu, la liberté devient l'objet même du gouvernement: elle se définit comme la sûreté dans laquelle chacun est que le caprice d'un gouvernement ne viendra pas lui ôter ses biens ou sa vie et n'a donc pas encore la portée que nous donnons aujourd'hui aux libertés[26]. L'auteur de *L'Esprit des Lois* n'en sème pas moins, après Locke, une idée révolutionnaire car, comme l'écrit Olivier-Martin, «les anciens Français n'ont jamais eu l'idée, avant la fin du XVIIIe siècle, qu'ils pouvaient revendiquer des droits intangibles, opposables à l'autorité du Roi»[27]. Les droits de l'homme viennent ainsi à la fois renforcer l'État de droit et exiger de celui-ci une protection toujours plus grande pour l'individu. Cependant, ces idées ne se sont pas imposées du jour au lendemain: dans l'ensemble de l'Europe, au XVIIIe siècle, les institutions autoritaires sont bien ancrées et il faudra, dans plusieurs États, attendre les révolutions libérales du XIXe siècle pour qu'elles s'inclinent devant des règles supérieures. Il ne manque pas de philosophes à cette époque pour faire l'éloge du «despotisme éclairé» d'un Frédéric II, par exemple, et certaines «Lumières» paraissent aujourd'hui plus conservatrices que libérales. En outre, si Montesquieu a montré que, pour qu'on ne puisse abuser du pouvoir, «il faut que par la disposition des choses, le pouvoir arrête le pouvoir», il confie cette tâche, en France du moins, aux institutions traditionnelles, qui doivent faire contrepoids au monarque exerçant à la fois les pouvoirs exécutif et législatif. La «disposition des choses» est différente en Angleterre, con-

---

[25] ORDONNANCE, titre XVI, art. V, XI, XVIII et 31; titre XIX, reproduite, dans: J.-Y. MORIN et J. WOEHRLING, LES CONSTITUTIONS DU CANADA ET DU QUÉBEC DU RÉGIME FRANÇAIS À NOS JOURS, Thémis, Montréal, 2e éd. (1994), vol. II, p. 25.

[26] DE L'ESPRIT DES LOIS (1748), éd. G. Truc, Garnier, Paris (1956), t. Ier, XII, I et II, pp. 196–197.

[27] *Supra* note 23, p. 340.

state-t-il, puisque le pouvoir législatif y appartient au Parlement. Or, dans la conception qu'il s'en fait, les lois sont par définition libératrices, de sorte que Montesquieu n'a guère aperçu le rôle que le juge pourrait être appelé à exercer en tant que protecteur des libertés à l'encontre du législateur même.

Ce n'est pas la Révolution française qui modifiera cet état de choses. S'inspirant des *Bill of Rights* américains, particulièrement celui de la Virginie (1776), les Constituants proclament les droits de l'homme, mais la France de l'époque n'a pas dans ses tribunaux – les Parlements d'Ancien Régime – la confiance que les Américains, à l'imitation de la Grande-Bretagne, placent dans leurs juges. Certes, la *Déclaration des droits de l'homme et du citoyen* de 1789 énonce plusieurs exigences caractéristiques de l'État de droit: «Nul homme ne peut être arrêté, ni détenu que dans les cas déterminés par la Loi, et selon les formes qu'elle a prescrites»; la non-rétroactivité des lois, la présomption d'innocence et l'égalité devant la loi sont garanties[28]. En outre, la Constitution de 1791 précise le rôle du pouvoir judiciaire en matière criminelle: par exemple, nul ne peut être arrêté ou détenu sans mandat ou ordonnance, l'instruction est publique, l'accusé a droit au secours d'un conseil et toute accusation doit être reçue par des jurés[29]. Cependant, ces garanties seront bientôt remplacées par la Constitution montagnarde de 1793 et les régimes plus ou moins autoritaires qui se succéderont pendant la majeure partie du XIXe siècle tarderont à doter les citoyens des recours et institutions nécessaires au contrôle du pouvoir. Par la Constitution de l'An VIII (1799), Bonaparte crée le Conseil d'État, appelé, trois quarts de siècle plus tard, à jouer un rôle majeur dans la construction de l'État de droit, mais le pouvoir du Premier Consul n'est restreint par aucune déclaration de droits.

Lorsque, sous la IIIe République, on parviendra à limiter le pouvoir de l'Exécutif, ce sera pour affirmer la suprématie du législateur, à la manière des institutions britanniques. Nous touchons ici à un débat fondamental sur la nature et la portée de l'État de droit dans la tradition des pays occidentaux: ce «droit» se réfère-t-il à des normes supérieures aux lois «positives», comme dans la tradition médiévale, pour laquelle des règles d'origine morale et divine – ce qu'on appellait en anglais la *higher law* – s'imposaient aux gouvernants comme aux gouvernés, ou bien le droit renvoie-t-il simplement à la loi? La ruine des institutions médiévales et de la *Civitas christiana* soulevaient la question dans toute son ampleur et le XVIIe siècle avait tenté d'y répondre par la laïcisation du droit naturel, de Grotius à Locke. On peut

---

28 Articles 5, 6, 8 et 9, reproduits, dans: M. DUVERGER, CONSTITUTIONS ET DOCUMENTS POLITIQUES, PUF, Paris, 13e éd. (1992), p. 17.

29 Articles 9, 10, 11, 14, 15 et 16, reproduits, dans: *ibid.* p. 18.

considérer que les colonies américaines, en adoptant leurs déclarations de droits, de 1776 à 1784, puis le *Bill of Rights* fédéral de 1789–1791, ont voulu résoudre la question en *constitutionnalisant*, pour la première fois, les droits supérieurs et le *due process of law* (qui est la version américaine de la prééminence du droit)[30]. Le constitutionnalisme, aujourd'hui si répandu, est-il autre chose qu'une forme laïcisée et démocratisée de *higher law*?

Telle n'est cependant pas la solution qui s'imposera au législateur français pendant plus d'un siècle et demi après la Déclaration de 1789, pourtant fortement influencée par l'exemple américain. Sans doute plusieurs révolutionnaires ont-ils pensé qu'en plaçant la Déclaration au frontispice de la Constitution de 1791, ils imposaient des règles fondamentales à toute forme d'État; certains étaient même persuadés de légiférer pour l'humanité entière[31]. Cependant, une autre influence se révéla plus déterminante: celle de J.-J. Rousseau qui, dans sa tentative d'inventer un nouveau «contrat social», fonde la loi sur la «volonté générale»[32]. Idée séduisante pour les représentants de la nation, qui se voyaient volontiers comme interprètes de la volonté générale (alors que le Genevois Rousseau pensait plutôt à la démocratie directe de sa ville natale). Or, pour «Jean-Jacques», la volonté générale est infaillible, de sorte que la loi est par définition juste et tend toujours à l'utilité publique. Mais si la loi s'en prend à la liberté ou devient despotique? Notre philosophe répond à la question posée par Aristote par une nouvelle forme d'idéalisme platonicien: «sous la loi de raison», volonté générale et loi sont intrinsèquement «vertueuses» et on doit leur obéir à l'instant; par définition, le souverain qui exprime cette volonté ne saurait menacer la liberté. Rousseau ne parle des «bornes du pouvoir» que pour affirmer que le souverain seul en est juge[33]. On dérive ainsi, dans la France des XVIIIe et XIXe siècles, comme en Angleterre, vers la «souveraineté de la loi», qui n'est autre que le pouvoir juridiquement illimité du législateur lui-même, dont la Révolution américaine avait voulu s'affranchir.

Un débat aussi crucial ne pouvait demeurer sans suite; ce n'est cependant qu'au début du XXe siècle qu'il reprit pour de bon en France. Pour le p^r^ A. Esmein, la Déclaration de 1789 énonçait des principes philosophiques ou moraux sans valeur juridique, qui n'avaient d'autre objet que d'inspirer

30 *Voir* les Constitutions de la Virginie et du Massachusetts, dans: S. RIALS, LA DÉCLARATION DES DROITS DE L'HOMME ET DU CITOYEN, Hachette, Paris (1988), pp. 495 et 512; le BILL OF RIGHTS (les dix premiers amendements à la *Constitution des États-Unis*) est reproduit, dans: R.E. CUSHMAN, LEADING CONSTITUTIONAL DECISIONS, Appleton, N.Y., 10e éd. (1955), p. 448.

31 *Voir* P. BASTID, L'IDÉE DE CONSTITUTION, Économica, Paris (1985), pp. 145–162.

32 POLITIQUE DU CONTRAT SOCIAL OU PRINCIPES DU DROIT POLITIQUE (1762); éd. H. Guillemin, Paris, Unoin gén., (1966), II, VI, p. 81.

33 *Ibid.* II, IV et V, pp. 253–256.

le législateur; pour d'autres, comme le pr P. Bastid, l'intention des hommes de 89 était bien de faire oeuvre constitutionnelle. Le doyen L. Duguit allait plus loin: il estimait que la Déclaration liait les constituants eux-mêmes, ayant pour ainsi dire une valeur supra constitutionnelle[34]. Ce débat ne sera tranché que plus tard; en tout cas, la Révolution n'a pu asseoir l'État de droit théorique qu'elle a conçu pour la France sur des recours pratiques ou une sanction effective, surtout à l'égard de la législation. Il faudra attendre les années 1970 pour que la Déclaration de 1789 entre dans le droit positif de façon indubitable. Depuis la Seconde Guerre mondiale, la principale contribution à l'élaboration du principe européen de la prééminence du droit, dans sa formulation moderne, est venue d'Allemagne, que l'expérience de l'entre-deux-guerres a amenée à constitutionnaliser les droits de l'homme et à se donner les moyens de contrôler l'ensemble des actes du pouvoir étatique.

3. Origines du *Rechtsstaat* allemand

Comme plusieurs pays d'Europe, l'Allemagne a connu au Moyen-Âge l'idée de la soumission du pouvoir au droit: même si l'autorité de l'Empereur sur les nombreuses principautés est plus nominale que réelle, il instaure au XVe siècle le tribunal de la *Reichskammergericht*, qui ouvre à certains sujets de l'Empire la possibilité d'un recours contre leurs gouvernements respectifs[35]. Cependant, après la Guerre de Trente ans et la Paix de Westphalie (1648), l'autorité de princes se fait plus absolue; au XVIIIe siècle prévaut «l'État de police» (*Polizeistaat*), exerçant des pouvoirs administratifs de plus en plus étendus et dans lequel le Chef d'État et ses agents ne sont pas liés eux-mêmes par les règles qu'ils ont établies, à moins qu'il ne s'agisse, comme en Prusse, de «lois de droit» (*Rechtsgesetze*), beaucoup moins fréquentes. Ce régime, conséquence du développement économique, est parfois «éclairé», selon une certaine philosophie politique, mais fait ressortir l'originalité de la pensée d'Emmanuel Kant, sujet de Frédéric II. Malgré le contexte de ce régime césarien, c'est lui qui recueille les héritages laissés par Locke, Montesquieu, Rousseau et la Révolution française, pour en donner une synthèse nouvelle, qui anticipe l'État de droit moderne.

L'État kantien est subordonné à l'Idée de droit car l'un des impératifs de la conscience morale et de la raison de l'homme exige qu'il sorte de l'état de nature, dans lequel personne n'est assuré contre la violence, pour entrer dans «l'état juridique» (*rechtlicher Zustand*), c'est-à-dire dans «une com-

---

34 A. ESMEIN, ÉLÉMENTS DE DROIT CONSTITUTIONNEL ET COMPARÉ, 4e éd. (1906), p. 456; P. BASTID, *op. cit.*, *supra* note 31, p. 158; L. DUGUIT, TRAITÉ DE DROIT CONSTITUTIONNEL, Boccard, Paris, 2e éd. (1921), pp. 22–36.

35 *Voir* O. MAYER, LE DROIT ADMINISTRATIF ALLEMAND (1903), vol. Ier, p. 32.

mune soumission à une contrainte publique, légale, extérieure», permettant que le droit de chacun soit légalement défini et assuré. Le Pacte par lequel le peuple se constitue en État lie le souverain puisque les lois ainsi établies sont obligatoires pour tous, reposant sur un rapport entre hommes libres qui exclut toute soumission d'une personne à la volonté absolue d'une autre. Kant insiste sur l'égalité universelle et «innée» des sujets, qui ne sauraient se contraindre mutuellement que par l'autorité de la loi; est donc exclu tout pouvoir arbitraire et le peuple souverain peut déposer le prince ou réformer son administration[36]. Cela ne va pas jusqu'à l'obligation d'établir la démocratie – qui n'existe nulle part à la fin du XVIIIe siècle –, mais la souveraineté du peuple en découlera nécessairement et les juristes disciples du philosophe de Königsberg franchiront bientôt le pas qui sépare «l'état juridique» de l'État de droit. Si les citoyens ne peuvent, pour l'heure, faire appel aux tribunaux à l'encontre des actes arbitraires du *Polizeistaat*, Kant a compris que l'existence de pareille justice «peut être considérée, parmi toutes les questions d'ordre juridique, comme la plus importante»[37].

Les prérequis du *Rechtsstaat* étant ainsi posés – même si le mot n'apparaît pas dans l'oeuvre du philosophe –, la doctrine juridique allemande du XIXe siècle ne tardera pas à en tirer les conséquences. Les juristes de la tradition germanique, qui est également celle du droit romain, sont en effet perméables aux principes premiers, dont ils déduisent volontiers des normes subsidiaires et des règles plus précises. C'est là une démarche bien différente de celle des juristes anglais, qui ont plutôt tendance à commencer par les recours concrets, les *remedies*, pour en «induire» les droits et libertés du sujet. Ce n'est pas que l'esprit juridique anglais soit fermé aux principes, ni que la doctrine allemande soit insensible aux exigences concrètes du *Rechtsstaat*, mais leurs attitudes respectives demeurent divergentes: elles ne sont pas étrangères au fait que la Grande-Bretagne n'a pas de constitution formelle tandis que l'Allemagne, depuis la Révolution libérale de 1848, et surtout depuis la *Loi fondamentale* de 1949, donne l'exemple le plus achevé de protection des droits et libertés par les techniques du constitutionnalisme et du contrôle juridictionnel des actes de l'État.

Le *Rechtsstaat* à ses débuts exprime le libéralisme de la bourgeoisie allemande, chez R. von Mohl (1829)[38], par exemple, et se préoccupe des problèmes créés par l'État de police: on y puisera les éléments d'un nouveau droit administratif (*Verwaltungsrecht*), en vue de contrôler un appareil

---

36 *Die Metaphysic des Sitten* (1797), dans: B. KELLERMANN (dir.), WORKS (1922), vol. VII, p. 123, § 49.

37 DOCTRINE DU DROIT, Vrin, Paris (1988), p. 188, § 41.

38 DIE POLIZEIWISSENSCHAFT NACH DEN GRUNDSÄTZEN DES RECHTSSTAAT (1832–1834, Tubingen); *voir* E. FORSTHOFF, TRAITÉ DE DROIT ADMINISTRATIF ALLEMAND, Fromont, trad. (1969), p. 94.

étatique qui prend toujours plus d'ampleur à l'époque, comme dans la plupart des pays en voie d'industrialisation. La création de la Cour administrative suprême de Prusse, en 1875, témoigne de cette évolution. Bientôt, cependant, apparaissent les inégalités croissantes du *bürgerlicher Rechtsstaat* et L. von Stein se fait l'avocat, sous l'influence des idées socialistes, d'un *sozialer Staat* qui compléterait le *Rechtsstaat*[39]. Si répandue chez les juristes est l'idée de la soumission de l'État au droit que même un homme de droite comme F.J. Stahl, partisan de l'autorité de droit divin, s'en remet au *Rechtsstaat* pour «déterminer avec précision les moyens et les limites de son activité ainsi que la sphère de liberté de ses citoyens, à la manière du droit»[40]. Les fondements des développements ultérieurs sont presque tous déjà réunis. Avant d'en traiter, jetons un coup d'oeil sur le dialogue qui se noue à cette époque entre juristes allemands, anglais et français au sujet de la prééminence du droit.

4. Premiers éléments d'une notion européenne de l'État de droit

La grande préoccupation des juristes du XIXe siècle est de mettre fin à l'arbitraire de l'Éxécutif et de l'administration; ce n'est qu'au XXe que la théorie juridique voudra imposer le *Rechtsstaat* et l'État de droit au législateur. Les juristes allemands, R. von Gneist par exemple, ont étudié le système anglais et proposent que les actes administratifs soient contrôlés selon les formes applicables devant les tribunaux de droit commun[41]; d'autres, comme O. Mayer, «véritable créateur» du droit administratif allemand, s'inspirent plus volontiers à la fin du siècle de la solution française d'une juridiction née de l'administration elle-même mais qui affirme graduellement son indépendance depuis que la IIIe République a remis la justice déléguée au Conseil d'État (1872), qui n'a pas tardé à poser le principe de la responsabilité de l'État et à élargir les recours pour excès de pouvoir[42].

Le juriste anglais A.V. Dicey ne partage pas du tout cet intérêt pour les institutions françaises: dans son célèbre ouvrage de droit constitutionnel, publié en 1885, il exprime sa méfiance à l'endroit des juridictions administratives spécialisées et particulièrement d'un Conseil d'État qui, à ses yeux, porte le poids de son origine napoléonienne; pour lui, rien n'est plus étranger aux «règne, prééminence et suprématie de la loi» que le droit administratif

---

39 DIE VERWALTUNGSLEHRE (1865), 8 tomes.

40 RECHTS – UND STAATSLEHRE AUF DER GRUNDLAGE CHRISTLICHER WELTANSCHAUUNG (1837), v. II, p. 37.

41 DES RECHTSSTAAT UND DIE VERWALTUNGSGERICHTE IN DEUTSCHLAND (2e éd. 1879), pp. 158–190.

42 LE DROIT ADMINISTRATIF ALLEMAND (1908), vol. Ier, pp. 38–41.

à la française et tout pouvoir ou agent public doit être assujetti à la loi ordinaire appliquée par les tribunaux de droit commun (*ordinary courts*)[43]. Dans les éditions ultérieures de cet ouvrage, Decey se laisse convaincre, notamment par G. Jèze, de l'évolution du Conseil d'État vers un système de règles fixes qui en font un «véritable tribunal», mais il persiste à croire qu'il n'en est pas moins incompatible avec le *rule of law* «rigide» du droit anglais. Son influence persistera en Angleterre jusqu'après la Seconde Guerre mondiale, bien que d'autres juristes, tels C.K. Allen et W.A. Robson, se soient portés à la défense du droit administratif français[44]. Aussi n'est-il pas sans intérêt de noter qu'en 1983 l'autorité judiciaire elle-même, dans un rapprochement significatif avec les méthodes françaises, ait établi au sein de la *High Court* une «division administrative», composée de juges versés en la matière[45]; en revanche, on observe que le droit prétorien élaboré par le Conseil d'État n'est pas sans rappeler les méthodes anglaises.

Cependant, le rapprochement ainsi esquissé ne s'étend pas au contrôle des lois elles-mêmes au nom des libertés. Sur ce point, la doctrine française va pencher, après de longs débats, vers le constitutionnalisme. En Angleterre, aux critiques qui auraient vu dans la tradition du pays la possibilité de voir le «despotisme du Parlement» succéder à la prérogative royale, Dicey répondait que «l'esprit de légalité» dans lequel le législateur exerçait sa suprématie excluait toute dérive de cette sorte. Sur le continent, au contraire, l'instauration de régimes républicains en France (1870), en Allemagne, en Autriche et ailleurs (notamment en 1919), secouant les traditions, soulèvera éventuellement la question du contrôle de constitutionnalité des lois.

En France, le débat se déroule en deux phases distinctes: dès avant la Première Guerre mondiale un premier courant de pensée, illustré par L. Duguit et M. Hauriou, plaide pour la reconnaissance du caractère constitutionnel, donc juridiquement obligatoire, de la Déclaration de 1789. Hauriou est séduit par le système américain et Duguit n'est «pas éloigné d'accepter» l'idée de son collègue, bien qu'il hésite devant le pouvoir ainsi accordé aux juges[46]. Dans une seconde phase, le débat porte, à compter de 1921, sur le

---

[43] INTRODUCTION TO THE STUDY OF THE LAW OF THE CONSTITUTION, Macmillan, Londres, 10e éd. (1961), pp. 188, 193, 195, 203, 329 n. 2, 331 n. 1; il existe une traduction française de cet ouvrage par A. BATUT et G. JÈZE: INTRODUCTION À L'ÉTUDE DU DROIT CONSTITUTIONNEL, Giard et Brière, Paris (1902).

[44] C.K. ALLEN, BUREAUCRACY TRIUMPHANT (1931), pp. 3, 105; W.A. ROBSON, JUSTICE AND ADMINISTRATIVE LAW (3e éd 1951), pp. 28–34, 453–456.

[45] Déclaration de Lord Denning, MASTER OF THE ROLLS, dans: *O'Reilly* v. *Mackman* (1983) 2 A.C. 237, p. 259.

[46] L. DUGUIT, MANUEL DE DROIT CONSTITUTIONNEL, Boccard, Paris, 2e éd., (1911), pp. 101–103, et TRAITÉ DE DROIT CONSTITUTIONNEL, Boccard, Paris, 2e éd., (1921), pp. 22–36; M. HAURIOU,

meilleur moyen d'organiser le contrôle juridictionnel: y participeront É. Lambert, pionnier du droit comparé et grand critique du «gouvernement des juges», et les disciples du juriste autrichien H. Kelsen.

On ne saurait cependant comprendre la portée de ce vaste débat pour l'État de droit sans souligner l'importance de l'apport de R. Carré de Malberg dans sa *Contribution à la théorie générale de l'État* (1920–1922). Pour ce juriste parfaitement au fait de la doctrine allemande, la souveraineté de la loi à la française ne constitue pas un État de droit, notion dérivée du *Rechtsstaat*, mais un «État légal». Or, l'esprit du régime de l'État de droit, son «développement naturel», conduisent à lier le législateur lui-même à «un principe de respect du droit individuel qui doive s'imposer à lui de façon absolue»; sous la IIIe République, le système constitutionnel protège sans doute les citoyens contre l'arbitraire administratif, mais la Constitution «ne s'est pas élevée jusqu'à la perspective de l'État de droit»[47].

Comment atteindre cette perspective sans l'existence d'un organe de contrôle constitutionnel, qui ne saurait être ni l'Exécutif, ni le législateur? Lambert redoute le «gouvernement des juges» à l'américaine, qui ne pourrait séduire que ceux qui veulent ligoter le législateur au moment où s'imposent des réformes économiques peu compatibles avec une conception individualiste du droit. L'influence de cette critique, bientôt confirmée par la crise du *New Deal* aux États-Unis, sera durable: on ne trouve guère d'auteur, aujourd'hui encore, qui ne s'y réfère. Cependant, Lambert ne dit rien de ce que pourrait être un contrôle de constitutionnalité à la française; sur ce point, l'inspiration allait venir d'Autriche et d'Allemagne.

Reconnaissant l'influence des idées du maître de Vienne, répandues en France dans les années trente par ses disciples, notamment Chs Eisenmann[48], le pr L. Favoreu écrit: «Au commencement était Kelsen»[49]. C'est bien là, en effet, l'un des exemples les plus probants de l'européanisation de la prééminence du droit entendue dans son sens le plus large, qui postule désormais le contrôle de la constitutionnalité des lois, et des mécanismes institutionnels qui permettent de l'assurer. La logique kelsénienne de la hiérarchie des

---

PRINCIPES DE DROIT PUBLIC, Sirey, Paris, (1916), p. 645, et PRÉCIS DE DROIT CONSTITUTIONNEL, Sirey, Paris, 2e éd., (1929), pp. 137, 296, 303–307; le point de vue contraire est exprimé par G. JÈZE, *Le contrôle constitutionnel des lois*, R.D.P. (1924), pp. 385, 403, 412–413.

47 CONTRIBUTION À LA THÉORIE GÉNÉRALE DE L'ÉTAT, Sirey, Paris (1921–1922), vol. Ier, pp. 488, 490, 492.

48 LA JUSTICE CONSTITUTIONNELLE ET LA HAUTE COUR CONSTITUTIONNELLE D'AUTRICHE, Economica, Paris (1928); le pr Eisenmann traduit l'ouvrage de Kelsen, REINE RECHTSLEHRE (1927), sub. tit. THÉORIE PURE DU DROIT, Dalloz, Paris (1962).

49 *Actualité et légitimité du contrôle juridictionnel des lois en Europe occidentale*, R.D.P. (1984), pp. 1147, 1174.

normes exclut la souveraineté du législateur, qui est un organe constitué; c'est l'ordre constituant qui doit exercer cette souveraineté dans l'État. Le Parlement ne saurait, «par nature», être restreint dans l'exercice de son pouvoir à moins que ce ne soit par «un organe différent de lui, indépendant de lui et de toute autre autorité étatique». Cependant, Kelsen s'éloigne délibérément du modèle américain en proposant que l'organe de contrôle prenne la forme d'une cour spécialisée dans les questions constitutionnelles, composée de telle sorte que ce «législateur négatif» soit parfaitement indépendant, déterminé en tout par la seule constitution[50]. La Cour constitutionnelle autrichienne établie en 1920 devait beaucoup à ces idées et a servi plus tard de modèle dans plusieurs pays européens. En France, le raisonnement de Kelsen sur la pyramide des normes a fini par l'emporter, mais a été adapté aux circonstances des années cinquante.

Le Conseil constitutionnel créé par la Constitution de 1958 se voit confier au départ le rôle plutôt limité de «chien de garde» des règles par lesquelles le constituant de la Ve République entend protéger le pouvoir réglementaire de l'Exécutif. C'est pourquoi le contrôle de constitutionnalité des lois s'exerce *a priori*, c'est-à-dire avant leur promulgation, à la demande du Président de la République, du Président de l'Assemblée nationale ou du Président du Sénat, qui nomment d'ailleurs les membres de ce Conseil[51]; en outre, rien n'indique que la protection constitutionnelle s'étend aux droits et libertés énoncés dans les Déclarations de droits antérieures. Aussi, à la lumière de ces faits, l'affirmation par le Conseil de la valeur constitutionnelle des Déclarations de 1789 et 1946, au début des années 70, a-t-elle une signification considérable, qui déborde le cadre français pour s'inscrire dans la mouvance européenne. Deux courtes phrases, conforme à la *brevitas* en usage dans les arrêts des tribunaux français, consacrent ce changement: «Vu la Constitution et notamment son préambule» et «Considérant qu'au nombre des principes reconnus par les lois de la République et solennellement réaffirmés par le préambule de la Constitution, il y a lieu de ranger le principe de la liberté d'association»[52]. Grâce au préambule de 1958, qui renvoie aux Déclarations et aux «principes fondamentaux reconnus par les lois de la République», le Conseil constitutionnel se dote, à la lumière des droits de l'homme et des garanties qui forment l'État de droit, d'une faculté d'appréciation de la validité des lois qui lui a permis

---

[50] *La garantie constitutionnelle de la Constitution (La justice constitutionnelle)*, R.D.P. (1928), pp. 197, 224, 227, 233, 247, 252.

[51] Constitution du 4 oct. 1958, art. 56 à 63 dans: Duverger, *op. cit.*, *supra* note 28, p. 261.

[52] Décision 71–44 DC (Liberté d'association), 16 juil. 1971, REC., p. 29, et dans: L. FAVOREU et L. PHILIP, LES GRANDES DÉCISIONS DU CONSEIL CONSTITUTIONNEL, Sirey, Paris, 4e éd. (1986), pp. 239, 241.

depuis lors de déclarer non conformes à la Constitution, sans se fonder directement sur le texte de 1958, plusieurs dispositions législatives[53]. Certes, la légitimité de cette démarche prétorienne a parfois été contestée, surtout depuis que l'élargissement de la saisine, en 1974, permet à un certain nombre de membres de l'Assemblée nationale de soumettre les projets de lois à l'examen du Conseil, mais le dénouement des crises suscitées par les nationalisations (1982), puis par les privatisations (1986) a montré qu'en définitive, les décisions du Conseil ont contribué à apaiser ces turbulences et favorisé l'acceptation du changement[54]. L'argument du «gouvernement des juges», entendu à l'occasion, ne paraît pas entamer l'intérêt croissant de l'opinion française pour les questions liées à l'État de droit et aux libertés, mais la proposition visant à permettre la saisine du Conseil par les justiciables, qui conduirait sans doute à l'examen des lois après leur entrée en vigueur, se heurte pour l'instant à l'opposition d'une partie de la classe politique, notamment au Sénat[55]. On aura noté, cependant, que la décision du Conseil constitutionnel élargissant le «bloc de constitutionnalité» précède de peu la ratification par la France de la Convention européenne de sauvegarde des droits de l'homme (1974) et le comportement du Conseil constitutionnel depuis ce moment montre qu'il existe une interaction entre sa jurisprudence et celle de la Cour européenne: comme le fait observer le p^r^ F. Sudre, sous couvert des principes constitutionnels le Conseil procède à une «transfusion» en droit interne des solutions consacrées par la Cour[56].

Revenons à la Grande-Bretagne: elle n'a pas parcouru le même itinéraire que la France, n'ayant pas de constitution «à principes», encore que la jurisprudence de ses tribunaux en contienne plus d'un. Nombreux sont les juristes qui demeurent réticents devant la perspective d'incorporer telle quelle la Convention européenne, ou d'adopter un *Bill of Rights* détaillé, comme d'autres l'ont proposé[57]. Les juges eux-mêmes sont partagés: en 1977 dans

---

[53] *V.g.* décisions 88-248 DC, 17 janv. 1989, consid. 29, Rec., p. 18; 89-260 DC, 28 juil. 1989, consid. 44, Rec., p. 71; 93-326, 11 août 1993, consid. 12 et 15, Rec., p. 217; *voir* D. TURPIN, DROIT CONSTITUTIONNEL, PUF, Paris (1992), p. 96.

[54] Décisions 81-132 DC, 16 janv. 1982; 82-139, 11 fév. 1982, Rec., pp. 18 et 31; 86-207 DC, 25–26 juin 1986, REC., p. 61; *voir* L. FAVOREU, *Crise du juge et contentieux constitutionnel en droit français*, dans: J. LENOBLE (dir.), LA CRISE DU JUGE, L.G.D.J., Paris (1990), pp. 61, 64.

[55] La proposition en a été faite par R. BADINTER, alors Président du Conseil constitutionnel: LE MONDE, 3 mars 1989, p. 1; *voir* la réaction du Président du Sénat, A. POHER, LE MONDE, 26 mai 1990, p. 8.

[56] DROIT INTERNATIONAL ET EUROPÉEN DES DROITS DE L'HOMME, PUF, Paris, (2e éd.) (1995), p. 331.

[57] *Voir* M. ZANDER, *The British Experience – The Effort to Have the European Convention Incorporated*, dans: L.A. REHOF et C. GULMANN (dir.), HUMAN RIGHTS IN DOMESTIC LAW AND DEVELOPMENT ASSISTANCE POLICIES IN THE NORDIC COUNTRIES (1989), pp. 143–151.

l'affaire *Gouriet*, lord Denning, peut-être influencé par la Convention européenne, a voulu déduire directement de la notion de *rule of law*, invoquée comme principe général du droit anglais, le pouvoir des tribunaux de contrôler l'exercice d'une compétence discrétionnaire attribuée par le Parlement au Procureur général; selon le juge, la décision du Procureur paraissait déraisonnable à la lumière de ce principe. La Chambre des Lords a renversé cette décision, estimant qu'on ne pouvait de la sorte «pousser jusqu'au dernier degré le pouvoir d'innovation des juges»[58]. Les méthodes déductives «continentales» se heurtent ici aux méthodes d'interprétation restrictive des *statutes*. Ce signal d'arrêt montre que la différence entre cette tradition et celle de la plupart des pays européens est toujours d'actualité. Toutefois, cette attitude et le refus d'incorporer la Convention comportent un grave inconvénient pour le Royaume-Uni: depuis qu'il a accepté la juridiction des institutions de Strasbourg, celles-ci lui servent en quelque sorte de Cour constitutionnelle…

Aussi a-t-on vu naître depuis quelques années divers projets de constitution formelle, assortis d'un contrôle juridictionnel. Le plus important a été publié en 1991 par l'*Institute for Public Policy Research* après qu'un groupe de juristes, de politiques, de gens d'affaires et de syndicalistes, parmi lesquels les p[rs] R. Dworkin, J. Jowell, A. Bradley et Sir William Goodhart, y eût consacré trois ans de réflexion. Intitulé *The Constitution of the United Kingdom*, le projet comporte un chapitre sur les droits fondamentaux (articles 2 à 29) et se substituerait à la suprématie du Parlement: il rendrait inopérantes les lois et règles de *common law* non conformes, le contrôle étant exercé par les cours supérieures, avec appel à une Cour suprême[59]. Les rédacteurs redoutent cependant que pareil système, semblable à celui des États-Unis, n'entraîne la politisation du recrutement des juges et le projet contient des dispositions très élaborées en vue de soustraire leur nomination à toute ingérence politique. La Convention et la Cour européennes ne sont sûrement pas étrangères à cette évolution des idées, qui exigerait une sorte de mutation dans la culture juridique britannique. Celle-ci est peut-être inévitable à moyen ou à long terme, compte tenu du processus d'intégration en cours en Europe. Entre-temps, l'Allemagne continuera d'élaborer les corollaires et conséquences du *Rechtsstaat* et d'influencer la jurisprudence européenne relative à la prééminence du droit, comme nous allons maintenant le constater.

---

[58] *Gouriet* v. *Union of Post Office Workers* (1977), 1 ALL E.R. 697, aux pp. 715–716 (C.A.); *Gouriet* v. *Post Office Engineering*, A.C. 435 (1978), à la p. 478 (lord Wilberforce).

[59] L'Institut (I.P.P.R.) est un organisme indépendant voué à l'étude des questions sociales, économiques et politiques: *voir* le projet d'articles, n°s 102–113.

B. Le *Rechtsstaat* constitutionnalisé de l'Allemagne

Le sort des libertés et droits fondamentaux sous le régime qu'un auteur a appelé le *Führesstaat* explique dans une large mesure la volonté bien arrêtée des constituants allemands de 1949 de renouer avec leur tradition philosophique et juridique et de se doter d'un *Rechtsstaat* garanti par la *Loi fondamentale*. Désormais, les droits et libertés seront non seulement constitutionnalisés, mais «directement applicables» par tous les organes de l'État sour la surveillance des tribunaux. La Constitution de Bonn proclame en effet que la loi est assujettie à l'ordre constitutionnel, que l'Exécutif et les tribunaux sont soumis «au droit et à la justice» et que l'ordre juridique des États membres (*Länder*) doit se conformer aux principes de «l'État de droit social» (*socialer Rechtsstaat*)[60].

La tâche de faire respecter cet ordre constitutionnel revient à tous les pouvoirs, mais c'est la nouvelle Cour constitutionnelle de la Fédération (*Bundesverfassungsgericht*) qui est chargée d'interpréter la *Loi fondamentale* et de régler les litiges constitutionnels, y compris ceux qui naîtraient de l'accès direct reconnu par l'article 93 § 4a à tout individu alléguant la violation de ses droits fondamentaux; en outre, tout tribunal qui estime qu'une loi n'est pas conforme à la Constitution doit s'adresser à cette Cour spécialisée pour obtenir une décision sur ce point avant de rendre jugement[61]. Ce système se situe pour ainsi dire au carrefour de la tradition libérale issue de Kant, du constitutionnalisme américain et des idées kelséniennes. C'est cependant la jurisprudence de la Cour constitutionnelle qui va lui imprimer son cachet d'originalité et exercer une influence considérable sur la notion européenne de prééminence du droit. Non seulement a-t-elle interprété libéralement les dispositions garantissant de façon spécifique les diverses règles de l'État de droit (justiciabilité des droits fondamentaux, accès aux tribunaux, procès équitable, droits de la défense et réparation des violations), mais la notion de *Rechtsstaat* elle-même est devenue en quelque sorte une source de droit autonome, la Cour n'hésitant pas à en déduire des règles lorsque l'affaire examinée s'y prête. De l'abondante jurisprudence ainsi accumulée depuis bientôt un demi-siècle, retenons quelques points saillants: 1° l'interprétation des droits fondamentaux garantis par les articles 1er à 19 de la Constitution à la lumière du principe des *Rechtsstaat*; 2° les règles «non écrites» déduites directement de ce concept; enfin, 3° le principe de proportionnalité, à titre d'exemple particulièrement important des méthodes d'interprétation pratiquées par la Cour.

---

60 DAS BONNER GRUNDGESETZ, 23 mai 1949, art. 1 à 20 et 28 § 1.

61 *Ibid.* art. 93 § 1 et 100 § 1.

1. Les *Grundrechte* à la lumière du *Rechtsstaat*

Le mot *Rechtsstaat* n'apparaît qu'une fois dans la *Loi fondamentale*: l'article 28 l'applique aux *Länder*. La Cour a décidé, cependant, que «l'ordre constitutionnel» imposé au législateur fédéral par l'article 20 ainsi que l'obligation qui est faite aux organes exécutif et juridictionnel de respecter «le droit et la justice» correspondaient au *Rechtsstaatprinzip*[62]. La suprématie du droit s'applique donc de façon très générale à toute la structure de l'État allemand et la Cour s'appuie sur ce principe dans son interprétation des droits fondamentaux (*Grundrechte*) spécifiquement garantis, comme si le *Rechtsstaat* constituait une valeur constitutionnelle fondamentale liant les uns aux autres l'ensemble de ces droits. Dans l'arrêt sur la *Loyauté des fonctionnaires*, par exemple, la Cour décide que la liberté d'expression et l'égalité devant la loi (articles 3 et 5), jointes au principe de la *Rechtsstaatlichkeit*, imposaient aux autorités le devoir d'entendre équitablement l'intéressé et de respecter son droit de réfuter les accusations portées contre lui[63]. De même, une personne dont l'état de santé est si précaire qu'une poursuite pénale pouvait mettre sa vie en danger ou aggraver sa condition peut invoquer à la fois son droit à la vie (article 2) et le principe du *Rechtsstaat*; l'interdiction préventive trop absolue d'une démonstration peut violer à la fois la liberté de réunion (article 8) et l'État de droit; un mandat de perquisition exécuté sans indication de l'infraction qui fait l'objet de l'enquête ou des preuves recherchées, enfreint l'inviolabilité du domicile (article 13) concurremment avec le *Rechtsstaat*[64]. Comme le fait observer le p^r^ U. Karpen, les droits fondamentaux et le principe de la limitation du pouvoir vont de pair «comme le piston et le cylindre»[65].

2. Les «principes non écrits» déduits de l'État de droit

La *Loi fondamentale* énonce plusieurs principes qui font traditionnellement partie de l'État de droit, tel celui qui exige que toute loi restreignant les droits individuels soit d'application générale, sans acception de personne (article 19 § 1), ou la règle *Nulla poena sine lege* (article 103), mais elle s'abstient de définir la notion de *Rechtsstaat*. La Cour constitutionnelle n'a pas voulu non plus s'enfermer dans une description exhaustive et il n'est pas interdit de penser qu'elle a agi ainsi dans l'intention de se réserver la lati-

---

62 Article 20 § 3; *voir* BVerfGE, vol. 35, pp. 41, 47.

63 BVerfGE (1975), v. 39, pp. 334, 386–389.

64 *Ibid.* (1979), vol. 51, p. 324; *ibid.* (1976), vol. 42, p. 212.

65 *Rule of Law*, dans: U. Karpen (dir.), The Constitution of the Federal Republic of Germany (1988), pp. 185–186.

tude nécessaire pour faire face aux problèmes nouveaux suscités sans cesse par l'évolution de la société. Cela lui a permis de déduire du *Rechtsstaats-prinzip* un certain nombre de règles «non écrites», parfois détaillées. C'est ainsi, par exemple, qu'elle exige que la législation soit aussi claire et précise que possible: la loi national-socialiste de 1934 interdisant les réunions a été déclarée inconstitutionnelle par manque de précision parce qu'elle attribuait au gouvernement un pouvoir discrétionnaire exorbitant[66].

Les principes de la sécurité juridique et de la prévisibilité des règles découlent également du *Rechtsstaat* dans la jurisprudence de la Cour constitutionnelle, en vue d'assurer la confiance des citoyens dans la stabilité des situations créées par la loi. Non seulement la Cour s'est-elle prononcée contre les lois rétroactives ou rétrospectives, mais elle a appliqué une règle analogue aux tribunaux, lesquels sont contraints, au moment de modifier leur jurisprudence au détriment d'une partie, de mesurer l'impact de leur décision sur les droits individuels de cette partie par rapport à l'intérêt public: la nouvelle règle doit être suffisamment importante de ce point de vue pour écarter la confiance que les particuliers ont placé dans la jurisprudence antérieure[67]. Bien d'autres exemples pourraient être donnés de ces principes non écrits, définissant notamment les conditions du procès équitable. Aucun n'est plus important que le principe de proportionnalité (*Verhältnismässigkeit*), tant parce qu'il pénètre l'ensemble du droit constitutionnel et administratif allemand qu'en raison de l'influence qu'il exerce sur la jurisprudence européenne et sur celle de plusieurs pays.

3. Le principe de proportionnalité

Bien que la Cour de Karlsruhe mentionne encore à l'occasion que ce principe est un corollaire ou tire son origine du *Rechtsstaat*, il a acquis dans sa jurisprudence une sorte d'existence autonome. Sa signification générale est celle-ci: toute atteinte à la sphère des droits fondamentaux de l'individu doit se révéler indispensable à la protection des droits d'autrui ou de l'intérêt public. La Cour a été amenée dès 1957, dans l'arrêt *Lüth*, à mettre en balance les droits et intérêts opposés et, en l'espèce, à mesurer l'importance de la liberté d'expression par rapport aux autres intérêts protégés par la loi[68]. Elle a défini avec plus de précision, notamment dans l'affaire de la *Loi*

---

[66] BVERFGE (1966), v. 20, p. 150.

[67] *Ibid.* (1981), vol. 59, pp. 128, 165; *voir* G. GRASSMAN, *La constitutionnalité des règles de droit rétroactives et rétrospectives dans la jurisprudence allemande: Règlement du conflit entre la confiance digne de protection des sujets de droit ... et l'intérêt public*, 4 REV. INTERNATIONALE DR. COMPARÉ (1989), 1017, à la p. 1022.

[68] BVERFGE (1957), vol. 7, pp. 198, 208 et s.

bavaroise sur les pharmacies, les critères lui permettant de juger les restrictions à la liberté à l'aune de l'objectif poursuivi, en l'occurrence le droit de choisir une profession, par rapport à la protection du public: le législateur doit s'assurer que les restrictions sont absolument nécessaires à la protection d'un intérêt social important; il doit user des moyens appropriés à l'objectif visé et qui restreignent le moins possible les droits fondamentaux[69].

L'affaire de la *Pneumoencéphalographie* (1963) illustre bien la portée du principe de proportionnalité: un tribunal ayant ordonné de soumettre l'accusé à un test médical destiné à établir son degré de responsabilité dans l'acte incriminé, la Cour constitutionnelle décide que la ponction du canal vertébral n'était pas sans risque pour l'intéressé et qu'il existait d'autres méthodes moins dangereuses pour son intégrité physique; il n'était pas établi avec certitude qu'une telle atteinte à sa liberté fût proportionnée à la gravité de l'infraction et l'ordre du tribunal allait donc à l'encontre des droits garantis[70]. Des cas nombreux et variés ont été jugés selon le même principe: par exemple, dans les *Expropriations de Hambourg* (1968), la Cour a estimé que le danger que présentaient pour la ville les raz-de-marée comme celui de 1962 justifiait au regard de la Constitution l'expropriation d'espaces destinés à la construction de digues; l'acquisition de gré à gré eût exigé trop de temps et l'atteinte à la propriété privée était proportionnée aux exigences de la protection publique[71]. Les libertés économiques n'ont pas échappé au critère de proportionnalité: dans l'affaire de la *Représentation des employés de grandes entreprises* (1979) la Cour a décidé que la participation des travailleurs à des comités de surveillance répondait à des objectifs sociaux valables et ne portait pas indûment atteinte aux droits des actionnaires; le principe de proportionnalité permettait d'établir un certain équilibre entre le libéralisme économique et les intérêts légitimes des travailleurs[72].

Les «principes non écrits» permettent à la Cour constitutionnelle de poursuivre en quelque sorte le dessein des constituants de 1949 et de donner de la *Loi fondamentale* une interprétation telle qu'elle soit constamment compatible avec «l'ordre de valeurs» qui la sous-tend[73]. La prééminence du droit et la limitation du pouvoir, sous la forme du *Rechtsstaat*, sont la source de ces principes et insufflent en quelque sorte à la Constitution allemande l'esprit des traditions du droit naturel et de l'*Aufklärung*.

---

69 *Ibid.* (1957), pp. 377, 405 et s.

70 *Ibid.* (1963), vol. 17, pp. 108, 117–119; *voir* également vol. 22, pp. 180, 219 (1967).

71 *Ibid.* (1968), vol. 24, pp. 367, 412.

72 *Ibid.* (1974), vol. 50, pp. 290, 340–352.

73 *Ibid.* (1970), vol. 30, pp. 1, 19.

Quelques autres Constitutions d'Europe occidentale, celles du Portugal, de l'Espagne et de la Turquie, énoncent expressément le principe de l'État de droit[74]. La chose est plus répandue encore dans les pays d'Europe centrale et orientale: la plupart des nouvelles Constitutions proclament le principe, habituellement dans leurs tout premiers articles, y ajoutant quelquefois les mots «démocratique» ou «social»; les États baltes font exception[75]. L'influence du Conseil de l'Europe se fait ici sentir et, dans bien des cas, il s'agit d'un grand projet à réaliser et non d'un acquis, mais la propagation de la notion d'État de droit dans «l'autre Europe» n'en est pas moins un phénomène frappant, un signe des temps.

Mais avant de répandre l'idée de la prééminence du droit, les institutions européennes ont dû «intérioriser» le principe énoncé dans leurs traités constitutifs, en préciser la portée et lui donner sa dimension internationale. C'est vers cette démarche que nous nous tournons maintenant.

II. LE PRINCIPE DE LA PRÉÉMINENCE DU DROIT DANS LA JURISPRUDENCE DES INSTITUTIONS EUROPÉENNES

Il eût été étonnant que les jurisprudences des Cours européennes de Strasbourg et de Luxembourg ne reflètent point, du moins à la longue, les comportements économiques et sociaux ainsi que les idiosyncrasies juridiques des États parties à la Convention de sauvegarde des droits de l'homme et au Traité de Rome[76]. Aussi ne peut-on s'étonner de voir ces tribunaux consacrer un grand nombre de leurs arrêts à divers aspects de l'État de droit, tels que les principes et règles portant sur l'accès à la justice, les contrôles de constitutionnalité et de légalité, le procès équitable, les droits de la défense, la réparation des violations des droits et libertés et la suspension des garanties; la Convention européenne énonce d'ailleurs là-dessus des règles nombreuses

---

[74] Constitutions du Portugal (1976), art. 2; de l'Espagne (1978), préambule et art. Ier § 1; de la Turquie (1982), art. 2 et 5; *voir* également l'Andorre (1993), art. 1er § 1, et Monaco (1962), art. 2 § 2.

[75] Albanie (projet), art. 2 § 1; Bulgarie (1991), art. 4 § 1; Constitutions du Bélarus (1994), préambule; Croatie (1990), art. 3; Georgie (1994), préambule; Hongrie (1989), préamb. et art. 2 § 1; Macédoine (1991), préamb. et art. 8 § 1; Moldavie (1994), préamb. et art. 1 § 3; Pologne (1952, 1992), art. 1er; République Tchèque (1992), préamb. et art. 1er; Roumanie (1991), art. 1 § 3 et 37 § 2; Russie (1993), art. 1er § 1; Slovaquie (1992), art. 1er; Slovénie (1991), préamb. et art. 2; Ukraine (projet), préamb. et art. 2; Yougoslavie (1992), art. 9 § 1.

[76] Convention *supra* note 1; Traité instituant la Communauté économique européenne, 25 mars 1957, 298:11 R.T.N.U. (1958), tel que modifié par la suite, reproduit, dans: J.-Y. MORIN, F. RIGALDIES et D. TURP, DROIT INTERNATIONAL PUBLIC. NOTES ET DOCUMENTS, Thémis, Montréal, 2e éd. (1992), pp. 373 et s.

et détaillées que la Cour de Strasbourg avait le devoir d'appliquer, au besoin en les interprétant. En revanche, il n'était pas évident que les Cours européennes feraient appel à des concepts plus généraux – et plus «flous» – comme la «prééminence du droit», mentionnée dans le préambule de la Convention de sauvegarde et dans le Statut du Conseil de l'Europe, ou le principe de proportionnalité, qui n'apparaît nulle part dans ces instruments. Le sens et la portée de ces notions, dans leur dimension européenne, ne pouvaient résulter que d'une construction prétorienne et donc de l'action de tribunaux suffisamment sûrs de leurs arrières pour s'aventurer, à la manière de certaines juridictions nationales, dans les sentiers de l'interprétation innovatrice. Pour mesurer le chemin parcouru, nous étudierons avant tout la jurisprudence de la Cour européenne des droits de l'homme (A) pour ensuite exposer quelques arrêts majeurs de la Cour de justice des Communautés (B).

A. La «prééminence du droit» dans la jurisprudence de la Cour européenne des droits de l'homme

Selon l'expression de W.B. Gallie, les concepts de portée très générale, comme l'est indubitablement la prééminence du droit, sont «par essence contestés», en ce sens qu'il n'existe pas qu'un usage de l'expression qui puisse être considéré comme «correct»[77]. C'est le cas également de termes comme le *rule of law*, la liberté, la justice, l'égalité, la nature, le procès équitable, le comportement raisonnable ou la démocratie. Ce sont là des notions «appréciatives» (*appraisive*) qui font appel à des systèmes de valeurs pouvant faire l'objet de divergences parfaitement légitimes, appuyées sur des arguments tout à fait respectables de part et d'autre. Le mérite de la Cour européenne des droits de l'homme est d'avoir su dégager peu à peu des acceptions nationales et des dispositions de la Convention portant sur la prééminence du droit un sens et une portée communs auxquels tous les États parties puissent adhérer, non sans sourciller parfois. Il est vrai qu'elle a pu faire appel pour cela à l'héritage partagé de limitation du pouvoir issu de la civilisation de l'Europe médiévale et au droit naturel des Lumières, sans le dire expressément, mais il lui a fallu, pour y accéder, se garder d'un certain positivisme, qui fait également partie du patrimoine européen. Cette démarche vaut qu'on l'étudie 1° dans ses sources et 2° dans les conséquences qu'elle comporte pour l'interprétation de la Convention et du droit des États.

---

[77] *Essentially Contested Concepts*, 56 PROCEEDINGS OF THE ARISTOTELIAN SOC. (1956), pp. 167–168.

1. Les sources de la jurisprudence strasbourgeoise en matière de prééminence du droit

Si la Convention de sauvegarde et le Statut du Conseil de l'Europe reconnaissent la «prééminence du droit», les deux instruments dans leur préambule et le second également à l'article 3, l'expression ne fait l'objet d'aucune définition ou description dans ces traités. Certes, on trouve dans la Convention de nombreuses garanties concrètes de l'État de droit, notamment aux articles 5, 6, 7 et 8, mais quelle idée se faisaient les négociateurs de la notion abstraite de prééminence lorsqu'ils affirmaient que les États parties, «animés d'un même esprit et possédant un patrimoine commun d'idéal et de tradition politiques, de respect de la liberté et de prééminence du droit», étaient résolus à assurer la garantie collective des droits de l'homme? La réponse à cette question n'était pas évidente en 1949, au sortir d'une période qui avait si profondément divisé les pays européens au sujet du respect des droits de l'homme; elle n'en a pas moins une grande importance pour l'interprétation que la Cour européenne sera appelée à donner des dispositions de la Convention.

L'examen du contexte de celle-ci, auquel le droit international coutumier et la Convention sur le droit des traités renvoient pour l'interprétation des traités[78], montre bien qu'il s'agit de la protection des droits individuels, mais ne permet guère de préciser le contenu de la notion de prééminence. Lorsque le sens d'une disposition est obscur, on peut avoir recours à des moyens complémentaires d'interprétation notamment aux travaux préparatoires: ceux-ci peuvent-ils nous guider? Le premier projet, rédigé par la Section juridique du Mouvement européen, propose dans son préambule «d'assurer le respect de la loi», termes dont la portée paraît très restreinte, voisine de celle du *rule of law* dans son acception britannique, c'est-à-dire compatible avec la souveraineté de la loi[79]. Cette rédaction est soumise au Comité des ministres du Conseil de l'Europe en juillet 1949, mais la Commission nommée par les ministres pour examiner la possibilité d'instaurer une garantie collective des droits fondamentaux, ne retient pas dans son projet la prééminence du droit, quoique le rapporteur, P.-H. Teitgen, souligne au passage le fait que l'article 3 du Statut du Conseil reconnaît ce principe et s'interroge: «N'était-ce là qu'un souhait, une affirmation théorique, une sorte de clause de style dont on pourrait dire qu'elle n'engage pas réellement?».

---

[78] Convention du 22 mai 1969, 1155 R.T.N.U. (1980), 353, articles 31 à 33.

[79] Commission préparatoire du Conseil de l'Europe, Comité des ministres et Assemblée consultative, RECUEIL DES «TRAVAUX PRÉPARATOIRES», Nijhoff, La Haye (1975–1985), vol. Ier, p. 297: les termes «respect de la loi» pourraient être une traduction littérale de l'expression *rule of law*.

La Commission ne l'a pas pensé, répond le rapporteur qui ajoute que la garantie proposée «manifesterait clairement la volonté commune des États de bâtir l'Union européenne selon les principes du droit naturel, de l'humanisme et de la démocratie»[80]. À défaut d'indication quant au sens précis attribué à la prééminence du droit dans le Statut du Conseil, la Commission se réfère en quelque sorte à l'ensemble de la tradition occidentale.

L'Assemblée consultative, saisie du projet par le Comité des ministres, approuve après débat un texte qui protège les droits et libertés, mais ne mentionne pas la prééminence du droit. Le Comité d'experts nommés par les gouvernements pour établir le texte de la future Convention n'en parle pas davantage dans son avant-projet de février 1950; il ne propose d'ailleurs aucun préambule[81]. Il faut attendre que M. Mitchison, représentant du Royaume-Uni, propose un préambule à la Commission des questions juridiques de l'Assemblée consultative pour qu'apparaisse le principe de la prééminence du droit (août 1950). Celle-ci l'approuve sans que les procès-verbaux nous indiquent si le sens ou la portée du principe a été discutée; de même, l'assemblée adopte, sans débat semble-t-il, un préambule affirmant que les parties contractantes possèdent «un patrimoine de la liberté et de prééminence du droit» (*rule of law* dans la version anglaise)[82]. C'est ce texte, légèrement modifié quant à la forme par un comité d'experts constitué par les Ministres, qui apparaît au paragraphe 5 du préambule de la Convention de sauvegarde signée le 4 novembre 1950.

Si l'on s'en tenait à ces données, on pourrait être tenté de conclure que le principe de la prééminence du droit constitue une sorte d'ajout adventice, d'accessoire inspiré sans doute du Statut du Conseil, mais auquel les Parties n'entendaient pas accorder une force contraignante. Ce serait faire fi de la motivation profonde des rédacteurs, pour lesquels la prééminence du droit paraît aller de soi en tant qu'élément intrinsèque de la tradition libérale de l'Europe. Tel est le fondement de l'opinion de la Cour européenne dans l'arrêt *Golder* (1975)[83], dans lequel elle a pour la première fois fait appel au principe de la prééminence du droit en tant que tel.

Les juges de Strasbourg avaient à interpréter l'article 6 § 1 de la Convention, qui garantit à toute personne le droit de faire entendre sa cause équitablement, mais n'établit pas en termes exprès le droit d'accès aux tribunaux.

---

80 *Ibid.* vol. Ier, pp. 193–215, 267 (5 sept. 1949).

81 *Ibid.* vol. II, p. 275 (recommandation no 38 de l'Assemblée); v. III, p. 237 (avant-projet des experts, doc. A 833); *voir* également le projet adopté par le Comité des ministres, 7 août 1950, doc. A 1937, qui ne comporte aucune allusion à la prééminence du droit.

82 *Ibid.* vol. VI, pp. 29, 41, 67, 239–240 et 273 (doc. A 2158 et A 2838 août 1950).

83 Arrêt du 21 fév. 1975, série A, n° 18, p. 1 et s.

Le ministre de l'Intérieur du Royaume-Uni avait refusé d'autoriser un détenu à intenter une poursuite civile contre un gardien qui l'avait accusé d'agression pour ensuite admettre qu'il y avait peut-être erreur sur la personne. Selon le gouvernement britannique, l'article 6 garantissait l'audition équitable d'une cause seulement une fois que celle-ci était engagée: interprétée strictement, la disposition ne garantissait pas le droit à un tribunal[84]. La Cour a estimé, au contraire, que la garantie de procès équitable ne se concevait pas sans droit d'accès à un tribunal. Elle eût sans doute pu s'appuyer sur l'article 13, qui garantit un «recours effectif» en cas de violation des droits et libertés reconnus dans la Convention, mais on eût pu lui répondre que le droit revendiqué par le requérant n'était pas de ceux-là. Les juges ont donc préféré faire appel au contexte global du traité, à la lumière de son objet et de son but, tels qu'ils ressortent notamment du préambule.

Sans entrer dans l'examen des travaux préparatoires – nous avons constaté que la Cour n'y eût pas trouvé de réponse précise –, elle décide que la prééminence du droit n'a pas été incluse dans le texte comme «rappel plus ou moins théorique», mais comme principe propre à éclairer l'interprétation de la Convention tout entière. Or, la prééminence du droit ne se conçoit guère sans la possibilité d'accéder aux tribunaux[85]: que signifierait en effet le *rule of law* sans possibilité pour l'individu de faire valoir ses droits?

La méthode déductive ainsi appliquée par la Cour s'apparente fortement au raisonnement familier à la tradition civiliste et c'est pour ainsi dire toute la tradition «continentale», non seulement juridique, mais philosophique, qui se trouve de la sorte incorporée dans la Convention. On pouvait donc s'attendre à ce que cette solution libérale marquât l'interprétation de toutes ces dispositions, comme le faisait observer R. Pelloux au lendemain de l'arrêt *Golder*[86]. Aussi ne peut-on s'étonner outre mesure de l'opinion séparée du juge G. Fitzmaurice, révélatrice de la différence entre l'esprit de la *common law* et celui de la tradition romaine. Selon le juge britannique, la Cour a accordé trop d'importance au principe de la prééminence du droit; elle aurait du donner de l'article 6 § 1 une interprétation plus prudente, pour ne pas imposer aux États des obligations qu'ils n'ont pas eu conscience d'assumer[87]. Cette approche serait effectivement plus conforme à l'interprétation restrictive des *statutes* familière aux juristes anglais et il pourrait paraître singulier que le préambule de la Convention ait été proposé par un représentant du

---

84 *Ibid.* p. 12, § 25; p. 18, § 36.

85 *Ibid.* p. 16, § 34.

86 *L'affaire Golder devant la Cour européenne des droits de l'homme*, 21 A.F.D.I. (1975), p. 330.

87 *Ibid.* p. 53, § § 38 et 39.

Royaume-Uni; seulement, on ne doit pas perdre de vue que le *rule of law* n'est pas constitutionnalisé dans le pays qui l'a vu naître et que, strictement parlant, il renvoie à la souveraineté du législateur. Il faut cependant constater que le Parlement britannique a pris soin de modifier sa législation lorsque la Cour a constaté, à diverses reprises, qu'elle n'était pas conforme aux engagements du pays[88]. La Convention de sauvegarde sert en quelque sorte de constitution au Royaume-Uni et le tribunal de Strasbourg, de Cour constitutionnelle.

L'arrêt *Golder* donne le ton à une jurisprudence importante, qui vient encore élargir la portée de la notion de prééminence du droit dans l'interprétation de la Convention de sauvegarde.

2. Développement du principe de la prééminence du droit par la Cour européenne des droits de l'homme

Depuis 1975, la cour de Strasbourg a eu l'occasion de faire appel à la prééminence du droit dans une vingtaine d'arrêts dont certains comptent parmi les plus importants de sa jurisprudence. Ils traitent avant tout de requêtes alléguant des violations des articles 5 (privation de liberté), 6 (procès équitable) et 8 (respect de la vie privée et de la correspondance), c'est-à-dire de règles rattachées traditionnellement à l'État de droit. Récemment, la Cour a étendu le champ d'application du principe à l'une des grandes libertés fondamentales, la liberté d'expression (article 10) et en a profité pour diversifier quelque peu sa terminologie: elle emploie en effet les expressions «primauté du droit» et «État de droit».

a) Privation de liberté et prééminence du droit

L'article 5 de la Convention affirme le principe de la liberté personnelle et indique dans quelles circonstances et selon quelles «voies légales» un individu peut en être privé. S'il refuse, par exemple, de se soumettre à une ordonnance rendue par un tribunal en vue de garantir une obligation prescrite par la loi, l'arrestation ou la détention serait «régulière» (§ 1b); s'il a été arrêté parce qu'il existe des raisons plausibles de soupçonner qu'il a commis une infraction ou des motifs raisonnables de croire qu'il s'apprête à la commettre, il doit être traduit aussitôt devant le magistrat compétent (§ § 1c et 3); enfin, la détention peut être régulière dans certains cas, comme ceux de l'«aliéné», du toxicomane ou d'une personne susceptible de propager une maladie

---

88 En ce qui concerne les suites données à l'arrêt *Golder*, *voir* Pelloux, *op. cit.*, *supra* note 86, 338. Les arrêts MALONE ET SUNDAY TIMES, *infra* notes 98 et 101, sont à l'origine du *Interception of Communications Act* (1985), c. 56, et du Contempt of Court Act (1981), c. 49.

contagieuse (§ 1e). Cependant, des termes comme «détention régulière», «obligation prescrite par la loi» et «aussitôt» sont susceptibles d'une interprétation plus ou moins extensive ou, au contraire, restrictive, et la Cour a dû rechercher des critères lui permettant d'appliquer correctement les règles aux situations concrètes.

Dans l'affaire *Engel* (1976), le gouvernement néerlandais soutenait que les arrêts imposés à un militaire répondaient aux exigences de l'article 5 § 1b puisque cette mesure de rigueur visait à «garantir l'exécution d'une obligation prescrite par la loi». Une interprétration large de la disposition conventionnelle eût peut-être donné raison à l'autorité militaire, mais la Cour, qui venait de faire appel à la prééminence du droit dans l'arrêt *Golder*, a estimé que le principe était également pertinent ici: une interprétation extensive, a-t-elle décidé, serait contraire au principe «dont s'inspire la Convention tout entière» et pourrait justifier, par exemple, l'internement administratif d'un citoyen, tendant à le contraindre de s'acquitter d'un vague devoir général d'obéissance à la loi et non d'une «obligation spécifique et concrète» qu'il a négligé d'accomplir[89]. Peut-être la Cour eût-elle pu parvenir à la même conclusion par un raisonnement différent, mais on doit constater qu'elle fait de la prééminence du droit le fondement de sa décision sur ce point.

Quand la détention d'une personne atteinte de maladie mentale est-elle «régulière»? La Cour eurpéenne répond, dans l'arrêt *Winterwerp* (1979) qu'on ne saurait interner une personne comme «aliéné» sans des preuves médicales «propres à justifier une hospitalisation forcée». Le bon sens eût suffi à dicter cette interprétation, mais la Cour ajoute, sans doute pour faire bonne mesure, que «dans une société adhérant à la prééminence du droit, une détention arbitraire ne peut jamais passer pour régulière»[90]. En l'espèce, les preuves médicales étaient suffisantes et la détention, régulière, de sorte que la référence au principe paraît relever de ce que la *common law* appelle un «obiter dictum». On peut en dire autant de l'allusion à la prééminence du droit dans l'arrêt *Kemmache* (1994): le refus d'une cour d'assise de mettre l'accusé en liberté, en vue d'éviter sa fuite, paraît justifié aux yeux de la Cour de Strasbourg et la détention est donc régulière au regard de l'article 5 § 1[91]. Ici encore, le principe ne joue pas un rôle déterminant, mais la Cour a jugé utile de le rappeler.

La célérité exigée par l'article 5 § 3 pour la comparution de toute personne arrêtée demande également à être appréciée, d'autant que les mots «aussitôt»

---

[89] Arrêt *Engel et autres* c. *Pays-Bas*, 8 juin 1976, série A, nº 22, p. 28, § 69.

[90] Arrêt du 24 oct. 1979, série A, nº 33, pp. 17–19, § 39 et 43; cependant, il y avait eu violation de l'art. 5 § 4.

[91] Arrêt (nº 3), 24 nov. 1994, série A, nº 296-C, pp. 88–89, § 42 et 45.

et «promptly» des deux versions officielles de la Convention n'ont pas tout à fait la même signification. La Cour s'est penchée sur la question dans l'affaire *Brogan* (1988). Les événements d'Irlande du Nord avaient mis à rude épreuve les engagements ratifiés par le Royaume-Uni et la Cour a estimé que la durée de la garde à vue d'un individu soupçonné de terrorisme pouvait, dans une certaine mesure, être étendue sans violer ces engagements; cependant, la Convention de sauvegarde ne pouvait aller jusqu'à autoriser une période de détention de 4 à 6 jours sans comparution. La célérité exigée doit s'apprécier, dit la Cour, à la lumière de l'objet et du but de l'article 5, lesquels font du contrôle judiciaire un élément essentiel dans la réduction du risque d'arbitraire. Ce contrôle, ajoute-t-elle, «va de pair avec la prééminence du droit», principe auquel «se réfère expressément au préambule de la Convention»[92]. L'arrêt est ainsi rédigé qu'il est difficile d'établir si le principe en constitue la *ratio decidendi*; du moins joue-t-il le rôle d'argument d'appoint.

b) Procès équitable et prééminence du droit

De toutes les dispositions de la Convention européenne, l'article 6 est, dans la jurisprudence de la Cour, le plus étroitement lié à l'État de droit. Il garantit le droit de toute personne à un procès équitable devant un tribunal indépendant et impartial, tant en matière civile qu'en matière pénale (§ 1). La disposition conventionnelle précise en outre, en cas de procès pénal, les droits de la défense (§ 3).

Dans l'arrêt *Golder*, mentionné plus haut, la Cour avait déjà souligné le lien entre l'article 6 § 1 et la prééminence du droit, pour en tirer le «droit à un tribunal». La disposition ne paraissait pas garantir formellement ce droit, mais le principe a fait pencher la balance en faveur d'une interprétation libérale du texte. Mais quel doit être le *degré* d'accès au tribunal assuré par la législation nationale? Dans l'affaire *Ashingdane* (1985), la Cour fait appel de nouveau au principe de la prééminence du droit pour résoudre la question. Comme dans l'arrêt *Winterwerp*, déjà mentionné, une personne internée dans une institution psychiatrique n'avait pas réussi à faire juger la régularité de sa détention. Les juges de Strasbourg estiment que le degré d'accès doit être mesuré à la lumière de la prééminence du droit dans une société démocratique: d'un part, ce droit peut être assujetti à des limitations car il appelle, de par sa nature même, une réglementation par l'État, mais, d'autre part, il ne doit pas être atteint dans sa substance même. Comment concilier ces deux propositions? La Cour fait appel à un critère découlant de l'État de droit dans certains droits nationaux: les limitations ne sont com-

---

92 Arrêt du 23 nov. 1988, série A, n° 145-B, pp. 32–33, § 58 et 62.

patibles avec l'article 6 § 1 (interprété selon la prééminence du droit) que «s'il existe un rapport raisonnable de proportionnalité entre les moyens employés et le but visé»[93]. La prééminence du droit dicte ainsi à la Cour une règle d'interprétation «non écrite».

Il en va de même dans l'affaire *Fayed* (1994), où le droit au tribunal avait été soumis à des limitations que les requérants considéraient comme incompatibles avec l'article 6 § 1. La Cour estime qu'il serait contraire à la prééminence du droit «qu'un État puisse sans réserve ... soustraire à la compétence des tribunaux toute une série d'actions civiles ou exonérer de toute responsabilité civile de larges groupes ou catégories de personnes». Toutefois, appliquant le critère du «rapport raisonnable de proportionnalité», elle en vient à la conclusion qu'en l'espèce, la limitation imposée aux requérants ne constituait pas un déni injustifié de leur droit à un tribunal[94].

Le principe de la prééminence du droit et le critère de proportionnalité qui en découle apparaissent également dans l'arrêt *Poitrimol* (1993). L'accusé dans cette affaire, s'étant abstenu de comparaître, s'était vu privé par le tribunal du droit d'avoir l'assistance d'un défenseur de son choix, garanti par l'article 6 § 3c de la Convention. La Cour décide qu'il s'agit là d'une «sanction disproportionnée», eu égard «à la place primordiale que les droits de la défense et le principe de la prééminence du droit occupent dans une société démocratique»[95].

Comme il arrive souvent en droit interne, la Cour a eu à trancher la question de savoir si les accusations à caractère disciplinaire et les sanctions administratives sont soumises aux garanties du procès équitable. L'arrêt *Engel*, précité, se fonde sur la prééminence du droit pour affirmer que «ressortissent à la matière pénale les privations de liberté susceptibles d'être infligées à titre répressif, hormis celles qui par leur nature, leur durée ou leurs modalités d'exécution ne sauraient causer un préjudice important». Il en découle que le huis-clos devant un tribunal militaire viole le droit d'être entendu publiquement, garanti par l'article 6 § 1[96]. De même, dans l'affaire *Deweer* (1980), le requérant avait été acculé au paiement d'une amende par l'administration sous la menace de fermeture de son commerce: la Cour décide que cette mesure relève de la matière pénale au regard de la Convention et déclare qu'elle doit se montrer vigilante devant les contraintes qui tendent à priver une personne de son droit à un procès équitable. Elle entend donc s'assurer qu'il

---

93 Arrêt du 28 mai 1985, série A, nº 93, pp. 25–26, § 56 et 57.
94 Arrêt du 21 sept. 1994, série A, nº 294-B, p. 49, § 65.
95 Arrêt du 23 nov. 1993, série A, nº 277-A, p. 15, § 35, 38.
96 Arrêt *supra* note 89, pp. 35–36, § 82 et 85.

y a absence de contrainte, comme «le veut un instrument international fondé sur les idées de prééminence du droit et de liberté»[97].

Quelle est l'étendue de l'autorité du juge selon les exigences du procès équitable? La Cour a eu à considérer le pouvoir attaché à la notion de *contempt of court* (outrage à magistrat, traduit parfois par l'expression «mépris de cour») dans la pratique judiciaire anglaise. Citant l'arrêt *Golder*, la Cour s'appuie sur le principe «fondamental» de la prééminence du droit, consacré, dit-elle, par l'article 6 de la Convention, pour conclure que les règles de *common law* dans ce domaine y sont conformes car elles visent à garantir l'autorité du pouvoir judiciaire, élément clé de l'État de droit. Notons également que la Cour, examinant la question de savoir si le *contempt*, création prétorienne, est prévu par la loi, décide que la «loi» englobe à la fois le droit écrit et la *common law*. Cependant, le citoyen doit disposer de renseignements suffisants sur les règles juridiques applicables à un cas donné: la «loi» doit être *accessible et prévisible*, comme c'est d'ailleurs le cas en l'espèce[98]. Sans le dire expressément, la Cour invoque ici une exigence de l'État de droit tel qu'il est conçu dans les traditions de plusieurs pays d'Europe.

c) Respect de la vie privée et prééminence du droit

Parmi les arrêts les plus importants de la Cour de Strasbourg, il s'en trouve qui portent sur le droit au respect de la vie privée, du domicile et de la correspondance, garanti par l'article 8 de la Convention. Cette disposition, cependant, n'en fait pas un droit absolu: il peut y avoir ingérence d'une autorité publique à condition qu'elle soit prévue par la loi et qu'il s'agisse d'une mesure «qui, dans une société démocratique, est nécessaire» à la sûreté publique, à la défense de l'ordre, à la prévention des infractions pénales, etc. Les bornes et le contrôle de ce qui est nécesssaire en pareil cas ont soulevé – et soulèvent encore – des difficultés dans de nombreux pays et la Cour n'y a pas échappé. Or, dans sa recherche de critères d'interprétation lui permettant de définir les mesures «nécessaires», elle a fait appel au principe de la prééminence du droit.

L'arrêt *Klass* (1978) porte sur les écoutes téléphoniques: quelle sorte de contrôle l'article 8 § 2 exige-t-il sur ce type d'ingérence secrète dans la vie privée? L'Allemagne avait organisé une surveillance par un comité de cinq parlementaires élus par le *Bundestag*, comprenant des députés de l'opposition, et par une commission indépendante. L'accord de cette commision était requis avant que le gouvernement ne procédât aux écoutes: elle pouvait

---

[97] Arrêt du 27 fév. 1980, série A, n° 35, p. 25, § 49, et p. 27, § 51.

[98] Arrêt du 26 avril 1979, série A, n° 30, p. 32, § 49, et p. 34, § 55–56.

alors les déclarer illégales ou non nécessaires. Ce système était-il conforme aux garanties de la Convention? En réponse, la Cour s'est appuyée à nouveau sur la prééminence du droit et particulièrement sur son arrêt *Golder*. Le principe implique qu'une ingérence de cette sorte soit soumise à un contrôle «efficace» et les juges estiment souhaitable que celui-ci soit exercé par un juge, «en un domaine où les abus sont potentiellement si aisés». Cependant, la Cour admet la légitimité de pouvoirs de surveillance secrète dans une société démocratique et estime que la nature du contrôle et des sauvegardes prévus dans la législation allemande ne transgresse pas les limites de ce qui peut passer pour nécessaire dans une société fondée sur la prééminence du droit[99]. Le facteur déterminant de cet arrêt se trouve dans l'indépendance des organes de contrôle, pouvant être considérés, «dans les circonstances de la cause», comme propres à statuer de manière objective.

Le même principe, appliqué à l'interception de la correspondance d'un détenu, produit le résultat opposé dans l'affaire *Silver* (1983). Le «contrôle efficace» exigé par la prééminence du droit n'existe plus lorsque la loi investit l'Exécutif d'amples pouvoirs discrétionnaires, «échappant à tout examen au Parlement». Cette immixtion des autorités dans la vie privée est donc contraire aux garanties de l'article 8 § 1. La Cour fait également appel, sans mentionner l'État de droit, à deux critères qui en relèvent traditionnellement: une loi comportant une telle ingérence doit être suffisamment accessible et précise pour permettre au citoyen de prévoir à un degré raisonnable les conséquences de sa conduite, condition qui n'est pas respectée en l'espèce. En outre, la surveillance de la correspondance doit correspondre à un «besoin social impérieux» et être «proportionnée au but légitime poursuivi»[100]. On voit ainsi se préciser graduellement la portée du principe de la prééminence du droit.

S'il y avait quelque doute là-dessus, l'arrêt *Malone* (1984) en disposerait. Dans cette affaire d'interception de communications postales et téléphoniques, la Cour s'est appuyée essentiellement sur la prééminence du droit pour interpréter l'article 8. Tout d'abord, les mots «prévue par la loi» se réfèrent à une loi d'une «qualité» telle qu'elle soit compatible avec notre principe, c'est-à-dire offre une «certaine protection contre les atteintes arbitraires de la puissance publique aux droits garantis», particulièrement là où le pouvoir de l'Exécutif s'exerce en secret. La loi doit donc user de «termes assez clairs» pour indiquer à tous de manière suffisante en quelles circonstances et à quelles conditions elle habilite le gouvernement à procéder à des

---

99 Arrêt du 6 sept. 1978, série A, n° 28, p. 28, § 48 et pp. 25–26, § 53, 55, 56.

100 Arrêt du 25 mars 1983, série A, n° 61, pp. 32, 34, 37–38, § 85–88, 90 et 98.

mesures d'interception. En second lieu, la prééminence du droit exige que la loi définisse l'étendue et les modalités d'exercice du pouvoir d'appréciation accordé aux autorités, cela avec une netteté suffisante pour que tout individu y trouve le «degré minimal de protection» voulu par le principe[101].

Quelques années plus tard, les arrêts *Huvig* et *Kruslin* (1990) procèdent du même raisonnement. La Cour européenne se fait cependant plus ferme dans l'affirmation du principe et plus précise dans la détermination de ses conséquences. Les écoutes téléphoniques dont se plaignaient les requérants étaient-elles «prévues par la loi»? La Cour déclare qu'il lui faut apprécier celle-ci «au regard des impératifs du principe fondamental de la prééminence du droit». Il s'agit en l'occurrence d'une atteinte grave au respect de la vie privée et les écoutes doivent donc être autorisées par une loi «d'une précision particulière». L'existence de règles «claires et détaillées» est donc indispensable, d'autant, ajoute l'arrêt, que «les procédés techniques utilisables ne cessent de se perfectionner». En conséquence, la Cour énumère certaines sauvegardes que tout système d'écoutes devrait comporter: définition des catégories de personnes susceptibles d'y être assujetties et de la nature des infractions pouvant y donner lieu, fixation d'une limite à la durée de la mesure par le juge, établissement de procès-verbaux consignant les conversations interceptées aux fins de contrôle éventuel par le juge et la défense, enfin, effacement ou destruction des bandes magnétiques, notamment après non-lieu ou relaxe[102]. Le tribunal de Strasbourg en arrive ainsi, à l'instar de certaines Cours constitutionnelles européennes, à indiquer au législateur les conditions auxquelles ses actes seraient conformes aux normes fondamentales, à la lumière du principe de la prééminence du droit.

Ces précautions législatives deviennent essentielles lorsque l'ingérence vise des personnes internées dans les institutions psychiatriques, le courrier étant souvent le seul contact de ces détenus avec le monde extérieur. Selon l'arrêt *Herczegfalvy* (1992), la prééminence du droit exige alors, en vue d'éviter que les intéressés ne soient à la merci des autorités, que la loi donne des précisions quant au type de restrictions autorisées, leur durée, leur étendue et leur contrôle[103].

d) Liberté d'expression et prééminence du droit

L'interprétation des dispositions de la Convention de sauvegarde portant sur les restrictions à la liberté d'expression soulève des questions assez

---

101 Arrêt du 2 août 1984, série A, nº 92, pp. 32–33, 36, § 67, 68 et 79.

102 Arrêt *Huvig* c. *France*, 24 avril 1990, série A, nº 176-A, pp. 55–57, § 31–35; arrêt *Kruslin*, *ibid.* nº 176-B, pp. 23–24, § 32–35.

103 Arrêt du 24 sept. 1992, série A, nº 244, pp. 27–28, § 88–91.

semblables à celles que nous avons rencontrées à l'article 8 et c'est sans doute pour cette raison que la Cour européenne a eu recours, une fois de plus, au principe de la prééminence du droit. L'exercice de cette liberté, garantie par l'article 10 § 1 de la Convention, peut en effet «être soumis à certaines formalités, conditions, restrictions ou sanctions *prévues par la loi*, qui constituent des mesures *nécessaires*, dans une société démocratique», à la protection des intérêts collectifs ou des droits d'autrui (§ 2). Sont mentionnées entre autres la sécurité nationale, la défense de l'ordre, la protection de la réputation d'autrui et celle de l'autorité du pouvoir judiciaire. Quand les mesures ainsi autorisées sont-elles nécessaires et quelles en sont les limites?

L'affaire *Vereniging Weekblad Bluf!* (1995) portait sur cette question, dans le contexte du secret requis par la sécurité nationale: les autorités néerlandaises, inquiètes de la publication d'un rapport confidentiel dans un hebdomadaire, l'avaient saisi et, après sa réimpression, avaient tenté d'obtenir son retrait de la circulation. Les éditeurs plaidaient que ces mesures n'étaient «conformes au principe fondamental de la prééminence du droit» que si elles s'inscrivaient dans le cadre d'une procédure pénale régulière, la seule offrant des garanties suffisantes contre l'arbitraire; or, le ministère public avait obtenu saisie et retrait sans avoir dû prouver contradictoirement la nécessité du secret. Cette argumentation n'était pas sans rappeler les cas d'ingérence jugés contraires à la Convention dans les arrêts *Silver, Malone* et *Huvig*. Les juges de Strasbourg, cependant, ont estimé que le principe de la «primauté du droit» pouvait exiger, dans le contexte des services de sécurité, la protection du secret et l'adoption de mesures «décidées en dehors d'une instance pénale», décision à rapprocher de l'arrêt *Klass*. En d'autres termes, le principe, qui tend généralement à la protection des particuliers contre l'arbitraire des autorités, peut être invoqué par celles-ci lorsque «le bon fonctionnement d'une société démocratique» l'exige. Un État, dit la Cour, «peut ainsi se protéger contre les agissements des individus et groupes qui tentent de porter atteinte aux valeurs essentielles d'une société démocratique». En l'espèce, cependant, le tribunal de Strasbourg estime que le retrait de la publication, après sa réimpression et sa diffusion, n'était plus justifié, les renseignements confidentiels ayant été largement divulgués. Faute de «nécessité» dans une société démocratique, il y avait eu violation de l'article 10[104].

---

[104] Arrêt du 9 fév. 1995, série A, n° 306-A, pp. 12–16, § 30, 32, 35, 43 et 46. La notion d'«État de droit» apparaît également dans l'arrêt *Prager et Oberschlick* c. *Autriche*, 26 avril 1995 (13/1994/460/541), portant sur le même article de la Convention. Elle n'y figure cependant qu'à titre accessoire, la Cour rappelant au passage le *rôle éminent* joué par la presse dans un État de droit.

Cet emploi de la notion de la prééminence du droit, tantôt pour la protection de la liberté, tantôt pour celle du secret, n'est paradoxale qu'en apparence: les deux démarches ont en effet pour objet la défense de la conception libérale de la société. Cela fait néanmoins ressortir la marge d'appréciation considérable laissée aux tribunaux dans l'application du principe de prééminence et montre comment les «valeurs» qui sous-tendent l'État de droit et la démocratie peuvent s'inscrire dans le droit positif grâce à un ensemble de règles «non écrites».

B. La prééminence du droit dans la jurisprudence de la Cour de justice des Communautés européennes

La seule prééminence dont il soit question dans les Traités instituant la CECA (1951), la CEEA ou la CEE (1957) est celle du droit communautaire par rapport à l'ordre juridique interne des États membres: il n'existe pas dans ces dispositions conventionnelles de garantie des droits fondamentaux, à l'exception de quelques libertés de nature économique, comme les libertés de circulation et d'établissement[105]. Cet esprit utilitaire contraste avec la Convention de sauvegarde des droits de l'homme et le Traité instituant l'Union de l'Europe Occidentale (1948), dont le préambule rappelait l'attachement des Membres aux droits fondamentaux et à «la dignité et la valeur de la personne humaine»[106]. Très tôt, cependant, sont apparues des contradictions entre les actes pris par les Communautés et les garanties constitutionnelles reconnues aux individus par chacun des États membres. Comme le faisait observer G. Cohen-Jonathan, une situation paradoxale était ainsi apparue: des compétences soumises à des normes limitatives chez les Membres n'étaient plus restreintes dès qu'elles passaient dans l'ordre communautaire[107]. Ce phénomène, menaçant à la fois les libertés et l'effectivité du droit communautaire, explique l'obligation dans laquelle s'est trouvée la CJCE, chargée d'assurer l'interprétation et l'application correcte des Traités, de compléter le droit communautaire en matière d'État de droit.

N'étant pas tenue, comme le tribunal de Strasbourg, à un énoncé de droits, libertés et recours, la Cour de Luxembourg s'est tournée, dans un premier

---

105 Traité instituant la Communauté économique européenne, Rome, 25 mars 1957, 298 RTNU 11 (1958), art. 48–58.

106 Traité instituant l'UEO, Bruxelles, 17 mars 1948, modifié par les Accords de Paris, 23 oct. 1954; *voir* C.-A. COLLIARD, INSTITUTIONS DES RELATIONS INTERNATIONALES, Dalloz, Paris, 6e éd. (1974), p. 473, § 461.

107 *La Cour des Communautés européennes et les droits de l'homme*, R.M.C. (1978), pp. 74 et s.

temps du moins, vers les principes communs aux droits des États membres des Communautés. Dans son arrêt *Stauder* (1969), elle s'est reconnue la responsabilité de veiller au respect des droits fondamentaux par les institutions communautaires[108]; en l'absence de normes communes, ce sont en effet les règles nationales, comme la Constitution allemande (y compris le principe du *Rechtsstaat*) qui auraient servi à vérifier la validité des actes de la Commission de Bruxelles. La Cour s'engage alors dans une démarche qui va lui permettre de dégager des garanties analogues, «inhérentes» au droit communautaire: la sauvegarde de ces garanties, «tout en s'inspirant des traditions constitutionnelles communes des États membres, doit être assurée dans le cadre de la structure et des objectifs de la Communauté»[109]. Démarche prétorienne dont est né un droit communautaire non écrit, protecteur des libertés dans le domaine relevant des Communautés. Pareille évolution soulevait cependant diverses interrogations: pourquoi la CJCE n'appliquait-elle pas la Convention de sauvegarde, à laquelle étaient parties tous les Membres des Communautés? Le principe de la prééminence du droit était-il pertinent et s'appliquait-il aux Communautés elles-mêmes?

Les arrêts *Nold* (1974) et *Hauer* (1979) ont vu la Cour préciser le mécanisme de détermination des normes nationales transposables dans l'ordre communautaire[110]. Comparant entre elles les règles respectives des États, elle a décidé de retenir celles qui assurent la protection la plus poussée puisque la simple superposition de l'ensemble des règles l'eût conduite plutôt à rechercher le plus petit commun dénominateur; on aboutit ainsi à un ensemble de «principes généraux du droit» qu'on a qualifié de «standard maximum»[111]. La Cour se réfère également aux engagements internationaux des États, lesquels peuvent «fournir des indications dont il convient de tenir compte dans le cadre du droit communautaire»; la Convention de sauvegarde, en particulier, lui permet d'établir en quelque sorte un standard minimum européen. Ces techniques vont permettre à la Cour de mettre en oeuvre dans l'Union européenne des règles apparentées au principe de la prééminence du droit et de définir ainsi ce que nous pourrions appeler un «État de droit communautaire» qui n'est pas sans ressembler à celui du Conseil de l'Europe, tout en étant adapté aux préoccupations économiques des Communautés. Pour nos fins, deux catégories de règles peuvent être distingués: 1° celles

---

108 Arrêt du 12 nov. 1969, aff. 22/69, REC. (1969), pp. 419, 425, § 7.

109 *Internationale Handelsgesellschaft mbH* c. *Einfurh-und Vorrattsstelle für Getreide und Futtermittel*, 17 déc. 1970, aff. 11/70, REC. (1970), pp. 1125, 1135, § 4.

110 *Nold*, 14 mai 1974, aff. 4/73, REC. (1974), p. 508, § 13; *Hauer*, 13 déc. (1979), aff. 44/79, REC. (1979), p. 3744, § 15.

111 G. ISAAC, DROIT COMMUNAUTAIRE GÉNÉRAL, Masson, Paris 3e éd. (1980), p. 147.

qui découlent de l'État de droit classique, comme le «droit au juge», les droits de la défense et le principe de la confidentialité des rapports entre l'avocat et son client; 2° celles qui ont dû être façonnées en fonction d'une union de nature économique, comme le principe de la «sécurité juridique», celui de la «confiance légitime» et celui de la protection contre les interventions arbitraires des pouvoirs publics.

1. Règles déduites de l'État de droit classique

Le principe du recours effectif ou du «droit au juge» a été affirmé à diverses reprises par la CJCE, notamment dans l'affaire *Johnston* (1986), où une directive communautaire était contredite par la loi nationale, privant le particulier de toute possibilité de faire valoir son droit devant les tribunaux. Selon l'arrêt de la Cour, le contrôle exigé par la directive n'était que l'expression d'un principe général de droit commun aux traditions constitutionnelles des Membres, également consacré par la Convention de sauvegarde[112]. La Cour donne ainsi raison à l'avocat général, qui soutenait dans ses conclusions la thèse selon laquelle la CEE, étant une «communauté de droit», ne saurait priver l'individu du droit au juge.

Le caractère contradictoire de la procédure devant les tribunaux est un autre principe traditionnel de l'État de droit en Europe. La Cour l'a appliqué très tôt, même aux procédures devant les organes administratifs, comme la Commission de la CEEA, qui avait engagé une action disciplinaire contre un fonctionnaire[113]. D'autres droits de la défense ont également été affirmés: par exemple, les Communautés ont l'obligation de motiver toute résiliation d'un contrat de travail, pour ne pas que le contrôle de légalité en soit gêné[114]. On peut même affirmer que, depuis l'arrêt *Hoffmann-Laroche* (1979), l'ensemble des droits de la défense reconnus dans les pays membres de l'Union européenne doivent être respectés par la Commission dans toutes les affaires entraînant des sanctions ou astreintes[115]. Parfois, l'application devra en être nuancée: le principe *Non bis in idem*, par exemple, n'interdit pas, dans le contexte de la réglementation économique, le cumul des sanctions communautaires et nationales à l'encontre des infractions aux règles

---

112 Arrêt du 15 mai 1986, aff. 222/84, REC. 1986, p. 1656, § 3 et 4; p. 1682, § 18.

113 *Snupat*, 22 mars 1961, aff. 42 et 49/59, REC. (1951), p. 156; *Van Eick*, 11 juil. 1968, aff. 35/67, REC. (1968), pp. 481, 501.

114 *Lachmuller*, 15 juil. 1960, aff. 43, 45 et 48/59, REC. (1960), pp. 939, 956; *Fiddelaar*, 16 déc. (1960), aff. 44/59, REC. (1960), pp. 1083, 1099.

115 Arrêt du 13 fév. 1979, aff. 85/76, REC. 1979, pp. 508, 511–512, § 9 et 11; *voir* L. GOFFIN, *La jurisprudence de la Cour de justice sur les droits de la défense*, 16 CDE 127 (1980), à la p. 132.

de la concurrence; néanmoins, la Commission doit tenir compte, lorsqu'elle impose une amende, de la sanction infligée pour les mêmes faits par les autorités nationales.

Comme on l'a constaté plus haut, la jurisprudence allemande a déduit du *Rechtsstaat* un principe de proportionnalité dont l'influence se fait sentir dans plusieurs autres pays, parfois sous des dénominations différentes. La CJCE l'a intégré par étape dans le droit communautaire, à partir des dispositions du Traité portant sur la politique agricole commune: celle-ci pouvant faire l'objet de «toutes les mesures nécessaires» (article 40 § 3), la Cour a décidé que le législateur communautaire ne pouvait mettre en oeuvre que ce qui était nécessaire pour la réalisation des objectifs agricoles fixés. La Cour a ensuite appliqué le principe à d'autres domaines relevant des organes communautaires, ceux-ci devant veiller «à ce que les charges imposées aux opérateurs économiques ne dépassent pas ce qui est nécessaire pour atteindre les objectifs»[116]. Cette règle de proportionnalité s'applique aux actes législatifs, réglementaires ou administratifs, du moins lorsque l'autorité communautaire exerce un pouvoir d'appréciation; elle a également été appliquée par la Cour aux mesures prises par les États membres. Dans le premier cas, elle en fait une application très large, mais nuancée, exigeant dans certains cas que la disproportion soit «manifeste»[117]. Dans le second, elle y fait systématiquement appel pour contrôler les restrictions nationales imposées aux droits que le Traité reconnaît aux individus, notamment en matière de libre circulation des personnes et des marchandises. Par exemple, dans l'affaire *Commission* c. *Italie* (1979), la Cour a décidé que les règles douanières ne doivent pas faire obstacle inutilement à la libre circulation des marchandises en imposant des formalités qui ne seraient pas nécessaires pour l'exercice correct des contrôles[118]. Le même souci de proportionnalité oriente la jurisprudence portant sur les sanctions imposées par les États à l'inobservation de leurs prescriptions en matière de circulation des personnes: celles-ci doivent être non seulement compatibles avec le droit communautaire, mais raisonnables.

L'arrêt *Johnston*, précité, montre que le principe de proportionnalité s'applique de façon très large: la Cour y déclare qu'en déterminant la portée de toute dérogation à un droit individuel tel que l'égalité du traitement entre hommes et femmes – il s'agissait en l'espèce de savoir si l'État pouvait refuser de renouveler les contrats de femmes policiers du fait de la nécessité de leur

---

116 *Balkan*, 24 oct. 1973, aff. 5/73, REC. (1973), p. 1091.

117 *Voir* J.-P. SPITZER, *Les principes généraux de droit communautaire dégagés par la CJCE*, GP (1986), pp. 732, 735.

118 Arrêt du 25 oct. 1979, aff. 159/78, REC. (1979), p. 3747.

faire porter une arme à feu –, le respect du principe de proportionnalité «exige de concilier, dans toute la mesure du possible, le principe de l'égalité de traitement avec les exigences de la sécurité publique»[119].

2. La prééminence du droit appliquée spécifiquement aux questions économiques

Avec le critère de proportionnalité, tel qu'appliqué par la CJCE, nous sommes déjà témoins de l'adaptation d'un principe de droit constitutionnel et administratif emprunté aux États à la dimension économique de l'Europe. La Cour de Luxembourg a su pousser très loin cette adaptation des principes découlant de la prééminence du droit aux objectifs économiques des Communautés. Certes, le Traité de Rome est fondé sur des principes libéraux, tels les droits de propriété et de libre exercice du commerce, et interdit explicitement, par exemple, la discrimination exercée en raison de la nationalité (article 7)[120], mais c'est la Cour qui a dû expliciter la plupart des droits et libertés que requiert le libéralisme économique à l'européenne.

C'est ainsi que l'exigence de clarté et de précision des textes, caractéristique de l'État de droit, s'applique aux actes communautaires, particulièrement en matière fiscale, ce qui n'est pas sans rappeler la règle *Nullum crimen sine lege*. Tout acte doit faire l'objet d'une publicité suffisante sous peine d'être inopposable aux intéressés et la Cour exige que la communication d'une décision soit effectuée dans une langue comprise du destinataire[121]. Ce principe de «sécurité juridique», emprunté à la jurisprudence de quelques États membres, signifie également que l'entrée en vigueur d'un acte communautaire ne saurait être fixée à une date antérieure à sa publication, sauf cas exceptionnels, règle semblable à la non-rétroactivité assurée par les droits de l'homme en matière pénale[122]. Autre conséquence: les institutions doivent exercer leurs compétences dans un délai raisonnable car «l'exigence fondamentale de la sécurité juridique» s'oppose à ce que la Commission puisse retarder indéfiniment l'exercice de son pouvoir d'infliger des amendes[123].

Étroitement associé à ce principe est celui de la «confiance légitime» que les acteurs économiques doivent pouvoir placer dans les actes législatifs

---

119 Arrêt *supra* note 112, p. 1651.

120 Sur le principe de l'égalité de traitement, *voir* J.-P. SPITZER, *op. cit.*, *supra* note 117, p. 733.

121 *Racke*, aff. 98/78, REC. (1979), p. 69; *Société Gondrand*, 19 juil. 1981, aff. 169/80, REC. (1981), p. 1931; *Farranto*, 18 fév. 1975, aff. 66/74, REC. (1975), p. 157.

122 *Kent Kirk*, 10 juil. 1984, aff. 63/83, REC. 1984, p. 2689.

123 *Cnta*, 15 mai 1975, aff. 74/74, REC. (1975), p. 533.

communautaires, en vue d'éviter que des mesures imprévisibles et unilatérales ne viennent perturber les transactions. Ce principe ne signifie pas que les entreprises ont un droit acquis au maintien des avantages obtenus de l'organisation du marché commun à un moment donné, mais que les modifications des règles doivent être assorties d'un délai ou de mesures transitoires[124]. La Cour de Luxembourg s'assujettit elle-même au principe de la confiance légitime dans l'élaboration de ses décisions, attitude qui n'est pas rappeler la jurisprudence allemande[125].

La CJCE a donc défini un ensemble de principes fondamentaux à caractère économique, mais les «barrières immanentes» protégeant les droits des particuliers[126] découlent en fait des traditions européennes de prééminence du droit. La Cour considère ces principes comme faisant partie intégrante du droit communautaire et il s'ensuit, par l'application d'autres principes propres aux Communautés, comme ceux de l'effet direct et de la primauté du droit communautaire, que sa jurisprudence fait pénétrer les règles de l'État de droit dans les systèmes juridiques internes, d'où la Cour les a parfois tirés. Ainsi s'établit une sorte d'osmose entre l'Union européenne et ses Membres, favorisée par leurs traditions constitutionnelles communes, parmi lesquelles la Cour choisit souvent les normes les plus avancées.

La Cour s'est également référée à la Convention de sauvegarde dans la construction de l'État de droit communautaire et cela n'a pas manqué de soulever dans la doctrine la question de l'adhésion des Communautés en tant que telles à la Convention, certains préférant cependant l'adoption d'une Charte des droits de l'homme distincte pour l'Union européenne[127]. La première solution offrirait l'avantage d'«unifier» le droit européen en matière de droits fondamentaux, mais soumettrait les Communautés à la juridiction de la Cour de Strasbourg dans ce domaine, le rôle de la CJCE y devenant plutôt incertain. Or, la prééminence du droit appliquée aux questions économiques présente des exigences particulières, illustrées, on l'a vu, par une jurisprudence originale et spécialisée. Quant au projet de Charte, il pourrait sans doute combler certaines lacunes du droit communautaire, mais comporterait le risque, dans le cadre du Parlement européen, d'aboutir à des principes représentant le plus petit commun dénominateur, susceptible d'édulcorer les principes déjà posés par la CJCE. Comme l'écrit le p^r C. Philip, dans la

---

124 *Eridania*, 27 sept. 1979, aff. 23/78, REC. (1979), p. 2479.

125 *Voir supra* note 67.

126 *Voir* les arrêts *Internationale Handelsgesellschaft*, *Nold* et *Hauer*, *supra* notes 109 et 110.

127 *Voir* H. MONET, *La Communauté européenne et la Convention européenne des droits de l'homme*, RTDH (1994), pp. 501, 518.

mesure où la Cour déclare s'appuyer sur le plus grand dénominateur commun, aucun texte ne peut garantir une protection plus grande ou mieux assurée[128]. À Maastricht, l'Union européenne a retenu sur ce point une solution qui permet de rendre les deux régimes de protection compatibles: l'article F § 2 du Traité prescrit en effet que l'Union «respecte les droits fondamentaux, tels qu'ils sont garantis par la Convention européenne de sauvegarde ... et tels qu'ils résultent des traditions constitutionnelles communes aux États membres en tant que principes généraux du droit communautaire»[129].

Si la «prééminence du droit» n'est pas garantie comme telle dans les textes constitutifs de l'Union, elle fait partie du «patrimoine commun» mentionné dans le préambule de la Convention de sauvegarde: verra-t-on maintenant la CJCE faire appel explicitement à cette notion fondamentale, dont elle a su tirer jusqu'ici les conséquences implicites? Une telle orientation serait également conforme aux traditions de l'État de droit, du *Rechtsstaat*, du *Stato di diritto*, du *Retstat*, de l'*Estado de derecho* et même d'un *rule of law* qui s'imposerait à la souveraineté du législateur britannique.

* * *

Le sens et la portée de la notion de «prééminence du droit» ont été établis, dans un premier temps, par les traditions particulières des pays de l'Europe, encore que celles-ci aient été influencées par l'héritage commun de la philosophie grecque, de la *civitas christiana* et du droit romain. Du début des Temps modernes au XIXe siècle, chaque État cherche par et pour lui-même les moyens de discipliner le pouvoir politique et de réduire les risques de l'arbitraire, non sans se comparer à ses voisins à l'occasion. Cette évolution est composite, mais en simplifiant les choses, on peut dire que la tradition qui en résulte accepte la nécessité sociale du pouvoir politique, tout en cherchant inlassablement à limiter ses prérogatives en fonction de la sûreté des sujets et à contrôler ses abus éventuels par la loi et des recours effectifs, tendant du même coup à le légitimer. L'État de droit européen est, historiquement, celui qui organise son ordre juridique et ses institutions en vue d'atteindre cet objectif, lequel ne cesse cependant d'accroître ses exigences, à mesure que l'État étend ses compétences et son emprise sur la plupart des aspects de la vie en société.

---

128 *La Cour de justice des Communautés européennes et la protection des droits fondamentaux dans l'ordre juridique communautaire*, 383 AFDI (1975), à la p. 389.

129 On a vu dans cette disposition l'intégration *formelle* de la Convention dans l'ordre juridique communautaire: L.B. KROGSGAARD, *Fundamental Rights in the European Community After Maastricht*, dans: LEGAL ISSUES OF EUROPEAN INTEGRATION (1993), pp. 99, 108.

Une telle idée-force, en effet, constamment nourrie aux sources anciennes et contestée le plus souvent par le pouvoir, ne s'arrête pas en chemin: elle déploie avec le temps tout un arsenal de voies de droit contre l'arbitraire des gouvernants. De la *Grande Charte* et de l'*habeas corpus* aux constitutions modernes, les règles et les contrôles embrassent successivement le prince et ses agents, puis l'ensemble de l'administration publique, enfin, le législateur lui-même, pourtant longtemps considéré – et encore de nos jours dans quelques pays – comme l'autorité ultime. L'État de droit, qui a tant misé sur «la loi» pour circonscrire l'arbitraire du pouvoir, s'appuie maintenant sur «le droit», c'est-à-dire une loi supérieure imprégnée des valeurs du milieu, qui prend la forme de garanties constitutionnelles devant lesquelles la loi même doit céder le pas. Quelques États vont encore plus loin: les droits et libertés ainsi hypostasiés ne sauraient être modifiés et s'imposent donc au constituant lui-même, comme le veut par exemple l'article 79 § 3 de la *Loi fondamentale* allemande; la Constitution française fait de même à l'égard de la forme républicaine de gouvernement (article 89).

L'évolution socio-économique des pays occidentaux, sur laquelle viennent se greffer les mentalités et les idées, n'est évidemment pas étrangère au développement de l'État de droit. Celui-ci, dont on peut retrouver les origines au Moyen-Âge, précède et prépare les idées libérales du XVIIIe siècle. Les Lumières et l'*Aufklärung*, de Locke à Kant, en passant par Montesquieu et Rousseau, font de la liberté individuelle l'objet même du pouvoir: l'État de droit n'est plus seulement un moyen de circonscire l'arbitraire, il devient alors l'ensemble des recours et des institutions propres à garantir et à favoriser la liberté et les droits fondamentaux. Telle est aujourd'hui la portée d'une notion à laquelle les grands juristes anglais, allemands et français de la fin du XIXe siècle et de la première moitié du XXe, de von Gneist, Mayer et Kelsen à Dicey, en passant par Carré de Malberg, Duguit et Hauriou, pour ne mentionner que ceux-là, donneront à nouveau une dimension européenne. La primauté de la liberté appelle la prééminence du droit.

Cette évolution, qui a souvent pris la forme de révolutions, fût demeurée impossible sans la constitution d'une autorité capable d'imposer les normes fondamentales à l'Exécutif et au législateur. Sans doute fut-ce l'étape la plus délicate. L'Angleterre, qui a été la première à confier ce «contre-pouvoir» aux tribunaux, ne l'a pas admis à l'encontre du Parlement. Il a fallu que les États-Unis naissants aient un bien grand respect pour leurs juges pour accepter le contrôle de constitutionnalité et en donner l'exemple. Il a fallu plus d'un siècle aux États de l'Europe continentale pour admettre que le constitutionnalisme et la protection des libertés ne pouvaient être fondés pratiquement que sur un pouvoir juridictionnel indépendant. Encore a-t-il fallu que Kelsen trouvât un moyen d'écarter les tribunaux ordinaires au profit de Cours constitutionnelles spécialisées. Une fois franchie cette étape, la notion d'État de droit pouvait, à titre de critère d'interprétation, puis de principe fondamental, prendre la place qu'elle occupe aujourd'hui dans la jurisprudence nationale de nombreux États européens, avant de passer dans celles des Cours de Strasbourg et de Luxembourg.

L'Allemagne donne l'exemple le plus poussé de cette démarche prétorienne: non seulement le *Rechtsstaat* sert-il à renforcer les droits fondamentaux mentionnés dans la *Loi fondamentale*, il devient un principe philosophico-juridique doté en quelque sorte d'existence autonome et d'une portée croissante. La Cour constitutionnelle allemande en a tiré par déduction le critère de proportionnalité et les exigences de clarté, de précision et de prévisibilité de la loi (principes de la sécurité juridique et de la confiance légitime). Cette audace judiciaire trouve sa légitimation dans la volonté des constituants de 1949 de revenir, après la longue éclipse des libertés au temps du *Führerstaat*, au *Rechtsstaat* du libéralisme allemand, et dans l'appui que cette démarche a reçu de la population. D'autres tribunaux constitutionnels européens poursuivent un dessein semblable, en usant de concepts ou de techniques différents. Le Conseil constitutionnel français, par exemple, fait appel aux «principes fondamentaux reconnus par les lois de la République», qui lui fournissent également une large faculté d'interprétation. Il n'y a guère que le Royaume-Uni qui ignore le contrôle de constitutionnalité et limite la «faculté d'innovation» des juges, mais le débat amorcé dans ce pays depuis quelques années au sujet de l'adoption d'une constitution formelle ou d'un *Bill of Rights* montre que le *rule of law* n'a peut-être pas dit son dernier mot. Dans l'ensemble de l'Europe, cependant, le constitutionnalisme s'est imposé et consolide l'État de droit; son application par les tribunaux nationaux, plus ou moins développée selon les pays, vient le parachever.

Depuis quelques années, cette dynamique s'est communiquée aux Cours de Strasbourg et de Luxembourg et nous passons ainsi du droit comparé au droit européen, avant que celui-ci n'influence en retour les ordres juridiques nationaux.

C'est à l'époque où les constituants allemands inscrivaient le *Rechtsstaat* dans la *Loi fondamentale* et, semble-t-il, pour des raisons du même ordre que les fondateurs du Conseil de l'Europe et les rédacteurs de la Convention européenne de sauvegarde des droits de l'homme ont inclus le *rule of law* et la prééminence du droit parmi les principes propres à inspirer l'action des institutions nationales et européennes. Certes, il est difficile d'établir quelle a été exactement l'intention des négociateurs de ces instruments puisque les travaux préparatoires ne permettent pas de définir le sens des notions de *rule of law* et de prééminence du droit, d'autant que la proposition formelle est venu d'un représentant du Royaume-Uni, pour qui le principe ne pouvait avoir la même portée que dans les traditions des pays du continent. Le plus probable est qu'il s'agissait d'une référence très générale aux traditions libérales que l'histoire récente de plusieurs pays européens avait occultées. Il s'agissait davantage de donner aux Parties un projet commun à réaliser que de constater l'existence d'un acquis: à l'époque, plusieurs pays, comme l'Espagne et le Portugal, manquaient d'ailleurs à l'appel des États libéraux et démocratiques.

Il aura tout de même fallu un quart de siècle pour que la Cour de Strasbourg s'avisât de l'importance que pouvait présenter le principe de la prééminence du droit pour l'interprétation de la Convention. Quant à la Cour de Luxembourg, elle n'a fait appel aux corollaires de l'État de droit que vers la même époque, à compter des années 70, et depuis Maastricht, un lien pour ainsi dire officiel a été établi entre elle et la Convention de sauvegarde. L'évolution de l'État de droit dans les ordres juridiques des Parties, mais également l'esprit d'initiative des deux Cours expliquent ce tournant dans l'ordre européen, dont l'ampleur n'a fait que se confirmer depuis lors.

Ce tournant a été pris à l'occasion de l'arrêt *Golder* (1975) et ce n'est pas sans paradoxe que la Cour a appliqué le principe du *rule of law* pour la première fois à l'encontre d'une loi britannique alors que le Royaume-Uni ne l'applique pas au législateur souverain. Nous avons constaté que les méthodes déductives en usage dans la majorité des pays du continent expliquent cette démarche qui n'a pas manqué d'étonner le juge Fitzmaurice. Il faut ajouter que le Parlement et le gouvernement britanniques se sont inclinés devant l'arrêt du tribunal qui, en définitive, leur sert de Cour constitutionnelle. Ils ont agi de même à la suite des arrêts *Silver* et *Malone*, également fondés en partie sur la prééminence du droit.

À Strasbourg, le principe a servi avant tout à expliciter les garanties données aux articles 5, 6 et 8 de la Convention, tous liés de près à la notion classique de l'État de droit, c'est-à-dire aux recours destinés à protéger les libertés fondamentales plutôt qu'aux libertés elles-mêmes. La prééminence du droit s'est ainsi détachée des contextes nationaux pour acquérir un sens et une portée autonomes qui se sont révélés fort utiles pour trancher certains cas limites, qui sont les plus difficiles, comme ceux de la détention et des droits des personnes atteintes de maladie mentale; elle a également servi à expliciter les nombreuses exigences du procès équitable et à fixer les bornes que l'État ne doit pas franchir lorsqu'il autorise diverses formes d'ingérence dans les communications des particuliers. Récemment, la Cour l'a appliqué directement à la liberté d'expression, sous la forme de la «primauté du droit» et du principe de proportionnalité, dans sa recherche d'un juste équilibre entre cette liberté et les exigences de la sécurité intérieure de l'État dans une société démocratique. Il ne serait pas étonnant de la voir maintenant appliquer de semblables critères aux autres libertés fondamentales chaque fois qu'elle doit tenir la balance entre celles-ci et l'intérêt public ou les droits d'autrui.

Le sens et la portée donnés à la notion polysémique de prééminence du droit sont sans doute appelés à sous-tendre des secteurs entiers de l'ordre juridique européen: la Cour de Luxembourg, qui fait déjà appel aux corollaires de l'État de droit en s'inspirant à la fois des principes communs aux Membres de l'Union européenne et de la Convention de sauvegarde, y trouvera une source intarissable de normes propres à gérer équitablement le libre marché de l'Europe économique. Les nouveaux Membres du Conseil de l'Europe qui ont inscrit l'État de droit dans leurs constitutions respectives et accepté la juridiction de la Cour de Strasbourg pourront, à la lumière de la jurisprudence, mesurer les exigences de cet impératif catégorique et préparer ainsi en connaissance de cause leur entrée dans l'Union européenne. La Convention pourra ainsi devenir, selon l'expression de la Cour dans l'affaire *Loizidou*, «l'instrument constitutionnel de l'ordre public européen».

Davantage, la jurisprudence européenne commence à servir de référence et de modèle aux tribunaux nationaux dans leur recours à l'État de droit en tant que principe fondamental garantissant l'ensemble des libertés et droits fondamentaux, et même à la Cour interaméricaine des droits de l'homme dans ses efforts pour limiter les effets des déclarations d'état d'urgence. Cette jurisprudence ne peut manquer non plus d'exercer une influence plus large dans les forums internationaux, notamment dans le cadre des Nations Unies, où se noue depuis quelques décennies un dialogue interculturel sur les droits de l'homme et, plus récemment, sur le renforcement de l'État de droit comme moyen par excellence de «remédier aux violations des droits de l'homme».

Basic Distinctions in the Law of International Organizations: Practice versus Legal Doctrine

by

Finn Seyersted

I. INHERENT VERSUS DELEGATED POWERS. "IMPLIED POWERS" – AN UNNECESSARY FICTION OFFERING ESCAPE BUT NO GUIDANCE

Writers on the law of intergovernmental organizations (IGOs) start out from the premise that an intergovernmental organization – in contradistinction to States and other self-governing communities – can do only what is provided in its constitution (the treaty establishing it). (In its pure form, this is referred to as the doctrine of "attributed" or "delegated powers" – meaning powers given to the particular organisation by its member States.) This concept is applied indiscriminately to all types of acts – from transacting on an equal and voluntary basis with external parties (legal **capacity**) to making decisions binding upon member States and other types of parties (**jurisdiction**).

Seeing that this is not so in practice[1] – and that perhaps most of the acts performed by IGO's have not been authorized by constitutional provisions (other than by falling within its defined purposes) – writers resort to the fiction of "**implied powers**". In theory, this concept starts out from an interpretation of what the authors of the constitution of the organization concerned are supposed to have had in mind when they drafted that particular convention. In the absence of criteria other than the fictitious intention of the authors, the concept is in fact applied flexibly whenever the need is felt. As has been stated: "The most fascinating aspect of the doctrine of implied powers is its flexibility."[2] Indeed, it offers no guidance,[3] merely an escape from a false point of departure.

---

[1] *See e.g.* the practice reported by the present writer in IV Indian Journal of International Law (1964) at 74 and 233–265, and by Schermers and Blokker, International Institutional Law, den Haag (1995), §§ 1594–1598.

[2] *Ibid.* § 236.

[3] *See e.g.* Royer-Hameray, Les compétences implicites des organisations internationales, Paris (1962).

Even the **International Court of Justice** resorted to this fiction during its first years, when it held that the U.N. could claim reparation under international law for damage suffered by its officials and representatives in the performance of their mission for the Organization,[4] and when it held that power to establish an administrative tribunal to adjudicate disputes between the Organization and its officials "arises by necessary intendment out of the Charter."[5] However, in 1962, the Court turned the presumption around,[6] adopting the principle of "**inherent power**" advanced by the present writer in an article written for use in that case and circulated to the judges by one of them.[7] However, the latter advisory opinion appears to have escaped the attention of legal writers. Or they have not noticed its diametrically opposed point of departure: "the presumption is that the Organization **has** the power" (*in casu* to establish military forces other than those provided for in chapter VII of the U.N. Charter), which implies that it is any **limitation** of the power that requires a legal basis.

If one also in legal theory would turn the presumption around and **make the relevant distinctions between different types of "powers"** – on the basis of consistent practice described in earlier articles[8] and in a forthcoming book[9] by the present writer – the problems fall into place. It then becomes clear that there are firm principles of general customary law, common to all IGO's, which determine what an IGO can and cannot do in the absence of specific authorization in its constitution or otherwise, and that there is no need for "implied powers" as a fictitious escape.

In the first place, there is no requirement in international law practice that the **legal personality** (external legal **capacity**) of an international or-

4 Reparation for injuries suffered in the service of the United Nations, ICJ REPORTS 1949 at 182.

5 Effect of awards of compensation made by the United Nations Administrative Tribunal, ICJ REPORTS 1954 at 56–57.

6 Certain Expenses of the United Nations, ICJ REPORTS 1962 at 168.

7 *Can the United Nations Establish Military Forces and Perform Other Acts Without Specific Basis in the Charter?*, XIII ÖSTERREICHISCHE ZEITSCHRIFT FÜR ÖFFENTLICHES RECHT (1962) at 188 ff., esp. at 201 ff., reprinted in F. SEYERSTED, UNITED NATIONS FORCES IN THE LAW OF PEACE AND WAR, Leiden (1966), Chapter IV.

8 *International Personality of Intergovernmental Organizations*, IV INDIAN JOURNAL OF INTERNATIONAL LAW (1964) at 1–74 and 233–265; *Jurisdiction over Organs and Officials of States, the Holy See and Intergovernmental Organizations*, INTERNATIONAL AND COMPARATIVE LAW QUARTERLY IV (1964) at 1–74 and 493–527; *Settlement of Internal Disputes of International Organizations by Internal and External Courts*, XXIV ZEITSCHRIFT FÜR AUSLÄNDISCHES ÖFFENTLICHES RECHT UND VÖLKERRECHT (1964) at 1–121; *Applicable Law in Relations Between Intergovernmental Organizations and Private Parties*, III RECUEIL DES COURS DE L'ACADÉMIE DE DROIT INTERNATIONAL DE LA HAYE (1967) at 433–612.

9 COMMON LAW OF INTERNATIONAL ORGANIZATIONS to be published by MARTINUS NIJHOFF, den Haag.

ganization in national and international law shall be laid down in its constitution or other express treaty provision. All intergovernmental organizations have – and exercise – **inherent capacity** to act externally as subjects of national and international law in all relations where they are in a practical position to do so (international personality follows from well established customary international law). Any **limitation** upon that personality requires a legal basis in the national law concerned or in the constitution of the organization, respectively. Examples of such limitations are hard to find[10] – even harder than it is to find provisions **stating** international personality. The tendency among legal writers to seek authorization in the constitution of each organization concerned may be understandable in the case of Continental European lawyers, as their national legal systems require a basis in statute for legal personality of associations and companies under national law. But even writers from Anglo-Saxon countries, which, like Scandinavian countries, require no such basis in their national law – tend to start from the opposite (and false) point of departure in **international** law. Indeed, it was the American judge Hackworth who took the most restrictive view (delegated powers) in the first ICJ advisory opinion (Reparation for Injuries 1949). A parallel position was taken by communist countries – as a non-communist majority.

In the second place, every intergovernmental organization exercises **inherent** jurisdiction over its **organs and their members** as such. This **organic jurisdiction** is never stated generally in the constitution. It includes legislative, administrative and judicial power, but not power of enforcement, which is an aspect of **territorial** jurisdiction. The inherent organic jurisdiction includes the power to establish new organs[11] – unless it should follow from the constitution that the organs established by its express provisions are to be the only ones. In practice this means that organizations cannot establish new organs to perform the decision-making powers which the written constitution has vested in specified (principal) organs, but that organizations are free to establish subsidiary organs under the principal organs, as well as judicial organs to evaluate the acts of principal and other organs. The latter was held by the International Court of Justice in its advisory opinion on the U.N. Administrative Tribunal of 1954, although at that time still relying upon

---

[10] An enumeration in the constitution of the organization of its **purposes** is, in principle, limitative internally, subject to developments by internal customary law. But it is doubtful whether the organization **externally** (*vis-à-vis* non-members) – or an external party – on this basis can claim invalidity of *e.g.* a treaty concluded with a state or another IGO. This has its parallel in international law on relations between **States** if they *e.g.* enter into treaties in violation of constutitional provisions (Art. 46 of the 1969 Vienna Convention on the Law of Treaties).

[11] *See* the second (and third) of the articles listed, *supra* note 8.

the fiction of "implied powers." The inherent power to establish other subsidiary organs (*in casu* military forces) was recognized by the International Court of Justice in 1962, despite the fact that the U.N. Charter did contain provisions for the establishment of military forces by different organs and methods. The inherent organic jurisdiction comprises also jurisdiction over the representatives of member States **as members of the organs**, although there is so far no known precedent for **judicial** (only administrative) settlement of disputes in this regard.

Both the inherent international personality and the inherent organic jurisdiction are subject to any **limitations** contained in the constitution of the particular organization concerned.[12] However, this is not a very practical situation. In some cases, an enumeration of specific external capacities or of specific acts of internal jurisdiction could by interpreted *a contrario* to exclude other types. But even this is not very practical – normally any such enumeration must be considered either as examples or as provisions destined to specify procedures or modalities concerning the specific acts or organs concerned. This, too, was confirmed by the International Court of Justice in its advisory opinion of 1962 on **Certain Expenses of the United Nations**, when it held that the U.N. could establish military forces other than those provided for in Chapter VII of the Charter.

On the other hand, intergovernmental organizations do not have "implied power" to **impose new obligations upon member States or external parties (States or private persons)**. In accordance with the principle of the sovereignty of States, this requires a specific treaty provision or a unilateral commitment by the States concerned – but even this does not have to be stated in the **constitution** of the organization. Organizations do not even have an "**implied** power" to do this in substantive – or even in most organizational[13] (as opposed to procedural)[14] matters – unless, in exceptional cases, there has been a **genuine** or a **necessary** implication. An example of the latter could be the provision of Art. 34 of the U.N. Charter that "the Security Council may investigate any dispute, or any situation which might lead to international friction or give rise to a dispute, in order to determine whether the continuance of the dispute or situation is likely to endanger the maintenance of international peace and security." This must probably imply a right of access to the territories involved for the representatives of the Security Council.

---

12 *See* the third article listed in *supra* note 8, and ICJ REPORTS 1954 at *supra* note 5.

13 The organization cannot without legal basis impose upon member states *e.g.* an obligation to pay financial contributions to the organization.

14 The organization can impose upon the representatives of member states on its deliberative organs *e.g.* restrictions on their right to speak (closure of debate, limited speaking time).

Reference may also by made to some of the opinions and cases reported by Skubiszewski, *op. cit. infra.*

Thus, legal theory – if it is to conform with practice – must distinguish between the **inherent** external legal **capacity** to act on a voluntary basis as an equal partner and inherent **internal jurisdiction over organs and their members as such** – on the one hand – and **extended** power to exercise functional jurisdiction over or in (*i.e.* to make decisions binding upon) member States or private individuals and (other) external parties, on the other hand. The former exist automatically in all IGO's as a matter of common customary law for all self-governing communities. The latter – and only they – must be conferred upon the organization concerned; and thus exist only when so provided in the constitution or other treaty or unilateral act for the specific organization concerned – such power is **delegated** to the organization by the member (or non-member) States concerned.

Only a few writers tend in this directionn – and only part of the way. Thus Skubiszewski, in an article on *Implied Powers of International Organizations*,[15] makes the basic distinction indicated above, although not as sharply as I do, when he underlines that more latitude can be given to implication "in the internal sphere of the organization" than when "rights and duties of Member States are at stake". Moreover, he realistically points out that "the process of implication should not be identified with the discovery of the intention of the parties" – indeed, he speaks of a "useless fiction", as I do. He also cites Professor Bernhard (and the present writer) who goes all the way, admitting that inherent powers "follow directly from the existence of the organization".[16] However, in contradiction to me, Skubiszewski concludes that "it is impossible to state a general and abstract rule". He contents himself with stating that the application of the doctrine of implication becomes **easier** "if obligations of States are not directly at state".

As for **terminology**, Skubiszewski appropriately points out that inherence is a factor different from **implication**. However, many writers do not distinguish dearly between the traditional concept of "implied powers" and the term "inherent" powers which I used in articles in the 1960's and which **in substance** was applied by the International Court of Justice in the Expenses Case. It should therefore, in conclusion of this Part, be reemphasized that my term "inherent powers" does **not** start out from the common point of

---

15 INTERNATIONAL LAW AT A TIME OF PERPLEXITY, ESSAYS IN HONOUR OF SHABTAI ROSENNE, Dordrecht (1989) at 855–868.

16 R. BERNHARDT, QUALIFIKATION UND ANWENDUNGSBEREICH DES INTERNEN RECHTS INTERNATIONALER ORGANISATIONEN, BERICHTE DER DEUTSCHEN GESELLSCHAFT FÜR VÖLKERRECHT, 7, at 27–28 (12. Tagung (1971) Karlsruhe 1973).

departure that an IGO has only such powers as follow from its constitution. Indeed, the terms "implied" and "inherent" are diametrically opposed in their points of departure. And they apply **in different fields** according to the basic distinctions made above: "Inherent" applies **generally** to internal (organic) jurisdiction and to external capacity – while "implied" may apply **exceptionally** to extended jurisdiction.

II. ORGANIC JURISDICTION AND ORGANIC CONNECTING FACTOR. AN INDISPENSABLE ADDITION TO TERRITORIAL AND PERSONAL DITTO

Books on **public international law** describe in their parts on jurisdiction the **territorial jurisdiction** of States over their land, sea and air territory and the **personal jurisdiction** of States over their nationals and inhabitants in personal matters even when they are abroad. There are rules of public (and private) international law on which of these two types of jurisdiction shall take precedence in what respects.

However, there is also, as explained above, a third type of jurisdiction, the **organic jurisdiction**, which not only States, but also other subjects of international law (self-governing communities, including insurgents, the Holy See and, above all, IGO's) exercise over their organs and their members as such. This jurisdiction, although apparently ignored in legal literature, is a strong jurisdiction which, like the other two, comprises legislative, administrative and judicial competence. Like the personal jurisdiction, it does not comprise the power of enforcement. It is fairly clearly delimited in practice. It is exclusive within its field – *i.e.*, it takes precedence over both territorial and personal jurisdiction, even if both of these are combined in a(nother) State, as they are in respect of officials who are both nationals of and working in the State where the organization has its headquarters or its mission.

The organic jurisdiction does show its effects not only in the internal law of the organization and in **public** international law, but also in **conflict of laws**. Here, too, one traditionally distinguishes between territorial and personal jurisdiction by applying either **territorial or personal connecting factors**. However, there is also the **organic connecting factor** which – within the field of organic jurisdiction – is exclusive and is applied by national courts to determine the applicable law under national conflict of law rules; this is even a duty **under public international law**: it would be a violation of that law if *e.g.* a State were to impose its law governing public or private employment upon foreign state or IGO officials working in its territory, unless they were engaged as local personnel under local private law. – The internal law of an IGO may even be the applicable law pursuant to territorial or personal connecting factors in those special cases where an IGO has **extended jurisdiction** – over territory or over special categories of individuals, *e.g.* refugees – but this is a different matter.

* * *

There is thus no need to establish whether the constitution of any particular IGO authorizes it to perform specific external acts on an equal footing with other subjects of international law, such as concluding treaties, claiming reparation, settling disputes by courts of arbitration, or other external acts. Nor is there need to explore the constitution in order to establish the organization's power to legislate and to make binding administrative and judicial decisions on relations with and between its organs and their members as such, because that power, too, is a well established customary law, common to all IGO's. It corresponds to a basic principle in the national law of Nordic democratic States, referred to as the **principle of legality** (*legalitetsprinsippet*). The latter implies that the government may impose new duties upon – or reduce existing rights of – private physical or legal persons only by statute or under authority delegated by statute, whereas the executive branch of government in principle has the authority to make both general regulations and administrative acts binding upon – and to establish (administrative) tribunals or other bodies to settle disputes with – members of administrative State organs as such. Thus, there is a parallel between the powers of a government to act without basis in statute and those of an IGO to act without basis in treaty. The limit is drawn in principle the same way: only infringement of rights and freedoms of persons existing as legal subjects outside the organization or State concerned requires specific legal basis. Other acts do not: the government or the IGO has inherent internal **power** (jurisdiction) and external **capacity** – but no inherent **external jurisdiction**.

III. INTERNAL LAW OF IGO's DISTINCT LEGAL SYSTEMS – PARALLEL TO NATIONAL RATHER THAN TO PUBLIC INTERNATIONAL LAW – ALSO IN CONFLICT OF LAWS

When I studied international law in Paris after World War II, I was told that there are only two types of law and that any law that was not national law is (public) international law (fortunately, my objections were accepted subsequently). This was maintained, partly emphatically, by prominent writers at that time (including Battifol and Mann).[17] But if one regards practice, it becomes obvious that public international law and the internal law of IGO's are different systems of law.[18] Another matter is that IGO's are **also** subject to public and private international law (and thereby to national law) – in their **external** relations; that law applies externally to IGO's in essentially the same manner as it does to States, deviations are found more frequently in legal literature than in practice.

The term "internal law" of an IGO was used by the Administrative Tribunal of the League of Nations in 1929. It differs from public international law and resembles (public) national law in nearly all respects:

1. It is a **separate system** of law for each organization.

2. Its **sources are hierarchical**: a constitution in the form of a treaty, which takes precedence over the legislative acts in the form of "regulations." The latter are mostly administrative regulations addressed to members of the organs, but in some organizations – having extended jurisdiction over territory, individuals and/or States – they are comparable to genuine national legislation under the principle of legality referred to above. Customary internal law also comes in at both levels: the constitutional[19] and the (lower) regular customary law. All this is, at both, supplemented by general principles of law, which may be drawn from all types of legal systems – including both national and international law – but above all from the common law of IGO's. Even so, such principles become part of the particular internal law of the organization concerned. In public international law, however, the sources are **equal** – the later supersedes the earlier, whatever its nature.

3. While the primary (and the only general) **subjects** of public **international law** are the self-governing communities (States, organizations of States [IGO's], insurgents, the Holy See) the subjects (persons) of the internal law are the organization, its member States as such and their representatives on the organs of the organization as such, its several organs and their members, including its officials as such. Experts on mission for the organization, however, are usually more in the nature of independent external contractors, who may have accepted some of the regulations enacted by the organization in their contracts.

---

[17] *The Proper Law of Contracts Concluded by International Persons*, XXI BRITISH YEARBOOK OF INTERNATIONAL LAW (1944) at 11 ff.

[18] On internal law of international organizations, *see* III RECUEIL DES COURS (1967) cited *supra* note 8, at 529 ff. and 536–8.

[19] *E.g.* the practice introduced in the Security Council by Soviet Ambassador Gromyko in the 1940's, that an abstention is not a veto, despite the words of Art. 27,3 of the U.N. Charter.

4. Most important, the **effects** of the internal law **in** the **national law** of the member States is twofold. First, the **constitution** is normally embodied in a written convention, which has the same effect as other treaties (public international law) in the law of the contracting States – *i.e.* it is incorporated into the national law of **member** States in accordance with the constitutional rules of the State concerned. Second, in addition, the **entire** internal law – including the constitutional treaty, all regulations, customary law developed within the organization and general principles of the internal law – is applied by national and other courts in member **and non-member** States alike when the applicable rule of **conflict of laws** refers to the law of the organization: *i.e.* in the same manner as they apply foreign **national** law. Early writers submitted that in such cases a substitute national law must be sought, *e.g.* the law of the host State. However, in practice this is not so. If the reference is by a territorial connecting factor (*e.g.* the place of contract or delict), it refers directly to the national law governing the territory concerned. But if the connecting factor is organic (*e.g.* employment of officials), the organization has its own law – and the administrative law of the host country has no relation to the matter.[20] Personal connecting factors are less relevant to IGO's (family law, law of succession, law of minors) – but when they are relevant (legal capacity, competent organs) the answer is usually found in the internal public law of the organization or in international law. Finally, if the organization has **extended** territorial and/or personal jurisdiction, it also has its own relevant territorial and personal law.[21]

* * *

There are thus not two, but **three** types of legal systems, **three** types of jurisdiction (in internal, national and public international law), and **three** types of connecting factors (in conflict of laws).

*

A full discussion of the problems summarized above may be found in the articles cited in note 7, which, in updated and revised form, will be included in a forthcoming book on *Common Law of International Organizations*.

---

20 *See* III RECUEIL DES COURS (1967), notably at 442 ff.

21 *See* III RECUEIL DES COURS (1967), notably at 448 ff.

CONTEMPORARY EUROPEAN LAW: EXCLUSIVISM, PATERNALISM AND PARTNERSHIP

by

RENATA SZAFARZ

"...common resolve and our growing interdependence will help to overcome the mistrust of decades, to increase stability and to build the united Europe..."

(CHARTER OF PARIS FOR A NEW EUROPE, 1990).

Challenges of Change

(OSCE. HELSINKI DOCUMENT 1992).

Towards a Genuine Partnership in a New Era

(OSCE. BUDAPEST DOCUMENT 1994).

This essay is devoted on one hand to the phenomena of some kind of exclusivism and paternalism and on the other – to the phenomenon of genuine partnership in the intra-European relations and European law.

On this background and in this context it is pertinent to emphasise the role of Krzysztof Skubiszewski as a statesman – Foreign Minister of the reborn Polish State in the period 1989–1993, *i.e.* the one which is generally considered to be historic both in Polish and European terms.[1]

I. THE ORIGIN AND CHARACTERISTICS OF THE EUROPEAN LAW

In the post-war history of international relations one may distinguish the phenomena of both the globalisation and regionalisation of certain international issues. At present it seems that the clear predominance of the regionalisation process can be observed, in particular as far as security, military, economic, human rights and environmental domains are concerned.

The following all-European (or nearly all-European) norm-creating centres can be identified: the OSCE, the Council of Europe and the U.N. Economic Commission for Europe. Furthermore, it is necessary to mention at this point the important international organisations, including supranational ones, comprising only certain West European States and – by the same

---

1 KRZYSZTOF SKUBISZEWSKI was the Foreign Minister of the Republic of Poland from 12 September 1989 to 26 October 1993.

token – still having a sub-regional character. In particular, the importance of the European Union/Communities and NATO (which is in actual fact a Euro-Atlantic organisation) could be highlighted in this respect.

Sometimes the regional approach has a real advantage over undertakings of universal character, since it very often makes possible the adoption of solutions which are farther reaching and better serve civilisation as well as particularities of closer common interests shared by States belonging to a given region.

The regional international law constitutes just one outcome of the more general regionalisation process of international affairs and sometimes results from specific problems arising in a given region.[2]

Regional international law is being created on different continents, yet it is in Europe and in (the) America(s) that it is most developed. Thus, it seems that only an *advocatus diaboli* intention can dictate the opinion that "the European idea [which is in fact the basis of European law – R.S.] is nothing more than only a greater and worse nationalism."[3] The author of this opinion, Karlheinz Deschner, is wrong for two fundamental reasons. First, let us remember that it is in Europe that the two criminal totalisms and two most devastating world wars occurred; it is in and for Europe that the Teheran, Yalta and Potsdam conferences took place. The admonishment of those facts should serve as a sufficient justification for the interest shown in Europe as such, in relations among European States as well as in European law – in other words – in promoting the European idea.

The second fact, perhaps more important today, is that the whole outside world including, above all, developing countries, can only profit from a stable, democratic, peaceful, prosperous and united Europe.

A. Bleckmann, the author of the entry *European Law* contained in the *Encyclopedia of Public International Law* gives the following characteristics of this notion:

> "The notion of European law has been developed by scholars, not by the practice of States. It includes in its narrowest meaning the law of the European Communities only. In a wider sense it extends to the conventions of the Council of Europe and particularly to the European Convention on Human Rights. In an even broader meaning, we might extend the no-

---

[2] Generally, on regionalism and regional law, including Inter-American Law *see* S. GONZALEZ GALVEZ, *The Future of Regionalism in an Asymmetrical International Society*, (in:) R.ST.J. MACDONALD, D.M. JOHNSTON (eds.), THE STRUCTURE AND PROCESS OF INTERNATIONAL LAW, Dordrecht (1986) at 661 ff.

[3] K. DESCHNER (quoted by A. OLSZEWSKI, *Pan Arcydiabeł*, WPROST (1995 – 29 January), at 70.

> tion to the law of the other European organisations such as the Western European Union, the Benelux Economic Union, the Organisation for Economic Cooperation and Development (OECD), the North Atlantic Treaty Organisation and even to other bilateral and multilateral conventions, as well as to European customary law."[4]

The above definition rightly presents three possible levels of perception of European law, yet it comes as a surprise that no clear mention is made in it of the U.N. Economic Commission for Europe which appears to be an important European treaty-making centre. Among the achievements of this Commission there have been 54 all-European treaties, so far.[5] The conclusion of further treaties in the near future has been officially declared.[6]

Moreover, mention of the OSCE should also be made in this context because the first treaty has already been concluded within its framework. This was the Convention on Conciliation and Arbitration within the OSCE of 15 December 1992.[7] Hopefully, this was a good beginning and in the future more treaties will be concluded within the framework of the OSCE.

The very subject of this essay is the European law in its broadest sense. However, the clarity of the forthcoming reasoning can benefit from the introductory remarks explaining the mutual relationship between the notions of "European law" and "the international law of Europe." The above mentioned author, A. Bleckmann maintains that "all European law is public international law, applying to the international relations between European countries. This is generally considered also to apply even for the law of the European Communities."[8]

However, in these days the opposite view, according to which the secondary law of the European Communities (*droit communautaire*) is an autonomous legal order alongside public international law (also of Europe) and the internal legal orders of States, prevails both in the judicature[9] and in doc-

---

[4] A. BLECKMANN, *European Law*, (in:) 6 ENCYCLOPEDIA OF PUBLIC INTERNATIONAL LAW, Amsterdam–New York–London (1983) at 176.

[5] For the enumeration and presentation of the status of these treaties, as well as the discussion of some of them *see* R. SZAFARZ, ROZWÓJ PRAWA MIĘDZYNARODOWEGO EUROPY. Z PROBLEMATYKI "EUROPEJSKIEJ PRZESTRZENI PRAWNEJ", Warszawa (1994) at 130–149 (the titles of treaties are cited both in Polish and English).

[6] This is announced in the official ECE document – *see* ECE, ENVIRONMENTAL CONVENTIONS ELABORATED UNDER THE AUSPICES OF THE UNITED NATIONS ECONOMIC COMMISSION FOR EUROPE (UN – ECE), United Nations, New York (1992) at 1.

[7] For the text *see* XXXII:2 INTERNATIONAL LEGAL MATERIALS (1993) at 557 ff.

[8] A. BLECKMANN, *op. cit., supra* note 4 at 176; also *see* the argumentation presented there.

[9] For example, the following judgments of the Court of Justice of the European Communities may be quoted: The CJ Judgment in the case concerning *N.V. Algemene Transport – en Expeditie Onderneming Van Gend and Loos v. Nederlandse Administratie der Belastingen*, ECR

trine.[10] The secondary law of European Communities due to its specific characteristics should be treated as a new quality in European law.

Consequently, only the treaty law of the European Union/Communities should be treated as part of the public international law of Europe.[11] In addition, the very core of the public international law of Europe consists, at present, of more than 220 all-European/Eurocentric treaties (see *infra*) as well as European customary norms.[12]

In the light of the above presented remarks it is evident that the European law in its broadest sense is not a uniform legal system. *Inter alia*, this is significant while applying different methods of the interpretation of the law in question. Indeed, the possibility of the application of analogy and systemic interpretations is very limited.

Contemporarily, in the process of the formation and functioning of European law the phenomena of exclusivism, paternalism and partnership, with different scope and intensity can be encountered. In particular, this is striking today, when for the first time in the post-war period there has arisen a chance and perspective of creating unified Europe.

(1963) (it opened the way for recognizing the secondary law of European Communities as an autonomous legal order); The CJ Judgment in the case concerning *Flaminio Costa v. ENEL*, ECR (1964) (the autonomous character of the secondary law of European Communities was directly and definitely recognized by the CJ); *The CJ Judgment in the case concerning Internationale Hand elsgesellschaft GmbH v. Einfuhr – und Vorratsstelle für Getreide und Futtermittel*, ECR (1970) (it was acknowledged that the validity of measures applied by the Communities' institutions might only be assessed in the light of *droit communautaire*). Also *see* the CJ judicature quoted by D. WYATT, A. DASHWOOD, EUROPEAN COMMUNITY LAW, London (1993) at 54–55.

[10] *See e.g.* M. SCHWEITZER, W. HUMMER, EUROPARECHT. DAS INSTITUTIONELLE RECHT DER EUROPÄISCHEN GEMEINSCHAFTEN. DAS MATERIELLE RECHT DER EWG, Frankfurt a. M. (1985) at 194; D. LASOK, J. W. BRIDGE, LAW AND INSTITUTIONS OF THE EUROPEAN COMMUNITIES, London (1991) at 82–86, in particular at 83; J. RIDEAU, *Les accords internationaux dans la jurisprudence de la Cour de justice des Communautes européennes: Reflections sur les relations entre les ordres juridiques international, communautaire et nationaux*, 94:2 REVUE GENERALE DE DROIT INTERNATIONAL PUBLIC (1990); P. MENGOZZI, EUROPEAN COMMUNITY LAW, London–Dordrecht–Boston (1992) at 58 ff.; TH. OPPERMANN, EUROPARECHT, München (1991) at 152.

[11] All these treaties as well as many others, including all-European ones, are enumerated and generally discussed by S. OSCHINSKY, P. JENARD, L'ESPACE JURIDIQUE ET JUDICIAIRE EUROPÉEN. EXAMEN DE 250 CONVENTIONS, Bruxelles (1993). On one hand "the European legal space" has been treated very extensively in this book. Namely, many treaties binding for European States but universal in scope have also been discussed. On the other hand it is surprising that 54 all-European treaties adopted under the auspicies of the U.N. Economic Commission for Europe have been omitted (except for the European Convention on International Commercial Arbitration. Done at Geneva on 21 April 1961 – *ibid.* at 399).

[12] On European customary law *see* A. BLECKMANN, *op. cit.*, *supra* note 4 at 180 ff. and R. SZAFARZ, *Towards All-European International Law*, XX POLISH YEARBOOK OF INTERNATIONAL LAW (1993) at 10–11.

II. WILL EXCLUSIVISM IN EUROPEAN LAW SURVIVE 2000?

It is well known that the "Founding Fathers" of the European integration, and the European Communities, namely: K. Adenauer, R. Schuman and A. de Gasperi thought in the 1950s – in perspective – about the whole European continent. It is precisely due to the then prevailing political and economic situation, *i.e.* the division of Europe into opposite and rival blocs, that the treaties establishing the European Coal and Steel Community, the European Atomic Energy Community and the European Economic Community comprised only the West European States. The number of members of the European Communities has been gradually increasing from 6 to 12, and after the conclusion of the treaty on the European Union of February 1992 (Treaty of Maastricht) – to 15. Thus, the European Union based on Communities is still of a subregional character.

In virtue of art. 0 of the Treaty of Maastricht the European Union (and Communities) is formally open for all European States. However, in practice the Union has been showing a great restraint as far as the admission of new members is concerned. When, following the democratic changes in Central and Eastern Europe there appeared for the first time the possibility of admission to European Communities (and afterwards – to the Union) of, at least, some of the States from this region of Europe, the reaction of those organisations (and the Union) as well as their member States has been ambivalent. The benevolent words of interest in our aspirations were, in actual fact, accompanied by the disinclination to determine which States, when and on which conditions will be admitted to the European Union. At present, as far as the States of the former Eastern bloc are concerned, only the former GDR as part of reunited Germany enjoys membership in the European Union. Other Central and East European States have been offered different status in relation to the Union/Communities. Namely, the European Communities have concluded association agreements with 11 States in question. In the light of the declared intentions these agreements are meant to be the first step of these States on their way to the full integration with the Union/Communities.[13] Moreover, 6 Central and East European States, *i.e.* Hungary, Poland, Slovakia, Romania, Latvia and Estonia have formally applied to the European Union Council for admission to the Union on the basis of art. 0 of the Maastricht Treaty (Poland applied on 8 April 1994). Krzysztof

---

[13] *See e.g.* the Europe Agreement establishing an association between the Republic of Poland of the one part, and the European Communities and their member States of the other part, signed in Brussels on 16 December 1991 (Dz. U. 1994, N° 11, item 38).

Skubiszewski, the founder of the Western and European orientation in the foreign policy of the Republic of Poland has correctly emphasised that

> "While discussing the ties with the European Union, there is, rightly, much talk about economic affairs. But we should remember that the crux of the matter lies in the political sphere, as it concerns our security in its broad sense... Our association with the Union and our striving for membership, are primarily of a political character... In fact, the goal is to guarantee Poland a lasting and safe position in Europe."[14]

The negotiations concerning the admission of new members from Central and Eastern Europe can start only after the 1996 intergovernmental conference of the member States of the Union, *i.e.* after the review of the treaties establishing the Union/Communities. Besides, certain conditions are addressed to the States-candidates to the Union, for example, real progress in developing democracy and market economy, as well as the adjustment of internal law to the Community law.

The Central and East European States have been making efforts to meet the Union's conditions and expectations since, according to the opinion of Krzysztof Skubiszewski, they treat this organisation as the most successful response – at the end of the 20th century – to the challenges of the future.[15] Furthermore, Krzysztof Skubiszewski has emphasised that "Within the confines of the Community, there can be no return to totalitarianism, and indeed there is constant support for democracy. All hegemony is alien to the Community."[16]

These are *inter alia* the reasons why, because of the membership of, at least, some Central and East European States in the Union/Communities is in the best conceived interest of both States-candidates and member States of the Union. The risk connected with the Union's ignoring this challenge is shared since one cannot expect that in case of non-meeting it the area of instability or even conflicts can be separated from the Western part of Europe by a new tightly closed border. All temporary economic obstacles as regards the admission of new Central European States to the Union should be viewed from this perspective. Consequently, the issue is a far-sighted and

---

[14] K. SKUBISZEWSKI, *Perspectives of Poland's Foreign Policy in Europe*, YEARBOOK OF POLISH FOREIGN POLICY (1993–1994) at 27.

[15] K. SKUBISZEWSKI, POZYCJA POLSKI W EUROPIE, Warszawa (1994) at 10.

[16] K. SKUBISZEWSKI, *Poland's Political Dialogue with the European Community*, (in:) K. GINTHER, G. HAFNER, W. LANG, H. NEUHOLD, L. SUCHARIPA-BEHRMANN (eds.), VÖLKERRECHT ZWISCHEN NORMATIVEM ANSPRUCH UND POLITISCHER REALITÄT. FESTSCHRIFT FÜR KARL ZEMANEK ZUM 65 GEBURSTAG, Berlin (1994) at 416.

"enlightened self-interest"[17] of the Union's member States. Simply, it is the self-interest arising from the wise and deep understanding of Europe's interdependence which is at stake. Obviously, as Krzysztof Skubiszewski has ascertained,

> "Poland is fully aware of the fact that she must bear the brunt of the adjustment. However, the task is too big for us to be left alone... It is not a question of aid but that of treating us as true partners. Our priorities are access to markets, knowledge (including technology transfers), institutions, and capital. A more active policy lies equally in the Western interest. It is not an exercise in philantrophy."[18]

Thus, will the exclusivism of the European Union and Community law survive 2000?

At present, it is difficult to answer this question unequivocally. At any rate, it seems that assuming good political will of the West, the so-called Iberian or Spanish model of membership in the Union would be possible at that time, at least for some Central and East European States.

The Treaty of Maastricht provides that the Western European Union (WEU) which originated from the Brussels Treaty of 17 March 1948 and was finally established in virtue of the Paris Agreements of 23 October 1954, "is an integral part of the development of the Union" (art. J. 4(2)). This European military – defence organisation has also become the subject of vivid interest for Central and East European States at the beginning of the 1990s. So far, the efforts of these States to become members of WEU have been usuccessful. However, since 1994 these States, including Poland, have had the status of associated partners of the WEU. Consequently, in the contemporary practice of the WEU, the phenomenon of exclusivism is also present, though one may hope that it is a transitional one. However, a realistic approach dictates an expectation that the admission of Central and East European States to the WEU will be parallel to the admission of those States to the European Union. By the same token, the question concerning the year 2000 posed above is also relevant in relation to the WEU.

The North Atlantic Treaty Organisation established in virtue of the North Atlantic Treaty of 4 April 1949 is still another European, or more precisely Euro-Atlantic organisation practicing exclusivism towards the Central and

---

17 K. SKUBISZEWSKI, *ibid.* at 415.

18 K. SKUBISZEWSKI, *Poland, Germany and Europe after 1989*, (in:) U. BEYERLIN, M. BOTHE, R. HOFMANN, E.-U. PETERSMANN (eds.), RECHT ZWISCHEN UMBRUCH UND BEWAHRUNG. VÖLKERRECHT – EUROPARECHT – STAATSRECHT, FESTSCHRIFT FÜR RUDOLF BERNHARDT, Berlin–Heidelberg–New York–London–Paris (1995) at 1307.

East European States. NATO is the only efficient defence alliance in Europe based on the system of values which as of 1989 have been fully shared by Poland and many other Central and East European States. Because of her historical experiences Poland's turn to the North Atlantic Alliance is quite natural. To be situated in the gray zone which is, in fact, the present situation of Poland means a growing anxiety and sense of hopelessness. Undoubtedly, such a status of a State cannot and should not last long. Therefore the best conceived Polish *raison d'état* is a leitmotiv of our efforts – undertaken officially for the first time in 1993 by the then Polish Foreign Minister, Krzysztof Skubiszewski – to join NATO. The Polish interest in extending the area of stability and security in Europe, as well as to become part of this area is self-evident and unequivocal; this is a genuine imperative of our foreign policy. It is clear and understandable that we attach a great importance to the crucial art. 5 of the North Atlantic Treaty. As Krzysztof Skubiszewski has rightly underlined "There are different security levels in Europe. Poland's historical experience and the state of relations in Central and Eastern Europe make us seek the highest of these levels"[19] *i.e.* NATO. At the same time, as Krzysztof Skubiszewski put it "A broader Union and NATO is the answer to the self-destruction of Europe which was the feature of the first half of our century. That spectre is back with us in the Yugoslav crisis."[20]

The response of member States of NATO to the aspirations of Central and East European States is full of restraint. On the one hand they have been trying to assure us that the real problem is not if, but when and how to admit these States to the North Atlantic Alliance. On the other hand different conditions and objections have been formulated. All these conditions do not provoke reservations and are, as such, acceptable but at the same time they constitute the reason for a certain brown study, since NATO does not seem to treat the violation of human rights and the rights of minorities in Turkey as an essential problem and nobody expected to find a fully fledged democracy in Spain and Portugal at the moment of the admission of those States to NATO.

In connection with the sometimes heard objection that in the West nobody wants "to die for Cracow or Bratislava" one has to point out that the

---

[19] K. SKUBISZEWSKI, *Perspectives of Poland's…, op. cit., supra* note 14, at 29. While further developing this idea, K. Skubiszewski has added: "How, in view of the different levels of security on the European continent, are we to implement the principle of indivisibility of European security? That is why Poland raised the problem of her future membership in the North Atlantic Alliance" (*Poland, Germany and Europe…, op. cit., supra* note 18, at 1308).

[20] *Ibid.* at 1307.

recent polls show significant support of the Western societies for the idea of an extension of NATO and Poland's membership in this organisation.[21] In this context it seems that it is precisely the political elites of the Western States who are hampering the extension of NATO to the East. And in spite of intensive denials it is crystal clear that this attitude of the political elites of the West is the result of strong Russian objection. So far, the Russian veto – *i.e.* a veto of a third State – against the extension of NATO to Central and Eastern Europe has been successful.[22] It seems, as in the well known saying of Lord Ismay, the first Secretary-General of NATO (quoted in the press), that the mission of this organisation has been: "To keep Russians out, Americans in and Germans down" has recently been supplemented by the phrase: "and Central Europe at the door."

In the shadow of all objections/pretexts presented above, and, in particular, in the long shadow of Moscow, NATO and its members have recently undertaken certain efforts to partially meet the expectations of Central European States. The North Atlantic Cooperation Council (NACC) was established in 1991. Also the "Partnership for Peace" programme has been worked out, on U.S. initiative. Of course, all documents signed on these occasions by the interested States are of political and not legal character. The contents of documents connected with the "Partnership for Peace" programme indicate some paternalism on the part of NATO and its member States. The final appraisal of NACC and the "Partnership for Peace" programmes which are, at present, only palliative measures, depends on future developments. If they are the first step preparing for full membership in NATO they should be assessed positively, but if the intention of the West is to perpetuate these palliative measures, *i.e.* to perpetuate exclusivism and paternalism on the part of NATO, the result will be only greater uncertainty as regards the future of Europe.

Today we may only hope that around 2000 it will be clear which one of the two possibilities presented above is more realistic. Poland's firm goal is

---

[21] *See* the Study *The New European Security Architecture* U.S. Information Agency, September 1995. According to this Study 80 per cent of the British people, 70 per cent of the French and more than 60 per cent of the Germans support the prospective membership of Poland in NATO.

[22] J. EYAL, the director of the Royal Institute of Defence Studies in London, commenting on this fact has openly stated: "I have always been hearing assurances that the West will not discuss the price of Central Europe's security with Russia. However, no one in the West believes it. Such is the truth. NATO should extend to the East before and not after the setting of partnership with Russia" (quoted by M. RYBARCZYK, *Zachodowi brak woli*, GAZETA WYBORCZA (1995 – 4 May). *See* also the different points of view on the issue of NATO-Central Europe relations, (in:) CH.L. BARRY (ed.), THE SEARCH FOR PEACE IN EUROPE. PERSPECTIVES FROM NATO AND EASTERN EUROPE, Washington (1993).

to become the member of NATO on the basis of legally regulated partnership.

Let us remember that in the history of Europe the sin of negligence has too often proved to be costly.

III. PATERNALISM AS A CONTEXT OF CONTEMPORARY EUROPEAN LAW

An element of paternalism inherent in the Partnership for Peace programme has already been indicated above. In this section it is pertinent to focus attention on the Pact of Stability in Europe, signed in Paris on 20–21 March 1995. It has recently been the most prominent exercise in paternalism in the context of European law.

An initiative concerning this Pact was presented in 1993 by the French Prime Minister E. Balladur. It was based on the diagnosis that the great hopes of 1989 for freedom, democracy, social progress and overcoming historical divisions had not become a reality, since "carrying out the changes in the East proved to be more difficult and costly than one had thought."[23] In this connection his proposal – not free from patronising overtones – was that

> "the European Union and all countries interested in stability on our continent, and in particular the United States of America and Russia, set the political framework for the Central and East European countries, in which it would be easier to solve problems connected with their good-neighbourliness to the effect that the issues of frontiers and minorities would not arise any more."[24]

The initiative and proposals launched by E. Balladur were accepted by the European Council in Copenhagen on 21–22 June 1993 and in Brussels on 10–11 December 1993.

According to the idea launched by E. Balladur, accepted by the European Union, an all-European conference devoted to the draft Pact on Stability in Europe was held in Paris on 26 and 27 May 1994. The conference resulted in establishing two regional round-tables: the round-table of Baltic States (Estonia, Latvia, Lithuania, Poland and those invited by them) and the round-table of other Central and East European States (Bulgaria, Hungary, Poland,

---

23 E. BALLADUR, *Pour un Pacte de Stabilité en Europe, Recueil de Documents*, 1 Institut Polonais des Affaires Internationales (1994) at 146.

24 *Ibid.* at 147. In another part of this article a clear *iunctim* between the participation in the proposed Pact and possible success of efforts to become members of the European Union has been underlined.

Romania, Slovakia, the Czech Republic and those invited by them, including Slovenia). An invitation to participate in those round-tables was also extended to the OSCE, the Council of Europe and the Council of the Baltic Sea States. The round-tables in question were chaired by the European Union.

The actual purpose of these round-tables was to bring about the conclusion of a network of bilateral treaties concerning State frontiers and minorities. For such States like Poland, which had earlier regulated – in a treaty form – all these problems with all their neighbour States, participation in the round-tables in question was devoid of much sense.

Generally, the results of the negotiations conducted at the round-tables proved to be less than moderate: the "Baltic table" was totally unsuccessful and the success of the "Central European table" was only one – an agreement between Hungary and Slovakia. All efforts to conclude a similar agreement between Romania and Hungary failed. In spite of this state of affairs a political document entitled "The Pact on Stability in Europe" was adopted by 52 European States at the Paris conference held on 20–21 March 1995. Scores of different bilateral treaties, agreements, arrangements and declarations concerning good-neighbourliness, friendship, co-operation, frontiers and minorities, which had earlier been concluded by European States among themselves, have been included into the Pact.

The Pact was deposited with the OSCE which would monitor the implementation of obligations included into the Pact.

The representatives of the Western States have defined the Pact on Stability in Europe as "the first great exercise in preventive diplomacy after the cold war."[25] The Pact itself declares that "one aim is to direct this evolution (of Europe) towards building a more united Europe based on greater solidarity..."[26] In connection with this ascertainment doubt arises whether the form in which – in the context of the Pact – the said "solidarity" has manifested itself, still deserves this name. First of all an asymmetry of obligations is striking in spite of the fact that on the part of the Western States which played the role of collective patron and teacher there have also been such conflicts like the one in Northen Ireland, in the Basque Provinces and in Corsica. Therefore, the Central and East European States showed no enthusiasm as regards the Pact which has been both a legal and political

---

[25] The Foreign Minister of France, Alain Juppe – quoted by R. SOŁTYK, *Po balu Balladura*, GAZETA WYBORCZA (1995 – 22 March).

[26] The Pact on Stability in Europe, Paris 20 -21 March 1995 (text provided by the Polish Ministry of Foreign Affairs). Generally on this Pact *see* F. BENOIT-ROHMER, *Le Pacte de Stabilité: la première action "diplomatique" commune d'envergure de l'Union europeénne*, 30:4 REVUE TRIMESTRELLE DE DROIT EUROPÉEN (1994) at 566 ff.

undertaking marked by the evident paternalism of the member States of the European Union. The press even used the term "tutelage of 15" in this context. If, nevertheless, the Central and East European States participated in this undertaking and signed the Pact, they did so above all for the sake of their perspectives of future membership in the European Union.

All the remarks presented above make it difficult to describe the Pact on Stability in Europe as a success. No doubt, it would be beneficial for Europe as a whole if this Pact were the last expression of paternalism in the European law context. Certainly, this is not the way to a genuine unity of Europe. Besides, perceived on a deeper level, paternalism never serves well the dignity of either people or States. By the same token it cannot serve well the merits of the ultimate goals.

IV. PARTNERSHIP – A REAL RESPONSE TO THE REAL NEEDS OF EUROPE

When discussing below the phenomenon of partnership I have in mind, in particular, partnership between the States of the West and East of Europe, though this does not mean that all States of a given region have to automatically be treated uniformly on all accounts. The crucial point is to eliminate – from mutual relations of States of both parts of Europe – the regional considerations, as such, to the benefit of considerations always based on merits of the matter.

The U.N. Economic Commission for Europe has been the first and for a long time the only all-European political, economic and legal forum based on the principle of partnership. The U.N. ECE was established in 1947 in virtue of the resolution 36 (IV) of the U.N. Economic and Social Council. At present 53 States are members of this Commission. The very survival of the ECE during the cold war period was the most important initial success of this organ. In addition, since 1950 it has become the first treaty-making centre on an all-European scale. From 1950 to 1992 a total 57 treaties were concluded under the auspices of the ECE, including three treaties of a universal scope and 54 basically all-European treaties.[27] These treaties concerned the following fields: commercial arbitration, customs, road traffic, transport by rail, water transport, multimodal transport, navigation and environment. They addressed specific needs of Europe as a whole, and its infrastructure.

---

[27] For details *see* R. SZAFARZ, *op. cit.*, *supra* note 5, at 127–149.

The second European forum based on the idea of all-European partnership has been the OSCE (formerly CSCE) established in accordance with the OSCE Final Act of Helsinki in 1975. The Helsinki Final Act, as such, is not a treaty, but a document of a political nature. Nevertheless, the principles contained in the Declaration of Principles Guiding Relations between Participating States, contained in the "first basket" of the Helsinki Final Act include legally binding provisions as well as provisions of a political character, with the former prevailing.[28] The principles of the Helsinki Declaration, the so-called Helsinki Decalogue, contain numerous provisions binding the States participating in the OSCE, because they reflect the principles of general international law. In fact, they repeat those principles, confirm them, and strengthen them.[29]

Though in the whole OSCE process political documents have been prevailing, mention must be made of the first treaty adopted within its framework, namely the Convention on Conciliation and Arbitration within the OSCE signed at Stockholm on 15 December 1992.[30] This Convention signed on behalf of Poland by the Foreign Minister, Krzysztof Skubiszewski, entered into force on 5 December 1994.

Since the OSCE has changed from a heterogeneous forum to a homogeneous one, it could have been expected that more legal documents, *i.e.* treaties would be adopted within this organisation. However, so far, these expectations have not materialised. Moreover, in spite of many achievements in different fields, the serious failure of this organisation is its perplexity as regards the Yugoslav conflict. If, at present, the role of the OSCE may still be assessed positively it is precisely because of the fact that this forum which includes 53 States in total, is counteracting the division of Europe.

---

[28] For details *see* R. SZAFARZ, *CSCE Contribution to the Establishment of the European Legal Order*, XXI POLISH YEARBOOK OF INTERNATIONAL LAW (1994) at 11–22.

[29] In this connection *see* the references to two principles contained in the OSCE Declaration of the Principles of the Helsinki Final Act made by the International Court of Justice in its judgment concerning the *Nicaragua case* (ICJ REPORTS 1986 at 100, para. 189 and at 107, para. 204).

[30] For the text of the Convention *see* XXXII INTERNATIONAL LEGAL MATERIALS (1993) at 557 ff. On this Convention *see* R. BADINTER, *L'Europe du droit, Annex: Convention on Conciliation and Arbitration within the CSCE*, 4:1 EUROPEAN JOURNAL OF INTERNATIONAL LAW (1993) at 15 (*Annex* – at 24); G.J. TANJA, *Peaceful Settlement of Disputes within the Framework of the CSCE: A Legal Novelty in a Political-Diplomatic Environment*, (in:) A. BLOED (ed.), THE CHALLENGES OF CHANGE. THE HELSINKI SUMMIT OF THE CSCE AND ITS AFTERMATH, Dordrecht–Boston–London (1994) at 67 ff.; A. PELLET, *Notes sur la Cour de conciliation et d'arbitrage de la CSCE*, (in:) E. DECAUX, L.-A. SICILIANOS (eds.), LA CSCE: DIMENSION HUMAINE ET RÈGLEMENT DES DIFFÉRENDS, Paris (1993) at 189 ff.; P.-M. EISEMAN, *La Convention de Stockholm relative à la conciliation et à l'arbitrage au sein de la CSCE. Quelques observations iconoclastes*, (in:) E. DECAUX, L.-A. SICILIANOS (eds.), La CSCE: dimension humaine et règlement des différends, Paris (1993) at 219 ff.

It is the Council of Europe that has been the only West European international organisation which after 1989 has widely – though not unconditionally – admitted the Central and East European States. At present 14 following States from the East of Europe are members of this organisation: Albania, Bulgaria, the Czech Republic, Estonia, Hungary, Latvia, Lithuania, Moldova, Poland, Romania, Slovakia, Slovenia, Tfyromacedonia and Ukraine.[31] Moreover, as many as 18 Central and East European States are parties to some of 159 conventions (agreements) protocols adopted within the Council of Europe. These States, of course, include all the above mentioned members of the Council of Europe as well as Bosnia-Herzegovina, Croatia, Belarus and Russia.[32] Consequently, all Central and East European States are already parties to (some) Council of Europe's treaties, with the wholly understandable exception of new Yugoslavia (Serbia and Montenegro). In view of this fact and to the best of my belief it is possible to ascertain that the treaty law of the Council of Europe, which was mainly created as a West European law, has recently been transformed into an all-European treaty law. Due to this process the idea of an authentic all-European partnership was applied to the fullest extent precisely in the Council of Europe's practice.

It may be added that the instrument of accession of Poland to the Statute of the Council of Europe was deposited on 26 November 1991. On the same day the Polish Foreign Minister, Krzysztof Skubiszewski, signed the Convention for the Protection of Human Rights and Fundamental Freedoms of 4 November 1950.

The treaty law of the Council of Europe is one of the forms in which the European civilisation manifests itself very clearly and distinctly. As is well known the basic values of this civilisation are democracy, political pluralism, rule of law, market economy and protection of human rights, which have at their roots the triad: Greek philosophy, Roman law and Christian ethics. And it is a most positive and felicitous fact that the Central and East European States which are now sharing these values and are trying to put them into practice, could relatively quickly – and according to the principle of genuine partnership – find themselves under the influence of the law of the Council of Europe.

If the above issue is considered in the categories of interests one has to admit that in this case the West has pertinently recognized the direct benefits for itself from the transferring of an emphasis – as far as, *inter alia*, the

---

31 *See* the Council of Europe Doc.: Chart of Signatures and Ratifications of European Treaties. Updating as 21 November 1995 at 3–4. At present, 38 European States are members of the Council of Europe.

32 All data – according to the Council of Europe document quoted in *supra* note 31.

promotion of democracy and human rights in the East is concerned – from the political plane (OSCE) to the legal one (Council of Europe).

The OECD is another Western international organisation, which has recently begun the process of the admission of some Central and East European States. Full membership based on the partnership principle is at stake. On 28 November 1995 the Czech Republic – as the first State from the East – concluded the relevant agreement with the OECD, in virtue of which it would become (after ratification) the 26th member of this organisation. Poland will probably become a member of the OECD in mid-1996. It seems that some other States from our region will sooner or later follow suit.

When discussing the all-European law based by its very nature on the idea of partnership, it is also purposeful to mention some individual treaties which are not formally connected with either the U.N. ECE, the OSCE or the Council of Europe. So far, six following treaties of this kind have been concluded:

- Convention on the Recognition of Studies, Diplomas and Degrees Concerning Higher Education in the States Belonging to the Europe Region, adopted in Paris on 21 December 1979.[33]
- Treaty on Conventional Armed Forces in Europe, signed in Paris on 19 November 1990.[34]
- Treaty on Open Skies, signed in Helsinki on 24 March 1992.[35]
- Agreement Establishing the European Bank for Reconstruction and Development, signed in Paris on 29 May 1990.[36]
- Energy Charter Treaty, signed in Lisbon on 17 December 1994.[37]
- Energy Charter Protocol on Energy Efficiency and Related Environmental Aspects, signed in Lisbon on 17 December 1994.[38]

One may expect that in the future more such all-European treaties – concerning different fields – will be concluded.

The idea of partnership is present not only in the all-European treaty law but also in the process of the formation of all-European customary law. It is

---

[33] The text of the Convention provided by the Secretariat of UNESCO.

[34] For the text *see* XXX:1 INTERNATIONAL LEGAL MATERIALS (1991) at 6 ff.

[35] The text of the Treaty provided by the Polish Ministry of Foreign Affairs.

[36] For the text of the Agreement *see* P.A. MENKVELD, ORIGIN AND ROLE OF THE EUROPEAN BANK FOR RECONSTRUCTION AND DEVELOPMENT, London (1991) at 105 ff. and I.F.I. SHIHATA, THE EUROPEAN BANK FOR RECONSTRUCTION AND DEVELOPMENT. A COMPARATIVE ANALYSIS OF THE CONSTITUENT AGREEMENT, London–Dordrecht–Boston (1991) at 109 ff.

[37] The text of the Treaty provided by the Polish Ministry of Foreign Affairs. This Treaty can be defined as a "Eurocentric" one. The very title of the Final Act of the Lisbon Conference reads: "Final Act of the European Energy Charter Conference".

[38] As far as the text of the Protocol is concerned *see supra* note 37.

possible to identify such customary norms *in statu nascendi* which concern the following fields:
- democracy (democratic entitlement), including free elections;[39]
- fundamental rights of minorities;[40]
- right to environment.[41]

In addition, A. Bleckmann identifies the European customary norms – developed before 1945 – in the law of aliens and the law of expropriation and confiscation.[42]

Undoubtedly, a genuine partnership in the context of European relations and European law manifests itself also in certain plurilateral and even bilateral undertakings. According to Krzysztof Skubiszewski "Winning over the West to partnership with us will long remain an important component of our policy. This component consisits of many elements, one of them being the Weimar Triangle, *i.e.* collaboration between France, Germany and Poland."[43]

Other multilateral undertakings of this kind include: the Central European Initiative and the Council of the Baltic Sea States.

As far as bilateral undertakings are concerned, mention should be made, in particular, of many treaties concerning good-neighbourliness, solidarity, friendship and co-operation. Poland has recently concluded treaties of this kind with all her new neighbour States as well as with some other States. These States include: Belarus, Bulgaria, the Czech and Slovak Republics, Estonia, France, Germany, Hungary, Italy, Latvia, Romania, the Russian Federation and Ukraine. The respective treaties concluded with these States within the period 1991–1993 were signed on behalf of Poland by the then Polish Foreign Minister, Krzysztof Skubiszewski.

In the light of above presented considerations – as a whole – it is evident that Krzysztof Skubiszewski both as the Foreign Minister of Poland and an eminent international lawyer, *i.e.* both in practice and in theory, was strongly committed to the idea of genuine partnership among all European States as

---

[39] While it has rightly been pointed out that the customary norm concerning democratic entitlement is also *in statu nascendi* in the universal system and in some other regional systems (in the Inter-American system), in Europe the custom formation process is most advanced. Indirectly to this effect *see* the reasoning of T.M. FRANCK, *The Emerging Right to Democratic Governance*, 86:1 AMERICAN JOURNAL OF INTERNATIONAL LAW (1992) at 66–69. *See* also A. BLECKMANN, *op. cit.*, *supra* note 4, at 180 (this author also mentions the rule of law principle as a European customary norm) and R. SZAFARZ, *op. cit.*, *supra* note 28, at 29–32.

[40] On this subject *see* R. SZAFARZ, *ibid.* at 32–34.

[41] The conclusion to this effect has resulted, *inter alia*, from the discussions which took place at the International Congress on the Fundamental Rights of Man and Environment in the Context of Changes in Central and Eastern Europe, held in Warsaw from 2 to 4 June 1995.

[42] A. BLECKMANN, *op. cit.*, *supra* note 14, at 180.

[43] K. SKUBISZEWSKI, *op. cit.*, *supra* note 14, at 27.

well as in the context of European law. Moreover, he personally contributed to a significant extent to the establishment of a new European architecture, at the same time serving the Polish *raison d'état* very well. It deserves particular emphasis that in the understanding of Minister Krzysztof Skubiszewski the Polish *raison d'état* was also based on moral imponderables. According to Krzysztof Skubiszewski's own declaration "Our policy rests on the foundation of the Polish *raison d'état* which honours law and morality."[44]

Undoubtedly, Krzysztof Skubiszewski has found a firm place in the modern history of Poland as a distinguished statesman of the reborn Polish State.

V. FUTURE PROSPECTS

Certainly, in the years 1994–1995 it was no longer necessary to "put an end to the facile millenarianism that was an immediate product of 1989."[45] The euphoria of 1989 and the Paris Charter for a New Europe of 1990 disappeared very quickly and their great optimism has become less than moderate. The great hopes have been substituted by the awareness of great challenges, ever increasing disillusionment and even bitterness (in the East). The happily solved great problems (the collapse of communism, totalism) have unexpectedly given rise to new uneasy problems: the lack of a sense of stability, the predictability of the situation for the West and the new lack of a sense of security and even rejection in the East. In addition, both East and West have been shocked by the tremendous costs of indispensable transformation in Central and Eastern Europe. However, it was only the Yugoslav conflict that has shown the whole truth about the shamefully low degree of Europe's commitment to the declared values and principles. It has also been evidence that the idea of all-European solidarity was still a diplomatic euphemism. Why has this happened?

Many contemporary intellectuals, political analysts and statesmen have tried to diagnose the situation and answer this question. Both the diagnoses and answers are not indifferent for the appraisal of the drawbacks of exclusivism and paternalism as well as the merits of partnership in the context of European relations and European law. If, as J. Crawford has put it "international law [and European law as well – R.S.] in its relationship with practice

---

44 *Ibid.* at 22.

45 J. CRAWFORD, *Democracy and International Law*, THE BRITISH YEAR BOOK OF INTERNATIONAL LAW (1993) at 132.

is better described as an intellectual activity, carried out for practical purposes, though in more or less literary form,"[46] the relevant appraisal should also be based on deeper factors which influence this "intellectual activity."

Peter Nadas, a Hungarian intellectual, has presented his diagnosis and answered the above asked question – with painful sincerity – on the occasion of receiving a prize for his "contribution to promoting the idea of mutual European understanding" (at the *Book Fare*, Leipzig 1995).

Peter Nadas said, *inter alia*: "I was to speak about the beautiful daydream: about mutual understanding. To my regret, I find that I can only speak about the lack of understanding, appearances of understanding, the painful reality of the grey and hopeless everyday life."[47]

The subtitles of P. Nadas's lecture speak for themselves: "Basic calm," "Europe of cripples," "Temptation and punishment." While developing his passionate reasoning P. Nadas stated:

> "... Nobody would convince me that two Europes exist. There is only one Europe – a Europe of cripples. Limits of mutual understanding are not geographic ... If we had been able to speak about mutual understanding in Europe and not only about its lack and appearances, we would not have been asking the question, why nations more acquainted with democracy and governments elected democratically had not helped the new democracies to rise to their feet though this had been their moral duty. Why do they constrain them to stay on their knees... The actual question would be: Why are the leading European thinkers not able to awake and eventually manage to pronounce the sentence understandable for all: I cannot help you because the principles of the functioning of my political system prevent me from doing so, but I will analyse its functional drawbacks, since the scale of danger is directly proportional to the scale of my negligence; therefore I ask you, if you have concepts or ideas on how we should organise our common life, to speak up... The nations more acquainted with democracy and governments elected democratically do not aim at strenghthening the democratic tradition, correcting the errors of the democratic system, eliminating its drawbacks. They try to build a new hierarchical relationship. They do not exercise a dialogue – and they even do not wish to conduct one. Instead of natural integration they offer the new democracies controlled isolation and for themselves – controlled separation. And they do not leave any doubt as to who is in control, who is to influence the turn of events, where the limits of the binding etiquette are, and generally, who is to govern here.

---

[46] *Ibid.*

[47] P. NADAS, *U mętnych źródeł pozorów*, GAZETA WYBORCZA (GAZETA ŚRODKOWOEUROPEJSKA) (1995 – 20–21 May). The lecture of P. NADAS is also quoted below according to this source.

> Of course, things are always right as they are. Though it may be seen that as the chaos becomes greater, information coming from outside is more carefully strained. We know this very well. The spirit of the Congress of Vienna and Kremlin returns to the Baroque halls."

Moreover, the German political analyst, Ch. Royen, has stated quite bluntly: "It is true that many politicians in my country would prefer the changes of 1989 to end definitely on the unification of Germany."[48] This is a bitter and painful ascertainment. However, should it come as a surprise, if a poet describes the State of the spirit of contemporary Western Europe as "nihility,"[49] that a philosopher adds "vacancy"[50] and the Church sums it all up as "nihilism" or "the spiritual homelessness." It seems as if somewhere on the way a genuine European has lost the power of imagination, spirit and will.

Obviously, the language of all the opinions quoted above is not a diplomatic one. Neither am I a diplomat while identifying the atrophy of the European imagination on both sides of the former "iron courtain." This phenomenon is not understandable after all the European experiences of the 20th century.

The same or similar problems, concerns and dangers have been indicated by Krzysztof Skubiszewski – in more diplomatic language – as follows:

> "Naturally, we should keep explaining to the West, in various ways, that if it fails to face up to the situation developing since 1989, it will soon have unstable countries at its doorstep. That would not be a safe Europe. If the West turns it on itself, it will soon see that the situation develops itself to its detriment and against its own vital interests. This line of reasoning should be confronted with the Western tendency to seek calmness – which is not always peace – in the first place. But we should also go further, and seek to convince the West about the need, even necessity, of jointly working out a strategy for democratic transformation... There can be no doubt that the West initially committed itself to supporting radical changes in this part of Europe. But confronted with the enormity of needs and with the growing problems and obstacles involved in transformation, and finding that this is just the beginning of a long-term process – not a one-off, relatively simple operation resembling the Marshall Plan – the West may gradually move away from a policy of wide and costly sup-

---

[48] CH. ROYEN in the interview entitled *Spawanie kontynentu* [The Welding of the Continent], WPROST (1995 – 12 November) at 83.

[49] CZ. MIŁOSZ (the Nobel Prize winner in poetry), the poem entitled *Sarajevo* – in the collection of poems *Na brzegu rzeki*, Kraków (1994) at 46.

[50] A. FINKIELKRAUT in the interview entitled *Polityka i samotność* [Politics and Loneliness], TYGODNIK POWSZECHNY (1995-3 September).

> port to systemic changes, and turn towards laying emphasis on calm and stability in the region, irrespective of progress in systemic transformation."[51]

Central and East Europeans may also be said to feel lost and overwhelmed by the new reality which is not always understandable for them. At the same time they still experience the burden of newly gained freedom and corresponding personal responsibility. They are also disappointed that no actual and genuine all-European solidarity has arisen. All these factors are reasons for the dangerous frustrations which manifest themselves, *inter alia*, in the phenomena of populism, demagogy and a return of post-communists to power.

So, what are we to do now?

It seems that truly common efforts are needed on many planes. First, the consciousness and conscience of European nations should be awakened, as well as a sense of the common fate of Europe as a whole ("we all are in the same boat"). The horizons of imagination should be broadened in order to show the fallacy of the conviction that "this horror does not affect me." A moral source of politics, including foreign policy, should be emphasised. It is also worth trying to define "the European common good" and to courageously undertake the relevant actions to protect and promote it. The result will be the vision of a common goal and the determination to achieve it by the common efforts of the West and the East. And this will be possible only on the basis of genuine partnership both in relations of European States and in the context of European law. The genuine partnership among all European States is the means as well as one of the essential purposes. The sphere of partnership in Europe should be systematically extended as a result of an elimination of exclusivism (for example, the "concentric circles" as regards the security relations) and paternalism phenomena from European life. Furthermore, European law/European treaties, in principle, should not be overgrown with palliative political documents.

As far as the concept of different speeds of European integration is concerned, it is not contrary to the idea of partnership to the extent in which it is realized within the European Union/Communities.

I wish to belive that the future of European law will be determined by the idea of genuine partnership among States of all regions of Europe. It is only on partnership that the all-European "house on rock"[52] can be built.

---

51 K. SKUBISZEWSKI, *op. cit.*, *supra* note 14, at 27 and 28.

52 . MATTHEW 7, BIBLE at 24.

La politique étrangère et de sécurité commune de l'Union européenne (la PESC) dans l'optique du 5 ème élargissement. Comment la renforcer?

par

Daniel Vignes

Conscients peut-être de l'imperfection de leur oeuvre, persuadés qu'ils ne pouvaient immédiatement réformer complètement les traités européens et les Communautés, les négociateurs du Traité sur l'Union européenne (TUE) signé à Maastricht le 7 février 1992, avaient prévu qu'en 1996 une conférence intergouvernementale de révision (CIG 96) se tiendrait. Ceci amena les instances de l'Union au second semestre 1995 à faire le point de ce qui avait été fait et à dresser les plans de cette révision. Il peut être intéressant dans des Mélanges en l'honneur d'une personnalité qui a longuement et avec éclat dirigé les Affaires étrangères d'un futur Etat membre d'en parler.

En 1992, quatre points figuraient sur la liste de ce que ferait la CIG 96, de ceux-ci la PESC était l'un d'eux. Pourquoi? Autant les négociateurs en 1991 avaient des idées claires sur ce que devait être une politique extérieure commune et l'avaient exprimé, autant ils étaient flous sur ce que serait à terme certes, une politique de "sécurité de l'Union" et l'éventuelle définition dans le futur d'une "défense commune". A l'égard de la première, un des négociateurs d'importance – nous en tairons le nom – estimait: "la PESC, c'est la création en quelques années d'un Ministère des Affaires étrangères de l'Union"; en revanche, celle d'un Ministère de la Défense de l'Union avait été complètement laissée de côté, sans doute temporairement car les bouleversements en cours de l'Europe de l'Est risquaient de renouveler le problème.

L'exercice intellectuel de préparation de la CIG 96 a ainsi tout au cours de l'année 1995 donné aux Etats membres et aux Institutions de l'Union l'occasion de se concentrer sur un bilan de la PESC et d'avancer des projets de réforme. On soulignera toutefois que s'agissant de bilan, il ne porte pas sur un temps bien long: 26 mois, ce qui est dérisoire pour juger. On s'attachera dès lors plus dans une première section à décrire ce qu'est la PESC, en l'examinant d'après les textes et en enrichissant cet examen de quelques remarques voire critiques sur ce qui a été fait, en réservant à une seconde section ce que la CIG 96 pourrait être appelée à faire pour renforcer la PESC.

I. LA PESC, CE QU'ELLE EST

Le Titre V du Traité de l'Union, intitulé *Dispositions concernant la Politique étrangère et de sécurité commune* est probablement des six grandes réformes que comprenait le Traité de 1992, ce qui a été reçu avec le plus d'étonnement et de controverses. Alors que quatre des autres grandes réformes s'inscrivaient dans le prévisible ou la continuité, il n'en était pas de même des Titres V et VI (celui-ci consacré à la coopération en matière de Justice et d'Affaires intérieures et appelé encore IIIème pilier ou en abrégé JAI).

S'inscrivait dans la continuité, l'augmentation des pouvoirs du Parlement européen, même si la réforme était importante puisqu'on lui donnait avec le Conseil de ministres un pouvoir véritable de co-décision normative sur pas mal de questions; était tout à fait dans la continuité une augmentation des pouvoirs d'action de la Communauté tant dans quelques domaines déjà régentés, que dans des secteurs nouveaux, notamment ceux intéressant la société civile; n'avait rien non plus d'imprévu que l'on décide de réaliser rapidement la mise en place d'une monnaie unique appelée à se substituer à celles des Etats membres dès avant la fin du siècle, l'article 102A CE rédigé en 1986 l'annonçait; également la création d'une citoyenneté européenne était un aboutissement prévisible prenant acte de la réalisation de la libre circulation des personnes et de ce que les ressortissants des Etats membres constituaient depuis 1976 le corps électoral du Parlement européen, leur donner le titre de citoyen de l'Union n'était que la reconnaissance officielle de ce double acquis.

Au contraire, les Titres V et VI du Traité de l'Union avaient une toute autre dynamique. Ils se construisaient en dehors de la Communauté la "complétant" (art. A.3 TUE) par une politique et une forme de coopération inédite. Inédite parce que de nature intergouvernementale et non supranationale comme les traités originaires. La plupart des Etats membres – sauf peut-être la Belgique et l'Italie – n'étaient en effet pas disposés à retenir le module communautaire pour la PESC et les affaires judiciaires et intérieures. Ils désiraient des mécanismes purement intergouvernementaux, des décisions d'un commun accord et non à la majorité, une place réduite pour les Institutions communautaires, les acteurs seraient les Etats membres et nuls autres, même pas la Commission. Sur ce dernier point, un compromis cosmétique fut toutefois passé pour ne pas désespérer la Commission et ses défenseurs et surtout éviter l'effet de dispersion, ce fut la création pour l'Union d'un cadre décisionnel unique chargé de gérer la Communauté mais aussi de s'occuper de la PESC et de la coopération dans les domaines de la Justice et des Affaires intérieures, tout en assurant entre tous ces domaines et acteurs disparates l'indispensable cohésion (art. C). Cette structure complexe fut appelée à trois piliers, un pilier central qui est la Communauté, flanqué de deux autres piliers, le deuxième, la PESC, le troisième, Justice et les Affaires intérieures, la JAI. On emploie fréquemment le terme de troisième pilier, peu ceux de premier et deuxième piliers, même si la Commission émule de Procuste ne perd pas une occasion dans ses rapports pour critiquer sévèrement cet éclatement contre nature et réclamer la rentrée dans le rang des deuxième et troisième piliers.

A. La PESC, son cadre d'activité

Répétons-le, il est intergouvernemental et pas supranational.

1. Une demie-douzaine d'idées-force à titre d'objectifs (TUE, art. J.1)

Ces idées-force rédigées sobrement, complètent les objectifs de l'Union exposés à l'article B du TUE; l'un de ceux-ci (art. B, deuxième tiret) vise plus spécialement la PESC en affirmant l'identité de l'Union sur la scène internationale.

Une première idée pour la PESC serait l'universalisme de son objet: elle couvre tous les domaines de la politique étrangère et de sécurité (TUE, art. J.1.1.); évidemment, ce qui est de la compétence communautaire, l'économique, lui échappe, restant aux soins de la Communauté.

Les objectifs sont cinq, on se contentera de les énumérer:
- l'idée de valeurs communes, d'intérêts fondamentaux, d'indépendance de l'Union;
- celle de sécurité de l'Union et des Etats membres à renforcer;
- les principes de la société internationale, maintien de la paix et de la sécurité internationale, respect de la Charte des Nations Unies, de la CSCE;
- la promotion de la coopération internationale;
- le renforcement de la démocratie, de l'Etat de droit et le respect des droits de l'homme et libertés fondamentales.

2. Deux moyens d'action privilégiés: l'action commune et la position commune

Tous deux, exprimés dans les articles J.2. et J.3., correspondent à la mise en commun par les Etats membres d'activités, de biens matériels, d'attitudes, de moyens financiers, d'appuis politiques, de formulation de déclarations, de façon à ce que cette mise en commun, proclamée voire médiatisée ***una voce***, ait un impact plus fort que ne le serait les mêmes éléments mis en oeuvre isolément par chacun des Etats membres. Au vrai, cet impact supérieur d'une action commune à celui d'activités isolées ne figure pas au texte du moins du Titre V mais se trouve dans Titre VI, art. K.3. Rien n'indique toutefois par son évidence que l'idée n'est pas valable également pour la PESC.

Le texte ne définit d'ailleurs que rapidement le contenu de ces moyens; on peut toutefois en rassemblant diverses idées relever que les **positions communes** sont destinées à deux bénéfices: il faut que les Etats membres conforment leurs politiques nationales aux positions communes (art. J.2.2.2.), et que les Etats membres défendent ces positions communes dans les conférences et organisations internationales (art. J.2.3.).

Quant à l'**action commune**, il semble qu'elle est surtout immatérielle, un appui politique et moral, une médiation, une négociation (nous pensons à celle du pacte de stabilité en Europe), un rapprochement voire une unification de services ou actes, une simplification administrative; mais elle peut aussi être matérielle, de l'argent, des aides financières ou humaines voire humanitaires, des soldats. L'article J.3. est général sur le contenu que le Conseil pourra lui donner, sur ses objectifs et sa durée (§ 1), son adaptation si nécessaire (§ 3), sa procédure d'urgence (§ 6), ses incidents (§ 7).

Ainsi, se trouvent créés deux actes spécifiques aux contours assez larges, propres à la PESC et ayant un début de parallélisme avec les actes communautaires, ces règlements, directives, décisions … énumérés à l'article 189 CE. Devrait-on si, on faisait de la théorie du droit, dire que ces actes font de la coopération intergouvernementale une structure particulièrement dualiste: sans doute sont-ils élaborés dans un ordre international, le cadre institutionnel unique de l'Union reposant sur le Conseil de Ministres de l'Union, mais ils sont exécutés à l'échelon inférieur des Etats membres, par chacun de ceux-ci; voilà de quoi réjouir outre-tombe les professeurs H. Triepel et D. Anzilotti.

3. Méthodes de la PESC

Nous visons par cela l'obligation d'information mutuelle et de concertation au sein du Conseil que pose l'article J.2.1: les Etats membres avaient une vieille habitude de ces consultations entre eux. En fait, elle remontait à 1960 où, par exemple pour préparer l'action extérieure communautaire notamment les pratiques d'embargos réalisées dans le cadre des Nations Unies, telle celui de la Rhodésie, les Directeurs des affaires politiques des Etats membres étaient présents aux sessions du Conseil CEE.

C'est lors de l'entrée en vigueur de l'Acte Unique (1986) que cette obligation s'est trouvée affirmée dans le cadre de la Coopération politique (AUE, article 30, abrogé par le TUE).

Un réseau d'information mutuelle a au surplus été créé sous le nom de COREU: chaque ministère des Affaires étrangères, par l'intermédiaire d'un "correspondant européen", met en commun les informations les plus variées que lui ont procurées ses postes diplomatiques et ses propres analystes (AUE, art. 30.10.e). Ce réseau sert aussi à l'élaboration de déclarations communes, une centaine par an.

4. Sécurité et défense

On a indiqué que le Traité de l'Union avait, en 1992, été particulièrement discret en son article J.4. sur ces questions, les Etats membres n'étaient pas prêts. D'autres paramètres que l'Union européenne étaient d'ailleurs en cause. La défense de l'Europe était pour beaucoup assurée dans le cadre de l'Alliance atlantique et de l'OTAN. Sans doute, existait-il un organisme proprement européen, l'Union de l'Europe occidentale (UEO) reposant sur le Traité de Bruxelles de 1948, plusieurs fois révisé et élargi, mais tous les Etats membres n'en étaient pas parties: on y distingue actuellement parmi les Etats membres de l'Union, certains Etats pleinement membres (dix), plus des "associés" (cinq); par ailleurs, trois "observateurs" non membres de l'Union, et enfin parmi les candidats à l'adhésion neuf partenaires "associés" et deux "dialoguant" avec l'UEO; faut-il rappeler que certains Etats membres étaient d'ailleurs plutôt réticents à l'Alliance atlantique, voire avaient une politique de neutralité, quatre (sur les actuels quinze) sont dans ce cas, avec des variantes. Compte tenu d'un engagement de garantie mutuelle en cas d'agression souscrit entre Etats membres de l'UEO (article 5 du Traité de Bruxelles, texte de 1954) et conclu pour cinquante ans, la CIG 96 doit justement avoir mission d'étudier les progrès réalisés dans un rapprochement avec l'UEO et de réviser à cet égard le Titre V. Au sujet de ce rapprochement UEO-UE et de conversations avec l'OTAN, une "déclaration commune des Etats membres de l'UE simultanément membres de l'UEO" avait d'ailleurs été annexée au Traité de l'UE sous le double thème du développement de l'UEO comme **composante** de défense de l'Union européenne et comme **moyen** de renforcer le pilier européen de l'Alliance atlantique" (déclaration n° 30).

5. Financement de la PESC

Evidemment, les dépenses administratives entraînées pour les Institutions de la Communauté par la PESC sont à la charge de celles-ci, c'est une application banale de l'unicité des Institutions. Quant aux dépenses opérationnelles – spécialement celles entraînées par des actions communes – elles sont soit à la charge des Etats membres, éventuellement selon les termes d'une répartition à convenir, soit à la charge du budget de la Communauté, sur décision unanime du Conseil; dans un tel cas les dispositions budgétaires du Traité sont d'application. Signalons que très couramment depuis 1993 les Etats membres ont eu tendance – même si les actions communes ont été modestes – à prévoir une telle imputation au budget communautaire, avec une certaine inconséquence de raisonnement, le Parlement européen exerçant dès lors un contrôle sur ces activités beaucoup plus étroit qu'il ne l'eut fait si elles n'avaient relevé que de la PESC *stricto sensu.*

6. Une lacune?

On relèvera que l'Union n'a pas la personnalité juridique, qu'elle ne peut de ce fait passer un traité avec des Etats tiers ou avec d'autres organisations. Est-ce un oubli? Une conséquence de ce que puisqu'il s'agit de coopération entre les Etats membres ce serait à ceux-ci seuls de contracter? Est-ce enfin une parade des Etats membres pour empêcher la Cour de Justice de considérer comme conséquence de ce que l'Union aurait la personnalité juridique, qu'elle aurait aussi la possibilité de passer des accords internationaux (application extrapolée de la jurisprudence AETR), ce à quoi en 1992 on n'était pas prêt? Les premières raisons paraissent les plus pertinentes. Quoiqu'il en soit, notamment dans ses actions communes en ex Yougoslavie, la Présidence de l'Union a, par anticipation, eu l'occasion de passer avec les serbes des mémorandums d'accord au nom de l'Union[1].

7. Force obligatoire des actes de la PESC

Les Etats membres appuient "activement et sans réserve" la PESC et "s'abstiennent de toute action contraire" (article J.1.4.).

---

[1] A ce sujet, *voir* une curieuse note de D. LOPANDIC, à la 392 RMCUE (1995), pp. 557–562.

8. Répercussion de la PESC dans la Communauté

Au titre de la cohérence entre la PESC et le régime communautaire, certaines décisions de la PESC se répercutent pour leur exécution dans la Communauté (celui-là est juridiquement subordonné à celles-ci). Ainsi, une mesure d'embargo décidée politiquement dans le cadre de la PESC sera exécutée par la Communauté dans son cadre à elle (art. 228A CE).

B. Les acteurs de la PESC

C'est évidemment le Conseil de l'Union européenne qui est l'organe essentiel de décision de la PESC (art. J.8.2.). Il le fait sur base des orientations générales arrêtées par le Conseil européen, c'est-à-dire les chefs d'Etat et de gouvernement des Etats membres. De même, il veille à l'unité, la cohérence et l'efficacité de cette action de l'Union. Il se prononce à l'unanimité, sauf en matière de décisions de procédure et sauf possibilité, une fois prise la décision de base sur une action commune d'arrêter les décisions d'application à la majorité qualifiée pondérée de soixante-deux voix, exprimant l'accord de dix Etats membres (chiffres et procédure habituels). Il est enfin prévu dans une déclaration annexée au Traité que pour éviter autant que possible d'empêcher qu'il y ait unanimité, les Etats membres réticents à une décision chercheront à se rallier à l'unanimité (ou à s'abstenir) lorsqu'il y a déjà une majorité qualifiée favorable (déclaration n° 27), c'est ce qu'on a appelé l'abstention constructive.

Si le Comité des Représentants permanents n'en conserve pas moins en matière de PESC, sa compétence générale de préparation du Conseil, celui-ci est en outre, dans sa préparation et dans la surveillance de la situation internationale, assisté par les Directeurs des Affaires politiques des Ministères des Affaires étrangères, réunis en un Comité politique (voir art. J.8.5. et en outre la Déclaration 28 annexée au TUE).

Le Conseil européen a dans la définition des principes et des orientations générales de la PESC un rôle essentiel et déploie son autorité dans la lancée de toute action.

La présidence du Conseil – en tant que besoin assisté des deux autres membres de la Troïka, c'est-à-dire le représentant de l'Etat membre qui immédiatement l'a précédé et de celui qui le suit – assure une tâche de représentation à l'extérieur de la PESC, ainsi qu'une tâche d'exécution. Dans cette tâche, elle est assistée du Secrétariat du Conseil lequel comprenait dans son sein de 1986 à 1993 une petite unité composée non pas de fonctionnaires communautaires mais de fonctionnaires détachés par les Etats membres pour assurer le secrétariat de la Coopération politique européenne. Cette unité a été intégrée plus intimement au Secrétariat général et élargie, elle a également établi des liens exploratoires avec le Secrétariat de l'UEO.

Une concertation spéciale sur tous les sujets de PESC a lieu entre missions diplomatiques et consulaires des Etats membres et délégations de la Commission tant dans les capitales étrangères qu'à l'occasion des travaux des organisations internationales ou des conférences diplomatiques.

Sans doute le rôle des autres Institutions est-il moindre dans le cadre de la PESC que dans celui de la Communauté.

La Commission, par exemple, perd son droit d'initiative de la proposition qui est à la base de la décision communautaire (art. 148 et 189A), elle n'en a pas moins la possibilité de saisir le Conseil de toute question. D'une manière générale, elle est associée à tous les travaux, notamment d'exécution, de représentation extérieure, de contact avec le Parlement ...

Le Parlement européen est consulté sur les principaux aspects et les choix fondamentaux de la PESC; ses vues sont à la diligence de la Présidence du Conseil et de la Commission prises en compte par le Conseil; il est régulièrement tenu au courant de l'évolution de la PESC, il procède annuellement à un débat sur les progrès de celle-ci et peut faire des recommandations et poser des questions (art. J.7.). Son rôle est, on le voit, nettement moindre que dans le cadre communautaire où il est consulté spécifiquement sur presque tous les actes en élaboration, mais n'est-on pas dans un cadre intergouvernemental, voire extra-communautaire?

La Cour de Justice enfin n'est pas mentionnée au Titre V.

* * *

Si on examine les activités entre novembre 1993 et décembre 1995 (vingt-six mois) de la PESC, on ne peut qu'être frappé de la modestie des opérations et des résultats. Dans son Rapport sur le fonctionnement du Traité sur l'Union européenne, présenté en mai 1995 par la Commission, celle-ci est des plus critiques estimant que la méthode intergouvernementale a montré son inefficacité totale. Elle préconise dès lors – comme elle l'avait déjà proposé en 1991, *voir* Supplément 2-91 au Bulletin des Communautés, Contributions de la Commission aux CIG, *e.g.,* p. 87 – une communautarisation quasi-complète, par suppression du deuxième pilier avec toutefois quelques dispositions extracommunautaires particulières pour la politique commune de sécurité. Il est difficile de se ranger à toutes les remarques de ce Rapport dont certaines sentent le dépit de ne pas l'être vu attribué un meilleur rôle. Avec des nuances entre eux, les Etats membres réunis au sein du Groupe de réflexion en cours du deuxième semestre 1995, inclinent nettement à un renforcement de la PESC mais à ce qu'on lui garda sa spécificité. De quoi s'agit-il?

II. RENFORCER LA PESC. QU'EST-CE À DIRE?

Jusqu'ici les réalisations de la PESC n'auraient pas été brillantes. Certes, elle a fréquemment agi en Yougoslavie avec une quinzaine de positions et actions communes, plus encore autant dans d'autres domaines.

Mais on ne peut pas dire en Yougoslavie que son action y ait été couronnée de succès: la plupart de ses interventions y ont concerné des mesures d'embargo ou des actions humanitaires *largo sensu* (administration de la ville de Mostar); quant au principal, sa médiation n'a pas réussi, ses essais d'interposition non plus; elle a certes suivi l'action du Groupe de contact des Nations Unies qui sur cinq membres était composé de trois Etats membres; elle a dû laisser la main aux Nations Unies, à l'OTAN, aux Etats-Unis ... Certes après Dayton, son médiateur, le suédois C. Bildt a reçu d'importantes fonctions dans l'administration de la paix ...Mais tout cela n'est aucunement marqué au coin du succès ...

Hors Yougoslavie, si on met à part des positions communes concernant un abaissement des relations économiques et commerciales avec des Etats en crise (Haïti deux fois, Soudan et Libye, une fois chacun); d'autres relatives à des réfugiés (Rwanda et Burundi); une action concernant la relance économique au Moyen-orient; par deux fois un soutien à la démocratisation du pays par l'envoi d'observateurs à des élections (Russie et Afrique du Sud), on relèvera comme actions diplomatiques réelles une position commune sur les objectifs et les priorités de l'Union européenne à l'égard de l'Ukraine et surtout six actions communes sur le maintien de la paix et le désarmement: d'une part sa réussite dans la négociation d'un Pacte de stabilité en Europe (deux actions communes) et d'autre part, plus particulières, celle concernant le contrôle des exportations de bien à double usage, et celles préparant la conférence de réexamen du Traité sur la non-prolifération des armes nucléaires, une sur les lasers aveuglants, une sur les mines antipersonnelles.

Le pacte de stabilité serait son seul franc succès, même si depuis sa conclusion en avril 1995 il a peut-être perdu un peu de son panache.

Sans doute ajoutera-t-on pour expliquer un peu son insuccès yougoslave, qu'elle a, en juin – juillet 1991, pris de plein fouet, avant même son baptême de Maastricht, l'éclatement des hostilités en Yougoslavie; que ses Etats membres avaient à l'égard de ce problème des attirances opposées (mais est-ce une excuse?); que l'acharnement des parties au conflit ne lui a pas facilité la tâche (même remarque). Dans d'autres directions, non plus. Que faire?

Conceptuellement, la PESC était destinée à constituer, à terme, une sorte de Ministère commun des relations étrangères, auquel progressivement dans le cadre d'une Union européenne politique en devenir, serait dévolu le service des relations extérieures communes des Etats membres et de l'Union. Une démarche très progressive, l'ouverture à tous les Etats membres de la PESC commandaient évidemment un usage prolongé de l'unanimité. Jusqu'ici la PESC n'a pas vraiment eu de problème à cet égard, mais doit-on pour autant renoncer à l'unanimité? Certains le pensent, d'autres ne le veulent absolument pas.

On a beaucoup parlé au groupe préparatoire de la CIG 96 de deux réformes pour permettre son envol. Par ailleurs, l'élargissement de l'Union réalisé au début 1995 et simultanément le bouleversement du panorama politique européen depuis 1990, commandent qu'on repense le volet défense/sécurité à peine ébauché pour la PESC dans le texte de 1992.

Deux innovations administrativo-institutionnelles sont annoncées avec une certaine constance (A), plus un réexamen du volet sécurité (B).

A. Innovations administrativo-institutionnelles

D'abord, on créerait une cellule d'analyse et de préparation pour permettre la réalisation de la PESC. On envisage que celle-ci occupe une soixantaine d'agents, pour partie détachés temporairement des Etats membres, pour partie appartenant aux services du Secrétariat du Conseil de l'Union, pour partie enfin venant de la Commission (à moins que cette partie ne fasse que coopérer intimement; de toute façon, la Communauté occupe pour tout le volet économique de la PESC une place majeure). Cette cellule analyserait les situations politiques sur base d'une documentation émanant de tous les Etats membres et de leurs ambassades ainsi que de la Commission, il faudrait que ceux-là et celle-ci concourrent à son travail; elle ébaucherait des solutions, le tout en étroite relation avec les Ministères des Affaires étrangères. Quant au nombre de soixante de ces agents, disons qu'il soutiendrait la comparaison avec celui des agents correspondants du Ministère des Affaires étrangères d'un pays important: le chiffre de soixante agents n'est pas substantiellement différent du nombre des fonctionnaires de grade A du Ministère français des Affaires étrangères, Direction des affaires politiques et Directions géographiques confondues.

Pour assurer le caractère opérationnel de cette cellule, il serait nécessaire – et c'est la seconde innovation – de la doter d'un chef; on parle d'un monsieur (ou d'une madame) PESC. Comment le choisir? Quel serait son statut? Sa responsabilité? Quatre candidatures sont possibles. Le Secrétaire Général du Conseil, mais celui-ci a déjà un rôle administratif et politique important. Peut-on le dédoubler? Un Secrétaire général politique pour la PESC et un Secrétaire général pour la Communauté? Si un Secrétaire général unique peut être d'un niveau politique (Luns ou Spaak à l'OTAN), un co-Secrétaire général ou un Secrétaire général délégué le sera moins. Sera-ce encore un Commissaire, celui dont relève la Direction générale des relations extérieures politiques, mais cela semble difficile, la Commission a en effet pour essence d'être indépendante du Conseil et des Etats membres, de n'en recevoir aucune instruction? L'autonomie de la Commission semble dès lors en absolue contradiction avec le statut intergouvernemental de cette politique; il faut quelqu'un en qui le Conseil ait une parfaite confiance opérationnelle, auquel il donne des mandats, et qui fasse corps avec lui. Sera-ce alors le Secrétaire général de l'UEO? Une assez grande incertitude sur ce qui se passera pour celle-ci en 1998 amènerait à rejeter cette candidature (*cf. infra*); au surplus le Secrétaire général de l'UEO sera peut-être le Secrétaire d'Etat futur de la Défense, mais pas le Secrétaire d'Etat aux Affaires étrangères. Alors quelqu'un, d'un haut niveau politique, désigné à long terme, 5 ans? par le Conseil européen ou par le Conseil de Ministres de l'Union, et responsable devant ceux-ci; ce serait probablement là la solution? Un tel personnage ne risque-t-il pas toutefois de porter ombrage au Président du Conseil UE, c'est-à-dire au Ministre des Affaires étrangères de l'Etat membre assurant semestriellement cette présidence. La question est évidemment liée au statut de cette présidence dont par ailleurs les Etats membres souhaitent à la CIG 96 le renforcement.

Sans doute tout cela semble-t-il un peu mièvre. Evidemment plusieurs Etats membres demandront à nouveau que de plus en plus on décide tout à la majorité, mais il est peu probable qu'on bouge beaucoup à cet égard, sauf dans le cas où le Conseil européen aurait dès la première discussion dégagé une grande unanimité sans faille et où le reste ne serait plus qu'intendance et exécution; sinon la doctrine de "l'intérêt vital" chère au Général de Gaulle ne manquerait pas de s'imposer à nouveau: rappelons que ce qu'on a appelé l'unanimité moins une voix a été caricaturé par la Grèce comme permettant à l'Union de tout faire en faveur de la Turquie.

Peut-être sera-t-on plus heureux sur la nécessité d'une reconnaissance de la personnalité juridique de l'Union; certains toutefois y sont très opposés.

B. CIG 96, sécurité et UEO

A côté de ces deux innovations dont on parle beaucoup, même si elles semblent mineures, d'autres réflexions dérivent de l'évolution de la structure internationale du continent Europe depuis trois ou quatre ans. Il a été une constante au cours de l'année 1991 que la PESC devait à terme être dirigée vers une politique de sécurité extérieure, voire de défense. A cet égard, dès juin 1991 (Conseil européen de Luxembourg), on pense déjà qu'elle se réalisera dans le cadre de l'UEO. Aussi l'article J.4.6. du Traité de 1992 prévoit à la fois comme étapes la révision de 1996 et évoque le renouvellement en 1998 de l'UEO. C'est ce qui figure dans son texte. Mais il y a une large marge d'inconnu.

Trois mois après la signature de Maastricht, à Lisbonne, l'horizon a déjà changé.

Sans doute, poursuivra-t-on le rapprochement UE et UEO; celle-ci émigrera de Londres à Bruxelles; les secrétariats de ces deux organisations se feront des risettes.

Mais l'optique est dans les élargissements immédiats de l'Union vers le reste de l'AELE et vers les PECOs. Cela peut-être plus dans les mobiles de l'Allemagne pour laquelle 1991 a été l'année du dépouillement de l'habit fédéral et qui s'installe dans sa politique post-réunification, que pour les autres Etats membres. L'adhésion de trois pays de l'AELE (sur sept, quatre n'adhèrent pas pour des raisons ou d'autres, la Norvège, l'Islande, la Suisse et le Liechstenstein, leurs raisons sauf peut-être celles de la Suisse ne semblent en rien avoir à faire avec les questions de sécurité) est conclue au printemps 1994. Elle a toutefois l'inconvénient de donner trop de poids aux voix neutres dans l'Union: quatre Etats membres sur quinze, c'est-à-dire treize voix à la majorité qualifiée pondérée de l'article 148 CE, alors qu'il n'en faut que vingt-trois pour bloquer.

Par ailleurs, la Russie, qui n'est plus celle de Gorbatchev, mais celle d'Elstine voire de … ne voit pas d'un bon oeil l'entrée des PECOs dans le système militaire de l'Occident, que ce soit à l'UEO à long terme ou à l'OTAN à plus bref délai.

Toujours par ailleurs, les Américains, tant en esquissant un mouvement d'abandonner l'Europe pour des raisons principalement budgétaires, réussissent trois opérations sécuritaires majeures, celle d'Irak, la paix au Moyen-Orient et un désarmoçage apparent (temporaire) du conflit en ex-Yougoslavie. Leur *leadership* retrouvé?

Des Etats membres originaires ou du premier élargissement plus tentés par l'OTAN que par la PESC?

Tout cela vide de son contenu PESC la CIG 1996 où ne figurerait plus que les thèmes mineurs de la création de la cellule de planification et d'analyse et de la nomination de M. PESC. Et puis, l'UEO avec des contours identiques à l'UE est-elle vraiment adéquate comme élément de défense de l'Union européenne et comme pilier européen de l'Alliance atlantique? En un mot, si le nombre de membres de l'Union européenne va d'ici la fin du siècle passer de quinze à presque trente, tous ces nouveaux membres sont-ils aptes à occuper une place entière dans l'UEO et désireux de le faire ou simplement ne voient-ils pas pour certains d'entre-eux leur activité en faveur de la sécurité commune se confiner à des actions non pas seulement humanitaires mais purement pacifiques (dites du type Petersberg), à l'exclusion d'actions de défense? L'Europe de la Sécurité extérieure et de la Défense ne doit-elle pas être alors à deux vitesses et en outre construite sur un mode moins égalitaire que l'Union en reconnaissant aux grands Etats d'Europe occidentale qui en ont la capacité matérielle (la bombe atomique) ou financière (l'Allemagne) ou l'Italie si elle en a la volonté, une priorité que le Benelux voire d'autres Etats sont peut être disposés, tout en participant pleinement à l'UEO, à reconnaître à ceux-là.

Le Traité sur l'Union européenne a dit que la CIG 96 ferait le point, compte tenu de l'échéance de 1998 du Traité de Bruxelles (UEO)[2], ainsi que de "l'évaluation des progrès réalisés et de l'expérience acquise" jusque-là. Il ne dit toutefois pas que le volet sécurité de la PESC doit en 1996 être révisé, il dit seulement qu'il **peut** l'être. Il est évident que la géométrie 1996 est différente de la géométrie 1991. L'Europe de la défense ne va-t-elle pas être à deux vitesses tout en s'ouvrant pleinement à tous ceux qui veulent y participer – voire sont prêts à participer à la garantie mutuelle – mais non autant aux neutres? Il resterait à fixer les modalités des relations entre Etats pleinement participants à la PESC et ceux n'y participant que partiellement – c'est ce qu'on appelle introduire un élément de flexibilité – et évidemment à mettre en forme les relations entre l'Union et l'UEO (fusion, intégration, partenariat renforcé, dépendance, convergence institutionnelle)? Les Communautés et l'Union en ont vu bien d'autres, même si souvent cela prendra du temps.

De toute façon, comme il est exclu qu'on recule – la fuite en avant est une règle d'or de la Communauté – on devra faire quelque chose.

---

2 L'UEO, rappelons-le, est comptable d'un engagement mutuel entre ses membres „d'aide et d'assistance, par tous les moyens en leur pouvoir: militaires et autres" en cas d'agression armée (art. 4 originaire du Pacte de l'Union occidentale du 17 mars 1948, devenu art. 5 lors de la révision du 23 octobre 1954, qui en outre change le nom d'Union occidentale en Union de l'Europe occidentale; le Pacte de 1948 avait été conclu pour cinquante ans à partir de son entrée en vigueur, soit le 25 août 1998).

Fourth Part

Adjudication

QUELQUES OBSERVATIONS SUR LE RECOURS AU RÈGLEMENT JURIDICTIONNEL DES DIFFÉRENDS INTERÉTATIQUES

par

DANIEL BARDONNET

1. La possibilité de soumettre certains différends interétatiques au règlement arbitral ou judiciaire, impliquant par conséquent une décision obligatoire fondée sur le droit et rendue par des personnalités indépendantes, est justement considérée comme une étape importante dans le développement du droit international. L'arbitrage obligatoire et la juridiction obligatoire, même s'ils ont toujours été assortis de nombreuses restrictions, devenaient, sinon une réalité, du moins un espoir. Néanmoins, les résistances individualistes des Etats à ce que l'on a parfois appelé, avec une vision quelque peu euphorisante du droit international, une «véritable justice», demeurent aussi fortes en cette fin du XXème siècle qu'elles l'ont été dès ses premiers balbutiements, tant elles sont inhérentes à la structure même de la société internationale.

Aussi bien, en hommage au dédicataire de ces pages – dont on n'oubliera pas qu'il a, le 21 septembre 1990, en tant que Ministre des Affaires étrangères, souscrit, au nom du Gouvernement polonais, une déclaration d'acceptation de la juridiction obligatoire de la Cour Internationale de Justice, conformément à l'article 36 par. 2 de son Statut[1] – voudrait-on présenter quelques observations sur le recours au règlement juridictionnel. Avant d'analyser quelques-unes des précautions qui doivent être prises par les Gouvernements décidés à soumettre un différend interétatique, par voie de compromis ou accessoirement par voie de requête unilatérale, à un Tribunal d'arbitrage ou à la Cour (II), on rappellera brièvement les conditions nécessaires pour recourir à ces modes de règlement pacifique des différends qui en circonscrivent et en limitent étroitement la portée (I).

I

2. Le recours au règlement arbitral ou judiciaire suppose que trois conditions soient réunies. En premier lieu, il suppose la paix. Comme Nicolas

---

[1] C.I.J., ANNUAIRE 1993–1994, n° 48, pp. 118–119.

Politis l'observait déjà en 1924, c'est-à-dire à l'apogée de ce qu'il appelait «l'esprit international», «on se figurait que la justice amènerait la paix, parce qu'on la croyait capable de tuer la guerre. Mais l'histoire montre que c'est plutôt le contraire qui est vrai; la justice suppose la paix»[2]. Et tout récemment, un Juge à la Cour internationale de Justice, M. Gilbert Guillaume, remarquait dans le même sens: «The problem of peace cannot be reduced to the settlement of disputes and even to the settlement of certain kinds of disputes. Certainly the judiciary may make a very valuable contribution to the maintenance of peace. But resort to the Court is not the 'miraculous' remedy which will wipe violence from the face of the Earth»[3]. Il est bien vrai en effet qu'on ne résoud les différends interétatiques ni par l'invocation de formules plus ou moins incantatoires ni par la multiplication des mécanismes juridictionnels[4]. Ce n'est pas le nombre des institutions qui importe mais la qualité de l'engagement des Etats.

3. Le recours au règlement arbitral ou judiciaire suppose en second lieu le consentement des Etats parties au différend, que ce consentement ait été donné avant ou après la naissance du conflit. Le droit de refuser d'être attrait devant un tiers est toujours considéré comme l'un des apanages de la souveraineté et les Tribunaux d'arbitrage[5] tout comme la Cour internationale de Justice[6] font du principe du consensualisme, c'est-à-dire de la volonté des Parties, le fondement de leur compétence.

La récente affaire relative au Timor oriental en constitue une illustration particulièrement significative. Malgré la force de l'argumentation sur les rapports du droit – ou plus précisément des règles régissant la compétence

---

[2] LA JUSTICE INTERNATIONALE, Paris, Hachette, 1924, pp. 253–254. *Cf.* CH. DE VISSCHER, THÉORIES ET RÉALITÉS EN DROIT INTERNATIONAL PUBLIC, Paris, Pedone, 2e éd., 1955, p. 409; A. GROS, ANNUAIRE DE L'INSTITUT DE DROIT INTERNATIONAL 1979, vol. 58-II, p. 27.

[3] *The Future of International Judicial Institutions*, THE INTERNATIONAL AND COMPARATIVE LAW QUARTERLY 1995, vol. 44, pp. 848–862, à la p. 860. A n'en pas douter, comme l'a remarqué le Juge GUILLAUME, la Cour a apporté une contribution importante à la paix par son arrêt du 3 février 1994 en l'affaire du différend territorial Libye/Tchad, d'autant que la Libye s'est retirée, trois mois après la décision de la Cour, de la bande d'Aouzou (LES GRANDES CRISES INTERNATIONALES ET LE DROIT, Seuil, 1994, pp. 297–315).

[4] Sur les risques qu'entraîne la prolifération des juridictions, *voir* les observations du Juge GUILLAUME, *ibid.* pp. 861–862 et sa suggestion de transposer dans l'ordre international un mécanisme rappelant celui qui a été institué, en droit communautaire, par l'article 177 du Traité de Rome.

[5] Dans l'affaire Ambatielos (arrêt du 19 mai 1953), la Cour s'est référée «au principe bien établi en droit international», d'après lequel «un Etat ne saurait être obligé de soumettre ses différends à l'arbitrage sans son consentement» (C.I.J., REC. 1953, p. 19).

[6] Déjà la Cour permanente, dans l'affaire de l'usine de Chorzów (arrêt du 13 septembre 1928), avait proclamé que sa juridiction «dépend de la volonté des Parties» (Série A, n° 17, pp. 37–38). Ce principe a été réaffirmé par la suite dans l'affaire de l'Or monétaire pris à Rome en 1943 et constamment énoncé depuis lors, notamment dans les affaires d'intervention.

et la recevabilité – et de la justice, telle qu'elle a été brillamment développée dans l'opinion dissidente qui suit l'arrêt du 30 juin 1995[7], la Cour a fait prévaloir ce qu'elle a appelé «l'un des principes fondamentaux de son Statut», d'après lequel «elle ne peut trancher un différend entre des Etats sans que ceux-ci aient consenti à sa juridiction»[8]. Cette jurisprudence constante ne fait que traduire la répugnance fondamentale des Etats à l'égard du règlement obligatoire des différends fondé sur le droit.

4. Le recours au règlement arbitral ou judiciaire suppose enfin, en troisième lieu, que les différends portés devant l'organe tiers soient de nature juridique, comme l'impliquent l'article 37 de la Convention de La Haye de 1907 pour le règlement pacifique des conflits internationaux et l'article 38 du Statut de la Cour internationale de Justice. Sans doute l'artificialité de la distinction entre les différends juridiques soumis à des moyens juridictionnels de règlement et les différends politiques soumis à des moyens non juridictionnels a été souvent dénoncée. Il est bien vrai en effet qu'un différend juridique dans son essence, au sujet duquel «les Parties se contesteraient réciproquement un droit»[9], peut comporter une dimension politique tout comme un différend de nature politique peut comporter des aspects juridiques[10]. En d'autres termes, le Secrétaire général des Nations Unies, M. Boutros Boutros-Ghali, remarquait, dans le discours qu'il a prononcé, le 17 mars 1995, au Congrès du droit international: «les différends juridiques qui sont soumis [à la Cour] ne sont souvent que la traduction normative de conflits politiques plus profonds»[11].

Quelle que soit l'évolution des analyses relatives à la classification précitée des différends, l'idée prédominante, qui irrigue la politique juridique des Chancelleries, demeure que l'arbitre et le juge ne doivent être saisis que des différends «exclusivement juridiques», c'est-à-dire, en définitive, des différends le plus souvent mineurs. Le Président de la Cour internationale de Justice, M. Mohamed Bedjaoui, ne disait rien d'autre lorsqu'il s'interrogeait dans les termes suivants: «Pourquoi la Cour paraît-elle ... trop

---

7 C.I.J., REC. 1995, pp. 237–255, par. 40–96.

8 C.I.J., REC. 1995, p. 101, par. 26. En plus de la jurisprudence citée, on rappellera que, dans l'affaire de la délimitation maritime et des questions territoriales entre Qatar et Bahreïn (compétence et recevabilité, arrêt du 15 juin 1995), la Cour a également souligné que «sa compétence ne peut être établie qu'en recherchant la volonté des Parties, telle qu'elle résulte des textes pertinents» (C.I.J., REC. 1995, p. 23, par. 43).

9 Pour reprendre la formule bien connue de l'Acte général d'arbitrage du 26 septembre 1928.

10 Comme en témoignent notamment l'affaire du personnel diplomatique et consulaire à Téhéran (C.I.J., REC. 1980, p. 20, par. 35) ou l'affaire des activités militaires ou paramilitaires au Nicaragua (C.I.J., REC. 1984, p. 435, par. 95).

11 SG/SM/5583, L/2710, p. 5.

souvent en retrait de l'actualité? Pourquoi n'est-elle pas saisie de certains différends particulièrement graves, qui appellent une solution rapide, juste et durable, et auxquels le règlement judiciaire pourrait apporter toutes les vertus apaisantes?»[12].

5. Ainsi, le «champ opératoire»[13], dans lequel peut se déployer le règlement arbitral ou judiciaire international, demeure-t-il, malgré tous les efforts qui ont été faits pour l'élargir, étroitement balisé. Il en est ainsi par la volonté même des Etats, comme en témoignent les multiples réserves aux déclarations d'acceptation de la juridiction obligatoire de la Cour. Aussi bien, dans le cadre des limites structurelles précédemment rappelées, convient-il d'examiner maintenant quelques-unes des précautions que doit prendre le Gouvernement qui a décidé de recourir à ces procédures juridictionnelles pour résoudre un différend qui l'oppose à un autre Gouvernement, afin non seulement d'assurer au mieux la défense de ses intérêts, mais aussi le meilleur exercice possible de la fonction juridictionnelle.

II

6. Dans la plupart des contentieux, il existe un risque, communément appelé le risque judiciaire, qui est inhérent au règlement des différends par les procédures juridictionnelles et qui est, en général, égal pour les deux Parties. Toute décision motivée dispose certes de l'autorité de la chose jugée et il faut rappeler à cet égard la formule souvent citée de la sentence arbitrale rendue le 11 mars 1941 dans l'affaire du Trail Smelter, «That the sanctity of *res judicata* attaches to a final decision of an international tribunal is an essential and settled rule of international law»[14]. Mais il est tout aussi vrai que, bien souvent, cette décision aurait pu être autre sur le plan de la détermination du droit comme sur le plan de l'appréciation des faits. Comme l'a remarqué avec une grande finesse le Professeur Paul Reuter, «c'est la libre

---

[12] Conférence donnée, le 16 janvier 1995, à l'Institut des Hautes Etudes internationales de Paris sur «La contribution de la Cour internationale de Justice au maintien et au rétablissement de la paix».

[13] Pour reprendre la formule du Professeur MICHEL VIRALLY dans son étude bien connue sur *Le champ opératoire du règlement judiciaire international*, REVUE GÉNÉRALE DE DROIT INTERNATIONAL PUBLIC 1983, t. 87, pp. 281–314.

[14] N.U., RECUEIL DES SENTENCES ARBITRALES, vol. III, p. 1950. On peut lire également dans la sentence arbitrale rendue, le 21 octobre 1994, dans l'affaire de la Laguna del Desierto: «Una sentencia con autoridad de cosa juzcada (*res judicata*) es judicamente vinculante para las Partes en el litigio. Este es un principio fundamental del derecho de gentes invocado reiteradamente por la jurisprudencia, que considera la autoridad de cosa juzcada como un principio de derecho internacional, universal y absoluto» (par. 68). La traduction en français de cette Sentence se trouve dans la REVUE GÉNÉRALE DE DROIT INTERNATIONAL PUBLIC 1996, t. 100, pp. 520–597.

acceptation de ce risque judiciaire qui est la source la plus profonde de l'autorité des sentences», et le même auteur ajoutait: «quoi que l'on fasse, quelle que soit la qualité du recrutement des arbitres ou des juges, quelle que soit la multiplication des degrés de juridiction et des recours, le risque subsiste»[15]. Il faut ajouter que, pour certains types d'affaires, par exemple en matière de délimitations maritimes[16], la prévisibilité du résultat de l'instance[17] – qui constitue cependant l'une des vertus majeures du processus judiciaire – est pratiquement impossible. Outre ces interrogations préalables fondamentales sur l'issue du contentieux, tout Gouvernement décidé à s'engager dans cette voie doit prendre un certain nombre de décisions, particulièrement délicates et lourdes de conséquences, qui concernent, pour s'en tenir aux plus importantes, le choix de l'organe, le choix des hommes et le choix des mots, sur lesquels on souhaiterait faire quelques observations.

* * *

7. A partir du moment où l'instance politique constitutionnellement compétente a convenu de rechercher la solution d'un différend interétatique, alors que les négociations diplomatiques ont échoué, par la voie juridictionnelle, la première décision à prendre concerne l'organe à saisir d'un commun accord avec l'autre Partie[18]. Il s'agit de savoir d'abord si le différend considéré doit être porté devant un Tribunal d'arbitrage ou devant la Cour internationale de Justice.

Ces deux modalités de règlement pacifique des différends que sont le règlement arbitral et le règlement judiciaire comportent naturellement des points communs puisque, ainsi qu'on l'a déjà rappelé, l'un et l'autre débouchent sur une décision obligatoire fondée sur le droit et rendue par des personnalités indépendantes des Parties. Elles comportent néanmoins des différences qui doivent demeurer présentes à l'esprit de ceux qui opèrent ce premier choix. Le règlement judiciaire se distingue de l'arbitrage à un pre-

---

15 La motivation et la révision des sentences arbitrales à la Conférence de la Paix de 1899 et le conflit frontalier entre le Royaume-Uni et le Venezuela, MÉLANGES ANDRASSY, La Haye, M. Nijhoff, 1968, p. 245.

16 *Cf.* tout particulièrement, la sentence arbitrale rendue le 10 juin 1992 dans l'affaire de la délimitation des espaces maritimes de Saint-Pierre-et-Miquelon entre le Canada et la France (REVUE GÉNÉRALE DE DROIT INTERNATIONAL PUBLIC 1992, t. 96, pp. 673–751) et les commentaires d'E. ZOLLER (ANNUAIRE FRANÇAIS DE DROIT INTERNATIONAL 1992, vol. XXXVIII, pp. 480–500) qui parle notamment de «l'anarchie qui prévaut depuis 1982 dans le droit des délimitations maritimes» (*ibid.* p. 484).

17 Sur la nécessaire "predictability in the legal process", *voir* D.W. BOWETT, *Contemporary Developments in Legal Techniques in the Settlement of Disputes*, RECUEIL DES COURS DE L'ACADÉMIE DE DROIT INTERNATIONAL 1983-II, t. 180, pp. 191–203.

18 Pour ne pas allonger démesurément cette étude, elle ne portera que sur la saisine de l'organe juridictionnel par voie de compromis, et non par voie de requête unilatérale.

mier point de vue, par le fait que ceux qui sont appelés à statuer ne sont pas désignés par les Parties[19], en d'autres termes, que le tribunal est préconstitué. Mais règlement judiciaire et arbitrage se distingueraient également à un second point de vue, en ce sens que seule la justice serait rendue en droit strict, alors que l'arbitrage demeurerait imprégné de considérations extrajuridiques. La question est controversée mais, même si le débat demeure ouvert, il ne faut pas oublier, au moins sur le plan des principes, qu'aux termes de l'article 37 déjà cité de la Convention de La Haye de 1907 pour le règlement pacifique des conflits internationaux, «l'arbitrage international a pour objet le règlement des litiges entre les Etats ... sur la base du respect du droit». En fait, chaque cas constitue un unicum; tout dépend des termes mêmes du compromis.

8. Le choix entre le règlement arbitral et le règlement judiciaire peut faire l'objet de discussions, plus ou moins longues, lors de la négociation du compromis, entre les Parties qui ne sont pas nécessairement d'accord sur la procédure à instaurer. On voudrait rappeler à cet égard que, dans l'affaire de la délimitation du plateau continental entre la France et le Royaume-Uni, le Gouvernement britannique avait d'abord proposé que le différend soit porté devant la Cour internationale de Justice, alors que le Gouvernement français avait avancé, dans un premier temps, que soit saisie la Cour de Justice des Communautés européennes. Aucune de ces propositions n'avait soulevé, comme on s'en doutera aisément, l'enthousiasme de l'autre Partie et finalement les deux Gouvernements sont parvenus, sans grandes difficultés, à un accord, dans le compromis qu'ils ont signé le 10 juillet 1975, en convenant de résoudre le différend «par une procédure d'arbitrage»[20].

D'une façon plus générale, le choix entre le règlement arbitral et le règlement judiciaire peut correspondre pour un Gouvernement, à une véritable position de principe dans sa politique juridique[21]. Tel est le cas, bien connu, de la France, bien qu'elle ait été, jusqu'en 1973, l'Etat à saisir le plus fréquemment la Cour de La Haye[22]. En effet, à la suite des affaires des essais nucléaires

---

19 *Voir* parmi d'autres, P. REUTER, DROIT INTERNATIONAL PUBLIC, Paris, Themis, 6e éd., 1983, pp. 437–438.

20 N.U., RECUEIL DES SENTENCES ARBITRALES, vol. XVIII, p. 132.

21 Sur les avantages et inconvénients respectifs de l'arbitrage et du règlement judiciaire et le développement de l'arbitrage depuis 1945; *voir* L. CAFLISCH, *L'avenir de l'arbitrage interétatique*, ANNUAIRE FRANÇAIS DE DROIT INTERNATIONAL 1979, vol. XXV, pp. 17–25; D.H.M. JOHNSON, *International Arbitration Back in Favour*, YEARBOOK OF WORLD AFFAIRS 1980, pp. 305–328; CHR. GRAY & B. KINGSBURY, *Developments in Dispute Settlements: Inter-State Arbitration since 1945*, THE BRITISH YEAR BOOK OF INTERNATIONAL LAW 1992, vol. LXIII, pp. 97–134 etc.

22 *Voir* A. GROS, *Cinquante années de justice internationale*, REVUE GÉNÉRALE DE DROIT INTERNATIONAL PUBLIC 1972, t. 76, pp. 6–7.

portées devant la Cour par l'Australie et la Nouvelle-Zélande, la France a retiré sa déclaration d'acceptation de la juridiction obligatoire de la Cour[23] et depuis lors elle n'a plus porté de différends devant la Haute Juridiction[24]. Elle a choisi délibérement de déterminer, cas par cas, la méthode de règlement pacifique qui lui paraît la plus appropriée et a eu recours, comme on le sait, à la voie arbitrale pour régler les litiges juridiques qui l'ont opposée successivement au Royaume-Uni, aux Etats-Unis, au Canada et à la Nouvelle-Zélande[25]. Le fait que le Gouvernement français ait accepté de faire connaître ses vues devant la Cour à la suite de la demande d'examen de la situation par la Nouvelle-Zélande au titre du paragraphe 63 de l'arrêt rendu par la Cour le 20 décembre 1974 dans l'affaire des essais nucléaires (*Nouvelle-Zélande c. France*) ne permet pas de dire, à la présente date, qu'il a modifié sa position antérieure sur ce point[26].

9. Si les Parties écartent le recours à l'arbitrage et conviennent de porter le différend qui les oppose devant la Cour, elles doivent alors décider du point de savoir si l'affaire sera jugée par la Cour en plénière ou par une Chambre *ad hoc*. La possibilité de saisir une Chambre peut présenter un incontestable intérêt pour certains Gouvernements, dans la mesure où elle réunit les avantages, notamment financiers, du recours à la Haute Juridiction et où, en même temps, elle réintroduit dans la justice internationale certains éléments de l'arbitrage[27]. Le recours à une Chambre *ad hoc*, tel qu'il a été prévu dans

---

23 *Cf.* le LIVRE BLANC SUR LES EXPÉRIENCES NUCLÉAIRES, Paris, juin 1973, et les commentaires de G. DE LACHARRIÈRE et DE J.P. COT, ANNUAIRE FRANÇAIS DE DROIT INTERNATIONAL 1973, vol. XIX, pp. 235–251 et 252–271.

24 *Voir* J.P. PUISSOCHET, *Affaires étrangères et affaires juridiques*, REVUE FRANÇAISE D'ADMINISTRATION PUBLIQUE 1994, n° 69, *Les affaires étrangères*, pp. 84–85.

25 *Voir* E. DECAUX, *La pratique française en matière d'arbitrage (1969–1978)*, ANNUAIRE FRANÇAIS DE DROIT INTERNATIONAL 1978, vol. XXIV, pp. 352–372. *Cf.* également les décisions du 30 juin 1977 et du 14 mars 1978 dans l'affaire de la délimitation du plateau continental avec le Royaume-Uni (N.U., RECUEIL DES SENTENCES ARBITRALES, vol. XVIII, pp. 130–268 et 339–413); la sentence du 9 décembre 1978 dans l'affaire concernant l'accord relatif aux services aériens du 27 mars 1946 avec les Etats-Unis (*ibid.* vol. XVIII, pp. 454–493); la sentence du 17 juillet 1986 dans l'affaire concernant le filetage à l'intérieur du golfe du Saint-Laurent avec le Canada (*ibid.* vol. XIX, pp. 225–296); la sentence du 30 avril 1990 dans l'affaire du *Rainbow Warrior avec la Nouvelle-Zélande* (REVUE GÉNÉRALE DE DROIT INTERNATIONAL PUBLIC 1990, t. 94, pp. 838–878) et la sentence, citée *supra* (note 16), du 10 juin 1992 dans l'affaire de délimitation des espaces maritimes avec le Canada.

26 *Voir* l'ordonnance de la Cour du 22 septembre 1995 (C.I.J., REC. 1995, pp. 288–421).

27 *Voir* ST. SCHWEBEL, *Ad hoc Chambers of the International Court of Justice*, AMERICAN JOURNAL OF INTERNATIONAL LAW 1987, vol. 81, pp. 832–854; SH. ODA, *Further Thoughts on the Chamber, Procedure of the International Court of Justice* 1988, *ibid.* vol. 82, pp. 556–562; H. MOSLER, *The ad hoc Chambers of the International Court of Justice, Evaluation after Five Years of Experience*, INTERNATIONAL LAW OF A TIME OF PERPLEXITY, ESSAYS IN HONOUR OF SHABTAI ROSENNE, Dordrecht, Nijhoff, 1989, pp. 449–460; Sir R. JENNINGS, *The Collegiate Responsibility and Authority of the International Court of Justice*, *ibid.* pp. 343–353 et, du même auteur, *Cham-*

l'article 26 par. 2 du Statut et développé en 1978 lors de la révision du Règlement[28] soulève en effet le problème du choix de ses membres.

Aux termes des articles 17 et 18 du Règlement, si le Président de la Cour doit s'informer «des vues» des Parties «au sujet de la composition de la Chambre», c'est la Cour en plénière qui procède, au scrutin secret, à l'élection de ses membres. Ce qui signifie que si, juridiquement, la Cour conserve cette fonction de désignation, les Parties peuvent exercer ou chercher à exercer une influence prépondérante dans ce choix. Ainsi, il est bien connu que, dans l'affaire du Golfe du Maine, le Canada et les Etats-Unis se sont assuré le plein contrôle de la composition de la Chambre *ad hoc*, qui a été déterminée par l'ordonnance du 20 janvier 1982[29]. Tous ses membres appartenant au même groupe régional, on peut facilement imaginer que cette décision a suscité quelques réserves de la part des autres membres de la Cour. Des considérations extrajuridiques n'étaient pas étrangères, de toute évidence, à ce choix. Comme l'ont remarqué, en termes choisis, trois membres de l'équipe américaine – parmi lesquels se trouvent l'agent et l'agent-adjoint du Gouvernement des Etats-Unis – la composition de la Chambre avait été le résultat d'un «process of reaching a balance of experienced jurists that both sides could propose»[30].

On doit remarquer cependant que, dans les autres affaires qui ont été soumises, par la suite, à des Chambres *ad hoc*, les juges élus ont été choisis dans des groupes régionaux différents. Il en a été ainsi, en effet, dans l'affaire Burkina Faso/Mali ainsi que dans les affaires Elsi et El Salvador/Honduras[31].

---

bers of the International Court of Justice and Courts of Arbitration, in HUMANITÉ ET DROIT INTERNATIONAL, MÉLANGES RENÉ-JEAN DUPUY, Paris, Pedone, 1991, pp. 197–201; M. LACHS, *Some Comments on ad hoc Chambers of the International Court of Justice*, *ibid.*, pp. 203–230; D.W. BOWETT, J. CRAWFORD, I. SINCLAIR, A.D. WATTS, *Report of the Study Group Established by the British Institute of International and Comparative Law as a Contribution to the U.N. Decade of International Law, The International Court of Justice Efficiency of Procedures and Working Methods*, THE INTERNATIONAL AND COMPARATIVE LAW QUARTERLY, vol. 45, January 1996, Supplement, S21–S22, par. 70–73 etc.

[28] *Cf.* les observations du Juge E. JIMENEZ DE ARECHAGA, *Les amendements au Règlement de la Cour internationale de Justice*, Conférence commémorative Gilberto Amado, Genève, N.U., 1972, 29 p.; *The Amendments to the Rules of Procedure of the International Court of Justice*, AMERICAN JOURNAL OF INTERNATIONAL LAW 1973, vol. 67, pp. 1–22, aux pp. 2–4.

[29] C.I.J., REC. 1982, pp. 2–13, aux pp. 8–9. *Cf.* les commentaires de G. GUYOMAR, ANNUAIRE FRANÇAIS DE DROIT INTERNATIONAL 1981, vol. XXVII, pp. 213–221 et de E. ZOLLER, REVUE GÉNÉRALE DE DROIT INTERNATIONAL PUBLIC 1982, t. 86, pp. 302–324.

[30] D.R. ROBINSON, D.A. COLSON & B.C. RASHKOW, *Some Perspectives on Adjudicating before the World Court: The Gulf of Maine Case*, AMERICAN JOURNAL OF INTERNATIONAL LAW 1985, pp. 578–597, à la p. 583. *Cf.* les observations de A. PILLEPICH, *Les chambres in S.F.D.I., Colloque de Lyon*, LA JURIDICTION INTERNATIONALE PERMANENTE, Paris, Pedone, 1987, pp. 45–72, aux pp. 68–69, par. 66–68.

[31] Sur la base respectivement des ordonnances du 3 avril 1985 (C.I.J., REC. 1985, p. 7; *cf.* l'arrêt du 22 avril 1986, C.I.J., REC. 1986, pp. 558–559, par. 5–7); du 2 mars 1987 (C.I.J., REC.

De toutes manières, le mécanisme des Chambres *ad hoc*, sur lequel l'accent avait été mis à un moment où la Cour traversait une crise profonde, n'a guère été utilisé que pendant quelques années, dans la période comprise entre 1982 et 1987 et, depuis lors, les Etats plaideurs n'y ont plus eu recours. Compte tenu du nombre, jamais atteint, d'affaires inscrites au rôle de la Cour, on ne saurait que se féliciter de cette tendance des Etats à ne plus saisir que la plénière. Ainsi, évite-t-on tout risque de remise en cause de l'unité de la jurisprudence de la Cour.

* * *

10. Avec la compsition des Chambres *ad hoc* de la Cour, on a déjà abordé le problème du choix des hommes, dont l'importance est essentielle pour la constitution des Tribunaux d'arbitrage. Les chances de gagner ou de perdre un contentieux de ce genre sont naturellement fonction du dossier, mais elles sont également fonction de la composition de l'organe arbitral qui connaîtra du différend. L'histoire de l'arbitrage en donne quelques exemples significatifs, dont le plus célèbre est sans doute celui de l'affaire de la détermination de la frontière de la Guyane britannique, entre le Royaume-Uni et le Vénézuela, qui a donné lieu à la sentence rendue le 3 octobre 1899 par le Tribunal arbitral présidé par Frédéric de Martens. Par les révélations posthumes, un demi-siècle plus tard, de Mallet-Prévost, secrétaire de la délégation américaine qui représentait le Vénézuela devant le Tribunal[32], la sentence non motivée aurait été rendue sur la base d'un marchandage purement politique et sans tenir compte des dispositions de l'article IV du compromis du 2 février 1897 relatives au droit applicable[33].

Le choix des arbitres qui doivent être désignés d'un commun accord par les deux Parties doit par conséquent être traité avec une attention particulière

---

1987, p. 4; *cf.* l'arrêt du 20 juillet 1989, C.I.J., REC. 1989, p. 18, par. 4) et du 8 mai 1987 (C.I.J., REC. 1987, p. 12; *cf.* l'arrêt du 11 septembre 1992, C.I.J., REC. 1992, p. 359, par. 7).

32 V.O. SCHOENRICH, *The Venezuela-British Guiana Boundary Dispute*, AMERICAN JOURNAL OF INTERNATIONAL LAW 1949, vol. 43, pp. 523–530; CL.J. CHILD, *The Venezuela-British Guiana Boundary Arbitration of 1899*, AMERICAN JOURNAL INTERNATIONAL LAW 1950, vol. 44, pp. 682–693; W.C. DENIS, *The Venezuela-British Guiana Boundary Arbitration of 1899*, *ibid.* pp. 720–727. *Cf.* également J. GILLIS WETTER, THE INTERNATIONAL ARBITRAL PROCESS: PUBLIC AND PRIVATE, New York, Oceana Pub., 1979, vol. III, 470 p. et F. MARTENS, RUSIA E INGLATERRA EN ASIA CENTRAL, Traduccion y Estudio preliminar de H. Gros Espiell, Caracas, Ediciones de la Presidencia de la Republica, 1981, 185 p.

33 MARTENS, NOUVEAU RECUEIL GÉNERAL DE TRAITÉS, 2e série, t. 28, pp. 328–332, aux pp. 330–331. De surcroît, le surarbitre aurait imposé le tracé frontalier finalement retenu aux deux arbitres américains, sous la menace, en cas de refus, d'attribuer la totalité du territoire contesté au Royaume-Uni (*cf.* P. REUTER, *op. cit.*, *La motivation et la révision des sentences arbitrales à la Conférence de la Paix de 1899 et le conflit frontalier entre le Royaume-Uni et le Venezuela*, p. 238, note 2).

par les Gouvernements et on comprend qu'il soit susceptible de soulever de grandes difficultés pratiques et de se poursuivre pendant de longs mois avant de parvenir à un résultat. C'est ce qui peut se passer, dans l'hypothèse d'un Tribunal arbitral composé de trois membres, pour la désignation du Président, comme en ont témoigné les négociations en vue de la conclusion du compromis du 12 mars 1985 dans le différend relatif à la détermination de la frontière maritime entre la Guinée-Bissau et le Sénéga[34]. C'est ce qui peut se passer également, dans l'hypothèse d'un Tribunal arbitral composé de cinq membres, pour la désignation des trois arbitres autres que les arbitres nationaux, ce qui est survenu notamment au cours des négociations qui ont débouché sur la signature du compromis du 31 mars 1989 dans l'affaire précitée de la délimitation des espaces maritimes de Saint-Pierre-et-Miquelon[35].

11. Un tel état de choses n'a rien de surprenant. Il tient au fait que «la manière de concevoir la tâche» de l'arbitre ou du juge, pour reprendre la formule d'Anzilotti[36], est susceptible de varier. Le Professeur Paul De Visscher a remarqué naguère que, indépendamment des querelles doctrinales touchant les méthodes d'interprétation, deux conceptions de la fonction juridictionnelle peuvent s'affronter: «celle du juge 'engagé', qui n'hésitera pas à suppléer aux lacunes et insuffisances du droit face aux besoins nouveaux de la vie, et celle du juge serviteur d'un droit dont il appartient aux Etats eux-mêmes de provoquer la révision»[37]. On pourrait être tenté d'ajouter une troisième conception de «la manière de juger», qui correspondrait à celle du juge ou de l'arbitre conciliateurs, privilégiant l'amiable composition et la recherche de la paix, plutôt qu'une application stricte de la règle de droit[38]. Il ne s'agit donc pas seulement d'une affaire de science et d'expérience, mais

---

[34] Que l'on trouve dans la sentence arbitrale du 31 juillet 1989, publiée par la REVUE GÉNÉRALE DE DROIT INTERNATIONAL PUBLIC 1990, t. 94, pp. 206–209.

[35] Que l'on peut consulter dans la décision du 10 juin 1992, publiée par la REVUE GÉNÉRALE DE DROIT INTERNATIONAL PUBLIC 1992, t. 96, pp. 678–682.

[36] Dans son opinion dissidente jointe à l'affaire des prises d'eau à la Meuse, C.P.J.I., Série A/B, n° 70, p. 451.

[37] *Cours général de droit international public*, RECUEIL DES COURS DE L'ACADÉMIE DE DROIT INTERNATIONAL DE LA HAYE 1972-II, t. 136, p. 184. *Voir* les références citées à la note 19.

[38] En contrepoint de cette conception, on peut citer la sentence arbitrale, rendue le 8 février 1977, dans l'affaire du Canal de Beagle (INTERNATIONAL LAW REPORTS, vol. 52, pp. 93–285). Comme on le sait, cette conception du «juge conciliateur» a été vigoureusement attaquée par le Juge GROS dans ses opinions dissidentes jointes à plusieurs affaires de délimitation maritime, notamment dans l'affaire Tunisie/Libye (C.I.J., REC. 1982, pp. 143–156) et dans l'affaire du GOLFE DU MAINE (C.I.J., REC. 1984, pp. 360–389). *Cf.* du même auteur, *La recherche du consensus dans les décisions de la Cour internationale de Justice*, FESTCHRIFT FÜR HERMANN MOSLER, 1983, pp. 351–358 et les observations du professeur D. BOWETT sur la question de savoir si le

aussi de tempérament et peut-être surtout, en définitive, de caractère et d'intégrité. Le choix des arbitres «neutres» par les Gouvernements constitue une grande responsabilité dans la genèse d'un contentieux international et il doit être conduit avec un luxe de précautions et un soin qui n'est jamais assez minutieux. On peut même penser que, parfois, il serait préférable d'interrompre la procédure plutôt que d'accepter, après des mois d'échanges infructueux, en désespoir de cause, comme par lassitude, des noms ne réunissant pas, dans les limites toujours incertaines tant du risque judiciaire que de l'appréciation des hommes, les exigences requises. Mais il s'agirait là, pour ceux qui négocient la composition d'un Tribunal arbitral, d'une décision difficile à prendre, compte tenu des pressions, politiques ou autres, pas nécessairement inavouables, pour mettre en oeuvre, aussi rapidement que possible, le processus juridictionnel. Là encore, tout est cas d'espèce.

* * *

12. Si l'issue d'une procédure juridictionnelle se joue avec le choix des hommes, elle se joue tout autant avec le choix des mots. Les juristes, au sens large du terme, c'est-à-dire aussi bien ceux qui contribuent à la création du droit international que ceux qui contribuent à son interprétation, à son application, ou à sa diffusion, sont des «peseurs de mots»[39]. Ils vivent des mots, tant il est vrai que chaque vocable a son contenu propre et que, sous l'écorce terminologique, se trouve une réalité bien spécifique. Ils qualifient les faits par des concepts, par des catégories juridiques préexistantes. Ils luttent pour l'emploi d'un mot plutôt que d'un autre, lors de l'élaboration d'un texte et par l'emploi du mot juste, ils clarifient les idées et préviennent les équivoques[40]. Ils essaient de résoudre les multiples problèmes que soulève l'interprétation des mots et Vattel, dans le chapitre de son *Droit des gens* relatif à l'interprétation des traités, consacre un paragraphe aux «chicanes sur les mots»[41]. Et, pour ne citer qu'un exemple jurisprudentiel récent, on rappellera les difficultés qu'a soulevées, dans l'affaire de la délimitation maritime et des questions territoriales entre Qatar et Bahreïn (compétence et recevabilité),

"compromise is consistent with the judicial process" (*op. cit.*, pp. 198–201), étant entendu que, de son point de vue, "it is no part of the judicial function to simply 'split the difference' between conflicting claims" (*ibid.* p. 199).

39 Pour reprendre la formule que VALERY LARBAUD utilise pour les traducteurs dans SOUS L'INVOCATION DE SAINT JÉRÔME, OEUVRES COMPLÈTES, Gallimard, 1953, t. 8, p. 98.

40 *Cf.* les remarques de CH. DE VISSCHER, reprises par J. BASDEVANT dans la préface qu'il a donnée au DICTIONNAIRE DE LA TERMINOLOGIE DU DROIT INTERNATIONAL (Paris, Sirey, 1960, pp. V–VIII), ou celles de P. REUTER dans *Quelques réflexions sur le vocabulaire de droit international*, MÉLANGES LOUIS TROTABAS, Paris, L.G.D.J., 1970, p. 434.

41 LE DROIT DES GENS, t. II, Livre II, chap. XVII, pp. 9–10, par. 273.

l'interprétation de l'expression *al tarafan*, qu'on trouve dans l'accord international connu sous le nom de procès-verbal de Doha du 25 décembre 1990[42].

Le compromis étant l'«un des actes internationaux les plus difficiles à rédiger»[43], il convient donc d'être très attentif au choix des mots, dans le cadre des négociations qui doivent déboucher sur sa conclusion, tout spécialement pour formuler la question ou les questions posées à l'organe juridictionnel devant lequel le différend sera porté et déterminer le droit applicable. Il y faut de la clarté, de la précision et de la cohérence, car le compromis est non seulement la loi des Parties mais il oblige également le Tribunal. Il n'a de compétence que celle énoncée dans le compromis et il doit la respecter strictement, au risque d'être accusé d'avoir commis un excès de pouvoir.

13. L'observation du Professeur Pierre Lalive relative à l'arbitrage commercial, selon laquelle «les meilleurs arbitres du monde ne sauraient faire des miracles face à un compromis mal rédigé»[44] s'applique tout aussi bien à l'arbitrage interétatique. Elle se trouve illustrée de façon significative par l'affaire de la détermination de la frontière maritime entre la Guinée-Bissau et le Sénégal, dont on peut penser qu'une rédaction différente du compromis aurait à la fois facilité et accéléré le règlement définitif.

Dans cette affaire, les deux Parties étaient en désaccord sur la validité et la portée d'un échange de lettres, en date du 26 avril 1960, entre leurs Etats prédécesseurs, le Portugal et la France, relatif à la délimitation de la mer territoriale, de la zone contiguë et du plateau continental. Après de longues négociations, commencées en 1977 mais demeurées infructueuses, la Guinée-Bissau et le Sénégal décidèrent de recourir à une procédure arbitrale et signèrent, à cet effet, le 12 mars 1985, un compromis dont l'article 2 dispose: «Il est demandé au Tribunal de statuer conformément aux normes du droit international sur les questions suivantes: 1. L'accord conclu par un échange de lettres, le 26 avril 1960, et relatif à la frontière en mer, fait-il droit dans les relations entre la République de Guinée-Bissau et la République du Sénégal? 2. En cas de réponse négative à la première question, quel est le tracé de la ligne délimitant les territoires maritimes qui relèvent respectivement de la République de Guinée-Bissau et de la République du Sénégal?»[45].

---

[42] Qatar traduisait l'expression par «les parties» et Bahreïn par «les deux parties». *Cf.* l'arrêt de la Cour du 15 février 1995 (C.I.J., REC. 1995, pp. 18–19, par. 34–36).

[43] A. BALASKO, CAUSES DE NULLITÉ DE LA SENTENCE ARBITRALE EN DROIT INTERNATIONAL PUBLIC, Paris, Pedone, 1938, p. 106.

[44] Avantages et inconvénients de l'arbitrage ad hoc, in ETUDES OFFERTES À PIERRE BELLET, Paris 1991, p. 305.

[45] REVUE GÉNÉRALE DE DROIT INTERNATIONAL PUBLIC 1990, t. 94, p. 207.

Par sa sentence du 31 juillet 1989, le Tribunal arbitral décida que l'accord de 1960 était valable et opposable aux Parties mais qu'il ne pouvait naturellement pas délimiter les espaces maritimes qui, comme la zone économique exclusive, n'existaient pas à la date de sa conclusion. Il décida par ailleurs que la seconde question prévue dans l'article 2 du compromis n'appelait pas, compte tenu de son libellé, de réponse de sa part[46]. Le 23 août 1989, la Guinée-Bissau introduisit devant la Cour internationale de Justice une requête sur l'inexistence et la nullité de la sentence de 1989, déplorant notamment, parmi d'autres arguments, l'absence de réponse par le Tribunal arbitral à la seconde question qui lui était posée dans le compromis. La Cour, dans son arrêt du 12 novembre 1991, rejeta la requête de la Guinée-Bissau et considéra que la sentence de 1989 «était valable et obligatoire pour les deux parties»[47].

L'affaire ne se trouvait pas pour autant définitivement réglée car, entre temps, la Guinée-Bissau avait introduit, le 12 mars 1991, une nouvelle requête contre le Sénégal touchant «la délimination de l'ensemble des territoires maritimes» des deux Etats. Aucun délai ne fut cependant fixé par la Cour pour le dépôt des écritures, car des négociations s'étaient engagées entre les Parties. Négociations qui débouchèrent sur la signature de deux accords: d'une part, un accord de coopération et de gestion, signé le 14 octobre 1993, qui prévoyait notamment l'exploitation en commun d'une zone maritime située de part et d'autre de la ligne de 1960 et l'institution d'une agence internationale pour l'exploitation de la zone; et d'autre part, un protocole d'accord, signé le 12 juin 1995, portant sur l'organisation et le fonctionnement de l'agence de gestion et de coopération instituée par l'accord antérieur. La Guinée-Bissau renonça alors à la procédure qu'elle avait engagée par sa requête du 12 mars 1991 et la Cour, prenant acte de ce désistement, raya l'affaire du rôle par une ordonnance du 8 novembre 1995[48].

Or, ce retard considérable dans le règlement définitif de l'affaire – plus de 10 ans entre la signature du compromis d'arbitrage et l'ordonnance de désistement prise par la Cour – tout comme le fait que la sentence arbitrale de 1989 n'ait pas abouti à une délimitation complète des espaces maritimes relevant respectivement de la Guinée-Bissau et du Sénégal s'expliquent aisément. Comme l'a clairement indiqué la Cour dans son arrêt du 12 novembre 1991, «ce résultat trouve son origine dans la rédaction retenue à l'ar-

---

[46] *Ibid.* p. 273, par. 87.

[47] C.I.J., REC. 1991, p. 76, par. 69.

[48] C.I.J., REC. 1995, pp. 423–426. *Cf.* les observations d'I. DIAITE, *Le Règlement du contentieux entre la Guinée-Bissau et le Sénégal relatif à la délimitation de leur frontière maritime*, ANNUAIRE FRANÇAIS DE DROIT INTERNATIONAL 1995, vol. XLI, pp. 700–710.

ticle 2 du compromis»[49]. La formulation de la seconde question était telle qu'elle offrait au Tribunal arbitral la possibilité de n'y pas répondre et qu'il s'est naturellement saisi de cette possibilité. Comme l'a justement souligné un commentateur de l'arrêt de la Cour, «le Tribunal ne pouvait procéder à la délimitation maritime qu'à condition d'écarter l'accord de 1960; à partir du moment où il n'écartait pas celui-ci, il ne pouvait pas y avoir de délimitation maritime complète effectuée *ex novo*»[50]. Faute pour les Parties d'être parvenues, lors des négociations portant sur le compromis, à une formulation commune acceptable pour préciser la mission du Tribunal, la tentation était grande, pour elles, de juxtaposer, comme elles l'ont fait dans l'article 2 du compromis, deux questions, dont chacune d'elles reflétait les préoccupations de l'un des Etats, sans se soucier de la cohérence de l'ensemble. En fait, le Sénégal souhaitait que le contentieux soit limité à la première question et la Guinée-Bissau à la seconde. Ce sont donc les deux Etats eux-mêmes «qui ont, en définitive, créé l'impasse dans laquelle ils se sont trouvés»[51], suscitant de graves difficultés dans leurs relations et retardant le règlement final de leurs divergences pendant des années[52].

14. La rédaction du compromis est tout aussi décisive en ce qui concerne la détermination du droit applicable ou, plus généralement, la formulation des dispositions relatives à la voie selon laquelle le Tribunal doit se prononcer. Il est évident que les pouvoirs d'un Tribunal seront différents – et que, par conséquent, l'issue du litige pourra être tout autre – si le compromis dispose que l'arbitre statue en droit mais que, dans certaines conditions, il pourra statuer en équité ou si le compromis dispose exclusivement que l'arbitre statue en droit. A cet égard, la comparaison des compromis signés respectivement le 30 décembre 1902 entre la Bolivie et le Pérou et le 31 octobre 1991 entre l'Argentine et le Chili est significative dans deux affaires de même nature.

La Bolivie et le Pérou ont soumis, par une convention spéciale du 30 décembre 1902, au Gouvernement argentin, «en qualité d'arbitre, juge de droit (*juez de derecho*)» (art. 1er), la délimitation de tout un secteur de leur frontière commune, sur lequel les Parties n'avaient pu s'entendre à l'amiable. Par ailleurs, cette convention disposait que «toutes les fois que les actes ou

---

[49] C.I.J., REC. 1991, p. 74, par. 66.

[50] J.P. QUÉNEUDEC, ANNUAIRE FRANÇAIS DE DROIT INTERNATIONAL 1991, vol. XXXVII, p. 441.

[51] *Ibid.* p. 442.

[52] Comme l'a justement remarqué CH. DE VISSCHER, «Il est de l'intérêt général que les litiges ne recommencent pas indéfiniment relativement au même objet: *ut sit finis litium*» (*La chose jugée devant la Cour internationale de Justice*, REVUE BELGE DE DROIT INTERNATIONAL 1965-I, p. 5). Cette observation s'applique aussi bien pour l'affaire Guinée-Bissau/Sénégal que pour l'affaire de la Laguna del Desierto (*infra*, par. 14).

dispositions royales ne définiront pas clairement l'étendue d'un territoire, l'arbitre résoudra la question équitablement (*equitativamente*), en se rapprochant, dans la mesure du possible, du sens de ces actes ou dispositions, et de l'esprit qui les a dictés» (art. 4)[53]. Or, précisément, le tracé retenu par l'arbitre, dans la sentence du 9 juillet 1909, a été fondé sur l'équité et a débouché sur un partage de la zone contestée, car les cédules et ordonnances royales, les ordonnances des intendants, les cartes espagnoles ou les descriptions officielles – en un mot, le principe de l'*uti possidetis* de 1810 – ne permettaient pas de trancher le différend. Dans ces conditions, l'arbitre s'est considéré comme tenu d'appliquer strictement l'article 4 de la convention spéciale précitée et de statuer en équité: «Considérant que de ce qui précède il résulte que je dois résoudre équitablement la question qui m'est soumise...»[54].

La contre-épreuve de la précédente affaire est très exactement fournie par la récente affaire de la Laguna del Desierto entre l'Argentine et le Chili. Le différend portait sur l'interprétation et l'application d'un passage de la sentence arbitrale rendue, le 20 novembre 1902, par le Roi Edouard VII touchant la définition de la frontière entre les deux Pays dans la Cordillière des Andes entre la borne 62 et le Mont Fitz Roy[55]. Le compromis du 31 octobre 1991 disposait, dans son article 2 par. 1er, que «Le Tribunal décidera en interprétant et en appliquant la Sentence de 1902, conformément au droit international», ce qui excluait pour lui la possibilité de se prononcer comme amiable compositeur et impliquait l'éventualité de l'attribution de la totalité de la zone contestée à l'une des Parties. Si le Chili n'a jamais prétendu que le Tribunal arbitral avait été investi des pouvoirs de statuer *ex aequo et bono*, il a néanmoins considéré l'équité *infra legem*, sinon *contra legem*, comme faisant «partie intégrante du droit international» et soutenu que, contrairement à la lettre même de la sentence de 1902 à interpréter qui se référait, pour le tronçon de frontière considéré, au critère de la ligne de partage des eaux, un tracé équitable devait couper différents cours d'eau, voire la Laguna del Desierto. Ce point de vue a été rejeté par le Tribunal arbitral dans sa sentence du 24 octobre 1994 qui a attribué la totalité de la zone revendiquée par le Chili à l'Argentine[56]. On peut penser que la seule référence, dans le

---

53 N.U., RECUEIL DES SENTENCES ARBITRALES, vol. XI, p. 139.

54 *Ibid.*, p. 143.

55 N.U., RECUEIL DES SENTENCES ARBITRALES, vol. IX, p. 37.

56 Le Tribunal de Rio a ainsi statué par trois voix contre deux. (*Voir* la tradiction en français de la sentence dans la REVUE GÉNÉRALE LE DROIT INTERNATIONAL PUBLIC 1996, t. 100, p. 597). *Cf.* le commentaire de L.I. SANCHEZ RODRIGUEZ, ANNUAIRE FRANÇAIS DE DROIT INTERNATIONAL 1994, vol. XL, pp. 465–483.

compromis, au droit international explique que le Tribunal ait rejeté toute solution de conciliation tendant à «couper la poire en deux»[57].

* * *

15. Ces quelques observations suffisent pour rappeler, si besoin en était, combien il est nécessaire d'apporter la plus grande attention à la rédaction du compromis, tout spécialement dans le choix de l'organe, dans le choix des hommes et dans le choix des mots. Cette attention n'est-elle pas d'ailleurs la condition même de «la commune confiance» que les Parties qui ont décidé de confier le règlement d'un différend qui les oppose à un Tribunal d'arbitrage ou à la Cour internationale de Justice doivent avoir dans ce que le Président Basdevant appelait «la sagesse et l'impartialité de leur justice?»[58].

---

57 Le recours en révision et en interprétation, déposé par le Chili le 31 janvier 1995, a été rejeté par le Tribunal de Rio dans une nouvelle sentence du 13 octobre 1995 (par quatre voix contre une pour le recours en révision et à l'unanimité pour le recours en interprétation).

58 Dans la péroraison de la plaidoirie qu'il a prononcée devant la Cour permanente de Justice internationale, dans l'affaire des Phosphates du Maroc. Cité par CH. CHAUMONT, préface à L'HOMMAGE D'UNE GÉNÉRATION DE JURISTES AU PRÉSIDENT BASDEVANT, Paris, Pedone, 1960, p. XIX.

The Caveat Ruling in Case A18

by

Bengt Broms

On 6 March 1996 Chamber Two of the Iran-United States Claims Tribunal made an award in case N° 419, that of *Rouhollah Karubian*, as Claimant, and *the Government of the Islamic Republic of Iran*, as Respondent.[1] The Chairman of Chamber Two is Judge Krzysztof Skubiszewski, to whom this collection of essays is dedicated. This is also why I decided to take up the problem of the **Caveat** in the ruling on case **A18**, which was one of the most important legal issues discussed by Chamber Two.[2]

I. THE FACTS OF CASE N° 419

In case N° 419 the Claimant sought compensation from the Government of the Islamic Republic of Iran for the value of four properties in Iran, alleging that these properties had been expropriated by the Respondent or subjected to other measures affecting the property rights of the Claimant within the meaning of Article II, paragraph 1, of the Claims Settlement Declaration.

The Algiers Declarations of 19 January 1981 established an agreement between the Governments of the Islamic Republic of Iran and the United States to the effect that the Iranian assets held by the United States Federal Reserve Bank, the United States private banks and by United States institutions and nationals would be released in return for a promise by the Islamic Republic of Iran to release the fifty-two United States nationals held in Teheran. In addition, the Islamic Republic of Iran promised to co-operate in setting up the Security and Escrow Accounts, the aim of which was to improve the efficacy of the separate Claims Settlement Declaration which was concluded on the same day.

---

[1] The Award will be published in a forthcoming volume of the Iran-United States Claims Tribunal Reports. In this article the references to the Award are made by indicating its paragraphs.

[2] Krzysztof Skubiszewski joined the Iran-United States Claims Tribunal in 1994 and he later became President of the Tribunal. The other members of Chamber Two are Judges G.H. Aldrich and K.H. Ameli.

The Claims Settlement Declaration provided a forum, the Iran-United States Claims Tribunal, to resolve all legal problems between the two States parties which had led to the severance of their economic relations. In case **A1**, which was decided in 1982, the Tribunal concluded that the Claims Settlement Declaration fulfilled all customary requirements and the rules of the Vienna Convention on the Law of Treaties. Article II(1) of the Claims Settlement Declaration includes the following provision: "An International Arbitral Tribunal (the Iran-United States Claims Tribunal) is hereby established for the purpose of deciding claims of nationals of the United States against Iran and claims of nationals of Iran against the United States." Article VII, paragraph 1, contains the specification that "A national of Iran or the United States, as the case may be, means a) a natural person who is a citizen of Iran or the United States..." The wording used in this provision leaves unanswered the question of the capacity of dual nationals to bring claims before the Tribunal and this omission has caused a difference of opinion between the parties to the Claims Settlement Declaration.[3]

In the *Karubian* case the Claimant submitted that his nationality was that of the United States, although he was born in Teheran on 21 March 1912 and held an Iranian Nationality Card issued in 1918. In 1934 the Claimant travelled to the United States as a student, completing his studies in 1940. He then returned during the same year to Iran where he resided with his wife and children until 1948 when he moved back to the United States. Thereafter he resided in the United States. In the period between 1948 and 1978 he visited Iran ten times at most on trips of an average duration of two weeks. On 6 April 1954 he was issued with a United States Certificate of Naturalization. Soon thereafter he obtained a United States passport. In 1968 he also obtained an Iranian passport, which he later lost, and in 1973 he acquired another Iranian passport.

The Respondent submitted that the Claimant was solely a national of Iran and could not as such bring a claim against Iran before the Tribunal. Alternatively, the Respondent argued that the Tribunal lacked jurisdiction in this case because the Claimant's dominant and effective nationality was Iranian or, at least, not that of the United States. As a further argument, the Respondent said that if the Claimant's dominant and effective nationality were found to be that of the United States, the caveat in case **A18** would bar the Claim-

[3] It should be pointed out that during the negotiations which led to the signing of the Claims Settlement Declaration the representatives of the two parties used an intermediary, the Republic of Algeria, in place of meetings between their own representatives. This procedure may be a partial reason for later differences of opinion in as far as some other legal issues are concerned, too.

ant's recovery. Finally, the Respondent denied expropriation of any of the four properties at issue or the contention that these properties had been subjected to other measures affecting the property rights of the Claimant.

Before turning to the final Award, it should be added that on 3 March 1989 the Tribunal had already issued an Order to the effect that, during the period between the time the alleged claims arose and 19 January 1981, it appeared that the Claimant was a national of both Iran and the United States.[4]

II. PROBLEMS RELATED TO THE NATIONALITY OF THE CLAIMANT

In the *Karubian* Award the Tribunal discussed, at great length, the Claimant's nationality.[5] Facts related to his birth, education, residence, employment, family, property in the United States, civic activities and other comparable matters were reviewed. Let it be mentioned that in dual nationality cases facts like these are usually brought out in determining the nationality issue.

The Tribunal decided that the relevant period for determining the dominant and effective nationality of the Claimant was the period between February 1979, when the claims were deemed to have arisen, and 19 January 1981. The starting-point of the Tribunal was that under Article 976 of the Iranian Civil Code the Claimant was an Iranian national by birth and that he had never relinquished or otherwise lost his Iranian nationality. The Tribunal went on to say, at the same time, that the Claimant had shown that from 1954 he had been a United States national and, during the relevant period, had maintained this nationality. The Tribunal concluded that during the relevant period the Claimant was a national of both Iran and the United States.[6]

The Tribunal then began to discuss the Claimant's dominant and effective nationality during the relevant period. It maintained that there was "little difficulty in reaching the conclusion that the Claimant has demonstrated that his dominant and effective nationality, during the relevant period, is that of the United States." Having said this, the Tribunal decided that the claims of

---

[4] On 6 April 1984 the Full Trbibunal had decided that the Tribunal had first to determine, on the basis of the evidence, whether the Claimant was, during the relevant period from the time a claim arose until 19 January 1981, when the Claims Settlement Declaration was issued, a national of the United States, of Iran, or of both States. If the Claimant were found to be a dual national, then the Tribunal had to determine his dominant and effective nationality.

[5] Paras. 8 to 25.

[6] Para. 95.

the Claimant were those of a national of the United States as defined in Article VII, paragraph 1, of the Claims Settlement Declaration.

III. THE BACKGROUND TO THE CAVEAT

Until the Award in case **A18** in 1984, the Government of the United States had argued that the jurisdiction of the Tribunal extended to claims of all nationals of Iran or the United States and that dual nationals were also included among those entitled to bring claims. The Government of Iran had never accepted this interpretation, arguing instead that the use of the disjunctive conjunction "or" in Article VII, paragraph 1, was intended to indicate that dual nationals were excluded. A further argument put forward by the Government of the Islamic Republic of Iran was that Iran did not recognize the concept of dual nationality. It was therefore quite impossible for Iran to have accepted the inclusion of dual nationals into the text of the Claims Settlement Declaration.[7]

In responding to the request of the Islamic Republic of Iran for an interpretation of the relevant provisions of the Algiers Declarations relating to the jurisdiction of the Tribunal over claims by dual nationals, the Full Tribunal pointed out that while dual nationals might benefit from their status, they could not avoid some disadvantages deriving from the dual nationality. The Full Tribunal decided that "in cases where the Tribunal finds jurisdiction based upon dominant and effective nationality of the claimant, the other nationality may remain relevant to the merits of the claim."[8] Since then the representatives of the Claimants and Respondents in dual nationality cases have submitted differing interpretations as to what the relevance of the other nationality is to the merits of the cases they are parties to.

IV. ARGUMENTS OF THE CLAIMANT

The Claimant justified the acquisition of real property in Iran by various arguments. In so far as his United States nationality was concerned, he expressed the view that Iranian legislation did not prohibit Iranian nationals from applying for and acquiring a second nationality. He maintained that

---

7 These opinions had alread been expressed in the cases of *Nasser Esphahanian v. Bank Tejarat* Award N° 31-157–2 and *Atohollah Golpira* Award N° 32-211-2, *see* Vol. 2 IRAN-UNITED STATES CLAIMS TRIBUNAL 1 at 156, 178 ff.

8 Vol. 5 IRAN-UNITED STATES CLAIMS TRIBUNAL at 265–266.

the sole consequence of acquiring a second nationality was that in Iran only the Iranian nationality was recognized.[9] Furthermore, the Claimant was of the opinion that there was no legal provision rendering illegal the purchase of real property in Iran after an Iranian national had acquired another nationality. He referred also to Article 989 of the Iranian Civil Code and reminded the Tribunal of the fact that the proceeds of the sale of real estate by the Public Prosecutor had to be paid to the dual national. From this provision the Claimant drew the conclusion that it confirmed the right of a dual national to be compensated whenever the government made use of the statutory authority to sell real estate belonging to such a person. In reply to the Respondent's argument that the Claimant had concealed his United States nationality when acquiring real estate in Iran, he denied having done so.

Another argument of the Claimant was that prior to the Revolution of 1979, dual nationals had been recommended by the Government of Iran to invest in Iran so as to help the economy of the country.[10] On this ground the Claimant drew the conclusion that the doctrine of estoppel prevented the Government of Iran from arguing that he was not entitled to acquire real estate in Iran.[11] The Tribunal, however, rejected the contention that the Respondent was estopped from arguing that he had illegally purchased real property in Iran.[12] The Tribunal said that it did not, in this context, accept the evidence proffered by the Claimant and his son.

V. ARGUMENTS OF THE RESPONDENT

In the *Karubian* case the above-mentioned Order of 3 March 1989 had included a statement to the effect that in a case involving a dual national the Claimant's other nationality should be examined together with other issues "such as the facts and applicable laws relating to the alleged acquisition and ownership of the property which constitutes the basis of this Claim as well as the actions of the Respondent allegedly affecting them."[13]

---

9 *Ibid.* para. 149.

10 *Ibid.* para 150.

11 In this context the Claimant mentioned by name several Iranian government officials who had recommended him to invest in Iran as an Iranian national because he was born in Iran and he had remained an Iranian citizen under Iranian law. The Claimant's son, Mr. John F. Karubian, stated in his Affidavit of 8 May 1992 that he had participated, prior to the Revolution, in a committee to encourage Iranians living abroad to return to Iran in order to help the country to develop, paras. 151 and 152.

12 Para. 153.

13 Para. 146.

Throughout the proceedings the Respondent argued that the claims of the Claimant were barred by the *caveat* of case **A18**, along with other grounds, because the Claimant was presented as a United States national and because his claims concerned benefits which only belonged to Iranian nationals. It was further argued by the Respondent that, as a rule, according to Iranian legislation, foreign nationals were not entitled to own real property in Iran. It was admitted that there were limited exceptions to this rule, but that they did not exist in the present case. Furthermore, the Respondent pointed out that the Claimant had concealed his dual nationality when he registered the real properties he had acquired in Iran.

To support these arguments the Respondent referred to several provisions of the Iranian Civil Code including Article 988, which has a list of the conditions to be fulfilled by Iranian nationals if they want to abandon their nationality. This provision reads as follows:

> "1. That they have reached the full age of 25.
> 2. That the Council of Ministers has allowed the renunciation of their Iranian nationality.
> 3. That they have previously undertaken to transfer, by some means or other, to Iranian nationals, within one year from the date of the renunciation of their Iranian nationality, all the rights that they possess on landed properties in Iran or which they may acquire by inheritance although Iranian laws may have allowed the possession of the same properties in the case of foreign nationals. The wife and children of the person who renounces his nationality according to this Article do not lose their Iranian nationality, whether the children are minors of age, unless the permission of the Council of Ministers allows them to renounce their nationality; and
> 4. That they have terminated active military service."

According to a Note attached to Article 988, those who may venture to apply for the renunciation of their Iranian nationality according to this Article in favour of a foreign nationality must, besides carrying out the provisions of Clause 3 of Article 968, leave Iran within one year. Should they fail to do so, the proper authorities will issue orders to expel them and sell their properties. The Note ends with a mention that persons expelled from Iran must obtain special permission from the Council of Ministers if they wish to come to Iran in the future. Such permission will be only issued once and for a specified duration of time.

The Respondent also referred to Article 989 of the Iranian Civil Code which provides that where any Iranian subject has acquired a foreign nationality after the solar year 1280 (1901–1902) without observing the provisions of the Iranian law, "his foreign nationality will be considered null and void and he will be regarded as an Iranian subject." All landed properties of an Iranian subject who has acquired a foreign nationality will be sold under the supervision of the local Public Prosecutor and the proceeds of the sale will be paid to the person concerned after the deduction of the expenses of the sale.[14] Those Iranian subjects who may have personally, or whose fathers may have renounced Iranian nationality in accordance with the provisions of Iranian law, and who may wish to re-acquire their original nationality, can be reinstated in their Iranian nationality by mere application unless the Government deems the grant of their application to be unadvisable.[15]

VI. THE AWARD

Having investigated the arguments, the Tribunal went on to examine whether the right to acquire real estate in Iran was a benefit limited to those whose nationality was Iranian. In answering this question, the Tribunal referred to Articles 988 and 989 of the Iranian Civil Code. Then, the Tribunal discussed the Law of Nationality of Iran of 1906, which had also been mentioned by the Respondent as proof of the fact that the right of ownership of real property was exclusively reserved for Iranian nationals.

> "Section Eight: If an Iranian national living abroad wishes to acquire the nationality of another State, firstly, he/she must not be under criminal charges in the courts of Iran; secondly, he/she must not already have been on trial or have escaped such trial; thirdly, he/she must not have escaped military service; and fourthly, he/she must not be in debt and intend to escape such debt. Otherwise his/her change of nationality shall be null and void.
>
> ...
>
> Section Nine: Change of Iranian nationality, in spite of compliance with the stipulated requirements, is still subject to the permission and decision of the King. If an Iranian national living abroad acquires foreign nationality without obtaining such permission, he/she shall be barred entry into Iran. If he/she owns real estate or other property in Iran, he/she shall be forced to give up such property."

In the present context, the Tribunal paid particular attention to Section Fourteen which reads as follows:

---

14 As a further consequence, an Iranian subject who has acquired a foreign nationality is debarred from attaining the position of a Cabinet Minister or Assistant Minister or from membership of the Legislative Assemblies, Provincial and District Councils and Municipal Councils, or any other governmental position.

15 Article 990 of the Iranian Civil Code.

> "Those who come to Iran from foreign countries and during their residence in Iran concealed their nationality and were treated in all matters as Iranian nationals, or purchased real estate in Iran, which privilege is exclusively available to nationals of Iran, shall be treated as nationals of the State of Iran, and their claim to foreign nationality will not be accepted."

The Tribunal also referred to more recent Iranian laws and regulations addressing the issue of foreign ownership of real estate in Iran. Among these were the Foreign Nationals Immovable Properties Act, enacted on 6 June 1931, and providing for the forced sale of any lands in Iran, which might be owned by a foreign national and the Decree Law Concerning Landed Property Ownership by Foreign Nationals, approved by the Council of Ministers on 26 November 1948, and providing for the procedure to be followed by a foreign national wishing to obtain permission to own real estate in Iran. The Decree Law of 1948 mentions the requirements a foreign national must comply with to obtain permission to own real estate in Iran. To begin with, permission is granted only if the real estate becomes a residence or business of the foreign national. Furthermore, if Iran ceases to be his or her permanent residence, the real property must be transferred within six months from the date of his or her departure from Iran. The transfer can only be made to an Iranian national or to a foreign national who has retained the required permission to own real estate. A reference was also made to the Decree Concerning Landed Property Ownership by Foreign Nationals, approved on 25 September 1963. This Decree provides that persons who are not in possession of an Iranian permanent residence permit, but who regularly make seasonal trips to Iran to tour and use resort areas, are enabled to buy immovable properties for their personal residence.[16]

This review of the Iranian legislation led the Tribunal to conclude that the right to own real property in Iran by contract was reserved by relevant Iranian laws for Iranian nationals. Thus, the Tribunal decided that the Claimant could only have acquired his properties as an Iranian national.[17] In so far as the Claimant's right to compensation was concerned, the Tribunal pointed out that the Claimant, who was a dual national with dominant and effective United States nationality, had brought the claim as a United States national. For this reason, the use of the Claimant's other, that is, his Iranian nationality to purchase real property as an Iranian national, was relevant to the merits of the Claims in light of the *caveat* of case **A18**.[18]

---

16 Para. 158.

17 Para. 159.

18 Para. 160.

The final conclusion of the Tribunal was that as the right to own real property in Iran was reserved solely for Iranian nationals, the Tribunal had to assume that "the Claimant purchased all the properties that are the subjects of these Claims in his capacity as an Iranian national after he had acquired United States nationality. He now claims in respect of those properties as a national of the United States. If the Tribunal were to allow him to recover against the Respondent in these circumstances, it would be permitting an abuse of right. Consequently, the **A18** caveat must bar the Claimant's recovery. See J.M. SAGHI, et al. supra."[19] The Tribunal decided in the following paragraph 162 that in view of the foregoing considerations, "the Tribunal finds that the **A18** caveat bars the Claimant, who brings these Claims as a United States national, from recovering against the Respondent for interference with property rights that, under Iranian law, he could have acquired only as an Iranian national." Each party was ordered to bear its own costs of arbitration.[20]

Having reached this conclusion, the Tribunal decided in a short Award that the claim for expropriation of the Chaboksar property be dismissed for lack of proof during the period over which the Tribunal has jurisdiction.[21] The claims for expropriation of the other three properties were dismissed for lack of proof.[22] The claims for other measures attributable to the Respondent affecting the four properties were barred by the *caveat* ruling in case **A18**.

It may be added that the Award includes an interesting review of the Iranian land reform legislation and other official acts of the Respondent.[23] This section of the Award helps to understand the provisions of the 1979 Act Concerning Abolition of Ownership of Mawat (Undeveloped) Urban Lands and the Manner of their Development as well as the provisions of the Urban Lands Act of 1982. The section also includes references to newspaper reports on official statements and governmental action which the Claimant produced in order to prove the responsibility of the Respondent.[24]

On the whole, the Award in the *Karubian* case is an interesting Tribunal precedent. This is especially so when one takes into account the fact that Chamber Two was unanimous in reaching the Award. It is, however, necessary to keep in mind that the cases involving the implications of the *caveat*

---

19 Para. 161.
20 Para. 163.
21 Para. 164 A.
22 Para. 164 B.
23 Paras. 26–46.
24 As this article has been limited mainly to the effect of the *caveat* ruling in case **A18**, this part of the Award has been omitted here.

ruling in case **A18** have in the past been related to different types of property. This seems to be true as well for the relatively few remaining claims where this issue may have an effect on the final rulings of the Tribunal. These cases, therefore, will have to be decided in light of the specific circumstances involved.

SOME QUESTIONS CONCERNING THE APPLICABLE LAW IN INTERNATIONAL TRIBUNALS

by

IAN BROWNLIE

Introduction

It is a great pleasure to celebrate a friend's birthday and, in the present context, to celebrate also a distinguished career marked by a dedication both to scholarship and to the maintenance of standards of legality in practice. There are others, but Krzysztof Skubiszewski is undoubtedly a leading exponent of the tradition of public international law in Poland in this turbulent century.

My friendship with Skubiszewski began in 1961 or thereabouts when he visited Nottingham University, and it was at my prompting that he applied for a Visiting Fellowship at All Souls College, Oxford. This long relationship provided the background to my visits to Poland in 1976 (under the auspices of Skubiszewski), and in 1987 (under the auspices of the editor of this *Festschrift*).

The topic selected for this essay does not reflect the areas of international law on which Skubiszewski has written. However, it is thought to be of general interest and is not often examined outside the confines of the familiar theme of "delocalisation of contracts".

I. FISSILE TENDENCIES IN PUBLIC INTERNATIONAL LAW

It is beyond question that public international law constitutes an applicable law, and may be indicated as such or "played in," by the determination of a tribunal, to govern certain issues. The question addressed first of all is to what extent specialised areas of international law, such as "International Human Rights Law" or "International Environmental Law" may constitute discrete forms of applicable law, forming bodies of law independent of the parent body.

This question has become acute as a result of academic empire-building and the opportunism of those who need students and are unwilling to require a rigorous or, indeed, any knowledge of general international law. Thus it is common to see Master's degrees in specialised areas of international law awarded to students with little or no knowledge of the law of treaties or the principles of State responsibility. "International Environmental Law" has tended to develop as a wholly academic personality, developed in ignorance of the practice of States and organisations. If international tribunals are seduced by academic fashion, States may become shy of accepting jurisdiction in relation to environmental matters. After all the academic development, Chernobyl and the diplomatic aftermath indicated the large gap between State practice and the *lex ferenda* of the literature.

It is the principles of State responsibility which are applicable and which need developing. To encourage the fragmentation of international law will have retrograde effects. Neither in the sphere of teaching nor in the spheres of practice is it helpful to signal the relevance of a decision like the *Corfu Channel* case by indicating that it can be classified as a decision relating to the environment.

II. STANDARD-SETTING TREATIES AND THE APPLICABLE LAW

Multilateral standard-setting treaties concerning human rights do not contain provisions indicating the applicable law. This is true (for example) of the Genocide Convention (1948), the European Convention for the Protection of Human Rights and Fundamental Freedoms (1950), and the Convention on the Elimination of All Forms of Discrimination against Women (1979). No doubt such provisions are not thought to be necessary.

There is, however, a source of unease in relation to the European Convention. The "violations" which are indicated in the petitions, and in the determinations of the Commission and the Court, are, of course, violations by the Respondent States of their treaty obligations. For this and other reasons it is normal and, indeed, necessary to apply the provisions of the Convention taking into account any relevant general principles of international law. This is a well-recognised principle of treaty interpretation and it appears in Article 31(3)(c) of the Vienna Convention on the Law of Treaties. Why, then, the reference to a source of unease? The answer lies partly in the occasional reluctance of the Commission (in particular) to take on board critically relevant matters of public international law. A further element consists of the ambience in which such bodies work. This ambience is increasingly dominated by appointees with little or no knowledge of international law, and yet in its earlier stages (1953 to 1984) the Commission included senior international lawyers such as Waldock and Fawcett.

III. ECLECTIC APPLICABLE LAW PROVISIONS

On occasion the clause on applicable law in a negotiated agreement is eclectic and rather flexible. An example of such a clause is to be found in the Claims Settlement Declaration, dated 19 January 1981,[1] which governs the work of the Iran-United States Claims Tribunal. Article V of the Declaration provides as follows:

> "The Tribunal shall decide all cases on the basis of respect for law, applying such choice of law rules and principles of commercial and international law as the Tribunal determines to be applicable, taking into account relevant usages of the trade, contract provisions and changed circumstances."

This type of open-textured provision may have the effect of discouraging the parties and their representatives, together with the tribunal concerned, from focusing effectively upon the applicable law.[2] The consequences may include adverse effects on the development of the pleadings and arguments in appropriate stages.

IV. TRIBUNALS PERMITTED TO RESORT TO *DEPEÇAGE*

Different issues arising in a complex case may call for different choice of law rules, and this process is often described as *depeçage*. There is a logical determinism involved here and it is unhelpful to regard *depeçage* as though it is merely a form of opportunism. Several sets of standard arbitration rules permit, and indeed appear to encourage, resort to *depeçage*. This is true of the ICSID system: and thus Article 42 of the Convention provides (in paragraph 1):[3]

> "The Tribunal shall decide a dispute in accordance with such rules of law as may be agreed by the parties. In the absence of such agreement, the Tribunal shall apply the law of the Contracting State party to the dispute

---

1 20 INTERNATIONAL LEGAL MATERIALS (1981) at 230.

2 *See* S.T. TOOPE, MIXED INTERNATIONAL ARBITRATION, Cambridge (1990) at 361–383; and W. MAPP, THE IRAN-UNITED STATED CLAIMS TRIBUNAL, Manchester (1993) at 110–113.

3 4 INTERNATIONAL LEGAL MATERIALS (1965) at 532.

> (including its rules on the conflict of laws) and such rules of international law as may be applicable."

Similarly, the UNICITRAL Rules provide (in Article 33, paragraph 1):[4]

> "The arbitral tribunal shall apply the law designated by the parties as applicable to the substance of the dispute. Failing such designation by the parties, the arbitral tribunal shall apply the law determined by the conflict of laws rules which it considers applicable."

In the case of *Wintershall A.G. v. Government of Qatar*, decided under the UNICITRAL Rules (as agreed by the Parties), the Tribunal in its Order of 18 March 1987 had concluded that public international law would be applicable "in case the Tribunal should determine that it is relevant to an issue." In its Partial Award on Liability the Tribunal decided as follows:[5]

> "By paragraph 2. of its Order of March 18, 1987, the Tribunal provided that 'In the absence of a controlling choice of substantive governing law clause and in consideration of the close links of ... the EPSA ... to Qatar, the governing substantive law shall be the law of Qatar and, in case the Tribunal should determine that it is relevant to an issue, public international law.' The Tribunal, after reviewing the deposited authorities on public international law, has determined that public international law is not independently relevant to the issues before the Tribunal in this Partial Award on Liability, and that the governing substantive law on those issues is the law of Qatar."

V. ECCENTRIC POSSIBILITIES

Practice throws up eccentric possibilities which are not considered in the literature. In a case (not reported), decided by a court of arbitration, the special agreement provided that the applicable law was **either** the law of State A **or** the law of State B **or** the law of State C, without providing any indication of the method by which the selection of the applicable law was to be carried out. In such a case no doubt the general principles of conflict of laws must be applied.

An added problem occurs when the special agreement includes an acceptance of liability without any indication as to the putative applicable law to which this acceptance was related. Given that the issue of quantum of

---

4 G. WETTER, IV THE INTERNATIONAL ARBITRAL PROCESS, New York (1979) at 413.

5 28 INTERNATIONAL LEGAL MATERIALS (1989) at 798.

damages has a close connection with the cause of action, this creates acute difficulty for the tribunal.

VI. INTERNATIONAL LAW AS PART OF THE APPLICABLE LAW

A fairly common situation is the case in which there is no explicit choice of public international law, but it is pleaded on the basis that it forms a part of the choice of domestic system of applicable law. In the alternative a tribunal may accept that, as a matter of legal logic, public international law is applicable to certain types of issue. There are no *a priori* principles which inhibit such an approach and, as Dr. Mann has pointed out, municipal law is subordinate to public international law.[6] At the same time an express choice of municipal law should not be subverted by the insertion of public international law unless this is necessitated by the particular subject-matter.

VII. THE NEGATIVE CHOICE OF LAW AND THE PRINCIPLES OF NATURAL JUSTICE

The devices used by draftsmen to avoid reference to the national law of either of the parties are often described as the process of "delocalisation." The more useful analysis is to see the process as in two stages. The first is a negative choice of law. Thus the references to "the principles of good faith," "the principles of natural justice," or "the general principles of law," are, first and foremost, indications, that the national law of the respective parties is not to apply.[7]

The second stage is to translate this "negative choice of law" into a positive indication of the principles which are to be applied by the tribunal. Certain distinguished writers have pointed to the difficulty of establishing the content of "general principles of law"[8] or the so-called *lex mercatoria* and other variants of a delocalised proper law.[9]

---

6 F.A. MANN, STUDIES IN INTERNATIONAL LAW, Oxford (1973) at 14.

7 *Cf. Ruler of Qatar v. International Marine Oil Co. Ltd.* (1953), 20 INTERNATIONAL LAW REPORTS (ed. E. Lauterpacht) at 534; *Sapphire International v. NIOC* (1963), *ibid.* Vol. 35 at 136; *BP v. Libyan Arab Republic* (1974), *ibid.* Vol. 53 at 297; *Texaco v. Libyan Arab Republic* (1977), *ibid.* Vol. 53 at 389; *LIAMCO v. Libyan Arab Republic* (1977), *ibid.* Vol. 62 at 62.

8 *See* F.A. MANN, FURTHER STUDIES IN INTERNATIONAL LAW, Oxford (1990) at 264 and 268–269.

9 *See* Lord MUSTILL, (in:) M. BOS and I. BROWNLIE (eds.), LIBER AMICORUM FOR LORD WILBERFORCE, Oxford (1987) at 149–183.

The reasonable inference would be that the content of the general principles of law or of natural justice would be indicated by the expectations of the parties. On this basis, two constituents emerge. The first is negative: that natural justice does not involve a reference back to the law of one of the parties. The second is that natural justice involves the incorporation of general principles of conflicts of law. Both these constituents rest upon the assumption that the applicable law should be applied in a manner which is compatible with the shared expectations of the parties.

The general approach was supported by the Award of the distinguished Tribunal which decided *Government of Kuwait v. Aminoil* (1982).[10] The key passages in the Award stress the expectation of the parties that the applicable law would include reference to general principles of law. The relevant passages are as follows:

> "6. Respecting the law applicable to the substantive issues in the dispute, which is what is really at stake between the Parties regarding the applicable law, the question equally simple in the present case. It can hardly be contested but that the law of Kuwait applies to many matters over which it is the law most directly involved. But this conclusion, based on good sense as well as law, does not carry any all-embracing consequences with it, and this for two reasons. The *first* is that Kuwait law is a highly evolved system as to which the Government has been at pains to stress that 'established public international law is necessarily a part of the law of Kuwait' (GCM paragraph 3.97(5)). In their turn the general principles of law are part of public international law – *Article 38, 1(c) of the Statute of the International Court of Justice*, and that this specifically applies to Kuwait oil concessions duly results from the clauses included in these. For instance, in the 1973 Agreement between the Parties, First Annex, Second Part, XII CGM App.1.9) the following provision is to be found (punctuation of second sentence added):
>
> > 'The parties base their relations with regard to the agreements between them on the principle of goodwill and good faith. Taking account of the different nationalities of the parties, the agreements between them shall be given effect, and must be interpreted and applied, in conformity with principles common to the laws of Kuwait and of the State of New York, United States of America, and in the absence of such common principles, then in conformity with the principles of law normally recognised by civilised States in general, including those which have been applied by international tribunals.'
>
> Although the Parties did not, in the course of the present arbitral proceedings, make any reference to this particular text, it is of all the more interest

[10] 66 INTERNATIONAL LAW REPORTS (1982) at 518.

to note that the ideas it embodies are no isolated features of Kuwait practice.

7. Equally, the Offshore Concession Agreement of the Arabian Oil Company (AOC) (AR Vol. V1, Exh. 39), contains the same provision, except that reference is made to the principles common to Kuwait and to Japanese law (Article 39). The Oil Concession Agreement with the Kuwait National Petroleum Company and Hispanica de Petroleos, concluded in 1967 (AR *loc. cit.*), refer to the principles common to Kuwait and to Spanish law. Yet it would be quite unrealistic to suppose that these three Concessions were governed by three different régimes. Clearly, it must have been the general principles of law that were chiefly present to the minds of the Government of Kuwait and its associates.

8. But there is a *second* consideration which has greatly eased the task of the Tribunal, namely that the Parties have themselves, in effect, indicated in the Arbitration Agreement what the applicable law is. Article II, 2 of the Agreement provides that

> 'The law governing the substantive issues between the Parties shall be determined by the Tribunal, having regard to the quality of the Parties, the transnational character of their relations and the principles of law and practice prevailing in the modern world.'

Although it may in theory be possible for a litigation to be governed by an assemblage of rules different from that which, before the Arbitration, governed the situations and matters that are the object of the litigation, there must be a presumption that this is not the case. Thus, to the extent that Article III, 2 of the Arbitration Agreement calls for interpretation, such an interpretation ought to be based on that provision which not only was freely chosen by the Parties in 1973 (*see*, paragraph 6 *supra*), but also reflects the spirit which has underlain the carrying on of the oil concession in Kuwait.

9. Article III, 2, with good reason, makes it clear that Kuwait is a sovereign State entrusted with the interests of a national community the law of which constitutes an essential part of intra-community relations within the State. At the same time, by referring to the transnational character of relations with the concessionaire, and to the general principles of law, this Article bring out the wealth and fertility of the set of legal rules that the Tribunal is called upon to apply."[11]

Both in these passages and elsewhere in the Award, the Tribunal placed emphasis on the intentions and expectations of the parties. As the Tribunal expresses the matter:

> "Clearly, it must have been the general principles of law that were chiefly present to the minds of the Government of Kuwait and its associates."[12]

---

11 AWARD at 560–561.

12 *Ibid.* para. 7.

This approach, which in effect treats the agreement itself as the applicable law, is particularly appropriate to inter-State contracts not governed by the law of Treaties. The essential criterion is provided by the intentions of the parties. The reference to "natural justice" must necessarily be understood and applied as requiring equity in relation to the content of the agreements. The resort to "general principles of law" is thus not a straightforward recourse to a familiar department of public international law, as in the Statute of the International Court. Article 38(1)(c), but is a recourse modified so as to maintain equality and natural justice **within the framework of the contractual provisions**.

Sur des dimensions culturelles de l'arbitrage international

par

Pierre Lalive

Dans sa phase la plus récente, la carrière d'exception du destinataire du présent volume le voit présider, à La Haye, la résolution de litiges irano-américains par le Iran-US Claims Tribunal. Aussi cette circonstance justifie-t-elle sans doute, parmi bien d'autres, le choix de l'un des aspects les moins étudiés de l'arbitrage international comme thème de cet hommage.

Le domaine de l'arbitrage, fort ancien mais en pleine expansion, exerce aujourd'hui, on le sait, un attrait croissant chez les juristes, souvent praticiens, attrait suscité certes par ses enjeux matériels mais aussi, comme l'a fort bien noté Bruno Oppetit «par la séduction intellectuelle qu'exerce sur les esprits une notion située au carrefour de presque toutes les disciplines juridiques, de droit substantiel comme de méthodologie, ce qui interdit le cloisonnement qu'entraînent trop souvent à notre époque la spécialisation à outrance et l'étroite technicisation, devenues les tendances dominantes de la doctrine moderne»[1].

En effet, l'arbitrage international – devenu le moyen ordinaire de règlement des différends internationaux, au moins privés ou «semi-privés» – au-delà de son évidente importance pratique-nous «ouvre des perspectives philosophiques» en nous invitant sans cesse à «une réflexion sur les questions les plus fondamentales susceptibles de se poser dans le cadre d'un système juridique: la justice, ses formes et ses buts, la juridicité, ses sources et sa nature, la structure de l'ordre juridique, les fins du droit»[2].

Sans nourrir ici l'ambition de nous élever au niveau de la philosophie ou de la théorie générale du droit, nous souhaiterions attirer l'attention sur un aspect relativement négligé, parmi la multitude des études, colloques et conférences consacrés un peu partout à l'arbitrage international. Ce dernier est un phénomène dont «l'étonnant développement … dans les relations internationales depuis la dernière guerre mondiale n'a pas cessé de surprendre» et dont «nous n'avons pas fini de découvrir tous les aspects», comme

---

[1] B. Oppetit, *Philosophie de l'arbitrage commercial international*, Journal Clunet (1993), p. 811.

[2] *Ibid.*

l'observait naguère un autre grand connaisseur de la matière, le Premier Président Pierre Bellet[3], un prédécesseur du Professeur Krzysztof Skubiszewski à la tête de l'important Tribunal irano-américan de La Haye.

Il s'agira ici d'un aspect certes concret, mais souvent dissimulé, pour ne pas dire clandestin du règlement des différends: la dimension que l'on pourrait appeler «interculturelle». Aspect fort malaisé à percevoir et à analyser, pour une pluralité de raisons: d'une part le caractère en principe confidentiel de l'arbitrage (le Iran-US Claims Tribunal sortant clairement, de ce point de vue aussi, des schémas classiques); d'autre part, le fait que chaque espèce, ou presque, a sa singularité, peu favorable à des généralisations, pourtant indispensables. Aussi qui pourrait prétendre, même après des décennies d'expérience personnelle, avoir une vision globale et complète d'un phénomène aussi protéiforme?

Ces difficultés ne sauraient dispenser toutefois chaque observateur ou acteur de la vie juridique internationale d'apporter sa contribution à l'acquisition d'une telle vision globale. D'autant que, comme l'a écrit, dans un autre contexte, le destinataire du présent hommage collectif: «Tout le monde a besoin d'une vision qui corresponde à la réalité».

Or jusqu'ici l'essentiel de l'attention, chez les juristes et chez les praticiens en général, a été dirigé, de façon très compréhensible, vers les conflits d'intérêts, d'une part, et les conflits de lois, de l'autre. Beaucoup plus rarement s'est-on soucié de la «dimension culturelle» ou «interculturelle» ou de «l'influence», sur la solution des litiges, de ce que l'on peut appeler un peu schématiquement les «conflits de cultures», celles des parties en litige et, plus largement, celles de tous les acteurs de ce petit «drame» que constitue le règlement arbitral (donc y compris les arbitres et les conseils). Or ces conflits de cultures jouent un rôle tout sauf négligeable, et bien plus grand souvent que ne le soupçonnent et les intéressés eux-mêmes et les milieux d'affaires en général. Une chose est certaine en effet, ces conflits, ces oppositions de vue, de *Weltanschauungen* influent, le plus souvent négativement, sur le processus de règlement arbitral, et en ralentissent, voire en empêchent parfois la solution.

Mais de quoi parlons-nous exactement? Reconnaissons d'abord que l'adjectif «culturel» figure parmi les plus imprécis et les plus équivoques qui soient, ce qui découle sans doute de l'ambivalence essentielle du terme et de la notion même de «culture». Pense-t-on ici à la Culture au sens du XVIIIème siècle, à cet acquis de connaissances et d'expériences, à ce fonds commun ap-

---

[3] Dans: P. BELLET, ETUDES DE DROIT INTERNATIONAL EN L'HONNEUR DE P. LALIVE, Genève (1993), p. 399.

partenant à l'élite des hommes qui ont le plus d'éducation, d'intelligence et de sensibilité? Ou pensons-nous, plutôt, à la notion de «Culture» telle qu'elle est apparue au début du XIXème siècle (enrichie qu'elle a été des apports du Romantisme, du Marxisme et de la Sociologie), soit à un **donné**, à un ensemble de caractéristiques propres à certains groupes sociaux, à des valeurs collectives et des manières d'être, etc.? C'est en ce dernier sens, sociologique, que l'on distinguerait par exemple les cultures des Polonais et des Allemands, des Italiens et des Anglais ou, d'autre part, celles des paysans et des citadins, des civils et des militaires, des juristes et des non-juristes, et l'on en passe.

A ces quelques jalons introductifs, ajoutons simplement la mention de l'élément conflictuel que semblent impliquer nécessairement les définitions qui précèdent. A ce propos, M. Alain Plantey, de l'Institut de France, et Président de la «Cour Internationale d'Arbitrage» de la Chambre de Commerce International, observait naguère à juste titre que:

> «Entre les nations, les valeurs culturelles ne peuvent être facilement harmonisées. C'est même souvent en ce domaine que les peuples ont le mieux établi leurs caractéristiques spécifiques et authentiques. Ils ont en effet rarement les mêmes conceptions sociales, le même patrimoine historique. Entre eux règne facilement incompréhension ou ignorance réciproques»[4].

Il semblerait en résumé que l'arbitrage international implique en soi, de par son internationalité même, la possibilité ou, mieux, la probabilité d'oppositions de vues, de visions du monde, de «conflits de cultures» entre ses différents acteurs ou participants, des conflits qui, pour être le plus souvent implicites ou sous-jacents, n'en constituent pas moins un facteur important du processus du règlement des différends. C'est ce que nous voudrions illustrer en examinant un certain nombre de ces conflits ou différences de vues ou de visions, d'abord sur la notion même et la conception générale et l'esprit de l'arbitrage, ensuite à propos du rôle et des qualités requises des Arbitres eux-mêmes.

Avant d'analyser quelques différences d'attitudes d'ordre «culturel» – du début à la fin du règlement d'un différend international par l'arbitrage – il paraît nécessaire de situer le contexte général, par trois observations.

La première observation concerne le **concept** même d'arbitrage. Serait-il plus correct, ou plus opportun, de parler **des** concepts d'arbitrages, tant la diversité est grande en la matière, et cela déjà en droit interne, et *a fortiori* sur le terrain international, non seulement quant aux genres ou formes des

---

4 Dans: ETUDES EN L'HONNEUR DE O.A. GLOSSNER, p. 242.

arbitrages, mais encore quant à leurs buts et leurs critères. Aussi a-t-on pu parler de «notion à contenu variable», aux critères insaisissables et fuyants. Laissons ici de côté les controverses doctrinales, assez dépassées, sur la nature «contractuelle», «juridictionnelle» ou mixte de l'arbitrage et mentionnons seulement, *pro memoria*, la diversité des opinions sur l'arbitrage **en droit** et l'arbitrage **en équité** (ou sur l'identité, ou non, de ce dernier terme avec ceux d'amiable composition). On peut s'interroger aussi sur la question de savoir s'il s'agit d'une méthode tendant à faire **trancher** un litige par un tiers appelé à «dire le droit», ou plutôt d'un processus tendant à rétablir la paix pour l'avenir entre les parties, au besoin en modifiant et aménageant leur rapport contractuel. Dans cette optique, le juriste européen a tendance à opposer à la vision très, ou trop juridique de l'arbitrage qui semble prévaloir en Europe et en Amérique du Nord, une «vision asiatique» des choses (peut-être inexistante, du reste, vu la diversité, mal perçue en Europe, des points de vue entre les pays d'Asie), selon laquelle le souci de conciliation, d'éviter «la perte de face» l'emporterait nettement, au point qu'il conviendrait de voir alors l'arbitrage comme un phénomène extra-juridique. Et si l'on voit dans les «jeux de réflexion» les plus populaires le reflet de la culture d'un peuple, on serait tenté d'opposer le jeu d'échecs (pourtant d'origine indienne!) cher aux Occidentaux, avec son caractère de combat ou de tournoi médiéval, au jeu de go, cher aux Orientaux, qui est un jeu de construction beaucoup plus que de combat.

Pour notre part, nous restons convaincus par la thèse, chère à ce grand comparatiste qu'était René David[5] de **l'unité** fondamentale de la notion d'arbitrage, mais peu importe ici. Si la notion même, en droit interne déjà, est aussi multiforme et aussi controversée, comment s'étonnerait-on que, sur le plan international, donc dans un milieu hétérogène par excellence, règnent les opinions, les conceptions, les philosophies les plus diverses au sujet de la notion, de la fonction et des buts de l'arbitrage? Comment s'étonner, en d'autres termes, des **conflits de cultures**, qui, consciemment ou non, vont influencer le comportement des parties, de leurs avocats et des arbitres?

Une deuxième observation générale s'impose, qui est plus politique. L'arbitrage international semble jouir aujourd'hui d'une faveur quasi universelle, consacrée par la «Loi modèle» élaborée par la CNUDCI, si bien que l'arbitrage a pu apparaître comme l'«enfant gâté» de l'ONU, comme l'écrivait Philippe Fouchard, et bénéficier d'un véritable «engouement», qui est attesté par de nombreuses législations récentes, ainsi que par une prolifération de centres ou institutions d'arbitrage, de tout niveau et de tout acabit.

---

[5] R. DAVID, L'ARBITRAGE DANS LE COMMERCE INTERNATIONAL, Paris (1982) *passim*.

Ces faits ne doivent pas faire oublier les réticences et les méfiances, parfois profondes, qui subsistent, derrière les déclarations gouvernementales de circonstances ou les proclamations publicitaires.

Il y a encore une ou deux décennies à peine, il eut été de mode dans quelques pays en voie de développement et auprès de leurs défenseurs patentés, de dépeindre l'arbitrage international classique comme une sorte d'invention occidentale ou capitaliste, nécessairement défavorable aux pays non-industrialisés. On a pu sourire, mais à tort, de ce genre de généralisations. S'agissant de condamnations sommaires, il est plus constructif d'en rechercher les causes, dont la première est le plus souvent l'ignorance et l'inexpérience. Comment ne se méfierait-on pas d'une institution que l'on connaît mal et dont on ne maîtrise pas les mécanismes? Or le fait est que les cadres des pays en développement étaient souvent mal préparés, naguère, à l'art de la négociation et de la rédaction des contrats internationaux, de même qu'ils se sentaient désavantagés dans des procédures arbitrales parfois complexes, et où ils leur arrivait de se présenter mal conseillés, fût-ce par des avocats occidentaux, parfois mal choisis au hasard d'une amitié politique ou de leur capacité de «marketing».

Pour une partie (étatique ou privée) pour qui un arbitrage international est une expérience nouvelle, la perte de la cause laisse une impression amère, propre à susciter des réactions d'humeur (comme en témoigne le fameux décret de l'Arabie Saoudite interdisant l'arbitrage international aux organismes d'Etats après la sentence Aramco), et il est tentant d'en rendre responsable les «préjugés» d'arbitres occidentaux ou l'institution elle-même de l'arbitrage, plutôt que son propre comportement ou les lacunes et erreurs du contrat initial. On pense à ce propos à la si juste observation de ce grand connaisseur qu'était Lazare Kopelmanas qui, à propos de certains arbitrages importants, constatait que s'il y avait trop de juristes à la fin, c'est qu'il n'y en avait pas eu assez au début, c'est-à-dire lors de la négociation du contrat!

S'agissant d'arbitrages auxquels est partie soit un Etat, soit une grande société multinationale (deux situations entre lesquelles les analogies sont nombreuses, même d'ordre culturel), on comprend que la susceptibilité de la partie «perdante» soit d'autant plus grande qu'elle est surprise par le résultat, notamment quand personne n'avait osé le lui laisser prévoir. Compte tenu d'une tendance, très humaine, par exemple des cadres de l'Etat comme des cadres d'une grande société, à préférer dissimuler leurs erreurs et ne pas reconnaître leurs responsabilités, on comprend la fréquence d'un phénomène curieux, lui aussi d'ordre culturel, celui de la **mauvaise information** de tant de gouvernants ou de dirigeants de sociétés, soit sur les perspectives, soit sur l'état et les progrès d'une procédure arbitrale internationale dans laquelle leur pays ou leur société est engagé. Les exemples ne sont pas rares d'affaires importantes où un arbitrage international s'est prolongé, bien au-delà du nécessaire, du seul fait de mauvaises communications internes à une partie ou d'un refus de certains acteurs d'admettre leurs responsabilités.

La méfiance assez générale qui persiste en certains pays et en certains milieux arabes à l'égard de l'arbitrage international, il convient de le noter, ne semble pas due essentiellement à la nature de l'institution (qui est, on le sait, parfaitement reconnue par le Coran), mais plutôt due à son «internationalité», qui est parfois ressentie comme une intrusion ou une limitation imposée **par l'étranger** à l'indépendance ou à la souveraineté nationale. C'est ainsi que, il y a quelques années, à l'occasion de l'un des Congrès d'arbitrage «euro-arabes», nous avions l'occasion de découvrir, avec une surprise que certains jugeront naïve, que le caractère obligatoire d'une clause d'arbitrage international dans un contrat, et la reconnaissance des sentences arbitrales étrangères, rappelait à certains participants le régime des Capitulations! Et l'on sait que, sur un terrain politique analogue, bien des pays d'Amérique Latine se ressentent encore d'une vieille tradition hostile à l'arbitrage international, parfois expressément interdit dans leur Constitution, tradition assez aisément explicable par les souvenirs historiques du XIXème siècle, dont celui de la «diplomatie de la canonnière». Une évolution, lente mais certaine, se manifeste cependant, comme en témoignent les ratifications de la Convention de Washington de 1965 de la Banque Mondiale ou l'adhésion de l'Arabie Saoudite à la Convention de New York de 1958 sur la reconnaissance des sentences arbitrales.

Une troisième observation, beaucoup moins politique ou historique, contribue à expliquer la relative lenteur de ce reflux des réticences «politico-culturelles» à l'égard de l'arbitrage international, et le caractère très récent, soit d'un texte international comme la «Loi modèle» de la CNUDCI, soit des législations nationales les plus libérales, comme celles de la France, de la Suisse, des Pays-Bas – une lenteur assez étonnante si l'on pense à la pression des nécessités économiques et les besoins de la mondialisation des échanges. La lenteur de cette évolution et de ses progrès a aussi des causes à caratère intellectuel ou culturel, comme on ne l'a pas assez remarqué, à notre avis.

Dans la plupart des pays, aussi bien occidentaux qu'orientaux, aussi bien en Suisse qu'en Egypte par exemple, juristes et politiques semblent avoir éprouvé la plus grande difficulté à concevoir l'arbitrage du commerce international autrement que comme une simple variante, une sorte d'extension de l'arbitrage **interne**. Or ce dernier, ne l'oublions pas, constitue une exception au monopole étatique de la justice et une concurrence pour cette dernière; d'où sa définition sur la base d'un critère négatif, manifeste dans divers arrêts du Tribunal fédéral suisse par exemple, celui de la «soustraction d'un litige au juge ordinaire.» La conséquence logique en est que l'institution doit être strictement limitée et contrôlée, dans le cadre de dispositions impératives.

Tout à fait admissible, voire indiscutable **dans l'ordre juridique interne**, pareille conception est aussi injustifiée qu'inopportune sur le terrain international où précisément, vu la présence de conflits de juridictions et l'absence d'un véritable «juge ordinaire» (au moins à défaut de solutions précises résultant d'actes internationaux comme les Conventions de Bruxelles et de Lugano), l'arbitrage s'impose, **dans un contexte juridiquement et culturellement tout différent**, par de nombreuses raisons dont celle du maintien d'une véritable égalité entre les parties. C'est donc à pleine raison que, au moins depuis l'Acte final de la Conférence d'Helsinki de 1975, en passant par les recommandations de l'ONU sur la «Loi modèle» de la CNUDCI, et de nombreuses législations et jurisprudences nationales, on peut constater une tendance universelle favorable à l'arbitrage international et à sa libéralisation.

Si cette tendance se répand, ainsi que la connaissance de l'institution, assistée par les progrès de l'enseignement et la multiplication des colloques et des associations, on aurait tort de croire que toutes les réticences nationales ont disparu et que toute possibilité de régression est exclue[6]. Quoi qu'il en soit, il subsiste et il subsistera des «conflits de cultures» et bien des divergences plus ou moins conscientes, de vues et de sensibilités quant à la nature et aux fonctions de l'arbitrage international, au rôle, qualifications et devoirs de ses principaux acteurs. C'est à quelques-uns des ces aspects, moins généraux et plus concrets, que nous voudrions consacrer la seconde partie de notre contribution, en la limitant, faute de place, au seul cas des arbitres, malgré l'intérêt que présenterait un examen des différences culturelles séparant tant les parties elles-mêmes que les conseils de ces dernières.

On s'attachera d'abord et surtout au rôle de **l'arbitre choisi par une partie**, en se demandant s'il est différent de celui de l'arbitre unique ou président. C'est là un premier point – capital – sur lequel apparaissent de véritables «conflits de cultures».

Dans la conception dominante aujourd'hui, au moins en Occident, cet arbitre-là est un «juge», qui devrait réunir les **mêmes** qualités d'indépendance et d'impartialité que le magistrat étatique, et cela quand bien même (a) il existe une fonction temporaire et (b) il tient son pouvoir d'une partie ou plus exactement sans doute **des** parties (même s'il n'est choisi que par une).

---

6 *Cf.* G. WETTER, dans: LCIA Centenary *Looking Ahead to the Next Ten Years*, Londres (1995), pp. 85–106.

Ce n'est pas ici le lieu de discuter la définition ou la distinction, si souvent débattue, des notions d'**indépendance** et d'**impartialité**, notions très floues et ambiguës[7]. Certains systèmes et certains commentateurs les assimilent un peu vite. Disons simplement que la première, l'**indépendance**, constate une situation plus objective et plus aisée à vérifier que la seconde, l'**impartialité**, laquelle paraît plus subjective en ce qu'elle traduit une attitude ou une disposition d'esprit; attitude qui découle, pour partie, sans doute, d'un don naturel, mais aussi et surtout d'une volonté ou d'une technique acquise, par la formation juridique et par l'expérience.

Pareille esquisse des qualités requises de l'arbitre, si sommaire qu'elle soit, reflète déjà une certaine «philosophie de l'arbitrage», une certaine conception culturelle qui n'est pas universellement admise, pas plus, du reste, qu'elle n'est reconnue par tous les praticiens dans un seul et même pays, au moins en ce qui concerne le cas de l'**arbitre dit «de partie»**, c'est-à-dire choisi par elle.

Il serait tentant, mais simpliste, d'opposer sur ce point une conception «européenne» à une conception «arabe». L'arbitre «de partie» doit-il, et peut-il, être aussi neutre et impartial que l'arbitre unique ou Président d'un Tribunal arbitral de trois membres? C'est ce qu'affirment par exemple le Tribunal fédéral suisse et la jurisprudence française[8]. Pareille exigence relève d'un idéalisme fort sympathique mais, à notre avis, assez utopique; au-delà même des conflits culturels existant à ce sujet, et que cette conception veut ignorer, l'exigence manque à l'évidence de réalisme[9].

A l'opposé, il semble que, dans les pays arabes par exemple, l'idée prévale que l'arbitre choisi par une partie est, sinon à proprement parler l'avocat de cette dernière ou son représentant, au moins une sorte d'**intermédiaire**, de trait-d'union ou de «médiateur» entre la partie au litige et le Président neutre du Tribunal arbitral. Nous avons pu constater la force de cette tradition dans divers congrès «euro-arabes» et il y a là, assez clairement, un **donné** sociologique et culturel que l'on ne saurait méconnaître, ni écarter à la légère au nom d'une prétendue supériorité d'autres valeurs, plus «occidentales» ou ... plus récentes. Au demeurant, les juristes arabes semblent quelque peu partagés eux aussi sur le rôle de l'arbitre dit «de partie» et sur les limites dans lesquelles il doit se tenir. Ces divergences ou ces hésitations seraient dues au fait que le Coran, s'il admet l'arbitrage et lui est incontestablement favorable, semble envisager seulement le cas de l'arbitre unique

---

7 *Cf.* RAPPORT PL À LA CCI, 59, cité par P. BELLET, *op. cit.*, *supra* note 3, p. 401, note 13.

8 *Cf.* P. BELLET, *op. cit.*, *supra* note 3, p. 405, note 42.

9 Comme le note Robert Coulson, alors président de l'American Arbitration Association, cité par P. BELLET, *op. cit.*, *supra* note 3, p. 404.

et non pas celui, aujourd'hui de loin le plus fréquent en matière de commerce international, d'un Tribunal arbitral de plusieurs membres.

Une illustration frappante de ce conflit de cultures nous est fournie par le cas – interétatique mais il n'importe ici – de l'**Oasis de Buraimi**, entre la Grande-Bretagne et l'Arabie Saoudite, souvent cité par les commentateurs et souvent mal compris, dans lequel l'Arbitre saoudite, qui était en même temps Vice-Ministre des Affaires Etrangères en charge du dossier de Buraimi, entendait participer activement et ouvertement à la conduite de la procédure, par exemple en faisant passer des instructions aux avocats de «sa» partie. Cette attitude souleva les vives protestations du Conseil de la Grande-Bretagne, Sir Hartley Shawcross. Il fallut toute l'expérience et le sens de la diplomatie arbitrale du Président Charles De Visscher pour apaiser, temporairement, au cours d'une étonnante délibération *in camera* du Tribunal, un conflit de cultures aussi aigu. On notera en passant que la conception de l'«arbitre de partie» comme intermédiaire ou médiateur ne soulèverait guère d'objections fondamentales si elle était, d'entrée de cause, connue et, surtout, commune aux deux arbitres choisis par les parties, le principe d'égalité étant ainsi respecté.

Quoi qu'il en soit, peut-on conclure, sur la base d'exemples de ce genre, que ce conflit quant au rôle de l'arbitre oppose des traditions **nationales**, par exemple, une vision «arabe» à une vision «occidentale»? Une telle idée (encore qu'elle comporte sans doute une part de vérité, au moins en ce qui concerne l'arbitrage interne) serait trop simplificatrice, voire erronée, car l'expérience indique qu'il s'agit plutôt de différences **de degrés**.

En outre, à l'intérieur même du prétendu «bloc occidental», la diversité des points de vue est manifeste. C'est ainsi que, en 1977, l'**American Bar Association** et l'AAA publiaient ensemble un «Code of Ethics» à l'usage des arbitres, lequel dispensait expressément les arbitres «non-neutres» de certaines des obligations imposées au Président du Tribunal arbitral[10]. Or dix ans plus tard à peine, l'**International Bar Association** publiait son propre code de déontologie lequel (tout comme les règlements de la CCI, de la LCIA ou comme la Loi modèle et les jurisprudences française et suisse) imposent aux arbitres choisis par les parties les mêmes devoirs qu'au Président neutre, une conception «idéale» qui appelle, on l'a vu, quelques réserves. Elle semble être fondée sur l'idée que de telles règles protègeraient l'arbitre contre les pressions (et par exemple les demandes d'information) auxquelles il risquerait d'être soumis de la part de la partie qui l'a choisi. Le motif est louable, encore qu'il ne paraisse pas suffire à justifier l'assimilation totale de deux

---

10 *Ibid.*

situations qui, quoi que l'on dise, ne sont ni ne seront jamais identiques: celle des arbitres «de partie» et celle du président neutre.

Il est vrai que certains comportements, telle la violation du secret du délibéré, doivent à l'évidence être interdits à tous les arbitres. On peut dire en effet que, par-delà toutes différences culturelles, le règlement arbitral implique que les «règles du jeu» soient connues et les mêmes pour tous (plus exactement pour tous ceux qui se trouvent dans la même situation, soit les deux arbitres choisis par les parties). On pourrait transposer ici le mot fameux de Churchill, avant la dernière Guerre, à propos des relations diplomatiques avec l'Allemagne nazie: «on ne peut pas jouer au bridge avec des gens qui jouent au poker»!).

L'observation et l'expérience révèlent une très grande variété de situations, et il est fort difficile de généraliser[11]. Cela est si vrai que l'on en vient parfois à se demander s'il existe réellement des «conflits de cultures» en ce domaine, en tous les cas de «cultures nationales», ou si l'on ne se trouve pas plutôt, et seulement, devant des **oppositions de cultures ... individuelles**! Peut-on vraiment parler, quant aux rôles des arbitres, d'une «culture occidentale»?

Les praticients connaissent des cas où trois ressortissants de pays européens voisins, et de même tradition juridique, membres d'un même Tribunal arbitral, ne pouvaient s'entretenir en privé du déroulement des débats en cours sans que, quelques jours après, par une bizarre coïncidence, l'avocat d'une des parties en vienne à infléchir son argumentation précisément dans le sens ou sur un point où le Président avait observé une lacune ou une faiblesse au cours d'une conversation entre les arbitres! On a vu de même des arbitres européens, venant de pays de vieille tradition judiciaire et arbitrale, s'étonner de la demande qui leur était faite de démissionner alors que, en cours de procédure, l'un était entré au Conseil d'Administration d'une des sociétés partie au litige, et l'autre appartenait à un Cabinet d'avocats qui venait de fusionner avec celui du Conseil d'une des parties! D'autre part, on a vu de grandes sociétés occidentales, mécontentes d'avoir «perdu» une cause par une sentence unanime, boycotter à l'avenir l'arbitre qu'elles avaient précédemment choisi, pour son «manque d'efficacité» (idée que l'on pourrait traduire par «excès d'indépendance»)! Il y a là un phénomène qui n'est sans doute pas isolé et qui inciterait à compléter les définitions de l'indépendance de l'arbitre en y incluant l'idée du courage de déplaire, ou de l'absence de tout désir d'être choisi une seconde fois par la même partie!

---

[11] *Voir* à ce sujet, *e.g.* P. LALIVE, *Assurer l'exécution des sentences arbitrales*, dans: CCI 60 ANS APRÈS, REGARDS SUR L'AVENIR, Paris (1984), p. 338 et s.

Dans ce contexte, il faudrait mentionner aussi l'institution de l'**opinion dissidente**, proscrite ou inconnue dans certaines traditions, admise par d'autres et de plus en plus en matière internationale, où elle a des avantages «politiques» peu discutables, notamment pour l'arbitre désigné par un Etat ou un organisme étatique, ou provenant d'un pays à régime où domine la «pensée unique». Qui contesterait que tous les pays n'ont pas la même culture en matière de justice, ni la même compréhension de l'objectivité ou de l'indépendance judiciaire?

Une anecdote très peu, trop peu connue, mérite d'être citée à ce propos, bien qu'elle concerne non pas directement l'arbitrage international mais la Cour Internationale de Justice (où l'on sait, soit dit en passant, le rôle qu'ont joué des juges polonais éminents comme Bohdan Winiarski et Manfred Lachs). Il s'agit de l'affaire de l'Anglo-Iranian Oil Company où la Cour, suivant les conclusions de l'Iran, déclina sa compétence à la majorité de neuf voix contre cinq, en 1951 – une majorité comprenant non seulement, de manière assez prévisible, la voix du juge *ad hoc* iranien, mais aussi celle du juge anglais, Sir Arnold McNair (*as he then was*). Les faits sont connus mais l'on sait moins que, une fois l'affaire terminée, l'Ambassadeur d'Iran fit une visite de courtoisie au futur Lord McNair et entreprit de le remercier de son vote. A quoi McNair fit en substance cette belle et significative réponse: «M. l'Ambassadeur, ce n'est pas moi qu'il faut remercier: c'est plutôt le pays dont la culture reconnaît à un juge le droit de voter en toute indépendance, selon sa conscience»!

On est tenté de voir ici la manifestation toute naturelle des standards éthiques des juristes anglais, et donc d'une certaine culture juridique nationale. Pareille généralisation, peut-être hâtive, demanderait à être nuancée, notamment si l'on tient compte de la **perspective historique** car ce qui paraît normal aujourd'hui, dans une société donnée, ne l'a pas toujours été. Ainsi, nul internationaliste n'ignore le célèbre arbitrage dit de l'**Alabama**, qui se déroula à Genève entre 1872 et 1879, entre les Etats-Unis et la Grande-Bretagne après la Guerre de Sécession. On dit que le comportement de l'arbitre anglais fut alors assez loin des normes d'impartialité et de correction qui allaient de soi pour un Arnold McNair.

Si l'on interrogeait les praticiens de plusieurs pays sur ce qu'ils attendent exactement de l'arbitre qu'ils ont désigné, ou sur les critères qu'ils appliquent lors de son choix, on constaterait sans doute bien des différences culturelles, mais en même temps certaines préoccupations communes par-delà les frontières. Ainsi, un excellent praticien anglais avouait rechercher de préférence une personne qui, non seulement soit compétente, mais aussi «combine le maximum de prédispositions en faveur de la thèse de mon client avec le minimum d'apparence de partialité»! Un autre praticien, interrogé sur la possibilité de désigner un arbitre d'une certaine nationalité, déclinait vigoureusement cette proposition au motif, crûment déclaré, que le risque était trop grand de le voir accepter, selon les usages de son pays, un cadeau de la partie adverse!

En définitive, on doit faire ici la part du feu, avec un grand magistrat et arbitre français, le Premier Président Bellet, pour qui, tout en exigeant de tous les arbitres «un minimum d'honnêteté», il faut bien admettre que «l'arbitre partisan existe et l'on doit s'accommoder de son existence»[12]. Cette existence, avouons-le, est peut-être une condition de la confiance des parties dans l'institution de l'arbitrage international et elle peut parfois révéler son utilité, selon les circonstances, notamment dans les arbitrages proches de la conciliation.

Cela dit, les cas ne sont pas très rares où il se produit un «conflit de cultures» **entre les deux arbitres** choisis par les parties, dont l'un seulement se comporte en juge indépendant; il en résulte un déséquilibre qui pourrait compromettre le bon fonctionnement de l'arbitrage, à moins que le Président ne s'en avise et lui apporte les correctifs nécessaires.

Passons donc au cas à l'évidence le plus important, celui de l'**arbitre unique ou président** «neutre» par définition, qui va faire la majorité ou même, en l'absence de cette dernière, va trancher seul (selon les dispositions de règlements d'institutions comme la CCI ou la LCIA, ou de l'article 189 de la loi suisse de droit international privé). Et demandons-nous, compte tenu de la dimension culturelle ou «interculturelle» de l'arbitrage international, ce qu'il faut entendre précisément par cette «neutralité» de l'arbitre-président. Est-elle seulement synonyme d'indépendance ou d'impartialité, ou recouvre-t-elle quelque chose de plus?

Ce sont là des questions tout à fait fondamentales, où se révèlent à notre avis avec le plus d'acuité la dimension culturelle de l'arbitrage international et, en particulier, les oppositions de cultures. Le sujet appellerait des analyses approfondies mais l'on doit ici se contenter, sans trop schématiser, de quelques observations:

La première est que, quoi qu'aiment à prétendre certains, l'indépendance, l'impartialité, l'objectivité, la neutralité – notions voisines – sont des qualités qui **existent** et que l'on rencontre chez la majorité des arbitres d'expérience; non pas qu'elles soient innées, parfaites ou absolues, ou qu'elles n'exigent pas un effort et une discipline constante de l'intéressé, en même temps que des contrôles extérieurs. Mais elles existent.

---

12 P. BELLET, *op. cit., supra* note 3, p. 408.

A l'opposé, on a souvent laissé entendre, naguère, notamment chez certains représentants de pays en développement, que la nationalité politique conditionnait l'attitude de l'arbitre, si bien que les arbitres des pays occidentaux étaient présumés nourrir à l'égard du Tiers-Monde des préjugés hostiles – seule explication possible du fait que certaines sentences arbitrales ne leur avaient pas donné gain de cause! De manière quelque peu analogue, une certaine conception opposait alors au droit international dit classique, instrument de la domination capitaliste, un «droit du développement» correcteur des inégalités. Si cette controverse, au demeurant importante et intéressante, paraît quelque peu dépassée aujourd'hui, il n'en reste pas moins que l'idée de l'impartialité ou de l'objectivité de l'arbitre unique ou président «neutre», n'est pas universellement admise. Et l'on ne saurait ni s'en étonner ni s'en affliger car elle contraint à s'interroger en permanence et à ne rien tenir pour «allant de soi».

Un éminent juriste algérien, Mohamed Bedjaoui, aujourd'hui Président de la Cour de La Haye comme on le sait observait avec raison que «l'arbitre n'est pas un être désincarné et flottant, sans origines ni attaches, ethniques, culturelles, religieuses, sociales … et autres».

Cette vérité n'implique en aucune manière que l'arbitre international, toujours influencé en quelque mesure par son milieu et sa culture d'origine, soit encore modelé par ces derniers au point d'être incapable d'objectivité, comme certains l'on quelquefois laissé entendre, soit par tactique politique, soit par une certaine naïveté.

Cette conception simpliste reflète un curieux déterminisme, selon lequel la personnalité de l'arbitre serait moins importante que son «environnement social». Sans doute, chaque arbitre possède sa nationalité, son domicile, sa formation professionnelle, bref certaines attaches socio-culturelles qui ont contribué à façonner sa *Weltanschauung*, sa vision du monde; mais cela dans une mesure très variable pour chaque individu, et qui sera probablement plus grande si l'intéressé provient d'un pays où règne une religion officielle ou une idéologie d'Etat, et plus faible si l'arbitre appartient à une société pluraliste, laïque et libérale.

Cela rappelé, qui méritait de l'être, constatons les faits: l'arbitre-président ou unique est choisi dans l'immense majorité des cas parmi les ressortissants d'un pays tiers «neutre», c'est-à-dire étranger aux deux parties comme à l'affaire. Il y a là la conséquence d'un phénomène culturel intéressant et plus complexe qu'il n'y paraît. Il est lié au principe fondamental de l'égalité des parties dans l'arbitrage. On peut y voir une sorte de double présomption: présomption qu'une nationalité commune entre le Président et l'une des parties favoriseraient cette dernière et ensuite, négativement, l'idée qu'une nationalité tierce du Président offre une plus grande garantie d'impartialité. Cette «neutralité géographique», pour insuffisante qu'elle soit, apparaît aux parties comme un symbole rassurant, et l'idée semble profondément ancrée dans leurs psychologies.

Mais la vraie neutralité, à notre sens, est beaucoup plus que géographico-politique, elle est culturelle. Cette notion de «neutralité» doit s'entendre en son sens le plus large.

Si l'arbitrage, disait Jean Robert, est essentiellement «un état d'esprit», cela est particulièrement vrai pour la neutralité de l'arbitre international, dont l'impartialité implique certes l'idée d'égalité de traitement, mais encore et surtout, une ouverture d'esprit à la variété des cultures «nationales» des parties, donc une attitude comparative ou, si l'on préfère, «comparatiste», qui doit être aux antipodes du nationalisme, du chauvinisme ou du provincialisme juridiques.

C'est-à-dire le même état d'esprit qui devrait inspirer les négociateurs d'un contrat international et c'est justement son absence, voire une forme d'impérialisme culturel, qui est à l'origine de contrats déséquilibrés qui provoquent une partie des litiges soumis à l'arbitrage international!

C'est dire combien la conception purement géographique ou politique de la neutralité de l'arbitre-président est réductrice et insuffisante. Elle peut conduire à des malentendus ou des erreurs évidentes dans la pratique de l'arbitrage international. Ainsi, dans la célèbre affaire Westland, les représentants de la partie étatique crurent opportun, à un certain moment, de critiquer comme irrégulière, la composition du Tribunal au motif qu'il ne comportait que des Européens sans aucun ressortissant d'un pays en voie de développement. Une critique qui fut rejetée par le Tribunal fédéral suisse, comme totalement dénuée de pertinence, et avec d'autant plus de raison que le litige ne concernait en rien ce qu'on a pu appeler le «droit du développement».

On a dit souvent que «tant vaut l'arbitre, tant vaut l'arbitrage». Pour que l'arbitrage **international** atteigne ses objectifs, et remplisse sa fonction de justice et de pacification, il doit nécessairement être conduit par un arbitre lui aussi «international», neutre au plein sens du terme, c'est-à-dire ouvert à d'autres cultures que la sienne (d'un point de vue juridique comme d'un point de vue plus large, non juridique), apte à comprendre les différentes cultures des parties et de leurs conseils, et à surmonter ou apaiser les oppositions ou les conflits entre ces dernières. René David l'a fort bien dit[13]. Une partie ne peut guère considérer l'arbitrage comme un procédé adéquat de solution des litiges s'il est administré par un arbitre imbu des modes de pensée et des

---

[13] R. DAVID, *The Art of Arbitration*, (in:) MÉLANGES SANDERS (1982), p. 92.

préjugés d'une autre culture. L'arbitre doit donc être international par son état d'esprit «comparatiste», ce qui lui sera non seulement précieux mais indispensable aussi bien s'il s'agit de questions juridiques de fond que de procédure.

On peut penser que ce sont là des truismes: après tout, le système et l'ordre juridiques d'un peuple font partie intégrante de sa culture, d'où non seulement l'existence des conflits de lois, bien entendu, mais aussi la variété des attitudes et des sensibilités des juristes sur nombre de questions, comme l'étendue et les limites de l'autonomie de la volonté, l'influence des «lois de police», le recours au principe général de la bonne foi, l'admissibilité de la théorie de l'imprévision, l'existence ou non d'un ordre public transnational ou d'une *lex mercatoria*, et bien d'autres questions. Les différences sont peut-être plus marquées encore que dans le droit matériel dans le domaine de la procédure, qui a été façonné par l'histoire, les traditions, les usages autant, voire davantage que par des considérations rationnelles. D'où il résulte, assez souvent, de véritables «conflits de cultures», par exemple en matière de preuve, d'interrogation des témoins, pour ne pas parler d'exemples aussi classiques que ceux de la *discovery* ou de la *cross-examination*.

Certes, des rapprochements s'opèrent graduellement dans la pratique internationale, de par la coopération qui s'établit entre arbitres, entre conseils de formation différente. On a pu déceler de nombreux signes de convergences et d'harmonisation, voire parler, peut-être un peu prématurément, de l'apparition d'une culture internationale de l'arbitrage, selon un mouvement parallèle à l'apparition de ce que Berthold Goldman aimait à appeler la «société internationale des commerçants». L'évolution est certaine, avec la globalisation du commerce. Elle ne devrait pas conduire, cependant, à sous-estimer ou nier l'existence ou la possible résurgence de nombreux «conflits de cultures» dans l'arbitrage international, mais au contraire d'en prendre toujours une conscience exacte.

THE INTERNATIONAL JUDICIAL FUNCTION: SOME REFLECTIONS

by

JERZY MAKARCZYK

Introduction

After a long period of co-operation in legal research and diplomacy[1] both of us, I since May 1992, and Professor Skubiszewski since a year and a half later, serve as international judges. Accordingly, when I started considering the subject of my contribution to his Liber Amicorum, I thought that it would perhaps be fitting if I tried to make a few reflections on the international judicial function. The complexity of the task is obvious to me and naturally I intend to concentrate my comments on the position I know best, that of a judge of the European Court of Human Rights. I believe that a thorough study of what has become almost an international judicial profession, with close to a hundred international judges sitting in Europe alone (as compared to the fifteen of the International Court of Justice in 1946) – will soon be undertaken. If basic differences do exist between the various institutions, many problems are common to all, such as independence, status, incompatibilities and many others. But most of all, the role of international adjudication, its impact not only on national courts, but also on decisions of the executive and even on the lawmakers, is growing rapidly. It is then appropirate that the somewhat mysterious figures of those who make the decisions should be better known.

I. THE CANDIDATES

International judges are appointed to office either by elections, or by direct nomination by the Governments. Only in the case of the European Court of Human Rights a parliamentary body, the Parliamentary Assembly, consisting of members of national parliaments, is competent to elect judges by a majority vote from a list of persons nominated by the members of the Council of Europe. The European Community, which also possesses a parliamentary assembly, but consisting of members elected directly by the

---

[1] *See Introduction* at 11–34.

electorate in the member States, adopted perhaps the least democratic method of appointing judges to its judicial institution – by direct Government appointment. This example has been followed by the newly established EFTA tribunal. Only in the United Nations are two principal organs – Security Council and the General Assembly competent simultaneously.[2] The members of the Inter-American Court of Human Rights are elected by secret ballot by an absolute majority vote of the States Parties to the American Convention of Human Rights in the General Assembly of the Organization, from a panel of candidates proposed by those States. A new and interesting division of functions between the General Assembly and the Security Council has been established by the Security Council Resolution 808(1993) in respect of the election of judges of the International Tribunal for former Yugoslavia. According to § 75 of the Resolution, judges should be elected by the General Assembly from a list submitted by the Security Council. The initial list, of not less than 22 and no more than 33 candidates, shall be established by the Council on the basis of names proposed by States, and transmitted to the General Assembly for final election of 11 members of the Tribunal. Thus, both principal organs of the United Nations play a role – one of selector, and the other of elector of judges, a system which is certainly an improvement as compared to the elections to the International Court of Justice.

If the mode and procedures of final elections is of considerable importance, not less and perhaps more so is the process of the selection of candidates within the member States. No matter how good the mode of international election, a highly qualified person will occupy a seat in the international court only if the choice offered to the electing body by competent national organs contains the best names a State may offer. The presentation of a list of persons so qualified is nothing less but a treaty obligation of each member State. Let us consider this problem first.

A. The National Selection

According to art. 39 § 3 of the European Convention on the Protection of Human Rights and Fundamental Freedoms:

---

[2] H. ROLLIN proposed the suppression of the system of double election as early as in 1954: " Je préférerais également voir disparaître le système de double élection. Il n'a manifestement été imaginé que pour introduire dans le fait en faveur des principales puissances le privilège que l'on estimait ne pouvoir leur reconnaître oficiellement, à savoir de compter toujours un juge a la Cour", 2 ANNUAIRE DE L'INSTITUT DE DROIT INTERNATIONAL (1954) at 489.

> "The candidates shall be of high moral character and must either possess qualifications required for appointment to high judicial office or be jurisconsults of recognized competence."

This provision, basically taken from art. 2 of the Statute of the International Court of Justice, differs from its source in three ways. First, there is no mention here of nationality of the candidates; this matter is regulated in § 1 of the quoted article of the Convention, according to which each member State shall nominate three candidates, of whom two at least shall be its nationals. Second, the qualifications requirement is different, as it is enough to be qualified for "high judicial office", and not necessarily the highest one, as in the ICJ's Statute. Last but not least, a quality of being a jurisconsult of recognized competence suffices, as compared to the ICJ's requirements of being recognized as an expert in international law.

It is worth noting that, contrary to the European Convention, the American Convention of Human Rights not only requires that candidates shall be of the highest moral character, but also that they be "… of recognized competence in the field of human rights." So it would in principle not be possible for a member State to put forward a well known specialist in, say, the international law of the sea, who has never contributed in his writings to the development of the law of human rights. Furthermore, the American Convention links the two requirements, and candidates with prospects for election must be both known specialists, and possess qualifications required to occupy in their respective countries the highest judicial functions, which should normally mean that they should be able to sit in the supreme or constitutional courts.

This evolution is, of course, in part explained by historical factors – at the time of drafting or even entry into force of the European Convention it would have been very difficult to find candidates with internationally recognized expertise in the field of international human rights. But it can be further seen in the drafting of statutes of newly created international courts, like the International Criminal Tribunals for the Former Yugoslavia and Rwanda, where the notion of equitable geographic representation has been happily partly abandoned in the text (practice is another matter), and where emphasis was placed on a practical qualification, namely expertise in criminal law and international law, including humanitarian law and human rights law.[3]

---

[3] Only Art. 13 point c of the Statute of the International Tribunal for the Prosecution of Persons Responsible for Serious Violations of International Humanitarian Law Committed in the Territory of Former Yugoslavia since 1991 (later called International Criminal Tribunal for Former

Noting the importance of this evolution, which indicates the growing specialization of international courts, one should remember that one qualification is permanent and will certainly remain so. That is the exigency of the high, or highest as the case may be, moral stranding of the candidate.

This factor is fundamental for the authority of any court, but especially for an international one. It is at the same time the most difficult to grasp and evaluate. Still, no effort in this direction should, in my view, be spared.

One difficulty is – who is competent to proceed with the evaluation of a candidate in respect of his moral standing – the nominating State or the electing organ? Is the latter interfering in a domestic matters of a State if the candidates presented by the government find no approval in that organ, what is not a purely theoretical problem, considering the recent experience of the Consultative Assembly of the Council of Europe?[4] What test should be applied both domestically and internationally? To what extent should a candidate to the elucidation of potential difficulties? Should scrutiny apply only to new candidates or to judges seeking reelection as well, who could have changed during their long mandate not only as far as professional qualifications are concerned? Such examples could be multiplied.

It is understandable that the situation varies greatly depending of the kind of tribunal to which the candidate applies. For example, in the case of human rights courts, or international criminal courts, the requirement of experience granting access to the highest judicial organs may, for some countries, give rise to conflict with the moral standing criterion. Indeed, somebody who as a judge or prosecutor participated actively in his own country in the breaches of human rights, particularly in breaches made in the name of the law, manipulated to serve the political interests of the ruling party, should be excluded by his own State, and if he is not, should be ruled out at the international level. But this in turn requires the possession by the international organ of qualifications and knowledge to decide on matters which in fact and law should be determined internally. Some attempts in this direction undertaken by the Assembly of the Council of Europe will be discussed later.[5]

This problem, as recent experience has shown, is far from theoretical. When the judgment in *McCann and Others* case[6] was delivered in 1995, the less respectable sections of the British press published the *curricula vitae* of all

Yugoslavia) mentions the requirement of taking due account of the adequate representation of the principal legal systems of the world (IT/32 REV. 7).

4 *See infra*, note 19.

5 *See infra* at 798–799.

6 EUR. COURT H.R., *McCann and Others v. Great Britain Judgment of 1995 September 27th*, Series A, N° 324.

European Court's judges who voted for a violation by Great Britain of Art. 2 of the European Convention, intending of course to discredit them because of their alleged past activities under the communist or other totalitarian systems. There was not much to find, except that some judges got their education in universities in their respective countries or held one or other judicial or administrative position. But the press was obviously unable to know, and was not interested in knowing, how they performed their functions, since the aim was to discredit the judges and of course the judgment itself. This shows the importance of proper selection inside the countries and the responsibility of States to ensure that nobody who has been discredited under the *ancien régime* ever reaches the position of international judicial eligibility.

Next comes the equally important problem of professional qualifications. Here the criteria are perhaps more transparent, which does not mean that the issue is straightforward. It is, of course, quite different in various international judicial organs, even though the statutory provisions may be comparable or identical.

I do not intend in this short essay or am able to go into much detail, but perhaps some remarks concerning particular courts could usefully be made.

As far as the International Court of Justice is concerned, the problem, and especially the controversy between articles 2 and 9 of the Statute are sufficiently known to be further commented on here. The basic question remains: what would be the ideal composition of the world's highest judicial organ from the view point of those it is intended to serve, namely States but also, through advisory opinions, the United Nations system of organizations? It is in my view clear that to serve this purpose the ICJ should be elected not on the basis of the criteria of article 9, in other words geographic equitability, but exclusively on the basis of professional qualifications.[7] As to the latter, I do not think that the capacity of occupying the highest judicial function in the respective countries is, considering the development of international law and its specialization – relevant any longer. As Hersh Lauterpacht rightly stated forty-two years ago:

> "... it is necessary to bear in mind that unless a very substantial number of judges possess such expert knowledge of international law the efficacy and the authority of the Court are bound to suffer."[8]

---

[7] *See* J. MAKARCZYK, *The International Court of Justice in the Changing Political Environment*, (in:) PERSPECTIVES ON INTERNATIONAL LAW, Kluwer Law (1995), Chapter 14, at 302–304.

[8] *See* 2 ANNUAIRE DE L'INSTITUT DE DROIT INTERNATIONAL (1954), Vol. I at 478.

The difficulty lies in the definition of the expression "substantial number". If these words were true in 1954, when such domains of international law as the protection of the environment or human rights, to mention but two, did not in practice exist, the "substantial number" now should simply mean fifteen.

The qualifications of candidates for such courts as the Court of Justice of the European Communities or the EFTA judicial organ pose specific problems, but if expertise in international economic law, the Community Law and certainly constitutional and civil law of member States seems essential, there is also room for specialists in public international law. After all, both institutions have to interpret and apply international treaties.

This is also the case with the European Court of Human Rights, even if the essential requirement is a comparative knowledge of all branches of the domestic legal systems.

Let us concentrate briefly on the professional qualifications of its judges, taking into account not just the strictly formal criteria, but also the practical ones.

It should be stressed from the outset, that although the Convention does not specify a requirement of being a specialist in public international law, many judges were indeed prominent experts in our field, to mention just Lord Waldock, McNair, Fitzmaurice, Balladore Pallieri or Mosler.

Four of them sat, sometimes at the same time, in the International Court of Justice.[9] This was possible of course because of the much lighter workload of both tribunals, and would be hardly conceivable nowadays. That knowledge of public international law is essential in the European Court stems not only from the character of the international treaty it is bound to apply, but also from specific provisions of the Convention. For example according to Article 26, the Commission may only deal with the matter after all domestic remedies have been exhausted, accordingly to the generally recognized rules of international law. The same applies in the Court which must on several occasions deal with the question of admissibility.[10] It is true that views among international lawyers vary substantially in this respect and the greater their number, the more difficult it can be to reach a common standpoint. But speaking seriously, this problem, with which the Court is confronted more and more often cannot be properly solved and the right deci-

---

[9] In the actual Court, Judges BERNHARDT, FOIGHEL, MAKARCZYK, MATCHER, VALTICOS and WILDHABER are public international lawyers. Judge Valticos served twice as judge *ad hoc* at the ICJ.

[10] Among the most recent Judgments *see e.g. Akdivar and Others v. Turkey*, Judgment of September 16th, Reports of Judgments and Decisions of the ECHR, 1996, and *Louizidon v. Turkey*, of March 23rd 1995, Series A, N° 310.

sion taken by internal lawyers alone. Or, under Article 15, in time of war or other public emergency threatening the life of the nation any High Contracting Party may take measures derogating from its obligations under the Convention to the extent strictly required by the exigencies of the situation, provided that such measures are not inconsistent with its other obligations under international law. Also, the Court has with increased frequency dealt with matters concerning the extraterritorial application of the Convention, where States may be prohibited from expelling from their territory aliens who may than be exposed to torture or inhuman or degrading treatment prohibited under Article 3 of the Convention. Here we enter into the very core of State sovereignty.[11]

It is clear than that the European Court of Human Rights must include judges who are specialists in public international law, and that their role in the work of the Court is likely to increase. It will therefore be imperative to ensure that when the new Court is elected after the still hypothetical entry into force of Protocol N° 11 to the Convention, this need is duly taken into account. It must be added here that since May 1992 not a single judge elected by the Assembly has been a public international lawyer.

Unlike the World Court, the requirement of being capable of sitting in the high domestic judicial bodies is here fully justified. It is wise that the text speaks of "high" and not "highest" judicial offices, as it is better to have a younger judge but fulfilling all the conditions of the first part of art. 39 § 3 of the Convention. In fact, a predominant number of judges in the European Court before the rapid increase in membership after admission to the Council of Europe of countries from Eastern and Central Europe were either present or past judges or presidents of the highest domestic judicial bodies.

Now moving to the strictly practical aspects, one could well start at the beginning and mention the linguistic abilities. It may indeed be said that no one can pretend to compete in the Tour de France without first learning to ride a bicycle. Perfect knowledge in speaking and reading of at least one of the official languages of each court, normally English and French, is an essential requirement for any candidate. Judges should not only be able to participate freely in deliberations, and not just to read a prepared statement, but also be able to question the parties at hearings. The ability to draft a judgment or a dissenting opinion is another requirement. The national authorities have the responsibility of checking the linguistic aptitudes of candidates and the ways and means they do so is their internal affair, as long as the result

---

[11] *See e.g.* Judgments in the case of *Vilvarajah v. the United Kingdom* of October 30th, 1991, Series A, N° 215. *Cruz Varas & Others v. Sweden* of March 20th, 1991, *ibid.* N° 201, *Vijayanathan and Pusperajah v. France* of August 27th, 1992, N° 241-B.

proves satisfactory. Of course, a judge may become familiar with the particular legal terminology used in his court during the first months of his mandate, but otherwise his fluency is a prerequisite.

Other qualities to be verified during the selection process are perhaps less tangible, and it is indeed difficult even to enumerate them. Certainly it is good for any court to have members with some previous political experience. Particularly in the human rights courts, and international criminal courts, judges who have in the past held political or high administrative positions may be free of a certain complex sometimes present in the representatives of the *troisième pouvoir* against those who belong to the executive. Many judges are academics by profession and the lively debate in Great Britain concerning the ability of professors to be good judges is quite pertinent.[12] Another matter is the capacity of seeing things in a broad international perspective. As a well-known if controversial American author, speaking about the ability of serving well in the World Court puts it:

> "It involves shaping a frame of mind..., developing an ability to see things from another nation's point of view as well as from your own nation's, and then further refining this mental attitude to synthesize a new, objective point of view that transcends particularistic national myopia."[13]

Even if "synthesizing a new objective point of view" may seem slightly vague, this definition in my opinion synthesizes successfully the basic requirements which any international judge should fulfill. The European Court of Human Rights frequently stresses in its judgments that the Convention is a living instrument and must be interpreted and applied according to the social development of the region it covers. A judge, when deciding a case, especially concerning his own State, must be able to bear in mind that his decision should not only solve a particular human case, but serve to create a homogenous legal system in the enlarged democratic Europe. This ability is a basic requirement which applies to all judges, both from the old democracies and the new ones.

B. The Selectors

Candidates to all courts except the International Court of Justice are, at the domestic level, selected by their respective Governments. According to Art. 4 of its Statute, members shall be elected by the General Assembly and

---

[12] THE TIMES, 17 and 22 April 1996.

[13] A. D'AMATO, *Remarks* (in a discussion on the World Court), (in:) AMERICAN SOCIETY OF INTERNATIONAL LAW, PROCEEDINGS OF THE ANNUAL MEETING (1986).

by the Security Council from a list of persons nominated by the national groups in the Permanent Court of Arbitration. This exclusion of the administration of a State from the process has largely proved a fiction, even if some exceptions to the rule can be indicated.[14] So has also been the provision of Art. 6 of the Statute, which recommends that each national group consult its highest court of justice, its legal faculties and schools of law, and its national academies and national sections of international academies devoted to the study of the law before making the nominations.

But the general direction indicated by these provisions, at least the second of them, merits serious consideration and support. The second, because the first, which has largely proved unsuccessful in respect of the ICJ, would encounter fierce opposition from States as far as courts so important for their domestic legal systems as the courts of human rights, or the courts of integration institutions are concerned.

But none of the statutes of courts other than the World Court contains provisions about consulting national judicial organs and the academic community about possible candidates, even if in those courts such an opinion, considering the importance of the decisions for domestic courts, would be of great importance. It would be essential not only to reach the principal aim of selecting the very best, but also for the authority of the international judicial body within the member State and for its co-operation with national courts, the quality of which is vital for the success of both. Even Protocol N° 11 to the European Convention, a totally new document, simply reiterates the original provisions, without even introducing the requirement included in the American Convention on Human Rights, that candidates should be renowned specialists in human rights law. It is not because of lack of desire to innovate, as in further provisions the position of future judges is indeed significantly altered, not necessarily to their advantage.

In other words, States are totally free to proceed with the selection as they think fit. Methods vary from country to country; normally two administrative agencies are involved – justice and foreign affairs. Decisions on consultations with national courts and the academic community, if any, are left entirely up to each State.

---

14 *E.g.* to the knowledge of this author, the candidature of Professor Jessup was successfully supported by the American national group at the Permanent Court of Arbitration against the candidate of the Administration.

II. THE ELECTIONS

The motives for the inclusion of art. 9 into the Statutes of both the Permanent Court of International Justice and its successor, the International Court of Justice are well known. Still, it may be useful to repeat here the commendably frank statement made by the president of the Advisory Committee of Jurists in 1920:

> "The President thought that the clause which he had proposed with reference to the representation of civilizations and legal systems would ensure in so far as humanly possible the desired result, that is to say the representation of the Great Powers."[15]

Nothing has changed since then, nor for that matter in the lack of respect for the Art. 2 requirement that judges be elected regardless of their nationality. As Hudson puts it, this provision:

> "... can hardly be taken seriously ... for it might easily wreck an international judicial institution."[16]

Indeed, the results of elections held between 1921 and 1938 were largely determined by the nationality of the candidates, and those held after the Second World War, by the influence of the political blocks. The postulate that the judges of the World Courts be elected exclusively following the criterion of professional competence was always considered unrealistic. There are few indications that a change of attitude of States is to be expected.

The elections to the human rights courts poses other kinds of problems, as both in the European and the American Court the number of seats corresponds either to the membership of the Council of Europe or to the number of States bound by the American Convention on Human Rights. Under Protocol N° 11 to the European Convention, only States which have ratified the Convention will be entitled to have a seat at the Court.

The qualities required of a candidate have also been modified in the Protocol N° 11 so as to correspond to the permanent functioning of the Court. Under the old system, judges were prohibited from holding any position incompatible with their independence or impartiality as members of the Court or the demands of office. New provisions speak about independence, impartiality and availability required by a full-time activity.[17]

---

15 Permanent Court of International Justice, Advisory Committee of Jurists, PROCES-VERBAUX, The Hague (1920) at 371.

16 M. HUDSON, *ibid.* at 262.

17 Protocol N° 11, art. 21 para. 3.

A brief comment on the permanent character of the new Court seems to be appropriate at this point. In my opinion, and fully understanding the importance of accelerating the procedures, the transforming of the European Court of Human Rights into a permanent body, with an extremely heavy workload, including all the work done actually by the Commission, is a grave mistake. I do not have in mind here the fact that for some States the fulfillment by the same organ and by the same judges of functions of investigating judges, magistrates trying to encourage a friendly settlement between the parties and judges deciding the case is unconstitutional. Things differ in various legal systems. But one thing is common: in my view in the long run, to be a useful member of any human rights court, a judge cannot afford to lose touch with not only his own legal system, but also with political and social conditions prevailing in his State. What can a person know about such conditions after six or, as the case may be, twelve years of being permanently absent? What is quite feasible for tribunals such as the ICJ or the Luxembourg Court, is in my view not appropriate here.

Returning to the elections proper, a list of three candidates, established in order of preference, is transmitted by the Government to the Secretary General, who presents it to the Committee of Ministers,which is competent to deliberate and decide on the transmission of the document to the Assembly. The role of the Committee members is purely formal, as they are not competent to comment about a decision made by their equals.[18] So the whole responsibility of the election falls on the parliamentarians.

And this responsibility is quite heavy. The difficulty of the task also arises from the fact that the information on candidates consists formally only in documents obtained from the governments, which only provide a more or less detailed *curriculum vitae*. The desires of governments, expressed in the order of names, do not necessarily help to make a proper decision.

Still, the Assembly has recently taken its task very seriously, and the rejection of a whole list presented by Romania in 1994, is a precedent which raises the question as to whether the parliamentary organ is acting in accordance with the Convention when refusing to take a vote.[19]

In my view, such a right should be recognized if the election process is not to be considered as a mere formality. That such situations should be care-

---

[18] In a recent document of a Member State transmitted to the Secretary General of the Council of Europe one can find, among other ideas, the project of consultations to be carried out by governments in respect of potential candidates. Apparently, such a practice exists in the election of judges to the Court of Justice of the European Communities.

[19] Formally, the Assembly did not proceed to a vote in accordance with Art. 39 of the Convention, but refused to consider the coresponding agenda, item. A new list has been presented by Romania only two years later.

fully avoided is another matter. But perhaps a different interpretation of the words "shall be elected by the Consultative Assembly" could also be possible, according to the general rules of interpretation of treaties.

To ensure a better knowledge of candidates the Parliamentary Assembly voted on the 22 April 1996 a Resolution on the procedure for examining candidatures for the election of judges to the European Court of Human Rights.[20]

Paragraph 3 of the Resolution reads as follows:

> "Now that a new Court is to be set up on a fully professional basis, with judges residing permanently in Strasbourg, the Assembly wishes to improve its own procedure for the selection of candidates from the three proposed by the Contracting Party concerned."

For this purpose, it was considered useful for the information to be provided by the candidates to be presented systematically and on broadly similar lines to facilitate comparison amongst them. Consequently, a model *curriculum vitae* should be established and sent to each candidate who will complete the document as part of his or her submission of candidature. The model *curriculum vitae* is annexed to and forms an integral part of the Resolution.

According to paragraph 5, the Assembly shall undertake to call upon candidates to participate in a personal interview, to be organized in Strasbourg by the Sub-Committee on Human Rights or by an *ad hoc* sub-committee of the Committee on Legal Affairs and Human Rights.

It does not matter that this Resolution contains several errors, first of all in that it refers to the candidates as submitting their names for election. Of course, this is done by the respective governments, and not by the persons concerned. Second, when drafting and voting the document, the Assembly should normally know which of its subsidiary organs is empowered to conduct the interviews.

What is important on the contrary is that for the first time in the process of electing persons to such high and responsible position, the electing organ undertakes an attempt to check the qualifications of each candidate presented by the governments. Whether such a procedure will be effective is another matter. That will very much depend on the professional qualities of the interviewers. But the attempt, proposed many times in other contexts, is most certainly a constructive one, tending to make the election authentic.

---

20 Resolution 1082 (1996). *See* Doc. 7439, report of the Committee on Legal Affairs and Human Rights (Rapporteur: Lord KIRKHILL).

One might, however, have doubts as to some questions on the model *curriculum vitae* for candidates seeking election. It includes all the routine information as to personal details, education and academic and other qualifications, professional activities, including details of judicial activities, data on non-judicial legal activities and finally details of all non-legal professional activities. Also, questions on activities and experience in the field of human rights have to be answered, filling the gap left by article 21 of Protocol N° 11. But paragraph V of the questionnaire gives rise to serious doubts. The questions are as follows: posts held in a political party; duration; membership of parliament.

If the third question could well be answered under the heading "details of all not legal professional activities", the first too clearly indicates that the parliamentarians' choice could be dictated by their political preferences. Everybody knows that this consideration can hardly be avoided in a parliamentary organ. But making it an official part of a questionnaire serving to elect the best judges to a court of law is of course quite another matter.

The questionnaire closes with questions concerning other activities, publications and other works and finally the linguistic abilities, with special reference to the official languages of the Court.

Another question is – who will have to complete the questionnaire and attend the proposed interview – new candidates or also judges seeking re-election? The question is a delicate one and I would rather be tempted to leave it to be solved by practice.

III. THE ELECTED

According to Art. 6 of the European Convention, everybody is entitled to a fair and public hearing within a reasonable time by an independent and impartial tribunal established by law.

This principle obviously applies also to those appearing before international tribunals, even if some doubts are being voiced as to whether the last one to appear on the international arena was indeed so established.[21]

I will not dwell on this matter, and in this last part of these reflections concentrate on conditions of independence and impartiality which apply to international judges to be elected to the European Court of Human Rights under Protocol N° 11 to the Convention.

---

21 *See* Report of the Secretary-General Pursuant to Paragraph 2 of Security Council Resolution 808 (1993), in particular at I, THE LEGAL BASIS FOR THE ESTABLISHMENT OF THE INTERNATIONAL TRIBUNAL.

It is clear that independence and impartiality are above all a state of mind. A judge may have all objective conditions fulfilled and still be unable to be independent, whereas another judge may suffer the worst pressures and keep the highest standards of both. These things are very difficult to assess, as the experience of the European Court trying to decide on the so-called subjective impartiality of judges clearly shows. It would be tempting to deal with these matters more in detail, but there is no space, as it seems necessary to consider rather the conditions created by the international lawmakers as far as independence of judges is concerned. If this is essential in national courts, it is equally and perhaps more so in the international ones.

Let me start with a very difficult matter, which results from Art. 5 of the Protocol:

> " Without prejudice to the provisions of articles 3 and 4, the mandates of the judges, members of the Commission, registrar and deputy registrar expire on the date of the entry into force of the present Protocol."

According to article 40 of the Convention:

> "The members of the Court shall be elected for nine years. They may be reelected."

Although, under Art. 6 of the Protocol, the term of the mandate has been reduced to six years (and I will comment later on this) it may be said that the basic principle of the stability of the mandate has been violated here, and without any good reasons being given. Indeed, one would have thought that a system where a sitting judge would complete his term of nine years and the rotation would be progressive thus permitting a smooth transition from an old to the new court should be much more appropriate, respecting at the same time the mutual commitment of the judge and the parliamentary organ expressed in the act of election. It is maintained that Protocol N° 11, being in itself an international treaty signed and ratified by all member States, constitutes *lex posterioris* as against the Convention. That may well be so, but the situation has grave consequences firstly for the independence of the judges, and second, potentially for the stability of the Court's case law.

One can well imagine a situation where a judge, elected for nine years will in fact not sit in a single case, if the Protocol comes into force shortly after his election, or will sit for several months only. It is well known that every member of the Court, no matter which may have been his previous experience, needs a certain time to adapt to the ways and means of the Court's work. This period may vary, but half a year is a safe assessment. Protocol

N° 11 may well be *lex posterioris*, but in an organization whose main task is to induce member States to be democratic and to respect the rule of law the solution is at least strange.

But of even greater importance is the possible lack of continuity in the Court's case-law. It may be accepted that in all probability at least some experienced members of the Court will be again presented by their governments and re-elected; this is only a probability, and political changes in several countries may make it unrealistic. If that were to be the case, I can hardly imagine how a completely new institution, with the burden of fulfilling the duties of both the Commission and the Court, will be able to cope with its task.

Last but not least, the proposed solutions create within the Court the climate of uncertainty and of living in a period of transition. Newly elected judges have before them the formidable task of becoming acquainted with the details of the Court's enormous case-law.[22] Those elected in the early nineties do not know which part of their mandate they will be in practice able to serve. These are not the conditions in which the Court should perform its ever growing duties.[23]

A new article has been introduced by Protocol N° 11, which reads as follows:

> "A judge may be removed from his function only if other judges decide, by a two third majority that he no longer fulfills the conditions required."[24]

This rule, which in itself is another indication that a duly elected judge cannot be removed during the term of his mandate otherwise than by a decision of his peers, is modeled on article 18 § 1 of the ICJ's Statute. It may be mentioned that it did not exist in the original text of the Convention, but was included in the Rules of the Court, established by the Court itself, and that unanimity was required to remove a judge from his function. I would not argue with the fact that a unanimous decision is a very strong safeguard, perhaps too strong, but would on the contrary question the justification of this change offered in the Explanatory Report prepared by the Council of Europe. According to the Report, this measure tends to assure the independence of the Court!

---

22 Over 120 volumes.

23 If in 1995 the Court decided 85 cases, the prospects for 1996 may safely be estimated at more than one hundred.

24 Article 24.

Let us now return to the question of the term of the mandate, reduced as mentioned above by three years. It is true that the American Court of Human Right uses a 6-year term, but in the International Court of Justice it is 9, and even here proposals were made several times to increase this term to 12 or even 15 years, at the same time eliminating the possibility of re-election. There is no doubt that a relatively long mandate is a primary guarantee of judicial independence and the right of re-election may be potentially used by States to exercise undue pressure on the judge seeking it. I do not say that any judge would yield to such pressures. But the very existence of such an opportunity for a State, where a change of political regime can easily take place in the meantime, is improper and should be avoided. So this solution goes against the general trend and can only be explained with great difficulty, if one rejects as abhorrent the idea that perhaps some interests of the administrations are involved.

Also the justification for reducing the age limit for judges to 70 years is not convincing. In the Report quoted above it is said that this change (there was no age limit under the Convention) results from the fact that the Court will now sit permanently. This is no argument at all, and if some age limit is perhaps useful, considering the experience of this and other international tribunals the limit of 75 would seem more appropriate.

Let us briefly consider, to close these few remarks, the problem of taxation of the emoluments of the judges.

One could normally expect, that Protocol N° 11, creating a permanent Court, will deal with this delicate matter, which is now only regulated in an additional Protocol N° 5 to the Convention on Privileges and Immunities of the Council of Europe.[25] This Protocol has attracted ratification by less than half of the member States. Some have clearly displayed a determined intention never to ratify it.

When the Permanent Court of International Justice was created, it was decided that the judges must, as a statutory rule, be free as far as their emoluments are concerned, from all national taxes. This provision have been maintained in the Statute of the ICJ. It has never been the question of funding, as tax collected from one person by the State really does not have much impact on its budget. Rather, it is a question of principle; it has been considered that such a provision, formulated in an international treaty, will create for those called to solve disputes among States the necessary conditions of total independence from any influence from the State of origin. Let me say it quite clearly: it may be, just as the right to seek re-election, a potential

[25] Ratified by Poland on April 22, 1993.

weapon in the hands of the administration. Again, I am not saying any judge would yield to it or even that any State will ever try to use it. But its very existence is contrary to the principle of independence of an international judge. If the authors of the Protocol were so strongly inspired by the ICJ Statute, why did they not copy this model provision?

This is not just a matter of principle. It is well known that in the present Court the remuneration is normally not the main source of the income of the judges. But that will not be so in a permanent Court. The situation will then be, that some judges will in fact receive half of the salary of some of their colleagues.

Secondly, a State which taxes its judge in fact does nothing other than to reduce its contribution to the budget of the organizations, taking away with one hand what was given with the other. This puts States in a position of inequality.

Conclusion

These remarks are, as I have thought them to be, only an introduction to a subject which seems to be increasingly topical. Many important questions have been left aside, but perhaps some, addressed rather than answered, could be usefully discussed further. If my closing remarks concerning some specific aspects of Protocol N° 11 to the European Convention may seem somewhat severe, they are in my view largely deserved. I am an objective commentator, as I do not intend to serve as judge under its provisions. As I have said, a human rights judge detached from his environment could not, in my view, properly fulfill his mission.

THE GENERAL LIST OF THE INTERNATIONAL COURT OF JUSTICE

by

SHABTAI ROSENNE

The question of the General List of the International Court of Justice, not as a technical adminstrative matter but as a legal issue, has recently come into prominence. Its development is examined in this article.[1]

I

There is no mention of the General List in the Statute of the Court. Its legal significance is partly the outcome of successive versions of the Rules of Court, and partly originated in State practice in connection with the discontinuance of a case. More recently the presence of an "unwilling respondent" in a case has added a new dimension in connection with objections to the admissibility of an application or possibly to the jurisdiction of the Court.

The original organization of the Permanent Court as expressed in the Rules of 1922 was that the Court would meet in sessions each year, and that the Registry would maintain separate lists of contentious and advisory cases submitted to the Court, together with lists for each session (Rules of 1922/1926/1931, Article 23). This required the Registrar to maintain the archives in accordance with the arrangements laid down; and on the matter examined here required each case to have a "file number" (*numéro de dossier*). Other provisions dealt with the session lists and related matters.

The concept of the General List was introduced in Article 38 of the Rules of 1931. This required that:

> "The general list of cases submitted to the Court for decision or for advisory opinion shall be prepared and kept up to date by the Registrar on

---

1 The Rules of Court to which reference is made are as follows: PERMANENT COURT OF INTERNATIONAL JUSTICE [PCIJ] – Rules of 24 March 1922, International Intermediary Institute, The Hague (1922); Rules of 31 July 1926, PCIJ, Ser. D, N° 1 (1926); Rules of 21 February 1931, PCIJ, Ser. D, N° 1)2nd ed., 1926); Rules of 11 March 1936, *ibid.* (4th ed., 1940): INTERNATIONAL COURT OF JUSTICE [ICJ] – Rules of 6 May 1946, ICJ, ACTS AND DOCUMENTS CONCERNING THE ORGANIZATION OF THE COURT, N° 1 (2nd ed., 1947); Rules of 10 May 1972, *ibid.* N° 3 (1977); Rules of 14 April 1978, *ibid.* N° 5 (1989). The 1946, 1972 and 1978 RULES OF THE INTERNATIONAL COURT OF JUSTICE are reproduced in my compilation DOCUMENTS ON THE INTERNATIONAL COURT OF JUSTICE, First Bilingual Edition (1991).

> the instructions of and subject to the authority of the President. Cases shall be entered in the list and numbered successively according to the date of the receipt of the document submitting the case to the Court."

This was introduced on the proposal of Judge Fromageot who explained that his object in proposing the creation of a General List was to prevent it being possible to give one case preference over another which had been entered higher on the List.[2] The General List existed alongside the session lists. No further consequences were included in the 1931 revision of the Rules.

In 1936, Article 25 of the new Rules introduced the concept of the judicial year (*l'année judiciaire*) in place of sessions. Article 38 of the 1931 Rules was retained as Article 20, with drafting amendments. The session lists were abolished, and in their place Article 20, paragraph 2, set out 20 headings which the General List was to contain. Heading III was the date of registration; heading XVII was the result (nature and date), and heading XIX removal from list (cause and date). Paragraph 3 required the General List to contain a space for notes, if any, and spaces for the inscription, above the initials of the President and of the Registrar, of the dates of the entry of the case, of its result, or of its removal from the list, as the case may be.

At the same time, one of the functions of the General List was indicated in Article 46:

> "1. Subject to the priority resulting from Article 61 of the present Rules [relating to provisional measures of protection], cases submitted to the Court will be taken in the order in which they become ready for hearing. When several cases are ready for hearing, the order in which they shall be taken is determined by the position which they occupy in the General List.
>
> 2. Nevertheless, the Court may, in special circumstances, decide to take a case in priority to other cases which are ready for hearing, and which precede it in the General List.
>
> 3. If the parties to a case which is ready for hearing are agreed in asking for the case to be put after other cases which are ready for hearing and which follow in the General List, the President may grant an adjournment: if the parties are not in agreement, the President decides whether or not to submit the question to the Court."

This arrangement was retained as Articles 20 and 46 of the Rules of 1946 and Articles 20 and 50 of the Rules of 1972.

In 1978, however, the Rules were changed completely. The previous Article 20 was replaced by Article 16, paragraph 1, which sets out in gen-

---

2 PCIJ (1931), Ser. D, N° 2, Addendum 2 96.

eral terms the functions of the Registrar. Subparagraph 1(b) requires the Registrar to keep, under the supervision of the President, and in such form as may be laid down by the Court, a General List of all cases, entered and numbered in the order in which the documents instituting proceedings or requesting an advisory opinion are received in the Registry. This replaces the 20 headings of the previous Rules. That provision has to be read in conjunction with Article 14 of the Instructions for the Registry.[3] By this

> "... Any failure to conform to the directions of the Statute or Rules which may be noted by him [the Registrar] in a document instituting proceedings or in a pleading will be brought by him to the notice of the party or person from whom the document emanates."

This is an independent and autonomous power of the Registrar from which there is no appeal, and his decision holds until the Court takes the matter under its consideration. So far as is known, the Registrar has used this power only once to refuse to accept a document purporting to be an application instituting proceedings. In a letter of 18 February 1994 he informed the Government of Yugoslavia that

> "In exercise of my duty under the Statute and Rules of Court, I have carefully examined [a communication incorporating an application instituting proceedings against the member States of NATO] from the standpoint of formal compliance with the procedural requirements laid down by those texts.
>
> With regret I have to inform you that I am unable to regard your communication as constituting an 'application' justifying action by me under Article 40 of the Statute and Article 38 of the Rules of Court...
>
> I observe that no indication at all is given in your communication of any legal grounds of jurisdiction whatever; nor is any claim presented, as distinct from a request for the indication of provisional measures. Nor can the communication be accepted as a request, formally valid, for the indication of provisional measures ... No case exists until an application, formally valid, has been filed instituting proceedings."

He therefore did not propose taking any further action on that communication.[4]

At the same time, former Article 46 was completely recast as Article 54. The date for oral proceedings is to be fixed by the Court, or by the President

---

[3] YEARBOOK OF THE INTERNATIONAL COURT OF JUSTICE 1946–1947 at 66, amended in *ibid.* 1949–1950 at 74. Reproduced in my compilation of DOCUMENTS, *supra* note 1, at 453. Article 16 of the Instructions for the Registry of the Permanent Court was identical in this respect. *See* M.O. HUDSON, THE PERMANENT COURT OF INTERNATIONAL JUSTICE 1922–1942 (1943) at 762.

[4] M. BULAJIĆ, ALTERNATIVE YUGOSLAVIA TRIBUNAL (1995) at 209.

if the Court is not sitting; and the Court is to have regard for the priority required for cases of provisional measures of protection and to any other special circumstances, including the urgency of a particular case. There is no provision in the 1978 Rules dealing specifically with the contingency that several cases should be ready for hearing at the same time. Under general principle this should probably be a matter for the full Court, the decision to be taken in light not only of the dates upon which the different cases became ready for hearing, but also of their places in the General List, and subject to the priorities to be given to other cases under the Statute or other Rules of Court. There is no explanation why the Court cancelled the objective criterion for the taking of cases when more than one is ready for hearing at a given moment.[5]

The Rules of Court are supplemented by the Instructions for the Registry. For the present purpose it is sufficient to refer to the current Instructions, those issued in 1946 and still in force. Article 6 requires the Registrar in accordance with the relevant provision of the Rules to prepare and keep up to date the General List of cases submitted to the Court for judgment or advisory opinion. Article 46, on the archives, prescribes in paragraph 3 that the archives will contain the General List of cases, and that in case of doubt the Registrar will decide in which file a document shall be placed. That is all.

II

With regard to the termination of proceedings, in the Rules of 1936 Article 68, dealing with agreement to discontinue the proceedings, provided that the order recording the conclusion of the settlement or the discontinuance of the proceedings "will prescribe the removal of the case from the list". A similar provision appears in Article 69, paragraph 1, on the unilateral discontinuance of a case instituted by application. This has been repeated in Articles 68 and 69 of the Rules of 1946, Articles 73 and 74 of the Rules of 1972, and Articles 88 and 89 of the Rules of 1978.

It seems that the origin of this addition was a remark by Judge Fromageot, to the effect that there was no indication of how the discontinuance (in ei-

[5] This contingency occurred in January 1996. On 31 December 1995 the following cases were ready for hearing, their position in the General List and the date on which they became ready for hearing being indicated: *Aerial Incident of 4 July 1989* case (N° 79, 9 September 1992 – hearings had been fixed for this case in September 1994, but were suspended at the request of both parties in their attempt to settle the case); *Oil Platforms* case (N° 90, 1 July 1994); *Gabčikovo-Nagymaros Project* case (N° 92, 20 June 1995); *Application of Genocide Convention* case (N° 91, 14 November 1995); *Application of the Montreal Convention of 1971* cases (N°s 88, 89, 22 December 1995) – an unprecedented pile-up.

ther case) was to be done. The record goes on to report his remark that this was normally done by way of order. "It would be a good thing to say so in the Rules," adding that the Court would order the case to be struck out of the list.[6] A vote was taken on the question of the removal of the case from the list, and the proposal was adopted unanimously.[7] No further explanation was given for this addition. In fact that had been the practice of the Court in all cases of agreed termination or unilateral discontinuance of a case, with one exception.[8] The first instance of this was when the applicant (Belgium) requested the removal of the case from the List when it discontinued the *Denunciation of the Treaty of 2 November 1865 between China and Belgium* case, and the order of the Permanent Court included an appropriate operative paragraph.[9] The Permanent Court included such a paragraph even when it had not been directly requested.[10]

III

The versions of the Rules of 1936/1946/1972 do nothing to affect the administrative quality of the General List or its function in relation to the determination of the order in which cases ready for hearing shall be taken. They establish that a folio is opened with the receipt in the Registry of a document instituting proceedings, and is closed either by the termination of the proceedings through a judgment or an advisory opinion, or by an order in an instance of termination by agreement or unilateral discontinuance. While the opening of the folio is a matter for the Registrar, acting under the authority of the President (and subject to the Registrar's power under the

6 2 PCIJ (1935), Ser. D, Add. 3 at 313 (meeting of 22 February).

7 *Ibid.* at 317.

8 The exception was the first order terminating a case by agreement, in the *Chorzów Factory* case, 18/19 PCIJ, Ser. A, at 13. Here the Court simply declared that the proceedings "are terminated".That this differentiation was deliberate in a case terminated by agreement is demonstrated by the fact that this order was made on the same day – 25 May 1929 – as the order in the Belgium–China case mentioned in the next note.

9 18 PCIJ (1929), Ser. A. Followed by the Permanent Court at the request of one or both parties in *Delimitation of the Territorial Waters between the Island of Castellorizo and the Coasts of Anatolia* case, 51 PCIJ (1933), Ser. A/B; *Appeals from Certain Judgments of the Hungarian-Czechoslovak Mixed Arbitral Tribunal* case, 56 PCIJ (1933), Ser. A/B.

10 *Polish Agrarian Reform* case, 60 PCIJ (1933), Ser. A/B. In the *Borchgrave* case under the Rules of 1936, the Court included in its recitals a statement to the effect that under Article 68 of the Rules, if the parties inform the Court in writing that they are not going on with the proceedings, "it is for the Court to make an order officially recording the discontinuance of the case and prescribing the removal of the case from the list." This was followed by a formal operative clause ordering the case to be removed from the Court's list, 78 PCIJ (1938), Ser. A/B.

Instructions for the Registry), its closing is always a matter for the Court or, in the case of discontinuance, its President if the Court is not sitting.

No question about the entering of a case in the General List appears to have arisen until 1973. In the 1950s eight cases were introduced by application on the basis of the so-called *forum prorogatum* doctrine, that is in the application instituting the proceedings the respondent is invited to accept the jurisdiction of the Court. If the respondent refuses, that is the end of the matter. Those applications were entered in the General List like all other instruments instituting proceedings, and when the invitation to accept the jurisdiction was refused, the Court made orders directing the removal of the cases from the General List.[11]

The first indication that an entry in the General List could play a legal role in a case occurred in 1973. On receipt of the applications instituting the proceedings in the *Nuclear Tests* cases of that year (heard under the Rules of 1972, and duly entered in the List), the unwilling respondent, France, contesting the jurisdiction of the Court, informed the Court that in its view the Court was manifestly not competent in the case, that it could not accept the Court's jurisdiction, and that accordingly the French Government did not intend to appoint an agent and requested the Court to remove the case from its list. Opening the hearings on the request for the indication of provisional measures of protection, the President (Lachs) stated that the French request to remove the case from the List had been duly noted "and the Court will deal with it in due course, in application of Article 36, paragraph 6, of the Statute".[12] In its orders indicating provisional measures of protection the Court first found that the material submitted by the applicants appeared *prima facie* to afford a basis on which the Court's jurisdiction might be founded, and that accordingly the Court would proceed to examine the requests for the indication of provisional measures of protection. It went on to decide that the circumstances of the case did not permit the Court to accede "at the present stage of the proceedings" to the French request that the case be removed from

---

[11] *Treatment in Hungary of Aircraft and Crew of United States of America* (*U.S.A. v. Hungary*; *U.S.A. v. U.S.S.R.*), ICJ REPORTS 1954 at 99 and 103; *Aerial Incident of 10 March 1953* (*U.S.A. v. U.S.S.R.*), *ibid.* (1956) at 5; *Aerial Incident of 7 October 1952* (*U.S.A. v. U.S.S.R.*), *ibid.* at 9; *Antarctica* (*U.K. v. Argentina*; *U.K. v. Chile*), *ibid.* at 12 and 15; *Aerial Incident of 4 September 1954* (*U.S.A. v. U.S.S.R.*), *ibid.* (1958) at 158; *Aerial Incident of 7 November 1954* (*U.S.A. v. U.S.S.R.*), *ibid.* (1959) at 276.

[12] *Nuclear Tests* cases, I Pleadings at 165 (Australia) and II *ibid.* at 99 (*New Zealand*). Recited in the judgments in these case, ICJ REPORTS 1974 at 257 (para. 14) (*Australia*) and 460 (para. 14) (*New Zealand*).

the list.[13] None of the individual (separate or dissenting) opinions attached to those orders refer to this aspect.

In those orders, the Court required the issues of jurisdiction and admissibility to be pleaded first. In its 1974 judgments, the Court referred to the President's statement when opening the hearings in the provisional measures phase, and to the cited paragraphs of those orders, and concluded: "Having now had the opportunity of examining the request in the light of the subsequent proceedings, the Court finds that the present case is not one in which the procedure of summary removal from the list would be appropriate".[14] This statement does not throw much light on when it would be appropriate for the Court summarily to remove a case from the list: the only instances of this in the past had been cases in which there was manifestly no jurisdiction, which was not the situation here.

As in the case of the orders indicating provisional measures, none of the individual (separate or dissenting) opinions joined to the judgment in the next phase deal with this aspect, except for a glancing reference to it by *ad hoc* Judge Barwick in his dissent.[15]

Two years later, in the *Aegean Sea Continental Shelf* case, Turkey, the unwilling respondent, asked the Court to remove the case from the list on the ground that there was no jurisdiction. As before, in the phase of provisional measures of protection the Court stated that having regard to what had proceeded in the order of 11 September 1976, "the Court cannot, at the present stage of the proceedings, accede to the request of the Turkish Government ... that the case be removed from the list."[16] Judge Tarazi, in his separate opinion, gave an interpretation of that request: "it denied the Court's right – he said – to pronounce upon the Application by Greece or even to discuss it." Judge Tarazi continued with the following explanation of the Court's decision:

> "The request that the case be removed from the Court's list could not be acceded to in the present circumstances. According to the consistent jurisprudence of the Court, such removal is decided only in the event that the applicant State does not invoke in support of its Application any legal instrument conferring jurisdiction on the Court but contents itself with

---

13 INTERNATIONAL COURT OF JUSTICE, Reports 1973 at 102 (para. 17), 105 (para. 32) and 138 (para. 18), 141 (para. 33).

14 ICJ REPORTS 1974 at 257 (para. 14) (Australia) and 460 (para. 14) (*New Zealand*).

15 ICJ REPORTS 1974 at 400. And *see* SIR GARFIELD's very personal account of his participation in those cases, in his A RADICAL TORY: GARFIELD BARWICK'S REFLECTIONS AND RECOLLECTIONS (1995) at 254.

16 ICJ REPORTS 1976 at 13 (para. 46).

> leaving the respondent State the possibility of expressing its assent to the proceedings. If, on the other hand, the respondent State responds in the negative, by indicating its refusal to recognize the Court's jurisdiction, the Court orders the case to be removed from its list. Such in my view are the significance and legal scope of the Orders [referred to in note 11 above].
>
> It is clear that this situation is different in respect of the present case. That is why the Court has not decided to remove it from its list and has reserved its position on the question of jurisdiction for later consideration."[17]

Turkey also introduced a more openly political element in an informal communication to the Court in connection with that case. In one of its communications to Greece, the Turkish Government stated that the discontinuance of the proceedings and the removal of the case from the Court's list would be more conducive to the creation of a favourable political climate for an agreed settlement. The Court interpreted this as suggesting that the Court ought not to proceed with the case while the parties continue to negotiate, and that the existence of active negotiations in progress constitutes an impediment to the Court's exercise of jurisdiction in the present case.[18] This is a statement of principle which the Court limited to "the present case", in which it found that it was without jurisdiction.

In 1978 the Court introduced a new provision into the Rules of Court. Dealing with the institution of proceedings by unilateral application, Article 38, paragraph 5, reads:

> "When the applicant State proposes to found the jurisdiction of the Court upon a consent thereto yet to be given or manifested by the State against which such application is made, the application shall be transmitted to that State. It [the application] shall not however be entered in the General List, nor any action be taken in the proceedings, unless and until the State against which such application is made consents to the Court's jurisdiction for the purposes of the case."

By including this in the revised Rules, the Court adopted Judge Tarazi's interpretation of the implications of a request by the respondent for the case to be removed from the list. An authoritative comment on that provision suggests that the previous procedure of entering that type of case in the list was inconvenient. Cases which had no chance of being examined on their substance were entered on the list. As for the respondent, it was officially

---

17 *Ibid.* at 31 and 32.

18 ICJ REPORTS 1976 at 12.

cited without there being any basis for any such action by its opponent. Paragraph 5 remedies that situation.[19]

The issue was raised again by the unwilling respondent in the *Military and Paramilitary Activities in and against Nicaragua* case, in a slightly different form. Here, in acknowledging receipt of the application instituting the proceedings the United States indicated its firm conviction that the Court was without jurisdiction and requested the Court to remove the case from the list. A few days later the United States brought to the Court's notice further information which in its view established that the instruments relied upon by Nicaragua could not serve as a basis of jurisdiction, and requested the Court to "take an immediate decision which will preclude any further proceedings." The next day the Court, taking into account some observations received from Nicaragua, decided that it then had no sufficient basis for acceding to that request or the earlier request for removal of the case from the list.[20] The hearings on the request for provisional measures then followed. In the operative clause of the order indicating provisional measures the Court unanimously rejected the request the case be terminated by the removal of the case from the list – the most far-reaching pronouncement on this issue by the Court to date.[21]

This case confirms the previous interpretation placed upon the practice of the Court before the adoption of the 1978 Rule, and the interpretation given to that Rule.

New light was thrown on the significance of the General List in 1995, in connection with the application of New Zealand for an examination of the situation arising out of France's underwater nuclear tests in the Pacific region, in light of the 1974 judgment. The Registrar did not immediately enter this request on the General List.[22] On receipt of the request for examination,

---

[19] La procédure ainsi suivie n'était pas sans inconvénient: on inscrivait au rôle de la Cour des affaires qui n'avaient, en fait, aucune chance d'être mis en cause officiellement, alors qu'aucun fondement juridique ne pouvait être invoqué pour justifier une telle démarche de son adversaire. C'est à cette situation que le § 5 de l'article 38 entend porter remède. G. GUYOMAR, COMMENTAIRE DU RÈGLEMENT DE LA COUR INTERNATIONALE DE JUSTICE, ADOPTÉ LE 14 AVRIL 1978 (1983) at 246. *See* also G. WEGEN, VERFLEICH UND KLAGERÜCKNAME IM INTERNATIONALEN PROZEß (1987), especially at 159.

[20] ICJ REPORTS 1984 at 172 (para. 6). Repeated at 175 (para. 15).

[21] *Ibid.* at 186. To some extent Judge Schwebel at first sight thought that the United States request to strike the application from the List appeared to be justified were it not for some other facts "which did not come sufficiently to light in the course of the oral proceedings" (at 201). He found in those facts sufficient at that stage to provide the Court with a possible basis of jurisdiction, and therefore did not find it possible to vote to strike the application from the list (at 204).

[22] In fact there were two issues regarding the General List. One was whether the Court had been seised of a case at all; the second was, if it had been seised of a case, was it a continuation of the 1974 case (General List N° 59) or a new case.

together with New Zealand's request for further provisional measures, France replied on 28 August 1995 that France considered that the Court manifestly lacked jurisdiction and that France could not accept jurisdiction in this case. Consequently the choice of an *ad hoc* judge did not arise any more than that of the indication of provisional measures of protection. The message continued:

> "Hence, in its view, the action of New Zealand cannot properly be the object of an entry in the General List, pursuant to the provisions of Article 38, paragraph 5, of the Rules."

At the same time France agreed to be represented at a meeting with the President (Bedjaoui) by the Director of Legal Affairs of its Ministry for Foreign Affairs – who was not designated agent – on informal proceedings limited to the question of whether the New Zealand requests fell within the provisions of a cited paragraph from the 1974 judgment in the *Nuclear Tests* case between New Zealand and France. That meeting took place on 30 August, and it was agreed that each party would submit to the Court what was termed an *Aide-Mémoire* on certain procedural points, to be followed by a hearing at which each party would be given equal speaking-time. In its *Aide-Mémoire* France reiterated its view that the application could not be entered in the General List. It pointed out that in the cases mentioned in note 11 above, the Court had made use of its power of administration and by means of orders delivered without hearings and without the parties having been invited to take any procedural steps, had decided to remove them from the list. That was under the Rules of 1946. There was no difference under the later Rules: whether a "case" manifestly not lying within the jurisdiction of the Court has been removed from the List or not entered in it, no procedural steps can be taken (paras. 31, 32).

The issue of the entry in the General List occupied a prominent place in the hearings on 12 and 13 September 1995. Opening the hearing, the President referred to the *Aides-Mémoires* and stated that they confirmed that the parties held radically different views on the "preliminary and fundamental issue" whether, in the absence of an act expressly recognized by the Statute as capable of instituting proceedings, the Court is, in the circumstances, seised of a case."[23] Each side argued the matter in depth. In its order of 22 September the Court, after reciting the procedural developments and the principal contentions of the parties, included the following paragraph:

---

[23] CR 95/19 (1995) at 13 (11 September) (uncorrected translation by the Registry).

> "Whereas New Zealand has submitted a 'Request for an Examination of the Situation' under paragraph 63 of the Judgment delivered by the Court on 20 December 1974 in the *Nuclear Tests Case (New Zealand v. France)*; whereas such a request, even if it is disputed *in limine* whether it fulfils the conditions set forth in that paragraph, must nonetheless be the object of an entry in the General List of the Court for the sole purpose of enabling the latter to determine whether those conditions are fulfilled; and whereas, consequently, the Court has instructed the Registrar, pursuant to Article 26, paragraph 1(b) of its Rules, to enter that Request in the General List."

At the end of that order the Court wrote:

> "Whereas, as indicated in paragraph 44 above, the 'Request for Examination of the Situation' submitted by New Zealand in accordance with paragraph 63 of the 1974 Judgment has been entered in the General List for the sole purpose of allowing the Court to determine whether the conditions laid down in that text have been fulfilled in the present case; and whereas following the present Order, the Court has instructed the Registrar, acting pursuant to Article 26, paragraph 1(b), of the Rules, to remove that request from the General List as from 22 September 1995."

Accordingly, the case was entered in the General List under a new Number, Nº 97.[24] Given that the question whether the case should be entered in the General List or not was argued in the hearings (after being discussed also in the written communications to the Court), it is clear that the Court in the course of its deliberations decided on the entry in the General List, and dealt with the matter somewhat extensively in the two passages recited above. No reference to this aspect of the case appears in any of the individual opinions joined to the order.

One of the implications of this is that before any any decision can be given on a prejudicatory question of whether the Court has been seised of a case, even if some sort of written and oral proceedings have taken place, an appropriate entry has to be made in the General List. On the other hand, the fact that such an entry is made has no effect whatsoever on the basic question of whether the Court is seised of a case or not.

In one sense, the initial hesitation of the Registrar regarding the entry in the General List follows the general line established by the Court when it introduced Article 38, paragraph 5, into the Rules in 1978 – incidentally, a provision to which no reference is made in the order, although it was cited in the pleadings.

---

24 ICJ REPORTS 1995 at 302, 306 (paras. 44 and 66). It is interesting to note that Vice-President Schwebel, who in his declaration pointedly listed most of the actions taken by the Court to reach the conclusion that the Court had conducted oral hearings on a phase of a case, did not mention the entry in the General List.

There is really nothing unusual about this. Most if not all courts have what is sometimes known as a "cause list" – simply a list of cases on the tribunal's agenda, whether immediate or long-term, without any further implication. The case-law of the Court on this seemingly technical and administrative matter establishes that for the International Court of Justice, the General List is nothing more than an indication of its agenda, without any presumption, one way or the other, as to what the decision will be.[25]

[25] The General List used to be published in the Court's YEARBOOK. This practice was stopped in YEARBOOK (1964–1965). No explanation for this is furnished. However, the YEARBOOK (1964–1965) states that extracts from the General List are supplied by the Registry on request (at 92). The current issue of that publication is ambiguous. It states that extracts from the General List are supplied by the Registry on request "in the form of *Background Notes II and II bis: Synopsis of Cases Referred to the International Court of Justice (1947–1969 and 1969–1976)*, YEARBOOK (1993–1994) at 150. The same publication states that the General List is prepared and kept up to date by the Registrar in accordance with Articles 28, paragraph 1(b) and 38, paragraph 5, of the Rules of Court and Articles 6, paragraph 1 and Article 46, paragraph 3, of the Instructions for the Registry.

PLAIDOYER POUR UNE JURIDICTION INTERNATIONALE OBLIGATOIRE

par
HEINHARD STEIGER

I. KANT

A. Dans sa *Metaphysik der Sitten* Immanuel Kant caractérise l'état des relations entre les états comme «non juridique» [nicht rechtlich] ou «sans lois» [gesetzlos] et en conséquence comme un état «de guerre permanente» [Zustand des beständigen Krieges][1]. Pourquoi? Dans l'état naturel ou de celui de la liberté naturelle où les états se trouvent, tout droit des peuples, le mien et le tien [Mein und Dein], toute possession, tout droit sur l'avoir d'une chose, toute situation, toute relation personelle n'est que provisoire. Cela signifie qu'elle se trouve non définie, incertaine, conflictuelle. Dans l'état naturel, il n'existe, selon Kant qu'un «droit privé» parce que son interprétation, son application, sa réalisation dépendent exclusivement de la volonté et de la force subjectives privées des particuliers et des personnes concernées, mais non d'une autorité publique objective et générale[2]. Ainsi il existe aussi un droit des gens dans l'état naturel entre les états, qu'il appelle comme premier *Staatenrecht.* Mais celui-ci ne consiste qu'en un droit à la guerre, un droit dans la guerre et un droit à la paix[3], et c'est aussi un «droit privé», parce qu'il dépend de la seule volonté des états pris séparément. Il est dépourvu d'une décision objective et autoritaire. En conséquence, la guerre est le seul moyen de résoudre un conflit. Pour établir un état de paix entre les états il faut transformer le droit des gens provisoire et privé en droit péremptoire et public. Cette transformation ne peut se faire que dans un état civil [bürgerlicher Zustand]. Kant propose de conclure le *pactum pacis* pour fonder «un certain fédéralisme» ou «la société des nations» [Völkerbund][4]. Il ne décrit pas l'organisation de cette société des nations. Mais dans sa forme dévelop-

---

1 I. KANT, METAPHYSIK DER SITTEN, RECHTSLEHRE (1797), par. 53, 54.

2 *Ibid.* par. 41,42.

3 *Ibid.* par. 53, 56.

4 I. KANT, ZUM EWIGEN FRIEDEN, EIN PHILOSOPHISCHER ENTWURF (1795), Zweiter Definitivartikel; METAPHYSIK, RECHTSLEHRE, par. 61. *Voir* recemment V. GERHARDT, ***Immanuel Kants Entwurf Zum Ewigen Frieden***, EINE THEORIE DER POLITIK, Darmstadt (1995); M. LUTZ-BACHMANN et J. BOHMAN (éd.), FRIEDEN DURCH RECHT, Frankfurt/Main (1996).

pée cet état civil comprend un législateur public qui édicte les lois et fixe ainsi le droit, et le juge qui sur la base de ces lois publiques décide définitivement sur le mien et le tien[5].

Selon Kant c'est le juge qui assure l'édification et la force du droit par l'application des lois. Le juge décide impartialement sur la base des lois ou des normes, dans l'impartialité, sans considération de la force ou de l'inégalité de fait entre les parties. Cette décision sera définitive et aura l'autorité de la force jugée. Kant ne suit pas la pensée de Montesquieu lorsque ce dernier considère le juge comme «bouche qui prononce les paroles de la loi», un pouvoir «en quelque façon nul». C'est par le juge que la justice publique [öffentliche Gerechtigkeit – *iustitia distributiva*] se réalise.

B. Kant associe l'état naturel sans droit [rechtlos] à l'état de guerre permanente. A l'inverse, l'état civil et de droit assure l'état de paix permanente[6]. La paix présuppose le droit, qui se construit par l'élaboration du droit public édicté par le législateur et appliqué par le juge.

Ainsi l'état de droit représente l'état de paix. Selon Kant c'est une obligation de la raison [Vernunftgebot] a priori de quitter l'état de guerre permanente c'est-à-dire de la liberté naturelle et d'entrer dans l'état de paix permanente c'est-à-dire dans l'état civil [bürgerlicher Zustand], car la guerre représente l'injustice en soi, a priori. Ainsi la fondation de l'état civil ou de droit entre les états qui inclut l'établissement d'une juridiction, d'un tribunal est nécessaire pour parvenir à la paix. Elle est une *conditio sine qua non*. La juridiction internationale ne serait pas, selon Immanuel Kant, un instrument pour résoudre les différends en concurrence à discrétion avec d'autres instruments comme la médiation, la conciliation, l'arbitrage, etc.; elle est une obligation de la raison pour établir et assurer un ordre international fondé et dirigé vers la paix, le seul instrument valable, certain et définitif.

II. 1996

A. A l'époque de Kant c'était une utopie de penser à une cour internationale. A la fin du 18e siècle la souveraineté était en plein essor. Elle représentait l'idéal, le but politique de chaque état. La soumission d'un état souverain à une cour ou à un tribunal international était absolument incompatible avec cette conception d'une souveraineté absolue.

---

5 I. KANT, *op. cit.*, *supra* note 1, par. 41.

6 *Voir ibid.* par. 53 et surtout l'essai ZUM EWIGEN FRIEDEN, *op. cit.*, *supra* note 4; *voir* aussi H. STEIGER, *Frieden durch Institution*, dans: FRIEDEN DURCH RECHT, *op. cit.*, *supra* note 4.

Depuis lors la situation a beaucoup changé. Depuis 1921 l'ordre international juridique s'est doté d'une Cour internationale générale et mondiale, dénommée la CPJI puis en 1945 la CIJ. D'autres cours ou tribunaux internationaux ont également été instaurés: la Cour sur le droit de la mer, des Cours des droits de l'homme en Europe et en Amérique, la Cour de l'Union européenne (CJCE – Cour de justice des Communautés Européennes), des tribunaux réprimant les crimes de guerre commis lors de la deuxième guerre mondiale et de la guerre en ex-Yougoslavie et au Ruanda. Avons-nous quitté l'ère du droit international provisoire et privé et sommes-nous entrés dans l'ère du droit international péremptoire et public, du droit mondial interne?

L'analyse de la situation actuelle de la juridiction internationale ne donne pas une réponse tout à fait affirmative puisque la compétence de ces cours et tribunaux n'est généralement pas obligatoire. L'obligation pure et simple de soumettre un différend à une cour ou à un tribunal international ne constitue pas la règle mais l'exception. Mais c'est cette obligation qui transforme le droit provisoire en droit péremptoire.

B. Selon l'art. 92 de la Charte des Nations Unies, la CIJ est l'organe judiciaire de l'Organisation. Sa compétence selon l'art. 36 par. 2 du Statut concerne «tous les différends d'ordre juridique ayant pour objet:

a) l'interprétation d'un traité;

b) tout point de droit international;

c) la réalité de tout fait qui s'il était établi, constituerait la violation d'un engagement international;

d) la nature ou l'étendue de la réparation due pour la rupture d'un engagement international».

Ainsi la compétence *ratione materiae* s'avère très générale et étendue. Elle comprend au fond toutes les questions du droit. Le droit international dans sa totalité est soumis à son appréciation, à son jugement et à son contrôle. L'article précité dispose cependant que sa compétence en matière *ratione personae* n'est pas obligatoire mais seulement facultative. C'est-à-dire que les états peuvent déclarer au préalable soumettre les différends juridiques qui les opposent à d'autres états à la juridiction de la Cour, mais ils peuvent aussi bien renoncer à une telle déclaration et choisir d'autres voies pour résoudre leurs conflits, même s'il s'agit de conflits de droit. De plus ils peuvent y ajouter des réserves. A l'heure actuelle 58 états ont accepté de se soumettre à la juridiction obligatoire de la Cour pour juger les conflits qui les opposent entre eux. Mais toutes ces déclarations contiennent certaines réserves ou conditions. Bien que selon ces déclarations la juridiction de la CIJ soit en principe devenue obligatoire pour ces états, on ne peut être certain que dans un cas concret cette obligation ne soit pas écartée sur le fondement de ces réserves. En tout cas ce système ne peut fonctionner que si tous les états qui sont parties au conflit ont fait des déclarations convergeantes. Souvent de longues disputes sur des questions préliminaires en résultent.

La compétence *ratione personae* a été étendue par des engagements conventionels spécifiques pour soumettre des différends à la juridiction de la CIJ. On en trouve une longue liste dans l'Annuaire de la Cour mondiale. Mais les termes de ces engagements conventionnels diffèrent beaucoup. Il s'agit de traités bilatéraux et de traités et conventions multilatéraux. Souvent ces clauses ne concernent que les différends en relation avec le traité ou la convention. Cependent d'autres instruments de règlement pacifique se trouvent également en parallèle et en concurrence avec la juridiction de la Cour: conciliation, arbitrage, médiation ou des moyens convenus *ad hoc*. Les états essayent de garder une grande liberté d'action malgré leur acceptation de normes de droit régissant leur relation avec les autres *Hautes Parties contractantes*. La compétence obligatoire de la CIJ n'est donc pas la règle.

C. Il existe une exception intéressante. La Convention européenne pour le règlement pacifique des différends de 1957 contient dans son art. 1er l'obligation inconditionnelle, pure et simple des états parties de soumettre leurs différends de droit à la compétence de la Cour mondiale. Bien sûr, cette Convention ne concerne que les membres du Conseil de l'Europe qui l'ont ratifiée[7]. Il s'agit d'une juridiction obligatoire, mais régionale et ainsi limitée. La Convention donne très clairement la priorité à cette procédure judiciaire devant tout autre moyen de règlement pacifique, notamment le règlement arbitral[8]. La Convention ne prévoit pas de réserves. Dans ce sens elle a le mérite d'être stricte, claire et assez simple. Malgré une clause d'exception à l'art. 28, qui prévoit la possibilité pour les parties de se mettre d'accord sur un autre moyen pour résoudre un conflit, cette règle générale et étendue constitue un pas décisif vers une juridiction internationale obligatoire[9].

La Convention américaine sur le règlement pacifique des différends (*Bogota Treaty*) contient à l'art. 31 une clause similaire à l'art. 1 de la Convention européenne qui stipule que les états parties contractantes à cette Convention reconnaissent la compétence de juridiction de la Cour «in relation to any other American State[!] as compulsory *ipso facto*, without the necessity of any special agreement so long as the present Treaty is in force, in all

---

[7] Malheureusement ce ne sont que douze états qui ont ratifié cette convention (31.12.1994).

[8] L'art. 19.

[9] Il est intéressant de noter que cette juridiction obligatoire est régionale, mais la Cour est internationale, c'est-à-dire des juges des autres régions peuvent siéger dans un litige strictement européen.

disputes of a juridical nature that arise among them concerning[!]», suit le texte de l'art. 36 par. 2 Statut de la CIJ. Mais à la différence de la Convention européenne le recours à la CIJ est selon l'art. 32 subsidiaire même dans des conflits juridiques relatifs à la procédure de conciliation, la conclusion d'un traité ou la procedure d'arbitrage. En d'autres termes la soumission d'un conflit juridique aux juges internationaux réguliers n'est pas la règle ordinaire, normale.

Ainsi, la compétence de la juridiction de la Cour mondiale manque de certitude de prévisibilité ainsi que de clarté et souffre d'imprécision et surtout n'est pas obligatoire. Bien sûr, la Cour existe et rend des jugements; le nombre des affaires pendantes augmente, mais il est toujours minime[10]. Souvent d'autres moyens pour arriver à un règlement pacifique sont préférés par les parties au litige, et le recours à la compétence de la Cour semble être le moyen ultime. En résumé, il n'existe pas une juridiction internationale générale, effective, acceptée comme recours clair, certain et normal pour règler les litiges juridiques par la voie judiciaire.

D. La seule juridiction obligatoire à caractère international relève de la compétence de la Cour de justice des Communautés Européennes. Tous les différends juridiques entre états-membres, entre états-membres – et les Communautés, entre les particuliers et les Communautés, entre les organes des Communautés qui concernent le droit communautaire primaire et secondaire doivent être jugés par cette Cour. Elle contrôle aussi l'application du droit européen par les juridictions nationales. Sa juridiction est obligatoire, exclusive, bien définie et stricte. Le recours à une autre cour ou à un autre tribunal, ou bien encore à l'arbitrage est exclu pour toutes les questions qui concernent le droit communautaire primaire et secondaire. Ainsi la compétence de la Cour de justice des Communautés Européennes constitue l'exemple le plus avancé d'une juridiction supranationale. Ses jugements lient les états et leur exécution est, depuis 1993, assurée par une sanction pécuniaire. Elle exerce des fonctions semblables à celles d'un tribunal administratif et d'un tribunal constitutionel dans les ordres juridiques nationaux. Mais il s'agit d'un exemple très spécifique. La Cour fait partie d'une organisation de type supranational. Ces organisations *sui generis* se trouvent entre un état fédéral et les institutions ou organisations internationales normales. Le droit matériel des traités est obligatoire pour les états-membres et crée des droits et obligations directes pour leurs ressortissants. De plus elles détiennent des pouvoirs quasi législatifs et exécutifs directs dans certaines matières. La Cour doit contrôler ce droit, sa conformité avec le droit primaire

10 Jusqu'en 1994 la Cour a traité 93 affaires, 72 cas contentieux, 21 cas d'avis consultatifs.

aussi bien que son application par les états. La position de cette Cour européenne est donc très proche et presque identique à la position d'une cour nationale dans l'ordre interne.

Toutefois, sa compétence se trouve limitée au droit communautaire. Elle n'est pas compétente pour les autres conflits entre les états-membres des trois Communautés. Elle n'est même pas en droit la Cour de l'Union européenne. Les matières des deux autres piliers sont expréssement exclus de sa compétence. Les conflits «internationaux», c'est-à-dire les conflits entre états-membres hors du cadre des Communautés ne peuvent être portés devant cette Cour. C'est l'art. 1 de la Convention européenne pour le règlement pacifique des différends cité ci-dessus qui s'applique avec la juridiction obligatoire de la CIJ, mais seulement pour ceux qui l'ont ratifiée.

E. Entre ces deux extrêmes de la juridiction internationale il existe d'autres exemples de juridictions internationales: la Cour sur le droit de la mer, prévue par l'art. 286 de la Convention sur le droit de la mer de 1982, entrée en vigueur en 1994, et les deux Cours des droits de l'homme américaine et européenne. La première sera établie à Hambourg. Sa juridiction n'est ni obligatoire ni exclusive. L'art. 287 UNCLOS offre aux états un choix entre la juridiction de cette nouvelle cour spéciale, la Cour internationale de Justice et deux formes d'arbitrage juridique définies aux annexes VII et VIII pour resoudre leurs conflits par un vote judiciaire. Cette possibilité constitue un certain progrès puisqu'elle oblige les états à choisir au moins une procédure judiciaire. Mais puisque le choix entre ces trois voies est libre pour chaque état, il se peut que les états parties dans un différend, n'ont pas opéré le même choix. Cela veut dire que là, où il y a une procédure d'arbitrage selon l'art. 287 par. 5 et là, où les deux états ont choisi la méthode *ad hoc*, tout recours à la voie judiciaire peut-être exclu. En plus, ce système de choix crée une concurrence entre les deux cours et les procédures d'arbitrage. Cela peut conduire à des jugements ou à des décisions divergeants et des réponses contradictoires à une même question. De surcroît il n'existe pas de solution à un conflit de jugement qui ne pourra être tranché par aucune de l'une ou l'autre des institutions.

F. Un vrai changement fondamental de la position des états est survenu dans une matière centrale et fondamentale du droit des gens, la matière des droits de l'homme. Le Protocole 11 de la Convention européenne des droits de l'homme prévoit désormais dans son art. 33 que les états parties à cette convention devront se soumettre à la juridiction de la nouvelle Cour des droits de l'homme. Toute partie contractante peut saisir la Cour de tout manquement d'un état adhérent aux dispositions de la Convention. De plus la soumission obligatoire des états à la juridiction de la Cour a été élargie car l'art. 33 permet désormais l'introduction de requêtes individuelles[11]. Un règlement similaire a été adopté en par l'Organisation des Etats américains par la Charte américaine des droits de l'homme. Nous sommes là en présence d'un nouveau développement et d'un changement profond de la position des états vis-à-vis de la juridiction internationale obligatoire.

Il est important d'analyser la situation d'une manière plus approfondie. Matériellement il s'agit d'une matière d'une importance primordiale: les droits de l'homme. Depuis la Déclaration des droits de l'homme de l'Assemblée générale de l'ONU en 1948 l'importance de cette matière a grandi. Dans trois des plus grands continents du monde, une convention est entrée en force créant des droits immédiatement applicables aux habitants de ces continents respectifs: l'Europe, l'Amérique, l'Afrique. Des conventions internationales générales et spéciales ont été adoptées et mises en vigueur à l'échelon mondial. L'Assemblé génèrale de l'ONU et maintes organisations internationales et leurs organes ont souligné l'importance des droits de l'homme comme étant le coeur du droit international de la paix. Bien sûr, l'universalité des droits de l'homme n'est pas encore acceptée partout, ni en théorie ni en pratique. Même dans ces trois parties du monde, on constate fréquemment un mépris, une absence de mise en oeuvre et une violation des ces droits. Néanmoins les droits de l'homme, du moins les droits essentiels comme le droit à la vie et à la santé, le droit à la personnalité juridique, l'interdiction de l'esclavage, de la torture et du traffic d'êtres humains doivent être reconnus comme faisant partie du *ius cogens*.

L'importance de ces droits a débouché dès le début de leur mise en oeuvre à des procédures spéciales devant les organismes internationaux pour contrôler leur application. La Convention européenne, comme la Convention américaine ont à titre de premier pas établi un contrôle international par une Commission et une Cour internationale, indépendantes et liées seulement au droit, c'est-à-dire aux normes juridiques édictées par chacune de ces deux Conventions. Au début leur juridiction était également purement facultative. Les états ont par la suite reconnu l'un après l'autre cette juridiction. Il est devenu en quelque sorte quasi-obligatoire de l'accepter, de se soumettre à leur compétence. De plus les deux commissions comme les deux cours ont developpé une jurisprudence acceptée par les états comme par les particuliers. Ainsi une structure et même une culture du droit international s'est developée dans cette matière qui, au moins en Europe et en Amérique, correspondent à la culture de droit interne fondée sur la reconnaissance des

11 *Voir* R. BERNAHRDT, *Reform of the Control Machinery under the European Convention on Human Rights Protocol 11*, 89 AJIL (1995), pp. 145–154.

droits de l'homme comme droits fondamentaux. On pourrait même dire que grâce aux droits de l'homme une unité fondamentale de l'ordre juridique interne et de l'ordre juridique externe s'est constituée.

Ainsi l'acceptation de la juridiction internationale obligatoire comme deuxième étape du contrôle international en matière des droits de l'homme semble être le fruit d'un long développement matériel et institutionel.

G. Pour conclure l'analyse de la situation actuelle de la juridiction internationale il faut reconnaître que depuis 1921 les développements vers la reconnaissance et l'établissement de son autorité se poursuivent. Un certain progrès peut être constaté. Mais un système clair, simple, certain, effectif est surtout obligatoire n'existe pas encore. L'idée d'une juridiction internationale obligatoire se heurte toujours à l'idée de la souveraineté des états et à d'autres objections et résistances qui empêchent les états de se soumettre à une juridiction internationale obligatoire précise, claire, non ambiguë, effective et définitive. Les arguments soulevés dans la politique comme dans la doctrine contre la juridiction internationale obligatoire varient. Outre le concept de la souveraineté on mentionne la méfiance à l'égard de l'impartialité des juges, les différences des traditions juridiques et culturelles, l'hétérogénéité des structures économiques et sociales et autres[12], une conception des états plutôt politique que juridique des différends, pour lesquels la dimension juridique d'un litige paraît secondaire[13]. Mais tous ces arguments contre une juridiction obligatoire générale ne tiennent pas compte de certains changements profonds et fondamentaux des structures de la société internationale des états et de son droit.

III. GLOBALISATION

A. Le monde et avec lui la société des états et des peuples se trouvent dans un mouvement de globalisation. Cette notion décrit d'abord le développement vers un marché global, qui ne comprend pas seulement le commerce, comme autrefois, mais aussi les mouvements des capitaux, des services, des travaux intellectuels, des technologies, la globalisation des productions etc. La globalisation est en premier lieu économique. Mais elle est plus large. Font également partie de cette globalisation les mouvements de personnes, y inclus les grandes vagues d'immigration des ressortissants du tiers monde vers

---

12 *Voir e.g.* K. OELLERS-FRAHM, *Probleme und Grenzen der obligatorischen Gerichtsbarkeit*, 27 ADV (1989), pp. 442–454, 444 et s.

13 G.L. SCOTT, C.L. CARR, *The ICJ and Compulsory Jurisdiction: The Case for Closing the Clause*, 81 AJIL (1987), pp. 57–76, 73.

les pays du nord, le développement des voies de télécommunications et d'informations éléctroniques qui atteignent une nouvelle dimension avec l'internet et autres systèmes, mais aussi l'internationalisation grandissante et menaçante d'organisations internationales du crime. La globalisation change les structures traditionnelles mondiales des échanges entre les peuples et les états. Elle crée un filet d'interactions et d'interdépendances culturelles, scientifiques, sociales, technologiques, économiques, commerciales, financières, communicatives, criminelles etc. qui ne respectent pas les frontières des états et leur souveraineté. Les acteurs dans ce système de globalisation des interactions, ne sont plus les seuls états mais aussi les forces économiques, comme les grandes firmes et associations, mais aussi ceux qui exploitent les nouvelles possibilités de communication et d'information c'est-à-dire les universités et d'autres institutions ou organisations scientifiques et culturelles, les sociétés, les sociétés de télévisions, les medias, et même les particuliers qui utilisent l'internet, qui regardent la télévision via satellite etc., etc.

Si les états veulent encore influencer ce développement de globalisation, s'ils veulent le règler et le contrôler, s'ils veulent éviter certaines conséquences nuisibles pour les hommes, pour leur économie nationale, leurs systèmes sociaux, monétaire etc., ils doivent coordonner leurs activités, coopérer et prendre des mesures communes.

Nous assistons encore à d'autres formes de globalisation, la globalisation des problèmes de la conservation de l'environnement mondial, de la sécurité et de la sauvegarde de la paix mondiale, de la réalisation du respect des droits de l'homme, du développement des peuples du tiers monde et bien autres encore.

B. La globalisation résulte dans une réduction continue de la souveraineté politique ou de fait des états. La politique nationale doit suivre dans de nombreuses matières les exigences des marchés, des développements scientifiques et technologiques, des besoins d'une société mondiale. Aucun état n'a encore le pouvoir de décider sur le taux de change de sa monnaie; aucun état n'a assez de moyens pour combattre le crime organisé; aucun état n'est en mesure de contrôler actuellement d'une manière effective le courant d'informations.

Souveraineté n'est pas seulement une notion de droit mais aussi une notion de politique ou de pouvoir. En droit, elle signifie l'indépendance juridique de l'état par rapport à un autre état ou à une autre organisation publique. L'état souverain n'est pas juridiquement soumis aux normes ou aux ordres donnés par un tiers. En terme de pouvoir, la souveraineté signifie que l'état a la capacité matérielle, l'indépendance de fait, le pouvoir réel de prendre ses décisions selon ses intérêts, ses désirs, sa libre et indépendante volonté. La souveraineté au sens juridique existe pour presque tous les états. Mais la souveraineté au sens politique se perd de plus en plus. En d'autres termes, la souveraineté juridique perd son contenu politique de pouvoir, elle devient de plus en plus un cocon vide pour tous les états même les grands. Autrefois c'était souvent la dépendance politique des petits états vis-à-vis d'une grande puissance hégémonique qui a vidé la souveraineté des premiers. Aujourd'hui c'est l'interdépendance économique, financière, écologique, technologique, communicative, sociale, de sécurité des états entre eux par la globalisation dans toutes les matières qui vide la souveraineté de son pouvoir autonome et indépendant. Ces mouvements vers l'interdépendance s'accélèrent.

IV. LÉGIFÉRATION

A. La réduction de la souveraineté politique ou de fait des états a pour conséquence un développement accéléré de l'ordre international vers une concentration et une intensification. D'une part l'organisation internationale s'étend et s'approfondit, non pas d'une façon systématique mais par l'intermédiaire des institutions ou organisations internationales, globales et régionales, générales et spéciales. D'autre part, le droit international connaît un développement et une intensification énormes. La multiplication des normes se poursuit, mais aussi leur champ d'application et leur contenu juridique. Nous assistons à une extension et à une intensification du droit international par le développement du droit coutumier des conventions et la formation d'une masse énorme du *soft law*.

Le développement du droit coutumier se poursuit dans toutes les matières. Il conserve sa position fondamentale. Son rôle est nécessaire pour les fondements de l'ordre juridique du droit international, pour les matières qui restent en suspend, pour combler les lacunes du droit écrit, pour les états qui ne font pas partie des codifications ou des conventions internationales écrites. Nous assistons encore aujourd'hui à la création d'un droit coutumier dans toutes les matières, qu'elles soient classiques ou émergeantes.

De plus en plus de matières sont reglées par des conventions multilatérales, soit des matières classiques, comme le droit des traités, des ambassadeurs ou des consuls, soit des matières tout à fait récentes, comme la protection et l'utilisation de la biodiversité, la protection du climat, de certains animaux etc., etc. Les matières classiques du droit se transforment en raison des impératifs actuels et leur règlementation exige des solutions nouvelles tout en gardant quelques principes traditionnels, comme *e.g.* le droit de la mer. Nous pouvons continuer la description de ce développement et y ajouter bien d'autres matières et de conventions qui les concernent.

Ce développement matériel du droit international change profondément ses structures traditionnelles. Il devient de plus en plus un droit mondial interne. Bien qu'il utilise comme forme principale le traité ou la convention, les états ne sont souvent plus libres et souverains de refuser ou même d'influencer le texte. Les grandes codifications sont élaborées lors de conférences internationales. C'est souvent la majorité qui y décide, en fait, comme en droit. De plus en plus les états doivent se conformer à ces conventions, souvent malgré eux. Ils ne peuvent se permettre de s'en écarter.

B. Nous assistons donc à la transformation accélérée d'un ordre international politique ouvert, sans règles détaillées vers un ordre de plus en plus juridique. Cette transformation contient un développement de «l'état naturel» vers «l'état civil», de la liberté naturelle politique à la liberté civile et juridique. Cette transformation demande une détermination nouvelle de la relation entre la dimension politique et la dimension juridique des relations entre les états. Depuis la naissance de l'état moderne et souverain, c'est-à-dire depuis le 16e siècle, la dimension politique était prédominante dans les relations des états entre eux, dans l'ordre international. Le droit était un moyen, un instrument à la disposition de la politique, que celle-ci a utilisé à son gré. Même si des traités ont été conclus, même si des normes du droit coutumier étaient reconnues, les états ont toujours gardé leur souveraineté politique également vis-à-vis de ce droit. Au 19e siècle cette conception de la souveraineté atteignit son apogée jusqu'à la première guerre mondiale.

Même après les deux guerres mondiales cette conception de la primauté du politique vis-à-vis du droit n'a pas été abandonnée malgré l'établissement de la Cour mondiale et d'autres cours internationales, et malgré le développement important, essentiel et fondamental de la dimension juridique des rélations entre états.

Déjà aujourd'hui et plus encore à l'avenir, cette conception ne correspond plus au développement et à la fonction du droit dans l'ordre international. Celle-ci consiste dans l'établissement d'un ordre international durable, certain et sûr. La relation des dimensions politiques et juridiques de cet ordre peut être définie en deux phases ou en deux modes d'action des états. La phase de la politique est vis-à-vis du droit la phase de la création des normes. Elle n'est pas tout à fait libre car les normes des principes généraux et celles du droit coutumier l'encadrent[14]. Mais ce cadre est très large, indéfini, imprécis et très ouvert à l'interprétation et à l'action politique. Il connaît même

---

[14] Je laisse la question ouverte si un ordre juridique de droit naturel est présupposé. *Voir* pour la discussion au dix-neuvième siècle, H. STEIGER, *Völkerrecht und Naturrecht zwischen Christian Wolff und Adolf Lasson*, dans: D. KLIPPEL (éd.), NATURRECHT IM 19. JAHRHUNDERT – KONTINUITÄT – INHALT – FUNKTION – WIRKUNG, Frankfurt/Main (1996).

des lancunes en laissant de larges domaines où aucun droit n'existe ou des normes de droit ne se forment que très lentement. Ainsi la politique beneficie toujours d'un vaste champ et d'options infinies pour exercer son action. Cela constituerait une grave et profonde erreur de soumettre ces actions à une juridiction internationale. Mais si l'action politique touche à ces normes elle doit les respecter. Elle ne peut en disposer selon son gré et elle peut être contrôlée, comme par exemple dans le cas opposant le Nicaragua aux Etats-Unis. Si l'action politique est à l'origine de la création des normes du droit international coutumier, des conventions ou des traités elle s'est alors transformée en droit. Elle a abandonné sa liberté d'action. Désormais, c'est le droit qui détermine l'activité des états entre eux. La réalisation de la dimension juridique de l'ordre international ne peut dépendre de la politique. Par la création des règles de droit, par la transformation d'une politique en règles de droit se produit un changement de qualité des critères et des normes de l'activité des états. Ce n'est plus la volonté politique qui détermine le droit mais le droit qui détermine l'activité politique.

V. JURIDICTION OBLIGATOIRE

A. L'extension et le renforcement de la dimension juridique qui va jusqu'à la formation croissante d'un ordre juridique mondial interne nécessite comme clef de voûte une juridiction internationale obligatoire, claire, précise et sans ambiguïté.

L'argument de Kant dans sa *Metaphysik der Sitten* que j'ai cité plus haut est exagéré en ce sens que sa conséquence serait de nier le caractère juridique du droit des gens provisoire comme source de droit. Mais il est vrai sur ce point qu'un droit provisoire ne remplit pas vraiment sa fonction de droit. Celle-ci ne peut être atteinte que si les sujets de droit ont la confiance que tous se comportent les uns vis-à-vis des autres conformement à ces règles et que chacun d'eux s'engage à respecter ces règles, notamment en cas de conflit. Cette confiance réciproque constitue la condition fondamentale pour que chacun apporte son adhésion à ces normes juridiques. L'établissement d'un ordre juridique tant sur le plan de matières générales que spécifiques n'est pas pour autant achevé par la signature ou la mise en vigueur d'une convention. Il est indispensable que son application soit effective, stable et durable. Il appartient à la juridiction internationale de veiller à cette application.

B. Les premiers pas dans cette direction, bien que très hésitants, ont été accomplis. Ils demeurent toutefois insuffisants car les règles applicables à la résolution d'un différend juridique sont toujours très équivoques et s'inspirent la plupart du temps de l'idéologie de la primauté de la politique. La confiance nécessaire pour assurer le fonctionnement du droit ne peut vraiment s'installer et se renforcer si les états ne peuvent être sûrs qu'un éventuel différend ne pourra être resolu par la voie juridique. Le système actuel contient trop de possibilités de s'écarter de la voie juridique et dévalorise ainsi la fonction du droit et du développement vers un ordre juridique international.

L'expérience des siècles et la théorie ont révélé que le meilleur instrument de l'administration du droit pour résoudre les différends réside dans une juridiction obligatoire dont les compétences sont claires et définitives. Elle est indispensable pour assurer le développement et la mise en place du nouveau droit dans maintes matières, qui transforme le droit international de plus en plus en un ordre juridique mondial interne avec toute sa vigueur et toute sa rigueur. S'il en était autrement ce droit resterait provisoire, incertain dans sa fonction, toujours menacé de perdre sa capacité à diriger le comportement des états.

C. Si cette fonction de la juridiction internationale est assez claire concernant le droit conventionnel, beaucoup doutent de sa fonction concernant le droit coutumier, surtout après la décision de la CIJ dans l'affaire Nicaragua contre Etats-Unis. Des auteurs américains, tout comme le gouvernement, ont estimé que la juridiction obligatoire ne sera pas à même de résoudre les problèmes de ce droit souvent imprécis dans ces normes, incertain dans son contenu comme dans sa valeur juridique et dont l'acceptation par les états reste ambiguë[15]. A nouveau, ces auteurs se réfèrent à la doctrine de la souveraineté et à la création du droit coutumier dans le système décentralisé des états souverains. Ces auteurs oublient que le droit coutumier se crée toujours dans un système décentralisé dans des secteurs autonomes. C'est l'une des différences primordiales qui oppose le droit coutumier et la création du droit par le législateur. Ils oublient aussi que dans un tel ordre les cours ont toujours joué un rôle central pour la détermination et le développement du droit. Tout ordre juridique de droit coutumier a besoin des cours, tout comme l'ordre juridique international. La juridiction internationale confirme une norme nouvelle; elle clarifie une interprétation incertaine; c'est elle qui scelle des développements incertains et ambigus et les transforme en droit certain. C'est ce rôle joué surtout par la CIJ qui lui a valu beaucoup de critique notamment de la part des juristes américains après la décision dans l'affaire Nicaragua contre Etats-Unis. Mais c'est un rôle nécessaire et indispensable pour le développement du droit international coutumier.

---

[15] *Voir e.g.* J.P. KELLY, *The Changing Process of International Law and the Role of the World Court*, 11 MICHIGAN JOURNAL OF INTERNATIONAL LAW, pp. 129–166, 143 et s.

D. La juridiction internationale actuelle est marquée par un manque de conception cohérente, claire et différenciée. La CIJ comme Cour mondiale occupe une position centrale. Sa compétence est extrêmement large et générale. L'art. 36 du Statut, comme l'art. 1 de la Convention européenne définissent sa juridiction dans des termes très abstraits et généraux et soumettent d'une façon générale à sa compétence toute question générale du droit international. La formule très vaste, citée plus haut, a créé beaucoup de difficultés, que les états ont essayé de résoudre en n'adhérant pas tout de suite à la juridiction obligatoire ou en donnant à la déclaration définie à l'art. 36 par. 2 du Statut un contenu relatif et en y ajoutant beaucoup de réserves. Parmi celles-ci figurait la plus fameuse et équivoque, la «Connally-réserve» de la déclaration américaine. Ces réserves ont pour effet de faire naître une grande incertitude pour savoir si ou non un cas concret tombe dans le champ de compétence de la juridiction de la Cour. Des objections préliminaires soulevées sur la base de ces réserves pèsent sur la procédure et allongent les délais.

De plus sera-t-il possible de soumettre tous les différends à une seule cour mondiale de 15 juges? Il semble en effet difficile qu'elle puisse traiter et décider de toutes les affaires dans un délai convenable. La discussion actuelle ne concerne que la juridiction de la CIJ et l'on s'interroge sur sa capacité pour remplir seule la fonction d'une juridiction internationale obligatoire effective.

E. Il faut concevoir un système différencié selon deux critères, la compétence matérielle, *ratione materiae*, et la compétence territoriale. Déjà aujourd'hui ces deux critères sont utilisés. Des cours spéciales existent pour les droits de l'homme et les différends en matières du droit de la mer. Les deux Cours de droit de l'homme sont des cours avec une compétence régionale, européenne et américaine.

Ce système peut être développé. Depuis déjà quelques années le projet d'un tribunal international pour le droit de l'environnement a été développé et poursuivi par un groupe d'environnementalistes internationaux.

Il convient d'assurer l'unité et la cohérence du système judiciaire international ainsi qu'une détermination claire, précise et bien définie du domaine des compétences de ses éléments. Il faut en plus que les compétences soient exclusives. On peut constater que de nombreux traités et conventions prévoient entre outre la possibilité de soumettre un différend les concernant à la juridiction de la CIJ ou d'une autre cour, comme nous l'avons décrit. Le défaut de ce régime consiste d'une part, à laisser aux états la possibilité de recourir à d'autres instruments pour trouver une solution pacifique au règlement du conflit et d'autre part, dans l'absence d'une obligation pure et simple de recourir à la compétence de la Cour. On doit modifier les articles litigieux de telle façon à ce que le recours à la juridiction d'une cour ou d'un tribunal déterminé soit une obligation claire et précise au moins après un échec des autres instruments, et que cette juridiction reçoive une compétence exclusive et qu'aucune réserve ou condition ne puisse être opposée à cette exclusivité. Par un tel règlement on réduit considérablement les problèmes posés par les questions préliminaires dont le nombre sera considérablement diminué et les décisions de la cour gagneront en simplicité. La lecture des traités et des conventions dont les termes prévoient un règlement judiciaire des différends fait ressortir que les auteurs ne prennent pas en considération les autres règlementations déjà existantes et qu'ils ne réfléchissent pas sur les conséquences d'une nouvelle règlementation, *e.g.* concurrence entre la nouvelle Cour sur le droit de la mer et la CIJ introduite par l'art. 289 UNCLOS. Il n'existe pas encore de plan ou de conception pour un système mondial d'une juridiction internationale.

Dans un système de juridiction internationale différencié et mieux organisé la position de la CIJ doit être définie à nouveau. On peut lui reserver, une compétence pour juger des affaires de droit international général qui devront être bien définies, les relations des états avec l'ONU, pour une décision sur l'agrément spécial des états selon l'art. 36 par. 1. Dans un système mieux développé et organisé les problèmes de la clause d'option pour une juridiction obligatoire seront réduits. Lors, de l'instauration de la Cour Permanente de Justice internationale en 1921, cette clause représentait un progrès. Aujourd'hui elle ne suffit plus, surtout par son caractère facultatif et le droit des états d'y ajouter des réserves. Si les compétences des cours ou tribunaux étaient bien définies, les états ne devraient pas craindre une sorte d'usurpation du pouvoir par les juges ou un gouvernement international des juges. Le développement d'une conception d'un tel système de juridiction international est une tâche appartenant aux organismes internationaux gouvernementaux et non-gouvernementaux. La réalisation d'un tel système prendra certainement du temps et il conviendrait de se mettre à l'ouvrage aussitôt que possible.

Kant s'est interrogé sur le chemin vers l'établissement de la «société des nations» [Völkerbund]. Sa confiance dans la raison seule n'était pas absolue. Il s'est référé à deux mécanismes ou phénomènes de la nature: la détresse ou la pénurie [Not] qui naissent des guerres et l'esprit du commerce [Handelsgeist] qui a besoin de la paix et de la sécurité[16]. Le monde connaît beaucoup de détresse de toute part. Le commerce se globalise. Le moment semble être venu, de faire un pas définitif vers un système d'une juridiction internationale obligatoire.

---

[16] I. KANT, ZUM EWIGEN FRIEDEN, *op. cit.*, *supra* note 4, Von der Garantie.

F. Si ce n'est possible à l'échelon mondial, il faudra commencer par un échelon régional européen. L'Europe est à la recherche d'un nouvel ordre de paix, de sécurité et de coopération pour parvenir à un développement pacifique.

La division du continent européen en deux a disparu. L'homogénéité économique, sociale, culturelle, constitutionelle s'étend. Les questions fondamentales des frontières etc. sont résolues par des traités bilatéraux ou multilatéraux. Les états européens remplissent la condition posée par Kant pour un ordre de paix: ils ont une constitution républicaine. La transformation de l'ordre européen en ordre juridique est encore plus marquée que pour l'ordre mondial. Le Conseil de l'Europe et la Commission économique européenne de L'ONU sont très actifs pour préparer des conventions dans tous les domaines. Les interdépendences des états entre eux sont beaucoup plus denses que dans d'autres régions du monde. Le moment semble être propice pour établir une Cour européenne qui trancherait les différends des états selon le droit. Ses compétences pourraient être énumérées et spécialisées. Cela constituera un avantage d'avoir des compétences bien définies, précises et certaines. Elles pourront toujours être élargies et développées avec le développement du droit. Aux 17e et 18e siècles la notion d'un droit public européen ou de l'Europe était très courant[17]. Il existait une conception selon laquelle l'ordre juridique commun formait une unité européenne malgré l'existence d'états souverains. Elle était fondée sur le droit naturel, la tradition du droit romain, le droit coutumier des gens et les traités conclus entre les états depuis la Paix de Westphalie en 1648. Aujourd'hui cette conception d'un droit public européen a encore plus de réalité qu'à l'époque de l'âge des lumières. L'établissement d'une Cour européenne ayant une juridiction obligatoire donnera à ce droit public européen sa vigueur nécessaire.

On dirait que le plaidoyer pour une juridiction internationale obligatoire serait peut-être juste en théorie mais n'est pas apte en pratique politique. Kant a refusé cette objection en recourant à la nature humaine. Le respect, dit-il, du droit et du devoir y est toujours plus vivant. Ainsi la raison morale et pratique vaincra enfin le mal, et conduira après maintes essais échoués les dieux de la terre, c'est-à-dire les états, vers la réalisation de ce que la raison leur demande, parce qu'il est nécessaire. Il est encore plus nécessaire aujourd'hui[18].

---

[17] *E.g.* DE MABLY, G. DE BONNOT, LE DROIT PUBLIC DE L'EUROPE FONDÉ SUR LES TRAITÉS (1748).

[18] I. KANT, ÜBER DEN GEMEINSPRUCH: DAS MAG IN DER THEORIE RICHTIG SEIN, TAUGT ABER NICHT FÜR DIE PRAXIS (1793), III. VOM VERHÄLTNIS DER THEORIE ZUR PRAXIS IM VÖLKERRECHT, à la fin.

COMPÉTENCE ET SAISINE: UN NOUVEL ASPECT DU PRINCIPE DE LA JURIDICTION CONSENSUELLE

par

PROSPER WEIL[*]

Comme chacun le sait, la compétence de la Cour internationale de Justice pour connaître d'un différend une fois établie, la Cour peut, aux termes de l'article 40 de son Statut, être saisie de deux manières: conjointement par les deux parties, par la notification d'un compromis; unilatéralement par l'une d'elles, par le dépôt d'une requête. Que la compétence de la Cour dépende de la volonté des parties, là-dessus aucun doute n'est possible: le «principe de la juridiction consensuelle»[1] traverse la jurisprudence à la manière d'un fil d'or dont la pérennité défie le temps[2]. Ce principe s'étend-il au choix du mode de saisine? Ce choix dépend-il lui aussi de la volonté des parties? Tel est le problème que l'on se propose d'examiner ici.

Pour bien le comprendre, il importe d'en déterminer les contours.

Le problème

Lorsque les parties ont décidé qu'un différend fera l'objet d'un règlement par la Cour internationale de Justice et qu'elles ont précisé qu'à cet effet elles négocieront un compromis, aucun doute n'est possible: la Cour ne pourra être saisie que par la notification de ce compromis.

A l'inverse, lorsque les parties ont décidé qu'un différend fera l'objet d'un règlement par la Cour internationale de Justice et qu'elles ont précisé qu'à cet effet la Cour pourra être saisie par l'une ou l'autre d'entre elles, pas davantage le doute n'est-il permis: la saisine par voie de requête est possible. Tel est le cas des traités qui comportent une clause d'après laquelle tout

---

[*] La présente étude reprend et développe, à la lumière de la position prise par la Cour internationale de Justice dans son arrêt du 15 février 1995 en l'affaire de la *Délimitation maritime et questions territoriales entre Qatar et Bahreïn (compétence et recevabilité)* (CIJ RECEUIL (1995), p. 6), certains thèmes de la plaidoirie prononcée devant la Cour par l'auteur de ces lignes en sa qualité de conseil de Bahreïn (*voir* notamment CR 94/2, pp. 64–72).

[1] *Différend frontalier terrestre, insulaire et maritime (El Salvador/Honduras)*, CIJ RECUEIL (1991), p. 133, par. 94.

[2] Pour une réaffirmation récente, voir *Timor oriental (Portugal c. Australie)*, CIJ RECUEIL (1993), 101, par. 26 («l'un des principes fondamentaux de son Statut est qu'elle ne peut trancher un différend entre des Etats sans que ceux-ci aient consenti à sa juridiction»).

différend portant sur l'interprétation ou l'application du traité sera soumis à la Cour sur requête de l'une ou l'autre des parties. Tel est le cas également du système de la clause facultative de juridiction obligatoire institué par l'article 36, paragraphe 2, du Statut, dont l'un des traits caractéristiques, selon la Cour, réside dans le fait que «pour les différends qui en relèvent, la Cour peut être saisie par requête d'une des parties»[3].

C'est seulement lorsque les parties ont décidé de soumettre un différend au règlement par la Cour sans spécifier le mode de saisine que le problème se pose. Comme ce n'est pas la voie de la saisine conjointe qui peut faire difficulté, mais seulement celle de la saisine unilatérale, le problème se pose concrètement de manière plus simple encore: si les parties n'ont pas spécifié que la Cour serait saisie par voie de compromis, l'une d'entre elles peut-elle prendre l'initiative de lui soumettre le différend par une requête introductive d'instance?

L'intérêt juridique du problème est de taille. Le principe de la juridiction consensuelle régit-il seulement la compétence de la Cour, ou bien gouverne-t-il aussi sa saisine? Suffit-il, pour que la Cour puisse se prononcer sur un différend, que les parties aient consenti au règlement judiciaire, ou bien faut-il qu'elles aient consenti aussi au mode de saisine? En un mot, quelle est l'étendue du principe de la juridiction consensuelle? quels sont les rapports entre compétence et saisine?

L'enjeu politique n'est pas moins considérable. Il arrive assez fréquemment que, pour sortir d'une situation conflictuelle plus ou moins complexe, deux gouvernements décident, par un accord de principe, de soumettre un différend, ou certains aspects d'un différend, au règlement de la Cour internationale de Justice, sans aller plus loin, c'est-à-dire sans prendre parti sur la voie procédurale qu'ils entendent suivre. Un accord de ce genre peut reposer sur un malentendu, en ce sens que pour l'une des parties il implique de bonne foi que l'on va entreprendre la négociation d'un compromis tandis que l'autre y voit, avec une égale bonne foi, l'autorisation pour chacune des parties de porter le différend à la Cour de manière unilatérale, en déposant une requête. Mais un accord de ce genre peut tout aussi bien se limiter à la décision de principe de recourir au règlement par la Cour, la question du mode de saisine de la Cour restant ouverte pour la simple raison qu'elle n'aura pas été évoquée. Pareille situation se présentera fréquemment lorsque la décision de soumettre un différend à la Cour est prise à l'échelon politique, au bénéfice d'une rencontre à haut niveau entre chefs d'Etat ou de governement, ou entre ministres des affaires étrangères, et se trouve être l'objet d'une men-

---

[3] *Nottebohm (exception préliminaire)*, CIJ RECUEIL (1953), p. 122.

tion dans le communiqué final destiné à rendre compte à l'opinion des deux pays du progrès réalisé par leurs dirigeants sur la voie du règlement du conflit qui les oppose. Peut-on en pareil cas permettre à l'une des parties de se précipiter à la Cour pour y déposer une requête introductive d'instance, à peine séchée l'encre du communiqué final? Mieux encore: peut-on permettre à l'une des parties de saisir la Cour unilatéralement lorsque les négociations entreprises depuis un temps plus ou moins long en vue de la conclusion d'un compromis traînent en longueur ou sont dans l'impasse? C'est dire combien il est important que les gouvernements sachent à quoi s'en tenir. Si la décision de soumettre un différend à la Cour implique le droit pour chaque partie de porter ce différend à la Cour unilatéralement, plus d'un gouvernement hésitera à s'en tenir à une décision de principe de recourir au règlement judiciaire et exigera que l'on mette les points sur les i. Rarement la prévisibilité et la sécurité juridique auront été en jeu davantage.

Des précédents peu concluants

Pour étonnant que cela soit, ni la doctrine ni la jurisprudence ne paraissent avoir porté grand intérêt à ce problème jusqu'à une date récente.

Dans les quelques affaires où elle a été saisie par voie de requête alors que l'instrument lui conférant compétence n'avait pas spécifié la méthode de saisine, la Cour s'est bornée à rechercher l'intention des parties telle qu'est s'était exprimée dans les termes de cet instrument et ressortait des circonstances dans lesquelles ce dernier avait été conclu; selon le cas, elle a reconnu ou décliné sa compétence pour statuer sur la requête.

C'est ainsi que, confrontée à la clause, très courante dans les traités d'amitié ou d'établissement, d'après laquelle «Tout différend relatif à l'interprétation et à l'application du présent traité sera porté devant la Cour internationale de Justice...», elle a estimé que

> «cet article ne prévoit certes pas en termes exprès que l'une ou l'autre partie peut saisir la Cour par requête unilatérale, mais il est évident que ... c'est bien ainsi que les parties l'entendaient ... L'intention des parties, lorsqu'elles acceptent ces clauses, est sans aucun doute de se réserver ce droit de s'adresser à la Cour unilatéralement...»[4].

---

[4] *Personnel diplomatique et consulaire des Etats-Unis à Téhéran*, CIJ RECUEIL (1980), p. 27, par. 52. Les Etats-Unis avaient observé au cours de la procédure que les parties interprétaient traditionnellement de telles clauses comme autorisant la saisine unilatérale (*Mémoires*, 153 et 285). Dans le même sens, *Activités militaires et paramilitaires au Nicaragua et contre celuici*, CIJ RECUEIL (1984), p. 427, par. 81.

C'est ainsi, à l'inverse, que, saisie par une requête sur la base d'un communiqué conjoint par lequel les premiers ministres de Grèce et de Turquie avaient décidé de lui soumettre le conflit relatif au plateau continental de la mer Egée sans spécifier si la Cour devrait être saisie par compromis ou pourrait l'être par requête de l'une des parties, la Cour a procédé à l'interprétation de cet instrument et conclu qu'il «n'avait pas pour objet et n'a pas eu pour effet de constituer ... un engagement immédiat ... d'accepter inconditionnellement que le ... différend soit soumis à la Cour par requête unilatérale»[5].

Dans une affaire où elle était dans l'incertitude quant à l'intention des parties de permettre, ou de ne pas permettre, la saisine unilatérale, elle a refusé de voir dans l'instrument invoqué une base de compétence suffisante[6].

Il n'est certes par interdit de penser, à la lumière de ces précédents, qu'aux yeux de la Cour le choix du mode de saisine – et, plus concrètement, la saisine par voie de requête – relève de l'exigence consensuelle et constitue une question de compétence. Dans toutes ces affaires, en effet, la Cour paraît bien avoir subordonné sa compétence au consentement des parties à la saisine unilatérale, se reconnaissant compétente lorsqu'elle pouvait conclure à ce consentement, déclinant sa compétence dans le cas contraire.

Le problème aurait-il donc été résolu depuis longtemps? Il serait téméraire de tirer de ces précédents une conclusion aussi péremptoire. Dans aucune de ces affaires, en effet, ni le problème des rapports entre compétence et saisine ni celui de la portée de l'exigence consensuelle n'avaient été abordés de front par les parties et n'ont, en conséquence, été abordés de front par la Cour; celle-ci s'est contentée de se prononcer en termes de consentement et de compétence comme une chose allant de soi. Dans la plupart de ces affaires, la question du consentement à la saisine n'a en outre pas été débattue ou tranchée en tant que telle, à l'état pur si l'on peut s'exprimer ainsi, mais

---

5 *Plateau continental de la mer Egée*, CIJ RECUEIL (1978), p. 44, par. 107.

6 *Application de la convention pour la prévention et la répression du crime de génocide (mesures conservatoires)*, CIJ RECUEIL (1993), p. 18, par. 31. L'instrument en cause était une lettre dans laquelle le président de la Yougoslavie avait indiqué que, selon la vue de la Yougoslavie, les différends entre la nouvelle Yougoslavie et les républiques issues de l'ancienne Yougoslavie devraient être soumis au règlement de la Cour. La Cour a déclaré qu'«à ce stade de la procédure» – c'est-à-dire au stade préliminaire de la demande en indication de mesures conservatoires – elle était «dans la plus grande incertitude quant au point de savoir si le but de la lettre ... était de constituer, de la part des deux présidents, un 'engagement immédiat', ayant force obligatoire pour la Yougoslavie, d'accepter inconditionnellement que soient soumis à la Cour, par requête unilatérale, une grande diversité de différends juridiques...; ou si son but n'était rien d'autre que d'énoncer une politique générale visant à favoriser le règlement judiciaire, sans offre ni engagement». La valeur de ce précédent ne doit cependant pas être surestimée: non seulement s'agissait-il seulement, à ce stade, d'une compétence *prima facie*, mais cette lettre n'avaient été invoquée par l'Etat requérant comme base de compétence qu'à titre supplémentaire en cours de procédure.

était liée au problème de la nature de l'instrument par lequel les Etats en cause avaient accepté la compétence de la Cour: pour renforcer sa thèse que les parties avaient, en l'espèce, consenti à la saisine unilatérale, l'Etat requérant soutenait que l'instrument pertinent avait le caractère d'un accord international, et pour combattre cette thèse l'Etat défendeur prétendait que cet instrument n'avait pas le caractère d'un accord international et ne constituait qu'un acte politique sans portée juridique[7].

Une première: l'affaire Qatar c. Bahreïn

Aussi peut-on considérer que c'est dans l'affaire de la *Délimitation maritime et questions territoriales entre Qatar et Bahreïn (compétence et recevabilité)* que le problème a, pour la première fois, été discuté par les parties sur ses mérites propres et tranché par la Cour de manière explicite.

Sans doute ne s'est-il, cette fois encore, pas présenté à l'état pur. A l'appui de sa requête Qatar invoquait comme base de compétence le procès-verbal d'une réunion du Conseil de coopération des Etats arabes du Golfe à Doha en 1990 par lequel les parties avaient réaffirmé leur accord antérieur de faire régler l'ensemble de leurs différends par la Cour et convenu qu'à l'expiration d'un délai de cinq mois elles «pourront soumettre la question à la Cour internationale de Justice conformément à la formule bahreïnite[8], qui a été acceptée par Qatar, et à la procédure qui en résulte». Selon Qatar, le procès-verbal de Doha constituait un accord international par lequel les parties avaient accepté implicitement que chacune d'elles pourrait à l'expiration d'un délai de cinq mois saisir la Cour unilatéralement. Selon Bahreïn, au contraire, le procès-verbal de Doha ne constituait qu'un simple compte-rendu de négociation, qui n'avait pas valeur d'accord international, qui n'exprimait aucun consentement des parties à une saisine unilatérale et dont les travaux

---

[7] Pour la plupart des commentateurs, c'est parce qu'il n'aurait pas été regardé par la Cour comme un accord international que le communiqué conjoint gréco-turc se serait vu refuser, dans l'affaire du *Plateau continental de la mer Egée*, la qualité d'un «titre de compétence direct et complet» (CIJ RECUEIL (1978), p. 44, par. 106). Comme l'a montré H. THIRLWAY, cette analyse est probablement inexacte: ce n'est pas parce qu'il n'était pas un accord international que le communiqué s'est vu récusé comme titre de juridiction, mais parce qu'il n'était pas l'expression de la volonté commune des parties d'autoriser la saisine unilatérale: «Although the Court does not say so, it appears to have proceeded on the assumption that the communiqué was an agreement, to conclude that it was not an agreement of the kind claimed by Greece». The *Law and Procedure of the International Court of Justice 1960–1989*, BRITISH YEAR BOOK OF INTERNATIONAL LAW (1991), pp. 14–15.

[8] Il s'agissait d'une formule, proposée par Bahreïn et destinée à figurer dans le compromis alors en voie de négociation, dont l'objet était de permettre à chacune des parties de soumettre à la Cour les questions qui lui paraissaient appropriées.

préparatoires montraient, tout au contraire, que Bahreïn, pour sa part, s'était formellement opposé à la saisine unilatérale.

A nouveau, on le constate, la discussion avait porté essentiellement sur la nature juridique de l'instrument pertinent et sur l'existence ou l'absence, en fait, d'un consentement des parties à la saisine unilatérale. Mais cette fois-ci le problème des rapports entre compromis et saisine et celui de la soumission de la saisine à l'exigence consensuelle avaient été soulevés et débattus par les parties en toute clarté. Pour reprendre le résumé qu'en donne la Cour,

> «Qatar ... distingu(ait) la saisine de la compétence en expliquant que, si la volonté des parties, telle qu'exprimée dans les accords en vigueur, est déterminante aux fins d'établir la compétence, la validité de la saisine doit en revanche s'apprécier essentiellement au regard du Statut et du Règlement de la Cour, sous réserve de toute disposition spéciale dont les parties auraient pu convenir»[9].

Bahreïn, pour sa part, avait fait valoir, toujours selon le résumé que la Cour donne de sa thèse,

> «que la saisine n'est pas une simple question de procédure, mais une question de compétence, que le consentement à la saisine unilatérale est soumis aux mêmes conditions que le consentement au règlement judiciaire et doit donc être non équivoque et indiscutable; et que, dans le silence des textes, la saisine conjointe constitue la solution par défaut»[10].

La compétence est une chose, la saisine en est une autre

Acceptée comme une vérité d'évidence par les deux parties dans cette affaire, la distinction de principe entre compétence et saisine n'a cependant guère été creusée par elles. Elle se situe, semble-t-il, sur un triple plan.

Leur nature, tout d'abord, est différente.

La compétence est un pouvoir, une faculté, une habilitation. En conférant par leur volonté commune compétence à la Cour pour statuer sur un différend, les parties l'habilitent à examiner cette affaire, à régler ce différend. Le titre (ou base) de compétence réside dans l'accord des parties pour conférer ce pouvoir à la Cour. Dans l'immense majorité des cas, le *negotium* qui constitue le titre (ou base) de compétence s'exprime dans un *instrumentum* qui peut prendre les formes les plus variées: traité, échange de lettres, communiqué conjoint, conjonction de déclarations unilatérales d'acceptation de la juridiction obligatoire dans le cadre de l'article 36, paragraphe 2, du Statut, etc. Dans certains

---

9 CIJ RECUEIL (1995), p. 23, par. 43.

10 *Ibid.*

cas, ce titre prend la forme de simples «actes concluants»[11] dont la Cour peut déduire une acceptation «volontaire, indiscutable»[12] de sa juridiction, tel le fait de défendre au fond sans faire de réserve sur la compétence.

La saisine, quant à elle, est un acte de procédure qui permet à la Cour l'exercice de la compétence qui lui a été conférée par les parties. En effet, même une fois établie par l'accord des parties, la compétence de la Cour pour connaître d'un différend n'est qu'une potentialité à l'état de puissance; pour que cette virtualité devienne effective, il faut passer à l'acte, si l'on peut s'exprimer ainsi, en recourant à l'un ou l'autre des modes de saisine prévus par le Statut. La compétence n'est rien sans l'acte de saisine qui en rend possible l'exercice.

En conséquence, compétence et saisine ne sont pas seulement distinctes conceptuellement, elles sont séparées dans le temps. Normalement, la compétence précède la saisine. C'est seulement la compétence une fois établie par la volonté commune des parties que la Cour sera saisie soit par la notification d'un compromis soit par le dépôt d'une requête. Dans certains cas, cependant, la séquence peut se trouver inversée. Telle est l'essence de la théorie du *forum prorogatum* selon laquelle la Cour peut avoir été valablement saisie d'une requête alors même que sa compétence n'aurait pas existé au moment du dépôt de cette dernière et n'aurait été acquise qu'ultérieurement, grâce à l'assentiment du défendeur. Ainsi, dans l'affaire du *Détroit de Corfou* la compétence de la Cour n'était pas établie avec certitude au moment où l'Albanie a accepté cette compétence. En pareil cas, le titre de juridiction naît de «deux actes séparés et successifs»[13] – l'acte de saisine pour l'Etat demandeur, l'acceptation de la compétence de la Cour pour l'Etat défendeur.

L'expérience a toutefois montré que l'inversion chronologique provoquée par la doctrine du *forum prorogatum* pouvait conduire à une dénaturation des rapports normaux entre compétence et saisine. Tout en étant conscient de l'absence de tout titre de juridiction entre lui-même et un autre Etat, un gouvernement pouvait en effet être tenté de saisir la Cour par voie de requête en offrant au défendeur la possibilité d'accepter cette compétence. L'acte de saisine s'analysait alors en une simple offre de consentement à la compétence, que le défendeur pouvait accepter ou refuser. En attendant la décision du défendeur, l'affaire était inscrite au rôle et la procédure contentieuse commençait à se dérouler. Si le défendeur refusait l'offre qui lui était proposée et que le défaut de compétence devenait de ce fait définitif, l'affaire

---

11 *Certains droits de minorités en Haute-Silésie (écoles minoritaires)*, 15 CPIJ, série A, p. 24.

12 *Détroit de Corfou, exception préliminaire*, CIJ RECUEIL (1947–1948), p. 27.

13 *Ibid.* p. 28.

était rayée du rôle[14]. Pour mettre fin à cette pratique, le Règlement adopté par la Cour en 1978 dispose à présent en son article 38, paragraphe 5, que

> «lorsque le demandeur entend fonder la compétence de la Cour sur un consentement non encore donné ou manifesté par l'Etat contre lequel la requête est formée…, elle (la requête) n'est pas inscrite au rôle général de la Cour et aucun acte de procédure n'est effectué tant que l'Etat contre lequel la requête est formée n'a pas accepté la compétence de la Cour aux fins de l'affaire»[15].

Distinctes conceptuellement et chronologiquement, compétence et saisine sont, enfin, régies par des textes différents: la compétence est régie par l'article 36 du Statut, tandis que la saisine l'est par l'article 40 du Statut et les articles 38 et 39 du Règlement[16].

La saisine, question de compétence

Faut-il conclure de la distinction entre compétence et saisine à leur séparation radicale au regard de l'exigence consensualiste, en ce sens que seule la compétence serait subordonnée à cette exigence tandis que la saisine, quant à elle, y échapperait? Faut-il admettre que, si la compétence dépend de la volonté des deux parties, la saisine, quant à elle, serait d'une importance trop minime pour ne pas relever de la décision de chaque partie? Le principe de la juridiction consensuelle ne couvre-t-il que la compétence, à l'exclusion de la saisine, ou bien s'étend-il à la fois à la compétence et à la saisine? En d'autres termes, *la saisine est-elle une question de compétence au regard du principe de la juridiction consensuelle*, et ce alors même qu'à d'autres égards, on vient de le voir, elle doit à coup sûr être distinguée?

Selon la théorie exposée par Qatar, l'abîme entre les deux concepts à cet égard serait presque infranchissable.

Qatar ne contestait à vrai dire pas que lorsque, au moment d'accepter la compétence de la Cour, les parties ont précisé, par une disposition spéciale, par quel mode procédural cette compétence doit être exercée, la saisine doit respecter leur commune volonté. Mais, ajoutait-il, lorsque les parties ont

---

[14] Ce scénario s'est déroulé à plusieurs reprises: affaire du *Traitement en Hongrie d'un avion des Etats-Unis et de son équipage*, CIJ RECUEIL (1954), p. 99; affaires des *Incidents aériens*, CIJ RECUEIL (1956), pp. 6 et 9; (1958), p. 158; (1959), p. 276; affaires de *L'Antarctique*, CIJ RECUEIL (1956), pp. 12 et 15. *Cf.* S. ROSSENNE, THE LAW AND PRACTICE OF THE INTERNATIONAL COURT OF JUSTICE, Leiden, Sijthoff (1965), vol. I, p. 356.

[15] *Cf.* G. GUYOMAR, COMMENTAIRE DU RÈGLEMENT DE LA COUR INTERNATIONALE DE JUSTICE ADOPTÉ LE 14 AVRIL 1978. INTERPRÉTATION ET PRATIQUE, Pedone, Paris (1983), pp. 245–246.

[16] En ce sens, *voir* S. ROSENNE, *op. cit.*, *supra* note 14, p. 311.

accepté la compétence de la Cour pour statuer sur un différend sans prendre position expressément sur la voie procédurale par laquelle la Cour devra être saisie, le choix du mode de saisine reste ouvert et est laissé au libre choix des parties, tant et si bien que chacune d'elles peut saisir la Cour unilatéralement en déposant une requête introductive d'instance.

A cette liberté de choix Qatar tentait certes de conserver un certain fondement consensualiste: en gardant le silence sur le mode de saisine, exposait-il, les parties ont implicitement accepté que l'une comme l'autre des voies procédurales de saisine leur soient ouvertes; elles ont montré en quelque sorte que le choix leur est indifférent; en d'autres termes, par leur silence elles peuvent être présumées avoir consenti aussi bien à la saisine unilatérale qu'à la saisine conjointe.

Mais – et c'est cela qui importe ici – Qatar allait plus loin. Se plaçant sur un terrain résolument non consensuel, il soutenait que, s'il est certes requis pour établir la compétence de la Cour, le consentement n'est pas exigé pour le choix du mode de saisine. Dans cette approche extrême, le consentement n'est plus présumé, il devient tout simplement inutile. Ce qui signifie que lorsque, au moment de décider que tel différend sera soumis au règlement par la Cour internationale de Justice, les parties ne précisent pas, par une disposition spéciale, que l'affaire sera portée à la Cour par voie de compromis, chacune d'elles est libre de la lui soumettre par voie de requête unilatérale.

A l'appui de cette théorie, Qatar soutenait que la compétence est régie par l'article 36 du Statut alors que la saisine de la Cour est, quant à elle, gouvernée par l'article 40 du Statut. Or, si l'article 36 consacre le principe d'après lequel la compétence de la Cour dépend de la volonté des parties, l'article 40 se borne à définir les méthodes par lesquelles la Cour peut être saisie sans subordonner le choix entre elles à une commune volonté des parties. Ce choix, selon Qatar, est de caractère purement procédural, et il est entièrement indépendant de la compétence. En conséquence, une fois la compétence établie et l'objet du différend déterminé, la Cour peut être appelée à exercer cette compétence indifféremment par la voie de la notification d'un compromis ou par celle du dépôt d'une requête. Les parties peuvent certes s'accorder sur le recours à telle voie d'accès de préférence à l'autre; si elles ne l'ont pas fait, chacune d'elles est libre de recourir à la voie qui lui convient. Autrement dit, ce qui importe, selon la thèse de Qatar, c'est que les parties consentent toutes deux au règlement d'un différend déterminé par la Cour: c'est là le domaine du principe de la juridiction consensuelle. Ce consentement une fois donné, le choix entre la saisine conjointe et la saisine unilatérale n'est plus qu'une simple question de procédure, sur laquelle les parties ont certes la possibilité de prendre position mais qui, en l'absence d'une telle prise de position commune, demeure à la discrétion de chacune d'elles. Même s'il existe «un lien assez étroit entre les problèmes de compétence et de saisine», soutenait Qatar, «il s'agit de deux problèmes de nature différente ... La compétence de la Cour dépend de la volonté des parties ... Quant au mode de saisine, il n'a pas nécessairement la même base volontariste». Si la Cour a pu valablement être saisie dans cette affaire par voie de requête, ajoutait Qatar, «c'est parce que la compétence de la Cour avait été définitivement acceptée par les deux Etats et parce que ce mode de saisine n'était pas exclu par les textes pertinents en l'espèce, même si ces textes ne l'avaient pas expressément prévu»[17].

Cette analyse, comme Bahreïn l'a fait observer, se heurte à des objections décisives.

Il convient de remarquer, tout d'abord, qu'il y a une facilité de langage trompeuse à parler de libre choix entre les deux modes de saisine en les situant sur le même plan et en établissant entre eux une fausse symétrie. Il n'y a en effet jamais aucun obstacle à ce que les parties négocient, concluent et notifient à la Cour un compromis; seule fait problème, on l'a noté plus haut, la faculté pour l'une des parties de saisir la Cour unilatéralement en déposant une requête introductive d'instance. La véritable question n'est pas de savoir si, dans le silence des parties quant au mode de saisine, celles-ci ont le choix entre aller à la Cour conjointement et y aller unilatéralement; elle est de savoir si le silence des parties quant au mode de saisine laisse chacune d'entre elles libre de saisir la Cour unilatéralement – l'une ayant généralement plus intérêt à le faire que l'autre.

Mais là n'est évidemment pas l'essentiel. C'est sur le fond que la régularité de l'acte de saisine ne peut pas être tenue pour étrangère à la compétence, et qu'elle doit tout au contraire être regardée comme partie intégrante de la compétence au regard de l'exigence du consentement. A cela il est une raison majeure: les considérations qui sont à la racine de cette exigence pour ce qui est de la compétence et qui constituent le fondement et la raison d'être du principe de la juridiction consensuelle jouent tout autant, *mutatis mutandis*, à l'égard du mode de saisine.

Il est à peine besoin de rappeler pourquoi la compétence «dépend de la volonté des parties»[18], pourquoi elle a toujours une «base consensuelle»[19]. C'est parce que, comme l'a rappelé le président de la Cour, M. Mohammed

---

17 Plaidoirie du professeur QUÉNEUDEC, CR 94/2, pp. 62–64.

18 *Certains droits de minorités en Haute-Silésie*..., *op. cit.*, *supra* note 11, p. 22

19 *Délimitation maritime dans la région du golfe du Maine*, CIJ RECUEIL (1984), p. 292, par. 89.

Bedjaoui, dans une conférence au cours de la session de Lisbonne de l'Institut de Droit international en 1995, «la fonction judiciaire internationale est ... à l'image de la société dont elle a vocation à régler les différends: elle est consensuelle». Le principe de la juridiction consensuelle, a-t-il précisé, est

> «la conséquence naturelle et inévitable de la conception actuelle des relations internationales. Les Etats restent attachés à la liberté politique et diplomatique dont ils disposent pour régler leurs différends selon leurs intérêts propres et selon les circonstances. Ils veulent voir ouvertes toutes les procédures existantes en matière de règlement pacifique des différends».

Le règlement judiciaire est, on le sait, un moyen de règlement des différends parmi d'autres; il n'est pas le seul. D'autres mécanismes existent, et le principe demeure celui du libre choix, énoncé à l'article 33 de la Charte des Nations Unies et confirmé dans de nombreux instruments ultérieurs. Même si les juristes ont une inclinaison naturelle à privilégier le règlement judiciaire, une vue réaliste de choses conduit à se défaire de tout fétichisme judiciaire et à accepter que d'autres modes de règlement coexistent avec le règlement judiciaire. Comme l'a souligné le président Bedjaoui dans sa conférence précitée, «ce sont les Etats qui doivent faire leur choix» en fonction de leurs intérêts et des circonstances. C'est pourquoi le règlement judiciaire est entre les mains des Etats. Il intervient lorsque les Etats le veulent, il intervient avec l'ampleur que les Etats lui assignent, il intervient sous la forme que les Etats lui donnent.

Il faut prendre garde, on peut le noter au passage, de ne pas tomber dans le piège d'un vocabulaire approximatif, parce qu'imprégné de la comparaison avec l'image omniprésente du modèle national. On parle couramment de consentement à la juridiction, d'acceptation de la juridiction, comme s'il y avait là une concession ou un sacrifice de la part des Etats, une renonciation à leur souveraineté, une amputation de leurs pouvoirs. La vérité est tout autre, et la terminologie usuelle – à laquelle nous recourons ici, comme tout le monde, en raison de sa commodité – la reflète mal. En recourant au règlement judiciaire, les Etats ne concèdent rien, ne renoncent à rien, ne sacrifient rien. Ils choisissent librement, dans l'exercice de leur souveraineté, tel mode de règlement de préférence à tel autre, ou parallèlement à tel autre, et lui assignent l'étendue qu'ils estiment appropriée à leurs intérêts et aux circonstances. Les Etats ne consentent pas à la compétence de la Cour, ils lui confèrent compétence. Le principe de la juridiction consensuelle n'est pas l'expression négative d'un sacrifice mais l'expression positive d'un choix souverain.

Car – c'est là le coeur du problème – la décision de conférer compétence à la Cour pour régler un différend relève d'une option politique; elle est discrétionnaire, et nul ne saurait faire grief à un Etat de ne pas l'avoir prise, ou de l'avoir assortie de certaines conditions et réserves. La Cour a elle-même rappelé il y a peu que les déclarations optionnelles de l'article 36, paragraphe 2, du Statut «sont des engagements facultatifs, de caractère unilatéral, que les Etats ont toute liberté de souscrire ou de ne pas souscrire»[20]; cette analyse vaut pour toute décision étatique de conférer, ou de ne pas conférer, compétence à la Cour.

Si tel est le fondement du principe de la juridiction consensuelle, force est de constater que les considérations qui l'inspirent valent tout autant pour le choix du mode de saisine que pour la compétence. La décision d'autoriser chaque partie – donc aussi la partie adverse – à porter le différend à la Cour unilatéralement ou, tout au contraire, de subordonner l'exercice par la Cour de sa compétence à la conclusion d'un compromis dépasse de loin la simple technique procédurale et ne saurait, sous peine de trahir la réalité, être reléguée au rang mineur d'une simple modalité dépourvue d'importance.

Le choix entre les deux modes de saisine n'est, en effet, pas neutre; il est politiquement et juridiquement aussi important que la décision de principe de recourir au règlement judiciaire. Saisir la Cour en lui notifiant un compromis définissant d'un commun accord le contenu exact des questions sur lesquelles la Cour est invitée à se prononcer et réglant diverses autres questions importantes aux yeux de l'une ou l'autre des parties est une chose; laisser à l'une des parties le soin de déterminer seule les contours du différend en est une autre. Sans doute, même saisie par voie de requête, la Cour est-elle appelée à définir elle-même les véritables questions en cause et s'inspirera-t-elle pour ce faire des conclusions du défendeur en même temps que de celles du demandeur; il n'en demeure pas moins que le défendeur ne peut élargir substantiellement l'étendue des questions soumises à la Cour par la requête qu'au prix d'une demande reconventionnelle. A quoi s'ajoute qu'au cas, qui est loin d'être exceptionnel, où les parties n'ont pas exactement la même vision de l'objet du différend, la formule du compromis est assez flexible pour permettre de saisir la Cour du différend tel que le voient l'une et l'autre. Par ailleurs, même si la procédure contentieuse assure l'égalité des parties, et si la Cour a toujours à coeur de ne pas désavantager le défendeur, un gouvernement peut avoir des raisons politiques, ne serait-ce que vis-à-vis de son opinion publique, de chercher à apparaître comme se présentant devant la

---

20 *Activités militaires et paramilitaires au Nicaragua et contre celui-ci (Nicaragua c. Etats-Unis d'Amérique),* CIJ RECUEIL (1984), p. 418, par. 59.

Cour sur un pied de parfaite égalité avec son adversaire plutôt que de sembler avoir été en quelque sorte traîné en justice par lui. Bien qu'il soit de principe que le dépôt d'une requête ne doit pas être considéré comme un acte d'inimitié, il n'en reste pas moins qu'un gouvernement peut, pour des raisons politiques dont il est seul juge, préférer la saisine conjointe à la saisine unilatérale.

Encore une fois, il est essentiel que chaque Etat demeure libre de rechercher la solution d'un différend par le procédé qui lui paraît le plus approprié. Le succès de la Cour repose sur la confiance des Etats. Forcer la volonté des Etats en matière de saisine serait aussi désastreux pour l'avenir de la juridiction internationale que de la forcer en matière de compétence.

C'est pourquoi le choix de la voie procédurale par laquelle la Cour va être mise en mesure d'exercer la compétence que lui a conférée la volonté commune des parties est un aspect de cette compétence. Le consentement à la saisine – concrètement, à la saisine unilatérale par voie de requête – est une composante à part entière du principe général de la juridiction consensuelle. Le choix de la méthode de saisine ne relève pas de la simple technique procédurale; il relève de la compétence. Il n'y a pas de liberté de choix en matière de saisine: la saisine par voie de compromis est toujours possible, cela va de soi; la saisine par voie de requête ne l'est que si les parties y ont toutes deux consenti.

Certes, tous les aspects de la saisine ne peuvent-ils pas être regardés comme relevant de la compétence. La question de la régularité formelle de la requête – celle, par exemple, de savoir si telle ou telle mention ou condition de forme exigée par le Statut ou le Règlement se trouve remplie – n'est de toute évidence pas une question de compétence. Ce qui est une question de compétence, c'est la question de savoir si en l'espèce les parties avaient consenti de manière non équivoque et indiscutable à ce que l'une d'entre elles puisse saisir la Cour unilatéralement en déposant une requête, car à cet égard les considérations qui fondent le principe de la juridiction consensuelle jouent à plein. Pour que la Cour ait compétence pour se prononcer sur une requête, il ne suffit pas que les parties aient décidé d'un commun accord de lui soumettre un différend donné; il faut aussi qu'elles aient consenti à ce que chacune d'elles puisse la saisir unilatéralement. L'observation de Sir Gerald Fitzmaurice va au coeur du problème:

> «if a tribunal has not been duly seized, it is incompetent to hear the case»[21].

---

[21] G. FITZMAURICE, THE LAW AND PROCEDURE OF THE INTERNATIONAL COURT OF JUSTICE (1986), vol. II, p. 440.

Il semble bien que ce soit cette approche de l'intégration de la saisine dans la compétence que la Cour ait adoptée depuis longemps, sans pour autant s'expliquer sur ce point.

Dans l'affaire *Nottebohm*, par exemple, elle explique que «l'article 36, paragraphe 2, et les déclarations qui s'y rattachent ont pour objet de régler la saisine de la Cour»[22] – ce qui paraît impliquer que si l'article 36 gouverne la compétence, il gouverne aussi, et du même coup, la saisine. Entre la compétence de l'article 36 et la saisine de l'article 40 il n'y a pas de barrière étanche. La saisine unilatérale est un aspect de la compétence et, comme la compétence, elle est subordonnée à la volonté des Etats.

Comment aussi ne pas songer au passage de l'arrêt interprétatif en l'affaire *Tunisie/Libye* où la Cour rappelle la faculté pour les parties à un traité ou à un compromis d'assortir de certaines conditions «leur consentement à la saisine de la Cour, et donc à sa juridiction?»[23].

Il est frappant par ailleurs de constater que, tout en admettant aujourd'hui plus que par le passé la distinction entre compétence et recevabilité[24], la Cour traite avec une constance remarquable – même si elle ne s'explique pas là-dessus – la question de savoir si elle a pu être valablement saisie par voie de requête comme une question de compétence, et non pas comme une question de recevabilité. Dans l'affaire du *Plateau continental de la mer Egée*, par exemple, elle ne s'est pas demandé si, compte tenu de l'attachement de la Turquie à une saisine conjointe, la requête de la Grèce était recevable; elle s'est demandé s'il existait un titre de compétence suffisant. C'est en termes de compétence que la Cour a raisonné, et c'est en termes de compétence que l'arrêt est rédigé; et le dispositif ne déclare pas que la requête de la Grèce est irrecevable, mais que la Cour «n'a pas compétence pour [en] connaître»[25]. C'est exactement de la même manière qu'elle procédera en 1995 dans l'affaire *Qatar c. Bahreïn*: l'arrêt examine séparément et successivement les questions de compétence et celles de recevabilité[26], et le problème de savoir

---

22 CIJ RECUEIL (1953), p. 122.

23 CIJ RECUEIL (1985), p. 216, par. 43.

24 Les arrêts récents révèlent une tendance croissante à examiner séparément et successivement la compétence et la recevabilité, la recevabilité n'étant examinée que si la Cour a conclu d'abord à sa compétence (voir, par ex. *Actions armées frontalières et transfrontalières (Nicaragua c. Honduras)*, CIJ RECUEIL (1988), p. 75, par. 15, et p. 91, par. 52, ainsi que les nombreuses affaires, dont *Qatar c. Bahreïn*, où elle examine à titre préliminaire, mais séparément, ces deux types de questions). Dans l'affaire de la Compétence en matière de pêcheries (*Espagne c. Canada*) la Cour a décidé qu'il avait statue séparément, avant toute procédure sur le fond «sur la question de la compétence de la Cour pour connaître le différend» – aucune mention n'étant faite de la recevabilité de la requête (CIJ RECUEIL (1995), p. 87).

25 CIJ RECUEIL (1978), p. 45, par. 109.

26 *Voir* notamment CIJ RECUEIL (1995), p. 14, par. 23, et p. 24, par. 44.

si Qatar avait pu valablement saisir la Cour par voie de requête se trouve examiné dans le cadre des questions de compétence.

Le paragraphe 43 de l'arrêt du 15 février 1995

La Cour ne s'est toutefois pas contentée dans cette affaire de cette solution implicite et indirecte. Même si les parties avaient débattu longuement du problème des rapports entre compétence et saisine au regard du principe de la juridiction consensuelle, elle aurait pu se dispenser de l'aborder de front à partir du moment où elle interprétait le procès-verbal de Doha comme comportant le consentement des parties non seulement à la compétence mais aussi à la saisine unilatérale. Il faut lui rendre hommage pour ne pas avoir cédé à cette solution de facilité. Sans doute a-t-elle déclaré qu'elle «ne croit pas devoir consacrer de longs développements aux liens qui existent entre compétence et saisine» et a-t-elle en conséquence jugé inutile d'«examiner les arguments tirés par Bahreïn de la nature discrétionnaire du choix du mode de saisine ni des désavantages qu'il y aurait pour lui à être placé en position de défendeur». Elle n'en a pas moins, en trois phrases d'une concision, mais aussi d'une précision, remarquables, exposé au paragraphe 43 de l'arrêt une théorie complète de la matière:

Primo: «Comme acte introductif d'instance, la saisine est un acte de procédure autonome par rapport à la base de compétence invoquée». La distinction entre les deux concepts est clairement affirmée.

Secundo: «La Cour ne saurait cependant connaître d'une affaire tant que la base de compétence considérée n'a pas trouvé son complément nécessaire dans un acte de saisine: de ce point de vue, la question de savoir si la Cour a été valablement saisie apparaît comme une question de compétence». Chaque mot, ici, est pesé. L'acte de saisine est le «complément nécessaire» de la base de compétence: tant qu'aucun acte de saisine n'est intervenu, la compétence est une simple virtualité pour ainsi dire désincarnée. La Cour «ne saurait ... connaître d'une affaire» si elle n'a pas été saisie valablement. «De ce point de vue» – mais pas nécessairement à tous égards – la question de la régularité de la saisine est «une question de compétence».

Enfin, *tertio*: Tirant la conséquence logique de cette analyse, l'arrêt déclare qu'«il ne fait pas de doute que la compétence de la Cour ne peut être établie qu'en recherchant la volonté des parties, telle qu'elle résulte des textes pertinents». A l'instar de la compétence, dont il est un aspect et un élément, l'«acte de saisine» est en conséquence gouverné lui aussi par le principe de la juridiction consensuelle, et sa validité doit elle aussi s'apprécier «en recherchant la volonté des parties, telle qu'elle résulte des textes pertinents».

En l'espèce, conclut la Cour, le texte pertinent – à savoir le procès-verbal de Doha – tel qu'elle l'interprète, permettait la saisine unilatérale, et ce sont donc les dispositions du Statut et du Règlement régissant ce mode de saisine qui l'appliquent. Si la Cour était parvenue à la conclusion que le procès-verbal de Doha ne permettait pas la saisine unilatérale, elle se serait déclarée incompétente pour connaître de la requête de Qatar.

En quelques mots tout est dit[27]. Tous les gouvernements savent à présent que s'ils prennent la décision de principe de soumettre un différend à la Cour internationale de Justice, chacun ne s'expose à une requête unilatérale de l'autre partie que dans la mesure où il y aura consenti. Autant l'arrêt *Qatar c. Bahreïn* du 15 février 1995 est de nature à rassurer les Etats au niveau des principes, autant, malheureusement, la méthode mise en oeuvre en l'espèce par la Cour pour interpréter le procès-verbal de Doha peut les inquiéter au niveau de leur application. A chacun donc de prendre les précautions nécessaires pour éviter que le texte pertinent ne puisse être interprété comme exprimant un consentement à la saisine unilatérale qu'il n'aurait pas donné. Si un gouvernement ne veut pas s'exposer à une requête unilatérale de l'autre partie, mieux vaudra pour lui prévoir expressément la saisine conjointe. Nul gouvernement ne saurait se montrer trop prudent à cet égard.

[27] Le problème est examiné plus en détail dans l'opinion dissidente du juge SHABUDDEEN (CIJ RECUEIL (1995), p. 59), qui met en lumière tout à la fois la différence qui sépare la compétence et la saisine et le «lien fonctionnel» qui les unit. «Le consentement à la compétence, lit-on dans cette opinion, ne s'étend pas, en soi, à l'acceptation d'un mode de saisine ou d'un autre»: en conséquence, «le droit de déposer une requête unilatérale dépend d'un consentement autre que l'acceptation de la compétence». «Le rôle du consentement, conclut le juge SHABUDDEEN, n'est pas négatif, excluant un droit de requête unilatérale qui existerait dès lors que la compétence a été acceptée, mais plutôt positif, en créant un droit de requête unilatérale qui ne saurait exister autrement». *Cf.* op. diss. KOROMA, *supra*, p. 72.

Fifth Part

Issues of Theory in the Development of the Law in New Areas

INDIVIDUALS AS SUBJECTS OF INTERNATIONAL HUMANITARIAN LAW

by

GEORGE H. ALDRICH

> It is, in the present view, impossible to study "law in action" without relating the law not merely to the supposed interests and conduct of States, but also (and above all) to those of the men and women of particular times and places.
>
> *Julius Stone*[1]

International humanitarian law has always had as one of its principal objectives the protection of individual victims of armed conflicts – sick or wounded combatants, prisoners of war, and civilians – but it has traditionally (at least since the rise of positivism) pursued that objective by according rights to, and imposing duties upon, States, rather than individuals. Under that traditional law, violations of the law during armed conflicts gave rise to rights of redress by the State whose nationals were victims, not to the victims themselves and, with a few exceptions, those rights were against the State responsible in law for the violations, not against the individual perpetrators. This, of course, was consistent with the basic structure of public international law in general as a law among States to which only States and, for some purposes, international organizations are subjects. During the past half century, however, this traditional approach to international humanitarian law has begun to change in at least one respect, as individual responsibility for international crimes has become an accepted feature of the law. On the other hand, there has been only slight movement in the law toward granting individual victims any remedy other than such as their own State may choose to accord.

Prior to the second world war, international humanitarian law (or the law of war, as it was then more commonly called) did not include any rules identifying violations of the law as international crimes. Certainly, Article 1 of Hague Convention N° IV of 1907 obligated the States parties to issue instructions to their armed forces in conformity with the annexed Regulations, and

---

1 J. STONE, LEGAL CONTROLS OF INTERNATIONAL CONFLICT (1954).

such an obligation implied a duty to enforce those instructions by appropriate disciplinary or criminal sanctions; but such enforcement would be done by a State with respect to its own personnel as a matter of its national law, not with respect to nationals of other States or as a matter of international law.

Despite the fact that international humanitarian law did not characterize violations of it as international crimes, political pressures to ensure the punishment of individuals responsible for atrocities resulted in occasional trials of individuals for the violation of the "law of nations;" and early in the twentieth century, it resulted in the addition of provisions to the Treaty of Versailles[2] requiring the surrender for trial of Germans charged with violations of the law. Ultimately, however, none was surrendered, Germany undertook to try those charged, and only a relative few were convicted.[3] While these events suggest that the traditional approach was already then ripe for reconsideration, the new treaties of the inter-war era – the Geneva Conventions of 1929 on Prisoners of War and on the Wounded and Sick – continued the traditional approach by not designating even the most serious violations of them as criminal.[4] Similarly, nothing in the Geneva Gas Protocol of 1925 suggests that the use of poison gas in warfare was being criminalized, quite apart from the widespread reservations that made that treaty in essence one that prohibited only first use of gas. With respect to what later came to be called crimes against peace, it should by noted that the Briand-Kellogg Pact of 1928, in which virtually all States renounced resort to war as an instrument of national policy, said nothing about any criminal liability of individuals.

Nevertheless, when faced with the conduct of the leaders of Germany and Japan in planning and launching wars of aggression and, in the case of the Germans, in planning and carrying out genocide, and when faced with German and Japanese armed forces that committed gross violations of the laws designed to protect civilians and prisoners of war, the allied nations that ultimately won the second world war found no difficulty in charging and convicting the most serious perpetrators of these acts as criminals and punishing them accordingly. From at least 1942 onward, the allied powers stated publicly their determination to bring to justice those responsible for war crimes, and their collective efforts resulted in the establishment of international military tribunals in both Germany and Japan and in the trial and pun-

---

2 Articles 227 and 228.

3 *See* J. STONE, *op. cit.*, *supra* note 1, at 356.

4 The Wounded and Sick Convention did, however, in Article 29, require parties to make misuse in time of war of the Red Cross emblem a crime under national law.

ishment of many other war criminals by national tribunals.[5] As the International Military Tribunal at Nürnberg recognized in its Judgment of 30 September 1946: "Crimes against international law are committed by men, not by abstract entities..."[6]

In light of that experience, it is not surprising that the development of international humanitarian law since the second world war has made individual criminal liability an explicit part of the law. Thus, the U.N. General Assembly unanimously adopted the Genocide Convention on 9 December 1948 which defined genocide as a crime under international law and prescribed obligations of trial and extradition of persons charged with genocide. In 1949, the four Geneva Conventions defined certain violations of them as "grave breaches" and obligated the parties "to enact any legislation necessary to provide effective penal sanctions for persons committing, or ordering to be committed, any of [those] grave breaches..."[7] Moreover, in view of the fact that virtually all States are parties to the four Geneva Conventions of 1949, the obligations created by those Conventions to try or extradite persons alleged to have committed grave breaches constitute, in effect, a system of universal jurisdiction over such offenses.

The Hague Convention of 1954 for the Protection of Cultural Property in the Event of Armed Conflict obligated the parties to take all necessary steps "within the framework of their ordinary criminal jurisdiction" to prosecute and punish persons "of whatever nationality, who commit or order to be committed a breach of the present Convention."[8] Protocol I of 1977 to the four Geneva Conventions of 1949 continued the "grave breach" system of those Conventions and created a number of new grave breaches.[9]

Most dramatically, in the 1990s the atrocities attendent on the "ethnic cleansing" that fast became a tragic hallmark of the war that erupted in the territory of the former Yugoslavia and the genocidal nature of tribal warfare in Rwanda led to the creation by the United Nations Security Council of two international criminal tribunals for the trial and punishment of war crimes, crimes against humanity, and genocide.

Whether these developments will lead to the creation of a permanent international criminal tribunal of more general jurisdiction cannot presently be known, although the International Law Commission responded to requests by the United

---

[5] *See* 11 WHITEMAN, DIGEST OF INTERNATIONAL LAW at 874–953.

[6] Judgment of September 30, 1946, as quoted in H. LAUTERPACHT, INTERNATIONAL LAW AND HUMAN RIGHTS, London (1950) at 6.

[7] *See e.g.* Article 49 of the First Convention.

[8] Article 28 of the Convention.

[9] Articles 85–89 of the Protocol.

Nations General Assembly by drafting a statute for such a tribunal. For the purposes of the present paper, the relevance of these developments is simply that they are evidence of the speed and extent of the development of international humanitarian law in the imposition of international obligations, including criminal sanctions, directly upon individuals.

No such dramatic developments have occurred with respect to the other side of the issue – the according of rights to individuals by international humanitarian law in the sense of rights that give the individual the possibility of taking action himself to vindicate those rights. A Professor Hersh Lauterpacht wrote forty-five years ago, individuals have rights under international law even if they cannot by themselves take steps to enforce them.[10] He added that "... insofar as the availability of a remedy is the hallmark of legal rights, they are imperfect legal rights."[11] With specific reference to international humanitarian law, Professor Lauterpacht pointed out an implication of the concept of crimes against humanity as punished by the Nürnberg Tribunal for the question of the recognition of the fundamental rights of the individual under international law.

> "Crimes against humanity are crimes regardless of whether they were committed in accordance with and in obedience to the national law of the accused. Such acts were deemed to violate the sanctity of human personality to such a degree as to make irrelevant reliance upon the law of the State which ordered them. To lay down that crimes against humanity are punishable is, therefore, to assert the existence of rights of man grounded in a law superior to the law of the State. Thus, upon analysis, the enactment of crimes against humanity in an international instrument signifies the acknowledgment of fundamental rights of the individual recognised by international law. It is possible that this result did not occur to the authors of the Charter, nor, perhaps, to the Tribunal which applied it. Yet unless the Charter is conceived as an *ad hoc* piece of vindictive legislation enacted by the victor against the vanquished, this is its inevitable and logical result. In terms of law, with the conception of crimes against humanity there must correspond the notion of fundamental human rights recognised by international law and, as a further result, of an international status of the individual whose rights have thus been recognised."[12]

While Lauterpacht was clearly correct, it may nevertheless be cold comfort to the victim of a war crime to know that, as a matter of law, (a) his legal

---

10 H. LAUTERPACHT, *op. cit.*, *supra* note 6, at 27.
11 *Ibid.* at 34.
12 *Ibid.* at 34–35.

rights have been violated, (b) the individual perpetrator is subject to criminal punishment as a result, and (c) the perpetrator, as well as his State, may at least theoretically be liable in damages. What good, he may ask, are such "imperfect rights"?

In the first place, I would suggest, the existence of such "rights", with the possibility of unpleasant consequences attendant upon their violation, may help deter violations somewhat more effectively than rules of international humanitarian law that are not described as "criminal" or as serious violations of individual rights. Moreover, I believe there is an understandable, and perhaps inevitable tendency at work in the process of the progressive development of the law to perfect, over time, rights presently imperfect. First steps in that direction may be seen, for example, in Article 6 of the Geneva Convention of 1949 for the Protection of Prisoners of War, which prohibits the States parties from making special agreements that restrict the rights of prisoners of war provided in the Convention. Similar restrictions on the power of the States to compromise the protections of the Conventions are found in the other three Conventions.[13] Contrast that with the rule of customary international law that permits States to waive or settle in any manner they wish claims by their nationals against other States.[14]

Another example is the development of the practice by the States concerned and by the International Committee of the Red Cross (ICRC) of ensuring to each prisoner of war, at the end of an armed conflict, the right to refuse repatriation, if he so chooses, and the right to have a private interview with an ICRC official or some other impartial authority to confirm that his decision to reject repatriation to the power in whose armed services he was a member was a choice made freely, without coercion. This practice, which was strongly supported by the International Committee of the Red Cross, developed notably at the end of the Korean War in 1953, when many Korean and Chinese prisoners of war refused repatriation.[15] Unfortunately, there was evidence that coercion was employed to force some prisoners of war to accept and others to refuse repatriation.[16] While at the end of many wars the problem did not arise, the practice of respecting refusals of repatriation and impartial verification of free choice was followed most recently at the conclu-

---

[13] Article 6 in the First and Second Conventions and Article 7 in the Fourth Convention.

[14] In that connection, note 2 *Restatement of the Law, Foreign Relations Law of the United States*, § 713, states: "The claim derives from injury to an individual, but once espoused it is the state's claim, and can be waived by the State."

[15] *See* A. ROSAS, THE LEGAL STATUS OF PRISONERS OF WAR (1976) at 478–486 and H.S. LEVINE, *Prisoners of War in International Conflict* (1977), 59 INTERNATIONAL LAW STUDIES OF THE U.S. NAVAL WAR COLLEGE.

[16] As told to the author by a civilian adviser to the United Nations Forces.

sion of the Gulf War in 1991, when many Iraqi soldiers who had been captured by the armed forces of the coalition rejected repatriation and were interviewed individually by ICRC delegates. Certainly, the guarantee of free choice to released prisoners of war is a clear example of rights being accorded directly to individuals, rather than to their States.

Nevertheless, one must admit that these two examples, isolated as they are, cannot be more than straws in the wind, indicating hopefully the direction that may be taken in future developments in international humanitarian law. Certainly, if we look carefully at the most recent codification of the laws – Protocol I of 1977 – we are struck by the extent to which the rights of individuals have been stressed in the drafting of the treaty. While the Protocol largely follows tradition in the drafting of its protections in terms of the duties of the parties to the conflict or of the occupying power, or by the prohibition of certain acts and the requirement of other acts, the substance of many articles is, in effect, the creation of individual rights. In a few cases, even the drafting used the language of human rights. For example, one might consider Article 11, which prohibits endangering the physical or mental health of persons in the power of an adverse party by any unjustified medical act or omission, and which states explicitly in paragraph 5 that such persons "have the right to refuse any surgical operation." Another example would be Article 45, which grants procedural and substantive rights to all persons who have taken part in hostilities and have been captured by an adverse party. A further, and quite important, example would be Article 75, which lists fundamental guarantees to which all persons affected by an armed conflict are entitled – including a party's own nationals. The human rights nature of that Article may perhaps be most clearly demonstrated in its articulation of fair trial guarantees.

> "4. No sentence may be passed and no penalty may be executed on a person found guilty of a penal offence related to the armed conflict except pursuant to a conviction pronounced by an impartially and regularly constituted court respecting the generally recognized principles of regular judicial procedure, which include the following:
>
> (a) the procedure shall provide for an accused to be informed without delay of the particulars of the offence alleged against him and shall afford the accused before and during his trial all necessary rights and means of defence;
>
> (b) No one shall be convicted of an offence except of the basis of individual penal responsibility;
>
> (c) no one shall be accused or convicted of a criminal offence on account of any act or omission which did not constitute a criminal offence under the national or international law to which he was subject at the

time when it was committed; nor shall a heavier penalty be imposed than that which was applicable at the time when the criminal offence was committed; if, after the commission of the offence, provision is made by law for the imposition of a lighter penalty, the offender shall benefit thereby;

(d) anyone charged with an offence is presumed innocent until proved guilty according to law;

(e) anyone charged with an offence shall have the right to tried in his presence;

(f) no one shall be compelled to testify against himself or to confess guilt;

(g) anyone charged with an offence shall have the right to examine, or have examined, the witnesses against him and to obtain the attendance and examination of witnesses on his behalf under the same conditions as witnesses against him;

(h) no one shall be prosecuted or punished by the same party for an offence in respect of which a final judgement acquitting or convicting that person has been previously pronounced under the same law and judicial procedure;

(i) anyone prosecuted for an offence shall have the right to have the judgement pronounced publicly; and

(j) a convicted person shall be advised on conviction of his judicial and other remedies and of the time-limits within which they may be exercised."

I suggest that the future avocation of the developers of international humanitarian law should be to move beyond the many fundamental human rights already set forth in the law and to concentrate upon improving the prospects for these rights to be recognized and respected in practice. Part of that necessary effort is underway through the work of the United Nations Tribunals for the former Yugoslavia and for Rwanda to bring to justice at least some of the perpetrators of genocide and war crimes; but I see no serious effort underway or in immediate prospect to improve the ability of war victims to enforce their rights.

Clearly, the most important development that might be feasible in the years ahead would be to improve external scrutiny of performance by the parties to a conflict. The protecting power system was the method adopted by the 1949 Geneva Conventions to ensure that serious violations would be detected and reported to the party or parties whose nationals were the victims of the violation – thereby serving as a deterrent to violations – but that method has not worked because parties to recent armed conflicts have refused – or simply failed – to appoint or to accept the appointment and functioning of protecting powers. To the best of my knowledge, there has not been a single instance since 1949 where the protecting power system established by the Conventions has been permitted to function during an international armed conflict. In many conflicts, one or more parties have even refused access to the delegates of the International Committee of the Red Cross. This depressing history must make us skeptical of the prospects for early agreement to effective scrutiny of performance. And yet the presence in occupied territory, in prisoner of war camps, and in internment camps of representatives of protecting powers or of the International Committee of the Red Cross would provide by far the best conceivable opportunity for individual war victims to take direct, and perhaps even effective, action to protest violations of their rights.

Protocol I of 1977 made two efforts to improve scrutiny. It established an obligatory procedure to make it more difficult for a party to a conflict to avoid accepting either a protecting power or a substitute, such as the International Committee of the Red Cross,[17] and it created a new entity – the International Fact Finding Commission to investigate allegations of serious violations of the Conventions and the Protocol.[18] Thus far, the new obligatory procedure has not been used, and, although forty-six States have accepted in advance the competence of the Commission, it still has not been asked to make any investigations. If individuals, whether prisoners of war or civilians, are to have direct access to representatives of protecting powers or of the International Red Cross or of any other external body charged with scrutiny of the performance of international humanitarian law, the international community will have to find both the will and the means to impose meaningful sanctions upon parties to armed conflicts that refuse to permit such scrutiny of their performance. Until then, the rights of individuals accorded by international humanitarian law will indeed remain imperfect in the extreme. We must never forget the fundamental truth, as stated by Professor Lauterpacht, that "... in relation to both rights and duties, the individual is the final subject of all law."[19]

---

17 Article 5 of the Protocol.

18 Article 90 of the Protocol.

19 H. LAUTERPACHT, *op. cit.*, *supra* note 6, at 69.

Réflexions sur la création d'une cour criminelle internationale

par

Lucius Caflisch

Introduction

A. L'individu en tant que sujet partiel du droit des gens

Le droit international classique est appelé à régir le comportement de ses sujets traditionnels, les Etats souverains, ainsi que des sujets créés ou reconnus par lui, telles les organisations internationales. Il détermine notamment les conséquences juridiques qu'entraînent pour ces sujets les contraventions à ses règles, conséquences qui peuvent différer, selon le projet d'articles de la Commission du droit international relatif à la responsabilité des Etats, suivant que l'activité de ces derniers est ou non qualifiée de «criminelle»[1]. Quoi que l'on puisse penser de cette distinction, c'est incontestablement, dans les deux hypothèses, de la responsabilité **étatique** qu'il s'agit.

---

[1] L'article 19 du projet est ainsi libellé:

«1. Le fait d'un Etat qui constitue une violation d'une obligation internationale est un fait internationalement illicite quel que soit l'objet de l'obligation violée.

2. Le fait internationalement illicite qui résulte d'une violation par un Etat d'une obligation internationale si essentielle pour la sauvegarde d'intérêts fondamentaux de la communauté internationale que sa violation est reconnue comme un crime par cette communauté dans son ensemble constitue un crime international.

3. Sous réserve des dispositions du paragraphe 2 et d'après les règles du droit international en vigueur, un crime international peut notamment résulter:
   a) d'une violation grave d'une obligation internationale d'importance essentielle pour le maintien de la paix et de la sécurité internationales, comme celle interdisant l'agression;
   b) d'une violation grave d'une obligation internationale d'importance essentielle pour la sauvegarde du droit des peuples à disposer d'eux-mêmes, comme celle interdisant l'établissement ou le maintien par la force d'une domination coloniale;
   c) d'une violation grave et à une large échelle d'une obligation internationale d'importance essentielle pour la sauvegarde de l'être humain, comme celles interdisant l'esclavage, le génocide, l'*apartheid*;
   d) d'une violation grave d'une obligation internationale d'importance essentielle pour la sauvegarde et la préservation de l'environnement humain, comme celles interdisant la pollution massive de l'atmosphère ou des mers.

4. Tout fait internationalement illicite qui n'est pas un crime international conformément au paragraphe 2 constitue un délit international».

Annuaire de la Commission du droit international (ci-après: ACDI) 1978, vol. II/2, p. 90.

Tout autre est la question de savoir s'il existe en droit international contemporain, à côté de la responsabilité des Etats, une responsabilité internationale des **individus** qui se seraient rendus coupables d'actes particulièrement répréhensibles, sanctionnés par le droit des gens et susceptibles d'être examinés par une instance internationale. Dans l'affirmative, l'individu peut être considéré comme revêtant la qualité de sujet du droit des gens dans le domaine considéré.

En fait, le droit international évolue clairement vers un rétrécissement du domaine réservé des Etats en protégeant directement les **droits** de l'individu et en établissant, si nécessaire, des instances internationales qui en assurent le respect. Limitée avant la Seconde Guerre mondiale à la protection des droits patrimoniaux et, occasionnellement, de ceux découlant de systèmes de protection des minorités, cette tendance englobe aujourd'hui l'ensemble des droits fondamentaux de la personne humaine lorsque ceux-ci ont été violés sur le plan étatique.

A côté des droits dont elle jouit désormais sur le plan international, la personne humaine doit assumer des **obligations**. Celles-ci peuvent découler de la coutume, par exemple des règles coutumières relatives aux conflits armés (*jus in bello*) ou de celles réprimant le génocide. A ces devoirs imposés par le droit coutumier s'ajoutent ceux résultant du droit conventionnel, telles les obligations résultant des règles sur la piraterie aérienne ou sur le terrorisme international. Généralement, c'est aux juridictions étatiques qu'il incombe de veiller à ce que les individus se conforment à ces obligations[2]; il serait donc difficile d'affirmer que les individus ont la qualité de sujets du droit des gens dans ce contexte[3]. Souvent, cependant, ces instances ne remplissent pas ou ne remplissent qu'imparfaitement leur tâche, soit parce que les personnes en cause ont agi pour le compte et dans l'intérêt de l'Etat dont elles relèvent, soit parce que, à la suite d'opérations militaires ou de troubles intérieurs, les juridictions nationales ne sont plus en état de fonctionner. D'où l'idée de faire appel à des instances internationales.

B. Evolution historique

Les premiers organismes créés dans ce domaine étaient les Tribunaux militaires de Nuremberg et de Tokyo chargés de juger les grands criminels

---

2 *Voir* l'article premier commun aux quatre Conventions de Genève du 12 août 1949, NATIONS UNIES, RECUEIL DES TRAITÉS (ci-après: RTONU), vol. 75, p. 31.

3 On a parfois affirmé que cette qualité revient aux pirates, «ennemis du genre humain». C'est oublier que les personnes accusées d'actes de piraterie sont traduites devant des juridictions **nationales**.

de la Seconde Guerre mondiale[4], Les procès de Nuremberg reposaient sur la Charte jointe à l'Accord conclu à Londres le 8 août 1945 entre les Etats-Unis, la France, la Grande-Bretagne et l'Union soviétique[5], ainsi que sur la Loi no 10 du Conseil allié de contrôle[6]. La Charte du Tribunal de Tokyo, copie quasi conforme de la Charte de Nuremberg, fut promulguée unilatéralement, le 1er août 1946, par le Général MacArthur[7].

L'article 6 de la Charte accompagnant l'Accord de Londres retenait comme actes punissables: a) les crimes contre la paix, plus précisément la conduite de guerres d'agression en violation du droit international, en particulier du Pacte Briand-Kellogg du 27 août 1928[8]; b) les crimes de guerre, soit les violations des lois et coutumes de la guerre; et c) les crimes contre l'humanité, c'est-à-dire une série d'actes comprenant le meurtre, l'extermination et la déportation de la population civile. Etant donné que les instruments internationaux pertinents omettaient de qualifier de crimes **individuels** les actes figurant dans les catégories a) et c), l'article 6 spécifiait que les comportements en cause entraîneraient une responsabilité individuelle – une qualification *ex post* qui a été critiquée comme faisant fi du principe *Nullum crimen sine lege* (légalité de l'incrimination)[9]. D'autres dispositions de la Charte de Londres portaient sur l'instigation et la complicité (article 6 *in fine*), la levée de l'immunité des hauts dignitaires (article 7), les actes commis sur l'ordre d'un supérieur (article 8), ceux accomplis par des individus en tant que membres d'une organisation criminelle (articles 9 à 11) et la procédure par contumace (article 12). La Charte renfermait également des règles sur l'enquête pénale (articles 14 et 15), la protection des droits des

---

4 Parmi les nombreux écrits consacrés au procès de Nuremberg, on consultera les ouvrages énumérés par H.H. JESCHECK, *Nuremberg Trials*, in: R. BERNHARDT (éd.), ENCYCLOPEDIA OF PUBLIC INTERNATIONAL LAW, vol. 4, Amsterdam, North-Holland (1982), pp. 50–57, ainsi que le récent ouvrage de T. TAYLOR, THE ANATOMY OF THE NUREMBERG TRIALS, Londres, Bloomsbury (1993); pour les ouvrages relatifs au procès de Tokyo, *voir* B.V.A. RÖLING, *Tokyo Trial*, ENCYCLOPEDIA..., *op. cit.*, pp. 242–245.

5 RTONU, vol. 82, p. 279. Les 19 Etats suivants ont adhéré à l'Accord de Londres: Australie, Belgique, Danemark, Ethiopie, Grèce, Haïti, Honduras, Inde, Luxembourg, Norvège, Nouvelle-Zélande, Panama, Paraguay, Pays-Bas, Pologne, Tchécoslovaquie, Uruguay, Venezuela et Yougoslavie. On notera que l'Afrique du Sud et le Canada ne figurent pas sur cette liste.

6 JOURNAL OFFICIEL DU CONSEIL DE CONTRÔLE EN ALLEMAGNE, n° 3, p. 22.

7 Pour le texte de cet instrument, *voir* R.W. MINEAR, VICTOR'S JUSTICE. THE TOKYO WAR CRIMES TRIAL, Princeton, Princeton University Press (1971), p. 185.

8 Traité général de renonciation à la guerre comme instrument de politique nationale, SOCIÉTÉ DES NATIONS, RECUEIL DES TRAITÉS, vol. 94, p. 57.

9 *Voir* H.H. JESCHECK, *op. cit.*, note 4, p. 52; H. EHARD, *The Nuremberg Trial against the Major War Criminals and International Law*, 44 AMERICAN JOURNAL OF INTERNATIONAL LAW (1949), pp. 223–245 (230–236); H. KELSEN, *Collective and Individual Responsibility for Acts of State in International Law*, JEWISH YEARBOOK OF INTERNATIONAL LAW (1949), pp. 226–239 (237–239) (pour les crimes contre la paix).

accusés («fair trial», article 16), la procédure à suivre (articles 17 à 25), et le jugement et les peines (articles 26 à 29). A propos de ces dernières, le Tribunal pouvait imposer la peine de mort ou toute peine qu'il estimait appropriée (article 27). Cette solution peut être critiquée comme allant à l'encontre du principe *Nulla poena sine lege* (légalité de la peine), d'abord parce que les peines avaient été fixées postérieurement à la commission des actes incriminés[10], ensuite parce que l'échelle des peines prévues était vague au point de ne pas en être une.

Le mécanisme de Nuremberg, qui vient d'être décrit en raison de son importance pour l'avenir, présentait ainsi de sérieux défauts: adoption de la Charte constitutive par les seules Puissances victorieuses, à l'exclusion notamment de l'Allemagne; «criminalisation» *ex post* de certains comportements; fixation *ex post* d'une échelle de peines qui, du reste, ne méritait guère cette appellation. Ces trois éléments, on le verra, seront les *leitmotivs* de la discussion actuelle relative à l'établissement d'une cour criminelle internationale préconstituée (ci-après: CCI).

Malgré leurs imperfections, les «principes de Nuremberg» furent confirmés dans la Résolution 95 (I) adoptée le 11 décembre 1946 par l'Assemblée générale, acquérant ainsi un degré de reconnaissance qui allait conduire à leur réception graduelle en droit international coutumier[11]. Dans sa Résolution 260 B (III) du 9 décembre 1948, l'Assemblée invita la Commission du droit international des Nations Unies (ci-après: CDI) à examiner si l'établissement d'une cour pénale internationale permanente était souhaitable et possible. Dans sa Résolution 177 (II) du 21 novembre 1947, l'Assemblée chargea la CDI d'élaborer un «code des crimes contre la paix et la sécurité de l'humanité» qui devait renfermer les principes de Nuremberg. Etant donné que l'agression figurait parmi les crimes que l'on souhaitait retenir, qu'il fallait ainsi la définir et que cette tâche avait été dévolue à un comité *ad hoc* de l'Assemblée générale, la CDI, en 1957, suspendit ses travaux jusqu'à l'adoption par l'Assemblée, le 14 décembre 1974, de la Résolution 3314 (XXIX) définissant l'agression.

En 1982, la CDI reprit son travail sur le code sans se préoccuper de la création éventuelle d'une CCI. De 1983 à 1995, 13 rapports furent produits sur ce code[12]. En revanche, ce n'est que dans les Résolutions 808 et 827 du

---

[10] H. EHARD, *op. cit.*, note 9, pp. 236–239.

[11] H.H. JESCHECK, *op. cit.*, note 4, pp. 55–56.

[12] ACDI 1983, vol. II/1, p. 143; 1984, vol. II/1, p. 93; 1985, vol. II/1, p. 63; 1986, vol. II/1, p. 53; 1987, vol. II/1, p. 1; 1988, vol. II/1, p. 199; 1989, vol. II/1, p. 87; 1990, vol. II/1, p. 27; 1991, vol. II/1, p. 39; NATIONS UNIES, documents A/CN.4/442 (1992), A/CN.4/449 (1993), A/CN.4/CN.4/460 (1994) et A/CN.4/466 (1995).

Conseil de sécurité, relatives à la mise en place du Tribunal international *ad hoc* pour juger des crimes de guerre commis en ex-Yougoslavie[13], que l'idée d'une CCI de caractère permanent refit surface, d'abord au sein de l'Assemblée générale[14], puis dans le contexte de la CDI qui, en 1993, adopta en première lecture un projet de statut d'une telle cour[15]. A la lumière des observations des Etats[16], un projet modifié vit le jour en 1994, année où fut également établi, par la Résolution 955 du Conseil de sécurité, le Tribunal *ad hoc* pour juger des crimes de guerre commis au Rwanda[17].

Bien que la présente étude ne porte pas directement sur ces deux juridictions *ad hoc*, il convient de leur consacrer quelques développements, car elles forment des précédents importants pour la création d'une CCI de caractère permanent.

C. Les Tribunaux internationaux *ad hoc* pour l' ex-Yougoslavie et le Rwanda

1. Historique

L'épicentre du conflit en ex-Yougoslavie, qui avait éclaté en 1991, se déplaça progressivement d'une partie de ce territoire à d'autres (Slovénie, Slavonie orientale, Bosnie-Herzégovine, Kraijna). Au cours de ce conflit, militaires et civils affichaient un comportement particulièrement brutal, procédant à des exécutions en masse, pratiquant la torture, le viol et l'internement dans des camps de concentration, l'ensemble de ces mesures concourant à ce que l'on a convenu d'appeler «purification ethnique».

---

13 Résolution 808 du 22 février 1993; Résolution 827 du 25 mai 1993. La première Résolution contient la décision de principe de créer ce Tribunal; la seconde, dont l'Annexe renferme le Statut du Tribunal, procède à l'établissement de ce dernier et demande la coopération de «tous les Etats», y compris ceux qui ne sont pas membres des Nations Unies. Le 2 février 1994, le Conseil fédéral suisse décida d'appliquer la Résolution 827 de façon autonome, *voir Pratique suisse 1993*, nº 9.3, REVUE SUISSE DE DROIT INTERNATIONAL ET DE DROIT EUROPÉEN (1994), vol. 4, p. 627.

14 Résolution 46/54 du 9 décembre 1991.

15 *Voir* le Rapport de la CDI sur les travaux de sa quarante-cinquième session, 3 mai–23 juillet 1993 (document A/48/10), p. 269.

16 Nations Unies, document A/CN.4/458 et Add. 1 à 8.

17 Pour le texte de ce projet, *cf.* le Rapport de la CDI sur les travaux de sa quarante-sixième session, 2 mai–22 juillet 1994 (document A/49/10), 47. L'Annexe de la Résolution 955 établissant le Tribunal *ad hoc* pour le Rwanda contient le Statut de cet organisme. A l'instar de la Résolution 827 (relative à l'ex-Yougoslavie, *voir supra*, note 13), la Résolution 955 exhorte «tous les Etats» à coopérer avec le Tribunal. Ici encore, le Conseil fédéral suisse décida, en date du 20 mars 1995, d'appliquer la Résolution à titre autonome, *cf.* JURISPRUDENCE DES AUTORITÉS ADMINISTRATIVES DE LA CONFÉDÉRATION (1995), fasc. 59/IV, nº 153.

Dans sa Résolution 780 du 6 octobre 1992, le Conseil de sécurité demanda au Secrétaire général des Nations Unies de mettre sur pied une commission d'experts pour établir si de graves violations du droit international humanitaire (DIH) avaient effectivement été commises en ex-Yougoslavie. La réponse affirmative donnée par la Commission[18] amena le Conseil de sécurité à décider, dans sa Résolution 808 adoptée le 22 février 1993, la création d'un tribunal pénal international *ad hoc* pour juger les coupables et à charger le Secrétaire général de préparer le statut du tribunal. Le Rapport du Secrétaire général, accompagné d'un projet de statut, fut présenté au Conseil le 3 mai 1993[19]. Ce projet, joint à la Résolution 827 du 25 mai 1993 établissant le Tribunal *ad hoc*, fut adopté sans changement par le Conseil. Le projet est accompagné d'un exposé des motifs sous forme de commentaire.

En élaborant ce projet, le Secrétaire général – en réalité le Bureau du Conseiller juridique des Nations Unies – devait notamment résoudre deux questions fondamentales. La première était celle de savoir si – à l'instar, par exemple, de la pratique suivie à Nuremberg en l'affaire *Bormann*[20] – le Tribunal *ad hoc* devait pouvoir juger par contumace. Le fait que les suspects se trouvaient généralement en territoire ex-yougoslave et, partant, ne pouvaient être traduits devant le Tribunal international aurait pu plaider en faveur d'une réponse affirmative. La réponse négative finalement donnée dans le Statut du Tribunal (ci-après: STY)[21] pouvait, quant à elle, s'appuyer sur deux considérations: un argument juridique d'après lequel les instruments relatifs à la protection internationale des droits de l'homme interdiraient les procès *in absentia*, et un argument politique aux termes duquel un tribunal appelé essentiellement à juger des absents ne serait pas pris au sérieux, ce qui porterait une atteinte sensible à l'idée d'instituer d'autres juridictions pénales internationales. Si le second argument apparaissait parfaitement fondé, le premier l'était moins: pour légitimer des procédures par contumace sous l'angle de la protection des droits de l'homme, il suffit de permettre au condamné de relever le défaut.

La seconde question à résoudre était celle de la nature juridique à attribuer à l'instrument constitutif du nouveau Tribunal. Deux possibilités s'offraient: la création du Tribunal au moyen soit d'un traité, soit d'une résolution du

---

18 *Voir* le RAPPORT INTÉRIMAIRE DE LA COMMISSION, (1993 – 10 février), NATIONS UNIES, document S/25274, 3. Pour le RAPPORT FINAL, du 27 mai 1994, *cf.* document S/1994/674, 3.

19 NATIONS UNIES, document S/25704 du 3 mai 1993.

20 PROCÈS DES GRANDS CRIMINELS DE GUERRE DEVANT LE TRIBUNAL MILITAIRE INTERNATIONAL, Nuremberg (1949), vol. XXII, p. 628.

21 Cette réponse résulte implicitement de l'article 20 du Statut et, explicitement, du paragraphe 101 du commentaire du Secrétaire général (*voir supra*, note 19).

Conseil de sécurité fondée sur le chapitre VII de la Charte des Nations Unies. La première solution aurait comporté l'avantage de l'orthodoxie juridique mais également le défaut de n'obliger que les Etats qui deviendraient Parties au traité – et il fallait s'attendre à ce que les pays impliqués dans le conflit ou du moins certains d'entre eux refuseraient de le faire. La seconde solution ne recelait pas cet inconvénient, puisque tous les Etats ou du moins tous les Etats membres de l'Organisation[22] sont liés par les résolutions formulées en des termes contraignants dans le cadre du chapitre VII; on pouvait en revanche se demander si la création d'un tribunal pour crimes de guerre relevait bien de ce chapitre. Pour terminer, le souci d'efficacité l'emporta sur ce scrupule juridique: le Statut du Tribunal *ad hoc* pour l'ex-Yougoslavie fait partie intégrante d'une résolution obligatoire adoptée par le Conseil de sécurité en application du chapitre VII de la Charte.

Le scénario suivi dans le cas du Rwanda était identique: création d'une commission d'enquête (Résolution 935 du Conseil de sécurité, du 1er juillet 1994) qui conclut à de massives violations du DIH; et établissement du Tribunal *ad hoc* sur la base d'une décision (Résolution 955 du 8 novembre 1994) prise par le Conseil de sécurité en application du chapitre VII de la Charte et comprenant le Statut du Tribunal (ci-après: STR), modelé sur celui du Tribunal pour l'ex-Yougoslavie. A vrai dire, la base juridique ainsi invoquée pouvait paraître ténue, car les violations du DIH visées avaient été commises dans le contexte d'un conflit interne. Le chapitre VII fut toutefois jugé applicable, vu les incidences du conflit sur les pays voisins et la menace à la paix et la sécurité internationales qui en résultait.

A l'issue de cet aperçu historique, il convient d'examiner sommairement le contenu des Statuts des Tribunaux *ad hoc* en abordant successivement cinq points:

i) organisation des Tribunaux;
ii) compétence;
iii) droit applicable;
iv) procédure; et
v) coopération entre Etats et Tribunaux.

2. Organisation des Tribunaux

Le Tribunal international *ad hoc* pour l'ex-Yougoslavie est composé de onze membres, élus pour des mandats de quatre ans par l'Assemblée générale

---

22 Comme cela a été expliqué (*supra*, notes 13 et 17), la Suisse, qui n'est pas membre de l'Organisation, décida d'appliquer les Résolutions 827 et 955 de manière autonome. Elle procéda ainsi parce qu'elle n'estimait pas être juridiquement liée par les deux textes.

après filtrage des candidatures par le Conseil de sécurité (articles 12 et 13 STY). Les juges doivent posséder, dans leurs pays respectifs, «les qualifications requises ... pour être nommés aux plus hautes fonctions judiciaires»; de plus faut-il tenir compte, pour la composition des chambres de jugement et du Tribunal dans son ensemble, «de l'expérience des juges en matière de droit pénal et de droit international, notamment de droit international humanitaire et des droits de l'homme» (article 13 STY). Ces formules sont habilement conçues, car elles ont la souplesse nécessaire – qualité que l'on cherchera en vain dans le projet de statut de la CCI[23]. Tout aussi ingénieuse est l'idée de faire élire les membres du Tribunal par l'Assemblée générale afin de compenser, en quelque sorte, le fait que le Tribunal avait été établi par le seul Conseil de sécurité; une telle compensation était d'autant plus judicieuse que c'est l'Assemblée qui, conformément à l'article 17 de la Charte, exerce l'autorité budgétaire en la matière.

Le Tribunal pour l'ex-Yougoslavie, dont le siège a été fixé à La Haye, comprend deux chambres de jugement, composées de trois membres chacune, et une chambre d'appel de cinq membres dirigée par le Président du Tribunal (articles 12 et 14, paragraphe 2, STY). Si ces arrangements semblent acceptables sur le plan financier – le nombre de juges prévu est inférieur à celui des membres de la Cour internationale de Justice – il aurait été possible de réduire à trois le nombre des membres de la chambre d'appel, ce qui aurait permis de ramener à neuf le nombre total des juges ou, alternativement, de donner au Tribunal la possibilité de remplacer les membres indisponibles d'une chambre de jugement. Outre ses trois chambres, le Tribunal comprend le Greffe, géré par un greffier désigné par le Secrétaire général des Nations Unies après consultation du Président du Tribunal (articles 11 et 17 STY), ainsi que l'Office du Procureur, ce dernier étant nommé par le Conseil de sécurité (articles 11 et 16 STY). Mais la subordination du Procureur au Tribunal est largement formelle, car le paragraphe 2 de l'article 16 du Statut précise que

> «le Procureur, qui est un organe distinct au sein du Tribunal international, agit en toute indépendance. Il ne sollicite ni ne reçoit d'instructions d'aucun gouvernement ni d'aucune autre source».

Le précédent établi par le Tribunal pour l'ex-Yougoslavie fut suivi lors de l'établissement du Tribunal *ad hoc* pour le Rwanda, dont le siège se trouve à Arusha (Tanzanie). Quatre aspects particuliers du Statut de ce dernier organe méritent cependant d'être relevés. Premier aspect, la Chambre d'ap-

---

[23] Sur ce point, *voir* ci-dessous, pp. 875–876.

pel du Tribunal *ad hoc* pour l'ex-Yougoslavie, avec ses cinq membres, remplira la même fonction dans le cadre du Tribunal pour le Rwanda (article 12, paragraphe 2, STR), ce qui a eu pour conséquence que seuls les six juges faisant partie des chambres de jugement de ce Tribunal ont dû être élus par l'Assemblée générale. En second lieu, contrairement à ce qui est prévu pour l'ex-Yougoslavie (article 14, paragraphe 2, STY), le Président du Tribunal pour le Rwanda n'est pas membre et président de la Chambre d'appel; s'il en était allé différemment, la même personne aurait présidé les deux Tribunaux, ce qui n'est pas le cas[24]. Troisième élément à mettre en relief, le Procureur du Tribunal pour l'ex-Yougoslavie assume la même fonction auprès du Tribunal pour le Rwanda, tout en disposant, dans le cadre de ce dernier, d'un procureur adjoint et de personnel supplémentaire (article 15, paragraphe 3, STR). Quatrième et dernier aspect à mentionner, le Règlement de procédure et de preuve de ce Tribunal doit, dans toute la mesure du possible, s'aligner sur celui du Tribunal pour l'ex-Yougoslavie (article 14 STR), afin que la plus grande unité possible soit assurée.

3. Compétence

i. Tribunal pour l'ex-Yougoslavie

Ratione temporis, loci et *materiae*, le Tribunal pour l'ex-Yougoslavie est habilité à juger les auteurs de crimes commis, après le 1er janvier 1991, sur le territoire de l'ex-Yougoslavie, plus précisément les auteurs d'infractions graves aux Conventions de Genève de 1949 (article 2 STY), de violations des lois ou coutumes de la guerre sur terre (article 3 STY), d'actes de génocide (article 4 STY) et de crimes contre l'humanité (article 5 STY). Sauf en ce qui concerne ces derniers[25], les infractions rentrant dans chacune de ces catégories font l'objet d'énumérations détaillées et exhaustives pour satisfaire au principe *Nullum crimen sine lege*. On notera en outre la volonté des auteurs du Statut de ne retenir que des comportements individuels réprimés par le droit international *coutumier*[26]. Cela semblait indispensable en raison du caractère contraignant que la Résolution 827 et le Statut annexé

---

[24] Le Tribunal pour l'ex-Yougoslavie et la Chambre d'appel sont actuellement présidés par M. A. CASSESE; le Président du Tribunal pour le Rwanda est M. K. LAITY .

[25] Les lettres a à h de l'article 5 STY énumèrent diverses infractions relevant de la catégorie «crimes contre l'humanité». La liste est complétée par la lettre i de l'article 5, qui se réfère à d'«autres actes inhumains», sans spécifier ceux-ci, suivant en cela la technique utilisée à l'article 6, lettre a, de la Charte de Nuremberg et à l'article 5, lettre a, de celle de Tokyo.

[26] C'est ce qui ressort des paragraphes 37, 41, 42, 44 et 45 du commentaire du Secrétaire général (*supra*, note 19). On notera qu'aucun de ces passages ne se rapporte aux crimes contre l'humanité.

étaient censés revêtir pour l'ensemble des Etats membres des Nations Unies, voire tous les Etats.

Ratione personae, la compétence du Tribunal est limitée aux individus, contrairement à ce qui avait été prévu à Nuremberg[27]. Ces individus ne sont pas habilitées à se prévaloir, au cours des procédure engagées contre eux, de leur qualité de chef d'Etat ou de gouvernement, ou de celle de haut fonctionnaire (article 7, paragraphe 2, STY)[28]. De plus, le Statut précise que la responsabilité pénale individuelle découlant d'un comportement interdit incombe non seulement à son auteur direct, mais aussi aux instigateurs et complices (article 7, paragraphe premier, STY). Le fait d'avoir suivi l'ordre d'un supérieur ne permet pas davantage à l'accusé de se disculper, bien qu'un tel ordre puisse «être considéré comme un motif de diminution de la peine si le Tribunal international l'estime conforme à la justice». Cette solution est identique à celle retenue à l'article 8 de la Charte de Nuremberg.

La définition de la compétence du Tribunal *ad hoc* pour l'ex-Yougoslavie résout également les problèmes de la compétence concurrente (article 9 STY) et ceux inhérents au précepte *Ne bis in idem* (article 10 STY).

L'article 9 fait ressortir que si les compétences des instances nationales et du Tribunal international sont concurrentes, le Tribunal peut en tout temps mettre un terme à cette concurrence en se saisissant d'une affaire. Cela revient à affirmer la primauté du Tribunal et, partant, à faire irruption dans le domaine étatique, irruption que ne justifie que partiellement la nature du conflit en cause[29]. Pour ôter à cette règle ce qu'elle a d'excessif, l'article 9 du Règlement de procédure et de preuve du 14 mars 1994 (ci-après: RTY)[30] dispose que le Tribunal attirera à lui des affaires dans trois situations:

1) si l'organe national saisi a qualifié à tort l'acte incriminé d'infraction de droit commun;

---

[27] L'on se souviendra (*voir* ci-dessus, p. 861) que les articles 9 à 11 de la Charte de Nuremberg permettaient la poursuite d'individus en raison de leur appartenance à des organisations criminelles. La Charte de Tokyo ne contenait pas de dispositions semblables.

[28] Par décision du 9 septembre 1992, le Conseil fédéral suisse accorda aux participants à la Conférence de Genève sur l'ex-Yougoslavie, conjointement organisée par les Nations Unies et la Communauté Européenne, les privilèges et immunités prévues par la Convention de New York sur les missions spéciales, du 8 décembre 1969 (RECUEIL SYSTÉMATIQUE DU DROIT FÉDÉRAL SUISSE (ci-après: RS) 0.191.2). Cette décision, antérieure à l'établissement du Tribunal *ad hoc* pour l'ex-Yougoslavie et à l'adoption de son Statut, fut ensuite nuancée par le Conseil fédéral qui précisa, le 2 octobre 1995, que les privilèges et immunités en cause ne s'étendraient pas aux personnes faisant l'objet d'un mandat d'arrêt du Tribunal.

[29] Elle cesse d'être justifiée lorsque l'affaire en cause est examinée par les tribunaux d'un Etat étranger au conflit.

[30] NATIONS UNIES, document IT/3, du 14 mars 1994.

2) si la procédure déjà engagée sur le plan national «ne serait ni impartiale ni indépendante, viserait à soustraire l'accusé à sa responsabilité pénale internationale ou n'aurait pas été exercée avec diligence»; ou

3) si cette procédure porte sur des points de fait ou de droit liés à des poursuites en cours devant le Tribunal *ad hoc*. Autrement dit, l'article 9 du Règlement de procédure et de preuve consacre la «complémentarité» plutôt que la primauté de ce Tribunal. Il en résulte, en effet, que la question de la compétence concurrente est résolue en appliquant le principe de la litispendance, sauf là où, de l'avis du Tribunal, l'instance étatique n'a pas fait ou a mal fait son travail et dans les cas liés à des affaires pendantes devant lui, dans l'intérêt d'une bonne administration de la justice.

Un problème connexe est celui de la portée du principe *Ne bis in idem*. Selon l'article 10 du Statut, un individu ne peut être traduit devant une instance nationale pour des faits déjà examinés par le Tribunal *ad hoc*. A l'inverse, ce dernier est habilité à revoir des affaires déjà jugées sur le plan interne si l'infraction en cause a été qualifiée à tort de crime de droit commun ou si l'organe national n'a pas ou a mal accompli sa tâche, étant entendu toutefois que, pour fixer la sanction, il tiendra compte de la peine que le coupable pourrait déjà avoir purgée sur le plan national pour les mêmes faits. C'est donc à nouveau l'idée de la complémentarité qui prévaut, en ce sens que le problème est réglé sur la base de l'autorité de la chose jugée, à moins que le travail n'ait pas été fait ou ait été mal fait au niveau national.

ii. Tribunal pour le Rwanda

Comme on l'a expliqué[31], la différence entre le Tribunal *ad hoc* pour le Rwanda et celui pour l'ex-Yougsolavie est que le premier, contrairement au second, doit connaître d'infractions commises dans le cadre d'une guerre civile. Cette différence a notamment affecté la définition de la compétence *ratione materiae* du Tribunal. Celle-ci comprend le génocide, les crimes contre l'humanité et les violations de l'article 3 commun aux Conventions de Genève de 1949 ainsi que du Protocole additionnel II à ces Conventions, du 8 juin 1977 (articles 2 à 4 STR). La double référence à l'article 3 et au Protocole II permet d'affirmer que les infractions punissables étaient effectivement, au moment de leur commission, réprimées en tant que crimes individuels. La mention du Protocole II, dont la nature coutumière a été mise en doute, a été rendue possible par l'adhésion du Rwanda à cet instrument en 1984[32].

---

31 Ci-dessus, p. 865.
32 RS 0.518.522.

4. Peines

Le principe *Nulla poena sine lege*, pilier du droit pénal moderne, doit aussi régir la responsabilité pénale internationale des individus. C'est pourquoi, aux termes des Statuts des Tribunaux *ad hoc* (article 24, paragraphe premier, STY; article 23, paragraphe premier, STR), «[le Tribunal] a recours à la grille générale des peines d'emprisonnement appliquée par les tribunaux de l'ex-Yougoslavie [du Rwanda]», sauf que la peine de mort est proscrite[33].

Dans le cas de l'ex-Yougoslavie, la solution retenue a été rendue possible par le fait que les infractions réprimées étaient également sanctionnées par le Code pénal yougoslave[34], resté en vigueur dans tout le territoire de l'ex-Fédération et prévoyant des peines minimum et maximum; et la même solution a pu être adoptée dans le cas du Rwanda (article 23 STR). On verra que la question sera plus difficile à résoudre dans le cadre d'une CCI de caractère permanent.

Il est également prévu (article 24, paragraphe 3, STY et article 23, paragraphe 3, STR) que les Tribunaux *ad hoc* peuvent ordonner la restitution à leurs propriétaires de tous biens acquis de manière illicite. Comme le rappelle le commentaire du Statut du Tribunal pour l'ex-Yougoslavie, ces dispositions reflètent un principe qui figure à la Résolution 779 du Conseil de sécurité du 6 octobre 1992, suivant lequel «toutes les déclarations faites et tous les engagements pris sous la contrainte, particulièrement ceux concernant la terre et la propriété, sont entièrement nuls et non avenus». Les mesures de restitution ordonnées par les Tribunaux sur la base de ces dispositions sont de nature **pénale**; demeurent réservées les revendications civiles, que les victimes devront porter devant les tribunaux nationaux compétents.

5. Procédure

Les règles de procédure prévues pour les deux Tribunaux *ad hoc* sont identiques.

L'enquête est déclenchée et menée par le Procureur, qui peut se fonder sur des informations reçues, notamment de la part de gouvernements et d'organisations intergouvernementales ou non gouvernementales. Dans le cadre de son enquête, le Procureur peut solliciter le concours des autorités locales, procéder lui-même à des investigations sur place ou faire les deux (article 18, paragraphes premier et 2, STY; article 17, paragraphes premier et 2,

---

33 Le Rwanda s'opposa à l'adoption de la Résolution 955 notamment parce que le Statut du Tribunal *ad hoc* joint à la Résolution excluait la peine de mort. Conseil de sécurité, 49e année, 3453e séance, 8 novembre 1994, document S/PV. 3453, pp. 3 et 16.

34 Code pénal yougoslave de 1977, révisé en 1990.

STR). Si les présomptions recueillies lui paraissent suffisantes, il dresse un acte d'accusation qu'il soumet à un juge du Tribunal[35]. Ce dernier l'examine et, le cas échéant, le confirme; il peut alors décerner les ordonnances et mandats requis – notamment d'éventuels mandats d'arrêt – pour permettre au procès d'avoir lieu (article 19 STY; article 18 STR).

Le procès se déroule devant l'une des chambres de jugement suivant des règles qu'il est impossible de décrire et d'analyser dans le cadre limité de la présente étude. On doit ainsi se contenter de quelques remarques générales. En premier lieu, le fait d'être saisis de violations brutales du DIH n'autorise nullement les Tribunaux *ad hoc* à faire fi des droits fondamentaux des accusés, victimes et témoins. Bien au contraire, ils doivent se montrer particulièrement vigilants dans ce domaine. C'est pourquoi les droits des accusés sont amplement protégés (articles 21 STY et 20 STR). En ce qui concerne la protection «des victimes et des témoins», il est prévu (articles 22 STY et 21 STR) que les Tribunaux *ad hoc*, dans leurs Règlements de procédure et de preuve[36], envisagent la prise de mesures protectrices, notamment la tenue d'audiences à huis clos et la protection de l'identité des victimes. La liste des mesures possibles est précisée par les Règlements de procédure et de preuve (articles 75 RTY et du Règlement du Tribunal pour le Rwanda (ci-après: RTR). Vu la nature des deux conflits et les circonstances qui les caractérisent, les principaux moyens de preuve seront les témoignages. Ceux-ci seront refusés si les témoins sont imparfaitement protégés, donc exposés à des actes de vengeance. Les dispositions en cause sont ainsi justifiées. Tout au plus peut-on se demander pourquoi il y est question de la protection **des victimes** et des témoins; si les victimes sont appelées à témoigner, elles seront, en effet, protégées en tant que témoins. Une explication possible réside dans la nécessité de protéger leur personnalité.

La procédure se termine par un arrêt rendu en public par la majorité des membres de la chambre de jugement saisie. Cet arrêt doit être motivé et peut être accompagné d'opinions dissidentes ou individuelles (article 22, paragraphe 2, STY; article 21, paragraphe 2, STR). Inspirées par le Statut de la Cour internationale de Justice (article 57) et la pratique arbitrale, ces dispositions feront apparaître les divergences qui ont séparé les membres des Tribunaux *ad hoc*. Par là-même, elles portent atteinte à l'autorité de ces juridictions, alors que cette autorité ne devrait souffrir aucune discussion, vu le domaine particulier où elle est appelée à s'exercer. La décision

---

35 Aux termes des Règlements de procédure et de preuve (articles 28 RTY et du Règlement du Tribunal pour le Rwanda (ci-après: RTR)), ce juge est désigné mensuellement par le Président du Tribunal parmi les membres des chambres de jugement.

36 Le RTR date du 29 juin 1995 (NATIONS UNIES, document ITR/3/RÉV. 1).

en l'affaire *Tadic* prise par la Chambre d'appel du Tribunal international pour l'ex-Yougoslavie en fournit la parfaite illustration: trois opinions individuelles dans le cadre d'une chambre composée de cinq juges[37]. Où est, dans cette situation, l'autorité de la décision?

Toute condamnation prononcée par une chambre de jugement peut faire l'objet d'un appel de la part du Procureur ou du condamné alléguant des erreurs de fait entraînant un déni de justice (*a miscarriage of justice*) ou des erreurs de droit qui «invalident la décision», c'est-à-dire essentielles. La Chambre d'appel peut confirmer, annuler ou réviser l'arrêt de la chambre de jugement (article 25 STY; article 24 STR)[38], mais non renvoyer l'affaire à celle-ci.

Les décisions émanant d'une chambre de jugement ou de la Chambre d'appel sont en outre susceptibles de révision, à l'initiative du condamné ou du Procureur (article 26 STY; article 25 STR), lorsqu'est découvert un fait nouveau qu'ignorait la partie intéressée au cours de la procédure initiale sans qu'il y ait eu faute de sa part (articles 119 RTY et 120 RTR). C'est la chambre qui a rendu la décision qui déterminera s'il y a fait nouveau et si celui-ci, s'il avait été connu, aurait motivé une décision différente. En cas de double réponse affirmative, la chambre en question, après avoir entendu les parties, prononce un nouvel arrêt (articles 120 RTY et 121 RTR). Ce dernier est à son tour susceptible d'appel, sauf s'il émane de la Chambre d'appel (articles 121 RTY et 122 RTR).

6. Coopération entre Etats et Tribunaux

Les Statuts des Tribunaux *ad hoc* vouent une attention particulière à la coopération avec les Etats. En effet, les personnes recherchées se trouvent forcément sur le territoire d'un Etat et ne peuvent être remises aux Tribunaux que sur la base d'un traité d'extradition ou d'un texte législatif. Mais les traités et législations existants portent sur l'extradition *stricto sensu*, d'Etat à Etat. Ici une forme différente d'entraide doit être envisagée: la remise d'individus à une juridiction internationale, créée par l'ensemble de la communauté des Etats, y compris le pays qui détient l'individu recherché, pour juger de crimes d'une gravité particulière entraînant une responsabilité pénale internationale. En raison de cette différence, les traités et lois actuels relatifs à l'extradition ne sauraient s'appliquer. Des considérations analogues valent

---

37 Décision du 2 octobre 1995, accompagnée des opinions individuelles de MM. LI, ABI-SAAB et SIDHWA.

38 Cette définition du mandat de la Chambre d'appel fait ressortir que la *reformatio in pejus* est possible.

pour la «petite entraide», soit le rassemblement de documents et de témoignages: La coopération de l'Etat concerné se justifie par la gravité des infractions visées, leur caractère international et l'intérêt que porte l'ensemble de la communauté étatique à leur répression. Pour ces mêmes raisons, le Procureur doit pouvoir enquêter sur place et entendre des témoins; il serait difficile de prétendre qu'en tolérant de telles activités, l'Etat sacrifie une parcelle de sa souveraineté.

Ce qui précède fait ressortir qu'il n'existe aucun conflit entre les obligations conventionnelles ou légales des Etats en matière d'entraide pénale et celles découlant des Statuts des Tribunaux *ad hoc*, car les deux catégories de règles couvrent des domaines différents. Autrement dit, les dispositions des Statuts forment une *lex specialis* par rapport aux obligations traditionnelles en matière d'entraide. Si cette conclusion devait être mise en doute, on pourrait en outre soutenir que les Statuts des Tribunaux *ad hoc* l'emportent en vertu de l'article 103 de la Charte des Nations Unies[39].

Toujours est-il que l'entraide qui vient d'être décrite est un concept nouveau, ce qui a amené un nombre d'Etats à compléter leurs législations nationales[40], en particulier sur les points suivants:

1) l'identification et la recherche de personnes;

2) la recherche de témoignages et d'autres preuves; et

3) l'arrestation, la détention et le transfert de prévenus ou accusés (articles 29 STY et 28 STR).

A ces éléments s'ajoutent:

1) la possibilité d'autoriser le Procureur à enquêter lui-même en territoire national (article 18, paragraphe 2, STY; article 17, paragraphe 2, STR); et

2) celle de faire exécuter les décisions restituant des biens illicitement acquis à leurs propriétaires (article 24, paragraphe 3, STY; article 23, paragraphe 3, STR).

D. Conclusions

Les Statuts des Tribunaux pour l'ex-Yougoslavie et pour le Rwanda sont similaires, sauf en ce qui concerne certains aspects institutionnels et la définition des infractions relevant de la compétence de chacun des deux organes.

---

39 Cette disposition a la teneur suivante: «En cas de conflit entre les obligations des membres des Nations Unies en vertu de la présente Charte et leurs obligations en vertu de tout autre accord international, les premières prévaudront».

40 C'est ainsi que la Suisse vient de créer les bases légales nécessaires pour coopérer avec les Tribunaux *ad hoc* en adoptant l'Arrêté fédéral urgent, du 18 octobre 1995, relatif à la coopération avec les Tribunaux internationaux chargés de poursuivre les violations du droit international humanitaire. Pour l'exposé des motifs, *voir* FEUILLE FÉDÉRALE (SUISSE) (1996) I 1. Le texte de l'Arrêté est reproduit *ibid.* p. 28.

L'idée de fonder l'établissement des Tribunaux *ad hoc* sur le chapitre VII de la Charte a pu être retenue parce que le Conseil de sécurité agissait dans le cadre de deux conflits précis rentrant dans le cadre de ce chapitre. Mais il sera impossible de continuer sur cette voie, non seulement parce qu'elle risque d'encourager des jurisprudences contradictoires, mais aussi parce qu'elle provoquera un gaspillage de temps, d'argent et de personnel.

Ce gaspillage serait évité par la création d'une instance permanente, prête à intervenir à tout moment. L'instance en question devrait, d'une part, pouvoir être saisie par des Etats et, éventuellement, par d'autres organes ou personnes; elle devrait également se tenir à la disposition du Conseil de sécurité lorsque celui-ci veut y faire appel dans le cadre d'un conflit dont il s'occupe en vertu du chapitre VII.

Le recours à des organismes internationaux *ad hoc* a indubitablement stimulé les travaux visant l'établissement d'une CCI de caractère permanent. Cet effet de stimulation serait encore amplifié si les Tribunaux *ad hoc* réussissaient à s'acquitter convenablement de leur tâche. Mais, quoi qu'il en soit, les travaux en cours seront facilités par les deux Statuts existants. Sur certains points, toutefois, la création d'une CCI de caractère permanent soulèvera des problèmes différents de ceux qui ont surgi lors de la mise en place des deux institutions temporaires.

L'ÉTABLISSEMENT D'UNE COUR PERMANENTE

A. Problèmes inhérents à la création d'une CCI et à sa composition

1. Création de la Cour

Il est admis désormais que le Conseil de sécurité peut instituer des tribunaux *ad hoc* pour juger des crimes commis au cours de conflits traités par lui dans le cadre du chapitre VII. Sans doute pourrait-il également conférer des compétences à une cour permanente sur des infractions commises dans le contexte de tels conflits. On ne saurait en revanche prétendre que la communauté internationale se trouve dans une situation d'urgence permanente au sens du chapitre VII, qui permettrait au Conseil de se fonder sur ce chapitre pour imposer la juridiction de la Cour à l'ensemble des Etats par la voie d'une résolution contraignante. Ainsi, l'établissement d'une CCI de caractère permanent passe par la conclusion d'un traité multilatéral. A ce propos, deux possibilités peuvent être envisagées.

La première serait de concevoir la nouvelle Cour comme un organe principal des Nations Unies, ce qui nécessiterait une révision de la Charte conformément à l'article 108 de celle-ci[41]. Cette solution présenterait l'avantage que l'accord portant révision de la Charte, une fois ratifié par une majorité des deux tiers, y compris les membres permanents du Conseil de sécurité, s'appliquerait à **tous** les Etats membres. Son inconvénient principal serait que l'accord créant la CCI ne pourrait entrer en vigueur qu'après sa ratification par plus de 120 pays. A cela s'ajoute que l'indépendance d'une cour étroitement liée aux Nations Unies, particulièrement importante dans le domaine qui sera le sien, pourrait paraître compromise. On peut également craindre que les Etats soient tentés de transiger à bas niveau dans le but d'assurer rapidement le nombre nécessaire de ratifications.

La seconde voie serait celle de l'établissement de la CCI par un traité multilatéral *ad hoc*. La nouvelle Cour serait alors gérée par l'assemblée des Etats Parties au traité, encore qu'elle puisse être reliée aux Nations Unies par un accord de coopération (article 2 du projet CDI). Cette manière de procéder, favorisée par la majorité des Etats et par la CDI, comporterait elle aussi un inconvénient: seuls les Etats qui deviendront Parties au traité seront liés par celui-ci. Or il est facile à prévoir que ce sont les pays qui n'ont rien à se reprocher qui entreront dans cette catégorie, tandis que les pays pour lesquels un tel traité serait particulièrement nécessaire refuseront d'y souscrire. Ainsi l'instrument en question deviendrait un accord applicable à ceux qui n'en ont guère besoin.

2. Composition de la Cour

D'après le projet de la CDI (article 6, paragraphes 2, 3 et 6), la future Cour sera composée de 18 juges élus par les Etats Parties pour des mandats de neuf ans parmi les candidats proposés par ces Etats. Quoique «permanente», la Cour ne se réunira que lorsqu'elle aura été saisie (article 4, paragraphe premier). Dix de ses membres doivent avoir «de l'expérience en matière de justice pénale», alors qu'on demande aux huit autres «une compétence notoire en matière de droit international» (article 6, paragraphe premier). Le souci des auteurs du projet de garantir la présence d'un nombre suffisant de praticiens pénalistes ressort également de l'article 9, paragra-

[41] L'article 108 de la Charte des Nations Unies dispose: «Les amendements à la présente Charte entreront en vigueur pour tous les membres des Nations Unies quand ils auront été adoptés à la majorité des deux tiers des membres de l'Assemblée générale et ratifiés, conformément à leurs règles constitutionnelles respectives, par les deux tiers des membres de l'Organisation, y compris tous les membres permanents du Conseil de sécurité».

phe 5, qui dispose que chacune des deux chambres de jugement doit comprendre une majorité de tels praticiens. Les règles ainsi proposées sont critiquables à plus d'un titre.

On peut d'abord estimer que le nombre des personnes appelées à siéger au sein de la CCI est excessif. Pourquoi ne pas se limiter au nombre de onze, retenu pour les Tribunaux *ad hoc*, ou éventuellement à treize, afin de disposer d'une certaine marge de manoeuvre? Pour une série de raisons, dont des motifs financiers, un organe dont le nombre de membres dépasse celui des juges à la Cour internationale de Justice paraît inopportun.

Un autre doute porte sur le nombre prescrit de praticiens pénalistes (dix) et d'internationalistes (huit). Comme on l'a indiqué[42], les Statuts des Tribunaux *ad hoc* ont retenu, sur ce point, une formule simple, souple et générale selon laquelle il faut tenir compte de l'expérience que chaque membre peut apporter dans les domaines du droit pénal, du droit des gens, y compris le DIH, et des droits de l'homme. Cette formule flexible et équilibrée a permis de constituer les Tribunaux *ad hoc* sans trop de difficultés. Le texte élaboré par la CDI, en revanche, pêche par excès de dogmatisme; plus dogmatique encore est l'attitude de quelques Etats, qui voudraient complètement exclure les internationalistes. Mais, pour en revenir au projet de la Commission, pourquoi cette subdivision en deux catégories, et pourquoi faire abstraction du DIH et des droits de l'homme, dont le respect est l'enjeu principal? Et pourquoi exiger une majorité de praticiens pénalistes alors que la tâche principale de la Cour consistera à décider si des individus ont transgressé des règles du droit **des gens** (génocide, crimes de guerre, crimes contre l'humanité et, peut-être, actes d'agression)? A ces objections s'ajoute la difficulté pratique d'assurer l'élection du nombre prescrit de pénalistes et d'internationalistes. La réponse appropriée à ces multiples questions serait l'abandon de l'exigence en cause et son remplacement par une formule plus souple modelée sur les Statuts des Tribunaux *ad hoc*.

Troisième et dernier point à aborder dans la présente rubrique, certains pays du Tiers-Monde estiment que la composition de la future CCI doit tenir compte du principe de la «représentation géographique équitable», qu'ils avaient déjà prôné lors des négociations aboutissant à la création du Tribunal du droit international de la mer[43]. Cette exigence va au-delà de ce qui est prévu à l'article 9 du Statut de la Cour internationale de Justice de La Haye, qui demande que les juges élus «assurent dans l'ensemble la représentation

[42] Ci-dessus, p. 866.

[43] A cette occasion, leur revendication avait été retenue, comme en témoigne l'article 2, paragraphe 2, de l'Annexe VI de la Convention des Nations Unies sur le droit de la mer, du 30 avril 1982, Nations Unies, document A/CONF. 62/122 du 7 octobre 1982. *Cf.* également l'article 35, paragraphe 2, de l'Annexe VI.

des grandes formes de civilisation et des principaux systèmes juridiques du monde». D'autres pays demandent que les membres de la CCI soient élus par l'Assemblée générale et le Conseil de sécurité (ou par l'Assemblée sur préavis du Conseil, suivant le précédent établi pour les Tribunaux *ad hoc*). Ces deux thèses sont mal fondées.

Contrairement à la plupart des autres organismes internationaux, les tribunaux n'ont pas de caractère représentatif au sens habituel de ce terme. Le juge, dont l'indépendance doit être une des principales qualités, ne représente que lui-même, sa conscience et, comme le montre l'article 9 du Statut de la Cour internationale de Justice, la civilisation juridique dont il relève. Vu le genre de cas dont la CCI aura à traiter, l'indépendance totale du juge, ici, est plus essentielle encore qu'au sein d'autres tribunaux internationaux.

Quant à l'idée d'une élection des juges par l'Assemblée générale, le Conseil de sécurité ou les deux, elle ne pourrait être retenue que dans l'hypothèse – improbable – de l'établissement de la Cour au moyen d'une révision de la Charte des Nations Unies conformément à l'article 108 de celle-ci. Si la CCI était mise sur pied par un traité *ad hoc*, en revanche, une telle solution n'aurait pas la moindre justification: on ne voit pas, en effet, pourquoi des Etats non Parties au Statut de cette Cour participeraient à l'élection des membres de celle-ci.

B. Compétence de la Cour

1. «Complémentarité» ou primauté?

En règle générale, l'examen et la répression des violations du droit des gens commises par des individus incombe aux tribunaux étatiques. On en a déduit que la CCI ne serait appelée à intervenir que dans les cas où les instances nationales n'auraient pas fait ou auraient mal fait leur devoir. Cette conception, qui forme la base des activités des Tribunaux *ad hoc*[44], a été désignée par l'expression «complémentarité». Y voyant un reflet du concept de la subsidiarité, les Etats réservés à l'égard de la création d'une CCI ont repris cette expression avec empressement. Toutefois, la concrétisation de l'idée de la complémentarité n'ira pas sans difficultés, puisqu'il faudra notamment résoudre les questions suivantes: A partir de quel moment peut-on affirmer que les instances nationales ont failli à leurs devoirs? A l'endroit des autorités de quel pays une telle détermination doit-elle être intervenue avant que la CCI puisse être saisie? Quel est l'organe qui y procède? La Cour

---

44 Du moins si l'on se réfère à leurs Règlements de procédure et de preuve, *voir* les articles 9 RTY et RTR.

devrait-elle pouvoir – et, si oui, dans quelles conditions – examiner des actes dont les auteurs ont déjà été poursuivis sur le plan national et, le cas échéant, prononcer des peines ou des compléments de peine?

Ce catalogue de questions – auxquelles on ne saurait tenter de répondre dans le cadre restreint de la présente étude – montre que l'idée de la complémentarité est plus complexe qu'il n'y paraît. Souvent, il est vrai, elle rejoint celle de la subsidiarité, par exemple lorsqu'on affirme que la CCI ne peut intervenir que si les instances nationales n'ont pas fait leur travail, encore que la subsidiarité ainsi constatée soit relativisé par le fait que c'est à la Cour qu'il appartiendra de constater l'insuffisance des efforts entrepris au niveau national. Qui plus est, les tribunaux étatiques n'auront sans doute pas compétence pour revoir les arrêts de la CCI; ici la complémentarité se traduit donc par la primauté de la CCI. Une primauté de celle-ci pourrait aussi résulter d'un pouvoir conféré à la Cour de réexaminer, dans certaines circonstances, les arrêts rendus par des juridictions nationales (article 42 du projet de la CDI).

Ainsi la complémentarité n'équivaut-elle pas toujours à la primauté des tribunaux internes, et la CCI sera appelée, dans certaines circonstances, à exercer des fonctions de contrôle. Il s'ensuit que le terme «complémentarité» évoque l'idée d'un partage de compétences entre les tribunaux nationaux et la Cour sans toutefois indiquer comment ce partage doit être effectué. Il sera donc essentiel de préciser le terme en question en s'assurant, d'une part, que l'instance internationale ne pourra intervenir que si elle juge que les organes nationaux ont failli à leur tâche et, d'autre part, qu'elle pourra le faire de manière efficace si cette condition est remplie. Le succès des négociations dépendra largement du contenu donné à la notion de complémentarité. Si ce contenu déborde du cadre qui vient d'être suggéré, dans le sens de compétences accrues attribuées à la CCI, bien des pays auront des difficultés à accepter la création de celle-ci.

Il est cependant des domaines où le concept de la complémentarité ne suffira pas. Ainsi la nouvelle Cour devrait, pour certains Etats, jouir d'une compétence exclusive en matière de punition des actes d'agression – au cas où ces actes seraient retenus comme crimes individuels. Une compétence exclusive de la CCI viendrait, ici, se substituer à l'idée de la complémentarité. Une telle compétence pourrait aussi être admise lorsque la Cour, dans l'hypothèse envisagée à l'article 23, paragraphe premier, du projet de la CDI, exercera des fonctions sur la base de résolutions adoptées par le Conseil de sécurité dans le cadre du chapitre VII de la Charte[45].

---

45 *Voir* ci-dessous, p. 881.

2. Infractions

Un deuxième secteur-clé de la négociation sera la définition de la compétence *ratione materiae* de la CCI, autrement dit des actes punissables sur le plan international et relevant de sa compétence. L'article 30 du projet de la CDI comprend les catégories suivantes: génocide, agression, violations du droit de la guerre (droit de La Haye) et crimes contre l'humanité, en tant qu'actes réprimés par le droit coutumier, ainsi que la violation de certains accords internationaux (Conventions de Genève de 1949 et Protocole additionnel I de 1977; conventions contre le terrorisme et le trafic des drogues; Convention sur la sécurité du personnel des Nations Unies et du personnel associé, du 9 décembre 1994[46]; etc.).

Plus la liste des infractions sera étendue, plus la négociation sera difficile; plus cette liste sera limitée, plus la négociation sera facile et plus il y aura de chances de faire admettre pour les crimes retenus une compétence inhérente de la Cour, c'est-à-dire une compétence qui découle directement du Statut de la CCI sans qu'il soit nécessaire que les Etats Parties concerné saient émis des déclarations d'acceptation. Pour cette raison, une tendance s'est dessinée en faveur d'une limitation de la compétence du nouveau tribunal aux catégories d'infractions les plus importantes (*core crimes*), réprimées par le droit international coutumier: génocide, violations du droit de la guerre (y compris les infractions graves au droit de Genève) et crimes contre l'humanité, soit les types d'actes visés par le Statut du Tribunal *ad hoc* pour l'ex-Yougoslavie[47]. Il est évident qu'à l'intérieur de chacune de ces rubriques, les comportements réprimés doivent être énumérés avec précision pour assurer le respect du principe *Nullum crimen sine lege*, comme le fait le Statut du Tribunal pour l'ex-Yougoslavie (articles 2 à 5), et comme la CDI a malheureusement omis de le faire à l'article 20 de son projet. Est également critiquable, sous l'angle de ce principe, la formule «autres actes inhumains» incluse dans la disposition de ce Statut consacrée aux «Crimes contre l'humanité» (article 5, lettre i), bien qu'une formule semblable eût figuré à l'article 6, lettre c, de la Charte de Nuremberg et à l'article 5, lettre c, de celle de Tokyo.

La tendance vers une simplification du catalogue des crimes a également dominé les débats, en 1995, lorsque la CDI a tenté de déterminer les infrac-

---

46 NATIONS UNIES, document A/49/724. Cet instrument n'est pas encore entré en vigueur.

47 La seule différence étant que, dans le Statut du Tribunal pour l'ex-Yougoslavie (articles 2 et 3), les violations du droit de La Haye et les infractions graves au droit de Genève forment deux catégories séparées, tandis qu'elles seraient, ici, réunies au sein d'une seule et même rubrique. Cette approche aurait l'avantage de retirer les infractions graves aux Conventions de Genève de la catégorie des «crimes conventionnels» pour les faire entrer dans celle des crimes réprimés par le droit coutumier – ce qui, d'ailleurs, correspond à la réalité.

tions à inclure dans son projet de code des crimes contre la paix et la sécurité de l'humanité. Ces débats ont débouché sur une proposition très voisine à celle qui vient d'être décrite, à savoir la limitation aux crimes réprimés par le droit international général, soit l'agression, le génocide, les violations graves du DIH, les crimes de guerre et les crimes contre l'humanité. Seraient notamment écartées les violations de certains traités multilatéraux («crimes conventionnels»). Cette proposition réductrice doit être saluée pour deux raisons. Premièrement, l'idée d'élaborer un code pénal international et celle d'établir une CCI ont des racines communes[48]; il serait à la fois surprenant et regrettable que les listes des crimes figurant dans le code et dans le Statut de la Cour diffèrent de manière sensible. En second lieu, le code sera appelé à énoncer des règles matérielles dont la mise en oeuvre est confiée aux tribunaux internes et internationaux en général, tandis que le Statut de la CCI formulera le droit pénal matériel à appliquer par cette juridiction particulière. Il serait toutefois gênant – ne serait-ce que sous l'angle de la «complémentarité» – que les règles matérielles appliquées par la CCI soient différentes de celles régissant les autres tribunaux pénaux internationaux et les organes judiciaires nationaux. Bien au contraire, un parallélisme aussi poussé que possible entre le code et le Statut paraît souhaitable. En fait, on pourrait même se demander si ces règles ne devraient pas être identiques.

Une question particulière à examiner se rapporte au crime de l'agression. De nombreux Etats ont demandé que l'agression disparaisse de la liste des actes punissables, cela pour trois motifs:

1) Contrairement à ce que prévoyaient les Chartes de Nuremberg et de Tokyo (articles 6, lettre a, respectivement 5, lettre a), qui se référaient à la conduite d'une *guerre* d'agression, il s'agirait, ici, de punir les *actes* d'agression, notion infiniment plus vaste;

2) ces actes, traditionnellement, revêtent un caractère étatique plutôt qu'individuel et seraient ainsi à ranger, si l'on suivait l'article 19 du projet de la CDI sur la responsabilité des Etats, dans la catégorie des «crimes d'Etat»[49];

3) la question de savoir si un comportement donné est un acte d'agression relèverait de la compétence exclusive du Conseil de sécurité agissant sur la base de l'article 39 de la Charte des Nations Unies – la CCI en serait ainsi réduite à se prononcer sur l'imputabilité de l'acte à un individu donné et, une fois cette identification accomplie, à fixer la peine, ce qui réduirait de manière considérable la fonction juridictionnelle de la Cour.

---

48 *Voir* ci-dessus, p. 862–863.

49 Ci-dessus, p. 859.

Ces trois objections rendent le maintien du crime individuel de l'agression – exigé notamment par la Russie et la République fédérale d'Allemagne – problématique sur le plan de la théorie autant que sous l'angle pratique.

Pour être complet, on ajoutera qu'en matière d'instigation, de complicité et d'ordre supérieur, rien n'est prévu dans le projet de la CDI, contrairement aux Statuts des Tribunaux pour l'ex-Yougoslavie et le Rwanda (articles 7 STY et 6 STR) qui reprennent les règles contenues dans les Chartes de Nuremberg et de Tokyo (articles 6 à 8 de la Charte de Nuremberg et 5 à 6 de celle de Tokyo). Tout comme les Statuts en question, le projet rejette la notion d'association de malfaiteurs, qui avait été admise à Nuremberg (article 10).

3. Compétence inhérente?

L'article 23, paragraphe premier, du projet de la CDI habilite la Cour à connaître de crimes «comme suite au renvoi d'une question devant elle par le Conseil de sécurité agissant dans le cadre du chapitre VII de la Charte des Nations Unies»: le Conseil de sécurité pourra ainsi faire appel à la CCI, instance préconstituée, lorsqu'il est saisi d'un conflit particulier. Ici la compétence de la Cour serait donc automatique ou inhérente; elle découlerait, non du traité multilatéral qui a donné naissance à la CCI, mais de la résolution pertinente du Conseil. Cette solution permettra d'économiser du temps, du personnel et des moyens financiers, et elle favorisera l'éclosion d'une jurisprudence cohérente.

De sérieux problèmes surgissent à propos des activités exercées par la Cour en dehors de l'hypothèse particulière qui vient d'être évoquée: La Cour doit-elle être nantie d'une compétence inhérente à son Statut, c'est-à-dire indépendante de tout consentement, ou faudrait-il exiger un acte spécial de consentement et, si oui, de la part de qui? Pour quel(s) type(s) de crimes faut-il, le cas échéant, prévoir une compétence inhérente?

L'article 21, paragraphe premier, du projet de la CDI investit la Cour d'une compétence inhérente en matière de génocide, ce qui signifie qu'une procédure en cette matière pourrait être déclenchée unilatéralement par tout Etat Partie au Statut de la CCI[50]. Pour ce qui est des autres crimes (actes d'agression, violations du droit de la guerre, crimes contre l'humanité, «crimes conventionnels»), le projet exige que l'Etat plaignant aussi bien que l'Etat territorial, ainsi que le pays qui détient le prévenu, soient non seulement Parties au Statut de la Cour (et, pour les «crimes conventionnels», Parties au traité pertinent), mais qu'ils aient tous accepté, au moyen de déclarations écrites, la compétence de la Cour pour la catégorie d'infractions en

---

[50] Sur ce point, *voir* ci-dessous, p. 885.

cause (articles 21, 22 et 25 du projet de la CDI). Il est à prévoir que les cas où ces conditions cumulatives vont effectivement être réunies seront rares, cela d'autant plus que les déclarations d'acceptation peuvent être assorties de réserves et que celles-ci sont susceptibles d'être invoquées, sur la base de la réciprocité[51], par les autres Etats concernés. Pour certains pays, même ces conditions draconiennes sont insuffisantes; selon eux, il faudrait que l'Etat national de l'accusé ait également déclaré accepter la compétence de la Cour. Cette accumulation d'exigences, issue d'un prétendu souci de préserver la souveraineté étatique, viderait le champ d'action de la future CCI d'une grande partie de son contenu et pourrait, en fin de compte, sonner le glas de l'idée d'une cour criminelle préconstituée.

A cette conception restrictive s'oppose un courant plus libéral, représenté par des pays moyens et petits de l'Europe, par la République fédérale d'Allemagne, la France et la Russie, ainsi que par quelques pays africains (Sénégal, Afrique du Sud) et latino-américains (Argentine, Venezuela). Ces Etats favorisent une compétence inhérente de la Cour pour tous les crimes graves réprimés par le droit international coutumier et limiteraient l'exigence d'une déclaration d'acceptation aux «crimes conventionnels» qui pourraient éventuellement être retenus.

Si le courant libéral paraît plutôt dominant, il ne l'emportera pas nécessairement. Le futur Statut de la CCI devra être adopté par consensus – ne serait-ce que pour assurer l'efficacité de la Cour à travers l'universalité de son Statut – et les consensus ont une fâcheuse tendance à s'établir autour du dénominateur commun le plus bas. Pour que ce dernier ne soit pas trop bas, il faudrait, on l'a dit[52], se limiter à retenir les infractions les plus importantes, ce qui pourrait permettre de conférer à la Cour une compétence inhérente sur **l'ensemble** de ces crimes. Cela est crucial, car, pour les raisons indiquées, une Cour à compétence largement facultative risquerait d'être mort-née.

C. Droit applicable

Les Tribunaux *ad hoc* pour l'ex-Yougoslavie et le Rwanda doivent appliquer leurs Statuts et leurs Règlements de procédure et de preuve, ainsi que les règles du droit international général définissant les infractions qui relèvent de leur compétence. Il devrait en aller de même pour la future Cour per-

---

51 *Voir* à ce propos, à titre d'exemple, l'arrêt de la CIJ du 10 juillet 1957 en l'affaire des *Emprunts norvégiens* (France c. Norvège), CIJ, RECUEIL 1957, p. 9 .

52 Ci-dessus, p. 879.

manente. Cela a paru si évident que ni les Statuts des Tribunaux *ad hoc* ni le projet de statut d'une CCI ne contiennent des dispositions expresses à ce sujet.

Il reste toutefois de nombreuses matières qui, sur le plan interne, seraient réglées par des «dispositions générales» du code pénal: intention, responsabilité et culpabilité, pour n'en citer que deux. Ces matières, n'étant pas couvertes par des règles du droit international général, devront dès lors être envisagées par le traité multilatéral appelé à donner naissance à la Cour permanente ou par le règlement de celle-ci. Parmi les questions ici visées se trouve la fixation des peines. En ce qui concerne les Tribunaux pour l'ex-Yougoslavie et le Rwanda, les grilles des peines sont celles prévues par les législations de ces deux pays en vigueur lors de la commission des crimes[53]. Ainsi le principe *Nulla poena sine lege* est pleinement respecté: la peine correspondra à celle qui menaçait l'auteur du crime au moment de la commission de l'acte et dans le territoire où il a agi, sauf que la peine de mort est exclue. Cette exclusion, bien qu'elle contredise *Nulla poena sine lege*, est légitime parce qu'elle profite au coupable. La solution relativement simple qui vient d'être décrite a été rendue possible par le fait qu'il s'agit généralement de crimes perpétrés sur le territoire d'un Etat par des ressortissants de cet Etat.

Les situations dont la CCI aura à s'occuper ne seront pas toujours aussi simples. Le crime relevant de la compétence de la Cour peut avoir été commis par un ressortissant de A contre un ressortissant de B sur le territoire de C, le détenteur de l'auteur du crime étant l'Etat D. Quelle loi la Cour va-t-elle appliquer en ce qui concerne la grille des peines? La prédominance du principe de la territorialité en droit pénal[54] aussi bien que le principe de la légalité des peines semble militer en faveur de la législation de l'Etat territorial. On peut en effet estimer qu'au moment de commettre le crime, l'auteur de celui-ci savait ou devait savoir qu'il était passible des sanctions pénales prévues par la loi de cet Etat.

La solution proposée à l'article 47 du projet de la CDI s'écarte de ces considérations et du précédent établi par les Statuts des Tribunaux *ad hoc*. Le paragraphe premier de l'article en question dispose que la Cour «peut infliger … une ou plusieurs des peines ci-après: a) peine d'emprisonnement à vie ou d'emprisonnement à temps d'un nombre spécifié d'années; b) amende». En fixant l'étendue de la peine privative de liberté ou de l'amende, la Cour «peut», aux termes du paragraphe 2 de l'article 47, «tenir compte des peines prévues par la loi» de l'Etat national du coupable, de l'Etat territorial ou de l'Etat qui «avait la garde de l'accusé ou avait compétence à son égard», par exemple sur la base

---

53 Ci-dessus, p. 870.

54 Sur ce principe, *voir* par exemple S. TRECHSEL, SCHWEIZERISCHES STRAFRECHT. ALLGEMEINER TEIL, I, 4e éd., Zurich, Schulthess (1994), p. 49.

des principes de la personnalité passive ou de l'universalité. Rien n'est prévu, enfin, en ce qui concerne la restitution des biens acquis au cours d'activités criminelles. Les dispositions ainsi résumées appellent quelques commentaires.

On voit mal, d'abord, pourquoi les peines privatives de liberté seraient nécessairement débitées en tranches annuelles et pourquoi il serait interdit de les nuancer davantage. On voit mal aussi, s'agissant de crimes graves proscrits par le droit international, comment la CCI pourrait se contenter de les sanctionner par de simples peines pécuniaires.

On notera ensuite qu'aux termes de l'article 47, paragraphe 2, la future Cour fixera librement la peine d'emprisonnement. Celle-ci peut aller d'une année à la perpétuité, la Cour ayant la faculté mais non l'obligation de «tenir compte» des grilles de peines prévues par une série de législations nationales. Ainsi le coupable, au moment de commettre son crime, n'avait même pas une idée approximative de la peine qui l'attendait. C'est dire que l'article 47 du projet de la CDI contrevient au principe de la légalité de la peine. Comment corriger ce défaut? Fondamentalement, deux approches sont possibles.

La première consisterait à préciser dans le Statut même de la Cour les peines maximum et minimum pour chaque crime ou catégorie de crimes. Cela présenterait l'inconvénient de provoquer d'interminables négociations qui aboutiraient à transformer le Statut en un code pénal international complet. La communauté des Etats ne peut guère attendre l'issue de telles négociations pour mettre en place la CCI.

La seconde approche est celle suivie par les Statuts des Tribunaux *ad hoc*: s'arrêter à une seule législation nationale et imposer à la Cour **l'obligation** d'en tenir compte, tout en excluant la peine de mort. Mais laquelle des législations nationales mentionnées à l'article 47, paragraphe 2, du projet de la CDI choisir? Les Statuts des Tribunaux pour l'ex-Yougoslavie et le Rwanda se prononcent en faveur de la loi de l'Etat territorial. Il serait judicieux de reprendre cette solution pour le compte de la CCI, peut-être en ajoutant une clause excluant les peines manifestement inhumaines, dégradantes ou déraisonnables.

La question des peines est liée à celle du sort des biens acquis au cours de l'activité criminelle. On rappellera à ce propos que les Statuts des Tribunaux *ad hoc* pour l'ex-Yougoslavie et le Rwanda permettent la restitution de tels biens à leurs légitimes propriétaires à titre de mesure pénale, les conséquences civiles des crimes commis continuant à relever des tribunaux nationaux[55]. Pourquoi la CDI a-t-elle refusé de suivre cette voie? Peut-être a-t-elle pensé que les Etats n'accepteraient pas de confier pareille compétence à la future Cour. Il est difficile de s'associer à ce raisonnement, d'abord parce

[55] *Voir* ci-dessus, p. 870.

que la compétence en question est indissolublement liée à l'exercice de la juridiction pénale, ensuite parce que l'on voit mal pourquoi les Etats refuseraient à une cour préconstituée un pouvoir qu'ils ont déjà dû concéder à des tribunaux internationaux *ad hoc.*

D. Procédure

La rubrique «procédure» englobe une vaste gamme de questions qui vont certainement se trouver au centre des négociations. Elle comprend des matières telles que le déclenchement des poursuites, l'examen de l'acte d'accusation et le déroulement du procès, y compris la protection des droits de l'accusé et des témoins, la décision, l'appel et la révision. Pour des raisons de sécurité juridique, il semble indispensable d'insérer une série de règles de procédure dans le Statut de la future Cour; on ne peut, en effet, renvoyer à une législation nationale particulière dans ce domaine.

Sur cette vaste liste, on choisira deux questions pour examen: le déclenchement de la procédure et les procès *in absentia.*

1. Déclenchement de la procédure

Devant les Tribunaux pour l'ex-Yougoslavie et le Rwanda, seul le Procureur peut mettre en mouvement la procédure, après avoir reçu, le cas échéant, des renseignements de la part d'Etats ou d'organisations ou individus quelconques. Le projet de statut d'une CCI élaboré par la CDI préconise une solution différente.

D'après l'article 25, paragraphe 2, du projet, une instance peut être ouverte sur plainte d'un Etat Partie au Statut ayant accepté la compétence de la CCI pour l'une ou l'autre des catégories de crimes ressortissant à sa compétence. Dans le cas du crime de génocide, une telle acceptation n'est pas requise; en revanche, l'Etat plaignant doit être Partie au Statut de la Cour aussi bien qu'à la Convention du 9 décembre 1948 sur la prévention et la répression du crime de génocide[56] (article 25, paragraphe premier, du projet de la CDI). S'il s'agit d'un acte d'agression, enfin, une déclaration d'acceptation de la compétence de la CCI est nécessaire; de plus, la plainte étatique n'est recevable que si le Conseil de sécurité a préalablement constaté l'existence d'une agression. Elle n'est pas davantage recevable si le crime se rattache à une situation soumise au Conseil en vertu du chapitre VII (article 23, paragraphes 2 et 3). La procédure peut en outre être déclenchée par le

[56] NATIONS UNIES, RECUEIL DES TRAITÉS, vol. 78, p. 277.

Conseil de sécurité lui-même, lorsque les activités criminelles qui doivent en faire l'objet sont liées à une situation que le Conseil est en train d'examiner dans le contexte du même chapitre VII (article 23, paragraphe premier)[57].

Ces dispositions ont suscité des objections d'ordre politique et technique. Les pays du Tiers-Monde voient d'un mauvais oeil le rôle actuellement joué par le Conseil de sécurité au détriment d'une Assemblée générale qui, pendant de longues années, avait dominé l'Organisation. Pour cette raison, ils voudraient refuser au Conseil toute initiative en la matière. Etant donné que la constatation d'une agression **par le Conseil** est une prémisse pour le déclenchement de toute procédure relative à des actes d'agression, certains de ces pays préféreraient en outre que le crime de l'agression ne soit pas retenu.

D'autres Etats estiment que la mise en mouvement de la procédure ne doit pas être réservée aux Etats Parties au Statut et, éventuellement, au Conseil de sécurité. Le Procureur devrait lui aussi pouvoir agir, comme il peut le faire auprès des Tribunaux *ad hoc*, car autrement ses fonctions seraient réduites à recevoir et exécuter les ordres des Etats et du Conseil, ce qui démentirait de l'affirmation, faite à l'article 12, paragraphe premier, du projet de la CDI, que «le Parquet est un organe indépendant au sein de la Cour».

L'article 25, paragraphe premier, du projet prévoit que l'Etat plaignant doit non seulement être Partie au Statut de la CCI, mais aussi à la Convention de 1948 sur le génocide; il n'est pas nécessaire, en revanche, que cet Etat ait fait une déclaration acceptant la compétence de la Cour. Cette règle soulève des problèmes techniques. Premièrement, étant donné que le génocide, tout comme les trois autres catégories d'infractions énumérées à l'article 20, lettres b à d, du projet de la CDI, relève du droit international coutumier, on ne voit pas pourquoi un Etat souhaitant porter plainte pour des actes de génocide devrait être Partie à la Convention de 1948, alors qu'aucune exigence similaire n'est formulée pour ces trois autres catégories[58]. En second lieu, on comprend mal pourquoi un droit de plainte (et la compétence de la Cour) seraient admis dans le cas du génocide et non dans les trois autres. La meilleure solution serait un droit de plainte et une compétence inhérents pour tous les crimes réprimés par le droit international coutumier et visés par le Statut de la CCI.

En ce qui concerne le problème du déclenchement des procédures à prévoir dans le futur Statut, la solution préférable serait celle qui attribuerait un droit de plainte à tout Etat Partie du Statut de la CCI, au Procureur de celle-

---

57 *Voir* ci-dessus, p. 881.

58 La solution suggérée est préjudiciable à des Etats tels que la Suisse, qui sont liés par l'interdiction coutumière du génocide sans pour autant être Parties à la Convention.

ci et au Conseil de sécurité si ce dernier est saisi du conflit générateur des crimes en cause dans le cadre du chapitre VII de la Charte.

2. Procédures *in absentia*

On se souviendra que les Statuts des Tribunaux *ad hoc* demandent la présence de l'accusé pour des motifs touchant à la protection des droits de l'homme et, surtout, pour ne pas mettre en cause l'effectivité de ces Tribunaux[59]. Si la présence de l'accusé est également exigée au paragraphe premier de l'article 37 du projet de la CDI, le paragraphe 2 de cette disposition permet d'y renoncer:

1) lorsque cette présence est indésirable pour des raisons de sécurité;

2) lorsque l'accusé a troublé de manière persistante le déroulement du procès; et

3) lorsqu'il s'est évadé. L'article 37, paragraphe 4, ajoute que lorsque l'absence de l'accusé est délibérée, une chambre d'accusation constituée *ad hoc* peut réunir et examiner les preuves et, si celles-ci le justifient, décerner un mandat d'arrêt, afin que l'affaire puisse passer en jugement une fois que l'accusé aura été appréhendé et remis à la CCI.

Il est raisonnable d'admettre que si un accusé trouble de manière persistante les audiences, celles-ci puissent continuer sans lui; sinon, il lui suffirait de perturber les audiences pour éviter d'être jugé. En revanche, les deux autres exceptions consacrées à l'article 37, paragraphe 2 – présence de l'accusé jugée indésirable pour des motifs de sécurité, évasion – semblent difficiles à justifier. Le cas de l'évasion devrait relever du paragraphe 4 de l'article 37, puisqu'il s'agit d'une absence délibérée de l'accusée. L'existence de problèmes de sécurité, quant à elle, ne permet pas de renoncer à la présence de l'accusé, car celui-ci n'est pas nécessairement responsable de la situation. Ici la solution appropriée consisterait à suspendre l'instance jusqu'à la disparition de ces problèmes; en attendant, la procédure prévue à l'article 37, paragraphe 4, pourrait être suivie.

E. Entraide judiciaire internationale

Les Statuts des Tribunaux *ad hoc* ont, dans ce domaine, défriché un champs vierge. La coopération et l'assistance judiciaire des Etats sont existentielles pour ces Tribunaux, comme elles le seront pour la CCI. Les tribunaux pénaux internationaux ne peuvent condamner sans preuves; celles-ci

---

[59] *Voir* ci-dessus, p. 864.

sont localisées sur le territoire des Etats et doivent être obtenues soit par la voie de l'entraide judiciaire, soit par celle d'enquêtes sur place. De plus, ces tribunaux ne peuvent juger sans avoir obtenu des autorités nationales la remise des accusés.

L'article 51 du projet de la CDI oblige les Etats Parties au Statut de la CCI à coopérer avec celle-ci s'ils en ont accepté la compétence[60], et il cherche même à étendre ce devoir aux pays tiers. L'article 53 du projet, quant à lui, demande aux Etats Parties de s'emparer des accusés et de les transférer à la Cour.

Ces dispositions soulèvent des questions complexes, dont deux seulement vont être examinées.

La première est celle du sort, face aux obligations mentionnées, des devoirs découlant pour les Etats de leurs traités d'entraide internationale en matière pénale. Plusieurs solutions sont envisageables. Une première solution serait d'admettre qu'il ne s'agit pas, ici, de devoirs d'entraide judiciaire envers des Etats qui sollicitent une assistance pour pouvoir exercer leur souveraineté en matière pénale, mais d'obligations à l'égard d'un organisme juridictionnel qui agit au nom et pour le compte de la communauté internationale dans son ensemble, y compris l'Etat dont la coopération est demandée. Les obligations en cause différant ainsi des devoirs d'entraide classiques, il n'y aurait aucun conflit, de sorte que seules les dispositions du Statut seraient applicables. Une autre construction, qui aboutirait toutefois au même résultat, consisterait à qualifier les devoirs nés du Statut de *lex specialis* par rapport aux devoirs ordinaires d'entraide pénale entre Etats. Enfin et en troisième lieu, on pourrait donner la priorité aux accords d'entraide en invoquant la «complémentarité» de la CCI. Ce sont là trois manières possibles d'expliquer les relations entre le droit conventionnel classique de l'entraide internationale en matière pénale et les obligations que le Statut de la future Cour imposera à ses Etats Parties. Quelle que soit, en définitive, la solution retenue, il est certain que la situation sera bien plus complexe, ici, qu'elle ne l'est pour les Tribunaux *ad hoc*: La primauté des devoirs que les Etats membres des Nations Unies se voient attribuer par les Statuts de ces instances peut en effet s'appuyer sur l'article 103 de la Charte de l'Organisation[61]. L'analyse sommaire qui précède demanderait du reste à être élargie en y ajoutant les problèmes que susciteront les relations entre la CCI ou un Etat Partie à son Statut et des Etats qui n'ont pas cette qualité.

---

[60] Cette condition tomberait bien évidemment si et dans la mesure où la CCI devait jouir d'une compétence générale inhérente vis-à-vis de tous les Etats Parties à son Statut, comme cela est suggéré en p. 882.

[61] Ci-dessus, p. 873.

L'obligation la plus importante dans le domaine de l'entraide internationale en matière pénale est la remise des personnes recherchées. En règle générale, un Etat n'extrade pas ses propres ressortissants, à moins que ceux-ci n'aient donné leur accord[62]. En ira-t-il de même vis-à-vis de la CCI? En gardant le silence sur ce point, le projet de la CDI semble exiger la remise même des nationaux. La solution ainsi proposée pourrait s'appuyer sur le fait qu'il s'agit du transfert d'une personne, non à un Etat étranger, mais à une instance qui juge au nom et pour le compte de la communauté internationale, y compris l'Etat transférant. Cette situation diffère fondamentalement de celle d'un Etat qui extrade une personne à un autre Etat pour permettre à celui-ci d'exercer sa souveraineté pénale. Ainsi l'obligation de transfert pourrait englober les ressortissants de l'Etat requis même si la législation de ce dernier interdit l'extradition des nationaux[63], à moins, bien entendu, que le Statut de la future Cour ne permette aux Etats Parties de formuler des réserves sur ce point.

Conclusions

Sérieusement envisagée à l'issue de la Seconde Guerre mondiale, l'idée de traduire devant une instance internationale les individus accusés de crimes réprimés par le droit des gens a refait surface. Ce développement résulte de l'augmentation du nombre de conflits générateurs de tels crimes et de l'incapacité ou du refus des tribunaux nationaux de poursuivre et punir leurs auteurs.

Pour savoir si l'évolution décrite se poursuivra, il faudra attendre les résultats de l'expérience en cours en ex-Yougoslavie et au Rwanda. Une issue positive de cette expérience faciliterait l'établissement d'une CCI de caractère permanent. Mais, quoi qu'il en soit, les discussions sont d'ores et déjà très avancées, et la pression exercée par l'opinion publique contribuera de façon significative à la création d'une telle cour. De plus, les Statuts des Tribunaux *ad hoc* pour l'ex-Yougoslavie et le Rwanda ont déjà résolu quelques-uns parmi les problèmes qui allaient surgir. On pourrait donc convenir, dès

---

62 C'est le cas de la Suisse, par exemple, *voir* l'article 7 de la Loi fédérale du 20 mars 1981 sur l'entraide internationale en matière pénale (EIMP), RS 351.1.

63 La législation suisse tient compte de cette différence. Alors que l'EIMP (*voir* la note précédente) interdit l'extradition de ressortissants suisses sans leur consentement écrit, l'article 10, alinéa 2, de l'Arrêté fédéral urgent relatif à la coopération avec les tribunaux internationaux chargés de poursuivre les violations graves du droit international humanitaire, du 18 octobre 1995 (*voir supra*, note 40), autorise leur remise aux Tribunaux *ad hoc* pour l'ex-Yougoslavie et le Rwanda, à condition qu'ils soient restitués à la Suisse à l'issue de la procédure, le cas échéant pour y purger leurs peines.

à présent, que les solutions fournies par ces textes ne seront écartées qu'en cas de nécessité absolue.

Il y a toutefois des problèmes qui ne peuvent être réglés en se fondant sur les modèles existants. C'est le cas des questions relatives à la compétence de la future Cour, en particulier à la «complémentarité» de celle-ci. Si ces questions peuvent faire l'objet d'un *package deal* raisonnable – intervention de la CCI limitée aux carences sur le plan national et aux crimes les plus graves, réprimés par le droit coutumier, compétence inhérente de la Cour pour ce type d'actes – le succès de la négociation sera à portée de main.

Il existe d'autres problèmes encore qui ne peuvent être résolus simplement en reprenant les dispositions des Statuts des Tribunaux *ad hoc*, notamment celui du sort des traités ou lois relatifs à l'entraide judiciaire internationale en matière pénale. On relèvera à ce propos qu'à l'occasion de la création des Tribunaux pour l'ex-Yougoslavie et le Rwanda, plusieurs pays ont édicté des lois devant permettre ou faciliter l'application des Résolutions 827 et 955 du Conseil de sécurité sur le plan interne. Ces lois ont sensibilisé les autorités nationales et le public aux difficultés que suscite l'établissement de juridictions pénales internationales et préparé ainsi le terrain pour l'adoption des lois internes nécessaires au fonctionnement d'une CCI préconstituée.

Le plus grand obstacle à la création d'une telle Cour résulte du fait que celle-ci doit être établie par la voie d'un traité multilatéral général. Réunir un consensus autour d'un tel instrument ne sera pas chose facile. Ou bien ce consensus sera atteint au prix d'une érosion inacceptable du contenu du traité, ce qui réduirait l'efficacité de la future Cour; ou bien le traité sera ratifié par un nombre insuffisant d'Etats, ce qui aurait également pour effet de diminuer cette efficacité. Il sera difficile d'éviter les deux écueils. Il faudra pourtant y parvenir, car jamais les conditions n'ont été aussi propices pour faire triompher l'idée d'une justice pénale véritablement internationale et permanente.

Crimes against Humanity

by

Yoram Dinstein

I. THE ORIGIN OF CRIMES AGAINST HUMANITY IN INTERNATIONAL LAW

The *locus classicus* for the definition of crimes against humanity is Article VI(c) of the 1945 Charter of the International Military Tribunal, annexed to the London Agreement for the Prosecution and Punishment of the Major War Criminals of the European Axis (initially adopted by the four Big Powers – the United States, the Soviet Union, the United Kingdom and France – later joined by many other allied nations which acceded to the instrument). This provision reads (in the original version, the punctuation of which was amended subsequently):

> "The following acts, or any of them, are crimes coming within the jurisdiction of the Tribunal for which there shall be individual responsibility:
>
> ...
>
> (c) **Crimes against humanity**: namely, murder, extermination, enslavement, deportation, and other inhumane acts committed against any civilian population, before or during the war; or persecutions on political, racial or religious grounds in execution of or in connection with any crime within the jurisdiction of the Tribunal, whether or not in violation of the domestic law of the country where perpetrated."[1]

Article VI(c) of the London Charter constitutes a veritable landmark, being the first instance in which a legally binding international treaty employs (let alone defines) the specific phrase "crimes against humanity".[2] There had been earlier usages of the phrase in non-binding declarations,[3] as in literary and journalistic writings, but only in 1945 was the terminology embraced by positive international law.

---

1 Charter of the International Military Tribunal, Annexed to the London Agreement for the Prosecution and Punishment of the Major War Criminals of the European Axis, 1945, 1 The Law of War: A Documentary History (1972) at 883, 887.

2 *See* M.C. Bassiouni, Crimes against Humanity in International Criminal Law (1992) at 1–2.

3 *See* R.S. Clark, *Crimes against Humanity at Nuremberg*, (in:) G. Ginsburgs & V.N. Kudriavtsev (eds.), The Nuremberg Trial and International Law (1990) at 177, 177–179.

In the 1946 Judgment of the International Military Tribunal, rendered at Nuremberg, the theme of crimes against humanity was somewhat de-emphasized, as compared to crimes against peace or ordinary war crimes.[4] Nevertheless, what is of singular import is that two of the defendants – Streicher and Von Schirach – were convicted exclusively of crimes against humanity (having been found not guilty on other counts),[5] and, indeed, the former was sentenced to death.[6]

Article VI(c) of the London Charter served as the model for two other texts pertaining to crimes against humanity perpetrated in the course of, or in connection with, World War II. The first is Article II(1)(c) of the 1945 Control Council Law N° 10 for the prosecution and punishment of the lower--echelon Nazi war criminals, which promulgates:

> "(c) **Crimes against Humanity**. Atrocities and offences, including but not limited to murder, extermination, enslavement, deportation, imprisonment, torture, rape, or other inhumane acts committed against any civilian population, or persecutions on political, racial or religious grounds whether or not in violation of the domestic laws of the country where perpetrated."[7]

This version differs from Article VI(c) of the London Charter in that (i) it relates to "[a]trocities and offences" in general, and the list of punishable acts is deliberately not exhaustive (instead of "namely", we encounter "including but not limited to");[8] (ii) the reference to time-frames ("before or during the war") is deleted, as is the linkage to "any crime within the jurisdiction of the Tribunal"; (iii) there is a specific addition of "imprisonment, torture, rape" to the catalogue of crimes against humanity.

The second text spawned by Article VI(c) of the London Charter is Article 5(c) of the Charter of the International Military Tribunal for the Far East, established in 1946 by Special Proclamation of General D. MacArthur, in his capacity as Supreme Commander for the Allied Powers in Tokyo.[9] This provision follows the original in every detail, except that the persecutions

---

4 *Ibid.* at 194–198.

5 Trial of Major War Criminals before the International Military Tribunal, Judgment (*Nuremberg*, 1946), 2 THE LAW OF WAR: A DOCUMENTARY HISTORY, *supra* note 1, at 922, 990, 1004.

6 *Ibid.* at 1025.

7 CONTROL COUNCIL LAW (1945), N° 10, 1 THE LAW OF WAR: A DOCUMENTARY HISTORY, *supra* note 1, at 908, 909.

8 It has been pointed out that the list of crimes enumerated in Article VI(c) is not truly exhaustive either, in light of the phrase "and other inhumane acts". *See* E. SCHWELB, *Crimes against Humanity*, 23 BRITISH YEAR BOOK OF INTERNATIONAL LAW (1946) at 178, 217.

9 Charter of the International Military Tribunal for the Far East, 1946, 1 THE LAW OF WAR: A DOCUMENTARY HISTORY, *supra* note 1, at 894, 897.

referred to here are only "on political or racial grounds",[10] whereas in Article VI(c) religious grounds are incorporated as well.

II. THE EVOLUTION OF CRIMES AGAINST HUMANITY

Considering the novelty of the international legal concept of "crimes against humanity" in the immediate post World War II period – and insofar as these crimes transcend the ambit of ordinary war crimes (see *infra*, para. 4) – it is arguable that Article VI(c) of the London Charter was not declaratory of customary international law at the time of its adoption.[11] However, in 1948, an American Military Tribunal (part of the "Subsequent Proceedings" at Nuremberg) held in the *Einsatzgruppen* case:

> "Although the Nuremberg trials represent the first time that international tribunals have adjudicated crimes against humanity as an international offense, this does not ... mean that a new offense has been added to the list of transgressions of man."[12]

Whatever the legal position was in the 1940s, it is virtually indisputable that – in the half-century that has elapsed since then – crimes against humanity have gained almost universal acknowledgement as an integral part of customary international law.[13] In 1995, in the *Tadic* case, the International Criminal Tribunal for the former Yugoslavia (Trial Chamber) held that "[t]here is no question but that crimes against humanity form part of customary international law."[14]

A survey of the relevant international legal texts firmly corroborates this conclusion. The International Law Commission first dealt with crimes against humanity in 1950, when it formulated (pursuant to instructions by the U.N. General Assembly) the Principles of I nternational Law recognized in the London Charter and in the Nuremberg Judgment. The "Nürnberg Principles", as presented by the Commission, include Principle VI(c) reading:

---

10 *Ibid.*

11 *See* G. SCHWARZANBERGER, THE LAW OF ARMED CONFLICT (1968) at 498.

12 *In re Ohlendorf and Others* (Einsatzgruppen Trial) (United States Military Tribunal, 1948), 15 INTERNATIONAL LAW REPORTS (1948) at 656, 665.

13 *See* H.S. LEVIE, *Violations of Human Rights in Time of War as War Crimes*, 24 ISRAEL YEARBOOK ON HUMAN RIGHTS (1994) at 119, 121.

14 International Tribunal for the Prosecution of Persons Responsible for Serious Violations of International Humanitarian Law Committed in the Territory of Former Yugoslavia since 1991, IT-94-1-T (Jurisdiction), DUSKO TADIC CASE (1995, 10 August) at 30 (mimeographed).

> "(c) **Crimes against Humanity**: Murder, extermination, enslavement, deportation and other inhuman acts done against any civilian population, or persecutions on political, racial or religious grounds, when such acts are done or such persecutions are carried on in execution of or in connexion with any crime against peace or any war crime."[15]

The text essentially reiterates the language of Article VI(c) of the London Charter, except that the phrase "before or during the war" is omitted. The Commission explained that the omission was due to the fact that "this phrase referred to a particular war, the war of 1939".[16]

In 1954, in its Draft Code of Offences against the Peace and Security of Mankind, the Commission adopted Article 2(11):

> "Inhuman acts such as murder, extermination, enslavement, deportation or persecutions, committed against any civilian population on social, political, racial, religious or cultural grounds by the authorities of a State or by private individuals acting at the instigation or with the toleration of such authorities."[17]

Earlier, the Commission explicitly stated that the original version of this Paragraph (then numbered 2(10)) "corresponds substantially" to the definition of crimes against humanity in Article VI(c) of the London Charter.[18] In 1954, however, the Commission decided "to enlarge the scope of the paragraph".[19] Thus, the new provision (i) underlines that the definition covers inhuman acts other than the ones specifically enumerated; (ii) includes persecutions on social and cultural grounds; (iii) is no longer linked to crimes against peace or war crimes; (iv) restricts the circumstances in which the crimes can be committed by private individuals to the framework of governmental instigation or toleration.

When the Commission returned to the Draft Code after a long interval, the Special Rapporteur, D. Thiam, in 1989 criticized the failure of Article 2 of the 1954 text to employ the words "crimes against humanity", taking the position that "it seems useful to give them their rightful place" and devoting Article 14 of his proposal to the subject.[20] By contrast, when the Commis-

---

15 Report of the International Law Commission to the General Assembly, 2nd Session, [1950] II YEARBOOK OF THE INTERNATIONAL LAW COMMISSION at 364, 377.

16 *Ibid.*

17 Report of the International Law Commission to the General Assembly, 6th Session, [1954] II YEARBOOK OF THE INTERNATIONAL LAW COMMISSION at 140, 150.

18 Report of the International Law Commission to the General Assembly, 3rd Session, [1951] II YEARBOOK OF THE INTERNATIONAL LAW COMMISSION at 123, 136.

19 *Supra* note 17, at 150.

20 D. THIAM, *Seventh Report on the Draft Code of Crimes against the Peace and Security of Mankind*, [1989] II:1 YEARBOOK OF THE INTERNATIONAL LAW COMMISSION at 81, 85–86.

sion adopted a Draft Code of Crimes against the Peace and Security of Mankind, in 1991, it moved in an opposite direction. The relevant provision, Article 21, is now entitled "Systematic or mass violations of human rights".[21] While it includes murder, enslavement, deportations and persecutions – as well as torture – there is no longer any reference to crimes against humanity.[22] This attempt to weave crimes against humanity within the growing fabric of the law of human rights has yet to stand the test of time. So far, human rights and crimes against humanity have pursued decidedly different paths.[23]

The Convention on the Non-Applicability of Statutory Limitations to War Crimes and Crimes against Humanity, adopted by the U.N. General Assembly in 1968, simply refers in Article I to crimes against humanity "as they are defined in the Charter of the International Military Tribunal".[24]

The Statute of the International Criminal Tribunal for the former Yugoslavia – proposed by the U.N. Secretary-General[25] and approved by the Security Council[26] in 1993, with a view to prosecuting "persons responsible for serious violations of international humanitarian law committed in the territory of the former Yugoslavia since 1991[27] – prescribes in Article 5:

> "**Crimes against humanity**. The International Tribunal shall have the power to prosecute persons responsible for the following crimes when committed in armed conflict, whether international or internal in character, and directed against any civilian population:
> (a) murder;
> (b) extermination;
> (c) enslavement;
> (d) deportation;
> (e) imprisonment;
> (f) torture;
> (g) rape;
> (h) persecutions on political, racial and religious grounds;
> (i) other inhumane acts."[28]

---

[21] Report of the International Law Commission, 43rd Session, [1991] II(2) YEARBOOK OF THE INTERNATIONAL LAW COMMISSION at 103.

[22] *Ibid.*

[23] *See* E. ZOLLER, *La Définition des Crimes contre l'Humanité*, 120 JOURNAL DU DROIT INTERNATIONAL (1993) at 549, 556–557.

[24] Convention on the Non-Applicability of Statutory Limitations to War Crimes and Crimes against Humanity, UNITED NATIONS JURIDICAL YEARBOOK (1968) at 160, 161.

[25] Report of the Secretary-General Pursuant to Paragraph 2 of Security Council Resolution 808 (1993), 32 INTERNATIONAL LEGAL MATERIALS (1993) at 1163, 1192.

[26] Security Council Resolution N° 827, 32 INTERNATIONAL LEGAL MATERIALS (1993) at 1203, 1204.

[27] *Supra* note 25, at 1170 (Article 1).

[28] *Ibid.* at 1193–1194.

This provision basically reverts to the mould of Article VI(c) of the London Charter, with some notable divergences: (i) whereas the crimes must be committed in armed conflict, that conflict can be either international or internal in nature; (ii) the list of inhumane acts (which is not exhaustive) specifically includes imprisonment, torture and rape.

In 1994, the Security Council decided to establish another International Tribunal for Rwanda.[29] Article 3 of the Statute of the Rwanda Tribunal includes the same enumeration of crimes (a) through (i) embodied in the 1993 Statute for the former Yugoslavia, but it substitutes the *chapeau* of the provision with:

> "The International Tribunal for Rwanda shall have the power to prosecute persons responsible for the following crimes when committed as part of a widespread or systematic attack against any civilian population on national, political, ethnic, racial or religious grounds."[30]

Thus, the linkage to armed conflict of whatever nature is replaced by a reference to widespread or systematic attacks against any civilian population on national, political, ethnic, racial or religious grounds. Interestingly, the new formula is derived word-for-word from the 1993 Report of the Secretary-General where, however, it was used in the commentary and not in the text of the Article itself.[31]

What plainly emerges from tracing these disparate texts is that, although the detailed contours of the definition of crimes against humanity are by no means agreed upon, the nucleus of the crimes is by now well established in customary international law.

III. THE LINKAGE BETWEEN CRIMES AGAINST HUMANITY AND ARMED CONFLICT

As indicated by the International Law Commission in formulating the "Nürnberg Principles", Article VI(c) of the London Charter distinguishes between two categories of crimes against humanity: murder, extermination, etc., on the one hand, and persecutions, on the other.[32] In the original English version of Article VI(c), as quoted above, a semicolon interposed be-

---

[29] Security Council Resolution N° 955, 33 INTERNATIONAL LEGAL MATERIALS (1994) at 1598, 1601.

[30] *Ibid.* at 1603.

[31] *Supra* note 25, at 1173.

[32] *Supra* note 15, at 377.

tween the two categories. It therefore appeared as if only the second category (persecutions) – but not the first (murder, extermination, etc.) – is subject to the caveat of a connection with crimes within the jurisdiction of the Tribunal. But in a special Protocol, done in Berlin in 1945, Paragraph (c) was amended in replacing the semicolon by a comma.[33] The thrust of the amendment is that crimes against humanity of both categories must be connected with crimes within the jurisdiction of the Tribunal. These crimes, as spelled out in the balance of Article VI of the London Charter, are crimes against peace and war crimes.[34]

By setting forth that crimes against humanity can only be committed in connection with crimes against peace or war crimes – hence with war – the framers of Article VI(c) introduced a serious rider on the proposition that crimes against humanity may be committed not only during but also before war (that is to say, in peacetime).[35] Not surprisingly, the International Military Tribunal at Nuremberg arrived at the conclusion that the Nazi persecutions of Jews (as well as political opponents) inside Germany – prior to the outbreak of World War II in September 1939 – could not be deemed crimes against humanity, inasmuch as they had not been connected with crimes against peace or war crimes.[36] It is true that in some special instances the Tribunal admitted a linkage between particular acts performed before September 1939 and crimes against peace or war crimes,[37] but as a rule it confined the applicability of crimes against humanity to the duration of the war.[38] Consequently, although it seems not to matter – under Article VI(c) – whether crimes against humanity are committed before or during war, in principle the Nuremberg precedent clearly requires that these crimes be committed in wartime.[39]

As mentioned, the "Nürnberg Principles", formulated by the International Law Commission, omit the phrase "before or during the war". The Commission stressed, however, that crimes against humanity may take place before war only "in connexion with crimes against peace".[40] This is the correct interpretation of the Charter (as amended) and the Judgment: crimes

---

33 International Military Tribunal, 1 NAZI CONSPIRACY AND AGGRESSION (1946) at 11–12 (Office of U.S. Chief of Counsel for Prosecution of Axis Criminality).

34 *Supra* note 1, at 886–887.

35 *See* E. SCHWELB, *supra* note 8, at 188, 193–195, 204.

36 *Supra* note 5, at 961.

37 *See* A. GOLDSTEIN, *Crimes against Humanity: Some Jewish Aspects*, JEWISH YEARBOOK OF INTERNATIONAL LAW (1948) at 206, 221.

38 *Supra* note 5, at 961.

39 *See* E. SCHWELB, *supra* note 8, at 204.

40 *Supra* note 15, at 377.

against humanity can be perpetrated before or during war; but if the former, there must exist a nexus between the punishable acts and the subsequent war.

Conversely, as noted, Article II(1)(c) of Control Council Law N° 10 for the prosecution of the lesser Nazi war criminals deleted both the words "before or during the war" and the linkage to "any crime within the jurisdiction of the Tribunal".[41] As a result, in the *Einsatzgruppen* case of 1948, an American Military Tribunal held:

> "The International Military Tribunal, operating under the London Charter, declared that the Charter's provisions limited the Tribunal to consider only those crimes against humanity which were committed in the execution of or in connection with crimes against peace and war crimes. The Allied Control Council, in its Law N° 10, removed this limitation so that the present Tribunal has jurisdiction to try all crimes against humanity as long known and understood under the general principles of criminal law."[42]

No wonder that B.V.A. Röling (who had served as a Judge in the Tokyo trial) maintained that the Nuremberg and Tokyo mandatory connection with crimes against peace or ordinary war crimes did not narrow the scope of crimes against humanity as such: the qualification applied only to the bounds of the International Military Tribunals' jurisdiction.[43] In other words, the Tribunals operating at Nuremberg and Tokyo had no jurisdiction to sit in judgment over crimes against humanity unless committed during or in connection with war. Yet, when certain acts directed against the civilian population are perpetrated, they amount to crimes against humanity irrespective of the incidence of war. Other tribunals not similarly hampered (such as the tribunals acting in conformity with Control Council Law N° 10) could and can exercise jurisdiction.

Over the years since the adoption of the seminal text of Article VI(c) of the London Charter, the term of art "crimes against humanity" seems to have acquired a standing less dependent on war. The International Law Commission itself, already in its 1950s Draft Code of Offences against the Peace and Security of Mankind, decided to eliminate initially the linkage to crimes against peace or war crimes,[44] and then the connection to any other crimes.[45] In 1989, the Commission's Special Rapporteur, Thiam, had this to say:

---

41 On the significance of this striking difference in language between Article II(1)(c) and Article VI(c), *see* E. SCHWELB, *supra* note 8, at 218.

42 *Supra* note 12, at 664.

43 B.V.A. RÖLING, THE TOKYO TRIAL AND BEYOND (1993) at 56.

44 *Supra* note 18, at 136.

45 *Supra* note 17, at 150.

> "First linked to a State of belligerency … the concept of crimes against humanity gradually came to be viewed as autonomous and is today quite separate from that of war crimes."[46]

Moreover, Article I of the 1968 General Assembly Convention on the Non--Applicability of Statutory Limitations to War Crimes and Crimes against Humanity, while referring to crimes against humanity as they are defined in the London Charter, adds the words: "whether committed in time of war or in time of peace".[47]

In the latest edition of Oppenheim (edited by R. Jennings and A. Watts), it is suggested:

> "While crimes against humanity are now generally regarded as a self-contained category, without the need for any formal link with war crimes, in practice those two categories are often treated together."[48]

Support for the "self-contained" status of crimes against humanity has been expressed by others in the legal literature, like T. Meron[49] and D.F. Orentlicher.[50]

A glaring illustration of the "self-contained" nature of crimes against humanity, as perceived in an international treaty, is the controversial International Convention on the Suppression and Punishment of the Crime of Apartheid,[51] adopted in 1973 by the U.N. General Assembly. Article I of the Convention proclaims that "apartheid is a crime against humanity."[52] Under Article II, the crime of apartheid pertains to inhuman acts such as murder of members of a racial group and various acts of persecution as practised in southern Africa at the time of the adoption of the Convention.[53] No connection to war is posited as a condition to the criminalization of these acts, although Article I states that the crimes constitute "a serious threat to international peace and security".[54]

---

46 D. THIAM, *supra* note 20, at 86.

47 *Supra* note 24, at 161.

48 1 OPPENHEIM'S INTERNATIONAL LAW (1992) (Part 2, 9th ed., by R. JENNINGS & A. WATTS) at 996.

49 T. MERON, *The Normative Impact on International Law of the International Tribunal for Former Yugoslavia*, 24 ISRAEL YEARBOOK ON HUMAN RIGHTS (1994) at 163, 174–175.

50 D.F. ORENTLICHER, *Settling Accounts: The Duty to Prosecute Human Rights Violations of a Prior Regime*, 100 YALE LAW JOURNAL (1990–1991) at 2537, 2590.

51 International Convention on the Suppression and Punishment of the Crime of Apartheid, UNITED NATIONS JURIDICAL YEARBOOK (1973) at 70.

52 *Ibid.* at 71.

53 *Ibid.*

54 *Ibid.*

The Statute of the International Criminal Tribunal for the former Yugoslavia takes an interesting and plausible position in retaining the linkage between crimes against humanity and armed conflict while clarifying that the character of the conflict – international or internal – is immaterial.[55] On the other hand, the Statute of the International Tribunal for Rwanda unties crimes against humanity from armed conflict and shifts the emphasis to widespread or systematic attacks against any civilian population on national, political, ethnic, racial or religious grounds.

In the *Tadic* case of 1995, the International Criminal Tribunal for the former Yugoslavia addressed the issue head-on. The Trial Chamber opined:

> "The nexus in the Nuremberg Charter between crimes against humanity and the two other categories, crimes against peace and war crimes, was peculiar to the context of the Nuremberg Tribunal established specifically 'for the just and prompt trial and punishment of the major war criminals of the European Axis countries'...
>
> That no nexus is required in customary international law between crimes against humanity and crimes against peace or war crimes is strongly evidenced by subsequent case law."[56]

The Trial Chamber relied on the *Einsatzgruppen* case, the Special Rapporteur of the International Law Commission (Thiam) and the latest edition of Oppenheim.[57]

The Appeals Chamber in the *Tadic* case (also in 1995) – grounding its decision on Control Council Law N° 10, the Genocide and the Apartheid Conventions – held:

> "It is by now a settled rule of customary international law that crimes against humanity do not require a connection to international armed conflict. Indeed, as the Prosecutor points out, customary international law may not require a connection between crimes against humanity and any conflict at all. Thus, by requiring that crimes against humanity be committed in either internal or international armed conflict, the Security

---

[55] Curiously enough, the Secretary-General commentary says: "Crimes against humanity are aimed at any civilian population and are prohibited regardless of whether they are committed in an armed conflict, international or internal in character." *Supra* note 25, at 1173. In light of the text of Article 5, which establishes that crimes against humanity must be "committed in armed conflict, whether international or internal in character" (*supra*, para. 2), this is a grossly misleading statement. *See* C. TOMUSCHAT, *Crimes against the Peace and Security of Mankind and the Recalcitrant Third State*, 24 ISRAEL YEARBOOK ON HUMAN RIGHTS (1994) at 41, 48–49.

[56] *Supra* note 14, at 30–31.

[57] *Ibid.*

Council may have defined the crime in Article 5 more narrowly than necessary under customary international law."[58]

Having concluded that in this case there existed an armed conflict, the Appeals Chamber did not hesitate in rejecting a challenge to its jurisdiction.[59]

While the position taken by the Appeals Chamber on the nexus issue is more tentative than that of the lower instance, the current trend aimed at releasing crimes against humanity from the bonds of any armed conflict has conspicuously been accelerated by the *Tadic* proceedings.

IV. CRIMES AGAINST HUMANITY VS. ORDINARY WAR CRIMES

The definition of crimes against humanity in Article VI(c) of the London Charter overlaps in many respects the definition of war crimes incorporated in Paragraph (b) of the same stipulation:

> "(b) **War crimes**: namely, violations of the laws or customs of war. Such violations shall include, but not be limited to, murder, ill-treatment or deportation to slave labor or for any other purpose of civilian population of or in occupied territory, murder or ill-treatment of prisoners of war or persons on the seas, killing of hostages, plunder of public or private property, wanton destruction of cities, towns or villages, or devastation not justified by military necessity."[60]

It is noteworthy that murder and deportation of civilian population are specified in both Paragraphs (b) and (c) of Article VI. Yet, Paragraph (b) applies only to the civilian population in occupied territories; whereas Paragraph (c) relates to any civilian population, not excluding that of the State whose armed forces commit the crimes (*e.g.* Jews in Germany).[61] The outcome is that murder or deportation of the civilian population in occupied territories is both a war crime and a crime against humanity, while murder or deportation of any other civilian population in time of – and in connection with – war is only a crime against humanity. On the other hand, crimes against humanity are strictly confined to acts detrimental to the civilian popu-

---

58 International Tribunal for the Prosecution of Persons Responsible for Serious Violations of International Humanitarian Law Committed in the Territory of Former Yugoslavia since 1991, IT-94-1-AR72 (Jurisdiction), DUSKO TADIC CASE (1995, 2 October) at 73 (mimeographed).

59 *Ibid.*

60 *Supra* note 1, at 887.

61 *See* E. SCHWELB, *supra* note 8, at 188–189.

lation.[62] This is in contradistinction to war crimes, which can be – and usually are – directed against members of the armed forces (by way of illustration, prisoners-of-war) no less than civilians.

The Four Geneva Conventions of 1949 for the Protection of War Victims brand prescribed acts as "grave breaches". These are defined in Article 50 of Geneva Convention (I) for the Amelioration of the Condition of the Wounded and Sick in Armed Forces in the Field;[63] Article 51 of Geneva Convention (II) for the Amelioration of the Condition of Wounded, Sick and Shipwrecked Members of Armed Forces at Sea;[64] Article 130 of Geneva Convention (III) Relative to the Treatment of Prisoners of War;[65] and Article 147 of Geneva Convention (IV) Relative to the Protection of Civilian Persons in Time of War.[66] The last clause includes such grave breaches committed against civilians as "wilful killing, torture or inhuman treatment" and "unlawful deportation".[67]

Article 85 of the 1977 Protocol Additional to the Geneva Conventions of 12 August 1949, and Relating to the Protection of Victims of International Armed Conflicts (Protocol I), adds to the list other items affecting civilians, while pronouncing categorically in Paragraph 5 that grave breaches of the Conventions as well as the Protocol "shall be regarded as was crimes".[68] Admittedly, the standing of Article 85 as a whole (where, *e.g.* apartheid is branded as a war crime) is doubtful, insofar as custominternational law law is concerned.[69] Strangely, also, in Article 2–3 of the Statute of the International Criminal Tribunal for the former Yugoslavia, grave breaches of the Geneva Conventions constitute a separate category from "violations of the laws or customs of war.'[70] In reality, of course, the phrase "violations of the laws or customs of war" is broad enough to encompass grave breaches of

---

[62] *See ibid.* at 190.

[63] Geneva Convention (I) for the Amelioration of the Condition of the Wounded and Sick in Armed Forces in the Field, 1 THE LAW OF WAR: A DOCUMENTARY HISTORY, *supra* note 1, at 525, 541.

[64] Geneva Convention (II) for the Amelioration of the Condition of Wounded, Sick and Shipwrecked Members of Armed Forces at Sea, 1 THE LAW OF WAR: A DOCUMENTARY HISTORY, *supra* note 1, at 570, 585.

[65] Genera Convention (III) Relative to the Treatment of Prisoners of War, 1 THE LAW OF WAR: A DOCUMENTARY HISTORY, *supra* note 1, at 589, 637.

[66] Geneva Convention (IV) Relative to the Protection of Civilian Persons in Time of War, 1 THE LAW OF WAR: A DOCUMENTARY HISTORY, *supra* note 1, at 641, 690.

[67] *Ibid.*

[68] Protocol Additional to the Geneva Conventions of 12 August 1949, and Relating to the Protection of Victims of International Armed Conflicts (Protocol I), 1977, DOCUMENTS ON THE LAWS OF WAR (1989) at 387, 437–439 (2nd ed., by A. ROBERTS & R. GUELFF).

[69] *See* C. TOMUSCHAT, *supra* note 55, at 46.

[70] *Supra* note 25, at 1192–1193.

the Geneva Conventions.[71] But irrespective of this peculiarity, one cannot deny that most of the grave breaches of the Geneva Conventions do constitute war crimes.[72]

In given settings, when the civilian population is the victim of grave breaches of the Geneva Conventions and Protocol I, the same punishable acts can be labeled not only as war crimes but also as crimes against humanity. All the same, caution is required in the juridical analysis of the grave breaches concerned, since the gist of crimes against humanity is that they are committed not against an individual civilian in isolation but against the civilian population as such.[73] In J.C. O'Brien's words, "crimes against humanity must be systematic or organized, not simply episodic and/or scattered attacks on individuals."[74] This central dimension of crimes against humanity is examined by Thiam, in his 1989 Report to the International Law Commission:

> "Does an act need to affect a mass of people in order to constitute a crime against humanity? The mass nature of an act is one criterion of a crime against humanity, but it is not the only one. On occasion, an inhuman act committed against a single person may also constitute a crime against humanity if it is part of a system, or is carried out according to a plan, or has a repetitive nature which leaves no doubt as to the intentions of the author."[75]

However –

> "The notion of system, plan and repetitiveness is necessary in order to categorize an act committed against an individual victim as a crime against humanity."[76]

A good case in point is that of deportations of civilians. Under Article 147 of Geneva Convention IV, "unlawful deportation or transfer or unlawful confinement of a protected person" constitute a grave breach.[77] The range

---

[71] *See* T. MERON, *War Crimes in Yugoslavia and the Development of International Law*, 88 AMERICAN JOURNAL OF INTERNATIONAL LAW (1994) at 78, 82.

[72] On the reasons for the use of the expression "grave breaches" in the Geneva Conventions in lieu of "war crimes", *see* J.A.C. GUTTERIDGE, *The Geneva Conventions of 1949*, 26 BRITISH YEARBOOK OF INTERNATIONAL LAW (1949), at 294, 304–305.

[73] *See In re Altstötter and Others* (Justice Trial) (United States Military Tribunal), 14 INTERNATIONAL LAW REPORTS (1947) at 278, 284.

[74] *See* J.C. O'BRIEN, *The International Tribunal for Violations of International Humanitarian Law in the Former Yugoslavia*, 87 AMERICAN JOURNAL OF INTERNATIONAL LAW (1993) at 639, 648.

[75] D. THIAM, *supra* note 20, at 88.

[76] *Ibid.* at 89.

[77] *Supra* note 66, at 690.

of this grave breach of the Convention surely extends to every isolated deportation of a protected civilian.[78] Yet, an isolated case of deportation does not, as a rule, amount to a crime against humanity. Indeed, only systematic or mass-scale deportations are criminalized in the relevant provision of the International Law Commission's 1991 Draft Code of Crimes against the Peace and Security of mankind.[79]

V. GENOCIDE

"Genocide" – a term originally coined by R. Lemkin against the background of the Holocaust[80] – is defined as follows in Article II of the Convention on the Prevention and Punishment of the Crime of Genocide (adopted by the U.N. General Assembly in 1948):

> "In the present Convention, genocide means any of the following acts committed with intent to destroy, in whole or in part, a national, ethnical, racial or religious group, as such:
> (a) Killing members of the group;
> (b) Causing serious bodily or mental harm to members of the group;
> (c) Deliberately inflicting on the group conditions of life calculated to bring about its physical destruction in whole or in part;
> (d) Imposing measures intended to prevent births within the group;
> (e) Forcibly transferring children of the group to another group."[81]

The same definition appears in Article 4 of the Statute of the International Criminal Tribunal for the former Yugoslavia,[82] and in Article 2 of the Rwanda Tribunal's Statute.[83] As asserted by the Secretary-General in his commentary, the Genocide Convention "is today considered part of international customary law".[84] Evidence is provided by the following dictum of the International

---

78 The Supreme Court of Israel, in a majority (4:1) decision in the *Abd el Afu* case, reached the conclusion that Geneva Convention (IV) prohibits only large-scale deportations and not individual ones. *H.C. 785/87 etc., Abd et Afu et al. v. Commander of the IDF Forces in the West Bank et al.*, 42(2) *Piskei Din*, 4, 24–33, 66–67. The Judgment is translated into English in 29 INTERNATIONAL LEGAL MATERIALS (1990) at 140. The majority clearly misinterpreted the Convention. *See* Y. DINSTEIN, *The Israel Supreme Court and the Law of Belligerent Occupation: Deportations*, 23 ISRAEL YEARBOOK ON HUMAN RIGHTS (1993) at 1, 12–17.

79 *Supra* note 21, at 103.

80 R. LEMKIN, AXIS RULE IN OCCUPIED EUROPE (1944) at 79.

81 Convention on the Prevention and Punishment of the Crime of Genocide, 1948, 1 THE LAW OF WAR: A DOCUMENTARY HISTORY, *supra* note 1, at 692, 693.

82 *Supra* note 25, at 1193.

83 *Supra* note 29, at 1602–1603.

84 *Supra* note 25, at 1172.

Court of Justice in its 1951 Advisory Opinion on Reservations to the Genocide Convention:

> "The principles underlying the Convention are principles which are recognized by civilized nations as binding on States, even without any conventional obligation."[85]

Since the crux of the crime of genocide is the extermination or persecution of a civilian population, it can be subsumed under the heading of crimes against humanity. Indeed, genocide may be looked upon as the most paradigmatic crime against humanity. The 1974 European Convention on the Non-Applicability of Statutory Limitation to Crimes against Humanity and War Crimes accentuates the close relationship of the two categories of crimes by referring in Article 1(1) to "the crimes against humanity specified in the Convention on the Prevention and Punishment of the Crime of Genocide."[86] Thiam, in his report to the International Law Commission, included genocide within the compass of the definition of crimes against humanity.[87]

It is precisely for this reason that one must underscore that, under Article I of the Genocide Convention:

> "The Contracting Parties confirm that genocide, whether committed in time of peace or in time of war, is a crime under international law which they undertake to prevent and to punish."[88]

In other words, whatever the true nature of crimes against humanity in general, a linkage to war is decidedly not a *conditio sine qua non* in the special case of genocide.

VI. PROSECUTION AND PUNISHMENT

Crimes against humanity, like other crimes, entail individual responsibility. Unlike crimes against peace, which can only be perpetrated by policy-makers,[89] crimes against humanity can be committed irrespective of status, even by private soldiers and unruly civilians. In its 1954 Draft Code of Of-

---

[85] *Reservations to the Convention on the Prevention and Punishment of the Crime of Genocide*, ICJ REPORTS 1951 at 15, 23.

[86] European Convention on the Non-Applicability of Statutory Limitation to Crimes against Humanity and War Crimes, 3 EUROPEAN CONVENTIONS AND AGREEMENTS (1974) at 212, 213.

[87] D. THIAM, *supra* note 20, at 85.

[88] *Supra* note 81, at 692.

[89] *See* Y. DINSTEIN, *The Distinctions between War Crimes and Crimes against Peace*, 24 ISRAEL YEARBOOK ON HUMAN RIGHTS (1994) at 1, 4–6.

fences against the Peace and Security of Mankind, the International Law Commission limited the possibility of the perpetration of crimes against humanity to the authorities of a State or private individuals acting at the instigation or with the toleration of such authorities (*supra*, para. 2). As the Special Rapporteur Thiam has suggested, the "plurality of victims" which characterizes typical crimes against humanity usually means also a plurality of perpetrators of the crimes and the use of "a State apparatus".[90] But the 1991 Draft Code rightly "does not rule out the possibility that private individuals with *de facto* power or organized in criminal gangs or groups might also commit ... systematic or mass violations of human rights."[91]

Ordinarily, breaches of international legal norms engender an obligation on the part of the State bearing responsibility to make reparation (meaning, primarily, restitution or the payment of financial compensation).[92] Yet, where crimes against humanity – like other crimes established by international law – are concerned, there is individual accountability (irrespective of State responsiblity). That is to say, the individuals perpetrating the acts constituting crimes against humanity are liable to face trial and punishment.

How is an individual to be punished for crimes against humanity? Rudimentary considerations of human rights and due process require that this be done only in a fair trial on the facts and the law before an impartial tribunal. In theory, the best option is to prosecute the individual before an international penal court. The trouble is that no such permanent international court with jurisdiction to try crimes against humanity exists at the present time. In 1994, after a long and arduous process, the International Law Commission adopted a Statute for an International Criminal Court.[93] Still, the prospects for the actual setting up of such a court on a permanent basis are unclear at the moment of writing.[94]

In the absence of a permanent international penal court, a crucial role can be played by *ad hoc* international tribunals. This is the case of the International Criminal Tribunals for the former Yugoslavia and for Rwanda, which follow in the footsteps of the two International Military Tribunals functioning at Nuremberg and at Tokyo after World War II.

When an international penal tribunal with jurisdiction over crimes against humanity is available, it stands to reason that the international pro-

---

90 D. THIAM, *supra* note 20, at 88.

91 *Supra* note 21, at 103.

92 *See Case Concerning the Factory at Chorzów* (Claim for Indemnity) (Merits) (A/17), 1 WORLD COURT REPORTS (1928) at 646, 664, 677–678.

93 *See* J. CRAWFORD, *The ILC Adopts a Statute for an International Criminal Court*, 89 AMERICAN JOURNAL OF INTERNATIONAL LAW (1995) at 404–416.

94 *See ibid.* at 414–416.

ceedings should have primacy over domestic courts. This is expressly stipulated by Article 9(2) of the Statute of the International Criminal Tribunal for the former Yugoslavia, and in Article 8(2) of the Statute of the Rwanda Tribunal.[95] As the Appeals Chamber pronounced in the *Tadic* case, unless an international tribunal is endowed with primacy over domestic courts, the very purpose of its creation can be defeated.[96]

In any event, in conformity with international law, universal jurisdiction as regards crimes against humanity is vested in all States. The principle of universality of jurisdiction over crimes against humanity has been recognized not only in theory but also in practice, the prime example being the Judgment of the Supreme Court of Israel in the *Eichmann Trial*.[97]

When no international tribunal is competent to sit in trial over the perpetrators of crimes against humanity, the domestic courts become the sole avenue for prosecution of persons accused of these crimes. But even where an international tribunal exists, the concurrent jurisdiction of domestic courts (subject to a provision of primacy of the international tribunal) is preserved.[98] Obviously, neither in their moral authority nor in their efficacy with a view to future deteterrence can domestic courts aspire to present an adequate alternative to an international tribunal. Nonetheless, justice can be done – always assuming that the domestic courts will strictly adhere to international law.

An important issue arises in respect of possible prescription of crimes against humanity. General international law does not by itself provide for any such prescription. The question is, to what extent a perpetrator of crimes against humanity prosecuted before domestic courts may benefit from the application of the regular statutes of limitations in force within the internal legislation of the local State. The problem was placed on the international agenda when twenty years elapsed after the end of World War II, while many of the Nazi war criminals were yet to stand trial. In 1968, the General Assembly adopted a Convention on the Non-Applicability of Statutory Limitations to War Crimes and Crimes against Humanity.[99] Under the first Article of this Convention, no statutory limitation is to apply to these crimes, regardless of the date of their commission.[100] It may be added that, accord-

---

[95] *Supra* note 25, at 1194; *supra* note 29, at 1605.

[96] *Supra* note 58, at 32.

[97] *Eichmann v. Attorney General* (1962), 16(3) *Piskei Din* (Israel Supreme Court Judgments) at 2033, 2048. The Judgment is translated into English in 36 INTERNATIONAL LAW REPORTS at 277 (*see* especially at 299).

[98] *See* Article 9(1) of the Statute of the International Tribunal for the former Yugoslavia and the commentary of the Secretary-General, *supra* note 25, at 1176–1177; Article 8(1) of the Statute of the Rwanda Tribunal, *supra* note 29, at 1605.

[99] *Supra* note 24, at 160.

[100] *Ibid.* at 161.

ing to at least one school of thought, the non-limitation principle is endorsed by customary international law.[101]

Conclusion

After many years of an almost purely theoretical appeal to scholars, crimes against humanity are now increasingly acquiring recognition as a grave and topical problem on the international agenda. The International Criminal Tribunal for the former Yugoslavia has already come to grips with the need to determine the range of these crimes, and there is reason to believe that recent experiences – not only in the Balkans – will intensify public interest in the subject-matter.

While crimes against humanity are clearly enshrined today in customary international law, their precise definition is not free of doubt. The paramount issue is whether crimes against humanity are "self-contained" or tied in an umbilical cord to armed conflict. Although the present tendency is to disconnect crimes against humanity from any armed conflict (international or even internal), more international judicial pronouncements are called for before the question can be laid to rest.

---

[101] *See* R.H. MILLER, *The Convention on the Non-Applicability of Statutory Limitations to War Crimes and Crimes against Humanity*, 65 AMERICAN JOURNAL OF INTERNATIONAL LAW (1971) at 476, 481–383.

The Contribution of Environmental Law to the Development of Modern International Law

by

Malgosia Fitzmaurice

Introductory

International environmental law has played a dual role in contributing to, and developing, international law. Firstly, international environmental law has enriched existing fields of international law, such as the laws of war, the law of State responsibility, the law of the sea and of human rights; and, secondly, it has given rise to the creation of unique concepts and principles, such as the principle of intergenerational equity. International environmental law has also contributed to the development of some existing principles, such as the precautionary principle, the concept of sustainable development and the "polluter-pays" principle, to the extent that the tendency exists very often to forget that their origins lay in other fields of law. This short essay will dwell on these two aspects of the role of international environmental law in modern times. However, choices must be made. Thus, as to the first category mentioned above – *i.e.* enrichment of the existing fields of international law – the areas of human rights and State responsibility will be examined; and within the second category – *i.e.* creation of new concepts and principles – attention will be focused on the theories of intergenerational equity and sustainable development, as being the most challenging.

PART I

A. Environmental Law and Human Rights

The first subject to be analysed is the contribution of environmental law to the development of the law of human rights, in particular as concerns the doctrine of a human right to a clean environment. It has to be said right from the outset that the whole problem of linking the environment with the issue human rights is very unclear and controversial. Despite the obvious doctrinal differences concerning the existence of such a right, it can be said that it could exist in several different forms, namely, as a substantive right, as a procedural right or as a constitutional right. Unfortunately, the massive existing literature on the subject is not very illuminating and stimulating, but if anything rather confusing. Despite the doctrinal attitudes, the problem of a human right to a clean environment exists and its importance is not only doctrinal but very practical; existence implies that it can be claimed.[1] However, having said that, the present author will not attempt to solve these problems, since this is not the subject matter of this essay, but will rather try to indicate how environmental law has enriched, even in this controversial way, the law relating to human right. We may say, in fact, that all the doctrinal aspects of this environmental rights appear confusing. Thus, even if we assume that there is such an environmental right, we do not know whether it is a "right to an environment", or to a "decent", "healthy", or "safe" environment.[2] There are broadly three main schools of thought relating to the relationship between human rights in general and an environmental human right.

The first school strongly supports the view that there are no human rights without an environmental right.[3] In short, the above mentioned school takes the stand that a right in relation to the environment is absolutely fundamental to the existence of the other human rights. Quite a large number of lawyers, on the other hand, represent the opposite view that an environmental right does not exist. Prof. Handl in a rather eloquent way tries to prove this point. Although the present essay is not primarily devoted to the issue of an environmental right, some of the arguments of the above mentioned author, who states that a "generic international environmental entitlement, both as an already existing and emerging human rights concept, is a highly questionable proposition",[4] may be worth presenting. He submits that the so-called "right to environment (with all the modifications such as the right to a "clean", or to a "safe" environment) would be difficult to conceptualise as an inalienable right. He takes into consideration the constant changes, or rather evolution, relating to environmental protection measures as being subject to the

---

1 Some authors claim that lack of justiciability does not prevent an environmental right from existing. The argument which underlines this theory is that human rights are not by themselves confrontational rights, so that actionability before a court is not a fundamental characteristic of a human right. PH. CULLET, *Definition of an Environmental Right in a Human Right Context*, 13 NQHR (1995) at 35.

2 *See* R. DESGAGNÉ, *Integrating Environmental Values into the European Convention On Human Rights*, 89 AJIL (1995) at 263.

3 *See* A.A. CANCADO TRINIDADE, *Environmental Protection and the Absence of Restrictions on Human Rights*, (in:) K.E. MAHONEY and P. MAHONEY (eds.), HUMAN RIGHTS IN THE 21ST CENTURY, Dordrecht (1993) at 561–594.

4 G. HANDL, *Human Rights and Protection of the Environment: A Mildly "Revisionist" Point of View*, (in:) A.A. CANCADO TRINIDADE, *op. cit., supra* note 3, at 120–121.

reordering of socio-economic priorities, and to adjustment to meet public policy objectives, such as ensuring continued "development" or "saving jobs". This author rightly points out that since a generic environmental entitlement would not be inalienable, it would therefore not "share either characteristic that is traditionally viewed as a hallmark of "natural rights".[5] Further, on a more practical level, according to the same author, there is not much evidence that States have in fact accepted the existence of a generic environmental right, which necessitates the claiming of an environmental entitlement in an indirect manner. Finally, the above author makes the very valid remark that environmental entitlements vary depending on the area where they arise, *i.e.* whether they relate to "North" or "South".[6] Finally, there is the most moderate group, which admits the existence of some environmental right, but derives its existence from other human rights.[7]

Another difficulty lies in the categorisation of the environmental right as being either a group right,[8] an individual right[9] or third generation rights.[10] Third generation rights are primarily viewed as being of a collective nature, with regard both to their objects and their subjects. Within this category of environmental rights belong as well the right to development, the right to peace, the right to the co-ownership of the common heritage of mankind and the right to communicate. The human rights experts consider these collective rights as immensely vague. Some express the view that these rights are so vast that they encompass anything and anybody. This approach to human rights is called sometimes "globalist", "third worldist" or "nationalist".[11] Human rights specialists try to find a link between human rights in general and environmental law, though it must be said that the theories presented are not always obvious or self-explanatory. For the want of a direct connection, an attempt is made to find some general common ground. This is found in the Preamble to the Universal Declaration on Human Rights: "the inherent dignity and inalienable rights of all members of the human family". The

---

5 *Ibid.* at 122.

6 *Ibid.* at 130.

7 S. WEBER, *Environmental Information and the European Convention on Human Rights*, 12:99 HUMAN RIGHTS JOURNAL (1991) at 177–185. More on the subject (in:) S. SCHIKOF, RIGHT TO CLEAN ENVIRONMENT (text unpublished).

8 *See e.g.* M. SIMON, *The Integration and Interdependence of Culture and the Environment*, (in:) K.E. MAHONEY and P. MAHONEY (eds.), *op. cit., supra* note 3, at 521–528.

9 M. KAMMINGA, *Mensrechten en millieubescherming – en nuttige combinatie*, NEDERLANDS TIJDSCHRIFT VOOR MENSRECHTEN, 18:3 NIJCM BULLETIN (1993) at 99.

10 PH. ALSTON, *A Third Generation of Solidarity Rights: Progressive Development of Obfuscation of International Human Rights Law*, XXIX NILR at 309.

11 M. GALEKAMP, *Individualism versus Collectivism. The Concept of Collective Rights*, RFS (1993) at 35.

right to environment, according to this theory, derives from this dignity.[12] Another approach seems to base the environmental right on the right to life and the right to health.[13]

Another of the problems relating to an environmental human right is that the contents of this right are not specified.[14] There are many questions without answers: is it a procedural right; is it a right enforceable through legal proceedings; is it merely a policy statement?[15] Some of most prominent environmental lawyers are of the view that procedural rights have the most important role to play in the protection of environmental rights. Thus, as it has been said, "... the existence of individual procedural rights helps shape domestic environmental policy and facilitates the resolution of transboundary conflicts through equal access to the same private law procedures."[16] The present author finds most convincing the view that human rights and environmental rights represent different but overlapping issues. The reasoning is based on a premise that although both fields share the same objectives, it would be artificial to link them forcibly together, since not all violations of human rights have an environmental context and likewise forcing all environmental issues into the framework of human rights may damage fundamentally their concept. Only this approach seems to take into account the possibility of these two fields coming into conflict. The proponents of this approach propose several solutions as to how to mould environment law from the perspective of human rights. Regrettably, the proposed solutions are not as novel or convincing as the basic concept. Firstly, environmental problems may be asserted through existing human rights (right to life, health etc.); secondly, a set of environmental rights is proposed, based upon the existing right to information; and, thirdly, a specific right to environment could be formulated and added to the current catalogue of human rights.[17] The link between human rights and the environment is not an entirely new phenomenon. As early as in 1972 the Stockholm Declaration on Human Environment stated that "... man has the fundamental right to freedom, equality and adequate conditions of life, in an environment of quality that permits

---

12 A. KISS, *Concept and Possible Implications of the Right to Environment*, (in:) K.E. MAHONEY and P. MAHONEY (eds.), *op. cit., supra* note 3, at 55.

13 *See e.g.* J. SYMONIDES, *The Human Right to a Clean Balanced and Protected Environment*, 20 INTERNATIONAL JOURNAL OF LEGAL INFORMATION (1991) at 29.

14 P. BIRNIE, A.E. BOYLE, INTERNATIONAL LAW AND THE ENVIRONMENT (1992) at 197.

15 *See e.g.* PH. ALSTON, *op. cit., supra* note 10, at 307–322.

16 P. BIRNIE, A.E. BOYLE, *op. cit., supra* note 14, at 196.

17 D. SHELTON, *Human Rights, Environmental Rights, and the Right to Environment*, 103 STANFORD JOURNAL OF INTERNATIONAL LAW (1991) at 104–105.

a life of dignity and well-being".[18] Interestingly, in contrast to the Stockholm Declaration, the Rio Declaration UNCED 1992 in its Principle 1 states only that "human beings are in the centre of concerns for sustainable development, entitled to a healthy and productive life in harmony with nature".[19] It is understood that the main reason for this formulation was the tension between the protection of environment and the right to economic development which reflected the conflict between "North" and "South" – the theme of the entire conference.[20] Recently, however, human rights and the environmental issue received more attention. In May 1994, an international group of experts produced a Draft Declaration of Principles on Human Rights and Environment (Draft Declaration). The same year the United Nations Special Rapporteur, Madame Fatma Zohra Ksentini, issued her final Report on Human Rights and the Environment (Final Report), to the sub-Commission on Prevention of Discrimination and Protection of Minorities. These two events are assessed as "remarkable progress in the field of human rights and the environment".[21] The Draft Declaration treats environmental rights as a comprehensive package which presents them not as a new type of a right but rather describes existing rights contained in the Draft Declaration consists of substantive rights and procedural rights. The list of substantive rights includes, *e.g.*: the right to safe food and water; the right to a safe and healthy working and living environment; the right to housing in an ecologically sound environment; rights of future generations (see *infra*); and the rights of indigenous peoples to control their environment. The procedural rights include, *e.g.*: the right to environmental information; the right to participation in environmental decision making; and the right to environmental and human rights education. The way the environmental rights were presented (as an existing human right) diminish political opposition to environmental rights by States. The presentation of the environmental rights as a package deal is considered as a novel feature. It is assumed that this catalogue of environmental rights can serve as a reference point for defining environmental harm in general.[22] The Special Rapporteur Madame Ksentini presented a very comprehensive Report. She discuses the relationship between human rights

---

[18] *Declaration of the United Nations Conference on Human Environment*, U.N. Doc. A/Conf./48/14, REV. 1.

[19] *Rio Declaration on Environment and Development*, U.N. Doc. A/Conf.151/5/, REV. 1, June 13, 1992, reprinted, (in:) 31:874 ILM (1992).

[20] D. SHELTON, *What Happened in Rio to Human Rights?*, 3 YEARBOOK OF INTERNATIONAL ENVIRONMENTAL LAW (1992) at 93.

[21] A.F. AGUILA, N.A.F. POPOVIÆ, *Law Making in the United: The U.N. Study on Human Rights and the Environment*, 3 RECIEL (1995) at 197.

[22] *Ibid.* at 201.

and environment, drawing examples from the link between indigenous peoples and the environment, protection of environment during armed conflict and the question of the environment and international peace and security. She also addressed the position of the most vulnerable groups: children, disabled, environmental refugees. Madame Ksentini emphasises a very important factor, namely, that development must evolve together with environmental protection. She also addressed the problem of the future generations.

The heated discussion on the doctrinal problems concerning environment and human rights goes on. Even if the answers are not ready yet, the arguments presented enriched the domain of human rights. The problem generated a rethinking of the general approaches to human rights. Moreover, the Convention on the Rights of the Child explicitly addresses environmental issues in Articles 24 and 29.[23] Thus, without much ado the issue entered into practice.

B. Environmental Law and State Responsibility

The next issue which the present author will discuss is the contribution of environmental law to the development of the doctrine of State responsibility. The issue is quite controversial; nevertheless, the International Law Commission (ILC) has occupied itself with a series of Draft Articles on "International Liability for Injurious Consequences of Acts not Prohibited by International Law" (the "Liability Draft").[24] The question whether there exists in international law a separate regime of "liability" for environmental damage which is conceptually different in its basis from the general regime of State responsibility arises because the ILC, when it came to cover topics of State responsibility, limited its work to responsibility for what it termed "wrongful acts," meaning acts which were in breach of duty imposed on a State by international law. The ILC expressly left out the problem of acts which international law does not prohibit. Thus, following this doctrinal distinction, the ILC produced two sets of drafts: one on State responsibility (for wrongful acts), and the other (later set) on responsibility for acts not

---

23 There is no consensus, however, as to the proper interpretation of the content of these articles. On the different interpretations, *see* S.E. BRICE, *Convention on the Rights of the Child: Using a Human Rights Instrument to Protect against Environmental Threats*, 7 GEORGETOWN INTERNATIONAL LAW REVIEW (1995) (Issue 2, Spring) in particular at 595–599. On the rights of the child generally, *see* G. VAN BUEREN, THE INTERNATIONAL LAW ON THE RIGHTS OF THE CHILD, Dordrecht & London (1995).

24 Quentin-Baxter's Special Report on International Liability "Schematic Outline," ILC YEARBOOK 1981-II) at 64; and Special Rapporteur Barbosa's Several Drafts (the most important Sixth Report, U.N. Doc. /A/CN.4/428 (1990).

wrongful in themselves in international law, which was called State liability. The draft on liability was conceptually limited to the environmental field and to physical consequences of activities which "cause, or create a risk of causing transboundary harm."[25] The present author will not dwell extensively on all the theoretical aspects of the ILC Drafts, since a vast body of literature exists on the subject.[26] It must be said from the outset that the main bases of the conceptual separation of the two topics have been subject to a widespread and fierce criticism, not to say condemnation. As a result of this, the Special Rapporteur Barboza, in his latest drafts, tried to accommodate his critics by abandoning some of the ideas of the liability draft in order to bring it closer to the responsibility draft. The success, however, of this operation is doubtful. The most important conceptual distinction introduced by the ILC Liability Draft was to abandon the distinction underlying the concepts of primary and secondary obligations, *i.e.* obligations to act in accordance with rules of international law and of consequences flowing from the breach of those rules. In the Liability Draft, the ILC attempted to construe a concept which is referred to as the "compound primary norm." This norm was construed to contain four individual duties: to prevent, to inform, to negotiate and to make reparation. The compound primary norm was considered to be a primary obligation; it was not, unlike the duty to compensate under the responsibility regime, based on a wrongful act. In order to bring the liability draft in line with the responsibility draft, it was considered, however, that the breach of the last element of the norm – *i.e.* that of compensation duty – was a breach of international law, and thus a wrongful act. The reasoning behind the separation of the ILC Drafts may be summarised as follows: some environmental activities which cause damage are not prohibited thus they do not constitute a wrongful act, some of them are even beneficial. Nevertheless, in case of damage done to another State, a new regime seemed to be in order, to enable the harmed State to obtain some compensation. Another perception of some members of the ILC was that wrongfulness was to be equated with fault or *culpa*. From this, it was inferred that the State responsibility regime was unable to support strict (*sine culpa*) liability and, because to introduce such a liability with respect to environmental damage was one

---

25 *See* Preliminary Report of Quentin-Baxter, ILC YEARBOOK (1980-II) at 248.

26 *See e.g.* M. AKEHURST, *International Liability for Injurious Consequences Arising out of Acts not Prohibited by International Law*, 16 NYIL (1985) at 3; A. BOYLE, *State Responsibility and International Liability for Injurious Consequences of Acts not Prohibited by International Law: A Necessary Distinction*, 39 ICLQ (1990) at 22; N.L.J.T. HORABACH, *The Confusion about State Responsibility and International Liability*, 4 NJIL (1991) at 47; I. BROWNLIE, STATE RESPONSIBILITY, Part I (1983) at 23; M. FITZMAURICE, *International Environmental Law as a Special Field*, 25 NYJL (1994) at 201–218.

of objectives of ILC, a separate regime was thought to be necessary. The reasoning presented by the ILC was met with the critical appraisal of international lawyers. The critics of the draft, based their arguments on the obligation of States regarding environmental damage done to other States as already firmly rooted in customary law regime of State responsibility. This long standing principle was first articulated in the *Trail Smelter* arbitration, where it was stated that "... no State has the right to use or permit to use of its territory in such a manner as to cause injury by fumes to the territory of another or the properties or persons therein, when the case is of serious consequence and injury is established by clear and convincing evidence."[27] This principle was endorsed by the ICJ in the *Corfu Channel* case.[28] Likewise, principle 22 of the Stockholm Declaration also emphasises the responsibility of States to ensure that "the activities within their jurisdiction or control do not cause damage to the environment of other States or beyond the limits of national jurisdiction."[29] Based on the above-mentioned considerations, the separation of the two regimes does not seem to be fully doctrinally justified; and this is, indeed, the prevailing view expressed in the literature. Out of the numerous publications on this topic, two may be cited, those of Brownlie and Boyle. Brownlie, basing his argument on the *Trail Smelter* case, treats the separation of the topics as "fundamentally misconceived." According to him, State responsibility relates also to harm caused by lawful activities. The distinction between lawful and unlawful activities is, therefore, without purpose and lacks support in either State practice or in jurisprudence. What is crucial is the contents of the rule.[30] A similar criticism is made by Boyle, according to whom "... the motion that activities incurring responsibility for harm are unlawful and prohibited can be seen as misconceived and oversimplified; the elements of harm, knowledge and control are drawn directly from comparable use in a State responsibility context."[31] We have to agree with the critics of the ILC Draft that in the case of the *Trail Smelter* arbitration (and this leads us to the more general conclusion), the operation of the plant was lawful but pollution caused by this operation was not, and was subject, therefore, to the responsibility regime.

Special Rapporteur Barboza, in order to take account of the many doctrinal criticisms which had been made, changed the conceptual basis of the

---

[27] 3 RIAA (1941) at 1911 and 1965. *See* also *Lac Lanoux* arbitration (*France v. Spain*), 55 AJIL (1959) at 156.

[28] In this case the Court stated that it is "every State's obligation not to allow knowingly its State territory to be used for acts contrary to the rights of other States." ICJ REPORTS 1949 at 22.

[29] 11 ILM (1972) at 1416.

[30] I. BROWNLIE, *op. cit, supra* note 26.

[31] A. BOYLE, *op. cit, supra* note 26, at 22.

Quentin-Baxter's Drafts, developing extensively, in his Draft, the principles both relating to State responsibility and liability. Unlike Quentin-Baxter, Barboza envisaged State responsibility in two cases, namely: when a State does not perform the primary obligation of prevention, information and negotiation; and when it does not perform the duty of reparation (the only case when State responsibility was foreseen in Quentin-Baxter's Draft). However, as a result of all these changes, Barboza blurred the theoretical distinction between the two drafts, and effectively obliterated the difference between primary and secondary rules. Another point of confusion is related to the problem of reparation for damage. A novel feature of Barboza's Draft, contrary to the Draft on State responsibility, relates to the lack (in the earlier Liability Drafts) of any obligation to discontinue the harmful activity, to restore the *status quo ante* or to compensate fully for harm. Barboza's Draft takes a different stand on the question of making reparation for appreciable harm.[32] Barboza, however, maintains the distinction between lawful and unlawful activities by varying the standard of compensation on the basis of the principle of the balance of interests, which limits the level of compensation. Under the responsibility doctrine for an internationally wrongful act, a State is under an obligation to pay compensation. According to the Barboza's Draft, a breach of a primary rule in the liability regime causes the same outcome, putting in doubt the necessity of the existence of two separate regimes. We may add that if a State does not pay compensation under the Liability Draft, it is also guilty of an internationally wrongful act, thus giving rise to State responsibility. On the basis of the theory contained in Barboza's Draft, the liability for environmental damage (wrongful act) (primary norm) changes into State responsibility (secondary norm). Notwithstanding the doctrinal differences, in both cases the final result will be the same. The only difference will be the amount of compensation, lower in case of the lawful act. From what has been said above on the Liability Draft, it may be hard to imagine how this draft could enrich the doctrine of State responsibility. The Draft on State Liability, however, is not entirely without merit. It must be stressed, on the positive side, that this Draft introduces some valid innovations: it strives towards a stricter liability standard; it covers conceptually both the results of unforeseeable accident and of continuing polluting activities; and it introduces the concept of balance of interest in relation to responsibility for environmental harm. The liability regime protects the victims of pollution which occurs through accident, whereas, if the unmodified regime of State responsibility was to be applied, the victim might well be left without any claim. Having taken

[32] Draft Arts. 8 and 9, (1989), UN Doc. A/CN./423.

all the circumstances into consideration, the present author agrees with the view that the positive elements of the Liability Draft should be incorporated into the existing responsibility regime; *i.e.* in terms of the definition of the obligations of States owed to other States in respect of environmentally harmful activities and taking into account the consequences of breaches of these obligations.[33]

PART II

A. The Concept of Sustainable Development

The concept of sustainable development is a result of the growing perception that environmental issues cannot be viewed in isolation from other issues such as poverty, development and trade. Recent years have brought an understanding that environmental protection is incompatible with unrestricted economic activity in developed States and unrestricted economic growth in developing States. The growing awareness concerning environmental issues was matched by the expanding claims of developing States asserting their right to development, even on an extreme view as a kind of collective right. The link between the environment and economic development was recognised in 1972 during the Stockholm Conference. The Stockholm Declaration set out the general obligation to preserve the environment, as well as stating obligations which recognise the necessity of economic growth and at the same time the need to provide assistance to developing countries to enable them both to meet their obligations towards the environment and, on the other hand, to secure their right to development (see *e.g.*, Principles 8, 9, and 11).

The conceptual summation of this problem has been recognised as the "concept of sustainable development." The classic definition of sustainable development is contained in the Brundland Report as a concept of development which meets the needs of present generations without compromising the ability of future generations to meet their own needs.[34] The essence of this concept is rather living off nature's "income" than squandering its "capital."[35] Since, the concept of sustainable development seems to provide the

---

33 K. ZEMANEK, *State Responsibility and Liability*, (in:) P.H. WINFIED, *et al.* (eds.), ENVIRONMENTAL PROTECTION AND INTERNATIONAL LAW (1991) at 2.

34 WORLD COMMISSION ON ENVIRONMENT AND DEVELOPMENT, OUR COMMON FUTURE (Brundtland Report), London (1987).

35 G. HANDL, *Environmental Security and Global Change: The Challenge of International Law*, YILE (1990) at 24.

solution to the problem of reconciliation of economic development and the environment, it has become the "key" word in the contemporary law of ecological protection. According to one expert, "not surprisingly, it has turned out to be a notion around which legally significant expectations regarding environmental conduct have begun to crystallise. This concept might turn into a mandatory standard of international legal evaluation."[36] The concept of sustainable development was a guiding principle during the UNCED Conference in Rio (the Earth Summit) in 1992. It was considered a readily available remedy for all the problems relating to environmental protection and economic growth. As a result, the concept has found its way into a substantial number of environmental documents of varying degrees of "hardness," and most notably, into the Rio Declaration and other instruments which were signed at the UNCED. The late Judge Nagendra Singh singled out three broad elements of sustainability: sustainability in relation to resources available for present and future generations; sustainability in relation to an adequate, healthy environment; and sustainability in relation to the community, to the concept of "international commons" and safeguarding the environmental "common heritage of mankind."[37]

As stated, however, by one author, "... the concept of sustainable development suffers from serious flaws."[38] The concept of sustainable development remains general and unspecified, an "umbrella concept." Although its formulation attempts to link two fields, development and environment, the mechanical linkage in itself has not proved to be sufficient to produce agreement on the fundamental theoretical questions relating to the concept. According to the same author, the basic weakness of the problem lies in the lack of definitions of the following: poverty and degradation, objectives of development, sustainability and participation. Another point at issue is how to proceed in view of incomplete knowledge.[39] This confusion relating to the fundamental definitions has not, however, been an obstacle to presenting some tentative principles relating to the concept of sustainable development, some of which were contained in the Brundland Report, and others of which were presented and adopted by the Expert Group appointed by

---

36 *Ibid.* at 33.

37 N. SINGH, *Right to Environment and Sustainable Development as a Principle of International Law*, ESSAYS IN HONOUR OF JUDGE TASLIM OLAWALE ELIAS, Dordrecht & London (1992), Vol. I, Professor E.G. BELLO and Prince BOLA A. AJIBOLA, SAN (eds.), at 186.

38 P. MALANCZUK, *Sustainable Development: Some Critical Thoughts in the Light of the RIO Conference*, (in:) K. GINTHER, E. DENTERS (eds.), SUSTAINABLE DEVELOPMENT AND GOOD GOVERNANCE, Dordrecht & London (1995), at 25.

39 *Ibid.* at 26.

WCED. This latter set of principles was not completely original, since they came partly from the Report, and thus only partly were adopted by the WCED as their own.[40] As a fundamental principle of sustainable development, the Expert Group singled out the fundamental human right to an environment adequate for health and well-being. The next general principle relates to conservation of environment for the benefit of present and future generations. The specific principles depict an acknowledged and accepted approach to reasonable management of natural resources and protection of the environment, involving such things as: development of environmental standards; prior environmental assessments; inclusion of the public in environmental planning. The next batch of principles concerns a general obligation on States to use transboundary or extraterritorial natural resources in a reasonable and equitable manner. These principles confirm a duty to cease, and provide compensation for, activities in breach of environmental obligations. The set of rules is completed by the Articles relating to peaceful settlement of environmental disputes. The commentary appended to the rules illustrates underlying principles with the decisions of the ICJ and international conventions. The draughtsmen of the principles based them on the Stockholm Declaration and World Charter for nature.[41] Some authors make a distinction between the "elements" underlying the notion of sustainable development and the "principles" relating to it. To the first group, the "elements," belong such concepts as the principle of intergenerational equity, the principle of sustainable use, the principle of equitable use and the principle of integration. Principles 21 and 22 of the Stockholm and Rio Declarations (sovereignty over natural resources and the responsibility not to cause environmental harm) as can be listed "principles" of sustainable development. Other principles which have been included as "principles" of sustainable development include the following: the principle of good neighbourliness and international cooperation; the principle of good governance, including participatory democracy; the principle of common but differentiated responsibility; the principle of preventive action; the precautionary principle; and the "polluter pays" principle. This catalogue lists all the known principles governing environmental protection.[42] The problem of this approach is rooted in the vagueness and generality of the above-mentioned principles. All of them suffer from the same

---

40 V. KOESTER, *From Stockholm to Brundland*, 20 EPL (1990) at 16.

41 *See ibid.* at 16; *see* also, J. LAMMERS and R. MUNROE, ENVIRONMENTAL PROTECTION AND SUSTAINABLE DEVELOPMENT (1987) at 36.

42 P. SANDS, *International Law in the Field of Sustainable Development: Emerging Legal Principles*, (in:) SUSTAINABLE DEVELOPMENT AND INTERNATIONAL LAW, Dordrecht & London (1995) at 53 ff.

affliction which is uncertainty as to their content. Thus, one vague notion is being explained by a whole catalogue of others. We are in the middle of a circular argument.

Another serious problem which arises in relation to the introduction of sustainable development as the guiding principle of environmental protection is the inherent contradiction between the objectives of development and those of environmental protection. Sustainable development as an international policy concept clearly implies some measure of international accountability; yet, as generally endorsed, it is also accompanied by an express disclaimer of any intended encroachment upon State sovereignty.[43] Thus, it has been said, on the one hand, that the concept is "inoperable" due to its inherent vagueness, whilst, one the other, that "emergence of a convenient definition which was found agreeable by all players would be an indication that the definition was inadequate, as the concept is too fundamental to be captured easily..." Reference to the concept of sustainable development may be found in many "soft law" documents as well as in recent conventions, coupled with other fashionable concepts (*e.g.* in the Climate Change Convention). This concept is used only in a mechanical manner – the provisions of these documents do not try to reconcile the inherent conflicts illustrated above; and it is thus difficult to see how these treaties can add to the clarification and development of the concept of sustainable development.

Sustainable development is one of most illusive doctrinal concepts of recent years. As evidenced above, the content of the concept is controversial and neither practitioner nor academic can really be expected on their own to present a satisfactory proposal. Sustainable development is a multi-disciplinary problem, so that the contribution of scientists seems to be inevitable. Certainly, searching for yet more principles does not seem to be a workable, constructive solution.

Be it as it may, sustainable development as a concept has revolutionized the law of environmental protection, and, without doubt, added a new dimension to international law and turned the attention of international lawyers to such problems as the conflict between "North" and "South," as well as having enriched the notion of State sovereignty. On a more practical level, the implementation of sustainable development has added much to the expansion of international financing and transfer of technology, in the context of "North" and "South." Finally, it should be added that, in order to specify what constitutes sustainable development, we must very carefully eliminate what does not. Thus we must try to avoid putting into the concept all the

---

43 G. HANDL, *op. cit., supra* note 35, at 25–26.

fashionable new theories of the day which substantially add very little but make the whole issue less clear.

B. Intergenerational Equity

The concept of intergenerational equity is treated very often as part and parcel of human rights. In the view of the present author, however, this concept merits a separate place in the development of modern international law, not only as an enrichment of human rights, since it was originally presented in the framework of environmental law by Professor E. Brown-Weiss.[44] There are several fundamental principles contained in this concept, and the present author will outline only the most basic ideas comprised in them. Brown-Weiss treats human beings as a part of nature. Degradation of nature has a direct influence on human beings. All generations are inherently linked to other generations, past and future. There are no generations which are more favoured or cherished; all of them are in a position of equality. The basis of the concept is to view human community as a partnership among all generations. Intergenerational equity is based on three basic principles. The first one is "conservation of options," which requires each generation to observe the diversity of the natural and cultural resource base. Future generations should be entitled to a degree of diversity comparable to that enjoyed by previous generations.[45] The second principle is that of "conservation of quality," the gist of which is that the next generation should enjoy the same quality of the planet as the previous generation.[46] Finally, the third principle is that of "conservation of access," which professes that each generation should provide its members with equitable rights of access to the legacy of past generations, and should conserve this access for future generations.[47] The proper summation of the complex system of intergenerational rights is found in the statement that each generation has "to pass the planet on in no worse condition than it received it and to provide equitable access to its resources and benefits."[48] Intergenerational rights are group rights, or "generational rights" which generations may enforce against each other.

Brown-Weiss constructs a whole system to implement these rights. First of all, she proposes the appointment of an ombudsman for future generations.

---

44 E. BROWN-WEISS, *In Fairness to Future Generations: International Law, Common Patrimony, and Intergenerational Equity*, UNITED NATIONS UNIVERSITY (1989); and *idem, Our Rights and Obligations to Future Generations for the Environment*, 84 AJIL (1990) at 198.

45 E. BROWN-WEISS, *Our Rights and Obligations to Future Generations for the Environment, op. cit., supra* note 44, at 202.

46 *Ibid.*

47 *Ibid.*

48 *Ibid.* at 200.

Other organs would be a Planetary Rights Commission to hear complaints, and the Commission for the Future of the Planet to assess the effects of present actions on future generations. She also foresees the creation of certain funds and trusts for maintaining the planet and for compensating future generations for the costs it imposes no them.

The Brown-Weiss theory has been the subject of fierce criticism. One author, indeed, goes so far as to claim that if we intervene to conserve the environment to protect future generations, we are doomed to disaster. D'Amato's main criticism is based on the so-called "Parfit's paradox", in combination with the new theory of chaos. He presents a dual argument: firstly, future generations cannot have any rights because they will consist of individuals who at the moment do not exist; and, secondly, there can be no *rationale* behind actions and interference taken by us at the present time in terms of the effect they will have on future generations, as we do not know what will be the requirements, or physical or psychological make-up, of these generations as a result of our input. The same author, further, assesses the whole concept as anthropocentric, thus not taking into account to a sufficient degree the rights of animals.[49] Brown-Weiss defends her approach by pointing out that intergenerational equity is a group right, thus the position of an individual is not important in the shaping of the rights of future generations. As to the other criticism, Brown-Weiss emphasises that the concept of intergenerational rights does place human beings together with other living creatures, thus not isolating them or doubting the importance of non human creations.[50] Other criticism derives from the human rights context. According to these critics Brown-Weiss wrongly conceptualised human rights in relation to intergenerational equity. She extends the human rights concept (which according to this author underlines her theory), across time, "... while at the same time embracing a generic human right to a decent environment."[51] The same author expresses doubts as to whether the human rights context is a proper forum in which to discuss intergenerational equity, since it is unclear if the environmental right exists at all. He argues for the possibility of the existence of such rights since they operate "... across space and time on behalf of broadly defined social and economic goods",[52] but sees as a valid point of criticism the problem relating to the needs of future generations – we do not know what future generations will be like, even less so

---

[49] A. D'AMATO, *Do We Owe a Duty to Future Generations to Preserve the Global Environment*, 84 AJIL (1990) at 192–194.

[50] E. BROWN-WEISS, *Our Rights and Obligations..., op. cit., supra* note 44, at 204.

[51] G.P. SUPANICH, *The Legal Basis of Intergenerational Responsibility: An Alternative View – The Sense of Intergenerational Identity*, 2 YIEL (1992) at 96–99.

[52] *Ibid.* at 97.

what will be the condition of our planet in some distant future.[53] Having said all this, the present author has to mention, however, that the much criticised concept of intergenerational equity has emerged as a basis for an environmental judgement in the *Oposa* claim.[54] The legal issues of the *Oposa* claim were very complicated. In this essay, we are only, however, interested in the manner in which the principle of intergenerational equity was implemented. For clarity, a short description will be given on the circumstances of the claim. The plaintiffs in this case were a number of minors and Philippine Ecological Network, Inc., a non-stock, non-profit-making organisation. The claim was tried at several instances in the Philippines. The original claim, which was filed as a taxpayers' class action, was to have all the existing Timber License Agreements cancelled.[55] Having had their claim dismissed at first instance, the claimants petitioned the Supreme Court to reverse the ruling. The Supreme Court reversed the ruling and the claim returned to a lower court. In the course of hearing the case, the Supreme Court made a very important pronouncement concerning the right to a healthful and balanced environment. This right is guaranteed by the Philippines Constitution. According to one author, "in interpreting these provisions, the Supreme Court recognised the primacy and centrality of the right to ecological security and health among many rights assured by the Constitution."[56] For the first time, the Court mentioned, explicitly, intergenerational equity and responsibility. The Court said that it was the responsibility of the Government that the nation should recognise, discharge and fulfil the responsibilities of each generation as a trustee and guardian of the environment for succeeding generations. Thus, though the Supreme Court did not incorporate globally the concept of intergenerational equity, the gist of it was preserved; and the judgement constitutes a novel, original and progressive approach in general to human rights and the environment.

Finally, in his Dissenting Opinion, Judge Weeramantry pointed out that the *Nuclear Test II* case,[57] raised the principle of intergenerational equity

---

53 *Ibid.* at 98.

54 *Minors Oposa et al. v. Secretary of the Environment and Natural Resources Fulgencio Factoran*, G.R.N° 101083, 30 July 1993. Reprinted, (in:) 33 ILM (1993), 173 (hereafter cited as the "*Oposa* claim"); *see* also, A. REST, *Implementing Principles of Intergenerational Equity and Responsibility*, 24 EPL (1994), at 314–320; A. LA VIÑA, THE RIGHT TO A SOUND ENVIRONMENT IN THE PHILIPPINES: THE SIGNIFICANCE OF THE MINORS OPOSA CASE, 3 RECIEL (1995) at 246.

55 *Ibid.* at 246.

56 *Ibid.* at 247.

57 Request for an Examination of the Situation in accordance with paragraph 63 of the Court's Judgement of 20 December, 1974 in the *Nuclear Test* case (*New Zealand v. France*), Order of the ICJ of 22 September, 1995.

(which had been pleaded by Professor Lauterpacht on behalf of New Zealand) as an important and rapidly developing principle of international law.[58] In relation to this principle, Judge Weeramantry saw the Court as being the trustee of intergenerational rights to the same degree as a domestic court is a trustee of the interests of an infant unable to speak for itself; and he took the view that the Court should not ignore the concept, which has found its way into the *corpus* of international law, only because of the lack of a precedent on which it may rest.

Concluding Remarks

This survey of the most recent developments in international environmental law clearly indicates that modern international law has been enriched. Even if we agree that not all the contributions are equally valid, we must admit that provoking a heated discussion in itself serves the purpose of stimulating the development of international law. The present essay focuses only on certain aspects of environmental law. As mentioned in the introduction, there are other concepts such as the "precautionary" principle and the "polluter pays" principle which have either entered the body of general international law, or been further developed through environmental law. The author of this study, however, is of the view that the contribution of environmental law is illustrated through the description of more general and theoretical concepts, such as that of State responsibility. It is important, however, to note that the whole discussion in not entirely doctrinal, and that certain concepts have actually entered into the practice of law such as intergenerational equity or the environmental human rights. International environmental law is one of the most energetic fields of international law. It appears that its contribution to international law will continue.

---

[58] *Nuclear Test* II case, Dissenting Opinion of Judge Weeramantry at 17.

On Cultural Differences, Levels of Societal Development and Universal Human Rights

by

Rein Müllerson

I feel greatly honoured to have been invited to contribute to the *Festschrift* for Krzysztof Skubiszewski whom I have been lucky to know in his capacity both as an eminent scholar and a diplomat of highest distinction. In autumn 1988, just shortly before Professor Skubiszewski became Foreign Minister of Poland, we both lectured at the Institute of International Law and Relations in Saloniki (Greece). I was struck by his erudition generally as well as by his detailed and profound knowledge of different areas of international law. One of such areas which developed positively in Poland during the years when Professor Skubiszewski was in the government is human rights. Therefore, I find it appropriate to devote my contribution to the volume in honour of Professor Skubiszewski to some controversial theoretical problems of human rights.

I. ON THE UNIVERSALITY OF HUMAN RIGHTS AND CULTURAL RELATIVISM

Practically all U.N. human rights documents, if not directly, then at least implicitly, proceed from the assumption of the universality of human rights, their indivisibility and equal importance. The Universal Declaration of Human Rights of 1948 sets as a goal to secure "universal and effective recognition and observance of all rights and freedoms enshrined in the Declaration."[1] The Vienna Declaration and Programme of Action adopted on 25 June 1993 by the World Conference on Human Rights, referring to the U.N. Charter and other U.N. instruments relating to human rights, reiterates that "the universal nature of these rights and freedoms is beyond question", and that "human rights and fundamental freedoms are the birthright of all human beings."[2]

---

[1] I. Brownlie (ed.), Basic Documents on Human Rights (3rd ed.), Clarendon Press, Oxford (1992) at 22.

[2] World Conference on Human Rights. The Vienna Declaration and Programme of Action, New York (1993) at 28.

However, the implementation of these rights and freedoms varies greatly from society to society and though there is no human rights paradise in the world there are quite a few human rights hells where none of the rights and freedoms solemnly proclaimed in U.N. documents are applied in practice.

Often the obvious cultural diversity of the world is given, if not as an excuse or justification, then at least as an explanation of the absence or violation of human rights in some societies. It is asserted that human rights are a Western concept which does not fit well with societies based on different values and traditions. Such voices come most often from the non-Western world, but interestingly enough, similar views are held by a number of people in the West as well.

Already in 1947 the *Statement on Human Rights* published on behalf of the executive board of the American Anthropological Association[3] and submitted to the U.N. Commission on Human Rights emphasised the Western cultural bias of the draft U.N. Declaration on Human Rights:

> "It will not be convincing to the Indonesian, the African, the Indian, the Chinese, if it lies on the same plane as like documents of an earlier period. The rights of man in the Twentieth Century cannot be circumscribed by the standards of any single culture or be dictated by the aspirations of any single people."[4]

Recently Bilahari Kausikan, a senior Singaporian diplomat, similarly questioned the values behind international human rights standards: "But what institutions and which values? The individualistic ethos of the West or the communitarian traditions of Asia? The consensus-seeking approach of East and South-East Asia or the adversarial institutions of the West?"[5]

Do, and if yes then to what extent, differences of values and traditions really constitute an obstacle to the universality of human rights? And are these traditions and values as different as they are sometimes asserted to be?

Obviously, there are no simple answers to these questions. Yes, there are different cultures which have different values. But, at the same time, there is more common in different cultures that a perfunctory glance would disclose. As Michael Walzer writes: "every human society is universal because it is human, particular because it is a society."[6] One of the most important and difficult questions in the domain of international promotion and pro-

---

3 49 AMERICAN ANTHROPOLOGIST (1947) at 539–543.

4 *Ibid.* at 543.

5 B. KAUSIKAN, *Asia's Different Standard*, FOREIGN POLICY FALL (1993) at 35.

6 M. WALZER, THICK AND THIN: MORAL ARGUMENT AT HOME AND ABROAD, University of Notre Dame Press (1994) at 8.

tection of human rights is the question of the relative influence of the factors which are common to different societies and of the particularities of their culture, history, traditions, religion, and economic development on the perception and acceptance of international human rights standards.

Though the idea of human rights as such emerged in the West, there were early precursors of human rights in different concepts of human dignity which can be traced both in the Eastern and Western thought as far back as 2000 years BC. As Arthur Henry Robertson and John Merrills wrote: "The idea of individual worth can be found in the work of sages, philosophers, prophets and poets from different countries and many faiths in all continents, including India, China, Japan, Persia, Russia, Turkey, Egypt, Israel, several countries of black Africa and pre-Columbian civilisations of South America."[7] This is definitely so and though human rights and especially their implementation may depend on cultural, religious or other traditions, these are not insurmountable obstacles for a universal acceptance of basic human rights, especially if we do not forget that cultures and values change.

Culture, certainly more slowly than economic and political structures of society, is capable of changing. Francis Fukuyama is correct that "we see evidence of cultural change all around us. Catholicism, for example, has often been held to be hostile to both capitalism and democracy ... yet there has been a 'Protestantization' of Catholic culture that makes differences between Protestant and Catholic societies much less pronounced than in times past."[8]

Moreover, societies themselves change. As Eric Hobsbawm observes, "in the 1980s, socialist Bulgaria and non-socialist Ecuador had more in common than either had with the Bulgaria or Ecuador of 1939."[9] A similar comment could be made about almost anywhere. If, for example, yesterday human rights were an unfamiliar concept in most Asian societies, today the peoples of Asian States are taking human rights more and more seriously.

That contemporary human rights standards are not immutable values, inherent only to Western countries can be proved also by the fact that these countries themselves, and others as well, came to the acceptance of these values through a long historic process. David Selbourne traces back the historic widening of claims-to-rights in liberal democratic civic orders:

> "from claims made by seventeenth-century property owners to the concomitant political rights to which they believed themselves entitled by

---

[7] A.H. ROBERTSON, J.G. MERRILLS, HUMAN RIGHTS IN THE WORLD (3rd ed.), Manchester University Press (1993) at 8.

[8] F. FUKUYAMA, TRUST, Hamish Hamilton, London (1995) at 41.

[9] E. HOBSBAWM, AGE OF EXTREMES, Michael Joseph, London (1994) at 9.

> virtue of their ownership; to claims made by non-property-owners in the nineteenth century to a variety of civic rights which should owe nothing to wealth or position; to claims made by all citizens (and even non-citizens) in the twentieth century to rights of protection from the consequences of misfortune, including the consequences of unemployment, old age, homelessness, and sickness."[10]

Sometimes it is asserted that some religions, for example, Christianity and Judaism contain more human rights roots than others, especially Islam.

Though international human rights standards protect the freedom of religion, and different religions or individual clergymen have quite often contributed to the protection of human rights, no religion in its fundamentalist form (which in terms of fundamentalists means, of course, the only true and genuine religion) is conducive to human rights. The Inquisition, especially the Spanish one as probably the most violent example, Torquemada as Grand Inquisitor, torture of Moors, Jews, Protestants and others who were called heretics are all fruits of fundamentalist Christianity.

Even in a liberal Church such as the Church of England the decision to allow the ordination of women, which from the human rights point of view is quite natural, was adopted in 1993 far from unanimously and has alienated many followers of that Church. Therefore, Arthur Schlesinger Jr., quite rightly observes:

> "As a historian, I confess to a certain amusement when I hear the Judeo-Christian tradition praised as the source of our concern for human rights. In fact, the great religious ages were notable for their indifference to human rights in the contemporary sense. They were notorious not only for acquiescence in poverty, inequality, exploitation and oppression but for enthusiastic justifications of slavery, persecution, abandonment of small children, torture and genocide. Religion enshrined and vindicated hierarchy, authority and inequality..."[11]

One may not be surprised with a finding, made by Adamantia Pollis, that in Orthodox theology "woman is considered morally inferior" or that her "inexorable conclusion ... is that individual human rights cannot be derived from Orthodox theology."[12] What may be surprising, from our point of view, is the underlying idea that human rights may be derived at all from a par-

---

10 D. SELBOURNE, THE PRINCIPLE OF DUTY, Sinclair-Stevenson, London (1994) at 57.

11 A. SCHLESINGER (Jr), *The Opening of the American Mind*, NEW YORK TIMES BOOK REVIEW (1989) at 26.

12 A. POLLIS, *Eastern Orthodoxy and Human Rights*, 15 HUMAN RIGHTS QUARTERLY (1993) at 344, 353.

ticular religion. Fred Halliday is right that "no derivation from any religion is ultimately possible."[13] Will Durant's comparison of two branches of Christianity in the Age of Faith is rather different from that of Adamantia Pollis:

> "While Western Europe was shrouded in darkness, misery and ignorance of the ninth and tenth centuries ... the Greek Church drew strength and pride from the revived wealth and power of the Byzantine State... To the Greeks of this age the Germans, Franks, and Anglo-Saxons of the contemporary West seemed crude barbarians, an illiterate and violent laity led by a worldly and corrupt episcopate."[14]

Therefore, while it is hardly possible to anchor contemporary human rights in any particular religion, practically all religions contain premises upon which can be built human rights ideas and practices. There are traditions, including religious ones, in all nations which can be supportive of the acceptance of human rights ideas.

It seems that sometimes it is rather the format, wording or details of international human rights standards than their substance which sounds Western. For example, Article 14 of the International Covenant on Civil and Political Rights contains detailed rules in relation to a fair trial. Its terminology is certainly Western, but the logic of these rules is rather simple and universal: to guarantee, as far as possible, that no innocent person is behind bars, or worse still, executed, and that there is no unnecessary suffering for those who may have committed crimes.

Jack Donnelly correctly observes that while human rights -inalienable entitlements of individuals held in relation to State and society – have not been a part of most cultural traditions, or even of the Western tradition, until quite recently, there is a striking similarity in many of the basic values of most cultures that today we seek to protect through human rights. This is particularly true when these values are expressed in relatively general terms:

> "Life, social order, protection from arbitrary rule, prohibition of inhuman and degrading treatment, the guarantee of a place in the life of the community, and access to an equitable share of the means of subsistence are central moral aspirations in nearly all cultures."[15]

---

13 F. HALLIDAY, ISLAM & THE MYTH OF CONFRONTATION: RELIGION AND POLITICS IN THE MIDDLE EAST, J.B. Tauris, London (1996) at 140.

14 W. DURANT, *Age of Faith*, Vol. 4 of THE STORY OF CIVILIZATION, Simon & Schuster, London (1950) at 544.

15 J. DONNELLY, *Cultural Relativism and Universal Human Rights*, 6:4 HUMAN RIGHTS QUARTERLY (1984) at 414–415.

In June 1995 *The Independent* published a table which showed the attitude of different religions (the Church of England, the Catholic Church, Judaism, Islam, Hinduism, Buddhism) as well as today's secular consensus to issues such as blasphemy, non-observance of religious events, murder, adultery, theft, lying, pre-marital sex, homosexual practices, divorce, masturbation, suicide and cruelty to animals.[16] The attitudes were categorised in terms of "sin", "wrong", "harmful", "permitted", "not a sin", "not harmful", "accepted", "not mentioned". Some of these practices (murder, lying, adultery, theft) are considered either as a sin, wrong or harmful by all religions and are condemned by secular morals. Others (*e.g.* pre-marital sex, homosexual practices, suicide, blasphemy) are considered wrong by all or most religions. Generally, the overlap in attitude is considerable. And it is also necessary to mention that even if some practices are not considered as wrong or sinful, especially by today's secular morals, they are often tolerated rather than encouraged or considered completely normal by the majority in different societies.

This comparison proves that there is much more in common in different societies than cultural relativists usually assume.

At the same time, one can hardly deny that there are cultural differences and historical or religious traditions which may make the implementation of at least some human rights problematic in certain countries. The equality of men and women and the freedom to choose and change one's religion are obvious examples of rights which are difficult to realize in some, especially Muslim, societies. Nor are historical traditions always supportive of the acceptance of the basic assumption of democracy – the one person, one vote principle.

Therefore, it would be wrong to ignore cultural or religious traditions when speaking of human rights in a particular country and these differences should be born in mind by individual States and international organizations when trying to promote human rights. We must equally admit that not all human rights, even those which are enshrined in various U.N. instruments, are universally accepted by or even equally important for every society. There may be periods in a given society when certain rights become particularly important either because they are manifestly violated (like the right to life or the freedom from torture in Uruguay or Argentina under the military dictatorships) or because at a certain level of implementation of basic rights people start to pay more attention to other rights and freedoms.

---

16 THE INDEPENDENT (1995) 8 June, at 15.

At the same time, in societies where people are arbitrarily killed, like in Rwanda or Bosnia, it is not an issue of priority whether accused and convicted persons are kept together or separately in places of detention, or whether victims of ethnic cleansing have the right to leave any country, including their own, respected. In such a case, the right of refugees to return to the places where they were evicted from becomes most important and even the importance of this right is conditioned by the observance of their right to life and the liberty and security of persons if they choose to and can return.

It may well be that difficulties rooted in the cultural or religious traditions of some societies inhibit full and immediate implementation of international human rights standards and also that for some countries a significant time period would be needed before full compliance with such standards would be achieved. Deeply rooted traditions, even when they are inexcusable from the point of view of international human rights standards, cannot be eradicated overnight. India, for example, has not yet succeeded in completely ridding itself of such vestiges of the past as the "dowry death" (where a wife is killed because of the insufficiency of her dowry) or *sati* (where a widow is expected and even encouraged to commit suicide after the death of her husband), but the government is certainly undertaking legislative and administrative measures aimed at overcoming these practices.[17] What is important, rather than the immediate insertion of the whole range of human rights into an unprepared soil, which sometimes may lead to social unrest, is a gradual effort by governments to implement universal human rights standards.

The arguments of those who deny the very possibility of the existence of universal human rights in the multi-cultural world overstate their case. I would agree, for example, with the Foreign Minister of Singapore, Wong Kan Seng, who in his statement at the World Conference on Human Rights in Vienna said that "universal recognition of the ideal of human rights can be harmful if universalism is used to deny or mask the reality of diversity."[18]

But is it? And does the recognition of the universality of human rights really mean that it is necessary to reject the obvious cultural diversity of the world? The Foreign Minister, as an example, stated that "Singaporeans, and people in many other parts of the world do not agree, for instance, that pornography is an acceptable manifestation of free expression or that a homo-

---

[17] The new offence of "dowry death" was included in the Indian Penal Code and there is the Commission of Sati (Prevention) Act of 1987 (SECOND PERIODIC REPORT OF INDIA TO THE U.N. HUMAN RIGHTS COMMITTEE (1989), 12 July, U.N. Doc. CCPR/C/137/Add. 13, paras. 117, 119).

[18] *The Real World of Human Rights*. Statement by Foreign Minister WONG KAN SENG of Singapore at the World Conference on Human Rights, Vienna, 16 June 1993, at 2.

sexual relationship is just a matter of lifestyle choice."[19] But here he is comparing the values of his own society not with universal human rights standards, but with values of some other societies. Neither the freedom of distribution of pornography nor equality between homosexuals and heterosexuals in all domains are universal human rights norms. There are still in force, though fallen somewhat to desuetude, the 1923 Convention for the Suppression of the Circulation of and Traffic in Obscene Publications[20] and Protocol to amend the said Convention of 1947.[21] Indeed, there are many controversial issues such as the death penalty, euthanasia, abortion, pornography, homosexuality, etc., which touch upon deeply rooted moral and religious sentiments and are considered differently in various societies. Though these issues may be closely related to human rights, there are no universal standards guaranteeing or prohibiting such acts.

The most important human rights and the gross and massive violations of them are not culturally conditioned. Genocide, other mass killings, torture (except, probably some forms of cruel punishment which may amount to torture), arbitrary arrests, and racial discrimination belong in this category. The experience of such culturally different countries as Nazi Germany, democratic Kampuchea, Bosnia, and Rwanda shows that there is no specific genocidal culture in the world, or to put it another way, that acts of genocide can be committed by people whose culture, traditions or religion differ widely. Most nations have had institutes such as slavery, serfdom, legalized social inequality, like the caste system in India or social stratification in Medieval Europe (which was a kind of social apartheid). The precise forms which such social structures have taken have been different and dependent, *inter alia*, on cultural factors. However, their substance has been culturally irrelevant.

Moreover, universal human rights standards are not rigid rules whose interpretation and application cannot be adapted to different cultural traditions. Although this is not always possible, there are many cases in which apparent contradictions can be reconciled. International human rights standards are rarely as detailed as domestic laws on the subject. Often they are framework norms which leave a room for States to adjust their implementation to the peculiarities of their domestic legal systems.

There is often room for what in the context of the European human rights system is called the "margin of appreciation". At the universal level this margin is even bigger. For example, Article 25 of the Covenant on Civil and

[19] *Ibid.* at 4.

[20] L.N.T.S. 2113.

[21] 46 U.N.T.S. 169.

Political Rights provides for free, regular elections by universal and equal suffrage and by secret ballot and stipulates that everybody should have the right to participate in the conduct of public affairs and to have access, on general terms of equality, to public service in the country. However, States may have different electoral systems (majoritarian or proportional); they may even have unelected heads of State like monarchs. Especially great is the margin of appreciation in issues concerning rights of ethnic and religious minorities. The reason for that is that individuals in different societies and their basic needs and interests are much more similar than minorities and their needs. Some of them are small, while others comprise millions; some are dispersed, while others live compactly and so forth. Even in the same country different minorities do not have similar needs and claims. For example, the problems of Gypsies and Hungarians in Slovakia differ substantially. That is why the European Charter for Regional or Minority Languages contains a special undertaking which provides that each State, at the time of ratification of the Charter, undertakes to apply a minimum of thirty-five paragraphs or sub-paragraphs chosen from among the provisions of Part III of the Charter. This means that States can, in principle, accommodate their own interests and capabilities as well as interests and demands of minorities, though in practice it may not be so easy to accomplish.

Most international human rights instruments also contain clauses of permissible derogations which try to balance different interests. For instance, several articles of the International Covenant on Civil and Political Rights contain a clause which provides that no restrictions may be placed on the exercise of the rights contained in the Covenant "other than those imposed in conformity with the law and which are necessary in a democratic society in the interests of national security or public safety, public order (*ordre public*), the protection of public health or morals or the protection of the rights and freedoms of others."[22] Though these clauses are open to abuse and, therefore, should not be easily resorted to, they show that there is often quite a large "margin of appreciation" for States to take care of interests of public health and morals (which really can differ significantly from society to society), national security and the rights and freedoms of others. Moreover, in exceptional cases of public emergency which threatens the life of the nation it is possible to suspend temporarily the application of certain rights.[23]

There are two recent documents, one regional and the other of universal character, which try to strike a balance between universality of human rights

---

[22] I. BROWNLIE (ed.), BASIC DOCUMENTS ON HUMAN RIGHTS at 132–133.
[23] *Ibid.* at 127.

on the one hand, and differences in cultural and historical traditions in their implementation on the other. One of them is tilted more towards cultural relativity, the other emphasizes more the universality of human rights. The Bangkok Inter-Governmental Declaration on Human Rights adopted in Spring 1993 at the regional conference of official representatives of countries of Asia and the Pacific region recognizes "that while human rights are universal in nature, they must be considered in the context of a dynamic and evolving process of international norm-setting, **bearing in mind the significance of national and regional particularities and various historical, cultural and religious backgrounds**"[24] (emphasis added). Somewhat different version of the relationship between the idea of universality and cultural relativity found its expression in the Vienna Declaration and Programme of Action adopted at the World Conference on Human Rights in Summer 1993 which, after stressing that "all human rights are universal, indivisible and interdependent and interrelated", admits that "while the significance of national and regional particularities and various historical, cultural and religious backgrounds must be born in mind, it is the duty of States, regardless of their political, economic and cultural systems, to promote and protect all human rights and fundamental freedoms."[25]

These statements, as to their wordings, do not really differ much. It seems that only the emphasis is put in a slightly different way: the Vienna document emphasises more the universality of human rights, whilst the Bangkok declaration stresses the necessity to take into account also national and regional particularities. But in order to understand the meaning of this slight difference in emphasis one has to know what is behind these seemingly innocuous and, when taken *in abstracto*, even quite correct wordings. And behind such statements and policies which emphasise the necessity to bear in mind national or regional particularities and historical, cultural or religious traditions when dealing with human rights are often attempts to justify human rights violations caused by political, economic or other interests. Jack Donnelly aptly observes that "while recognizing the legitimate claims of self-determination and cultural relativism, we must be alert to cynical manipulations of a dying, lost, or even mythical past."[26] Cultural and historical traditions of practically all societies tend to support inequality between men and women and discriminate on the basis of race, religion or ethnicity. Does this mean that we should respect such traditions? Does this mean, for

---

[24] *Bangkok Inter-Governmental Declaration on Human Rights* (in:) J. TANG (ed.), HUMAN RIGHTS AND INTERNATIONAL RELATIONS IN THE ASIA PACIFIC, Pinter, London (1995) at 205.

[25] World Conference on Human Rights. THE VIENNA DECLARATION AND PROGRAMME OF ACTION, New York (1993) at 30.

[26] J. DONNELLY, UNIVERSAL HUMAN RIGHTS IN THEORY AND PRACTICE, Cornell University Press, Ithaca (1989) at 119.

example, that Western societies are free to discriminate against Muslims or immigrants?

It is also necessary to clarify what is meant by saying that though human rights are universal, they must be considered in the context of dynamic and evolving norm-setting and that regional and national particularities have to be born in mind in the implementation of universal human rights standards.

The Bangkok NGO Declaration on Human Rights adopted by 110 NGOs in the Asia and Pacific region on 27 March 1993, just a few days before the adoption of the above-mentioned inter-governmental Declaration confirmed that it is not just cultural differences in societies which give rise to human rights violations in their countries; such violations largely take place as a result of the specific political interests of the ruling circles in some of these States. The Declaration further stressed that "cultural practices which derogate from universally accepted human rights, including women's rights, must not be tolerated."[27] It may be noted that this concern is not on this occasion being voiced by Western NGOs. Similarly, Aung San Suu Kyi, the Nobel Peace Prize winner of 1991 from Myanmar writes that "when democracy and human rights are said to run counter to non-Western culture, such culture is usually defined narrowly and presented as monolithic. In fact, the values that democracy and human rights seek to promote can be found in many cultures."[28]

It is necessary for experts and human rights activists from all over the world to become engaged in frank and open dialogue in order to clarify whether it is necessary, for example, to limit political or civil rights in order to promote economic and social ones, to what extent genuine concerns for political stability or stability of inter-ethnic relations require restriction of certain rights, for instance, freedom of the press and similar issues. It seems that really serious and concerted efforts are needed in order to separate deviations in the implementation of international human rights standards which may be genuinely caused by cultural, historical or religious peculiarities and which are generally supported by society, from abusive references by elites to these peculiarities in order to justify repressions caused by their interest in power. Such a "dialogue between cultures can seldom if ever be conducted as a dialogue between governments – if only because some governments just do not like human rights and other governments can't make them."[29]

---

[27] BANGKOK NGO DECLARATION ON HUMAN RIGHTS (1993 – 27 March) at 1.

[28] AUNG SAN SUU KYI, *Listen: the Culture of Human Rights and Democracy is Universal*, INTERNATIONAL HERALD TRIBUNE (1994 – 7 December) at 4.

[29] PH. WINDSOR, *Cultural Dialogue in Human Rights*, (in:) M. DESAI & P. REDFERN (eds.) GLOBAL GOVERNANCE: ETHICS AND ECONOMICS OF THE WORLD ORDER, Pinter, London (1995) at 185.

There are still some traditional practices occurring in the world today which can never be reconciled with universal human right norms, for example, death for apostasy in some fundamentalist Islamic countries or the caste system and *sati* in India. These practices, however, are no longer widely accepted even in Muslim or Hindu societies. Thus they are not only condemned from the point of view of other value systems and universal human right standards, but they do not find wide support in their own culture. Ann Elizabeth Mayer comes to the conclusion that "the common forms of oppression by Middle Eastern regimes are not just objectionable by Western standards but are perceived by people within these societies, especially the members of the educated elite, to be impermissibly harsh in their impact on society and culture."[30]

Roger Scruton may be too absolutist in observing that "in argument about moral problems, relativism is the first refuge of the scoundrel."[31] However, it is true that for many scoundrels relativism is a convenient excuse for the rejection of human rights allegedly as an alien phenomenon. The rejection of cultural relativism in arguments about human rights does not mean that cultural traditions do not matter at all in the human rights discourse or that all human rights can be applied immediately in every society. Being pushed by the ideal of human rights one has to be a realist in the implementation of international human rights standards in culturally different societies.

International human rights norms, in gradually helping to eradicate inhuman practices, do not undermine the cultural foundations of Asian or African societies in which such practices still occur, or impoverish them, like they did not undermine and impoverish the cultural foundations of Western societies when these societies rid themselves of the court of inquisition, death by hanging or guillotining or imprisonment for inability to fulfil contractual obligations. On the contrary, the introduction of human rights ideas and practices, often adjusted to local conditions, helps to make them more humane. The acceptance of universality of human rights certainly does not mean that the reality of cultural diversity is to be rejected.

II. HUMAN RIGHTS AND INDIVIDUALISM VERSUS COMMUNITARIANISM

A further aspect of the arguments of cultural relativists is the suggestion that as human rights stem from and are inherently linked with individual-

30 A.E. MAYER, ISLAM AND HUMAN RIGHTS: TRADITION AND POLITICS (2nd ed.), Westview Press, Boulder (1995) at 176.

31 R. SCRUTON, MODERN PHILOSOPHY, Sinclair-Stevenson, London (1994) at 32.

ism, they are not applicable in societies with different, that is to say – communitarian, traditions. However, it seems that references to communal or collectivist traditions to justify human rights violations often also miss the point. In addition, such references can be, and sometimes are, simply used to mask systematic violations of human rights in the interests of ruling elites.[32] Donnelly is right that "communitarian rhetoric too often cloaks the depredations of corrupt and often Westernized or deracinated elites."[33]

After the dissolution of the Soviet Union and the collapse of communism it has become clear practically for everybody even in former socialist countries that references to supreme interests of the collective, be it a State, society or party, were simply used to keep in power the communist elite or the new class, as Milovan Djilas called it.[34] Such a policy in the U.S.S.R., though probably helping to mobilize the population for the initial industrialization (an industrialization which coincidentally was achieved at quite inhumane costs) eventually led to the stagnation of society and the collapse of the whole economic, political and social system. Collectivist ideas were manipulated by the leaders in order to subordinate everybody to the interests of the communist party.

However, it is even more important to stress that not all collectivist or communitarian ideologies are inherently hostile to human rights. Respect for the rights of individuals does not necessarily mean that one needs to neglect families (even the most extended ones), larger communities or society as a whole. Nor does it even call for disrespect for authorities (especially if such respect is deserved). In fact, unbridled individualism may be as unfavourable a soil for the promotion of human rights as excessive communitarianism.

Though individualism as a philosophical doctrine and human rights are linked in their genesis this does not mean that the Western person is inherently individualist or that the Western society has always been and will necessarily remain individualistic. Both individualism and human rights ideas were aimed at liberating human beings from oppression by the State and church and at getting rid of feudal hierarchies which not only kept individuals in shackles but also stifled the development of society as a whole. Yash Ghai writes: "The 'communitarian' argument suffers from at least two weaknesses. First, it overstates the 'individualism' of Western societies and tradi-

---

32 R. HOWARD, *Evaluating Human Rights in Africa: Some Problems of Implicit Comparisons*, 6:2 HUMAN RIGHTS QUARTERLY (1984) at 175.

33 J. DONNELLY, UNIVERSAL HUMAN RIGHTS IN THEORY AND PRACTICE at 119.

34 M. DJILAS, THE NEW CLASS. AN ANALYSIS OF THE COMMUNIST SYSTEM, Praeger, New York (1965)

tions of thought. Even within Western liberalism there are strands of analysis which assert claims of community (*e.g.* Rousseau); and second, most Western human rights instruments allow limitations on and derogations from human rights in the public interest, or for reasons of State. Western courts regularly engage in the task of balancing the respective interests of the individual and the community."[35]

Currently, in the West we hear more and more criticism about excesses of individualism, abuse of rights and the erosion of communitarian bonds. Amitai Etzioni and the communitarian movement in the United States call for the restoration of a civil society and criticize "a major aspect of contemporary American civic culture: a strong sense of entitlement – that is, a demand that the community provide more services and strongly uphold rights – coupled with a rather weak sense of obligation to the local and national community."[36] The former U.S. Ambassador to the United Kingdom, Raymond Seitz, speaking of the U.S. and the U.K., said recently: "If a democracy becomes only a matter of asserting rights – merely an excuse for licence – then society can rapidly become a *mêlée* of self-indulgence."[37]

There is a serious call in the West to think more about duties of citizens. David Selbourne, in his book entitled *The Principle of Duty* writes:

> "For it is only on the basis of a reciprocity of obligation, in accord with the ethic of the civic bond and the principle of duty, that 'commodious and peaceable living' is possible in the civic order; that civic disaggregation can be arrested without recourse to draconian measures; and that life, health, and true liberty of the individual can be preserved."[38]

It is interesting to note in this regard that the Council of Europe convened in November 1994 a meeting of experts on the topic *Citizens' Responsibilities*. Different views were expressed during the meeting and the majority of experts rightly rejected the idea of any legally binding or even declaratory document emanating from the Council calling for implementation of citizens duties. However, the meeting concluded also that "modern democracies cannot survive unless their citizens assume active responsibility in their day to day lives, and in terms of participation."[39] Some experts called for draft-

---

35 Y. GHAI, *Asian Perspectives of Human Rights,* (in:) J. TANG (ed.), *op. cit.*, *supra* note 24, at 61.

36 A. ETZIONI, THE SPIRIT OF COMMUNITY, Simon & Schuster, London (1993) at 3.

37 THE TIMES (1995 – 3 June).

38 D. SELBOURNE, *op. cit., supra* note 10, at 83.

39 *Citizens' Responsibilities*, Discussion Seminar with Experts, Research and Planning Unit, 16 December 1994, at 2.

ing a reference document emanating from the Committee of Ministers which would highlight the values of morality, responsibility and participation.

Jack Shaw, the Shadow Home Secretary, speaking of a future Bill of Rights for the United Kingdom at the end of 1995, made a strong point about dangers of "me-first society", of over-emphasis on rights, to near exclusion of duties and responsibilities and he concluded by saying that we "need to break out of the language of dutiless rights, and begin insisting upon mutual responsibility. Rights and duties go hand in hand."[40]

However, this concern in the West with excessive individualism and the reminders that without duties and responsibilities the civic bonds of society could be damaged to such an extent that there may be a threat of a call for some kind of authoritarianism to restore these bonds, by no means supports the views of those who try to hide behind communitarian ideas in countries where it is not excessive individualism, but the absence of rights and freedoms of the individual which is the problem. Etzioni writes:

> "The people of China, Eastern Europe, and Japan for that matter may well need to move in the opposite direction: to make more room for self-expression, to slash excessive government control, and to roll back severely enforced codes that suppress creativity and impinge on individual rights."[41]

In short: societies need what they lack and different societies lack different things. Human beings, however, need rights and liberties to protect them from the State, which has a tendency to encroach upon individuals' freedoms, and even from society or its sometimes rather intrusive sub-structures (trade unions, local councils or neighbourhood watch). But they also need healthy and cohesive societies and good governments without which there would be an anarchy-easily-turned-into-dictatorship. Hamish McRae, who writes that it is difficult not to feel that both North America and Western Europe "have put themselves at an economic disadvantage by their quest for individual freedom", concludes: "Maybe the real message is that all modern industrial societies have to find a way of striking a balance between individualism and social control, and that somehow the democratic process has to maintain that balance, making the costs and benefits clear."[42]

Therefore, I believe that the argument put forward by some authors and politicians, that Asian or African values based on communitarian ideas are

---

40 The Times (1995 – 8 November) at 16.

41 A. Etzioni, *op. cit., supra* note 36, at 25.

42 H. McRae, The World in 2020. Power, Culture and Prosperity: A Vision of the Future, Harper-Collins Publishers, London (1994) at 204.

incompatible with individual human rights, is simply false. The West has had its own communitarian ideas and phases of development. Francis Fukuyama rightly observes that "the countries of medieval and early modern Europe were in many respects highly communitarian societies, with a large number of overlapping sources of communal authority – princely, ecclesiastical, seigniorial, and local – constraining the behaviour of individuals."[43] And currently many people in the West are thinking of how to put some limits on individualism, which while being necessary for human liberation and economic development may become excessive and indeed constitute a threat for both liberty and economic development. Therefore, it may even be the case that the realization of some so-called Asian communitarian values would be conducive to the development of human dignity and rights in Western societies. Asian as well as other developing societies, participating in the process of the promotion of human rights, are not only on the receiving end. Their experience and ideas on human rights, like their ideas and practices in the domain of economics, will inevitably enrich the whole human rights discourse.

III. HUMAN RIGHTS AND LEVELS OF SOCIETAL DEVELOPMENT

Besides some cultural practices which may influence the perception and implementation of human rights, there is another factor which is sometimes confused with cultural or historical traditions of a given society and which, in my view, provides a more realistic explanation of different human rights situations around the world. This factor is the level of its societal development, including its economic, social, political and cultural aspects.

The concept of human rights is not an immutable or ahistorical concept which always existed somewhere only waiting to be discovered by some advanced thinkers. The West, where the idea and practical implementation of the idea of human rights emerged, came, as we saw, to it through long historical development. In ancient Greece, both Aristotle and Demosthenes expressed the view that torture was the surest method for obtaining evidence.[44] In Western countries women were discriminated against (and in some of they them still are) and in many European countries heretics were burnt. In Spain the inquisition was abolished only in 1834[45] and in 1925 in

---

43 F. FUKUYAMA, *op. cit.*, *supra* note 8, at 157.

44 M.CH. BASSIOUNI (ed.), 1 INTERNATIONAL CRIMINAL LAW (1986) at 363.

45 LONGMAN'S ILLUSTRATED ENCYCLOPEDIA OF WORLD HISTORY, Ivy Least, London (1991) at 463.

Tennessee U.S. a school teacher was condemned by a local court for teaching Darwin's theory of the origin of the species.[46] In Denmark in 1770 King Christian VII's personal physician and minister, Struensee, introduced the freedom of speech by an Order of the Cabinet.[47] However, without any tradition supporting this declared freedom, the Order caused chaos and a smear campaign against Struensee himself (alleging his intimate relations with the Queen). After Struensee was executed in 1773, the freedom of speech, whose time had not yet come in Denmark or anywhere else, was not the order of the day for long.

As to the punishment of crimes, Western European countries have moved from such cruel forms of execution as hanging or guillotining to the complete abolition of death penalty at peace time. How people are executed (hanged, stoned, or guillotined) or tortured may, to a great extent, really depend on a specific culture, but whether people are executed or tortured at all depends more on the stage or level of societal development.[48]

In traditional societies (be they in the East or the West) the individual could realise his or her human dignity only according to his or her position in society. The very notion of the autonomy of the individual was absent. Most non-Western cultural and political traditions, like the pre-modern West, lacked not only the practice of human rights but also the very concept. It was the emergence of the modern State and market economy which called for liberal concepts of human rights and respective practices.[49] The emergence of the market economy made individuals autonomous not only *vis-à-vis* each other as owners, vendors or buyers, but also *vis-à-vis* society. This means that a degree of autonomy of the individual *vis-à-vis* the State was also needed. But the State has always had and still has a propensity to encroach upon the autonomy of the individual, especially in the absence of guarantees of such autonomy in the form of human rights and freedoms. Therefore, a modern State and human rights, as entitlements of the individual *vis-à-vis* the State, are mutually conditioned.

---

46 *Ibid.* at 410.

47 A. ROSS, STATSRET [STATE LAW], (3rd ed.), Copenhagen (1980) at 707. (I am thankful to my LLM student Kristina Miskowiak who drew my attention to this interesting fact.)

48 One may, of course, argue that death penalty is still used in some highly developed societies such as, for example, the U.S.A. However, the U.S. being a highly developed democratic society is at the same time a society which is developed very unevenly, especially in comparison with Western European democracies. Extreme richness and extreme poverty, the highest academic excellence and widespread illiteracy are to be found in the United States. Very high crime rate and the use of death penalty as a response seem to reflect this controversial character of the country.

49 J. DONNELLY, UNIVERSAL HUMAN RIGHTS IN THEORY AND PRACTICE at 70.

Today, in practically all societies, modern States have emerged with certain attributes – police, army, secret services, bureaucracy, etc. For the purposes of our analysis, it is not especially important whether some countries have accepted these attributes from Western societies or have developed them on their own. What matters is whether, having introduced institutions which have the tendency, in the absence of proper guarantees in the form of human rights, to suppress not only the individual freedoms but also to subordinate the whole society to the State apparatus, leaders of these States are free to leave human rights aside?

Rhoda Howard makes a strong point when she writes that "a comparison of human rights in Africa in the 1980s with human rights in the Western world at similar stages of national consolidation and economic development [*i.e.* a couple of hundred years ago] is, then, much more appropriate than a comparison of Africa with contemporary Western societies."[50]

However, there is one rather serious problem with this generally correct argument. Contemporary African societies, even if their levels of economic development and other societal characteristics are comparable to those of European ones some hundreds of years ago, are not isolated from contemporary European, American or Asian societies and are influenced by them in a variety of ways. Though the per capita GDP of some African countries may be comparable to that of the mediaeval England, their human rights situation cannot simply be judged by a yardstick of the seventeenth century Europe. And though not all of the standards applied by the European Court of Human Rights may easily be applicable in today's Africa, the Africans themselves would hardly be content with the seventeenth or even nineteenth century European human rights yardsticks.

Humankind, while remaining heterogeneous not only culturally, but also, and this is even more important from the point of view of the promotion of human rights, as to the level of societal development (including economic, social, political and cultural aspects of development) in different countries, is becoming at the same time closer and closer.

Though the world has always been diverse, it has never been so close. Today, post-industrial and feudal societies not only co-exist on the same planet, they closely interact and influence each other. This inevitably creates strains: on the one hand, there is a trend towards greater homogeneity (especially in the economic and technological spheres) and interpenetration of different cultures but, on the other hand, we face the continuing, and in some cases even widening, hiatus between the levels of development of dif-

[50] R. HOWARD, *op. cit.*, *supra* note 32, at 169–170.

ferent societies. The interpenetration of cultures also leads, as a counter--reaction, to an even stronger search for cultural identity and resistance to what is perceived as alien cultural challenges.

This situation is a major challenge for many societies and for human rights as well. Eric Hobsbawm writes that "perhaps the most striking characteristic of the end of the twentieth century is the tension between this accelerating globalization and the inability of both public institutions and the collective behaviour of human beings to come to terms with it."[51]

Closeness and interpenetration of societies create a pull towards universalization of human rights whilst the developmental gap and emphasis on historical cultural traditions is an obstacle for the acceptance of this universality. At the same time, today the world has become too small and interdependent to expect that only missile technology, computer hardware and software or narcotic drugs can transgress State boundaries. The Soviet leadership tried hard to close its society from outside influence: not only human rights, but also computers and photo-copying machines were considered dangerous for the regime and were kept out of the reach of ordinary Soviet citizens. However, if in a closed society it is possible to produce more steel than anybody else, it is impossible to compete in a world where success depends not so much on how many millions of tons of steel are produced by a country but on the knowledge and information held by its citizens.

The Soviet authorities could restrict distribution of foreign publications but they were only partly successful in jamming Western radio-stations. BBC, the Voice of America, Radio Liberty and Free Europe carried news to millions of listeners in the Soviet Union and Eastern Europe. It has been rightly observed that electronic media had contributed to the fall of the communist power in the Soviet Union.[52] Currently it is the Internet which is raising fears throughout the Middle East and Asia that their closed societies may be opened up to heretical ideas which threaten their governing cliques. *The Sunday Times*, speaking of Saudi Arabia, observes that "the Internet creates a poignant dilemma for the oil-rich kingdom. On the one hand it vaunts its capitalist and high-technology credentials, vital in the modern marketplace. At the same time the country is desperate to restrict access to the interloper from cyberspace with its seditiously irreverent ethos."[53] The same problem is haunting other Arab autocracies, Iran and China.

---

[51] E. HOBSBAWM, *op. cit.*, *supra* note 8, at 15.

[52] *See e.g.* S. SHANE, DISMANTLING UTOPIA: HOW INFORMATION ENDED THE SOVIET UNION (1994); G.D. GANBY, *Power of the People via Personal Electronic Media*, WASHINGTON QUARTERLY (1991) at 5–22.

[53] *News Review*, SUNDAY TIMES (1995 – 3 September) at 3.

Ideas and practices such as human rights, a market economy or the Internet, being Western discoveries at a certain level of development of Western societies, touch all societies, even those which have not yet come to these ideas, let alone practices, on their own.[54] They may affect these societies like a medicine: while curing and making some of them healthier and stronger, other societies, and especially their leaders may be rather allergic to human rights, market economy or Internet injections. Rapid introduction of human rights into such societies may sometimes make them rather ill and certain forces, whose power base is threatened by ideas and practices of modernity, including human rights, may become even more active and influential. Ideas of human rights, as we discussed above, have always been and still are subversive ideas in societies which are not based on them.

In the contemporary world we have not so much a clash of civilizations[55] as a clash of epochs and this clash is taking place not only between different societies but within many of them as well. Human rights and democracy are playing an important part in these clashes which are often about them or these notions are used and abused as tools in these conflicts.

I believe that human rights in the contemporary world are conditioned by three categories, or levels, of factors: anthropological, societal and international. These factors are not immutable in time or space. Whilst societal factors, that is, factors pertaining to the characteristics of a given society, have exercised the strongest influence on the content of rights and freedoms of members of society, international factors are of more recent origin, but their influence is rapidly growing. Some rights, like the right to life, freedom from torture and the right to found a family may be called of an anthropological nature, because they are closely related to the physical needs of human beings, though they, as with any other rights, can exist only in society. Robinson Crusoe could have had neither rights nor obligations before the appearance of Man Friday.

It seems that natural law approach to human rights asserting that all human rights are birth-rights of every human being immutable in time and place

---

[54] The fact that certain ideas, practices or discoveries, originating in some societies, are taken over by others does not mean that the former are inherently superior to the latter. Societies and civilizations develop unevenly. The West borrowed not only gun-powder from China and a lot of mathematics from the Arab world but the very *homo sapiens*, to all appearance, originated in Africa. It seems quite plausible that in the foreseeable future the West will have to borrow rather heavily from the East.

[55] In summer 1993 Samuel Huntington wrote: "The great divisions among humankind and the dominating source of conflict will be cultural. Nation States will remain the most powerful actors in world affairs, but principal conflicts of global politics will occur between nations and groups of different civilizations" – S. HUNTINGTON, *The Clash of Civilizations*, 72:3 FOREIGN AFFAIRS (1993) at 22.

is simply wrong. The *Virginian Bill of Rights* was authored by George Mason, a slave-owner, who did not find that slavery contradicted to what the Bill found self-evident – that all men were endowed by their creator with certain inalienable rights. This understanding of "all men" by progressive thinkers of the eighteenth century would be considered today as an example of extreme bigotry. Therefore, it is not possible to assert that there is such a thing as immutable human nature from which to draw rights and freedoms corresponding to that nature. Richard Rorty is right that "since no useful work seems to be done by insisting on a purportedly ahistorical human nature, there probably is no such nature, or at least, nothing in that nature that is relevant to our moral choices."[56] Human rights, as Philip Windsor writes, should be seen not in terms of "being" but in terms of "becoming."[57]

Usually this "becoming" is driven by endogenous factors though exogenous forces are becoming more and more important. Rorty emphasizes two factors which play important role in the spread and development of human rights: security and sympathy. He writes:

> "Foundationalists [Plato, Aquinas, Kant] think of these people [bad people who do not respect human rights] as deprived of truth, moral knowledge. But it would be better – more specific, more suggestive of possible remedies – to think of them as deprived of two more concrete things: security and sympathy. By 'security' I mean conditions of life sufficiently risk-free as to make one's difference from others inessential to one's self-respect, one's sense of worth. These conditions have been enjoyed by Americans and Europeans – the people who dreamed up the human rights culture – much more than they have been enjoyed by anyone else. By 'sympathy' I mean the sort of reaction that the Athenians had more of after seeing Aeschylus' *The Persians* than before, the sort that white Americans had more of after reading *Uncle Tom's Cabin* than before, the sort that we have more of after watching TV programmes about the genocide in Bosnia."[58]

And Rorty is right that security and sympathy usually go together. The tougher things are, the more you have to be afraid of, the more dangerous your situation, the less you can afford the time and effort to think what things might be like for people with whom you do not immediately identify. Senti-

---

56 R. Rorty, *Human Rights, Rationality, and Sentimentality*, (in:) S. Shute & S. Hurley (eds.), On Human Rights, Oxford Amnesty Lectures 1993, Basic Books, New York (1993) at 1919.

57 P. Windsor, *Cultural Dialogue in Human Rights*, (in:) M. Desai & P. Redfern (eds.), Global Governance. Ethics and Economics of the World Order, Pinter, London (1995) at 177–178.

58 R. Rorty, *op. cit., supra* note 56, at 128.

mental education only works on people who can relax long enough to listen.[59] And it is not surprising that for Rorty, like probably for millions other men and women and certainly for me, Harriet Blecher Stowe's *Uncle Tom's Cabin* is a more important contribution to the moral philosophy than Kant's categorical imperative.

Growing interdependence of the world as a whole and the transparency of most societies mean that international factors, not only through purposeful efforts of individual States, international organizations and human rights NGOs, but also through inter-penetration of cultures, ideas and knowledge, are influencing the perception of human rights concepts as well as the practices in different societies. It seems that no government is able to stop this process indefinitely. *The Economist* comments that "the Saudi royal family – and lesser rulers in the area – have already watched with alarm as their south-eastern neighbours in Yemen played with democracy. As education spreads, oil revenues shrink and Islamic fundamentalists become bolder, they have enough to make them nervous without anyone else trying the same game."[60] Michael Freeman is right when he says that "the human rights culture is no longer Western. It is no longer a matter of agreement among State élites. It is a global politico-cultural movement."[61]

However, this spread of human rights does not and should not lead to the cultural uniformity of the world. Neither does this mean that all societies develop and change in the same manner or that they inevitably pass through similar stages of development. It means that there are some things which human societies need because they are human, though remaining different as societies.

One of the rational points amongst the ideas of realists' approach to international relations seems to be that States, out of necessity, have to become more and more similar to each other in different (not in all of course) respects, taking over those characteristics and features which make some societies more successful than others. Kenneth Waltz writes that "one has to be impressed with the functional similarity of States and, now more than ever before, with the similar lines their development follows. From the rich to the poor States, from the old to the new ones, nearly all of them take a larger hand in matters of economic regulation, of eduction, health, and housing, of culture and arts, and so on almost endlessly."[62]

---

59 *Ibid.*

60 ECONOMIST (1995 – 1 July) at 54.

61 M. FREEMAN, *Human Rights: Asia and the West*, (in:) J. TANG (ed.), *op. cit.*, *supra* note 24, at 16–17.

62 K. WALTZ, THEORY OF INTERNATIONAL POLITICS, Addison Wesley Publishing Company, London (1979) at 97.

Societies which self-isolate (*e.g.* Albania until recently) or obstinately try to retain traditional ways of life which inhibit development or attempt to go back to basics (*e.g.* Iran, Sudan) are doomed to fail in the eternal world-wide competition. Therefore, as Fred Halliday writes, "as a result of international pressures, States are compelled more and more to conform to each other in their internal arrangements."[63] That is why Halliday, in studying international relations, rightly pays considerable attention to what happens within States and societies, and examines the interaction of international activity with domestic legitimacy and stability.

Human rights as a historical and developing phenomenon have become an important part of the concept of development. In some rapidly developing parts of the world, for example, in Asian countries such as South Korea, Taiwan or Thailand[64] positive changes in the field of human rights are coming about not so much because the West or international bodies, "infected" with Western views on human rights, are pressing for changes, but because domestic constituencies developing alongside the economic growth are starting to demand not only bread and butter and more of it; they are also demanding a say in the distribution of bread and butter. Francis Fukuyama writes that it is, of course, possible for a capitalist economy to coexist with an authoritarian system, as in the PRC today or as previously existed in Germany, Japan, South Korea, Taiwan, and Spain. But, as he points out, "in the long run, the industrialization process itself necessitates a more highly educated population and more complex division of labour, both of which tend to be supportive of democratic political institutions."[65] William Brands makes a strong point, reiterating that "the key factor in the political evolution of Asian countries will be the efforts of the people in the countries themselves rather than the actions or non-actions of the United States or other external powers."[66] The key factor – certainly, but often external efforts may not be superfluous.

One of the factors negatively affecting human rights is extreme poverty. It is not often recognized in the West that in certain cases poverty may really be the most important cause of the absence of human rights. A poor democratic country with high degree of observance of human rights is simply an

---

63 F. HALLIDAY, *International Society as Homogeneity: Burke, Marx, Fukuyama*, 21:3 MILLENNIUM (1992) at 435.

64 M. GABALLERO-ANTHONY writes that "Thailand's economic growth resulted in a growing middle class which eventualy played a crucial role in breaking the monopoly of military power ... towards a more stable and sustainable democratic system." (M. GABALLERO-ANTHONY, *Human Rights, Economic Change and Political Development*, (in:) J. TANG (ed.), *op. cit., supra* note 24, at 44.

65 F. FUKUYAMA, *op. cit., supra* note 8, at 356.

66 W. BRANDS, *Human Rights and US Policy Towards Asia*, (in:) J. TANG (ed.), *op. cit., supra* note 24, at 81.

oxymoron. Yash Ghai is right that "poverty is a great cause of the denial of human rights. The international system refuses to accept this reality – for largely political reasons."[67] However, the recognition that poverty destroys human dignity does not of course mean that all rich countries (there are some rich under-developed societies, like oil-rich Arab States) are democratic and human rights friendly. Neither does it refute the thesis that some poor countries are poor, at least to some extent, because of their corrupt authoritarian regimes, and thus due to the lack of democracy and human rights.

As it was argued above, human rights are conditioned by three categories, or levels, of factors (anthropological, societal and international). In addition to that, it seems that the spread of human rights is conditioned by two different pairs of factors. The first pair is internal and external factors. As I have just shown, though internal factors may be predominant, it would be wrong to ignore, in our interdependent world, the influence exerted on human rights by external factors. The second pair consists of ideas of human rights and democracy on the one hand, and economic, social and political conditions, which either facilitate acceptance and development of human rights ideas in society or inhibit this process, on the other.

Though economic, social and political conditions, as we have tried to show, exert great influence on the human rights situation in a country, and human rights are even one of the indicators of the development of society, it is necessary to admit that ideas about human rights are also very important. They can become a material force when held and supported by millions.

However, it is not enough to have ideas. As has been mentioned, there were precursors to human rights in different faiths and philosophies. Everywhere where there were oppressed human beings there often were also ideologues who, instead of dreaming of changing the places with the oppressors, dreamed of getting rid of the very oppression. But ideas need material conditions for their development and realization.

Ideas and dreams about liberty, freedom and human dignity indeed could be found in different cultures. But what the West had earlier than anybody else was the market economy and the modern State, which not only gave a push for the development of these ideas but also created the conditions for and even necessitated the realization of ideas of human rights and freedoms. Ideas, struggle for rights and freedoms plus material conditions in the form of the market economy and the modern State were necessary and sufficient preconditions for the emergence of human rights.

Therefore, I tend to agree with Robert Bartley that "the dominant flow of historical forces in the 21st century could well be this: economic deve-

[67] Y. GHAI, *op. cit.*, *supra* note 24, at 65.

lopment leads to demands for democracy and individual (or family) autonomy; instant worldwide communications reduce the power of oppressive governments; the spread of democratic States diminishes the potential for conflict."[68]

All what was said above seems to indicate that the receptiveness of different societies to international human rights standards is less conditioned by cultural peculiarities of a given society than by a level of its social, economic and political development.

IV. IS THE NORTH-SOUTH DIVIDE ON HUMAN RIGHTS REPLACING THE EAST-WEST ONE?

The end of the Cold War has considerably changed the context of human rights diplomacy. On the surface, it may be seen that the North-South confrontation on human rights has substituted for the East-West one. During the 51st session of the U.N. Commission on Human Rights, in Spring 1995, there was rather clear-cut division between developed and developing countries in voting on most sensitive issues. For instance, the draft resolution presented by Western countries criticising Chinese human rights record was narrowly defeated by 21 votes to 20 with 12 abstentions;[69] and the draft resolution critical of the situation in Nigeria was rejected by 21 votes to 17, with 17 abstentions.[70] No Third World country voted to condemn human rights violations in Nigeria[71] and of these countries only Nicaragua and Guinea-Bissau voted for the resolution on China. At the same time, the draft resolution "Human rights and universal coercive measures" presented by Cuba, alleging that some countries abuse their dominant position in the world economy and continue to intensify the adoption of unilateral coercive measures against developing countries – measures which, the draft says, are in clear contra-

---

68 R.L. BARTLEY, *The Case for Optimism. The West Should Believe in Itself*, 72:4 FOREIGN AFFAIRS (1993) at 17.

69 U.N. Doc. E/1995/23; E/CN.4/1995/176 at 391.

70 *Ibid.* at 417.

71 In this context, it is interesting to note that half a year later, after the military regime had executed nine activists for the independence of Ogoniland, including writer Ken SARA-WIVA, the Commonwealth suspended Nigeria's membership. These developments show that certain events related to human rights which thanks to mass-media are able to "shock the conscious of mankind" may trigger even some sanctions, while more important developments remain without any response. The execution of Ken SARA-WIVA was only one episode in the whole chain of massive human rights violations in Nigeria. Obviously, the most important among them, causing many other violations, occurred when the military regime in 1993 annulled the result of the elections which gave victory to Chief Abiola.

diction with international law, such as trade restrictions, blockades, embargoes and freezing of assets, with the purpose of preventing those countries from exercising their right fully to determine their own political, economic and social system, was adopted by 24 votes to 17, with 12 abstentions.[72] It goes without saying that it was mainly developing States which were in favour of this resolution, while developed countries voted against it.

However, the current North-South divide is not at all a mirror image of the Cold War era East-West clash over human rights. The East-West confrontation, as it related to human rights, was about two alternative ways for the development of humankind, both of which – liberal democracy and marxism-leninism – emerged in the framework of the Western social thought and practice. It was a dispute between two incompatible (market *versus* planned economy, State totalitarianism *versus* democracy, privileges for conformism versus human rights) ways for society to proceed. At the end of the day, one had to lose. Communism lost not just because of its ineffective economic system. It lost also because it did not satisfy the needs of men and women for human dignity and freedom.

Now the dispute, in which, once more, human rights play a substantial role is basically between societies which are at different levels of societal development. It is not only and not so much about whether humankind has to go to the left or to the right, or whether it can choose a middle way. To some extent the dispute is now about whether to go at all or stay where one stands, or even to try to find a way back (*e.g.* religious fundamentalists or extreme nationalists whose call is usually "back to basics"). In the East-West dispute the question was: how to modernize? Now the essential question for some societies seems to be: whether to modernize at all?

The East-West struggle over human rights was a struggle between natural development of society, including development of human rights and freedoms, and an artificial one, imposed according to the marxist-leninist social theory. The communist system, which was the result of an attempt to put into practice a social theory, was the only widespread artificial social system that has ever existed in reality. It is not surprising that it brought about violence and finally failed. One could hardly squeeze rich tapestry of societal life into the Procrustean bed of any social theory without violence.

Now the divide on human rights between the North and the South is one which exists, to a great extent, between societies which have reached the stage of societal development where human rights and freedoms can be guaran-

---

72 *Ibid.* at 351.

teed and societies where conditions for the acceptance of human rights could be said to be still rather embryonic.

This divide is not an artificial one which could be overcome by pulling down an imaginary "Berlin wall" (though even the cleaning up of the debris of the real Berlin wall will take time and is not an easy task). Human rights situations in most countries which belong to what is called the South can be significantly improved only as a part of larger societal change including eradication of poverty and management of inter-ethnic relations as components of social, and political reforms. The root cause of many current human rights emergencies is not so much that something somewhere has gone badly wrong, but that in some societies nothing is going on, while other societies are rapidly developing.

These considerations should be taken into account when choosing responses to human rights problems in different societies. However, one should not forget also that in some cases it is not so much cultural differences or even low levels of societal development (which may, of course, constitute a breeding ground for all kinds of warlords and dictators), but thirst for power, which is at the basis of certain human rights emergencies.

L'ÉVOLUTION DU DROIT PÉNAL INTERNATIONAL

par

KRZYSZTOF POKLEWSKI-KOZIEŁŁ

I

Le procès devant le Tribunal militaire international de Nuremberg, terminé par un jugement prononcé le 1er octobre 1946, fait certainement époque pour le droit pénal international. On parle même, dans cet ordre d'idées, de ce droit «d'avant» et «d'après» la deuxième guerre mondiale, englobant dans la seconde notion le «droit de Nuremberg» (y compris aussi le procès de Tokyo, 29 IV 1946–12 XI 1948). Il a fallu un autre cataclysme dans cette partie de l'Europe où avait commencé la première guerre mondiale, pour démontrer que le concept de la responsabilité pénale des auteurs des méfaits liés à la guerre, y compris les gouvernants, est de nouveau judiciairement réalisable[1]. La tragédie même de la Yougoslavie et tout ce qui a abouti au triste succès qu'on peut voir dans l'instauration du Tribunal Pénal International pour l'ex-Yougoslavie, a ravivé les discussions sur le «droit de Nuremberg» et a donné un certain éclat au cinquantenaire du fameux jugement.

L'importance du «droit de Nuremberg» pourrait, à ce qu'il semble, être rapprochée aux théoriciens du droit à l'aide d'un jeu de mots: sans contredire la justesse de l'adage «il n'y a rien d'aussi utile pour la pratique qu'une bonne théorie», il faut lui juxtaposer son inverse: «il n'y a rien d'aussi utile pour la théorie qu'une bonne pratique». Nuremberg c'est la pratique. Ce procès a permis de présenter aux spécialistes de l'illustre, ancienne doctrine du droit international une alliance spectaculaire en son sein de l'«international» et du «pénal».

Il est vrai que Nuremberg a pu profiter de l'expérience apportée par certaines solutions prises à l'issue de la première guerre mondiale, mais celles-ci avaient servi surtout à manifester les bonnes intentions et, en fin de compte, à dissiper les illusions. Le Traité de Versailles a consacré quatre

---

[1] Un autre Tribunal International a été aussi établi – pour juger les auteurs du génocide et autres violations du droit humanitaire international commis en Rwanda (et sur le territoire d'autres Etats voisins) depuis le 1er janvier jusqu'au 31 décembre 1994, résolution du Conseil de Sécurité N° 955 du 8 novembre 1994 (qui a adopté également le statut du Tribunal).

articles (227–230) aux sanctions et distingué entre deux sortes de coupables: Guillaume II, ancien empereur d'Allemagne devait être soumis à un droit d'exception, tandis que les combattants, auteurs des crimes de guerre – à une procédure proche de l'ordinaire. Avant de formuler ces articles du Traité d'éminents juristes avaient été consultés. Ils se prononcèrent pour la possibilité des poursuites mais sur la base du droit international, et non sur celle du droit pénal. «Le distinguo très significatif – écrit C. Lombois – est l'aveu qu'à ce moment il n'existe pas un droit qui soit à la fois international et pénal. En conséquence, la poursuite devra s'accomoder de l'absence d'incrimination préalable»[2]. La teneur de l'article 229 du Traité de Versailles avait une haute portée morale mais, à présent, elle peut paraître un peu naïve. Guillaume II fut inculpé «d'offense suprême contre la morale internationale et l'autorité sacrée des traités». Le gouvernement des Pays-Bas où l'ancien empereur a trouvé asile, refuse son extradition, en invoquant diverses raisons, parmi lesquelles l'objection que l'accusation viole la règle *nullum crimen nulla poena sine lege*, privait les autres de signification. Cette argumentation d'antan, faisant observer la carence de légalité d'une inculpation de ce genre, reste instructive.

L'article 228 du Traité a reconnu aux alliés la liberté de traduire devant leurs tribunaux militaires les auteurs des crimes de guerre. L'Allemagne a cependant bien vite obtenu la délégation du droit de juger par les tribunaux allemands ses ressortissants. La proportion des acquittements ou des condamnations à des peines très légères devrait servir d'avertissement aux auteurs des actes normatifs instaurant une juridiction internationale pénale. C'est seulement une cour internationale qui, semble-t-il, devrait avoir la compétence de juger les grands criminels «internationaux» sans pouvoir la déléguer aux autorités de l'Etat dont les ressortissants sont des inculpés.

Dans l'entre-les-deux-guerres la question des principes de la responsabilité pénale pour des crimes de guerre et internationaux faisait objet d'ouvrages, publications et délibérations. Ces dernières surtout dans l'Association Internationale de Droit Pénal, Union Interparlementaire et International Law Association qui – on allait le voir plus tard – ouvraient la voie des jugements de Nuremberg et de Tokyo. Parmi les éminents juristes savants il faut mentionner surtout les professeurs: Vespasien Pella[3], Jean

---

2 C. LOMBOIS, DROIT PÉNAL INTERNATIONAL, Paris (1971).

3 V. PELLA, LA CRIMINALITÉ COLLECTIVE DES ETATS ET LE DROIT PÉNAL DE L'AVENIR, Bucarest (1925); *Plan d'un code répressif mondial*, REVUE INTERNATIONALE DU DROIT PÉNAL (1935), n° 12.

Dumas[4], Emil S. Rappaport[5], Cezary Berezowski[6] et, je cite ce nom à la fin, mais c'est pour le rehausser, Henri Donnedieu de Vabres[7]. Ce distingué professeur de la Sorbonne[8] représentait la France au Tribunal Militaire International de Nuremberg composé de quatre juges (assisté chacun d'un suppléant): de France, de Grande Bretagne, des Etats-Unis et de l'Union Soviétique. Il est entré dans le Tribunal avec tout le bagage de son savoir, et a pu certainement apporter sa contribution à la formation du «droit de Nuremberg».

II

Une énorme littérature mondiale commente, critique et loue, discute et dissèque: la teneur de l'accord conclu à Londres le 8 août 1945 par les quatre puissances, établissant un Tribunal Militaire International, le contenu de son statut qui formule les fameuses notions – crimes contre la paix, crimes de guerre, crimes contre l'humanité (et son article 27 – «Le Tribunal pourra prononcer contre les accusés convaincus de culpabilité la peine de mort ou tout autre châtiment qu'il estimera être juste»), enfin toutes les subtilités légales qui en découlent.

Le professeur Donnedieu de Vabres, revenu à sa chaire de Paris, a donné un cours sur les fondements du procès de Nuremberg et, dans la troisième édition de son «Traité», a ajouté dans un nouveau chapitre consacré au droit pénal international des observations qu'on peut considérer déjà comme celles d'un théoricien devenu praticien pour une étape de sa carrière. Il souligne le caractère absolument exceptionnel de la situation dans laquelle se déroulait le procès de Nuremberg. Certains problèmes devenaient caducs, tels celui de la responsabilité pénale des Etats.

---

4 J. Dumas, De la responsabilité internationale des Etats à raison des crimes ou délits commis sur leur territoire au préjudice d'étrangers. Essai sur l'évolution qui conduit du droit pénal international au droit international pénal, Paris (1930).

5 E.S. Rappaport, Zagadnienie prawa karnego międzypaństwowego [Le problème du droit pénal interétatique], Warszawa (1930).

6 C. Berezowski, O polskim projekcie międzynarodowego prawa karnego [Au sujet du projet de droit international pénal], Warszawa (1927).

7 H. Donnedieu de Vabres, Introduction à l'étude du droit pénal international, Paris (1922); Les principes modernes du droit pénal international, Paris (1928).

8 Je me permets de rendre ici un hommage personnel à la mémoire de mon Maître. J'ai eu l'honneur de lui être présenté au cours du procès de Nuremberg et, ensuite, j'avais le privilège de lui soumettre en 1948 ma thèse de doctorat.

> «La capitulation sans conditions de l'Allemagne, l'occupation intégrale de son territoire avaient suspendu, sinon aboli, l'exercice de sa souveraineté. A l'infliction d'un châtiment collectif frappant la personne morale publique fut substituée la mise en oeuvre des sanctions individuelles»[9].

Le principe de la compétence territoriale fut écarté.

La révolution apportée par le procès de Nuremberg au droit international et pénal ne devait-elle pas introduire une nouveauté au moins dans le domaine de la terminologie?

Dans son «Traité» H. Donnedieu de Vabres donne la définition suivante du droit pénal international: [ce droit] «est la science que détermine la compétence des juridictions pénales de l'Etat vis-à-vis des juridictions étrangères, l'application de ses lois criminelles – lois de fond et lois de forme – par rapport aux lieux et aux personnes qu'elles régissent, l'autorité, sur son territoire, des jugements répressifs étrangers»[10]. Et il ajoute que «l'intérêt pratique de cette science s'accroît en proportion de la fréquence des relations internationales». Il mentionne toutefois à la page suivante la formation d'un droit pénal «interétatique» et reconnaît aux promoteurs de ce droit que le procès des «grands criminels de guerre» a donné à leur thèse une première illustration. Mais il écrit tout de suite après (p. 1022) qu'«il n'est guère à prévoir ni à souhaiter que le procès de Nuremberg serve de modèle, ou de précédent, à l'administration future de la justice pénale internationale. Comment supposer que se représentent, dans un avenir même lointain, les circonstances qui ont déterminé les modalités actuelles touchant la composition du tribunal, la procédure, les sanctions...?»

III

C'est justement l'acceptation de l'opinion que «Nuremberg» est un phénomène sans pareil qui semble ne pas forcer à changer, sous l'influence de ce cas isolé, les définitions générales du droit pénal international ou l'appelation de ce droit.

Par exemple en Pologne, le professeur Lech Gardocki appelle droit pénal international

---

[9] H. DONNEDIEU DE VABRES, TRAITÉ DE DROIT CRIMINEL ET DE LÉGISLATION PENALE COMPARÉE, 3ème édition, Paris (1947).

[10] *Ibid.* p. 919.

«une branche de droit comprenant des normes du droit international public qui forment directement ou indirectement le champ de la pénalisation, les principes de la responsabilité pénale et de la procédure pénale, ainsi que les normes du droit international et interne concernant les infractions avec un élément étranger ou les instruments de la coopération internationale en matière pénale»[11].

Il convient de rappeler ici les discussions et controverses au sujet des termes – et de leurs significations – tels que celui déjà signalé dans les définitions citées, opposé au «droit international pénal», ou encore d'autres termes, tels que: «droit pénal des peuples», «droit pénal *juris gentium*», «droit pénal interétatique». Il serait vain sans doute de vouloir chercher à exprimer dans une définition ou appellation, une part au moins de ce qu'a apporté le procès de Nuremberg à la pensée juridique et à la morale publique (nationale?)[12]. Toutefois, une quelconque modification pourrait-elle peut-être contribuer à donner satisfaction...

IV

La tragédie commencée en Yougoslavie, et la nécessité de créer, ensuite, de nouveau un tribunal international pour juger les auteurs des atrocités de la guerre, dispersaient la belle illusion de ceux qui, comme Donnedieu de Vabres, croyaient que les circonstances qui avaient déterminé les modalités du procès de Nuremberg ne pouvaient revenir. La réalité a démontré le contraire et le précédent de Nuremberg pouvait être utile. L'analogie essentielle entre les deux tribunaux consiste en ce que l'un et l'autre sont des organes judiciaires créés *ad hoc* et sans base «législative» solide. En effet, malgré les efforts des organes, organisations et spécialistes très compétents, et ensuite, des Nations Unies[13] il n'y avait toujours pas de juridiction internationale pénale permanente ni de code pénal international. La différence fondamentale entre ces juridictions repose dans le fait qu'en 1946 les puis-

---

11 *Cf.* L. GARDOCKI, ZARYS PRAWA KARNEGO MIĘDZYNARODOWEGO [Précis de droit pénal international], Warszawa (1985), p. 19; ZAGADNIENIA INTERNACJONALIZACJI ODPOWIEDZIALNOŚCI KARNEJ ZA PRZESTĘPSTWA POPEŁNIONE ZA GRANICĄ [Les problèmes que pose l'internationalisation de la responsabilité pénale pour les infractions commises à l'étranger], Warszawa (1979).

12 *Cf.* NUREMBERG and VIETNAM: An American Tragedy by Telford Taylor, U.S. Chief Counsel at Nuremberg. Sous-titre: IS THE U.S. GUILTY OF WAR CRIMES IN VIETNAM? (1970). Cet ouvrage a été écrit quand le général Taylor était déjà professeur de droit à Columbia University.

13 *Cf.* B. GRAEFRATH, *Die Verhandlungen der U.N.-Völkerrechtskommission zur Schaffung eines Internationalen Strafgerichtshofs*, 104 ZSTW (1992) Heft 1: *voir* aussi un rapport très instructif U.N. Report of the International Law Commission on the work of its 46th session 22 May–23 July 1994, Off. Rec. A/49/10.

sances victorieuses créait «leur» cour pour juger les vaincus, alors que le Tribunal pour l'ex-Yougoslavie est établi par les Nations Unies et au moment où les hostilités se poursuivaient, ce qui provoquait un vrai désarroi. Notamment sur le point de savoir à quel moment les criminels devenaient victimes ou inversement.

Le Tribunal a été établi en vertu de la résolution du Conseil de Sécurité N° 808 du 22 février 1993 fondée sur le Chapitre VII de la Charte des Nations Unies[14]. Composé de onze juges de différentes nationalités il a tenu sa première session en son siège à La Haye en novembre 1993. Un statut établissait les règles juridictionnelles et sa compétence porte sur des actes criminels perpétrés à partir de 1991.

Les opinions sur le Tribunal étaient naturellement divergentes. Au début les Serbes se montraient très critiques à l'égard du projet de créer une juridiction internationale pénale car c'étaient eux qui étaient considérés comme les principaux coupables. Cette opinion a été modifiée plus tard, surtout après que le Rapporteur Spécial de Nations Unies, Tadeusz Mazowiecki (ancien premier ministre polonais) a officiellement condamné les crimes perpétrés par les Musulmans sur les Serbes[15]. Mais les experts serbes en droit pénal international maintenaient l'opinion que le Conseil de Sécurité n'était pas autorisé à instituer un tribunal indépendant, et que la résolution N° 808 manifestait la suprématie de grandes puissances sur les petites nations et violait le principe de souveraineté des Etats.

D'après une opinion différente, le Tribunal marque un progrès considérable en établissant un mécanisme international impartial pour juger les inspirateurs et auteurs de graves infractions internationales. Il peut devenir un paradigme pour une cour pénale internationale permanente si la communauté internationale pouvait être persuadée de prendre cette décision.

V

L'activité du Tribunal même a été précédée par celle d'une Commission d'Experts constituée en vertu de la Résolution du Conseil de Sécurité

---

[14] F.L. KIRGIS, Jr., *The Security Council's First Fifty Years*, 3 AJIL (1995), p. 522, constate que «No legislative authority for statutes such as these of Yugoslav and Rwanda Tribunals is to be found in the Dumbarton Oaks or San Francisco plans. Nevertheless, it is not farfetched to find an implied power to create war crimes tribunals if the conditions for applying chapter VII are met and principles of fundamental adjudicatory fairness are followed».

[15] *Cf.* CH. BASSIOUNI, *The Commission of Experts Established Pursuant to Security Council Resolution 780: Investigating Violations of International Humanitarian Law in the Former Yugoslavia*, CRIMINAL LAW FORUM. AN INTERNATIONAL JOURNAL (p. 304). Editor in Chief, prof. R.S. CLARK. Ce numéro (vol. 5 Numbers 2–3) (1994) de 523 pages porte le sous-titre *A Critical Study of the International Tribunal for the former Yugoslavia.*

N° 780 du 6 octobre 1992 en vue de recueillir des preuves des plus graves violations des conventions de Genève et des droits humanitaires.

Elle est parvenu, sous la présidence du professeur Cherif Bassiouni, à réaliser parfaitement la tâche dont elle était chargée. L'activité de M. Bassiouni a joué un rôle des plus importants dans l'élaboration du concept même d'une juridiction pénale internationale. Il a une claire vision de cette juridiction et a présenté ses idées et thèses dans de nombreuses publications contenant notamment des projets d'actes normatifs très concrets[16]. Dans son rapport sur l'activité de la Commission, il a su mettre en relief toute la spécificité de la situation et des faits examinés. On a cru, répétons-le, après la deuxième guerre mondiale que l'horreur que l'humanité s'est infligée à elle-même a atteint le sommet ne pouvant plus être dépassé. Encore une illusion dissipée, et une déception qui, on voudrait le croire, secouera l'opinion publique mondiale boulversée et la mobilisera en faveur d'une juridiction pénale internationale permanente.

Des agissements inexistants jusque-là ont été mis en oeuvre, et surtout les épurations ethniques et les viols ou autres atrocités sexuelles considérés comme des armes de guerre. Dans son rapport précité M. Bassiouni distingue diverses catégories de cette criminalité perverse:

- atteintes sexuelles (y compris castrations) perpétrées par des individus ou groupes d'individus suivant la politique d'épurations ethniques; les femmes étaient arrêtées pour être violées et n'étaient libérées qu'après la constatation qu'elles étaient enceintes;
- individus ou groupes d'individus – soldats, gardiens, civils aussi – étaient autorisés à ravir des femmes des camps où elles étaient casées pour les violer, et (souvent) torturer et tuer;
- atteintes sexuelles et viols comme moyen d'intimidation dans certaines régions encore avant le déclenchement des hostilités; les actes barbares commis souvent en présence des membres de la famille de la victime;
- détention des femmes dans des hôtels ou *homes* pour des soldats sortant de la ligne de front.

VI

L'expérience fournie par la guerre en ex-Yougoslavie et les actes juridictionnels du Tribunal jettent une nouvelle lumière sur certains problèmes

---

16 *Voir e.g.* M.CH. BASSIOUNI, INTERNATIONAL CRIMINAL LAW. A DRAFT INTERNATIONAL CRIMINAL CODE, Sijthoff and Noordhoff (1980); DRAFT INTERNATIONAL CRIMINAL CODE AND DRAFT STATUTE FOR AN INTERNATIONAL CRIMINAL TRIBUNAL (1987).

intéressant en premier lieu le droit international public, tel la question de la souveraineté de l'Etat[17] qui pourrait être limitée par une responsabilité pénale particulière.

Manfred Mohr[18] emploie une expression *souveränitätsauflösende Verantwortlichkeit*. Il signale aussi la possibilité d'admettre *eine Doppelbestrafung* – double condamnation (rejetée, en général, avec indignation par la doctrine de droit pénal) lorsque une cour internationale est saisie d'un fait dont l'auteur a déjà été condamné pour une infraction ordinaire (*gewöhnliches Verbrechen*). En réfléchissant sur la relation entre une juridiction internationale et le droit interne des Etats il constate que ces rapports devraient refléter *ein echtes Völkerstrafrecht* – un droit pénal international «authentique». Cette notion un peu vague ouvre de larges possibilités d'interprétation.

Dans cet ordre d'idées il semble indiqué de signaler la définition du droit pénal international proposé par le professeur Otto Triffterer qui donne dans son étude une intéressante classification des crimes devant relever de la compétence d'une juridiction pénale internationale. Il constate que le droit pénal international établit la responsabilité individuelle directe conformément au droit international, et souligne que cette responsabilité est indépendante du fait que la réglementation nationale considère l'acte incriminé comme punissable, non repréhensible ou même légal[19].

C'est aussi la multitude de sujets et actes ayant trait à l'actuelle notion du droit pénal international, réglementés par une pléthore des traités, conventions, accords (M. Bassiouni évalue le nombre de ces actes à plus de trois cents – comptés, il est vrai, depuis le Traité de Vienne, 1815), qui fait que le

---

[17] *Cf.* J. KRANZ, *Państwo i jego suwerenność* [l'Etat et sa souveraineté], PAŃSTWO I PRAWO (1996), nº 7. L'auteur remarque que contrairement à certaines opinions, la souveraineté ne disparaît pas simultanément avec l'intensification des relations internationales. Il faut plutôt croire qu'avec l'évolution du droit international c'est la manière de concevoir la souvaraineté et sa fonction qui change.

[18] *Cf.* M. MOHR, *Strafrechtliche Verantwortlichkeit und Staatenverantwortlichkeit für internationale Verbrechen – Wechselwirkung statt Konfusion*, (in:) STRAFGERICHTE GEGEN MENSCHHEITSVERBRECHEN. ZUM VÖLKERSTRAFRECHT 50 JAHRE NACH DEN NÜRNBERGER PROZESSEN, Gerd Hankel/Gerhard Stuby (Hg.), Hamburg (1995).

[19] «Völkerstrafrecht ist das Strafrecht der Völkergemeinschaft, das diese als Teil ihrer eigenständigen Rechtsordnung des Völkerstrafrechts im Rahmen ihrer Rechtssetzungkompetenz zum Schutze ihrer Rechtsgüter gegen besonders schwerwiegende Verletzungen schaffen und einsetzen kann. Da es von seinem Gegenstand her Strafrecht ist, begründen seine Normen eine unmittelbare individuelle Verantwortlichkeit nach Völkerrecht. Diese ist unabhängig davon, ob staatliche Regelungen ein solches Verhalten ebenfalls für strafbar, für zulässig oder gar für rechtmässig erklären». *Cf.* O. TRIFFTERER, *Bestandsaufnahme zum Völkerstrafrecht*, (in:) *ibid.* p. 172.

«droit de Nuremberg» – associé du «droit de l'ex-Yougoslavie» et de celui «de Rwanda» – ne trouve plus, semble-t-il, de place confortable dans les définitions ou appellations traditionnelles du droit pénal international. L'évolution de ce droit demande probablement des changements dans ce domaine aussi.

AUX CONTOURS DES FONDEMENTS DU DROIT INTERNATIONAL HUMANITAIRE

par

*CHRISTOPHE SWINARSKI**

I. REMARQUES LIMINAIRES

La question des fondements du droit international n'est pas exactement celle qui de nos jours semble préoccuper beaucoup les juristes. Le formidable développement du droit positif à tous ses étages et sous toutes ses formes[1] d'une part, et les certitudes, et parfois les confusions qu'engendre l'ordre fondé sur la Charte des Nations Unies, de l'autre, ont quelque peu relégué en arrière la réflexion sur les bases organiques, formelles ou matérielles, de la normative internationale contemporaine.

Pour certains domaines du droit international, cette question semble tout de même revenir encore dans les créneaux principaux de la doctrine juridique contemporaine, ne serait-ce parce qu'ils sont politiquement plus complexes à manier sur le plan idéologique et susceptibles de générer des controverses dans la pratique.

Telle est en tout cas, avant tout, la situation des fondements du droit international des droits de l'homme. Bien que ses instruments constituent aujourd'hui un *corpus iuris* substantiel, sur le plan régional et universel, les fondements de ce droit continuent à être sujets à contestation, tantôt sous l'angle de leur alléguée incompatibilité avec certains concepts de la souveraineté étatique, tantôt sous celui de leur prétendue inadéquation aux valeurs de certaines civilisations et cultures.

Il n'est pas fortuit pas que le problème de fondements hétéronomes du droit se pose plus souvent en ce qui concerne les règles qui servent en premier lieu à la protection directe de l'individu en droit international sans passer par les mécanismes de médiation du droit interne.

Le droit international humanitaire (DIH) participe à cette même occurrence. Même si son appartenance au droit de la guerre, dans la conception

---

* Les opinions de l'auteur n'engagent pas le CICR.

1 Dans le sens d'observations sur le «seuil de la normativité», publiées dans: RGDIP (1982), vol. 5, n° 1, citées ici selon la version anglaise, de P. WEIL, *Towards Relative Normativity in International Law*, AJIL (1983), vol. 77, n° 3, p. 415.

classique du droit des gens, reste fermement établie, sa fonction actuelle, dans la communauté internationale, et les références qu'on y fait, ne satisfont plus aujourd'hui tout-à-fait aux défis des réponses attendues. Bien sûr, cette insuffisance de réponses est, en premier lieu, imputable à la modification substantielle de la nature des situations auxquelles ce droit est censé s'appliquer, mais l'on ne peut point exclure qu'il s'agisse aussi d'une mutation, tout au moins partielle, de sa nature profonde, à la lumière des exigences de ces situations.

> «... les guerres traditionnelles étaient le fait du Prince et avaient pour l'objet la conquête territoriale. Aujourd'hui, la majorité des guerres proviennent de troubles internes non maîtrisables ayant leur racine dans la misère, le sous-développement ou des confrontations ethniques qui, souvent, débordent des frontières. Dans de nombreux cas, les Gouvernements paraissent entraînés dans la guerre davantage qu'ils l'y conduisent leur peuple, dans une dynamique qui paraît échapper à tout contrôle»[2].

Dès lors, il ne semble pas inutile de revenir sur la question de fondements du droit humanitaire, au vu de ses récents développements normatifs et des performances qu'on est en train d'en solliciter dans la communauté internationale contemporaine.

L'occasion de cet hommage s'y prête parfaitement. La vaste contribution de K.J. Skubiszewski à la doctrine couvre plusieurs domaines du droit international, sous les aspects de leur développement et de leurs transformations, mais aussi sous ceux de leur adaptation aux réalités. Dans cette contribution le droit des conflits armés occupe une place de choix: depuis sa monographie sur la situation de la monnaie sur les territoires occupés[3], à travers de ses ouvrages sur les relations germano-polonaises après la Seconde Guerre mondiale[4], jusqu'aux écrits de doctrine générale, les différents éléments de ce droit y ont été souvent abordés et traités avec la même rigueur, lucidité et esprit novateur qui caractérisent toute son oeuvre. A cet égard, il convient de rappeler son chapitre sur l'usage de la force par les Etats, la sécurité collective, les lois de la guerre et la neutralité, préparé pour le «Ma-

---

2 Y. SANDOZ, *Pertinence et permanence du droit international humanitaire*, dans: A.J.M. DELISSEN et G.F. TANJA (éds.), HUMANITARIAN LAW OF ARMED CONFLICT; CHALLENGES AHEAD, ESSAYS IN HONOR OF FRITS KALSHOVEN (1991), p. 36.

3 *Cf.* K.J. SKUBISZEWSKI, PIENIĄDZ NA TERYTORIUM OKUPOWANYM [La monnaie sur le territoire occupé, en polonais], Poznań (1960).

4 *Cf.* surtout K.J. SKUBISZEWSKI, WYSIEDLENIE NIEMCÓW PO DRUGIEJ WOJNIE ŚWIATOWEJ [Le déplacement des Allemands après la Seconde Guerre Mondiale, en polonais], Poznań (1968), ainsi que ZACHODNIA GRANICA POLSKI W ŚWIETLE TRAKTATÓW [La frontière occidentale de la Pologne à la lumière des traités, en polonais], Poznań (1975).

nual of Public International Law»[5], à l'aide duquel plusieurs générations de juristes, tout autour du monde, ont abordé les rudiments du droit de la guerre – tout autant que sa contribution à l'«Encyclopedia of Public International Law»[6] sur la paix et la guerre.

La défininion selon laquelle le DIH est un ensemble de normes internationales, d'origine conventionnelle et coutumière, spécifiquement destiné à s'appliquer à des conflits armés, internationaux ou non-internationaux, qui limite, pour des raisons humanitaires, le droit des parties au conflit à choisir librement les méthodes et les moyens utilisés au combat et qui protègent les personnes et les biens affectés par les conflits[7] a rendu perplexe plus d'un juriste.

C'est surtout la référence à ces «raisons humanitaires» qui, le plus fréquemment, a sous-tendu certains scepticismes à l'égard d'une normative se référant si directement à des valeurs juridiquement mal définies et pour certains même carrément confuses. En effet, que convient-on entendre par les «raisons humanitaires»? Seraient-elles une référence aux fondements du droit? Représenteraient-elles simplement sa *ultima ratio legis*? Tenderaient-elles, enfin, à mettre l'accent sur les finalités de la fonction juridique du droit international humanitaire dans la société internationale? En voilà autant d'interrogations que des réponses possibles.

Il est indéniable que la signification du mot «humanitaire» n'est pas très précise[8]. En français, dans son sens courant, ce terme connote une attitude envers l'autrui, inspirée d'émotions éthiques ou des sentiments de solidarité[9]. Il est d'ailleurs incontestable que l'adjectif «humanitaire» a été admis dans le langage juridique international pour qualifier le droit des conflits armés, avant tout sous l'influence de la Croix-Rouge et plus spécifiquement du Comité international de la Croix-Rouge (CICR), qui l'utilise aux fins de mettre en relief parmi ses normes, celles dont l'objet est de protéger et d'assister les victimes de la violence armée («droit de Genève»)[10]. Est-on alors en droit de soutenir – comme le semblent soupçonner d'aucuns – qu'une telle référence dans la définition de ce droit déborderait ses simples conséquences

---

5 M. SÖRENSEN (éd.), MANUAL OF PUBLIC INTERNATIONAL LAW (1968), pp. 739–854.

6 R. BERNHARDT (éd.), ENCYCLOPEDIA OF PUBLIC INTERNATIONAL LAW (EPIL), Vol. 4 (1982), pp. 74–78.

7 J. PICTET, DÉVELOPPEMENT ET PRINCIPES DU DROIT INTERNATIONAL HUMANITAIRE, Genève-Paris (1983), pp. 7–10.

8 J.L. BLONDEL, *The Meaning of the Word Humanitarian in Relation to the Fundamental Principles of the Red Cross and Red Crescent*, 273 INTERNATIONAL REVIEW OF THE RED CROSS (1989), pp. 508–523.

9 LE PETIT LAROUSSE ILLUSTRÉ, PARIS (1979), p. 517.

10 Confirmé formellement, dans: J. PICTET, *op. cit.*, *supra* note 7, p. 7.

sémantiques, pour déboucher sur un lien direct entre le DIH et des systèmes de valeurs extra-juridiques; en d'autres mots, qu'au-delà de pur qualificatif, elle véhicule un contenu de caractère axiologique, situant l'ensemble de normes en question à cheval entre un système de droit positif et une échelle de préceptes de comportement d'une provenance éthique ou morale.

II. RÉTROSPECTIVES D'APPROCHES

Il est certain que la place particulière qu'a occupée la guerre en tant que relation internationale dans toute la trajectoire de développement du droit international public, tout autant que le fait que les premières normes de ce dernier, au niveau du droit positif, avaient été formulées à partir des préoccupations philosophiques (ou éthiques), notamment celles sur la légitimité du recours à la force, à l'instant même, où le conflit armé devint matière de l'étude des juristes et l'objet d'un système normatif fondé sur la distinction entre le «licite» et l'«illicite», situèrent d'emblée le problème de la nature du DIH dans un contexte d'une ambiguïté certaine.

Il est aujourd'hui impossible de se contenter de caractériser le conflit armé en tant qu'une relation internationale, par des définitions trop générales, telle, par exemple, la fameuse phrase de Jean-Jacques Rousseau disant que:

> «la guerre n'est point une relation d'homme à homme, mais une relation d'Etat à Etat, dans laquelle les particuliers ne sont ennemis qu'accidentellement, non point comme hommes, mais comme citoyens, non point comme membres de la Patrie, mais comme défenseurs»[11].

Bien de réalités du monde échappent de nos jours à une pareille simplicité conceptuelle.

On se souvient aussi, bien sûr, que les fondateurs du droit international réservèrent dans leur première réflexion juridique une place privilégiée à la guerre et à des régles conçues pour la régir. Sous des inspirations diverses, pour ce qui eût été pour chacun d'entre eux le critère suprême de l'assiette extra-juridique de cette relation internationale, ils étaient tous bien d'accord qu'un tel critère existât et qu'il convienne de le rechercher, au-delà du droit même, dans des valeurs intrinsèques de la nature humaine ou de l'ordre social[12].

---

[11] J.J. ROUSSEAU, DU CONTRAT SOCIAL (1762), (livre I, chapitre IV).

[12] *Cf. e.g.* H. GROTIUS, DE JURE BELLI AC PACIS (1625); F. DE VITORIA, DE JURE BELLI (1557); A. GENTILI, DE JURE BELLI (1598); E. DE VATTEL, LE DROIT DES GENS (1758); en général *cf.* J.H.W. VERZIJL, INTERNATIONAL LAW IN HISTORICAL PERSPECTIVE, vol. IX-A, Leiden (1978).

Par ailleurs, l'existence d'une telle référence extra-juridique semblait se confirmer dans la frappante similitude des premières normes connues, applicables aux situations de la violence armée, apparues spontanément dans les civilisations procédantes des systèmes de valeurs très diverses et peu convergentes, où les bases sur lesquelles on a fait reposer les principes de droit de la guerre avaient, pour la plupart d'entre elles, des fondements résolument idéologiques. Le caractère universel et l'apparition spontanée des premiers principes du droit de la guerre corroboraient ainsi leur transcendance par rapport à des pures règles de consentement ou de réciprocité, issues d'accords entre les acteurs de la communauté internationale et fondatrices de la coutume et des traités internationaux[13].

L'universalité du régime juridique de la violence armée témoignerait-elle du caractère extra-juridique des valeurs qui l'inspire et ferait placer les fondements du droit qui la régit au-delà du domaine du droit positif?

Les protagonistes d'une telle thèse étaient à la recherche des fondements du DIH à l'intérieur des systèmes de valeurs, dans lesquels se formèrent les premiers us et coutumes de la guerre au sein des diverses civilisations. On a très bien démontré l'existence des régimes très similaires de la guerre dans des civilisations aussi éloignées l'une de l'autre que celles de l'Afrique avant la conquête coloniale[14], de l'Inde antique[15], ou de vieilles civilisations du bassin méditerranéen[16], avant leurs contacts respectifs avec le monde extérieur. De surcroît, cette origine extra-juridique des fondements du droit de la guerre semblait se trouver confirmée dans le langage de premiers instruments multilatéraux qui en codifient les principes. Ainsi, par exemple, la Déclaration de Saint-Pétersbourg, de 1868 – premier instrument multilatéral du «droit de La Haye» – invoque, dans son préambule «les exigences de l'humanité et le progrès de la civilisation»[17]. Une autre preuve en aurait été encore la référence au concept de «nations civilisées» dans la fameuse clause de Martens, remplacées dans sa version plus moderne par une autre, de

---

13 B. SIMMA, *Reciprocity*, dans: EPIL, vol. 7, *supra* note 6, pp. 400–404.

14 E. BELLO, AFRICAN CUSTOMARY HUMANITARIAN LAW, Geneva (1980), aussi A. NDAM MJOYA, *La conception africaine*, dans: LES DIMENSIONS INTERNATIONALES DU DROIT HUMANITAIRE, Paris (1986), pp. 21–31.

15 N. SINGH, *Armed Conflicts and Humanitarian Law in Ancient India*, dans: CH. SWINARSKI (éd.), ETUDES ET ESSAIS SUR LE DROIT INTERNATIONAL HUMANITAIRE ET LES PRINCIPES DE LA CROIX-ROUGE EN L'HONNEUR DE JEAN PICTET, Genève–La Haye (1984), pp. 531–537.

16 K.J. PARTSCH, *La conception occidentale*, *ibid.* pp. 81–89 et H. SULTAN, *La conception islamique*, *ibid.* pp. 47–61.

17 D. SCHINDLER, J. TOMAN (éds.), THE LAWS OF ARMED CONFLICTS (1981), pp. 95–96; *cf.* également H.P. GASSER, *The International Legal Standards Applicable to Warfare and Some Lessons Drawn from Recent Conflicts*, dans: N. BORSINGER (éd.), 125TH ANNIVERSARY OF 1868 DECLARATION OF ST. PETERSBURG, Geneva (1994), pp. 58–69.

résonance tout aussi jusnaturaliste, aux «exigences de la conscience publique»[18].

En ce qui concerne cette dernière, il est révélateur de noter combien le concept de la «nation civilisée»[19] – avec celui de la conscience publique – ont-ils évolués depuis le commencement de ce siècle[20]. Frits Kalshoven le relève fort à propos, faisant état d'hésitations autour de la possibilité d'étendre le régime juridique international de guerre aux peuples qui n'eussent pas eu le même concept de cette conscience publique, en l'illustrant par des propos d'un délégué britannique à la Conférence de la Paix, à La Haye de 1907, lequel disait:

> «Dans la guerre civilisée, un soldat pénétré par un petit projectile est blessé; il se retire à l'ambulance, il n'avance plus. Le sauvage est bien différent. Quoique transpercé deux ou trois fois, il ne cesse pas de marcher en avant, il n'appelle pas les infirmiers, il avance toujours, et avant qu'on ait eu le temps de lui expliquer qu'il est en contradiction flagrante avec les décisions de la Conférence de La Haye, il vous tranche la tête»[21].

En juxtaposition, dans ce même contexte, on pourrait rappeler l'attitude des premières Autorités soviétiques en 1917, qui, tout en rejetant en bloc les engagements internationaux du régime précédent, afin d'affirmer la rupture totale de tout lien juridique qui eût pu exister entre le nouvel ordre social et la société qu'il a remplacée, maintint en vigueur les obligations des Conventions de La Haye et des Conventions de Genève d'alors, en tant que faisant «partie du patrimoine commun de l'humanité»[22].

Même le positivisme orthodoxe ne va pas à l'encontre – on le sait – de la possibilité d'existence des fondements extra-juridiques d'un ordre normatif, mettant seulement l'accent sur le fait que ceux-ci se placent au-delà de l'objet de la science du droit. Par conséquent, les définitions d'inspiration positiviste de la guerre mettent primordialement l'accent sur l'objectivité de l'état de

---

18 F. MÜNCH, *Die Martens'sche Klausel und die Grundlagen des Völkerrecht*, dans: 36 ZAÖRV (1976), pp. 347–373; aussi S. MIYAZAKI, *The Martens Clause and International Humanitarian Law*, dans: CH. SWINARSKI (éd.), *op. cit.*, *supra* note 15, pp. 433–444.

19 *Cf.* G. SCHWARZENBERGER, *The Law of Armed Conflict: A Civilized Interlude?*, dans: 28 THE YEARBOOK OF WORLD AFFAIRS, London (1974), pp. 293–309.

20 *Cf.* Protocole Additionnel II de 1977 aux Conventions de Genève de 1949, art. 1, par. 2, et Y. SANDOZ, CH. SWINARSKI, B. ZIMMERMANN (éds.), COMMENTARY ON THE ADDITIONAL PROTOCOLS, Geneva (1987), pp. 52–56.

21 F. KALSHOVEN, *The Solidier and His Clubs*, dans: CH. SWINARSKI (éd.), *op. cit.*, *supra* note 15, p. 375.

22 L.A. MOJORYAN, *Neutrality in Present-Day International Law*, dans: G. TUNKIN, CONTEMPORARY INTERNATIONAL LAW, Moscou (1969), pp. 216–233.

faits qui la constituent. C'est dans ce sens que Charles Rousseau affirme qu'elle peut être définie:

> «... en fonction de la croissance des mesures prises, à savoir de cet élément matériel qu'est l'utilisation de la violence ou le recours à la contrainte armée sans limitation d'espace ou de temps ...»[23].

Les instruments de Genève dégagent, quant à eux, ce caractère objectif des situations, où le DIH est applicable, avec une plus grande netteté encore[24].

Toujours en demeure-t-il que cette objectivité des conditions d'applicabilité du DIH ne permet pas, par elle-même, de répondre à la question de fond qui est celle de savoir sur quoi reposent en définitive les normes juridiques régissant la guerre – situation, où coexistent organiquement le droit et la force, d'une façon que certains auteurs n'hésitent pas de qualifier de «mystère»[25].

A l'ombre du principe de la Charte des Nations Unies (article 2(4)), qui interdit l'usage de la force dans les relations internationales, ce «mystère» ne devient que plus opaque, bien que la portée exacte dudit principe semble loin encore d'être clairement circonscrite[26]. Dans ce contexte, l'approche positiviste visant à exclure des références hétéronomes ne paraît guère entièrement élucider, elle non plus, le «mystère» de cette coexistence.

Les ambiguïtes du problème de fondements n'échappent pas aux principaux auteurs du DIH. Ainsi, Jean Pictet, en traitant de ses origines et fondements, dit tout d'abord que:

> «... en raison de leur caractère désintéressé et des valeurs suprérieures qu'elles défendent, en raison aussi de leur ancienneté et de leur extension dans le monde, on peut aujourd'hui affirmer que les Conventions de Genève et de La Haye ont, dans une large mesure, perdu leur aspect de traités réciproques et limités au cadre des relations étatiques pour devenir des engagements absolus»[27].

Mais, ajoutera-t-il ensuite, en nuançant quelque peu son opinion sur le problème:

---

[23] CH. ROUSSEAU, LE DROIT DES CONFLITS ARMÉS, Paris (1983), p. 4.

[24] *Cf.* les articles 2 et 3 communs des quatre Conventions de Genève de 1949 et les articles 1, par 4 et 1, par 1 de leurs Protocoles additionnels de 1977, respectivement.

[25] G. SCHWARZENBERGER, INTERNATIONAL LAW AS APPLIED BY INTERNATIONAL COURTS AND TRIBUNALS, vol. II: THE LAW OF ARMED CONFLICT, London (1968), p. 13.

[26] K.J. SKUBISZEWSKI, *Quelques remarques sur la notion de la force dans la Charte des Nations Unies*, dans: MÉLANGES OFFERTS À GEORGES PERRIN, Lausanne (1984).

[27] J. PICTET, LE DROIT HUMANITAIRE ET LA PROTECTION DES VICTIMES DE LA GUERRE, Leiden–Geneva (1973), p. 18.

> «... Le droit humanitaire est fondé, comme son nom l'indique, sur l'humanité. Or, ne peut être humain qu'un être de chair et de sang. L'Etat est un organisme abstrait, une sorte de robot. Affectant souvent des attitudes d'humanité, ne cessant d'invoquer la justice et les plus nobles sentiments, il offre la parfaite image de l'hypocrisie au service de l'égoïsme. Aussi le droit international n'est-il d'abord matériellement que la résultante des intérêts des parties, c'est-à-dire des Etats»[28].

Pourtant, le concept de compromis d'intérêts d'Etat qui s'attache principalement à évacuer les éléments jusnaturalistes du débat sur les fondements du DIH, en y substituant, dans la mesure du possible, des références au consentement des Etats, en tant que substrat de toute norme internationale, n'arrive pas, lui non plus, à répondre entièrement à la question soulevée.

Elle reste toujours valable pour ce qui est de savoir si la réglementation juridique de la guerre, c'est-à-dire de la violence armée, a, sur le plan international, la nature d'un véritable régime juridique, ou bien, si l'on doit avoir recours, en ultime ressort, aux moyens des prémisses axiologiques, afin d'expliquer son existence.

Or, la question revêt une importance cruciale dans le processus d'application de la normative humanitaire. Celle-ci est, en effet, tout à fait incapable d'assurer des effets de protection, de servir d'un véritable *temperamentum* des conflits armés, sans avoir réussi à s'assurer une acceptation universelle, libre des considérations idéologiques ou éthiques, de quelles origines qu'elles fussent; en bref, l'universalité du DIH apparaît comme une condition *sine qua non* de son effectivite[29].

III. PERSPECTIVES DE RÉPONSE

Une solution est proposée, à cet égard, par Henri Meyrowitz. Afin de pallier l'ambivalence inhérente aux fondements du DIH, cet auteur prend pour point de départ l'analyse du concept même de l'humanité. Il existe, affirme-t-il, deux sens de ce concept, lesquels, complémentaires, correspondent aux deux teneurs sensiblement différentes.

Le premier de ces sens est celui de *Menschlichkeit*:

> «... La raison pour laquelle on ne peut voir dans le principe d'humanité le concept fondateur du droit de la guerre, c'est que cette expression est

[28] J. PICTET, DÉVELOPPEMENT ET PRINCIPES DU DROIT INTERNATIONAL HUMANITAIRE, *op. cit., supra* note 7, p. 104.

[29] *Cf.* G. ABI-SAAB, *The Specifities of Humanitarian Law*, dans: CH. SWINARSKI (éd.), *op. cit., supra* note 15, p. 269.

> traditionnellement entendue dans un sens qui ne représente qu'une moitié de la signification que comporte le mot humanité. Et la moitié non couverte par l'acceptation traditionnelle est celle qui est, aujourd'hui, la plus importante. Pour rendre les deux sens, pertinents en droit international, du mot humanité, l'allemand emploi deux noms différents: *Menschlichkeit* et *Menscheit*. Au premier correspond le sens de sentiment de pitié active, de compassion. C'est dans ce sens, exprimé jadis par le mot 'philanthropie', que le nom 'humanité' est employé par l'Article 4, al. 2 du Règlement de La Haye, à propos du traitement des prisonniers de guerre. A cette acception, à laquelle s'applique l'adjectif humanitaire en usage aujourd'hui, se rattache aussi la notion de dignité humaine»[30].

Il s'agirait d'une attitude à contenu éthique (solidarité humaine) à l'égard des circonstances auxquelles s'applique le droit humanitaire, en relation évidente avec des systèmes de valeurs à multiples bases axiologiques possibles.

Dans le second sens, celui de *Menscheit*:

> «... signification du nom humanité est celle du genre humain, expression qui doit être entendue dans sa double dimension, spatiale et temporelle»[31].

On y viserait-là l'ensemble d'êtres humains, actuel ou futur, qui, en tant qu'un bien constitué, nécessite une protection juridique. La disparition de l'humanité serait, à ce point de vue, un désastre à éviter et sa protection établirait un intérêt juridique commun pour tous, surtout dans la situation de la guerre. Les fondements du droit qui y est applicable ne sauraient alors plus être recherchés dans les références extra-juridiques, mais procéderaient plutôt de la substance de biens protégés, à savoir des finalités réelles, propres au système même, tout comme c'est le cas pour d'autres branches de droit international ou pour l'ordre juridique interne. Ces fondements se confondraient ici avec *ultima ratio legis*, c'est-à-dire avec les objectifs dont la mise en oeuvre est garantie, de façon autonome, par le système normatif lui-même.

La protection de la *Menscheit* n'élimine pas du tout, dans cette conception, d'attitudes de *Menschlichkeit*, permettant seulement de différencier sa finalité proprement juridique des critères d'ordre moral ou idéologique, sans y créer pour autant des contradictions.

Au-delà des distinguo lexicales, il s'agit d'une tentative de résoudre le problème par une proposition qui démarque le contenu du DIH de sa facture sémantique, laquelle demeure à jamais sous l'influence de l'époque, où ses

---

30 H. MEYROWITZ, *Réflexions sur le fondement du droit de la guerre*, dans: CH. SWINARSKI (éd.), *op. cit.*, *supra* note 15, p. 428.

31 *Ibid. passim.*

formulations sont intervenues. La même facture sémantique, spécifique se trouve d'ailleurs, en grande partie, à l'origine des réserves à l'égard du DIH, de la part des Etats qui n'ont pas pris part active à ses premières codifications, lui reprochant, pour cette raison, de procéder d'un discours exagérément europo-centré, teinté d'inspiration judéo-chrétienne démesurément accentuée.

Il appert qu'une conception semblable, reprenant pratiquement tous les éléments principaux de l'approche aux fondements du DIH, est en train de se profiler en droit international de l'environnement.

Le débat sur les fondements de ce droit fait notamment appel à la notion de *commonness* dont le critère principal englobe l'intérêt de l'humanité toute entière. Le concept du *common concern of mankind* y est introduit, s'articulant comme suit:

> «... The term mankind from the start disclosed the link with the human rights framework (infra) and the long-term temporal dimension (encompassing also future generations)»[32].

Pour les tenants de cette approche, les menaces pour l'environnement, d'une part – à l'instar des conflits armés – deviennent d'intérêt commun (*common concern*) pour toute l'humanité, produisant en conséquence des règles à effets *erga omnes*. D'autre part, il est significatif que les éléments constitutifs d'une telle approche relèvent des mêmes doctrines par lesquelles on a tenté d'expliciter les fondements et la nature du DIH, à savoir celle de *res communis*, celle du «domaine public international", ainsi que celle de l'«intérêt public général»; l'idée de la protection d'un bien commun et l'extension de cette protection aux générations futures se trouvant au premier plan dans cette dernière. Le même terme de *common* y est employé dans une acception analogue, sinon identique à la manière dont on le retrouve dans la notion de l'ordre public.

> «... the notion of common concern appeared thus closely related to such concepts as obligations *erga omnes*, *jus cogens*, common heritage and global commons»[33].

On ne peut pas s'empêcher de noter que la parallèle entre l'environnement et l'humanité (*Menscheit*), en tant que biens protégés par le droit, n'est

---

32 A.A. CANÇADO TRINDADE, D. ATTARD, *Report on the 1st Meeting of the UNEP Group of Legal Experts to Examine the Implications of the Common Concern of Mankind, Concept of Global Environmental Issues*, dans: A.A. CANÇADO TRINDADE, DIREITOS HUMANOS E MEIO-AMBIENTE; PARALELO DOS SISTEMAS DE PROTEÇAO INTERNACIONAL, Porto Alegre (1993).

33 *Ibid. passim.*

pas une simple coïncidence et que l'éclairage qu'elle jette sur la question qui nous intéresse, offre un paradigme de valeur pour le DIH.

IV. PARALLÈLES ET CONVERGENCES

Il existe maintes autres confluences, liées surtout à des mécanismes de son fonctionnement, qui méritent une attention dans le cadre de discussion sur les fondements du DIH.

Sans reprendre ici les débats des années quarante et cinquante sur les relations qui existent entre le droit international des Droits de l'Homme et le DIH[34], il y a lieu de se souvenir, à ce propos, que le DIH se caractérise par l'absence virtuelle des possibilités pour ses bénéficiaires de faire directement valoir leurs droits par les voies procédurales à leur propre disposition. Sous cet aspect, les destinataires des normes du DIH demeurent, presque exclusivement, des Etats, les individus n'y apparaissant qu'en posture de ses bénéficiaires[35]. Le caractère «interétatique» du DIH ne saurait ne pas avoir d'incidence sur la question de ses fondements; il fournit un argument pour ceux qui affirment la parfaite identité des fondements du DIH à ceux du droit international public général[36].

Bien entendu, la question de fondements du DIH est de même organiquement liée à la discussion sur la nature et le contenu de *jus cogens*, ne serait-ce parce qu'on ne peut passer outre la situation particulière des normes humanitaires conventionnelles que leur réservent les dispositions des articles 53 et 60, par. 5, de la Convention de Vienne sur le droit des traités. Il serait évidemment hors-propos d'en analyser ici à fond tout impact sur la question; qu'on signale seulement son actualité à la lumière des développements jurisprudentiels récents[37], qui y ouvrent de nouvelles perspectives. Mais l'on ne saurait être plus d'accord avec Georges Abi-Saab, que:

> «The *jus cogens* character is however a mere technical classification, a short-hand description or synthesis of some of the above-mentioned

---

[34] *Cf.* M. EL-KOUHÈNE, LES GARANTIES FONDAMENTALES DE LA PERSONNE EN DROIT HUMANITAIRE ET DROITS DE L'HOMME, Dordrecht–Boston (1985).

[35] *Cf.* CH. SWINARSKI, *Las relaciones entre el derecho internacional humanitario y el derecho internacional de los derechos humanos*, (in:) ESTUDIOS BASICOS DE DERECHOS HUMANOS II, Instituto Interamericano de Derechos Humanos (IIHD) – Comision de la Union Europea, San José (1995), pp. 169–185.

[36] M. SASSÒLI, *Mise en oeuvre du droit international humanitaire et du droit international des droits de l'homme; une comparaison* dans: ANNUAIRE SUISSE DE DROIT INTERNATIONAL, vol. XCIII (1987).

[37] *Cf.* notamment *Cas Nicaragua v. Etats-Unis*, ICJ REPORTS 1986, pp. 112–115 et 125.

characteristics, which is itself deduced from their cumulative existence. It thus indicates the existence of certain characteristics of the norms, but does not explain why they attach to these norms.

In other words, the *jus cogens* character is the result and not the cause; and the cause has to be sought beyond any technical consideration or classification of the legal instruments, into their objects and purposes, in the social values and common interests they are intended to protect and promote, *i.e.* in the social ends for which law serves as a vehicle and an instrument»[38].

Il est aussi pertinent de tenir compte des conséquences pour le DIH découlant des considérations sur les Droits de l'Homme en tant que partie intégrante de l'«ordre public international»[39]. S'appliqueraient-elles, telles quelles, au DIH? Il est loisible d'argumenter que le concept de l'ordre public international puisse apparaître même, *prima facie*, beaucoup plus utile pour ce qui est du DIH, du fait de l'application de ce droit dans les situations de restrictions considérables, de fait ou de droit, de l'efficacité de l'ordre public interne et de la nécessité subséquente d'y suppléer par des normes internationales[40]. Il est au moins fort plausible que ce soit par cette voie qu'on arrive à conclure que les fondements du DIH prennent racine dans les exigences d'organiser juridiquement le minimum de la protection de l'être humain, face aux défaillances d'autres ordres normatifs opérant dans des situations «normales».

Aux termes des remarques, subtiles et un tant soit peu désabusées, de Roberto Vernengo, dans son essai sur les fondements des Droits de l'Homme:

> «... Il s'avère que les droits de l'homme en tant que phénomène juridique, loin d'avoir rencontré les fondements de leur existence dans la morale, mettent plutôt à nu les cartes du jeu, révélant la situation réelle; ce n'est pas la morale qui est l'ordre justificateur et fondateur des valeurs du droit, mais plutôt cette morale représente seulement, dans le monde contemporain, un mode subalterne du droit, comme une manière dont se manifeste le pouvoir social»[41].

---

38 *Cf.* G.ABI-SAAB, *The Specifities of Humanitarian Law*, dans: CH. SWINARSKI (éd.), *op. cit.*, *supra* note 15, p. 271.

39 *Cf.* D. EVRIGENIS, *Institutionnalisation des droits de l'homme et droit universel*, dans: INTERNATIONALES COLLOQUIUM ÜBER MENSCHRECHTE, Berlin (1966), pp. 26–34.

40 *Cf.* E. RAUCH, *Le concept de nécessité militaire* dans: *le droit de la guerre*, dans: 19 REVUE DE DROIT MILITAIRE ET DE DROIT DE LA GUERRE (1980), pp. 205–237.

41 R.J. VERNENGO, *Dos ensayos sobre problemas de fundamentacion de los derechos humanos*, dans: CUADERNOS DE INVESTIGACIONES 13, Instituto de Investigaciones Juridicas y Sociales «Ambrosio Gioja», Buenos Aires (1989), p. 40 (notre traduction).

Toutefois, il convient de ne pas oublier que l'origine, le développement et les institutions du DIH sont bien distincts de ceux des Droits de l'Homme[42], même s'il existe une relation de complémentarité entre ces deux branches de droit et une concurrence possible de leurs champs respectifs d'application; il ne faudrait pas, pour autant, perdre de vue la différence de nature de ces deux normatives[43]. Quoique toutes les deux régissent par des normes internationales la position de l'individu, elles l'organisent dans des circonstances distinctes et avec des conséquences différentes. Comme le résume bien Héctor Gros Espiell:

> «... dans les situations spécifiques prévues par le DIH, les personnes auxquelles ce droit s'applique jouissent *ab initio* des garanties propres de ce droit, sans pour autant préjuger qu'elles ne soient, en même temps, sous la protection des normes du droit international de droits de l'homme, lesquelles demeurent en vigueur dans les mêmes situations pour les individus, qui en tant que personnes humaines ne seraient pas expressément protégées par le droit international humanitaire»[44].

Ces complémentarité et concurrence du champ d'application ont, certes, elles aussi, des répercussions directes dans le débat sur les fondements respectifs de ces deux branches de droit international contemporain.

V. REMARQUES FINALES

En revenant au point de départ de ces observations, force est de constater que la fameuse expression «pour des raisons humanitaires» apparaît beaucoup plus indicative de *ratio juris* présidant à la formation et au développement du DIH, que de la nature de ses fondements extra-juridiques éventuels, ou encore de son prétendu caractère de normative issue d'un système axiologique, d'origine éthique ou morale. Il s'agirait plutôt d'une indication des finalités de ce droit, plutôt que d'une preuve de sa nature hétéroclite par rapport à d'autres corps de normes internationales.

L'état présent de la réponse à la question se trouve bien résumé par Antonio Augusto Cançado Trindade, lorsqu'il dit:

---

[42] Certains auteurs estiment que l'évolution irait aujourd'hui vers l'effacement progressif de ces différences, *cf. e.g.* R.-J. DUPUY, *L'action humanitaire*, dans: A.J.M. DELISSEN, G.J. TANJA (éds.), *op. cit.*, *supra* note 2, p. 71.

[43] *Cf.* CH. SWINARSKI, A NORMA E A GUERRA, Porto Alegre (1991), p. 20 ss.

[44] H. GROS ESPIELL, *Derechos humanos, derecho internacional humanitario y derecho internacional de los refugiados*, dans: CH. SWINARSKI (éd.), STUDIES AND ESSAYS IN HONOUR OF JEAN PICTET, *op. cit.*, *supra* note 15, p. 707 (notre traduction).

«... Il en ressort de ces quelques observations que, malgré les développements considérables du droit international humanitaire dans ces dernières années, il lui reste un long et nécessaire chemin à parcourir. La recherche du perfectionnement et du renforcement du droit international humanitaire s'impose comme une nécessité, puisqu'il y va d'un domaine juridique fort empreint du sentiment de l'humanité. Sous-jacent à ce fait, l'on y rencontre – comme il a été déjà souligné – le problème fondamental de trouver un équilibre entre les impératifs humanitaires et ce qu'on convient d'appeler les 'nécessités militaires', ou bien – comme il a déjà été proclamé, en 1868, dans les paragraphes premier et dernier de la Déclaration de Saint-Pétersbourg – de rechercher à réconcilier les 'nécessités de la guerre' avec les exigences de l'humanité, ces premières devant céder le pas aux secondes. Ce propos humanitaire mit à jour un objectif suprême et prédominant, qui est celui de la prévention même des conflits armés, aux bénéfices du genre humain et de l'avancement de la civilisation»[45].

Finalement, les fondements du DIH méritent une étude approfondie qui, bien au-delà de son intérêt académique, se doit de pouvoir contribuer à en renforcer le respect dans une communauté internationale, laquelle continue, toujours davantage, d'en avoir grand besoin, tout autant que la protection de l'individu au sein de celle-ci, dans des circonstances actuelles, où tant d'autres protections s'avèrent inexistantes, insuffisantes voire inacceptables.

45 A.A. CANÇADO TRINDADE, *A Evoluçao do Direito Internacional Humanitario e As Posiçoes do Brazil*, dans: BOLETIM DA SOCIEDADE BRASILEIRA DE DIREITO INTERNACIONAL, anos XXXIX et XLI, nº 69/71, pp. 106–107 (notre traduction).

English Index

A

B

C

D

E

H

I

M

N

R

S

T

U

V

W

Index Français

A

D

R

List of Contributors

ABI-SAAB, Georges M., Egypte, professeur de droit international à l'Institut universitaire de Hautes Etudes Internationales, Genève, membre de l'Institut de Droit international.

ALDRICH, George H., United States, Judge at the Iran-United States Claims Tribunal.

AMERASINGHE, Chittharanjan F., Sri Lanka, Honorary Professor of International Law, University of Colombo, Member of the Institut de Droit international.

BARDONNET, Daniel, France, professeur à l'Université de Paris II, membre de l'Institut de Droit international.

BERNHARDT, Rudolf, Germany, Professor of law (emeritus) of the University of Heidelberg, Member of the Institut de Droit international, Vice-President of the European Court of Human Rights.

BOS, Maarten, The Netherlands, professeur émérite de droit international public de l'Université d'Utrecht, membre de l'Institut de Droit international.

BOUTROS-GHALI, Boutros, Egypte, professeur honoraire de l'Université de Caire, Secretaire général de l'Organisation des Nations Unies, membre de l'Institut de Droit international.

BROMS, Bengt, Finland, Professor of Public International Law and Constitutional Law of the University of Helsinki, Member of the Institut de Droit international.

BROWNLIE, Ian, Great Britain, Chichele Professor of International Law in the University of Oxford, All Souls College, Member of the Institut de Droit international.

BURDEAU Geneviève, France, professeur aux Facultés de droit des Universités de Dijon et Paris I.

CAFLISCH, Lucius, Suisse, professeur à l'Institut universitaire de Hautes Etudes Internationales, membre de l'Institut de Droit international.

CAHIER, Philippe, France, professeur à l'Institut universitaire de Hautes Etudes Internationales à Genève.

CHARPENTIER, Jean, France, professeur à la Faculté de droit de l'Université de Nancy.

D'AMATO, Anthony, United States, Leighton Professor of Law, Northwestern University School of Law.

DEGAN, Vladimir-Djuro, Croatia, Professor of Public International Law at the University of Rijeka, Member of the Institut de Droit international.

DETTER, DE LUPIS FRANKOPAN Ingrid, Sweden, Professor at the University of Stockholm.

DINSTEIN, Yoram, Israel, President of Tel Aviv University, Member of the Institut de Droit international.

DOMINICÉ, Christian, Suisse, professeur à l'Institut universitaire de Hautes Études Internationales, membre de l'Institut de Droit international.

DUPUY, René Jean, France, professeur au College de France, membre de l'Institut de Droit international.

FITZMAURICE, Malgosia, Great Britain, Senior Lecturer, University of London.

FROWEIN, Jochen Abr., Germany, Professor at the University of Heidelberg.

HIGGINS, Rosalyn, Great Britain, Judge of the International Court of Justice, Member of the Institut de Droit international.

JENNINGS, Sir Robert, Great Britain, sometime Whewell Professor of International Law, University of Cambridge, Honorary Member of the Institut de Droit international, Former President of the International Court of Justice.

KOLASA, Jan, Poland, Professor of International Law at the University of Wrocław.

KOOIJMANS, Peter H., The Netherlands, Professor of Public International Law at the University of Leiden, Member of the Institut de Droit international.

KRANZ, Jerzy, Pologne, docteur en droit, Centre des Affaires internationales, Varsovie.

KWIATKOWSKA, Barbara, The Netherlands, Professor at the University of Utrecht.

LALIVE, Pierre, Suisse, docteur en droit, avocat au Barreau de Genève, membre de l'Institut de Droit international.

LAUTERPACHT, Elihu, Great Britain, Professor at the Cambridge University, Member of the Institut de Droit international, Judge *ad hoc* at the International Court of Justice.

LUKASHUK, Igor I., Ukraine, Professor at the Institute of State and Law of the Russian Academy of Sciences.

MAKARCZYK, Jerzy, Poland, Professor of International Law at the Institute of Legal Sciences of the Polish Academy of Sciences, associé de l'Institut de Droit international, Judge at the European Court of Human Rights.

McWHINNEY, Edward, Canada, Professor at the Simon Fraser University, Vancouver, Member of the Institut de Droit international.

MONACO, Riccardo, Italie, professeur émérite de droit international à l'Université de Rome, membre de l'Institut de Droit international.

MORIN, Jacques-Yvan, Canada, professeur à l'Université de Montreal, associé de l'Institut de Droit international.

MÜLLERSON, Rein, Estonie, Professor at the University of London School of Law, associé of the Institut de Droit international.

NASCIMENTO E SILVA, Gerardo Eulalio do, Brésil, Professor of International Law, Member of the Institut de Droit international.

PERRIN, Georges, Suisse, professeur honoraire à la Faculté de droit de l'Université de Lausanne.

PINTO, Moragodage C.W., Sri Lanka, Professor of International Law, associé of the Institut de Droit international.

POKLEWSKI-KOZIEŁŁ, Krzysztof, Pologne, docteur en droit.

REZEK, Francisco, Brasil, professeur de droit international.

ROSENNE, Shabtai, Israel, Member of the Institut de Droit international.

ŠAHOVIĆ, Milan, Yougoslavie, professeur de droit international, membre de l'Institut de Droit international.

SCHACHTER Oscar, United States, Hamilton Fish Professor of Law and Diplomacy, Columbia University School of Law, Member of the Institut de Droit international

SCHWEBEL, Stephen M., United States, Vice-President of the International Court of Justice, Member of the Institut de Droit international.

SEYERSTED, Finn, Norway, Professor emeritus of the University of Oslo.

SOHN, Louis B., United States, Bemis Professor of International Law, Emeritus, Harvard Law School, Member of the Institut de Droit international.

STEIGER, Heinhard, Allemagne, professeur de Justus-Liebig-Universität Giesen.

SUCHARITKUL, Sompong, Thailand, Distinguished Professor of Public International Law and Comparative Law, Golden Gate University, Member of the Institut de Droit international.

SWINARSKI, Christophe, Suisse, Chef de délégation du Comité International de la Croix Rouge, Hong Kong.

SZAFARZ, Renata, Poland, Professor of International Law at the Institute of Legal Sciences of the Polish Academy of Sciences.

TOMUSCHAT, Christian, Germany, Professor of the Faculty of Law, Humboldt-Universität zu Berlin.

VALTICOS, Nicolas, Grèce, President du Curatorioum, Académie de Droit international de La Haye, juge à la Cour européenne des Droits de l'Homme, membre de l'Institut de Droit international.

VIGNES, Daniel, France, professeur de droit de la mer à la Faculté de droit de l'Université de la Bruxelles, membre de l'Institut de Droit international.

WASILKOWSKI, Andrzej, Poland, Professor of International Law at the Institute of Legal Sciences of the Polish Academy of Sciences.

WEIL, Prosper, France, professeur émérite à l'Université de droit, d'économie et de sciences sociales de Paris, membre de l'Institut de Droit international.

WOLFKE, Karol, Poland, Professor of International Law at the University of Wrocław.

† ZIEMBIŃSKI, Zygmunt, Poland, Professor of the Theory of Law, University of Poznań.